Stan Lee PRESENTS

ESSENTIAL X-MEN VOL. 2

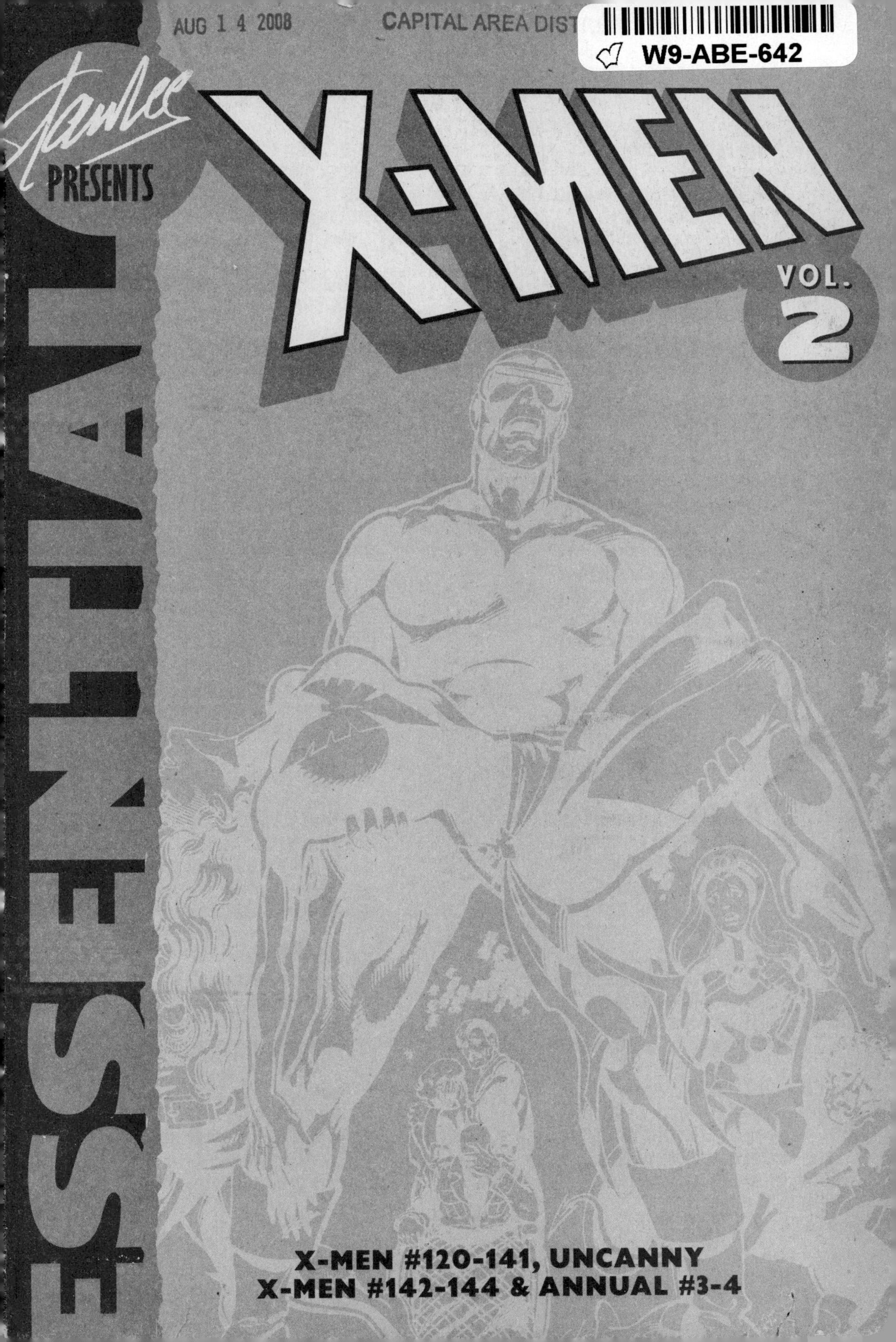

X-MEN #120-141, UNCANNY X-MEN #142-144 & ANNUAL #3-4

X-MEN #120
WRITER: **CHRIS CLAREMONT**
PENCILER & CO-PLOTTER: **JOHN BYRNE**
INKER: **TERRY AUSTIN**
LETTERER: **TOM ORZECHOWSKI**

X-MEN #121
WRITER: **CHRIS CLAREMONT**
PENCILER & CO-PLOTTER: **JOHN BYRNE**
INKER: **TERRY AUSTIN**
LETTERER: **DIANA ALBERS**

X-MEN #122
WRITER: **CHRIS CLAREMONT**
BREAKDOWNS & CO-PLOTTER: **JOHN BYRNE**
FINISHED ART: **TERRY AUSTIN**
LETTERER: **TOM ORZECHOWSKI**

X-MEN #123
WRITER: **CHRIS CLAREMONT**
PENCILER & CO-PLOTTER: **JOHN BYRNE**
INKER: **TERRY AUSTIN**
LETTERER: **TOM ORZECHOWSKI**

X-MEN #124
WRITER: **CHRIS CLAREMONT**
PENCILER & CO-PLOTTER: **JOHN BYRNE**
INKER: **TERRY AUSTIN**
LETTERER: **TOM ORZECHOWSKI**

X-MEN ANNUAL #3
WRITER: **CHRIS CLAREMONT**
PENCILER: **GEORGE PÉREZ**
INKER: **TERRY AUSTIN**
LETTERER: **TOM ORZECHOWSKI**

X-MEN #125
WRITER: **CHRIS CLAREMONT**
PENCILER: **JOHN BYRNE**
INKER: **TERRY AUSTIN**
LETTERER: **TOM ORZECHOWSKI**

X-MEN #126
WRITER: **CHRIS CLAREMONT**
PENCILER: **JOHN BYRNE**
INKER: **TERRY AUSTIN**
LETTERER: **TOM ORZECHOWSKI**

X-MEN #127
WRITER: **CHRIS CLAREMONT**
PENCILER & CO-PLOTTER: **JOHN BYRNE**
INKER: **TERRY AUSTIN**
LETTERER: **TOM ORZECHOWSKI**

X-MEN #128
WRITER: **CHRIS CLAREMONT**
PENCILER & CO-PLOTTER: **JOHN BYRNE**
INKER: **TERRY AUSTIN**
LETTERER: **TOM ORZECHOWSKI**

X-MEN #129
WRITER: **CHRIS CLAREMONT**
PENCILER & CO-PLOTTER: **JOHN BYRNE**
INKER: **TERRY AUSTIN**
LETTERER: **TOM ORZECHOWSKI**

X-MEN #130
WRITER: **CHRIS CLAREMONT**
PENCILER & CO-PLOTTER: **JOHN BYRNE**
INKER: **TERRY AUSTIN**
LETTERER: **TOM ORZECHOWSKI**

X-MEN #131
WRITER: **CHRIS CLAREMONT**
PENCILER & CO-PLOTTER: **JOHN BYRNE**
INKER: **TERRY AUSTIN**
LETTERER: **TOM ORZECHOWSKI**

X-MEN #132
WRITER: **CHRIS CLAREMONT**
PENCILER & CO-PLOTTER: **JOHN BYRNE**
INKER: **TERRY AUSTIN**
LETTERER: **TOM ORZECHOWSKI**

X-MEN #133
WRITER: **CHRIS CLAREMONT**
PENCILER & CO-PLOTTER: **JOHN BYRNE**
INKER: **TERRY AUSTIN**
LETTERER: **TOM ORZECHOWSKI**

X-MEN #134
WRITER: **CHRIS CLAREMONT**
PENCILER & CO-PLOTTER: **JOHN BYRNE**
INKER: **TERRY AUSTIN**
LETTERER: **TOM ORZECHOWSKI**

X-MEN #135
WRITER: **CHRIS CLAREMONT**
PENCILER & CO-PLOTTER: **JOHN BYRNE**
INKER: **TERRY AUSTIN**
LETTERER: **TOM ORZECHOWSKI**

X-MEN #136
WRITER: **CHRIS CLAREMONT**
PENCILER & CO-PLOTTER: **JOHN BYRNE**
INKER: **TERRY AUSTIN**
LETTERER: **TOM ORZECHOWSKI**

X-MEN #137
WRITER: **CHRIS CLAREMONT**
PENCILER & CO-PLOTTER: **JOHN BYRNE**
INKER: **TERRY AUSTIN**
LETTERER: **TOM ORZECHOWSKI**

X-MEN #138
WRITER: **CHRIS CLAREMONT**
PENCILER & CO-PLOTTER: **JOHN BYRNE**
INKER: **TERRY AUSTIN**
LETTERER: **TOM ORZECHOWSKI**

X-MEN ANNUAL #4
WRITER: **CHRIS CLAREMONT**
PENCILER: **JOHN ROMITA, JR.**
INKER: **BOB MCLEOD**
LETTERER: **TOM ORZECHOWSKI**

X-MEN #139
SCRIPT: **CHRIS CLAREMONT**
PENCILER & PLOT: **JOHN BYRNE**
INKER: **TERRY AUSTIN**
LETTERER: **TOM ORZECHOWSKI**

X-MEN #140
SCRIPT: **CHRIS CLAREMONT**
PENCILER & PLOT: **JOHN BYRNE**
INKER: **TERRY AUSTIN**
LETTERER: **TOM ORZECHOWSKI**

X-MEN #141
WRITER: **CHRIS CLAREMONT**
PENCILER & CO-PLOTTER: **JOHN BYRNE**
INKER: **TERRY AUSTIN**
LETTERER: **TOM ORZECHOWSKI**

UNCANNY X-MEN #142
WRITER: **CHRIS CLAREMONT**
PENCILER & CO-PLOTTER: **JOHN BYRNE**
INKER: **TERRY AUSTIN**
LETTERER: **TOM ORZECHOWSKI**

UNCANNY X-MEN #143
WRITER: **CHRIS CLAREMONT**
PENCILER & CO-PLOTTER: **JOHN BYRNE**
INKER: **TERRY AUSTIN**
LETTERER: **TOM ORZECHOWSKI**

UNCANNY X-MEN #144
WRITER: **CHRIS CLAREMONT**
PENCILER: **BRENT ANDERSON**
INKER: **JOSEF RUBENSTEIN**
LETTERER: **TOM ORZECHOWSKI**

REPRINT CREDITS

MARVEL ESSENTIAL DESIGN:
JOHN "JG" ROSHELL OF COMICRAFT
COVER ART:
JOHN BYRNE
FRONT COVER COLORS:
AVALON'S ANDY TROY
COLLECTION EDITOR:
MARK D. BEAZLEY
ASSISTANT EDITORS:
JENNIFER GRÜNWALD & MICHAEL SHORT
SENIOR EDITOR, SPECIAL PROJECTS:
JEFF YOUNGQUIST

PRODUCTION:
JERRON QUALITY COLOR
DIRECTOR OF SALES:
DAVID GABRIEL
BOOK DESIGNER:
TERNARD SOLOMON
CREATIVE DIRECTOR:
TOM MARVELLI
EDITOR IN CHIEF:
JOE QUESADA
PUBLISHER:
DAN BUCKLEY
SPECIAL THANKS TO NATHAN DOYLE, TOM BREVOORT, RALPH MACCHIO, TERRY AUSTIN, JAMES CHAN, WILL GABRI-EL, AND POND SCUM

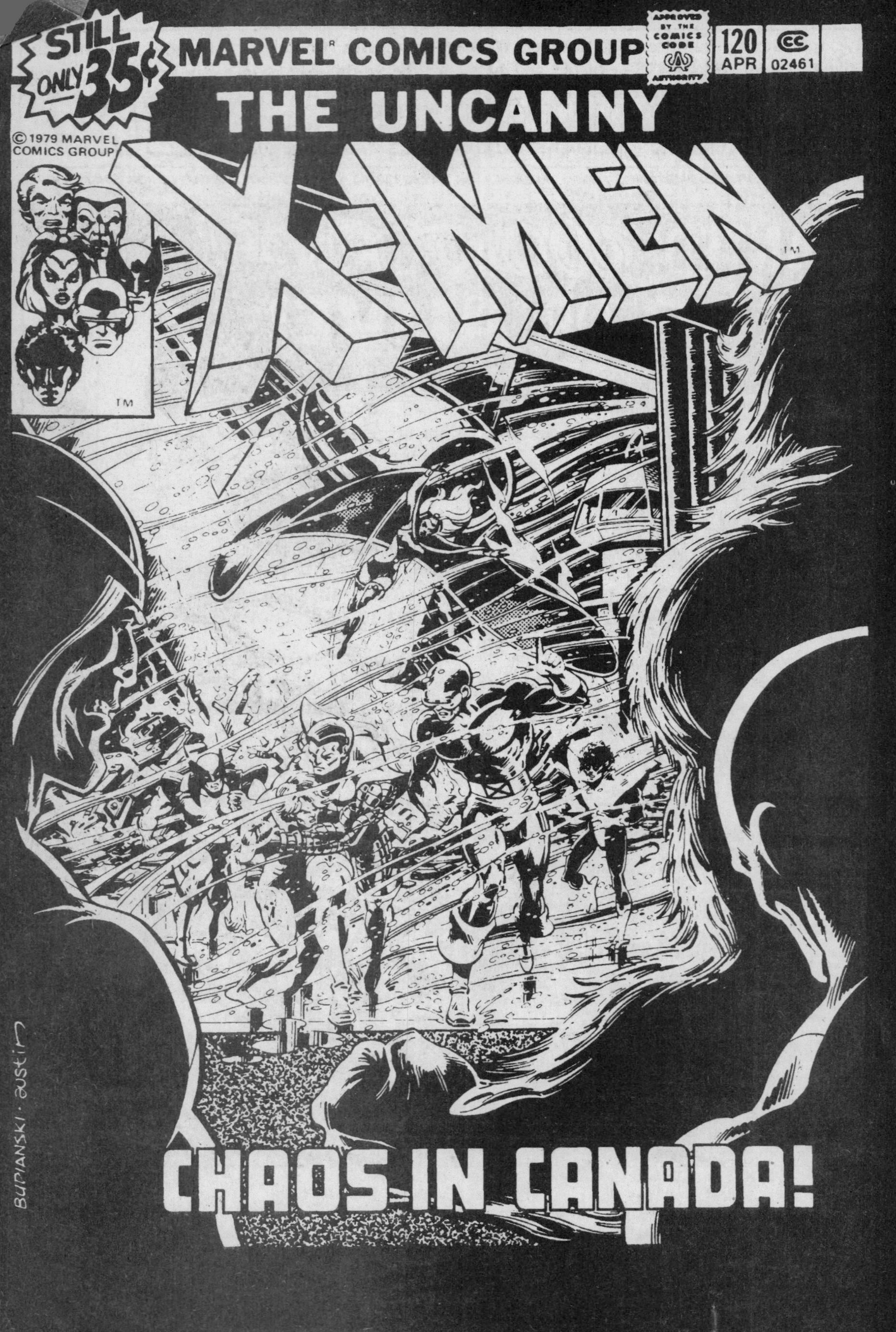

STILL ONLY 35¢
MARVEL COMICS GROUP
APPROVED BY THE COMICS CODE AUTHORITY
120 APR
CC 02461
THE UNCANNY
©1979 MARVEL COMICS GROUP
X-MEN
TM
CHAOS IN CANADA!
BUDIANSKI · austin

Cyclops. Storm. Banshee. Nightcrawler. Wolverine. Colossus. Children of the atom, students of Charles Xavier, MUTANTS--feared and hated by the world they have sworn to protect. These are the STRANGEST heroes of all!

STAN LEE PRESENTS: THE UNCANNY X-MEN!™

CHRIS CLAREMONT & JOHN BYRNE, AUTHOR/CO-PLOTTERS/PENCILER ✱ TERRY AUSTIN, INKER | TOM ORZECHOWSKI, letterer | ROGER STERN, EDITOR | JIM SHOOTER, EDITOR-IN-CHIEF

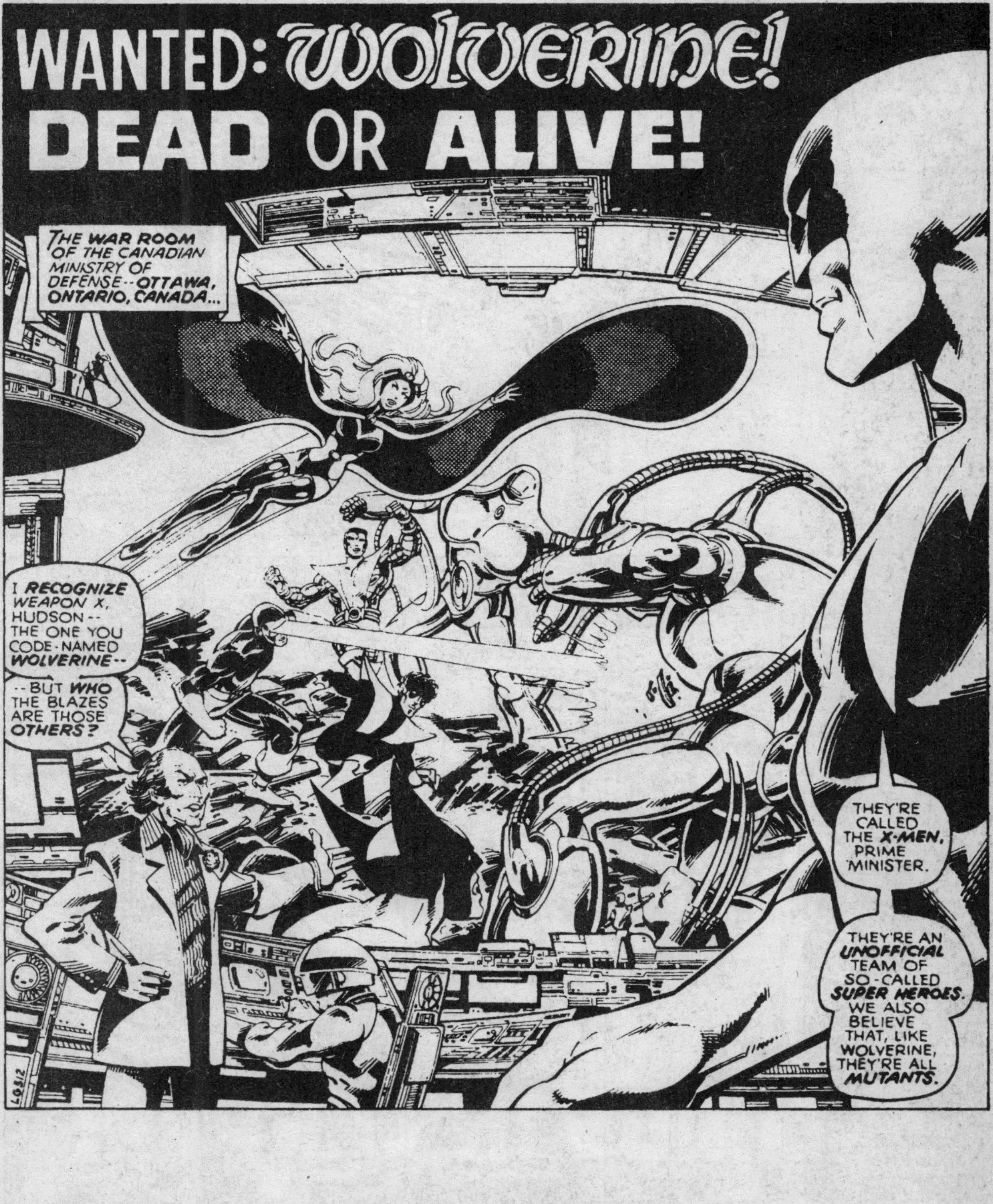
WANTED: WOLVERINE! DEAD OR ALIVE!
THE WAR ROOM OF THE CANADIAN MINISTRY OF DEFENSE--OTTAWA, ONTARIO, CANADA...
I RECOGNIZE WEAPON X, HUDSON--THE ONE YOU CODE-NAMED WOLVERINE--
--BUT WHO THE BLAZES ARE THOSE OTHERS?
THEY'RE CALLED THE X-MEN, PRIME MINISTER.
THEY'RE AN UNOFFICIAL TEAM OF SO-CALLED SUPER HEROES. WE ALSO BELIEVE THAT, LIKE WOLVERINE, THEY'RE ALL MUTANTS.

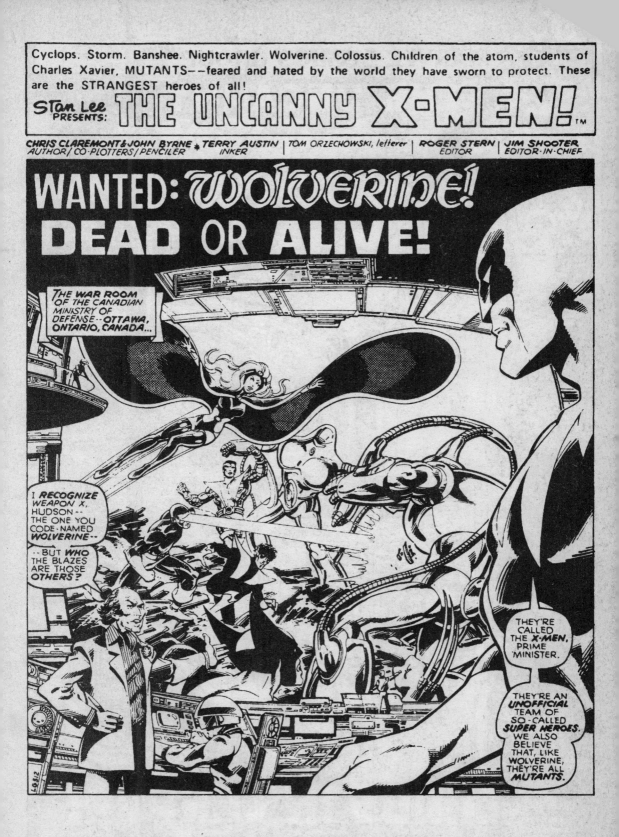

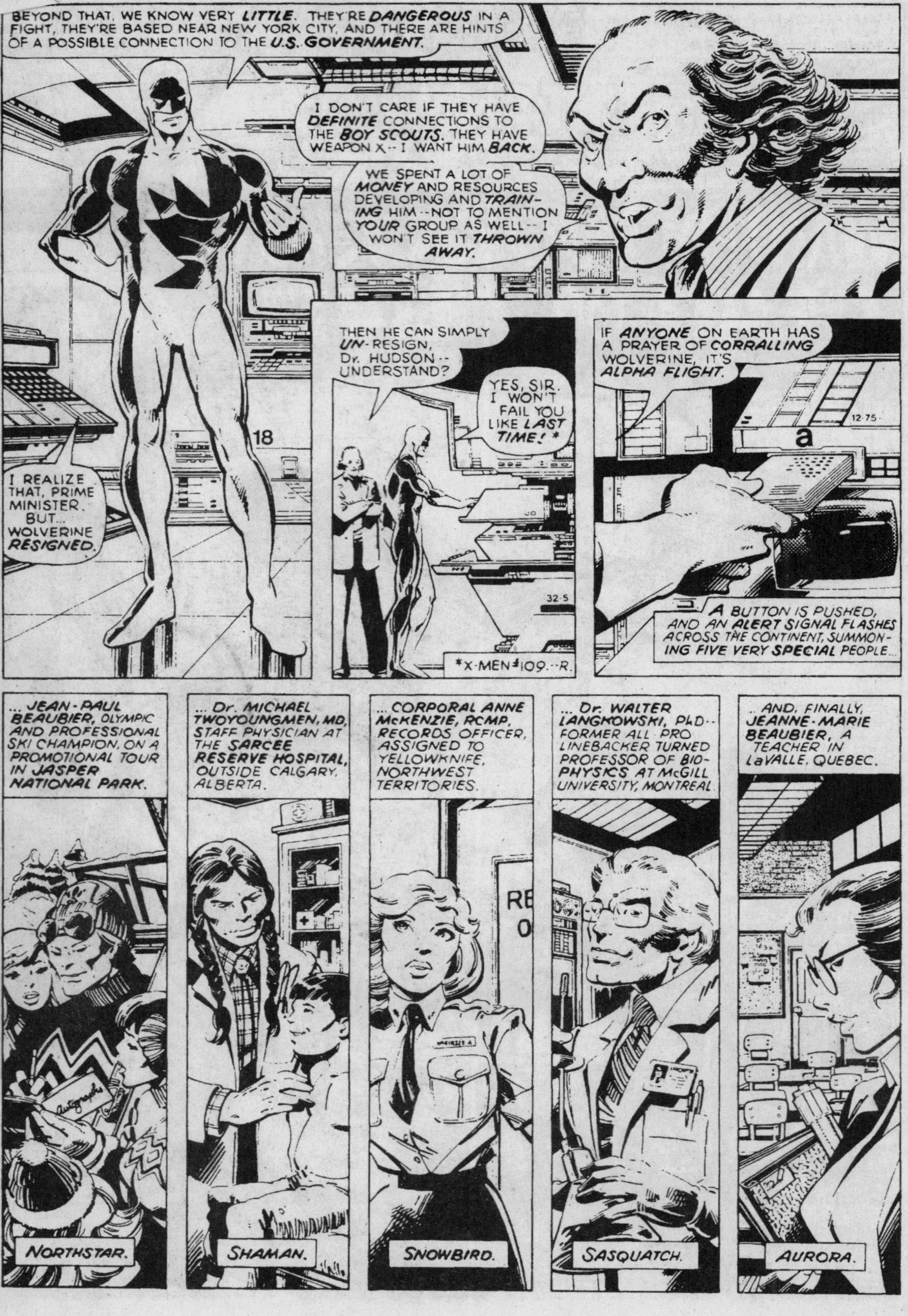

BEYOND THAT, WE KNOW VERY LITTLE. THEY'RE DANGEROUS IN A FIGHT, THEY'RE BASED NEAR NEW YORK CITY, AND THERE ARE HINTS OF A POSSIBLE CONNECTION TO THE U.S. GOVERNMENT.
I DON'T CARE IF THEY HAVE DEFINITE CONNECTIONS TO THE BOY SCOUTS. THEY HAVE WEAPON X-- I WANT HIM BACK.
WE SPENT A LOT OF MONEY AND RESOURCES DEVELOPING AND TRAINING HIM --NOT TO MENTION YOUR GROUP AS WELL-- I WON'T SEE IT THROWN AWAY.
I REALIZE THAT, PRIME MINISTER. BUT... WOLVERINE RESIGNED.
18
THEN HE CAN SIMPLY UN-RESIGN, Dr. HUDSON-- UNDERSTAND?
YES, SIR. I WON'T FAIL YOU LIKE LAST TIME! *
*X-MEN #109.--R.
IF ANYONE ON EARTH HAS A PRAYER OF CORRALLING WOLVERINE, IT'S ALPHA FLIGHT.
A BUTTON IS PUSHED, AND AN ALERT SIGNAL FLASHES ACROSS THE CONTINENT, SUMMONING FIVE VERY SPECIAL PEOPLE...
... JEAN-PAUL BEAUBIER, OLYMPIC AND PROFESSIONAL SKI CHAMPION, ON A PROMOTIONAL TOUR IN JASPER NATIONAL PARK.
NORTHSTAR.
... Dr. MICHAEL TWOYOUNGMEN, MD, STAFF PHYSICIAN AT THE SARCEE RESERVE HOSPITAL, OUTSIDE CALGARY, ALBERTA.
SHAMAN.
... CORPORAL ANNE McKENZIE, RCMP, RECORDS OFFICER, ASSIGNED TO YELLOWKNIFE, NORTHWEST TERRITORIES.
SNOWBIRD.
... Dr. WALTER LANGKOWSKI, PhD-- FORMER ALL-PRO LINEBACKER TURNED PROFESSOR OF BIO-PHYSICS AT McGILL UNIVERSITY, MONTREAL.
SASQUATCH.
.. AND, FINALLY, JEANNE-MARIE BEAUBIER, A TEACHER IN LaVALLE, QUEBEC.
AURORA.

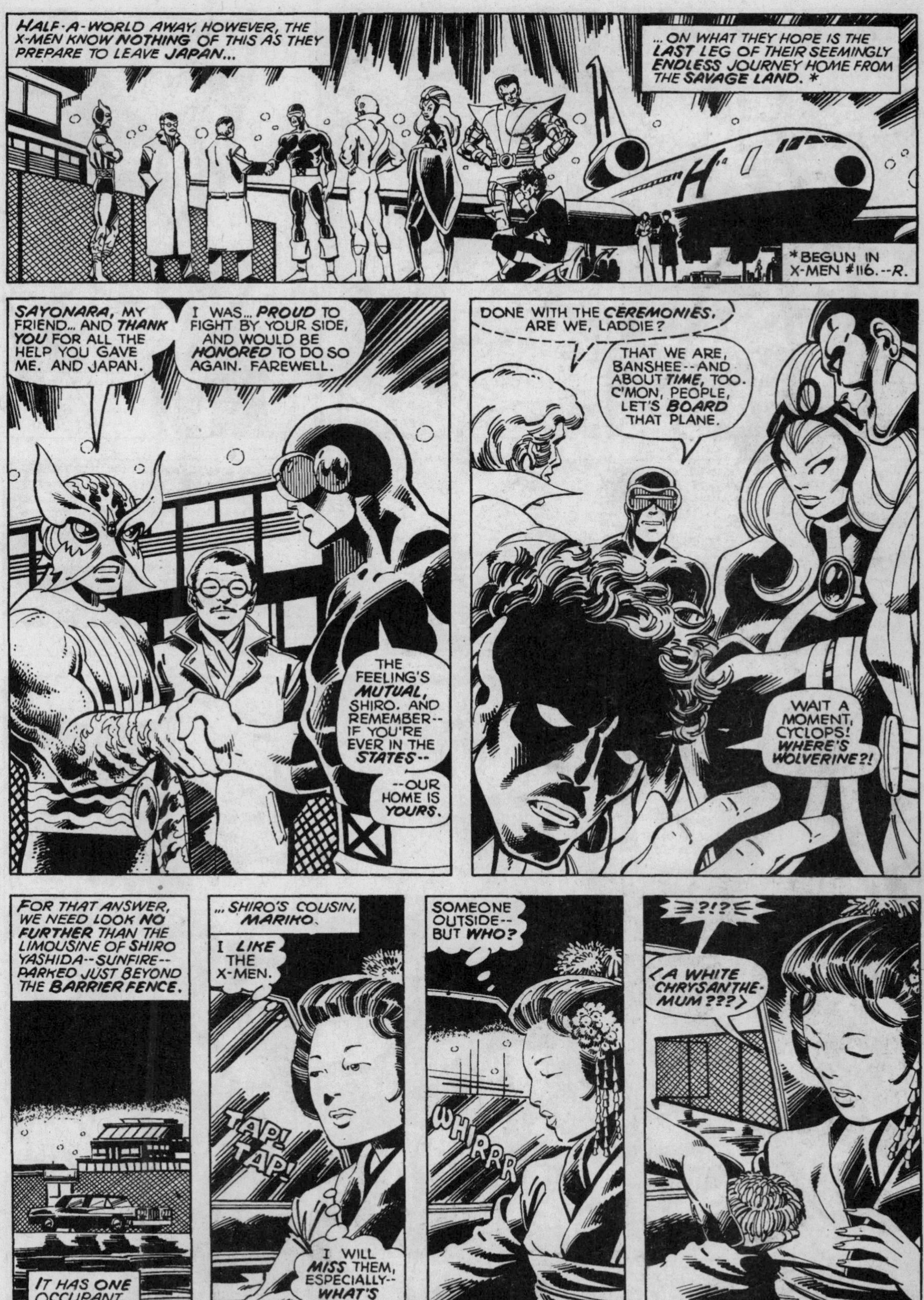
HALF-A-WORLD AWAY, HOWEVER, THE X-MEN KNOW NOTHING OF THIS AS THEY PREPARE TO LEAVE JAPAN...
...ON WHAT THEY HOPE IS THE LAST LEG OF THEIR SEEMINGLY ENDLESS JOURNEY HOME FROM THE SAVAGE LAND. *
*BEGUN IN X-MEN #116.--R.
SAYONARA, MY FRIEND... AND THANK YOU FOR ALL THE HELP YOU GAVE ME. AND JAPAN.
I WAS... PROUD TO FIGHT BY YOUR SIDE, AND WOULD BE HONORED TO DO SO AGAIN. FAREWELL.
THE FEELING'S MUTUAL, SHIRO. AND REMEMBER-- IF YOU'RE EVER IN THE STATES--
--OUR HOME IS YOURS.
DONE WITH THE CEREMONIES, ARE WE, LADDIE?
THAT WE ARE, BANSHEE--AND ABOUT TIME, TOO. C'MON, PEOPLE, LET'S BOARD THAT PLANE.
WAIT A MOMENT, CYCLOPS! WHERE'S WOLVERINE?!
FOR THAT ANSWER, WE NEED LOOK NO FURTHER THAN THE LIMOUSINE OF SHIRO YASHIDA--SUNFIRE--PARKED JUST BEYOND THE BARRIER FENCE.
IT HAS ONE OCCUPANT...
...SHIRO'S COUSIN, MARIKO.
I LIKE THE X-MEN.
TAP! TAP!
I WILL MISS THEM, ESPECIALLY-- WHAT'S THAT?!
SOMEONE OUTSIDE-- BUT WHO?
WHIRRR
?!?
<A WHITE CHRYSANTHEMUM???>

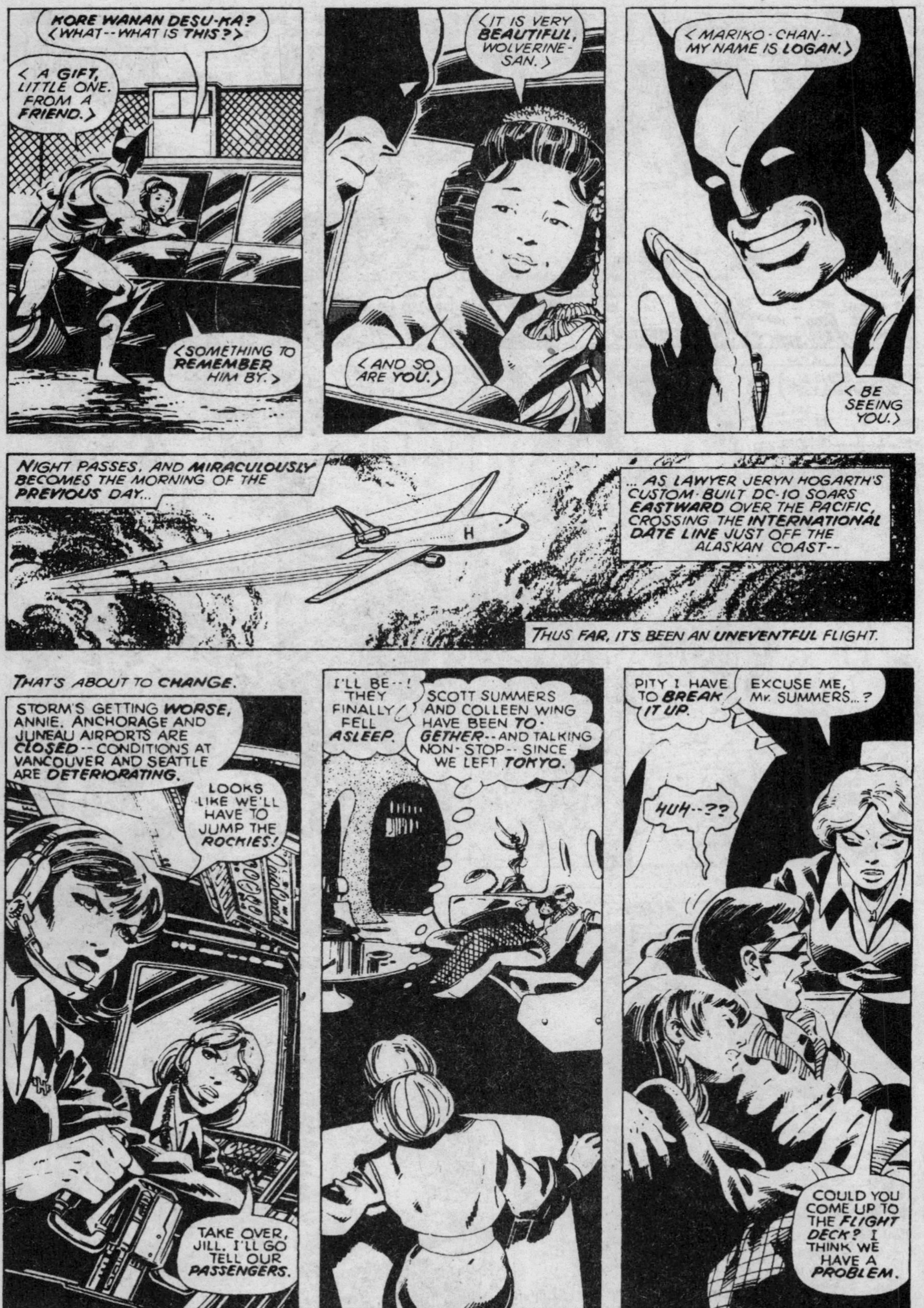
KORE WANAN DESU-KA? ⟨WHAT--WHAT IS THIS?⟩
⟨ A GIFT, LITTLE ONE. FROM A FRIEND.⟩
⟨SOMETHING TO REMEMBER HIM BY.⟩
⟨IT IS VERY BEAUTIFUL, WOLVERINE-SAN.⟩
⟨AND SO ARE YOU.⟩
⟨ MARIKO-CHAN-- MY NAME IS LOGAN.⟩
⟨ BE SEEING YOU.⟩
NIGHT PASSES, AND MIRACULOUSLY BECOMES THE MORNING OF THE PREVIOUS DAY...
...AS LAWYER JERYN HOGARTH'S CUSTOM-BUILT DC-10 SOARS EASTWARD OVER THE PACIFIC, CROSSING THE INTERNATIONAL DATE LINE JUST OFF THE ALASKAN COAST--
THUS FAR, IT'S BEEN AN UNEVENTFUL FLIGHT.
THAT'S ABOUT TO CHANGE.
STORM'S GETTING WORSE, ANNIE. ANCHORAGE AND JUNEAU AIRPORTS ARE CLOSED--CONDITIONS AT VANCOUVER AND SEATTLE ARE DETERIORATING.
LOOKS LIKE WE'LL HAVE TO JUMP THE ROCKIES!
TAKE OVER, JILL. I'LL GO TELL OUR PASSENGERS.
I'LL BE--! THEY FINALLY FELL ASLEEP.
SCOTT SUMMERS AND COLLEEN WING HAVE BEEN TO-GETHER--AND TALKING NON-STOP--SINCE WE LEFT TOKYO.
PITY I HAVE TO BREAK IT UP.
EXCUSE ME, Mr. SUMMERS...?
HUH--??
COULD YOU COME UP TO THE FLIGHT DECK? I THINK WE HAVE A PROBLEM.

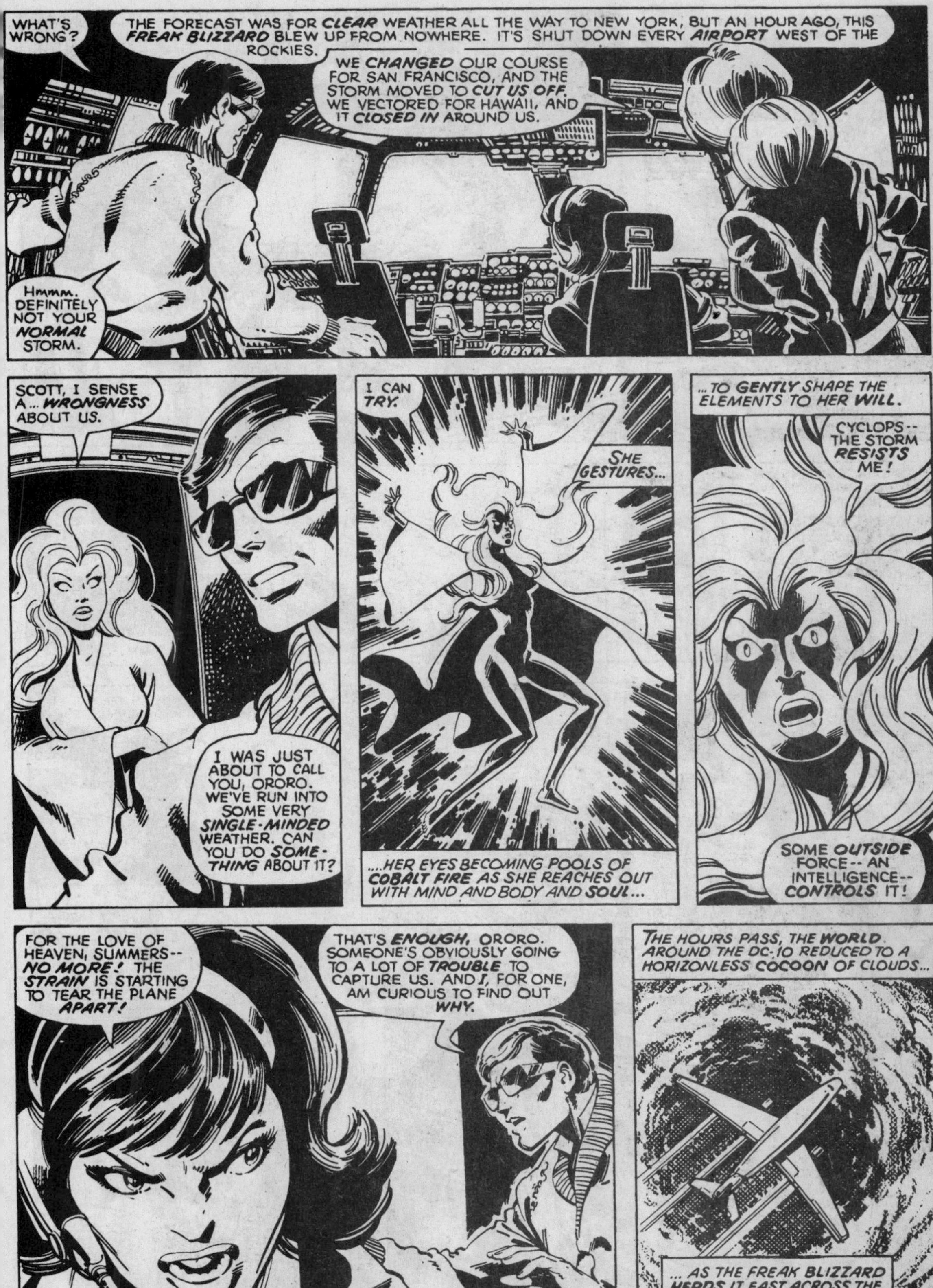
WHAT'S WRONG?
THE FORECAST WAS FOR CLEAR WEATHER ALL THE WAY TO NEW YORK, BUT AN HOUR AGO, THIS FREAK BLIZZARD BLEW UP FROM NOWHERE. IT'S SHUT DOWN EVERY AIRPORT WEST OF THE ROCKIES.
WE CHANGED OUR COURSE FOR SAN FRANCISCO, AND THE STORM MOVED TO CUT US OFF. WE VECTORED FOR HAWAII, AND IT CLOSED IN AROUND US.
Hmmm. DEFINITELY NOT YOUR NORMAL STORM.
SCOTT, I SENSE A... WRONGNESS ABOUT US.
I WAS JUST ABOUT TO CALL YOU, ORORO. WE'VE RUN INTO SOME VERY SINGLE-MINDED WEATHER. CAN YOU DO SOME-THING ABOUT IT?
I CAN TRY.
SHE GESTURES...
....HER EYES BECOMING POOLS OF COBALT FIRE AS SHE REACHES OUT WITH MIND AND BODY AND SOUL...
...TO GENTLY SHAPE THE ELEMENTS TO HER WILL.
CYCLOPS -- THE STORM RESISTS ME!
SOME OUTSIDE FORCE -- AN INTELLIGENCE -- CONTROLS IT!
FOR THE LOVE OF HEAVEN, SUMMERS -- NO MORE! THE STRAIN IS STARTING TO TEAR THE PLANE APART!
THAT'S ENOUGH, ORORO. SOMEONE'S OBVIOUSLY GOING TO A LOT OF TROUBLE TO CAPTURE US. AND I, FOR ONE, AM CURIOUS TO FIND OUT WHY.
THE HOURS PASS, THE WORLD AROUND THE DC-10 REDUCED TO A HORIZONLESS COCOON OF CLOUDS...
... AS THE FREAK BLIZZARD HERDS IT EAST ACROSS THE YUKON, THEN SOUTH INTO THE PROVINCE OF ALBERTA.

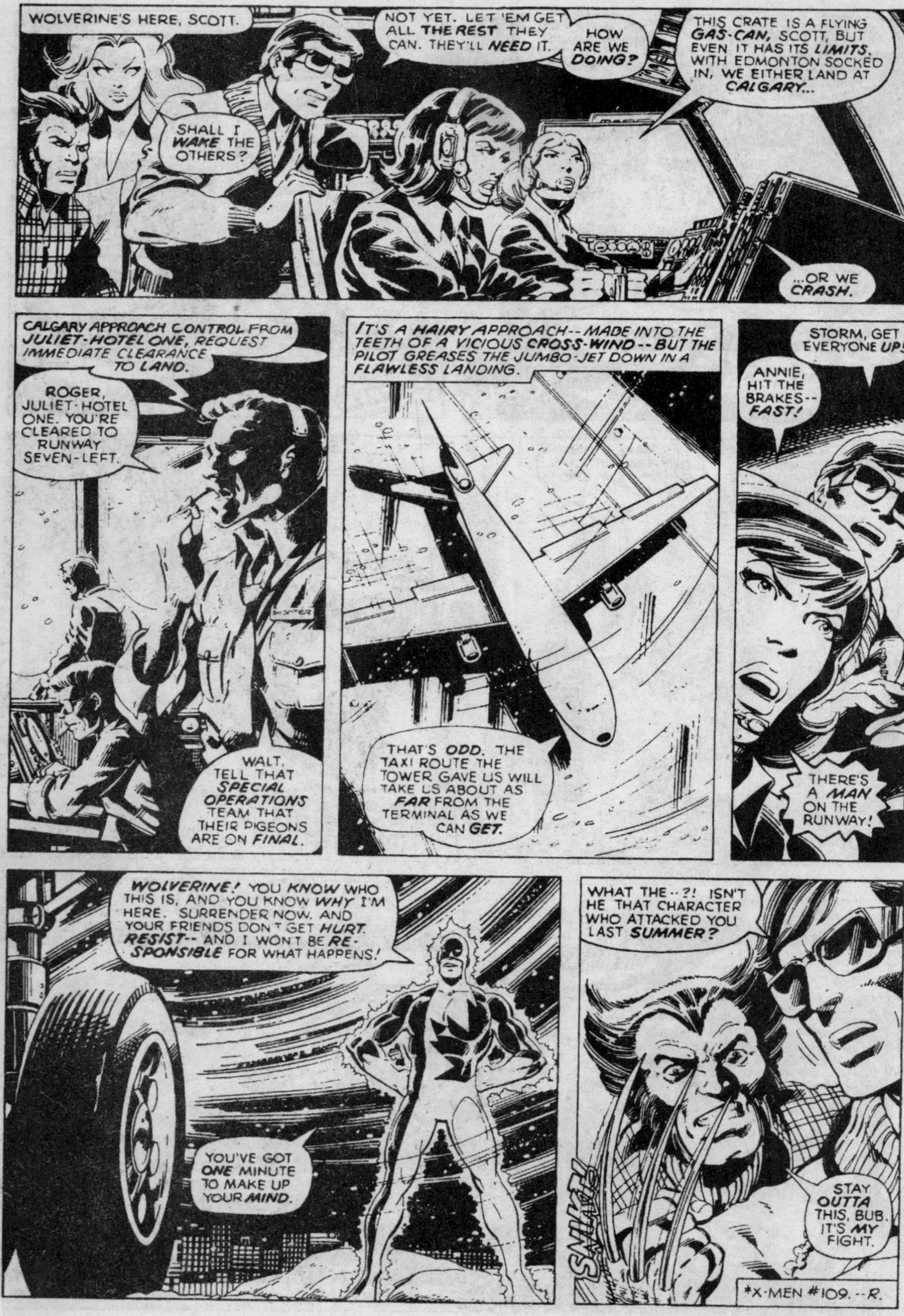
WOLVERINE'S HERE, SCOTT.
NOT YET. LET 'EM GET ALL THE REST THEY CAN. THEY'LL NEED IT.
SHALL I WAKE THE OTHERS?
HOW ARE WE DOING?
THIS CRATE IS A FLYING GAS-CAN, SCOTT, BUT EVEN IT HAS ITS LIMITS. WITH EDMONTON SOCKED IN, WE EITHER LAND AT CALGARY...
...OR WE CRASH.
CALGARY APPROACH CONTROL FROM JULIET-HOTEL ONE, REQUEST IMMEDIATE CLEARANCE TO LAND.
ROGER, JULIET-HOTEL ONE. YOU'RE CLEARED TO RUNWAY SEVEN-LEFT.
WALT, TELL THAT SPECIAL OPERATIONS TEAM THAT THEIR PIGEONS ARE ON FINAL.
IT'S A HAIRY APPROACH--MADE INTO THE TEETH OF A VICIOUS CROSS-WIND--BUT THE PILOT GREASES THE JUMBO-JET DOWN IN A FLAWLESS LANDING.
THAT'S ODD. THE TAXI ROUTE THE TOWER GAVE US WILL TAKE US ABOUT AS FAR FROM THE TERMINAL AS WE CAN GET.
STORM, GET EVERYONE UP!
ANNIE, HIT THE BRAKES--FAST!
THERE'S A MAN ON THE RUNWAY!
WOLVERINE! YOU KNOW WHO THIS IS, AND YOU KNOW WHY I'M HERE. SURRENDER NOW, AND YOUR FRIENDS DON'T GET HURT. RESIST-- AND I WON'T BE RESPONSIBLE FOR WHAT HAPPENS!
YOU'VE GOT ONE MINUTE TO MAKE UP YOUR MIND.
WHAT THE--?! ISN'T HE THAT CHARACTER WHO ATTACKED YOU LAST SUMMER?
SNIKT!
STAY OUTTA THIS, BUB. IT'S MY FIGHT.
*X-MEN #109.--R.

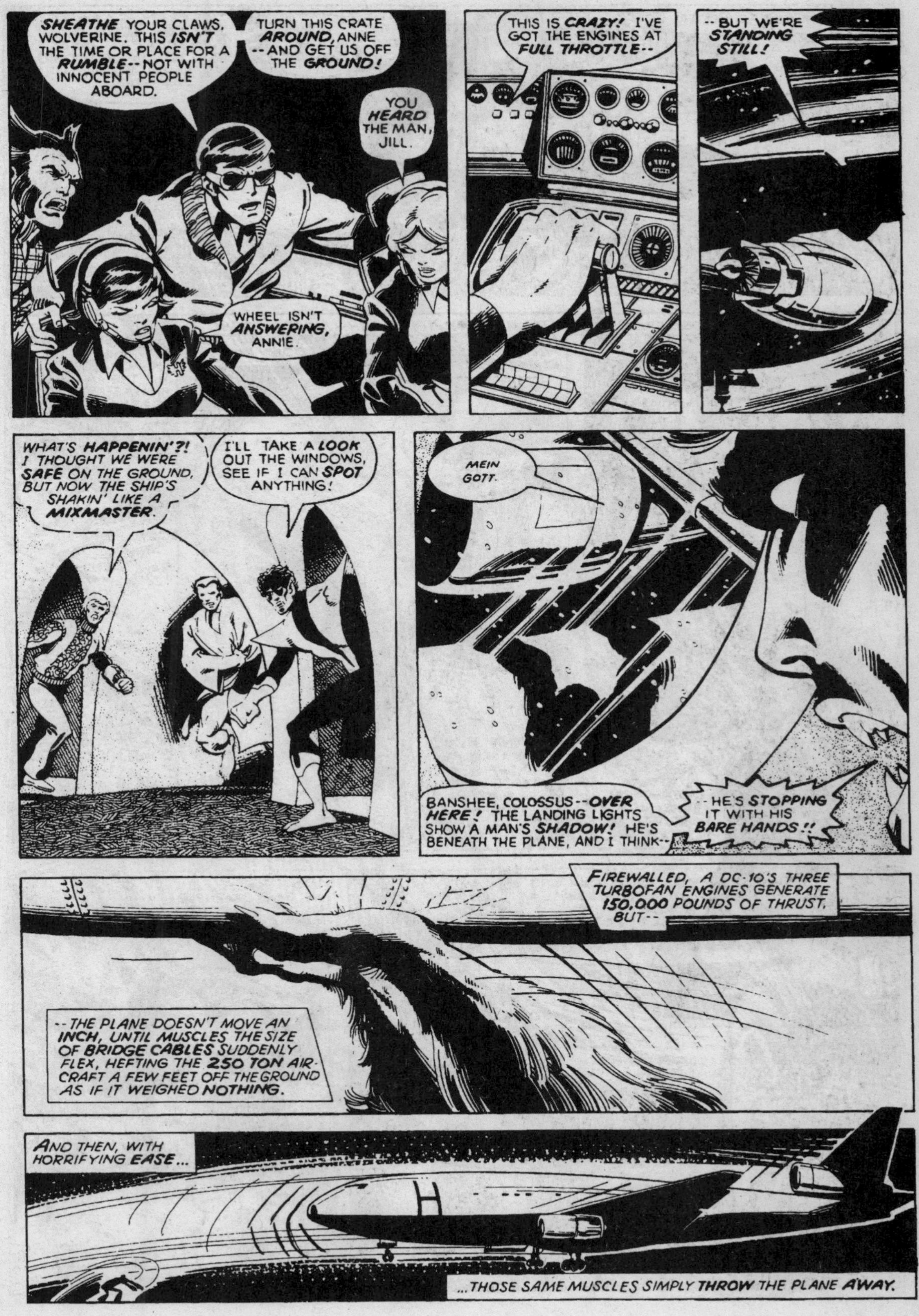
SHEATHE YOUR CLAWS, WOLVERINE. THIS ISN'T THE TIME OR PLACE FOR A RUMBLE--NOT WITH INNOCENT PEOPLE ABOARD.
TURN THIS CRATE AROUND, ANNE --AND GET US OFF THE GROUND!
YOU HEARD THE MAN, JILL.
WHEEL ISN'T ANSWERING, ANNIE.
THIS IS CRAZY! I'VE GOT THE ENGINES AT FULL THROTTLE--
--BUT WE'RE STANDING STILL!
WHAT'S HAPPENIN'?! I THOUGHT WE WERE SAFE ON THE GROUND, BUT NOW THE SHIP'S SHAKIN' LIKE A MIXMASTER.
I'LL TAKE A LOOK OUT THE WINDOWS, SEE IF I CAN SPOT ANYTHING!
MEIN GOTT.
BANSHEE, COLOSSUS--OVER HERE! THE LANDING LIGHTS SHOW A MAN'S SHADOW! HE'S BENEATH THE PLANE, AND I THINK--
--HE'S STOPPING IT WITH HIS BARE HANDS!!
FIREWALLED, A DC-10'S THREE TURBOFAN ENGINES GENERATE 150,000 POUNDS OF THRUST, BUT--
--THE PLANE DOESN'T MOVE AN INCH, UNTIL MUSCLES THE SIZE OF BRIDGE CABLES SUDDENLY FLEX, HEFTING THE 250 TON AIRCRAFT A FEW FEET OFF THE GROUND AS IF IT WEIGHED NOTHING.
AND THEN, WITH HORRIFYING EASE...
...THOSE SAME MUSCLES SIMPLY THROW THE PLANE AWAY.

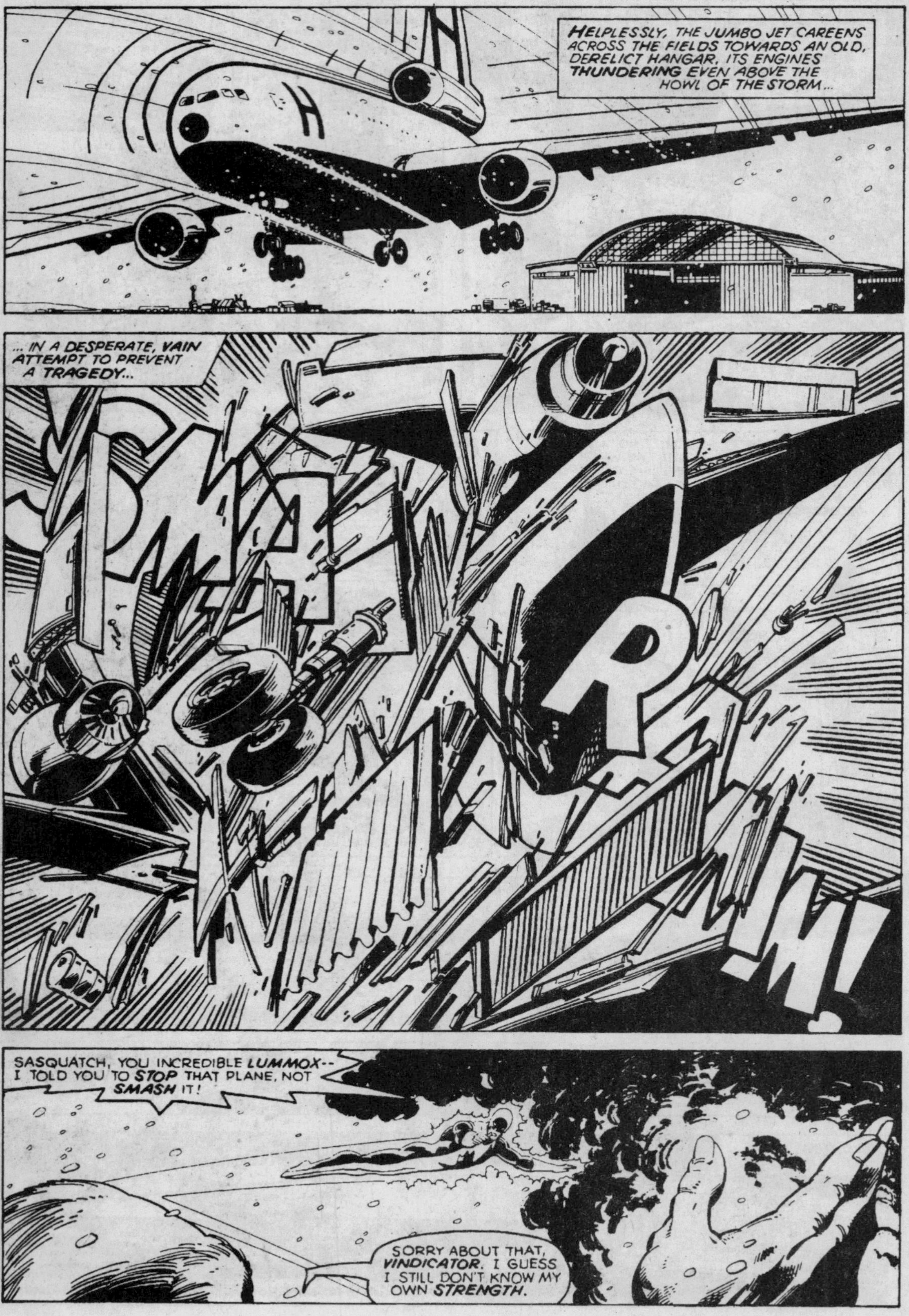
HELPLESSLY, THE JUMBO JET CAREENS ACROSS THE FIELDS TOWARDS AN OLD, DERELICT HANGAR, ITS ENGINES THUNDERING EVEN ABOVE THE HOWL OF THE STORM...
...IN A DESPERATE, VAIN ATTEMPT TO PREVENT A TRAGEDY...
SMARRM!
SASQUATCH, YOU INCREDIBLE LUMMOX-- I TOLD YOU TO STOP THAT PLANE, NOT SMASH IT!
SORRY ABOUT THAT, VINDICATOR. I GUESS I STILL DON'T KNOW MY OWN STRENGTH.

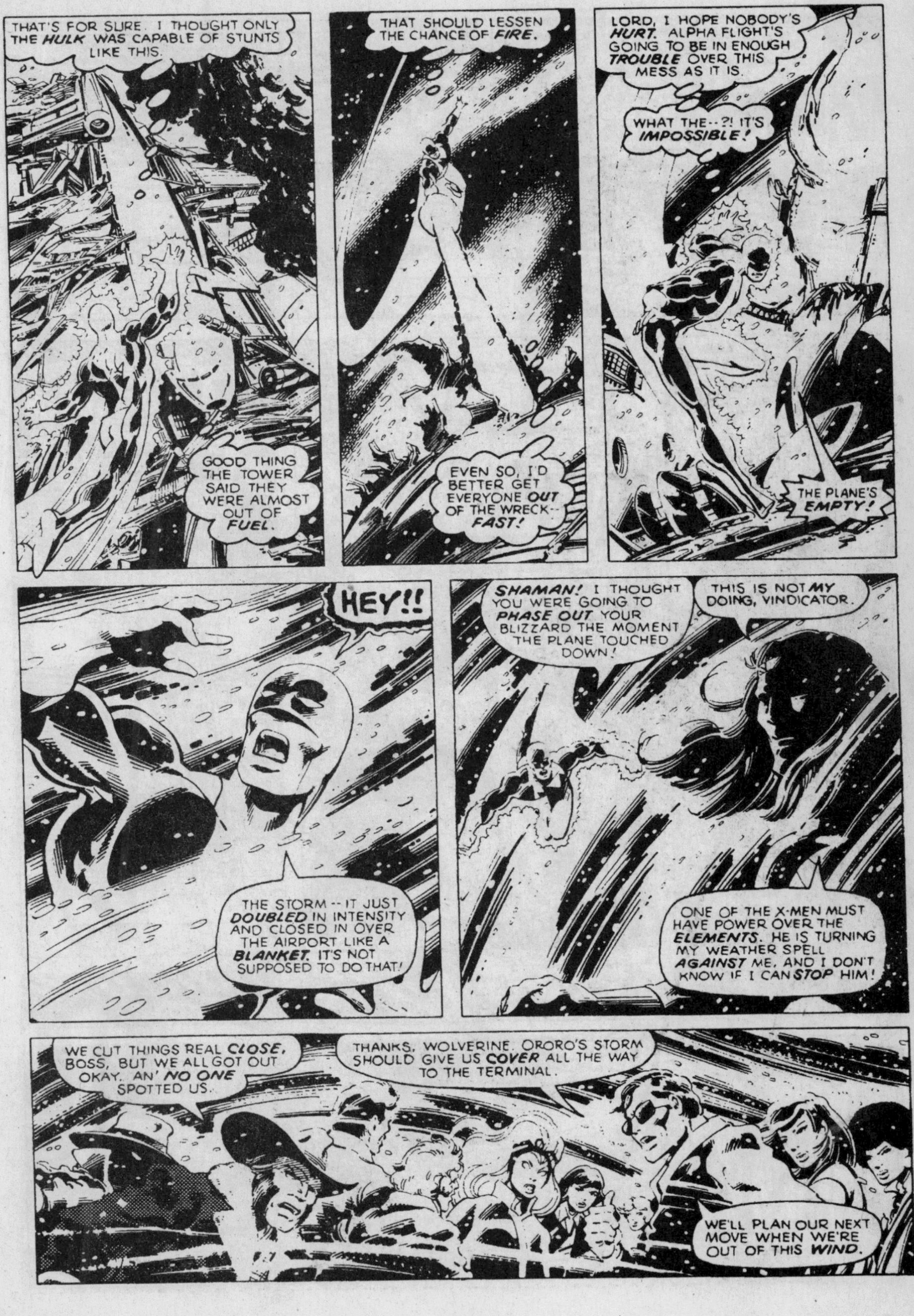
THAT'S FOR SURE. I THOUGHT ONLY THE HULK WAS CAPABLE OF STUNTS LIKE THIS.
GOOD THING THE TOWER SAID THEY WERE ALMOST OUT OF FUEL.
THAT SHOULD LESSEN THE CHANCE OF FIRE.
EVEN SO, I'D BETTER GET EVERYONE OUT OF THE WRECK-- FAST!
LORD, I HOPE NOBODY'S HURT. ALPHA FLIGHT'S GOING TO BE IN ENOUGH TROUBLE OVER THIS MESS AS IT IS.
WHAT THE--?! IT'S IMPOSSIBLE!
THE PLANE'S EMPTY!
HEY!!
THE STORM -- IT JUST DOUBLED IN INTENSITY AND CLOSED IN OVER THE AIRPORT LIKE A BLANKET. IT'S NOT SUPPOSED TO DO THAT!
SHAMAN! I THOUGHT YOU WERE GOING TO PHASE OUT YOUR BLIZZARD THE MOMENT THE PLANE TOUCHED DOWN!
THIS IS NOT MY DOING, VINDICATOR.
ONE OF THE X-MEN MUST HAVE POWER OVER THE ELEMENTS. HE IS TURNING MY WEATHER SPELL AGAINST ME, AND I DON'T KNOW IF I CAN STOP HIM!
WE CUT THINGS REAL CLOSE, BOSS, BUT WE ALL GOT OUT OKAY. AN' NO ONE SPOTTED US.
THANKS, WOLVERINE. ORORO'S STORM SHOULD GIVE US COVER ALL THE WAY TO THE TERMINAL.
WE'LL PLAN OUR NEXT MOVE WHEN WE'RE OUT OF THIS WIND.

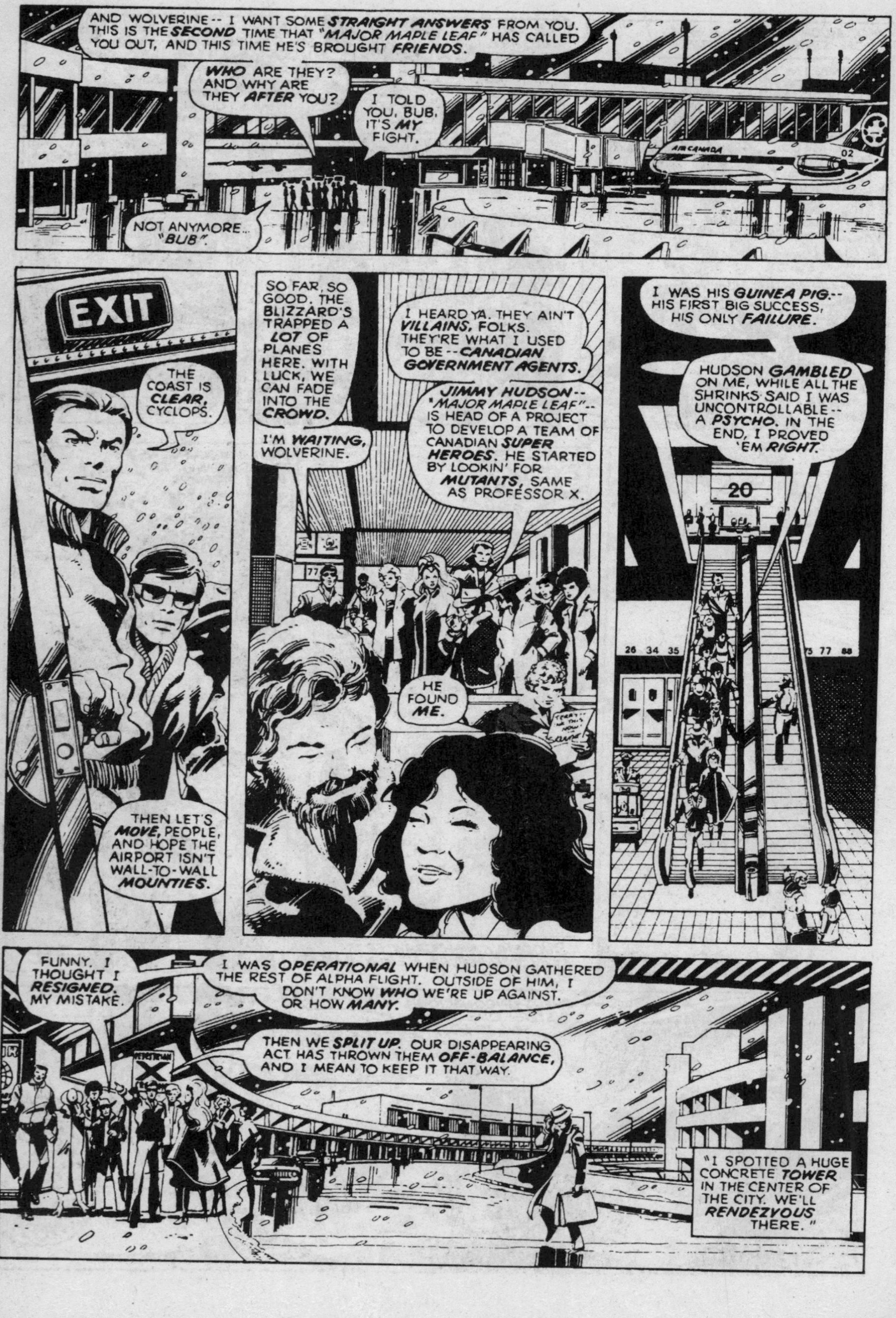
AND WOLVERINE-- I WANT SOME STRAIGHT ANSWERS FROM YOU. THIS IS THE SECOND TIME THAT "MAJOR MAPLE LEAF" HAS CALLED YOU OUT, AND THIS TIME HE'S BROUGHT FRIENDS.
WHO ARE THEY? AND WHY ARE THEY AFTER YOU?
I TOLD YOU, BUB. IT'S MY FIGHT.
NOT ANYMORE... "BUB".
AIR CANADA
EXIT
THE COAST IS CLEAR, CYCLOPS.
THEN LET'S MOVE, PEOPLE, AND HOPE THE AIRPORT ISN'T WALL-TO-WALL MOUNTIES.
SO FAR, SO GOOD. THE BLIZZARD'S TRAPPED A LOT OF PLANES HERE. WITH LUCK, WE CAN FADE INTO THE CROWD.
I'M WAITING, WOLVERINE.
I HEARD YA. THEY AIN'T VILLAINS, FOLKS. THEY'RE WHAT I USED TO BE--CANADIAN GOVERNMENT AGENTS.
JIMMY HUDSON-- "MAJOR MAPLE LEAF"-- IS HEAD OF A PROJECT TO DEVELOP A TEAM OF CANADIAN SUPER HEROES. HE STARTED BY LOOKIN' FOR MUTANTS, SAME AS PROFESSOR X.
HE FOUND ME.
I WAS HIS GUINEA PIG-- HIS FIRST BIG SUCCESS, HIS ONLY FAILURE.
HUDSON GAMBLED ON ME, WHILE ALL THE SHRINKS SAID I WAS UNCONTROLLABLE-- A PSYCHO. IN THE END, I PROVED 'EM RIGHT.
20
FUNNY. I THOUGHT I RESIGNED. MY MISTAKE.
I WAS OPERATIONAL WHEN HUDSON GATHERED THE REST OF ALPHA FLIGHT. OUTSIDE OF HIM, I DON'T KNOW WHO WE'RE UP AGAINST. OR HOW MANY.
THEN WE SPLIT UP. OUR DISAPPEARING ACT HAS THROWN THEM OFF-BALANCE, AND I MEAN TO KEEP IT THAT WAY.
"I SPOTTED A HUGE CONCRETE TOWER IN THE CENTER OF THE CITY. WE'LL RENDEZVOUS THERE."

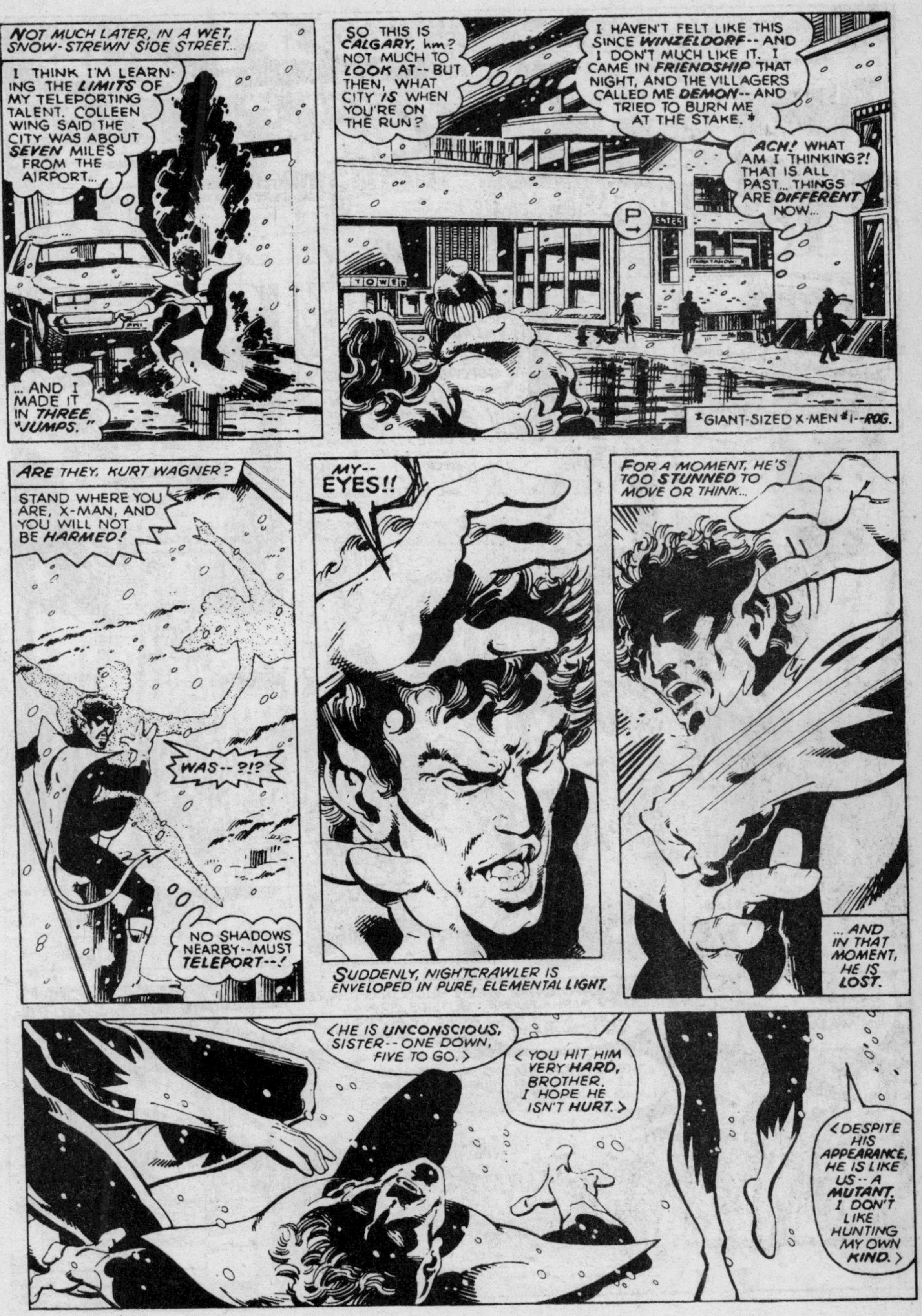

NOT MUCH LATER, IN A WET, SNOW-STREWN SIDE STREET...
I THINK I'M LEARNING THE LIMITS OF MY TELEPORTING TALENT. COLLEEN WING SAID THE CITY WAS ABOUT SEVEN MILES FROM THE AIRPORT...
...AND I MADE IT IN THREE "JUMPS."
SO THIS IS CALGARY, hm? NOT MUCH TO LOOK AT--BUT THEN, WHAT CITY IS WHEN YOU'RE ON THE RUN?
I HAVEN'T FELT LIKE THIS SINCE WINZELDORF--AND I DON'T MUCH LIKE IT. I CAME IN FRIENDSHIP THAT NIGHT, AND THE VILLAGERS CALLED ME DEMON--AND TRIED TO BURN ME AT THE STAKE.*
ACH! WHAT AM I THINKING?! THAT IS ALL PAST... THINGS ARE DIFFERENT NOW...
P
ENTER
TOWE
*GIANT-SIZED X-MEN #1--ROG.
ARE THEY, KURT WAGNER?
STAND WHERE YOU ARE, X-MAN, AND YOU WILL NOT BE HARMED!
WAS--?!?
NO SHADOWS NEARBY--MUST TELEPORT--!
MY--EYES!!
SUDDENLY, NIGHTCRAWLER IS ENVELOPED IN PURE, ELEMENTAL LIGHT.
FOR A MOMENT, HE'S TOO STUNNED TO MOVE OR THINK...
...AND IN THAT MOMENT, HE IS LOST.
<HE IS UNCONSCIOUS, SISTER--ONE DOWN, FIVE TO GO.>
<YOU HIT HIM VERY HARD, BROTHER. I HOPE HE ISN'T HURT.>
<DESPITE HIS APPEARANCE, HE IS LIKE US--A MUTANT. I DON'T LIKE HUNTING MY OWN KIND.>

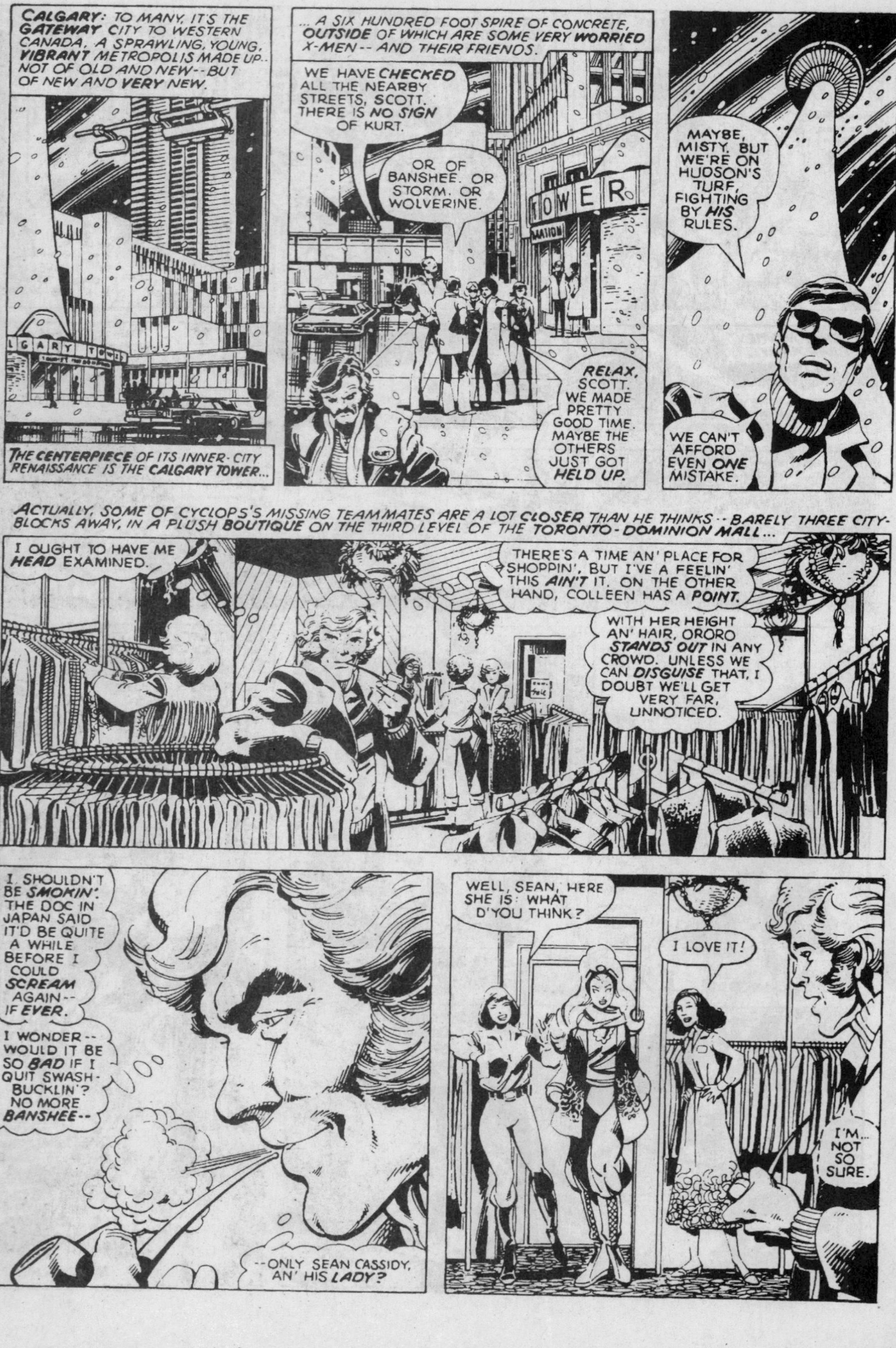
CALGARY: TO MANY, IT'S THE GATEWAY CITY TO WESTERN CANADA, A SPRAWLING, YOUNG, VIBRANT METROPOLIS MADE UP... NOT OF OLD AND NEW--BUT OF NEW AND VERY NEW.
THE CENTERPIECE OF ITS INNER-CITY RENAISSANCE IS THE CALGARY TOWER...
...A SIX HUNDRED FOOT SPIRE OF CONCRETE, OUTSIDE OF WHICH ARE SOME VERY WORRIED X-MEN -- AND THEIR FRIENDS.
WE HAVE CHECKED ALL THE NEARBY STREETS, SCOTT. THERE IS NO SIGN OF KURT.
OR OF BANSHEE. OR STORM. OR WOLVERINE.
TOWER
RELAX, SCOTT. WE MADE PRETTY GOOD TIME. MAYBE THE OTHERS JUST GOT HELD UP.
MAYBE, MISTY. BUT WE'RE ON HUDSON'S TURF, FIGHTING BY HIS RULES.
WE CAN'T AFFORD EVEN ONE MISTAKE.
ACTUALLY, SOME OF CYCLOPS'S MISSING TEAMMATES ARE A LOT CLOSER THAN HE THINKS -- BARELY THREE CITY-BLOCKS AWAY, IN A PLUSH BOUTIQUE ON THE THIRD LEVEL OF THE TORONTO-DOMINION MALL...
I OUGHT TO HAVE ME HEAD EXAMINED.
THERE'S A TIME AN' PLACE FOR SHOPPIN', BUT I'VE A FEELIN' THIS AIN'T IT. ON THE OTHER HAND, COLLEEN HAS A POINT.
WITH HER HEIGHT AN' HAIR, ORORO STANDS OUT IN ANY CROWD. UNLESS WE CAN DISGUISE THAT, I DOUBT WE'LL GET VERY FAR, UNNOTICED.
I SHOULDN'T BE SMOKIN'. THE DOC IN JAPAN SAID IT'D BE QUITE A WHILE BEFORE I COULD SCREAM AGAIN-- IF EVER.
I WONDER-- WOULD IT BE SO BAD IF I QUIT SWASH-BUCKLIN'? NO MORE BANSHEE--
--ONLY SEAN CASSIDY, AN' HIS LADY?
WELL, SEAN, HERE SHE IS: WHAT D'YOU THINK?
I LOVE IT!
I'M... NOT SO SURE.

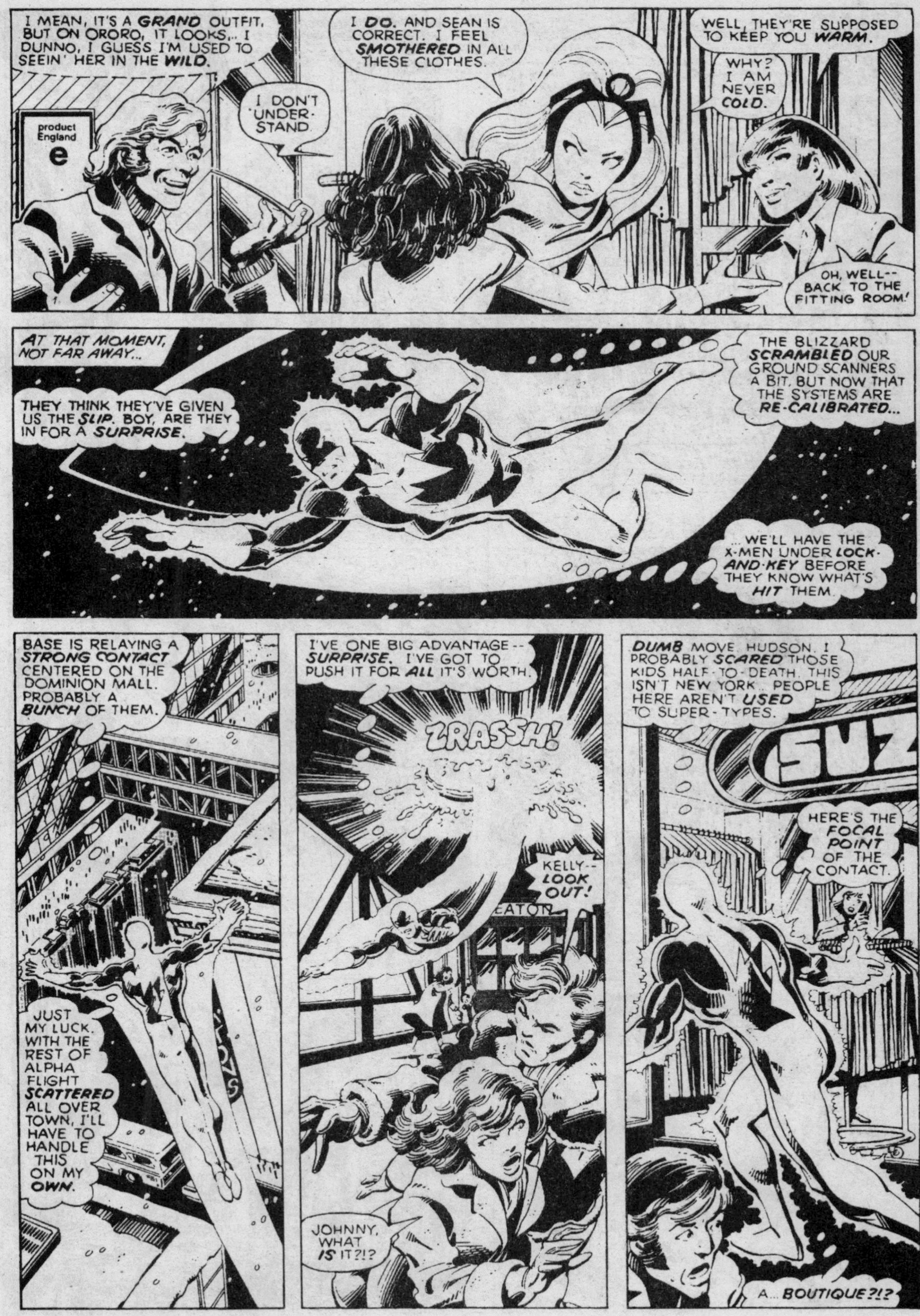

I MEAN, IT'S A GRAND OUTFIT, BUT ON ORORO, IT LOOKS... I DUNNO, I GUESS I'M USED TO SEEIN' HER IN THE WILD.
product England e
I DON'T UNDER-STAND.
I DO. AND SEAN IS CORRECT. I FEEL SMOTHERED IN ALL THESE CLOTHES.
WELL, THEY'RE SUPPOSED TO KEEP YOU WARM.
WHY? I AM NEVER COLD.
OH, WELL-- BACK TO THE FITTING ROOM!
AT THAT MOMENT, NOT FAR AWAY...
THEY THINK THEY'VE GIVEN US THE SLIP. BOY, ARE THEY IN FOR A SURPRISE.
THE BLIZZARD SCRAMBLED OUR GROUND SCANNERS A BIT, BUT NOW THAT THE SYSTEMS ARE RE-CALIBRATED...
...WE'LL HAVE THE X-MEN UNDER LOCK-AND-KEY BEFORE THEY KNOW WHAT'S HIT THEM.
BASE IS RELAYING A STRONG CONTACT CENTERED ON THE DOMINION MALL. PROBABLY A BUNCH OF THEM.
JUST MY LUCK. WITH THE REST OF ALPHA FLIGHT SCATTERED ALL OVER TOWN, I'LL HAVE TO HANDLE THIS ON MY OWN.
I'VE ONE BIG ADVANTAGE-- SURPRISE. I'VE GOT TO PUSH IT FOR ALL IT'S WORTH.
ZRASSH!
KELLY-- LOOK OUT!
EATON
JOHNNY, WHAT IS IT?!?
DUMB MOVE, HUDSON. I PROBABLY SCARED THOSE KIDS HALF-TO-DEATH. THIS ISN'T NEW YORK... PEOPLE HERE AREN'T USED TO SUPER-TYPES.
SUZ
HERE'S THE FOCAL POINT OF THE CONTACT.
A... BOUTIQUE?!?

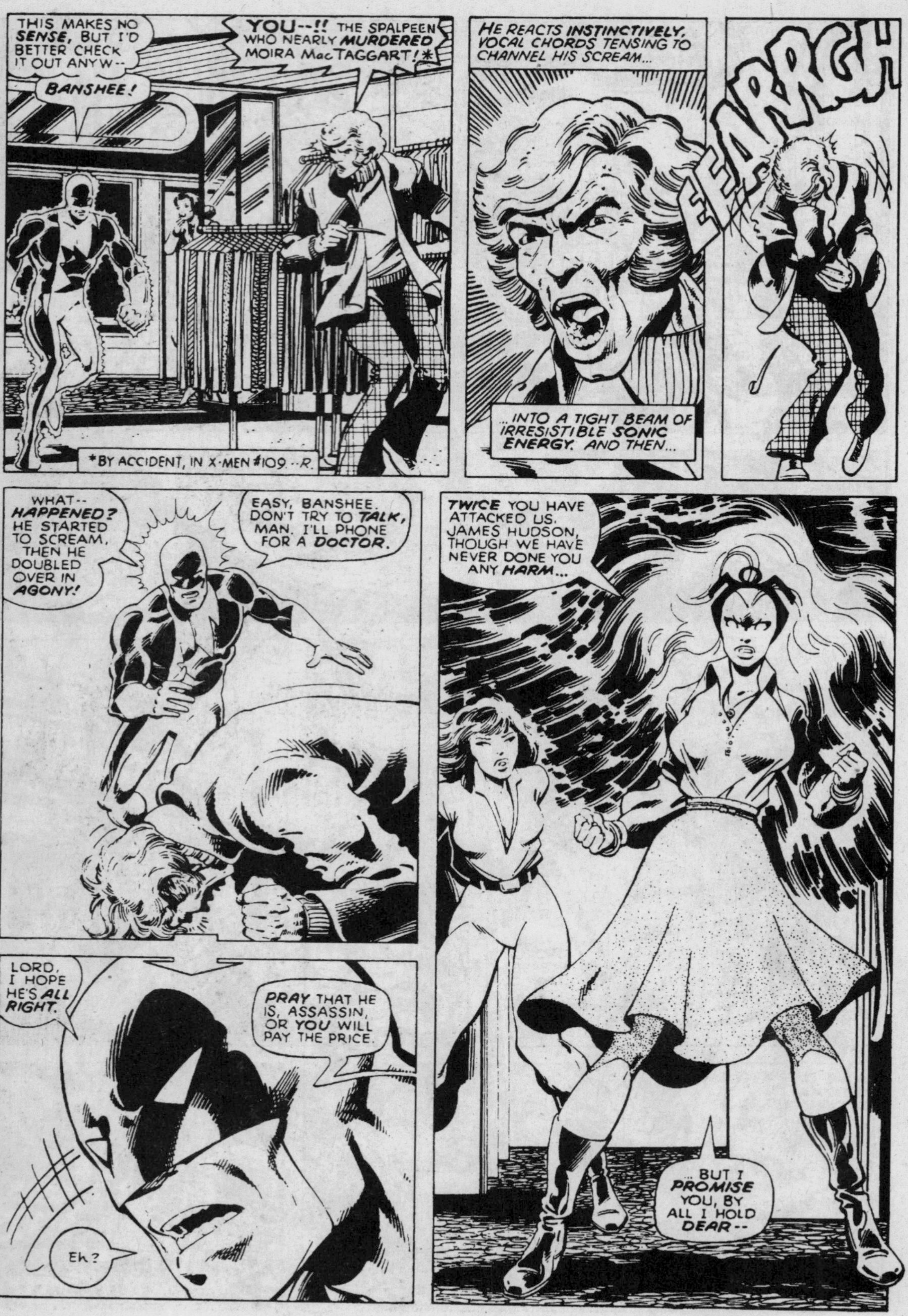
THIS MAKES NO SENSE, BUT I'D BETTER CHECK IT OUT ANYW--
BANSHEE!
YOU--!! THE SPALPEEN WHO NEARLY MURDERED MOIRA MacTAGGART!*
*BY ACCIDENT, IN X-MEN #109.--R.
HE REACTS INSTINCTIVELY, VOCAL CHORDS TENSING TO CHANNEL HIS SCREAM...
...INTO A TIGHT BEAM OF IRRESISTIBLE SONIC ENERGY. AND THEN...
EEARRGH
WHAT--HAPPENED? HE STARTED TO SCREAM, THEN HE DOUBLED OVER IN AGONY!
EASY, BANSHEE. DON'T TRY TO TALK, MAN. I'LL PHONE FOR A DOCTOR.
LORD, I HOPE HE'S ALL RIGHT.
PRAY THAT HE IS, ASSASSIN, OR YOU WILL PAY THE PRICE.
Eh?
TWICE YOU HAVE ATTACKED US, JAMES HUDSON, THOUGH WE HAVE NEVER DONE YOU ANY HARM...
...BUT I PROMISE YOU, BY ALL I HOLD DEAR--

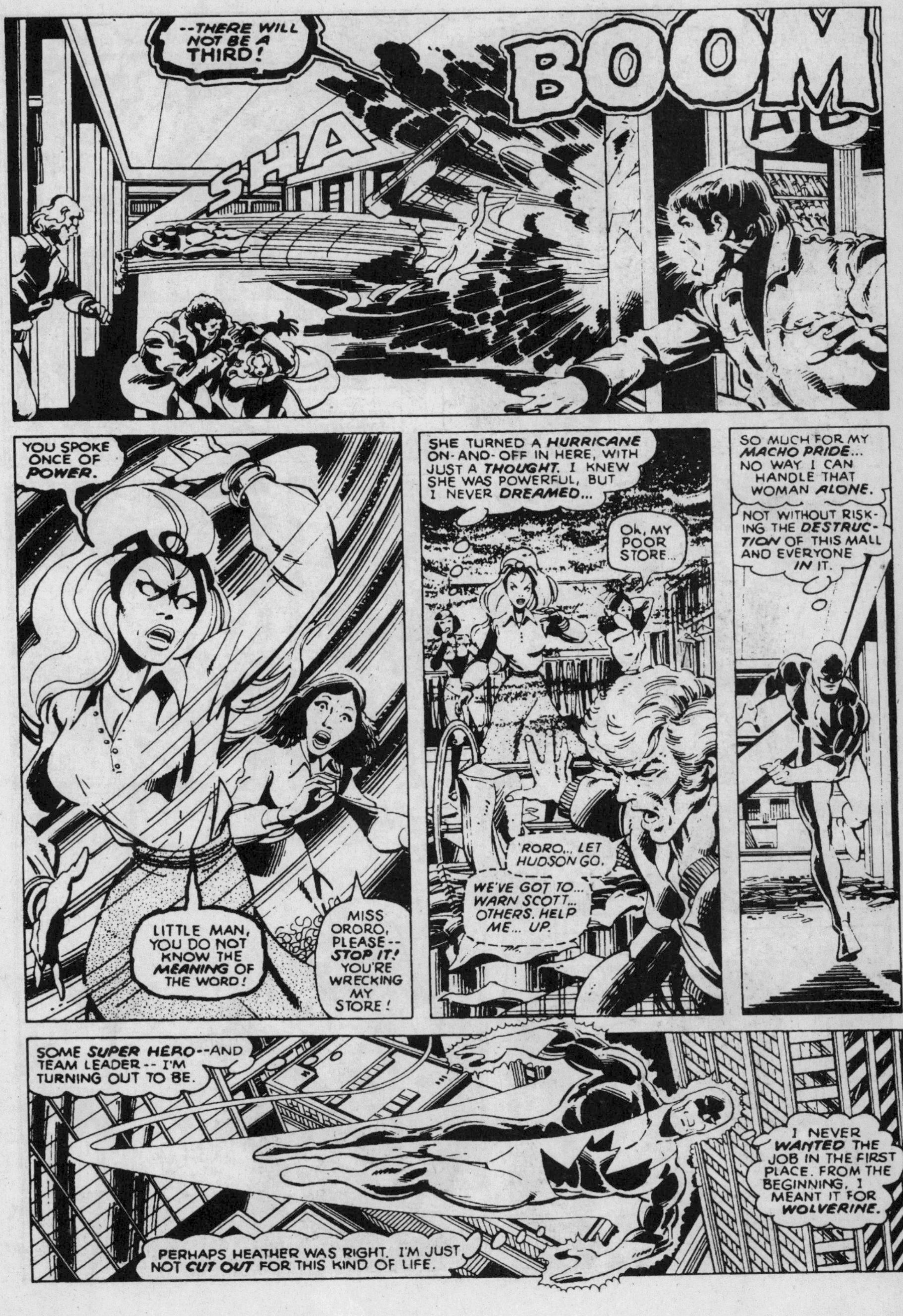
--THERE WILL NOT BE A THIRD!
SHA
BOOM
YOU SPOKE ONCE OF POWER.
LITTLE MAN, YOU DO NOT KNOW THE MEANING OF THE WORD!
MISS ORORO, PLEASE-- STOP IT! YOU'RE WRECKING MY STORE!
SHE TURNED A HURRICANE ON-AND-OFF IN HERE, WITH JUST A THOUGHT. I KNEW SHE WAS POWERFUL, BUT I NEVER DREAMED...
OH, MY POOR STORE...
'RORO... LET HUDSON GO.
WE'VE GOT TO... WARN SCOTT... OTHERS. HELP ME... UP.
SO MUCH FOR MY MACHO PRIDE... NO WAY I CAN HANDLE THAT WOMAN ALONE.
NOT WITHOUT RISKING THE DESTRUCTION OF THIS MALL AND EVERYONE IN IT.
SOME SUPER HERO--AND TEAM LEADER-- I'M TURNING OUT TO BE.
I NEVER WANTED THE JOB IN THE FIRST PLACE. FROM THE BEGINNING, I MEANT IT FOR WOLVERINE.
PERHAPS HEATHER WAS RIGHT. I'M JUST NOT CUT OUT FOR THIS KIND OF LIFE.

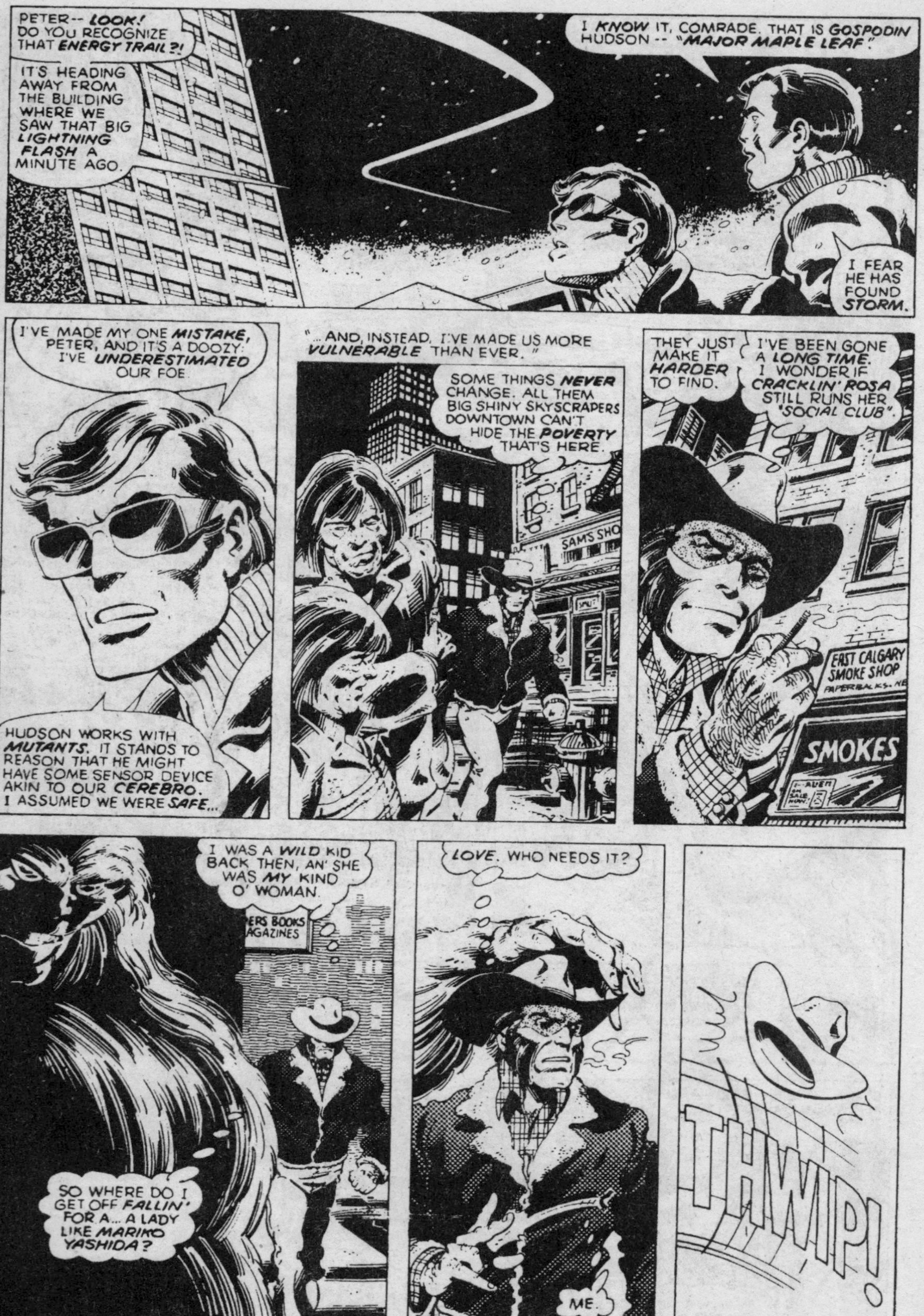

PETER-- LOOK! DO YOU RECOGNIZE THAT ENERGY TRAIL?!
IT'S HEADING AWAY FROM THE BUILDING WHERE WE SAW THAT BIG LIGHTNING FLASH A MINUTE AGO.
I KNOW IT, COMRADE. THAT IS GOSPODIN HUDSON -- "MAJOR MAPLE LEAF".
I FEAR HE HAS FOUND STORM.
I'VE MADE MY ONE MISTAKE, PETER, AND IT'S A DOOZY: I'VE UNDERESTIMATED OUR FOE.
HUDSON WORKS WITH MUTANTS. IT STANDS TO REASON THAT HE MIGHT HAVE SOME SENSOR DEVICE AKIN TO OUR CEREBRO. I ASSUMED WE WERE SAFE...
"... AND, INSTEAD, I'VE MADE US MORE VULNERABLE THAN EVER."
SOME THINGS NEVER CHANGE. ALL THEM BIG SHINY SKYSCRAPERS DOWNTOWN CAN'T HIDE THE POVERTY THAT'S HERE.
SAM'S SHO
THEY JUST MAKE IT HARDER TO FIND.
I'VE BEEN GONE A LONG TIME. I WONDER IF CRACKLIN' ROSA STILL RUNS HER "SOCIAL CLUB".
EAST CALGARY SMOKE SHOP
SMOKES
I WAS A WILD KID BACK THEN, AN' SHE WAS MY KIND O' WOMAN.
PERS BOOKS
AGAZINES
SO WHERE DO I GET OFF FALLIN' FOR A... A LADY LIKE MARIKO YASHIDA?
LOVE. WHO NEEDS IT?
ME.
THWIP!

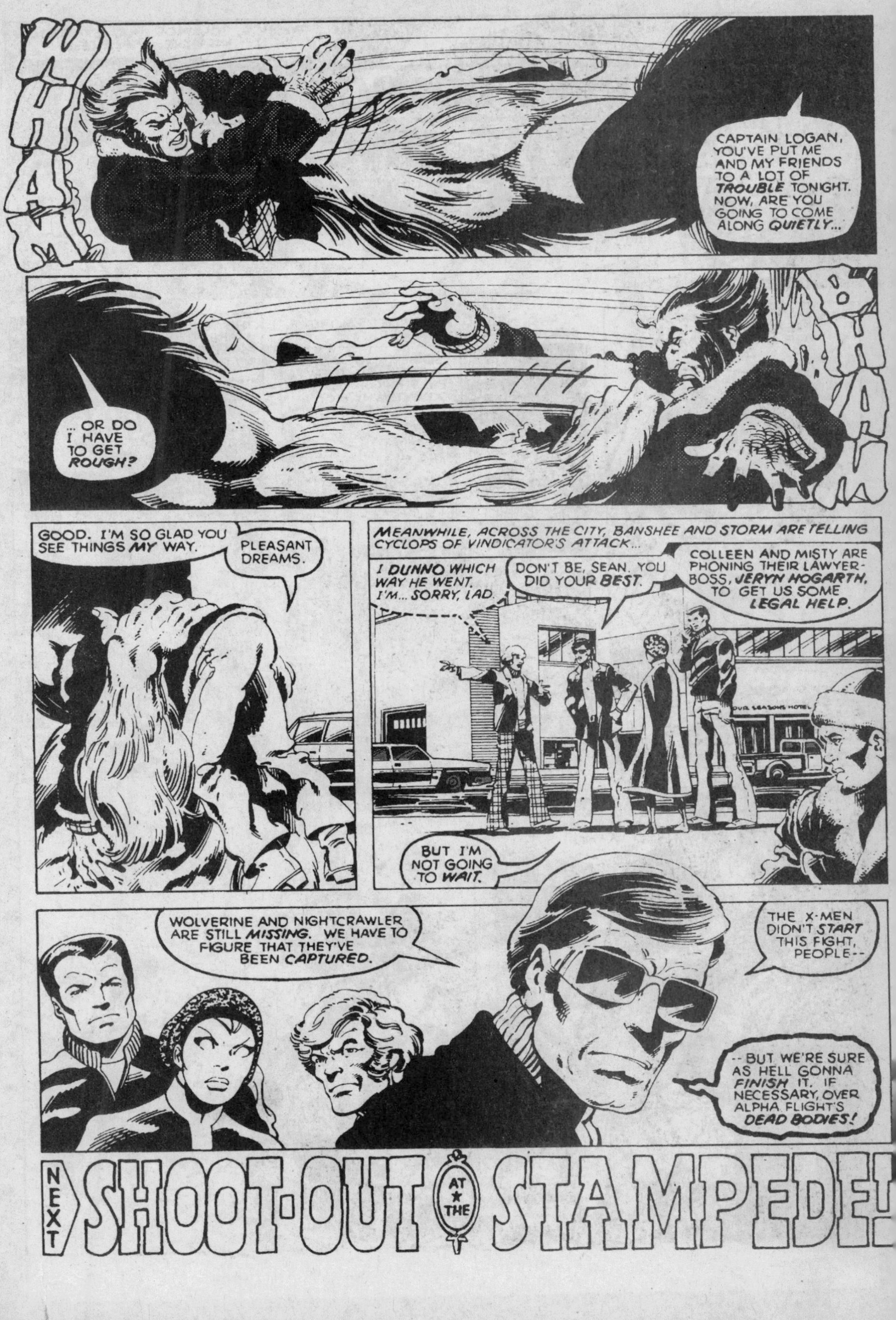
WHAM
CAPTAIN LOGAN, YOU'VE PUT ME AND MY FRIENDS TO A LOT OF TROUBLE TONIGHT. NOW, ARE YOU GOING TO COME ALONG QUIETLY...
...OR DO I HAVE TO GET ROUGH?
BHAM
GOOD. I'M SO GLAD YOU SEE THINGS MY WAY.
PLEASANT DREAMS.
MEANWHILE, ACROSS THE CITY, BANSHEE AND STORM ARE TELLING CYCLOPS OF VINDICATOR'S ATTACK...
I DUNNO WHICH WAY HE WENT. I'M... SORRY, LAD.
DON'T BE, SEAN. YOU DID YOUR BEST.
COLLEEN AND MISTY ARE PHONING THEIR LAWYER-BOSS, JERYN HOGARTH, TO GET US SOME LEGAL HELP.
BUT I'M NOT GOING TO WAIT.
WOLVERINE AND NIGHTCRAWLER ARE STILL MISSING. WE HAVE TO FIGURE THAT THEY'VE BEEN CAPTURED.
THE X-MEN DIDN'T START THIS FIGHT, PEOPLE--
--BUT WE'RE SURE AS HELL GONNA FINISH IT. IF NECESSARY, OVER ALPHA FLIGHT'S DEAD BODIES!
NEXT SHOOT-OUT AT THE STAMPEDE!

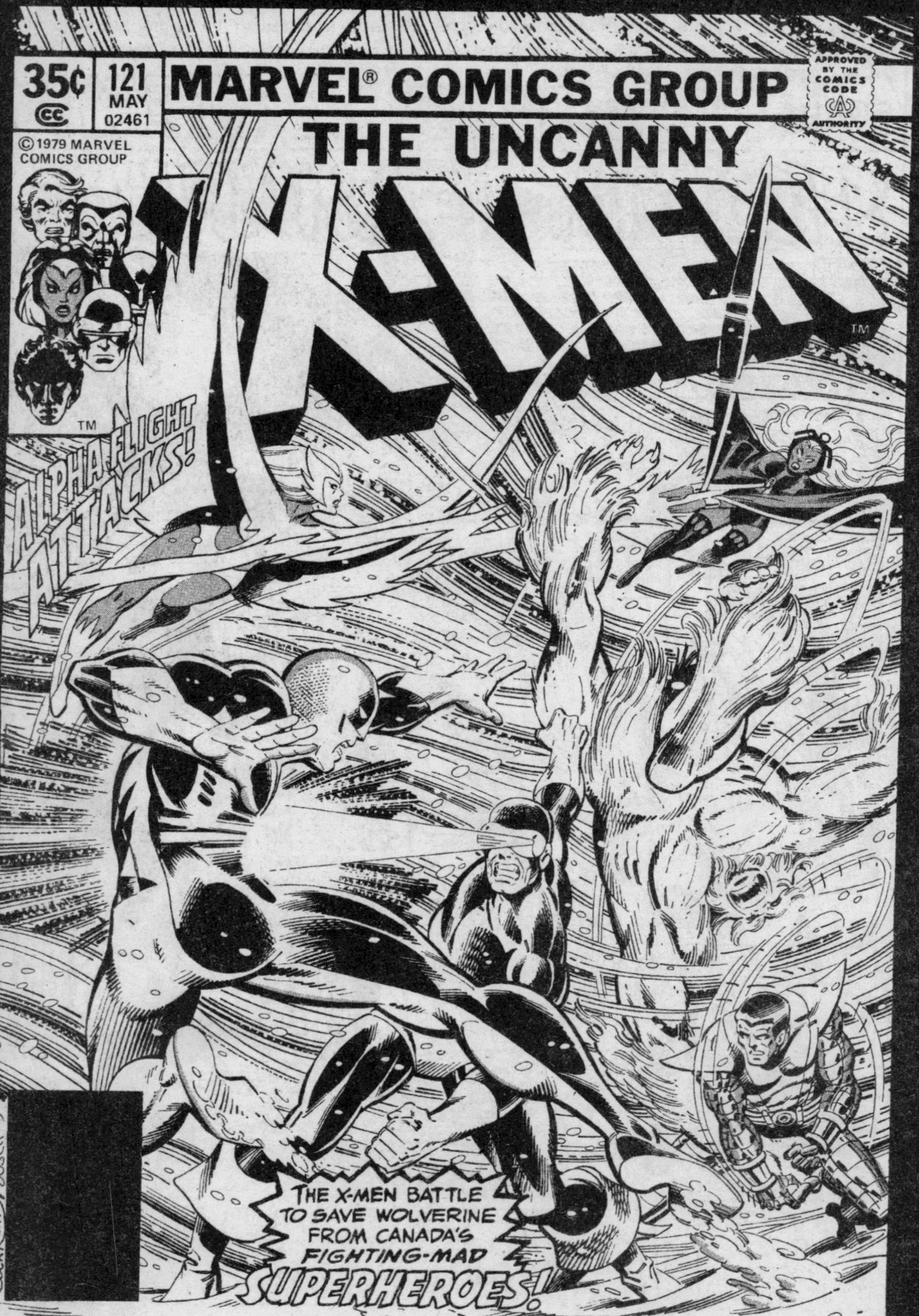
35¢
121
MAY
02461
CC
MARVEL® COMICS GROUP
APPROVED BY THE COMICS CODE AUTHORITY
©1979 MARVEL COMICS GROUP
THE UNCANNY
X-MEN™
ALPHA FLIGHT ATTACKS!
THE X-MEN BATTLE TO SAVE WOLVERINE FROM CANADA'S FIGHTING-MAD SUPERHEROES!

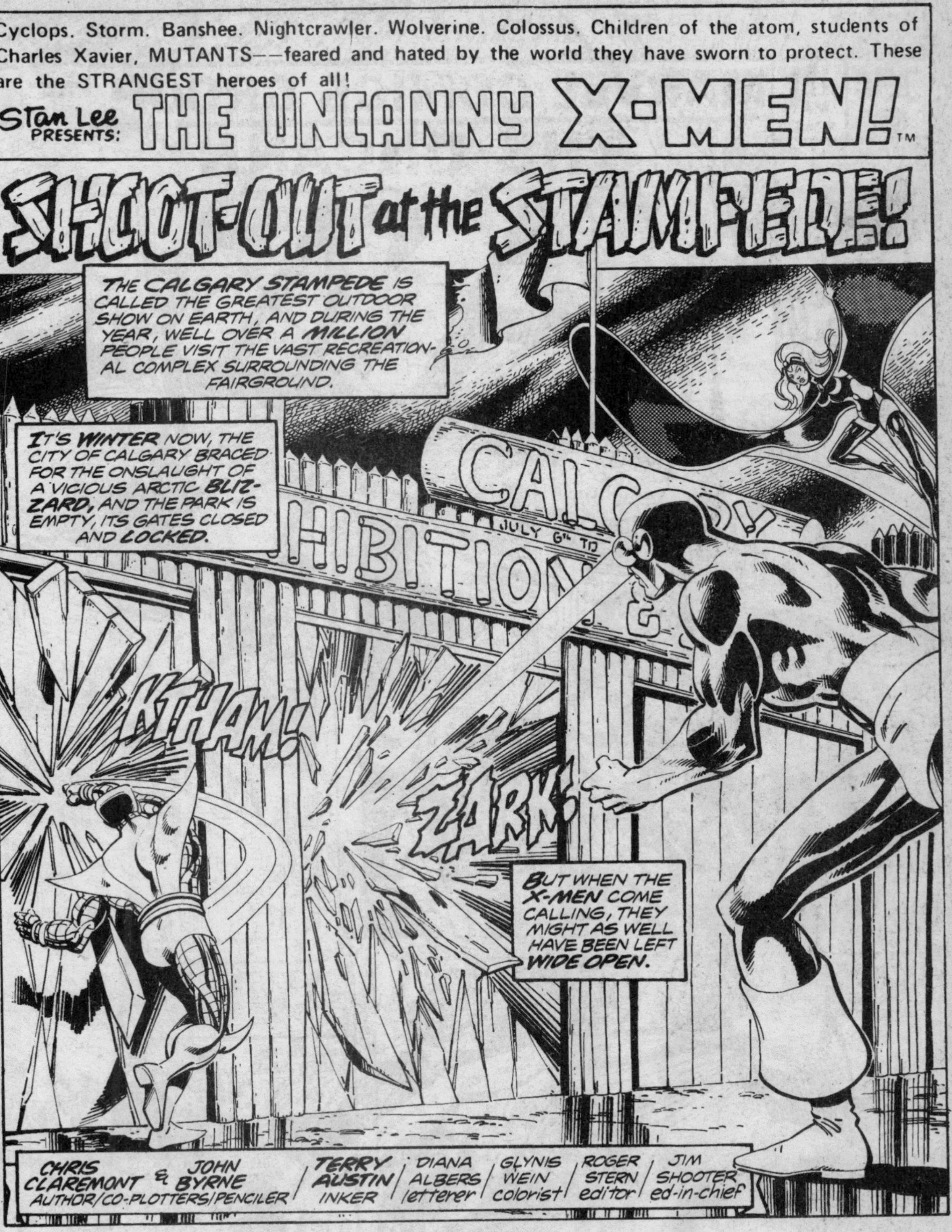
Cyclops. Storm. Banshee. Nightcrawler. Wolverine. Colossus. Children of the atom, students of Charles Xavier, MUTANTS--feared and hated by the world they have sworn to protect. These are the STRANGEST heroes of all!
Stan Lee PRESENTS: THE UNCANNY X-MEN!™
SHOOT-OUT at the STAMPEDE!
THE CALGARY STAMPEDE IS CALLED THE GREATEST OUTDOOR SHOW ON EARTH, AND DURING THE YEAR, WELL OVER A MILLION PEOPLE VISIT THE VAST RECREATIONAL COMPLEX SURROUNDING THE FAIRGROUND.
IT'S WINTER NOW, THE CITY OF CALGARY BRACED FOR THE ONSLAUGHT OF A VICIOUS ARCTIC BLIZZARD, AND THE PARK IS EMPTY, ITS GATES CLOSED AND LOCKED.
KTHAM!
ZARK!
BUT WHEN THE X-MEN COME CALLING, THEY MIGHT AS WELL HAVE BEEN LEFT WIDE OPEN.
CHRIS CLAREMONT & JOHN BYRNE AUTHOR/CO-PLOTTERS/PENCILER
TERRY AUSTIN INKER
DIANA ALBERS letterer
GLYNIS WEIN colorist
ROGER STERN editor
JIM SHOOTER ed-in-chief

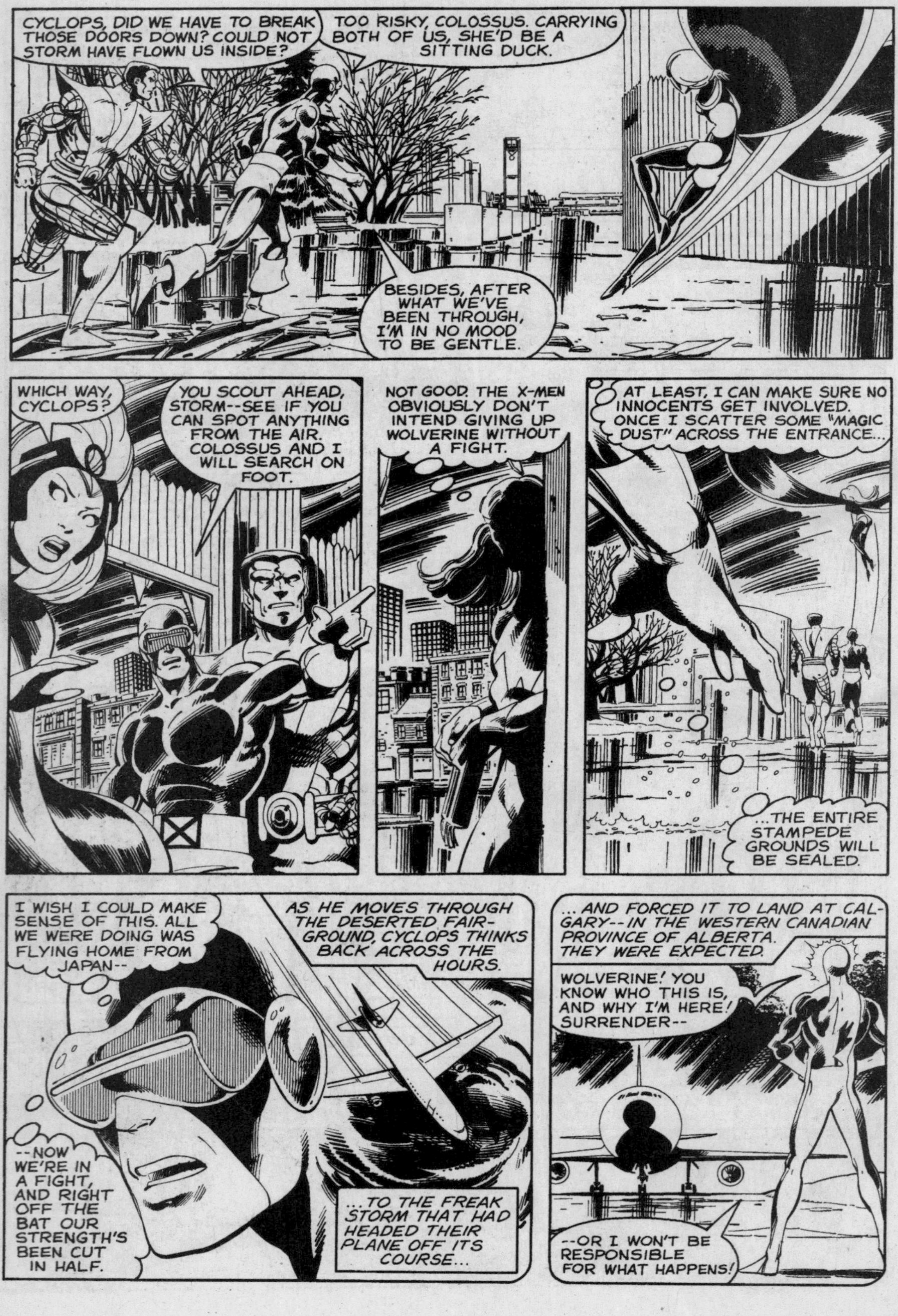
CYCLOPS, DID WE HAVE TO BREAK THOSE DOORS DOWN? COULD NOT STORM HAVE FLOWN US INSIDE?
TOO RISKY, COLOSSUS. CARRYING BOTH OF US, SHE'D BE A SITTING DUCK.
BESIDES, AFTER WHAT WE'VE BEEN THROUGH, I'M IN NO MOOD TO BE GENTLE.
WHICH WAY, CYCLOPS?
YOU SCOUT AHEAD, STORM--SEE IF YOU CAN SPOT ANYTHING FROM THE AIR. COLOSSUS AND I WILL SEARCH ON FOOT.
NOT GOOD. THE X-MEN OBVIOUSLY DON'T INTEND GIVING UP WOLVERINE WITHOUT A FIGHT.
AT LEAST, I CAN MAKE SURE NO INNOCENTS GET INVOLVED. ONCE I SCATTER SOME "MAGIC DUST" ACROSS THE ENTRANCE...
...THE ENTIRE STAMPEDE GROUNDS WILL BE SEALED.
I WISH I COULD MAKE SENSE OF THIS. ALL WE WERE DOING WAS FLYING HOME FROM JAPAN--
--NOW WE'RE IN A FIGHT, AND RIGHT OFF THE BAT OUR STRENGTH'S BEEN CUT IN HALF.
AS HE MOVES THROUGH THE DESERTED FAIR-GROUND, CYCLOPS THINKS BACK ACROSS THE HOURS.
...TO THE FREAK STORM THAT HAD HEADED THEIR PLANE OFF ITS COURSE...
...AND FORCED IT TO LAND AT CAL-GARY--IN THE WESTERN CANADIAN PROVINCE OF ALBERTA. THEY WERE EXPECTED.
WOLVERINE! YOU KNOW WHO THIS IS, AND WHY I'M HERE! SURRENDER--
--OR I WON'T BE RESPONSIBLE FOR WHAT HAPPENS!

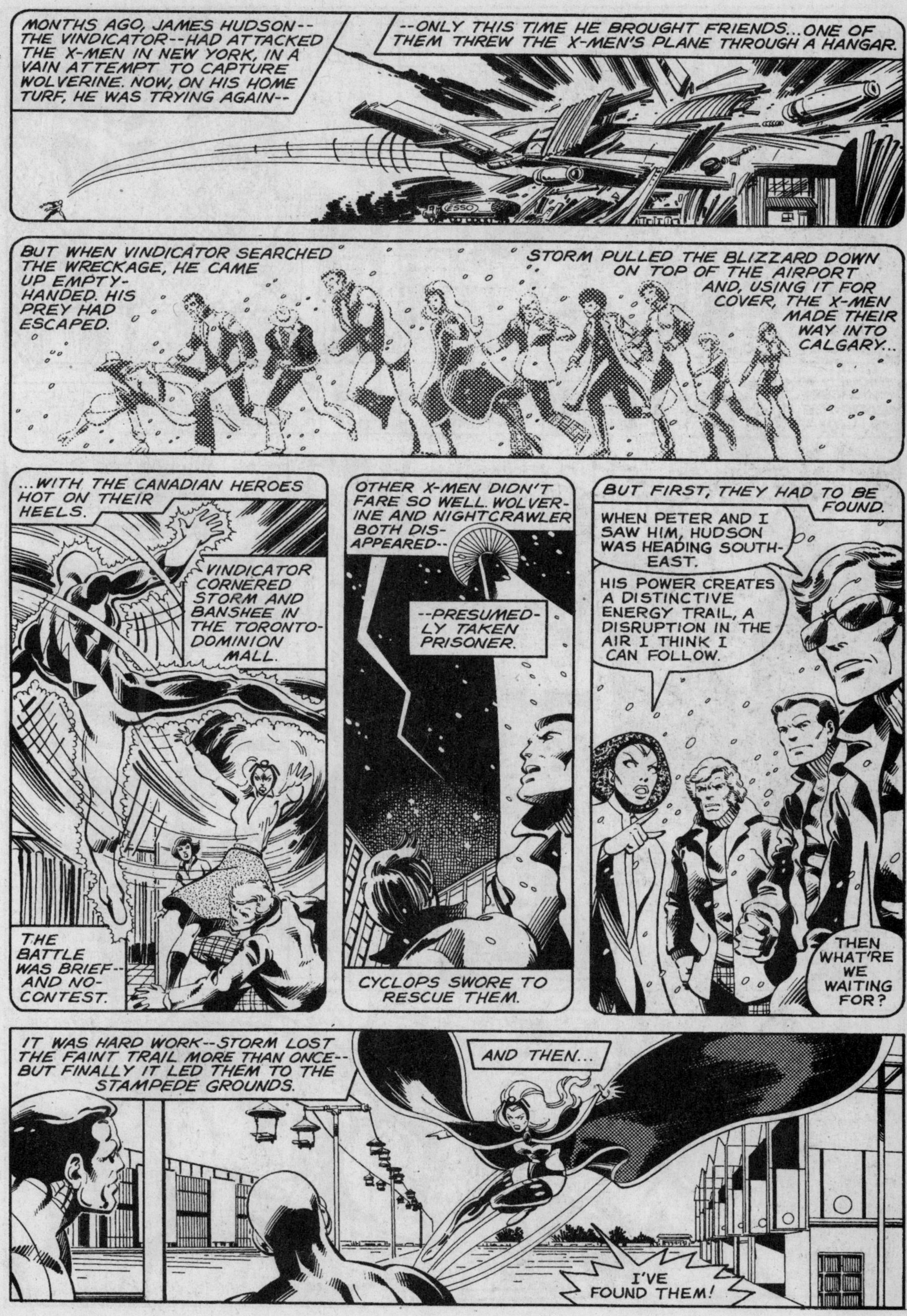
MONTHS AGO, JAMES HUDSON--THE VINDICATOR--HAD ATTACKED THE X-MEN IN NEW YORK, IN A VAIN ATTEMPT TO CAPTURE WOLVERINE. NOW, ON HIS HOME TURF, HE WAS TRYING AGAIN--
--ONLY THIS TIME HE BROUGHT FRIENDS... ONE OF THEM THREW THE X-MEN'S PLANE THROUGH A HANGAR.
ESSO
BUT WHEN VINDICATOR SEARCHED THE WRECKAGE, HE CAME UP EMPTY-HANDED. HIS PREY HAD ESCAPED.
STORM PULLED THE BLIZZARD DOWN ON TOP OF THE AIRPORT AND, USING IT FOR COVER, THE X-MEN MADE THEIR WAY INTO CALGARY...
...WITH THE CANADIAN HEROES HOT ON THEIR HEELS.
VINDICATOR CORNERED STORM AND BANSHEE IN THE TORONTO-DOMINION MALL.
THE BATTLE WAS BRIEF--AND NO-CONTEST.
OTHER X-MEN DIDN'T FARE SO WELL. WOLVERINE AND NIGHTCRAWLER BOTH DISAPPEARED--
--PRESUMEDLY TAKEN PRISONER.
CYCLOPS SWORE TO RESCUE THEM.
BUT FIRST, THEY HAD TO BE FOUND.
WHEN PETER AND I SAW HIM, HUDSON WAS HEADING SOUTH-EAST.
HIS POWER CREATES A DISTINCTIVE ENERGY TRAIL, A DISRUPTION IN THE AIR I THINK I CAN FOLLOW.
THEN WHAT'RE WE WAITING FOR?
IT WAS HARD WORK--STORM LOST THE FAINT TRAIL MORE THAN ONCE--BUT FINALLY IT LED THEM TO THE STAMPEDE GROUNDS.
AND THEN...
I'VE FOUND THEM!

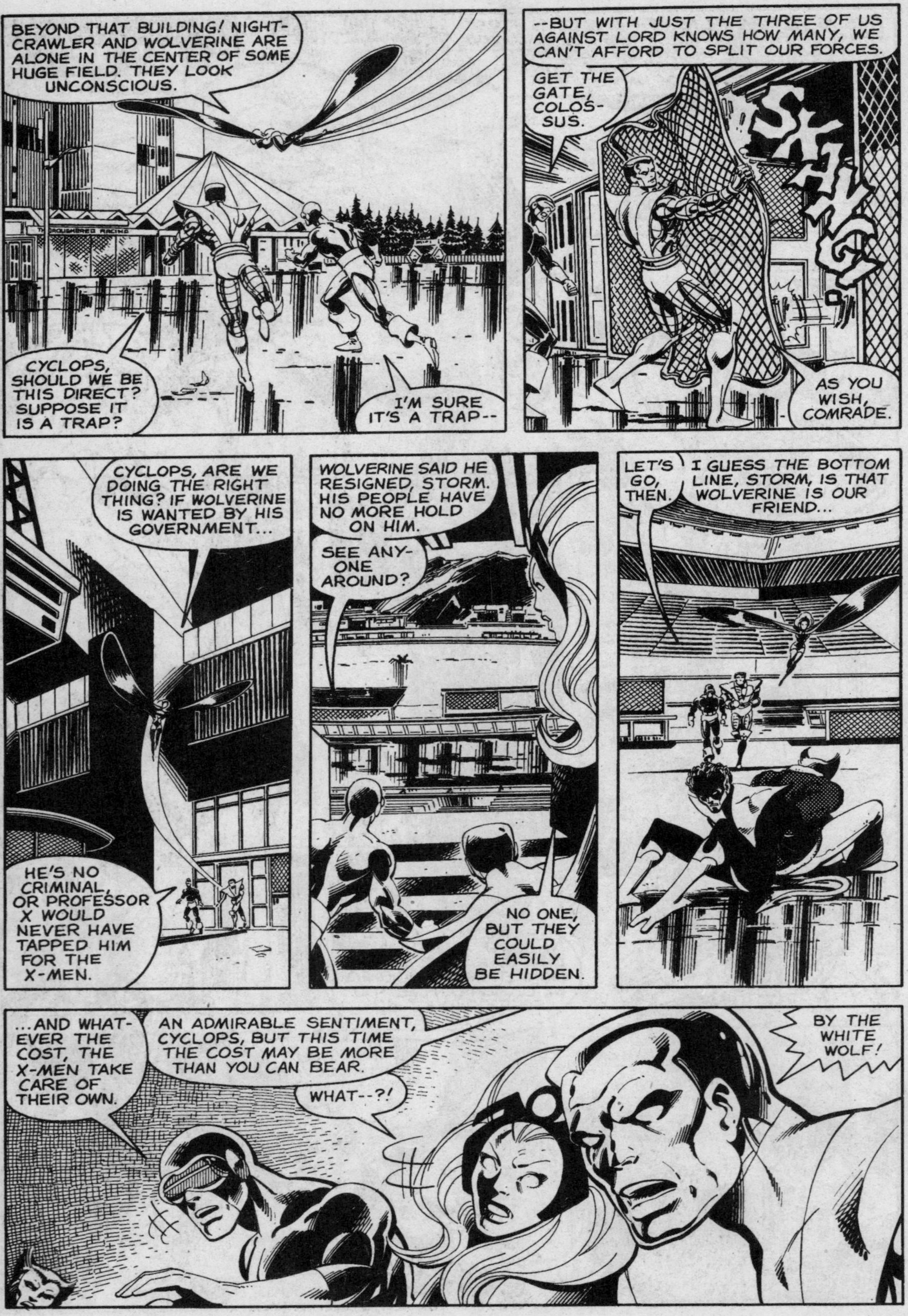

BEYOND THAT BUILDING! NIGHT-CRAWLER AND WOLVERINE ARE ALONE IN THE CENTER OF SOME HUGE FIELD. THEY LOOK UNCONSCIOUS.
CYCLOPS, SHOULD WE BE THIS DIRECT? SUPPOSE IT IS A TRAP?
I'M SURE IT'S A TRAP--
--BUT WITH JUST THE THREE OF US AGAINST LORD KNOWS HOW MANY, WE CAN'T AFFORD TO SPLIT OUR FORCES.
GET THE GATE, COLOS-SUS.
SKANG!
AS YOU WISH, COMRADE.
CYCLOPS, ARE WE DOING THE RIGHT THING? IF WOLVERINE IS WANTED BY HIS GOVERNMENT...
HE'S NO CRIMINAL, OR PROFESSOR X WOULD NEVER HAVE TAPPED HIM FOR THE X-MEN.
WOLVERINE SAID HE RESIGNED, STORM. HIS PEOPLE HAVE NO MORE HOLD ON HIM.
SEE ANY-ONE AROUND?
NO ONE, BUT THEY COULD EASILY BE HIDDEN.
LET'S GO, THEN.
I GUESS THE BOTTOM LINE, STORM, IS THAT WOLVERINE IS OUR FRIEND...
...AND WHAT-EVER THE COST, THE X-MEN TAKE CARE OF THEIR OWN.
AN ADMIRABLE SENTIMENT, CYCLOPS, BUT THIS TIME THE COST MAY BE MORE THAN YOU CAN BEAR.
WHAT--?!
BY THE WHITE WOLF!

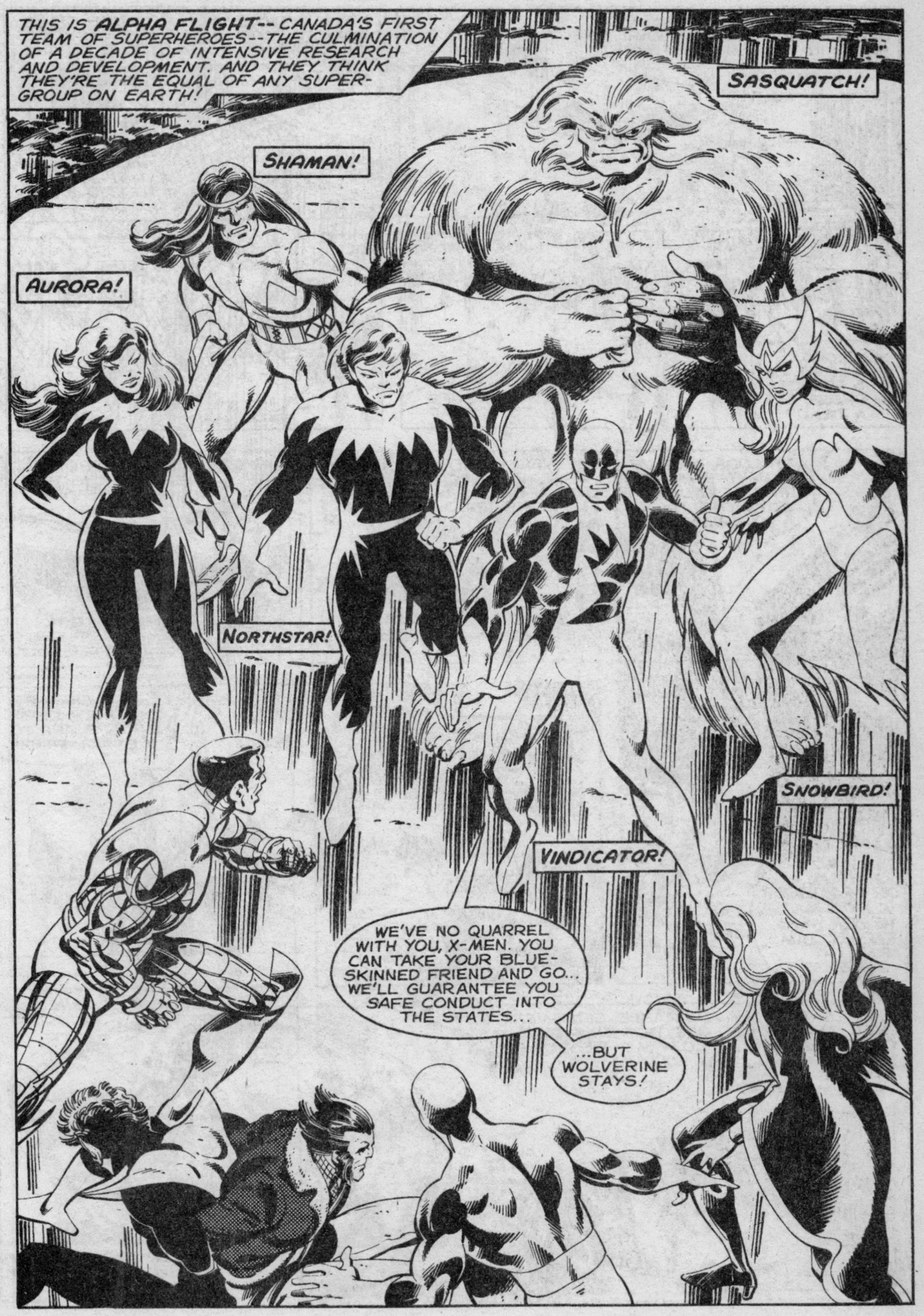
THIS IS ALPHA FLIGHT-- CANADA'S FIRST TEAM OF SUPERHEROES--THE CULMINATION OF A DECADE OF INTENSIVE RESEARCH AND DEVELOPMENT. AND THEY THINK THEY'RE THE EQUAL OF ANY SUPER-GROUP ON EARTH!
SASQUATCH!
SHAMAN!
AURORA!
NORTHSTAR!
SNOWBIRD!
VINDICATOR!
WE'VE NO QUARREL WITH YOU, X-MEN. YOU CAN TAKE YOUR BLUE-SKINNED FRIEND AND GO... WE'LL GUARANTEE YOU SAFE CONDUCT INTO THE STATES...
...BUT WOLVERINE STAYS!

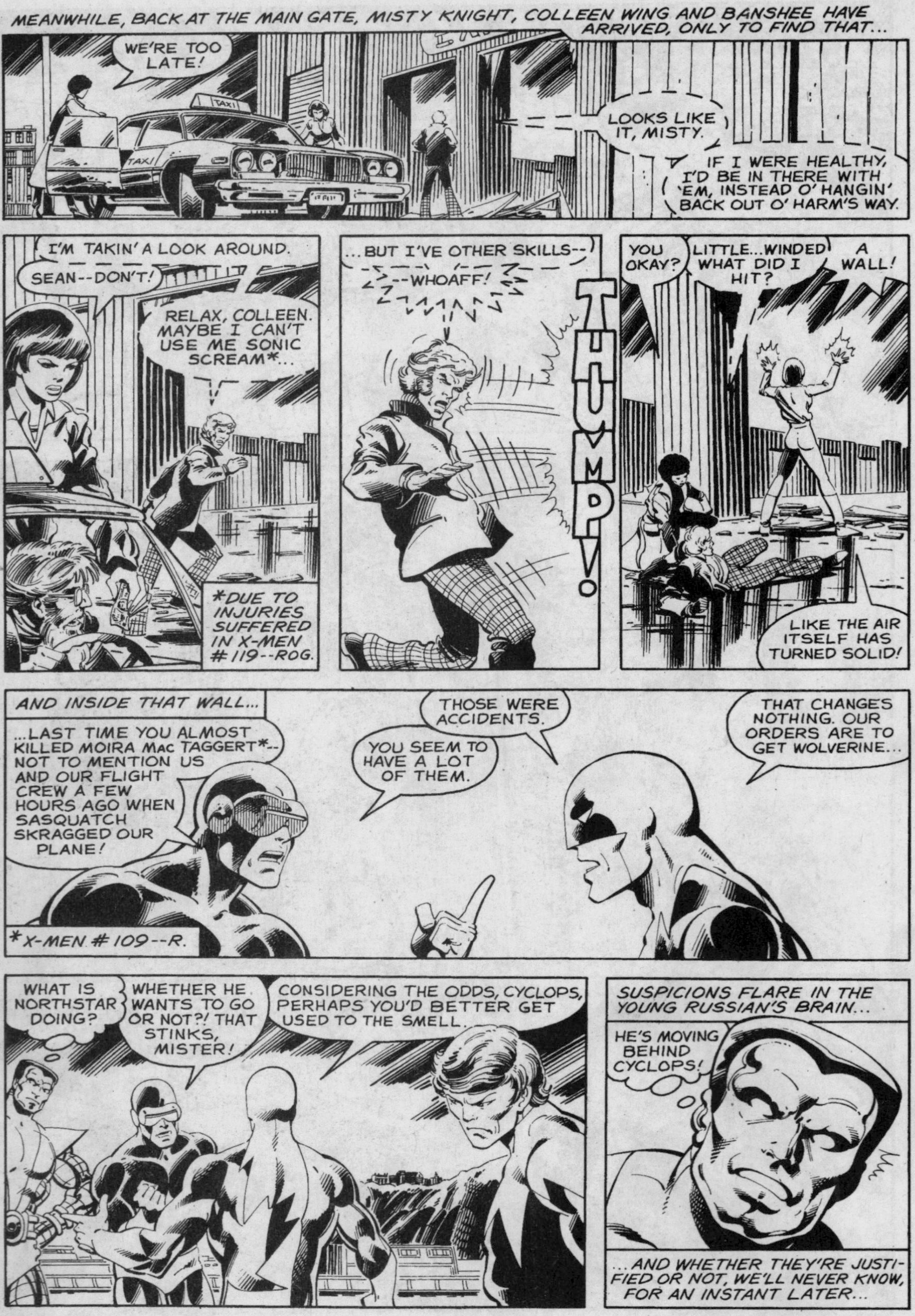
MEANWHILE, BACK AT THE MAIN GATE, MISTY KNIGHT, COLLEEN WING AND BANSHEE HAVE ARRIVED, ONLY TO FIND THAT...
WE'RE TOO LATE!
LOOKS LIKE IT, MISTY.
IF I WERE HEALTHY, I'D BE IN THERE WITH 'EM, INSTEAD O' HANGIN' BACK OUT O' HARM'S WAY.
I'M TAKIN' A LOOK AROUND.
SEAN--DON'T!
RELAX, COLLEEN. MAYBE I CAN'T USE ME SONIC SCREAM*...
*DUE TO INJURIES SUFFERED IN X-MEN #119--ROG.
...BUT I'VE OTHER SKILLS--
--WHOAFF!
THUMP!
YOU OKAY?
LITTLE...WINDED WHAT DID I HIT?
A WALL!
LIKE THE AIR ITSELF HAS TURNED SOLID!
AND INSIDE THAT WALL...
...LAST TIME YOU ALMOST KILLED MOIRA MacTAGGERT*-- NOT TO MENTION US AND OUR FLIGHT CREW A FEW HOURS AGO WHEN SASQUATCH SKRAGGED OUR PLANE!
*X-MEN #109--R.
THOSE WERE ACCIDENTS.
YOU SEEM TO HAVE A LOT OF THEM.
THAT CHANGES NOTHING. OUR ORDERS ARE TO GET WOLVERINE...
WHAT IS NORTHSTAR DOING?
WHETHER HE WANTS TO GO OR NOT?! THAT STINKS, MISTER!
CONSIDERING THE ODDS, CYCLOPS, PERHAPS YOU'D BETTER GET USED TO THE SMELL.
SUSPICIONS FLARE IN THE YOUNG RUSSIAN'S BRAIN...
HE'S MOVING BEHIND CYCLOPS!
...AND WHETHER THEY'RE JUSTIFIED OR NOT, WE'LL NEVER KNOW, FOR AN INSTANT LATER...

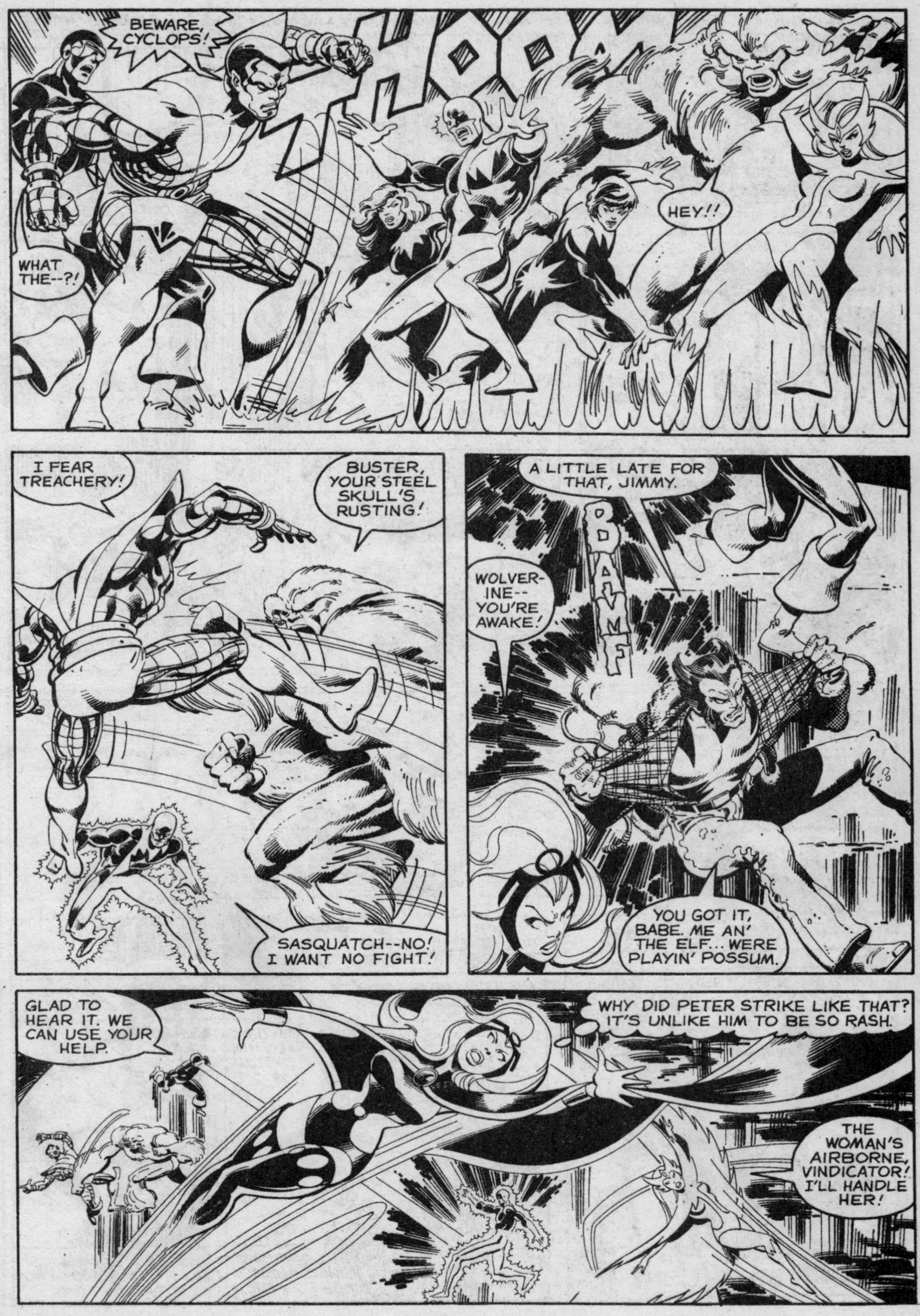
BEWARE, CYCLOPS!
WHAT THE--?!
HEY!!
I FEAR TREACHERY!
BUSTER, YOUR STEEL SKULL'S RUSTING!
SASQUATCH--NO! I WANT NO FIGHT!
A LITTLE LATE FOR THAT, JIMMY.
BAMF
WOLVERINE-- YOU'RE AWAKE!
YOU GOT IT, BABE. ME AN' THE ELF... WERE PLAYIN' POSSUM.
GLAD TO HEAR IT. WE CAN USE YOUR HELP.
WHY DID PETER STRIKE LIKE THAT? IT'S UNLIKE HIM TO BE SO RASH.
THE WOMAN'S AIRBORNE, VINDICATOR! I'LL HANDLE HER!

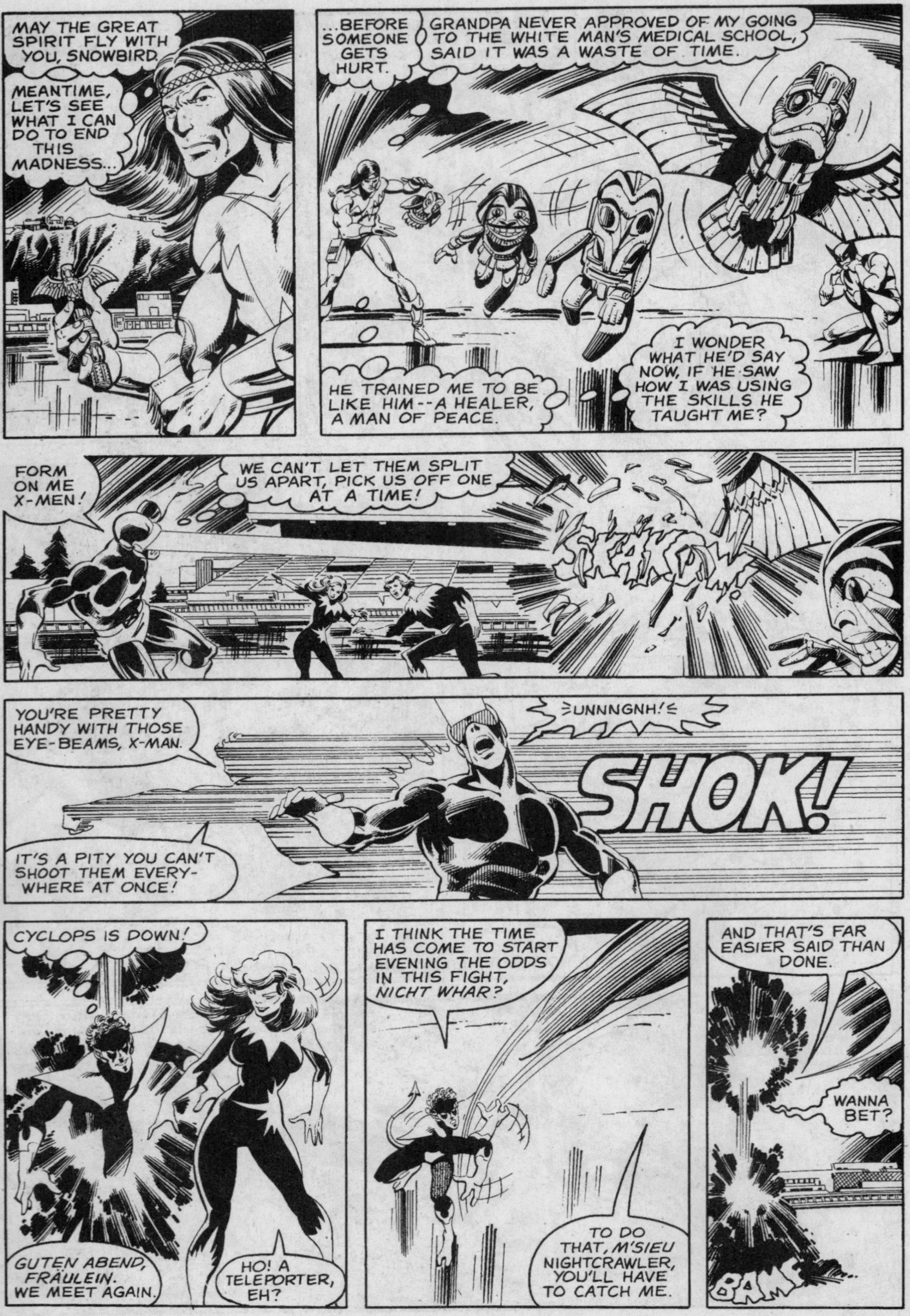
MAY THE GREAT SPIRIT FLY WITH YOU, SNOWBIRD.
MEANTIME, LET'S SEE WHAT I CAN DO TO END THIS MADNESS...
...BEFORE SOMEONE GETS HURT.
GRANDPA NEVER APPROVED OF MY GOING TO THE WHITE MAN'S MEDICAL SCHOOL, SAID IT WAS A WASTE OF TIME.
HE TRAINED ME TO BE LIKE HIM--A HEALER, A MAN OF PEACE.
I WONDER WHAT HE'D SAY NOW, IF HE SAW HOW I WAS USING THE SKILLS HE TAUGHT ME?
FORM ON ME X-MEN!
WE CAN'T LET THEM SPLIT US APART, PICK US OFF ONE AT A TIME!
SKAKOOM!
YOU'RE PRETTY HANDY WITH THOSE EYE-BEAMS, X-MAN.
UNNNGNH!
SHOK!
IT'S A PITY YOU CAN'T SHOOT THEM EVERY-WHERE AT ONCE!
CYCLOPS IS DOWN!
GUTEN ABEND, FRÄULEIN. WE MEET AGAIN.
HO! A TELEPORTER, EH?
I THINK THE TIME HAS COME TO START EVENING THE ODDS IN THIS FIGHT, NICHT WHAR?
TO DO THAT, M'SIEU NIGHTCRAWLER, YOU'LL HAVE TO CATCH ME.
AND THAT'S FAR EASIER SAID THAN DONE.
WANNA BET?
BAM

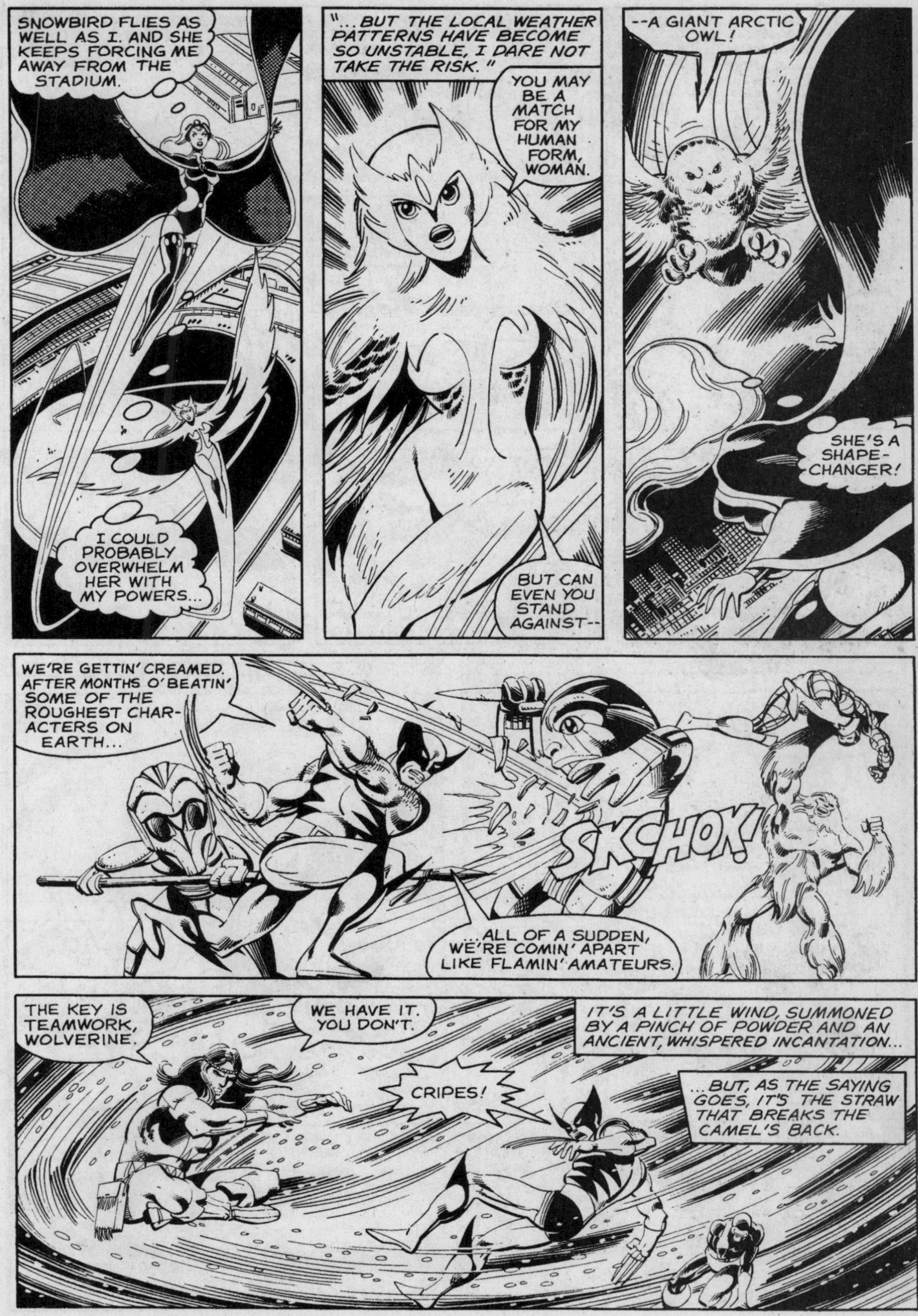

SNOWBIRD FLIES AS WELL AS I. AND SHE KEEPS FORCING ME AWAY FROM THE STADIUM.
I COULD PROBABLY OVERWHELM HER WITH MY POWERS...
"...BUT THE LOCAL WEATHER PATTERNS HAVE BECOME SO UNSTABLE, I DARE NOT TAKE THE RISK."
YOU MAY BE A MATCH FOR MY HUMAN FORM, WOMAN.
BUT CAN EVEN YOU STAND AGAINST--
--A GIANT ARCTIC OWL!
SHE'S A SHAPE-CHANGER!
WE'RE GETTIN' CREAMED. AFTER MONTHS O' BEATIN' SOME OF THE ROUGHEST CHARACTERS ON EARTH...
SKCHOK!
...ALL OF A SUDDEN, WE'RE COMIN' APART LIKE FLAMIN' AMATEURS.
THE KEY IS TEAMWORK, WOLVERINE.
WE HAVE IT. YOU DON'T.
IT'S A LITTLE WIND, SUMMONED BY A PINCH OF POWDER AND AN ANCIENT, WHISPERED INCANTATION...
CRIPES!
...BUT, AS THE SAYING GOES, IT'S THE STRAW THAT BREAKS THE CAMEL'S BACK.

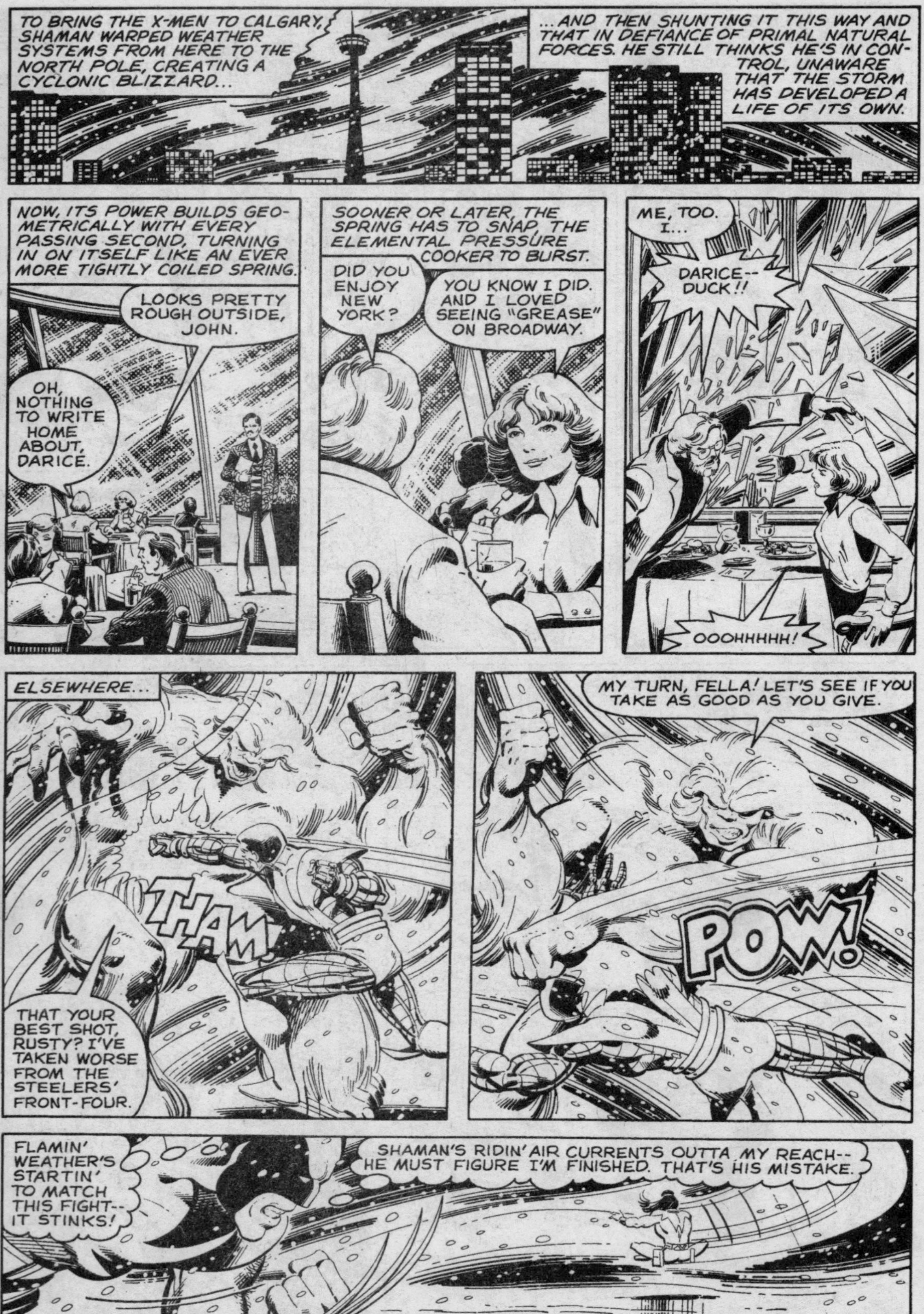
TO BRING THE X-MEN TO CALGARY, SHAMAN WARPED WEATHER SYSTEMS FROM HERE TO THE NORTH POLE, CREATING A CYCLONIC BLIZZARD...
...AND THEN SHUNTING IT THIS WAY AND THAT IN DEFIANCE OF PRIMAL NATURAL FORCES. HE STILL THINKS HE'S IN CONTROL, UNAWARE THAT THE STORM HAS DEVELOPED A LIFE OF ITS OWN.
NOW, ITS POWER BUILDS GEOMETRICALLY WITH EVERY PASSING SECOND, TURNING IN ON ITSELF LIKE AN EVER MORE TIGHTLY COILED SPRING.
LOOKS PRETTY ROUGH OUTSIDE, JOHN.
OH, NOTHING TO WRITE HOME ABOUT, DARICE.
SOONER OR LATER, THE SPRING HAS TO SNAP, THE ELEMENTAL PRESSURE COOKER TO BURST.
DID YOU ENJOY NEW YORK?
YOU KNOW I DID. AND I LOVED SEEING "GREASE" ON BROADWAY.
ME, TOO. I...
DARICE-- DUCK!!
OOOHHHHH!
ELSEWHERE...
THAM
THAT YOUR BEST SHOT, RUSTY? I'VE TAKEN WORSE FROM THE STEELERS' FRONT-FOUR.
MY TURN, FELLA! LET'S SEE IF YOU TAKE AS GOOD AS YOU GIVE.
POW!
FLAMIN' WEATHER'S STARTIN' TO MATCH THIS FIGHT-- IT STINKS!
SHAMAN'S RIDIN' AIR CURRENTS OUTTA MY REACH-- HE MUST FIGURE I'M FINISHED. THAT'S HIS MISTAKE.

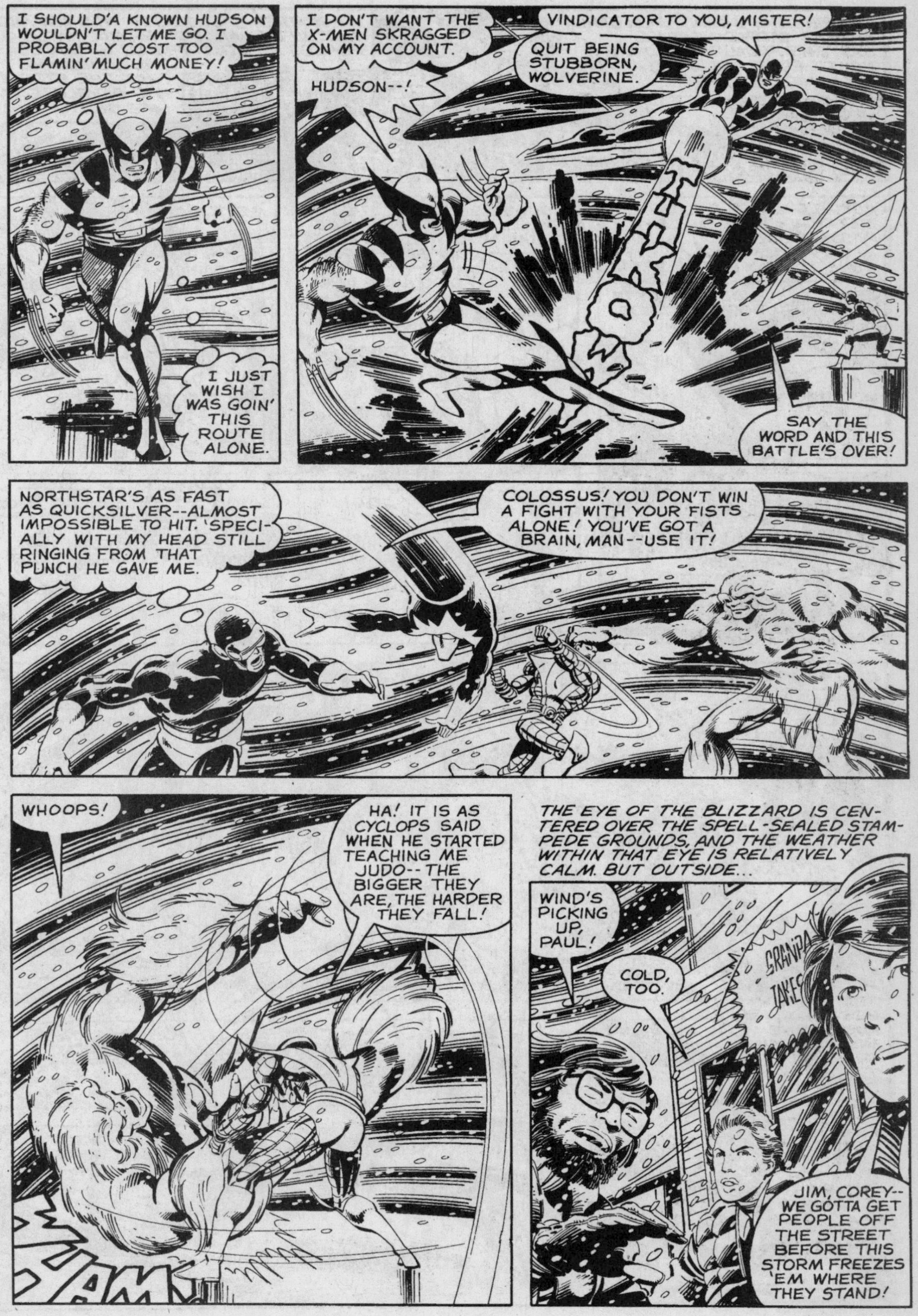
I SHOULD'A KNOWN HUDSON WOULDN'T LET ME GO. I PROBABLY COST TOO FLAMIN' MUCH MONEY!
I JUST WISH I WAS GOIN' THIS ROUTE ALONE.
I DON'T WANT THE X-MEN SKRAGGED ON MY ACCOUNT.
HUDSON--!
VINDICATOR TO YOU, MISTER!
QUIT BEING STUBBORN, WOLVERINE.
THOKK
SAY THE WORD AND THIS BATTLE'S OVER!
NORTHSTAR'S AS FAST AS QUICKSILVER--ALMOST IMPOSSIBLE TO HIT. 'SPECIALLY WITH MY HEAD STILL RINGING FROM THAT PUNCH HE GAVE ME.
COLOSSUS! YOU DON'T WIN A FIGHT WITH YOUR FISTS ALONE! YOU'VE GOT A BRAIN, MAN--USE IT!
WHOOPS!
HA! IT IS AS CYCLOPS SAID WHEN HE STARTED TEACHING ME JUDO-- THE BIGGER THEY ARE, THE HARDER THEY FALL!
WHAM!
THE EYE OF THE BLIZZARD IS CENTERED OVER THE SPELL-SEALED STAMPEDE GROUNDS, AND THE WEATHER WITHIN THAT EYE IS RELATIVELY CALM. BUT OUTSIDE...
WIND'S PICKING UP, PAUL!
COLD, TOO.
GRANPA JAKE'S
JIM, COREY-- WE GOTTA GET PEOPLE OFF THE STREET BEFORE THIS STORM FREEZES 'EM WHERE THEY STAND!

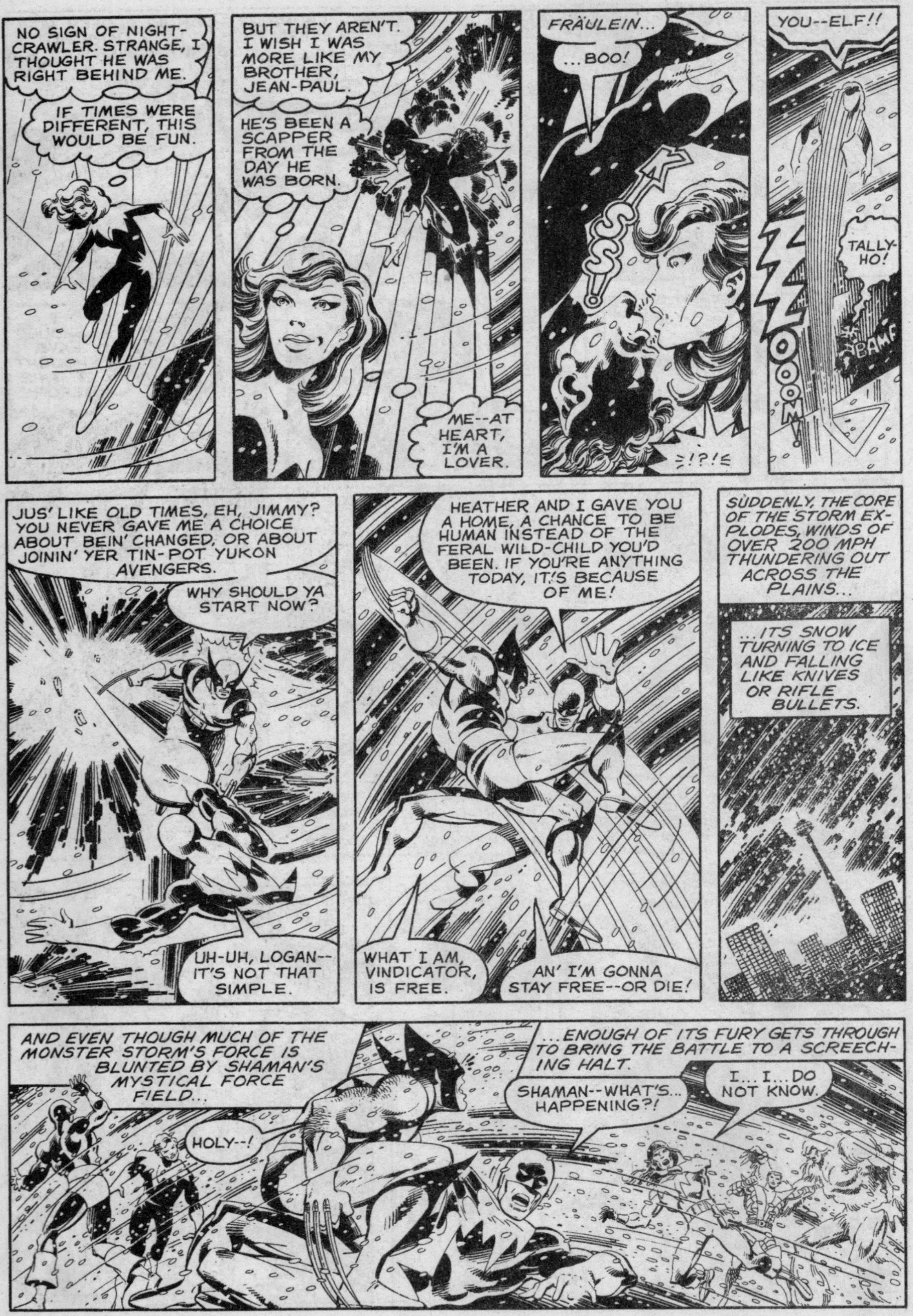

NO SIGN OF NIGHT-CRAWLER. STRANGE, I THOUGHT HE WAS RIGHT BEHIND ME.
IF TIMES WERE DIFFERENT, THIS WOULD BE FUN.
BUT THEY AREN'T. I WISH I WAS MORE LIKE MY BROTHER, JEAN-PAUL.
HE'S BEEN A SCAPPER FROM THE DAY HE WAS BORN.
ME--AT HEART, I'M A LOVER.
FRÄULEIN...
...BOO!
KISS!
!?!
YOU--ELF!!
ZOOOOOM!
TALLY-HO!
BAMF
JUS' LIKE OLD TIMES, EH, JIMMY? YOU NEVER GAVE ME A CHOICE ABOUT BEIN' CHANGED, OR ABOUT JOININ' YER TIN-POT YUKON AVENGERS.
WHY SHOULD YA START NOW?
UH-UH, LOGAN-- IT'S NOT THAT SIMPLE.
HEATHER AND I GAVE YOU A HOME, A CHANCE TO BE HUMAN INSTEAD OF THE FERAL WILD-CHILD YOU'D BEEN. IF YOU'RE ANYTHING TODAY, IT'S BECAUSE OF ME!
WHAT I AM, VINDICATOR, IS FREE.
AN' I'M GONNA STAY FREE--OR DIE!
SUDDENLY, THE CORE OF THE STORM EXPLODES, WINDS OF OVER 200 MPH THUNDERING OUT ACROSS THE PLAINS...
...ITS SNOW TURNING TO ICE AND FALLING LIKE KNIVES OR RIFLE BULLETS.
AND EVEN THOUGH MUCH OF THE MONSTER STORM'S FORCE IS BLUNTED BY SHAMAN'S MYSTICAL FORCE FIELD...
...ENOUGH OF ITS FURY GETS THROUGH TO BRING THE BATTLE TO A SCREECHING HALT.
HOLY--!
SHAMAN--WHAT'S... HAPPENING?!
I... I... DO NOT KNOW.

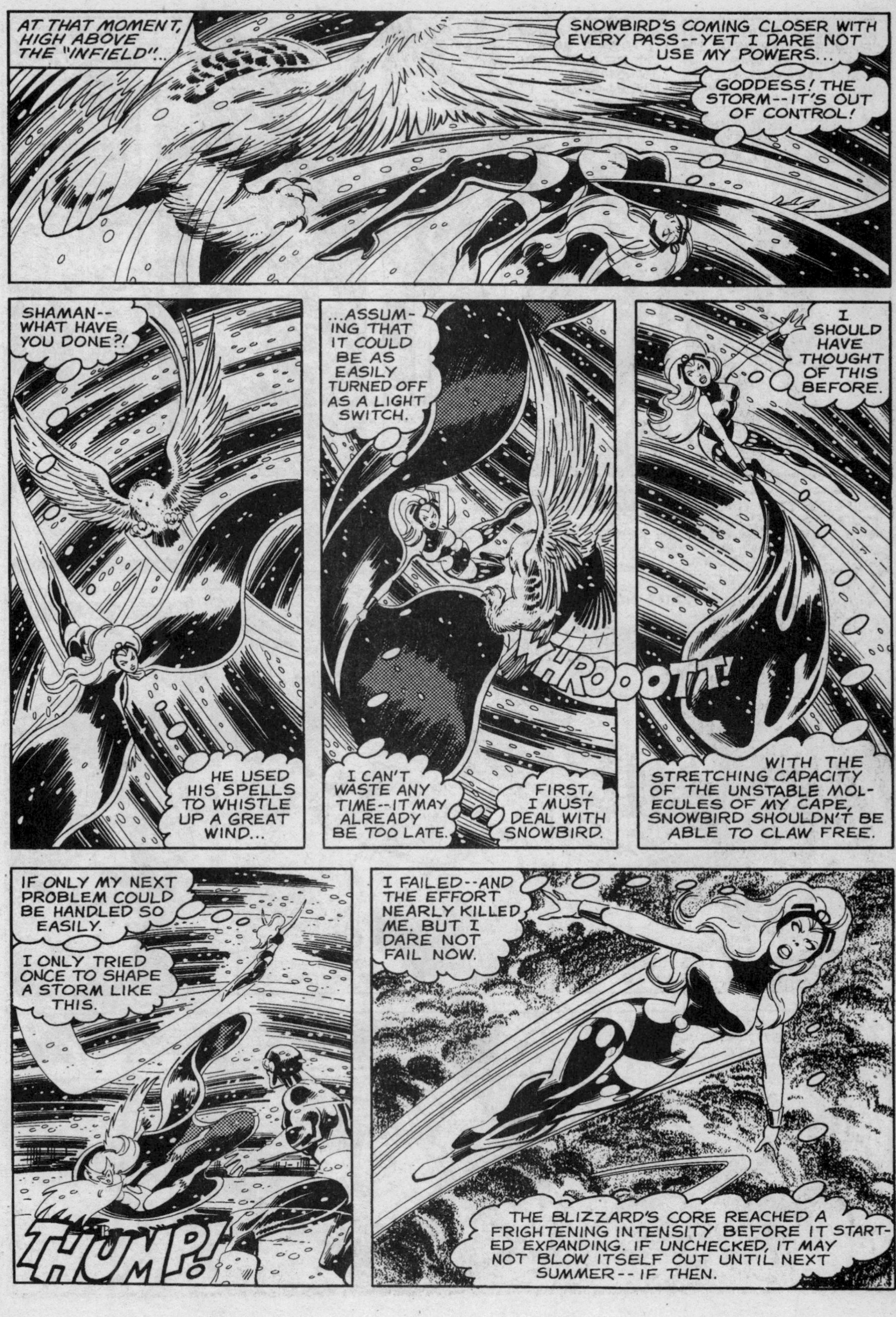

AT THAT MOMENT, HIGH ABOVE THE "INFIELD"...
SNOWBIRD'S COMING CLOSER WITH EVERY PASS--YET I DARE NOT USE MY POWERS...
GODDESS! THE STORM--IT'S OUT OF CONTROL!
SHAMAN--WHAT HAVE YOU DONE?!
HE USED HIS SPELLS TO WHISTLE UP A GREAT WIND...
...ASSUMING THAT IT COULD BE AS EASILY TURNED OFF AS A LIGHT SWITCH.
I CAN'T WASTE ANY TIME--IT MAY ALREADY BE TOO LATE.
FIRST, I MUST DEAL WITH SNOWBIRD.
WHROOOTT!
I SHOULD HAVE THOUGHT OF THIS BEFORE.
WITH THE STRETCHING CAPACITY OF THE UNSTABLE MOLECULES OF MY CAPE, SNOWBIRD SHOULDN'T BE ABLE TO CLAW FREE.
IF ONLY MY NEXT PROBLEM COULD BE HANDLED SO EASILY.
I ONLY TRIED ONCE TO SHAPE A STORM LIKE THIS.
THUMP!
I FAILED--AND THE EFFORT NEARLY KILLED ME. BUT I DARE NOT FAIL NOW.
THE BLIZZARD'S CORE REACHED A FRIGHTENING INTENSITY BEFORE IT STARTED EXPANDING. IF UNCHECKED, IT MAY NOT BLOW ITSELF OUT UNTIL NEXT SUMMER--IF THEN.

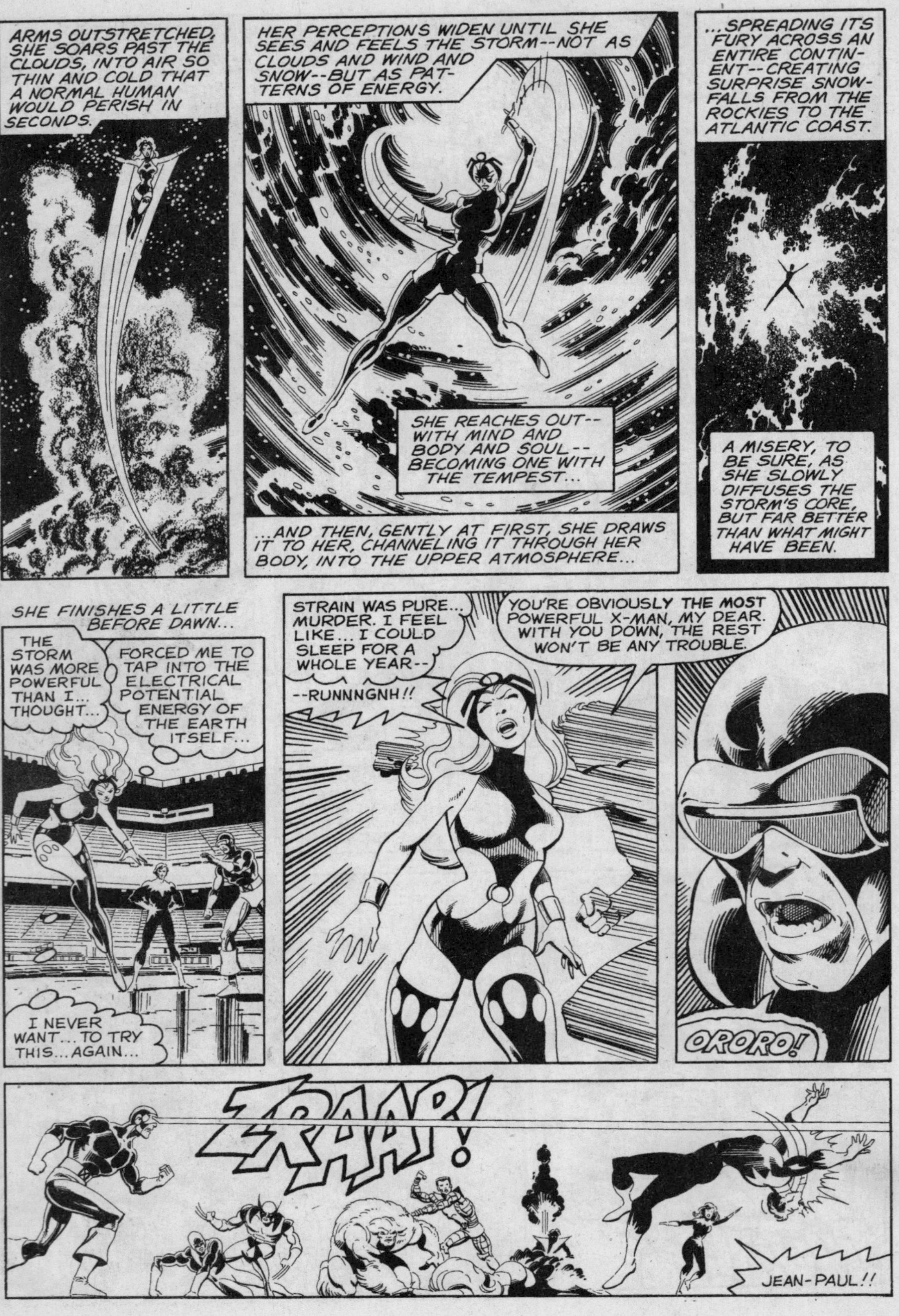
ARMS OUTSTRETCHED, SHE SOARS PAST THE CLOUDS, INTO AIR SO THIN AND COLD THAT A NORMAL HUMAN WOULD PERISH IN SECONDS.
HER PERCEPTIONS WIDEN UNTIL SHE SEES AND FEELS THE STORM--NOT AS CLOUDS AND WIND AND SNOW--BUT AS PATTERNS OF ENERGY.
SHE REACHES OUT--WITH MIND AND BODY AND SOUL--BECOMING ONE WITH THE TEMPEST...
...AND THEN, GENTLY AT FIRST, SHE DRAWS IT TO HER, CHANNELING IT THROUGH HER BODY, INTO THE UPPER ATMOSPHERE...
...SPREADING ITS FURY ACROSS AN ENTIRE CONTINENT--CREATING SURPRISE SNOWFALLS FROM THE ROCKIES TO THE ATLANTIC COAST.
A MISERY, TO BE SURE, AS SHE SLOWLY DIFFUSES THE STORM'S CORE, BUT FAR BETTER THAN WHAT MIGHT HAVE BEEN.
SHE FINISHES A LITTLE BEFORE DAWN...
THE STORM WAS MORE POWERFUL THAN I... THOUGHT...
FORCED ME TO TAP INTO THE ELECTRICAL POTENTIAL ENERGY OF THE EARTH ITSELF...
I NEVER WANT... TO TRY THIS... AGAIN...
STRAIN WAS PURE... MURDER. I FEEL LIKE... I COULD SLEEP FOR A WHOLE YEAR--
--RUNNNGNH!!
YOU'RE OBVIOUSLY THE MOST POWERFUL X-MAN, MY DEAR. WITH YOU DOWN, THE REST WON'T BE ANY TROUBLE.
ORORO!
ZRAAP!
JEAN-PAUL!!

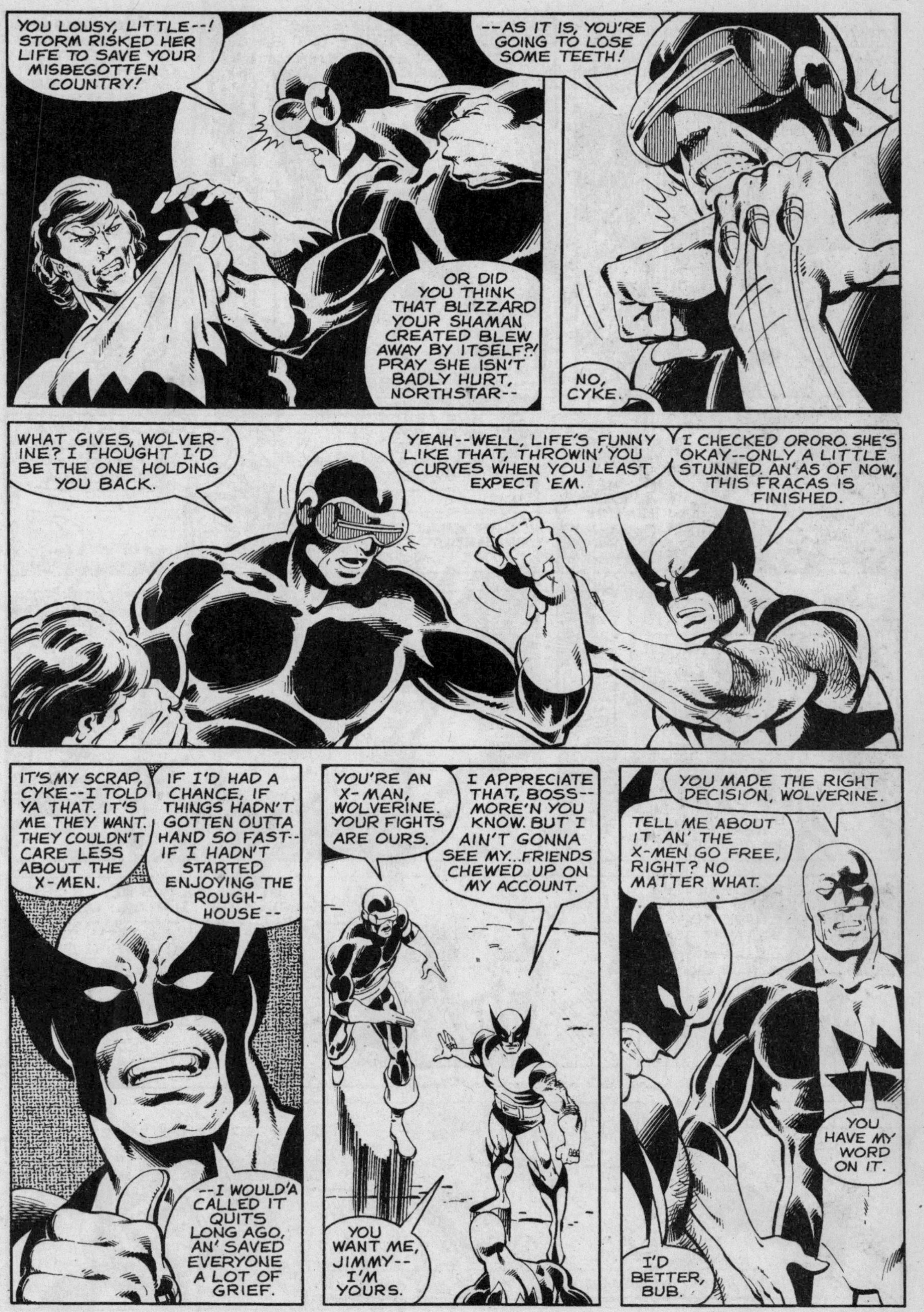
YOU LOUSY, LITTLE--! STORM RISKED HER LIFE TO SAVE YOUR MISBEGOTTEN COUNTRY!
OR DID YOU THINK THAT BLIZZARD YOUR SHAMAN CREATED BLEW AWAY BY ITSELF?! PRAY SHE ISN'T BADLY HURT, NORTHSTAR--
--AS IT IS, YOU'RE GOING TO LOSE SOME TEETH!
NO, CYKE.
WHAT GIVES, WOLVERINE? I THOUGHT I'D BE THE ONE HOLDING YOU BACK.
YEAH--WELL, LIFE'S FUNNY LIKE THAT, THROWIN' YOU CURVES WHEN YOU LEAST EXPECT 'EM.
I CHECKED ORORO. SHE'S OKAY--ONLY A LITTLE STUNNED. AN' AS OF NOW, THIS FRACAS IS FINISHED.
IT'S MY SCRAP, CYKE--I TOLD YA THAT. IT'S ME THEY WANT. THEY COULDN'T CARE LESS ABOUT THE X-MEN.
IF I'D HAD A CHANCE, IF THINGS HADN'T GOTTEN OUTTA HAND SO FAST--IF I HADN'T STARTED ENJOYING THE ROUGH-HOUSE--
--I WOULD'A CALLED IT QUITS LONG AGO, AN' SAVED EVERYONE A LOT OF GRIEF.
YOU'RE AN X-MAN, WOLVERINE. YOUR FIGHTS ARE OURS.
I APPRECIATE THAT, BOSS--MORE'N YOU KNOW. BUT I AIN'T GONNA SEE MY...FRIENDS CHEWED UP ON MY ACCOUNT.
YOU WANT ME, JIMMY--I'M YOURS.
YOU MADE THE RIGHT DECISION, WOLVERINE.
TELL ME ABOUT IT. AN' THE X-MEN GO FREE, RIGHT? NO MATTER WHAT.
YOU HAVE MY WORD ON IT.
I'D BETTER, BUB.

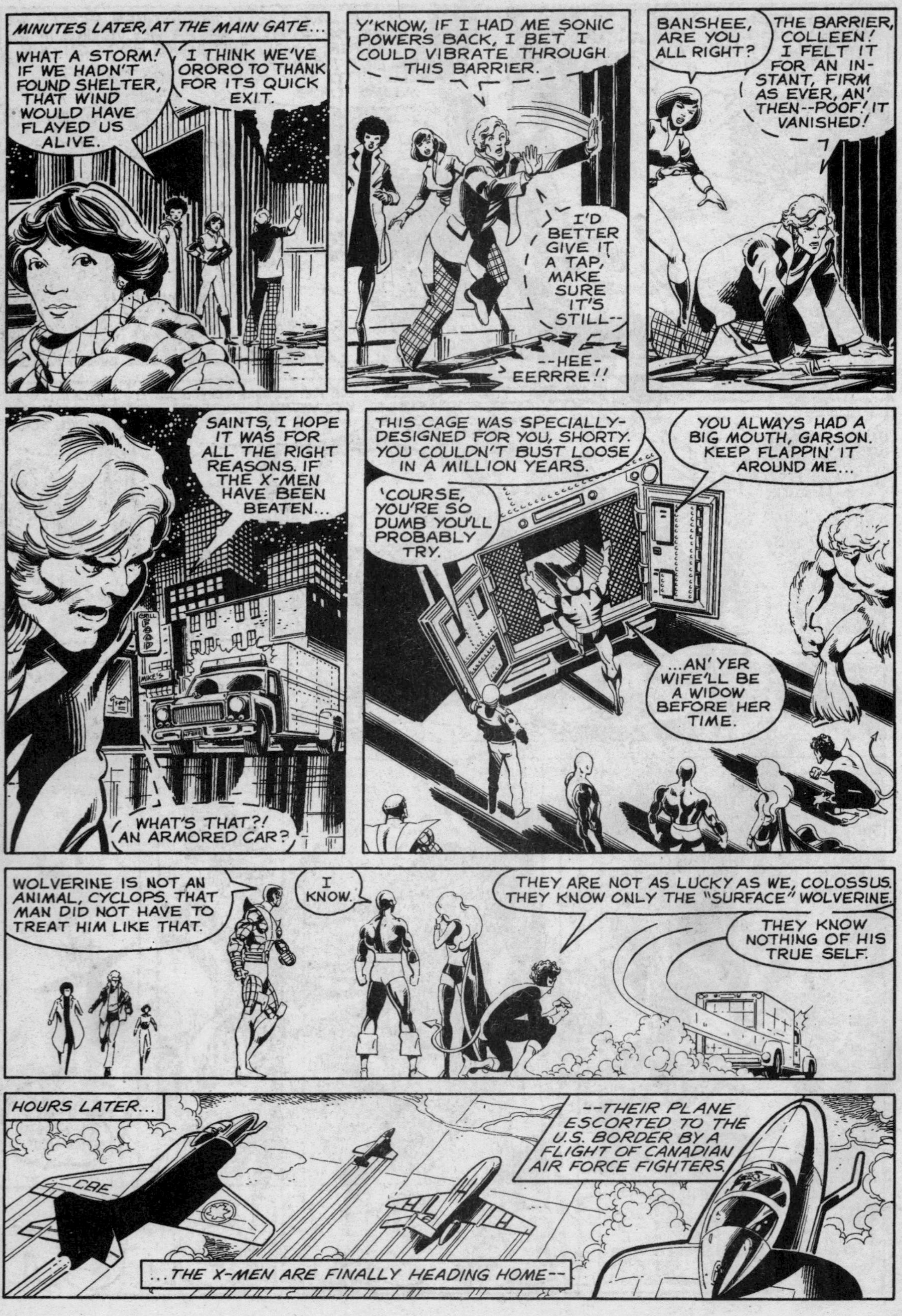
MINUTES LATER, AT THE MAIN GATE...
WHAT A STORM! IF WE HADN'T FOUND SHELTER, THAT WIND WOULD HAVE FLAYED US ALIVE.
I THINK WE'VE ORORO TO THANK FOR ITS QUICK EXIT.
Y'KNOW, IF I HAD ME SONIC POWERS BACK, I BET I COULD VIBRATE THROUGH THIS BARRIER.
I'D BETTER GIVE IT A TAP, MAKE SURE IT'S STILL--
--HEE-EERRRE!!
BANSHEE, ARE YOU ALL RIGHT?
THE BARRIER, COLLEEN! I FELT IT FOR AN INSTANT, FIRM AS EVER, AN' THEN--POOF! IT VANISHED!
SAINTS, I HOPE IT WAS FOR ALL THE RIGHT REASONS. IF THE X-MEN HAVE BEEN BEATEN...
WHAT'S THAT?! AN ARMORED CAR?
THIS CAGE WAS SPECIALLY-DESIGNED FOR YOU, SHORTY. YOU COULDN'T BUST LOOSE IN A MILLION YEARS.
'COURSE, YOU'RE SO DUMB YOU'LL PROBABLY TRY.
YOU ALWAYS HAD A BIG MOUTH, GARSON. KEEP FLAPPIN' IT AROUND ME...
...AN' YER WIFE'LL BE A WIDOW BEFORE HER TIME.
WOLVERINE IS NOT AN ANIMAL, CYCLOPS. THAT MAN DID NOT HAVE TO TREAT HIM LIKE THAT.
I KNOW.
THEY ARE NOT AS LUCKY AS WE, COLOSSUS. THEY KNOW ONLY THE "SURFACE" WOLVERINE.
THEY KNOW NOTHING OF HIS TRUE SELF.
HOURS LATER...
...THE X-MEN ARE FINALLY HEADING HOME--
--THEIR PLANE ESCORTED TO THE U.S. BORDER BY A FLIGHT OF CANADIAN AIR FORCE FIGHTERS.

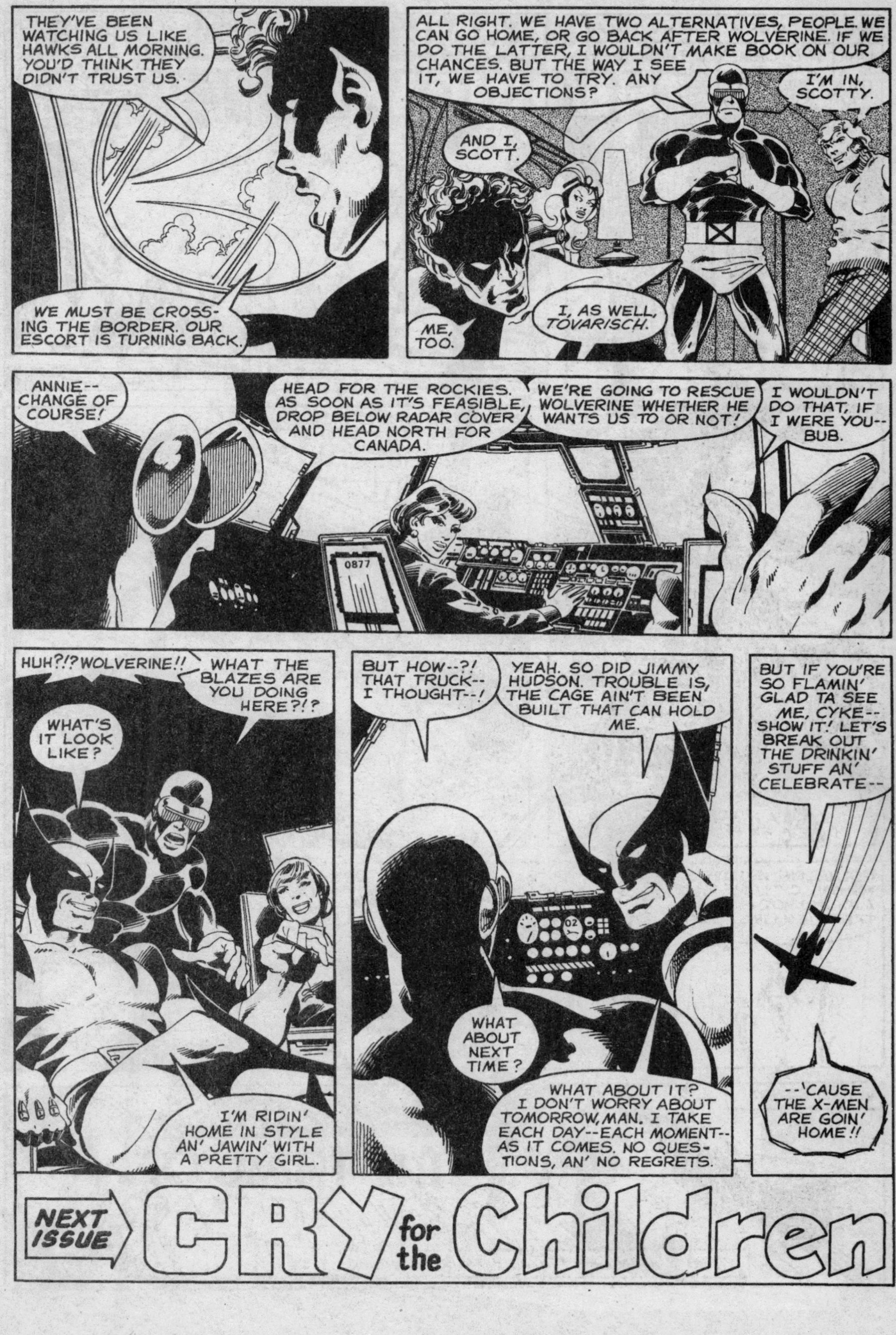
THEY'VE BEEN WATCHING US LIKE HAWKS ALL MORNING. YOU'D THINK THEY DIDN'T TRUST US.
WE MUST BE CROSSING THE BORDER. OUR ESCORT IS TURNING BACK.
ALL RIGHT. WE HAVE TWO ALTERNATIVES, PEOPLE. WE CAN GO HOME, OR GO BACK AFTER WOLVERINE. IF WE DO THE LATTER, I WOULDN'T MAKE BOOK ON OUR CHANCES. BUT THE WAY I SEE IT, WE HAVE TO TRY. ANY OBJECTIONS?
I'M IN, SCOTTY.
AND I, SCOTT.
ME, TOO.
I, AS WELL, TOVARISCH.
ANNIE-- CHANGE OF COURSE!
HEAD FOR THE ROCKIES. AS SOON AS IT'S FEASIBLE, DROP BELOW RADAR COVER AND HEAD NORTH FOR CANADA.
WE'RE GOING TO RESCUE WOLVERINE WHETHER HE WANTS US TO OR NOT!
I WOULDN'T DO THAT, IF I WERE YOU-- BUB.
0877
HUH?!? WOLVERINE!!
WHAT THE BLAZES ARE YOU DOING HERE?!?
WHAT'S IT LOOK LIKE?
I'M RIDIN' HOME IN STYLE AN' JAWIN' WITH A PRETTY GIRL.
BUT HOW--?! THAT TRUCK-- I THOUGHT--!
YEAH. SO DID JIMMY HUDSON. TROUBLE IS, THE CAGE AIN'T BEEN BUILT THAT CAN HOLD ME.
WHAT ABOUT NEXT TIME?
WHAT ABOUT IT? I DON'T WORRY ABOUT TOMORROW, MAN. I TAKE EACH DAY--EACH MOMENT-- AS IT COMES. NO QUESTIONS, AN' NO REGRETS.
BUT IF YOU'RE SO FLAMIN' GLAD TA SEE ME, CYKE-- SHOW IT! LET'S BREAK OUT THE DRINKIN' STUFF AN' CELEBRATE--
--'CAUSE THE X-MEN ARE GOIN' HOME!!
NEXT ISSUE
CRY for the Children

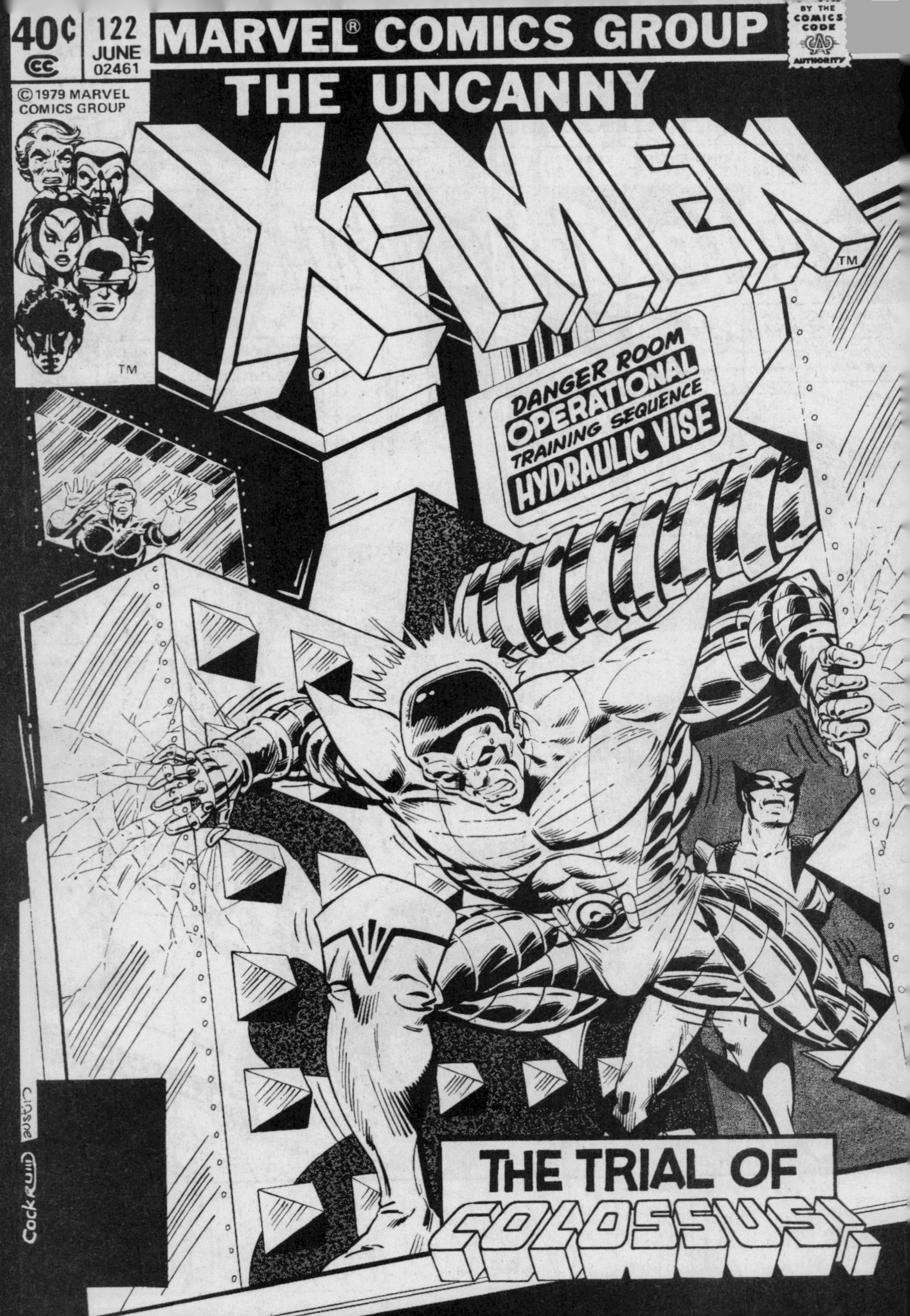

40¢
CC
122
JUNE
02461
MARVEL® COMICS GROUP
BY THE COMICS CODE AUTHORITY
© 1979 MARVEL COMICS GROUP
THE UNCANNY
X-MEN™
DANGER ROOM
OPERATIONAL
TRAINING SEQUENCE
HYDRAULIC VISE
THE TRIAL OF
COLOSSUS!

Cyclops. Storm. Banshee. Nightcrawler. Wolverine. Colossus. Children of the atom, students of Charles Xavier, MUTANTS––feared and hated by the world they have sworn to protect. These are the STRANGEST heroes of all!

Stan Lee PRESENTS: THE UNCANNY X-MEN!™

CHRIS CLAREMONT · JOHN BYRNE · TERRY AUSTIN | TOM ORZECHOWSKI, *letterer* | ROGER STERN * JIM SHOOTER
WRITER / CO-PLOTTERS / BREAKDOWNS · FINISHED ART | *GLYNIS WEIN, colorist* | *EDITOR* *EDITOR-IN-CHIEF*

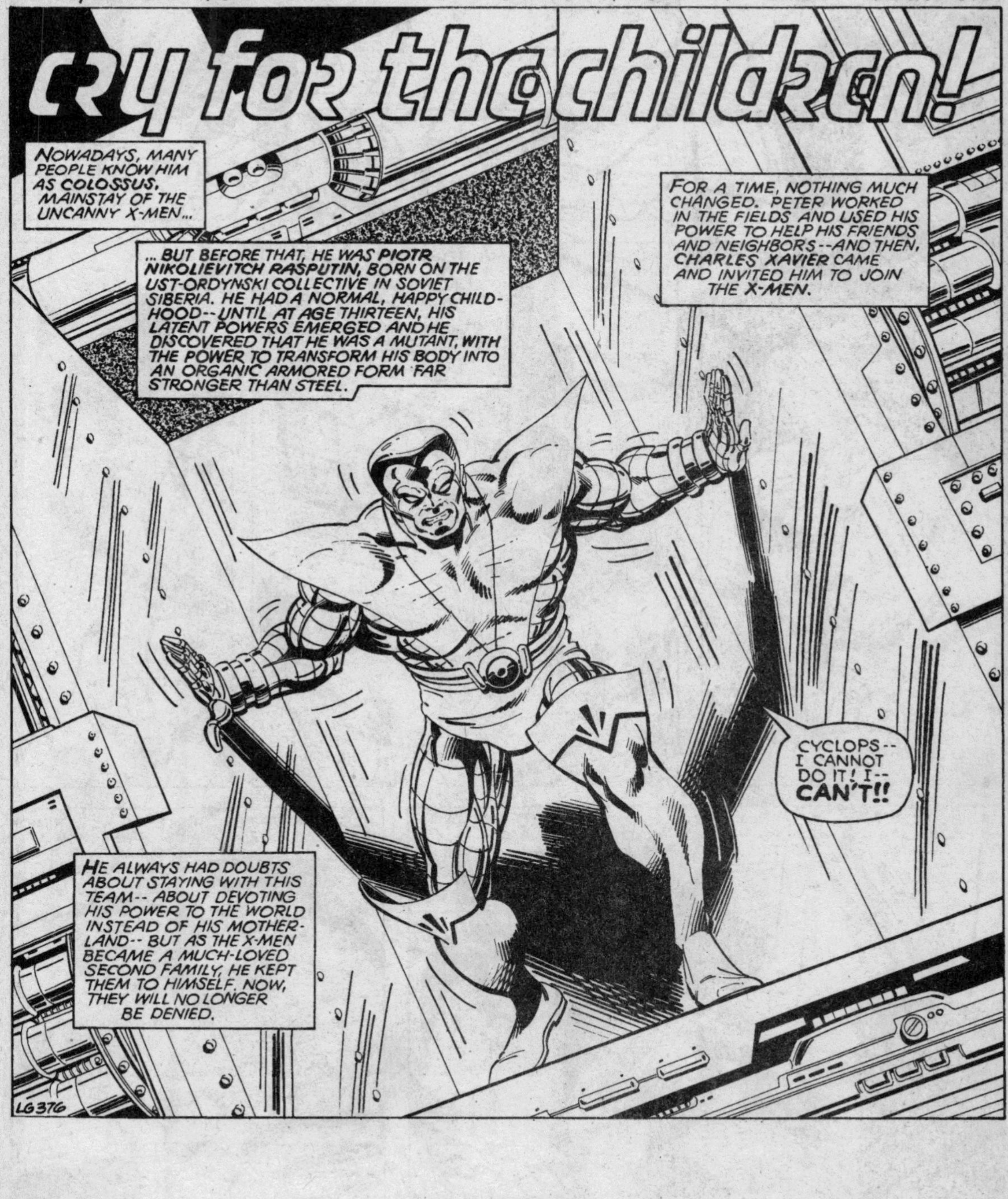
CRY FOR THE CHILDREN!
NOWADAYS, MANY PEOPLE KNOW HIM AS COLOSSUS, MAINSTAY OF THE UNCANNY X-MEN...
... BUT BEFORE THAT, HE WAS PIOTR NIKOLIEVITCH RASPUTIN, BORN ON THE UST-ORDYNSKI COLLECTIVE IN SOVIET SIBERIA. HE HAD A NORMAL, HAPPY CHILDHOOD-- UNTIL AT AGE THIRTEEN, HIS LATENT POWERS EMERGED AND HE DISCOVERED THAT HE WAS A MUTANT, WITH THE POWER TO TRANSFORM HIS BODY INTO AN ORGANIC ARMORED FORM FAR STRONGER THAN STEEL.
FOR A TIME, NOTHING MUCH CHANGED. PETER WORKED IN THE FIELDS AND USED HIS POWER TO HELP HIS FRIENDS AND NEIGHBORS--AND THEN, CHARLES XAVIER CAME AND INVITED HIM TO JOIN THE X-MEN.
CYCLOPS-- I CANNOT DO IT! I-- CAN'T!!
HE ALWAYS HAD DOUBTS ABOUT STAYING WITH THIS TEAM-- ABOUT DEVOTING HIS POWER TO THE WORLD INSTEAD OF HIS MOTHERLAND-- BUT AS THE X-MEN BECAME A MUCH-LOVED SECOND FAMILY, HE KEPT THEM TO HIMSELF. NOW, THEY WILL NO LONGER BE DENIED.
LG 376

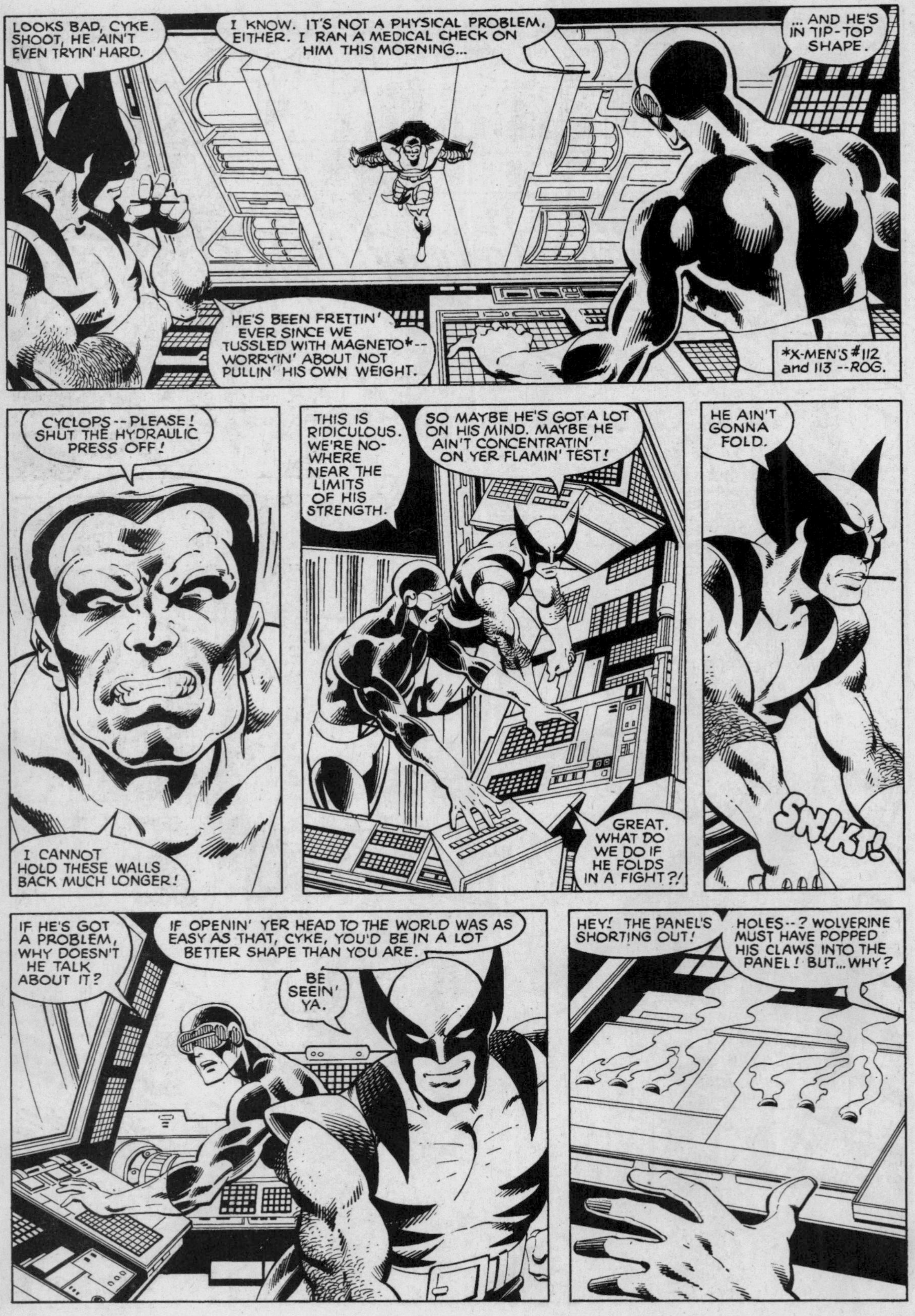
LOOKS BAD, CYKE. SHOOT, HE AIN'T EVEN TRYIN' HARD.
I KNOW. IT'S NOT A PHYSICAL PROBLEM, EITHER. I RAN A MEDICAL CHECK ON HIM THIS MORNING...
... AND HE'S IN TIP-TOP SHAPE.
HE'S BEEN FRETTIN' EVER SINCE WE TUSSLED WITH MAGNETO*-- WORRYIN' ABOUT NOT PULLIN' HIS OWN WEIGHT.
*X-MEN'S #112 and 113 --ROG.
CYCLOPS--PLEASE! SHUT THE HYDRAULIC PRESS OFF!
I CANNOT HOLD THESE WALLS BACK MUCH LONGER!
THIS IS RIDICULOUS. WE'RE NOWHERE NEAR THE LIMITS OF HIS STRENGTH.
SO MAYBE HE'S GOT A LOT ON HIS MIND. MAYBE HE AIN'T CONCENTRATIN' ON YER FLAMIN' TEST!
GREAT. WHAT DO WE DO IF HE FOLDS IN A FIGHT?!
HE AIN'T GONNA FOLD.
SNIKT!
IF HE'S GOT A PROBLEM, WHY DOESN'T HE TALK ABOUT IT?
IF OPENIN' YER HEAD TO THE WORLD WAS AS EASY AS THAT, CYKE, YOU'D BE IN A LOT BETTER SHAPE THAN YOU ARE.
BE SEEIN' YA.
HEY! THE PANEL'S SHORTING OUT!
HOLES--? WOLVERINE MUST HAVE POPPED HIS CLAWS INTO THE PANEL! BUT...WHY?

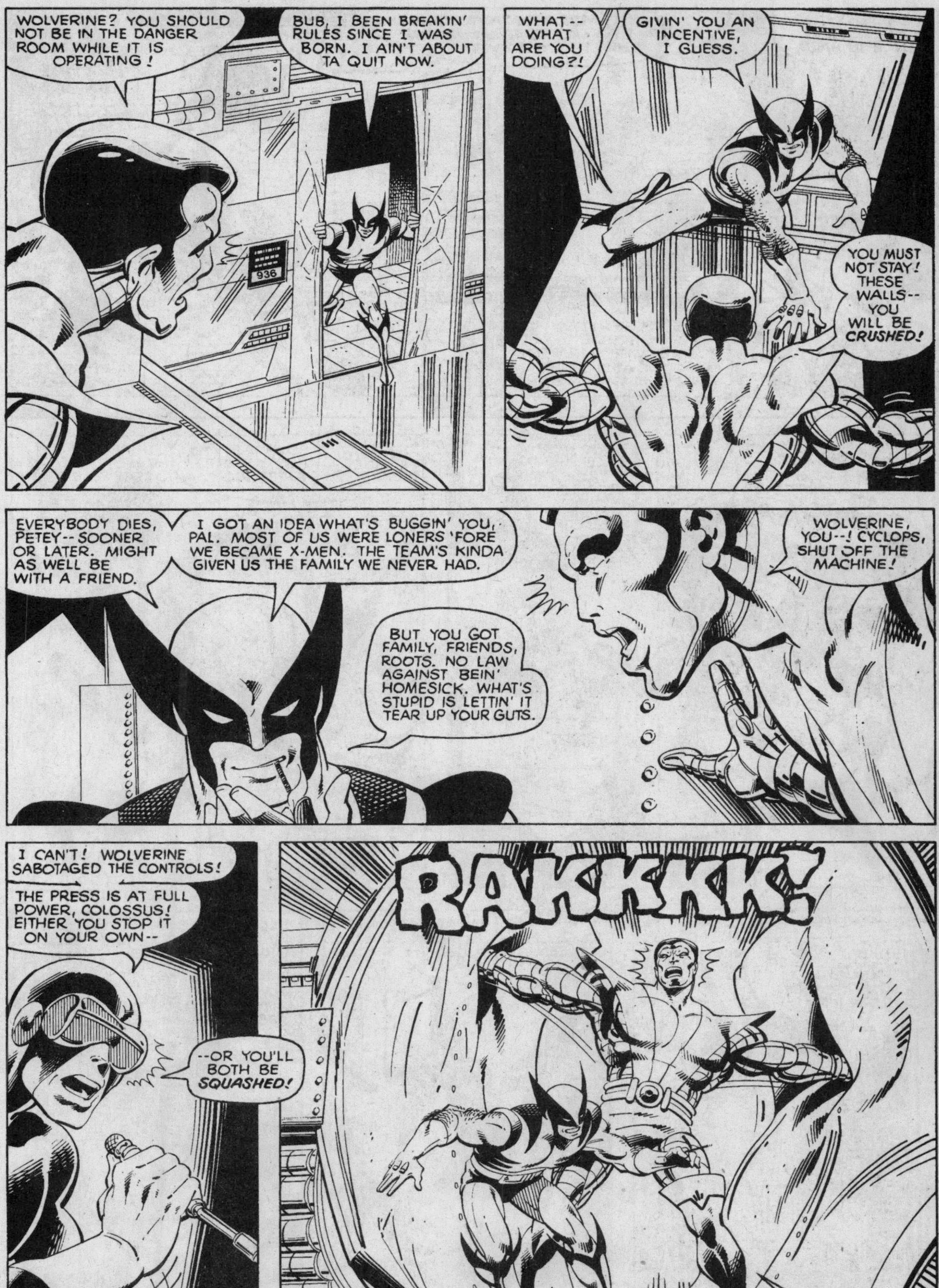
WOLVERINE? YOU SHOULD NOT BE IN THE DANGER ROOM WHILE IT IS OPERATING!
BUB, I BEEN BREAKIN' RULES SINCE I WAS BORN. I AIN'T ABOUT TA QUIT NOW.
936
WHAT--WHAT ARE YOU DOING?!
GIVIN' YOU AN INCENTIVE, I GUESS.
YOU MUST NOT STAY! THESE WALLS--YOU WILL BE CRUSHED!
EVERYBODY DIES, PETEY--SOONER OR LATER. MIGHT AS WELL BE WITH A FRIEND.
I GOT AN IDEA WHAT'S BUGGIN' YOU, PAL. MOST OF US WERE LONERS 'FORE WE BECAME X-MEN. THE TEAM'S KINDA GIVEN US THE FAMILY WE NEVER HAD.
BUT YOU GOT FAMILY, FRIENDS, ROOTS. NO LAW AGAINST BEIN' HOMESICK. WHAT'S STUPID IS LETTIN' IT TEAR UP YOUR GUTS.
WOLVERINE, YOU--! CYCLOPS, SHUT OFF THE MACHINE!
I CAN'T! WOLVERINE SABOTAGED THE CONTROLS!
THE PRESS IS AT FULL POWER, COLOSSUS! EITHER YOU STOP IT ON YOUR OWN--
--OR YOU'LL BOTH BE SQUASHED!
RAKKKK!
WAY TO GO, RUSSKIE!

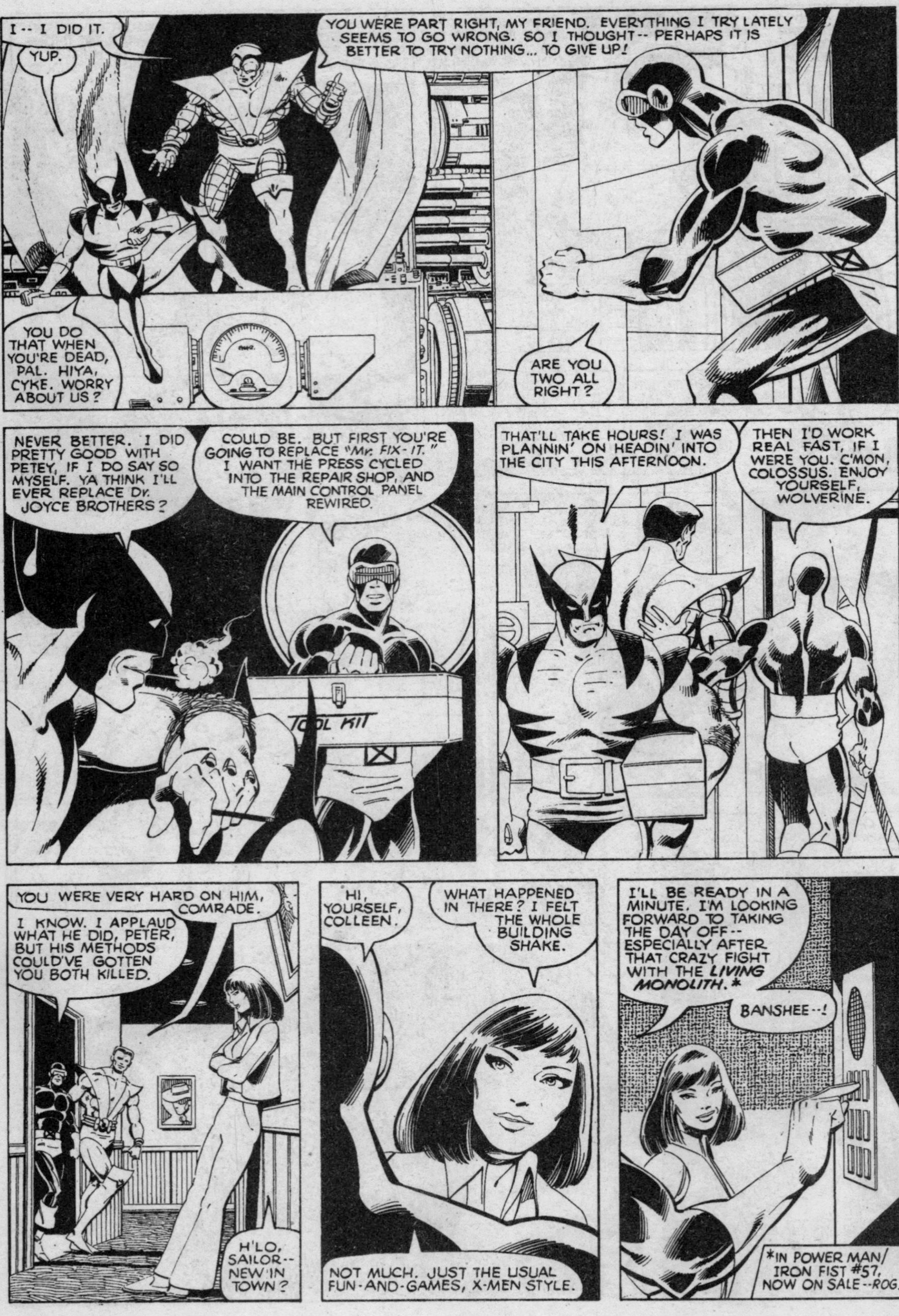
I -- I DID IT.
YUP.
YOU WERE PART RIGHT, MY FRIEND. EVERYTHING I TRY LATELY SEEMS TO GO WRONG. SO I THOUGHT -- PERHAPS IT IS BETTER TO TRY NOTHING... TO GIVE UP!
YOU DO THAT WHEN YOU'RE DEAD, PAL. HIYA, CYKE. WORRY ABOUT US?
ARE YOU TWO ALL RIGHT?
NEVER BETTER. I DID PRETTY GOOD WITH PETEY, IF I DO SAY SO MYSELF. YA THINK I'LL EVER REPLACE Dr. JOYCE BROTHERS?
COULD BE. BUT FIRST YOU'RE GOING TO REPLACE "Mr. FIX-IT." I WANT THE PRESS CYCLED INTO THE REPAIR SHOP, AND THE MAIN CONTROL PANEL REWIRED.
TOOL KIT
THAT'LL TAKE HOURS! I WAS PLANNIN' ON HEADIN' INTO THE CITY THIS AFTERNOON.
THEN I'D WORK REAL FAST, IF I WERE YOU. C'MON, COLOSSUS. ENJOY YOURSELF, WOLVERINE.
YOU WERE VERY HARD ON HIM, COMRADE.
I KNOW. I APPLAUD WHAT HE DID, PETER, BUT HIS METHODS COULD'VE GOTTEN YOU BOTH KILLED.
H'LO, SAILOR-- NEW IN TOWN?
HI, YOURSELF, COLLEEN.
WHAT HAPPENED IN THERE? I FELT THE WHOLE BUILDING SHAKE.
NOT MUCH. JUST THE USUAL FUN-AND-GAMES, X-MEN STYLE.
I'LL BE READY IN A MINUTE. I'M LOOKING FORWARD TO TAKING THE DAY OFF -- ESPECIALLY AFTER THAT CRAZY FIGHT WITH THE LIVING MONOLITH.*
BANSHEE--!
*IN POWER MAN/IRON FIST #57, NOW ON SALE--ROG.

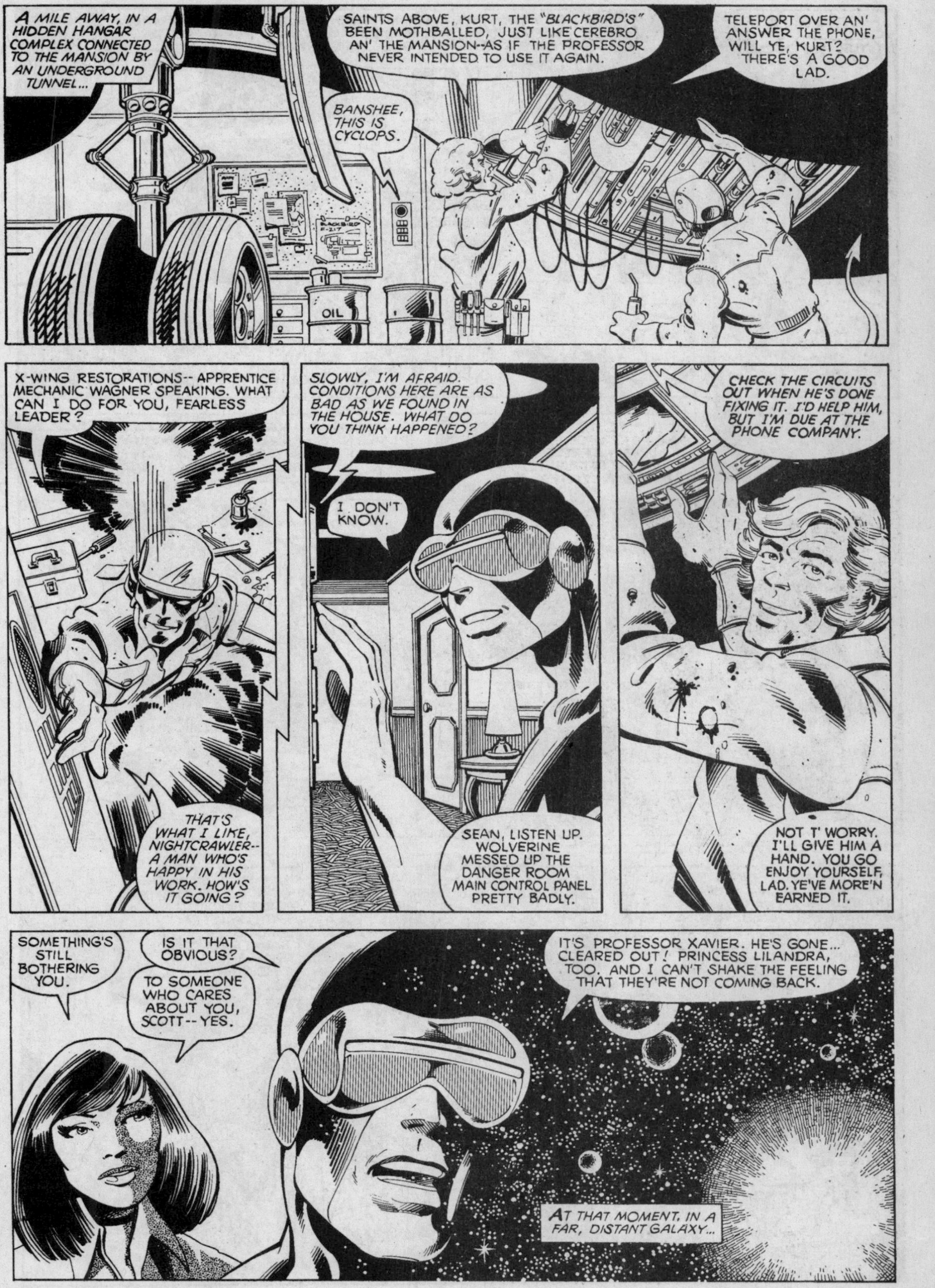

A MILE AWAY, IN A HIDDEN HANGAR COMPLEX CONNECTED TO THE MANSION BY AN UNDERGROUND TUNNEL...
SAINTS ABOVE, KURT, THE "BLACKBIRD'S" BEEN MOTHBALLED, JUST LIKE CEREBRO AN' THE MANSION--AS IF THE PROFESSOR NEVER INTENDED TO USE IT AGAIN.
TELEPORT OVER AN' ANSWER THE PHONE, WILL YE, KURT? THERE'S A GOOD LAD.
BANSHEE, THIS IS CYCLOPS.
OIL
X-WING RESTORATIONS-- APPRENTICE MECHANIC WAGNER SPEAKING. WHAT CAN I DO FOR YOU, FEARLESS LEADER?
THAT'S WHAT I LIKE, NIGHTCRAWLER-- A MAN WHO'S HAPPY IN HIS WORK. HOW'S IT GOING?
SLOWLY, I'M AFRAID. CONDITIONS HERE ARE AS BAD AS WE FOUND IN THE HOUSE. WHAT DO YOU THINK HAPPENED?
I DON'T KNOW.
SEAN, LISTEN UP. WOLVERINE MESSED UP THE DANGER ROOM MAIN CONTROL PANEL PRETTY BADLY.
CHECK THE CIRCUITS OUT WHEN HE'S DONE FIXING IT. I'D HELP HIM, BUT I'M DUE AT THE PHONE COMPANY.
NOT T' WORRY. I'LL GIVE HIM A HAND. YOU GO ENJOY YOURSELF, LAD. YE'VE MORE'N EARNED IT.
SOMETHING'S STILL BOTHERING YOU.
IS IT THAT OBVIOUS?
TO SOMEONE WHO CARES ABOUT YOU, SCOTT -- YES.
IT'S PROFESSOR XAVIER. HE'S GONE... CLEARED OUT! PRINCESS LILANDRA, TOO. AND I CAN'T SHAKE THE FEELING THAT THEY'RE NOT COMING BACK.
AT THAT MOMENT, IN A FAR, DISTANT GALAXY...

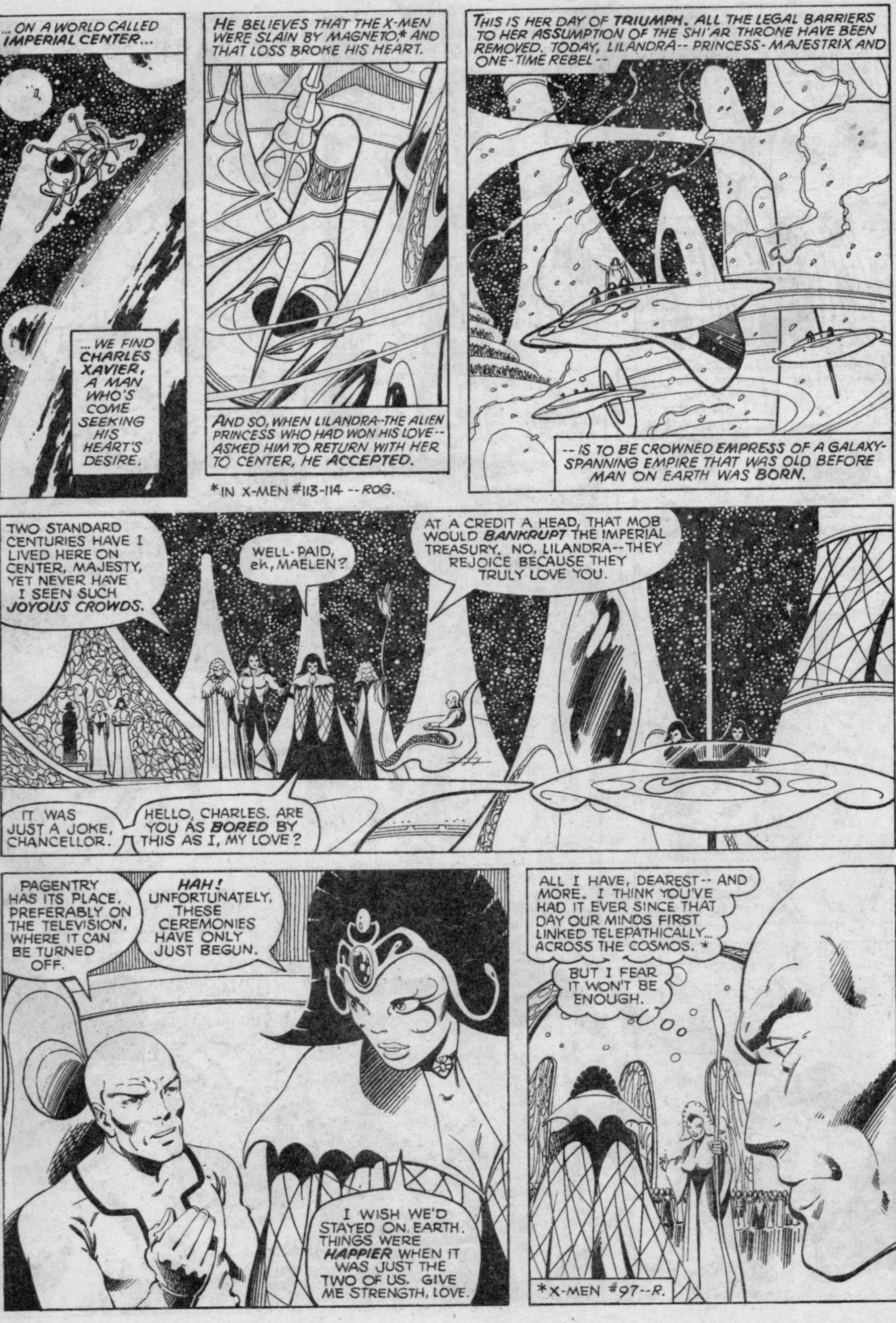
...ON A WORLD CALLED IMPERIAL CENTER...
...WE FIND CHARLES XAVIER, A MAN WHO'S COME SEEKING HIS HEART'S DESIRE.
HE BELIEVES THAT THE X-MEN WERE SLAIN BY MAGNETO,* AND THAT LOSS BROKE HIS HEART.
AND SO, WHEN LILANDRA--THE ALIEN PRINCESS WHO HAD WON HIS LOVE--ASKED HIM TO RETURN WITH HER TO CENTER, HE ACCEPTED.
*IN X-MEN #113-114 --ROG.
THIS IS HER DAY OF TRIUMPH. ALL THE LEGAL BARRIERS TO HER ASSUMPTION OF THE SHI'AR THRONE HAVE BEEN REMOVED. TODAY, LILANDRA-- PRINCESS-MAJESTRIX AND ONE-TIME REBEL--
--IS TO BE CROWNED EMPRESS OF A GALAXY-SPANNING EMPIRE THAT WAS OLD BEFORE MAN ON EARTH WAS BORN.
TWO STANDARD CENTURIES HAVE I LIVED HERE ON CENTER, MAJESTY, YET NEVER HAVE I SEEN SUCH JOYOUS CROWDS.
WELL-PAID, eh, MAELEN?
AT A CREDIT A HEAD, THAT MOB WOULD BANKRUPT THE IMPERIAL TREASURY. NO, LILANDRA--THEY REJOICE BECAUSE THEY TRULY LOVE YOU.
IT WAS JUST A JOKE, CHANCELLOR.
HELLO, CHARLES. ARE YOU AS BORED BY THIS AS I, MY LOVE?
PAGENTRY HAS ITS PLACE. PREFERABLY ON THE TELEVISION, WHERE IT CAN BE TURNED OFF.
HAH! UNFORTUNATELY, THESE CEREMONIES HAVE ONLY JUST BEGUN.
I WISH WE'D STAYED ON EARTH. THINGS WERE HAPPIER WHEN IT WAS JUST THE TWO OF US. GIVE ME STRENGTH, LOVE.
ALL I HAVE, DEAREST-- AND MORE. I THINK YOU'VE HAD IT EVER SINCE THAT DAY OUR MINDS FIRST LINKED TELEPATHICALLY... ACROSS THE COSMOS. *
BUT I FEAR IT WON'T BE ENOUGH.
*X-MEN #97--R.

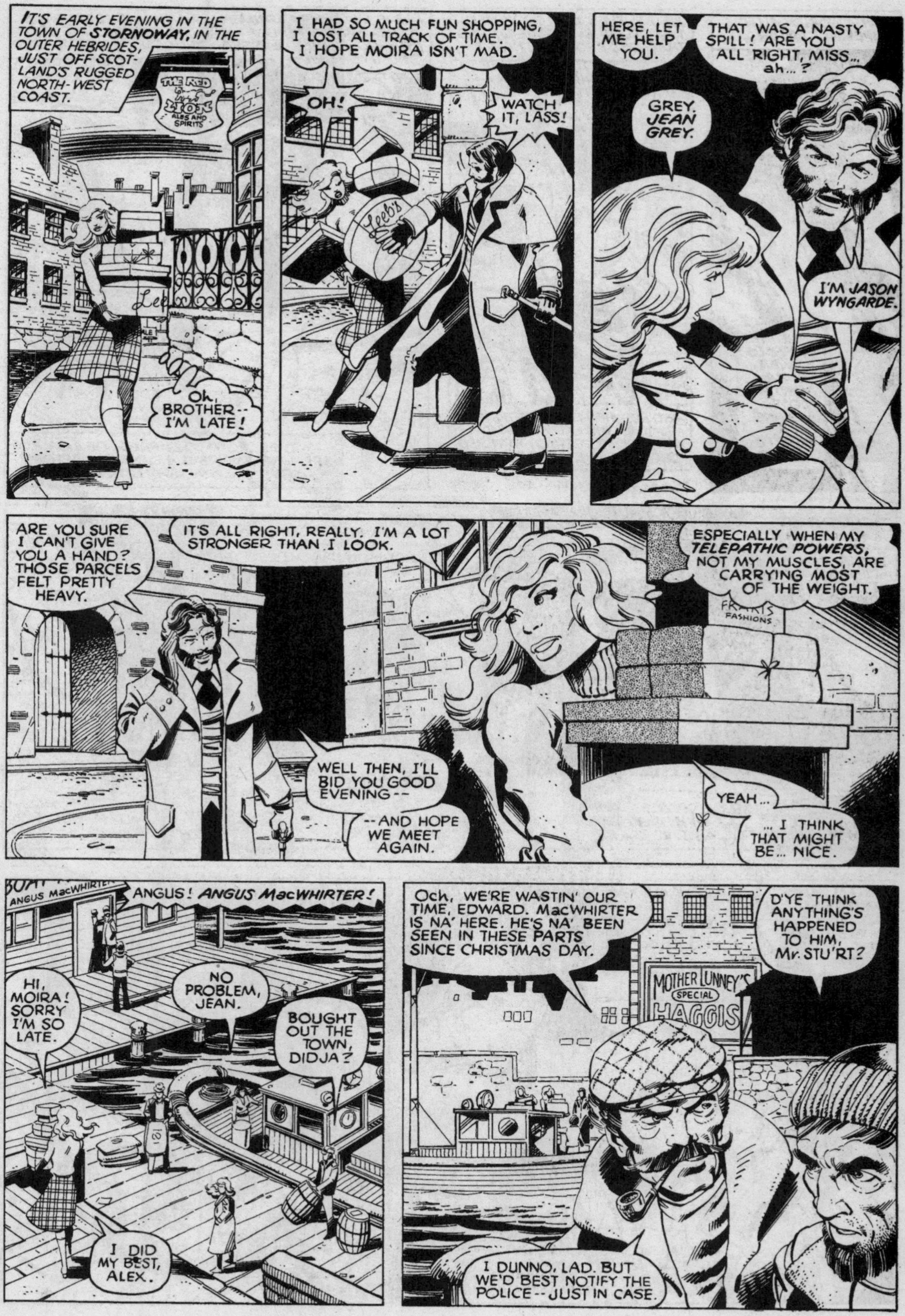

IT'S EARLY EVENING IN THE TOWN OF STORNOWAY, IN THE OUTER HEBRIDES, JUST OFF SCOTLAND'S RUGGED NORTH-WEST COAST.
THE RED LION ALES AND SPIRITS
Oh, BROTHER-- I'M LATE!
I HAD SO MUCH FUN SHOPPING, I LOST ALL TRACK OF TIME. I HOPE MOIRA ISN'T MAD.
OH!
WATCH IT, LASS!
HERE, LET ME HELP YOU.
THAT WAS A NASTY SPILL! ARE YOU ALL RIGHT, MISS... ah...?
GREY. JEAN GREY.
I'M JASON WYNGARDE.
ARE YOU SURE I CAN'T GIVE YOU A HAND? THOSE PARCELS FELT PRETTY HEAVY.
IT'S ALL RIGHT, REALLY. I'M A LOT STRONGER THAN I LOOK.
ESPECIALLY WHEN MY TELEPATHIC POWERS, NOT MY MUSCLES, ARE CARRYING MOST OF THE WEIGHT.
FRAKTS FASHIONS
WELL THEN, I'LL BID YOU GOOD EVENING--
--AND HOPE WE MEET AGAIN.
YEAH...
...I THINK THAT MIGHT BE... NICE.
ANGUS MacWHIRTER
ANGUS! ANGUS MacWHIRTER!
HI, MOIRA! SORRY I'M SO LATE.
NO PROBLEM, JEAN.
BOUGHT OUT THE TOWN, DIDJA?
I DID MY BEST, ALEX.
Och, WE'RE WASTIN' OUR TIME, EDWARD. MacWHIRTER IS NA' HERE. HE'S NA' BEEN SEEN IN THESE PARTS SINCE CHRISTMAS DAY.
D'YE THINK ANYTHING'S HAPPENED TO HIM, Mr. STU'RT?
MOTHER LUNNEY'S SPECIAL HAGGIS
I DUNNO, LAD. BUT WE'D BEST NOTIFY THE POLICE--JUST IN CASE.

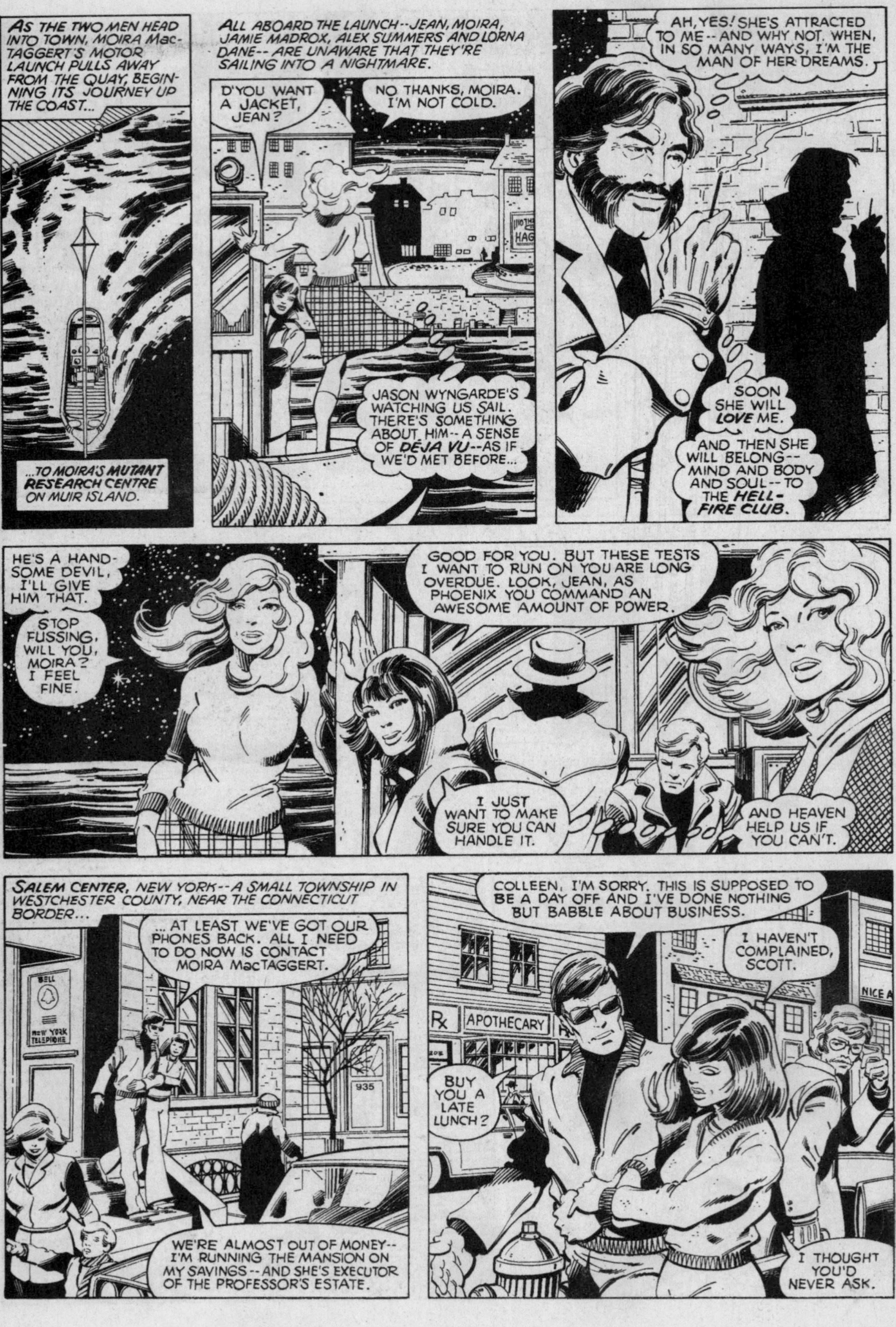
AS THE TWO MEN HEAD INTO TOWN, MOIRA MacTAGGERT'S MOTOR LAUNCH PULLS AWAY FROM THE QUAY, BEGINNING ITS JOURNEY UP THE COAST...
...TO MOIRA'S MUTANT RESEARCH CENTRE ON MUIR ISLAND.
ALL ABOARD THE LAUNCH--JEAN, MOIRA, JAMIE MADROX, ALEX SUMMERS AND LORNA DANE--ARE UNAWARE THAT THEY'RE SAILING INTO A NIGHTMARE.
D'YOU WANT A JACKET, JEAN?
NO THANKS, MOIRA. I'M NOT COLD.
JASON WYNGARDE'S WATCHING US SAIL. THERE'S SOMETHING ABOUT HIM--A SENSE OF DÉJA VU--AS IF WE'D MET BEFORE...
AH, YES! SHE'S ATTRACTED TO ME--AND WHY NOT. WHEN, IN SO MANY WAYS, I'M THE MAN OF HER DREAMS.
SOON SHE WILL LOVE ME.
AND THEN SHE WILL BELONG--MIND AND BODY AND SOUL--TO THE HELL-FIRE CLUB.
HE'S A HANDSOME DEVIL, I'LL GIVE HIM THAT.
STOP FUSSING, WILL YOU, MOIRA? I FEEL FINE.
GOOD FOR YOU. BUT THESE TESTS I WANT TO RUN ON YOU ARE LONG OVERDUE. LOOK, JEAN, AS PHOENIX YOU COMMAND AN AWESOME AMOUNT OF POWER.
I JUST WANT TO MAKE SURE YOU CAN HANDLE IT.
AND HEAVEN HELP US IF YOU CAN'T.
SALEM CENTER, NEW YORK--A SMALL TOWNSHIP IN WESTCHESTER COUNTY, NEAR THE CONNECTICUT BORDER...
...AT LEAST WE'VE GOT OUR PHONES BACK. ALL I NEED TO DO NOW IS CONTACT MOIRA MacTAGGERT.
BELL
NEW YORK TELEPHONE
935
WE'RE ALMOST OUT OF MONEY--I'M RUNNING THE MANSION ON MY SAVINGS--AND SHE'S EXECUTOR OF THE PROFESSOR'S ESTATE.
COLLEEN, I'M SORRY. THIS IS SUPPOSED TO BE A DAY OFF AND I'VE DONE NOTHING BUT BABBLE ABOUT BUSINESS.
I HAVEN'T COMPLAINED, SCOTT.
Rx
APOTHECARY
BUY YOU A LATE LUNCH?
I THOUGHT YOU'D NEVER ASK.

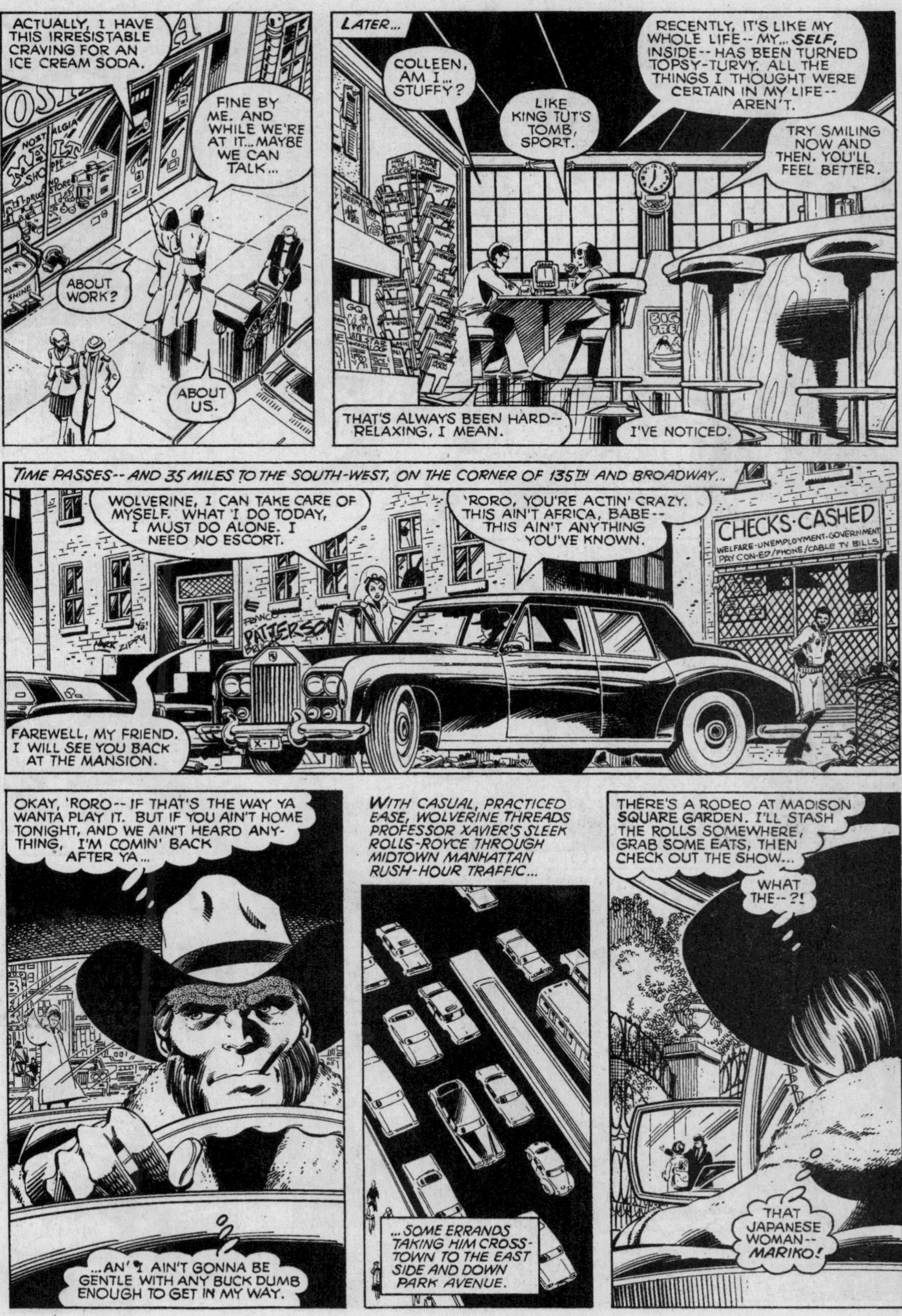
ACTUALLY, I HAVE THIS IRRESISTABLE CRAVING FOR AN ICE CREAM SODA.
FINE BY ME. AND WHILE WE'RE AT IT... MAYBE WE CAN TALK...
ABOUT WORK?
ABOUT US.
NOSTALGIA MALT SHOPPE AND DRUG STORE
LATER...
COLLEEN, AM I... STUFFY?
LIKE KING TUT'S TOMB, SPORT.
RECENTLY, IT'S LIKE MY WHOLE LIFE-- MY... SELF, INSIDE-- HAS BEEN TURNED TOPSY-TURVY. ALL THE THINGS I THOUGHT WERE CERTAIN IN MY LIFE-- AREN'T.
TRY SMILING NOW AND THEN. YOU'LL FEEL BETTER.
THAT'S ALWAYS BEEN HARD-- RELAXING, I MEAN.
I'VE NOTICED.
TIME PASSES-- AND 35 MILES TO THE SOUTH-WEST, ON THE CORNER OF 135TH AND BROADWAY...
WOLVERINE, I CAN TAKE CARE OF MYSELF. WHAT I DO TODAY, I MUST DO ALONE. I NEED NO ESCORT.
'RORO, YOU'RE ACTIN' CRAZY. THIS AIN'T AFRICA, BABE-- THIS AIN'T ANYTHING YOU'VE KNOWN.
CHECKS·CASHED
WELFARE·UNEMPLOYMENT·GOVERNMENT
PAY CON-ED/PHONE/CABLE TV BILLS
PATTERSON
X-1
FAREWELL, MY FRIEND. I WILL SEE YOU BACK AT THE MANSION.
OKAY, 'RORO-- IF THAT'S THE WAY YA WANTA PLAY IT. BUT IF YOU AIN'T HOME TONIGHT, AND WE AIN'T HEARD ANYTHING, I'M COMIN' BACK AFTER YA...
...AN' I AIN'T GONNA BE GENTLE WITH ANY BUCK DUMB ENOUGH TO GET IN MY WAY.
WITH CASUAL, PRACTICED EASE, WOLVERINE THREADS PROFESSOR XAVIER'S SLEEK ROLLS-ROYCE THROUGH MIDTOWN MANHATTAN RUSH-HOUR TRAFFIC...
...SOME ERRANDS TAKING HIM CROSS-TOWN TO THE EAST SIDE AND DOWN PARK AVENUE.
THERE'S A RODEO AT MADISON SQUARE GARDEN. I'LL STASH THE ROLLS SOMEWHERE, GRAB SOME EATS, THEN CHECK OUT THE SHOW...
WHAT THE--?!
THAT JAPANESE WOMAN-- MARIKO!

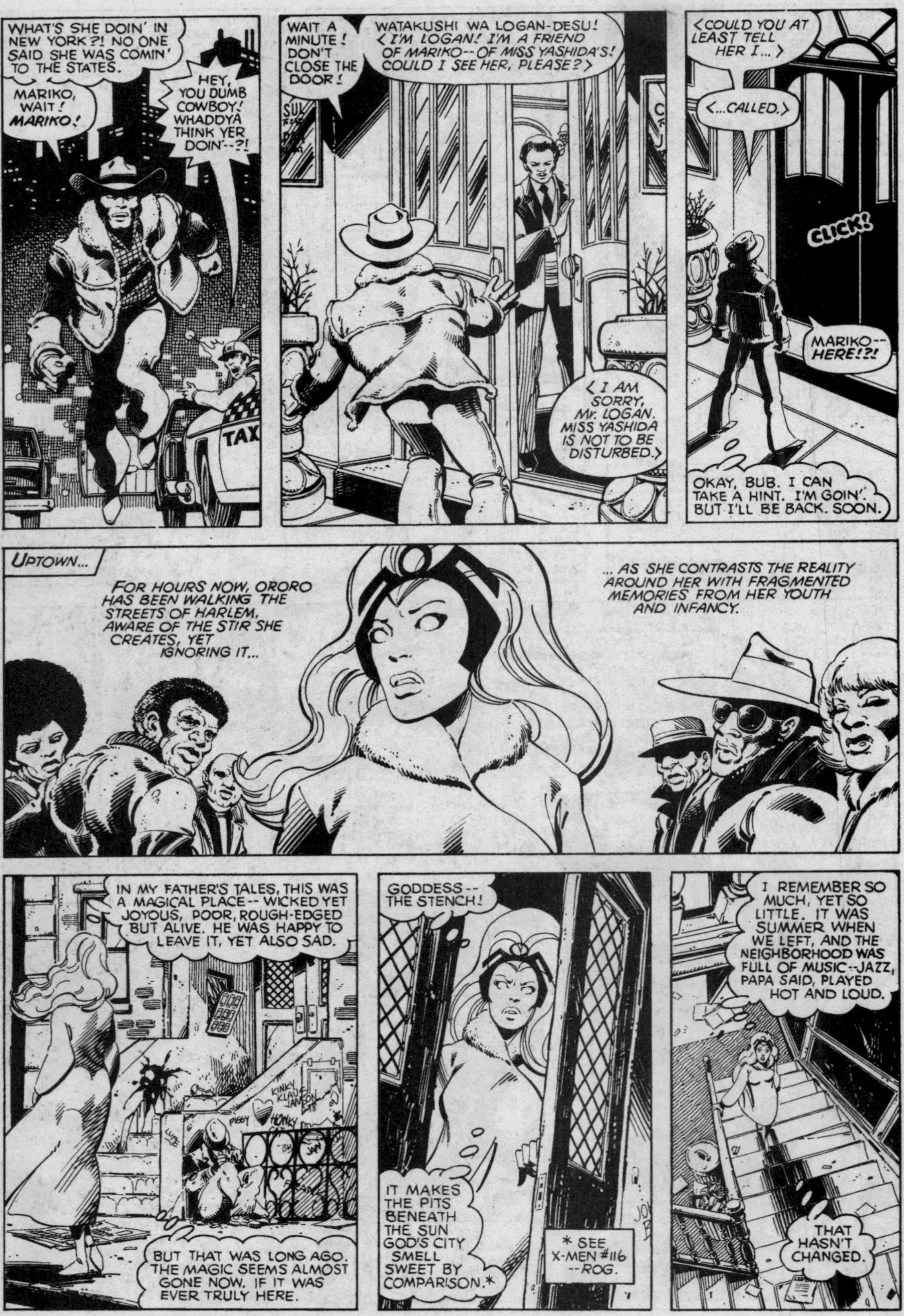

WHAT'S SHE DOIN' IN NEW YORK?! NO ONE SAID SHE WAS COMIN' TO THE STATES.
MARIKO, WAIT! MARIKO!
HEY, YOU DUMB COWBOY! WHADDYA THINK YER DOIN'--?!
WAIT A MINUTE! DON'T CLOSE THE DOOR!
WATAKUSHI WA LOGAN-DESU! <I'M LOGAN! I'M A FRIEND OF MARIKO--OF MISS YASHIDA'S! COULD I SEE HER, PLEASE?>
<I AM SORRY, Mr. LOGAN. MISS YASHIDA IS NOT TO BE DISTURBED.>
<COULD YOU AT LEAST TELL HER I...>
<...CALLED.>
CLICK!
MARIKO-- HERE!?!
OKAY, BUB. I CAN TAKE A HINT. I'M GOIN'. BUT I'LL BE BACK. SOON.
UPTOWN...
FOR HOURS NOW, ORORO HAS BEEN WALKING THE STREETS OF HARLEM, AWARE OF THE STIR SHE CREATES, YET IGNORING IT...
...AS SHE CONTRASTS THE REALITY AROUND HER WITH FRAGMENTED MEMORIES FROM HER YOUTH AND INFANCY.
IN MY FATHER'S TALES, THIS WAS A MAGICAL PLACE-- WICKED YET JOYOUS, POOR, ROUGH-EDGED BUT ALIVE. HE WAS HAPPY TO LEAVE IT, YET ALSO SAD.
BUT THAT WAS LONG AGO. THE MAGIC SEEMS ALMOST GONE NOW. IF IT WAS EVER TRULY HERE.
GODDESS-- THE STENCH!
IT MAKES THE PITS BENEATH THE SUN GOD'S CITY SMELL SWEET BY COMPARISON.*
* SEE X-MEN #116 --ROG.
I REMEMBER SO MUCH, YET SO LITTLE. IT WAS SUMMER WHEN WE LEFT, AND THE NEIGHBORHOOD WAS FULL OF MUSIC--JAZZ, PAPA SAID, PLAYED HOT AND LOUD.
THAT HASN'T CHANGED.

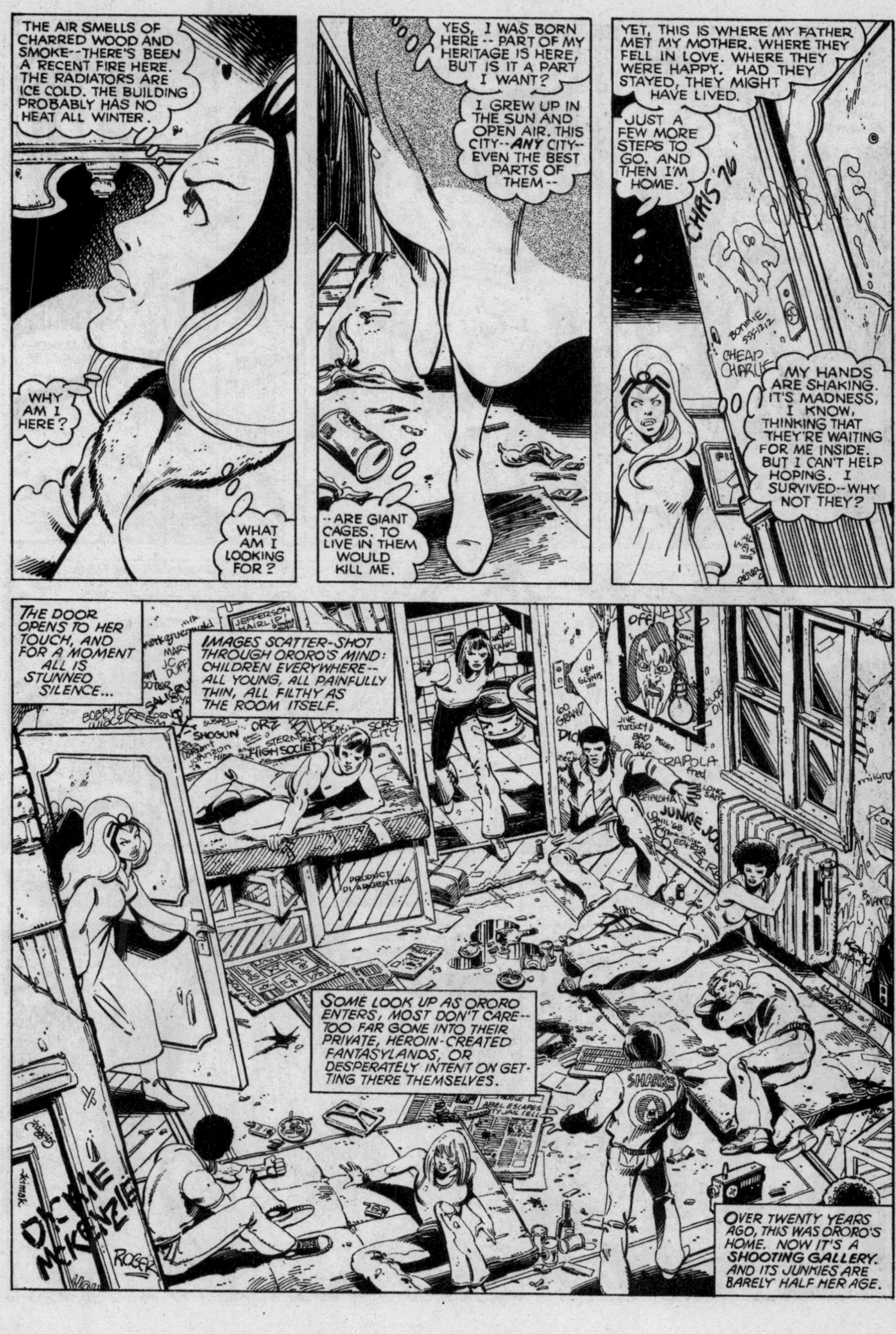
THE AIR SMELLS OF CHARRED WOOD AND SMOKE--THERE'S BEEN A RECENT FIRE HERE. THE RADIATORS ARE ICE COLD. THE BUILDING PROBABLY HAS NO HEAT ALL WINTER.
WHY AM I HERE?
WHAT AM I LOOKING FOR?
YES, I WAS BORN HERE -- PART OF MY HERITAGE IS HERE, BUT IS IT A PART I WANT?
I GREW UP IN THE SUN AND OPEN AIR. THIS CITY--ANY CITY--EVEN THE BEST PARTS OF THEM --
--ARE GIANT CAGES. TO LIVE IN THEM WOULD KILL ME.
YET, THIS IS WHERE MY FATHER MET MY MOTHER. WHERE THEY FELL IN LOVE. WHERE THEY WERE HAPPY. HAD THEY STAYED, THEY MIGHT HAVE LIVED.
JUST A FEW MORE STEPS TO GO. AND THEN I'M HOME.
CHRIS '76
CHEAP CHARLIE
MY HANDS ARE SHAKING. IT'S MADNESS, I KNOW, THINKING THAT THEY'RE WAITING FOR ME INSIDE. BUT I CAN'T HELP HOPING. I SURVIVED--WHY NOT THEY?
THE DOOR OPENS TO HER TOUCH, AND FOR A MOMENT ALL IS STUNNED SILENCE...
IMAGES SCATTER-SHOT THROUGH ORORO'S MIND: CHILDREN EVERYWHERE--ALL YOUNG, ALL PAINFULLY THIN, ALL FILTHY AS THE ROOM ITSELF.
JEFFERSON AIRLIP!
SHOGUN
HIGH SOCIETY
SCAG CITY
LEN GLYNIS
60 GRAND
CRAPOLA
JUNKIE JOE
PRODUCT DI ARGENTINA
SOME LOOK UP AS ORORO ENTERS; MOST DON'T CARE--TOO FAR GONE INTO THEIR PRIVATE, HEROIN-CREATED FANTASYLANDS, OR DESPERATELY INTENT ON GETTING THERE THEMSELVES.
SHARKS
DICKIE MCKENZIE
ROGER
OVER TWENTY YEARS AGO, THIS WAS ORORO'S HOME. NOW IT'S A SHOOTING GALLERY. AND ITS JUNKIES ARE BARELY HALF HER AGE.

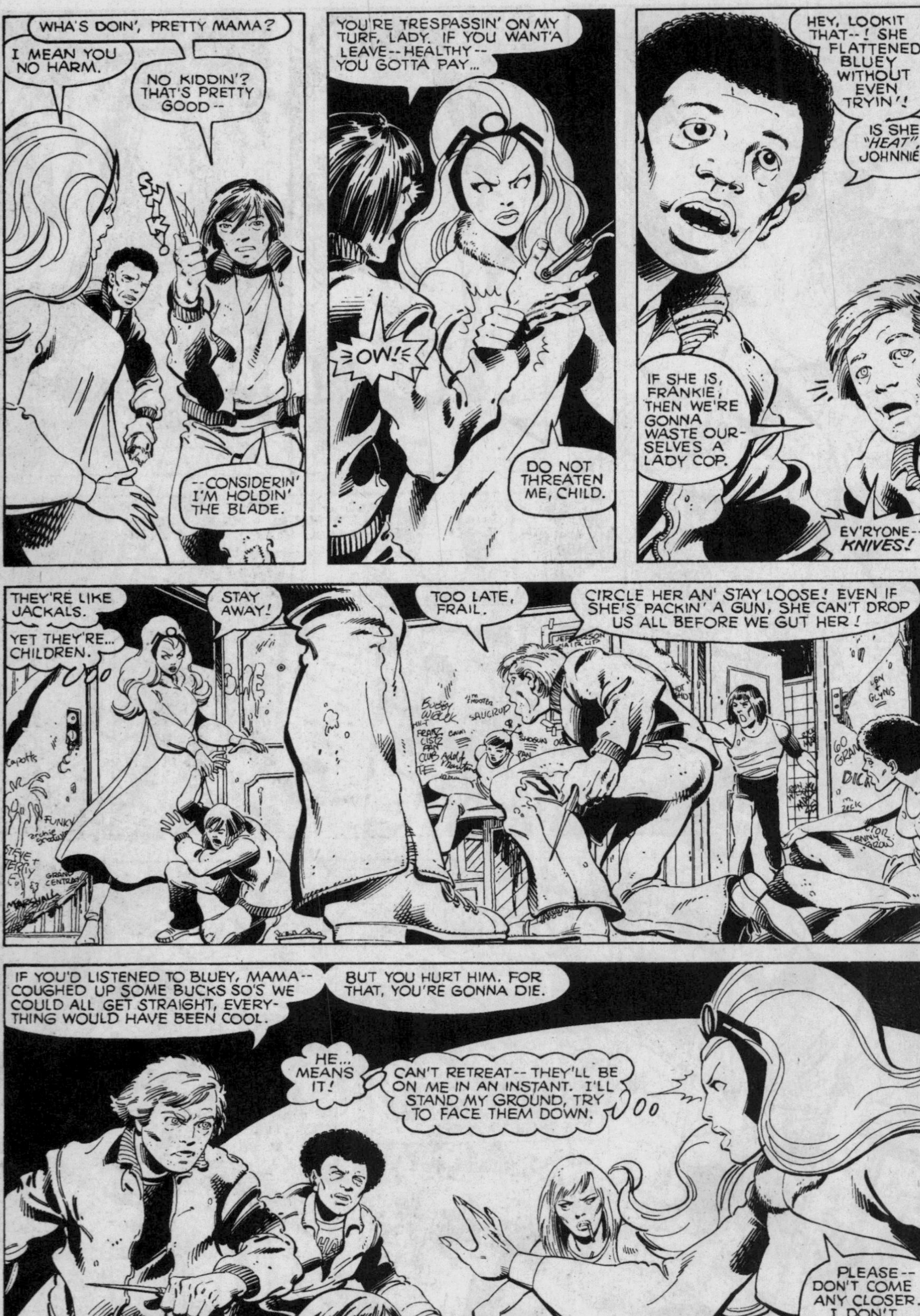

WHA'S DOIN', PRETTY MAMA?
I MEAN YOU NO HARM.
NO KIDDIN'? THAT'S PRETTY GOOD--
--CONSIDERIN' I'M HOLDIN' THE BLADE.
YOU'RE TRESPASSIN' ON MY TURF, LADY. IF YOU WANT'A LEAVE--HEALTHY--YOU GOTTA PAY...
OW!
DO NOT THREATEN ME, CHILD.
HEY, LOOKIT THAT--! SHE FLATTENED BLUEY WITHOUT EVEN TRYIN'!
IS SHE "HEAT" JOHNNIE?
IF SHE IS, FRANKIE, THEN WE'RE GONNA WASTE OURSELVES A LADY COP.
EV'RYONE--KNIVES!
THEY'RE LIKE JACKALS.
YET THEY'RE... CHILDREN.
STAY AWAY!
TOO LATE, FRAIL.
CIRCLE HER AN' STAY LOOSE! EVEN IF SHE'S PACKIN' A GUN, SHE CAN'T DROP US ALL BEFORE WE GUT HER!
IF YOU'D LISTENED TO BLUEY, MAMA--COUGHED UP SOME BUCKS SO'S WE COULD ALL GET STRAIGHT, EVERYTHING WOULD HAVE BEEN COOL.
BUT YOU HURT HIM. FOR THAT, YOU'RE GONNA DIE.
HE... MEANS IT!
CAN'T RETREAT--THEY'LL BE ON ME IN AN INSTANT. I'LL STAND MY GROUND, TRY TO FACE THEM DOWN.
PLEASE--DON'T COME ANY CLOSER. I DON'T WANT TO HARM YOU--!

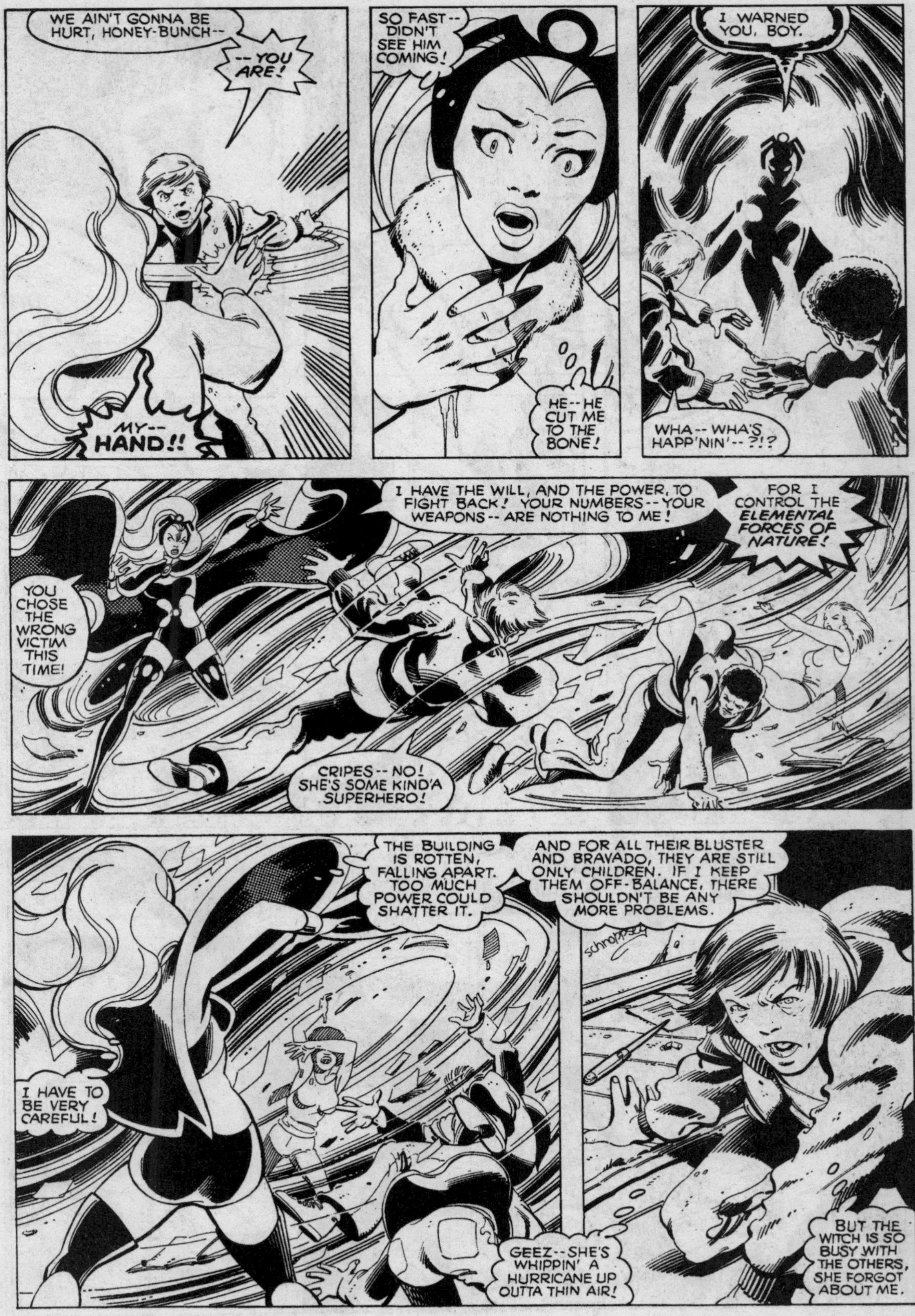

WE AIN'T GONNA BE HURT, HONEY-BUNCH--
--YOU ARE!
MY-- HAND!!
SO FAST-- DIDN'T SEE HIM COMING!
HE--HE CUT ME TO THE BONE!
I WARNED YOU, BOY.
WHA--WHA'S HAPP'NIN'--?!?
I HAVE THE WILL, AND THE POWER, TO FIGHT BACK! YOUR NUMBERS--YOUR WEAPONS--ARE NOTHING TO ME!
FOR I CONTROL THE ELEMENTAL FORCES OF NATURE!
YOU CHOSE THE WRONG VICTIM THIS TIME!
CRIPES--NO! SHE'S SOME KIND'A SUPERHERO!
THE BUILDING IS ROTTEN, FALLING APART. TOO MUCH POWER COULD SHATTER IT.
AND FOR ALL THEIR BLUSTER AND BRAVADO, THEY ARE STILL ONLY CHILDREN. IF I KEEP THEM OFF-BALANCE, THERE SHOULDN'T BE ANY MORE PROBLEMS.
I HAVE TO BE VERY CAREFUL!
GEEZ--SHE'S WHIPPIN' A HURRICANE UP OUTTA THIN AIR!
BUT THE WITCH IS SO BUSY WITH THE OTHERS, SHE FORGOT ABOUT ME.

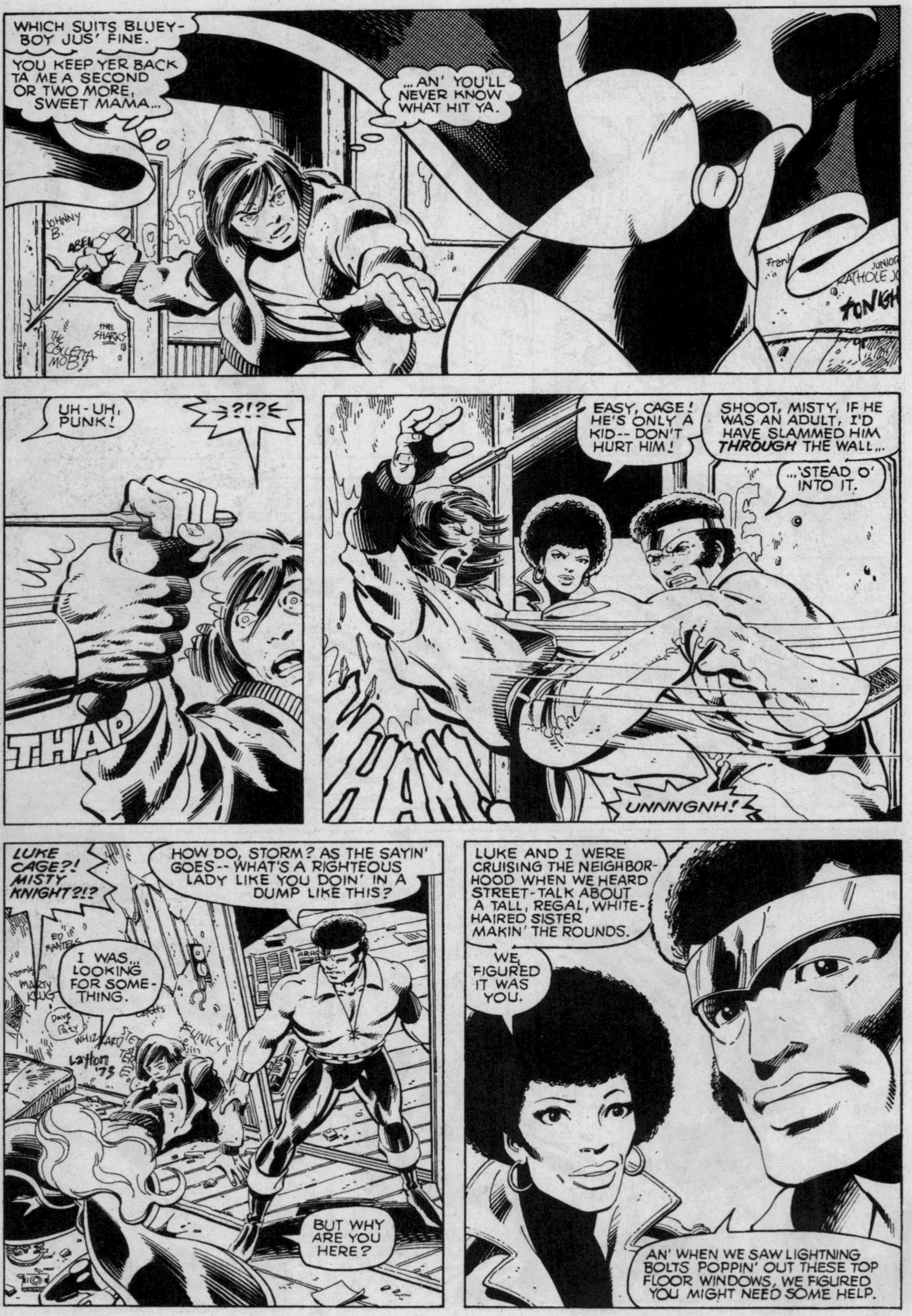
WHICH SUITS BLUEY-BOY JUS' FINE.
YOU KEEP YER BACK TA ME A SECOND OR TWO MORE, SWEET MAMA...
...AN' YOU'LL NEVER KNOW WHAT HIT YA.
UH-UH, PUNK!
?!!?
THAP
EASY, CAGE! HE'S ONLY A KID-- DON'T HURT HIM!
SHOOT, MISTY, IF HE WAS AN ADULT, I'D HAVE SLAMMED HIM THROUGH THE WALL...
...'STEAD O' INTO IT.
WHAM
UNNNGNH!
LUKE CAGE?! MISTY KNIGHT?!?
HOW DO, STORM? AS THE SAYIN' GOES-- WHAT'S A RIGHTEOUS LADY LIKE YOU DOIN' IN A DUMP LIKE THIS?
I WAS... LOOKING FOR SOME-THING.
BUT WHY ARE YOU HERE?
LUKE AND I WERE CRUISING THE NEIGHBOR-HOOD WHEN WE HEARD STREET-TALK ABOUT A TALL, REGAL, WHITE-HAIRED SISTER MAKIN' THE ROUNDS.
WE FIGURED IT WAS YOU.
AN' WHEN WE SAW LIGHTNING BOLTS POPPIN' OUT THESE TOP FLOOR WINDOWS, WE FIGURED YOU MIGHT NEED SOME HELP.

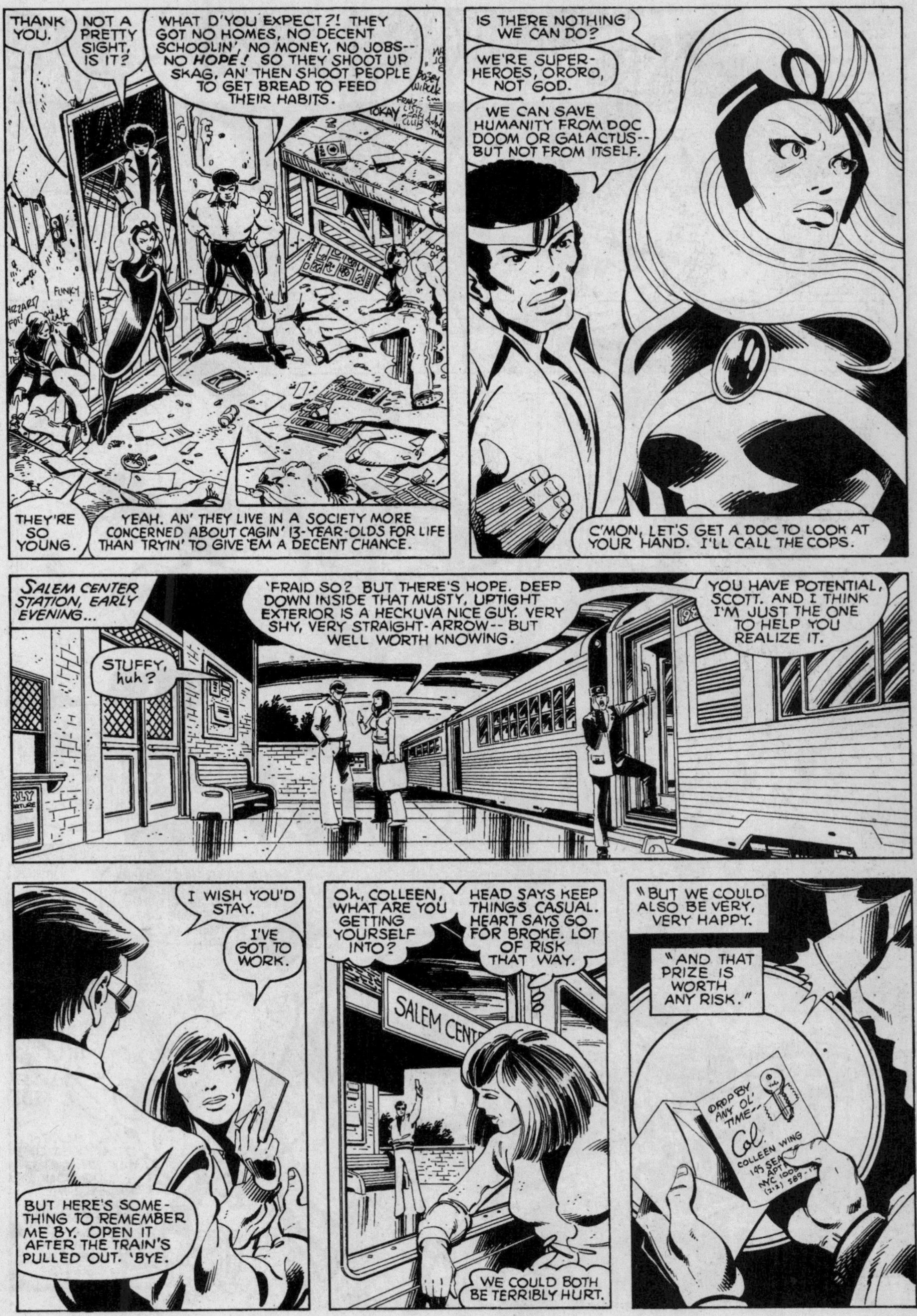
THANK YOU.
NOT A PRETTY SIGHT, IS IT?
WHAT D'YOU EXPECT?! THEY GOT NO HOMES, NO DECENT SCHOOLIN', NO MONEY, NO JOBS-- NO HOPE! SO THEY SHOOT UP SKAG, AN' THEN SHOOT PEOPLE TO GET BREAD TO FEED THEIR HABITS.
THEY'RE SO YOUNG.
YEAH. AN' THEY LIVE IN A SOCIETY MORE CONCERNED ABOUT CAGIN' 13-YEAR-OLDS FOR LIFE THAN TRYIN' TO GIVE 'EM A DECENT CHANCE.
IS THERE NOTHING WE CAN DO?
WE'RE SUPER-HEROES, ORORO, NOT GOD.
WE CAN SAVE HUMANITY FROM DOC DOOM OR GALACTUS-- BUT NOT FROM ITSELF.
C'MON, LET'S GET A DOC TO LOOK AT YOUR HAND. I'LL CALL THE COPS.
SALEM CENTER STATION, EARLY EVENING...
STUFFY, huh?
'FRAID SO? BUT THERE'S HOPE. DEEP DOWN INSIDE THAT MUSTY, UPTIGHT EXTERIOR IS A HECKUVA NICE GUY. VERY SHY, VERY STRAIGHT-ARROW-- BUT WELL WORTH KNOWING.
YOU HAVE POTENTIAL, SCOTT. AND I THINK I'M JUST THE ONE TO HELP YOU REALIZE IT.
I WISH YOU'D STAY.
I'VE GOT TO WORK.
BUT HERE'S SOMETHING TO REMEMBER ME BY. OPEN IT AFTER THE TRAIN'S PULLED OUT. 'BYE.
Oh, COLLEEN, WHAT ARE YOU GETTING YOURSELF INTO?
HEAD SAYS KEEP THINGS CASUAL. HEART SAYS GO FOR BROKE. LOT OF RISK THAT WAY.
SALEM CENTE
WE COULD BOTH BE TERRIBLY HURT.
"BUT WE COULD ALSO BE VERY, VERY HAPPY.
"AND THAT PRIZE IS WORTH ANY RISK."
DROP BY ANY OL' TIME-- Col.
COLLEEN WING

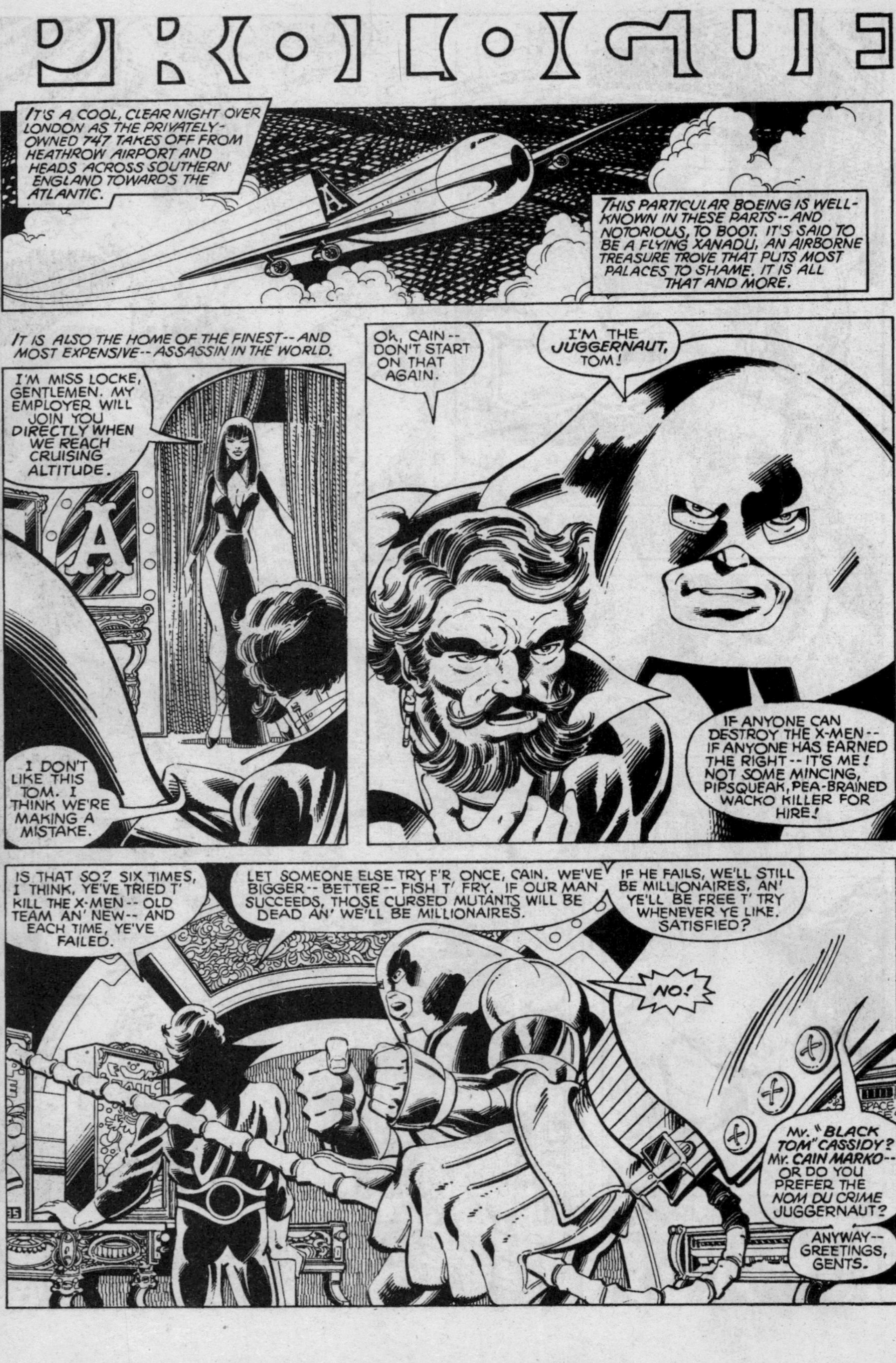
IT'S A COOL, CLEAR NIGHT OVER LONDON AS THE PRIVATELY-OWNED 747 TAKES OFF FROM HEATHROW AIRPORT AND HEADS ACROSS SOUTHERN ENGLAND TOWARDS THE ATLANTIC.
THIS PARTICULAR BOEING IS WELL-KNOWN IN THESE PARTS -- AND NOTORIOUS, TO BOOT. IT'S SAID TO BE A FLYING XANADU, AN AIRBORNE TREASURE TROVE THAT PUTS MOST PALACES TO SHAME. IT IS ALL THAT AND MORE.
IT IS ALSO THE HOME OF THE FINEST -- AND MOST EXPENSIVE -- ASSASSIN IN THE WORLD.
I'M MISS LOCKE, GENTLEMEN. MY EMPLOYER WILL JOIN YOU DIRECTLY WHEN WE REACH CRUISING ALTITUDE.
I DON'T LIKE THIS TOM. I THINK WE'RE MAKING A MISTAKE.
Oh, CAIN -- DON'T START ON THAT AGAIN.
I'M THE JUGGERNAUT, TOM!
IF ANYONE CAN DESTROY THE X-MEN -- IF ANYONE HAS EARNED THE RIGHT -- IT'S ME! NOT SOME MINCING, PIPSQUEAK, PEA-BRAINED WACKO KILLER FOR HIRE!
IS THAT SO? SIX TIMES, I THINK, YE'VE TRIED T' KILL THE X-MEN -- OLD TEAM AN' NEW -- AND EACH TIME, YE'VE FAILED.
LET SOMEONE ELSE TRY F'R ONCE, CAIN. WE'VE BIGGER -- BETTER -- FISH T' FRY. IF OUR MAN SUCCEEDS, THOSE CURSED MUTANTS WILL BE DEAD AN' WE'LL BE MILLIONAIRES.
IF HE FAILS, WE'LL STILL BE MILLIONAIRES, AN' YE'LL BE FREE T' TRY WHENEVER YE LIKE. SATISFIED?
NO!
Mr. "BLACK TOM" CASSIDY? Mr. CAIN MARKO -- OR DO YOU PREFER THE NOM DU CRIME JUGGERNAUT?
ANYWAY -- GREETINGS, GENTS.

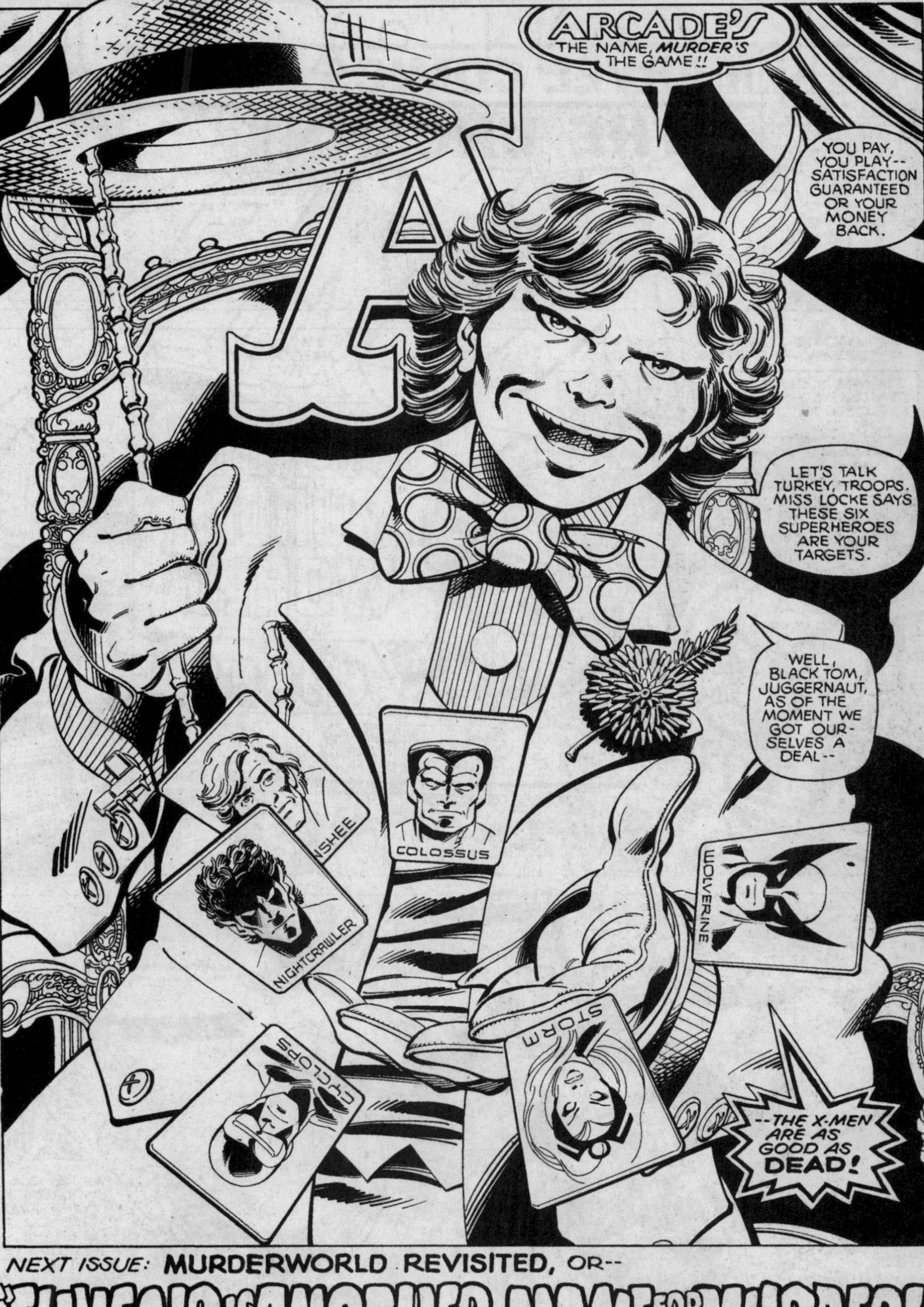
ARCADE'S THE NAME, MURDER'S THE GAME!!
YOU PAY, YOU PLAY--SATISFACTION GUARANTEED OR YOUR MONEY BACK.
LET'S TALK TURKEY, TROOPS. MISS LOCKE SAYS THESE SIX SUPERHEROES ARE YOUR TARGETS.
WELL, BLACK TOM, JUGGERNAUT, AS OF THE MOMENT WE GOT OUR-SELVES A DEAL--
--THE X-MEN ARE AS GOOD AS DEAD!
NSHEE
COLOSSUS
NIGHTCRAWLER
WOLVERINE
STORM
CYCLOPS

NEXT ISSUE: MURDERWORLD REVISITED, OR--

"FUNFAIR IS ANOTHER NAME FOR MURDER!"

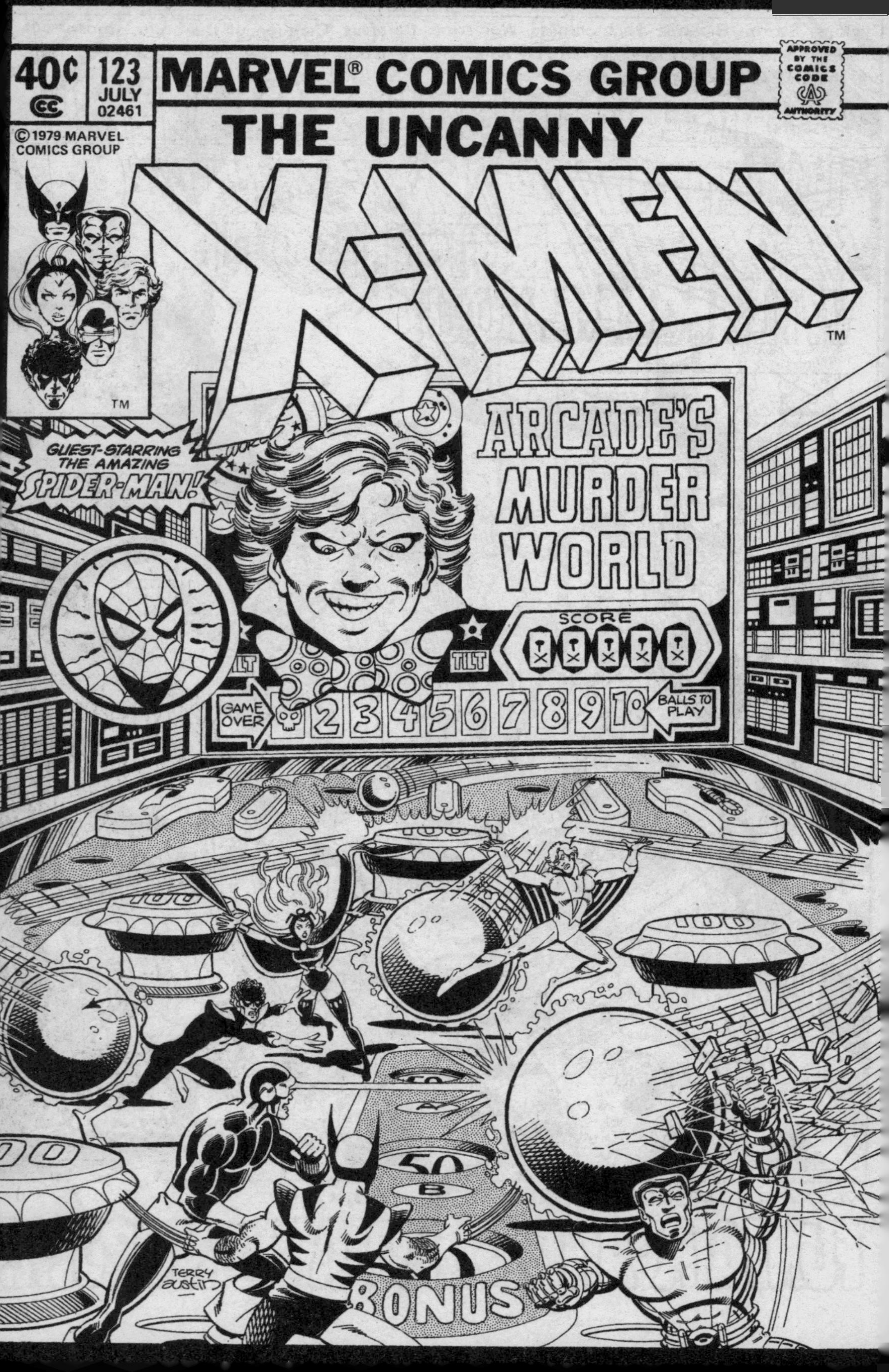
40¢
CC
123
JULY
02461
MARVEL® COMICS GROUP
APPROVED BY THE COMICS CODE AUTHORITY
©1979 MARVEL COMICS GROUP
THE UNCANNY
X-MEN
TM
TM
GUEST-STARRING THE AMAZING SPIDER-MAN!
ARCADE'S MURDER WORLD
SCORE
TILT
TILT
GAME OVER
2 3 4 5 6 7 8 9 10
BALLS TO PLAY
100
100
100
100
50
50
B
BONUS
TERRY AUSTIN

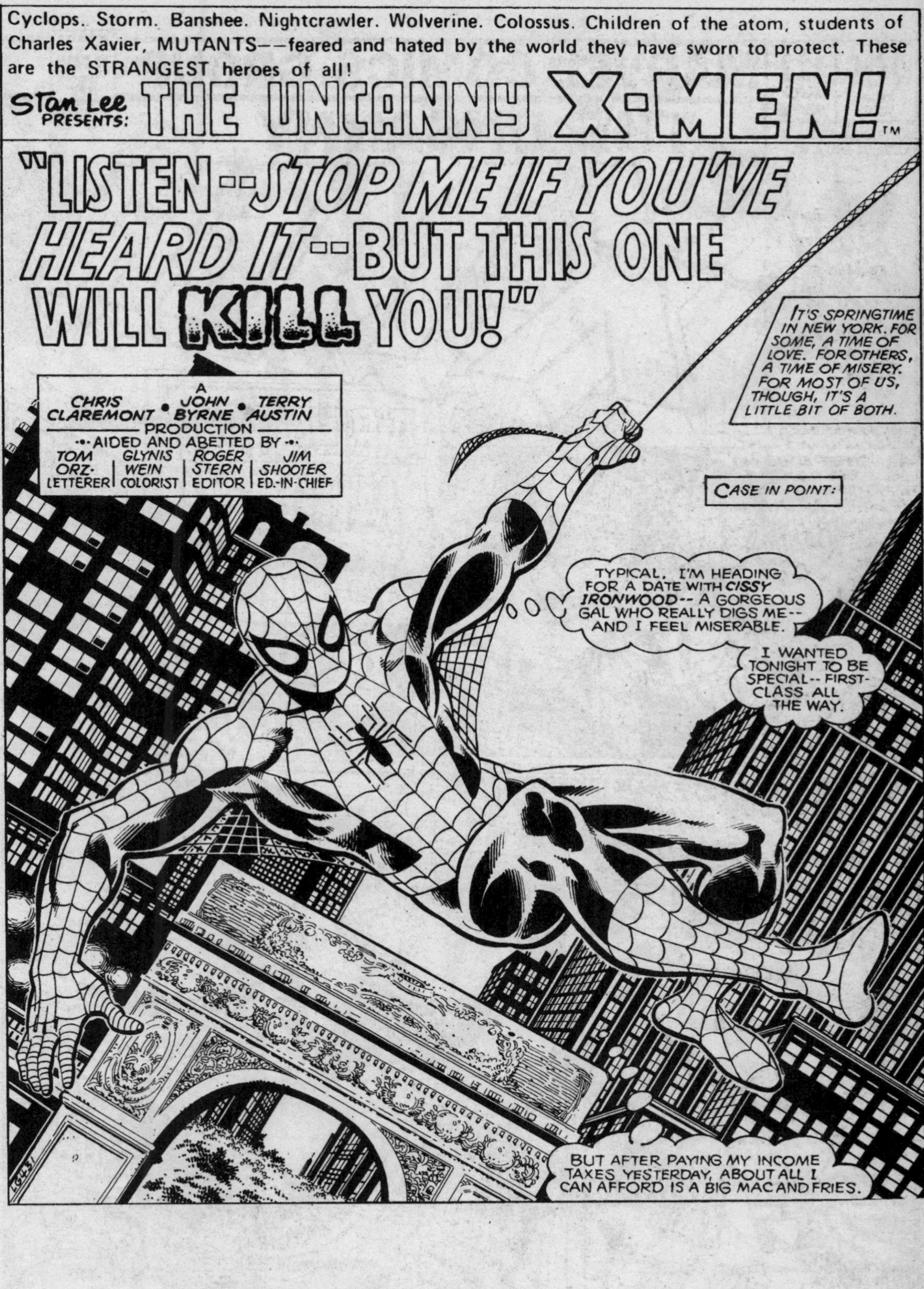

Cyclops. Storm. Banshee. Nightcrawler. Wolverine. Colossus. Children of the atom, students of Charles Xavier, MUTANTS--feared and hated by the world they have sworn to protect. These are the STRANGEST heroes of all!
Stan Lee PRESENTS: THE UNCANNY X-MEN! TM
"LISTEN--STOP ME IF YOU'VE HEARD IT--BUT THIS ONE WILL KILL YOU!"
A CHRIS CLAREMONT • JOHN BYRNE • TERRY AUSTIN PRODUCTION
AIDED AND ABETTED BY TOM ORZ. LETTERER | GLYNIS WEIN COLORIST | ROGER STERN EDITOR | JIM SHOOTER ED.-IN-CHIEF
IT'S SPRINGTIME IN NEW YORK. FOR SOME, A TIME OF LOVE. FOR OTHERS, A TIME OF MISERY. FOR MOST OF US, THOUGH, IT'S A LITTLE BIT OF BOTH.
CASE IN POINT:
TYPICAL. I'M HEADING FOR A DATE WITH CISSY IRONWOOD-- A GORGEOUS GAL WHO REALLY DIGS ME-- AND I FEEL MISERABLE.
I WANTED TONIGHT TO BE SPECIAL-- FIRST-CLASS ALL THE WAY.
BUT AFTER PAYING MY INCOME TAXES YESTERDAY, ABOUT ALL I CAN AFFORD IS A BIG MAC AND FRIES.

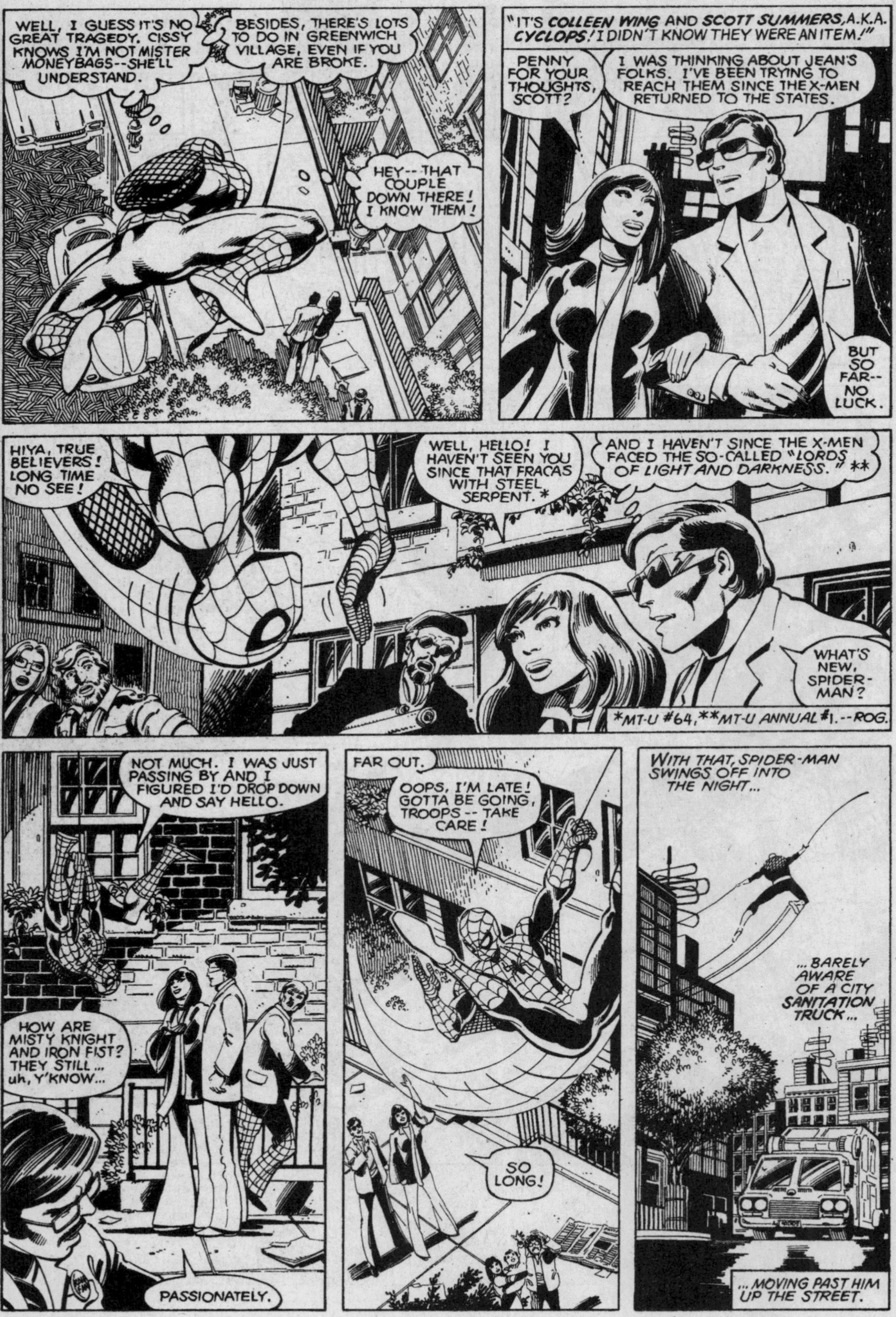
WELL, I GUESS IT'S NO GREAT TRAGEDY. CISSY KNOWS I'M NOT MISTER MONEYBAGS--SHE'LL UNDERSTAND.
BESIDES, THERE'S LOTS TO DO IN GREENWICH VILLAGE, EVEN IF YOU ARE BROKE.
HEY--THAT COUPLE DOWN THERE! I KNOW THEM!
"IT'S COLLEEN WING AND SCOTT SUMMERS, A.K.A. CYCLOPS! I DIDN'T KNOW THEY WERE AN ITEM!"
PENNY FOR YOUR THOUGHTS, SCOTT?
I WAS THINKING ABOUT JEAN'S FOLKS. I'VE BEEN TRYING TO REACH THEM SINCE THE X-MEN RETURNED TO THE STATES.
BUT SO FAR--NO LUCK.
HIYA, TRUE BELIEVERS! LONG TIME NO SEE!
WELL, HELLO! I HAVEN'T SEEN YOU SINCE THAT FRACAS WITH STEEL SERPENT.*
AND I HAVEN'T SINCE THE X-MEN FACED THE SO-CALLED "LORDS OF LIGHT AND DARKNESS." **
WHAT'S NEW, SPIDER-MAN?
*MT-U #64, **MT-U ANNUAL #1.--ROG.
NOT MUCH. I WAS JUST PASSING BY AND I FIGURED I'D DROP DOWN AND SAY HELLO.
HOW ARE MISTY KNIGHT AND IRON FIST? THEY STILL... uh, Y'KNOW...
PASSIONATELY.
FAR OUT.
OOPS, I'M LATE! GOTTA BE GOING, TROOPS -- TAKE CARE!
SO LONG!
WITH THAT, SPIDER-MAN SWINGS OFF INTO THE NIGHT...
...BARELY AWARE OF A CITY SANITATION TRUCK...
...MOVING PAST HIM UP THE STREET.

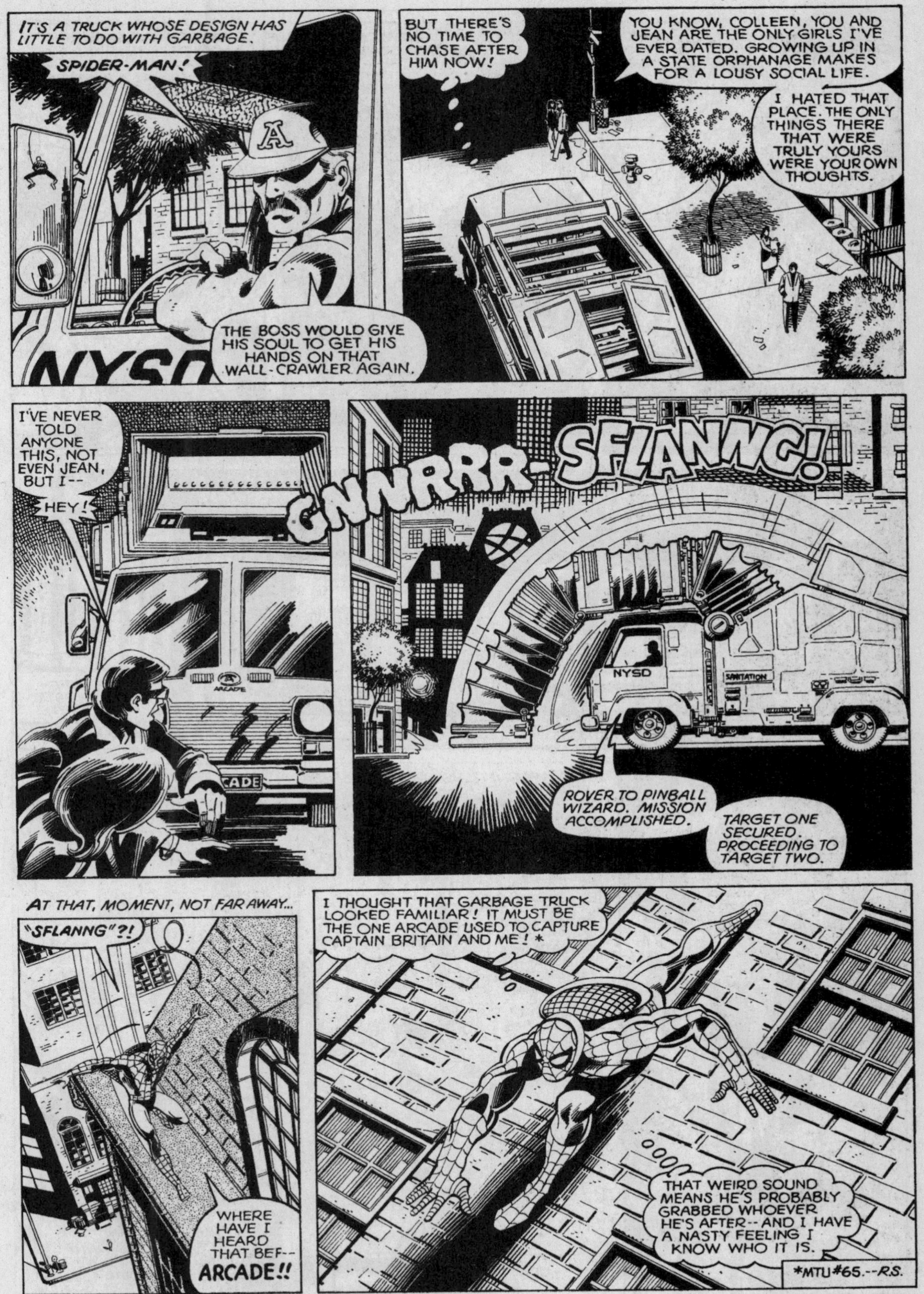
IT'S A TRUCK WHOSE DESIGN HAS LITTLE TO DO WITH GARBAGE.
SPIDER-MAN!
THE BOSS WOULD GIVE HIS SOUL TO GET HIS HANDS ON THAT WALL-CRAWLER AGAIN.
NYSD
BUT THERE'S NO TIME TO CHASE AFTER HIM NOW!
YOU KNOW, COLLEEN, YOU AND JEAN ARE THE ONLY GIRLS I'VE EVER DATED. GROWING UP IN A STATE ORPHANAGE MAKES FOR A LOUSY SOCIAL LIFE.
I HATED THAT PLACE. THE ONLY THINGS THERE THAT WERE TRULY YOURS WERE YOUR OWN THOUGHTS.
I'VE NEVER TOLD ANYONE THIS, NOT EVEN JEAN, BUT I--
HEY!
GNNRRR-SFLANNG!
NYSD
SANITATION
ROVER TO PINBALL WIZARD. MISSION ACCOMPLISHED.
TARGET ONE SECURED. PROCEEDING TO TARGET TWO.
AT THAT, MOMENT, NOT FAR AWAY...
"SFLANNG"?!
WHERE HAVE I HEARD THAT BEF-- ARCADE!!
I THOUGHT THAT GARBAGE TRUCK LOOKED FAMILIAR! IT MUST BE THE ONE ARCADE USED TO CAPTURE CAPTAIN BRITAIN AND ME! *
THAT WEIRD SOUND MEANS HE'S PROBABLY GRABBED WHOEVER HE'S AFTER-- AND I HAVE A NASTY FEELING I KNOW WHO IT IS.
*MTU #65.--R.S.

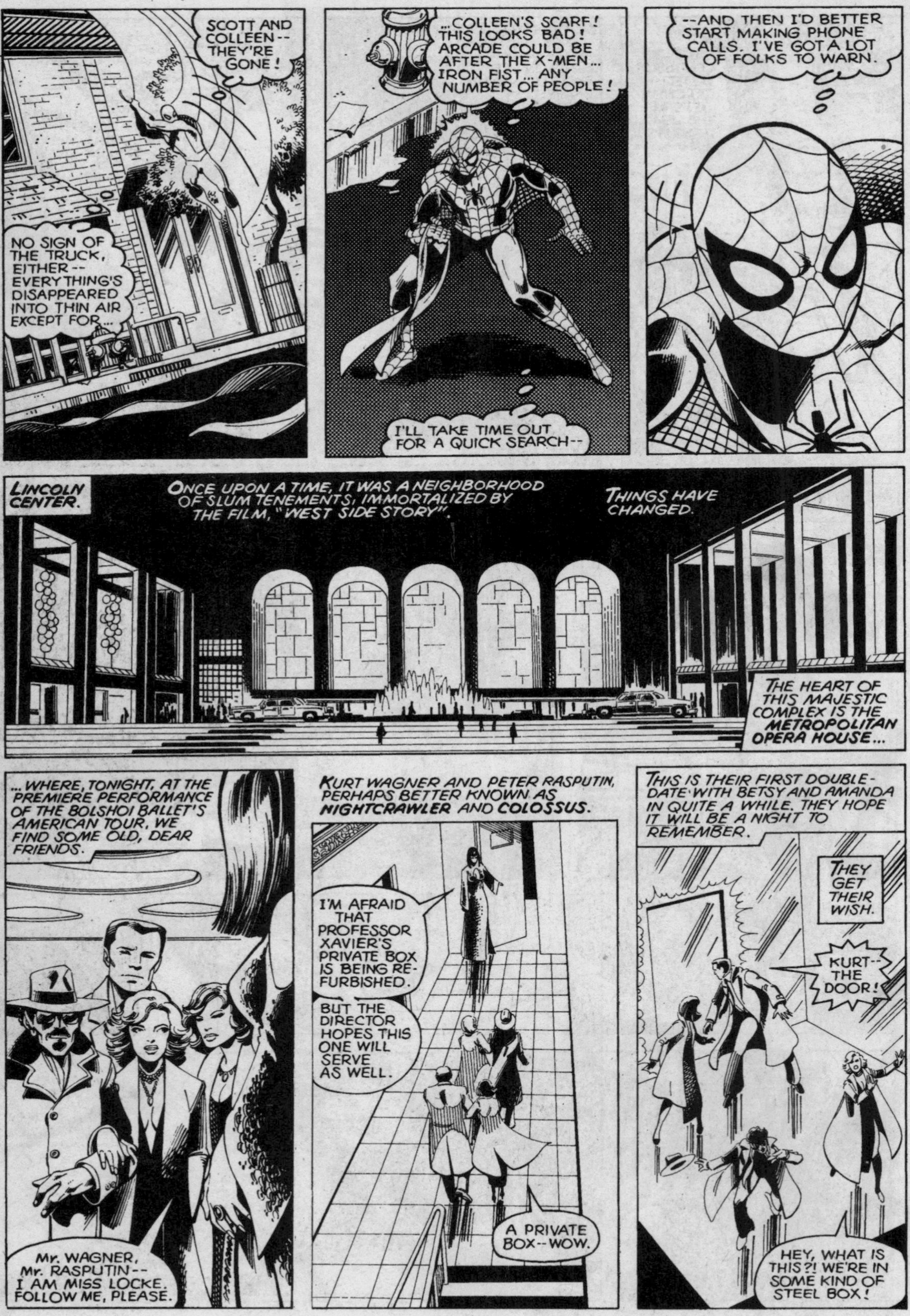
SCOTT AND COLLEEN-- THEY'RE GONE!
NO SIGN OF THE TRUCK, EITHER-- EVERYTHING'S DISAPPEARED INTO THIN AIR EXCEPT FOR...
...COLLEEN'S SCARF! THIS LOOKS BAD! ARCADE COULD BE AFTER THE X-MEN... IRON FIST... ANY NUMBER OF PEOPLE!
I'LL TAKE TIME OUT FOR A QUICK SEARCH--
--AND THEN I'D BETTER START MAKING PHONE CALLS. I'VE GOT A LOT OF FOLKS TO WARN.
LINCOLN CENTER.
ONCE UPON A TIME, IT WAS A NEIGHBORHOOD OF SLUM TENEMENTS, IMMORTALIZED BY THE FILM, "WEST SIDE STORY".
THINGS HAVE CHANGED.
THE HEART OF THIS MAJESTIC COMPLEX IS THE METROPOLITAN OPERA HOUSE...
...WHERE, TONIGHT, AT THE PREMIERE PERFORMANCE OF THE BOLSHOI BALLET'S AMERICAN TOUR, WE FIND SOME OLD, DEAR FRIENDS.
Mr. WAGNER, Mr. RASPUTIN-- I AM MISS LOCKE. FOLLOW ME, PLEASE.
KURT WAGNER AND PETER RASPUTIN, PERHAPS BETTER KNOWN AS NIGHTCRAWLER AND COLOSSUS.
I'M AFRAID THAT PROFESSOR XAVIER'S PRIVATE BOX IS BEING RE-FURBISHED.
BUT THE DIRECTOR HOPES THIS ONE WILL SERVE AS WELL.
A PRIVATE BOX--WOW.
THIS IS THEIR FIRST DOUBLE-DATE WITH BETSY AND AMANDA IN QUITE A WHILE. THEY HOPE IT WILL BE A NIGHT TO REMEMBER.
THEY GET THEIR WISH.
KURT-- THE DOOR!
HEY, WHAT IS THIS?! WE'RE IN SOME KIND OF STEEL BOX!

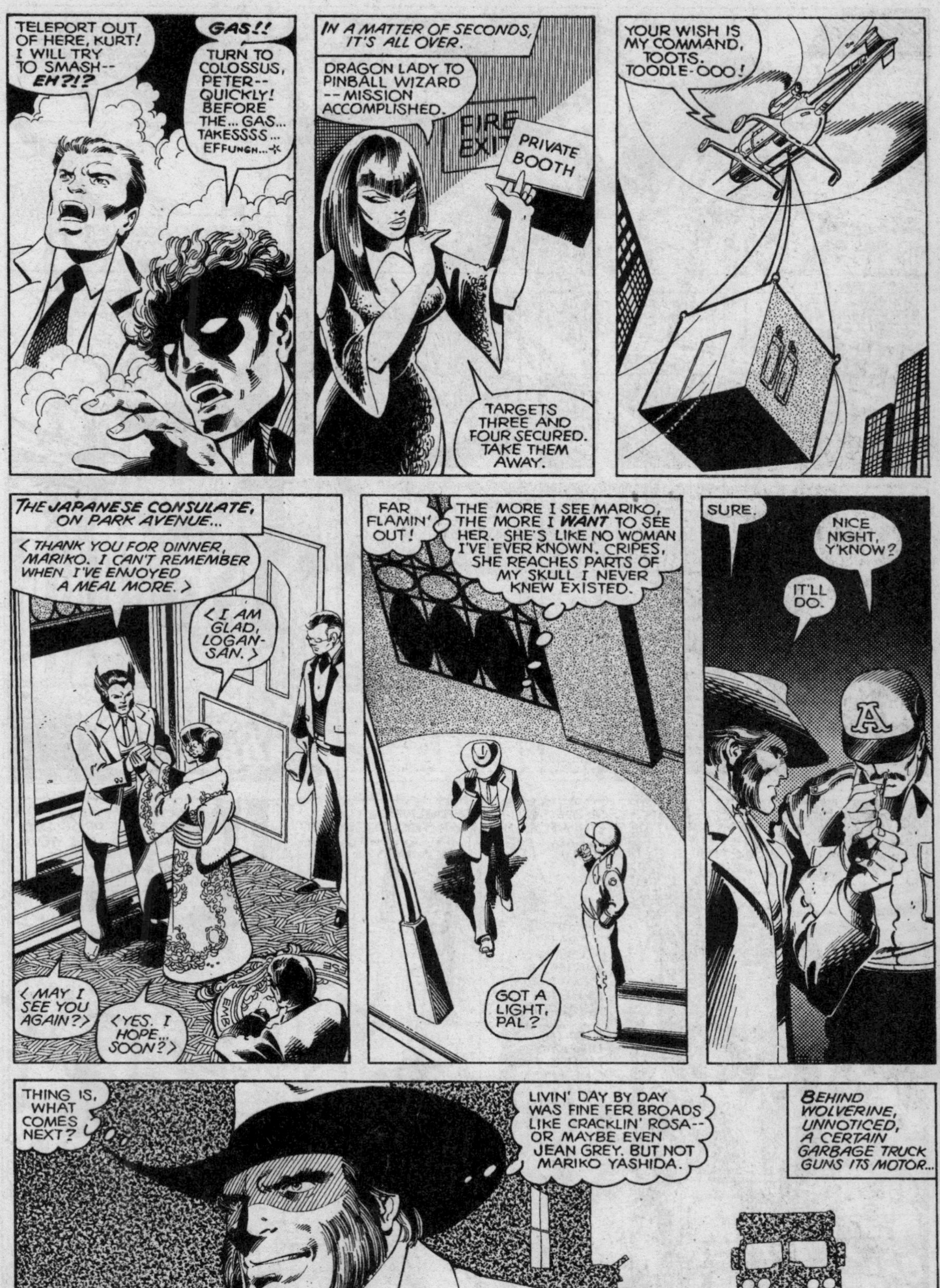
TELEPORT OUT OF HERE, KURT! I WILL TRY TO SMASH-- EH?!?
GAS!!
TURN TO COLOSSUS, PETER-- QUICKLY! BEFORE THE... GAS... TAKESSSS... EFFUNGH...
IN A MATTER OF SECONDS, IT'S ALL OVER.
DRAGON LADY TO PINBALL WIZARD --MISSION ACCOMPLISHED.
FIRE EXIT
PRIVATE BOOTH
TARGETS THREE AND FOUR SECURED. TAKE THEM AWAY.
YOUR WISH IS MY COMMAND, TOOTS. TOODLE-OOO!
THE JAPANESE CONSULATE, ON PARK AVENUE...
< THANK YOU FOR DINNER, MARIKO. I CAN'T REMEMBER WHEN I'VE ENJOYED A MEAL MORE. >
< I AM GLAD, LOGAN-SAN. >
< MAY I SEE YOU AGAIN? >
< YES. I HOPE... SOON? >
FAR FLAMIN' OUT!
THE MORE I SEE MARIKO, THE MORE I WANT TO SEE HER. SHE'S LIKE NO WOMAN I'VE EVER KNOWN. CRIPES, SHE REACHES PARTS OF MY SKULL I NEVER KNEW EXISTED.
GOT A LIGHT, PAL?
SURE.
NICE NIGHT, Y'KNOW?
IT'LL DO.
THING IS, WHAT COMES NEXT?
LIVIN' DAY BY DAY WAS FINE FER BROADS LIKE CRACKLIN' ROSA-- OR MAYBE EVEN JEAN GREY. BUT NOT MARIKO YASHIDA.
BEHIND WOLVERINE, UNNOTICED, A CERTAIN GARBAGE TRUCK GUNS ITS MOTOR...
...AND BEGINS MOVING DOWN THE STREET TOWARDS HIM.

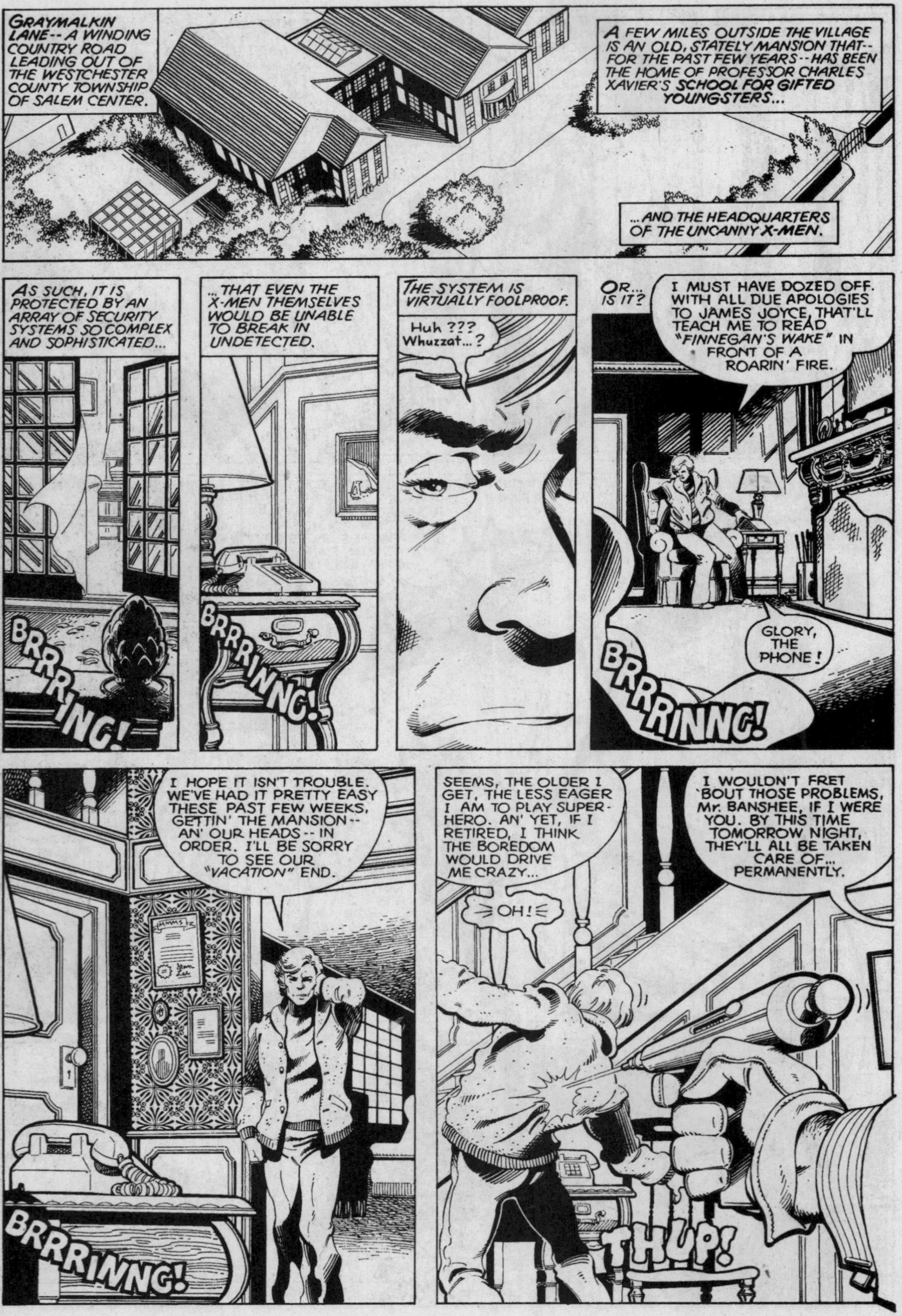
GRAYMALKIN LANE-- A WINDING COUNTRY ROAD LEADING OUT OF THE WESTCHESTER COUNTY TOWNSHIP OF SALEM CENTER.
A FEW MILES OUTSIDE THE VILLAGE IS AN OLD, STATELY MANSION THAT-- FOR THE PAST FEW YEARS-- HAS BEEN THE HOME OF PROFESSOR CHARLES XAVIER'S SCHOOL FOR GIFTED YOUNGSTERS...
...AND THE HEADQUARTERS OF THE UNCANNY X-MEN.
AS SUCH, IT IS PROTECTED BY AN ARRAY OF SECURITY SYSTEMS SO COMPLEX AND SOPHISTICATED...
BRRRRING!
...THAT EVEN THE X-MEN THEMSELVES WOULD BE UNABLE TO BREAK IN UNDETECTED.
BRRRINNG!
THE SYSTEM IS VIRTUALLY FOOLPROOF.
Huh ??? Whuzzat...?
OR... IS IT?
I MUST HAVE DOZED OFF. WITH ALL DUE APOLOGIES TO JAMES JOYCE, THAT'LL TEACH ME TO READ "FINNEGAN'S WAKE" IN FRONT OF A ROARIN' FIRE.
GLORY, THE PHONE!
BRRRINNG!
I HOPE IT ISN'T TROUBLE. WE'VE HAD IT PRETTY EASY THESE PAST FEW WEEKS, GETTIN' THE MANSION -- AN' OUR HEADS -- IN ORDER. I'LL BE SORRY TO SEE OUR "VACATION" END.
BRRRINNG!
SEEMS, THE OLDER I GET, THE LESS EAGER I AM TO PLAY SUPER-HERO. AN' YET, IF I RETIRED, I THINK THE BOREDOM WOULD DRIVE ME CRAZY...
I WOULDN'T FRET 'BOUT THOSE PROBLEMS, Mr. BANSHEE, IF I WERE YOU. BY THIS TIME TOMORROW NIGHT, THEY'LL ALL BE TAKEN CARE OF... PERMANENTLY.
OH!
THUP!

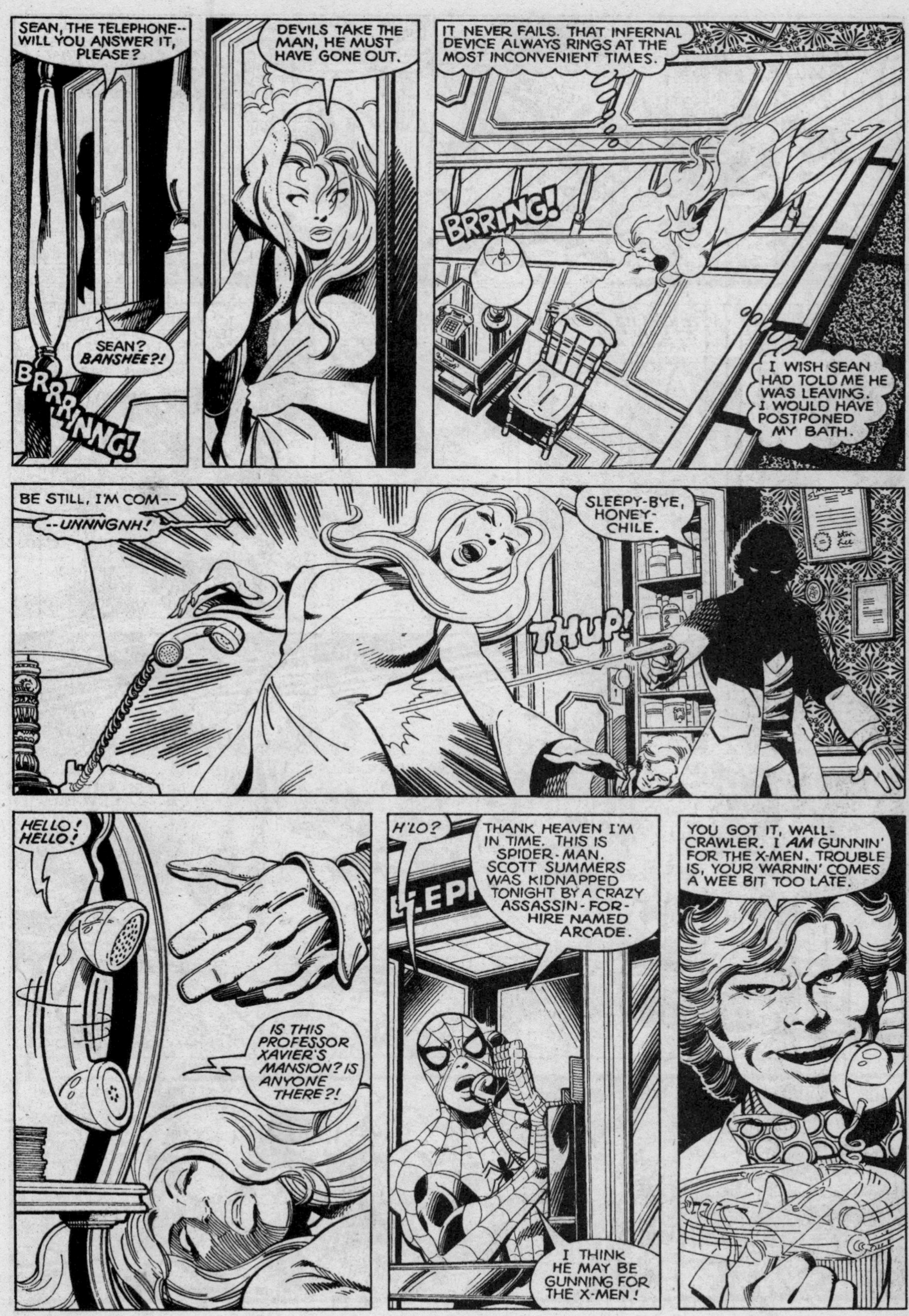
SEAN, THE TELEPHONE-- WILL YOU ANSWER IT, PLEASE?
SEAN? BANSHEE?!
BRRRRINNG!
DEVILS TAKE THE MAN, HE MUST HAVE GONE OUT.
IT NEVER FAILS. THAT INFERNAL DEVICE ALWAYS RINGS AT THE MOST INCONVENIENT TIMES.
BRRING!
I WISH SEAN HAD TOLD ME HE WAS LEAVING. I WOULD HAVE POSTPONED MY BATH.
BE STILL, I'M COM--
--UNNNGNH!
SLEEPY-BYE, HONEY-CHILE.
THUP!
HELLO! HELLO!
IS THIS PROFESSOR XAVIER'S MANSION? IS ANYONE THERE?!
H'LO?
THANK HEAVEN I'M IN TIME. THIS IS SPIDER-MAN. SCOTT SUMMERS WAS KIDNAPPED TONIGHT BY A CRAZY ASSASSIN-FOR-HIRE NAMED ARCADE.
I THINK HE MAY BE GUNNING FOR THE X-MEN!
YOU GOT IT, WALL-CRAWLER. I AM GUNNIN' FOR THE X-MEN. TROUBLE IS, YOUR WARNIN' COMES A WEE BIT TOO LATE.

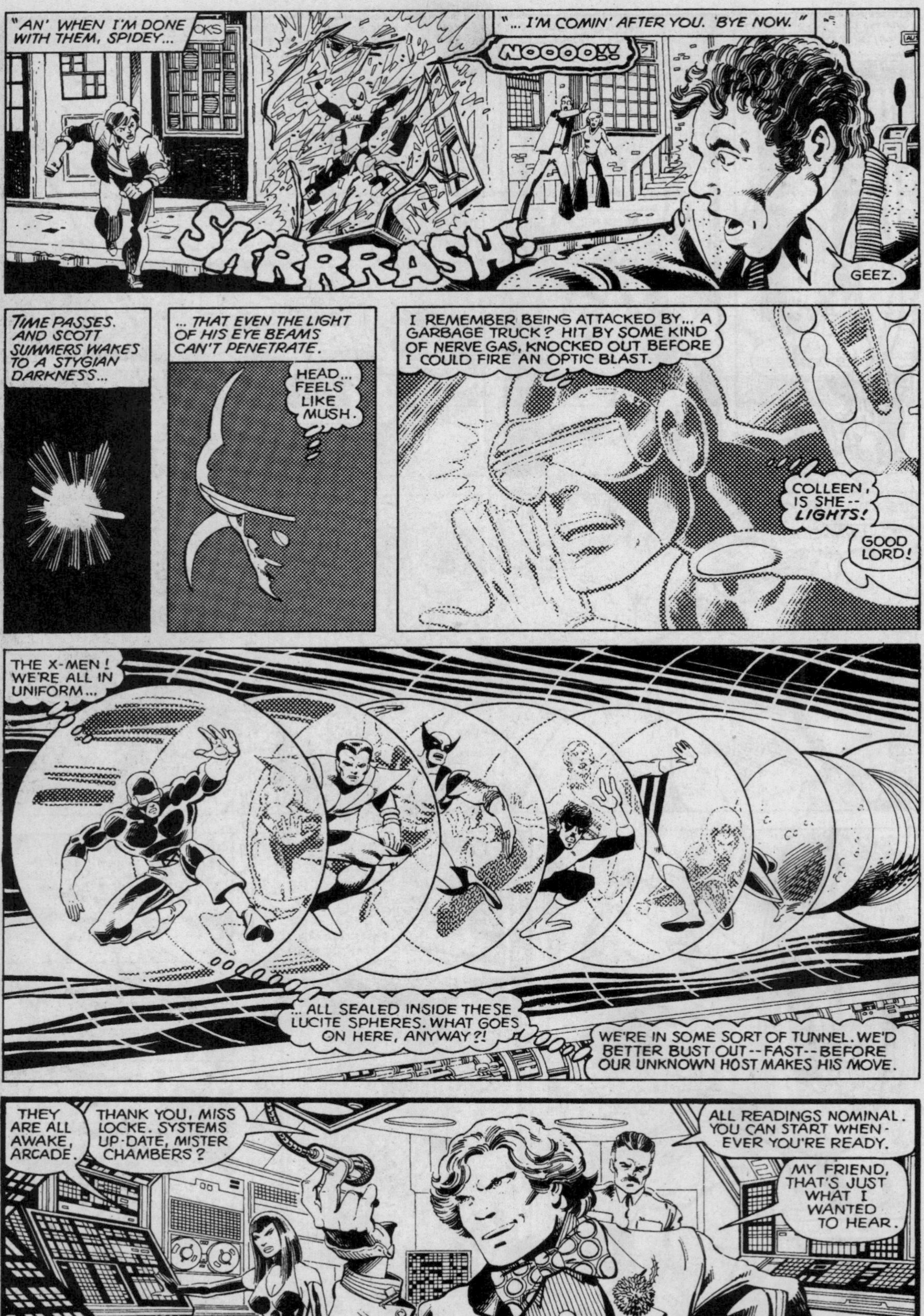
"AN' WHEN I'M DONE WITH THEM, SPIDEY...
OKS
"... I'M COMIN' AFTER YOU. 'BYE NOW."
NOOOO!!
SKRRRASH!
GEEZ.
TIME PASSES. AND SCOTT SUMMERS WAKES TO A STYGIAN DARKNESS...
... THAT EVEN THE LIGHT OF HIS EYE BEAMS CAN'T PENETRATE.
HEAD... FEELS LIKE MUSH.
I REMEMBER BEING ATTACKED BY... A GARBAGE TRUCK? HIT BY SOME KIND OF NERVE GAS, KNOCKED OUT BEFORE I COULD FIRE AN OPTIC BLAST.
COLLEEN, IS SHE-- LIGHTS!
GOOD LORD!
THE X-MEN! WE'RE ALL IN UNIFORM...
... ALL SEALED INSIDE THESE LUCITE SPHERES. WHAT GOES ON HERE, ANYWAY?!
WE'RE IN SOME SORT OF TUNNEL. WE'D BETTER BUST OUT--FAST--BEFORE OUR UNKNOWN HOST MAKES HIS MOVE.
THEY ARE ALL AWAKE, ARCADE.
THANK YOU, MISS LOCKE. SYSTEMS UP-DATE, MISTER CHAMBERS?
ALL READINGS NOMINAL. YOU CAN START WHEN-EVER YOU'RE READY.
MY FRIEND, THAT'S JUST WHAT I WANTED TO HEAR.

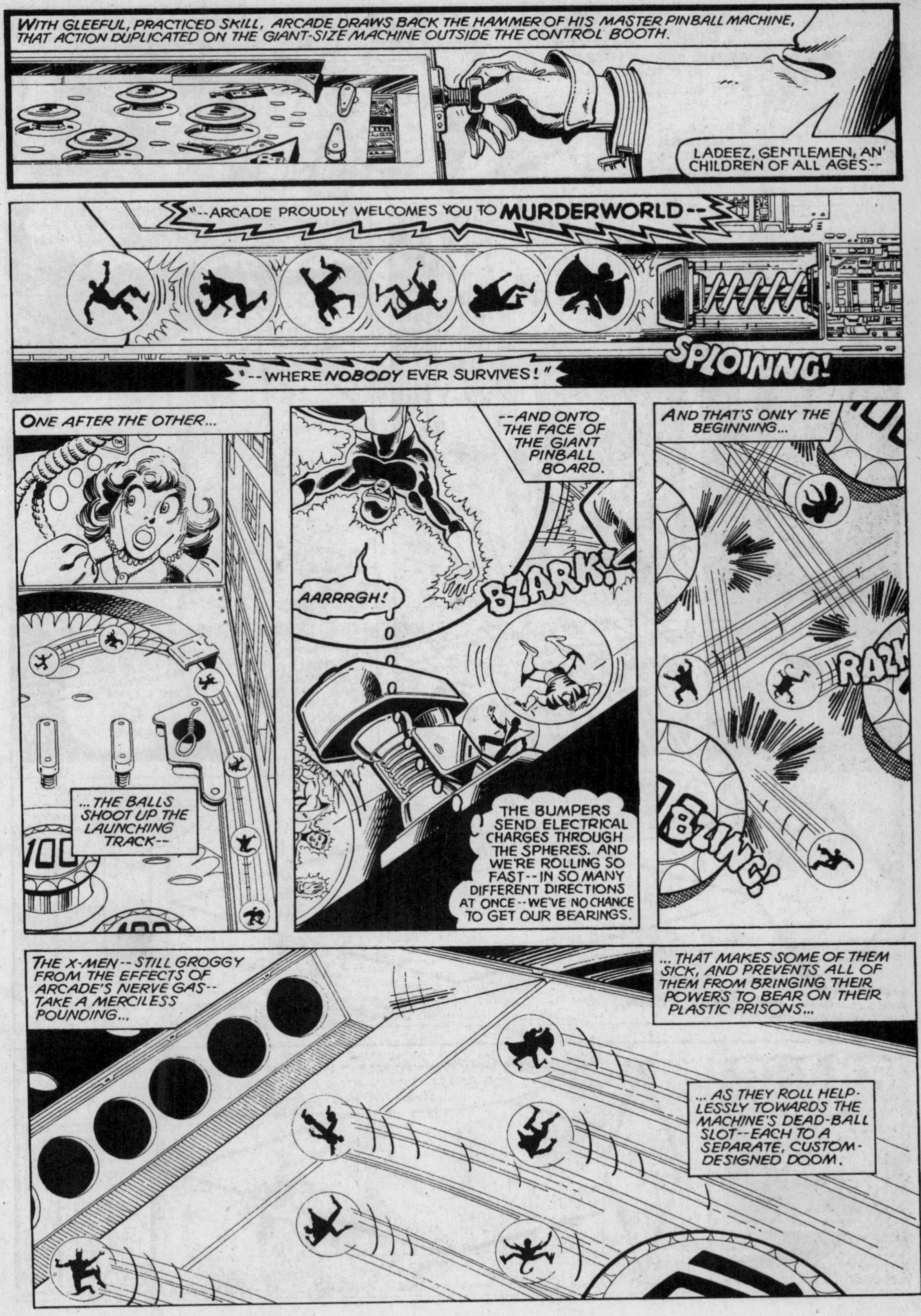

WITH GLEEFUL, PRACTICED SKILL, ARCADE DRAWS BACK THE HAMMER OF HIS MASTER PINBALL MACHINE, THAT ACTION DUPLICATED ON THE GIANT-SIZE MACHINE OUTSIDE THE CONTROL BOOTH.
LADEEZ, GENTLEMEN, AN' CHILDREN OF ALL AGES--
"--ARCADE PROUDLY WELCOMES YOU TO MURDERWORLD--
"--WHERE NOBODY EVER SURVIVES!"
SPLOINNG!
ONE AFTER THE OTHER...
...THE BALLS SHOOT UP THE LAUNCHING TRACK--
--AND ONTO THE FACE OF THE GIANT PINBALL BOARD.
AARRRGH!
BZARK!
THE BUMPERS SEND ELECTRICAL CHARGES THROUGH THE SPHERES. AND WE'RE ROLLING SO FAST--IN SO MANY DIFFERENT DIRECTIONS AT ONCE--WE'VE NO CHANCE TO GET OUR BEARINGS.
AND THAT'S ONLY THE BEGINNING...
BZING!
THE X-MEN--STILL GROGGY FROM THE EFFECTS OF ARCADE'S NERVE GAS--TAKE A MERCILESS POUNDING...
...THAT MAKES SOME OF THEM SICK, AND PREVENTS ALL OF THEM FROM BRINGING THEIR POWERS TO BEAR ON THEIR PLASTIC PRISONS...
...AS THEY ROLL HELPLESSLY TOWARDS THE MACHINE'S DEAD-BALL SLOT--EACH TO A SEPARATE, CUSTOM-DESIGNED DOOM.

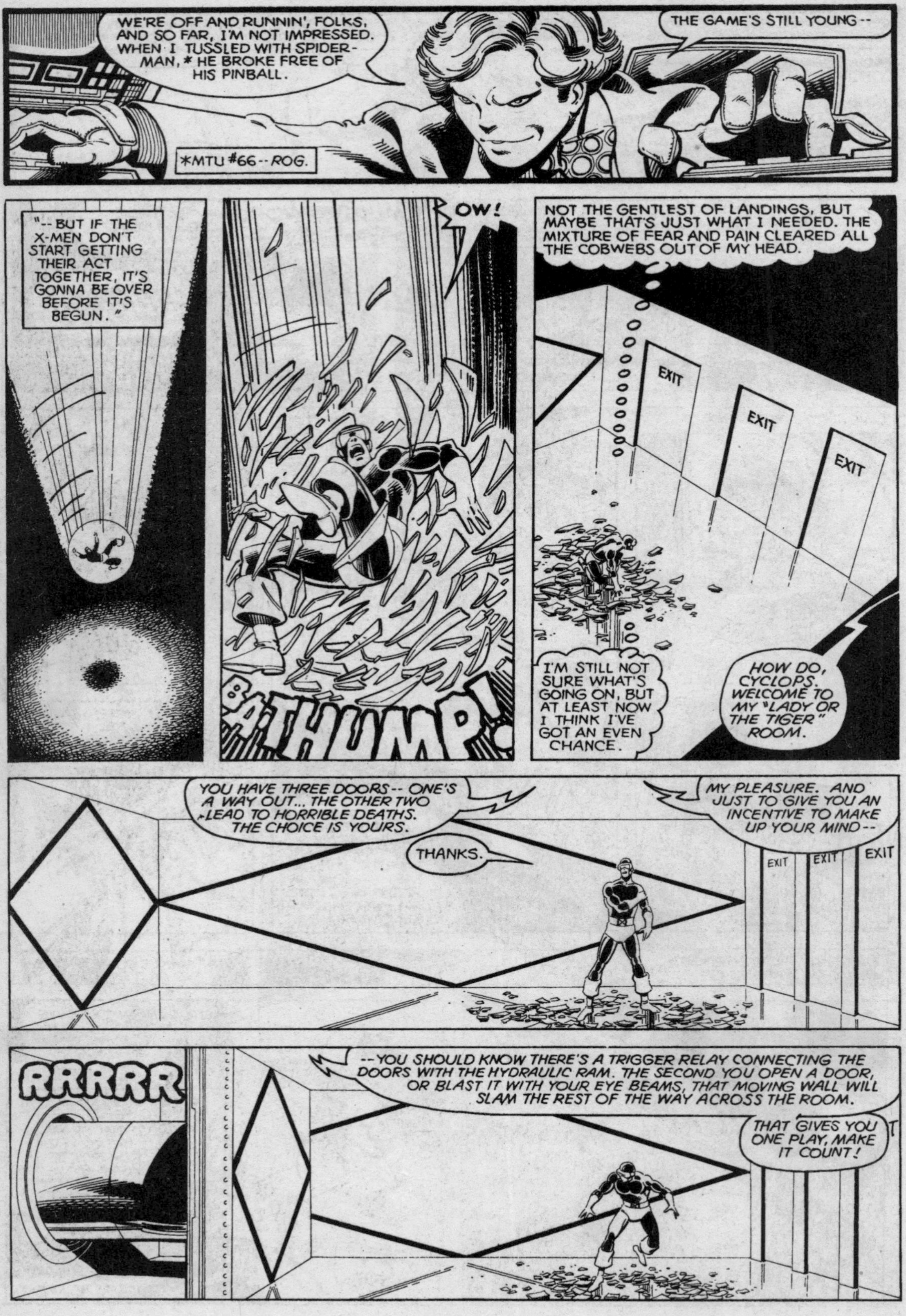
WE'RE OFF AND RUNNIN', FOLKS, AND SO FAR, I'M NOT IMPRESSED. WHEN I TUSSLED WITH SPIDER-MAN,* HE BROKE FREE OF HIS PINBALL.
*MTU #66 -- ROG.
THE GAME'S STILL YOUNG --
"-- BUT IF THE X-MEN DON'T START GETTING THEIR ACT TOGETHER, IT'S GONNA BE OVER BEFORE IT'S BEGUN."
OW!
BATHUMP!
NOT THE GENTLEST OF LANDINGS, BUT MAYBE THAT'S JUST WHAT I NEEDED. THE MIXTURE OF FEAR AND PAIN CLEARED ALL THE COBWEBS OUT OF MY HEAD.
EXIT
EXIT
EXIT
I'M STILL NOT SURE WHAT'S GOING ON, BUT AT LEAST NOW I THINK I'VE GOT AN EVEN CHANCE.
HOW DO, CYCLOPS. WELCOME TO MY "LADY OR THE TIGER" ROOM.
YOU HAVE THREE DOORS -- ONE'S A WAY OUT... THE OTHER TWO LEAD TO HORRIBLE DEATHS. THE CHOICE IS YOURS.
THANKS.
MY PLEASURE. AND JUST TO GIVE YOU AN INCENTIVE TO MAKE UP YOUR MIND --
EXIT
EXIT
EXIT
RRRRR
-- YOU SHOULD KNOW THERE'S A TRIGGER RELAY CONNECTING THE DOORS WITH THE HYDRAULIC RAM. THE SECOND YOU OPEN A DOOR, OR BLAST IT WITH YOUR EYE BEAMS, THAT MOVING WALL WILL SLAM THE REST OF THE WAY ACROSS THE ROOM.
THAT GIVES YOU ONE PLAY, MAKE IT COUNT!

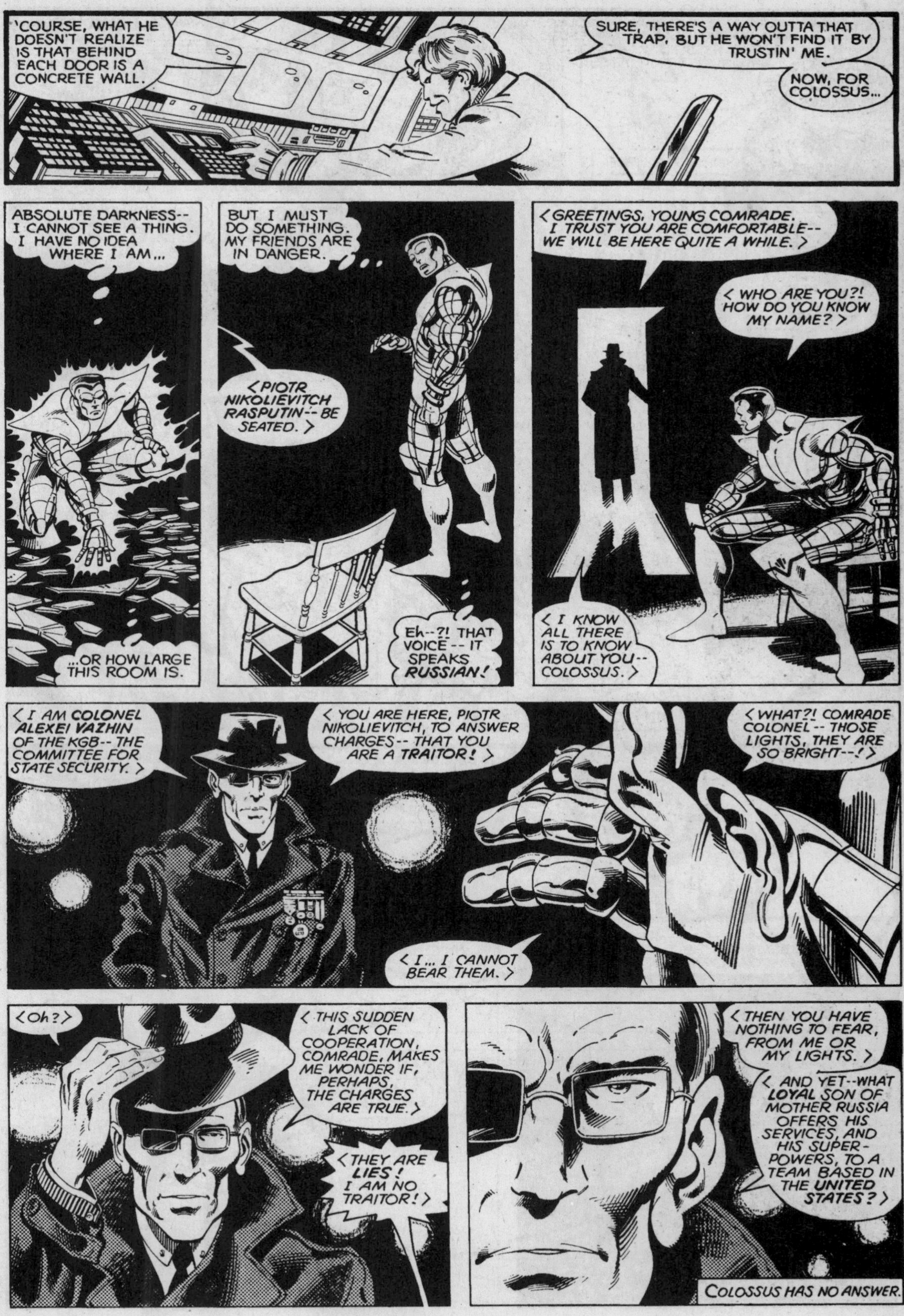

'COURSE, WHAT HE DOESN'T REALIZE IS THAT BEHIND EACH DOOR IS A CONCRETE WALL.
SURE, THERE'S A WAY OUTTA THAT TRAP, BUT HE WON'T FIND IT BY TRUSTIN' ME.
NOW, FOR COLOSSUS...
ABSOLUTE DARKNESS-- I CANNOT SEE A THING. I HAVE NO IDEA WHERE I AM...
...OR HOW LARGE THIS ROOM IS.
BUT I MUST DO SOMETHING. MY FRIENDS ARE IN DANGER.
< PIOTR NIKOLIEVITCH RASPUTIN-- BE SEATED. >
Eh--?! THAT VOICE -- IT SPEAKS RUSSIAN!
< GREETINGS, YOUNG COMRADE. I TRUST YOU ARE COMFORTABLE-- WE WILL BE HERE QUITE A WHILE. >
< WHO ARE YOU?! HOW DO YOU KNOW MY NAME? >
< I KNOW ALL THERE IS TO KNOW ABOUT YOU-- COLOSSUS. >
< I AM COLONEL ALEXEI VAZHIN OF THE KGB-- THE COMMITTEE FOR STATE SECURITY. >
< YOU ARE HERE, PIOTR NIKOLIEVITCH, TO ANSWER CHARGES-- THAT YOU ARE A TRAITOR! >
< WHAT?! COMRADE COLONEL -- THOSE LIGHTS, THEY ARE SO BRIGHT--! >
< I... I CANNOT BEAR THEM. >
< Oh? >
< THIS SUDDEN LACK OF COOPERATION, COMRADE, MAKES ME WONDER IF, PERHAPS, THE CHARGES ARE TRUE. >
< THEY ARE LIES! I AM NO TRAITOR! >
< THEN YOU HAVE NOTHING TO FEAR, FROM ME OR MY LIGHTS. >
< AND YET--WHAT LOYAL SON OF MOTHER RUSSIA OFFERS HIS SERVICES, AND HIS SUPER-POWERS, TO A TEAM BASED IN THE UNITED STATES? >
COLOSSUS HAS NO ANSWER.

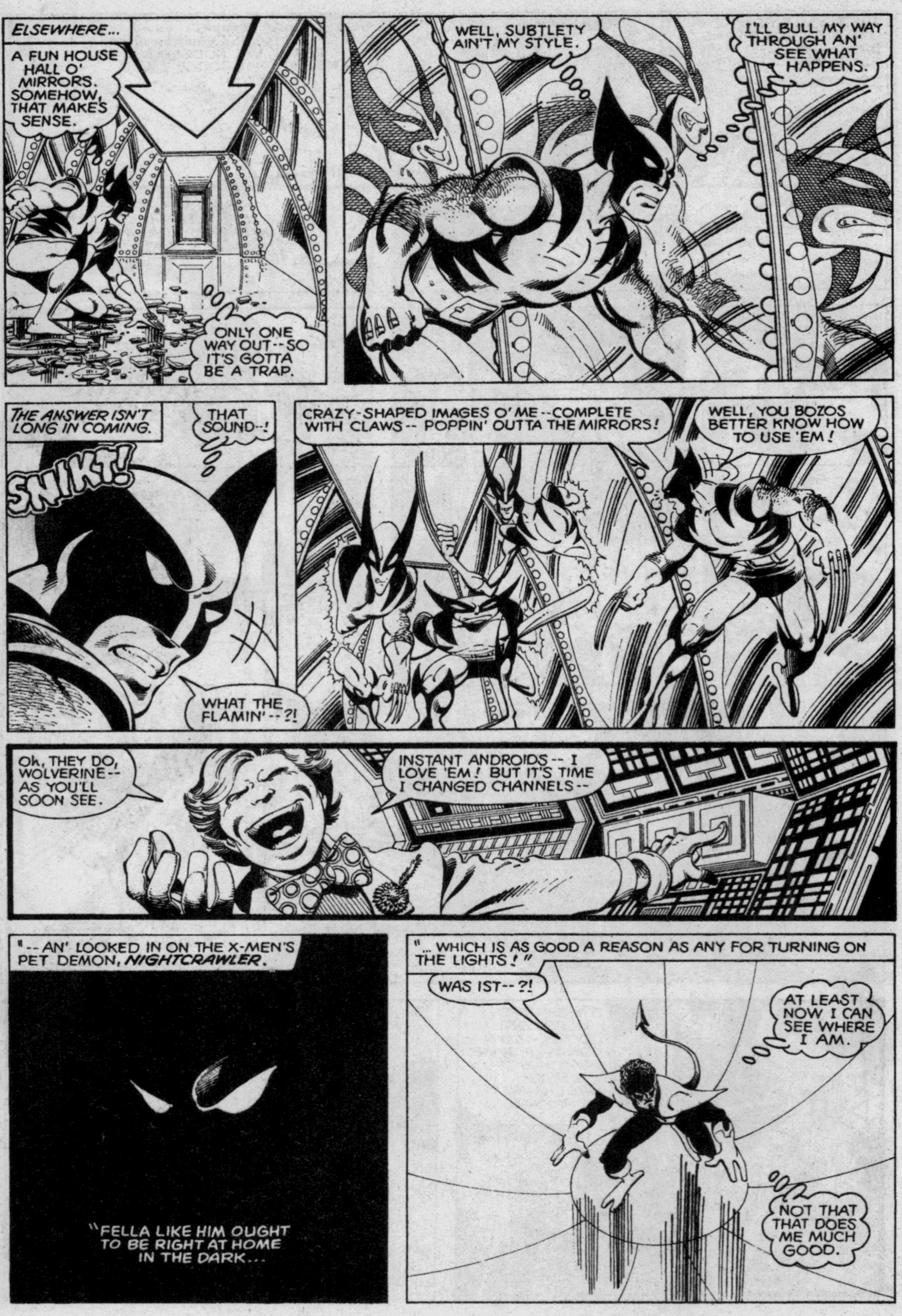
ELSEWHERE...
A FUN HOUSE HALL O' MIRRORS. SOMEHOW, THAT MAKES SENSE.
ONLY ONE WAY OUT--SO IT'S GOTTA BE A TRAP.
WELL, SUBTLETY AIN'T MY STYLE.
I'LL BULL MY WAY THROUGH AN' SEE WHAT HAPPENS.
THE ANSWER ISN'T LONG IN COMING.
THAT SOUND--!
SNIKT!
WHAT THE FLAMIN'--?!
CRAZY-SHAPED IMAGES O' ME--COMPLETE WITH CLAWS-- POPPIN' OUTTA THE MIRRORS!
WELL, YOU BOZOS BETTER KNOW HOW TO USE 'EM!
Oh, THEY DO, WOLVERINE-- AS YOU'LL SOON SEE.
INSTANT ANDROIDS-- I LOVE 'EM! BUT IT'S TIME I CHANGED CHANNELS--
"--AN' LOOKED IN ON THE X-MEN'S PET DEMON, NIGHTCRAWLER.
"FELLA LIKE HIM OUGHT TO BE RIGHT AT HOME IN THE DARK...
"...WHICH IS AS GOOD A REASON AS ANY FOR TURNING ON THE LIGHTS!"
WAS IST--?!
AT LEAST NOW I CAN SEE WHERE I AM.
NOT THAT THAT DOES ME MUCH GOOD.

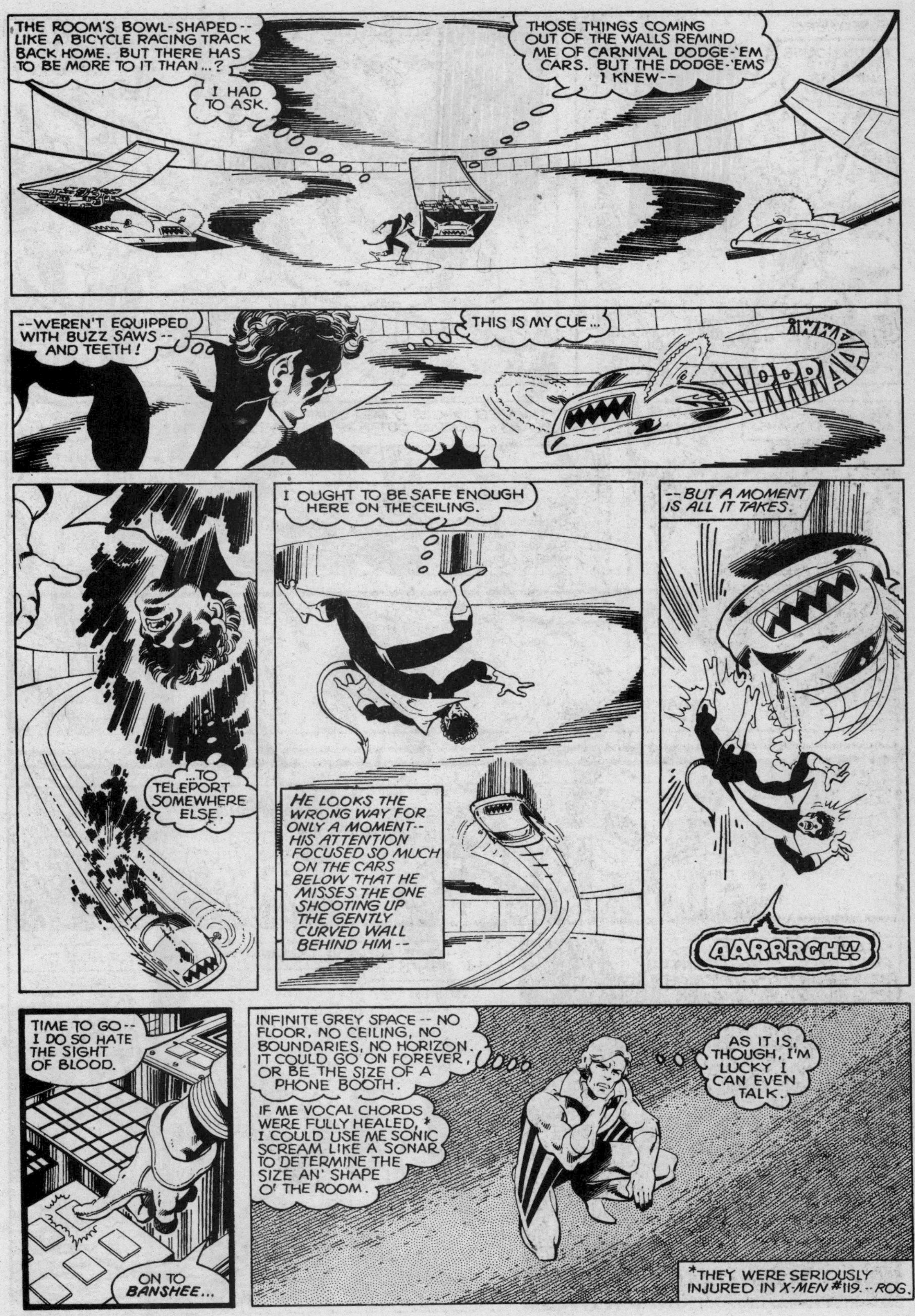
THE ROOM'S BOWL-SHAPED -- LIKE A BICYCLE RACING TRACK BACK HOME. BUT THERE HAS TO BE MORE TO IT THAN ...?
I HAD TO ASK.
THOSE THINGS COMING OUT OF THE WALLS REMIND ME OF CARNIVAL DODGE-'EM CARS. BUT THE DODGE-'EMS I KNEW--
--WEREN'T EQUIPPED WITH BUZZ SAWS -- AND TEETH!
THIS IS MY CUE...
VOOR
...TO TELEPORT SOMEWHERE ELSE.
I OUGHT TO BE SAFE ENOUGH HERE ON THE CEILING.
HE LOOKS THE WRONG WAY FOR ONLY A MOMENT-- HIS ATTENTION FOCUSED SO MUCH ON THE CARS BELOW THAT HE MISSES THE ONE SHOOTING UP THE GENTLY CURVED WALL BEHIND HIM --
--BUT A MOMENT IS ALL IT TAKES.
AARRRGH!!
TIME TO GO -- I DO SO HATE THE SIGHT OF BLOOD.
ON TO BANSHEE...
INFINITE GREY SPACE -- NO FLOOR, NO CEILING, NO BOUNDARIES, NO HORIZON. IT COULD GO ON FOREVER, OR BE THE SIZE OF A PHONE BOOTH.
IF ME VOCAL CHORDS WERE FULLY HEALED,* I COULD USE ME SONIC SCREAM LIKE A SONAR TO DETERMINE THE SIZE AN' SHAPE O' THE ROOM.
AS IT IS, THOUGH, I'M LUCKY I CAN EVEN TALK.
*THEY WERE SERIOUSLY INJURED IN X-MEN #119.--ROG.

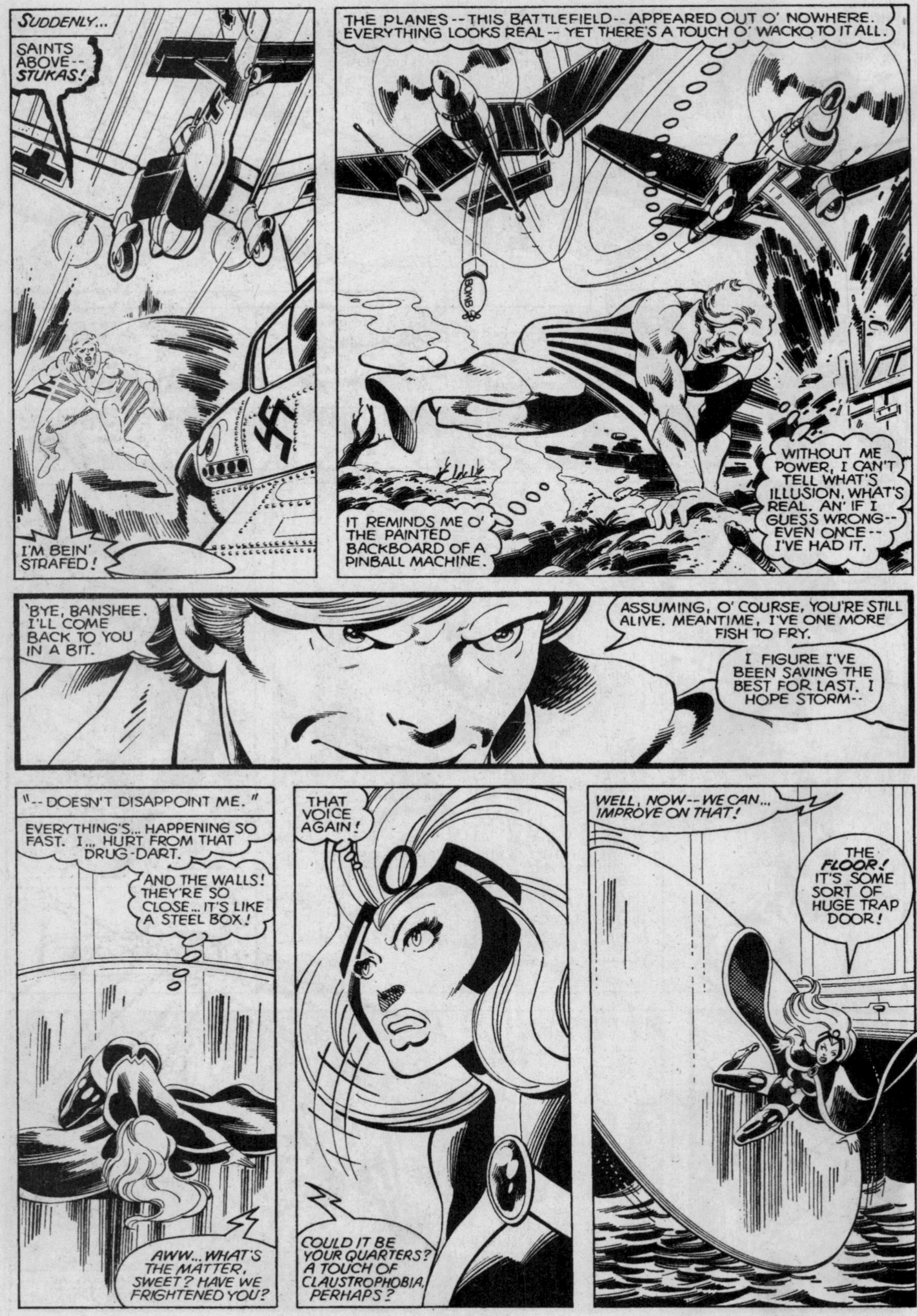

SUDDENLY...
SAINTS ABOVE-- STUKAS!
I'M BEIN' STRAFED!
THE PLANES--THIS BATTLEFIELD--APPEARED OUT O' NOWHERE. EVERYTHING LOOKS REAL--YET THERE'S A TOUCH O' WACKO TO IT ALL.
BOMB
IT REMINDS ME O' THE PAINTED BACKBOARD OF A PINBALL MACHINE.
WITHOUT ME POWER, I CAN'T TELL WHAT'S ILLUSION, WHAT'S REAL. AN' IF I GUESS WRONG-- EVEN ONCE-- I'VE HAD IT.
'BYE, BANSHEE. I'LL COME BACK TO YOU IN A BIT.
ASSUMING, O' COURSE, YOU'RE STILL ALIVE. MEANTIME, I'VE ONE MORE FISH TO FRY.
I FIGURE I'VE BEEN SAVING THE BEST FOR LAST. I HOPE STORM--
"--DOESN'T DISAPPOINT ME."
EVERYTHING'S... HAPPENING SO FAST. I... HURT FROM THAT DRUG-DART.
AND THE WALLS! THEY'RE SO CLOSE... IT'S LIKE A STEEL BOX!
AWW... WHAT'S THE MATTER, SWEET? HAVE WE FRIGHTENED YOU?
THAT VOICE AGAIN!
COULD IT BE YOUR QUARTERS? A TOUCH OF CLAUSTROPHOBIA, PERHAPS?
WELL, NOW--WE CAN... IMPROVE ON THAT!
THE FLOOR! IT'S SOME SORT OF HUGE TRAP DOOR!

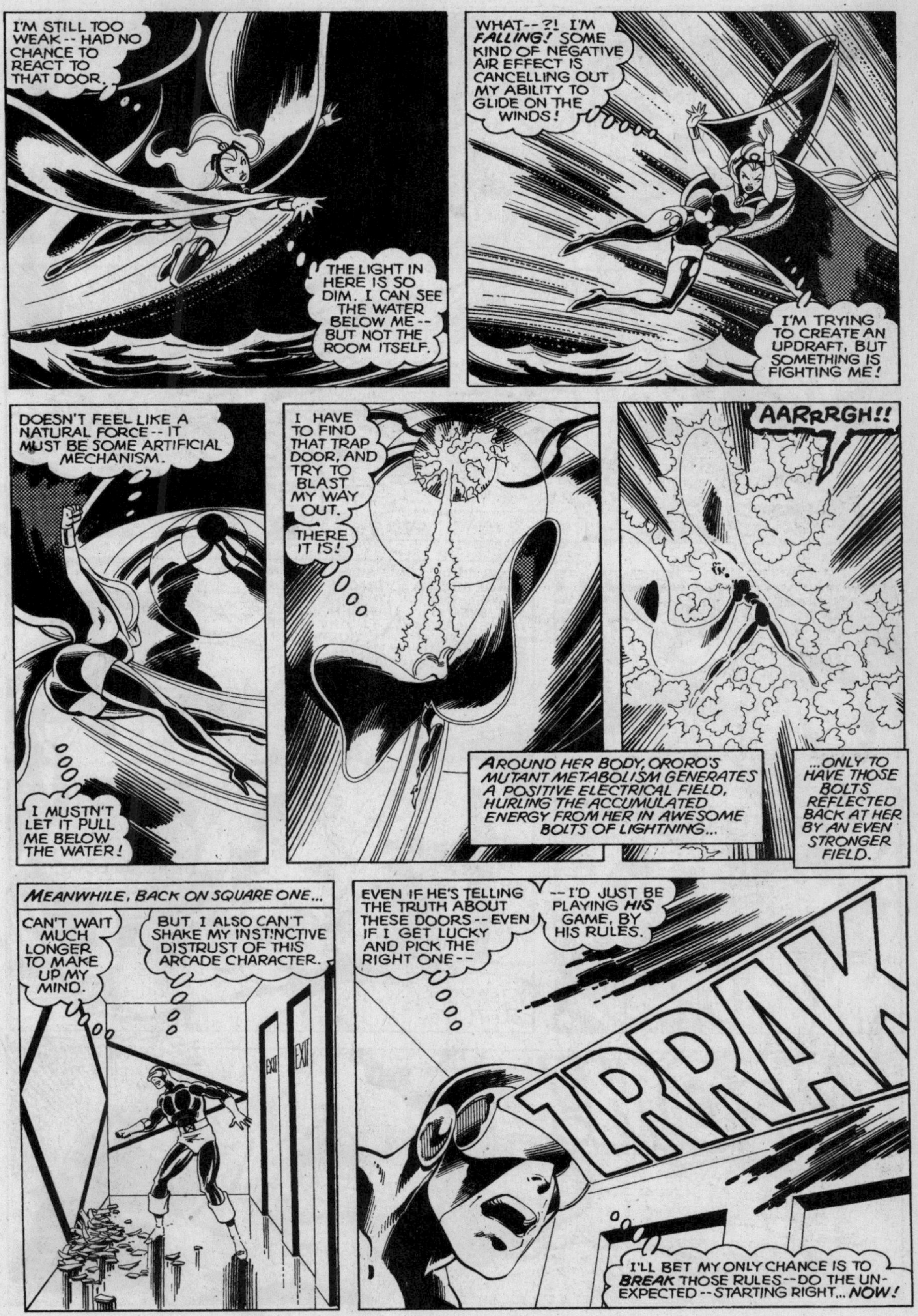
I'M STILL TOO WEAK -- HAD NO CHANCE TO REACT TO THAT DOOR.
THE LIGHT IN HERE IS SO DIM. I CAN SEE THE WATER BELOW ME -- BUT NOT THE ROOM ITSELF.
WHAT--?! I'M FALLING! SOME KIND OF NEGATIVE AIR EFFECT IS CANCELLING OUT MY ABILITY TO GLIDE ON THE WINDS!
I'M TRYING TO CREATE AN UPDRAFT, BUT SOMETHING IS FIGHTING ME!
DOESN'T FEEL LIKE A NATURAL FORCE -- IT MUST BE SOME ARTIFICIAL MECHANISM.
I MUSTN'T LET IT PULL ME BELOW THE WATER!
I HAVE TO FIND THAT TRAP DOOR, AND TRY TO BLAST MY WAY OUT.
THERE IT IS!
AARRRGH!!
AROUND HER BODY, ORORO'S MUTANT METABOLISM GENERATES A POSITIVE ELECTRICAL FIELD, HURLING THE ACCUMULATED ENERGY FROM HER IN AWESOME BOLTS OF LIGHTNING...
...ONLY TO HAVE THOSE BOLTS REFLECTED BACK AT HER BY AN EVEN STRONGER FIELD.
MEANWHILE, BACK ON SQUARE ONE...
CAN'T WAIT MUCH LONGER TO MAKE UP MY MIND.
BUT I ALSO CAN'T SHAKE MY INSTINCTIVE DISTRUST OF THIS ARCADE CHARACTER.
EXIT
EXIT
EVEN IF HE'S TELLING THE TRUTH ABOUT THESE DOORS -- EVEN IF I GET LUCKY AND PICK THE RIGHT ONE --
-- I'D JUST BE PLAYING HIS GAME, BY HIS RULES.
ZRRAK
I'LL BET MY ONLY CHANCE IS TO BREAK THOSE RULES -- DO THE UN-EXPECTED -- STARTING RIGHT... NOW!

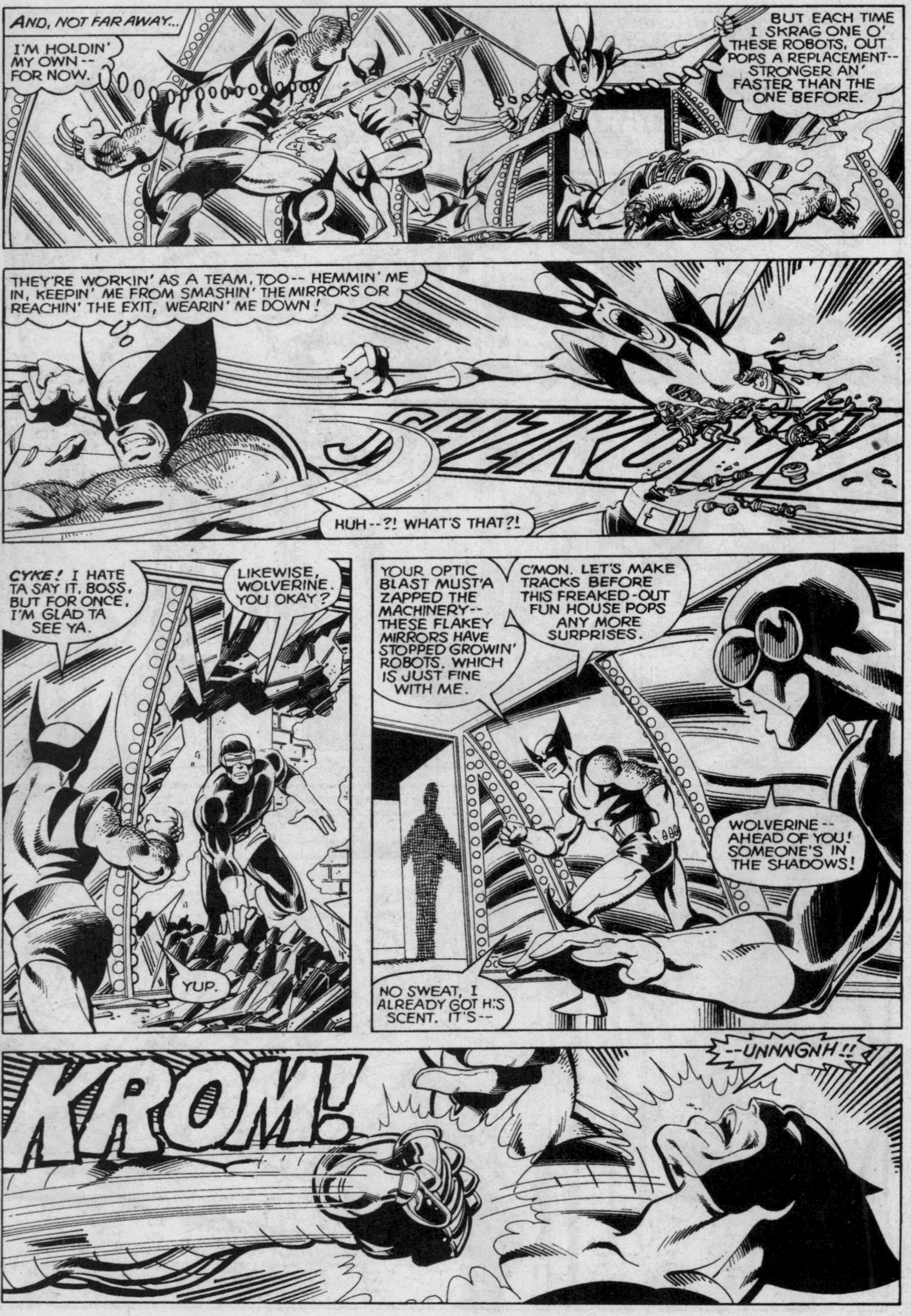
AND, NOT FAR AWAY...
I'M HOLDIN' MY OWN -- FOR NOW.
BUT EACH TIME I SKRAG ONE O' THESE ROBOTS, OUT POPS A REPLACEMENT-- STRONGER AN' FASTER THAN THE ONE BEFORE.
THEY'RE WORKIN' AS A TEAM, TOO-- HEMMIN' ME IN, KEEPIN' ME FROM SMASHIN' THE MIRRORS OR REACHIN' THE EXIT, WEARIN' ME DOWN!
SHKUNCH
HUH--?! WHAT'S THAT?!
CYKE! I HATE TA SAY IT, BOSS, BUT FOR ONCE, I'M GLAD TA SEE YA.
LIKEWISE, WOLVERINE. YOU OKAY?
YUP.
YOUR OPTIC BLAST MUST'A ZAPPED THE MACHINERY-- THESE FLAKEY MIRRORS HAVE STOPPED GROWIN' ROBOTS. WHICH IS JUST FINE WITH ME.
C'MON. LET'S MAKE TRACKS BEFORE THIS FREAKED-OUT FUN HOUSE POPS ANY MORE SURPRISES.
WOLVERINE-- AHEAD OF YOU! SOMEONE'S IN THE SHADOWS!
NO SWEAT, I ALREADY GOT HIS SCENT. IT'S--
KROM!
--UNNNGNH!!

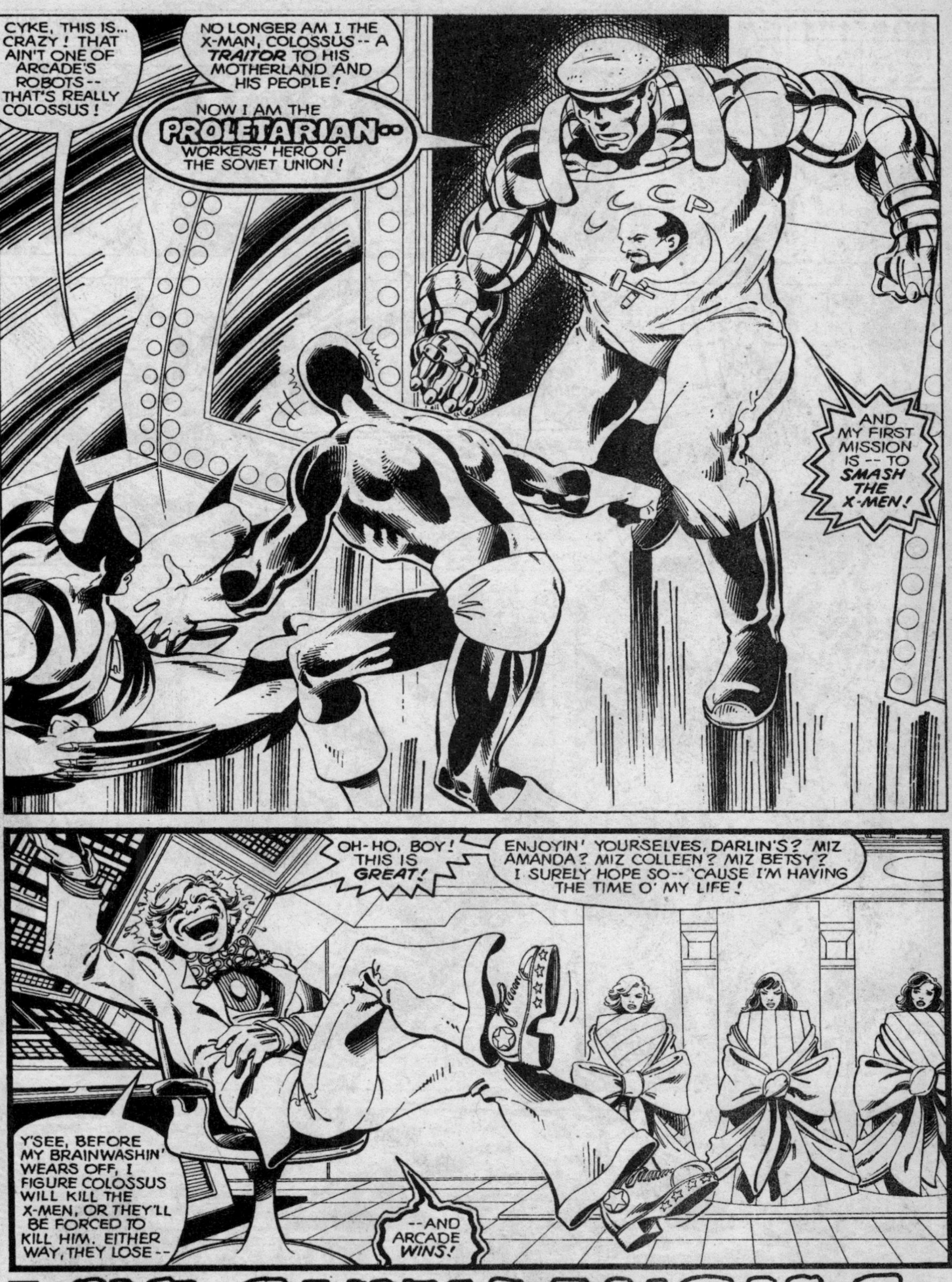
CYKE, THIS IS... CRAZY! THAT AIN'T ONE OF ARCADE'S ROBOTS-- THAT'S REALLY COLOSSUS!
NO LONGER AM I THE X-MAN, COLOSSUS-- A TRAITOR TO HIS MOTHERLAND AND HIS PEOPLE!
NOW I AM THE PROLETARIAN-- WORKERS' HERO OF THE SOVIET UNION!
CCCP
AND MY FIRST MISSION IS -- TO SMASH THE X-MEN!
OH-HO, BOY! THIS IS GREAT!
ENJOYIN' YOURSELVES, DARLIN'S? MIZ AMANDA? MIZ COLLEEN? MIZ BETSY? I SURELY HOPE SO-- 'CAUSE I'M HAVING THE TIME O' MY LIFE!
Y'SEE, BEFORE MY BRAINWASHIN' WEARS OFF, I FIGURE COLOSSUS WILL KILL THE X-MEN, OR THEY'LL BE FORCED TO KILL HIM. EITHER WAY, THEY LOSE--
--AND ARCADE WINS!

NEXT: HE ONLY LAUGHS WHEN I HURT!

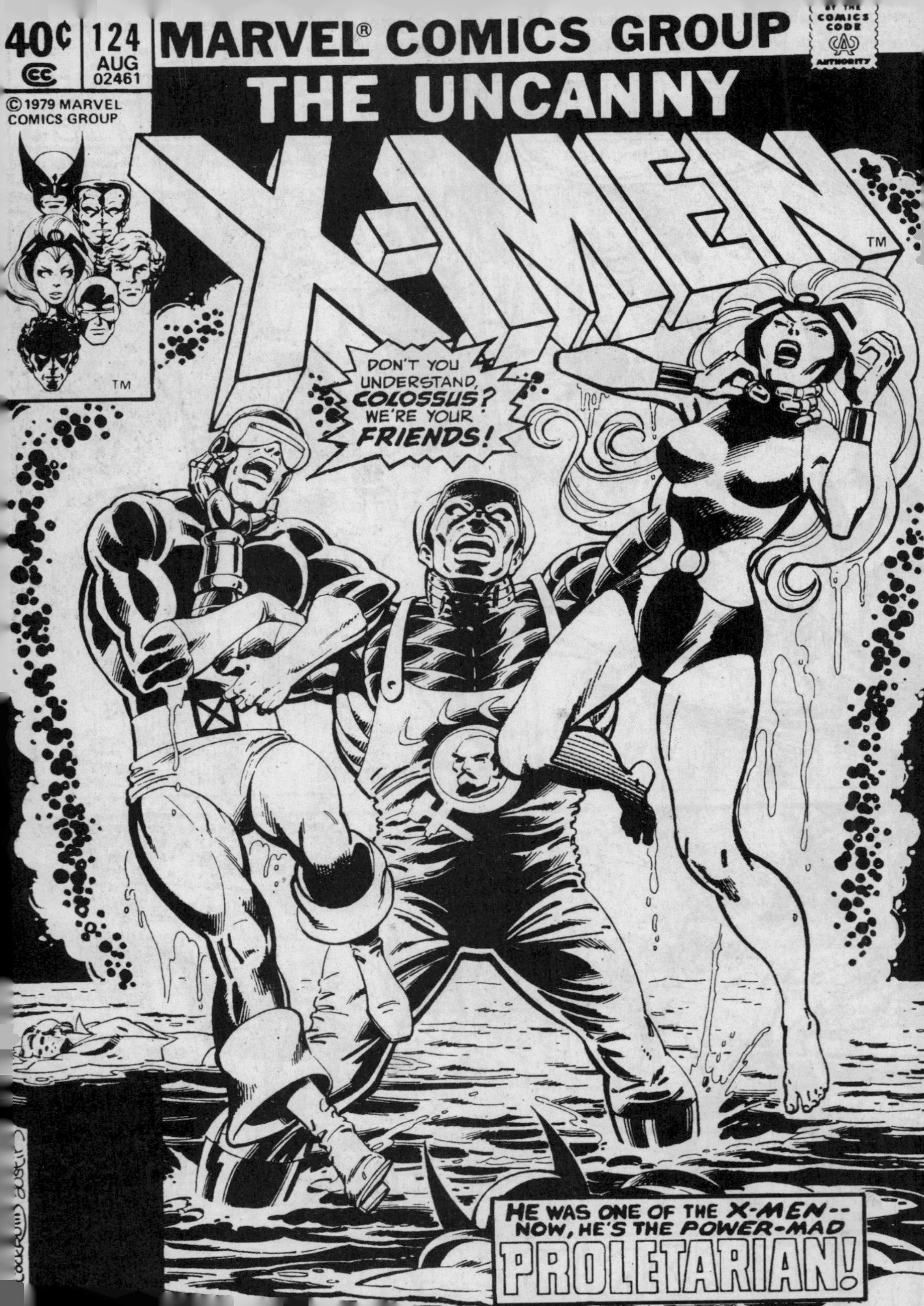

40¢
124
AUG
02461
MARVEL® COMICS GROUP
APPROVED BY THE COMICS CODE AUTHORITY
THE UNCANNY
©1979 MARVEL COMICS GROUP
X-MEN™
TM
DON'T YOU UNDERSTAND, COLOSSUS? WE'RE YOUR FRIENDS!
HE WAS ONE OF THE X-MEN-- NOW, HE'S THE POWER-MAD
PROLETARIAN!

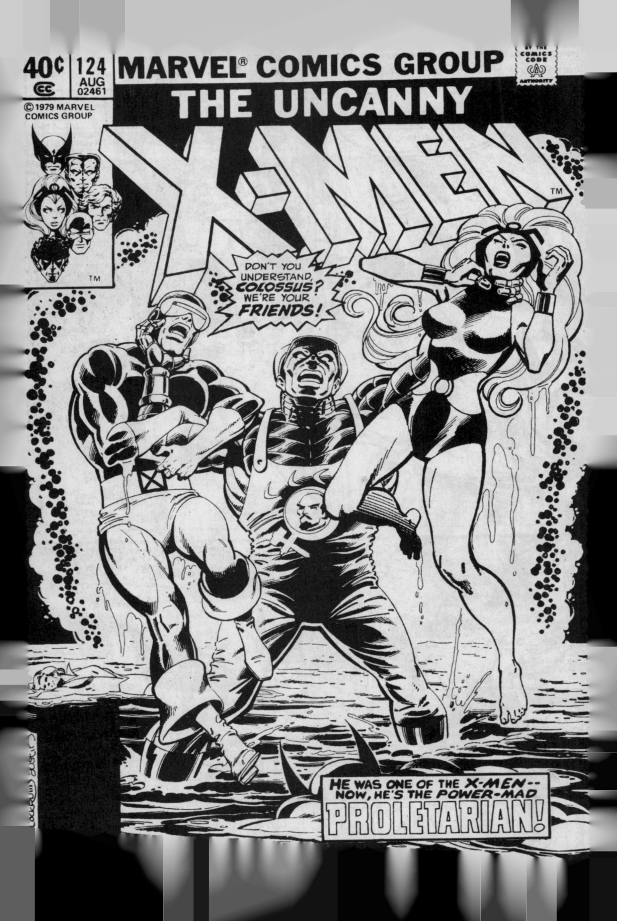

Cyclops. Storm. Banshee. Nightcrawler. Wolverine. Colossus. Children of the atom, students of Charles Xavier, MUTANTS--feared and hated by the world they have sworn to protect. These are the STRANGEST heroes of all!

Stan Lee PRESENTS: **THE UNCANNY X-MEN!** ™

CHRIS CLAREMONT & JOHN BYRNE, AUTHOR / CO-PLOTTERS / PENCILER | TERRY AUSTIN, INKER | TOM ORZECHOWSKI, *letterer* | GLYNIS WEIN, *colorist* | ROGER STERN, EDITOR | JIM SHOOTER, EDITOR-IN-CHIEF

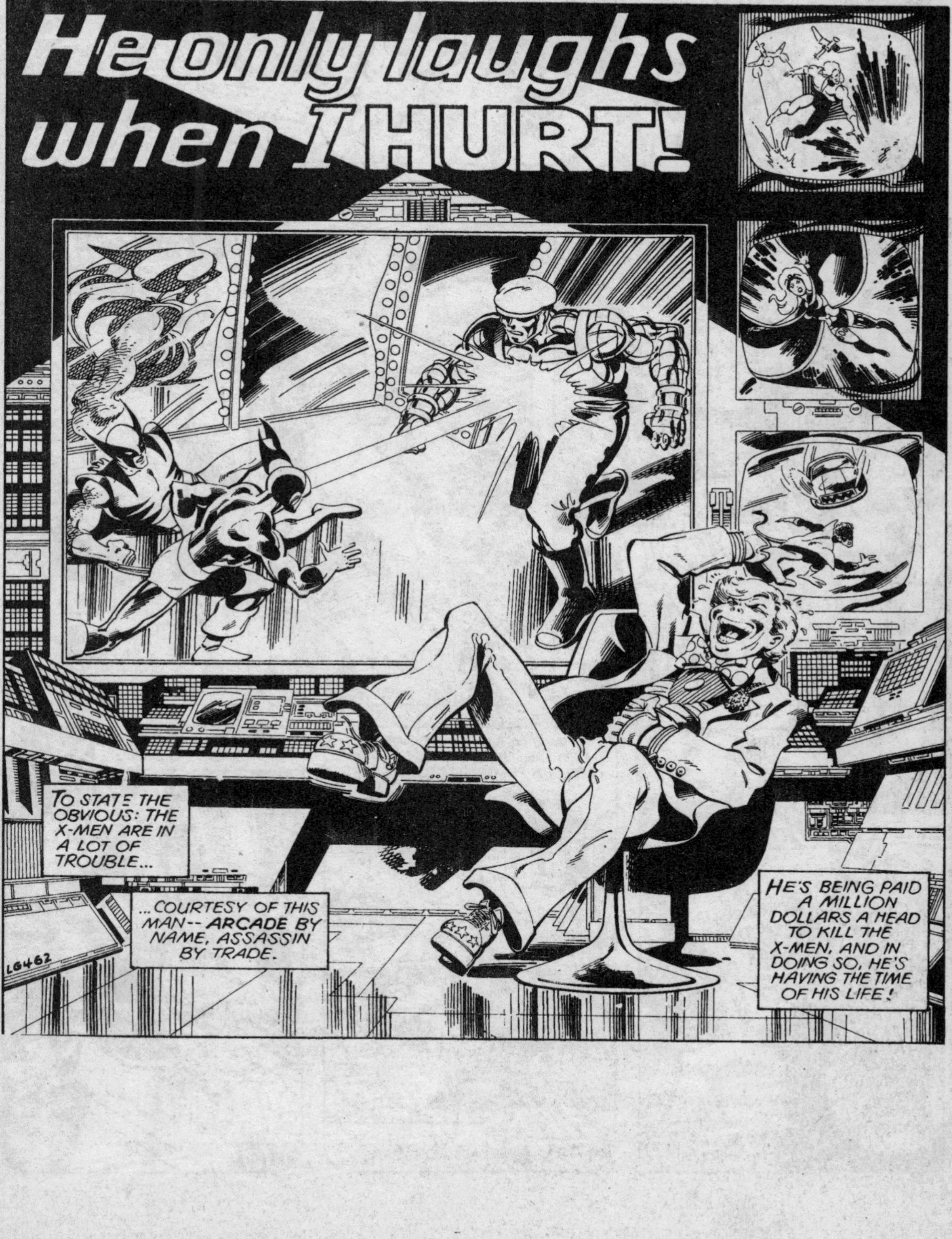
He only laughs when I HURT!
TO STATE THE OBVIOUS: THE X-MEN ARE IN A LOT OF TROUBLE...
...COURTESY OF THIS MAN-- ARCADE BY NAME, ASSASSIN BY TRADE.
HE'S BEING PAID A MILLION DOLLARS A HEAD TO KILL THE X-MEN, AND IN DOING SO, HE'S HAVING THE TIME OF HIS LIFE!
LG462

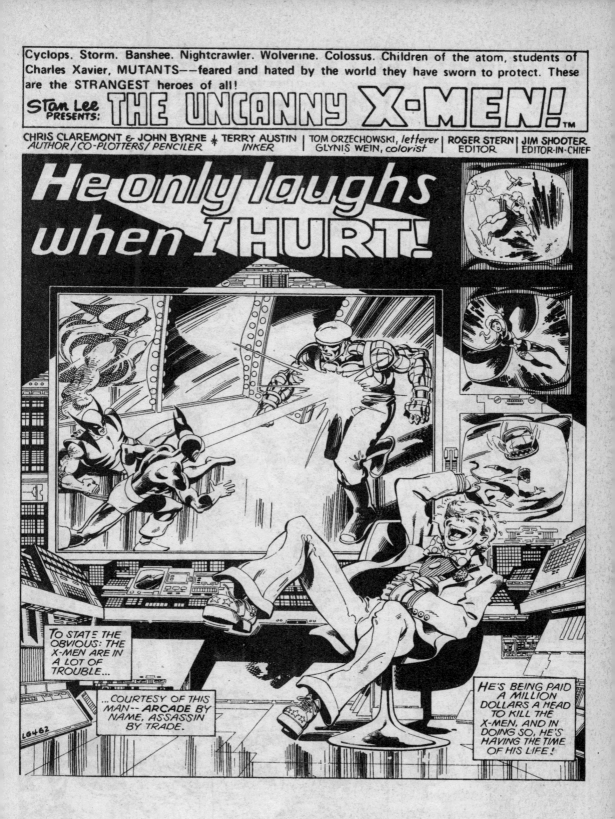

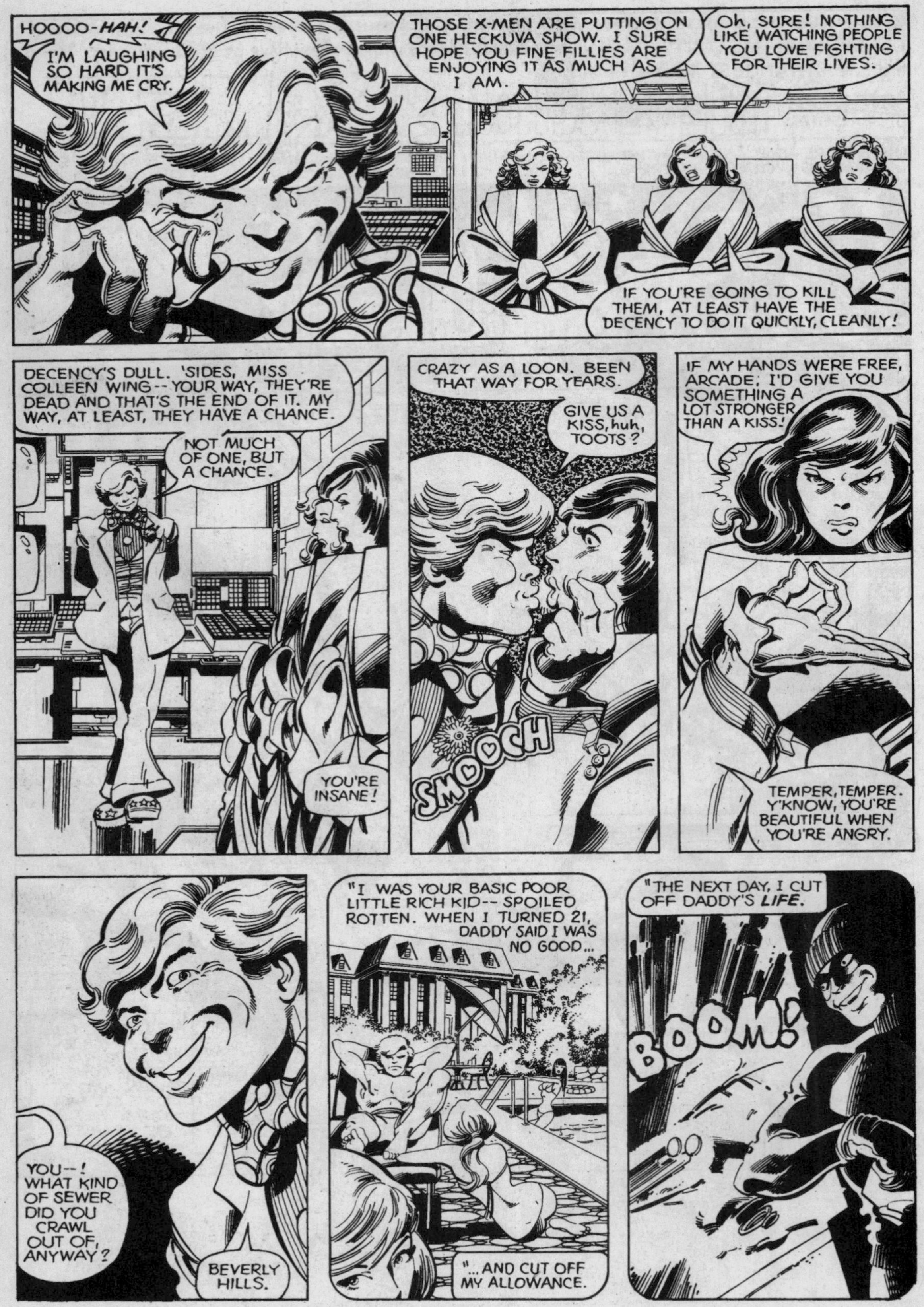
HOOOO-HAH!
I'M LAUGHING SO HARD IT'S MAKING ME CRY.
THOSE X-MEN ARE PUTTING ON ONE HECKUVA SHOW. I SURE HOPE YOU FINE FILLIES ARE ENJOYING IT AS MUCH AS I AM.
Oh, SURE! NOTHING LIKE WATCHING PEOPLE YOU LOVE FIGHTING FOR THEIR LIVES.
IF YOU'RE GOING TO KILL THEM, AT LEAST HAVE THE DECENCY TO DO IT QUICKLY, CLEANLY!
DECENCY'S DULL. 'SIDES, MISS COLLEEN WING-- YOUR WAY, THEY'RE DEAD AND THAT'S THE END OF IT. MY WAY, AT LEAST, THEY HAVE A CHANCE.
NOT MUCH OF ONE, BUT A CHANCE.
YOU'RE INSANE!
CRAZY AS A LOON. BEEN THAT WAY FOR YEARS.
GIVE US A KISS, huh, TOOTS?
SMOOCH
IF MY HANDS WERE FREE, ARCADE, I'D GIVE YOU SOMETHING A LOT STRONGER THAN A KISS!
TEMPER, TEMPER. Y'KNOW, YOU'RE BEAUTIFUL WHEN YOU'RE ANGRY.
YOU--! WHAT KIND OF SEWER DID YOU CRAWL OUT OF, ANYWAY?
BEVERLY HILLS.
"I WAS YOUR BASIC POOR LITTLE RICH KID-- SPOILED ROTTEN. WHEN I TURNED 21, DADDY SAID I WAS NO GOOD...
"...AND CUT OFF MY ALLOWANCE.
"THE NEXT DAY, I CUT OFF DADDY'S LIFE.
BOOM!

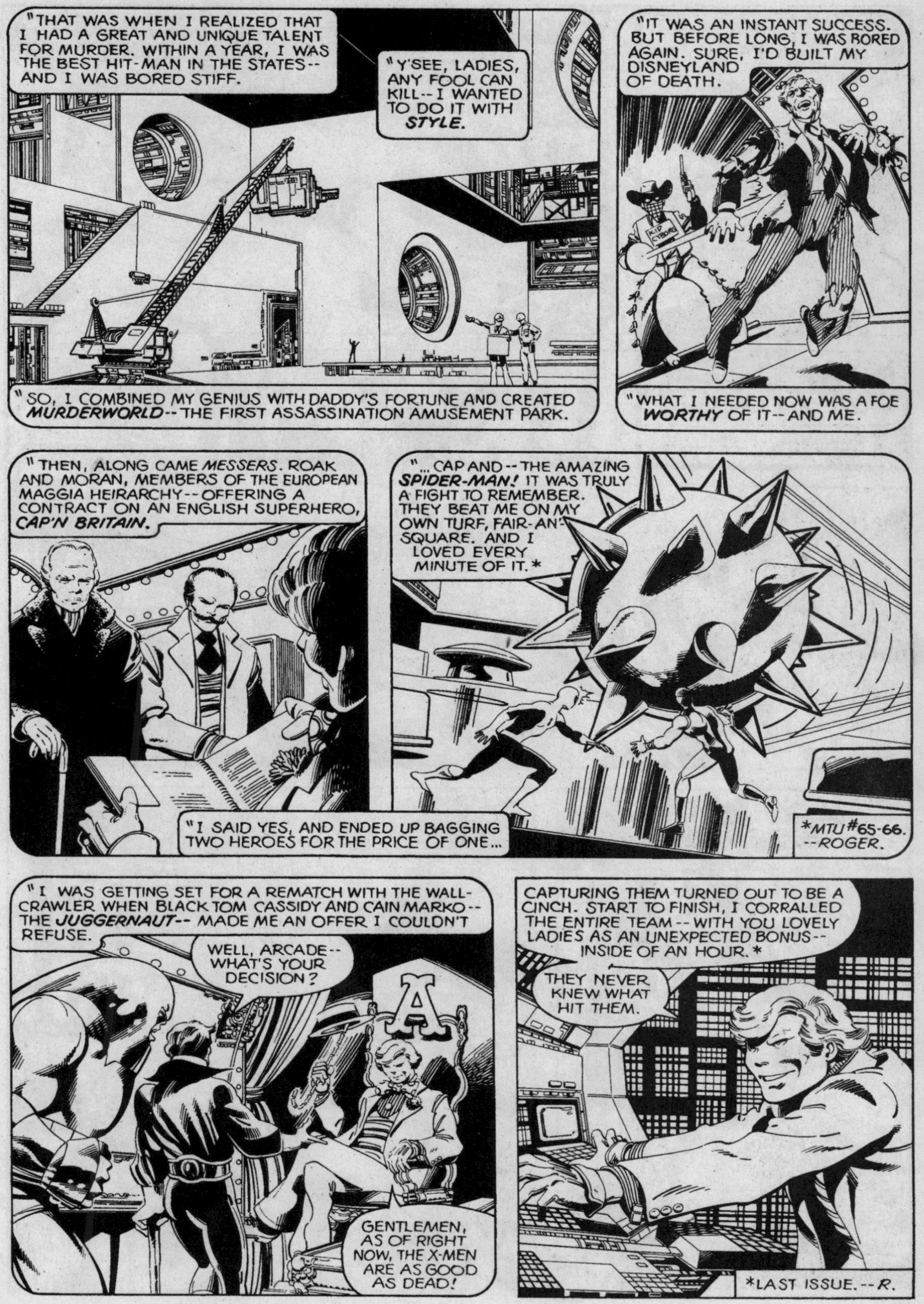
"THAT WAS WHEN I REALIZED THAT I HAD A GREAT AND UNIQUE TALENT FOR MURDER. WITHIN A YEAR, I WAS THE BEST HIT-MAN IN THE STATES -- AND I WAS BORED STIFF.
"Y'SEE, LADIES, ANY FOOL CAN KILL -- I WANTED TO DO IT WITH STYLE.
"SO, I COMBINED MY GENIUS WITH DADDY'S FORTUNE AND CREATED MURDERWORLD -- THE FIRST ASSASSINATION AMUSEMENT PARK.
"IT WAS AN INSTANT SUCCESS. BUT BEFORE LONG, I WAS BORED AGAIN. SURE, I'D BUILT MY DISNEYLAND OF DEATH.
KID CYBORG
"WHAT I NEEDED NOW WAS A FOE WORTHY OF IT -- AND ME.
"THEN, ALONG CAME MESSERS. ROAK AND MORAN, MEMBERS OF THE EUROPEAN MAGGIA HEIRARCHY -- OFFERING A CONTRACT ON AN ENGLISH SUPERHERO, CAP'N BRITAIN.
"... CAP AND -- THE AMAZING SPIDER-MAN! IT WAS TRULY A FIGHT TO REMEMBER. THEY BEAT ME ON MY OWN TURF, FAIR-AN'-SQUARE. AND I LOVED EVERY MINUTE OF IT.*
"I SAID YES, AND ENDED UP BAGGING TWO HEROES FOR THE PRICE OF ONE...
*MTU #65-66. --ROGER.
"I WAS GETTING SET FOR A REMATCH WITH THE WALL-CRAWLER WHEN BLACK TOM CASSIDY AND CAIN MARKO -- THE JUGGERNAUT -- MADE ME AN OFFER I COULDN'T REFUSE.
WELL, ARCADE -- WHAT'S YOUR DECISION?
A
GENTLEMEN, AS OF RIGHT NOW, THE X-MEN ARE AS GOOD AS DEAD!
CAPTURING THEM TURNED OUT TO BE A CINCH. START TO FINISH, I CORRALLED THE ENTIRE TEAM -- WITH YOU LOVELY LADIES AS AN UNEXPECTED BONUS -- INSIDE OF AN HOUR.*
THEY NEVER KNEW WHAT HIT THEM.
*LAST ISSUE. -- R.

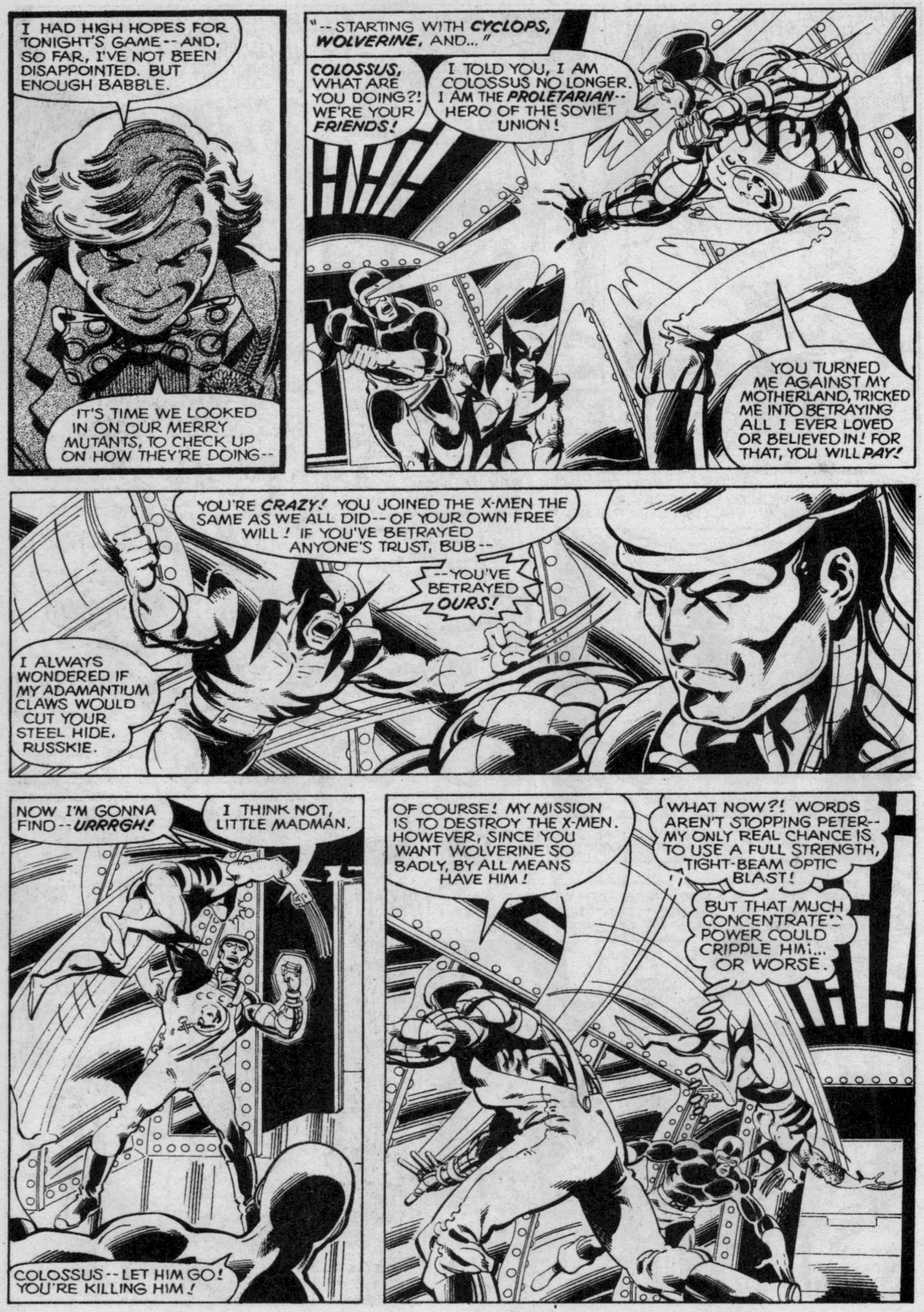
I HAD HIGH HOPES FOR TONIGHT'S GAME--AND, SO FAR, I'VE NOT BEEN DISAPPOINTED. BUT ENOUGH BABBLE.
IT'S TIME WE LOOKED IN ON OUR MERRY MUTANTS, TO CHECK UP ON HOW THEY'RE DOING--
"--STARTING WITH CYCLOPS, WOLVERINE, AND..."
COLOSSUS, WHAT ARE YOU DOING?! WE'RE YOUR FRIENDS!
I TOLD YOU, I AM COLOSSUS NO LONGER. I AM THE PROLETARIAN--HERO OF THE SOVIET UNION!
YOU TURNED ME AGAINST MY MOTHERLAND, TRICKED ME INTO BETRAYING ALL I EVER LOVED OR BELIEVED IN! FOR THAT, YOU WILL PAY!
YOU'RE CRAZY! YOU JOINED THE X-MEN THE SAME AS WE ALL DID--OF YOUR OWN FREE WILL! IF YOU'VE BETRAYED ANYONE'S TRUST, BUB--
--YOU'VE BETRAYED OURS!
I ALWAYS WONDERED IF MY ADAMANTIUM CLAWS WOULD CUT YOUR STEEL HIDE, RUSSKIE.
NOW I'M GONNA FIND--URRRGH!
I THINK NOT, LITTLE MADMAN.
COLOSSUS--LET HIM GO! YOU'RE KILLING HIM!
OF COURSE! MY MISSION IS TO DESTROY THE X-MEN. HOWEVER, SINCE YOU WANT WOLVERINE SO BADLY, BY ALL MEANS HAVE HIM!
WHAT NOW?! WORDS AREN'T STOPPING PETER--MY ONLY REAL CHANCE IS TO USE A FULL STRENGTH, TIGHT-BEAM OPTIC BLAST!
BUT THAT MUCH CONCENTRATED POWER COULD CRIPPLE HIM... OR WORSE.

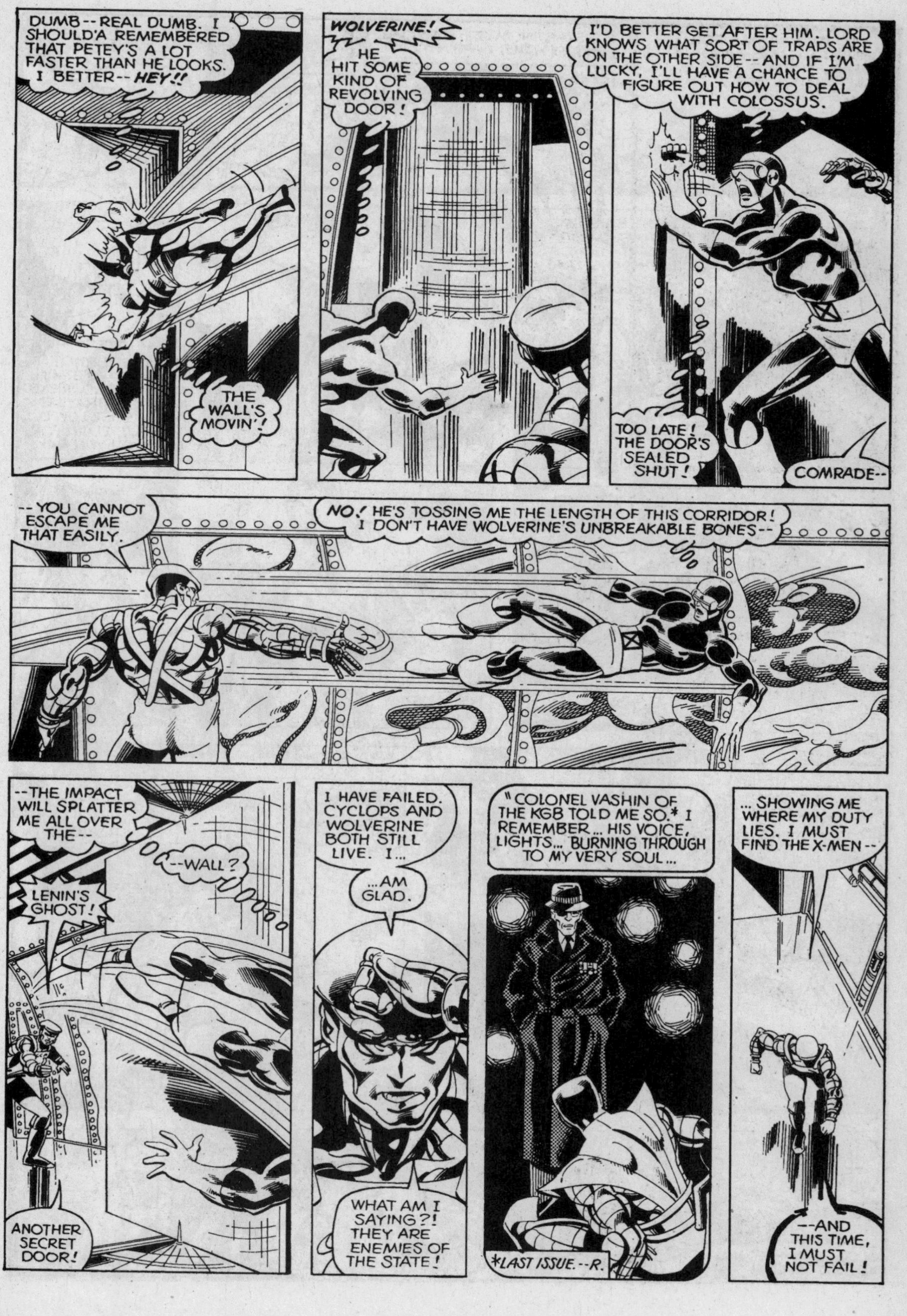
DUMB -- REAL DUMB. I SHOULD'A REMEMBERED THAT PETEY'S A LOT FASTER THAN HE LOOKS. I BETTER -- HEY!!
THE WALL'S MOVIN'!
WOLVERINE!
HE HIT SOME KIND OF REVOLVING DOOR!
I'D BETTER GET AFTER HIM. LORD KNOWS WHAT SORT OF TRAPS ARE ON THE OTHER SIDE -- AND IF I'M LUCKY, I'LL HAVE A CHANCE TO FIGURE OUT HOW TO DEAL WITH COLOSSUS.
TOO LATE! THE DOOR'S SEALED SHUT!
COMRADE--
-- YOU CANNOT ESCAPE ME THAT EASILY.
NO! HE'S TOSSING ME THE LENGTH OF THIS CORRIDOR! I DON'T HAVE WOLVERINE'S UNBREAKABLE BONES--
--THE IMPACT WILL SPLATTER ME ALL OVER THE--
--WALL?
LENIN'S GHOST!
ANOTHER SECRET DOOR!
I HAVE FAILED. CYCLOPS AND WOLVERINE BOTH STILL LIVE. I...
...AM GLAD.
WHAT AM I SAYING?! THEY ARE ENEMIES OF THE STATE!
"COLONEL VASHIN OF THE KGB TOLD ME SO.* I REMEMBER... HIS VOICE, LIGHTS... BURNING THROUGH TO MY VERY SOUL...
*LAST ISSUE. --R.
... SHOWING ME WHERE MY DUTY LIES. I MUST FIND THE X-MEN --
--AND THIS TIME, I MUST NOT FAIL!

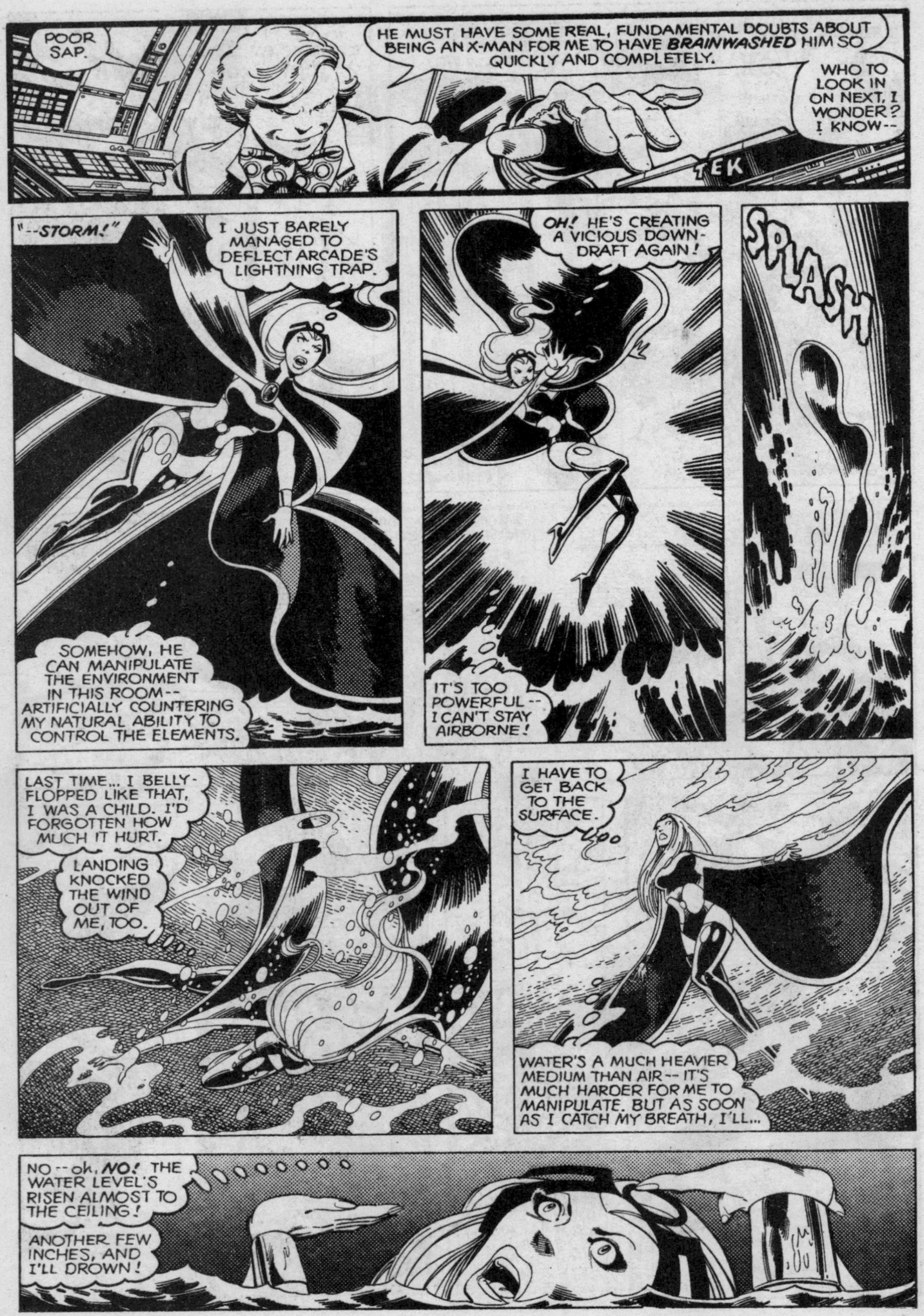

POOR SAP.
HE MUST HAVE SOME REAL, FUNDAMENTAL DOUBTS ABOUT BEING AN X-MAN FOR ME TO HAVE BRAINWASHED HIM SO QUICKLY AND COMPLETELY.
WHO TO LOOK IN ON NEXT, I WONDER? I KNOW--
TEK
"--STORM!"
I JUST BARELY MANAGED TO DEFLECT ARCADE'S LIGHTNING TRAP.
SOMEHOW, HE CAN MANIPULATE THE ENVIRONMENT IN THIS ROOM--ARTIFICIALLY COUNTERING MY NATURAL ABILITY TO CONTROL THE ELEMENTS.
OH! HE'S CREATING A VICIOUS DOWN-DRAFT AGAIN!
IT'S TOO POWERFUL--I CAN'T STAY AIRBORNE!
SPLASH
LAST TIME... I BELLY-FLOPPED LIKE THAT, I WAS A CHILD. I'D FORGOTTEN HOW MUCH IT HURT.
LANDING KNOCKED THE WIND OUT OF ME, TOO.
I HAVE TO GET BACK TO THE SURFACE.
WATER'S A MUCH HEAVIER MEDIUM THAN AIR--IT'S MUCH HARDER FOR ME TO MANIPULATE. BUT AS SOON AS I CATCH MY BREATH, I'LL...
NO--oh, NO! THE WATER LEVEL'S RISEN ALMOST TO THE CEILING!
ANOTHER FEW INCHES, AND I'LL DROWN!

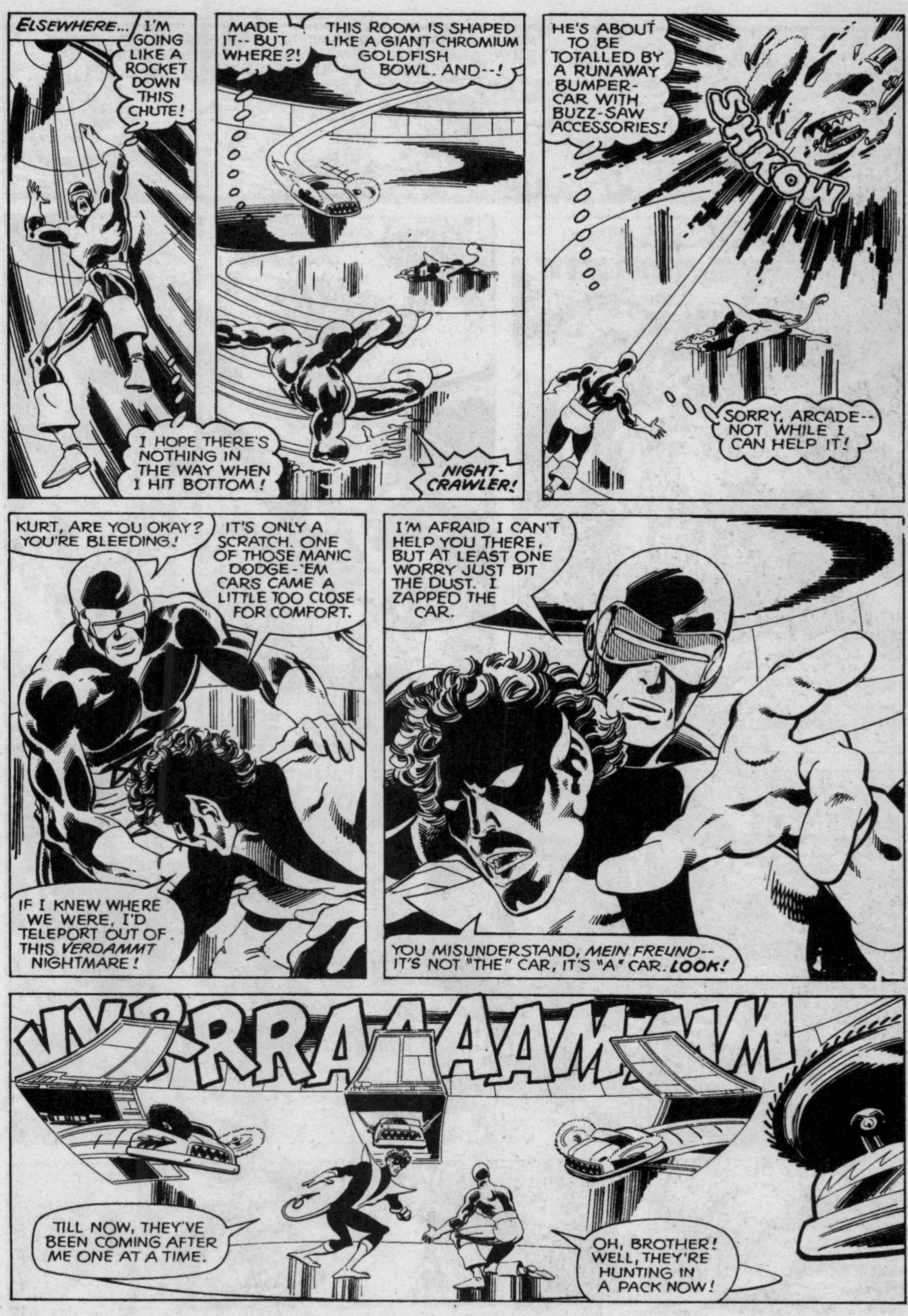
ELSEWHERE...
I'M GOING LIKE A ROCKET DOWN THIS CHUTE!
I HOPE THERE'S NOTHING IN THE WAY WHEN I HIT BOTTOM!
MADE IT-- BUT WHERE?!
THIS ROOM IS SHAPED LIKE A GIANT CHROMIUM GOLDFISH BOWL. AND--!
NIGHT-CRAWLER!
HE'S ABOUT TO BE TOTALLED BY A RUNAWAY BUMPER-CAR WITH BUZZ-SAW ACCESSORIES!
SHKOW
SORRY, ARCADE-- NOT WHILE I CAN HELP IT!
KURT, ARE YOU OKAY? YOU'RE BLEEDING!
IT'S ONLY A SCRATCH. ONE OF THOSE MANIC DODGE-'EM CARS CAME A LITTLE TOO CLOSE FOR COMFORT.
IF I KNEW WHERE WE WERE, I'D TELEPORT OUT OF THIS VERDAMMT NIGHTMARE!
I'M AFRAID I CAN'T HELP YOU THERE, BUT AT LEAST ONE WORRY JUST BIT THE DUST. I ZAPPED THE CAR.
YOU MISUNDERSTAND, MEIN FREUND-- IT'S NOT "THE" CAR, IT'S "A" CAR. LOOK!
VVV-RRRAAAAAMMMM
TILL NOW, THEY'VE BEEN COMING AFTER ME ONE AT A TIME.
OH, BROTHER! WELL, THEY'RE HUNTING IN A PACK NOW!

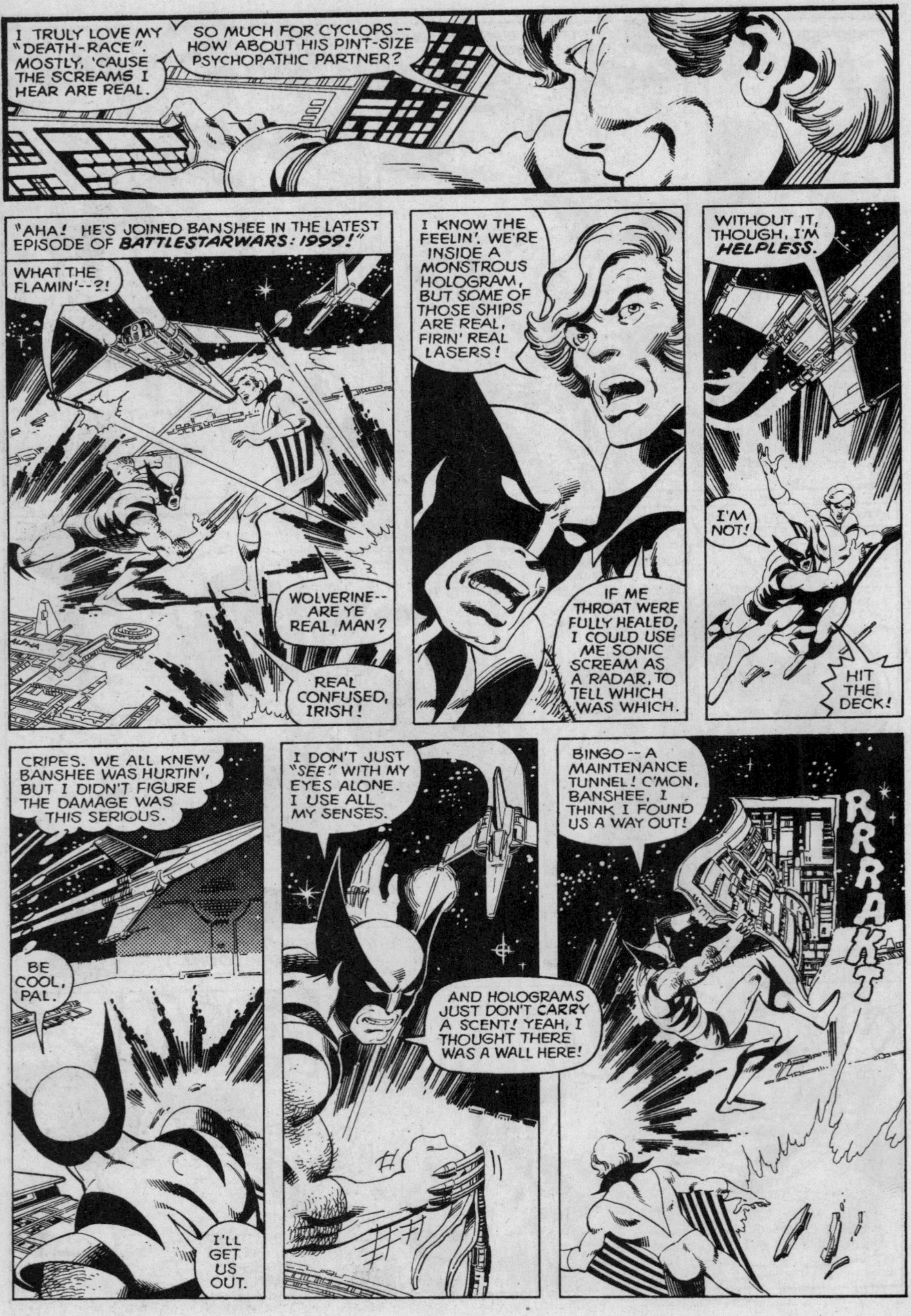
I TRULY LOVE MY "DEATH-RACE". MOSTLY, 'CAUSE THE SCREAMS I HEAR ARE REAL.
SO MUCH FOR CYCLOPS -- HOW ABOUT HIS PINT-SIZE PSYCHOPATHIC PARTNER?
"AHA! HE'S JOINED BANSHEE IN THE LATEST EPISODE OF BATTLESTARWARS: 1999!"
WHAT THE FLAMIN'--?!
WOLVERINE-- ARE YE REAL, MAN?
REAL CONFUSED, IRISH!
I KNOW THE FEELIN'. WE'RE INSIDE A MONSTROUS HOLOGRAM, BUT SOME OF THOSE SHIPS ARE REAL, FIRIN' REAL LASERS!
IF ME THROAT WERE FULLY HEALED, I COULD USE ME SONIC SCREAM AS A RADAR, TO TELL WHICH WAS WHICH.
WITHOUT IT, THOUGH, I'M HELPLESS.
I'M NOT!
HIT THE DECK!
CRIPES. WE ALL KNEW BANSHEE WAS HURTIN', BUT I DIDN'T FIGURE THE DAMAGE WAS THIS SERIOUS.
BE COOL, PAL.
I'LL GET US OUT.
I DON'T JUST "SEE" WITH MY EYES ALONE. I USE ALL MY SENSES.
AND HOLOGRAMS JUST DON'T CARRY A SCENT! YEAH, I THOUGHT THERE WAS A WALL HERE!
BINGO -- A MAINTENANCE TUNNEL! C'MON, BANSHEE, I THINK I FOUND US A WAY OUT!
RRRAKT

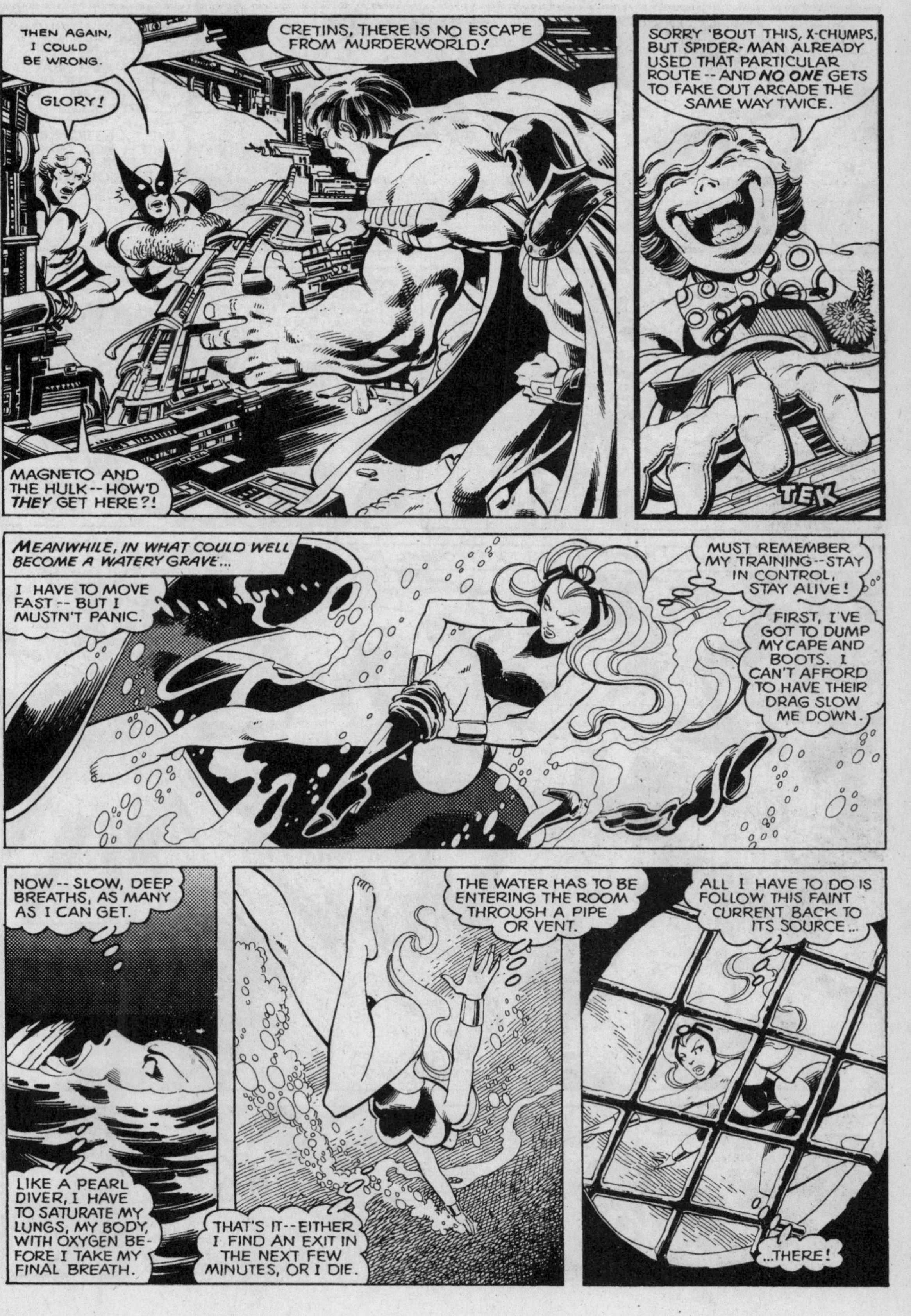
THEN AGAIN, I COULD BE WRONG.
GLORY!
CRETINS, THERE IS NO ESCAPE FROM MURDERWORLD!
MAGNETO AND THE HULK--HOW'D THEY GET HERE?!
SORRY 'BOUT THIS, X-CHUMPS, BUT SPIDER-MAN ALREADY USED THAT PARTICULAR ROUTE -- AND NO ONE GETS TO FAKE OUT ARCADE THE SAME WAY TWICE.
TEK
MEANWHILE, IN WHAT COULD WELL BECOME A WATERY GRAVE...
I HAVE TO MOVE FAST -- BUT I MUSTN'T PANIC.
MUST REMEMBER MY TRAINING--STAY IN CONTROL, STAY ALIVE!
FIRST, I'VE GOT TO DUMP MY CAPE AND BOOTS. I CAN'T AFFORD TO HAVE THEIR DRAG SLOW ME DOWN.
NOW -- SLOW, DEEP BREATHS, AS MANY AS I CAN GET.
LIKE A PEARL DIVER, I HAVE TO SATURATE MY LUNGS, MY BODY, WITH OXYGEN BEFORE I TAKE MY FINAL BREATH.
THE WATER HAS TO BE ENTERING THE ROOM THROUGH A PIPE OR VENT.
THAT'S IT--EITHER I FIND AN EXIT IN THE NEXT FEW MINUTES, OR I DIE.
ALL I HAVE TO DO IS FOLLOW THIS FAINT CURRENT BACK TO ITS SOURCE...
...THERE!

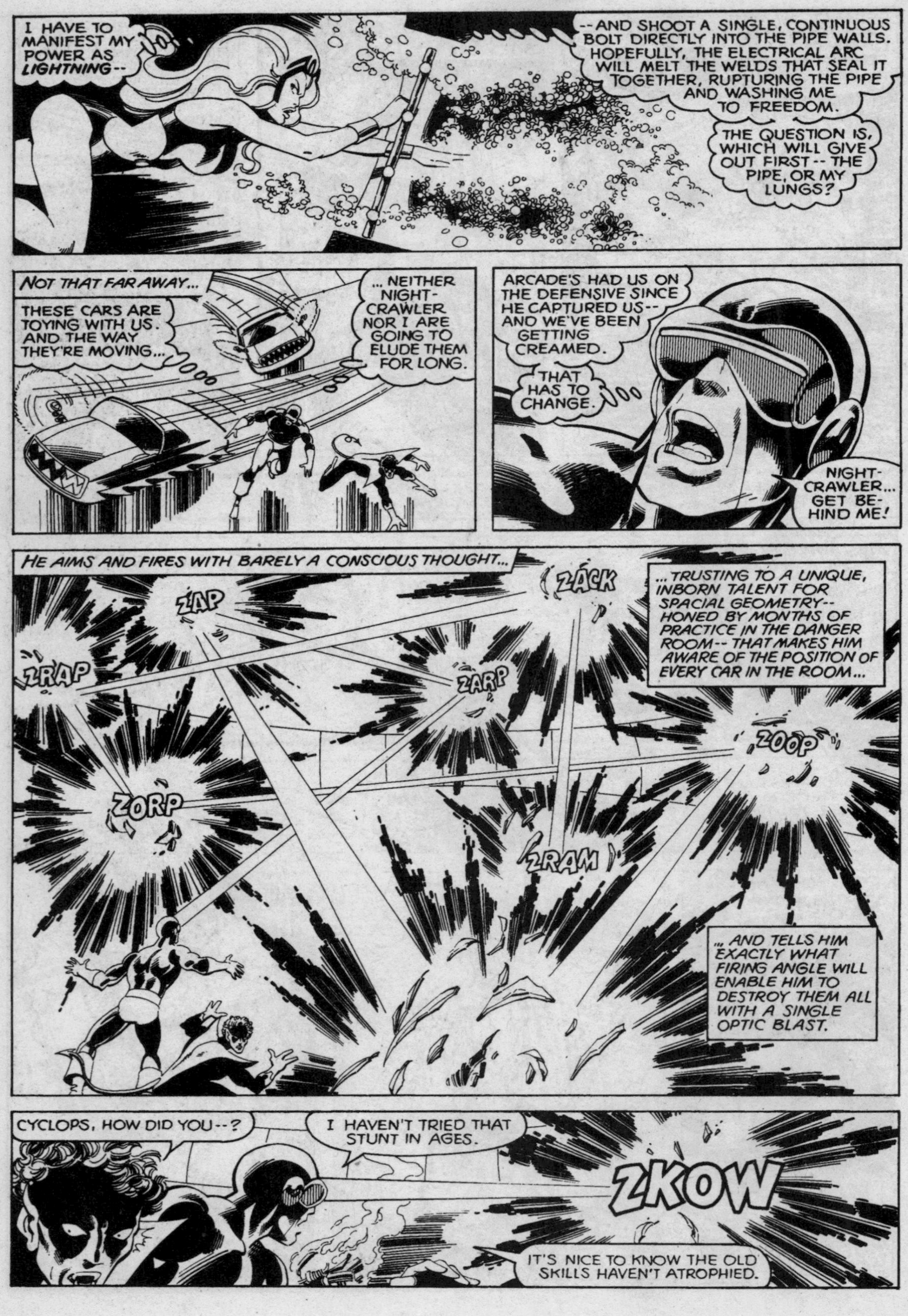
I HAVE TO MANIFEST MY POWER AS LIGHTNING--
--AND SHOOT A SINGLE, CONTINUOUS BOLT DIRECTLY INTO THE PIPE WALLS. HOPEFULLY, THE ELECTRICAL ARC WILL MELT THE WELDS THAT SEAL IT TOGETHER, RUPTURING THE PIPE AND WASHING ME TO FREEDOM.
THE QUESTION IS, WHICH WILL GIVE OUT FIRST -- THE PIPE, OR MY LUNGS?
NOT THAT FAR AWAY...
THESE CARS ARE TOYING WITH US. AND THE WAY THEY'RE MOVING...
...NEITHER NIGHT-CRAWLER NOR I ARE GOING TO ELUDE THEM FOR LONG.
ARCADE'S HAD US ON THE DEFENSIVE SINCE HE CAPTURED US-- AND WE'VE BEEN GETTING CREAMED.
THAT HAS TO CHANGE.
NIGHT-CRAWLER... GET BE-HIND ME!
HE AIMS AND FIRES WITH BARELY A CONSCIOUS THOUGHT...
...TRUSTING TO A UNIQUE, INBORN TALENT FOR SPACIAL GEOMETRY-- HONED BY MONTHS OF PRACTICE IN THE DANGER ROOM-- THAT MAKES HIM AWARE OF THE POSITION OF EVERY CAR IN THE ROOM...
ZACK
ZAP
ZRAP
ZARP
ZOOP
ZORP
ZRAM
...AND TELLS HIM EXACTLY WHAT FIRING ANGLE WILL ENABLE HIM TO DESTROY THEM ALL WITH A SINGLE OPTIC BLAST.
CYCLOPS, HOW DID YOU--?
I HAVEN'T TRIED THAT STUNT IN AGES.
ZKOW
IT'S NICE TO KNOW THE OLD SKILLS HAVEN'T ATROPHIED.

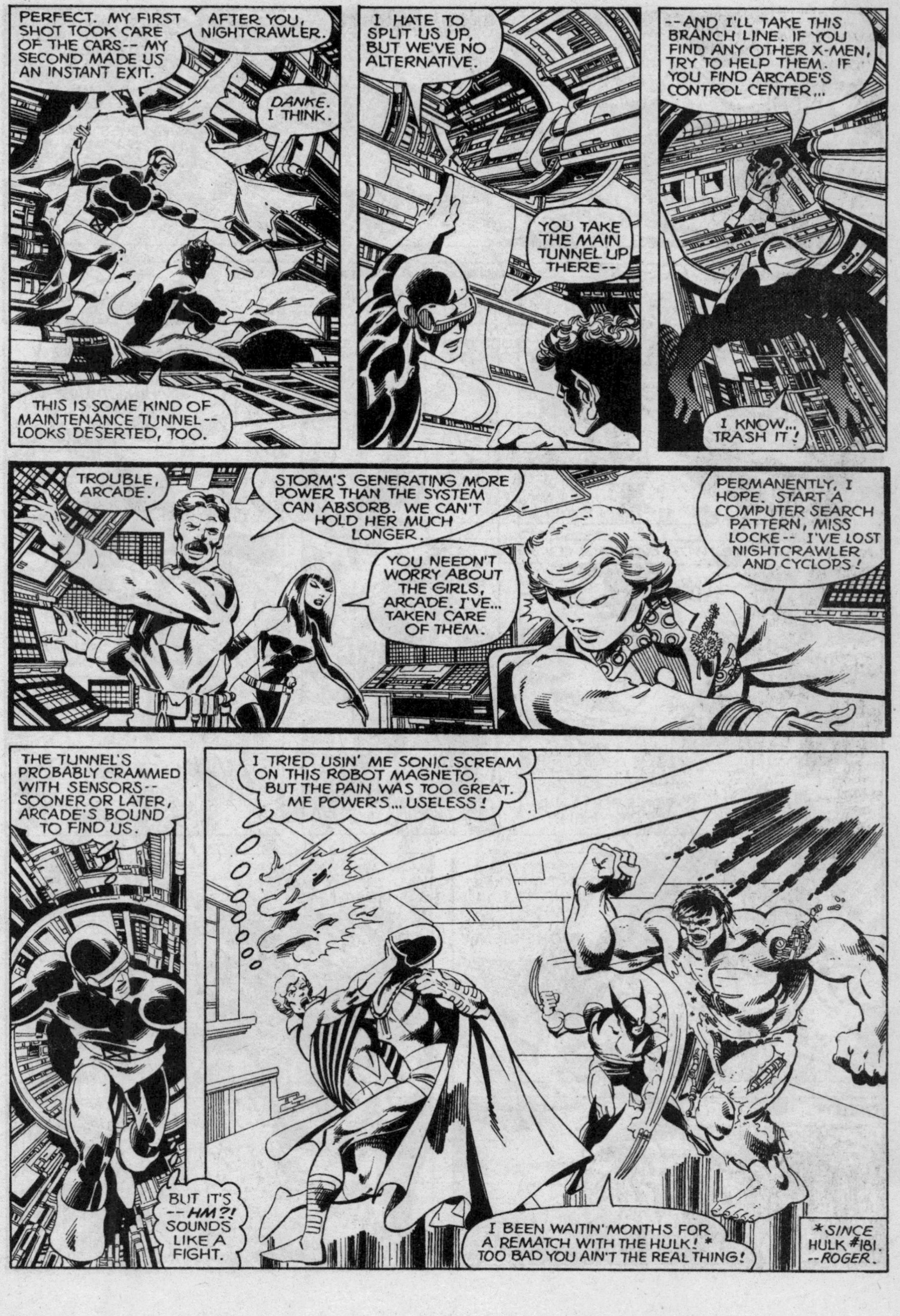
PERFECT. MY FIRST SHOT TOOK CARE OF THE CARS-- MY SECOND MADE US AN INSTANT EXIT.
AFTER YOU, NIGHTCRAWLER.
DANKE. I THINK.
THIS IS SOME KIND OF MAINTENANCE TUNNEL-- LOOKS DESERTED, TOO.
I HATE TO SPLIT US UP, BUT WE'VE NO ALTERNATIVE.
YOU TAKE THE MAIN TUNNEL UP THERE--
--AND I'LL TAKE THIS BRANCH LINE. IF YOU FIND ANY OTHER X-MEN, TRY TO HELP THEM. IF YOU FIND ARCADE'S CONTROL CENTER...
I KNOW... TRASH IT!
TROUBLE, ARCADE.
STORM'S GENERATING MORE POWER THAN THE SYSTEM CAN ABSORB. WE CAN'T HOLD HER MUCH LONGER.
YOU NEEDN'T WORRY ABOUT THE GIRLS, ARCADE. I'VE... TAKEN CARE OF THEM.
PERMANENTLY, I HOPE. START A COMPUTER SEARCH PATTERN, MISS LOCKE-- I'VE LOST NIGHTCRAWLER AND CYCLOPS!
THE TUNNEL'S PROBABLY CRAMMED WITH SENSORS-- SOONER OR LATER, ARCADE'S BOUND TO FIND US.
BUT IT'S --HM?! SOUNDS LIKE A FIGHT.
I TRIED USIN' ME SONIC SCREAM ON THIS ROBOT MAGNETO, BUT THE PAIN WAS TOO GREAT. ME POWER'S... USELESS!
I BEEN WAITIN' MONTHS FOR A REMATCH WITH THE HULK! * TOO BAD YOU AIN'T THE REAL THING!
*SINCE HULK #181. --ROGER.

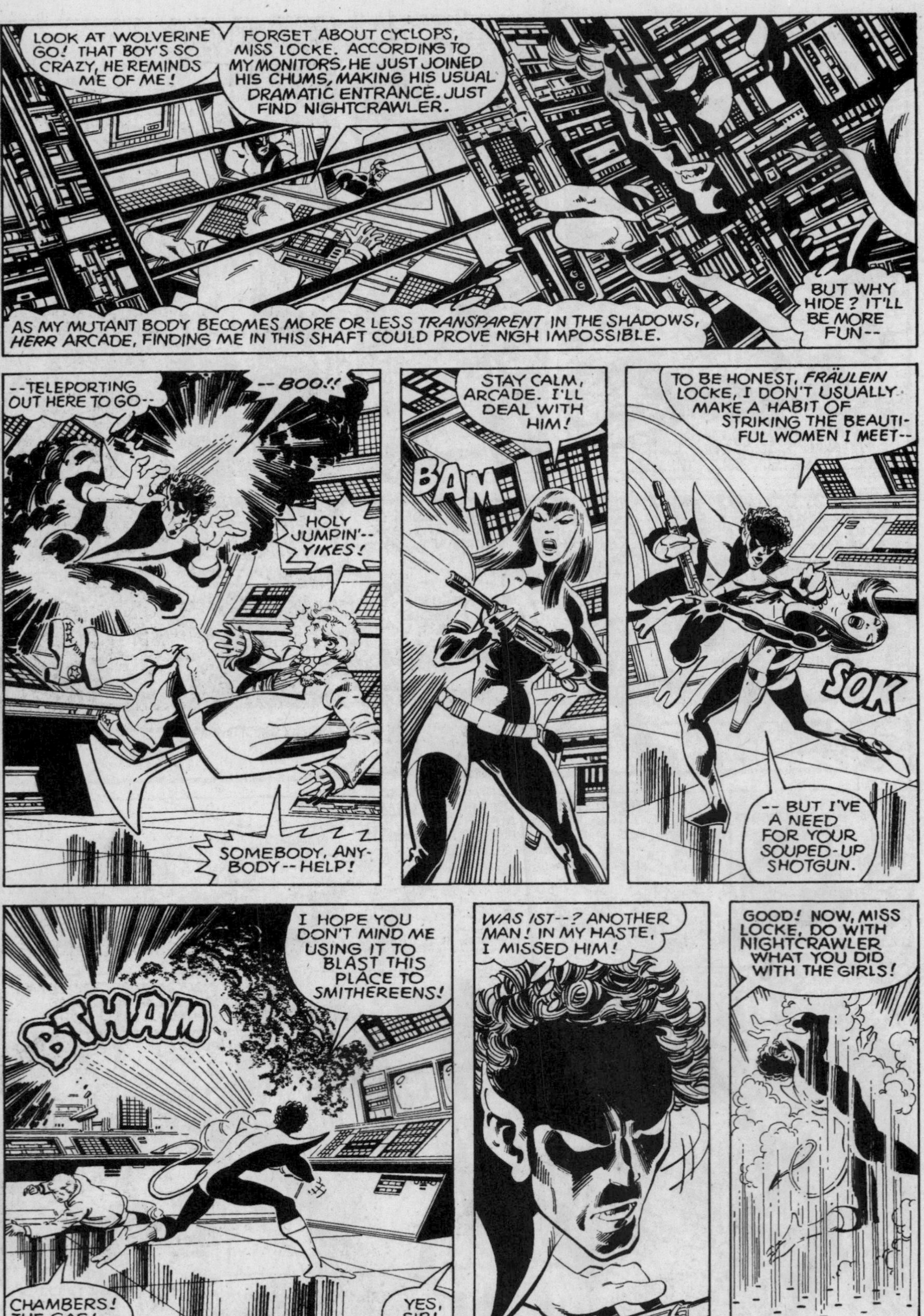
LOOK AT WOLVERINE GO! THAT BOY'S SO CRAZY, HE REMINDS ME OF ME!
FORGET ABOUT CYCLOPS, MISS LOCKE. ACCORDING TO MY MONITORS, HE JUST JOINED HIS CHUMS, MAKING HIS USUAL DRAMATIC ENTRANCE. JUST FIND NIGHTCRAWLER.
AS MY MUTANT BODY BECOMES MORE OR LESS TRANSPARENT IN THE SHADOWS, HERR ARCADE, FINDING ME IN THIS SHAFT COULD PROVE NIGH IMPOSSIBLE.
BUT WHY HIDE? IT'LL BE MORE FUN--
--TELEPORTING OUT HERE TO GO--
--BOO!!
HOLY JUMPIN'-- YIKES!
SOMEBODY, ANY-BODY--HELP!
STAY CALM, ARCADE. I'LL DEAL WITH HIM!
BAM
TO BE HONEST, FRÄULEIN LOCKE, I DON'T USUALLY MAKE A HABIT OF STRIKING THE BEAUTIFUL WOMEN I MEET--
SOK
--BUT I'VE A NEED FOR YOUR SOUPED-UP SHOTGUN.
I HOPE YOU DON'T MIND ME USING IT TO BLAST THIS PLACE TO SMITHEREENS!
BTHAM
CHAMBERS! THE GAS!
YES, SIR!
WAS IST--? ANOTHER MAN! IN MY HASTE, I MISSED HIM!
GOOD! NOW, MISS LOCKE, DO WITH NIGHTCRAWLER WHAT YOU DID WITH THE GIRLS!

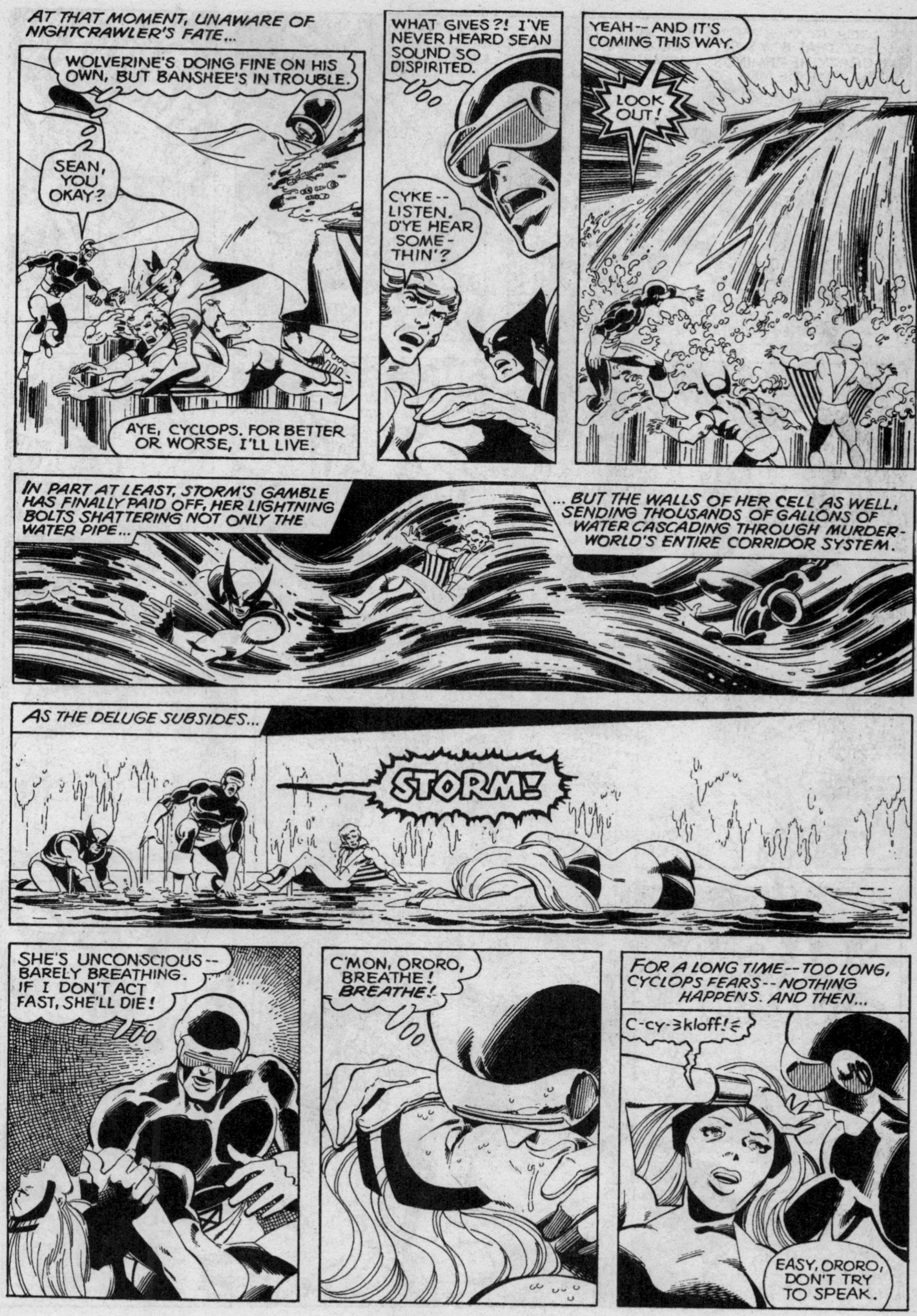
AT THAT MOMENT, UNAWARE OF NIGHTCRAWLER'S FATE...
WOLVERINE'S DOING FINE ON HIS OWN, BUT BANSHEE'S IN TROUBLE.
SEAN, YOU OKAY?
AYE, CYCLOPS. FOR BETTER OR WORSE, I'LL LIVE.
WHAT GIVES?! I'VE NEVER HEARD SEAN SOUND SO DISPIRITED.
CYKE -- LISTEN. D'YE HEAR SOME-THIN'?
YEAH -- AND IT'S COMING THIS WAY.
LOOK OUT!
IN PART AT LEAST, STORM'S GAMBLE HAS FINALLY PAID OFF, HER LIGHTNING BOLTS SHATTERING NOT ONLY THE WATER PIPE...
... BUT THE WALLS OF HER CELL AS WELL, SENDING THOUSANDS OF GALLONS OF WATER CASCADING THROUGH MURDER-WORLD'S ENTIRE CORRIDOR SYSTEM.
AS THE DELUGE SUBSIDES...
STORM!
SHE'S UNCONSCIOUS -- BARELY BREATHING. IF I DON'T ACT FAST, SHE'LL DIE!
C'MON, ORORO, BREATHE! BREATHE!
FOR A LONG TIME -- TOO LONG, CYCLOPS FEARS -- NOTHING HAPPENS. AND THEN...
C-cy- kloff!
EASY, ORORO, DON'T TRY TO SPEAK.

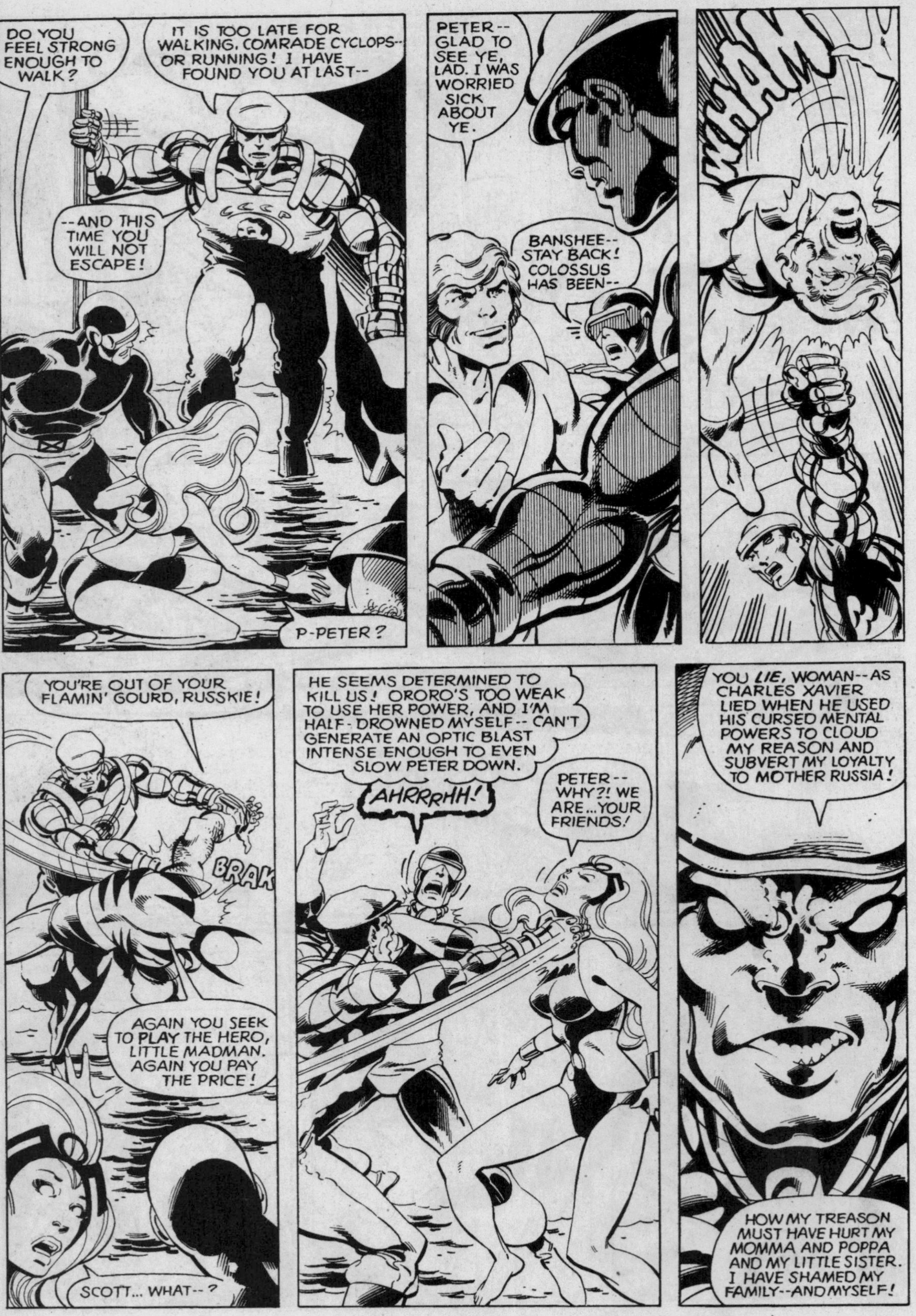
DO YOU FEEL STRONG ENOUGH TO WALK?
IT IS TOO LATE FOR WALKING, COMRADE CYCLOPS-- OR RUNNING! I HAVE FOUND YOU AT LAST--
--AND THIS TIME YOU WILL NOT ESCAPE!
CCCP
P-PETER?
PETER-- GLAD TO SEE YE, LAD. I WAS WORRIED SICK ABOUT YE.
BANSHEE-- STAY BACK! COLOSSUS HAS BEEN--
WHAM
YOU'RE OUT OF YOUR FLAMIN' GOURD, RUSSKIE!
BRAK
AGAIN YOU SEEK TO PLAY THE HERO, LITTLE MADMAN. AGAIN YOU PAY THE PRICE!
SCOTT... WHAT--?
HE SEEMS DETERMINED TO KILL US! ORORO'S TOO WEAK TO USE HER POWER, AND I'M HALF-DROWNED MYSELF-- CAN'T GENERATE AN OPTIC BLAST INTENSE ENOUGH TO EVEN SLOW PETER DOWN.
AHRRRHH!
PETER-- WHY?! WE ARE... YOUR FRIENDS!
YOU LIE, WOMAN-- AS CHARLES XAVIER LIED WHEN HE USED HIS CURSED MENTAL POWERS TO CLOUD MY REASON AND SUBVERT MY LOYALTY TO MOTHER RUSSIA!
HOW MY TREASON MUST HAVE HURT MY MOMMA AND POPPA AND MY LITTLE SISTER. I HAVE SHAMED MY FAMILY--AND MYSELF!

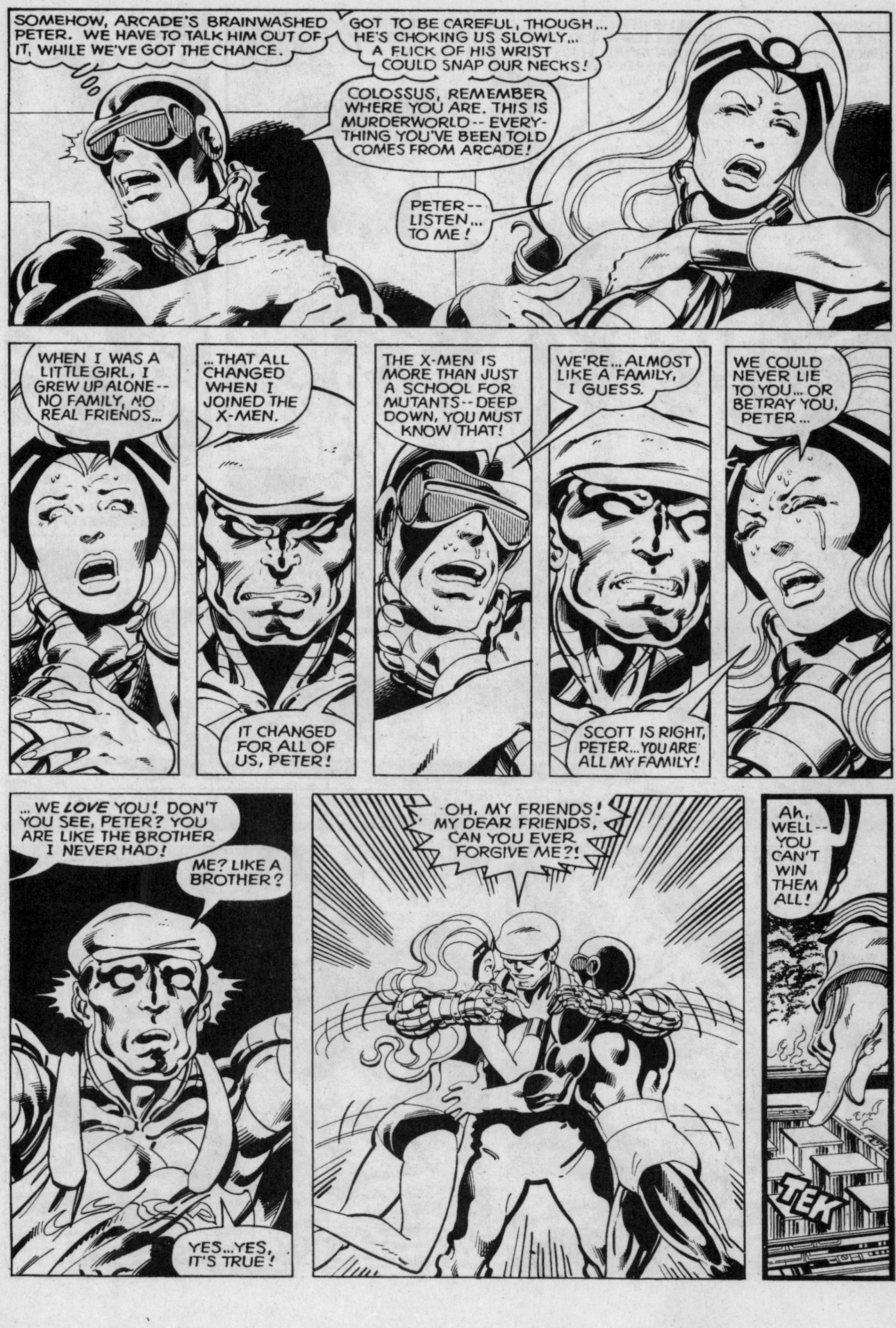
SOMEHOW, ARCADE'S BRAINWASHED PETER. WE HAVE TO TALK HIM OUT OF IT, WHILE WE'VE GOT THE CHANCE.
GOT TO BE CAREFUL, THOUGH... HE'S CHOKING US SLOWLY... A FLICK OF HIS WRIST COULD SNAP OUR NECKS!
COLOSSUS, REMEMBER WHERE YOU ARE. THIS IS MURDERWORLD -- EVERYTHING YOU'VE BEEN TOLD COMES FROM ARCADE!
PETER-- LISTEN... TO ME!
WHEN I WAS A LITTLE GIRL, I GREW UP ALONE -- NO FAMILY, NO REAL FRIENDS...
...THAT ALL CHANGED WHEN I JOINED THE X-MEN.
IT CHANGED FOR ALL OF US, PETER!
THE X-MEN IS MORE THAN JUST A SCHOOL FOR MUTANTS -- DEEP DOWN, YOU MUST KNOW THAT!
WE'RE... ALMOST LIKE A FAMILY, I GUESS.
SCOTT IS RIGHT, PETER... YOU ARE ALL MY FAMILY!
WE COULD NEVER LIE TO YOU... OR BETRAY YOU, PETER...
... WE LOVE YOU! DON'T YOU SEE, PETER? YOU ARE LIKE THE BROTHER I NEVER HAD!
ME? LIKE A BROTHER?
YES... YES, IT'S TRUE!
OH, MY FRIENDS! MY DEAR FRIENDS, CAN YOU EVER FORGIVE ME?!
Ah, WELL-- YOU CAN'T WIN THEM ALL!
TEK

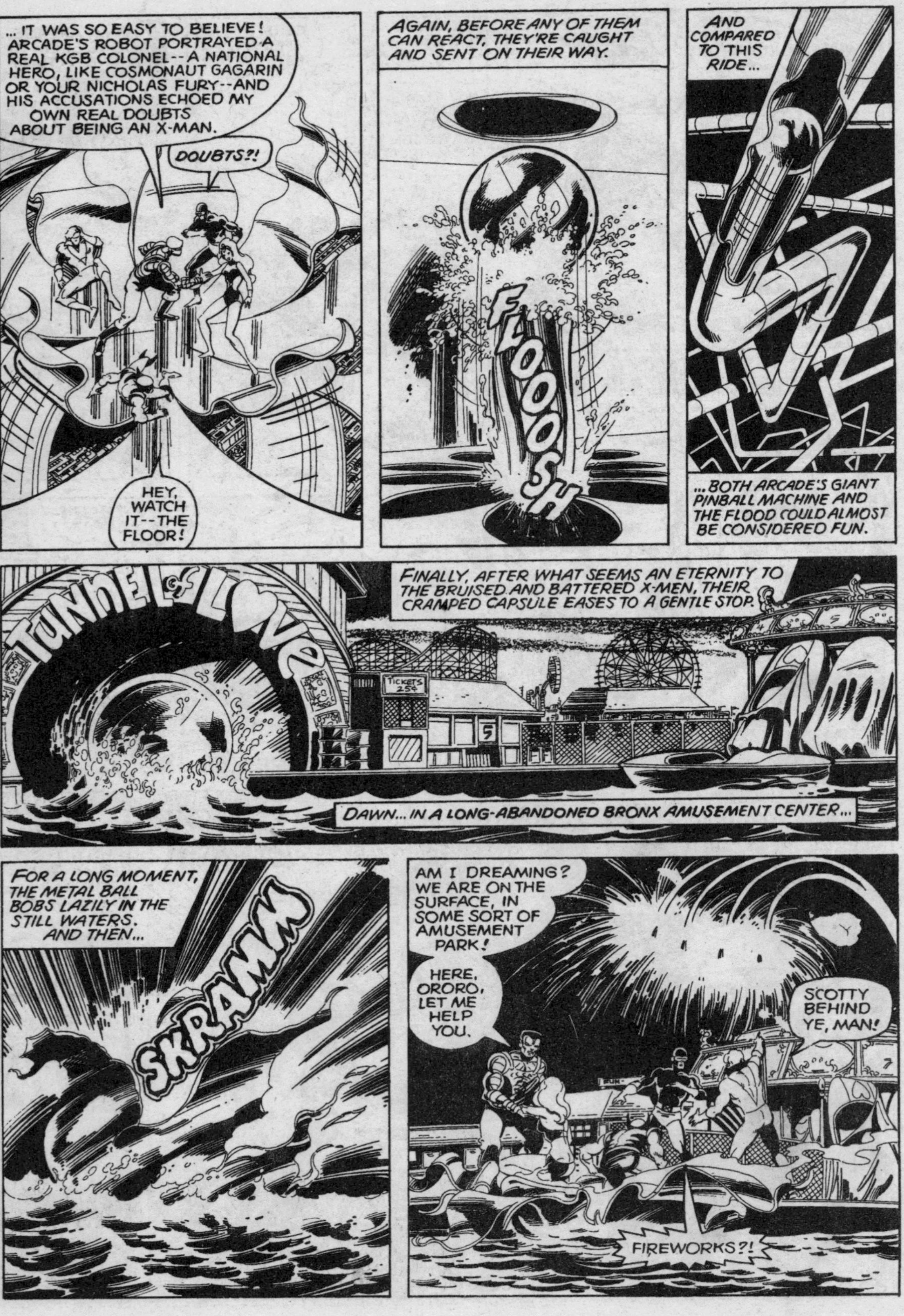
... IT WAS SO EASY TO BELIEVE! ARCADE'S ROBOT PORTRAYED A REAL KGB COLONEL-- A NATIONAL HERO, LIKE COSMONAUT GAGARIN OR YOUR NICHOLAS FURY--AND HIS ACCUSATIONS ECHOED MY OWN REAL DOUBTS ABOUT BEING AN X-MAN.
DOUBTS?!
HEY, WATCH IT--THE FLOOR!
AGAIN, BEFORE ANY OF THEM CAN REACT, THEY'RE CAUGHT AND SENT ON THEIR WAY.
FLOOOSH
AND COMPARED TO THIS RIDE...
...BOTH ARCADE'S GIANT PINBALL MACHINE AND THE FLOOD COULD ALMOST BE CONSIDERED FUN.
FINALLY, AFTER WHAT SEEMS AN ETERNITY TO THE BRUISED AND BATTERED X-MEN, THEIR CRAMPED CAPSULE EASES TO A GENTLE STOP.
TUNNEL of LOVE
TICKETS 25¢
DAWN... IN A LONG-ABANDONED BRONX AMUSEMENT CENTER...
FOR A LONG MOMENT, THE METAL BALL BOBS LAZILY IN THE STILL WATERS. AND THEN...
SKRAMM
AM I DREAMING? WE ARE ON THE SURFACE, IN SOME SORT OF AMUSEMENT PARK!
HERE, ORORO, LET ME HELP YOU.
SCOTTY BEHIND YE, MAN!
FIREWORKS?!

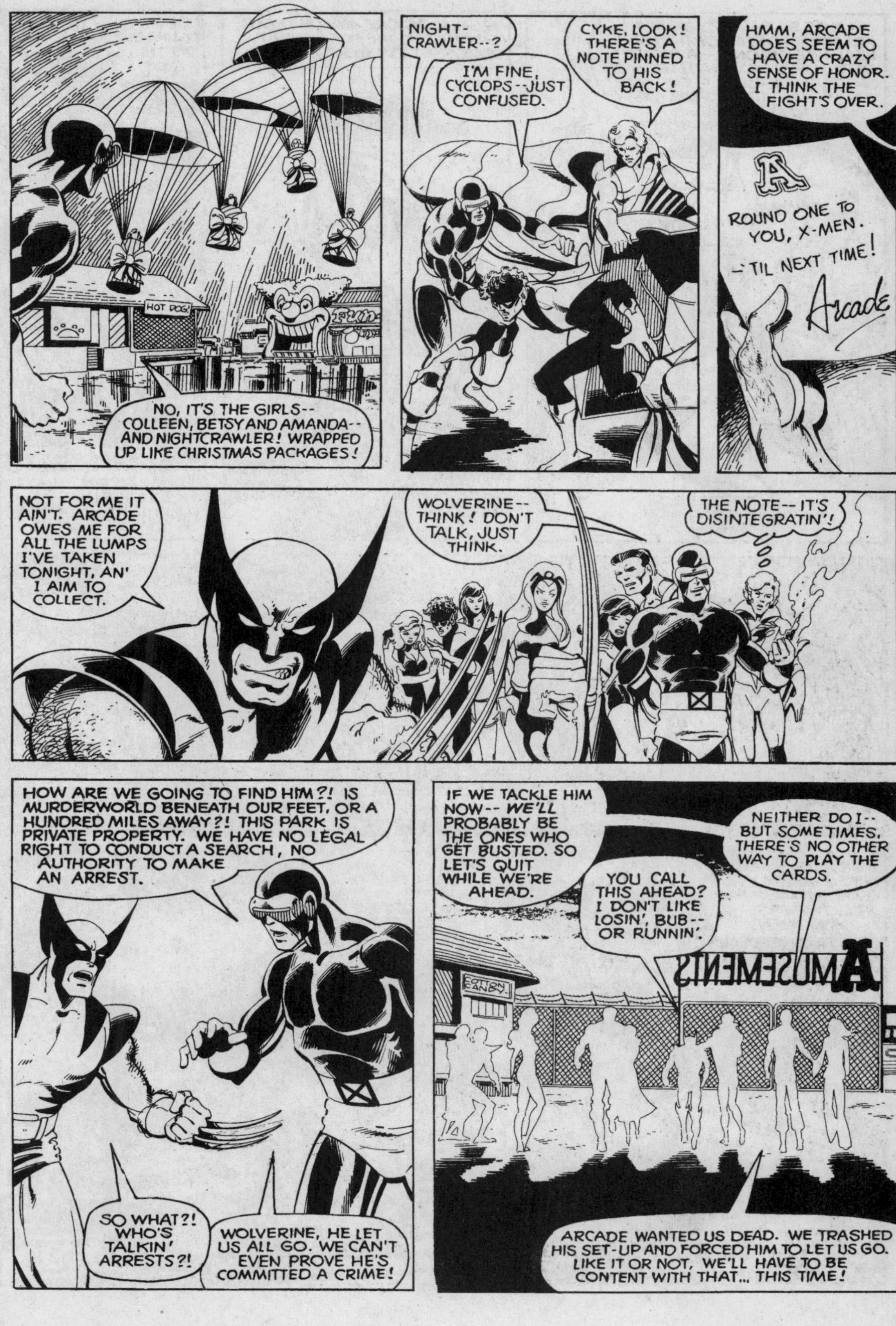
NO, IT'S THE GIRLS-- COLLEEN, BETSY AND AMANDA-- AND NIGHTCRAWLER! WRAPPED UP LIKE CHRISTMAS PACKAGES!
HOT DOG!
NIGHT-CRAWLER--?
I'M FINE, CYCLOPS--JUST CONFUSED.
CYKE, LOOK! THERE'S A NOTE PINNED TO HIS BACK!
HMM, ARCADE DOES SEEM TO HAVE A CRAZY SENSE OF HONOR. I THINK THE FIGHT'S OVER.
A
ROUND ONE TO YOU, X-MEN.
-'TIL NEXT TIME!
Arcade
NOT FOR ME IT AIN'T. ARCADE OWES ME FOR ALL THE LUMPS I'VE TAKEN TONIGHT, AN' I AIM TO COLLECT.
WOLVERINE-- THINK! DON'T TALK, JUST THINK.
THE NOTE--IT'S DISINTEGRATIN'!
HOW ARE WE GOING TO FIND HIM?! IS MURDERWORLD BENEATH OUR FEET, OR A HUNDRED MILES AWAY?! THIS PARK IS PRIVATE PROPERTY. WE HAVE NO LEGAL RIGHT TO CONDUCT A SEARCH, NO AUTHORITY TO MAKE AN ARREST.
SO WHAT?! WHO'S TALKIN' ARRESTS?!
WOLVERINE, HE LET US ALL GO. WE CAN'T EVEN PROVE HE'S COMMITTED A CRIME!
IF WE TACKLE HIM NOW-- WE'LL PROBABLY BE THE ONES WHO GET BUSTED. SO LET'S QUIT WHILE WE'RE AHEAD.
YOU CALL THIS AHEAD? I DON'T LIKE LOSIN', BUB-- OR RUNNIN'.
NEITHER DO I-- BUT SOMETIMES, THERE'S NO OTHER WAY TO PLAY THE CARDS.
COTTON CANDY
AMUSEMENTS
ARCADE WANTED US DEAD. WE TRASHED HIS SET-UP AND FORCED HIM TO LET US GO. LIKE IT OR NOT, WE'LL HAVE TO BE CONTENT WITH THAT... THIS TIME!

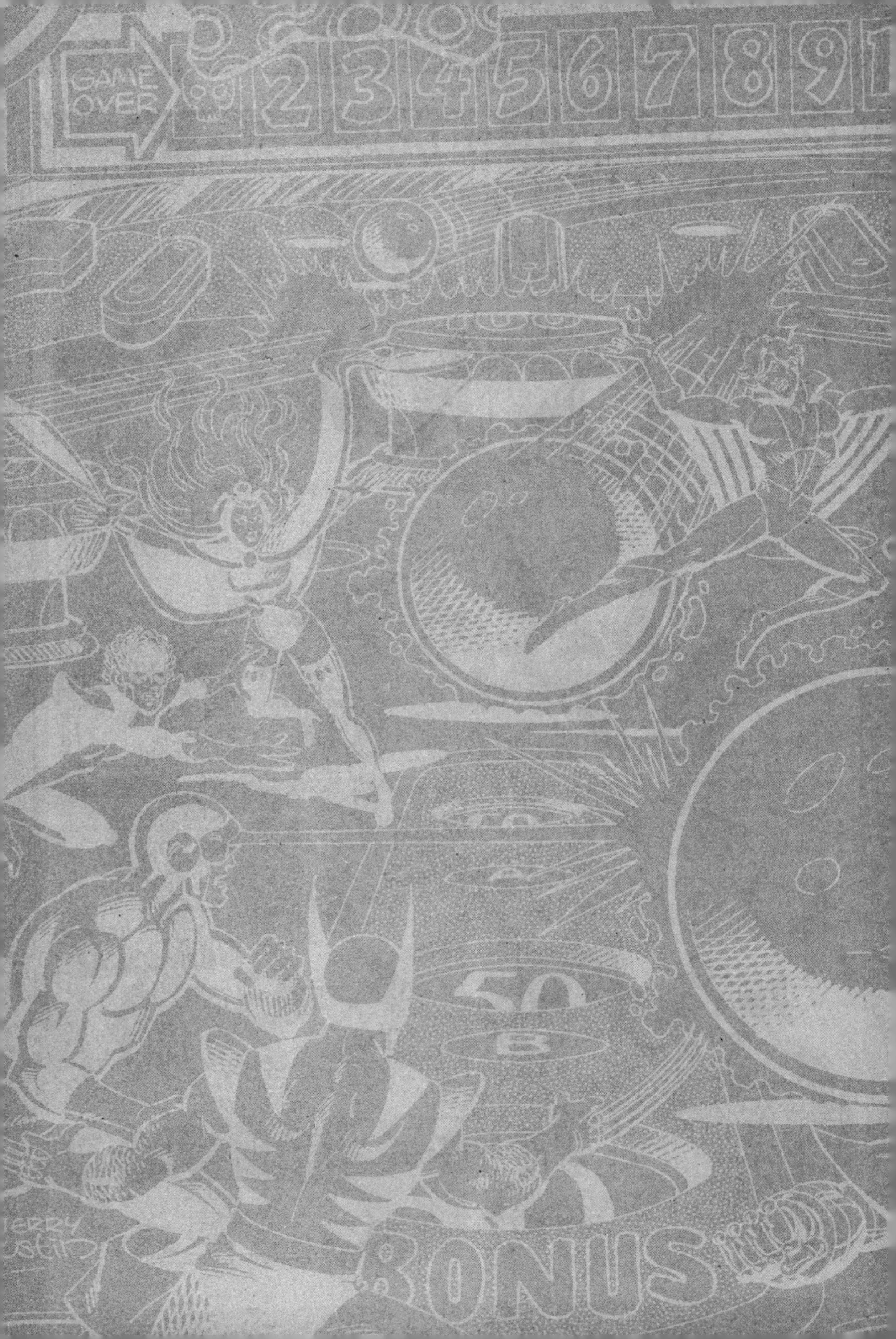
GAME OVER
2 3 4 5 6 7 8 9
50
B
BONUS

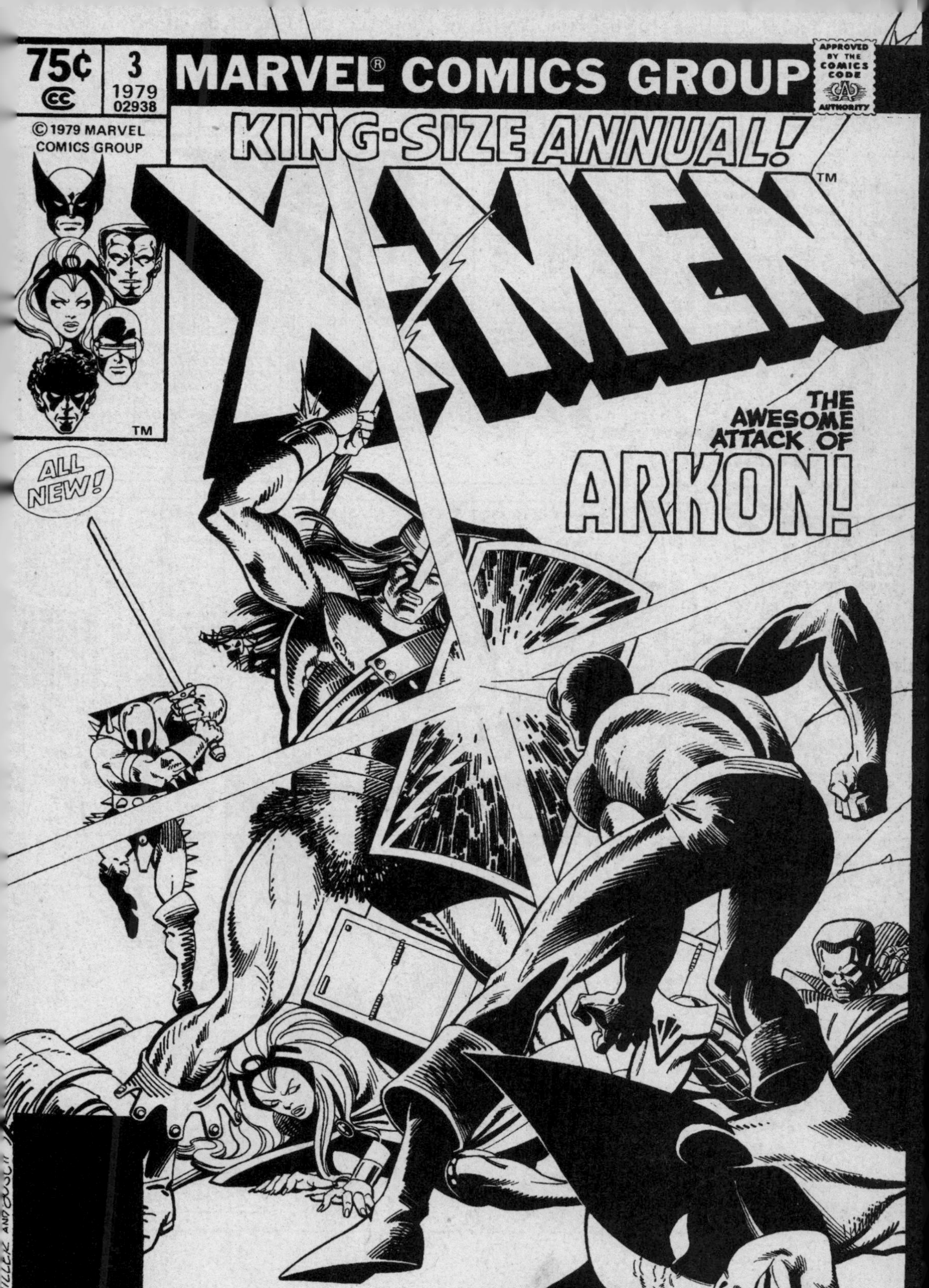
75¢
3
1979
02938
MARVEL® COMICS GROUP
APPROVED BY THE COMICS CODE AUTHORITY
© 1979 MARVEL COMICS GROUP
KING-SIZE ANNUAL!
X-MEN™
TM
ALL NEW!
THE AWESOME ATTACK OF
ARKON!

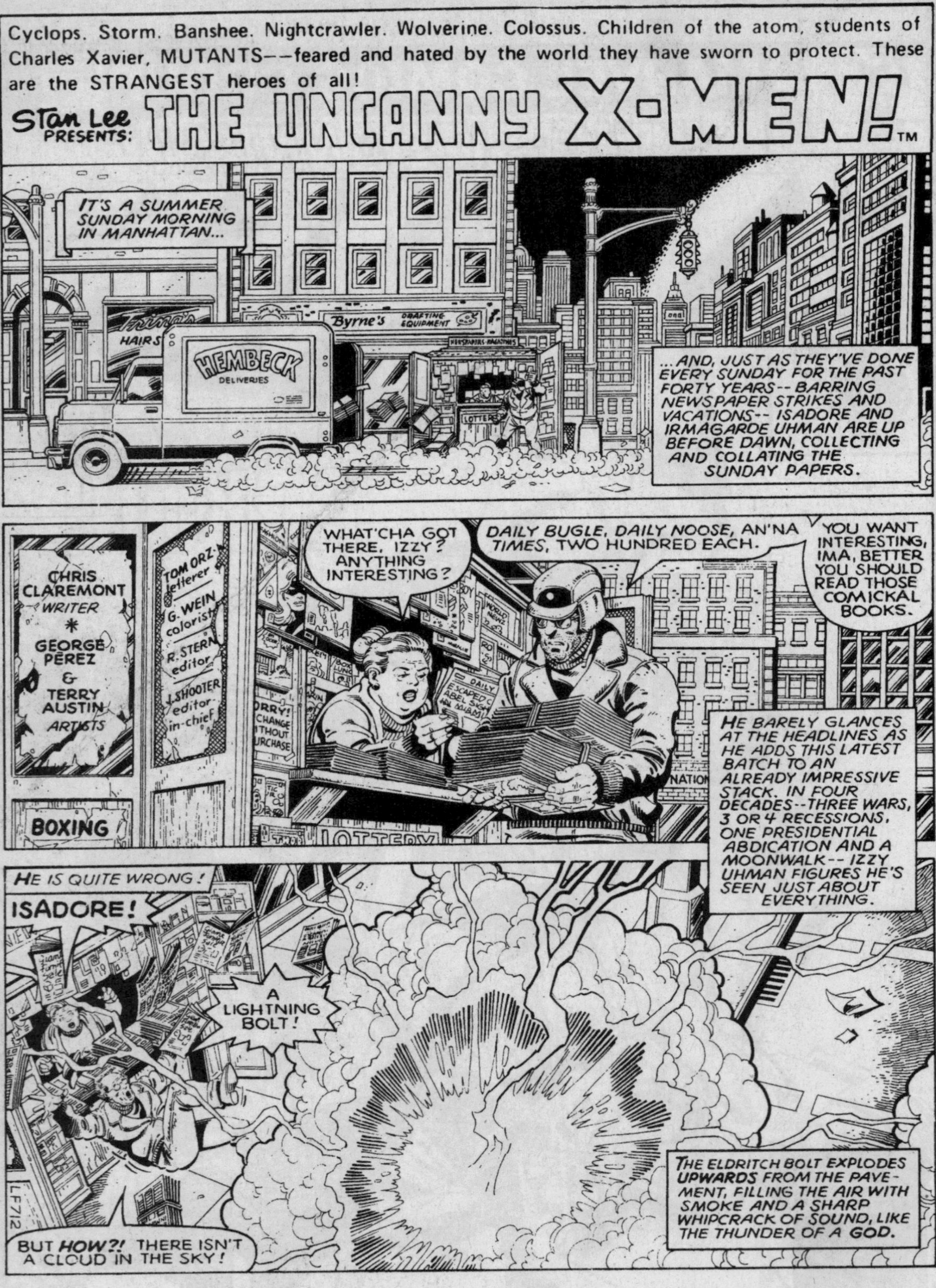
Cyclops. Storm. Banshee. Nightcrawler. Wolverine. Colossus. Children of the atom, students of Charles Xavier, MUTANTS--feared and hated by the world they have sworn to protect. These are the STRANGEST heroes of all!
Stan Lee PRESENTS: THE UNCANNY X-MEN!™
IT'S A SUMMER SUNDAY MORNING IN MANHATTAN...
Byrne's DRAFTING EQUIPMENT
HEMBECK DELIVERIES
...AND, JUST AS THEY'VE DONE EVERY SUNDAY FOR THE PAST FORTY YEARS-- BARRING NEWSPAPER STRIKES AND VACATIONS-- ISADORE AND IRMAGARDE UHMAN ARE UP BEFORE DAWN, COLLECTING AND COLLATING THE SUNDAY PAPERS.
CHRIS CLAREMONT WRITER
GEORGE PÉREZ & TERRY AUSTIN ARTISTS
TOM ORZ. letterer
G. WEIN colorist
R. STERN editor
J. SHOOTER editor-in-chief
WHAT'CHA GOT THERE, IZZY? ANYTHING INTERESTING?
DAILY BUGLE, DAILY NOOSE, AN'NA TIMES, TWO HUNDRED EACH.
YOU WANT INTERESTING, IMA, BETTER YOU SHOULD READ THOSE COMICKAL BOOKS.
BOXING
HE BARELY GLANCES AT THE HEADLINES AS HE ADDS THIS LATEST BATCH TO AN ALREADY IMPRESSIVE STACK. IN FOUR DECADES--THREE WARS, 3 OR 4 RECESSIONS, ONE PRESIDENTIAL ABDICATION AND A MOONWALK-- IZZY UHMAN FIGURES HE'S SEEN JUST ABOUT EVERYTHING.
HE IS QUITE WRONG!
ISADORE!
A LIGHTNING BOLT!
THE ELDRITCH BOLT EXPLODES UPWARDS FROM THE PAVEMENT, FILLING THE AIR WITH SMOKE AND A SHARP WHIPCRACK OF SOUND, LIKE THE THUNDER OF A GOD.
BUT HOW?! THERE ISN'T A CLOUD IN THE SKY!
LF712

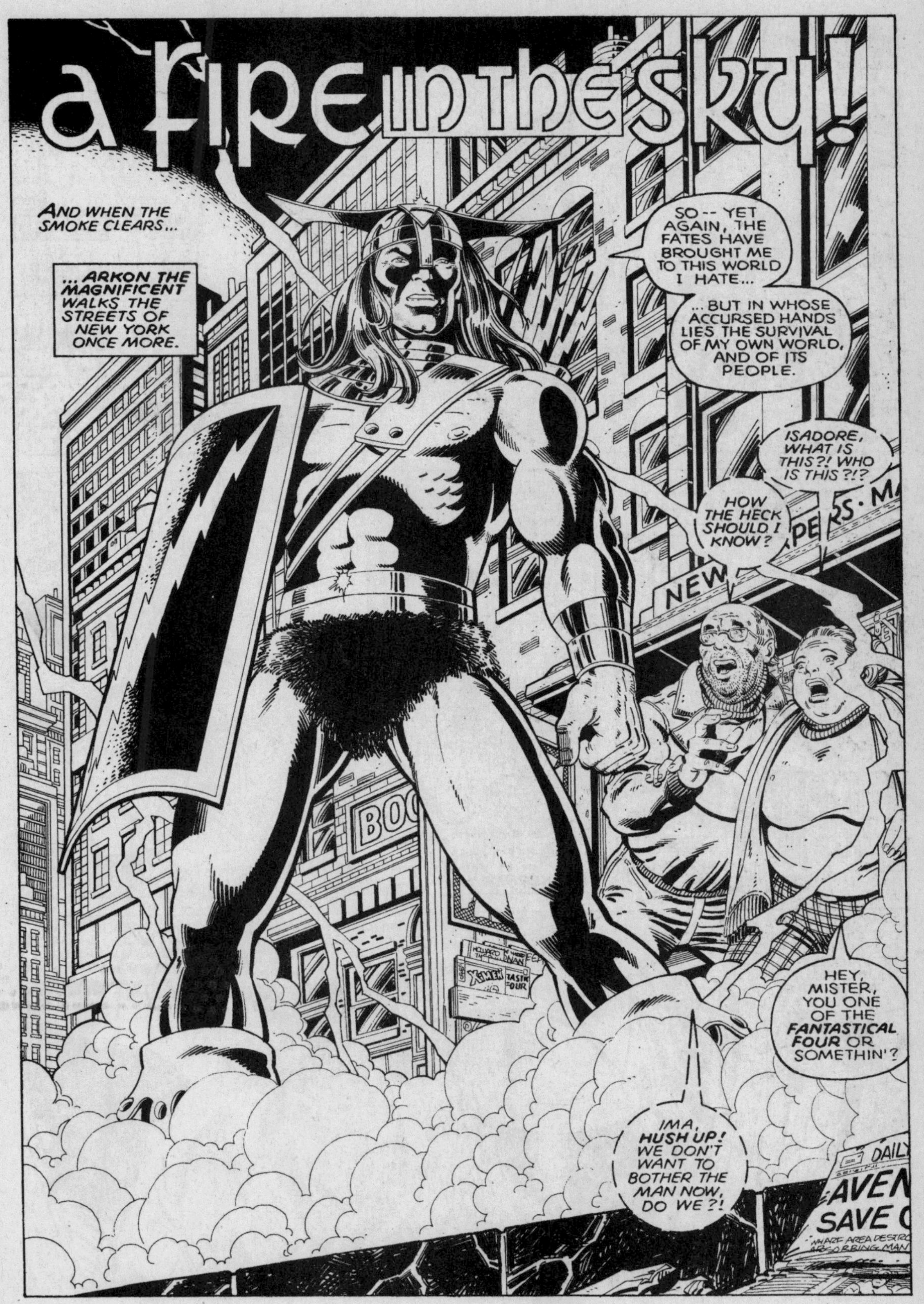

A FIRE IN THE SKY!
AND WHEN THE SMOKE CLEARS...
...ARKON THE MAGNIFICENT WALKS THE STREETS OF NEW YORK ONCE MORE.
SO -- YET AGAIN, THE FATES HAVE BROUGHT ME TO THIS WORLD I HATE...
...BUT IN WHOSE ACCURSED HANDS LIES THE SURVIVAL OF MY OWN WORLD, AND OF ITS PEOPLE.
ISADORE, WHAT IS THIS?! WHO IS THIS?!?
HOW THE HECK SHOULD I KNOW?
HEY, MISTER, YOU ONE OF THE FANTASTICAL FOUR OR SOMETHIN'?
IMA, HUSH UP! WE DON'T WANT TO BOTHER THE MAN NOW, DO WE?!

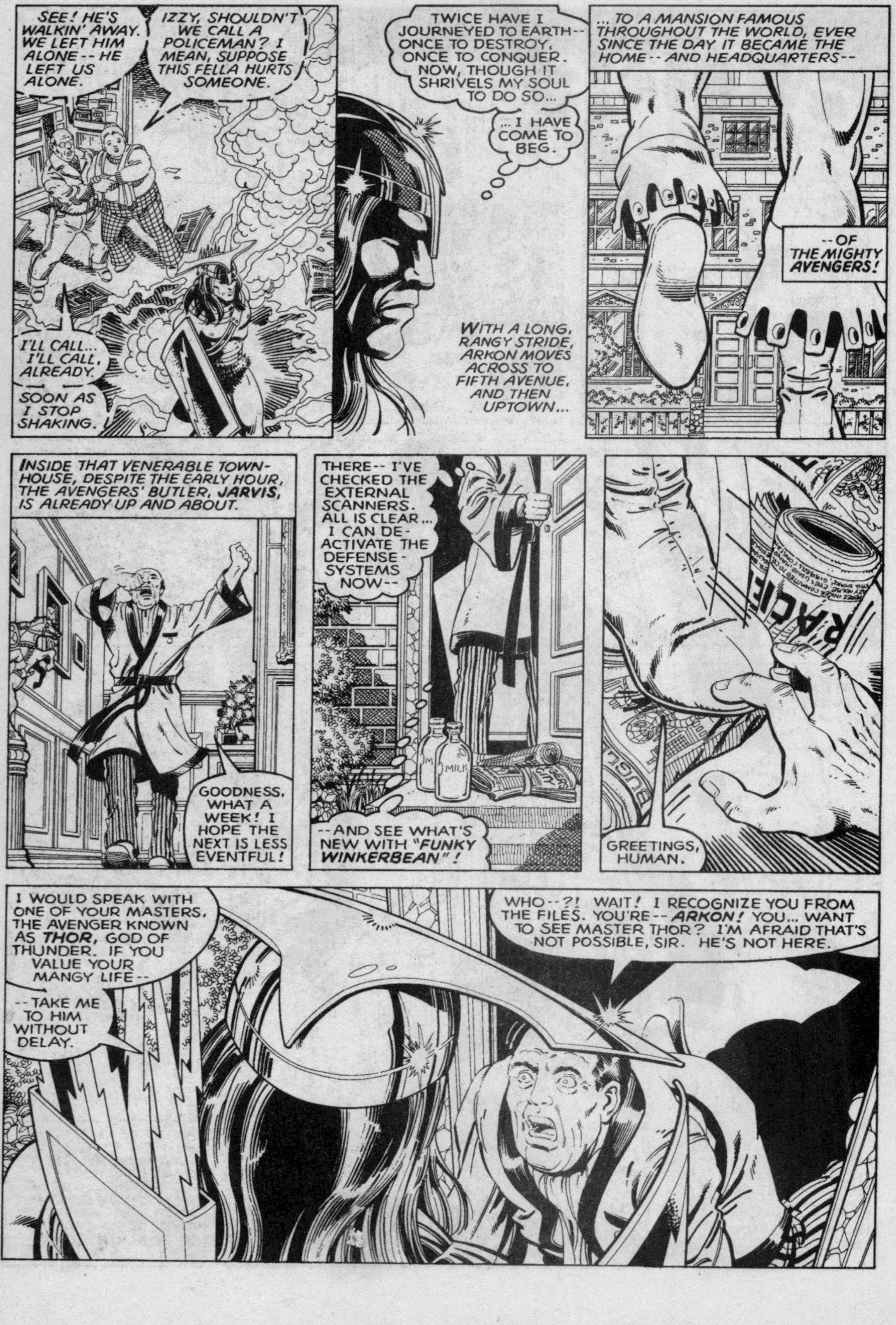
SEE! HE'S WALKIN' AWAY. WE LEFT HIM ALONE -- HE LEFT US ALONE.
IZZY, SHOULDN'T WE CALL A POLICEMAN? I MEAN, SUPPOSE THIS FELLA HURTS SOMEONE.
I'LL CALL... I'LL CALL, ALREADY.
SOON AS I STOP SHAKING.
TWICE HAVE I JOURNEYED TO EARTH -- ONCE TO DESTROY, ONCE TO CONQUER. NOW, THOUGH IT SHRIVELS MY SOUL TO DO SO...
... I HAVE COME TO BEG.
WITH A LONG, RANGY STRIDE, ARKON MOVES ACROSS TO FIFTH AVENUE, AND THEN UPTOWN...
... TO A MANSION FAMOUS THROUGHOUT THE WORLD, EVER SINCE THE DAY IT BECAME THE HOME -- AND HEADQUARTERS --
-- OF THE MIGHTY AVENGERS!
INSIDE THAT VENERABLE TOWN-HOUSE, DESPITE THE EARLY HOUR, THE AVENGERS' BUTLER, JARVIS, IS ALREADY UP AND ABOUT.
GOODNESS, WHAT A WEEK! I HOPE THE NEXT IS LESS EVENTFUL!
THERE -- I'VE CHECKED THE EXTERNAL SCANNERS. ALL IS CLEAR... I CAN DE-ACTIVATE THE DEFENSE-SYSTEMS NOW --
MILK
-- AND SEE WHAT'S NEW WITH "FUNKY WINKERBEAN"!
GREETINGS, HUMAN.
I WOULD SPEAK WITH ONE OF YOUR MASTERS, THE AVENGER KNOWN AS THOR, GOD OF THUNDER. IF YOU VALUE YOUR MANGY LIFE --
-- TAKE ME TO HIM WITHOUT DELAY.
WHO --?! WAIT! I RECOGNIZE YOU FROM THE FILES. YOU'RE -- ARKON! YOU... WANT TO SEE MASTER THOR? I'M AFRAID THAT'S NOT POSSIBLE, SIR. HE'S NOT HERE.

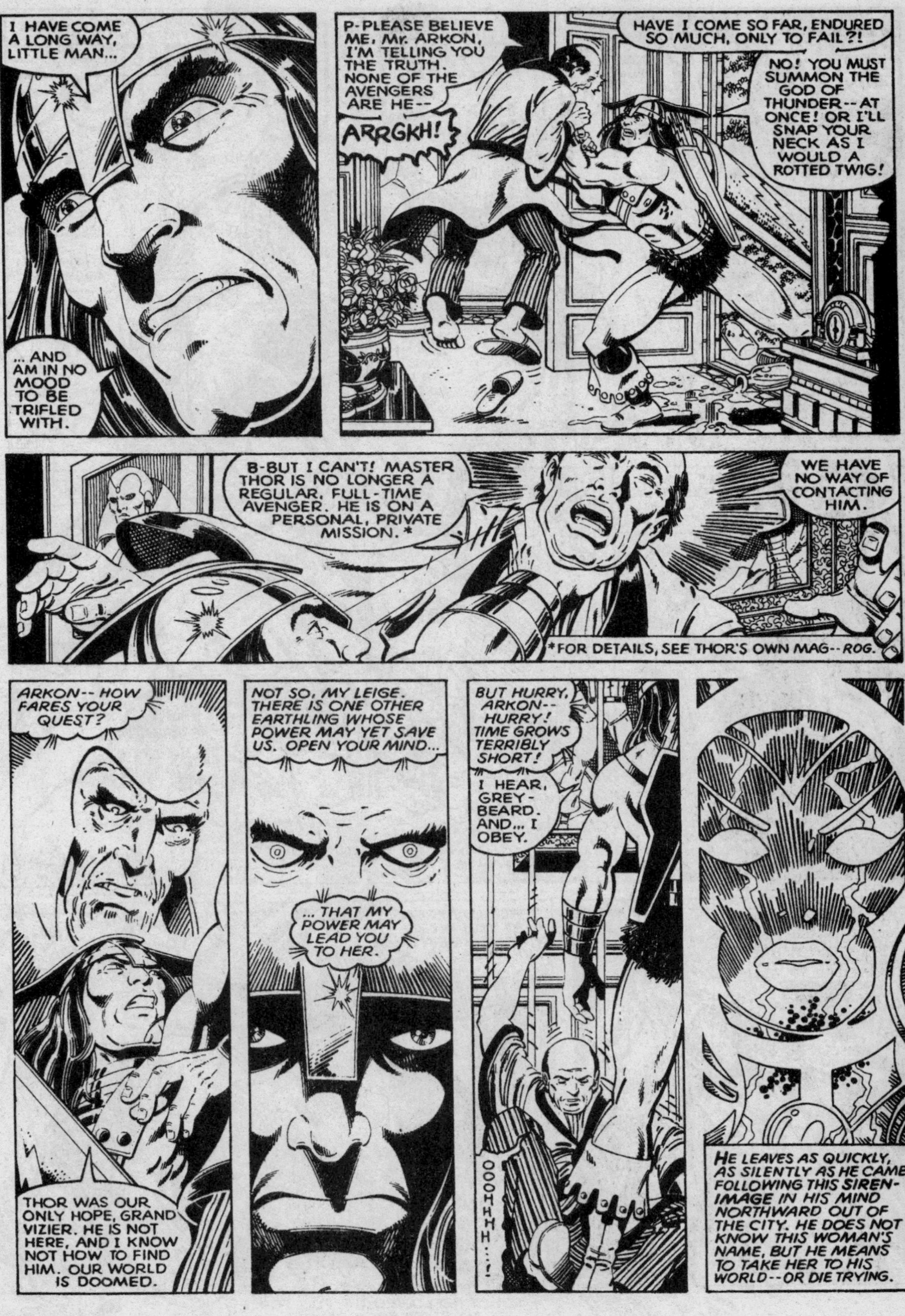
I HAVE COME A LONG WAY, LITTLE MAN...
... AND AM IN NO MOOD TO BE TRIFLED WITH.
P-PLEASE BELIEVE ME, Mr. ARKON, I'M TELLING YOU THE TRUTH. NONE OF THE AVENGERS ARE HE--
ARRGKH!
HAVE I COME SO FAR, ENDURED SO MUCH, ONLY TO FAIL?!
NO! YOU MUST SUMMON THE GOD OF THUNDER--AT ONCE! OR I'LL SNAP YOUR NECK AS I WOULD A ROTTED TWIG!
B-BUT I CAN'T! MASTER THOR IS NO LONGER A REGULAR, FULL-TIME AVENGER. HE IS ON A PERSONAL, PRIVATE MISSION.*
WE HAVE NO WAY OF CONTACTING HIM.
*FOR DETAILS, SEE THOR'S OWN MAG--ROG.
ARKON-- HOW FARES YOUR QUEST?
THOR WAS OUR ONLY HOPE, GRAND VIZIER. HE IS NOT HERE, AND I KNOW NOT HOW TO FIND HIM. OUR WORLD IS DOOMED.
NOT SO, MY LEIGE. THERE IS ONE OTHER EARTHLING WHOSE POWER MAY YET SAVE US. OPEN YOUR MIND...
... THAT MY POWER MAY LEAD YOU TO HER.
BUT HURRY, ARKON-- HURRY! TIME GROWS TERRIBLY SHORT!
I HEAR, GREY-BEARD. AND... I OBEY.
OOOHHHH...!
HE LEAVES AS QUICKLY, AS SILENTLY AS HE CAME FOLLOWING THIS SIREN-IMAGE IN HIS MIND NORTHWARD OUT OF THE CITY. HE DOES NOT KNOW THIS WOMAN'S NAME, BUT HE MEANS TO TAKE HER TO HIS WORLD--OR DIE TRYING.

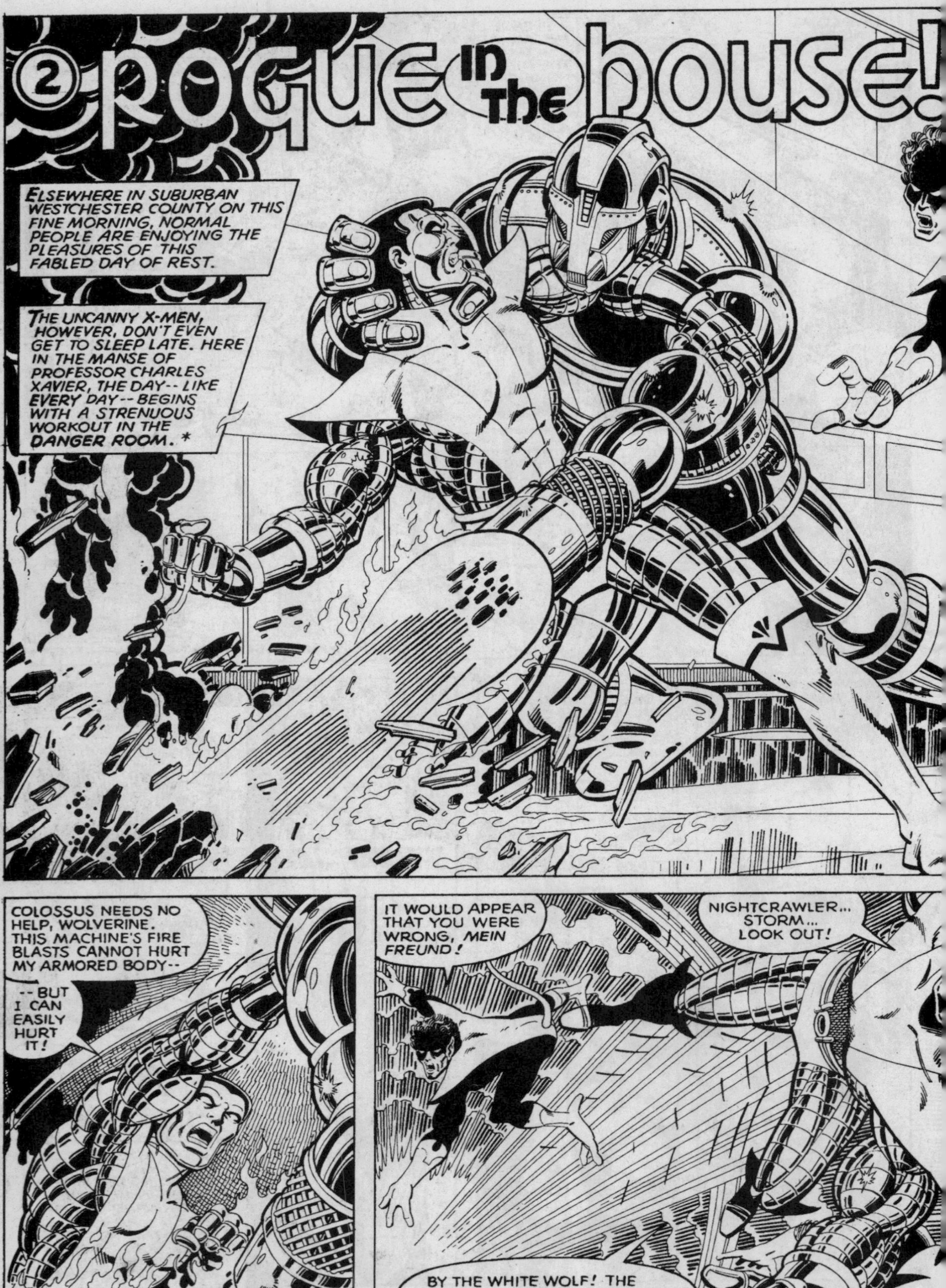

2 ROGUE in the HOUSE!
ELSEWHERE IN SUBURBAN WESTCHESTER COUNTY ON THIS FINE MORNING, NORMAL PEOPLE ARE ENJOYING THE PLEASURES OF THIS FABLED DAY OF REST.
THE UNCANNY X-MEN, HOWEVER, DON'T EVEN GET TO SLEEP LATE. HERE IN THE MANSE OF PROFESSOR CHARLES XAVIER, THE DAY-- LIKE EVERY DAY-- BEGINS WITH A STRENUOUS WORKOUT IN THE DANGER ROOM.*
COLOSSUS NEEDS NO HELP, WOLVERINE. THIS MACHINE'S FIRE BLASTS CANNOT HURT MY ARMORED BODY--
-- BUT I CAN EASILY HURT IT!
IT WOULD APPEAR THAT YOU WERE WRONG, MEIN FREUND!
NIGHTCRAWLER... STORM... LOOK OUT!
BY THE WHITE WOLF! THE ROBOT REFLECTED THE FULL FORCE OF MY BLOW BACK ON ME!

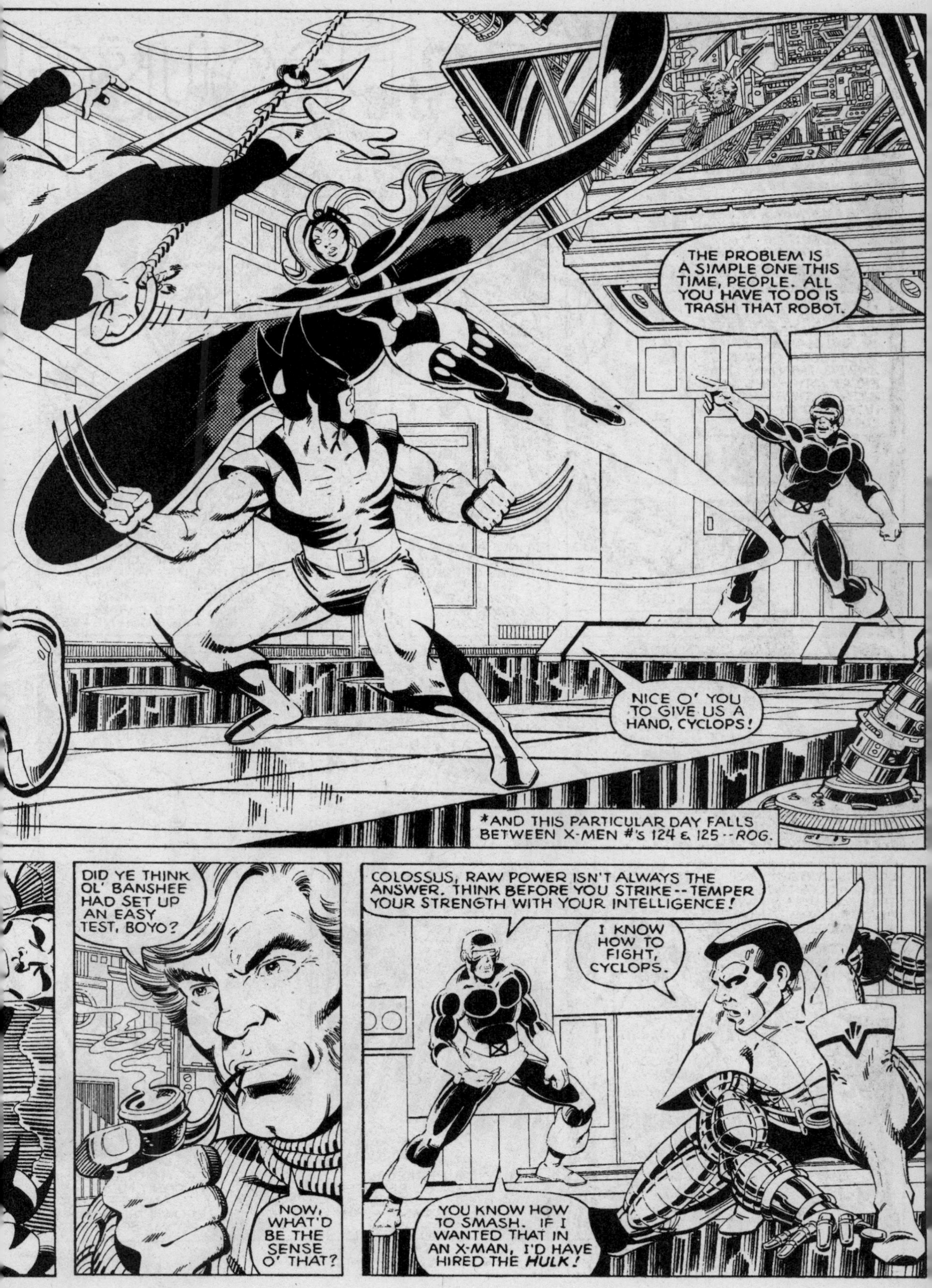
THE PROBLEM IS A SIMPLE ONE THIS TIME, PEOPLE. ALL YOU HAVE TO DO IS TRASH THAT ROBOT.
NICE O' YOU TO GIVE US A HAND, CYCLOPS!
*AND THIS PARTICULAR DAY FALLS BETWEEN X-MEN #'s 124 & 125 --ROG.
DID YE THINK OL' BANSHEE HAD SET UP AN EASY TEST, BOYO?
NOW, WHAT'D BE THE SENSE O' THAT?
COLOSSUS, RAW POWER ISN'T ALWAYS THE ANSWER. THINK BEFORE YOU STRIKE--TEMPER YOUR STRENGTH WITH YOUR INTELLIGENCE!
I KNOW HOW TO FIGHT, CYCLOPS.
YOU KNOW HOW TO SMASH. IF I WANTED THAT IN AN X-MAN, I'D HAVE HIRED THE HULK!

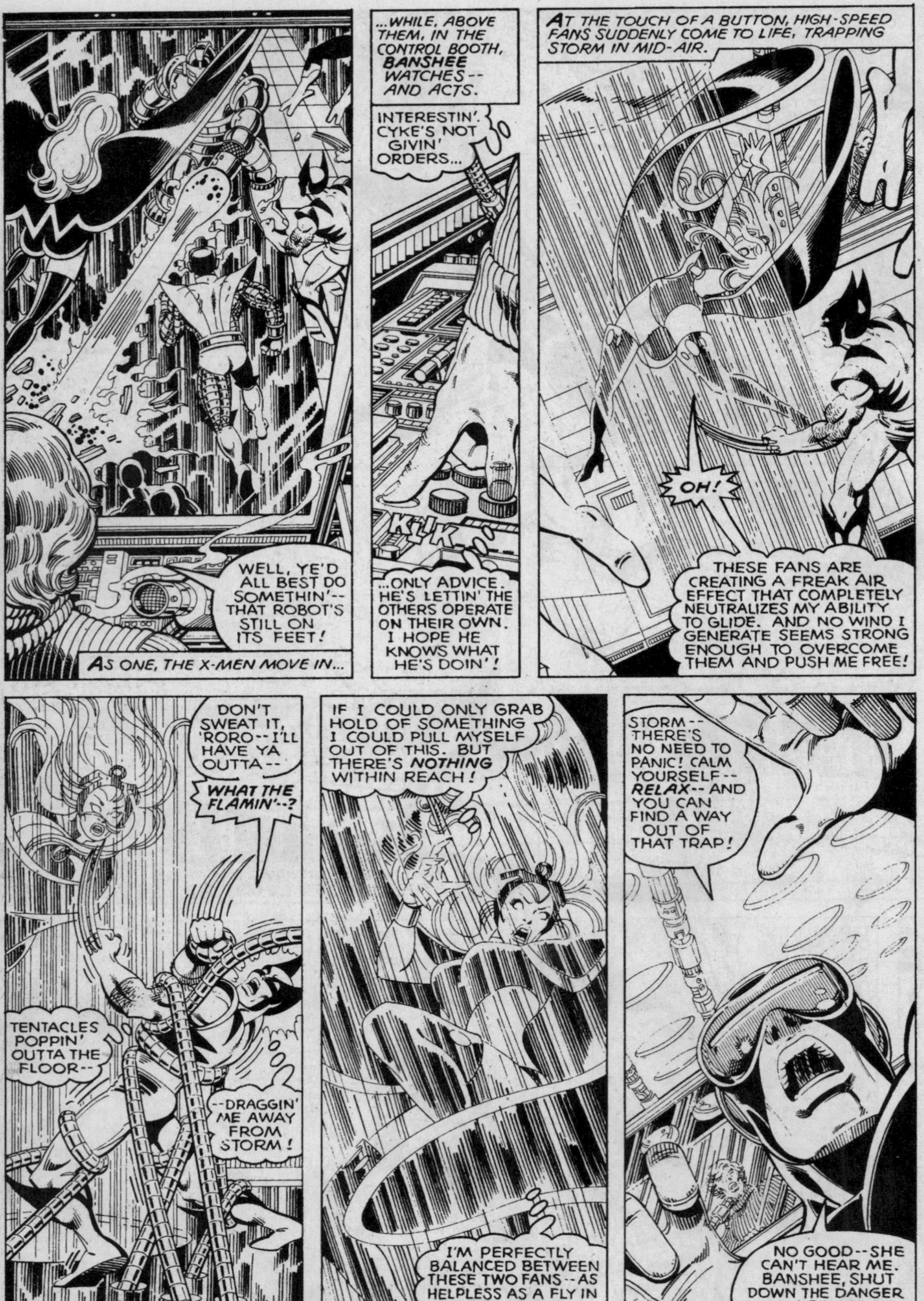
WELL, YE'D ALL BEST DO SOMETHIN'-- THAT ROBOT'S STILL ON ITS FEET!
AS ONE, THE X-MEN MOVE IN...
...WHILE, ABOVE THEM, IN THE CONTROL BOOTH, BANSHEE WATCHES-- AND ACTS.
INTERESTIN'. CYKE'S NOT GIVIN' ORDERS...
KLIK
...ONLY ADVICE. HE'S LETTIN' THE OTHERS OPERATE ON THEIR OWN. I HOPE HE KNOWS WHAT HE'S DOIN'!
AT THE TOUCH OF A BUTTON, HIGH-SPEED FANS SUDDENLY COME TO LIFE, TRAPPING STORM IN MID-AIR.
OH!
THESE FANS ARE CREATING A FREAK AIR EFFECT THAT COMPLETELY NEUTRALIZES MY ABILITY TO GLIDE. AND NO WIND I GENERATE SEEMS STRONG ENOUGH TO OVERCOME THEM AND PUSH ME FREE!
DON'T SWEAT IT, 'RORO-- I'LL HAVE YA OUTTA--
WHAT THE FLAMIN'--?
TENTACLES POPPIN' OUTTA THE FLOOR--
--DRAGGIN' ME AWAY FROM STORM!
IF I COULD ONLY GRAB HOLD OF SOMETHING I COULD PULL MYSELF OUT OF THIS. BUT THERE'S NOTHING WITHIN REACH!
I'M PERFECTLY BALANCED BETWEEN THESE TWO FANS-- AS HELPLESS AS A FLY IN A SPIDER-WEB!
STORM-- THERE'S NO NEED TO PANIC! CALM YOURSELF-- RELAX-- AND YOU CAN FIND A WAY OUT OF THAT TRAP!
NO GOOD-- SHE CAN'T HEAR ME. BANSHEE, SHUT DOWN THE DANGER ROOM! BEFORE IT'S--

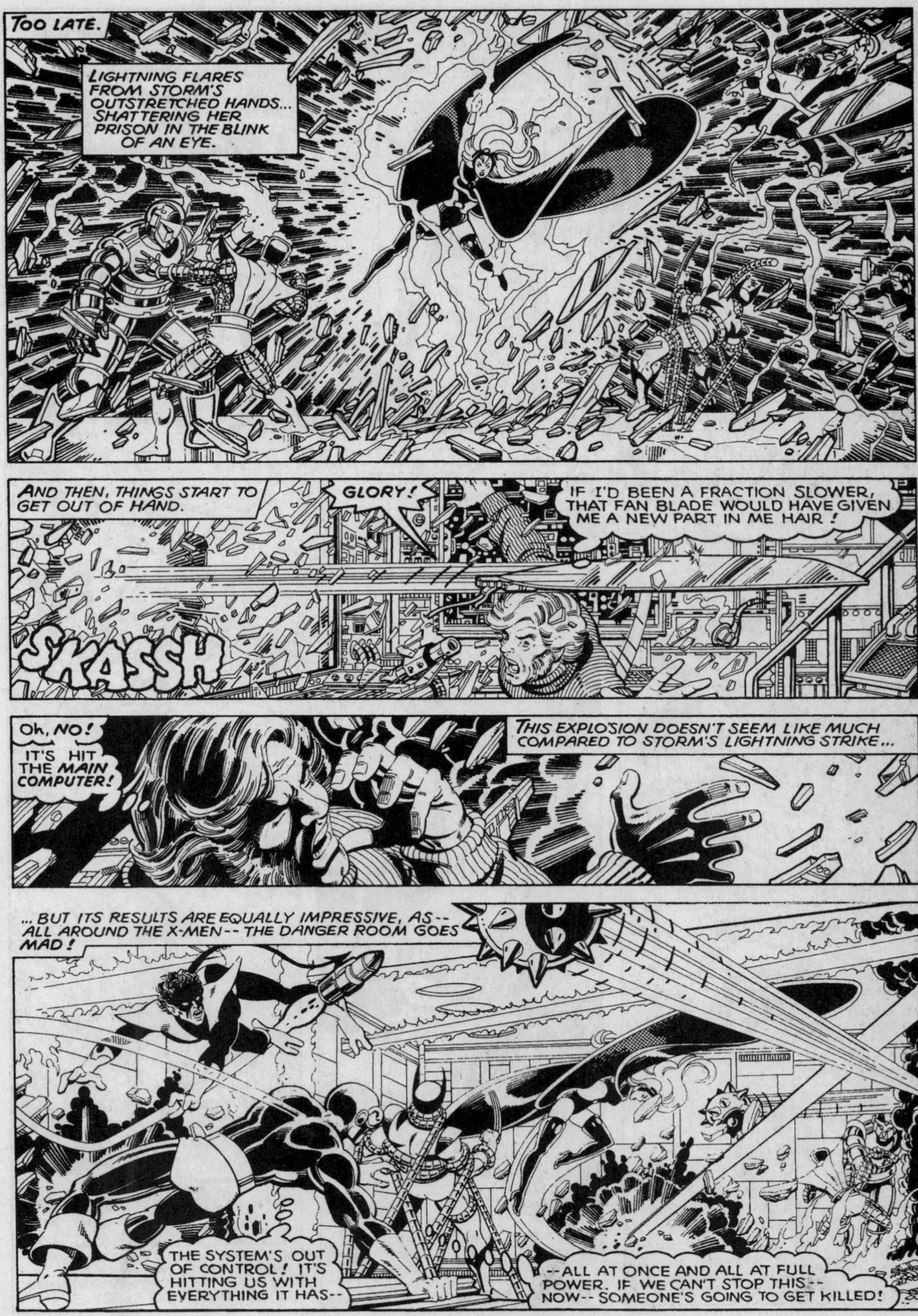
TOO LATE.
LIGHTNING FLARES FROM STORM'S OUTSTRETCHED HANDS... SHATTERING HER PRISON IN THE BLINK OF AN EYE.
AND THEN, THINGS START TO GET OUT OF HAND.
GLORY!
IF I'D BEEN A FRACTION SLOWER, THAT FAN BLADE WOULD HAVE GIVEN ME A NEW PART IN ME HAIR!
SKASSH
Oh, NO!
IT'S HIT THE MAIN COMPUTER!
THIS EXPLOSION DOESN'T SEEM LIKE MUCH COMPARED TO STORM'S LIGHTNING STRIKE...
...BUT ITS RESULTS ARE EQUALLY IMPRESSIVE, AS--ALL AROUND THE X-MEN--THE DANGER ROOM GOES MAD!
THE SYSTEM'S OUT OF CONTROL! IT'S HITTING US WITH EVERYTHING IT HAS--
--ALL AT ONCE AND ALL AT FULL POWER. IF WE CAN'T STOP THIS--NOW--SOMEONE'S GOING TO GET KILLED!

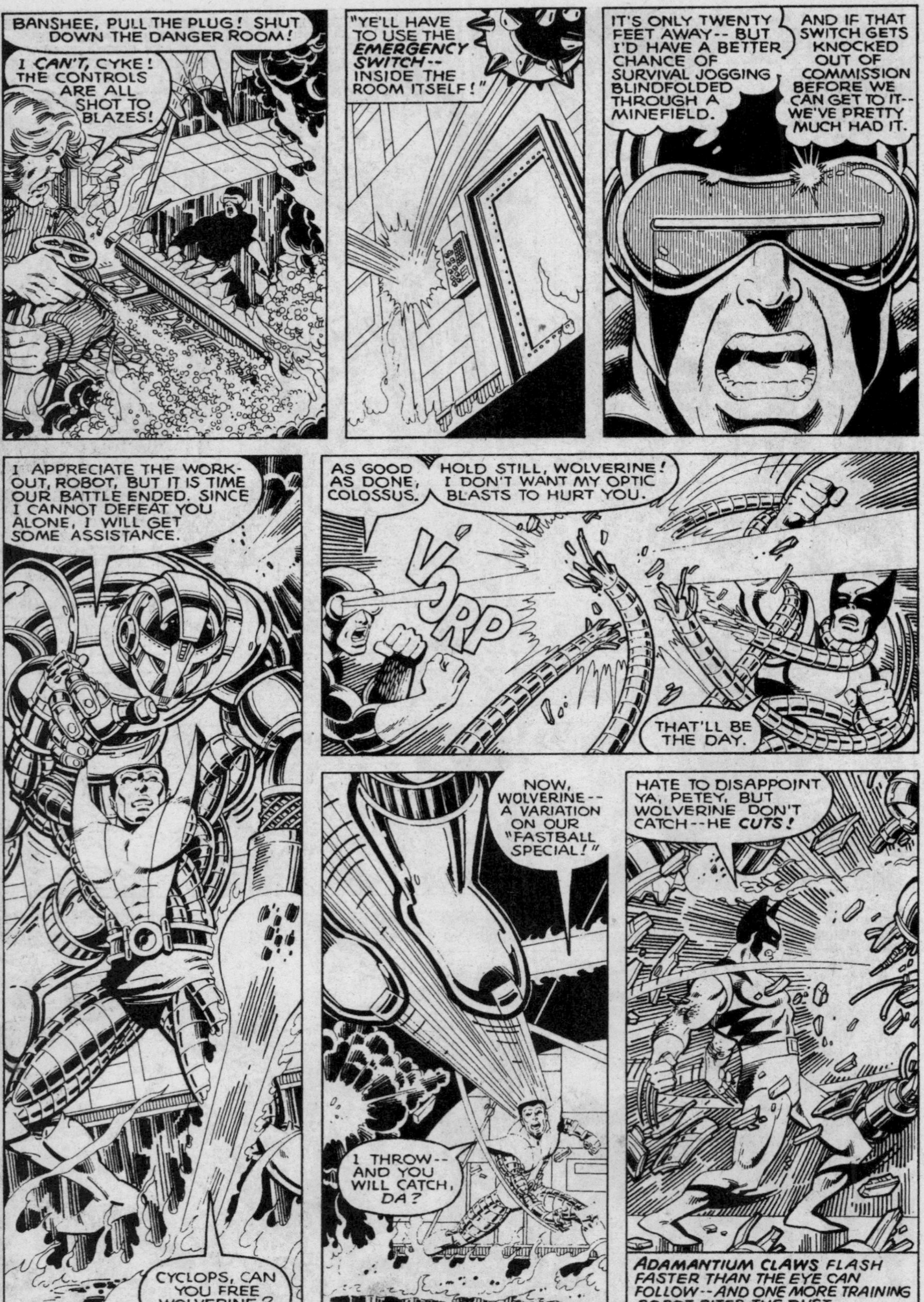

BANSHEE, PULL THE PLUG! SHUT DOWN THE DANGER ROOM!
I CAN'T, CYKE! THE CONTROLS ARE ALL SHOT TO BLAZES!
"YE'LL HAVE TO USE THE EMERGENCY SWITCH-- INSIDE THE ROOM ITSELF!"
IT'S ONLY TWENTY FEET AWAY-- BUT I'D HAVE A BETTER CHANCE OF SURVIVAL JOGGING BLINDFOLDED THROUGH A MINEFIELD.
AND IF THAT SWITCH GETS KNOCKED OUT OF COMMISSION BEFORE WE CAN GET TO IT-- WE'VE PRETTY MUCH HAD IT.
I APPRECIATE THE WORK-OUT, ROBOT, BUT IT IS TIME OUR BATTLE ENDED. SINCE I CANNOT DEFEAT YOU ALONE, I WILL GET SOME ASSISTANCE.
CYCLOPS, CAN YOU FREE WOLVERINE?
AS GOOD AS DONE, COLOSSUS.
HOLD STILL, WOLVERINE! I DON'T WANT MY OPTIC BLASTS TO HURT YOU.
VSORP
THAT'LL BE THE DAY.
NOW, WOLVERINE-- A VARIATION ON OUR "FASTBALL SPECIAL!"
I THROW-- AND YOU WILL CATCH, DA?
HATE TO DISAPPOINT YA, PETEY, BUT WOLVERINE DON'T CATCH--HE CUTS!
ADAMANTIUM CLAWS FLASH FASTER THAN THE EYE CAN FOLLOW--AND ONE MORE TRAINING ROBOT BITES THE DUST.

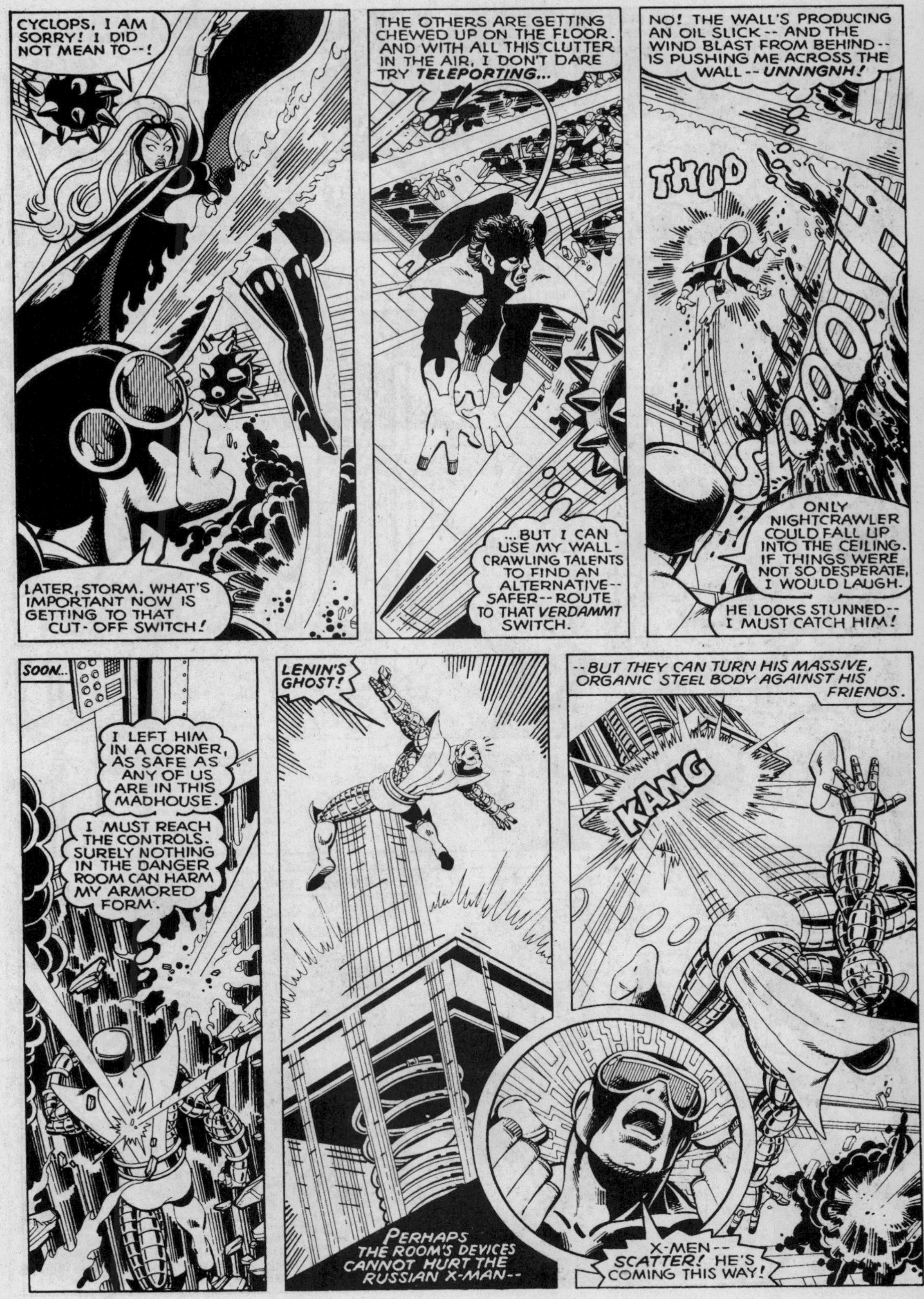
CYCLOPS, I AM SORRY! I DID NOT MEAN TO--!
LATER, STORM. WHAT'S IMPORTANT NOW IS GETTING TO THAT CUT-OFF SWITCH!
THE OTHERS ARE GETTING CHEWED UP ON THE FLOOR. AND WITH ALL THIS CLUTTER IN THE AIR, I DON'T DARE TRY TELEPORTING...
...BUT I CAN USE MY WALL-CRAWLING TALENTS TO FIND AN ALTERNATIVE--SAFER--ROUTE TO THAT VERDAMMT SWITCH.
NO! THE WALL'S PRODUCING AN OIL SLICK--AND THE WIND BLAST FROM BEHIND--IS PUSHING ME ACROSS THE WALL--UNNNGNH!
THUD
SLOOOSH!
ONLY NIGHTCRAWLER COULD FALL UP INTO THE CEILING. IF THINGS WERE NOT SO DESPERATE, I WOULD LAUGH.
HE LOOKS STUNNED--I MUST CATCH HIM!
SOON..
I LEFT HIM IN A CORNER, AS SAFE AS ANY OF US ARE IN THIS MADHOUSE.
I MUST REACH THE CONTROLS. SURELY NOTHING IN THE DANGER ROOM CAN HARM MY ARMORED FORM.
LENIN'S GHOST!
PERHAPS THE ROOM'S DEVICES CANNOT HURT THE RUSSIAN X-MAN--
--BUT THEY CAN TURN HIS MASSIVE, ORGANIC STEEL BODY AGAINST HIS FRIENDS.
KANG
X-MEN--SCATTER! HE'S COMING THIS WAY!

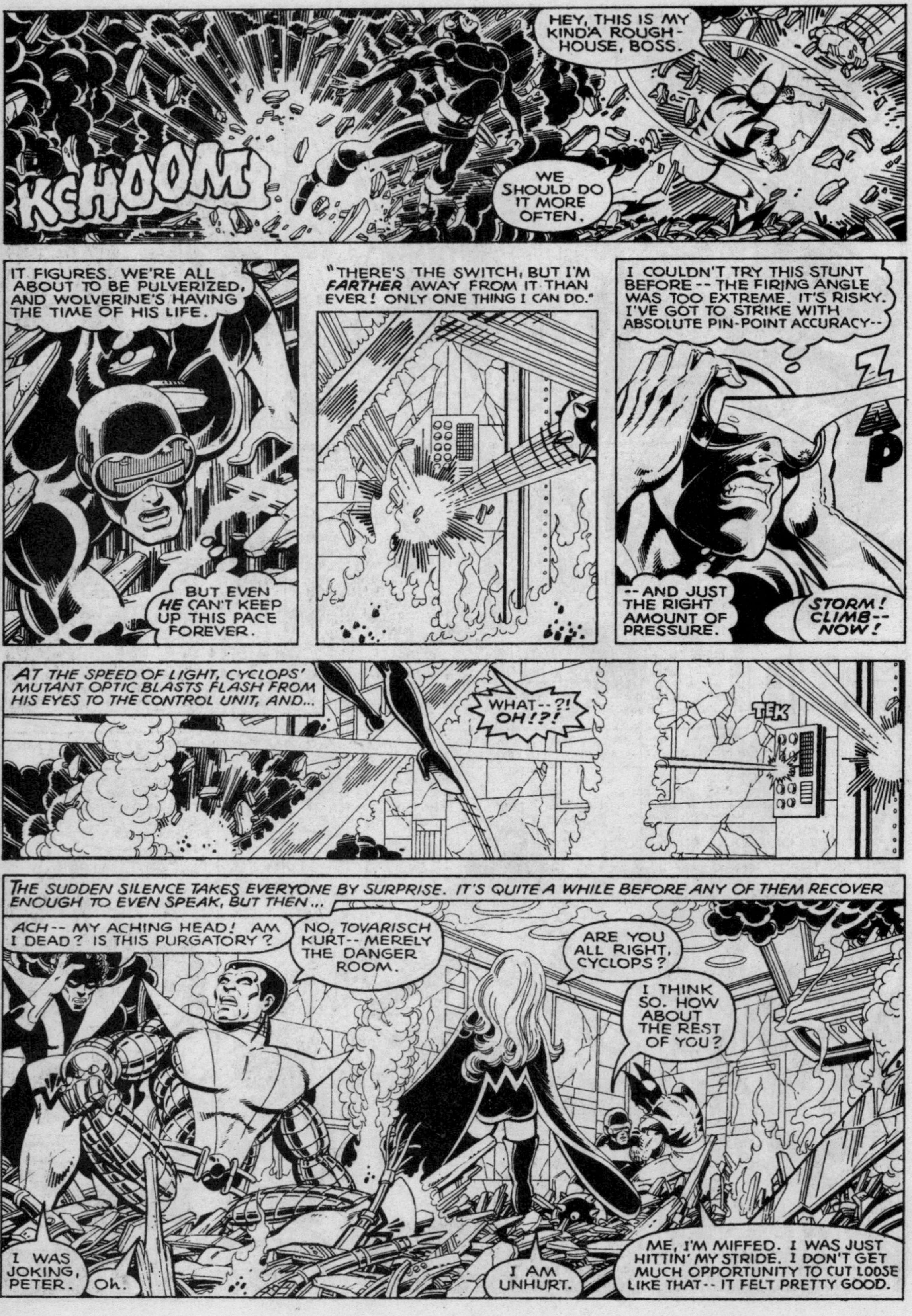
KCHOOM
HEY, THIS IS MY KIND'A ROUGH-HOUSE, BOSS.
WE SHOULD DO IT MORE OFTEN.
IT FIGURES. WE'RE ALL ABOUT TO BE PULVERIZED, AND WOLVERINE'S HAVING THE TIME OF HIS LIFE.
BUT EVEN HE CAN'T KEEP UP THIS PACE FOREVER.
"THERE'S THE SWITCH, BUT I'M FARTHER AWAY FROM IT THAN EVER! ONLY ONE THING I CAN DO."
I COULDN'T TRY THIS STUNT BEFORE -- THE FIRING ANGLE WAS TOO EXTREME. IT'S RISKY. I'VE GOT TO STRIKE WITH ABSOLUTE PIN-POINT ACCURACY--
ZAP
--AND JUST THE RIGHT AMOUNT OF PRESSURE.
STORM! CLIMB-- NOW!
AT THE SPEED OF LIGHT, CYCLOPS' MUTANT OPTIC BLASTS FLASH FROM HIS EYES TO THE CONTROL UNIT, AND...
WHAT--?! OH!?!
TEK
THE SUDDEN SILENCE TAKES EVERYONE BY SURPRISE. IT'S QUITE A WHILE BEFORE ANY OF THEM RECOVER ENOUGH TO EVEN SPEAK, BUT THEN...
ACH-- MY ACHING HEAD! AM I DEAD? IS THIS PURGATORY?
NO, TOVARISCH KURT-- MERELY THE DANGER ROOM.
ARE YOU ALL RIGHT, CYCLOPS?
I THINK SO. HOW ABOUT THE REST OF YOU?
I WAS JOKING, PETER.
Oh.
I AM UNHURT.
ME, I'M MIFFED. I WAS JUST HITTIN' MY STRIDE. I DON'T GET MUCH OPPORTUNITY TO CUT LOOSE LIKE THAT-- IT FELT PRETTY GOOD.

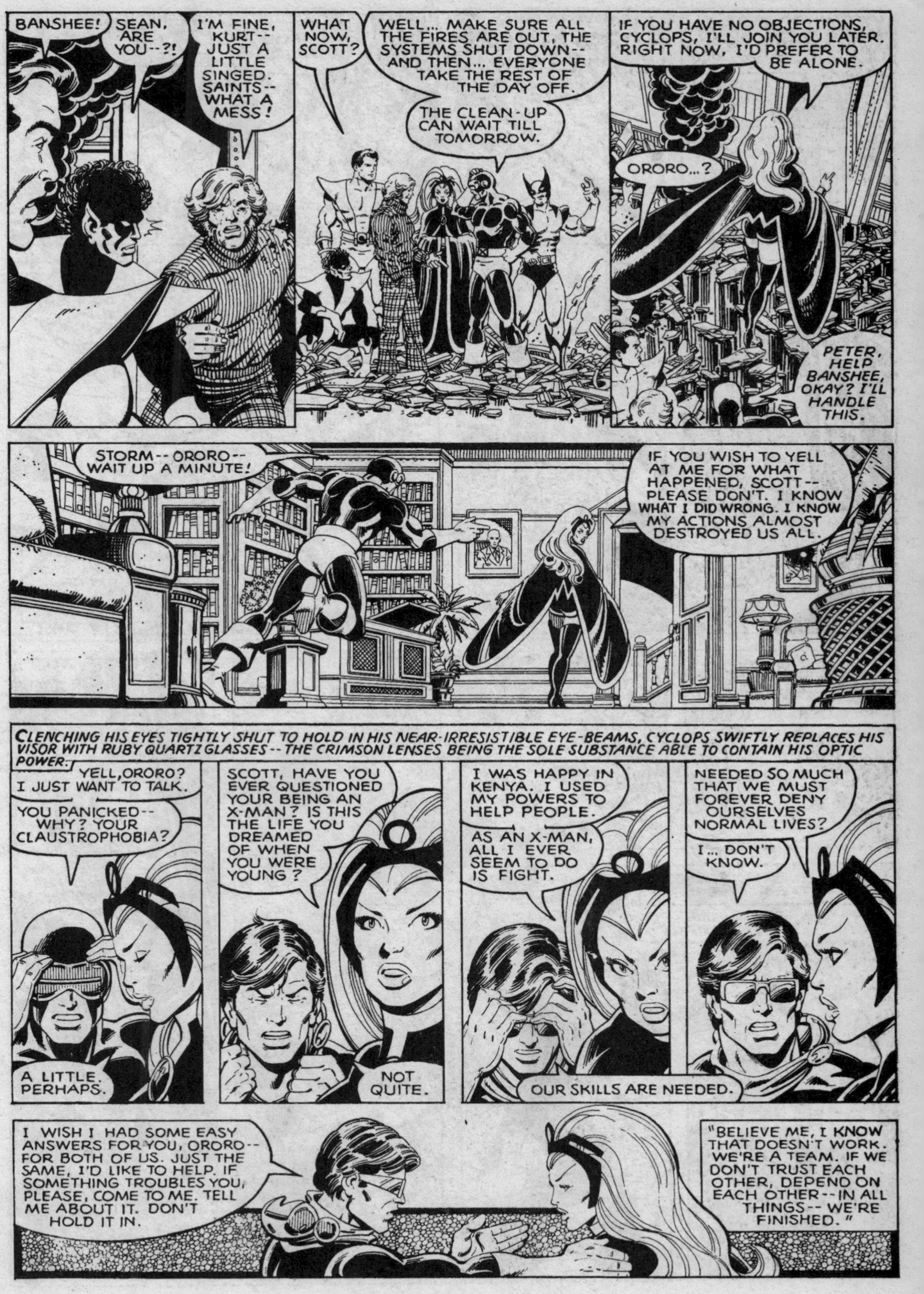
BANSHEE!
SEAN, ARE YOU--?!
I'M FINE, KURT-- JUST A LITTLE SINGED. SAINTS-- WHAT A MESS!
WHAT NOW, SCOTT?
WELL... MAKE SURE ALL THE FIRES ARE OUT, THE SYSTEMS SHUT DOWN-- AND THEN... EVERYONE TAKE THE REST OF THE DAY OFF.
THE CLEAN-UP CAN WAIT TILL TOMORROW.
IF YOU HAVE NO OBJECTIONS, CYCLOPS, I'LL JOIN YOU LATER. RIGHT NOW, I'D PREFER TO BE ALONE.
ORORO...?
PETER, HELP BANSHEE, OKAY? I'LL HANDLE THIS.
STORM-- ORORO-- WAIT UP A MINUTE!
IF YOU WISH TO YELL AT ME FOR WHAT HAPPENED, SCOTT-- PLEASE DON'T. I KNOW WHAT I DID WRONG. I KNOW MY ACTIONS ALMOST DESTROYED US ALL.
CLENCHING HIS EYES TIGHTLY SHUT TO HOLD IN HIS NEAR-IRRESISTIBLE EYE-BEAMS, CYCLOPS SWIFTLY REPLACES HIS VISOR WITH RUBY QUARTZ GLASSES -- THE CRIMSON LENSES BEING THE SOLE SUBSTANCE ABLE TO CONTAIN HIS OPTIC POWER.
YELL, ORORO? I JUST WANT TO TALK.
YOU PANICKED-- WHY? YOUR CLAUSTROPHOBIA?
A LITTLE. PERHAPS.
SCOTT, HAVE YOU EVER QUESTIONED YOUR BEING AN X-MAN? IS THIS THE LIFE YOU DREAMED OF WHEN YOU WERE YOUNG?
NOT QUITE.
I WAS HAPPY IN KENYA. I USED MY POWERS TO HELP PEOPLE.
AS AN X-MAN, ALL I EVER SEEM TO DO IS FIGHT.
OUR SKILLS ARE NEEDED.
NEEDED SO MUCH THAT WE MUST FOREVER DENY OURSELVES NORMAL LIVES?
I... DON'T KNOW.
I WISH I HAD SOME EASY ANSWERS FOR YOU, ORORO-- FOR BOTH OF US. JUST THE SAME, I'D LIKE TO HELP. IF SOMETHING TROUBLES YOU, PLEASE, COME TO ME. TELL ME ABOUT IT. DON'T HOLD IT IN.
"BELIEVE ME, I KNOW THAT DOESN'T WORK. WE'RE A TEAM. IF WE DON'T TRUST EACH OTHER, DEPEND ON EACH OTHER-- IN ALL THINGS-- WE'RE FINISHED."

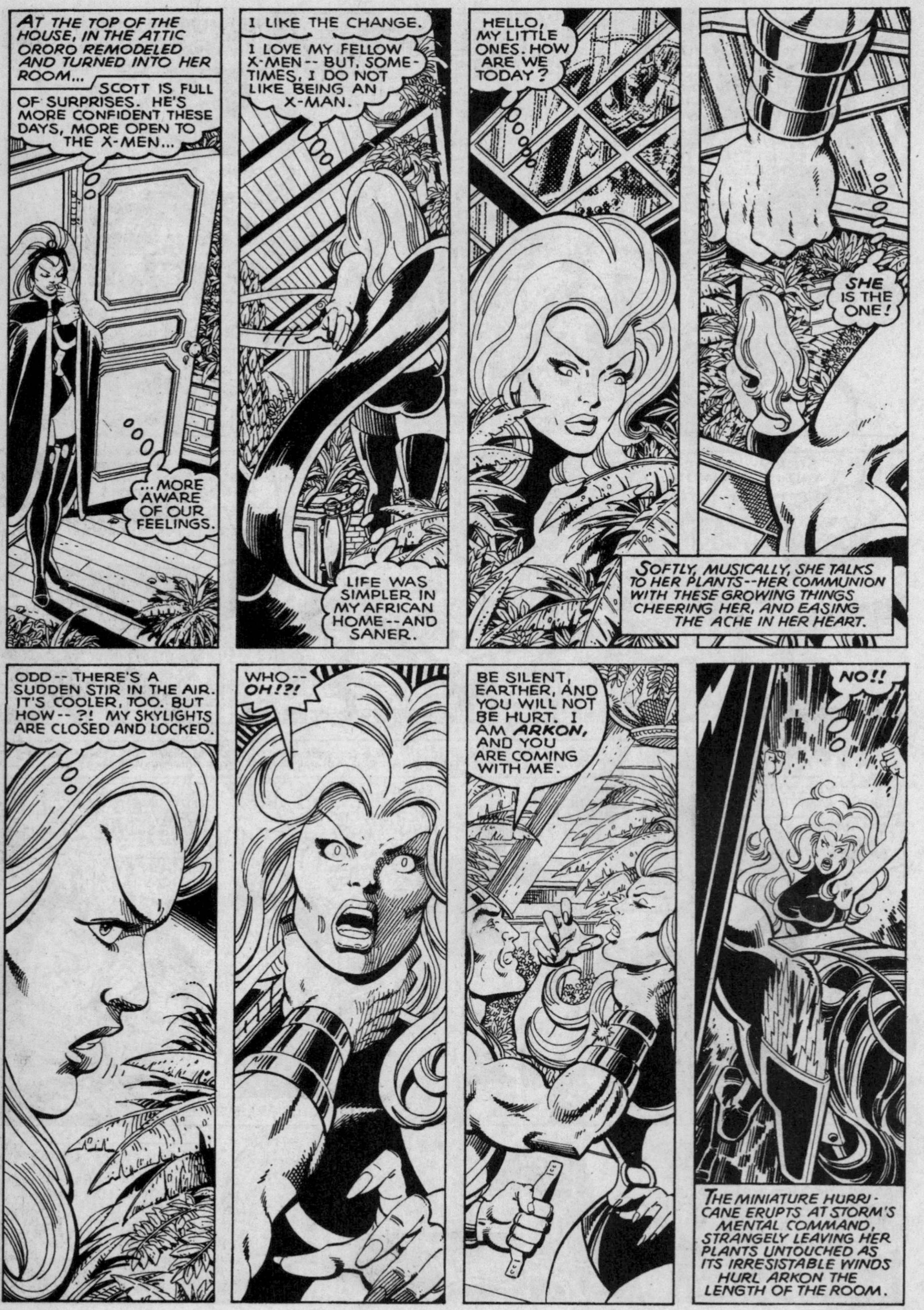

AT THE TOP OF THE HOUSE, IN THE ATTIC ORORO REMODELED AND TURNED INTO HER ROOM...
SCOTT IS FULL OF SURPRISES. HE'S MORE CONFIDENT THESE DAYS, MORE OPEN TO THE X-MEN...
...MORE AWARE OF OUR FEELINGS.
I LIKE THE CHANGE.
I LOVE MY FELLOW X-MEN -- BUT, SOMETIMES, I DO NOT LIKE BEING AN X-MAN.
LIFE WAS SIMPLER IN MY AFRICAN HOME -- AND SANER.
HELLO, MY LITTLE ONES. HOW ARE WE TODAY?
SOFTLY, MUSICALLY, SHE TALKS TO HER PLANTS -- HER COMMUNION WITH THESE GROWING THINGS CHEERING HER, AND EASING THE ACHE IN HER HEART.
SHE IS THE ONE!
ODD -- THERE'S A SUDDEN STIR IN THE AIR. IT'S COOLER, TOO. BUT HOW -- ?! MY SKYLIGHTS ARE CLOSED AND LOCKED.
WHO -- OH!?!
BE SILENT, EARTHER, AND YOU WILL NOT BE HURT. I AM ARKON, AND YOU ARE COMING WITH ME.
NO!!
THE MINIATURE HURRICANE ERUPTS AT STORM'S MENTAL COMMAND, STRANGELY LEAVING HER PLANTS UNTOUCHED AS ITS IRRESISTABLE WINDS HURL ARKON THE LENGTH OF THE ROOM.

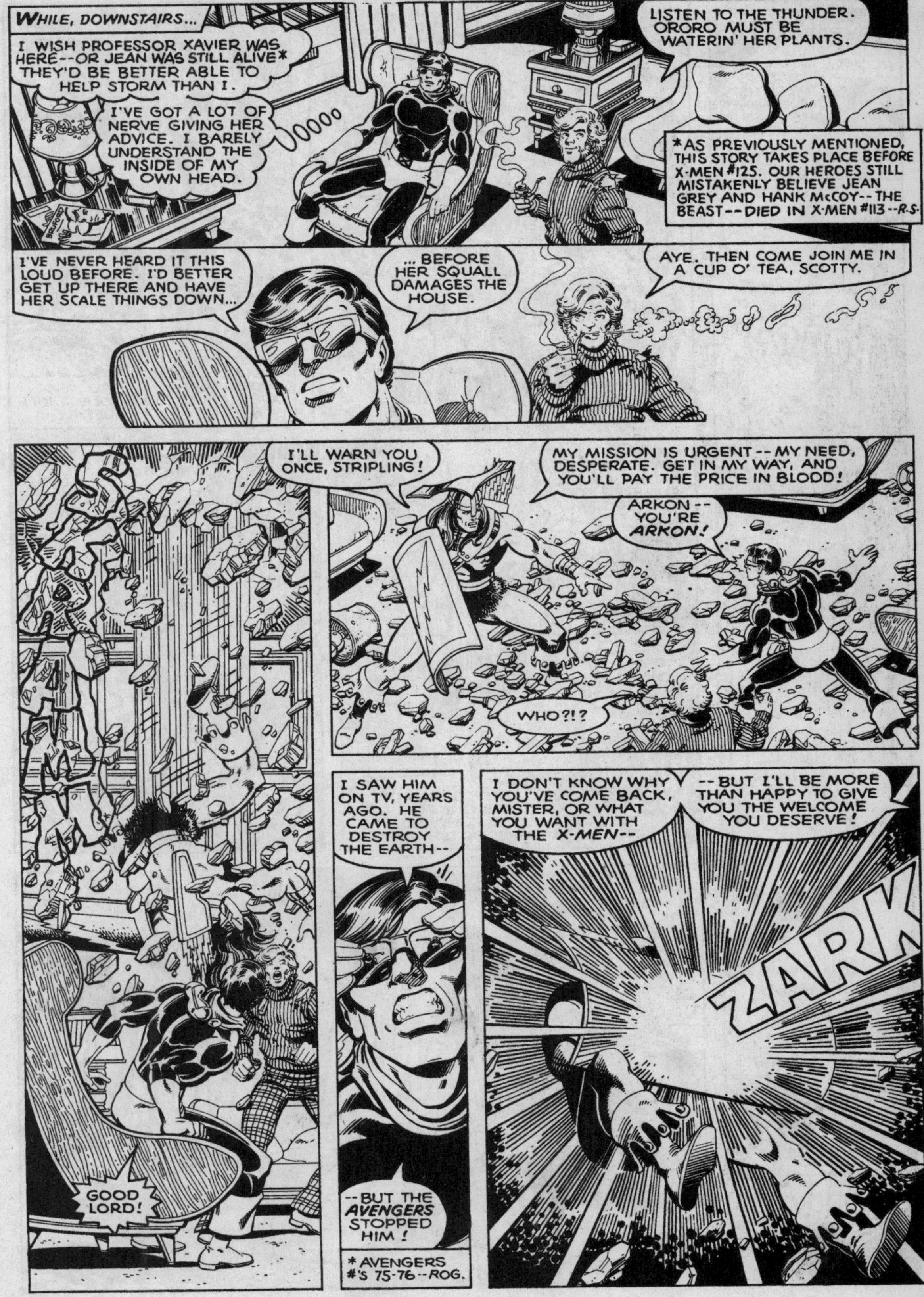
WHILE, DOWNSTAIRS...
I WISH PROFESSOR XAVIER WAS HERE--OR JEAN WAS STILL ALIVE* THEY'D BE BETTER ABLE TO HELP STORM THAN I.
I'VE GOT A LOT OF NERVE GIVING HER ADVICE. I BARELY UNDERSTAND THE INSIDE OF MY OWN HEAD.
LISTEN TO THE THUNDER. ORORO MUST BE WATERIN' HER PLANTS.
*AS PREVIOUSLY MENTIONED, THIS STORY TAKES PLACE BEFORE X-MEN #125. OUR HEROES STILL MISTAKENLY BELIEVE JEAN GREY AND HANK McCOY--THE BEAST--DIED IN X-MEN #113 --R.S.
I'VE NEVER HEARD IT THIS LOUD BEFORE. I'D BETTER GET UP THERE AND HAVE HER SCALE THINGS DOWN...
...BEFORE HER SQUALL DAMAGES THE HOUSE.
AYE. THEN COME JOIN ME IN A CUP O' TEA, SCOTTY.
GOOD LORD!
I'LL WARN YOU ONCE, STRIPLING!
MY MISSION IS URGENT--MY NEED, DESPERATE. GET IN MY WAY, AND YOU'LL PAY THE PRICE IN BLOOD!
ARKON--YOU'RE ARKON!
WHO?!?
I SAW HIM ON TV, YEARS AGO. HE CAME TO DESTROY THE EARTH--
--BUT THE AVENGERS STOPPED HIM!
*AVENGERS #'S 75-76--ROG.
I DON'T KNOW WHY YOU'VE COME BACK, MISTER, OR WHAT YOU WANT WITH THE X-MEN--
--BUT I'LL BE MORE THAN HAPPY TO GIVE YOU THE WELCOME YOU DESERVE!
ZARK

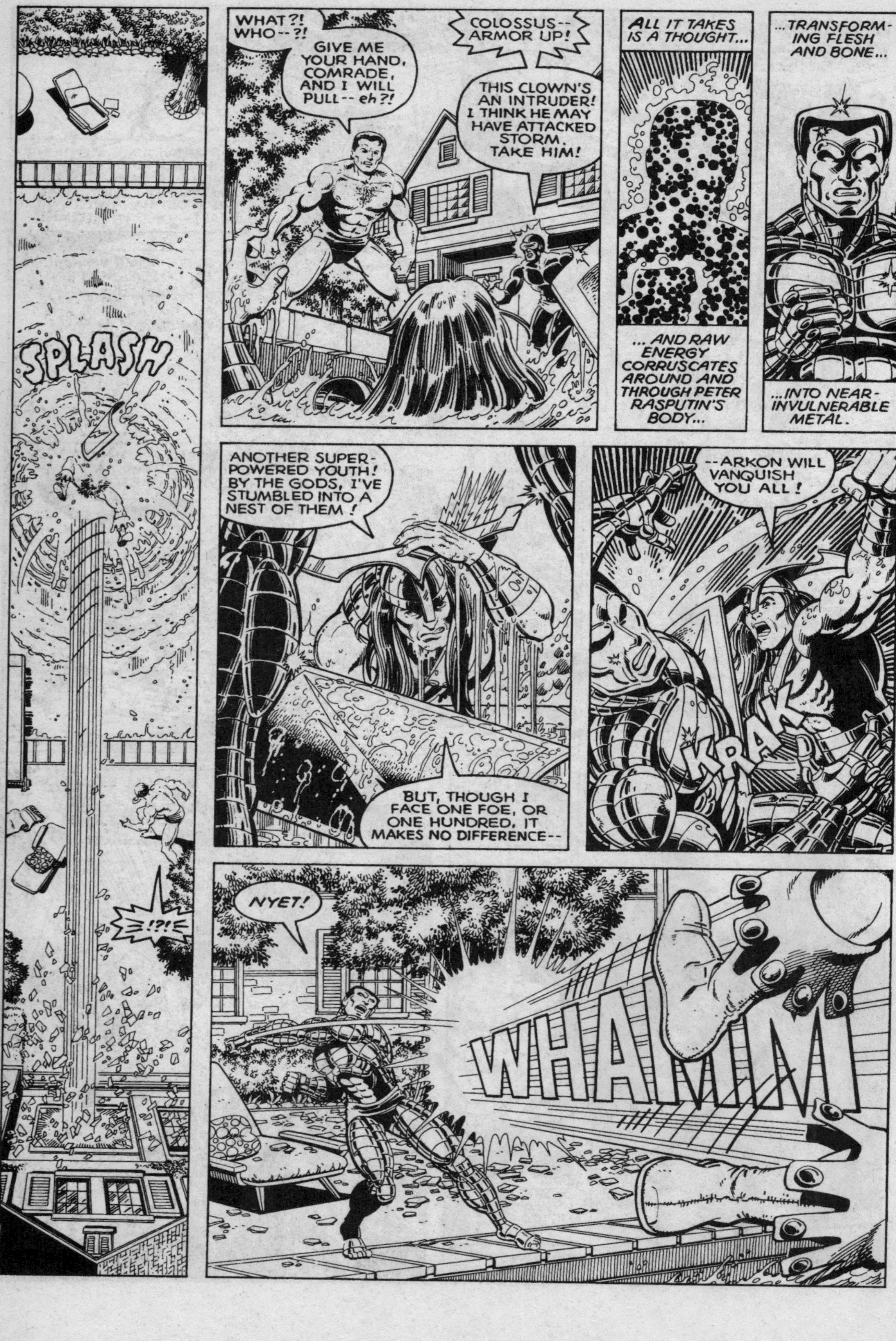
SPLASH
!?!
WHAT?! WHO--?!
GIVE ME YOUR HAND, COMRADE, AND I WILL PULL-- eh?!
COLOSSUS-- ARMOR UP!
THIS CLOWN'S AN INTRUDER! I THINK HE MAY HAVE ATTACKED STORM. TAKE HIM!
ALL IT TAKES IS A THOUGHT...
...AND RAW ENERGY CORRUSCATES AROUND AND THROUGH PETER RASPUTIN'S BODY...
...TRANSFORMING FLESH AND BONE...
...INTO NEAR-INVULNERABLE METAL.
ANOTHER SUPER-POWERED YOUTH! BY THE GODS, I'VE STUMBLED INTO A NEST OF THEM!
BUT, THOUGH I FACE ONE FOE, OR ONE HUNDRED, IT MAKES NO DIFFERENCE--
--ARKON WILL VANQUISH YOU ALL!
KRAK
NYET!
WHAMM

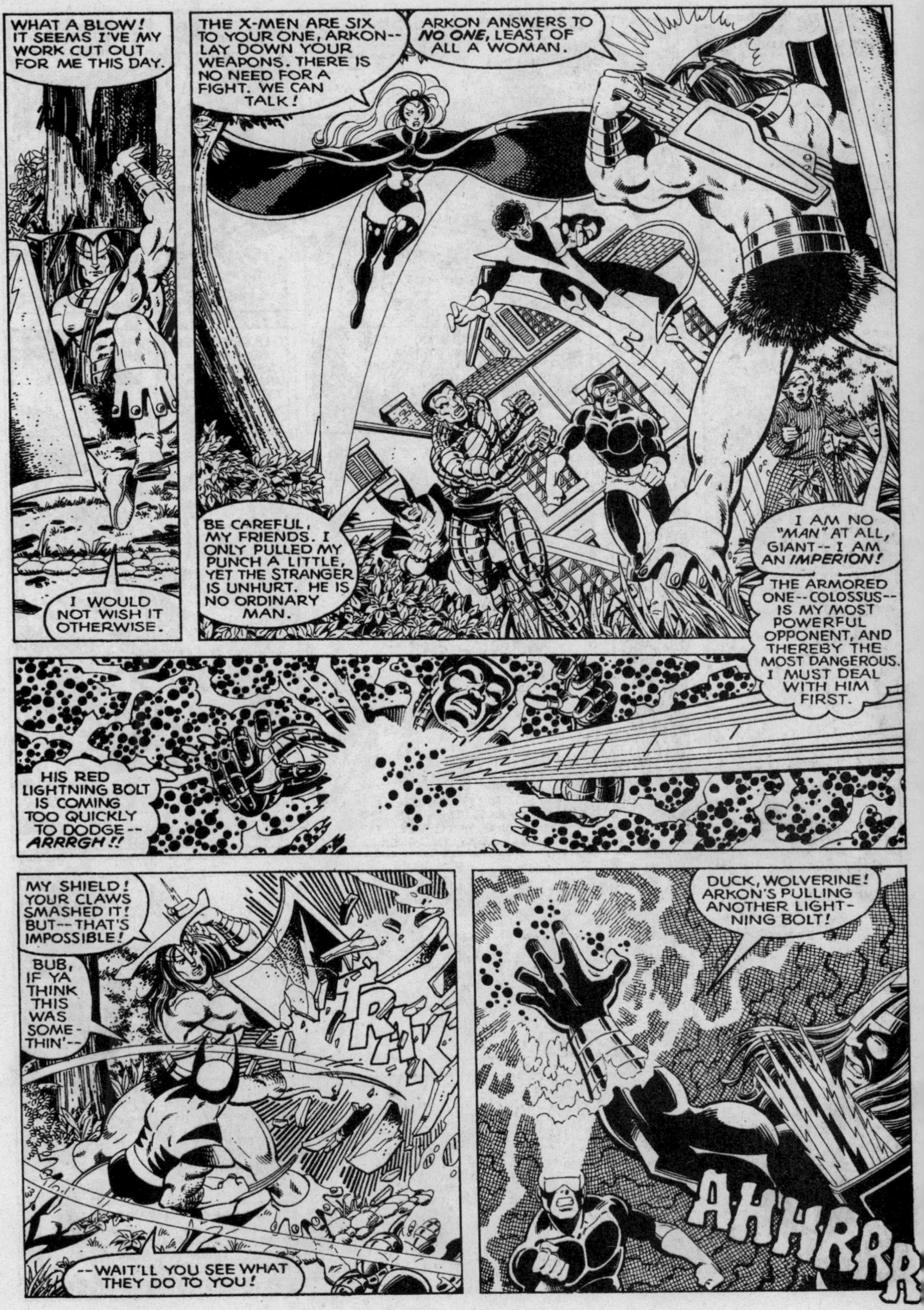
WHAT A BLOW! IT SEEMS I'VE MY WORK CUT OUT FOR ME THIS DAY.
I WOULD NOT WISH IT OTHERWISE.
THE X-MEN ARE SIX TO YOUR ONE, ARKON-- LAY DOWN YOUR WEAPONS. THERE IS NO NEED FOR A FIGHT. WE CAN TALK!
ARKON ANSWERS TO NO ONE, LEAST OF ALL A WOMAN.
BE CAREFUL, MY FRIENDS. I ONLY PULLED MY PUNCH A LITTLE, YET THE STRANGER IS UNHURT. HE IS NO ORDINARY MAN.
I AM NO "MAN" AT ALL, GIANT-- I AM AN IMPERION!
THE ARMORED ONE--COLOSSUS-- IS MY MOST POWERFUL OPPONENT, AND THEREBY THE MOST DANGEROUS. I MUST DEAL WITH HIM FIRST.
HIS RED LIGHTNING BOLT IS COMING TOO QUICKLY TO DODGE-- ARRRGH!!
MY SHIELD! YOUR CLAWS SMASHED IT! BUT--THAT'S IMPOSSIBLE!
BUB, IF YA THINK THIS WAS SOME-THIN'--
TRAK
--WAIT'LL YOU SEE WHAT THEY DO TO YOU!
DUCK, WOLVERINE! ARKON'S PULLING ANOTHER LIGHT-NING BOLT!
AHHRRR

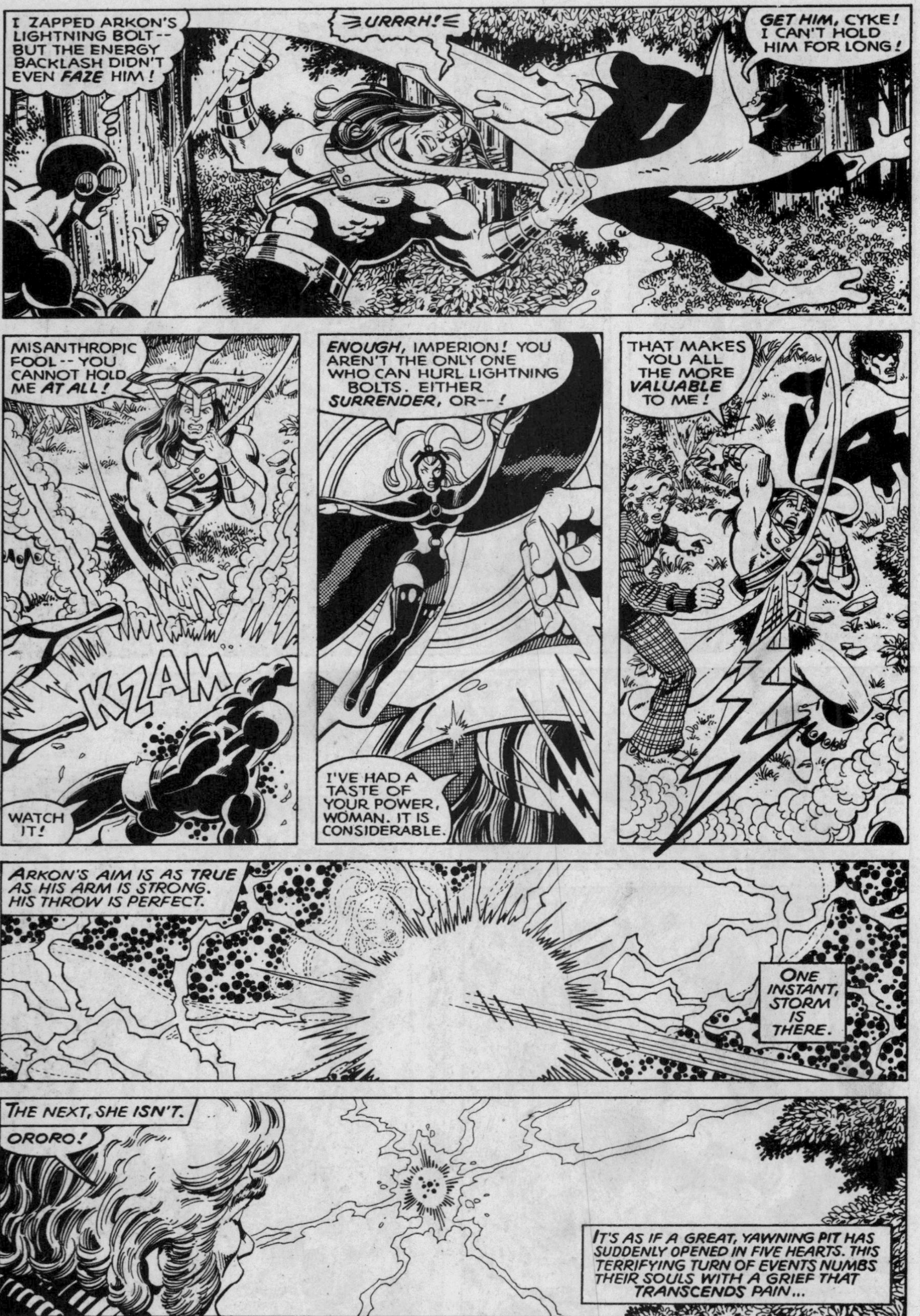
I ZAPPED ARKON'S LIGHTNING BOLT -- BUT THE ENERGY BACKLASH DIDN'T EVEN FAZE HIM!
URRRH!
GET HIM, CYKE! I CAN'T HOLD HIM FOR LONG!
MISANTHROPIC FOOL -- YOU CANNOT HOLD ME AT ALL!
KZAM
WATCH IT!
ENOUGH, IMPERION! YOU AREN'T THE ONLY ONE WHO CAN HURL LIGHTNING BOLTS. EITHER SURRENDER, OR--!
I'VE HAD A TASTE OF YOUR POWER, WOMAN. IT IS CONSIDERABLE.
THAT MAKES YOU ALL THE MORE VALUABLE TO ME!
ARKON'S AIM IS AS TRUE AS HIS ARM IS STRONG. HIS THROW IS PERFECT.
ONE INSTANT, STORM IS THERE.
THE NEXT, SHE ISN'T.
ORORO!
IT'S AS IF A GREAT, YAWNING PIT HAS SUDDENLY OPENED IN FIVE HEARTS. THIS TERRIFYING TURN OF EVENTS NUMBS THEIR SOULS WITH A GRIEF THAT TRANSCENDS PAIN...

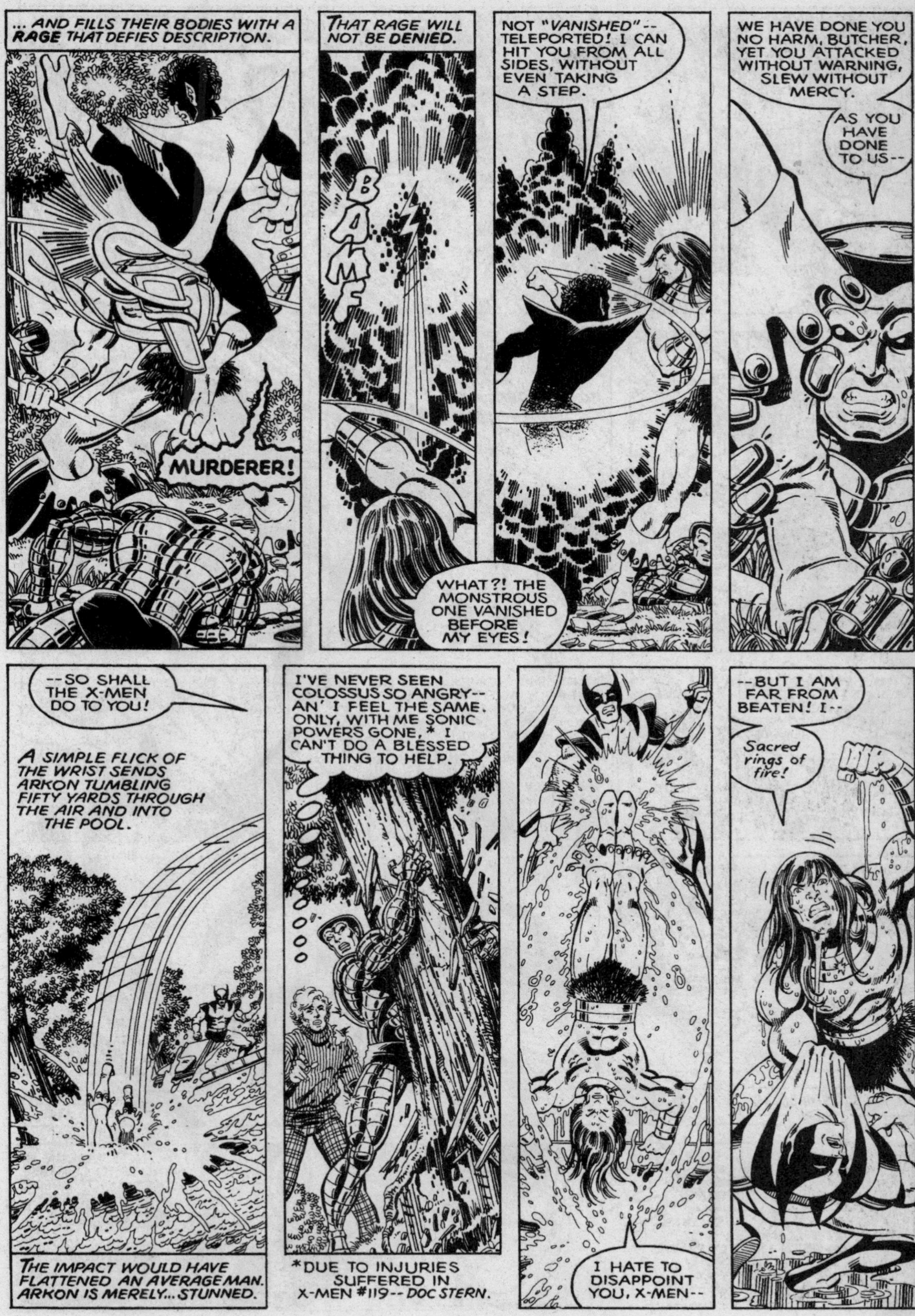
... AND FILLS THEIR BODIES WITH A RAGE THAT DEFIES DESCRIPTION.
MURDERER!
THAT RAGE WILL NOT BE DENIED.
BAMF
NOT "VANISHED"-- TELEPORTED! I CAN HIT YOU FROM ALL SIDES, WITHOUT EVEN TAKING A STEP.
WHAT?! THE MONSTROUS ONE VANISHED BEFORE MY EYES!
WE HAVE DONE YOU NO HARM, BUTCHER, YET YOU ATTACKED WITHOUT WARNING, SLEW WITHOUT MERCY.
AS YOU HAVE DONE TO US--
--SO SHALL THE X-MEN DO TO YOU!
A SIMPLE FLICK OF THE WRIST SENDS ARKON TUMBLING FIFTY YARDS THROUGH THE AIR AND INTO THE POOL.
THE IMPACT WOULD HAVE FLATTENED AN AVERAGE MAN. ARKON IS MERELY... STUNNED.
I'VE NEVER SEEN COLOSSUS SO ANGRY-- AN' I FEEL THE SAME. ONLY, WITH ME SONIC POWERS GONE,* I CAN'T DO A BLESSED THING TO HELP.
*DUE TO INJURIES SUFFERED IN X-MEN #119-- DOC STERN.
I HATE TO DISAPPOINT YOU, X-MEN--
--BUT I AM FAR FROM BEATEN! I--
Sacred rings of fire!

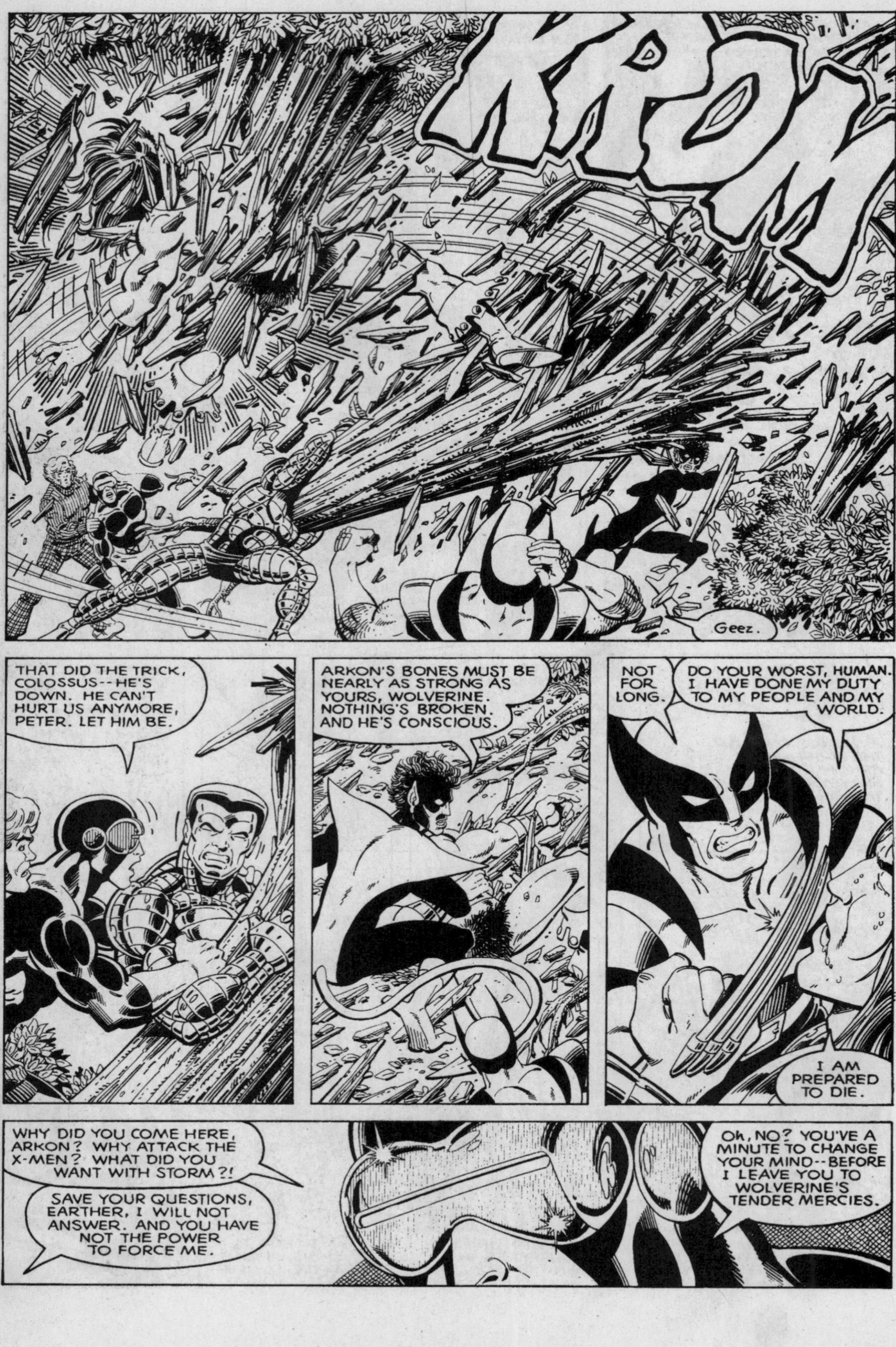
KROOM
Geez.
THAT DID THE TRICK, COLOSSUS--HE'S DOWN. HE CAN'T HURT US ANYMORE, PETER. LET HIM BE.
ARKON'S BONES MUST BE NEARLY AS STRONG AS YOURS, WOLVERINE. NOTHING'S BROKEN. AND HE'S CONSCIOUS.
NOT FOR LONG.
DO YOUR WORST, HUMAN. I HAVE DONE MY DUTY TO MY PEOPLE AND MY WORLD.
I AM PREPARED TO DIE.
WHY DID YOU COME HERE, ARKON? WHY ATTACK THE X-MEN? WHAT DID YOU WANT WITH STORM?!
SAVE YOUR QUESTIONS, EARTHER, I WILL NOT ANSWER. AND YOU HAVE NOT THE POWER TO FORCE ME.
Oh, NO? YOU'VE A MINUTE TO CHANGE YOUR MIND--BEFORE I LEAVE YOU TO WOLVERINE'S TENDER MERCIES.

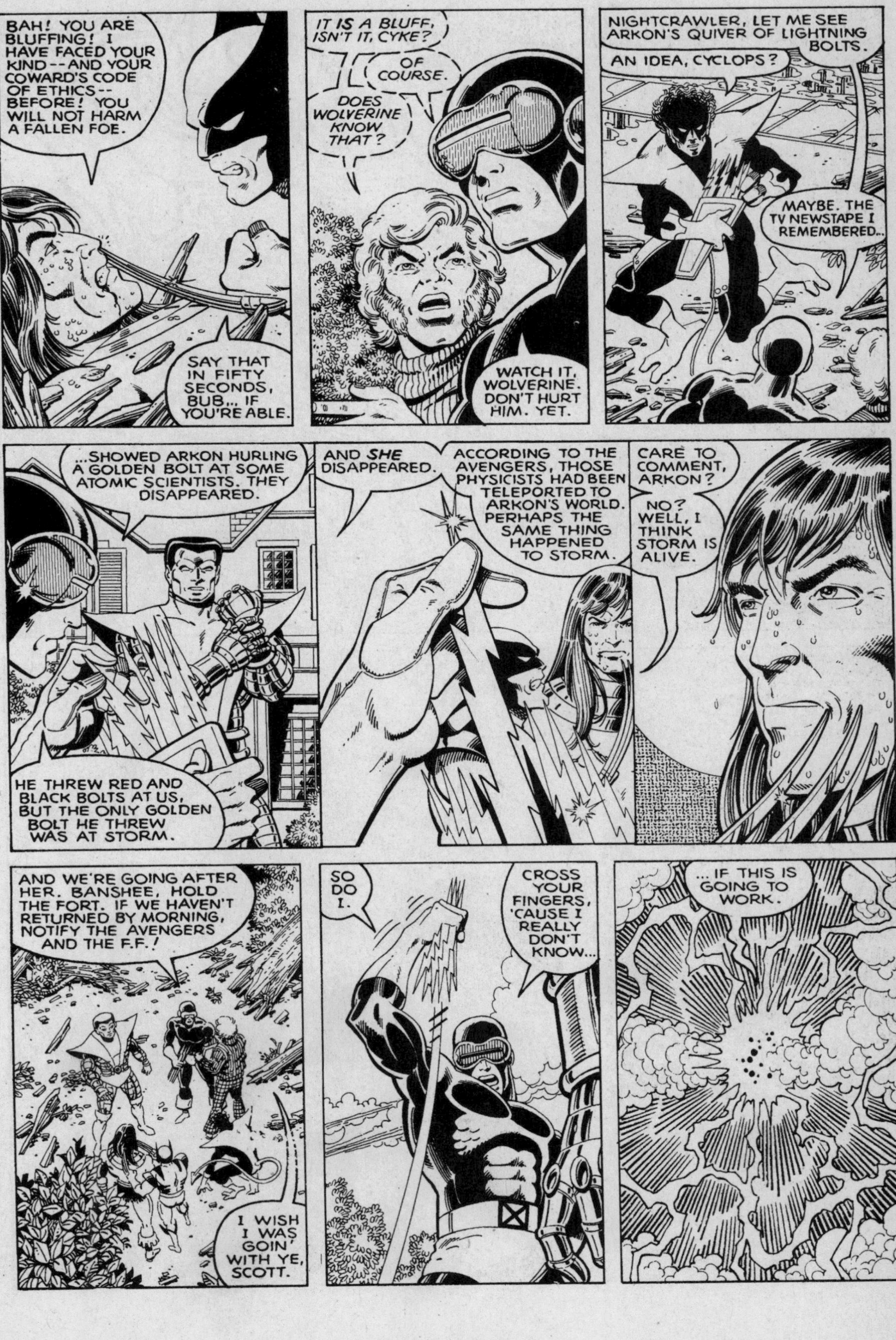
BAH! YOU ARE BLUFFING! I HAVE FACED YOUR KIND--AND YOUR COWARD'S CODE OF ETHICS--BEFORE! YOU WILL NOT HARM A FALLEN FOE.
SAY THAT IN FIFTY SECONDS, BUB... IF YOU'RE ABLE.
IT IS A BLUFF, ISN'T IT, CYKE?
OF COURSE.
DOES WOLVERINE KNOW THAT?
WATCH IT, WOLVERINE. DON'T HURT HIM. YET.
NIGHTCRAWLER, LET ME SEE ARKON'S QUIVER OF LIGHTNING BOLTS.
AN IDEA, CYCLOPS?
MAYBE. THE TV NEWSTAPE I REMEMBERED...
...SHOWED ARKON HURLING A GOLDEN BOLT AT SOME ATOMIC SCIENTISTS. THEY DISAPPEARED.
HE THREW RED AND BLACK BOLTS AT US, BUT THE ONLY GOLDEN BOLT HE THREW WAS AT STORM.
AND SHE DISAPPEARED.
ACCORDING TO THE AVENGERS, THOSE PHYSICISTS HAD BEEN TELEPORTED TO ARKON'S WORLD. PERHAPS THE SAME THING HAPPENED TO STORM.
CARE TO COMMENT, ARKON?
NO? WELL, I THINK STORM IS ALIVE.
AND WE'RE GOING AFTER HER. BANSHEE, HOLD THE FORT. IF WE HAVEN'T RETURNED BY MORNING, NOTIFY THE AVENGERS AND THE F.F.!
I WISH I WAS GOIN' WITH YE, SCOTT.
SO DO I.
CROSS YOUR FINGERS, 'CAUSE I REALLY DON'T KNOW...
...IF THIS IS GOING TO WORK.

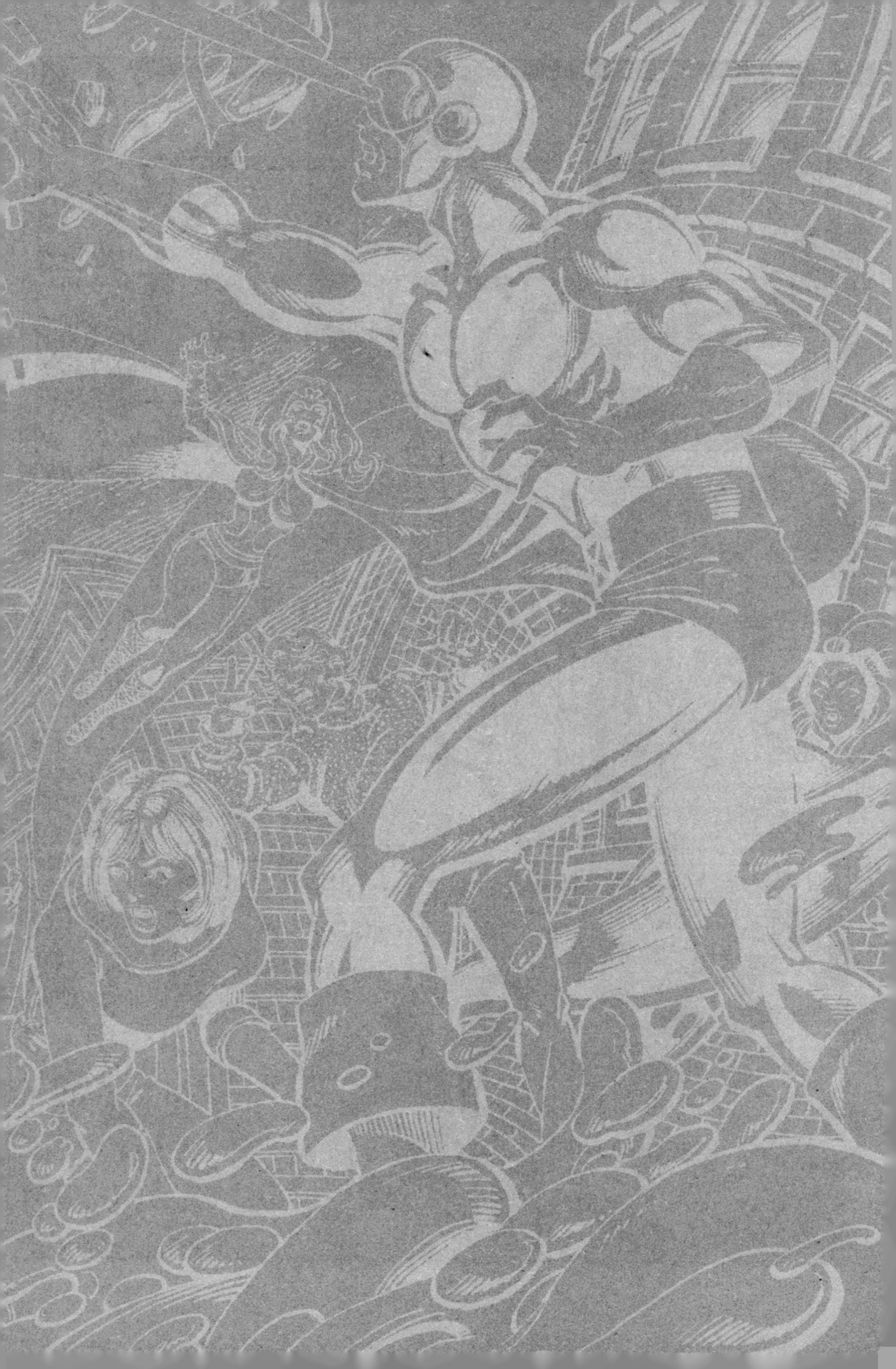

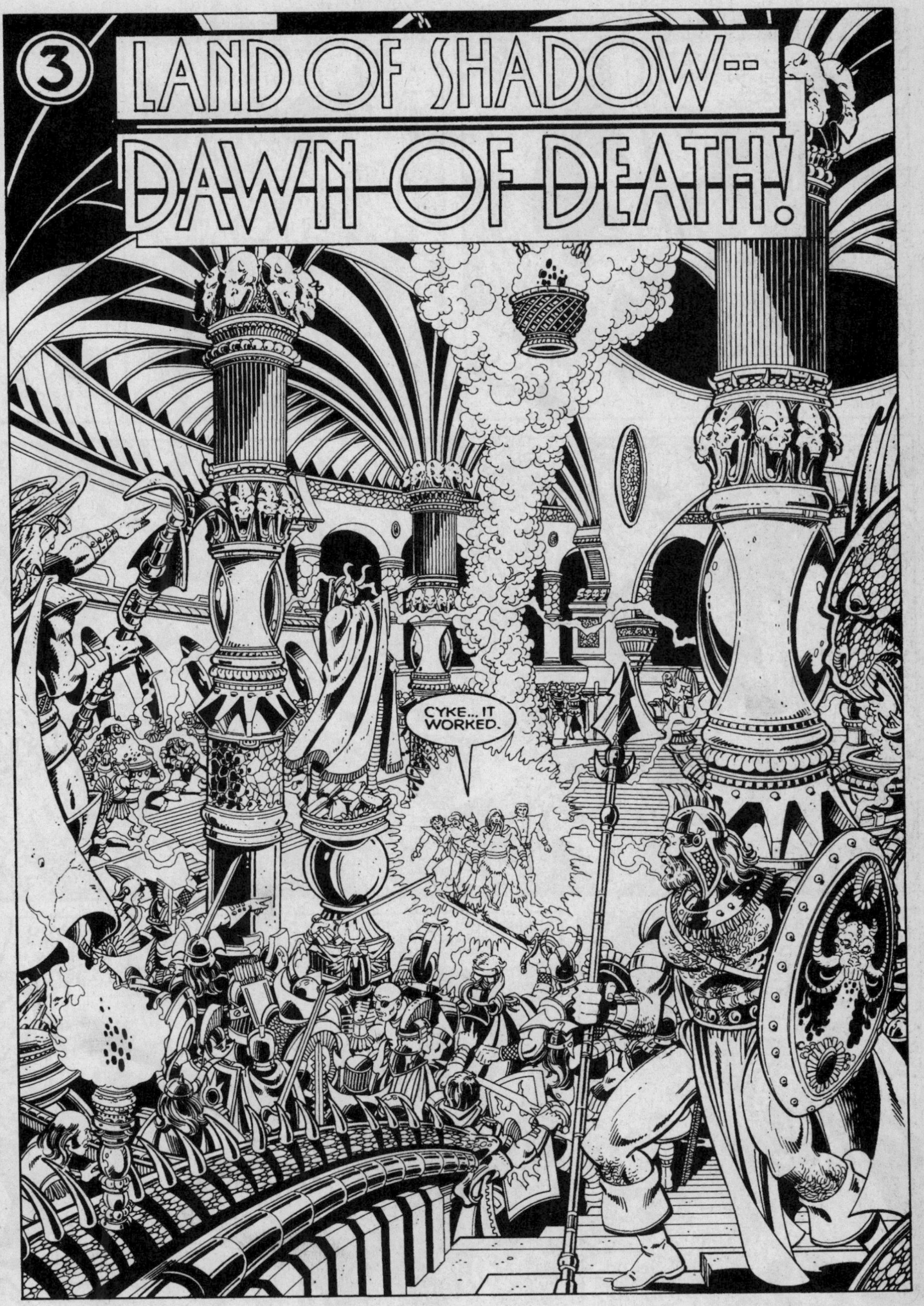
3
LAND OF SHADOW--
DAWN OF DEATH!
CYKE... IT WORKED.

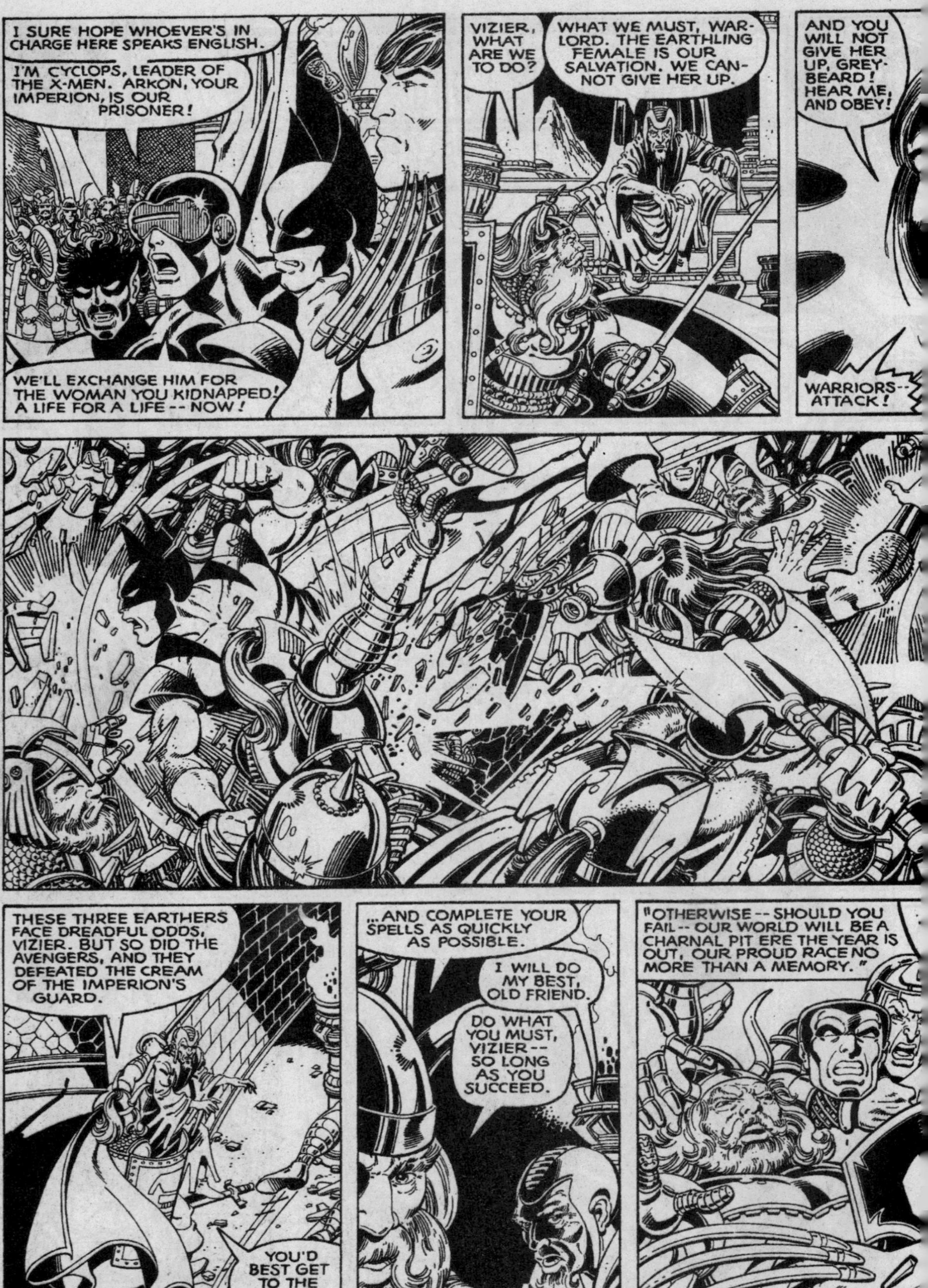
I SURE HOPE WHOEVER'S IN CHARGE HERE SPEAKS ENGLISH.
I'M CYCLOPS, LEADER OF THE X-MEN. ARKON, YOUR IMPERION, IS OUR PRISONER!
WE'LL EXCHANGE HIM FOR THE WOMAN YOU KIDNAPPED! A LIFE FOR A LIFE -- NOW!
VIZIER, WHAT ARE WE TO DO?
WHAT WE MUST, WARLORD. THE EARTHLING FEMALE IS OUR SALVATION. WE CANNOT GIVE HER UP.
AND YOU WILL NOT GIVE HER UP, GREYBEARD! HEAR ME, AND OBEY!
WARRIORS-- ATTACK!
THESE THREE EARTHERS FACE DREADFUL ODDS, VIZIER. BUT SO DID THE AVENGERS, AND THEY DEFEATED THE CREAM OF THE IMPERION'S GUARD.
YOU'D BEST GET TO THE TEMPLE...
...AND COMPLETE YOUR SPELLS AS QUICKLY AS POSSIBLE.
I WILL DO MY BEST, OLD FRIEND.
DO WHAT YOU MUST, VIZIER-- SO LONG AS YOU SUCCEED.
"OTHERWISE -- SHOULD YOU FAIL -- OUR WORLD WILL BE A CHARNAL PIT ERE THE YEAR IS OUT, OUR PROUD RACE NO MORE THAN A MEMORY."

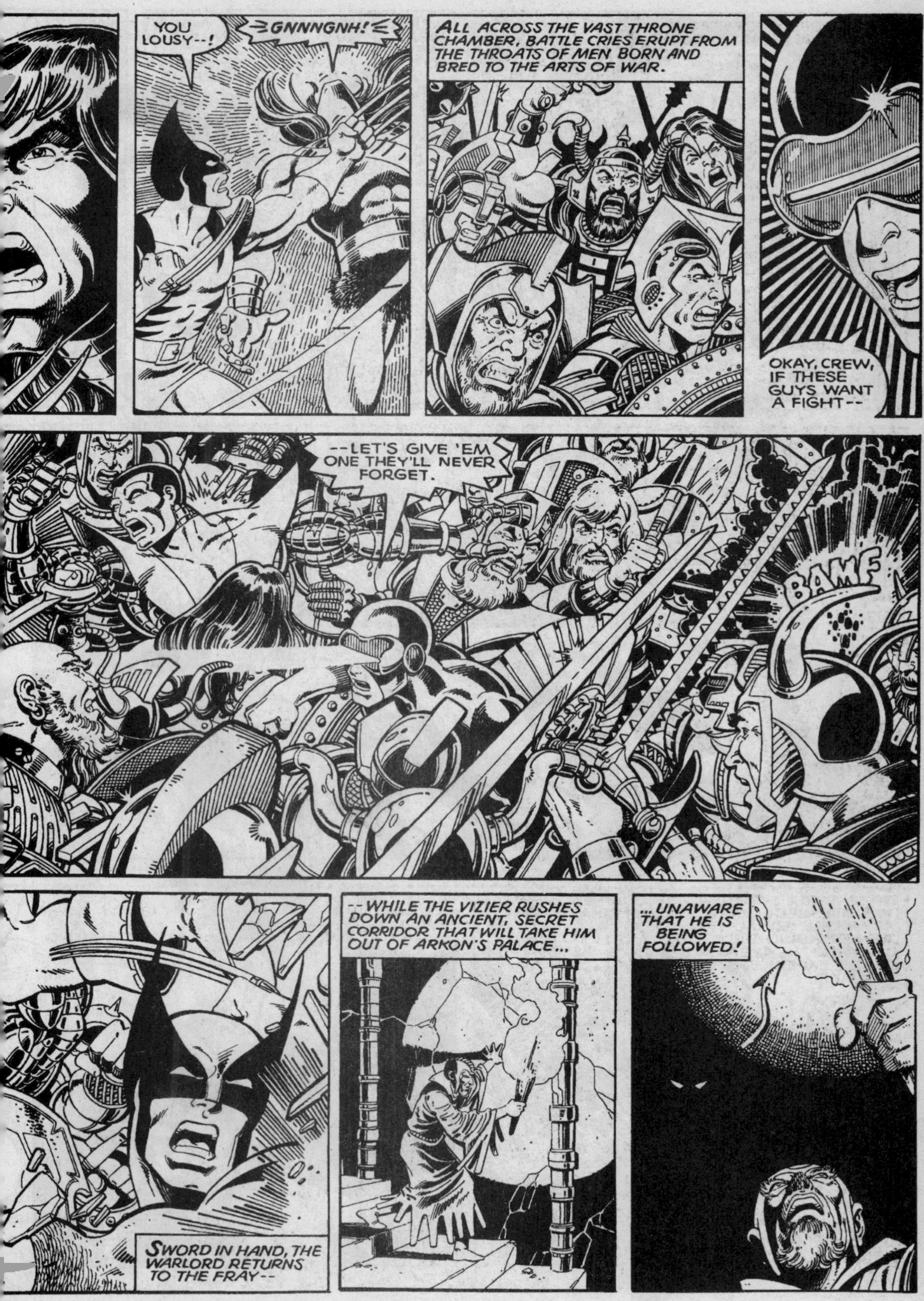

YOU LOUSY--!
GNNNGNH!
ALL ACROSS THE VAST THRONE CHAMBER, BATTLE CRIES ERUPT FROM THE THROATS OF MEN BORN AND BRED TO THE ARTS OF WAR.
OKAY, CREW, IF THESE GUYS WANT A FIGHT--
--LET'S GIVE 'EM ONE THEY'LL NEVER FORGET.
BAMF
SWORD IN HAND, THE WARLORD RETURNS TO THE FRAY--
--WHILE THE VIZIER RUSHES DOWN AN ANCIENT, SECRET CORRIDOR THAT WILL TAKE HIM OUT OF ARKON'S PALACE...
...UNAWARE THAT HE IS BEING FOLLOWED!

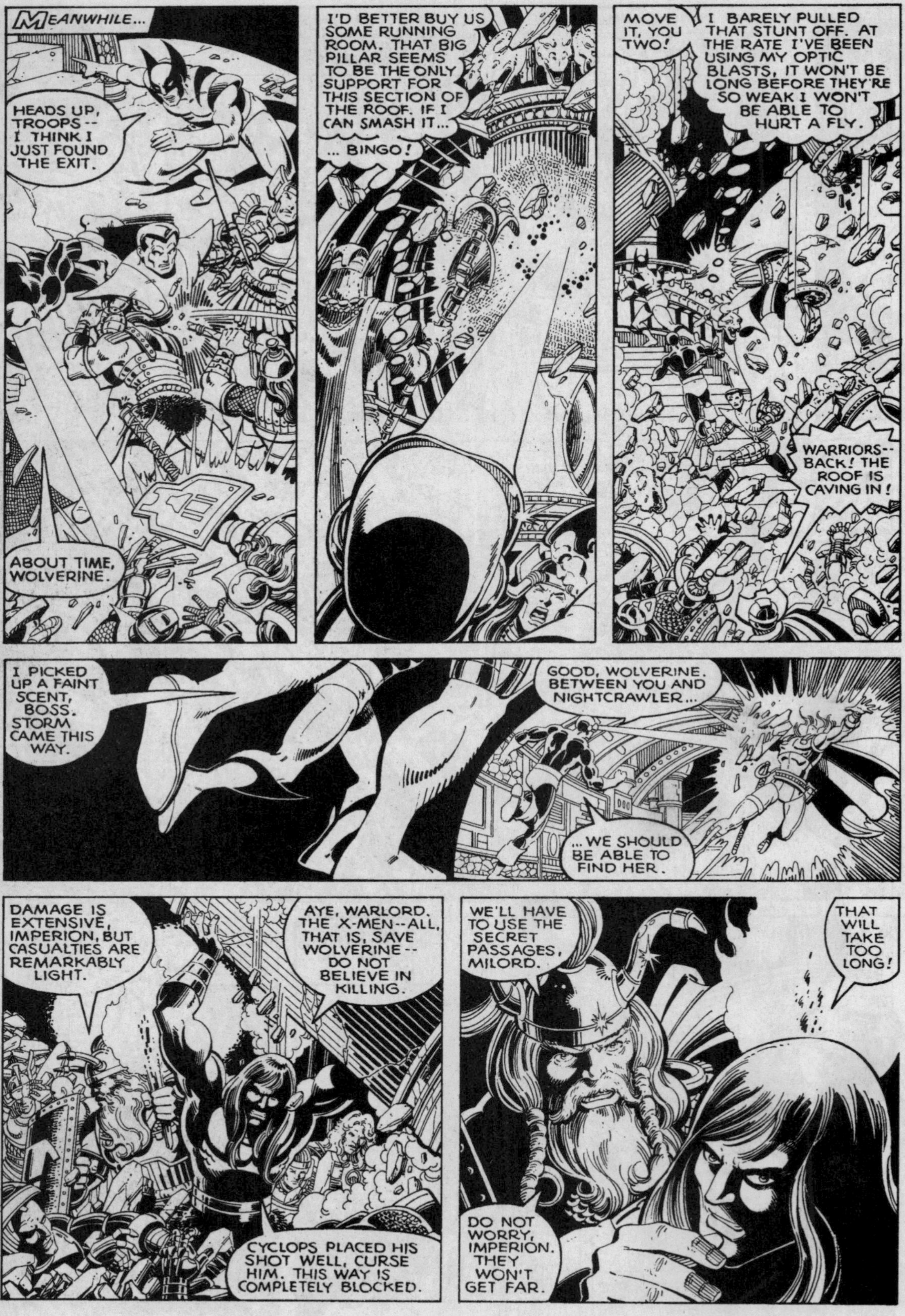
MEANWHILE...
HEADS UP, TROOPS -- I THINK I JUST FOUND THE EXIT.
ABOUT TIME, WOLVERINE.
I'D BETTER BUY US SOME RUNNING ROOM. THAT BIG PILLAR SEEMS TO BE THE ONLY SUPPORT FOR THIS SECTION OF THE ROOF. IF I CAN SMASH IT...
... BINGO!
MOVE IT, YOU TWO!
I BARELY PULLED THAT STUNT OFF. AT THE RATE I'VE BEEN USING MY OPTIC BLASTS, IT WON'T BE LONG BEFORE THEY'RE SO WEAK I WON'T BE ABLE TO HURT A FLY.
WARRIORS-- BACK! THE ROOF IS CAVING IN!
I PICKED UP A FAINT SCENT, BOSS. STORM CAME THIS WAY.
GOOD, WOLVERINE. BETWEEN YOU AND NIGHTCRAWLER...
... WE SHOULD BE ABLE TO FIND HER.
DAMAGE IS EXTENSIVE, IMPERION, BUT CASUALTIES ARE REMARKABLY LIGHT.
AYE, WARLORD. THE X-MEN--ALL, THAT IS, SAVE WOLVERINE -- DO NOT BELIEVE IN KILLING.
CYCLOPS PLACED HIS SHOT WELL, CURSE HIM. THIS WAY IS COMPLETELY BLOCKED.
WE'LL HAVE TO USE THE SECRET PASSAGES, MILORD.
THAT WILL TAKE TOO LONG!
DO NOT WORRY, IMPERION. THEY WON'T GET FAR.

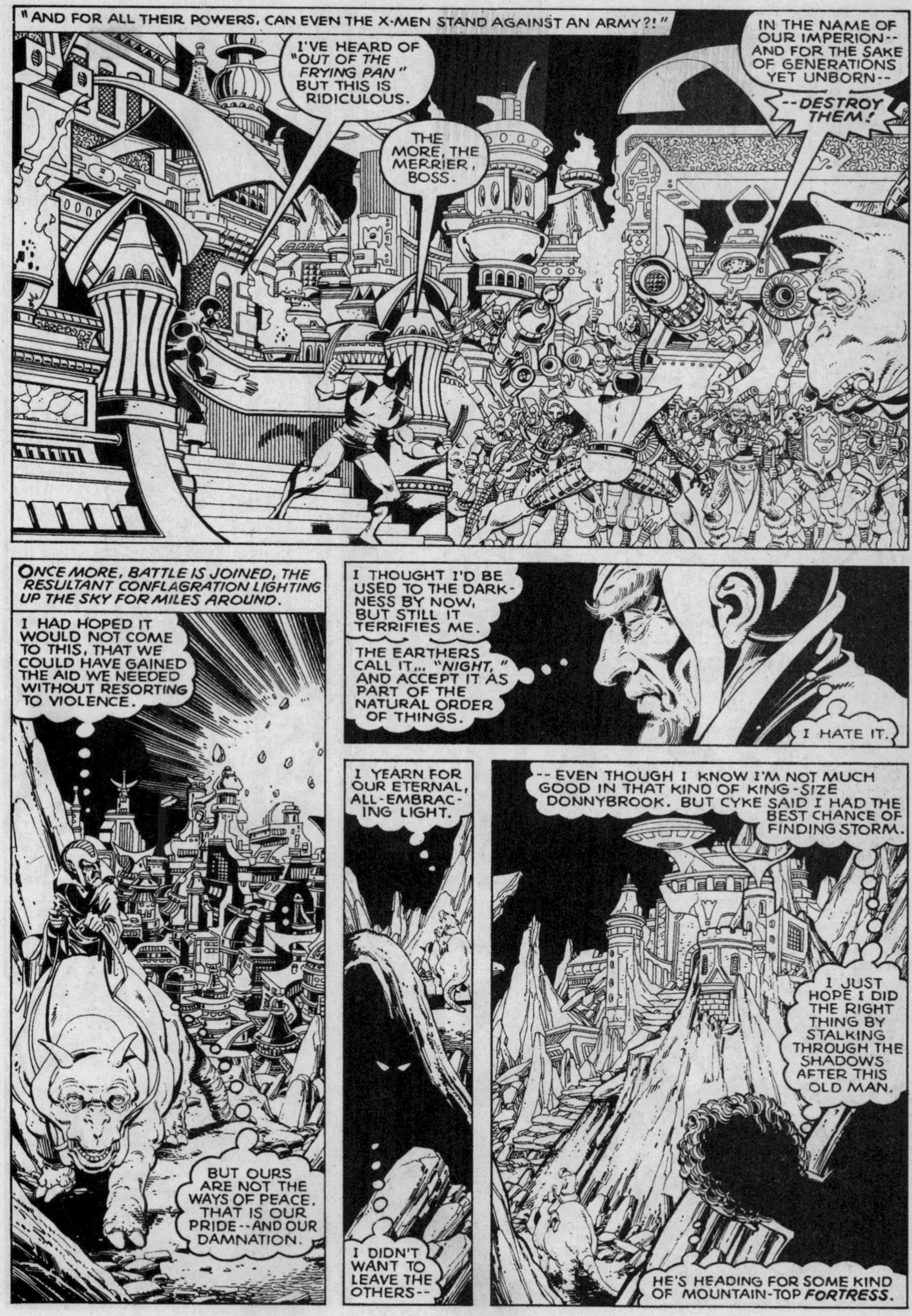
"AND FOR ALL THEIR POWERS, CAN EVEN THE X-MEN STAND AGAINST AN ARMY?!"
I'VE HEARD OF "OUT OF THE FRYING PAN" BUT THIS IS RIDICULOUS.
THE MORE, THE MERRIER, BOSS.
IN THE NAME OF OUR IMPERION-- AND FOR THE SAKE OF GENERATIONS YET UNBORN--
--DESTROY THEM!
ONCE MORE, BATTLE IS JOINED, THE RESULTANT CONFLAGRATION LIGHTING UP THE SKY FOR MILES AROUND.
I HAD HOPED IT WOULD NOT COME TO THIS, THAT WE COULD HAVE GAINED THE AID WE NEEDED WITHOUT RESORTING TO VIOLENCE.
BUT OURS ARE NOT THE WAYS OF PEACE. THAT IS OUR PRIDE--AND OUR DAMNATION.
I THOUGHT I'D BE USED TO THE DARKNESS BY NOW, BUT STILL IT TERRIFIES ME.
THE EARTHERS CALL IT... "NIGHT," AND ACCEPT IT AS PART OF THE NATURAL ORDER OF THINGS.
I HATE IT.
I YEARN FOR OUR ETERNAL, ALL-EMBRACING LIGHT.
I DIDN'T WANT TO LEAVE THE OTHERS--
--EVEN THOUGH I KNOW I'M NOT MUCH GOOD IN THAT KIND OF KING-SIZE DONNYBROOK. BUT CYKE SAID I HAD THE BEST CHANCE OF FINDING STORM.
I JUST HOPE I DID THE RIGHT THING BY STALKING THROUGH THE SHADOWS AFTER THIS OLD MAN.
HE'S HEADING FOR SOME KIND OF MOUNTAIN-TOP FORTRESS.

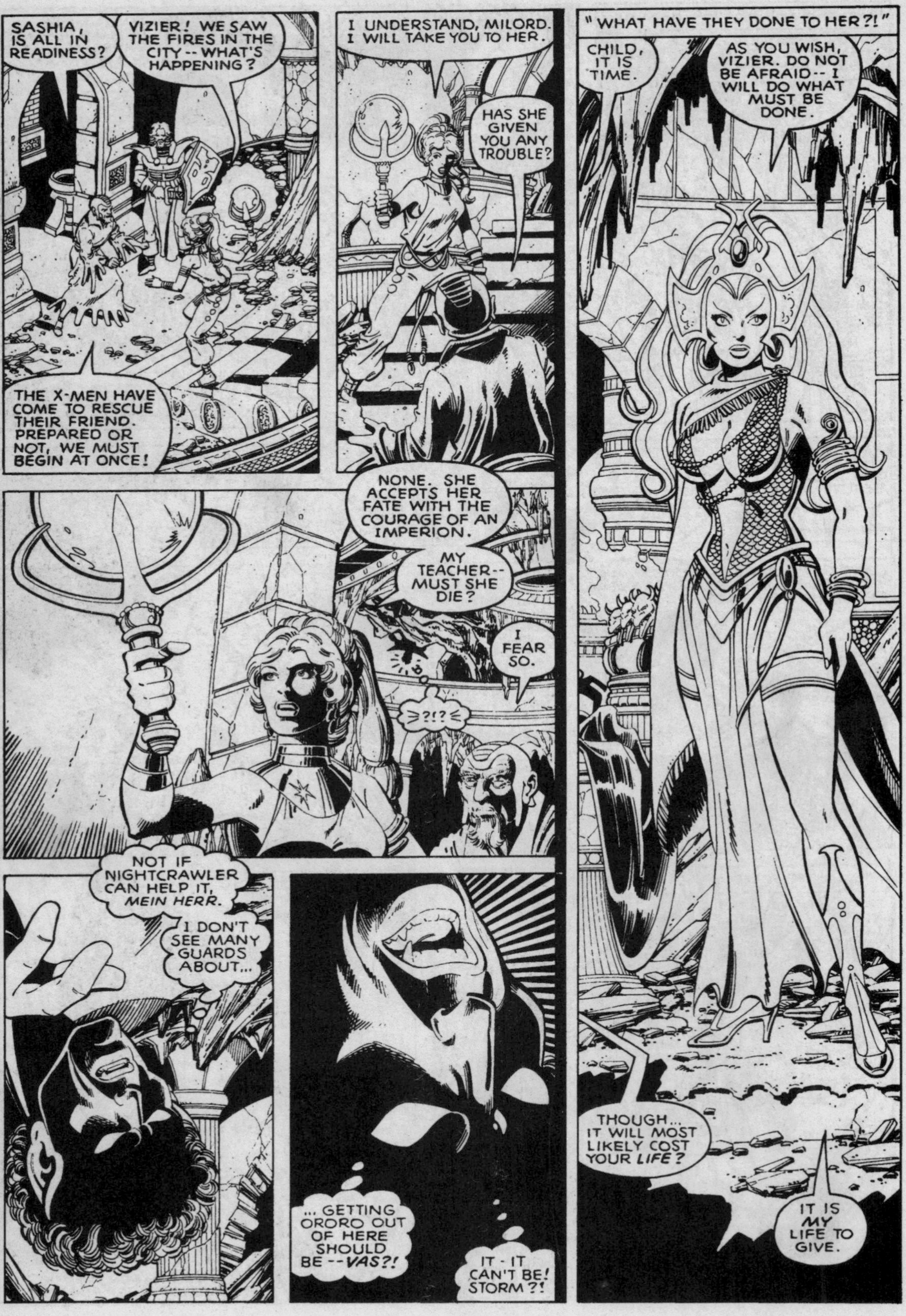
SASHIA, IS ALL IN READINESS?
VIZIER! WE SAW THE FIRES IN THE CITY -- WHAT'S HAPPENING?
THE X-MEN HAVE COME TO RESCUE THEIR FRIEND. PREPARED OR NOT, WE MUST BEGIN AT ONCE!
I UNDERSTAND, MILORD. I WILL TAKE YOU TO HER.
HAS SHE GIVEN YOU ANY TROUBLE?
NONE. SHE ACCEPTS HER FATE WITH THE COURAGE OF AN IMPERION.
MY TEACHER-- MUST SHE DIE?
I FEAR SO.
?!?
NOT IF NIGHTCRAWLER CAN HELP IT, MEIN HERR.
I DON'T SEE MANY GUARDS ABOUT...
... GETTING ORORO OUT OF HERE SHOULD BE --VAS?!
IT - IT CAN'T BE! STORM?!
"WHAT HAVE THEY DONE TO HER?!"
CHILD, IT IS TIME.
AS YOU WISH, VIZIER. DO NOT BE AFRAID-- I WILL DO WHAT MUST BE DONE.
THOUGH... IT WILL MOST LIKELY COST YOUR LIFE?
IT IS MY LIFE TO GIVE.

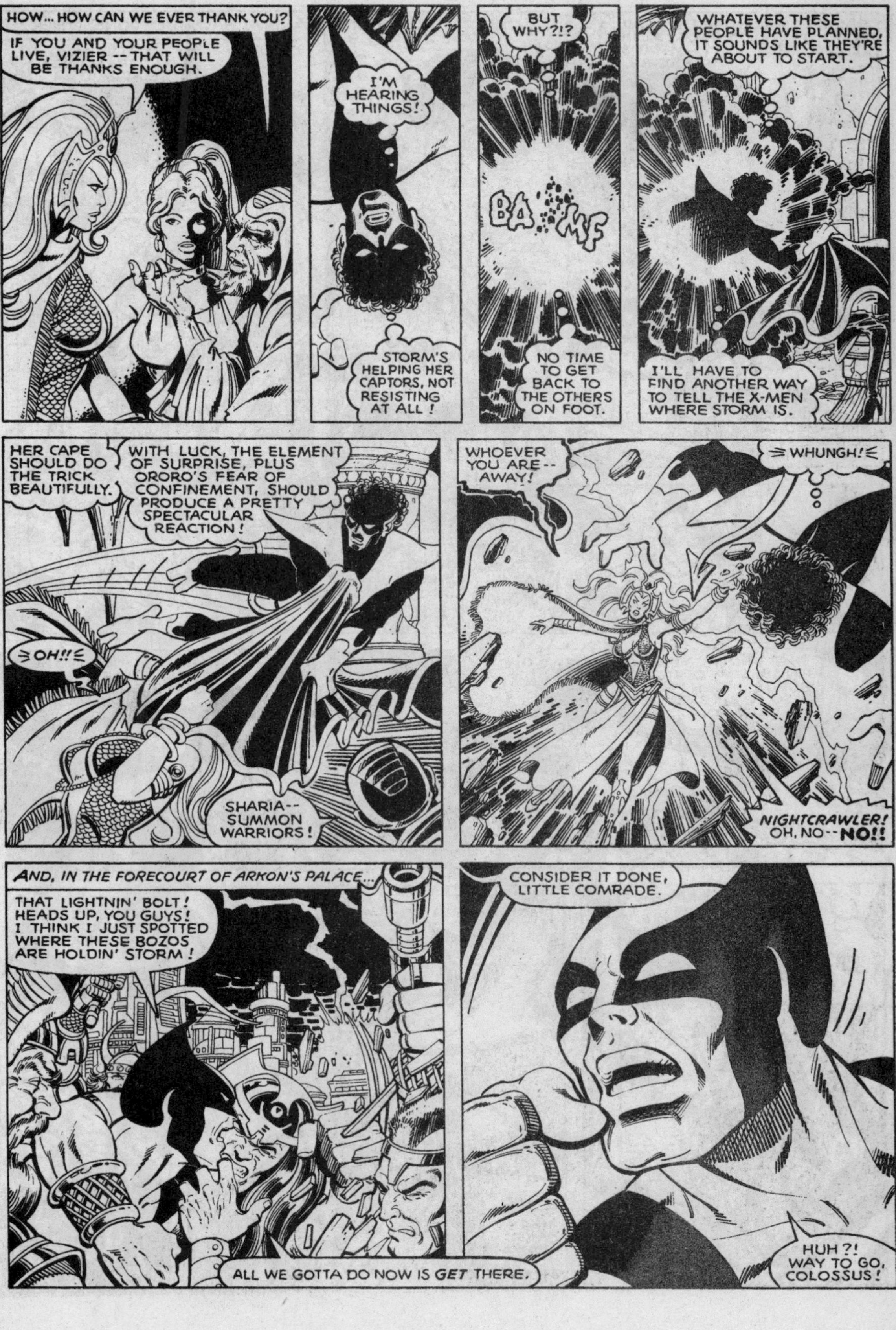

HOW... HOW CAN WE EVER THANK YOU?
IF YOU AND YOUR PEOPLE LIVE, VIZIER -- THAT WILL BE THANKS ENOUGH.
I'M HEARING THINGS!
STORM'S HELPING HER CAPTORS, NOT RESISTING AT ALL!
BUT WHY?!?
BAMF
NO TIME TO GET BACK TO THE OTHERS ON FOOT.
WHATEVER THESE PEOPLE HAVE PLANNED, IT SOUNDS LIKE THEY'RE ABOUT TO START.
I'LL HAVE TO FIND ANOTHER WAY TO TELL THE X-MEN WHERE STORM IS.
HER CAPE SHOULD DO THE TRICK BEAUTIFULLY.
WITH LUCK, THE ELEMENT OF SURPRISE, PLUS ORORO'S FEAR OF CONFINEMENT, SHOULD PRODUCE A PRETTY SPECTACULAR REACTION!
OH!!
SHARIA-- SUMMON WARRIORS!
WHOEVER YOU ARE-- AWAY!
WHUNGH!
NIGHTCRAWLER! OH, NO--NO!!
AND, IN THE FORECOURT OF ARKON'S PALACE...
THAT LIGHTNIN' BOLT! HEADS UP, YOU GUYS! I THINK I JUST SPOTTED WHERE THESE BOZOS ARE HOLDIN' STORM!
ALL WE GOTTA DO NOW IS GET THERE.
CONSIDER IT DONE, LITTLE COMRADE.
HUH?! WAY TO GO, COLOSSUS!

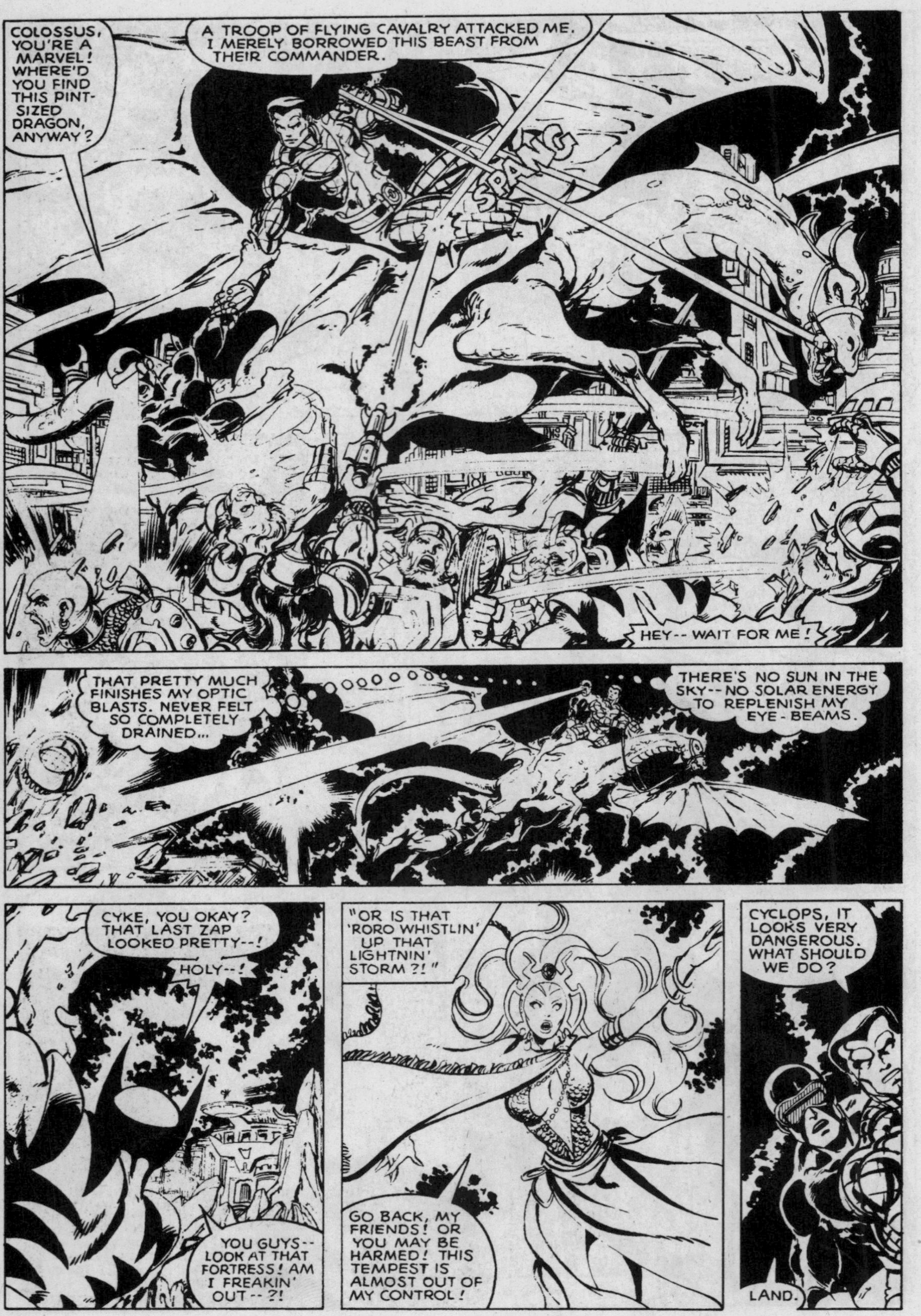
COLOSSUS, YOU'RE A MARVEL! WHERE'D YOU FIND THIS PINT-SIZED DRAGON, ANYWAY?
A TROOP OF FLYING CAVALRY ATTACKED ME. I MERELY BORROWED THIS BEAST FROM THEIR COMMANDER.
SPANG
HEY-- WAIT FOR ME!
THAT PRETTY MUCH FINISHES MY OPTIC BLASTS. NEVER FELT SO COMPLETELY DRAINED...
THERE'S NO SUN IN THE SKY--NO SOLAR ENERGY TO REPLENISH MY EYE-BEAMS.
CYKE, YOU OKAY? THAT LAST ZAP LOOKED PRETTY--!
HOLY--!
YOU GUYS-- LOOK AT THAT FORTRESS! AM I FREAKIN' OUT--?!
"OR IS THAT 'RORO WHISTLIN' UP THAT LIGHTNIN' STORM?!"
GO BACK, MY FRIENDS! OR YOU MAY BE HARMED! THIS TEMPEST IS ALMOST OUT OF MY CONTROL!
CYCLOPS, IT LOOKS VERY DANGEROUS. WHAT SHOULD WE DO?
LAND.

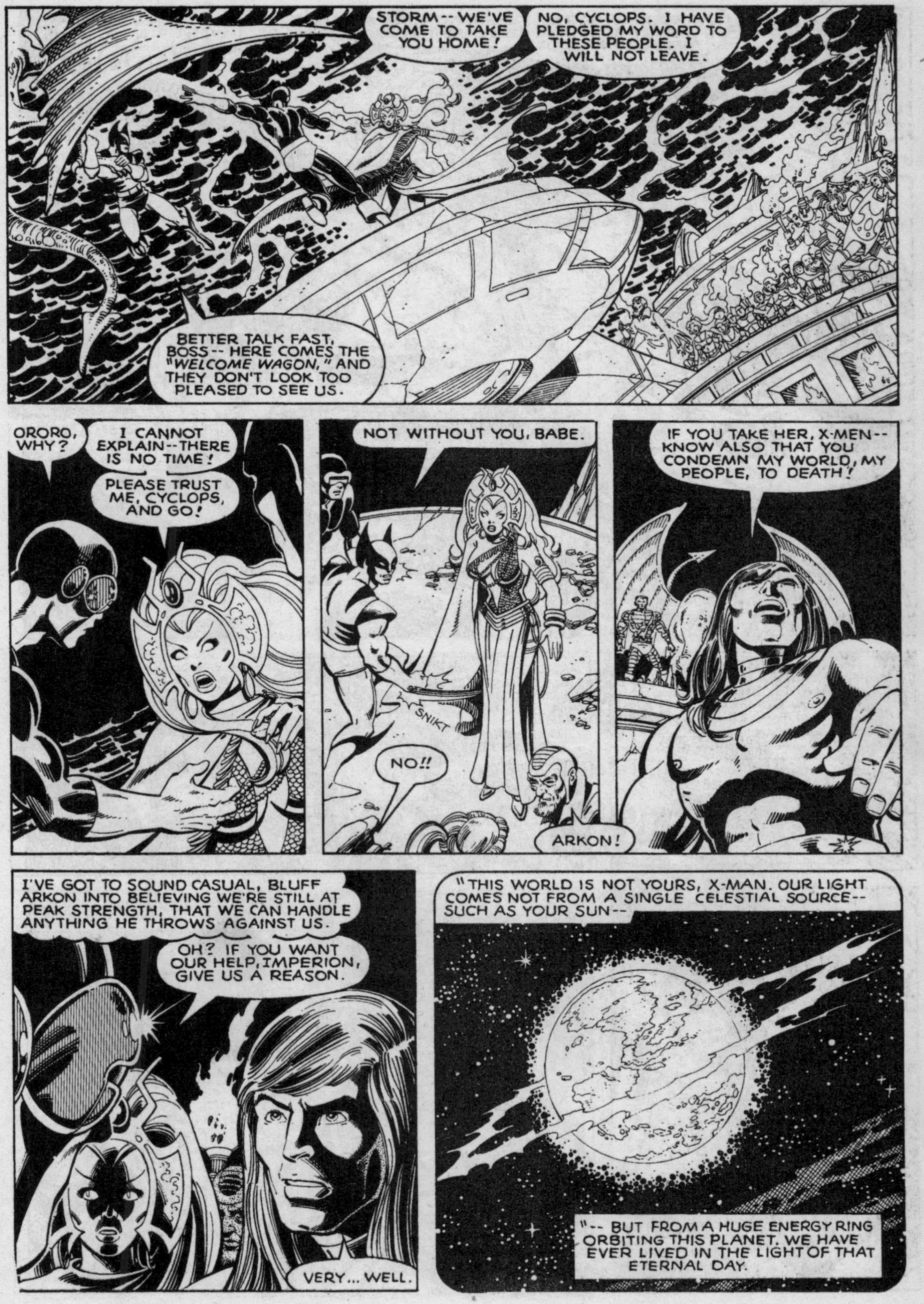
STORM-- WE'VE COME TO TAKE YOU HOME!
NO, CYCLOPS. I HAVE PLEDGED MY WORD TO THESE PEOPLE. I WILL NOT LEAVE.
BETTER TALK FAST, BOSS-- HERE COMES THE "WELCOME WAGON," AND THEY DON'T LOOK TOO PLEASED TO SEE US.
ORORO, WHY?
I CANNOT EXPLAIN--THERE IS NO TIME!
PLEASE TRUST ME, CYCLOPS, AND GO!
NOT WITHOUT YOU, BABE.
SNIKT
NO!!
ARKON!
IF YOU TAKE HER, X-MEN-- KNOW ALSO THAT YOU CONDEMN MY WORLD, MY PEOPLE, TO DEATH!
I'VE GOT TO SOUND CASUAL, BLUFF ARKON INTO BELIEVING WE'RE STILL AT PEAK STRENGTH, THAT WE CAN HANDLE ANYTHING HE THROWS AGAINST US.
OH? IF YOU WANT OUR HELP, IMPERION, GIVE US A REASON.
VERY... WELL.
"THIS WORLD IS NOT YOURS, X-MAN. OUR LIGHT COMES NOT FROM A SINGLE CELESTIAL SOURCE-- SUCH AS YOUR SUN--
"-- BUT FROM A HUGE ENERGY RING ORBITING THIS PLANET. WE HAVE EVER LIVED IN THE LIGHT OF THAT ETERNAL DAY.

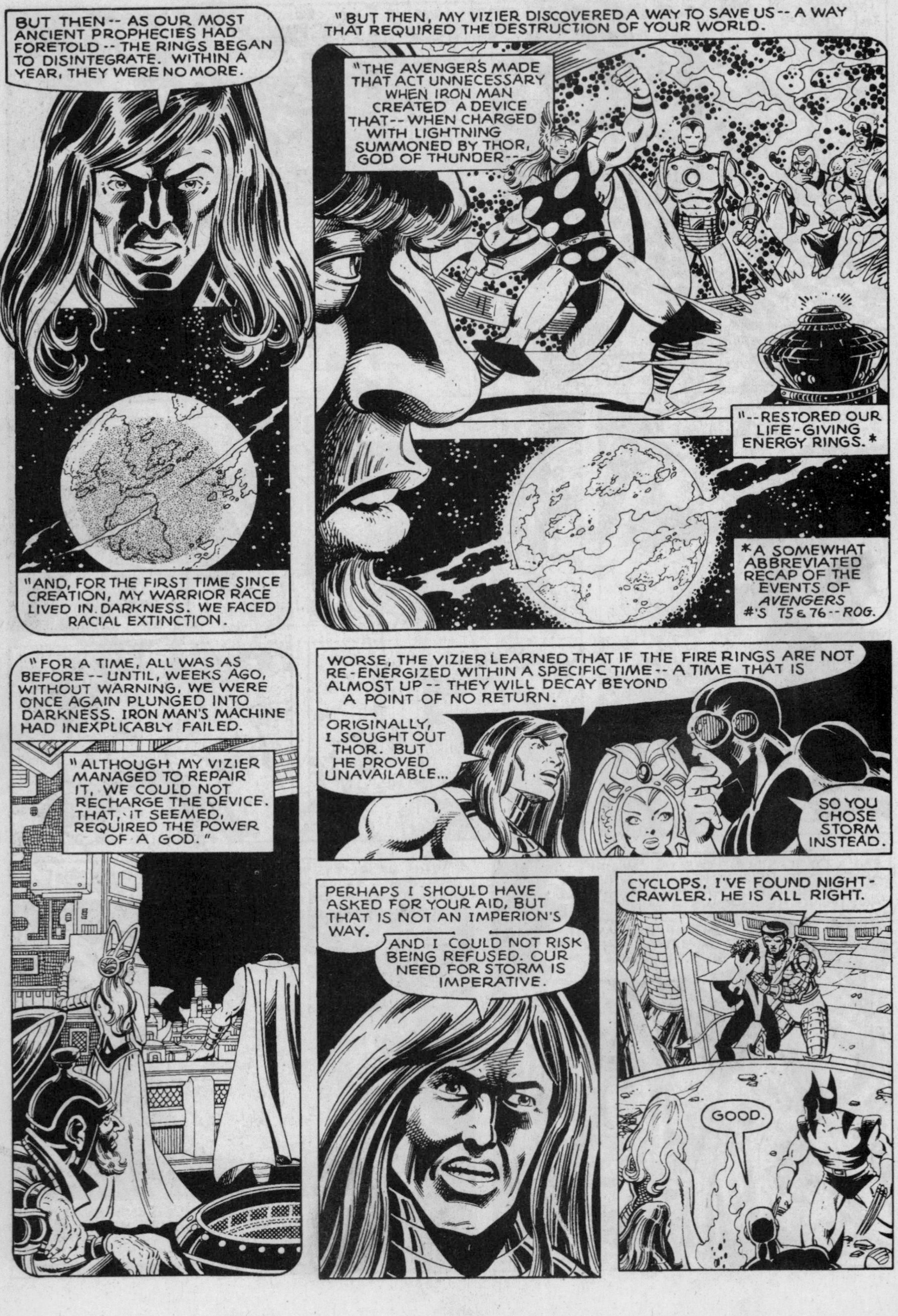

BUT THEN -- AS OUR MOST ANCIENT PROPHECIES HAD FORETOLD -- THE RINGS BEGAN TO DISINTEGRATE. WITHIN A YEAR, THEY WERE NO MORE.
"AND, FOR THE FIRST TIME SINCE CREATION, MY WARRIOR RACE LIVED IN DARKNESS. WE FACED RACIAL EXTINCTION.
"BUT THEN, MY VIZIER DISCOVERED A WAY TO SAVE US -- A WAY THAT REQUIRED THE DESTRUCTION OF YOUR WORLD.
"THE AVENGERS MADE THAT ACT UNNECESSARY WHEN IRON MAN CREATED A DEVICE THAT -- WHEN CHARGED WITH LIGHTNING SUMMONED BY THOR, GOD OF THUNDER --
"-- RESTORED OUR LIFE-GIVING ENERGY RINGS.*
*A SOMEWHAT ABBREVIATED RECAP OF THE EVENTS OF AVENGERS #'S 75 & 76 -- ROG.
"FOR A TIME, ALL WAS AS BEFORE -- UNTIL, WEEKS AGO, WITHOUT WARNING, WE WERE ONCE AGAIN PLUNGED INTO DARKNESS. IRON MAN'S MACHINE HAD INEXPLICABLY FAILED.
"ALTHOUGH MY VIZIER MANAGED TO REPAIR IT, WE COULD NOT RECHARGE THE DEVICE. THAT, IT SEEMED, REQUIRED THE POWER OF A GOD."
WORSE, THE VIZIER LEARNED THAT IF THE FIRE RINGS ARE NOT RE-ENERGIZED WITHIN A SPECIFIC TIME -- A TIME THAT IS ALMOST UP -- THEY WILL DECAY BEYOND A POINT OF NO RETURN.
ORIGINALLY, I SOUGHT OUT THOR. BUT HE PROVED UNAVAILABLE...
SO YOU CHOSE STORM INSTEAD.
PERHAPS I SHOULD HAVE ASKED FOR YOUR AID, BUT THAT IS NOT AN IMPERION'S WAY.
AND I COULD NOT RISK BEING REFUSED. OUR NEED FOR STORM IS IMPERATIVE.
CYCLOPS, I'VE FOUND NIGHT-CRAWLER. HE IS ALL RIGHT.
GOOD.

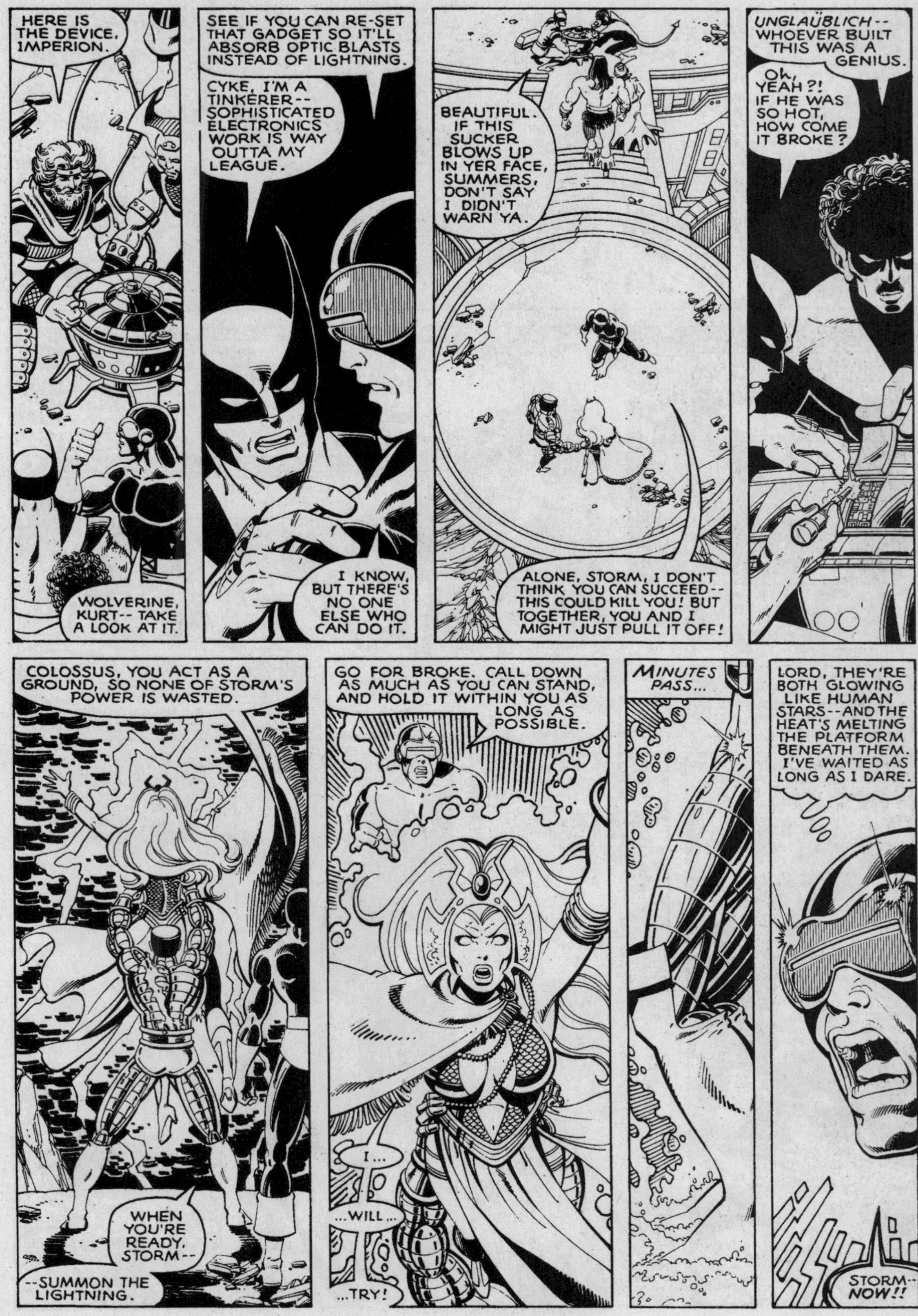
HERE IS THE DEVICE, IMPERION.
WOLVERINE, KURT-- TAKE A LOOK AT IT.
SEE IF YOU CAN RE-SET THAT GADGET SO IT'LL ABSORB OPTIC BLASTS INSTEAD OF LIGHTNING.
CYKE, I'M A TINKERER-- SOPHISTICATED ELECTRONICS WORK IS WAY OUTTA MY LEAGUE.
I KNOW, BUT THERE'S NO ONE ELSE WHO CAN DO IT.
BEAUTIFUL. IF THIS SUCKER BLOWS UP IN YER FACE, SUMMERS, DON'T SAY I DIDN'T WARN YA.
ALONE, STORM, I DON'T THINK YOU CAN SUCCEED-- THIS COULD KILL YOU! BUT TOGETHER, YOU AND I MIGHT JUST PULL IT OFF!
UNGLAÜBLICH-- WHOEVER BUILT THIS WAS A GENIUS.
OH, YEAH?! IF HE WAS SO HOT, HOW COME IT BROKE?
COLOSSUS, YOU ACT AS A GROUND, SO NONE OF STORM'S POWER IS WASTED.
WHEN YOU'RE READY, STORM--
--SUMMON THE LIGHTNING.
GO FOR BROKE. CALL DOWN AS MUCH AS YOU CAN STAND, AND HOLD IT WITHIN YOU AS LONG AS POSSIBLE.
I...
...WILL...
...TRY!
MINUTES PASS...
LORD, THEY'RE BOTH GLOWING LIKE HUMAN STARS--AND THE HEAT'S MELTING THE PLATFORM BENEATH THEM. I'VE WAITED AS LONG AS I DARE.
STORM-- NOW!!

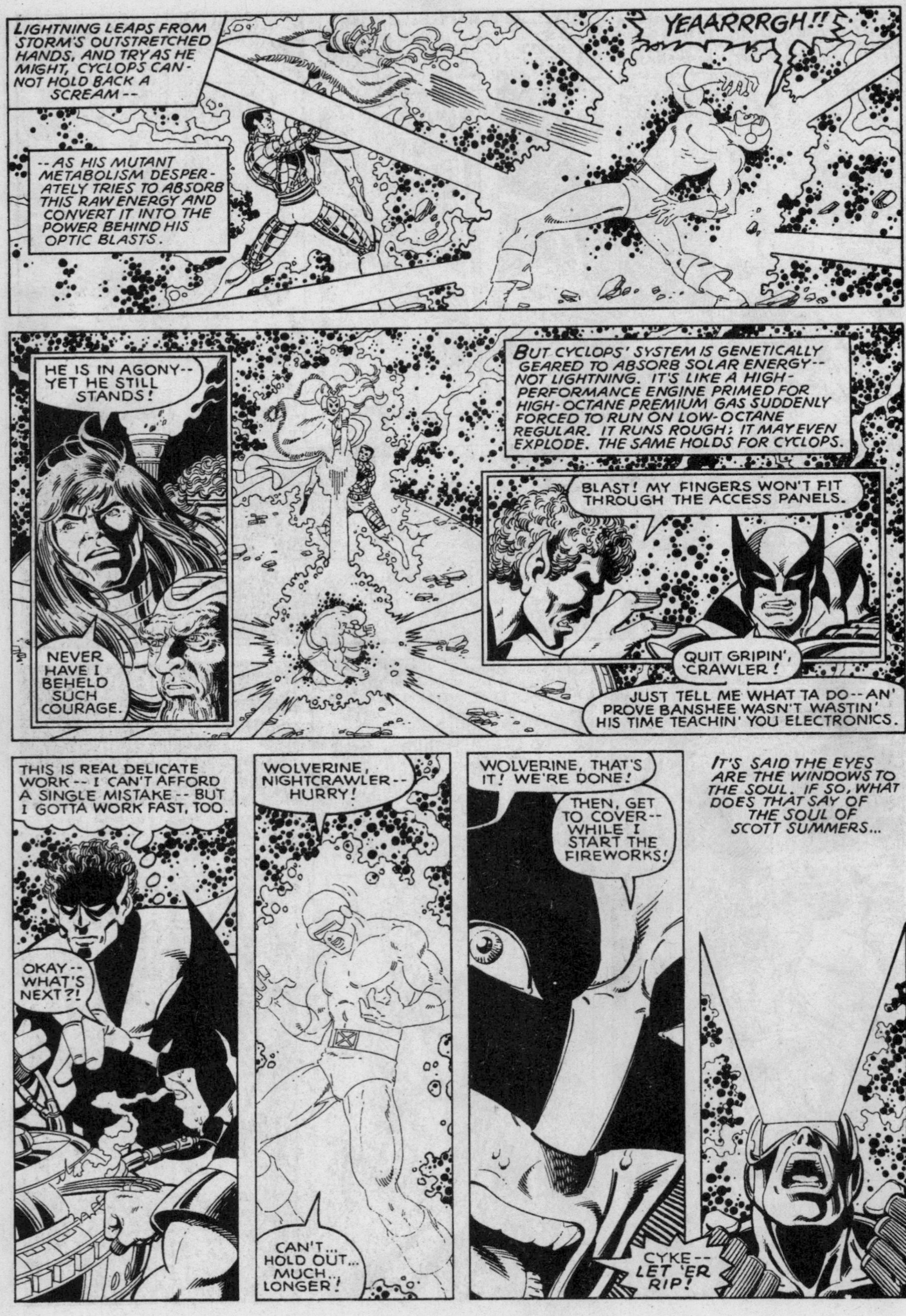

LIGHTNING LEAPS FROM STORM'S OUTSTRETCHED HANDS, AND TRY AS HE MIGHT, CYCLOPS CANNOT HOLD BACK A SCREAM --
YEAARRRGH!!
-- AS HIS MUTANT METABOLISM DESPERATELY TRIES TO ABSORB THIS RAW ENERGY AND CONVERT IT INTO THE POWER BEHIND HIS OPTIC BLASTS.
HE IS IN AGONY -- YET HE STILL STANDS!
NEVER HAVE I BEHELD SUCH COURAGE.
BUT CYCLOPS' SYSTEM IS GENETICALLY GEARED TO ABSORB SOLAR ENERGY -- NOT LIGHTNING. IT'S LIKE A HIGH-PERFORMANCE ENGINE PRIMED FOR HIGH-OCTANE PREMIUM GAS SUDDENLY FORCED TO RUN ON LOW-OCTANE REGULAR. IT RUNS ROUGH; IT MAY EVEN EXPLODE. THE SAME HOLDS FOR CYCLOPS.
BLAST! MY FINGERS WON'T FIT THROUGH THE ACCESS PANELS.
QUIT GRIPIN', 'CRAWLER!
JUST TELL ME WHAT TA DO -- AN' PROVE BANSHEE WASN'T WASTIN' HIS TIME TEACHIN' YOU ELECTRONICS.
THIS IS REAL DELICATE WORK -- I CAN'T AFFORD A SINGLE MISTAKE -- BUT I GOTTA WORK FAST, TOO.
OKAY -- WHAT'S NEXT?!
WOLVERINE, NIGHTCRAWLER -- HURRY!
CAN'T... HOLD OUT... MUCH... LONGER!
WOLVERINE, THAT'S IT! WE'RE DONE!
THEN, GET TO COVER -- WHILE I START THE FIREWORKS!
IT'S SAID THE EYES ARE THE WINDOWS TO THE SOUL. IF SO, WHAT DOES THAT SAY OF THE SOUL OF SCOTT SUMMERS...
CYKE -- LET 'ER RIP!

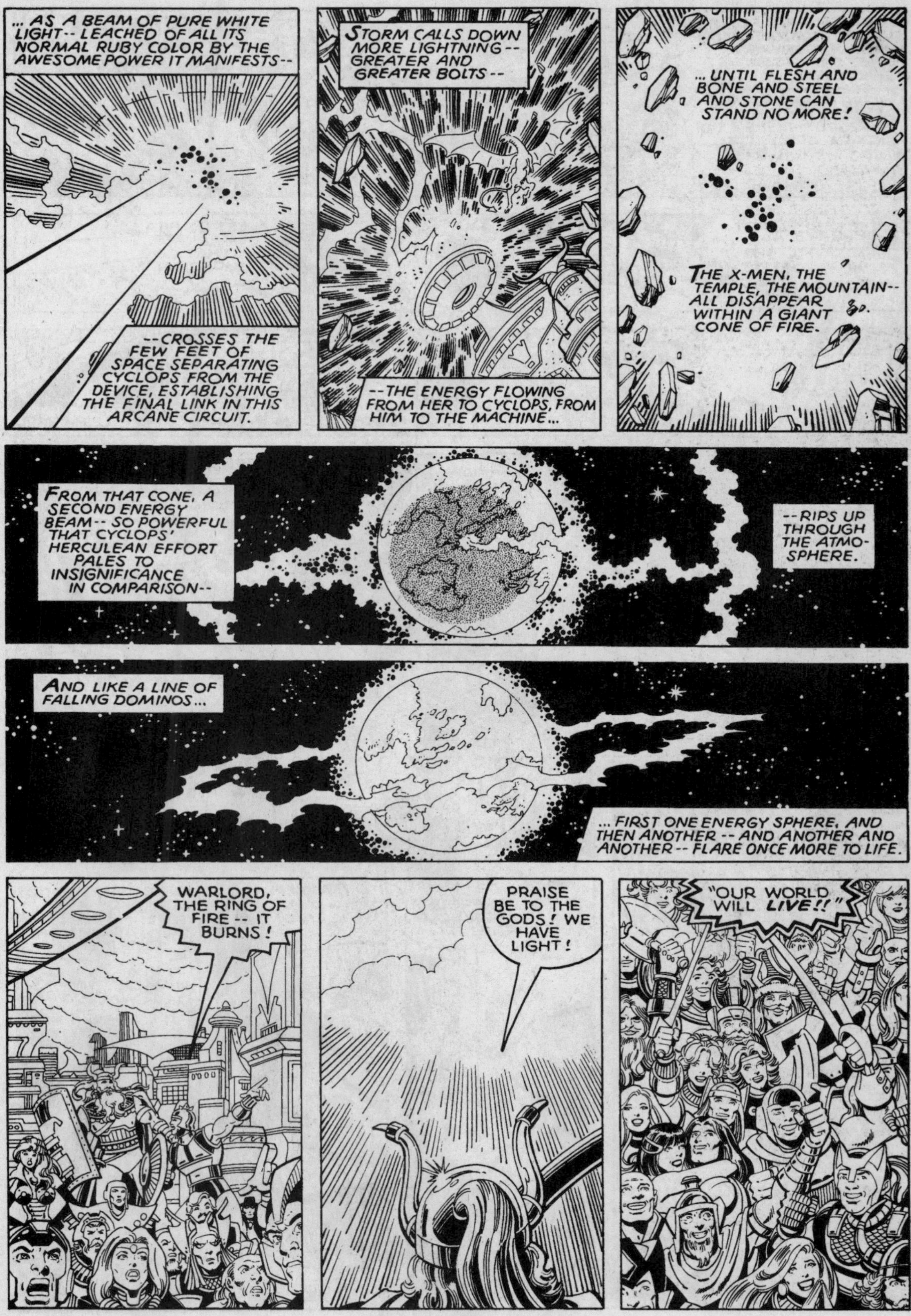

... AS A BEAM OF PURE WHITE LIGHT-- LEACHED OF ALL ITS NORMAL RUBY COLOR BY THE AWESOME POWER IT MANIFESTS--
--CROSSES THE FEW FEET OF SPACE SEPARATING CYCLOPS FROM THE DEVICE, ESTABLISHING THE FINAL LINK IN THIS ARCANE CIRCUIT.
STORM CALLS DOWN MORE LIGHTNING -- GREATER AND GREATER BOLTS --
--THE ENERGY FLOWING FROM HER TO CYCLOPS, FROM HIM TO THE MACHINE...
... UNTIL FLESH AND BONE AND STEEL AND STONE CAN STAND NO MORE!
THE X-MEN, THE TEMPLE, THE MOUNTAIN-- ALL DISAPPEAR WITHIN A GIANT CONE OF FIRE.
FROM THAT CONE, A SECOND ENERGY BEAM-- SO POWERFUL THAT CYCLOPS' HERCULEAN EFFORT PALES TO INSIGNIFICANCE IN COMPARISON--
--RIPS UP THROUGH THE ATMO-SPHERE.
AND LIKE A LINE OF FALLING DOMINOS...
... FIRST ONE ENERGY SPHERE, AND THEN ANOTHER -- AND ANOTHER AND ANOTHER -- FLARE ONCE MORE TO LIFE.
WARLORD, THE RING OF FIRE -- IT BURNS!
PRAISE BE TO THE GODS! WE HAVE LIGHT!
"OUR WORLD WILL LIVE!!"

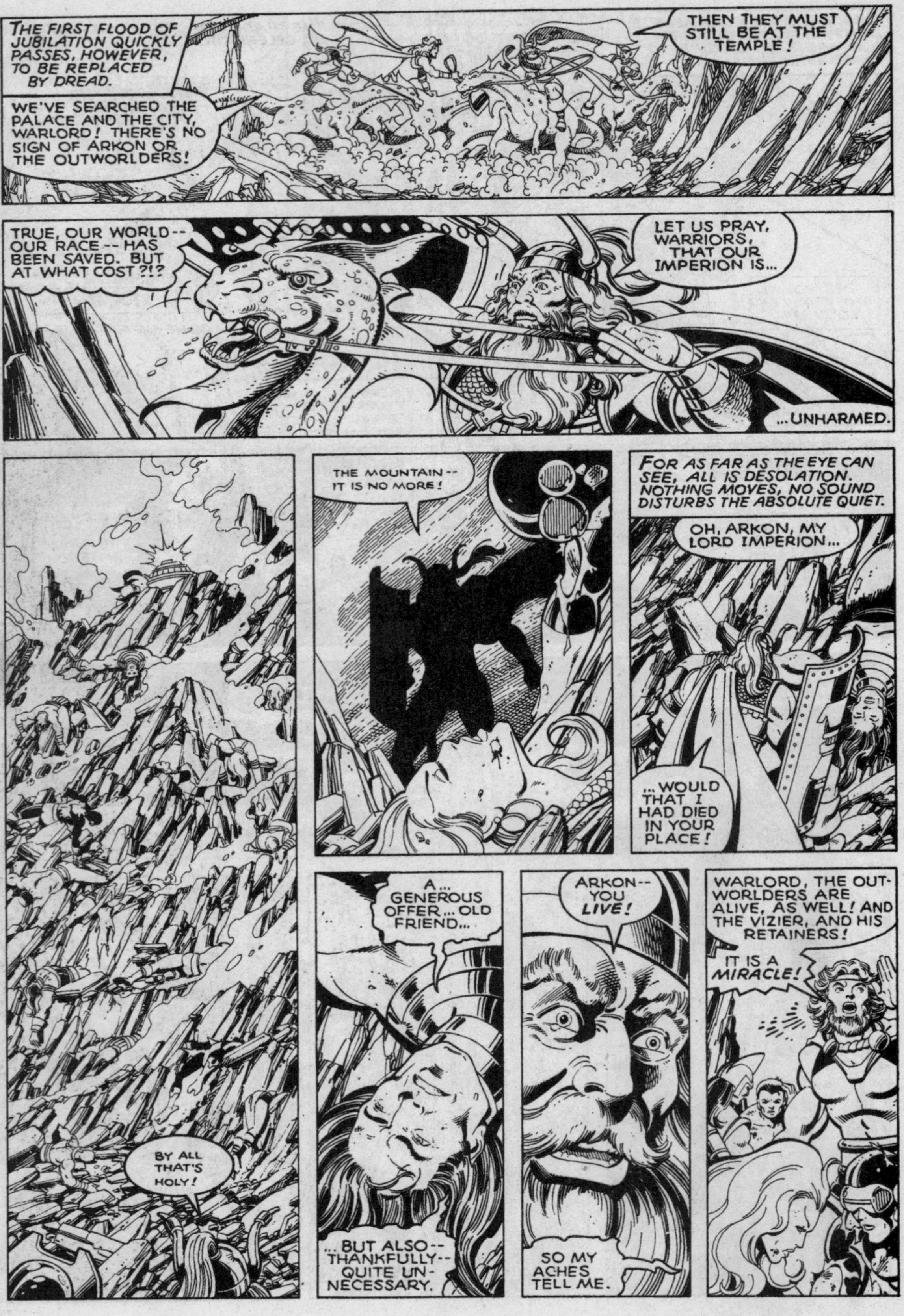

THE FIRST FLOOD OF JUBILATION QUICKLY PASSES, HOWEVER, TO BE REPLACED BY DREAD.
WE'VE SEARCHED THE PALACE AND THE CITY, WARLORD! THERE'S NO SIGN OF ARKON OR THE OUTWORLDERS!
THEN THEY MUST STILL BE AT THE TEMPLE!
TRUE, OUR WORLD-- OUR RACE-- HAS BEEN SAVED. BUT AT WHAT COST?!?
LET US PRAY, WARRIORS, THAT OUR IMPERION IS...
...UNHARMED.
BY ALL THAT'S HOLY!
THE MOUNTAIN-- IT IS NO MORE!
FOR AS FAR AS THE EYE CAN SEE, ALL IS DESOLATION. NOTHING MOVES, NO SOUND DISTURBS THE ABSOLUTE QUIET.
OH, ARKON, MY LORD IMPERION...
...WOULD THAT I HAD DIED IN YOUR PLACE!
A... GENEROUS OFFER... OLD FRIEND...
...BUT ALSO-- THANKFULLY-- QUITE UNNECESSARY.
ARKON-- YOU LIVE!
SO MY ACHES TELL ME.
WARLORD, THE OUTWORLDERS ARE ALIVE, AS WELL! AND THE VIZIER, AND HIS RETAINERS!
IT IS A MIRACLE!

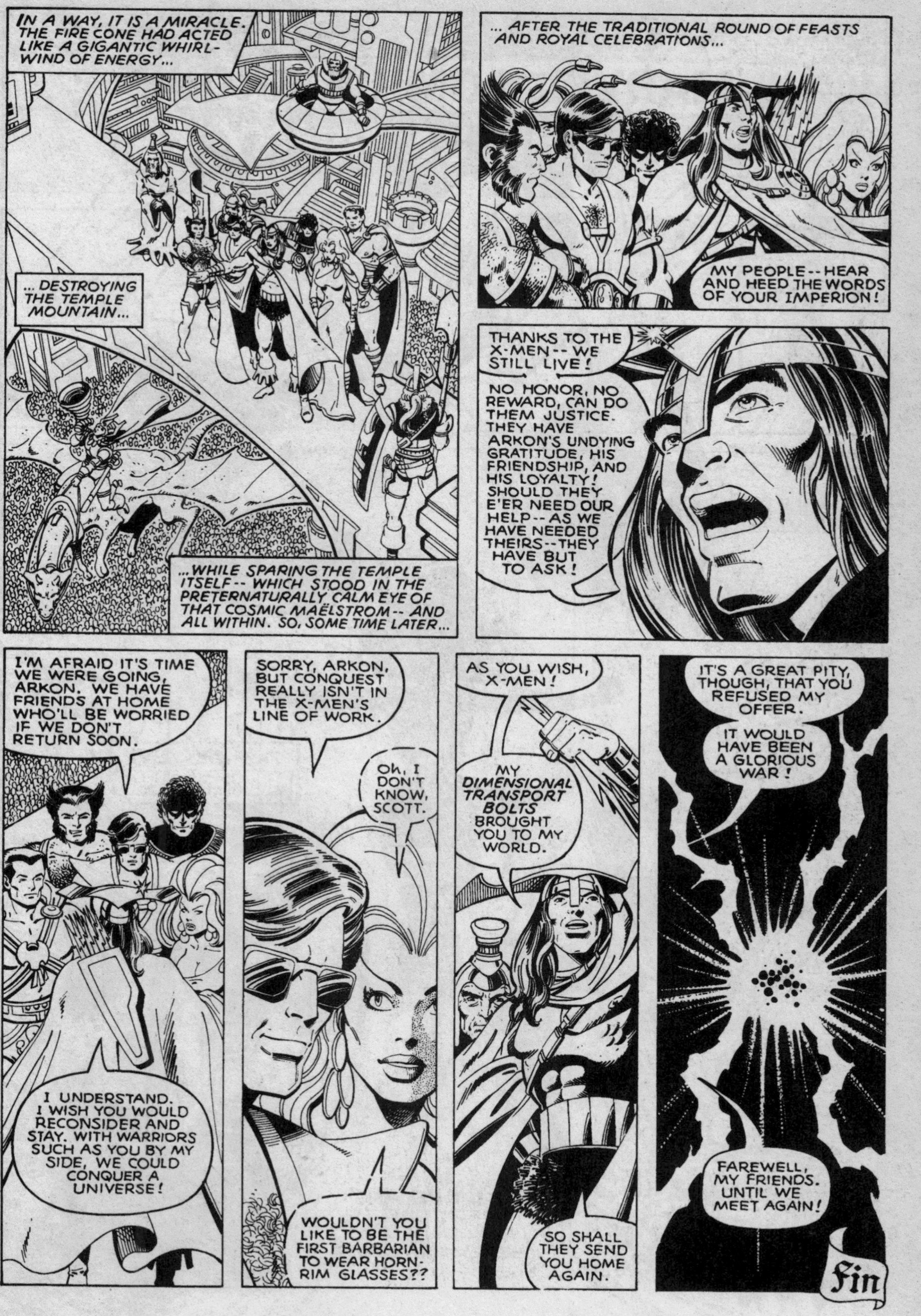

IN A WAY, IT IS A MIRACLE. THE FIRE CONE HAD ACTED LIKE A GIGANTIC WHIRL-WIND OF ENERGY...
...DESTROYING THE TEMPLE MOUNTAIN...
...WHILE SPARING THE TEMPLE ITSELF-- WHICH STOOD IN THE PRETERNATURALLY CALM EYE OF THAT COSMIC MAËLSTROM-- AND ALL WITHIN. SO, SOME TIME LATER...
...AFTER THE TRADITIONAL ROUND OF FEASTS AND ROYAL CELEBRATIONS...
MY PEOPLE--HEAR AND HEED THE WORDS OF YOUR IMPERION!
THANKS TO THE X-MEN-- WE STILL LIVE!
NO HONOR, NO REWARD, CAN DO THEM JUSTICE. THEY HAVE ARKON'S UNDYING GRATITUDE, HIS FRIENDSHIP, AND HIS LOYALTY! SHOULD THEY E'ER NEED OUR HELP-- AS WE HAVE NEEDED THEIRS-- THEY HAVE BUT TO ASK!
I'M AFRAID IT'S TIME WE WERE GOING, ARKON. WE HAVE FRIENDS AT HOME WHO'LL BE WORRIED IF WE DON'T RETURN SOON.
I UNDERSTAND. I WISH YOU WOULD RECONSIDER AND STAY. WITH WARRIORS SUCH AS YOU BY MY SIDE, WE COULD CONQUER A UNIVERSE!
SORRY, ARKON, BUT CONQUEST REALLY ISN'T IN THE X-MEN'S LINE OF WORK.
Oh, I DON'T KNOW, SCOTT.
WOULDN'T YOU LIKE TO BE THE FIRST BARBARIAN TO WEAR HORN-RIM GLASSES??
AS YOU WISH, X-MEN!
MY DIMENSIONAL TRANSPORT BOLTS BROUGHT YOU TO MY WORLD.
SO SHALL THEY SEND YOU HOME AGAIN.
IT'S A GREAT PITY, THOUGH, THAT YOU REFUSED MY OFFER.
IT WOULD HAVE BEEN A GLORIOUS WAR!
FAREWELL, MY FRIENDS. UNTIL WE MEET AGAIN!
Fin

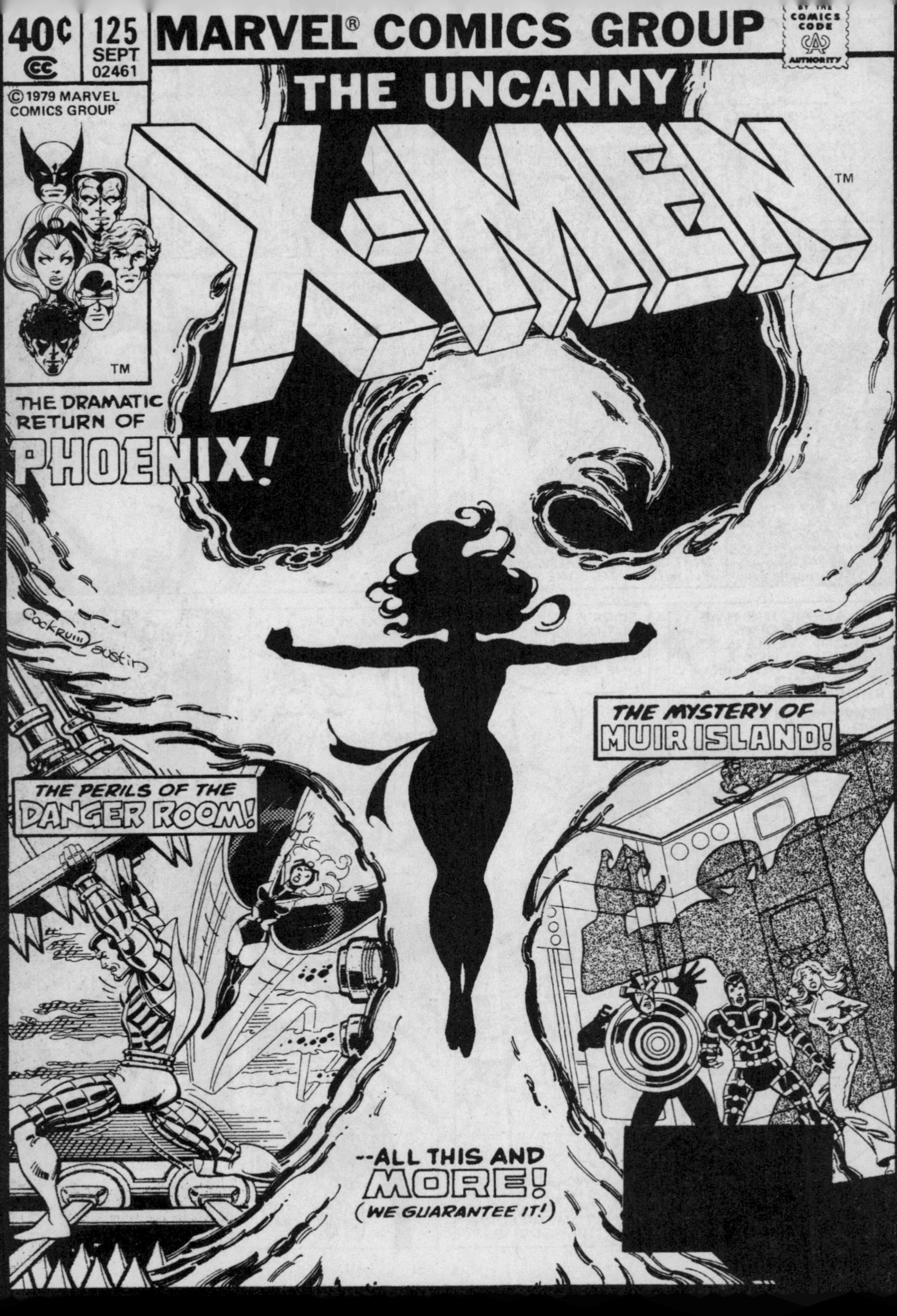
40¢
125
SEPT
02461
MARVEL® COMICS GROUP
APPROVED BY THE COMICS CODE AUTHORITY
© 1979 MARVEL COMICS GROUP
THE UNCANNY
X-MEN™
THE DRAMATIC RETURN OF
PHOENIX!
Cockrum / austin
THE MYSTERY OF
MUIR ISLAND!
THE PERILS OF THE
DANGER ROOM!
--ALL THIS AND
MORE!
(WE GUARANTEE IT!)

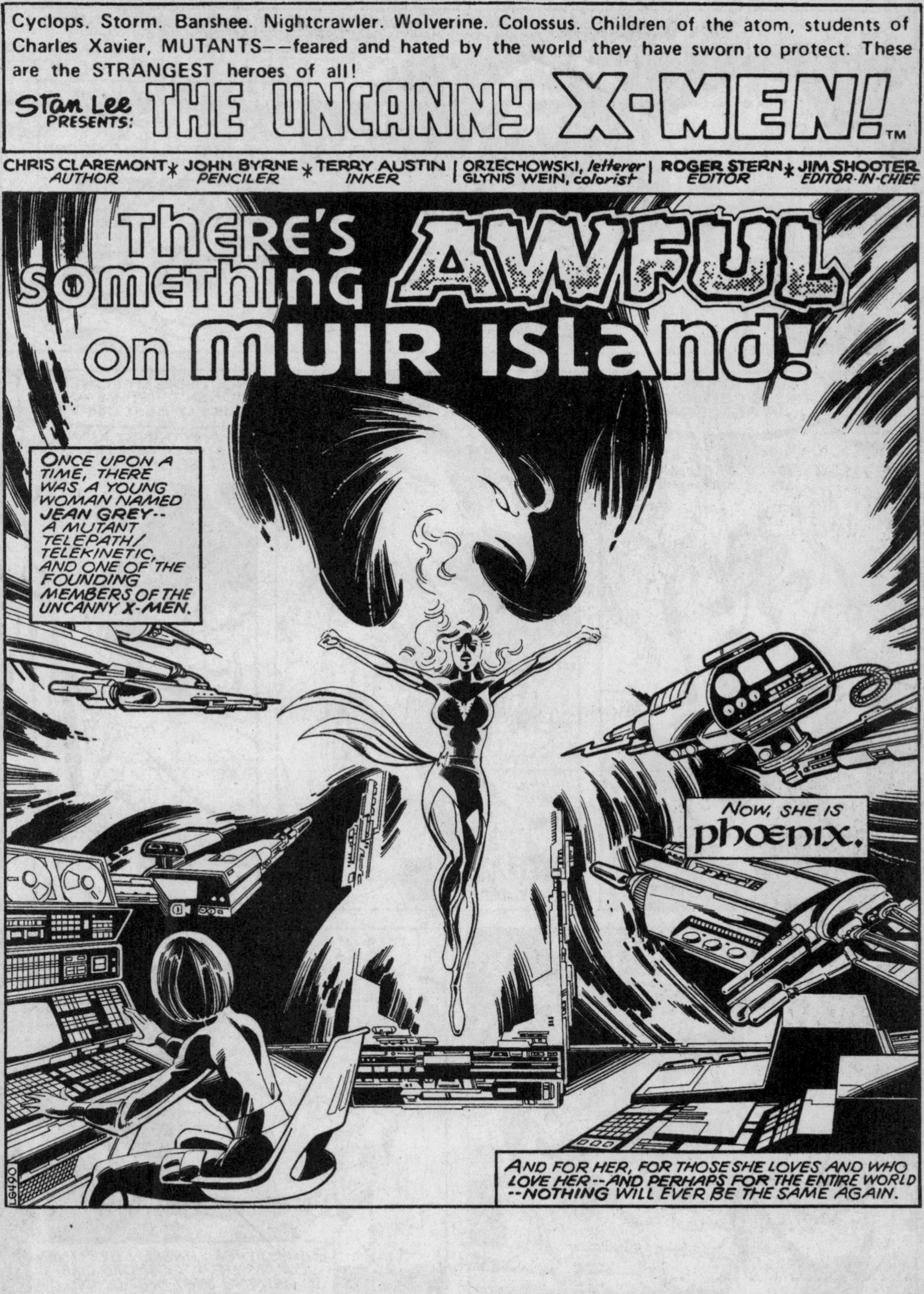
Cyclops. Storm. Banshee. Nightcrawler. Wolverine. Colossus. Children of the atom, students of Charles Xavier, MUTANTS--feared and hated by the world they have sworn to protect. These are the STRANGEST heroes of all!
STAN LEE PRESENTS: THE UNCANNY X-MEN!™
CHRIS CLAREMONT * AUTHOR
JOHN BYRNE * PENCILER
TERRY AUSTIN * INKER
ORZECHOWSKI, letterer | GLYNIS WEIN, colorist
ROGER STERN * EDITOR
JIM SHOOTER * EDITOR-IN-CHIEF
THERE'S SOMETHING AWFUL ON MUIR ISLAND!
ONCE UPON A TIME, THERE WAS A YOUNG WOMAN NAMED JEAN GREY-- A MUTANT TELEPATH/ TELEKINETIC, AND ONE OF THE FOUNDING MEMBERS OF THE UNCANNY X-MEN.
NOW, SHE IS PHOENIX.
AND FOR HER, FOR THOSE SHE LOVES AND WHO LOVE HER--AND PERHAPS FOR THE ENTIRE WORLD --NOTHING WILL EVER BE THE SAME AGAIN.

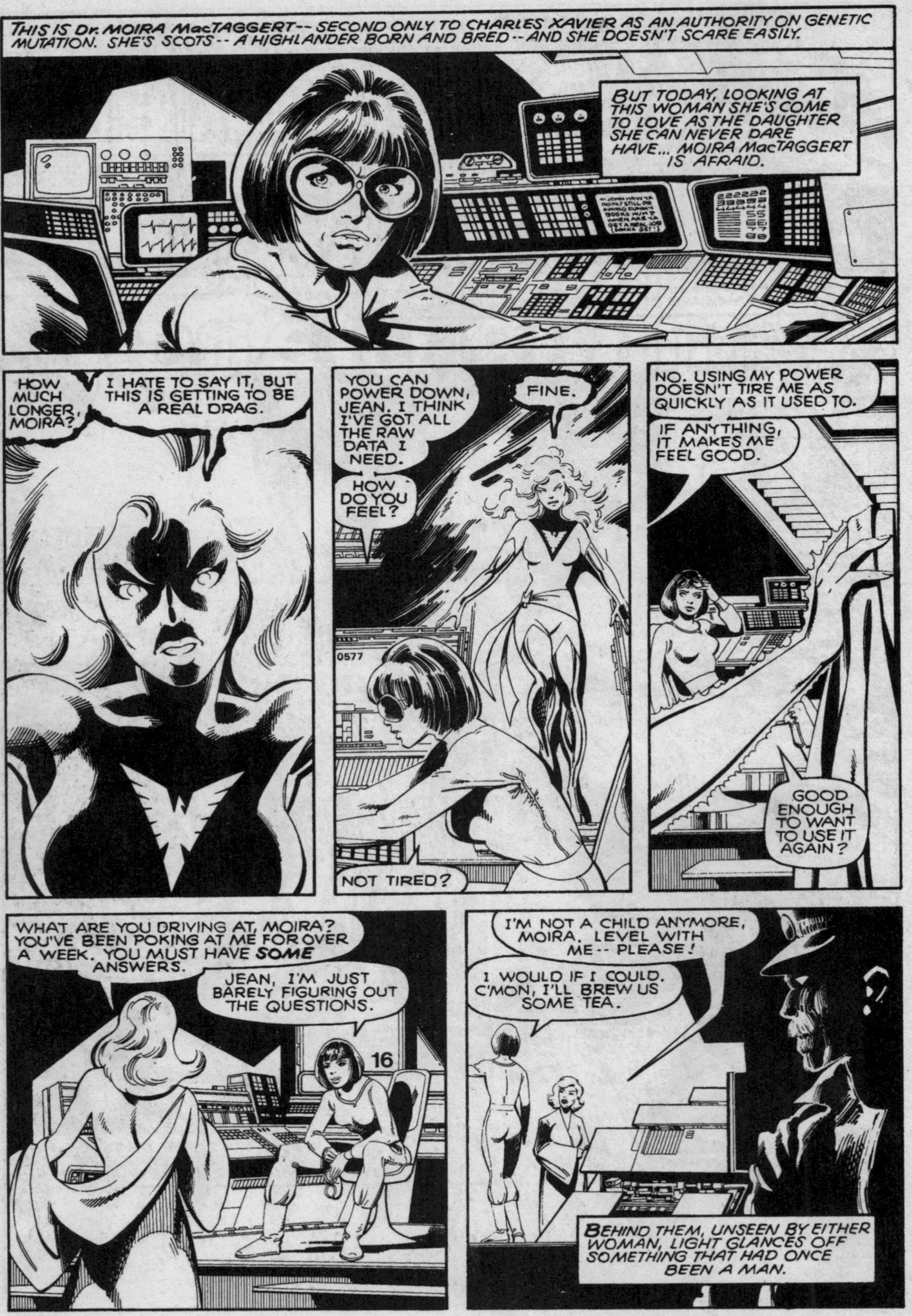
THIS IS Dr. MOIRA MacTAGGERT-- SECOND ONLY TO CHARLES XAVIER AS AN AUTHORITY ON GENETIC MUTATION. SHE'S SCOTS-- A HIGHLANDER BORN AND BRED-- AND SHE DOESN'T SCARE EASILY.
BUT TODAY, LOOKING AT THIS WOMAN SHE'S COME TO LOVE AS THE DAUGHTER SHE CAN NEVER DARE HAVE... MOIRA MacTAGGERT IS AFRAID.
HOW MUCH LONGER, MOIRA?
I HATE TO SAY IT, BUT THIS IS GETTING TO BE A REAL DRAG.
YOU CAN POWER DOWN, JEAN. I THINK I'VE GOT ALL THE RAW DATA I NEED.
FINE.
HOW DO YOU FEEL?
0577
NOT TIRED?
NO. USING MY POWER DOESN'T TIRE ME AS QUICKLY AS IT USED TO.
IF ANYTHING, IT MAKES ME FEEL GOOD.
GOOD ENOUGH TO WANT TO USE IT AGAIN?
WHAT ARE YOU DRIVING AT, MOIRA? YOU'VE BEEN POKING AT ME FOR OVER A WEEK. YOU MUST HAVE SOME ANSWERS.
JEAN, I'M JUST BARELY FIGURING OUT THE QUESTIONS.
16
I'M NOT A CHILD ANYMORE, MOIRA. LEVEL WITH ME-- PLEASE!
I WOULD IF I COULD. C'MON, I'LL BREW US SOME TEA.
BEHIND THEM, UNSEEN BY EITHER WOMAN, LIGHT GLANCES OFF SOMETHING THAT HAD ONCE BEEN A MAN.

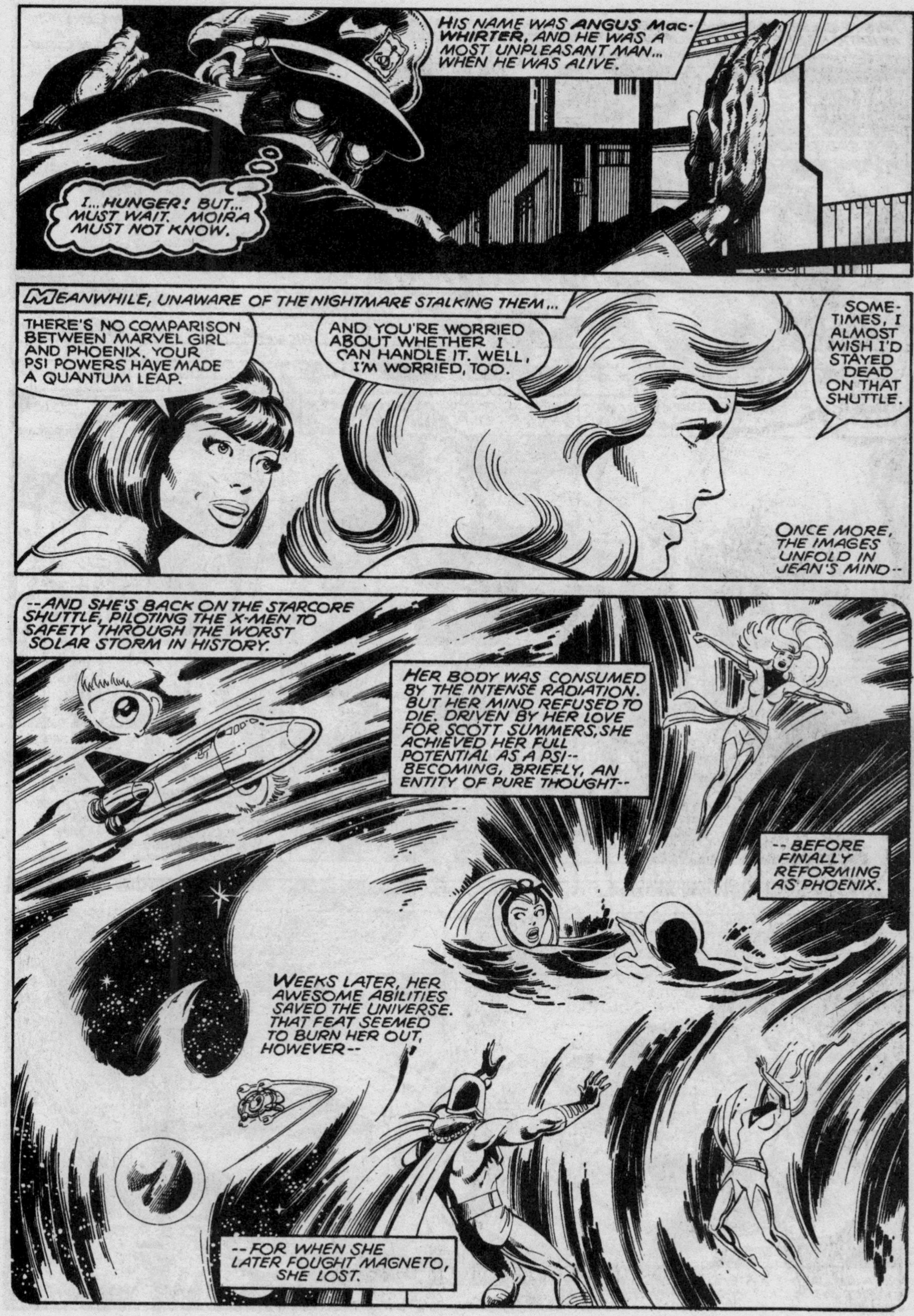
HIS NAME WAS ANGUS MacWHIRTER, AND HE WAS A MOST UNPLEASANT MAN... WHEN HE WAS ALIVE.
I... HUNGER! BUT... MUST WAIT. MOIRA MUST NOT KNOW.
MEANWHILE, UNAWARE OF THE NIGHTMARE STALKING THEM...
THERE'S NO COMPARISON BETWEEN MARVEL GIRL AND PHOENIX. YOUR PSI POWERS HAVE MADE A QUANTUM LEAP.
AND YOU'RE WORRIED ABOUT WHETHER I CAN HANDLE IT. WELL, I'M WORRIED, TOO.
SOMETIMES, I ALMOST WISH I'D STAYED DEAD ON THAT SHUTTLE.
ONCE MORE, THE IMAGES UNFOLD IN JEAN'S MIND--
--AND SHE'S BACK ON THE STARCORE SHUTTLE, PILOTING THE X-MEN TO SAFETY THROUGH THE WORST SOLAR STORM IN HISTORY.
HER BODY WAS CONSUMED BY THE INTENSE RADIATION. BUT HER MIND REFUSED TO DIE. DRIVEN BY HER LOVE FOR SCOTT SUMMERS, SHE ACHIEVED HER FULL POTENTIAL AS A PSI-- BECOMING, BRIEFLY, AN ENTITY OF PURE THOUGHT--
--BEFORE FINALLY REFORMING AS PHOENIX.
WEEKS LATER, HER AWESOME ABILITIES SAVED THE UNIVERSE. THAT FEAT SEEMED TO BURN HER OUT, HOWEVER--
--FOR WHEN SHE LATER FOUGHT MAGNETO, SHE LOST.

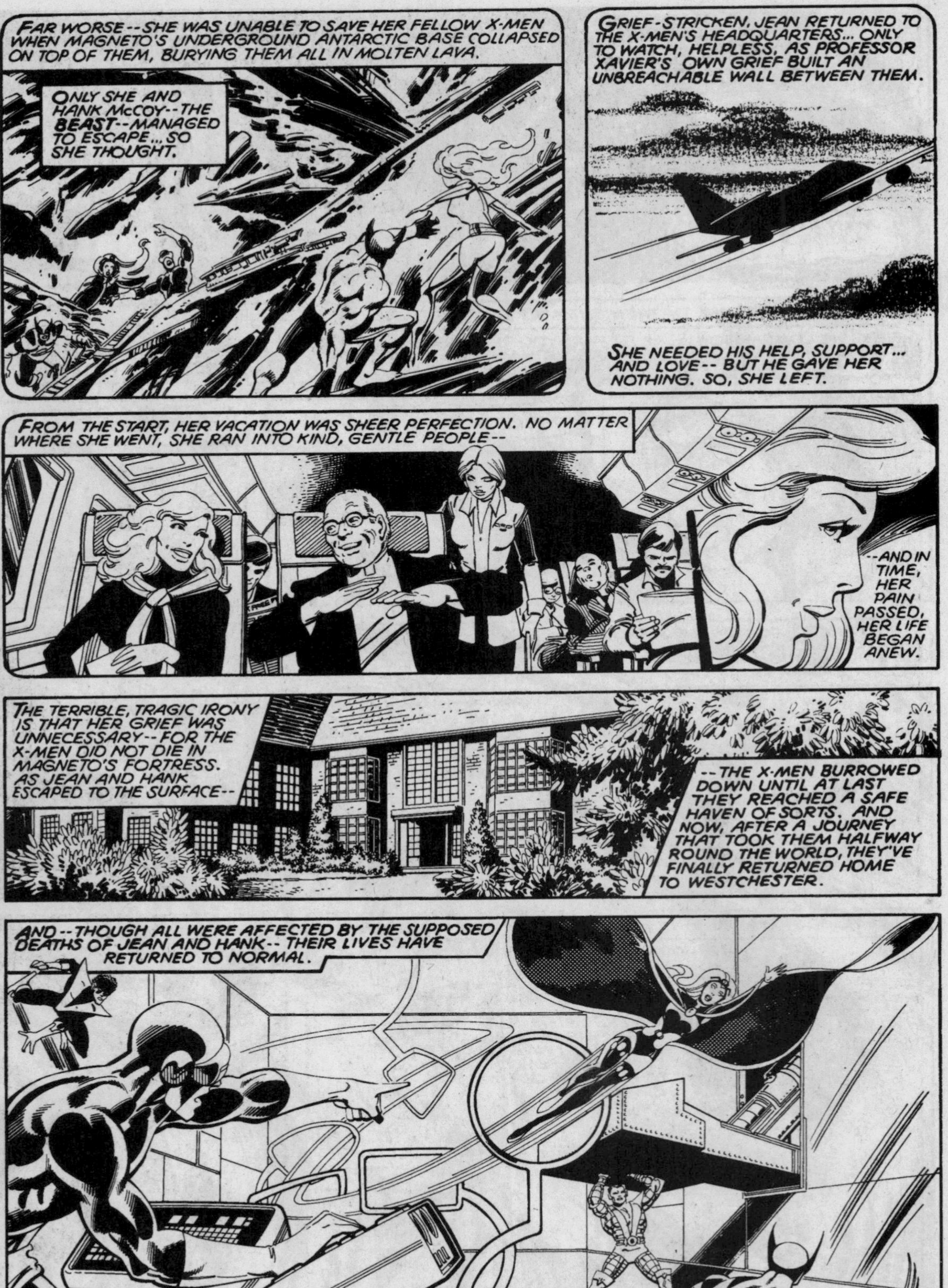
FAR WORSE--SHE WAS UNABLE TO SAVE HER FELLOW X-MEN WHEN MAGNETO'S UNDERGROUND ANTARCTIC BASE COLLAPSED ON TOP OF THEM, BURYING THEM ALL IN MOLTEN LAVA.
ONLY SHE AND HANK McCOY--THE BEAST--MANAGED TO ESCAPE... SO SHE THOUGHT.
GRIEF-STRICKEN, JEAN RETURNED TO THE X-MEN'S HEADQUARTERS... ONLY TO WATCH, HELPLESS, AS PROFESSOR XAVIER'S OWN GRIEF BUILT AN UNBREACHABLE WALL BETWEEN THEM.
SHE NEEDED HIS HELP, SUPPORT... AND LOVE--BUT HE GAVE HER NOTHING. SO, SHE LEFT.
FROM THE START, HER VACATION WAS SHEER PERFECTION. NO MATTER WHERE SHE WENT, SHE RAN INTO KIND, GENTLE PEOPLE--
--AND IN TIME, HER PAIN PASSED, HER LIFE BEGAN ANEW.
THE TERRIBLE, TRAGIC IRONY IS THAT HER GRIEF WAS UNNECESSARY--FOR THE X-MEN DID NOT DIE IN MAGNETO'S FORTRESS. AS JEAN AND HANK ESCAPED TO THE SURFACE--
--THE X-MEN BURROWED DOWN UNTIL AT LAST THEY REACHED A SAFE HAVEN OF SORTS. AND NOW, AFTER A JOURNEY THAT TOOK THEM HALFWAY ROUND THE WORLD, THEY'VE FINALLY RETURNED HOME TO WESTCHESTER.
AND--THOUGH ALL WERE AFFECTED BY THE SUPPOSED DEATHS OF JEAN AND HANK--THEIR LIVES HAVE RETURNED TO NORMAL.
WHICH, IN THE X-MEN'S CASE, MEANS A DAILY WORK-OUT IN THE DANGER ROOM.

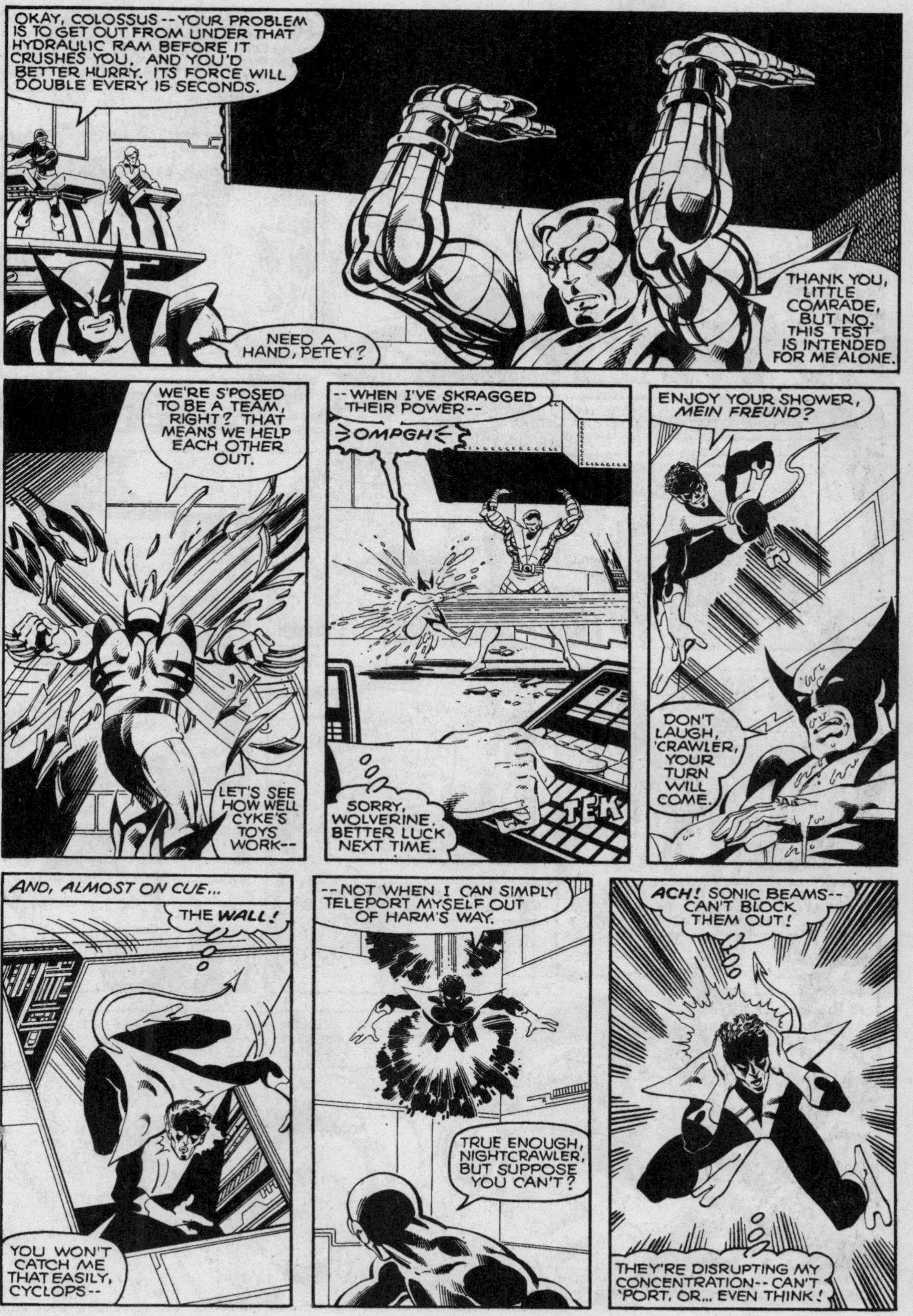

OKAY, COLOSSUS--YOUR PROBLEM IS TO GET OUT FROM UNDER THAT HYDRAULIC RAM BEFORE IT CRUSHES YOU. AND YOU'D BETTER HURRY. ITS FORCE WILL DOUBLE EVERY 15 SECONDS.
NEED A HAND, PETEY?
THANK YOU, LITTLE COMRADE, BUT NO. THIS TEST IS INTENDED FOR ME ALONE.
WE'RE S'POSED TO BE A TEAM, RIGHT? THAT MEANS WE HELP EACH OTHER OUT.
LET'S SEE HOW WELL CYKE'S TOYS WORK--
--WHEN I'VE SKRAGGED THEIR POWER--
OMPGH
SORRY, WOLVERINE. BETTER LUCK NEXT TIME.
TEK
ENJOY YOUR SHOWER, MEIN FREUND?
DON'T LAUGH, 'CRAWLER, YOUR TURN WILL COME.
AND, ALMOST ON CUE...
THE WALL!
YOU WON'T CATCH ME THAT EASILY, CYCLOPS--
--NOT WHEN I CAN SIMPLY TELEPORT MYSELF OUT OF HARM'S WAY.
TRUE ENOUGH, NIGHTCRAWLER, BUT SUPPOSE YOU CAN'T?
ACH! SONIC BEAMS--CAN'T BLOCK THEM OUT!
THEY'RE DISRUPTING MY CONCENTRATION--CAN'T 'PORT, OR... EVEN THINK!

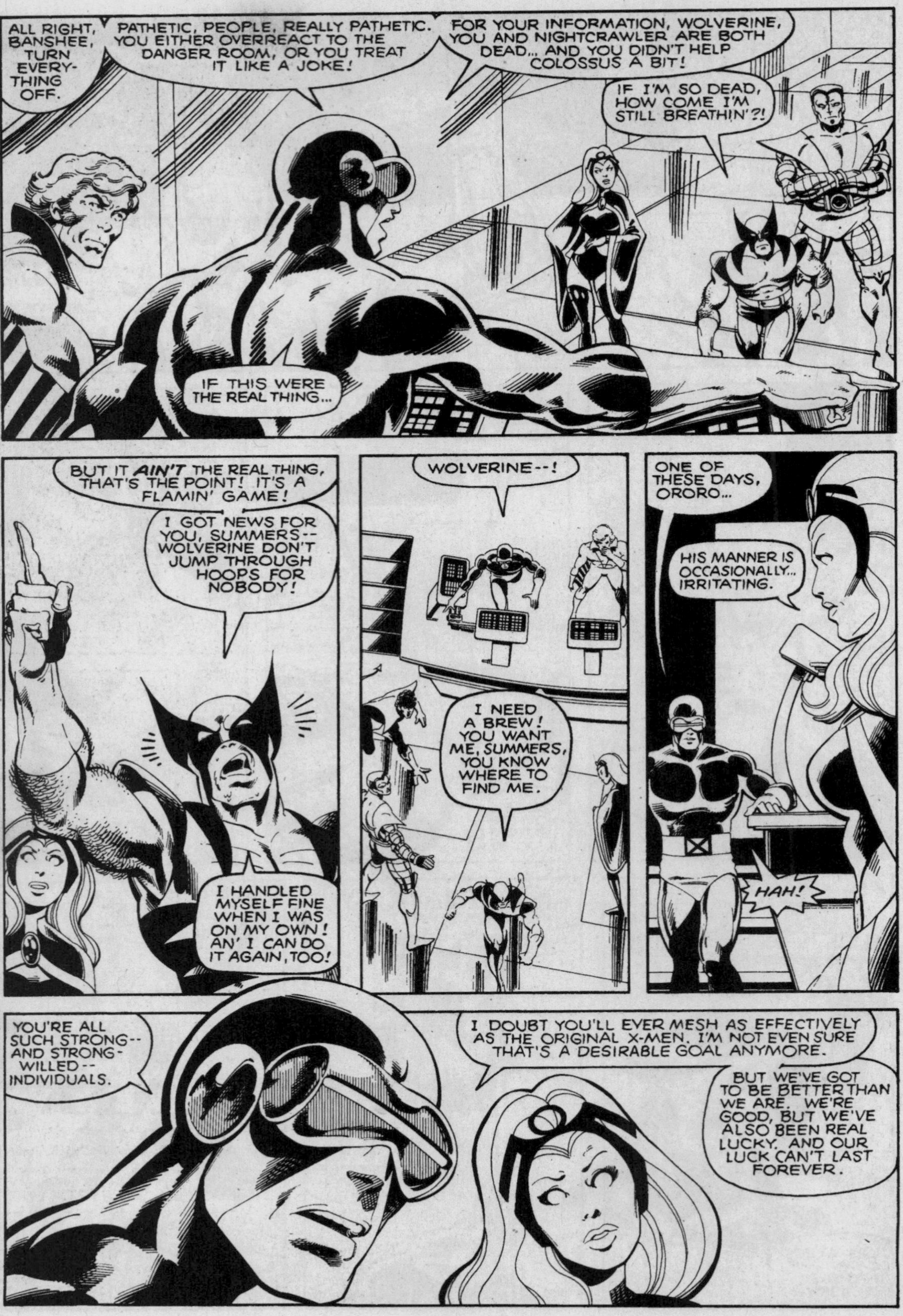
ALL RIGHT, BANSHEE, TURN EVERYTHING OFF.
PATHETIC, PEOPLE, REALLY PATHETIC. YOU EITHER OVERREACT TO THE DANGER ROOM, OR YOU TREAT IT LIKE A JOKE!
FOR YOUR INFORMATION, WOLVERINE, YOU AND NIGHTCRAWLER ARE BOTH DEAD... AND YOU DIDN'T HELP COLOSSUS A BIT!
IF THIS WERE THE REAL THING...
IF I'M SO DEAD, HOW COME I'M STILL BREATHIN'?!
BUT IT AIN'T THE REAL THING, THAT'S THE POINT! IT'S A FLAMIN' GAME!
I GOT NEWS FOR YOU, SUMMERS-- WOLVERINE DON'T JUMP THROUGH HOOPS FOR NOBODY!
I HANDLED MYSELF FINE WHEN I WAS ON MY OWN! AN' I CAN DO IT AGAIN, TOO!
WOLVERINE--!
I NEED A BREW! YOU WANT ME, SUMMERS, YOU KNOW WHERE TO FIND ME.
ONE OF THESE DAYS, ORORO...
HIS MANNER IS OCCASIONALLY... IRRITATING.
HAH!
YOU'RE ALL SUCH STRONG-- AND STRONG-WILLED-- INDIVIDUALS.
I DOUBT YOU'LL EVER MESH AS EFFECTIVELY AS THE ORIGINAL X-MEN. I'M NOT EVEN SURE THAT'S A DESIRABLE GOAL ANYMORE.
BUT WE'VE GOT TO BE BETTER THAN WE ARE. WE'RE GOOD, BUT WE'VE ALSO BEEN REAL LUCKY. AND OUR LUCK CAN'T LAST FOREVER.

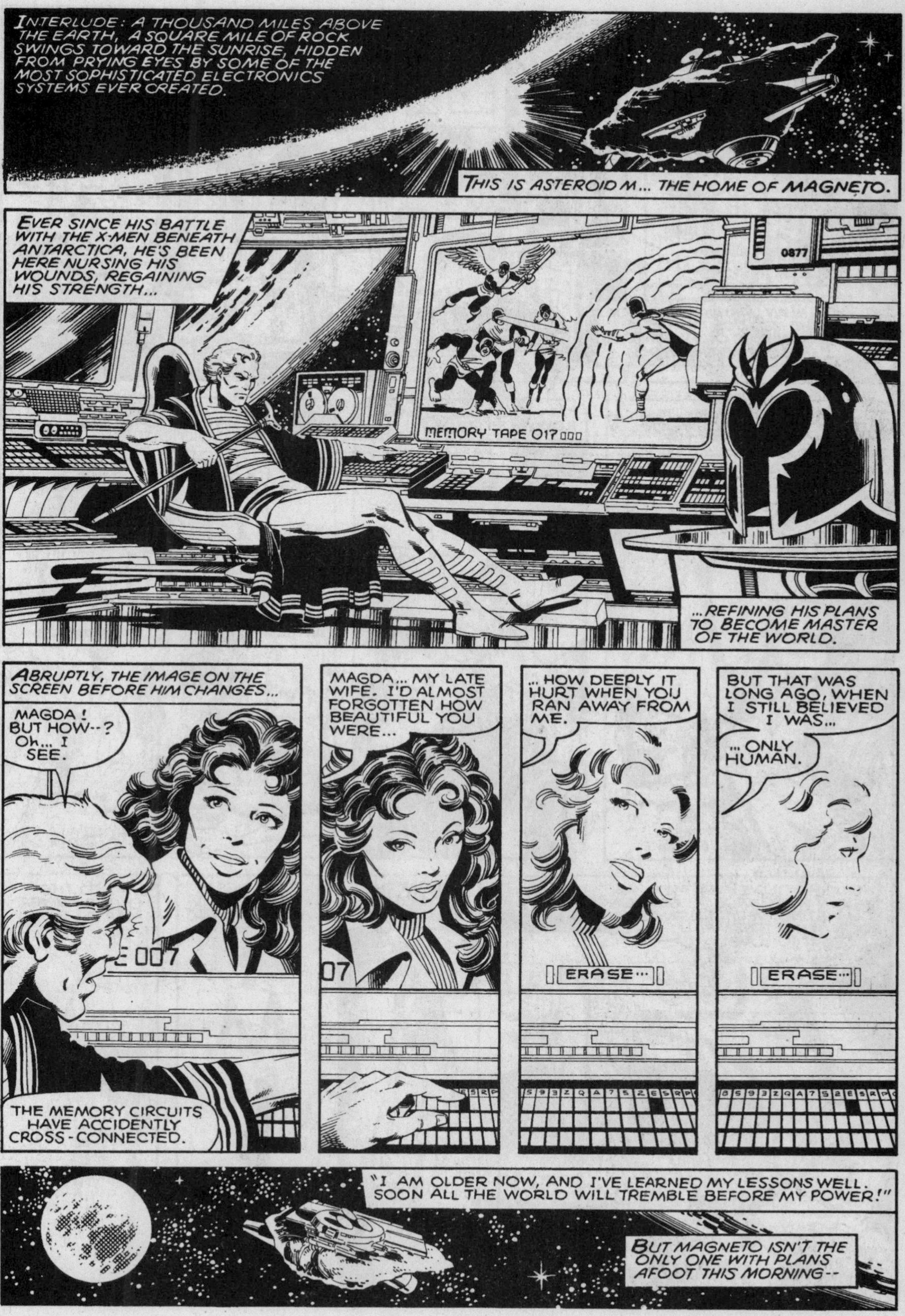
INTERLUDE: A THOUSAND MILES ABOVE THE EARTH, A SQUARE MILE OF ROCK SWINGS TOWARD THE SUNRISE, HIDDEN FROM PRYING EYES BY SOME OF THE MOST SOPHISTICATED ELECTRONICS SYSTEMS EVER CREATED.
THIS IS ASTEROID M... THE HOME OF MAGNETO.
EVER SINCE HIS BATTLE WITH THE X-MEN BENEATH ANTARCTICA, HE'S BEEN HERE NURSING HIS WOUNDS, REGAINING HIS STRENGTH...
0877
MEMORY TAPE 017
...REFINING HIS PLANS TO BECOME MASTER OF THE WORLD.
ABRUPTLY, THE IMAGE ON THE SCREEN BEFORE HIM CHANGES...
MAGDA! BUT HOW--? OH... I SEE.
THE MEMORY CIRCUITS HAVE ACCIDENTLY CROSS-CONNECTED.
MAGDA... MY LATE WIFE. I'D ALMOST FORGOTTEN HOW BEAUTIFUL YOU WERE...
... HOW DEEPLY IT HURT WHEN YOU RAN AWAY FROM ME.
ERASE...
BUT THAT WAS LONG AGO, WHEN I STILL BELIEVED I WAS...
... ONLY HUMAN.
ERASE...
"I AM OLDER NOW, AND I'VE LEARNED MY LESSONS WELL. SOON ALL THE WORLD WILL TREMBLE BEFORE MY POWER!"
BUT MAGNETO ISN'T THE ONLY ONE WITH PLANS AFOOT THIS MORNING--

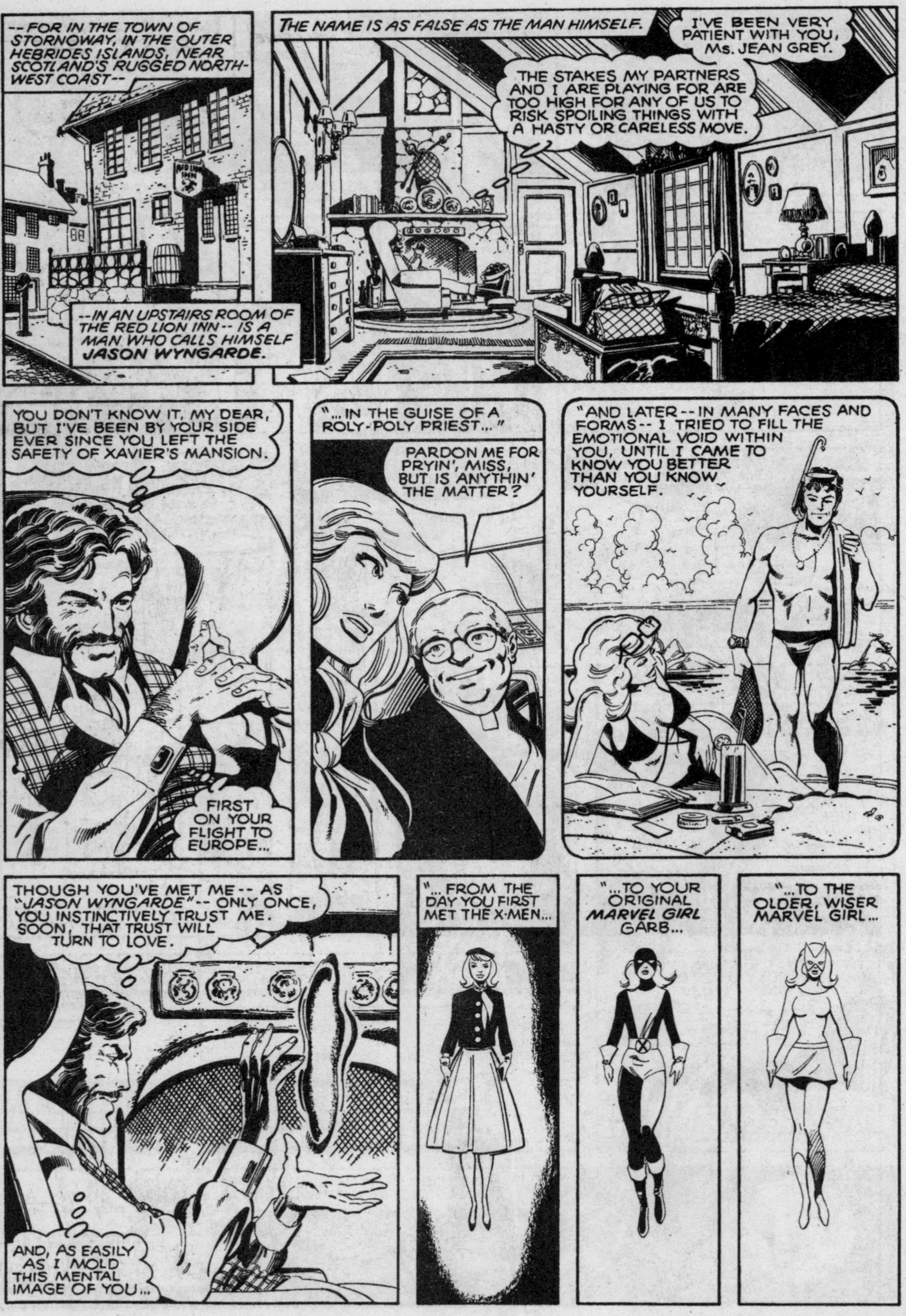
--FOR IN THE TOWN OF STORNOWAY, IN THE OUTER HEBRIDES ISLANDS, NEAR SCOTLAND'S RUGGED NORTH-WEST COAST--
RED LION INN
--IN AN UPSTAIRS ROOM OF THE RED LION INN-- IS A MAN WHO CALLS HIMSELF JASON WYNGARDE.
THE NAME IS AS FALSE AS THE MAN HIMSELF.
I'VE BEEN VERY PATIENT WITH YOU, Ms. JEAN GREY.
THE STAKES MY PARTNERS AND I ARE PLAYING FOR ARE TOO HIGH FOR ANY OF US TO RISK SPOILING THINGS WITH A HASTY OR CARELESS MOVE.
YOU DON'T KNOW IT, MY DEAR, BUT I'VE BEEN BY YOUR SIDE EVER SINCE YOU LEFT THE SAFETY OF XAVIER'S MANSION.
FIRST ON YOUR FLIGHT TO EUROPE...
"...IN THE GUISE OF A ROLY-POLY PRIEST..."
PARDON ME FOR PRYIN', MISS, BUT IS ANYTHIN' THE MATTER?
"AND LATER-- IN MANY FACES AND FORMS-- I TRIED TO FILL THE EMOTIONAL VOID WITHIN YOU, UNTIL I CAME TO KNOW YOU BETTER THAN YOU KNOW YOURSELF.
THOUGH YOU'VE MET ME-- AS "JASON WYNGARDE"-- ONLY ONCE, YOU INSTINCTIVELY TRUST ME. SOON, THAT TRUST WILL TURN TO LOVE.
AND, AS EASILY AS I MOLD THIS MENTAL IMAGE OF YOU...
"...FROM THE DAY YOU FIRST MET THE X-MEN...
"...TO YOUR ORIGINAL MARVEL GIRL GARB...
"...TO THE OLDER, WISER MARVEL GIRL...

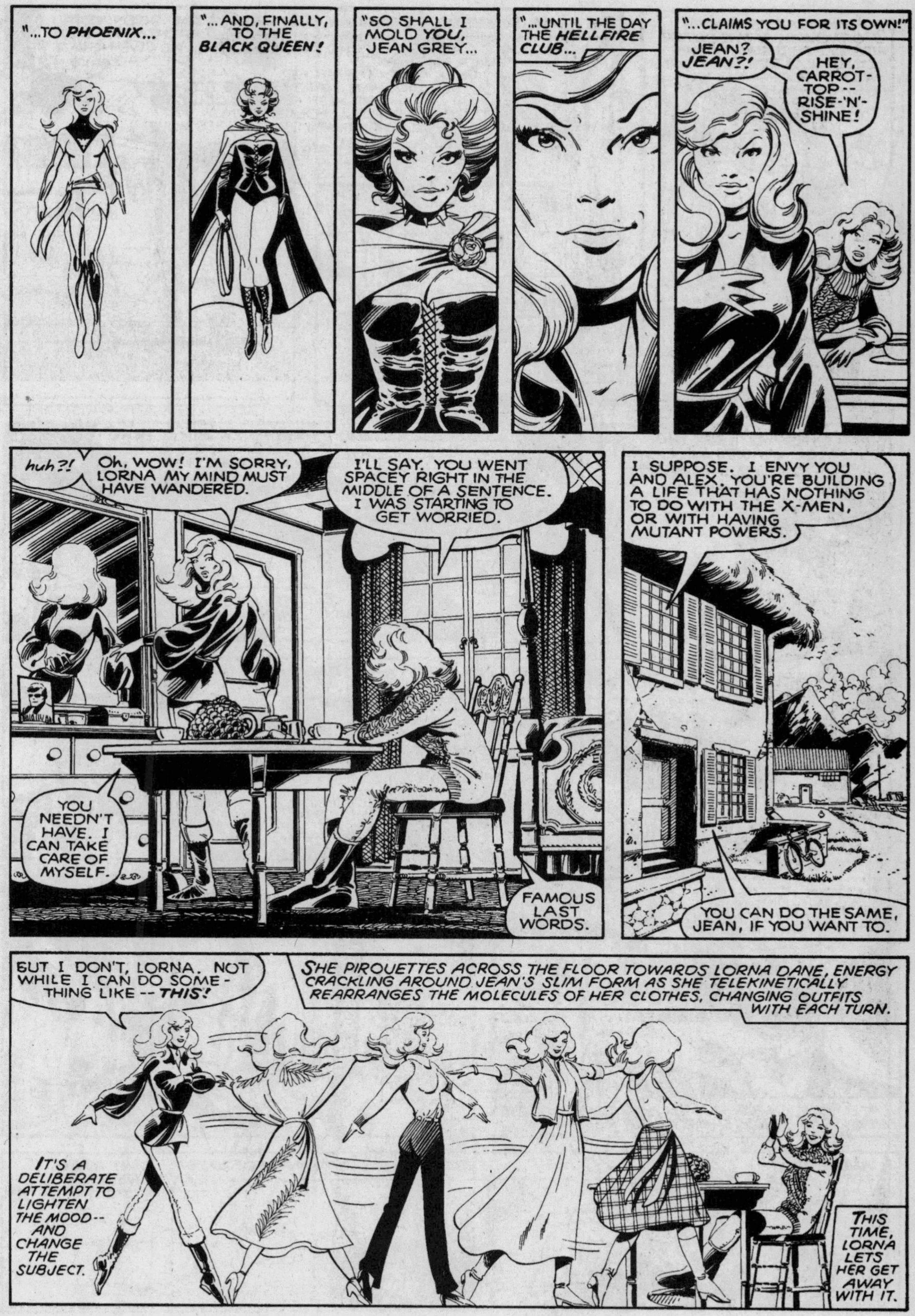

"...TO PHOENIX...
"...AND, FINALLY, TO THE BLACK QUEEN!
"SO SHALL I MOLD YOU, JEAN GREY...
"...UNTIL THE DAY THE HELLFIRE CLUB...
"...CLAIMS YOU FOR ITS OWN!"
JEAN? JEAN?!
HEY, CARROT-TOP -- RISE-'N'-SHINE!
huh?!
Oh, WOW! I'M SORRY, LORNA MY MIND MUST HAVE WANDERED.
I'LL SAY. YOU WENT SPACEY RIGHT IN THE MIDDLE OF A SENTENCE. I WAS STARTING TO GET WORRIED.
YOU NEEDN'T HAVE. I CAN TAKE CARE OF MYSELF.
FAMOUS LAST WORDS.
I SUPPOSE. I ENVY YOU AND ALEX. YOU'RE BUILDING A LIFE THAT HAS NOTHING TO DO WITH THE X-MEN, OR WITH HAVING MUTANT POWERS.
YOU CAN DO THE SAME, JEAN, IF YOU WANT TO.
BUT I DON'T, LORNA. NOT WHILE I CAN DO SOME-THING LIKE -- THIS!
SHE PIROUETTES ACROSS THE FLOOR TOWARDS LORNA DANE, ENERGY CRACKLING AROUND JEAN'S SLIM FORM AS SHE TELEKINETICALLY REARRANGES THE MOLECULES OF HER CLOTHES, CHANGING OUTFITS WITH EACH TURN.
IT'S A DELIBERATE ATTEMPT TO LIGHTEN THE MOOD-- AND CHANGE THE SUBJECT.
THIS TIME, LORNA LETS HER GET AWAY WITH IT.

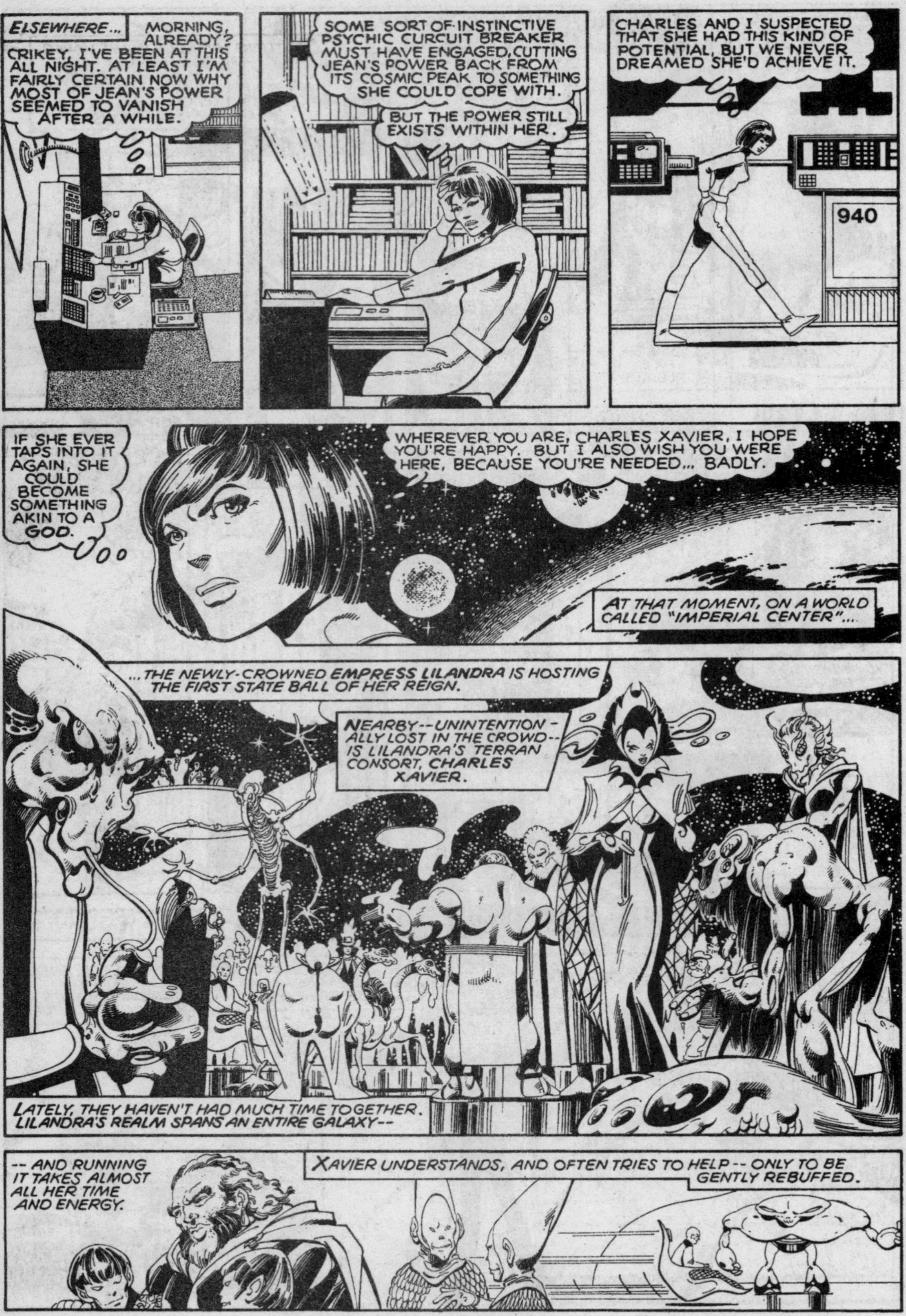
ELSEWHERE...
MORNING, ALREADY? CRIKEY, I'VE BEEN AT THIS ALL NIGHT. AT LEAST I'M FAIRLY CERTAIN NOW WHY MOST OF JEAN'S POWER SEEMED TO VANISH AFTER A WHILE.
SOME SORT OF INSTINCTIVE PSYCHIC CURCUIT BREAKER MUST HAVE ENGAGED, CUTTING JEAN'S POWER BACK FROM ITS COSMIC PEAK TO SOMETHING SHE COULD COPE WITH.
BUT THE POWER STILL EXISTS WITHIN HER.
CHARLES AND I SUSPECTED THAT SHE HAD THIS KIND OF POTENTIAL, BUT WE NEVER DREAMED SHE'D ACHIEVE IT.
940
IF SHE EVER TAPS INTO IT AGAIN, SHE COULD BECOME SOMETHING AKIN TO A GOD.
WHEREVER YOU ARE, CHARLES XAVIER, I HOPE YOU'RE HAPPY. BUT I ALSO WISH YOU WERE HERE, BECAUSE YOU'RE NEEDED... BADLY.
AT THAT MOMENT, ON A WORLD CALLED "IMPERIAL CENTER"...
...THE NEWLY-CROWNED EMPRESS LILANDRA IS HOSTING THE FIRST STATE BALL OF HER REIGN.
NEARBY--UNINTENTION-ALLY LOST IN THE CROWD--IS LILANDRA'S TERRAN CONSORT, CHARLES XAVIER.
LATELY, THEY HAVEN'T HAD MUCH TIME TOGETHER. LILANDRA'S REALM SPANS AN ENTIRE GALAXY--
--AND RUNNING IT TAKES ALMOST ALL HER TIME AND ENERGY.
XAVIER UNDERSTANDS, AND OFTEN TRIES TO HELP--ONLY TO BE GENTLY REBUFFED.

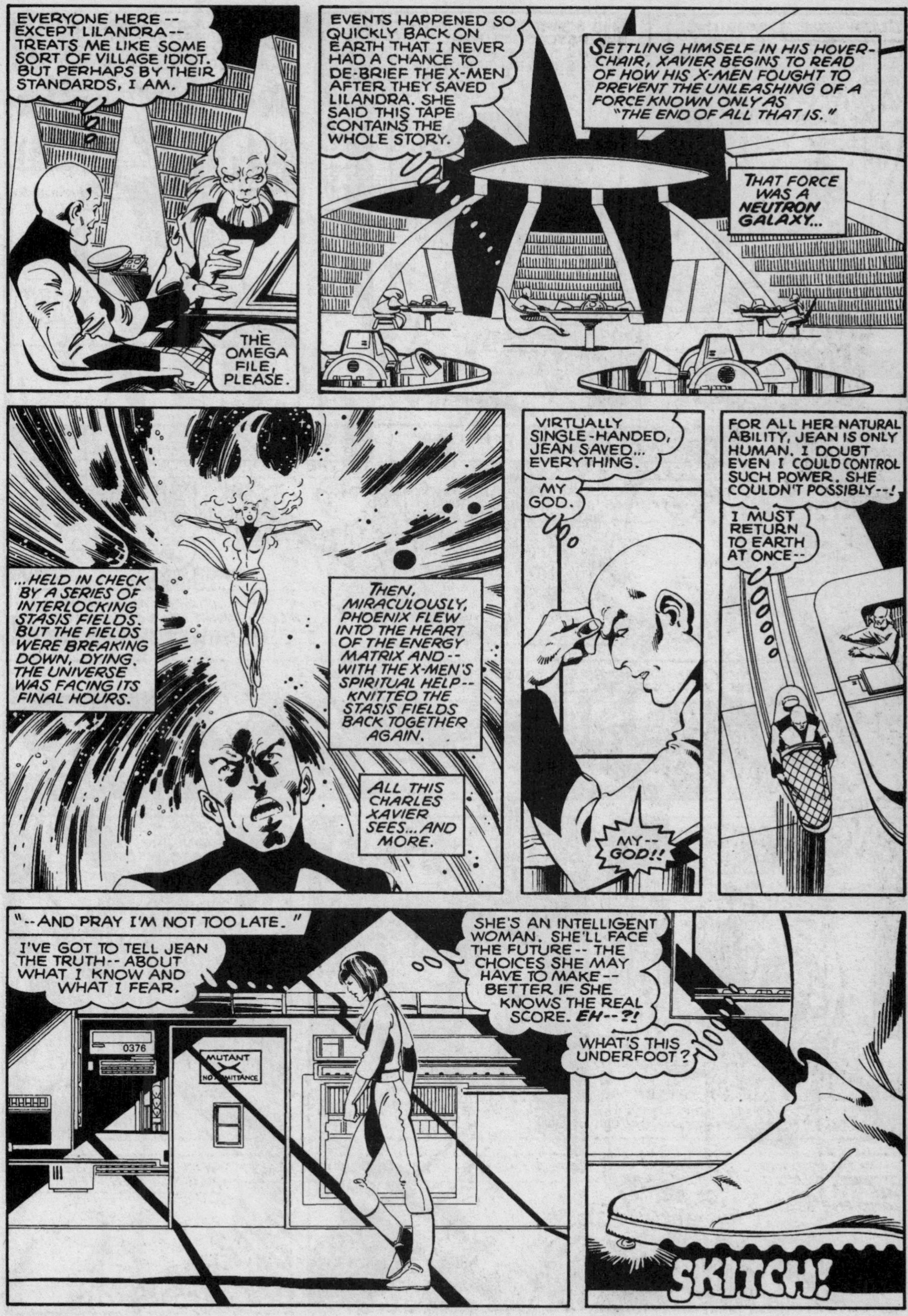
EVERYONE HERE -- EXCEPT LILANDRA -- TREATS ME LIKE SOME SORT OF VILLAGE IDIOT. BUT PERHAPS BY THEIR STANDARDS, I AM.
THE OMEGA FILE, PLEASE.
EVENTS HAPPENED SO QUICKLY BACK ON EARTH THAT I NEVER HAD A CHANCE TO DE-BRIEF THE X-MEN AFTER THEY SAVED LILANDRA. SHE SAID THIS TAPE CONTAINS THE WHOLE STORY.
SETTLING HIMSELF IN HIS HOVER-CHAIR, XAVIER BEGINS TO READ OF HOW HIS X-MEN FOUGHT TO PREVENT THE UNLEASHING OF A FORCE KNOWN ONLY AS "THE END OF ALL THAT IS."
THAT FORCE WAS A NEUTRON GALAXY...
...HELD IN CHECK BY A SERIES OF INTERLOCKING STASIS FIELDS. BUT THE FIELDS WERE BREAKING DOWN, DYING. THE UNIVERSE WAS FACING ITS FINAL HOURS.
THEN, MIRACULOUSLY, PHOENIX FLEW INTO THE HEART OF THE ENERGY MATRIX AND -- WITH THE X-MEN'S SPIRITUAL HELP -- KNITTED THE STASIS FIELDS BACK TOGETHER AGAIN.
ALL THIS CHARLES XAVIER SEES... AND MORE.
VIRTUALLY SINGLE-HANDED, JEAN SAVED... EVERYTHING.
MY GOD.
MY -- GOD!!
FOR ALL HER NATURAL ABILITY, JEAN IS ONLY HUMAN. I DOUBT EVEN I COULD CONTROL SUCH POWER. SHE COULDN'T POSSIBLY--!
I MUST RETURN TO EARTH AT ONCE--
"-- AND PRAY I'M NOT TOO LATE."
I'VE GOT TO TELL JEAN THE TRUTH -- ABOUT WHAT I KNOW AND WHAT I FEAR.
0376
MUTANT
NO ADMITTANCE
SHE'S AN INTELLIGENT WOMAN. SHE'LL FACE THE FUTURE -- THE CHOICES SHE MAY HAVE TO MAKE -- BETTER IF SHE KNOWS THE REAL SCORE. EH--?!
WHAT'S THIS UNDERFOOT?
SKITCH!

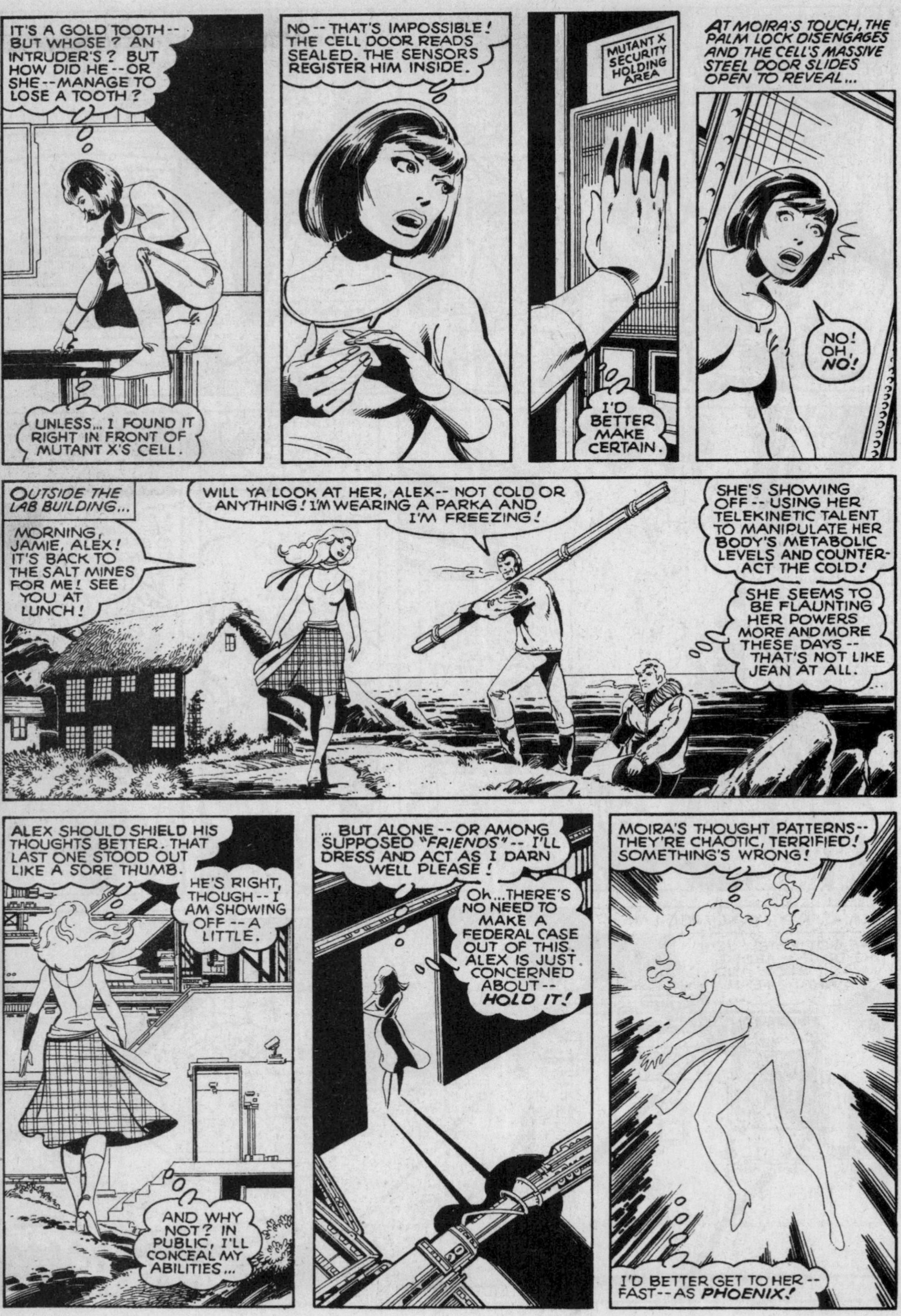
IT'S A GOLD TOOTH -- BUT WHOSE? AN INTRUDER'S? BUT HOW DID HE -- OR SHE -- MANAGE TO LOSE A TOOTH?
UNLESS... I FOUND IT RIGHT IN FRONT OF MUTANT X'S CELL.
NO -- THAT'S IMPOSSIBLE! THE CELL DOOR READS SEALED. THE SENSORS REGISTER HIM INSIDE.
MUTANT X SECURITY HOLDING AREA
I'D BETTER MAKE CERTAIN.
AT MOIRA'S TOUCH, THE PALM LOCK DISENGAGES AND THE CELL'S MASSIVE STEEL DOOR SLIDES OPEN TO REVEAL...
NO! OH, NO!
OUTSIDE THE LAB BUILDING...
MORNING, JAMIE, ALEX! IT'S BACK TO THE SALT MINES FOR ME! SEE YOU AT LUNCH!
WILL YA LOOK AT HER, ALEX-- NOT COLD OR ANYTHING! I'M WEARING A PARKA AND I'M FREEZING!
SHE'S SHOWING OFF -- USING HER TELEKINETIC TALENT TO MANIPULATE HER BODY'S METABOLIC LEVELS AND COUNTER-ACT THE COLD!
SHE SEEMS TO BE FLAUNTING HER POWERS MORE AND MORE THESE DAYS -- THAT'S NOT LIKE JEAN AT ALL.
ALEX SHOULD SHIELD HIS THOUGHTS BETTER. THAT LAST ONE STOOD OUT LIKE A SORE THUMB.
HE'S RIGHT, THOUGH -- I AM SHOWING OFF -- A LITTLE.
AND WHY NOT? IN PUBLIC, I'LL CONCEAL MY ABILITIES...
... BUT ALONE -- OR AMONG SUPPOSED "FRIENDS" -- I'LL DRESS AND ACT AS I DARN WELL PLEASE!
Oh... THERE'S NO NEED TO MAKE A FEDERAL CASE OUT OF THIS. ALEX IS JUST CONCERNED ABOUT -- HOLD IT!
MOIRA'S THOUGHT PATTERNS -- THEY'RE CHAOTIC, TERRIFIED! SOMETHING'S WRONG!
I'D BETTER GET TO HER -- FAST -- AS PHOENIX!

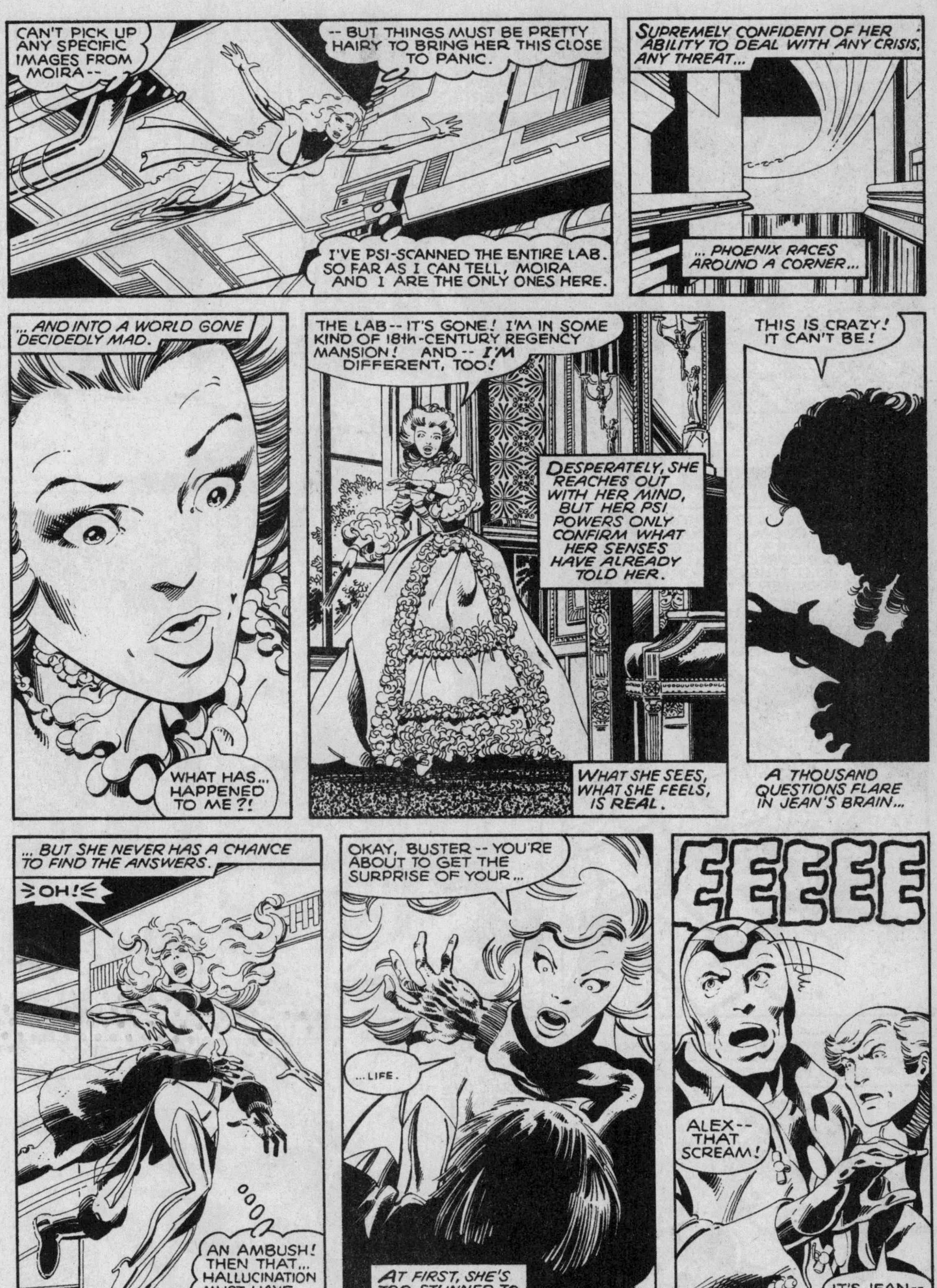
CAN'T PICK UP ANY SPECIFIC IMAGES FROM MOIRA --
-- BUT THINGS MUST BE PRETTY HAIRY TO BRING HER THIS CLOSE TO PANIC.
I'VE PSI-SCANNED THE ENTIRE LAB. SO FAR AS I CAN TELL, MOIRA AND I ARE THE ONLY ONES HERE.
SUPREMELY CONFIDENT OF HER ABILITY TO DEAL WITH ANY CRISIS, ANY THREAT...
... PHOENIX RACES AROUND A CORNER...
... AND INTO A WORLD GONE DECIDEDLY MAD.
WHAT HAS... HAPPENED TO ME?!
THE LAB -- IT'S GONE! I'M IN SOME KIND OF 18th-CENTURY REGENCY MANSION! AND -- I'M DIFFERENT, TOO!
DESPERATELY, SHE REACHES OUT WITH HER MIND, BUT HER PSI POWERS ONLY CONFIRM WHAT HER SENSES HAVE ALREADY TOLD HER.
WHAT SHE SEES, WHAT SHE FEELS, IS REAL.
THIS IS CRAZY! IT CAN'T BE!
A THOUSAND QUESTIONS FLARE IN JEAN'S BRAIN...
... BUT SHE NEVER HAS A CHANCE TO FIND THE ANSWERS.
OH!
OOO
AN AMBUSH! THEN THAT... HALLUCINATION MUST HAVE BEEN SOME WEIRD KIND OF DIVERSION!
OKAY, BUSTER -- YOU'RE ABOUT TO GET THE SURPRISE OF YOUR...
...LIFE.
AT FIRST, SHE'S TOO STUNNED TO REACT. THEN...
EEEEE
ALEX -- THAT SCREAM!
IT'S JEAN -- COME ON!

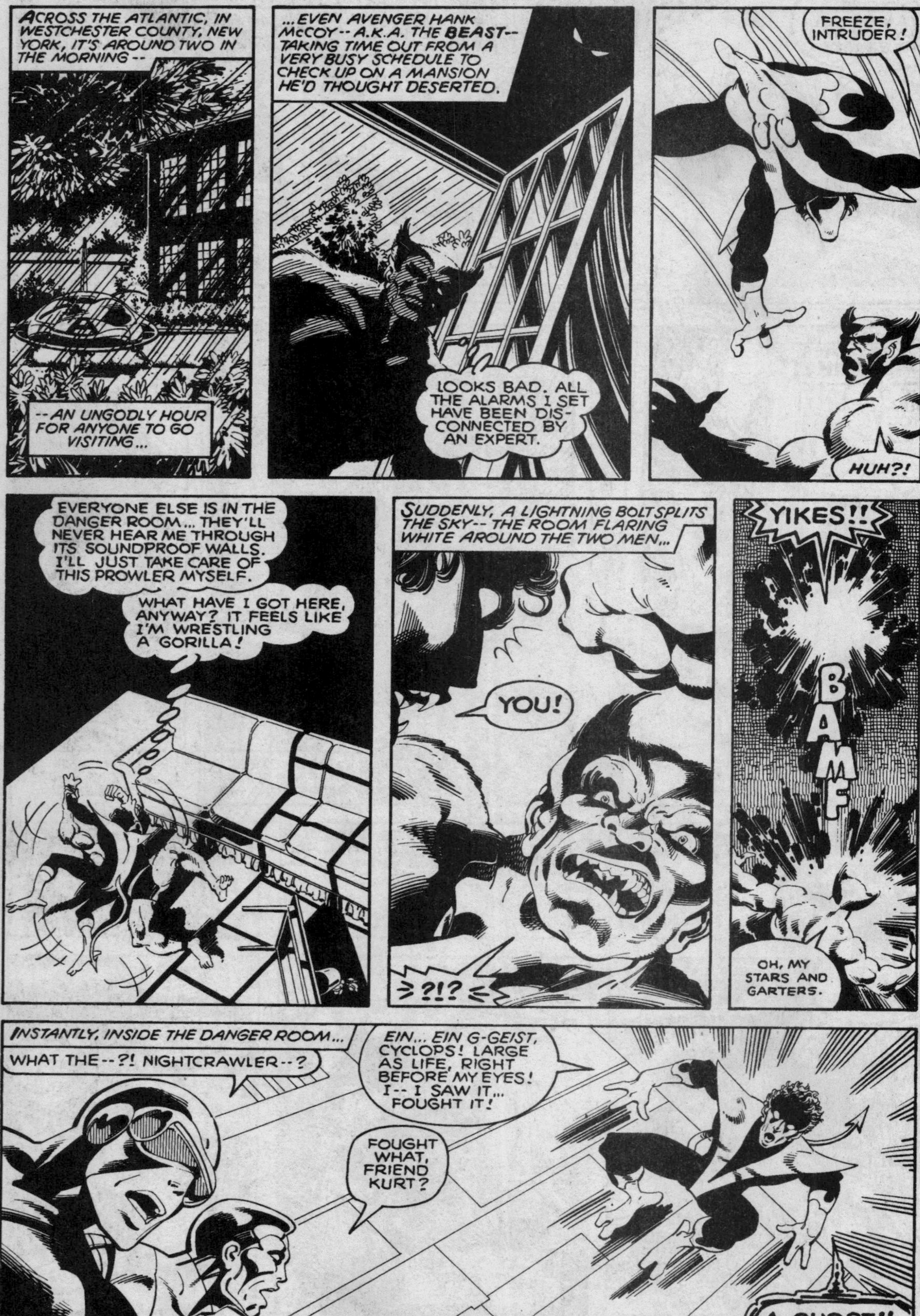
ACROSS THE ATLANTIC, IN WESTCHESTER COUNTY, NEW YORK, IT'S AROUND TWO IN THE MORNING --
-- AN UNGODLY HOUR FOR ANYONE TO GO VISITING...
...EVEN AVENGER HANK McCOY -- A.K.A. THE BEAST -- TAKING TIME OUT FROM A VERY BUSY SCHEDULE TO CHECK UP ON A MANSION HE'D THOUGHT DESERTED.
LOOKS BAD. ALL THE ALARMS I SET HAVE BEEN DISCONNECTED BY AN EXPERT.
FREEZE, INTRUDER!
HUH?!
EVERYONE ELSE IS IN THE DANGER ROOM... THEY'LL NEVER HEAR ME THROUGH ITS SOUNDPROOF WALLS. I'LL JUST TAKE CARE OF THIS PROWLER MYSELF.
WHAT HAVE I GOT HERE, ANYWAY? IT FEELS LIKE I'M WRESTLING A GORILLA!
SUDDENLY, A LIGHTNING BOLT SPLITS THE SKY -- THE ROOM FLARING WHITE AROUND THE TWO MEN...
YOU!
?!?
YIKES!!
BAMF
OH, MY STARS AND GARTERS.
INSTANTLY, INSIDE THE DANGER ROOM...
WHAT THE --?! NIGHTCRAWLER --?
EIN... EIN G-GEIST, CYCLOPS! LARGE AS LIFE, RIGHT BEFORE MY EYES! I -- I SAW IT... FOUGHT IT!
FOUGHT WHAT, FRIEND KURT?
A GHOST!!

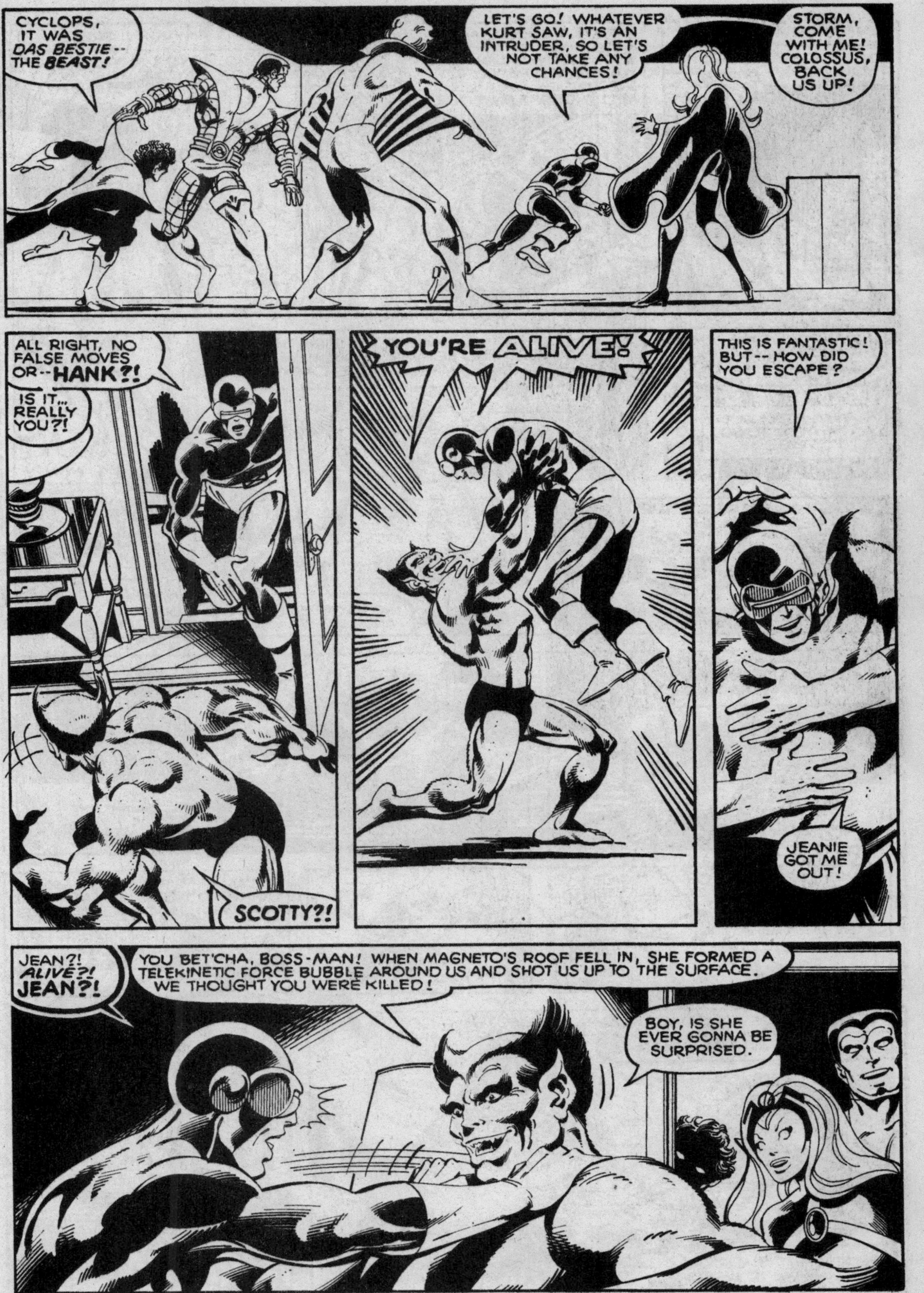
CYCLOPS, IT WAS DAS BESTIE -- THE BEAST!
LET'S GO! WHATEVER KURT SAW, IT'S AN INTRUDER, SO LET'S NOT TAKE ANY CHANCES!
STORM, COME WITH ME! COLOSSUS, BACK US UP!
ALL RIGHT, NO FALSE MOVES OR-- HANK?!
IS IT... REALLY YOU?!
SCOTTY?!
YOU'RE ALIVE!
THIS IS FANTASTIC! BUT-- HOW DID YOU ESCAPE?
JEANIE GOT ME OUT!
JEAN?! ALIVE?! JEAN?!
YOU BET'CHA, BOSS-MAN! WHEN MAGNETO'S ROOF FELL IN, SHE FORMED A TELEKINETIC FORCE BUBBLE AROUND US AND SHOT US UP TO THE SURFACE. WE THOUGHT YOU WERE KILLED!
BOY, IS SHE EVER GONNA BE SURPRISED.

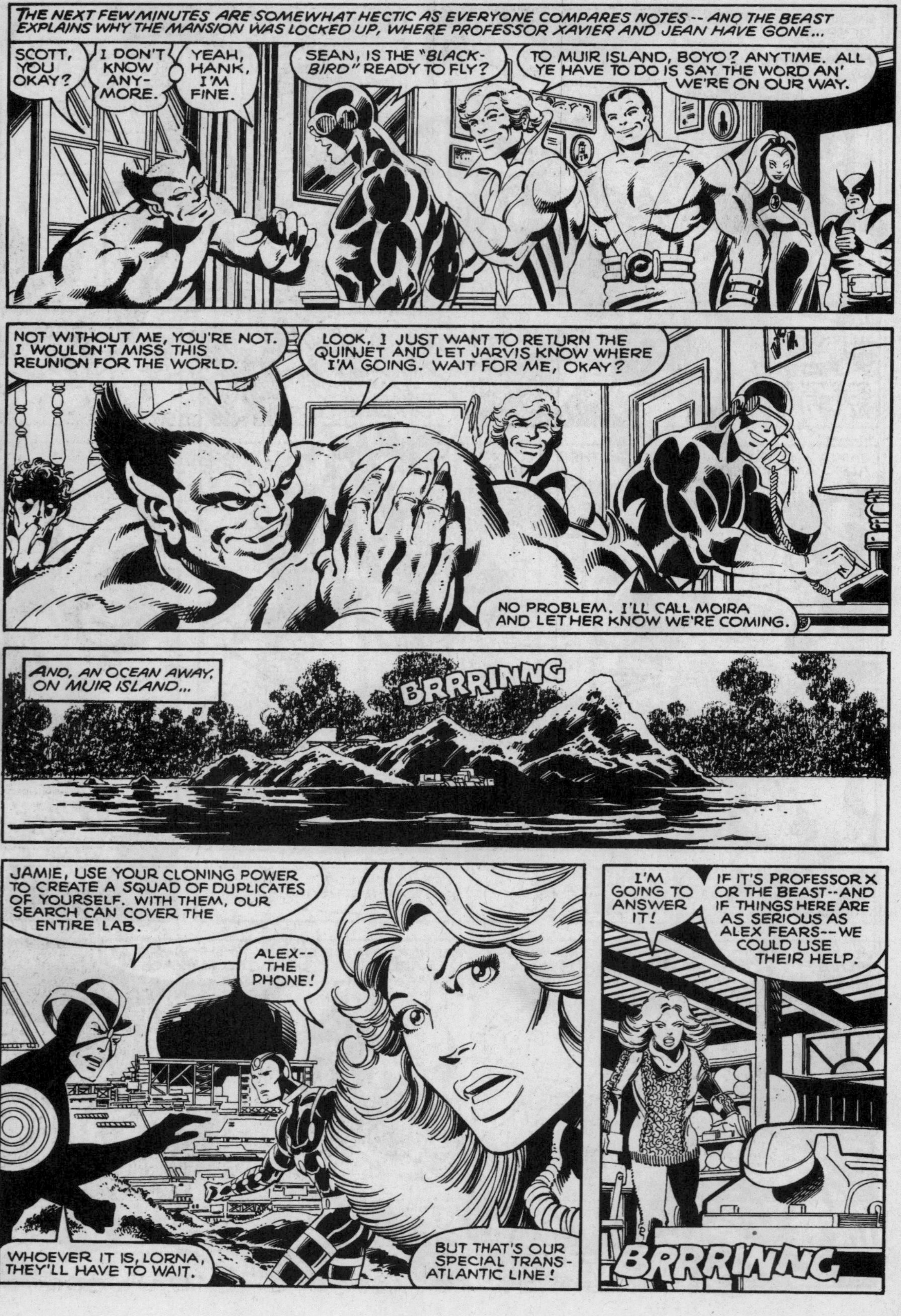
THE NEXT FEW MINUTES ARE SOMEWHAT HECTIC AS EVERYONE COMPARES NOTES -- AND THE BEAST EXPLAINS WHY THE MANSION WAS LOCKED UP, WHERE PROFESSOR XAVIER AND JEAN HAVE GONE...
SCOTT, YOU OKAY?
I DON'T KNOW ANY-MORE.
YEAH, HANK, I'M FINE.
SEAN, IS THE "BLACK-BIRD" READY TO FLY?
TO MUIR ISLAND, BOYO? ANYTIME. ALL YE HAVE TO DO IS SAY THE WORD AN' WE'RE ON OUR WAY.
NOT WITHOUT ME, YOU'RE NOT. I WOULDN'T MISS THIS REUNION FOR THE WORLD.
LOOK, I JUST WANT TO RETURN THE QUINJET AND LET JARVIS KNOW WHERE I'M GOING. WAIT FOR ME, OKAY?
NO PROBLEM. I'LL CALL MOIRA AND LET HER KNOW WE'RE COMING.
AND, AN OCEAN AWAY, ON MUIR ISLAND...
BRRRINNG
JAMIE, USE YOUR CLONING POWER TO CREATE A SQUAD OF DUPLICATES OF YOURSELF. WITH THEM, OUR SEARCH CAN COVER THE ENTIRE LAB.
ALEX-- THE PHONE!
WHOEVER IT IS, LORNA, THEY'LL HAVE TO WAIT.
BUT THAT'S OUR SPECIAL TRANS-ATLANTIC LINE!
I'M GOING TO ANSWER IT!
IF IT'S PROFESSOR X OR THE BEAST--AND IF THINGS HERE ARE AS SERIOUS AS ALEX FEARS--WE COULD USE THEIR HELP.
BRRRINNG

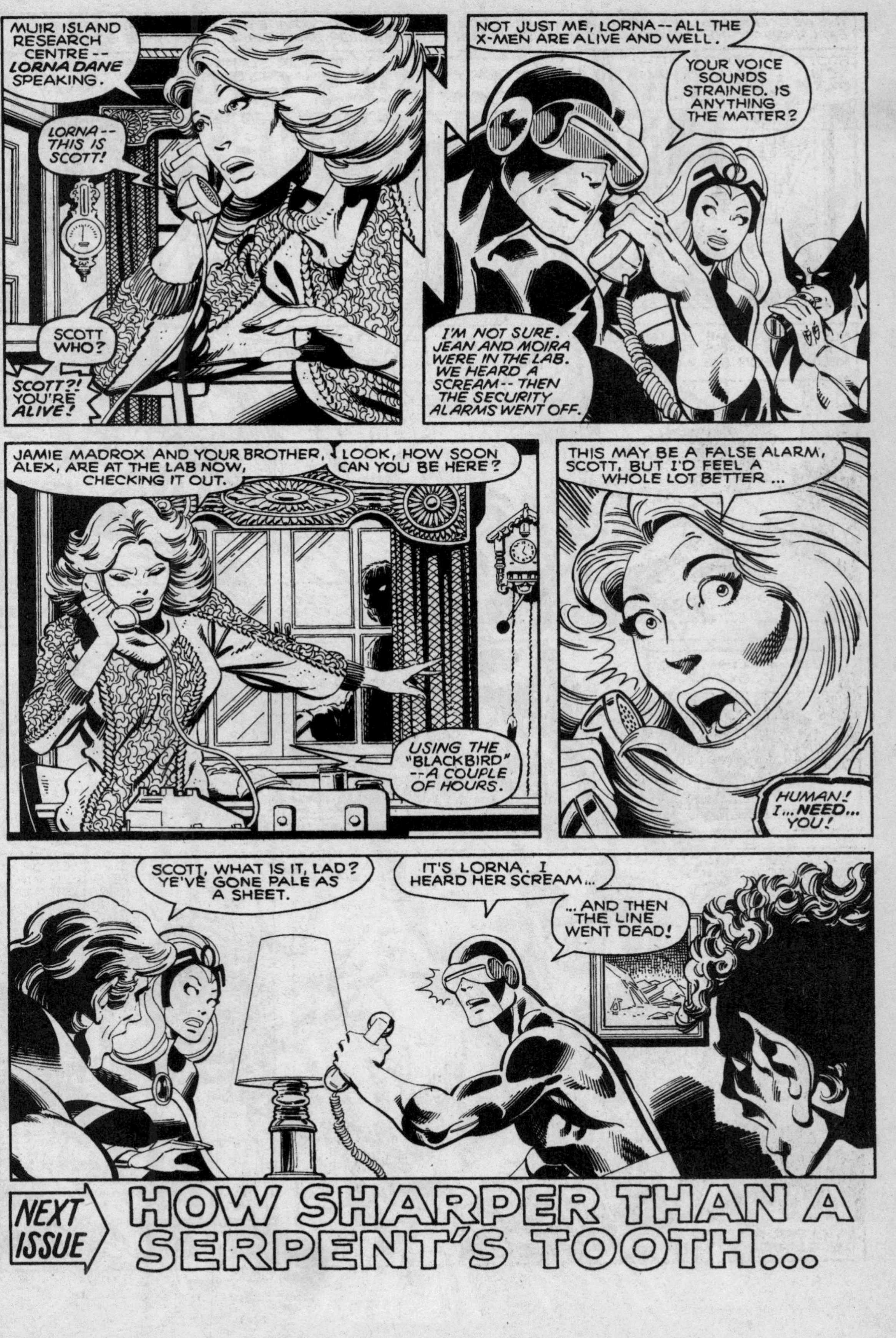
MUIR ISLAND RESEARCH CENTRE -- LORNA DANE SPEAKING.
LORNA -- THIS IS SCOTT!
SCOTT WHO?
SCOTT?! YOU'RE ALIVE!
NOT JUST ME, LORNA -- ALL THE X-MEN ARE ALIVE AND WELL.
YOUR VOICE SOUNDS STRAINED. IS ANYTHING THE MATTER?
I'M NOT SURE. JEAN AND MOIRA WERE IN THE LAB. WE HEARD A SCREAM -- THEN THE SECURITY ALARMS WENT OFF.
JAMIE MADROX AND YOUR BROTHER, ALEX, ARE AT THE LAB NOW, CHECKING IT OUT.
LOOK, HOW SOON CAN YOU BE HERE?
USING THE "BLACKBIRD" -- A COUPLE OF HOURS.
THIS MAY BE A FALSE ALARM, SCOTT, BUT I'D FEEL A WHOLE LOT BETTER ...
HUMAN! I... NEED... YOU!
SCOTT, WHAT IS IT, LAD? YE'VE GONE PALE AS A SHEET.
IT'S LORNA. I HEARD HER SCREAM...
... AND THEN THE LINE WENT DEAD!
NEXT ISSUE
HOW SHARPER THAN A SERPENT'S TOOTH...

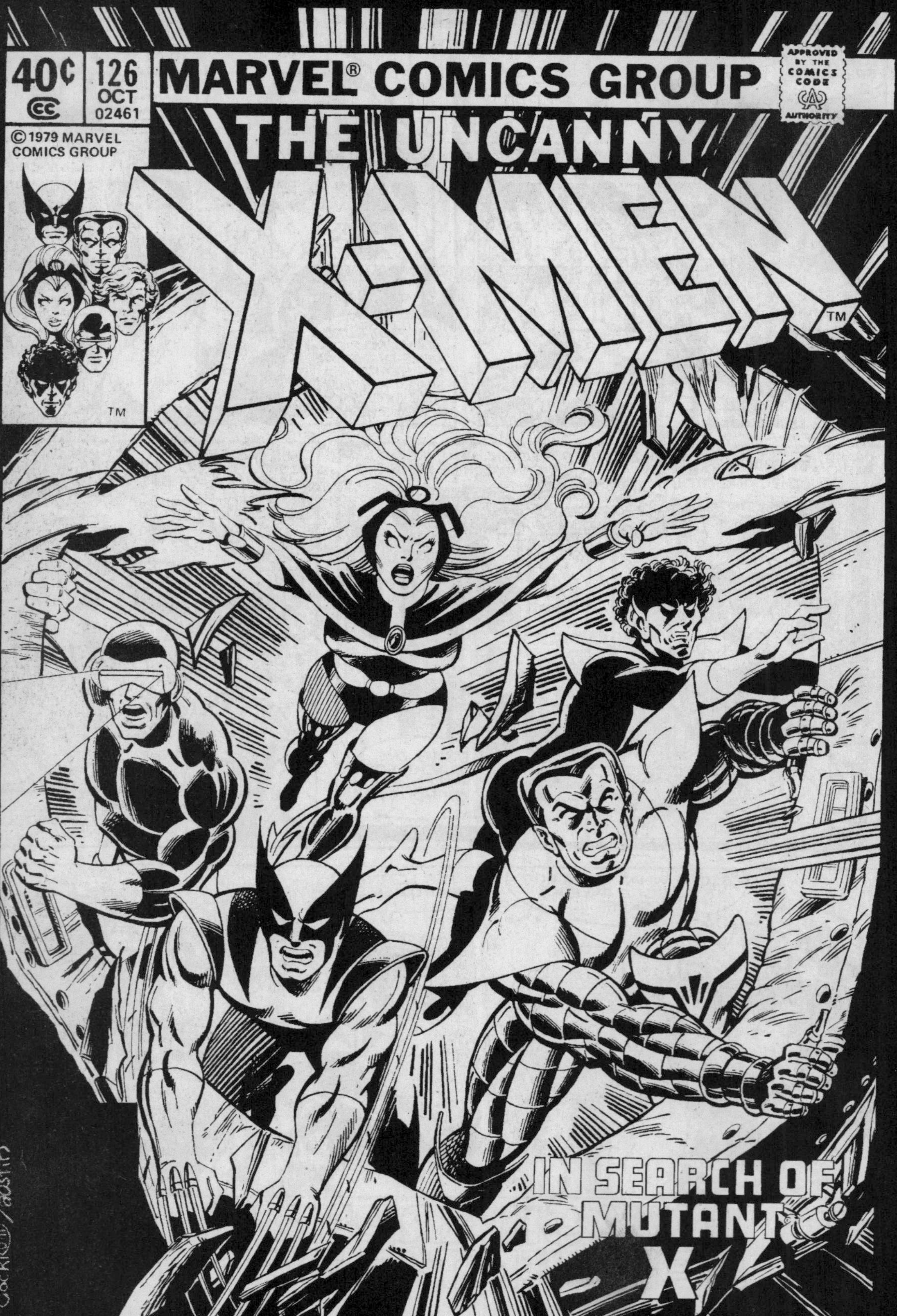
40¢
126
OCT
02461
MARVEL® COMICS GROUP
APPROVED BY THE COMICS CODE AUTHORITY
© 1979 MARVEL COMICS GROUP
THE UNCANNY
X-MEN™
IN SEARCH OF MUTANT X
Cockrum / austin

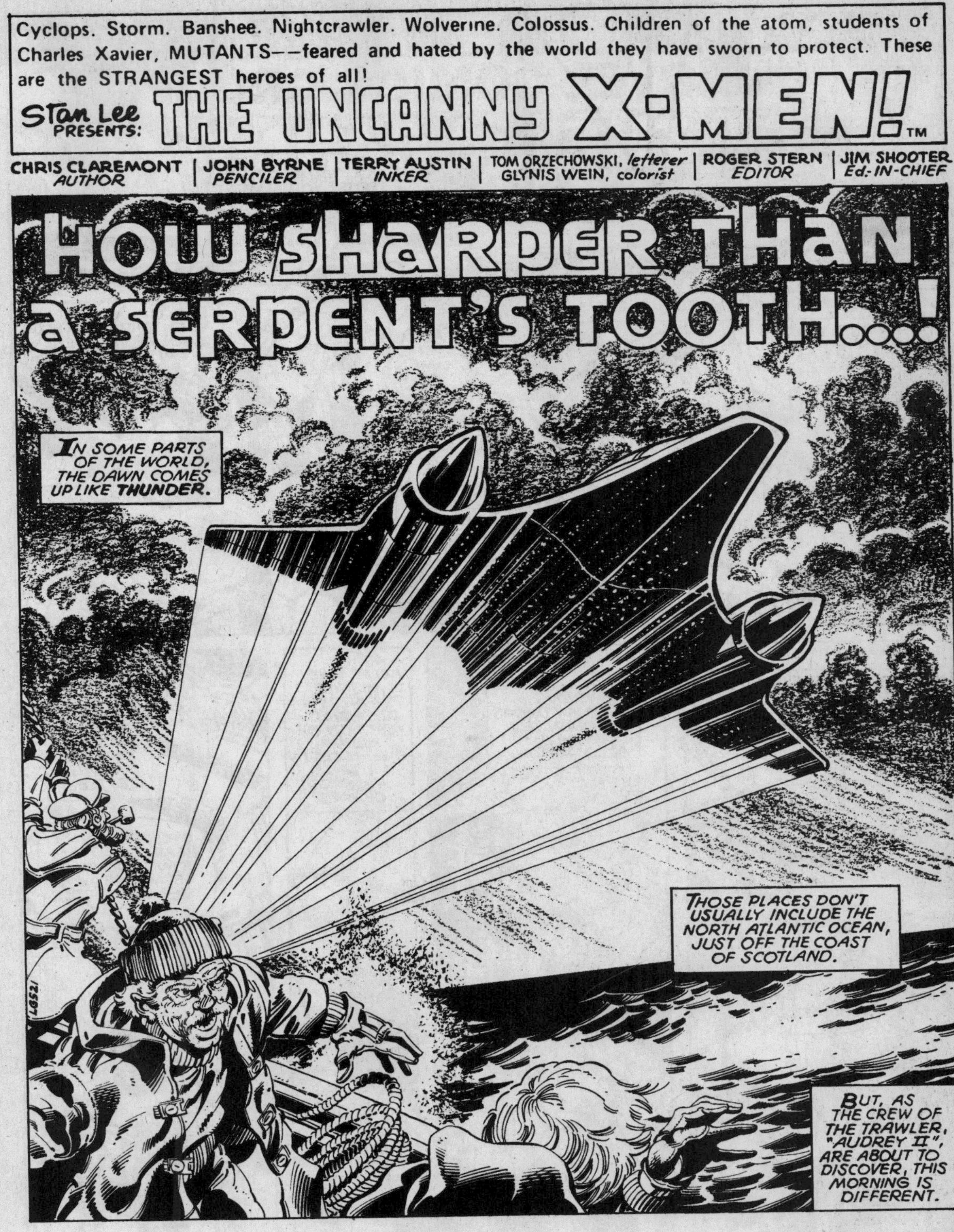
Cyclops. Storm. Banshee. Nightcrawler. Wolverine. Colossus. Children of the atom, students of Charles Xavier, MUTANTS--feared and hated by the world they have sworn to protect. These are the STRANGEST heroes of all!
Stan Lee PRESENTS: THE UNCANNY X-MEN! TM
CHRIS CLAREMONT AUTHOR
JOHN BYRNE PENCILER
TERRY AUSTIN INKER
TOM ORZECHOWSKI, letterer GLYNIS WEIN, colorist
ROGER STERN EDITOR
JIM SHOOTER Ed.-IN-CHIEF
HOW SHARPER THAN A SERPENT'S TOOTH...!
IN SOME PARTS OF THE WORLD, THE DAWN COMES UP LIKE THUNDER.
THOSE PLACES DON'T USUALLY INCLUDE THE NORTH ATLANTIC OCEAN, JUST OFF THE COAST OF SCOTLAND.
BUT, AS THE CREW OF THE TRAWLER, "AUDREY II", ARE ABOUT TO DISCOVER, THIS MORNING IS DIFFERENT.

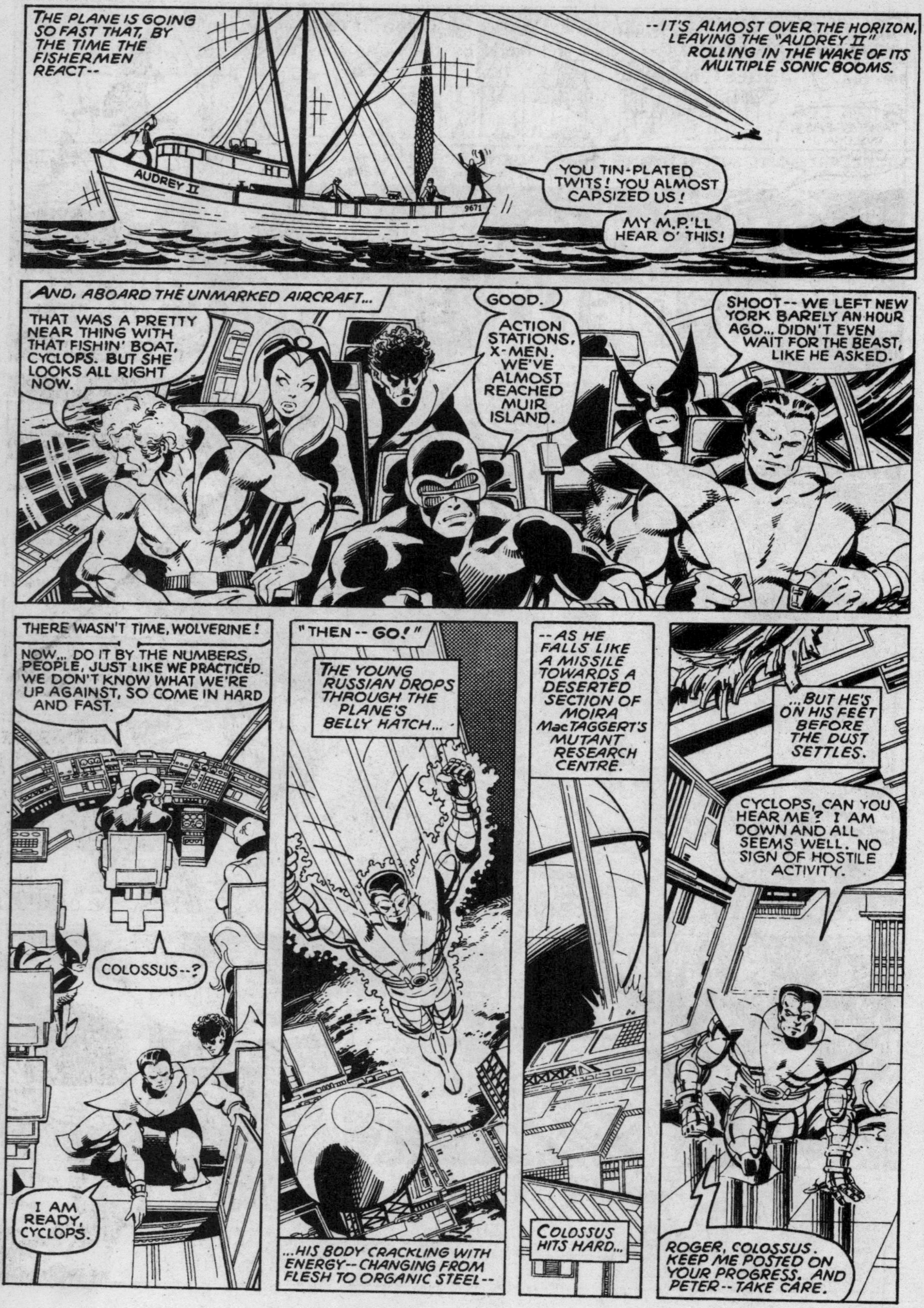
THE PLANE IS GOING SO FAST THAT, BY THE TIME THE FISHERMEN REACT--
--IT'S ALMOST OVER THE HORIZON, LEAVING THE "AUDREY II" ROLLING IN THE WAKE OF ITS MULTIPLE SONIC BOOMS.
AUDREY II
9671
YOU TIN-PLATED TWITS! YOU ALMOST CAPSIZED US!
MY M.P.'LL HEAR O' THIS!
AND, ABOARD THE UNMARKED AIRCRAFT...
THAT WAS A PRETTY NEAR THING WITH THAT FISHIN' BOAT, CYCLOPS. BUT SHE LOOKS ALL RIGHT NOW.
GOOD.
ACTION STATIONS, X-MEN. WE'VE ALMOST REACHED MUIR ISLAND.
SHOOT-- WE LEFT NEW YORK BARELY AN HOUR AGO... DIDN'T EVEN WAIT FOR THE BEAST, LIKE HE ASKED.
THERE WASN'T TIME, WOLVERINE!
NOW... DO IT BY THE NUMBERS, PEOPLE, JUST LIKE WE PRACTICED. WE DON'T KNOW WHAT WE'RE UP AGAINST, SO COME IN HARD AND FAST.
COLOSSUS--?
I AM READY, CYCLOPS.
"THEN -- GO!"
THE YOUNG RUSSIAN DROPS THROUGH THE PLANE'S BELLY HATCH...
...HIS BODY CRACKLING WITH ENERGY-- CHANGING FROM FLESH TO ORGANIC STEEL--
--AS HE FALLS LIKE A MISSILE TOWARDS A DESERTED SECTION OF MOIRA MacTAGGERT'S MUTANT RESEARCH CENTRE.
COLOSSUS HITS HARD...
...BUT HE'S ON HIS FEET BEFORE THE DUST SETTLES.
CYCLOPS, CAN YOU HEAR ME? I AM DOWN AND ALL SEEMS WELL. NO SIGN OF HOSTILE ACTIVITY.
ROGER, COLOSSUS. KEEP ME POSTED ON YOUR PROGRESS. AND PETER-- TAKE CARE.

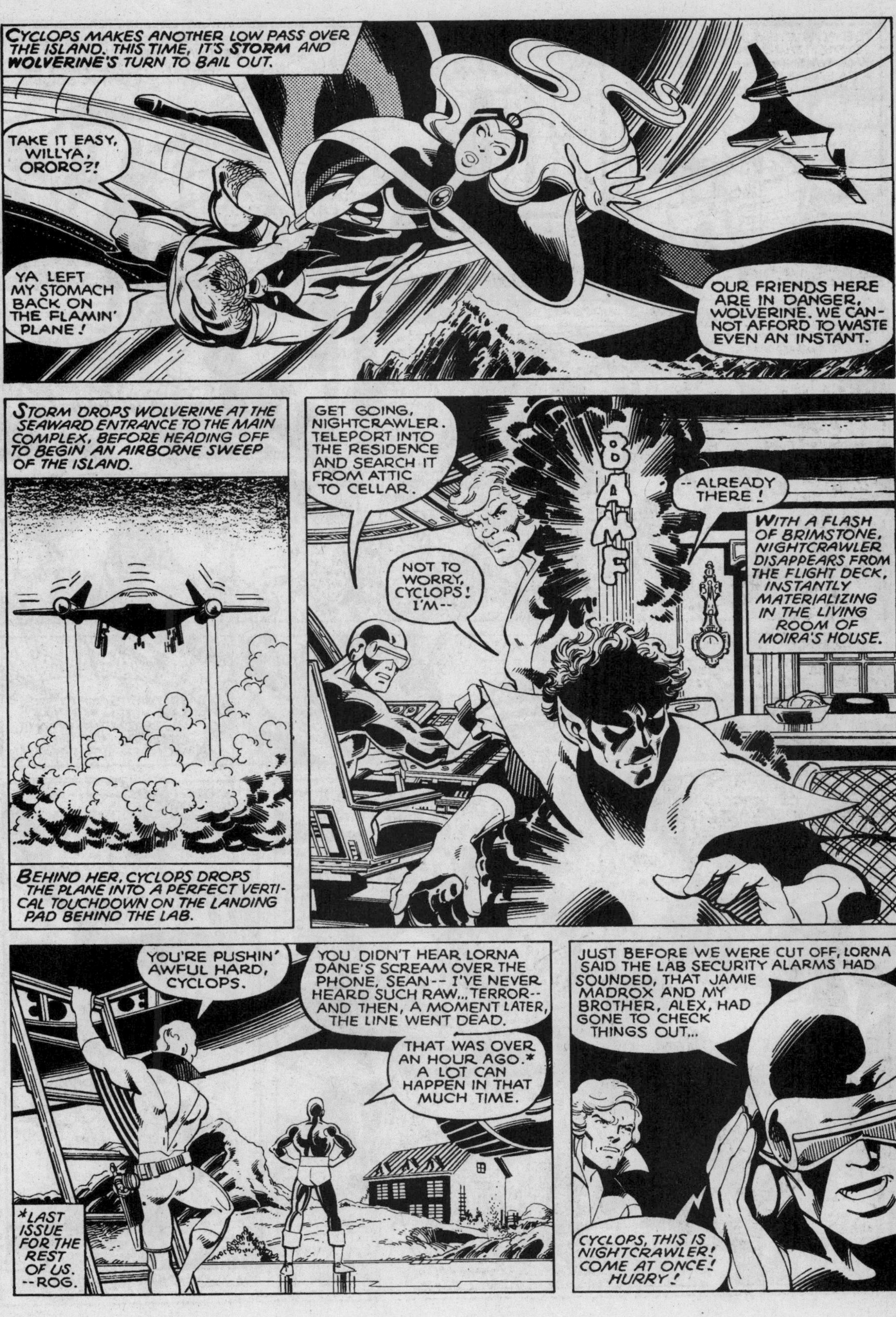

CYCLOPS MAKES ANOTHER LOW PASS OVER THE ISLAND. THIS TIME, IT'S STORM AND WOLVERINE'S TURN TO BAIL OUT.
TAKE IT EASY, WILLYA, ORORO?!
YA LEFT MY STOMACH BACK ON THE FLAMIN' PLANE!
OUR FRIENDS HERE ARE IN DANGER, WOLVERINE. WE CANNOT AFFORD TO WASTE EVEN AN INSTANT.
STORM DROPS WOLVERINE AT THE SEAWARD ENTRANCE TO THE MAIN COMPLEX, BEFORE HEADING OFF TO BEGIN AN AIRBORNE SWEEP OF THE ISLAND.
BEHIND HER, CYCLOPS DROPS THE PLANE INTO A PERFECT VERTICAL TOUCHDOWN ON THE LANDING PAD BEHIND THE LAB.
GET GOING, NIGHTCRAWLER. TELEPORT INTO THE RESIDENCE AND SEARCH IT FROM ATTIC TO CELLAR.
NOT TO WORRY, CYCLOPS! I'M--
BAMF
--ALREADY THERE!
WITH A FLASH OF BRIMSTONE, NIGHTCRAWLER DISAPPEARS FROM THE FLIGHT DECK, INSTANTLY MATERIALIZING IN THE LIVING ROOM OF MOIRA'S HOUSE.
YOU'RE PUSHIN' AWFUL HARD, CYCLOPS.
YOU DIDN'T HEAR LORNA DANE'S SCREAM OVER THE PHONE, SEAN-- I'VE NEVER HEARD SUCH RAW... TERROR-- AND THEN, A MOMENT LATER, THE LINE WENT DEAD.
THAT WAS OVER AN HOUR AGO.* A LOT CAN HAPPEN IN THAT MUCH TIME.
*LAST ISSUE FOR THE REST OF US. --ROG.
JUST BEFORE WE WERE CUT OFF, LORNA SAID THE LAB SECURITY ALARMS HAD SOUNDED, THAT JAMIE MADROX AND MY BROTHER, ALEX, HAD GONE TO CHECK THINGS OUT...
CYCLOPS, THIS IS NIGHTCRAWLER! COME AT ONCE! HURRY!

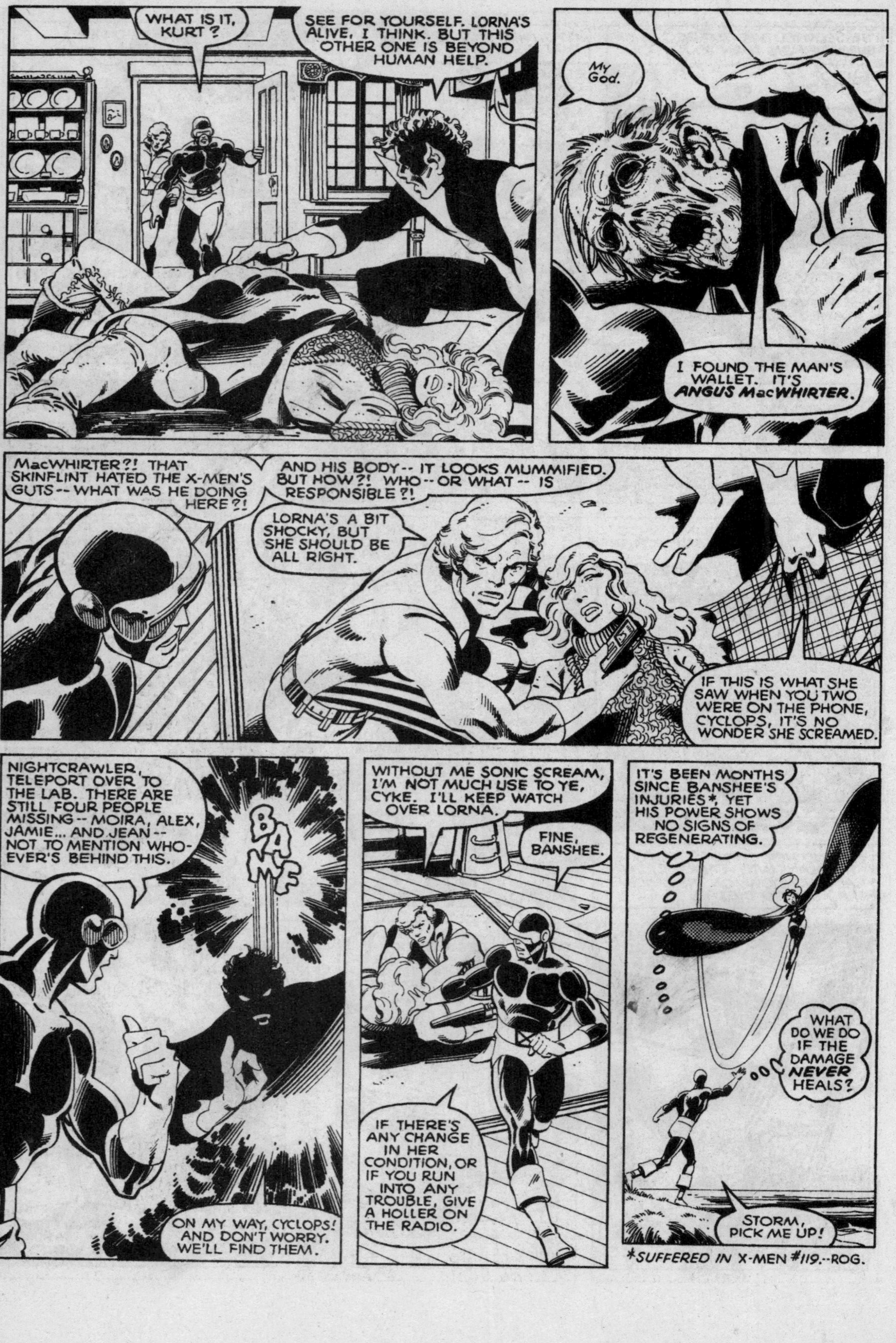
WHAT IS IT, KURT?
SEE FOR YOURSELF. LORNA'S ALIVE, I THINK. BUT THIS OTHER ONE IS BEYOND HUMAN HELP.
My God.
I FOUND THE MAN'S WALLET. IT'S ANGUS MacWHIRTER.
MacWHIRTER?! THAT SKINFLINT HATED THE X-MEN'S GUTS -- WHAT WAS HE DOING HERE?!
AND HIS BODY -- IT LOOKS MUMMIFIED. BUT HOW?! WHO -- OR WHAT -- IS RESPONSIBLE?!
LORNA'S A BIT SHOCKY, BUT SHE SHOULD BE ALL RIGHT.
IF THIS IS WHAT SHE SAW WHEN YOU TWO WERE ON THE PHONE, CYCLOPS, IT'S NO WONDER SHE SCREAMED.
NIGHTCRAWLER, TELEPORT OVER TO THE LAB. THERE ARE STILL FOUR PEOPLE MISSING -- MOIRA, ALEX, JAMIE... AND JEAN -- NOT TO MENTION WHO-EVER'S BEHIND THIS.
BAMF
ON MY WAY, CYCLOPS! AND DON'T WORRY. WE'LL FIND THEM.
WITHOUT ME SONIC SCREAM, I'M NOT MUCH USE TO YE, CYKE. I'LL KEEP WATCH OVER LORNA.
FINE, BANSHEE.
IF THERE'S ANY CHANGE IN HER CONDITION, OR IF YOU RUN INTO ANY TROUBLE, GIVE A HOLLER ON THE RADIO.
IT'S BEEN MONTHS SINCE BANSHEE'S INJURIES*, YET HIS POWER SHOWS NO SIGNS OF REGENERATING.
WHAT DO WE DO IF THE DAMAGE NEVER HEALS?
STORM, PICK ME UP!
*SUFFERED IN X-MEN #119.--ROG.

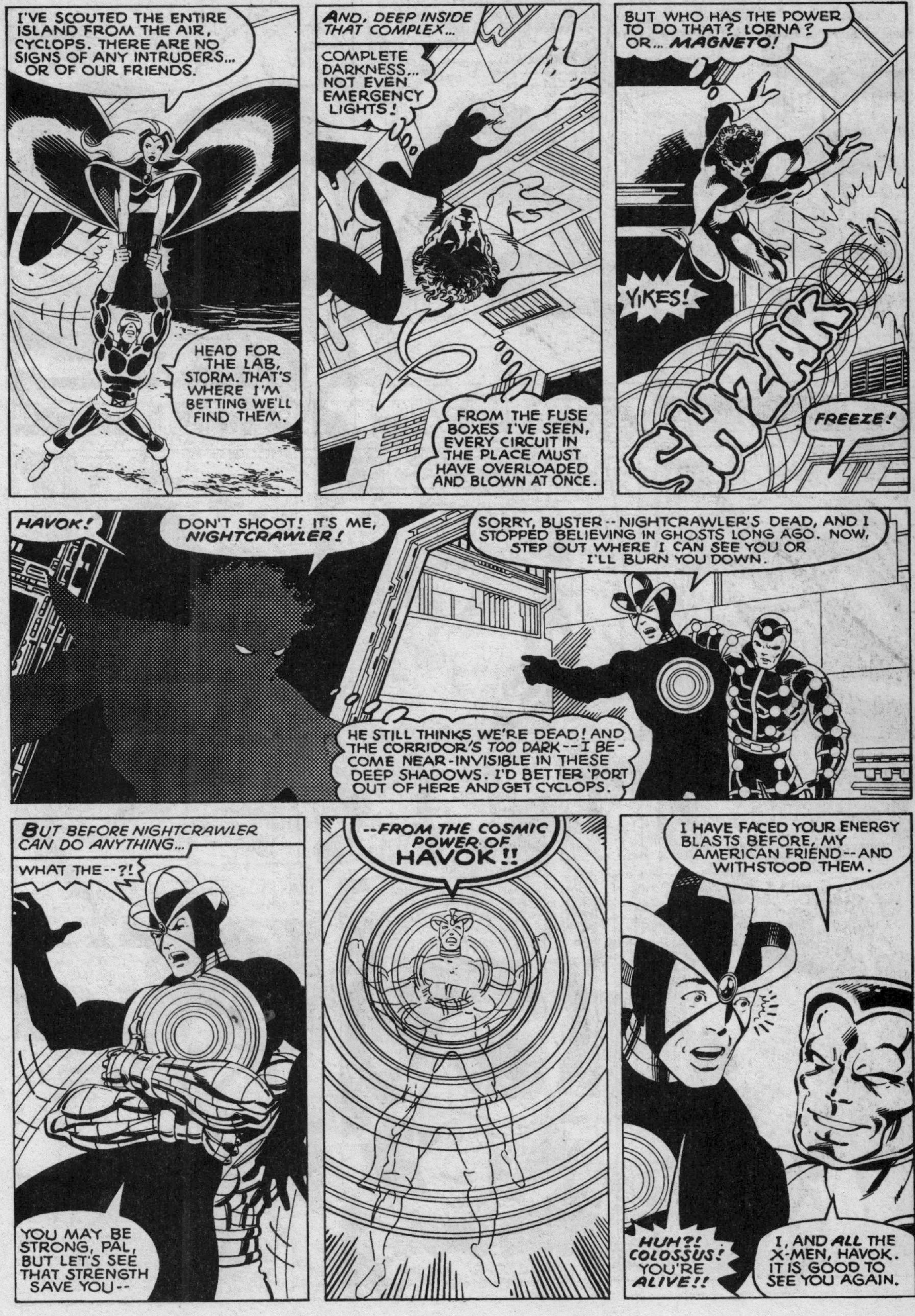
I'VE SCOUTED THE ENTIRE ISLAND FROM THE AIR, CYCLOPS. THERE ARE NO SIGNS OF ANY INTRUDERS... OR OF OUR FRIENDS.
HEAD FOR THE LAB, STORM. THAT'S WHERE I'M BETTING WE'LL FIND THEM.
AND, DEEP INSIDE THAT COMPLEX...
COMPLETE DARKNESS... NOT EVEN EMERGENCY LIGHTS!
FROM THE FUSE BOXES I'VE SEEN, EVERY CIRCUIT IN THE PLACE MUST HAVE OVERLOADED AND BLOWN AT ONCE.
BUT WHO HAS THE POWER TO DO THAT? LORNA? OR... MAGNETO!
YIKES!
SHZAK
FREEZE!
HAVOK!
DON'T SHOOT! IT'S ME, NIGHTCRAWLER!
SORRY, BUSTER--NIGHTCRAWLER'S DEAD, AND I STOPPED BELIEVING IN GHOSTS LONG AGO. NOW, STEP OUT WHERE I CAN SEE YOU OR I'LL BURN YOU DOWN.
HE STILL THINKS WE'RE DEAD! AND THE CORRIDOR'S TOO DARK--I BE-COME NEAR-INVISIBLE IN THESE DEEP SHADOWS. I'D BETTER 'PORT OUT OF HERE AND GET CYCLOPS.
BUT BEFORE NIGHTCRAWLER CAN DO ANYTHING...
WHAT THE--?!
YOU MAY BE STRONG, PAL, BUT LET'S SEE THAT STRENGTH SAVE YOU--
--FROM THE COSMIC POWER OF HAVOK!!
I HAVE FACED YOUR ENERGY BLASTS BEFORE, MY AMERICAN FRIEND--AND WITHSTOOD THEM.
HUH?! COLOSSUS! YOU'RE ALIVE!!
I, AND ALL THE X-MEN, HAVOK. IT IS GOOD TO SEE YOU AGAIN.

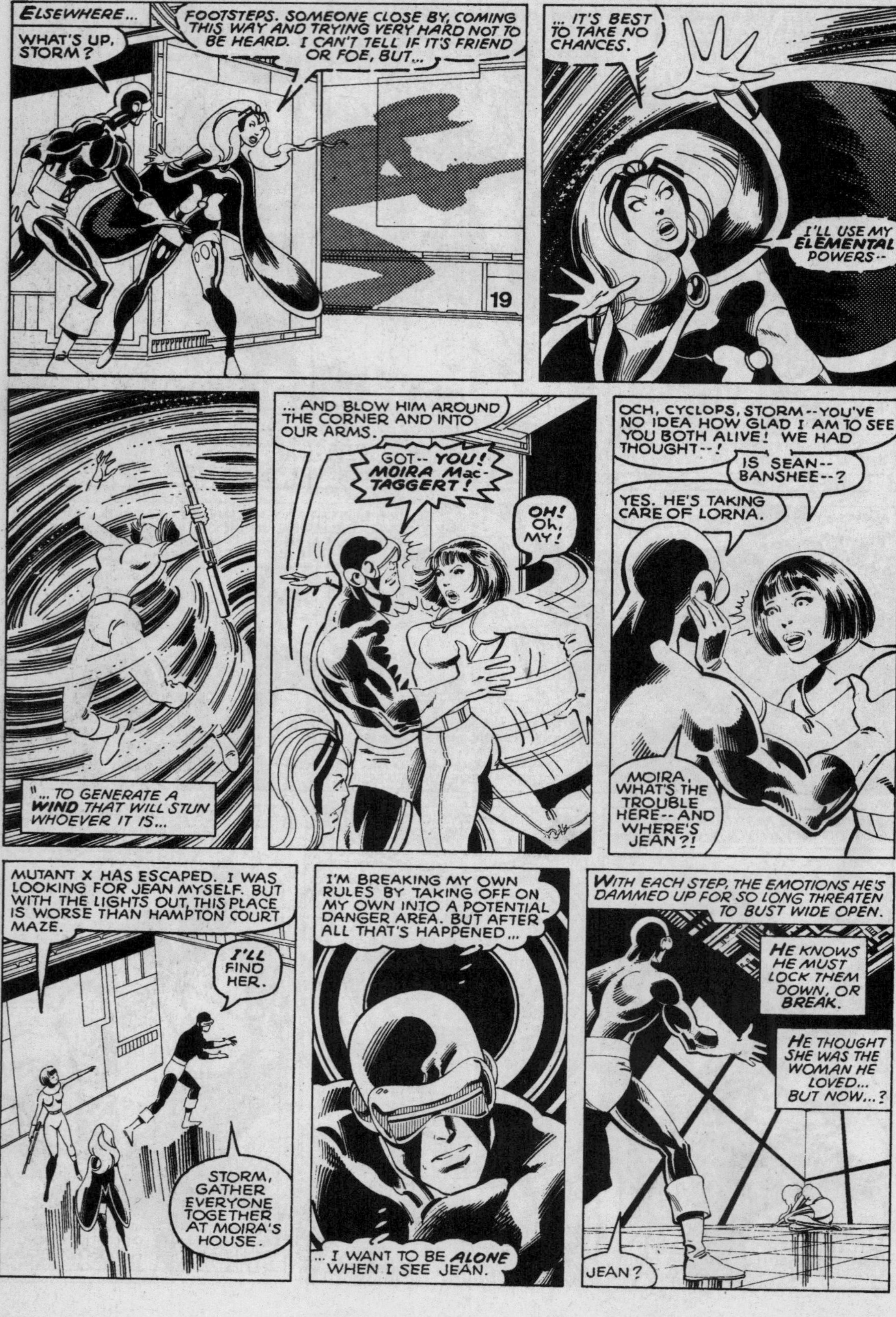

ELSEWHERE...
WHAT'S UP, STORM?
FOOTSTEPS. SOMEONE CLOSE BY, COMING THIS WAY AND TRYING VERY HARD NOT TO BE HEARD. I CAN'T TELL IF IT'S FRIEND OR FOE, BUT...
19
... IT'S BEST TO TAKE NO CHANCES.
I'LL USE MY ELEMENTAL POWERS--
"... TO GENERATE A WIND THAT WILL STUN WHOEVER IT IS...
... AND BLOW HIM AROUND THE CORNER AND INTO OUR ARMS.
GOT-- YOU! MOIRA MacTAGGERT!
OH! Oh, MY!
OCH, CYCLOPS, STORM--YOU'VE NO IDEA HOW GLAD I AM TO SEE YOU BOTH ALIVE! WE HAD THOUGHT--!
IS SEAN-- BANSHEE--?
YES. HE'S TAKING CARE OF LORNA.
MOIRA, WHAT'S THE TROUBLE HERE-- AND WHERE'S JEAN?!
MUTANT X HAS ESCAPED. I WAS LOOKING FOR JEAN MYSELF. BUT WITH THE LIGHTS OUT, THIS PLACE IS WORSE THAN HAMPTON COURT MAZE.
I'LL FIND HER.
STORM, GATHER EVERYONE TOGETHER AT MOIRA'S HOUSE.
I'M BREAKING MY OWN RULES BY TAKING OFF ON MY OWN INTO A POTENTIAL DANGER AREA. BUT AFTER ALL THAT'S HAPPENED...
... I WANT TO BE ALONE WHEN I SEE JEAN.
WITH EACH STEP, THE EMOTIONS HE'S DAMMED UP FOR SO LONG THREATEN TO BUST WIDE OPEN.
HE KNOWS HE MUST LOCK THEM DOWN, OR BREAK.
HE THOUGHT SHE WAS THE WOMAN HE LOVED... BUT NOW...?
JEAN?

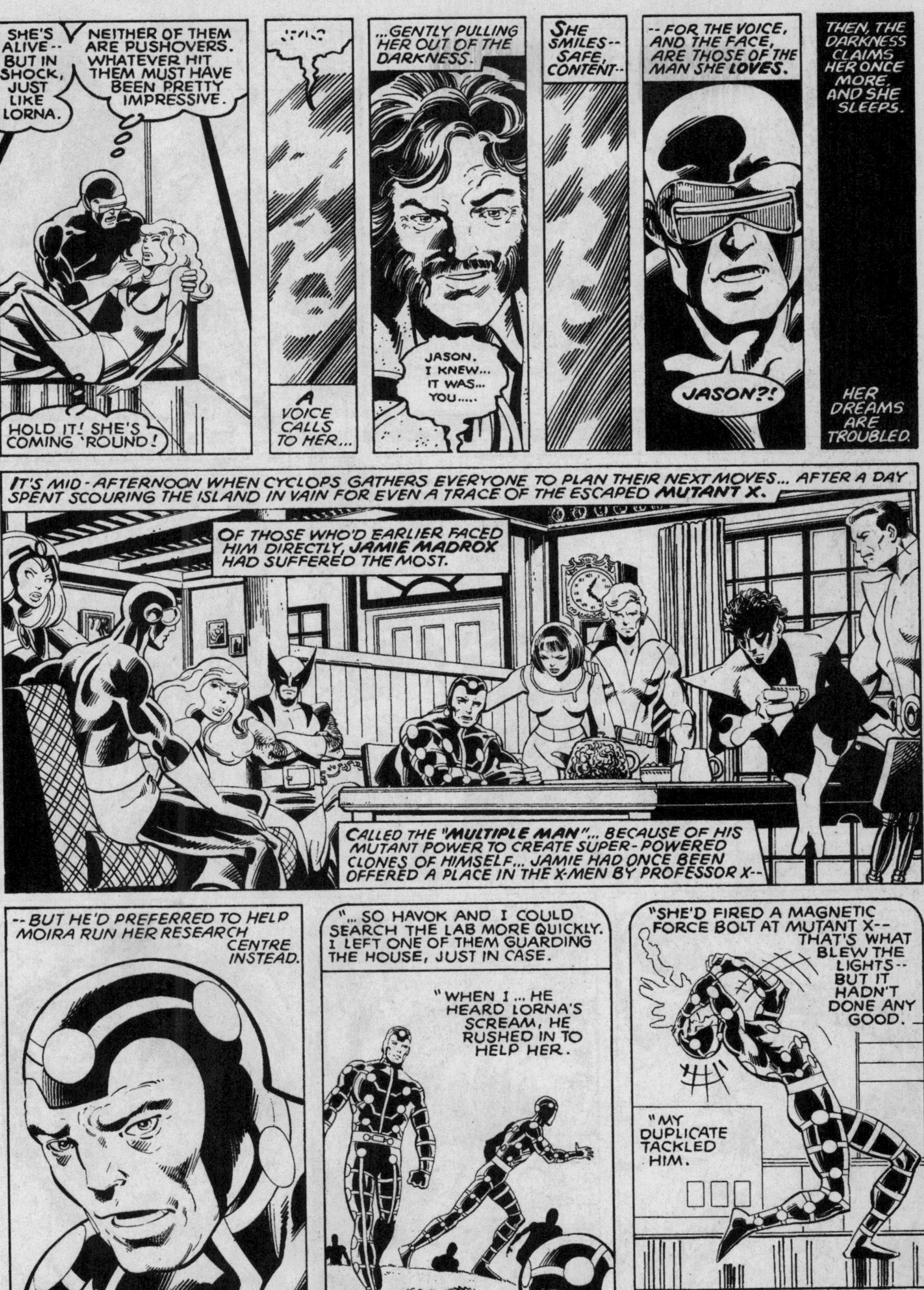
SHE'S ALIVE-- BUT IN SHOCK, JUST LIKE LORNA.
NEITHER OF THEM ARE PUSHOVERS. WHATEVER HIT THEM MUST HAVE BEEN PRETTY IMPRESSIVE.
HOLD IT! SHE'S COMING 'ROUND!
A VOICE CALLS TO HER...
...GENTLY PULLING HER OUT OF THE DARKNESS.
JASON. I KNEW... IT WAS... YOU.....
SHE SMILES-- SAFE, CONTENT--
--FOR THE VOICE, AND THE FACE, ARE THOSE OF THE MAN SHE LOVES.
JASON?!
THEN, THE DARKNESS CLAIMS HER ONCE MORE. AND SHE SLEEPS.
HER DREAMS ARE TROUBLED.
IT'S MID-AFTERNOON WHEN CYCLOPS GATHERS EVERYONE TO PLAN THEIR NEXT MOVES... AFTER A DAY SPENT SCOURING THE ISLAND IN VAIN FOR EVEN A TRACE OF THE ESCAPED MUTANT X.
OF THOSE WHO'D EARLIER FACED HIM DIRECTLY, JAMIE MADROX HAD SUFFERED THE MOST.
CALLED THE "MULTIPLE MAN"... BECAUSE OF HIS MUTANT POWER TO CREATE SUPER-POWERED CLONES OF HIMSELF... JAMIE HAD ONCE BEEN OFFERED A PLACE IN THE X-MEN BY PROFESSOR X--
--BUT HE'D PREFERRED TO HELP MOIRA RUN HER RESEARCH CENTRE INSTEAD.
WHEN THE ALARM SOUNDED, I CREATED A SQUAD OF DUPLICATES...
"... SO HAVOK AND I COULD SEARCH THE LAB MORE QUICKLY. I LEFT ONE OF THEM GUARDING THE HOUSE, JUST IN CASE.
"WHEN I ... HE HEARD LORNA'S SCREAM, HE RUSHED IN TO HELP HER.
"SHE'D FIRED A MAGNETIC FORCE BOLT AT MUTANT X-- THAT'S WHAT BLEW THE LIGHTS-- BUT IT HADN'T DONE ANY GOOD.
"MY DUPLICATE TACKLED HIM.
"AND SUDDENLY, I FELT AS IF MY SOUL WAS BEING TORN OUT OF ME.

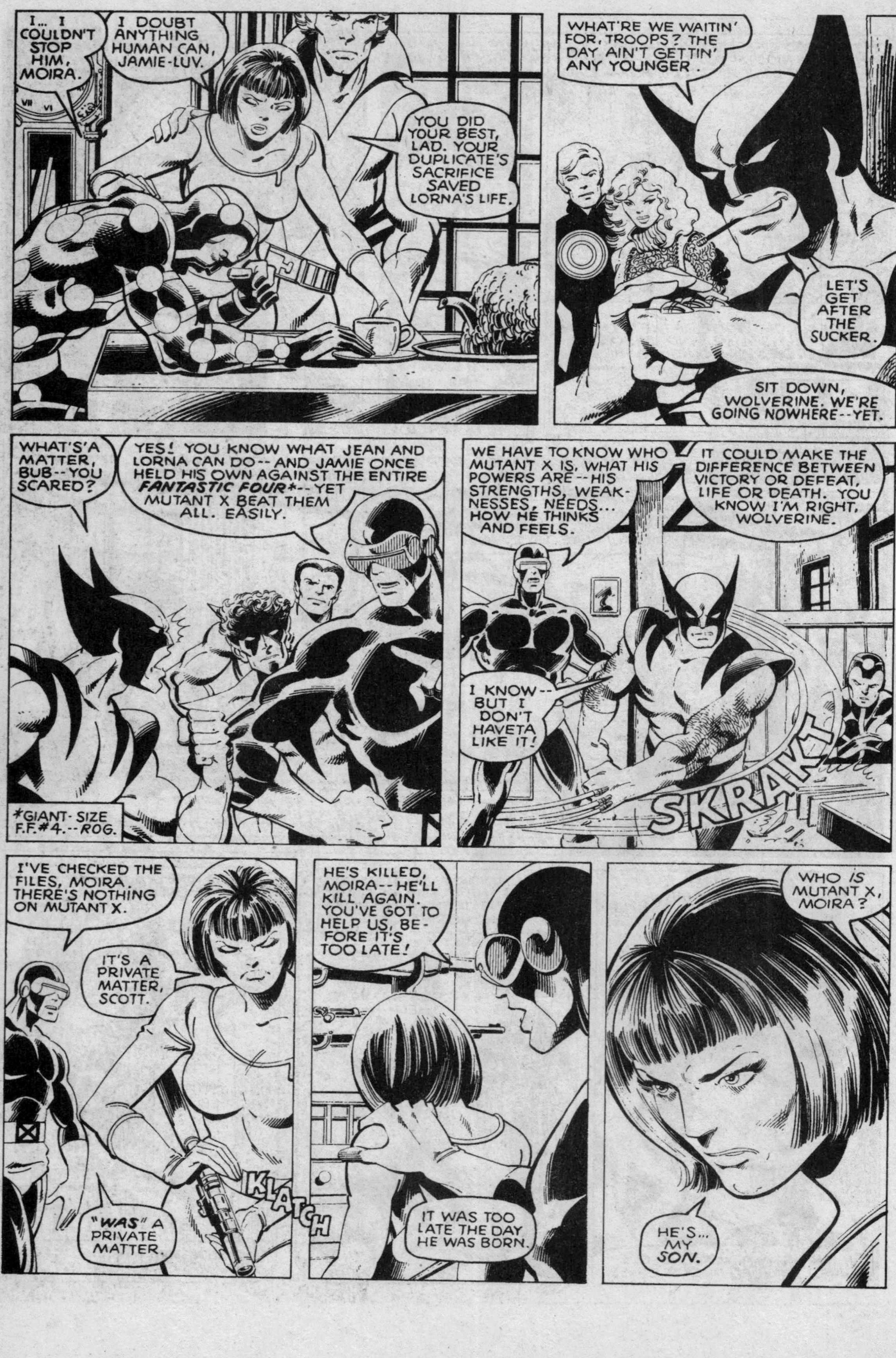
I... I COULDN'T STOP HIM, MOIRA.
I DOUBT ANYTHING HUMAN CAN, JAMIE-LUV.
YOU DID YOUR BEST, LAD. YOUR DUPLICATE'S SACRIFICE SAVED LORNA'S LIFE.
WHAT'RE WE WAITIN' FOR, TROOPS? THE DAY AIN'T GETTIN' ANY YOUNGER.
LET'S GET AFTER THE SUCKER.
SIT DOWN, WOLVERINE. WE'RE GOING NOWHERE--YET.
WHAT'S'A MATTER, BUB--YOU SCARED?
YES! YOU KNOW WHAT JEAN AND LORNA CAN DO--AND JAMIE ONCE HELD HIS OWN AGAINST THE ENTIRE FANTASTIC FOUR*--YET MUTANT X BEAT THEM ALL. EASILY.
*GIANT-SIZE F.F. #4.--ROG.
WE HAVE TO KNOW WHO MUTANT X IS, WHAT HIS POWERS ARE--HIS STRENGTHS, WEAKNESSES, NEEDS... HOW HE THINKS AND FEELS.
IT COULD MAKE THE DIFFERENCE BETWEEN VICTORY OR DEFEAT, LIFE OR DEATH. YOU KNOW I'M RIGHT, WOLVERINE.
I KNOW--BUT I DON'T HAVETA LIKE IT!
SKRAKT
I'VE CHECKED THE FILES, MOIRA. THERE'S NOTHING ON MUTANT X.
IT'S A PRIVATE MATTER, SCOTT.
"WAS" A PRIVATE MATTER.
KLATCH
HE'S KILLED, MOIRA--HE'LL KILL AGAIN. YOU'VE GOT TO HELP US, BEFORE IT'S TOO LATE!
IT WAS TOO LATE THE DAY HE WAS BORN.
WHO IS MUTANT X, MOIRA?
HE'S... MY SON.

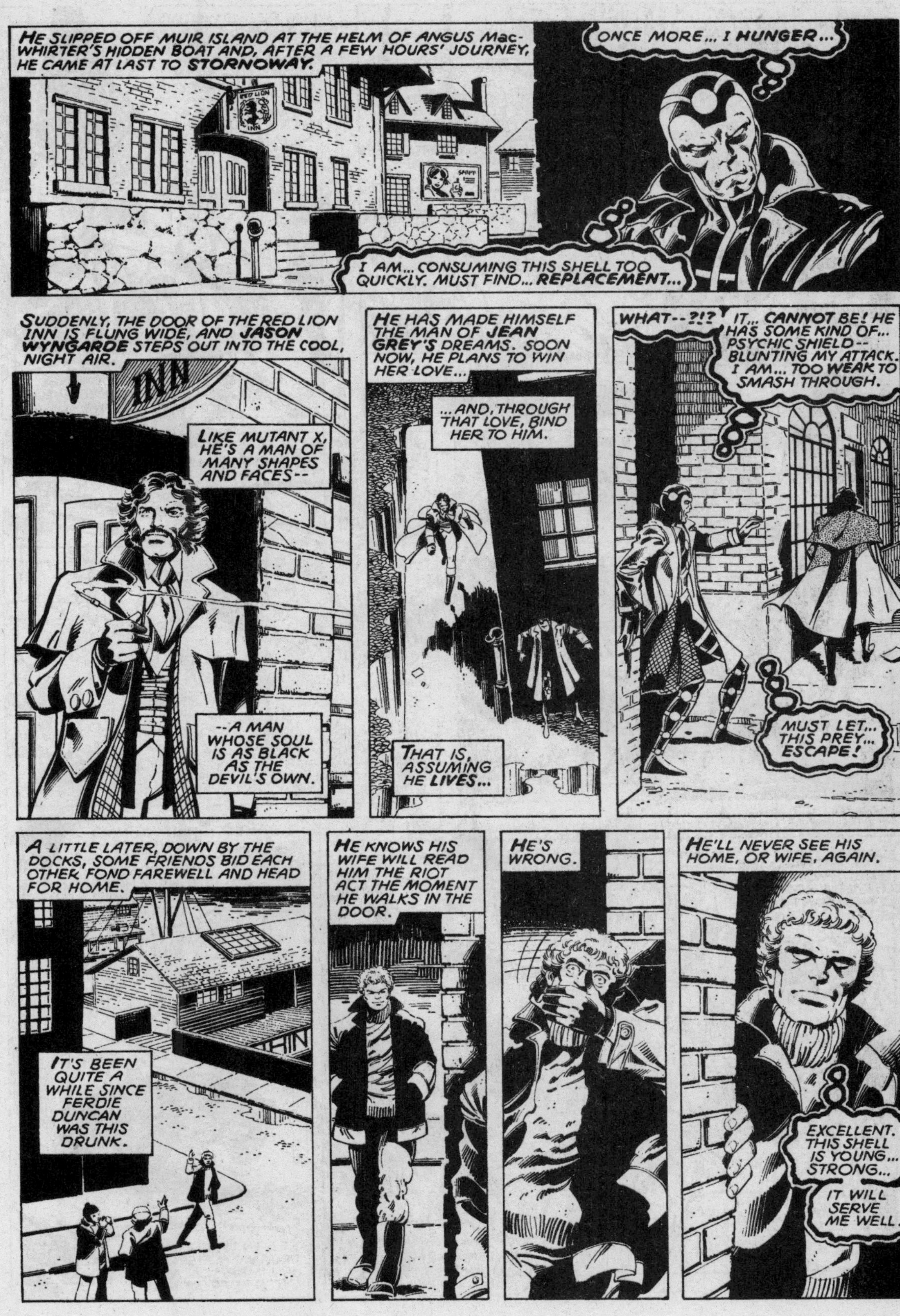

HE SLIPPED OFF MUIR ISLAND AT THE HELM OF ANGUS MacWHIRTER'S HIDDEN BOAT AND, AFTER A FEW HOURS' JOURNEY, HE CAME AT LAST TO STORNOWAY.
RED LION INN
ONCE MORE... I HUNGER...
I AM... CONSUMING THIS SHELL TOO QUICKLY. MUST FIND... REPLACEMENT...
SUDDENLY, THE DOOR OF THE RED LION INN IS FLUNG WIDE, AND JASON WYNGARDE STEPS OUT INTO THE COOL, NIGHT AIR.
INN
LIKE MUTANT X, HE'S A MAN OF MANY SHAPES AND FACES--
--A MAN WHOSE SOUL IS AS BLACK AS THE DEVIL'S OWN.
HE HAS MADE HIMSELF THE MAN OF JEAN GREY'S DREAMS. SOON NOW, HE PLANS TO WIN HER LOVE...
...AND, THROUGH THAT LOVE, BIND HER TO HIM.
THAT IS, ASSUMING HE LIVES...
WHAT--?!?
IT... CANNOT BE! HE HAS SOME KIND OF... PSYCHIC SHIELD--BLUNTING MY ATTACK. I AM... TOO WEAK TO SMASH THROUGH.
MUST LET... THIS PREY... ESCAPE!
A LITTLE LATER, DOWN BY THE DOCKS, SOME FRIENDS BID EACH OTHER FOND FAREWELL AND HEAD FOR HOME.
IT'S BEEN QUITE A WHILE SINCE FERDIE DUNCAN WAS THIS DRUNK.
HE KNOWS HIS WIFE WILL READ HIM THE RIOT ACT THE MOMENT HE WALKS IN THE DOOR.
HE'S WRONG.
HE'LL NEVER SEE HIS HOME, OR WIFE, AGAIN.
EXCELLENT. THIS SHELL IS YOUNG... STRONG...
IT WILL SERVE ME WELL.

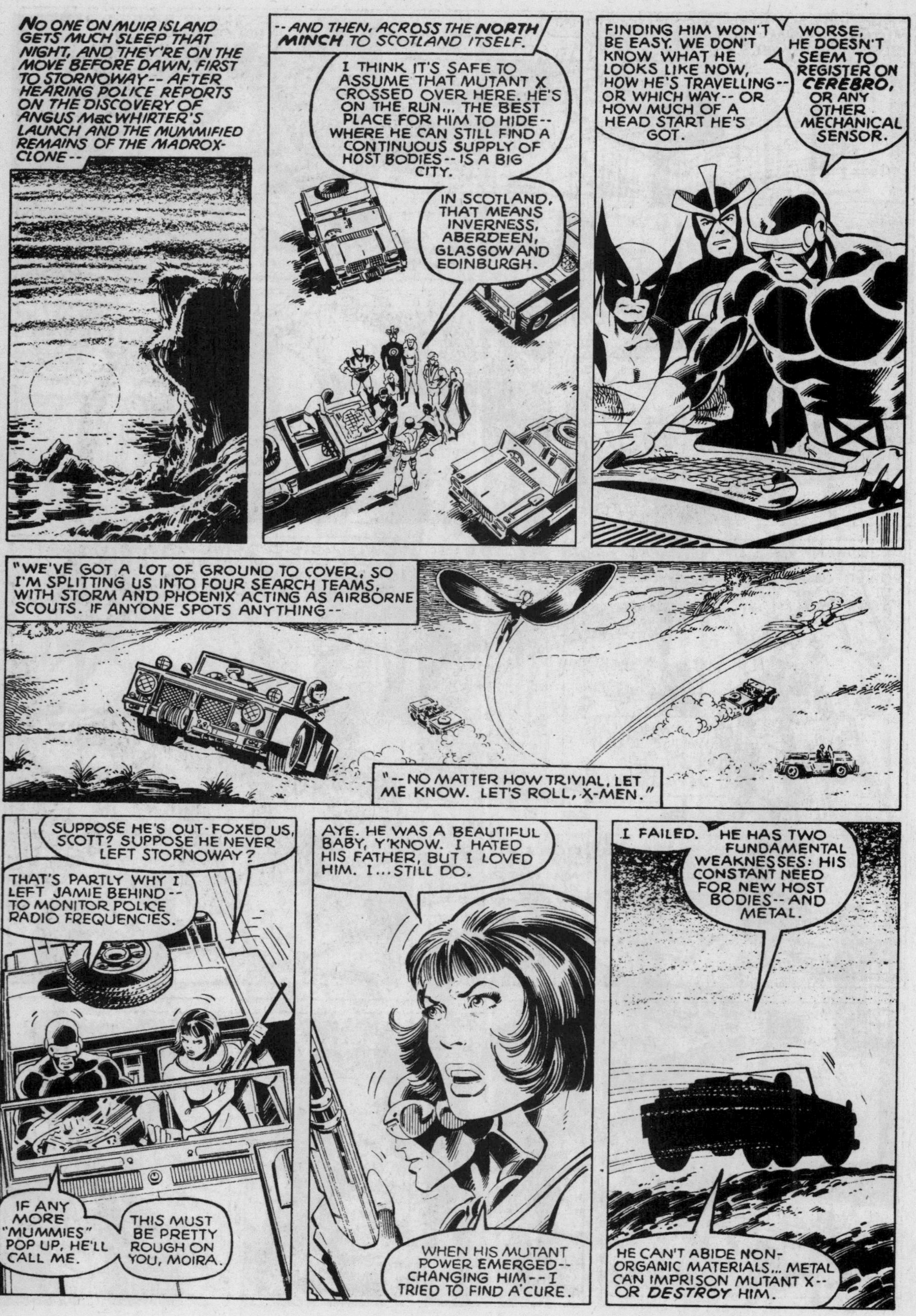
NO ONE ON MUIR ISLAND GETS MUCH SLEEP THAT NIGHT, AND THEY'RE ON THE MOVE BEFORE DAWN, FIRST TO STORNOWAY-- AFTER HEARING POLICE REPORTS ON THE DISCOVERY OF ANGUS MacWHIRTER'S LAUNCH AND THE MUMMIFIED REMAINS OF THE MADROX-CLONE--
--AND THEN, ACROSS THE NORTH MINCH TO SCOTLAND ITSELF.
I THINK IT'S SAFE TO ASSUME THAT MUTANT X CROSSED OVER HERE. HE'S ON THE RUN... THE BEST PLACE FOR HIM TO HIDE-- WHERE HE CAN STILL FIND A CONTINUOUS SUPPLY OF HOST BODIES-- IS A BIG CITY.
IN SCOTLAND, THAT MEANS INVERNESS, ABERDEEN, GLASGOW AND EDINBURGH.
FINDING HIM WON'T BE EASY. WE DON'T KNOW WHAT HE LOOKS LIKE NOW, HOW HE'S TRAVELLING-- OR WHICH WAY-- OR HOW MUCH OF A HEAD START HE'S GOT.
WORSE, HE DOESN'T SEEM TO REGISTER ON CEREBRO, OR ANY OTHER MECHANICAL SENSOR.
"WE'VE GOT A LOT OF GROUND TO COVER, SO I'M SPLITTING US INTO FOUR SEARCH TEAMS, WITH STORM AND PHOENIX ACTING AS AIRBORNE SCOUTS. IF ANYONE SPOTS ANYTHING--
"--NO MATTER HOW TRIVIAL, LET ME KNOW. LET'S ROLL, X-MEN."
SUPPOSE HE'S OUT-FOXED US, SCOTT? SUPPOSE HE NEVER LEFT STORNOWAY?
THAT'S PARTLY WHY I LEFT JAMIE BEHIND-- TO MONITOR POLICE RADIO FREQUENCIES.
IF ANY MORE "MUMMIES" POP UP, HE'LL CALL ME.
THIS MUST BE PRETTY ROUGH ON YOU, MOIRA.
AYE. HE WAS A BEAUTIFUL BABY, Y'KNOW. I HATED HIS FATHER, BUT I LOVED HIM. I... STILL DO.
WHEN HIS MUTANT POWER EMERGED-- CHANGING HIM-- I TRIED TO FIND A CURE.
I FAILED.
HE HAS TWO FUNDAMENTAL WEAKNESSES: HIS CONSTANT NEED FOR NEW HOST BODIES-- AND METAL.
HE CAN'T ABIDE NON-ORGANIC MATERIALS... METAL CAN IMPRISON MUTANT X-- OR DESTROY HIM.

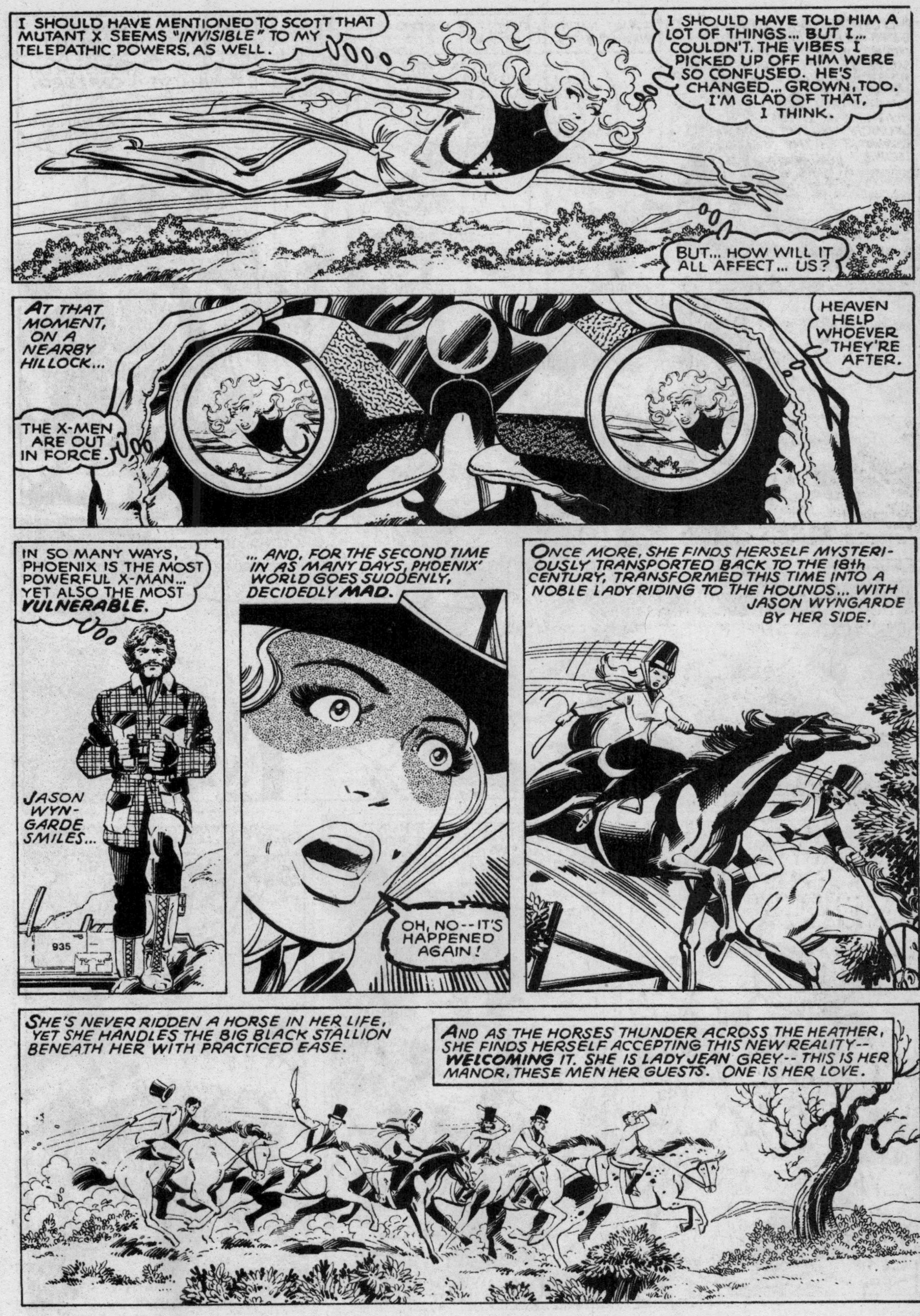
I SHOULD HAVE MENTIONED TO SCOTT THAT MUTANT X SEEMS "INVISIBLE" TO MY TELEPATHIC POWERS, AS WELL.
I SHOULD HAVE TOLD HIM A LOT OF THINGS... BUT I... COULDN'T. THE VIBES I PICKED UP OFF HIM WERE SO CONFUSED. HE'S CHANGED... GROWN, TOO. I'M GLAD OF THAT, I THINK.
BUT... HOW WILL IT ALL AFFECT... US?
AT THAT MOMENT, ON A NEARBY HILLOCK...
THE X-MEN ARE OUT IN FORCE.
HEAVEN HELP WHOEVER THEY'RE AFTER.
IN SO MANY WAYS, PHOENIX IS THE MOST POWERFUL X-MAN... YET ALSO THE MOST VULNERABLE.
JASON WYNGARDE SMILES...
935
... AND, FOR THE SECOND TIME IN AS MANY DAYS, PHOENIX' WORLD GOES SUDDENLY, DECIDEDLY MAD.
OH, NO--IT'S HAPPENED AGAIN!
ONCE MORE, SHE FINDS HERSELF MYSTERIOUSLY TRANSPORTED BACK TO THE 18th CENTURY, TRANSFORMED THIS TIME INTO A NOBLE LADY RIDING TO THE HOUNDS... WITH JASON WYNGARDE BY HER SIDE.
SHE'S NEVER RIDDEN A HORSE IN HER LIFE, YET SHE HANDLES THE BIG BLACK STALLION BENEATH HER WITH PRACTICED EASE.
AND AS THE HORSES THUNDER ACROSS THE HEATHER, SHE FINDS HERSELF ACCEPTING THIS NEW REALITY-- WELCOMING IT. SHE IS LADY JEAN GREY-- THIS IS HER MANOR, THESE MEN HER GUESTS. ONE IS HER LOVE.

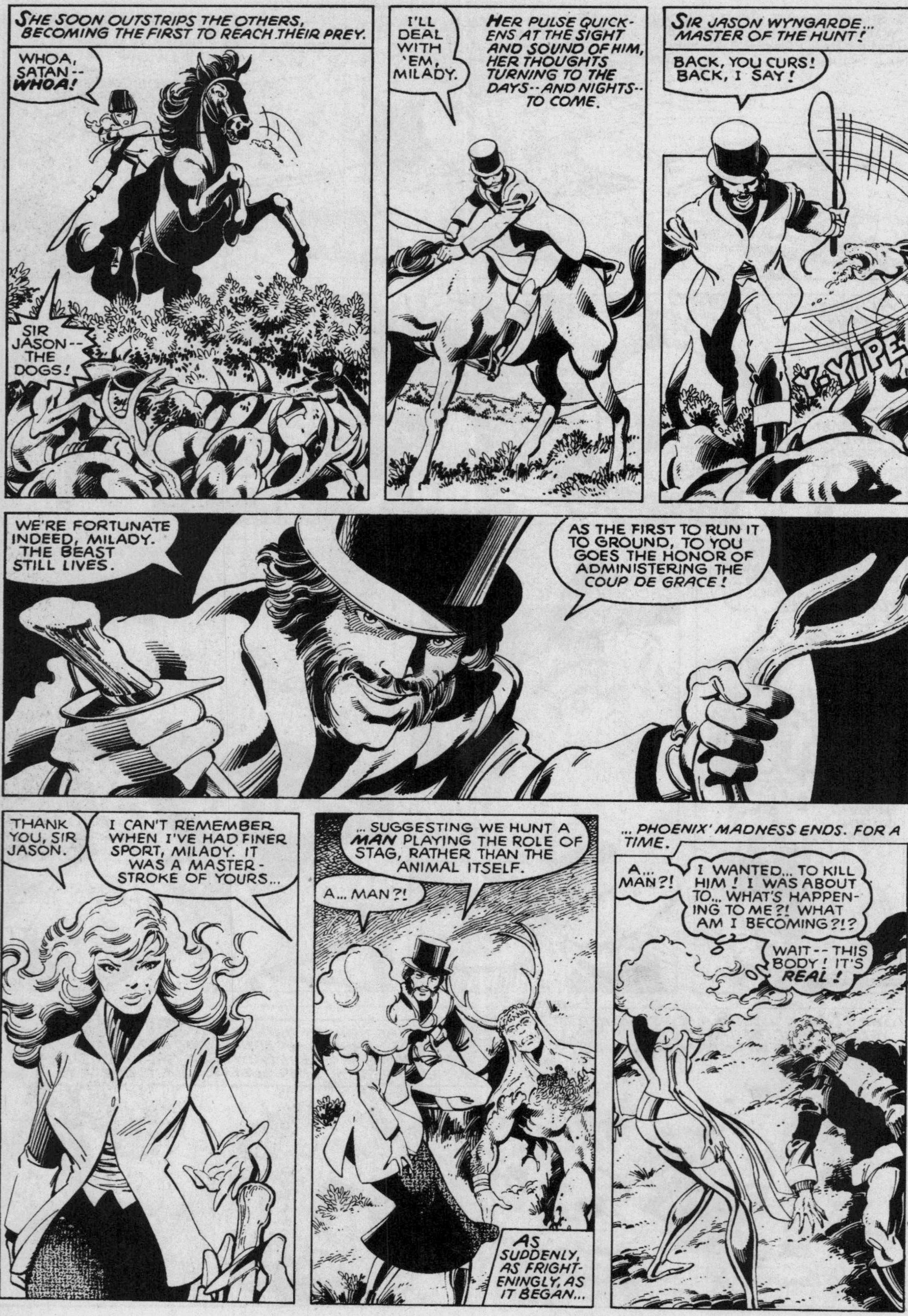
SHE SOON OUTSTRIPS THE OTHERS, BECOMING THE FIRST TO REACH THEIR PREY.
WHOA, SATAN-- WHOA!
SIR JASON-- THE DOGS!
I'LL DEAL WITH 'EM, MILADY.
HER PULSE QUICKENS AT THE SIGHT AND SOUND OF HIM, HER THOUGHTS TURNING TO THE DAYS--AND NIGHTS-- TO COME.
SIR JASON WYNGARDE... MASTER OF THE HUNT!
BACK, YOU CURS! BACK, I SAY!
Y-YIPE
WE'RE FORTUNATE INDEED, MILADY. THE BEAST STILL LIVES.
AS THE FIRST TO RUN IT TO GROUND, TO YOU GOES THE HONOR OF ADMINISTERING THE COUP DE GRACE!
THANK YOU, SIR JASON.
I CAN'T REMEMBER WHEN I'VE HAD FINER SPORT, MILADY. IT WAS A MASTER-STROKE OF YOURS...
... SUGGESTING WE HUNT A MAN PLAYING THE ROLE OF STAG, RATHER THAN THE ANIMAL ITSELF.
A... MAN?!
AS SUDDENLY, AS FRIGHTENINGLY, AS IT BEGAN...
... PHOENIX' MADNESS ENDS. FOR A TIME.
A... MAN?!
I WANTED... TO KILL HIM! I WAS ABOUT TO... WHAT'S HAPPENING TO ME?! WHAT AM I BECOMING?!?
WAIT-- THIS BODY! IT'S REAL!

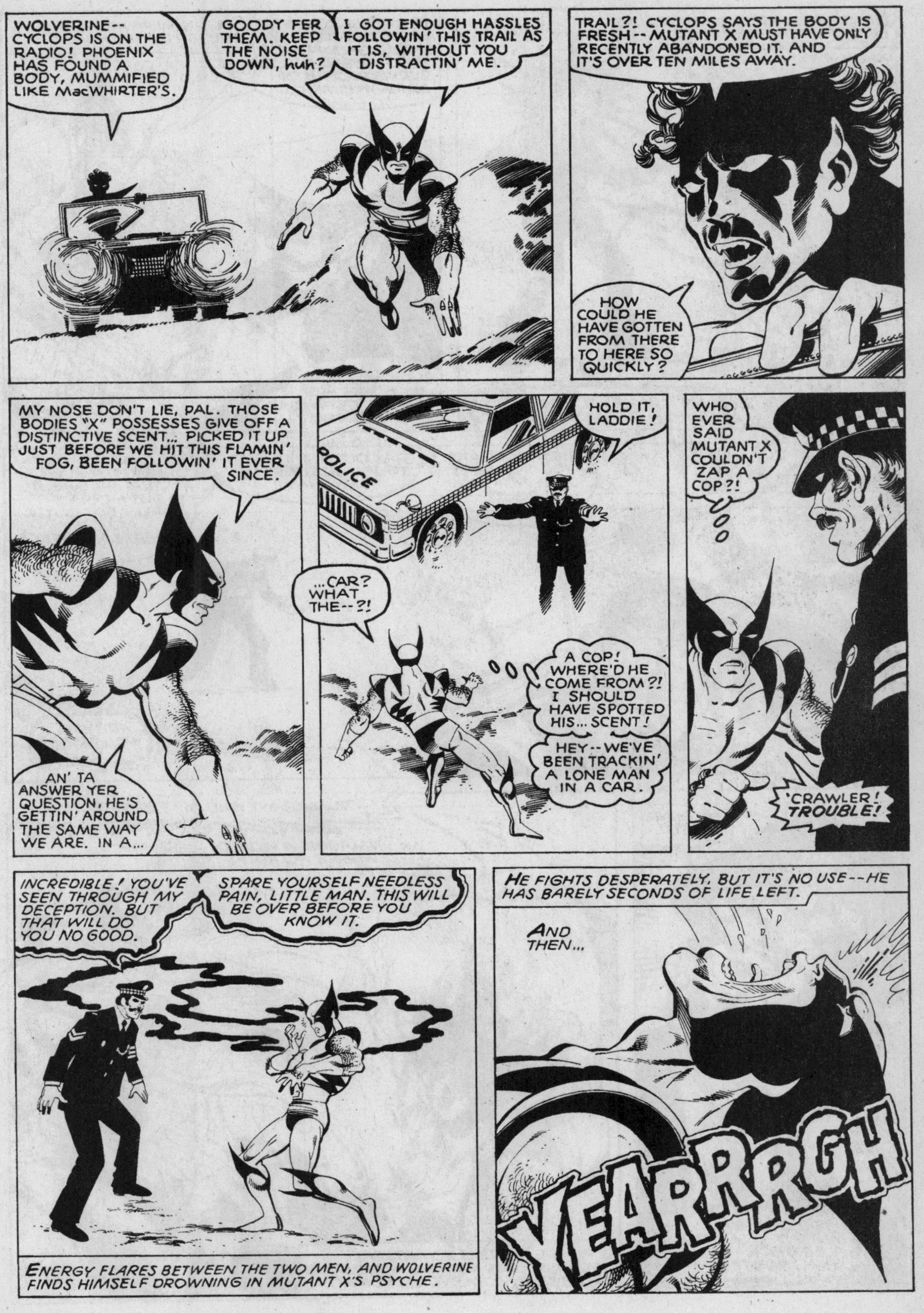
WOLVERINE-- CYCLOPS IS ON THE RADIO! PHOENIX HAS FOUND A BODY, MUMMIFIED LIKE MacWHIRTER'S.
GOODY FER THEM. KEEP THE NOISE DOWN, huh?
I GOT ENOUGH HASSLES FOLLOWIN' THIS TRAIL AS IT IS, WITHOUT YOU DISTRACTIN' ME.
TRAIL?! CYCLOPS SAYS THE BODY IS FRESH -- MUTANT X MUST HAVE ONLY RECENTLY ABANDONED IT. AND IT'S OVER TEN MILES AWAY.
HOW COULD HE HAVE GOTTEN FROM THERE TO HERE SO QUICKLY?
MY NOSE DON'T LIE, PAL. THOSE BODIES "X" POSSESSES GIVE OFF A DISTINCTIVE SCENT... PICKED IT UP JUST BEFORE WE HIT THIS FLAMIN' FOG, BEEN FOLLOWIN' IT EVER SINCE.
AN' TA ANSWER YER QUESTION, HE'S GETTIN' AROUND THE SAME WAY WE ARE. IN A...
POLICE
HOLD IT, LADDIE!
...CAR? WHAT THE--?!
A COP! WHERE'D HE COME FROM?! I SHOULD HAVE SPOTTED HIS... SCENT!
HEY--WE'VE BEEN TRACKIN' A LONE MAN IN A CAR.
WHO EVER SAID MUTANT X COULDN'T ZAP A COP?!
'CRAWLER! TROUBLE!
INCREDIBLE! YOU'VE SEEN THROUGH MY DECEPTION. BUT THAT WILL DO YOU NO GOOD.
SPARE YOURSELF NEEDLESS PAIN, LITTLE MAN. THIS WILL BE OVER BEFORE YOU KNOW IT.
ENERGY FLARES BETWEEN THE TWO MEN, AND WOLVERINE FINDS HIMSELF DROWNING IN MUTANT X'S PSYCHE.
HE FIGHTS DESPERATELY, BUT IT'S NO USE--HE HAS BARELY SECONDS OF LIFE LEFT.
AND THEN...
YEARRRGH

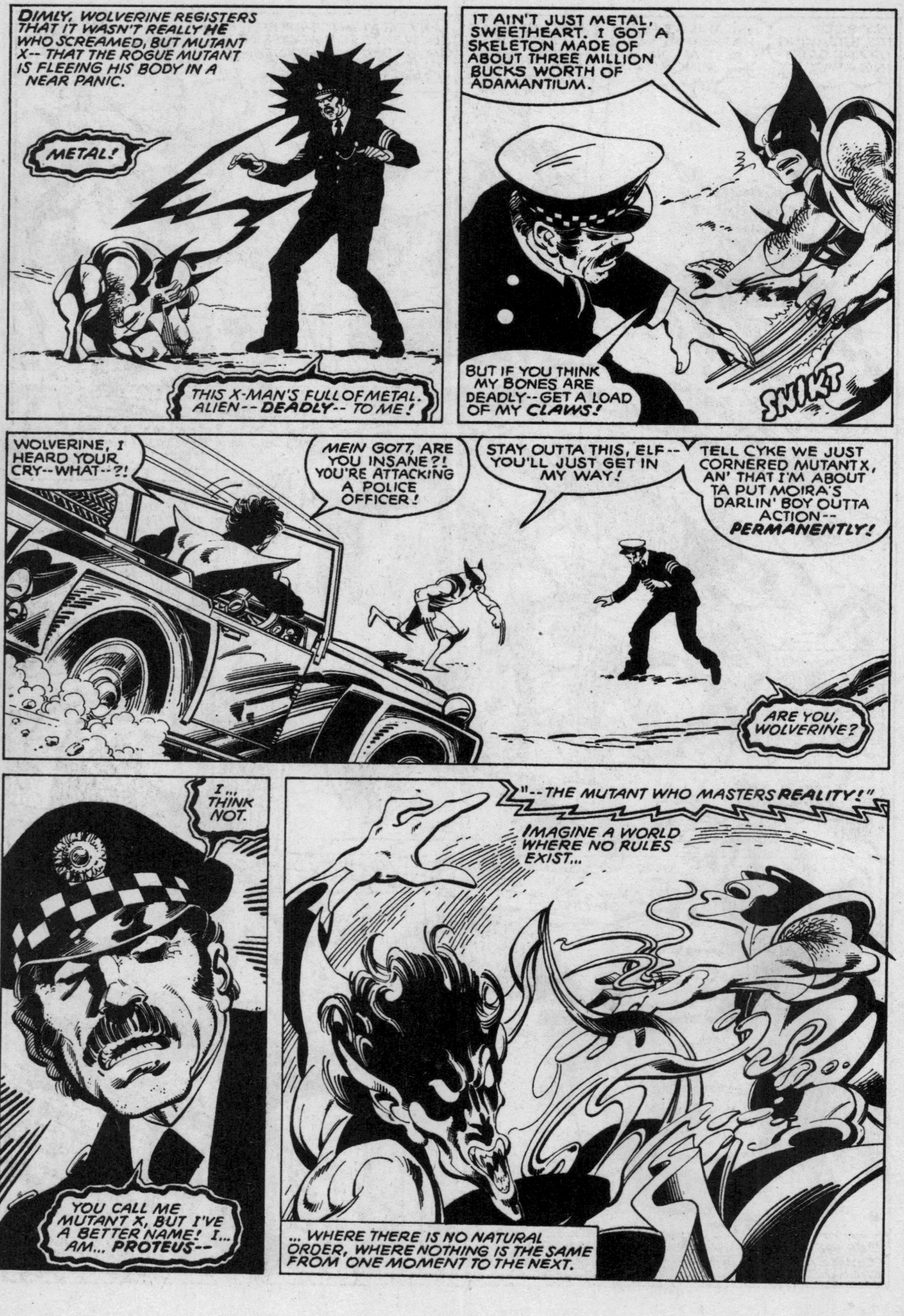
DIMLY, WOLVERINE REGISTERS THAT IT WASN'T REALLY HE WHO SCREAMED, BUT MUTANT X-- THAT THE ROGUE MUTANT IS FLEEING HIS BODY IN A NEAR PANIC.
METAL!
THIS X-MAN'S FULL OF METAL. ALIEN-- DEADLY-- TO ME!
IT AIN'T JUST METAL, SWEETHEART. I GOT A SKELETON MADE OF ABOUT THREE MILLION BUCKS WORTH OF ADAMANTIUM.
BUT IF YOU THINK MY BONES ARE DEADLY--GET A LOAD OF MY CLAWS!
SNIKT
WOLVERINE, I HEARD YOUR CRY--WHAT--?!
MEIN GOTT, ARE YOU INSANE?! YOU'RE ATTACKING A POLICE OFFICER!
STAY OUTTA THIS, ELF-- YOU'LL JUST GET IN MY WAY!
TELL CYKE WE JUST CORNERED MUTANT X, AN' THAT I'M ABOUT TA PUT MOIRA'S DARLIN' BOY OUTTA ACTION-- PERMANENTLY!
ARE YOU, WOLVERINE?
I... THINK NOT.
YOU CALL ME MUTANT X, BUT I'VE A BETTER NAME! I... AM... PROTEUS--
"--THE MUTANT WHO MASTERS REALITY!"
IMAGINE A WORLD WHERE NO RULES EXIST...
... WHERE THERE IS NO NATURAL ORDER, WHERE NOTHING IS THE SAME FROM ONE MOMENT TO THE NEXT.

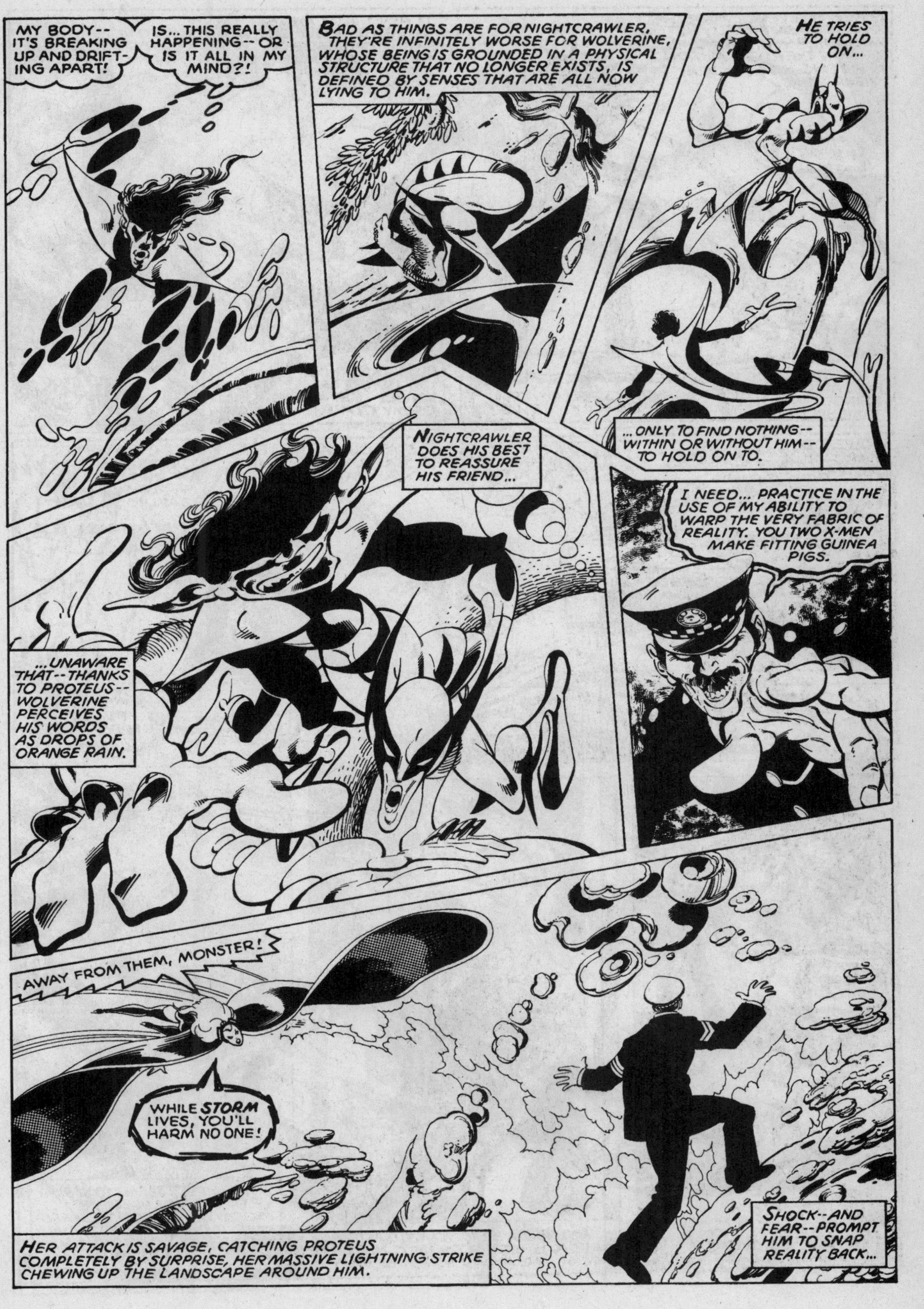
MY BODY-- IT'S BREAKING UP AND DRIFTING APART!
IS... THIS REALLY HAPPENING-- OR IS IT ALL IN MY MIND?!
BAD AS THINGS ARE FOR NIGHTCRAWLER, THEY'RE INFINITELY WORSE FOR WOLVERINE, WHOSE BEING IS GROUNDED IN A PHYSICAL STRUCTURE THAT NO LONGER EXISTS, IS DEFINED BY SENSES THAT ARE ALL NOW LYING TO HIM.
HE TRIES TO HOLD ON...
...ONLY TO FIND NOTHING-- WITHIN OR WITHOUT HIM-- TO HOLD ON TO.
NIGHTCRAWLER DOES HIS BEST TO REASSURE HIS FRIEND...
...UNAWARE THAT--THANKS TO PROTEUS--WOLVERINE PERCEIVES HIS WORDS AS DROPS OF ORANGE RAIN.
I NEED... PRACTICE IN THE USE OF MY ABILITY TO WARP THE VERY FABRIC OF REALITY. YOU TWO X-MEN MAKE FITTING GUINEA PIGS.
AWAY FROM THEM, MONSTER!
WHILE STORM LIVES, YOU'LL HARM NO ONE!
HER ATTACK IS SAVAGE, CATCHING PROTEUS COMPLETELY BY SURPRISE, HER MASSIVE LIGHTNING STRIKE CHEWING UP THE LANDSCAPE AROUND HIM.
SHOCK--AND FEAR--PROMPT HIM TO SNAP REALITY BACK...

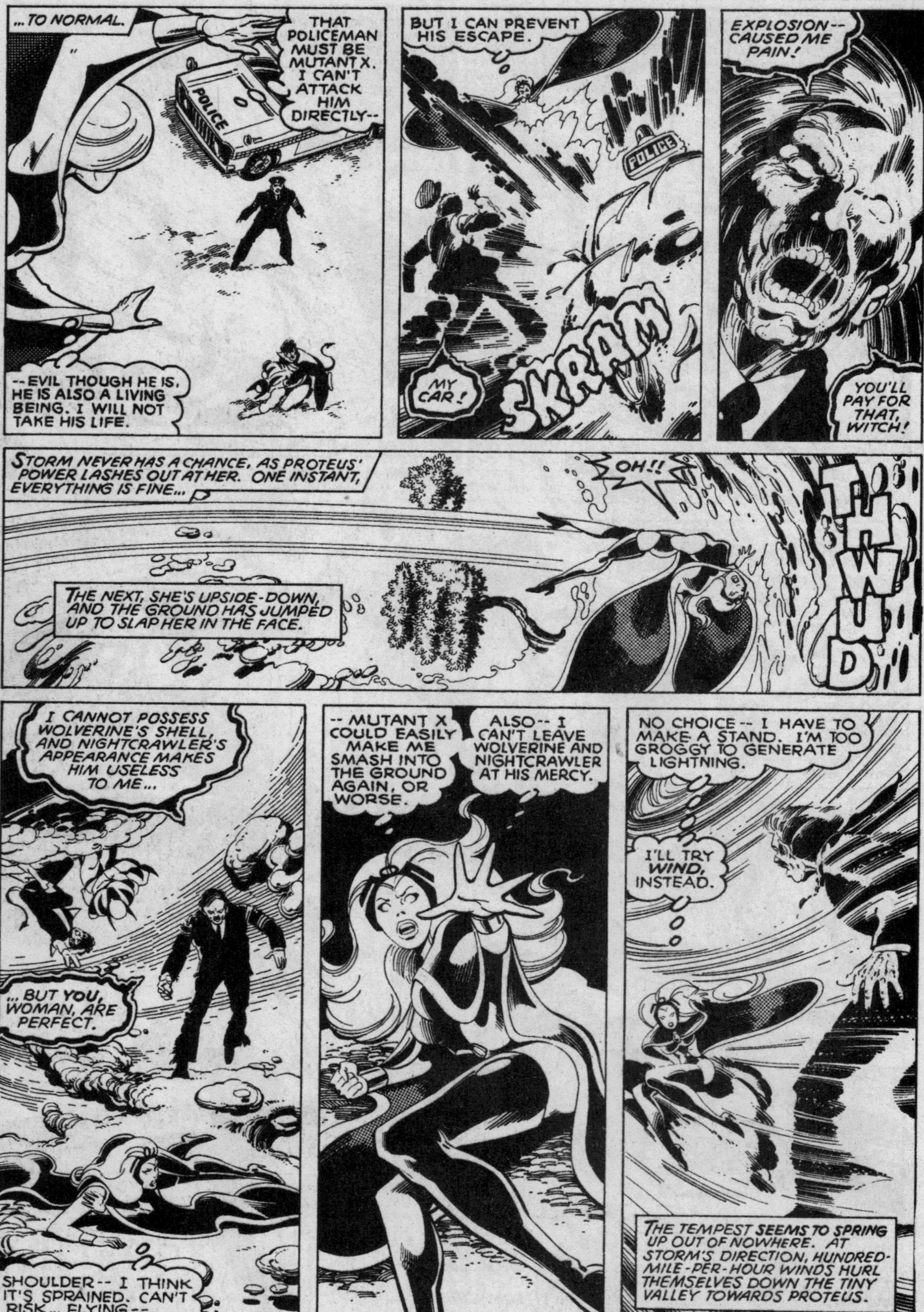
...TO NORMAL.
THAT POLICEMAN MUST BE MUTANT X. I CAN'T ATTACK HIM DIRECTLY--
POLICE
--EVIL THOUGH HE IS, HE IS ALSO A LIVING BEING. I WILL NOT TAKE HIS LIFE.
BUT I CAN PREVENT HIS ESCAPE.
POLICE
MY CAR!
SKRAM
EXPLOSION-- CAUSED ME PAIN!
YOU'LL PAY FOR THAT, WITCH!
STORM NEVER HAS A CHANCE, AS PROTEUS' POWER LASHES OUT AT HER. ONE INSTANT, EVERYTHING IS FINE...
OH!!
THWUD
THE NEXT, SHE'S UPSIDE-DOWN, AND THE GROUND HAS JUMPED UP TO SLAP HER IN THE FACE.
I CANNOT POSSESS WOLVERINE'S SHELL, AND NIGHTCRAWLER'S APPEARANCE MAKES HIM USELESS TO ME...
...BUT YOU, WOMAN, ARE PERFECT.
SHOULDER-- I THINK IT'S SPRAINED. CAN'T RISK... FLYING--
-- MUTANT X COULD EASILY MAKE ME SMASH INTO THE GROUND AGAIN, OR WORSE.
ALSO-- I CAN'T LEAVE WOLVERINE AND NIGHTCRAWLER AT HIS MERCY.
NO CHOICE -- I HAVE TO MAKE A STAND. I'M TOO GROGGY TO GENERATE LIGHTNING.
I'LL TRY WIND, INSTEAD.
THE TEMPEST SEEMS TO SPRING UP OUT OF NOWHERE. AT STORM'S DIRECTION, HUNDRED-MILE-PER-HOUR WINDS HURL THEMSELVES DOWN THE TINY VALLEY TOWARDS PROTEUS.

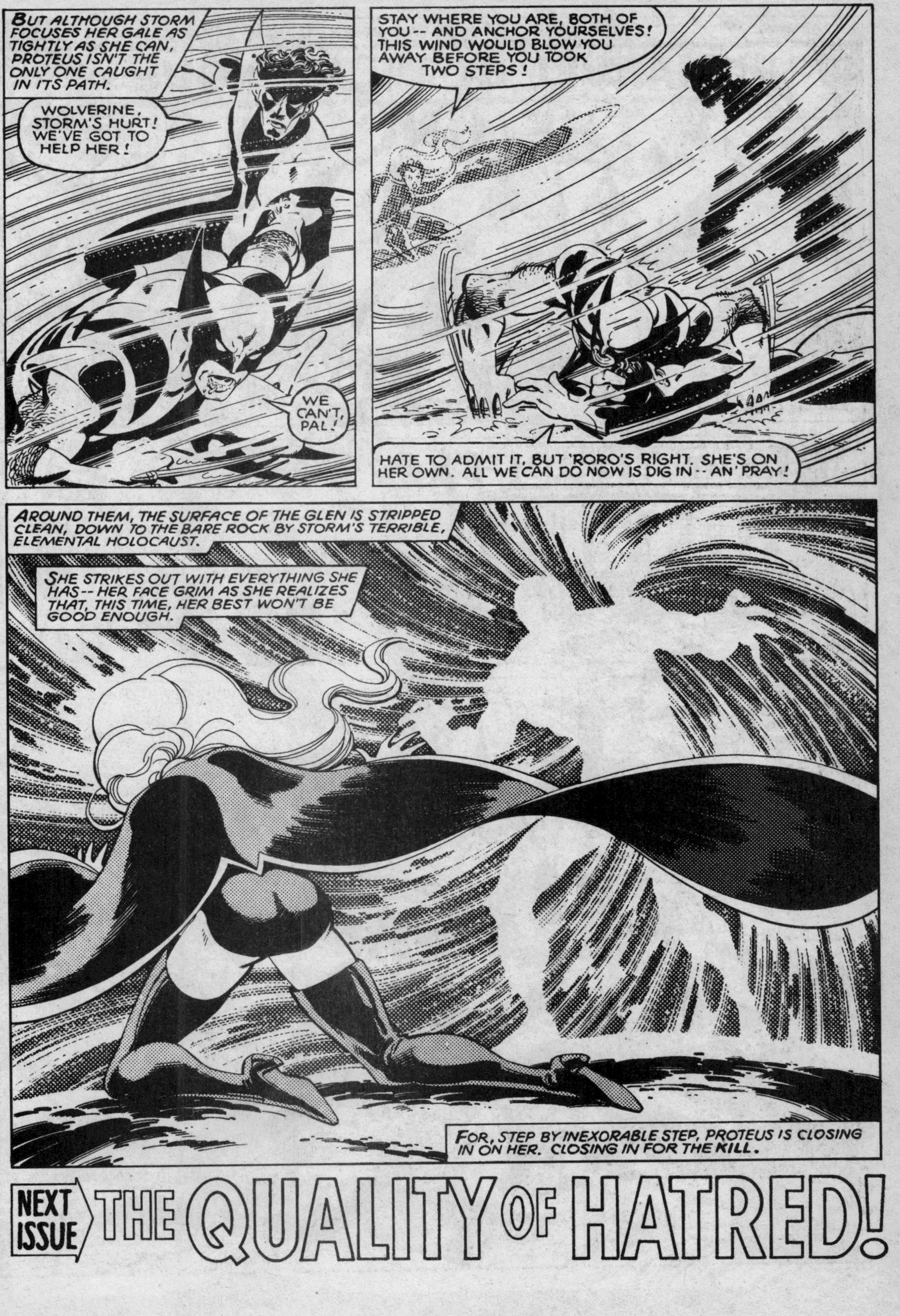

BUT ALTHOUGH STORM FOCUSES HER GALE AS TIGHTLY AS SHE CAN, PROTEUS ISN'T THE ONLY ONE CAUGHT IN ITS PATH.
WOLVERINE, STORM'S HURT! WE'VE GOT TO HELP HER!
WE CAN'T, PAL!
STAY WHERE YOU ARE, BOTH OF YOU-- AND ANCHOR YOURSELVES! THIS WIND WOULD BLOW YOU AWAY BEFORE YOU TOOK TWO STEPS!
HATE TO ADMIT IT, BUT 'RORO'S RIGHT. SHE'S ON HER OWN. ALL WE CAN DO NOW IS DIG IN -- AN' PRAY!
AROUND THEM, THE SURFACE OF THE GLEN IS STRIPPED CLEAN, DOWN TO THE BARE ROCK BY STORM'S TERRIBLE, ELEMENTAL HOLOCAUST.
SHE STRIKES OUT WITH EVERYTHING SHE HAS-- HER FACE GRIM AS SHE REALIZES THAT, THIS TIME, HER BEST WON'T BE GOOD ENOUGH.
FOR, STEP BY INEXORABLE STEP, PROTEUS IS CLOSING IN ON HER. CLOSING IN FOR THE KILL.
NEXT ISSUE
THE QUALITY OF HATRED!

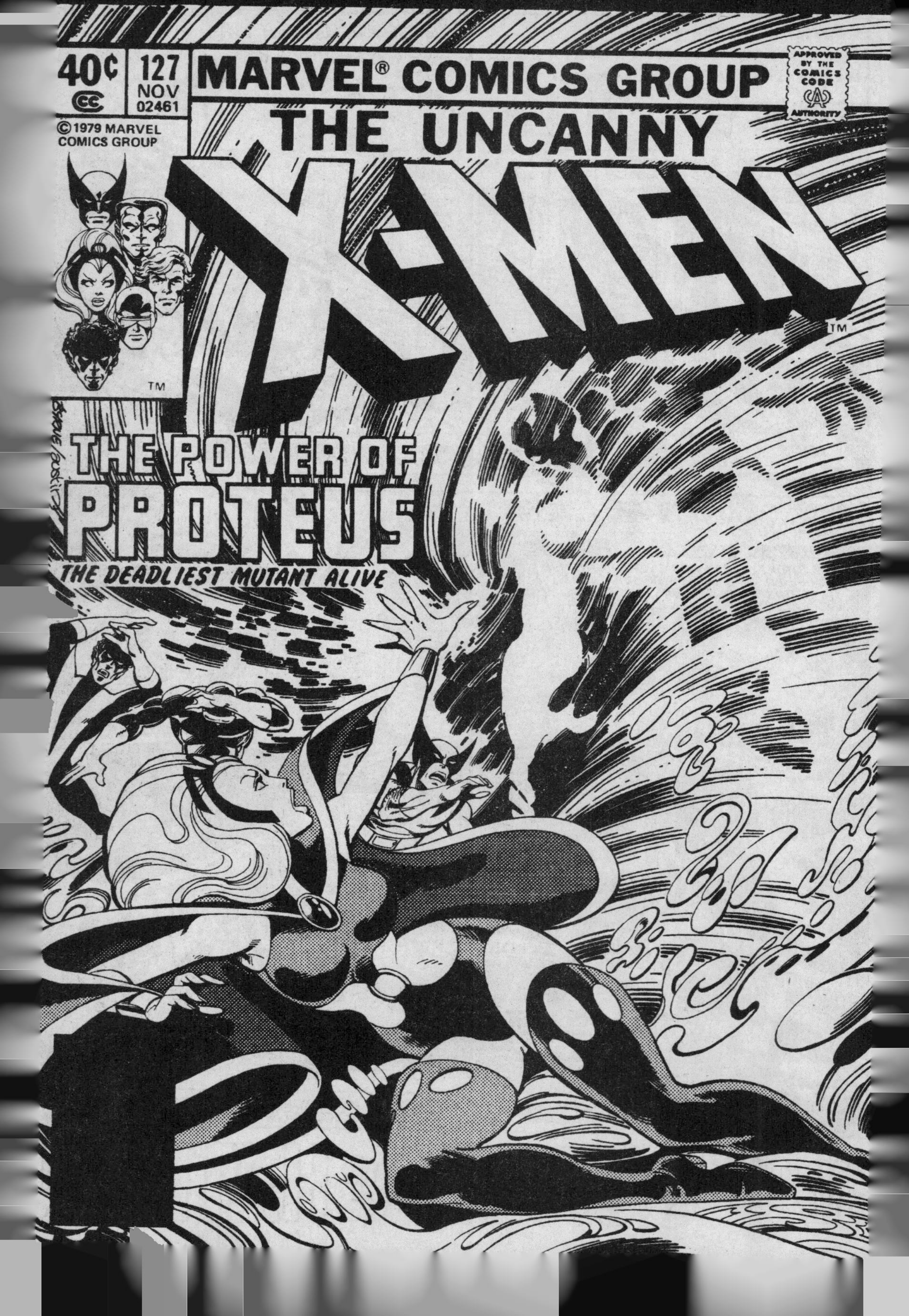

40¢
127
NOV
02461
MARVEL® COMICS GROUP
APPROVED BY THE COMICS CODE AUTHORITY
© 1979 MARVEL COMICS GROUP
THE UNCANNY
X-MEN™
THE POWER OF
PROTEUS
THE DEADLIEST MUTANT ALIVE

Cyclops. Storm. Banshee. Nightcrawler. Wolverine. Colossus. Children of the atom, students of Charles Xavier, MUTANTS––feared and hated by the world they have sworn to protect. These are the STRANGEST heroes of all!

Stan Lee PRESENTS: **THE UNCANNY X-MEN!**™

CHRIS CLAREMONT ✱ JOHN BYRNE *WRITER - PLOTTERS - PENCILER* | TERRY AUSTIN *INKER* | TOM ORZECHOWSKI, *letterer* GLYNIS WEIN, *colorist* | ROGER STERN *EDITOR* | JIM SHOOTER *Ed.-IN-CHIEF*

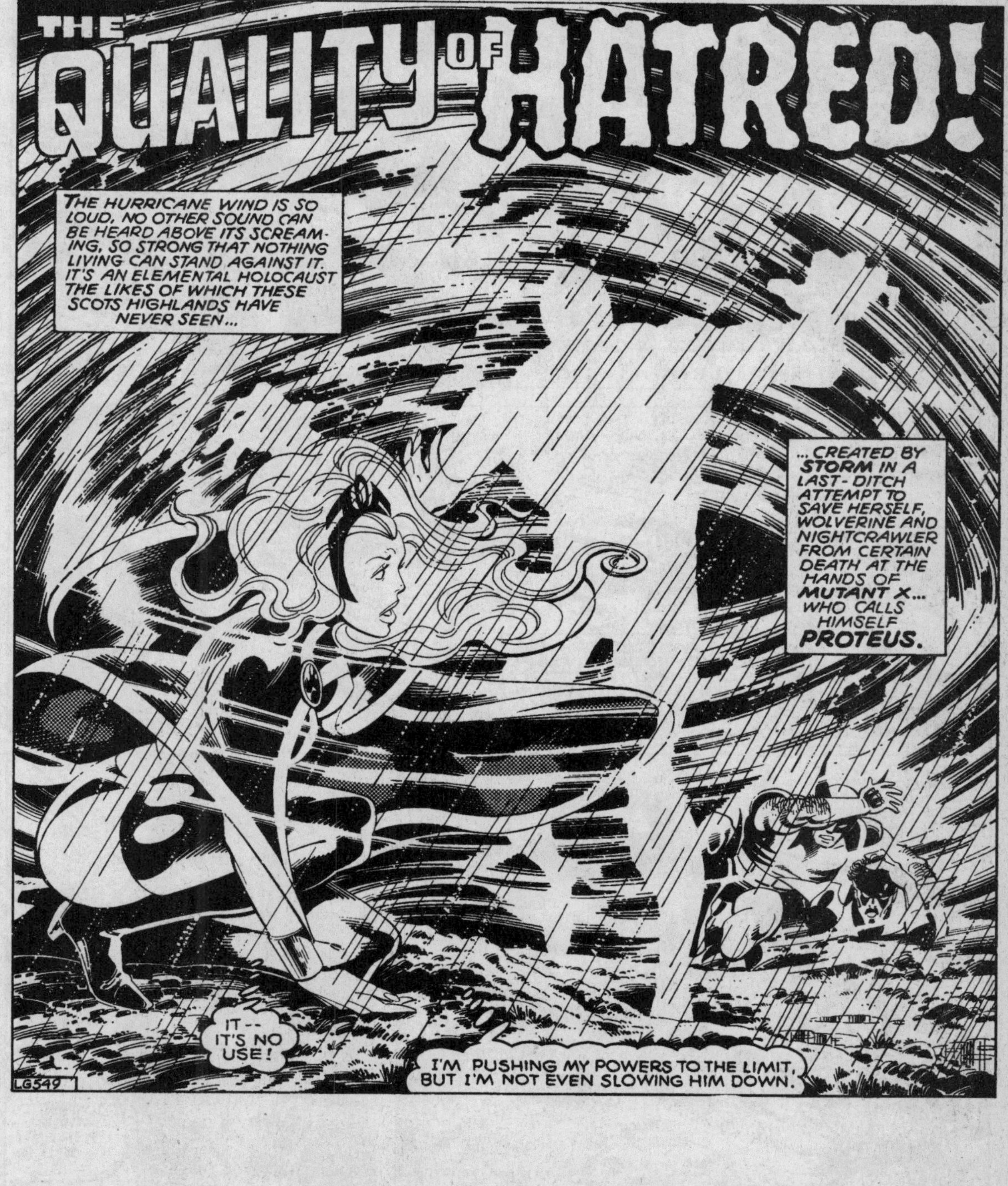
THE QUALITY OF HATRED!
THE HURRICANE WIND IS SO LOUD, NO OTHER SOUND CAN BE HEARD ABOVE ITS SCREAMING, SO STRONG THAT NOTHING LIVING CAN STAND AGAINST IT. IT'S AN ELEMENTAL HOLOCAUST THE LIKES OF WHICH THESE SCOTS HIGHLANDS HAVE NEVER SEEN...
...CREATED BY STORM IN A LAST-DITCH ATTEMPT TO SAVE HERSELF, WOLVERINE AND NIGHTCRAWLER FROM CERTAIN DEATH AT THE HANDS OF MUTANT X... WHO CALLS HIMSELF PROTEUS.
IT-- IT'S NO USE!
I'M PUSHING MY POWERS TO THE LIMIT, BUT I'M NOT EVEN SLOWING HIM DOWN.
LG549 1

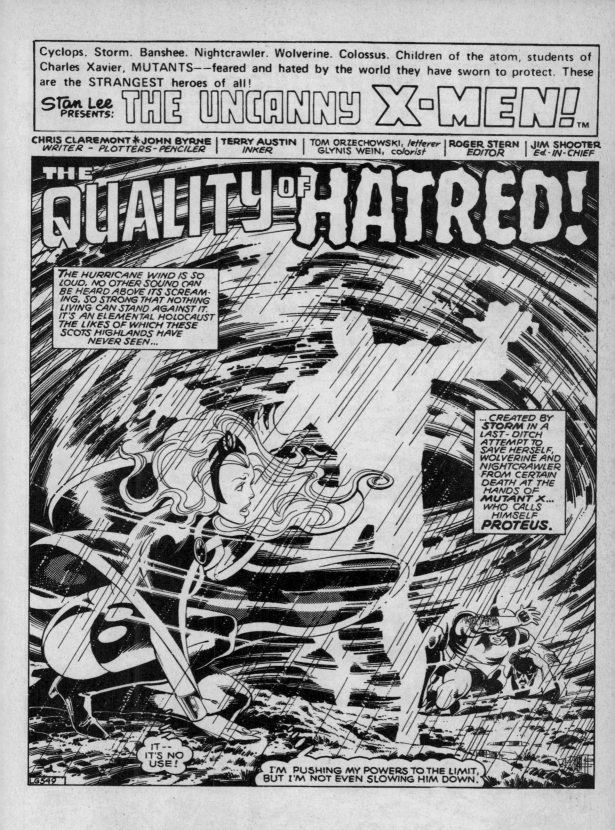

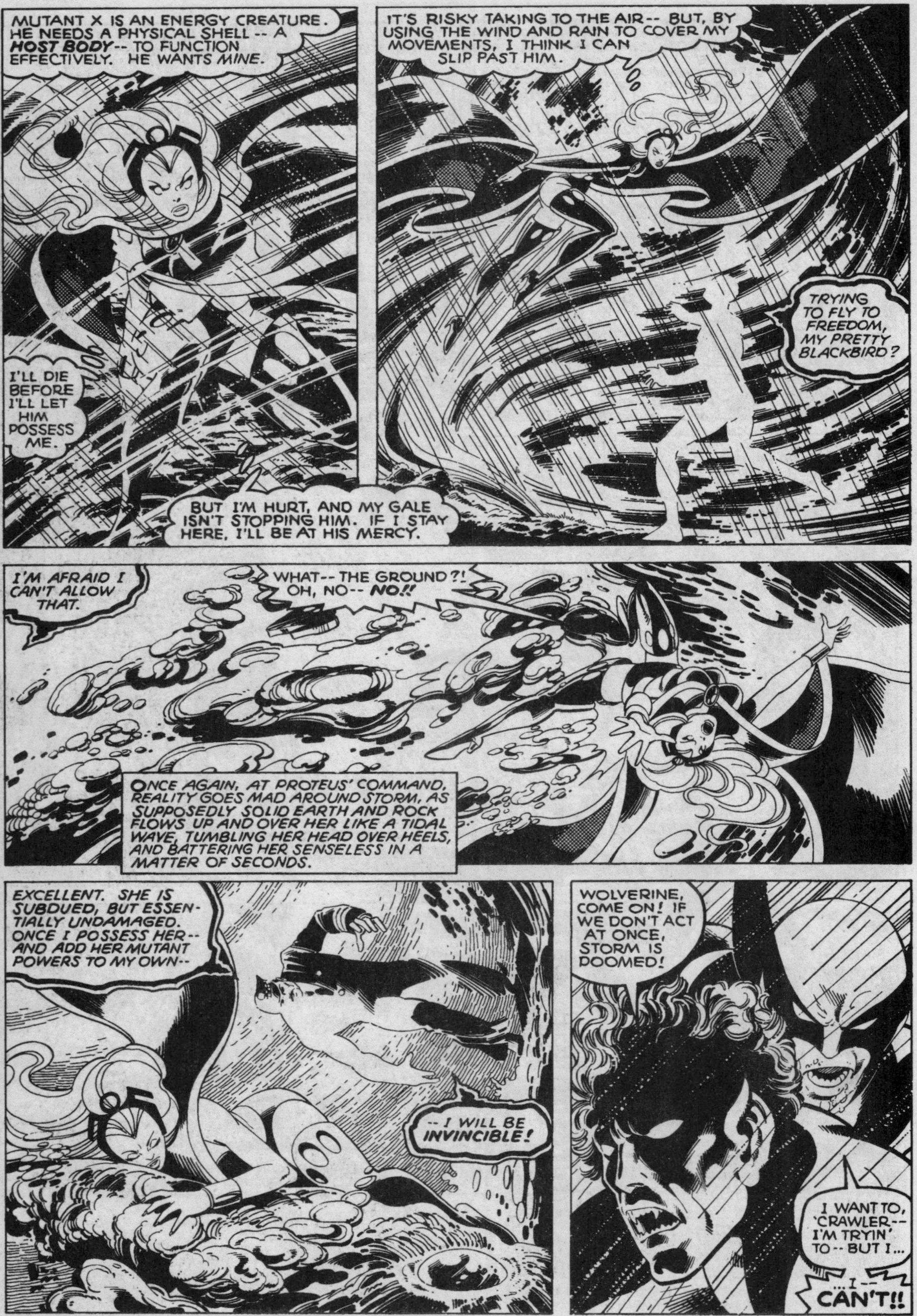
MUTANT X IS AN ENERGY CREATURE. HE NEEDS A PHYSICAL SHELL -- A HOST BODY -- TO FUNCTION EFFECTIVELY. HE WANTS MINE.
I'LL DIE BEFORE I'LL LET HIM POSSESS ME.
BUT I'M HURT, AND MY GALE ISN'T STOPPING HIM. IF I STAY HERE, I'LL BE AT HIS MERCY.
IT'S RISKY TAKING TO THE AIR -- BUT, BY USING THE WIND AND RAIN TO COVER MY MOVEMENTS, I THINK I CAN SLIP PAST HIM.
TRYING TO FLY TO FREEDOM, MY PRETTY BLACKBIRD?
I'M AFRAID I CAN'T ALLOW THAT.
WHAT -- THE GROUND?! OH, NO -- NO!!
ONCE AGAIN, AT PROTEUS' COMMAND, REALITY GOES MAD AROUND STORM, AS SUPPOSEDLY SOLID EARTH AND ROCK FLOWS UP AND OVER HER LIKE A TIDAL WAVE, TUMBLING HER HEAD OVER HEELS, AND BATTERING HER SENSELESS IN A MATTER OF SECONDS.
EXCELLENT. SHE IS SUBDUED, BUT ESSENTIALLY UNDAMAGED. ONCE I POSSESS HER -- AND ADD HER MUTANT POWERS TO MY OWN --
-- I WILL BE INVINCIBLE!
WOLVERINE, COME ON! IF WE DON'T ACT AT ONCE, STORM IS DOOMED!
I WANT TO, 'CRAWLER -- I'M TRYIN' TO -- BUT I...
...I -- CAN'T!!

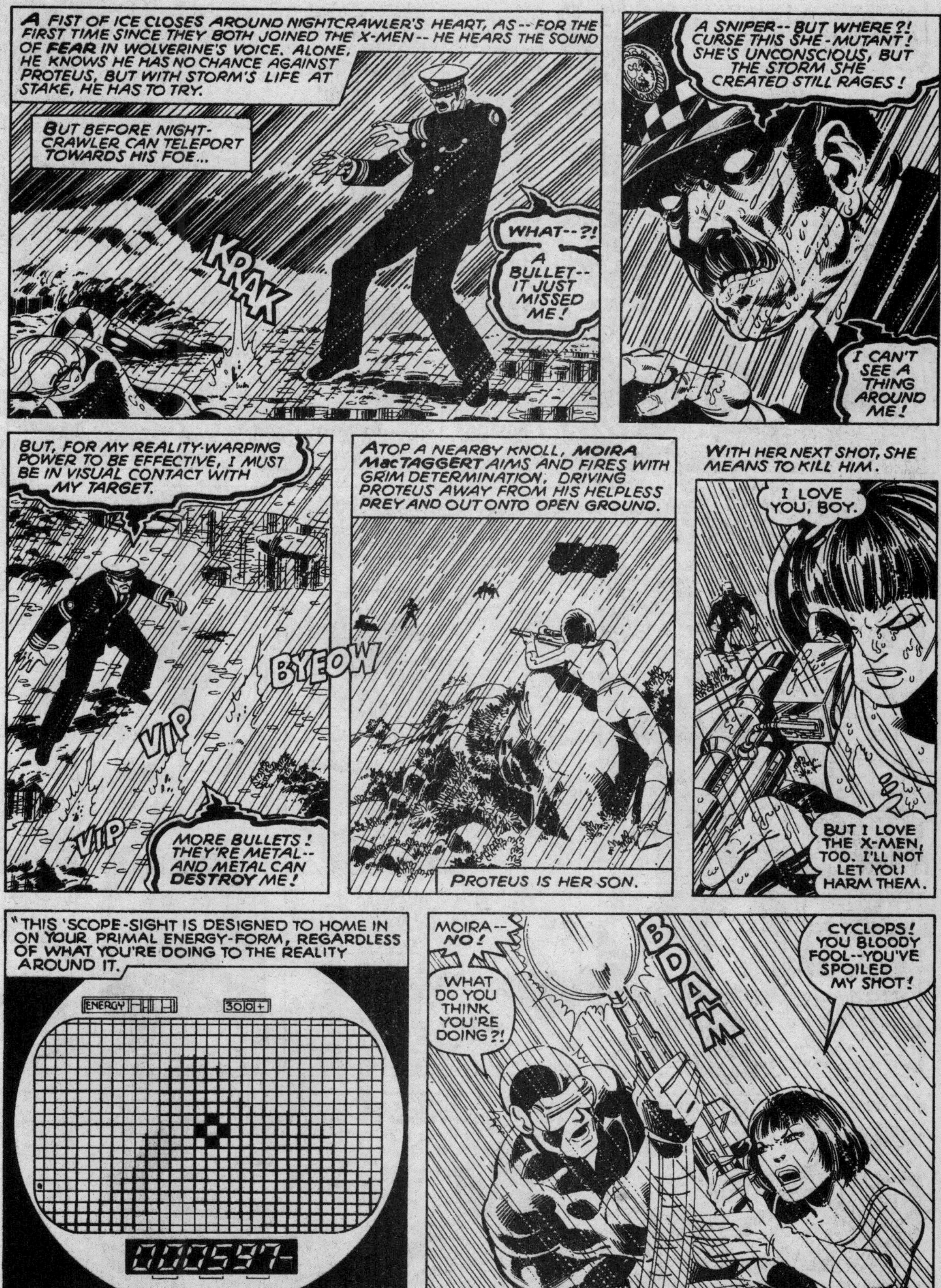

A FIST OF ICE CLOSES AROUND NIGHTCRAWLER'S HEART, AS--FOR THE FIRST TIME SINCE THEY BOTH JOINED THE X-MEN--HE HEARS THE SOUND OF FEAR IN WOLVERINE'S VOICE. ALONE, HE KNOWS HE HAS NO CHANCE AGAINST PROTEUS, BUT WITH STORM'S LIFE AT STAKE, HE HAS TO TRY.
BUT BEFORE NIGHT-CRAWLER CAN TELEPORT TOWARDS HIS FOE...
KRAK
WHAT--?! A BULLET--IT JUST MISSED ME!
A SNIPER--BUT WHERE?! CURSE THIS SHE-MUTANT! SHE'S UNCONSCIOUS, BUT THE STORM SHE CREATED STILL RAGES!
I CAN'T SEE A THING AROUND ME!
BUT, FOR MY REALITY-WARPING POWER TO BE EFFECTIVE, I MUST BE IN VISUAL CONTACT WITH MY TARGET.
BYEOW
VIP
VIP
MORE BULLETS! THEY'RE METAL--AND METAL CAN DESTROY ME!
ATOP A NEARBY KNOLL, MOIRA MacTAGGERT AIMS AND FIRES WITH GRIM DETERMINATION, DRIVING PROTEUS AWAY FROM HIS HELPLESS PREY AND OUT ONTO OPEN GROUND.
PROTEUS IS HER SON.
WITH HER NEXT SHOT, SHE MEANS TO KILL HIM.
I LOVE YOU, BOY.
BUT I LOVE THE X-MEN, TOO. I'LL NOT LET YOU HARM THEM.
"THIS 'SCOPE-SIGHT IS DESIGNED TO HOME IN ON YOUR PRIMAL ENERGY-FORM, REGARDLESS OF WHAT YOU'RE DOING TO THE REALITY AROUND IT.
ENERGY
300+
000597-
"I PRAYED IT WOULD NEVER COME TO THIS, BUT YOU'VE LEFT ME NO ALTERNATIVE."
MOIRA--NO!
WHAT DO YOU THINK YOU'RE DOING?!
BDAM
CYCLOPS! YOU BLOODY FOOL--YOU'VE SPOILED MY SHOT!

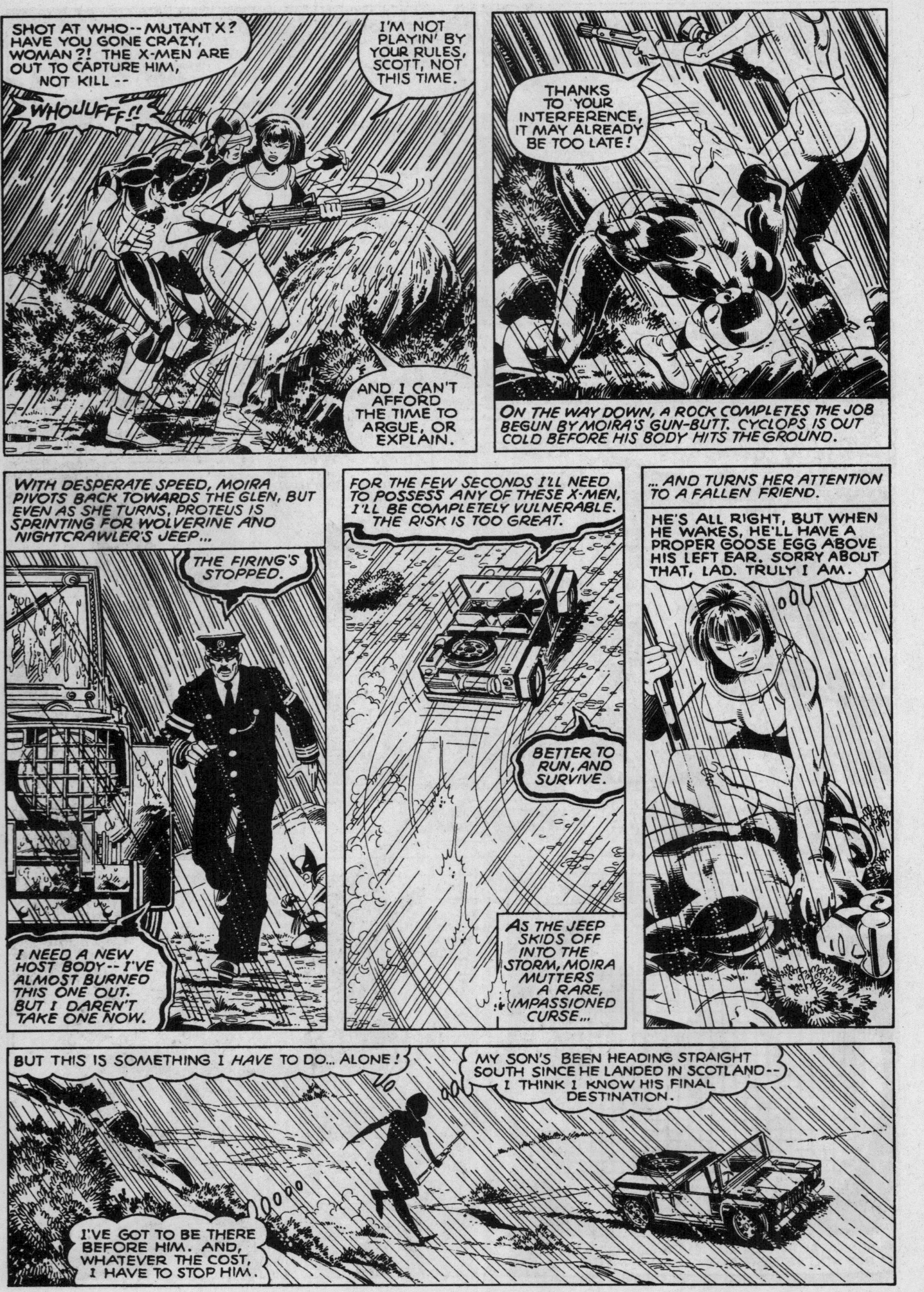
SHOT AT WHO-- MUTANT X? HAVE YOU GONE CRAZY, WOMAN?! THE X-MEN ARE OUT TO CAPTURE HIM, NOT KILL --
WHOUUFFF!!
I'M NOT PLAYIN' BY YOUR RULES, SCOTT, NOT THIS TIME.
AND I CAN'T AFFORD THE TIME TO ARGUE, OR EXPLAIN.
THANKS TO YOUR INTERFERENCE, IT MAY ALREADY BE TOO LATE!
ON THE WAY DOWN, A ROCK COMPLETES THE JOB BEGUN BY MOIRA'S GUN-BUTT. CYCLOPS IS OUT COLD BEFORE HIS BODY HITS THE GROUND.
WITH DESPERATE SPEED, MOIRA PIVOTS BACK TOWARDS THE GLEN, BUT EVEN AS SHE TURNS, PROTEUS IS SPRINTING FOR WOLVERINE AND NIGHTCRAWLER'S JEEP...
THE FIRING'S STOPPED.
I NEED A NEW HOST BODY -- I'VE ALMOST BURNED THIS ONE OUT. BUT I DAREN'T TAKE ONE NOW.
FOR THE FEW SECONDS I'LL NEED TO POSSESS ANY OF THESE X-MEN, I'LL BE COMPLETELY VULNERABLE. THE RISK IS TOO GREAT.
BETTER TO RUN, AND SURVIVE.
AS THE JEEP SKIDS OFF INTO THE STORM, MOIRA MUTTERS A RARE, IMPASSIONED CURSE...
... AND TURNS HER ATTENTION TO A FALLEN FRIEND.
HE'S ALL RIGHT, BUT WHEN HE WAKES, HE'LL HAVE A PROPER GOOSE EGG ABOVE HIS LEFT EAR. SORRY ABOUT THAT, LAD. TRULY I AM.
BUT THIS IS SOMETHING I HAVE TO DO... ALONE!
MY SON'S BEEN HEADING STRAIGHT SOUTH SINCE HE LANDED IN SCOTLAND-- I THINK I KNOW HIS FINAL DESTINATION.
I'VE GOT TO BE THERE BEFORE HIM. AND, WHATEVER THE COST, I HAVE TO STOP HIM.

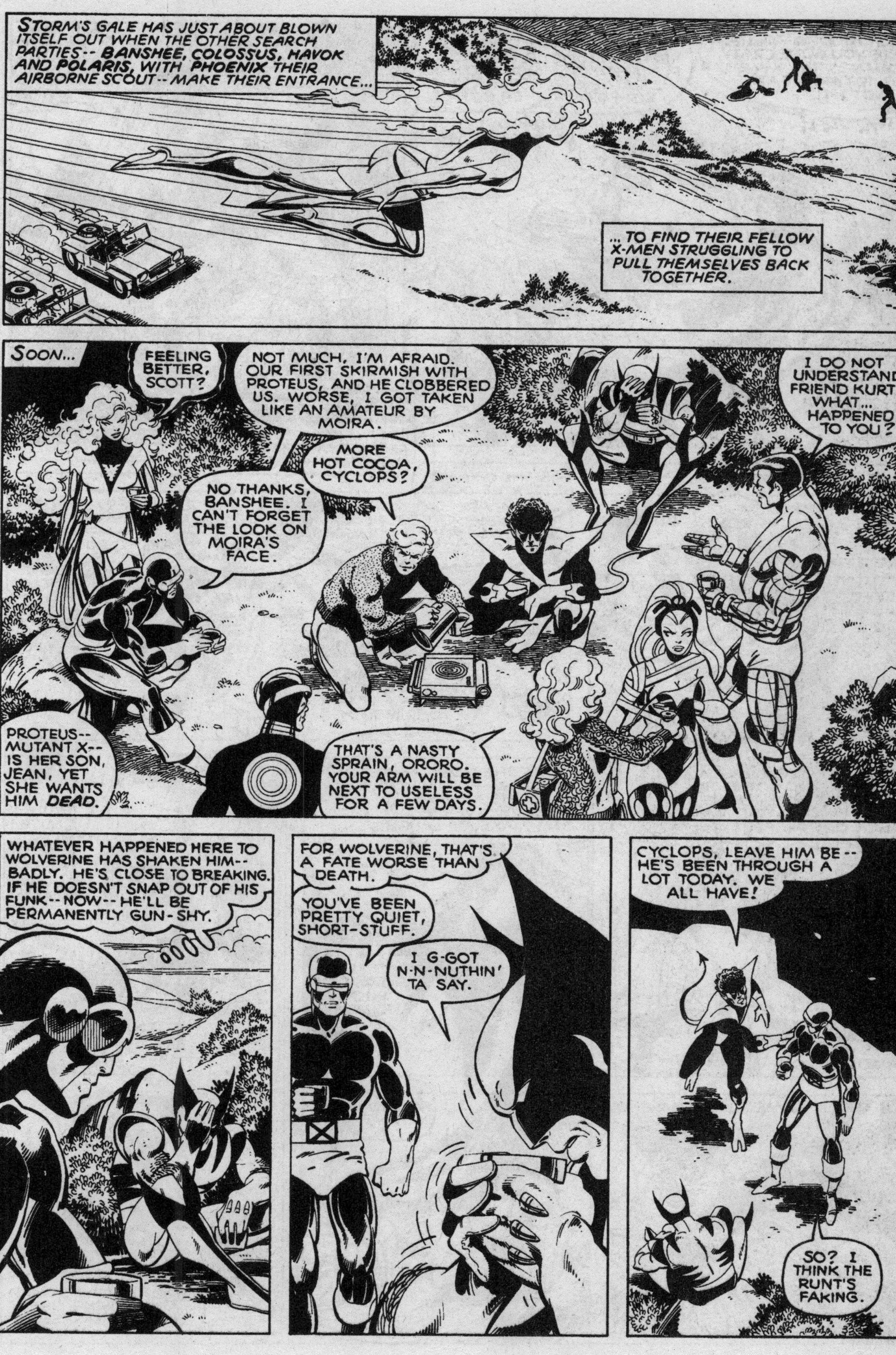
STORM'S GALE HAS JUST ABOUT BLOWN ITSELF OUT WHEN THE OTHER SEARCH PARTIES-- BANSHEE, COLOSSUS, HAVOK AND POLARIS, WITH PHOENIX THEIR AIRBORNE SCOUT-- MAKE THEIR ENTRANCE...
...TO FIND THEIR FELLOW X-MEN STRUGGLING TO PULL THEMSELVES BACK TOGETHER.
SOON...
FEELING BETTER, SCOTT?
NOT MUCH, I'M AFRAID. OUR FIRST SKIRMISH WITH PROTEUS, AND HE CLOBBERED US. WORSE, I GOT TAKEN LIKE AN AMATEUR BY MOIRA.
MORE HOT COCOA, CYCLOPS?
NO THANKS, BANSHEE. I CAN'T FORGET THE LOOK ON MOIRA'S FACE.
I DO NOT UNDERSTAND, FRIEND KURT. WHAT... HAPPENED TO YOU?
PROTEUS-- MUTANT X-- IS HER SON, JEAN, YET SHE WANTS HIM DEAD.
THAT'S A NASTY SPRAIN, ORORO. YOUR ARM WILL BE NEXT TO USELESS FOR A FEW DAYS.
WHATEVER HAPPENED HERE TO WOLVERINE HAS SHAKEN HIM-- BADLY. HE'S CLOSE TO BREAKING. IF HE DOESN'T SNAP OUT OF HIS FUNK-- NOW-- HE'LL BE PERMANENTLY GUN-SHY.
FOR WOLVERINE, THAT'S A FATE WORSE THAN DEATH.
YOU'VE BEEN PRETTY QUIET, SHORT-STUFF.
I G-GOT N-N-NUTHIN' TA SAY.
CYCLOPS, LEAVE HIM BE-- HE'S BEEN THROUGH A LOT TODAY. WE ALL HAVE!
SO? I THINK THE RUNT'S FAKING.

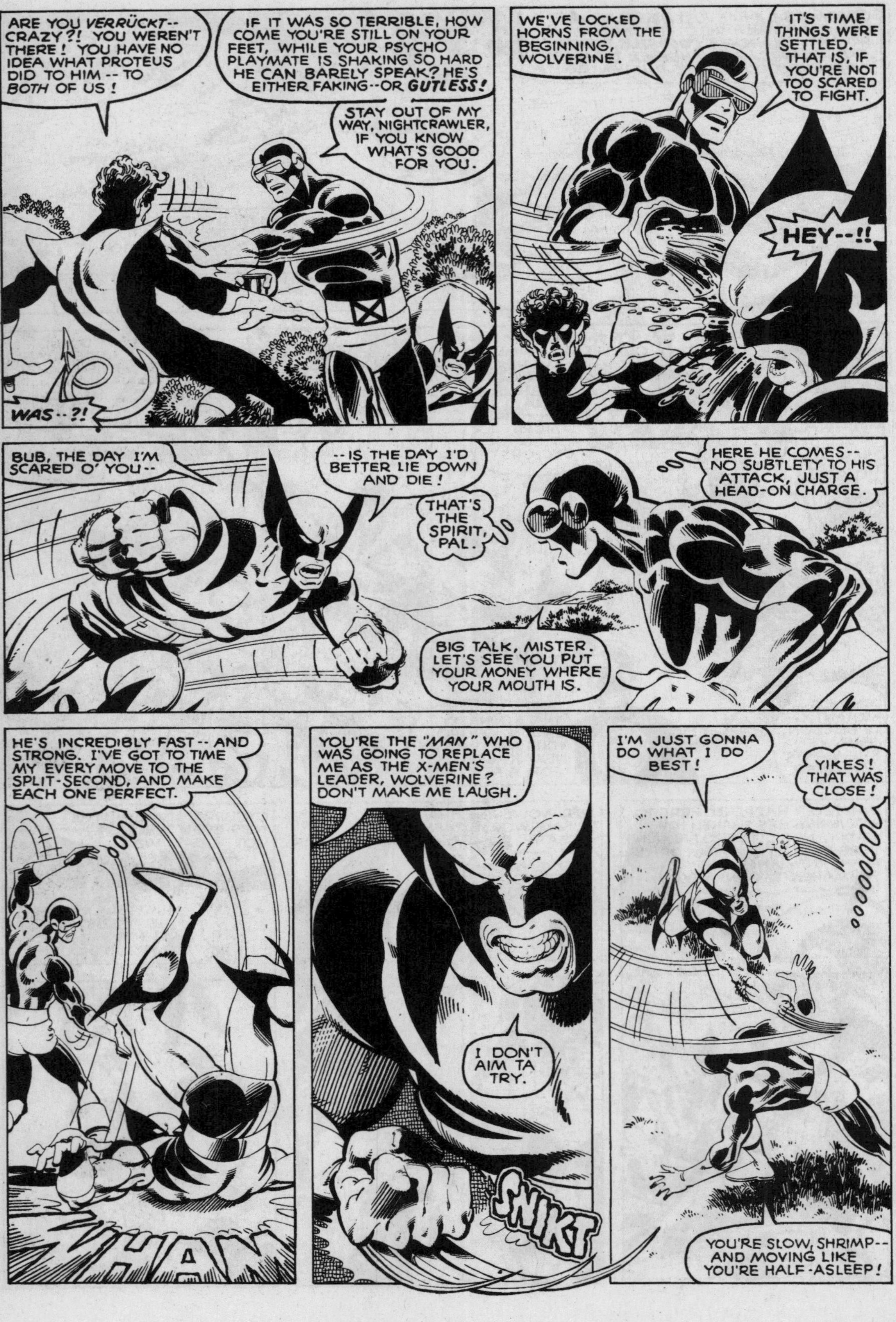
ARE YOU VERRÜCKT-- CRAZY?! YOU WEREN'T THERE! YOU HAVE NO IDEA WHAT PROTEUS DID TO HIM -- TO BOTH OF US!
IF IT WAS SO TERRIBLE, HOW COME YOU'RE STILL ON YOUR FEET, WHILE YOUR PSYCHO PLAYMATE IS SHAKING SO HARD HE CAN BARELY SPEAK? HE'S EITHER FAKING--OR GUTLESS!
STAY OUT OF MY WAY, NIGHTCRAWLER, IF YOU KNOW WHAT'S GOOD FOR YOU.
WAS--?!
WE'VE LOCKED HORNS FROM THE BEGINNING, WOLVERINE.
IT'S TIME THINGS WERE SETTLED. THAT IS, IF YOU'RE NOT TOO SCARED TO FIGHT.
HEY--!!
BUB, THE DAY I'M SCARED O' YOU--
--IS THE DAY I'D BETTER LIE DOWN AND DIE!
THAT'S THE SPIRIT, PAL.
HERE HE COMES-- NO SUBTLETY TO HIS ATTACK, JUST A HEAD-ON CHARGE.
BIG TALK, MISTER. LET'S SEE YOU PUT YOUR MONEY WHERE YOUR MOUTH IS.
HE'S INCREDIBLY FAST-- AND STRONG. I'VE GOT TO TIME MY EVERY MOVE TO THE SPLIT-SECOND, AND MAKE EACH ONE PERFECT.
ZHAN
YOU'RE THE "MAN" WHO WAS GOING TO REPLACE ME AS THE X-MEN'S LEADER, WOLVERINE? DON'T MAKE ME LAUGH.
I DON'T AIM TA TRY.
SNIKT
I'M JUST GONNA DO WHAT I DO BEST!
YIKES! THAT WAS CLOSE!
YOU'RE SLOW, SHRIMP-- AND MOVING LIKE YOU'RE HALF-ASLEEP!

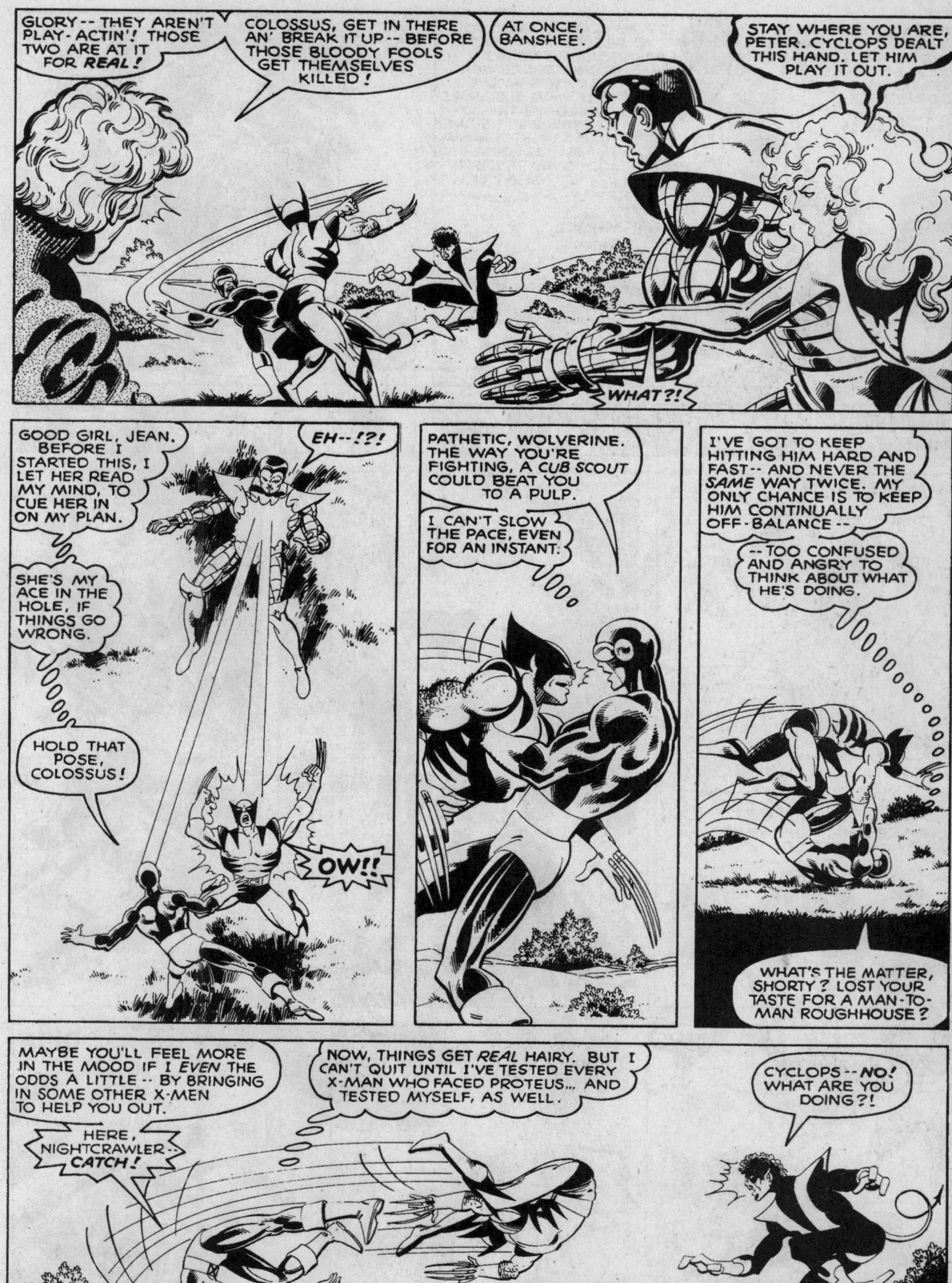
GLORY -- THEY AREN'T PLAY-ACTIN'! THOSE TWO ARE AT IT FOR *REAL!*
COLOSSUS, GET IN THERE AN' BREAK IT UP -- BEFORE THOSE BLOODY FOOLS GET THEMSELVES KILLED!
AT ONCE, BANSHEE.
STAY WHERE YOU ARE, PETER. CYCLOPS DEALT THIS HAND. LET HIM PLAY IT OUT.
WHAT?!
GOOD GIRL, JEAN. BEFORE I STARTED THIS, I LET HER READ MY MIND, TO CUE HER IN ON MY PLAN.
EH--!?!
SHE'S MY ACE IN THE HOLE, IF THINGS GO WRONG.
HOLD THAT POSE, COLOSSUS!
OW!!
PATHETIC, WOLVERINE. THE WAY YOU'RE FIGHTING, A *CUB SCOUT* COULD BEAT YOU TO A PULP.
I CAN'T SLOW THE PACE, EVEN FOR AN INSTANT.
I'VE GOT TO KEEP HITTING HIM HARD AND FAST -- AND NEVER THE *SAME* WAY TWICE. MY ONLY CHANCE IS TO KEEP HIM CONTINUALLY OFF-BALANCE --
-- TOO CONFUSED AND ANGRY TO THINK ABOUT WHAT HE'S DOING.
WHAT'S THE MATTER, SHORTY? LOST YOUR TASTE FOR A MAN-TO-MAN ROUGHHOUSE?
MAYBE YOU'LL FEEL MORE IN THE MOOD IF I *EVEN* THE ODDS A LITTLE -- BY BRINGING IN SOME OTHER X-MEN TO HELP YOU OUT.
HERE, NIGHTCRAWLER -- *CATCH!*
NOW, THINGS GET *REAL* HAIRY. BUT I CAN'T QUIT UNTIL I'VE TESTED EVERY X-MAN WHO FACED PROTEUS... AND TESTED MYSELF, AS WELL.
CYCLOPS -- *NO!* WHAT ARE YOU DOING?!

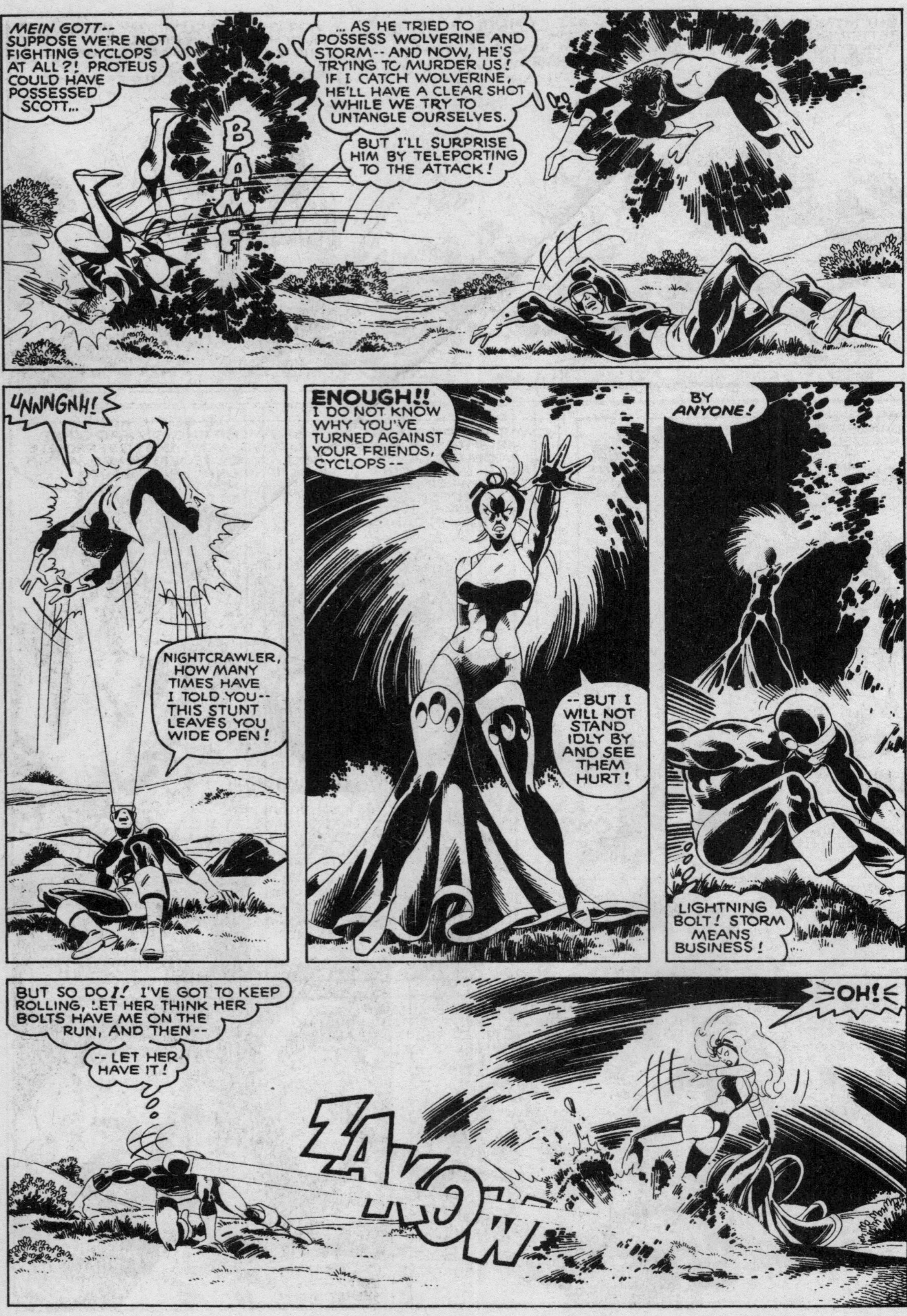

MEIN GOTT-- SUPPOSE WE'RE NOT FIGHTING CYCLOPS AT ALL?! PROTEUS COULD HAVE POSSESSED SCOTT...
BAMF
... AS HE TRIED TO POSSESS WOLVERINE AND STORM-- AND NOW, HE'S TRYING TO MURDER US! IF I CATCH WOLVERINE, HE'LL HAVE A CLEAR SHOT WHILE WE TRY TO UNTANGLE OURSELVES.
BUT I'LL SURPRISE HIM BY TELEPORTING TO THE ATTACK!
UNNNGNH!
NIGHTCRAWLER, HOW MANY TIMES HAVE I TOLD YOU-- THIS STUNT LEAVES YOU WIDE OPEN!
ENOUGH!! I DO NOT KNOW WHY YOU'VE TURNED AGAINST YOUR FRIENDS, CYCLOPS--
-- BUT I WILL NOT STAND IDLY BY AND SEE THEM HURT!
BY ANYONE!
LIGHTNING BOLT! STORM MEANS BUSINESS!
BUT SO DO I! I'VE GOT TO KEEP ROLLING, LET HER THINK HER BOLTS HAVE ME ON THE RUN, AND THEN--
-- LET HER HAVE IT!
OH!
ZAKOW

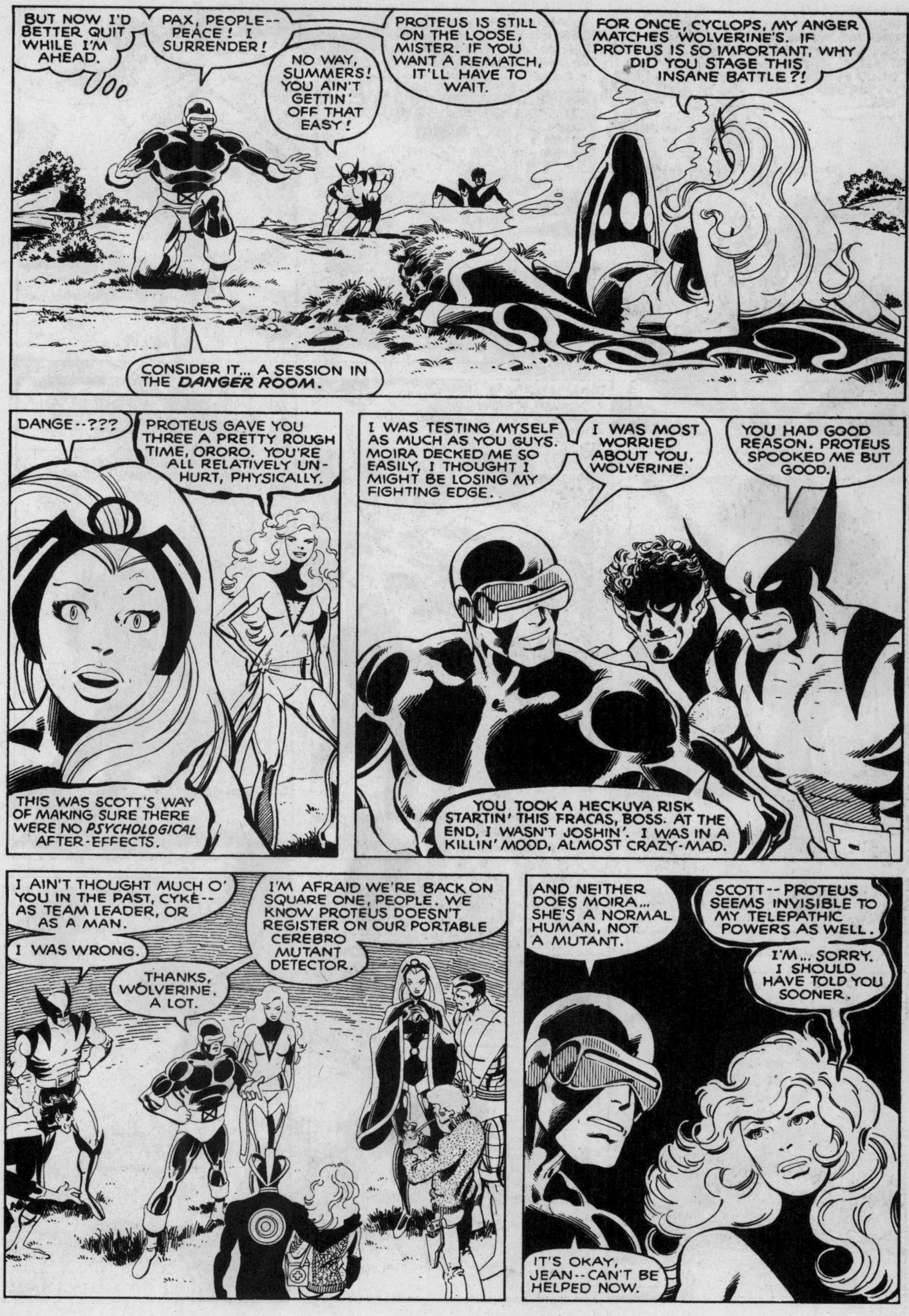

BUT NOW I'D BETTER QUIT WHILE I'M AHEAD.
PAX, PEOPLE-- PEACE! I SURRENDER!
UOO
NO WAY, SUMMERS! YOU AIN'T GETTIN' OFF THAT EASY!
PROTEUS IS STILL ON THE LOOSE, MISTER. IF YOU WANT A REMATCH, IT'LL HAVE TO WAIT.
FOR ONCE, CYCLOPS, MY ANGER MATCHES WOLVERINE'S. IF PROTEUS IS SO IMPORTANT, WHY DID YOU STAGE THIS INSANE BATTLE?!
CONSIDER IT... A SESSION IN THE DANGER ROOM.
DANGE--???
PROTEUS GAVE YOU THREE A PRETTY ROUGH TIME, ORORO. YOU'RE ALL RELATIVELY UN-HURT, PHYSICALLY.
THIS WAS SCOTT'S WAY OF MAKING SURE THERE WERE NO PSYCHOLOGICAL AFTER-EFFECTS.
I WAS TESTING MYSELF AS MUCH AS YOU GUYS. MOIRA DECKED ME SO EASILY, I THOUGHT I MIGHT BE LOSING MY FIGHTING EDGE.
I WAS MOST WORRIED ABOUT YOU, WOLVERINE.
YOU HAD GOOD REASON. PROTEUS SPOOKED ME BUT GOOD.
YOU TOOK A HECKUVA RISK STARTIN' THIS FRACAS, BOSS. AT THE END, I WASN'T JOSHIN'. I WAS IN A KILLIN' MOOD, ALMOST CRAZY-MAD.
I AIN'T THOUGHT MUCH O' YOU IN THE PAST, CYKE-- AS TEAM LEADER, OR AS A MAN.
I WAS WRONG.
THANKS, WOLVERINE. A LOT.
I'M AFRAID WE'RE BACK ON SQUARE ONE, PEOPLE. WE KNOW PROTEUS DOESN'T REGISTER ON OUR PORTABLE CEREBRO MUTANT DETECTOR.
AND NEITHER DOES MOIRA... SHE'S A NORMAL HUMAN, NOT A MUTANT.
SCOTT-- PROTEUS SEEMS INVISIBLE TO MY TELEPATHIC POWERS AS WELL.
I'M... SORRY. I SHOULD HAVE TOLD YOU SOONER.
IT'S OKAY, JEAN-- CAN'T BE HELPED NOW.

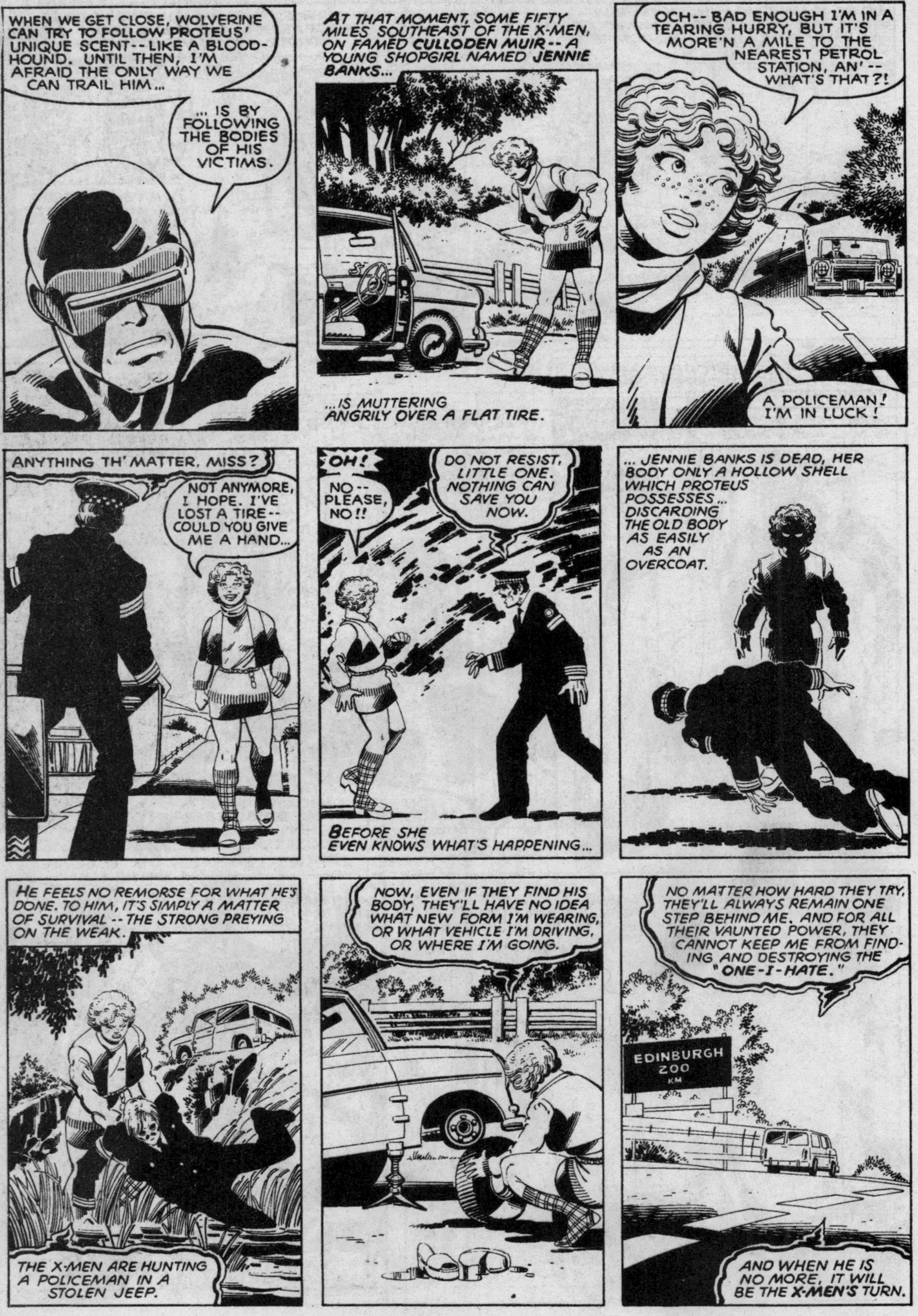
WHEN WE GET CLOSE, WOLVERINE CAN TRY TO FOLLOW PROTEUS' UNIQUE SCENT-- LIKE A BLOOD-HOUND. UNTIL THEN, I'M AFRAID THE ONLY WAY WE CAN TRAIL HIM...
... IS BY FOLLOWING THE BODIES OF HIS VICTIMS.
AT THAT MOMENT, SOME FIFTY MILES SOUTHEAST OF THE X-MEN, ON FAMED CULLODEN MUIR-- A YOUNG SHOPGIRL NAMED JENNIE BANKS...
...IS MUTTERING ANGRILY OVER A FLAT TIRE.
OCH-- BAD ENOUGH I'M IN A TEARING HURRY, BUT IT'S MORE'N A MILE TO THE NEAREST PETROL STATION, AN' -- WHAT'S THAT?!
A POLICEMAN! I'M IN LUCK!
ANYTHING TH' MATTER, MISS?
NOT ANYMORE, I HOPE. I'VE LOST A TIRE-- COULD YOU GIVE ME A HAND...
OH!
NO-- PLEASE, NO!!
DO NOT RESIST, LITTLE ONE. NOTHING CAN SAVE YOU NOW.
BEFORE SHE EVEN KNOWS WHAT'S HAPPENING...
... JENNIE BANKS IS DEAD, HER BODY ONLY A HOLLOW SHELL WHICH PROTEUS POSSESSES... DISCARDING THE OLD BODY AS EASILY AS AN OVERCOAT.
HE FEELS NO REMORSE FOR WHAT HE'S DONE. TO HIM, IT'S SIMPLY A MATTER OF SURVIVAL -- THE STRONG PREYING ON THE WEAK.
THE X-MEN ARE HUNTING A POLICEMAN IN A STOLEN JEEP.
NOW, EVEN IF THEY FIND HIS BODY, THEY'LL HAVE NO IDEA WHAT NEW FORM I'M WEARING, OR WHAT VEHICLE I'M DRIVING, OR WHERE I'M GOING.
NO MATTER HOW HARD THEY TRY, THEY'LL ALWAYS REMAIN ONE STEP BEHIND ME. AND FOR ALL THEIR VAUNTED POWER, THEY CANNOT KEEP ME FROM FINDING AND DESTROYING THE "ONE-I-HATE."
EDINBURGH ZOO KM
AND WHEN HE IS NO MORE, IT WILL BE THE X-MEN'S TURN.

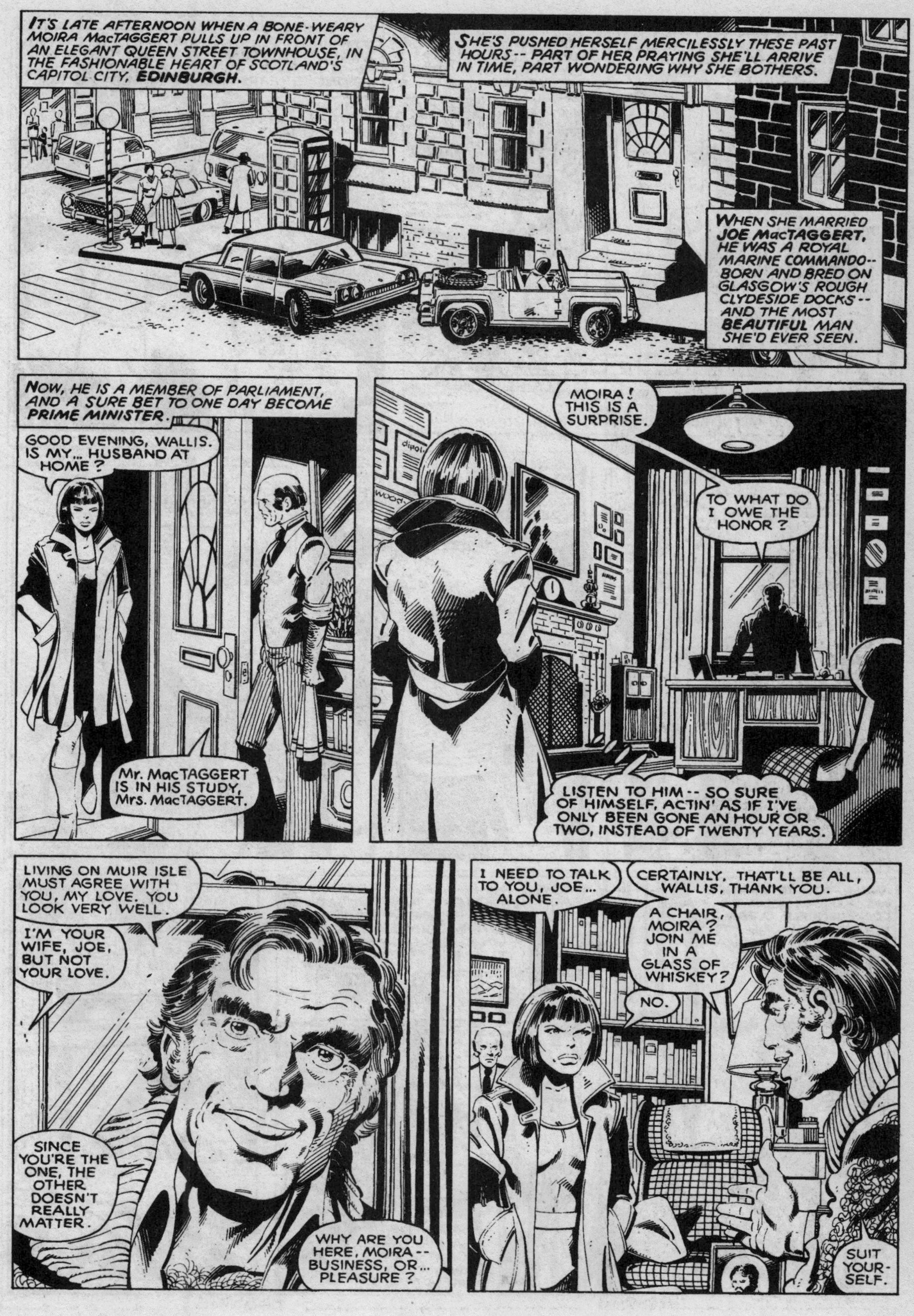
IT'S LATE AFTERNOON WHEN A BONE-WEARY MOIRA MacTAGGERT PULLS UP IN FRONT OF AN ELEGANT QUEEN STREET TOWNHOUSE, IN THE FASHIONABLE HEART OF SCOTLAND'S CAPITOL CITY, EDINBURGH.
SHE'S PUSHED HERSELF MERCILESSLY THESE PAST HOURS -- PART OF HER PRAYING SHE'LL ARRIVE IN TIME, PART WONDERING WHY SHE BOTHERS.
WHEN SHE MARRIED JOE MacTAGGERT, HE WAS A ROYAL MARINE COMMANDO-- BORN AND BRED ON GLASGOW'S ROUGH CLYDESIDE DOCKS -- AND THE MOST BEAUTIFUL MAN SHE'D EVER SEEN.
NOW, HE IS A MEMBER OF PARLIAMENT, AND A SURE BET TO ONE DAY BECOME PRIME MINISTER.
GOOD EVENING, WALLIS. IS MY... HUSBAND AT HOME?
Mr. MacTAGGERT IS IN HIS STUDY, Mrs. MacTAGGERT.
MOIRA! THIS IS A SURPRISE.
TO WHAT DO I OWE THE HONOR?
LISTEN TO HIM -- SO SURE OF HIMSELF, ACTIN' AS IF I'VE ONLY BEEN GONE AN HOUR OR TWO, INSTEAD OF TWENTY YEARS.
LIVING ON MUIR ISLE MUST AGREE WITH YOU, MY LOVE. YOU LOOK VERY WELL.
I'M YOUR WIFE, JOE, BUT NOT YOUR LOVE.
SINCE YOU'RE THE ONE, THE OTHER DOESN'T REALLY MATTER.
WHY ARE YOU HERE, MOIRA -- BUSINESS, OR... PLEASURE?
I NEED TO TALK TO YOU, JOE... ALONE.
CERTAINLY. THAT'LL BE ALL, WALLIS, THANK YOU.
A CHAIR, MOIRA? JOIN ME IN A GLASS OF WHISKEY?
NO.
SUIT YOURSELF.

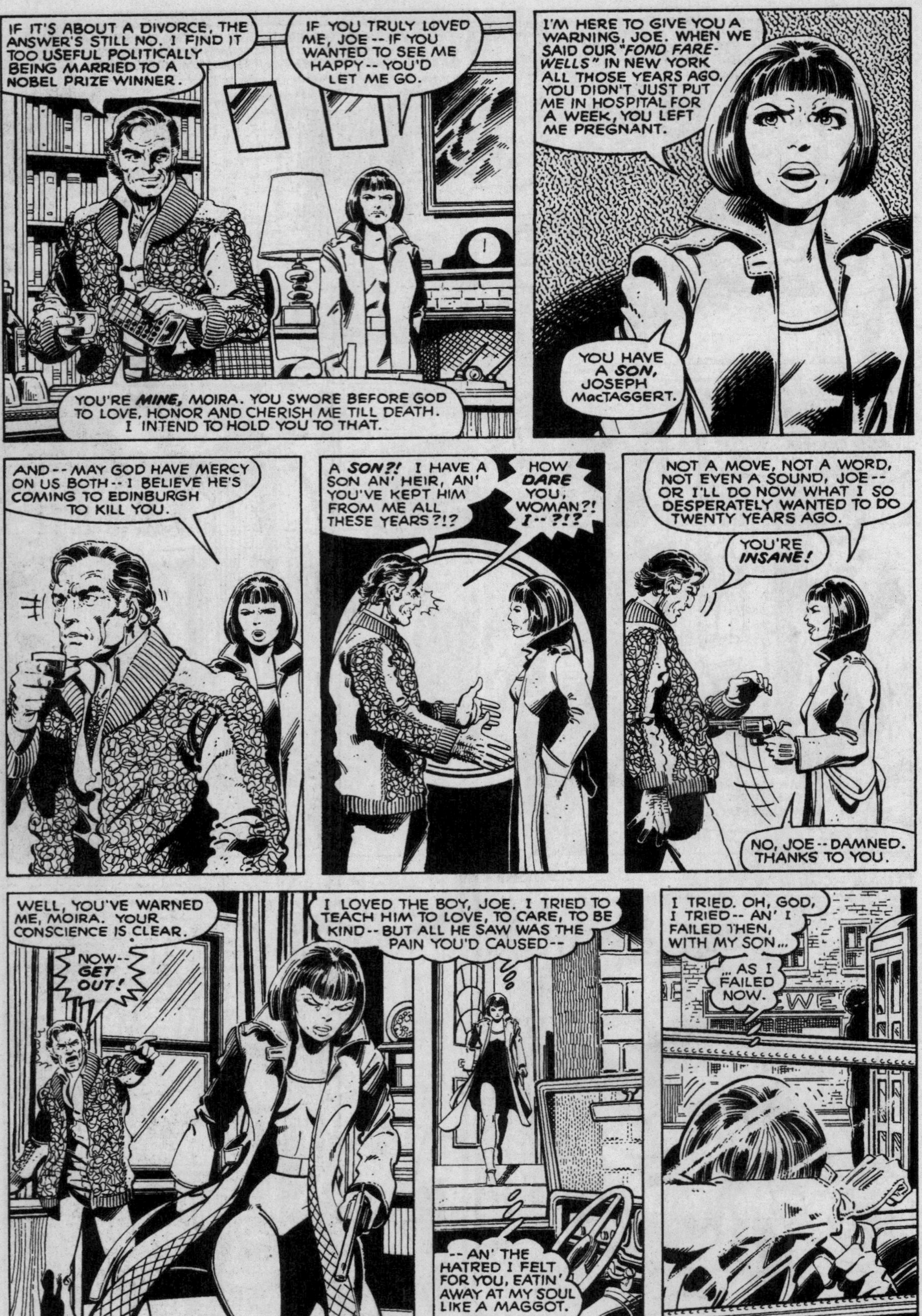

IF IT'S ABOUT A DIVORCE, THE ANSWER'S STILL NO. I FIND IT TOO USEFUL POLITICALLY BEING MARRIED TO A NOBEL PRIZE WINNER.
IF YOU TRULY LOVED ME, JOE -- IF YOU WANTED TO SEE ME HAPPY -- YOU'D LET ME GO.
YOU'RE MINE, MOIRA. YOU SWORE BEFORE GOD TO LOVE, HONOR AND CHERISH ME TILL DEATH. I INTEND TO HOLD YOU TO THAT.
I'M HERE TO GIVE YOU A WARNING, JOE. WHEN WE SAID OUR "FOND FAREWELLS" IN NEW YORK ALL THOSE YEARS AGO, YOU DIDN'T JUST PUT ME IN HOSPITAL FOR A WEEK, YOU LEFT ME PREGNANT.
YOU HAVE A SON, JOSEPH MacTAGGERT.
AND -- MAY GOD HAVE MERCY ON US BOTH -- I BELIEVE HE'S COMING TO EDINBURGH TO KILL YOU.
A SON?! I HAVE A SON AN' HEIR, AN' YOU'VE KEPT HIM FROM ME ALL THESE YEARS?!?
HOW DARE YOU, WOMAN?! I -- ?!?
NOT A MOVE, NOT A WORD, NOT EVEN A SOUND, JOE -- OR I'LL DO NOW WHAT I SO DESPERATELY WANTED TO DO TWENTY YEARS AGO.
YOU'RE INSANE!
NO, JOE -- DAMNED. THANKS TO YOU.
WELL, YOU'VE WARNED ME, MOIRA. YOUR CONSCIENCE IS CLEAR.
NOW -- GET OUT!
I LOVED THE BOY, JOE. I TRIED TO TEACH HIM TO LOVE, TO CARE, TO BE KIND -- BUT ALL HE SAW WAS THE PAIN YOU'D CAUSED --
-- AN' THE HATRED I FELT FOR YOU, EATIN' AWAY AT MY SOUL LIKE A MAGGOT.
I TRIED. OH, GOD, I TRIED -- AN' I FAILED THEN, WITH MY SON...
... AS I FAILED NOW.

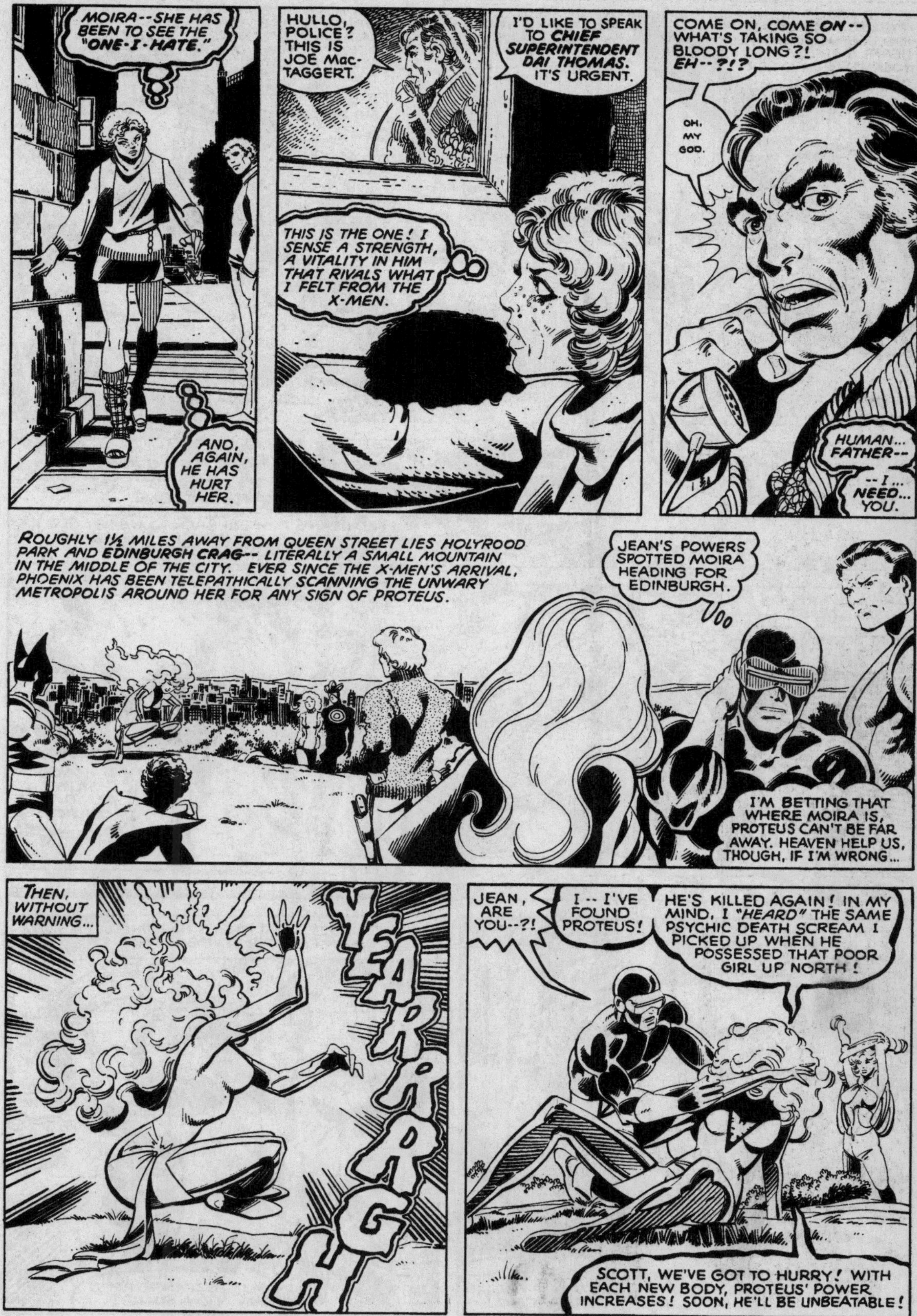
MOIRA--SHE HAS BEEN TO SEE THE "ONE-I-HATE."
AND, AGAIN, HE HAS HURT HER.
HULLO, POLICE? THIS IS JOE MacTAGGERT.
I'D LIKE TO SPEAK TO CHIEF SUPERINTENDENT DAI THOMAS. IT'S URGENT.
THIS IS THE ONE! I SENSE A STRENGTH, A VITALITY IN HIM THAT RIVALS WHAT I FELT FROM THE X-MEN.
COME ON, COME ON-- WHAT'S TAKING SO BLOODY LONG?! EH--?!?
OH, MY GOD.
HUMAN... FATHER--
--I... NEED... YOU.
ROUGHLY 1½ MILES AWAY FROM QUEEN STREET LIES HOLYROOD PARK AND EDINBURGH CRAG-- LITERALLY A SMALL MOUNTAIN IN THE MIDDLE OF THE CITY. EVER SINCE THE X-MEN'S ARRIVAL, PHOENIX HAS BEEN TELEPATHICALLY SCANNING THE UNWARY METROPOLIS AROUND HER FOR ANY SIGN OF PROTEUS.
JEAN'S POWERS SPOTTED MOIRA HEADING FOR EDINBURGH.
I'M BETTING THAT WHERE MOIRA IS, PROTEUS CAN'T BE FAR AWAY. HEAVEN HELP US, THOUGH, IF I'M WRONG...
THEN, WITHOUT WARNING...
YEARRRGH
JEAN, ARE YOU--?!
I -- I'VE FOUND PROTEUS!
HE'S KILLED AGAIN! IN MY MIND, I "HEARD" THE SAME PSYCHIC DEATH SCREAM I PICKED UP WHEN HE POSSESSED THAT POOR GIRL UP NORTH!
SCOTT, WE'VE GOT TO HURRY! WITH EACH NEW BODY, PROTEUS' POWER INCREASES! SOON, HE'LL BE UNBEATABLE!

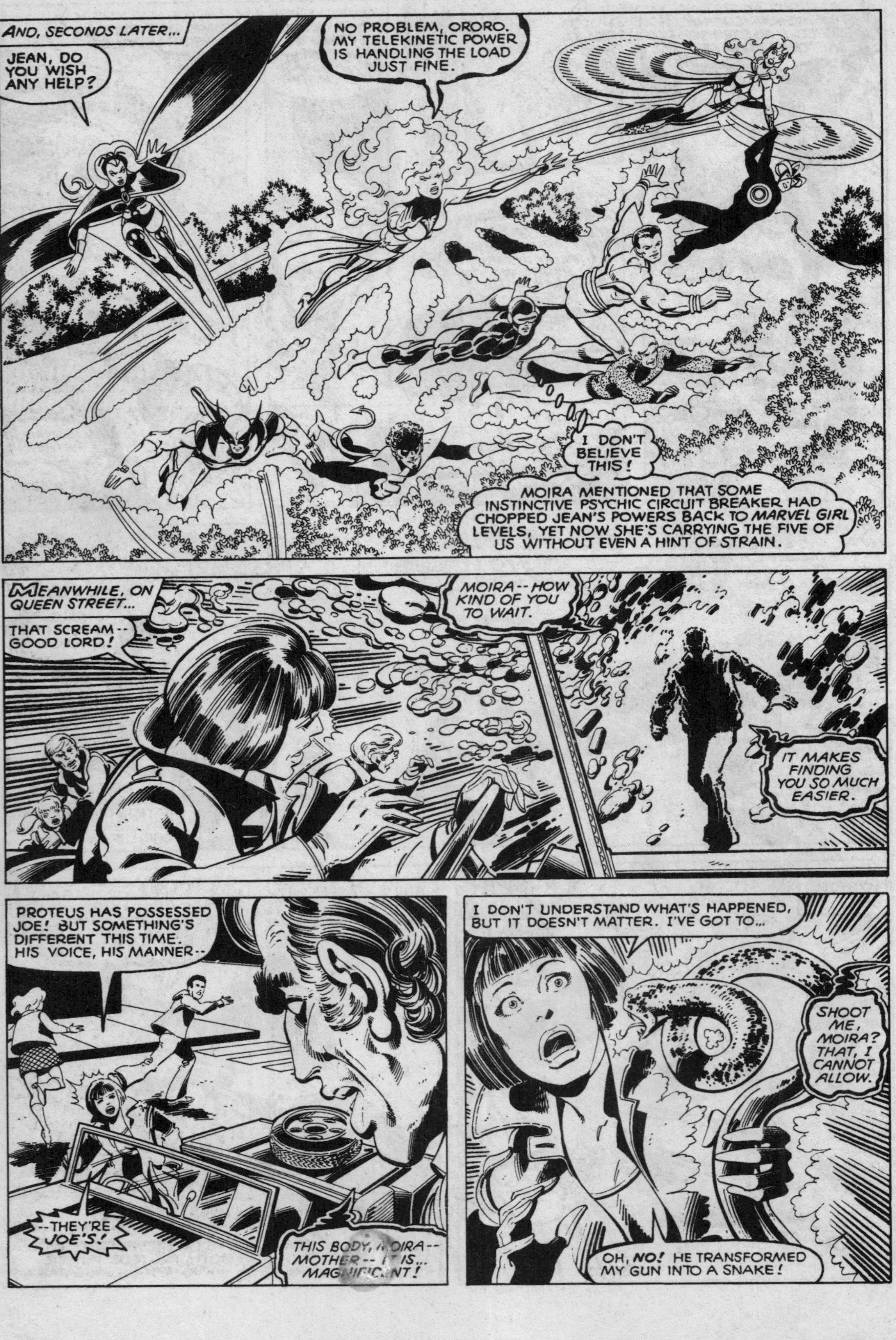
AND, SECONDS LATER...
JEAN, DO YOU WISH ANY HELP?
NO PROBLEM, ORORO. MY TELEKINETIC POWER IS HANDLING THE LOAD JUST FINE.
I DON'T BELIEVE THIS!
MOIRA MENTIONED THAT SOME INSTINCTIVE PSYCHIC CIRCUIT BREAKER HAD CHOPPED JEAN'S POWERS BACK TO MARVEL GIRL LEVELS, YET NOW SHE'S CARRYING THE FIVE OF US WITHOUT EVEN A HINT OF STRAIN.
MEANWHILE, ON QUEEN STREET...
THAT SCREAM -- GOOD LORD!
MOIRA -- HOW KIND OF YOU TO WAIT.
IT MAKES FINDING YOU SO MUCH EASIER.
PROTEUS HAS POSSESSED JOE! BUT SOMETHING'S DIFFERENT THIS TIME. HIS VOICE, HIS MANNER --
--THEY'RE JOE'S!
THIS BODY, MOIRA -- MOTHER -- IT IS... MAGNIFICENT!
I DON'T UNDERSTAND WHAT'S HAPPENED, BUT IT DOESN'T MATTER. I'VE GOT TO...
SHOOT ME, MOIRA? THAT, I CANNOT ALLOW.
OH, NO! HE TRANSFORMED MY GUN INTO A SNAKE!

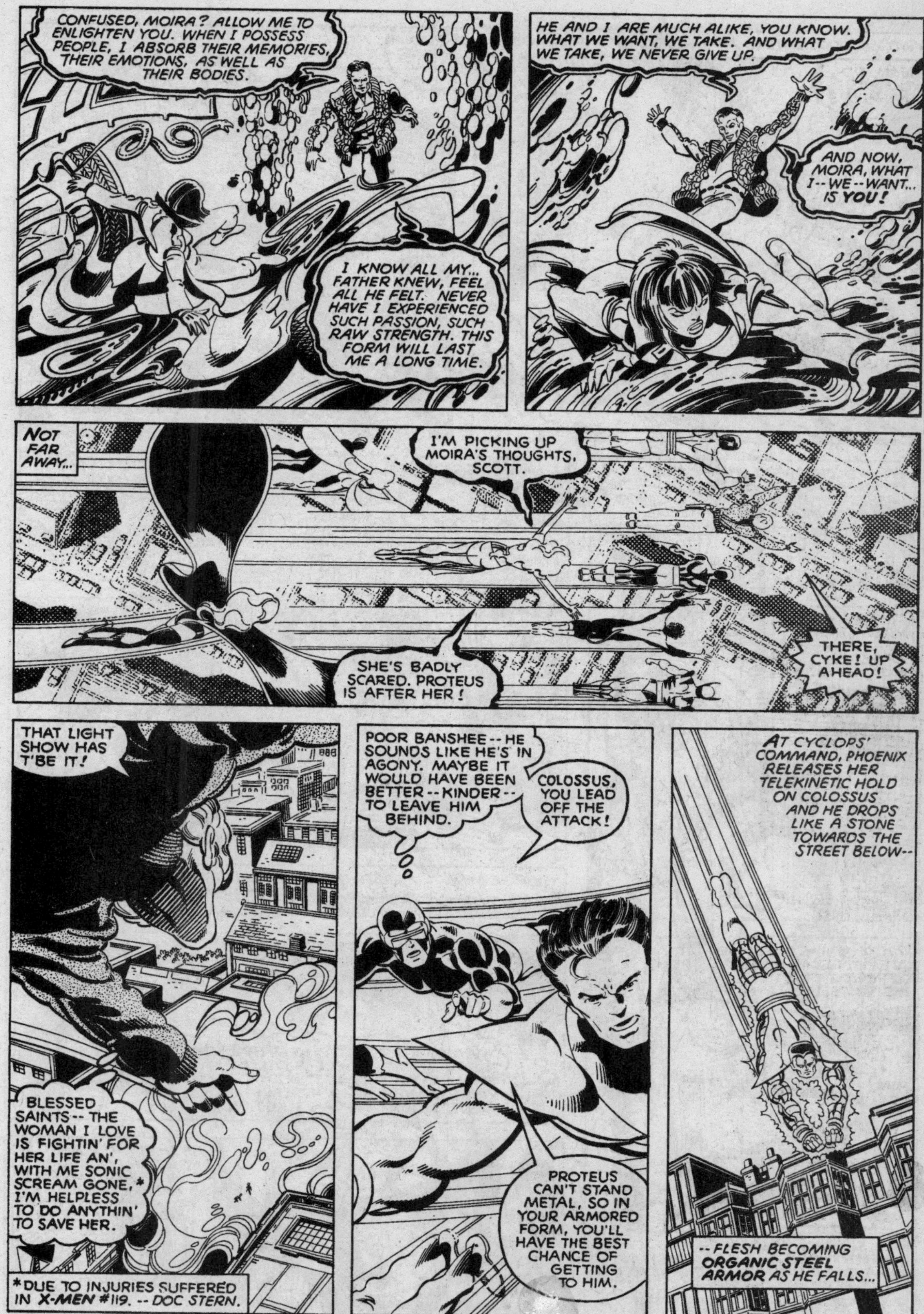
CONFUSED, MOIRA? ALLOW ME TO ENLIGHTEN YOU. WHEN I POSSESS PEOPLE, I ABSORB THEIR MEMORIES, THEIR EMOTIONS, AS WELL AS THEIR BODIES.
I KNOW ALL MY... FATHER KNEW, FEEL ALL HE FELT. NEVER HAVE I EXPERIENCED SUCH PASSION, SUCH RAW STRENGTH. THIS FORM WILL LAST ME A LONG TIME.
HE AND I ARE MUCH ALIKE, YOU KNOW. WHAT WE WANT, WE TAKE. AND WHAT WE TAKE, WE NEVER GIVE UP.
AND NOW, MOIRA, WHAT I--WE--WANT... IS YOU!
NOT FAR AWAY...
I'M PICKING UP MOIRA'S THOUGHTS, SCOTT.
SHE'S BADLY SCARED. PROTEUS IS AFTER HER!
THERE, CYKE! UP AHEAD!
THAT LIGHT SHOW HAS T'BE IT!
BLESSED SAINTS-- THE WOMAN I LOVE IS FIGHTIN' FOR HER LIFE AN', WITH ME SONIC SCREAM GONE,* I'M HELPLESS TO DO ANYTHIN' TO SAVE HER.
*DUE TO INJURIES SUFFERED IN X-MEN #119. --DOC STERN.
POOR BANSHEE--HE SOUNDS LIKE HE'S IN AGONY. MAYBE IT WOULD HAVE BEEN BETTER--KINDER--TO LEAVE HIM BEHIND.
COLOSSUS, YOU LEAD OFF THE ATTACK!
PROTEUS CAN'T STAND METAL, SO IN YOUR ARMORED FORM, YOU'LL HAVE THE BEST CHANCE OF GETTING TO HIM.
AT CYCLOPS' COMMAND, PHOENIX RELEASES HER TELEKINETIC HOLD ON COLOSSUS AND HE DROPS LIKE A STONE TOWARDS THE STREET BELOW--
--FLESH BECOMING ORGANIC STEEL ARMOR AS HE FALLS...

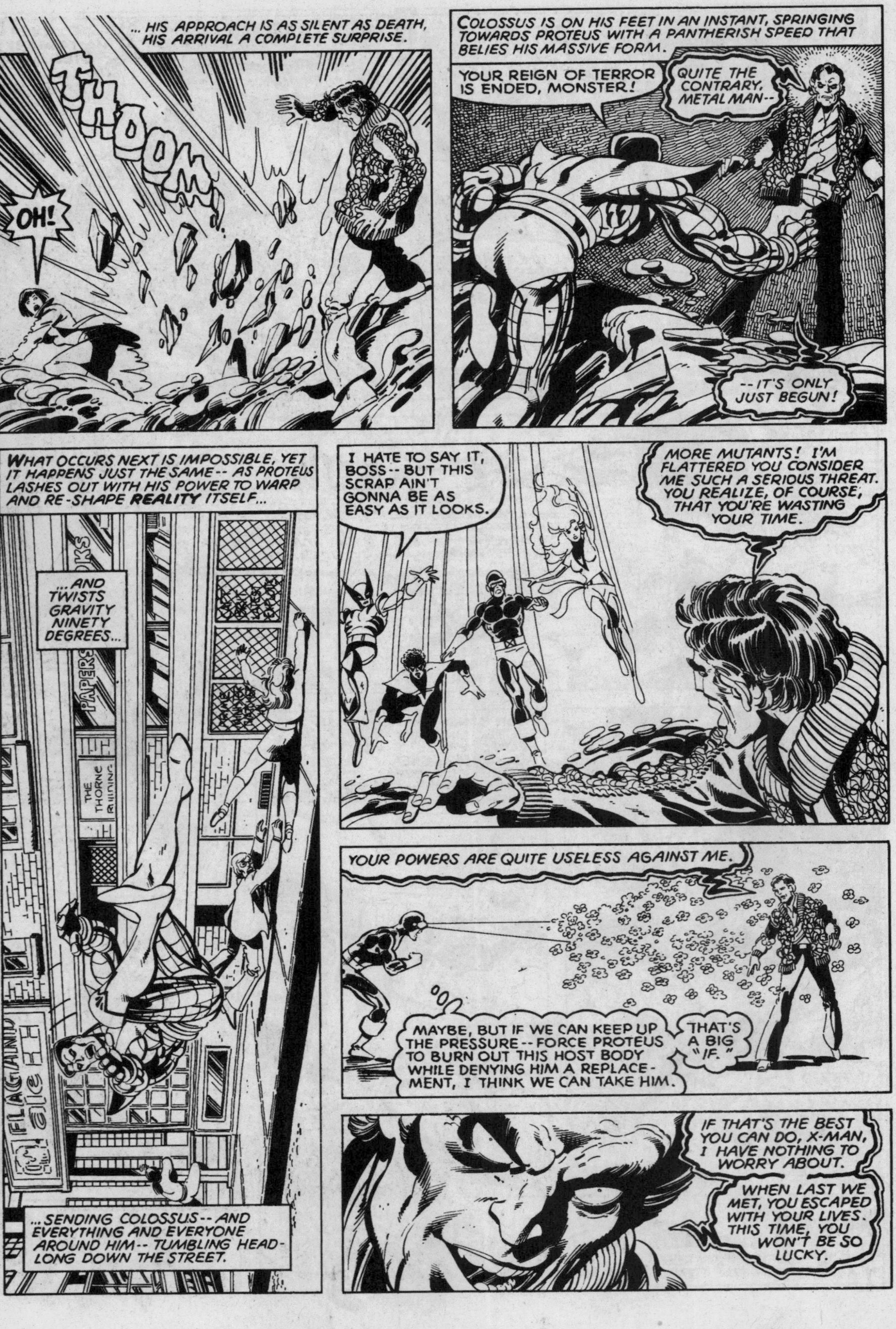

... HIS APPROACH IS AS SILENT AS DEATH, HIS ARRIVAL A COMPLETE SURPRISE.
THOOOM
OH!
COLOSSUS IS ON HIS FEET IN AN INSTANT, SPRINGING TOWARDS PROTEUS WITH A PANTHERISH SPEED THAT BELIES HIS MASSIVE FORM.
YOUR REIGN OF TERROR IS ENDED, MONSTER!
QUITE THE CONTRARY, METAL MAN--
--IT'S ONLY JUST BEGUN!
WHAT OCCURS NEXT IS IMPOSSIBLE, YET IT HAPPENS JUST THE SAME-- AS PROTEUS LASHES OUT WITH HIS POWER TO WARP AND RE-SHAPE REALITY ITSELF...
...AND TWISTS GRAVITY NINETY DEGREES...
PAPERS
...SENDING COLOSSUS-- AND EVERYTHING AND EVERYONE AROUND HIM-- TUMBLING HEAD-LONG DOWN THE STREET.
I HATE TO SAY IT, BOSS-- BUT THIS SCRAP AIN'T GONNA BE AS EASY AS IT LOOKS.
MORE MUTANTS! I'M FLATTERED YOU CONSIDER ME SUCH A SERIOUS THREAT. YOU REALIZE, OF COURSE, THAT YOU'RE WASTING YOUR TIME.
YOUR POWERS ARE QUITE USELESS AGAINST ME.
MAYBE, BUT IF WE CAN KEEP UP THE PRESSURE-- FORCE PROTEUS TO BURN OUT THIS HOST BODY WHILE DENYING HIM A REPLACE-MENT, I THINK WE CAN TAKE HIM.
THAT'S A BIG "IF."
IF THAT'S THE BEST YOU CAN DO, X-MAN, I HAVE NOTHING TO WORRY ABOUT.
WHEN LAST WE MET, YOU ESCAPED WITH YOUR LIVES. THIS TIME, YOU WON'T BE SO LUCKY.

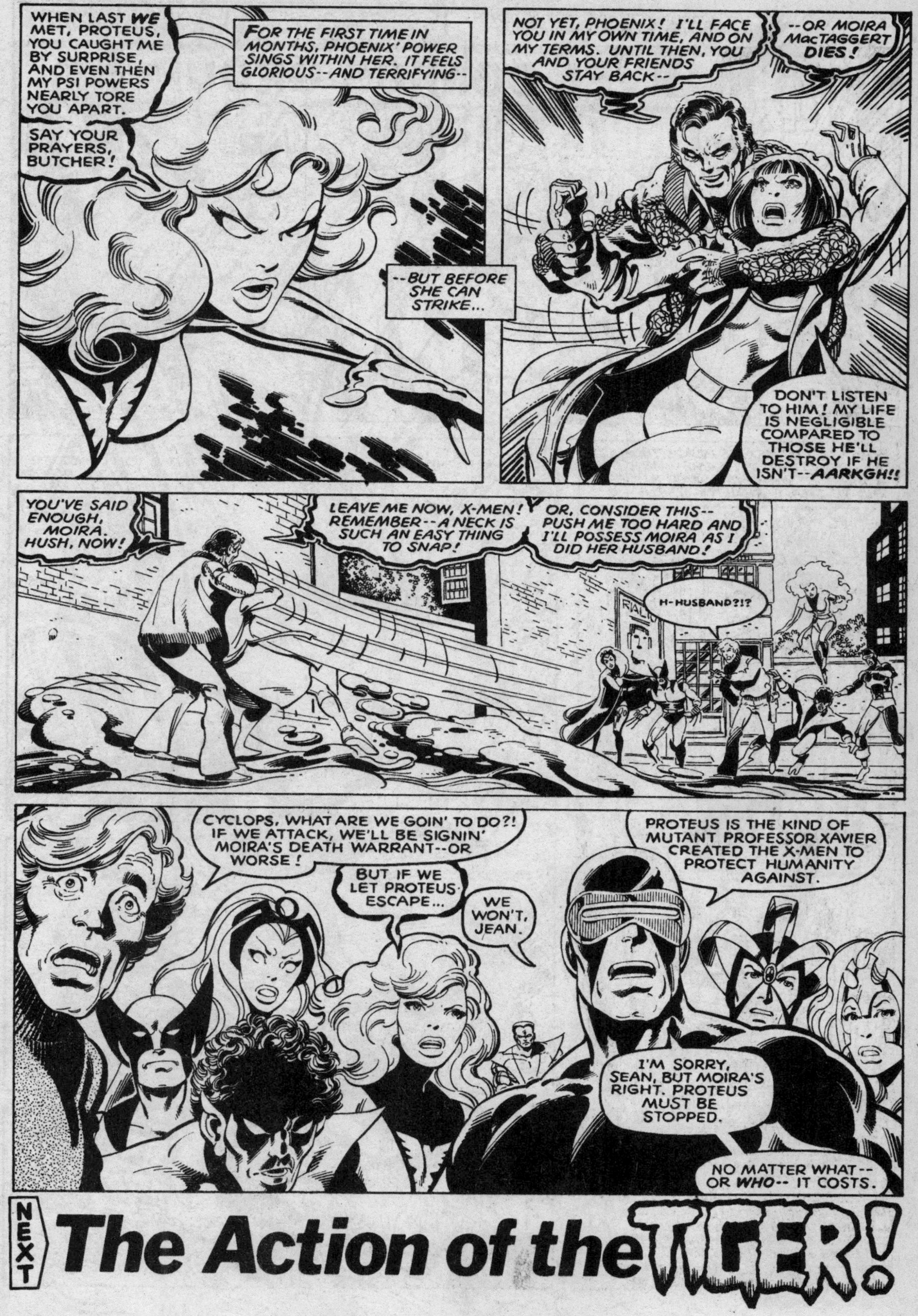

WHEN LAST WE MET, PROTEUS, YOU CAUGHT ME BY SURPRISE, AND EVEN THEN MY PSI POWERS NEARLY TORE YOU APART.
SAY YOUR PRAYERS, BUTCHER!
FOR THE FIRST TIME IN MONTHS, PHOENIX' POWER SINGS WITHIN HER. IT FEELS GLORIOUS--AND TERRIFYING--
--BUT BEFORE SHE CAN STRIKE...
NOT YET, PHOENIX! I'LL FACE YOU IN MY OWN TIME, AND ON MY TERMS. UNTIL THEN, YOU AND YOUR FRIENDS STAY BACK--
--OR MOIRA MacTAGGERT DIES!
DON'T LISTEN TO HIM! MY LIFE IS NEGLIGIBLE COMPARED TO THOSE HE'LL DESTROY IF HE ISN'T--AARKGH!!
YOU'VE SAID ENOUGH, MOIRA. HUSH, NOW!
LEAVE ME NOW, X-MEN! REMEMBER--A NECK IS SUCH AN EASY THING TO SNAP!
OR, CONSIDER THIS--PUSH ME TOO HARD AND I'LL POSSESS MOIRA AS I DID HER HUSBAND!
H-HUSBAND?!?
CYCLOPS, WHAT ARE WE GOIN' TO DO?! IF WE ATTACK, WE'LL BE SIGNIN' MOIRA'S DEATH WARRANT--OR WORSE!
BUT IF WE LET PROTEUS ESCAPE...
WE WON'T, JEAN.
PROTEUS IS THE KIND OF MUTANT PROFESSOR XAVIER CREATED THE X-MEN TO PROTECT HUMANITY AGAINST.
I'M SORRY, SEAN, BUT MOIRA'S RIGHT. PROTEUS MUST BE STOPPED.
NO MATTER WHAT--OR WHO--IT COSTS.
NEXT
The Action of the TIGER!

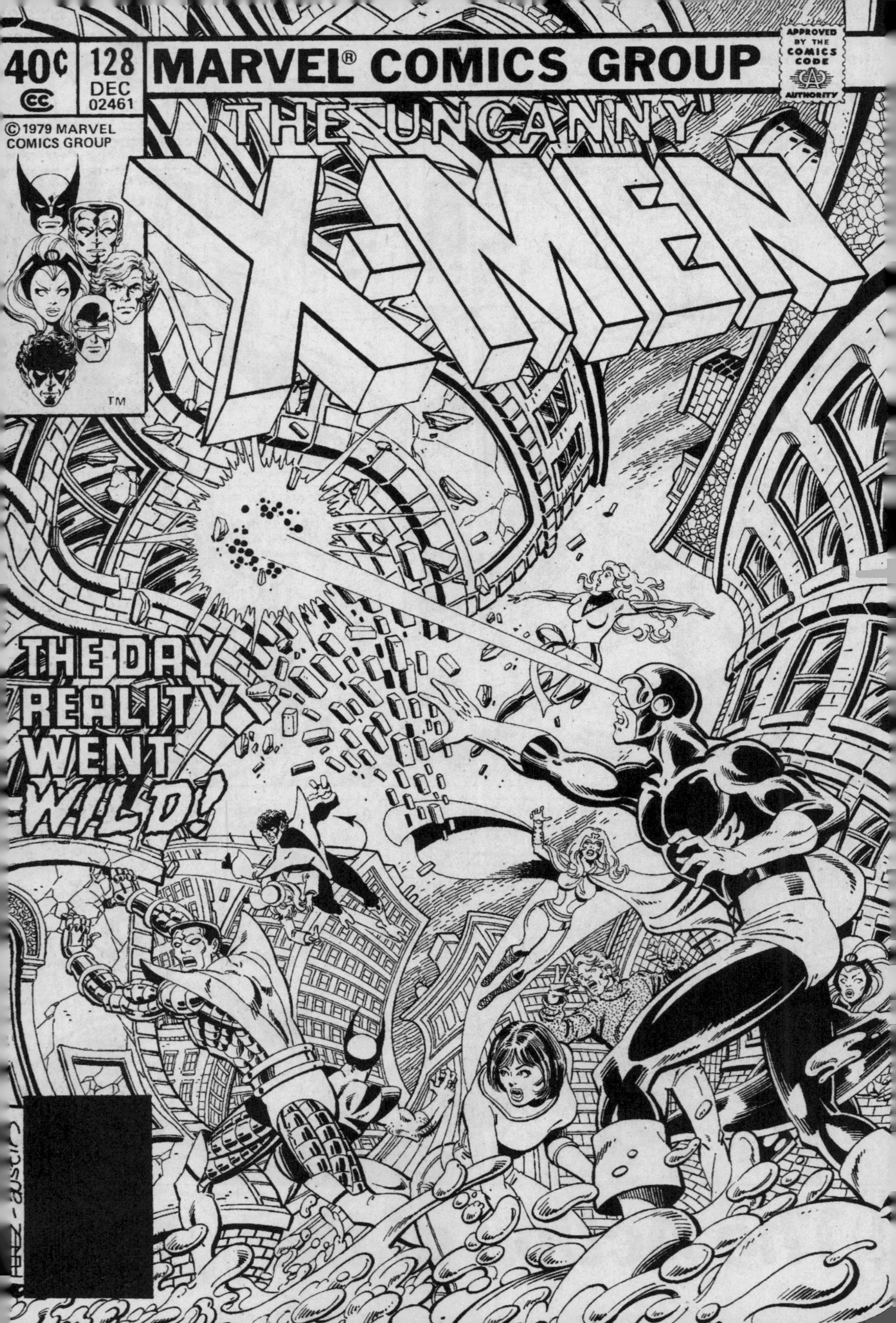
40¢
CC
128
DEC
02461
MARVEL® COMICS GROUP
APPROVED BY THE COMICS CODE AUTHORITY
© 1979 MARVEL COMICS GROUP
THE UNCANNY
X-MEN
TM
THE DAY REALITY WENT WILD!

Cyclops. Storm. Banshee. Nightcrawler. Wolverine. Colossus. Children of the atom, students of Charles Xavier, MUTANTS--feared and hated by the world they have sworn to protect. These are the STRANGEST heroes of all!

Stan Lee PRESENTS: **THE UNCANNY X-MEN!** TM

CHRIS CLAREMONT ✱ JOHN BYRNE, AUTHOR - PLOTTERS - PENCILER | TERRY AUSTIN, INKER | TOM ORZECHOWSKI, *letterer*, GLYNIS WEIN, *colorist* | ROGER STERN, EDITOR | JIM SHOOTER, Ed.-IN-CHIEF

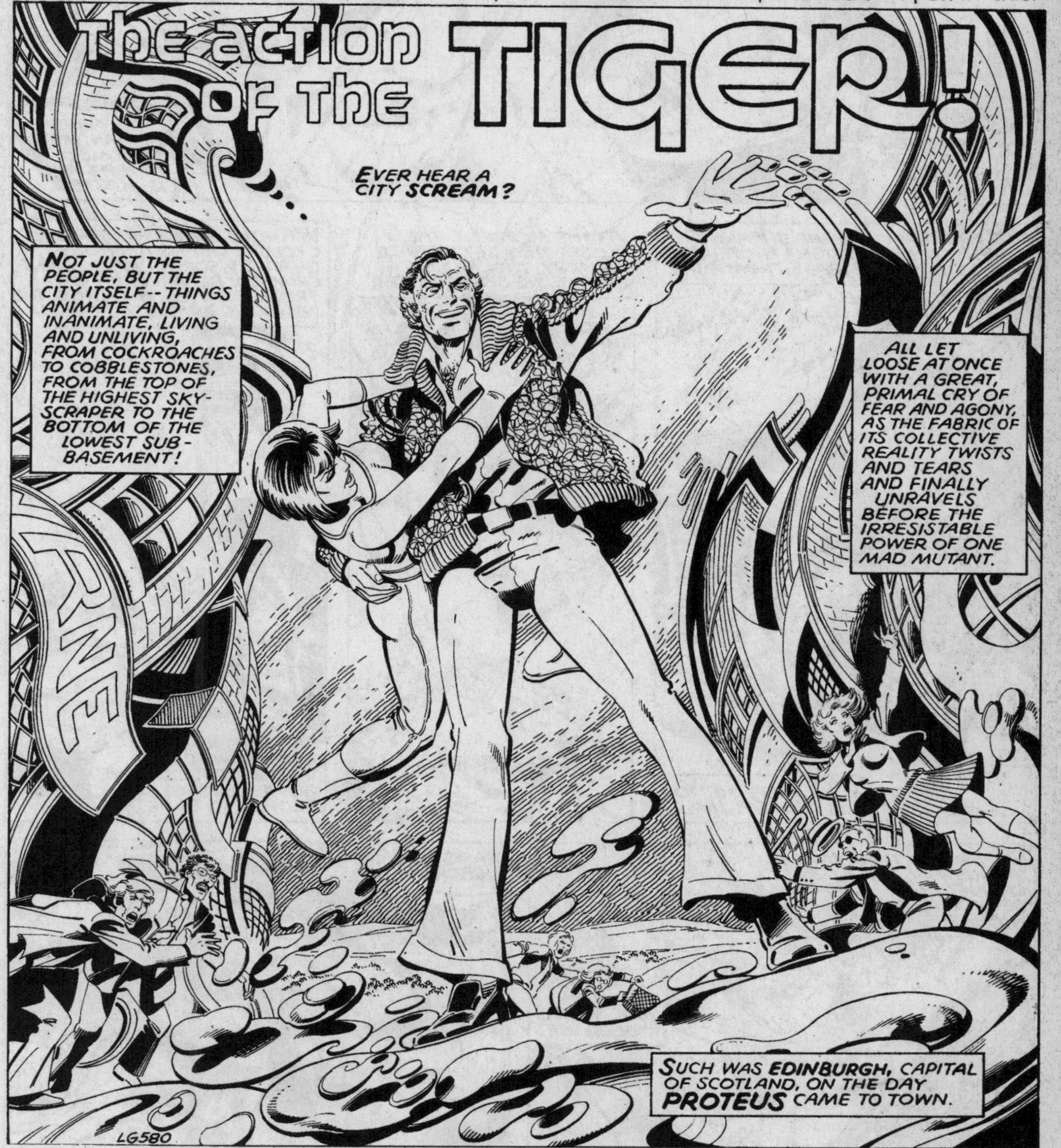
The action of the TIGER!
EVER HEAR A CITY SCREAM?
NOT JUST THE PEOPLE, BUT THE CITY ITSELF--THINGS ANIMATE AND INANIMATE, LIVING AND UNLIVING, FROM COCKROACHES TO COBBLESTONES, FROM THE TOP OF THE HIGHEST SKY-SCRAPER TO THE BOTTOM OF THE LOWEST SUB-BASEMENT!
ALL LET LOOSE AT ONCE WITH A GREAT, PRIMAL CRY OF FEAR AND AGONY, AS THE FABRIC OF ITS COLLECTIVE REALITY TWISTS AND TEARS AND FINALLY UNRAVELS BEFORE THE IRRESISTABLE POWER OF ONE MAD MUTANT.
SUCH WAS EDINBURGH, CAPITAL OF SCOTLAND, ON THE DAY PROTEUS CAME TO TOWN.
LG580

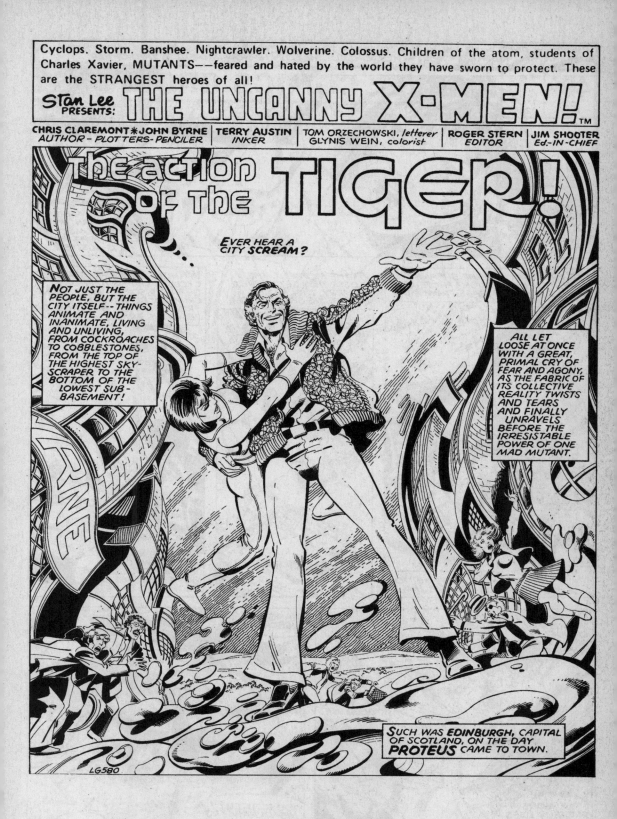

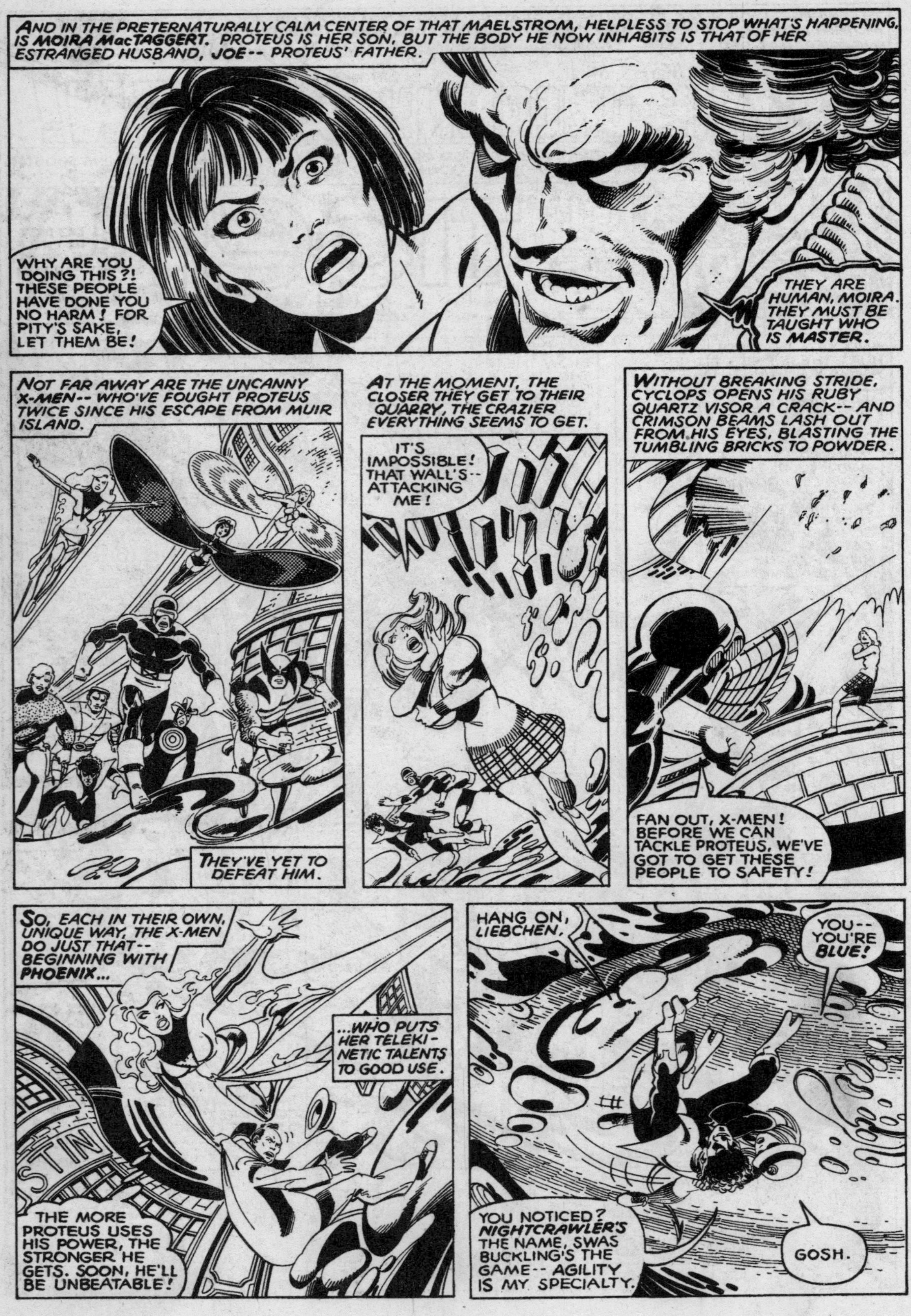
AND IN THE PRETERNATURALLY CALM CENTER OF THAT MAELSTROM, HELPLESS TO STOP WHAT'S HAPPENING, IS MOIRA MacTAGGERT. PROTEUS IS HER SON, BUT THE BODY HE NOW INHABITS IS THAT OF HER ESTRANGED HUSBAND, JOE-- PROTEUS' FATHER.
WHY ARE YOU DOING THIS?! THESE PEOPLE HAVE DONE YOU NO HARM! FOR PITY'S SAKE, LET THEM BE!
THEY ARE HUMAN, MOIRA. THEY MUST BE TAUGHT WHO IS MASTER.
NOT FAR AWAY ARE THE UNCANNY X-MEN-- WHO'VE FOUGHT PROTEUS TWICE SINCE HIS ESCAPE FROM MUIR ISLAND.
THEY'VE YET TO DEFEAT HIM.
AT THE MOMENT, THE CLOSER THEY GET TO THEIR QUARRY, THE CRAZIER EVERYTHING SEEMS TO GET.
IT'S IMPOSSIBLE! THAT WALL'S-- ATTACKING ME!
WITHOUT BREAKING STRIDE, CYCLOPS OPENS HIS RUBY QUARTZ VISOR A CRACK-- AND CRIMSON BEAMS LASH OUT FROM HIS EYES, BLASTING THE TUMBLING BRICKS TO POWDER.
FAN OUT, X-MEN! BEFORE WE CAN TACKLE PROTEUS, WE'VE GOT TO GET THESE PEOPLE TO SAFETY!
SO, EACH IN THEIR OWN, UNIQUE WAY, THE X-MEN DO JUST THAT-- BEGINNING WITH PHOENIX...
...WHO PUTS HER TELEKINETIC TALENTS TO GOOD USE.
THE MORE PROTEUS USES HIS POWER, THE STRONGER HE GETS. SOON, HE'LL BE UNBEATABLE!
HANG ON, LIEBCHEN.
YOU-- YOU'RE BLUE!
YOU NOTICED? NIGHTCRAWLER'S THE NAME, SWASHBUCKLING'S THE GAME-- AGILITY IS MY SPECIALTY.
GOSH.

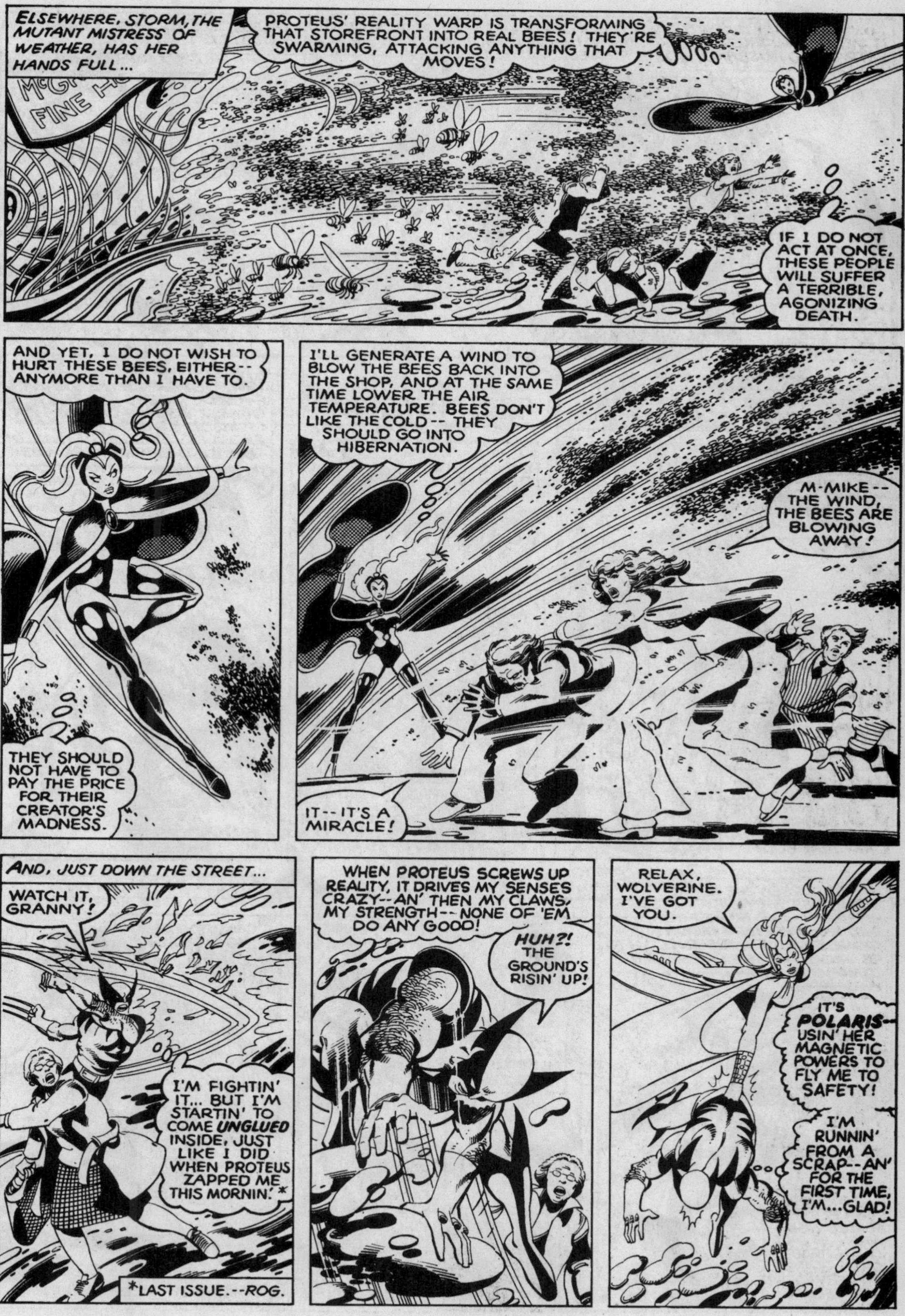
ELSEWHERE, STORM, THE MUTANT MISTRESS OF WEATHER, HAS HER HANDS FULL...
PROTEUS' REALITY WARP IS TRANSFORMING THAT STOREFRONT INTO REAL BEES! THEY'RE SWARMING, ATTACKING ANYTHING THAT MOVES!
IF I DO NOT ACT AT ONCE, THESE PEOPLE WILL SUFFER A TERRIBLE, AGONIZING DEATH.
AND YET, I DO NOT WISH TO HURT THESE BEES, EITHER-- ANYMORE THAN I HAVE TO.
THEY SHOULD NOT HAVE TO PAY THE PRICE FOR THEIR CREATOR'S MADNESS.
I'LL GENERATE A WIND TO BLOW THE BEES BACK INTO THE SHOP, AND AT THE SAME TIME LOWER THE AIR TEMPERATURE. BEES DON'T LIKE THE COLD -- THEY SHOULD GO INTO HIBERNATION.
M-MIKE -- THE WIND, THE BEES ARE BLOWING AWAY!
IT--IT'S A MIRACLE!
AND, JUST DOWN THE STREET...
WATCH IT, GRANNY!
I'M FIGHTIN' IT... BUT I'M STARTIN' TO COME UNGLUED INSIDE, JUST LIKE I DID WHEN PROTEUS ZAPPED ME THIS MORNIN'! *
*LAST ISSUE.--ROG.
WHEN PROTEUS SCREWS UP REALITY, IT DRIVES MY SENSES CRAZY--AN' THEN MY CLAWS, MY STRENGTH-- NONE OF 'EM DO ANY GOOD!
HUH?! THE GROUND'S RISIN' UP!
RELAX, WOLVERINE. I'VE GOT YOU.
IT'S POLARIS-- USIN' HER MAGNETIC POWERS TO FLY ME TO SAFETY!
I'M RUNNIN' FROM A SCRAP--AN' FOR THE FIRST TIME, I'M...GLAD!

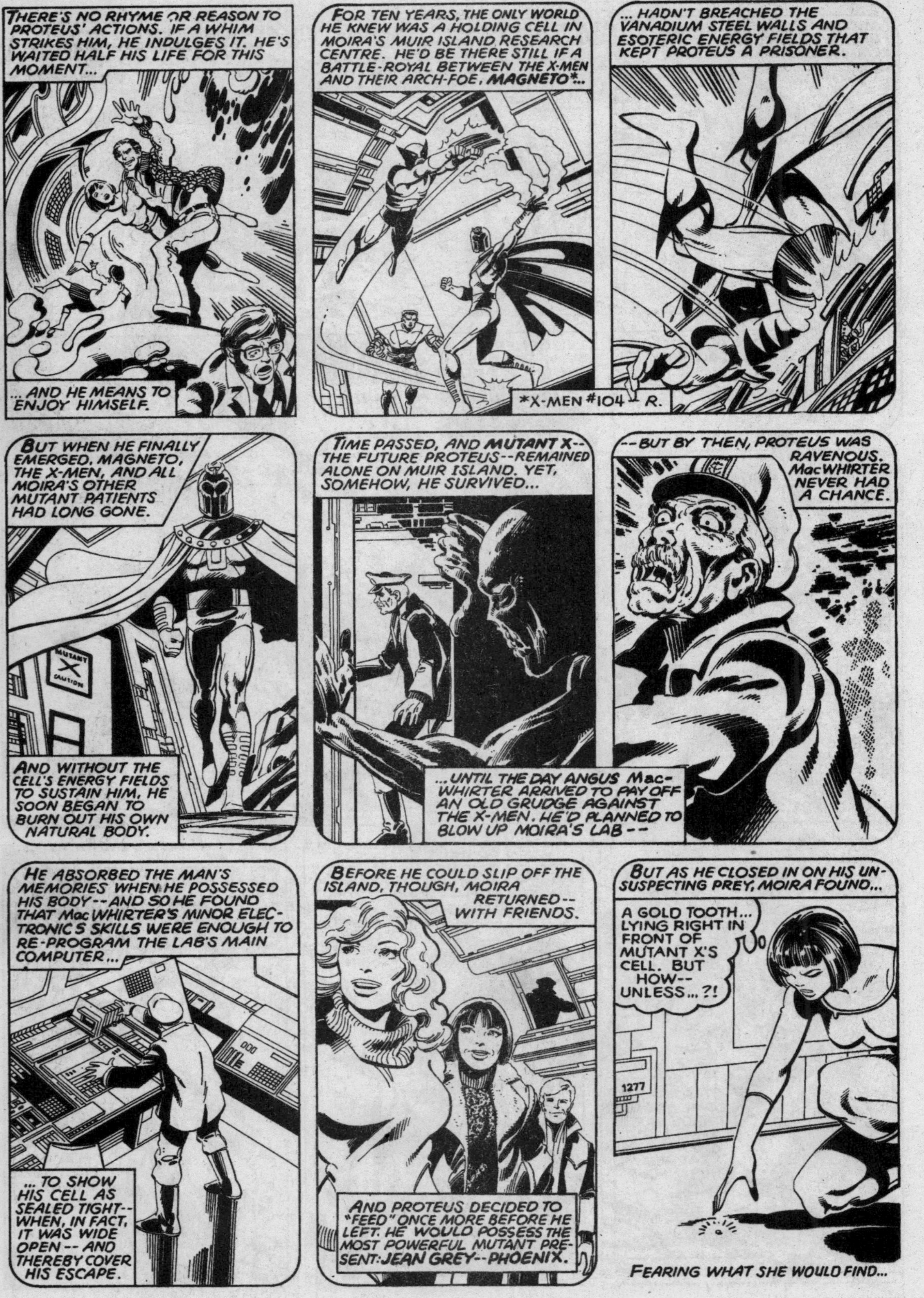

THERE'S NO RHYME OR REASON TO PROTEUS' ACTIONS. IF A WHIM STRIKES HIM, HE INDULGES IT. HE'S WAITED HALF HIS LIFE FOR THIS MOMENT...
...AND HE MEANS TO ENJOY HIMSELF.
FOR TEN YEARS, THE ONLY WORLD HE KNEW WAS A HOLDING CELL IN MOIRA'S MUIR ISLAND RESEARCH CENTRE. HE'D BE THERE STILL IF A BATTLE-ROYAL BETWEEN THE X-MEN AND THEIR ARCH-FOE, MAGNETO*...
*X-MEN #104 — R.
...HADN'T BREACHED THE VANADIUM STEEL WALLS AND ESOTERIC ENERGY FIELDS THAT KEPT PROTEUS A PRISONER.
BUT WHEN HE FINALLY EMERGED, MAGNETO, THE X-MEN, AND ALL MOIRA'S OTHER MUTANT PATIENTS HAD LONG GONE.
MUTANT X CAUTION
AND WITHOUT THE CELL'S ENERGY FIELDS TO SUSTAIN HIM, HE SOON BEGAN TO BURN OUT HIS OWN NATURAL BODY.
TIME PASSED, AND MUTANT X-- THE FUTURE PROTEUS--REMAINED ALONE ON MUIR ISLAND. YET, SOMEHOW, HE SURVIVED...
...UNTIL THE DAY ANGUS MacWHIRTER ARRIVED TO PAY OFF AN OLD GRUDGE AGAINST THE X-MEN. HE'D PLANNED TO BLOW UP MOIRA'S LAB--
--BUT BY THEN, PROTEUS WAS RAVENOUS. MacWHIRTER NEVER HAD A CHANCE.
HE ABSORBED THE MAN'S MEMORIES WHEN HE POSSESSED HIS BODY--AND SO HE FOUND THAT MacWHIRTER'S MINOR ELECTRONICS SKILLS WERE ENOUGH TO RE-PROGRAM THE LAB'S MAIN COMPUTER...
...TO SHOW HIS CELL AS SEALED TIGHT-- WHEN, IN FACT, IT WAS WIDE OPEN -- AND THEREBY COVER HIS ESCAPE.
BEFORE HE COULD SLIP OFF THE ISLAND, THOUGH, MOIRA RETURNED-- WITH FRIENDS.
AND PROTEUS DECIDED TO "FEED" ONCE MORE BEFORE HE LEFT. HE WOULD POSSESS THE MOST POWERFUL MUTANT PRESENT: JEAN GREY--PHOENIX.
BUT AS HE CLOSED IN ON HIS UNSUSPECTING PREY, MOIRA FOUND...
A GOLD TOOTH... LYING RIGHT IN FRONT OF MUTANT X'S CELL. BUT HOW-- UNLESS...?!
1277
FEARING WHAT SHE WOULD FIND...

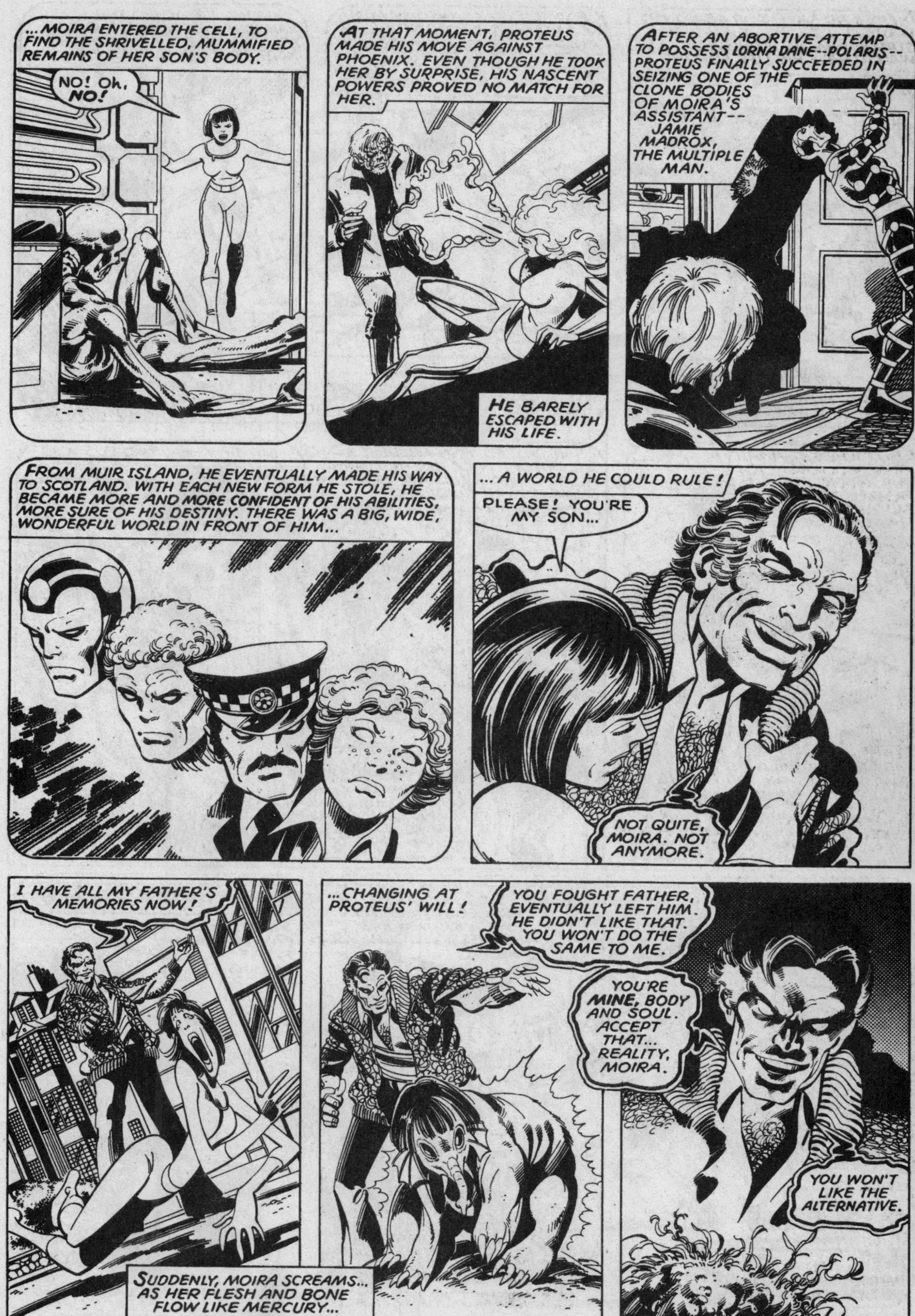
...MOIRA ENTERED THE CELL, TO FIND THE SHRIVELLED, MUMMIFIED REMAINS OF HER SON'S BODY.
NO! Oh, NO!
AT THAT MOMENT, PROTEUS MADE HIS MOVE AGAINST PHOENIX. EVEN THOUGH HE TOOK HER BY SURPRISE, HIS NASCENT POWERS PROVED NO MATCH FOR HER.
HE BARELY ESCAPED WITH HIS LIFE.
AFTER AN ABORTIVE ATTEMP TO POSSESS LORNA DANE--POLARIS--PROTEUS FINALLY SUCCEEDED IN SEIZING ONE OF THE CLONE BODIES OF MOIRA'S ASSISTANT--JAMIE MADROX, THE MULTIPLE MAN.
FROM MUIR ISLAND, HE EVENTUALLY MADE HIS WAY TO SCOTLAND. WITH EACH NEW FORM HE STOLE, HE BECAME MORE AND MORE CONFIDENT OF HIS ABILITIES, MORE SURE OF HIS DESTINY. THERE WAS A BIG, WIDE, WONDERFUL WORLD IN FRONT OF HIM...
...A WORLD HE COULD RULE!
PLEASE! YOU'RE MY SON...
NOT QUITE, MOIRA. NOT ANYMORE.
I HAVE ALL MY FATHER'S MEMORIES NOW!
SUDDENLY, MOIRA SCREAMS... AS HER FLESH AND BONE FLOW LIKE MERCURY...
...CHANGING AT PROTEUS' WILL!
YOU FOUGHT FATHER, EVENTUALLY LEFT HIM. HE DIDN'T LIKE THAT. YOU WON'T DO THE SAME TO ME.
YOU'RE MINE, BODY AND SOUL. ACCEPT THAT... REALITY, MOIRA.
YOU WON'T LIKE THE ALTERNATIVE.

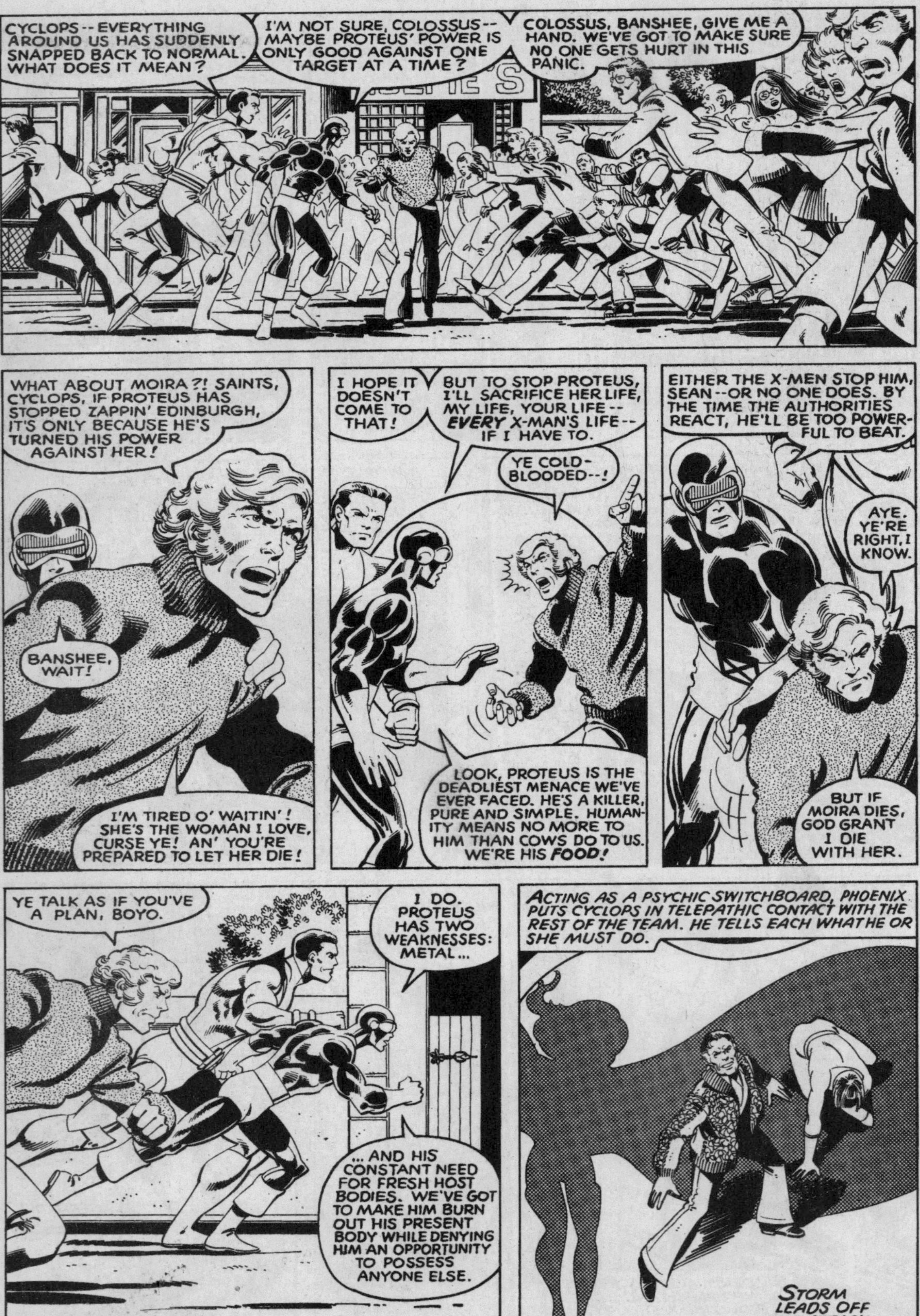

CYCLOPS -- EVERYTHING AROUND US HAS SUDDENLY SNAPPED BACK TO NORMAL. WHAT DOES IT MEAN?
I'M NOT SURE, COLOSSUS-- MAYBE PROTEUS' POWER IS ONLY GOOD AGAINST ONE TARGET AT A TIME?
COLOSSUS, BANSHEE, GIVE ME A HAND. WE'VE GOT TO MAKE SURE NO ONE GETS HURT IN THIS PANIC.
WHAT ABOUT MOIRA?! SAINTS, CYCLOPS, IF PROTEUS HAS STOPPED ZAPPIN' EDINBURGH, IT'S ONLY BECAUSE HE'S TURNED HIS POWER AGAINST HER!
BANSHEE, WAIT!
I'M TIRED O' WAITIN'! SHE'S THE WOMAN I LOVE, CURSE YE! AN' YOU'RE PREPARED TO LET HER DIE!
I HOPE IT DOESN'T COME TO THAT!
BUT TO STOP PROTEUS, I'LL SACRIFICE HER LIFE, MY LIFE, YOUR LIFE -- EVERY X-MAN'S LIFE -- IF I HAVE TO.
YE COLD-BLOODED--!
LOOK, PROTEUS IS THE DEADLIEST MENACE WE'VE EVER FACED. HE'S A KILLER, PURE AND SIMPLE. HUMANITY MEANS NO MORE TO HIM THAN COWS DO TO US. WE'RE HIS FOOD!
EITHER THE X-MEN STOP HIM, SEAN --OR NO ONE DOES. BY THE TIME THE AUTHORITIES REACT, HE'LL BE TOO POWERFUL TO BEAT.
AYE. YE'RE RIGHT, I KNOW.
BUT IF MOIRA DIES, GOD GRANT I DIE WITH HER.
YE TALK AS IF YOU'VE A PLAN, BOYO.
I DO. PROTEUS HAS TWO WEAKNESSES: METAL...
... AND HIS CONSTANT NEED FOR FRESH HOST BODIES. WE'VE GOT TO MAKE HIM BURN OUT HIS PRESENT BODY WHILE DENYING HIM AN OPPORTUNITY TO POSSESS ANYONE ELSE.
ACTING AS A PSYCHIC SWITCHBOARD, PHOENIX PUTS CYCLOPS IN TELEPATHIC CONTACT WITH THE REST OF THE TEAM. HE TELLS EACH WHAT HE OR SHE MUST DO.
STORM LEADS OFF THE ATTACK.

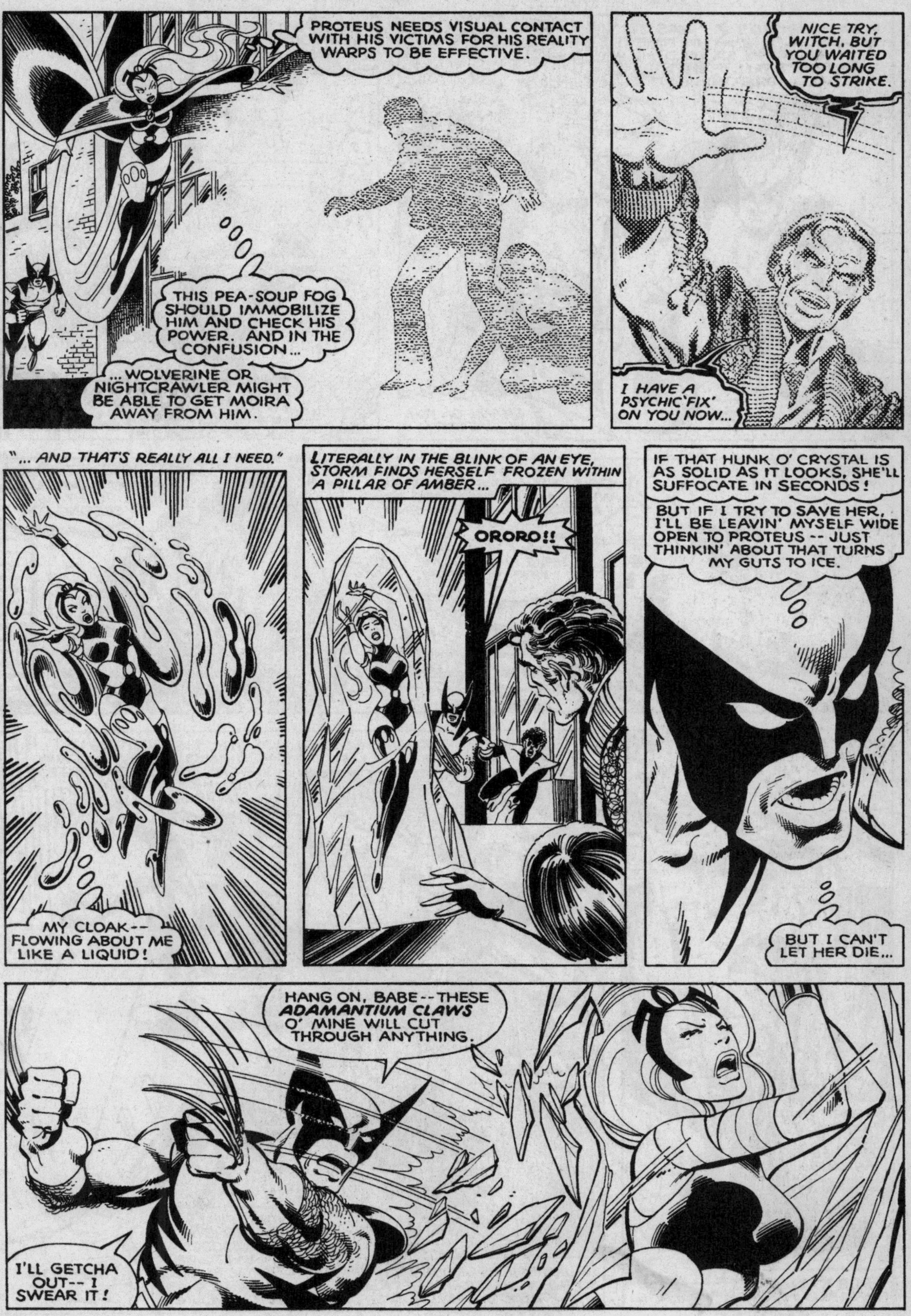
PROTEUS NEEDS VISUAL CONTACT WITH HIS VICTIMS FOR HIS REALITY WARPS TO BE EFFECTIVE.
THIS PEA-SOUP FOG SHOULD IMMOBILIZE HIM AND CHECK HIS POWER. AND IN THE CONFUSION...
...WOLVERINE OR NIGHTCRAWLER MIGHT BE ABLE TO GET MOIRA AWAY FROM HIM.
NICE TRY, WITCH, BUT YOU WAITED TOO LONG TO STRIKE.
I HAVE A PSYCHIC 'FIX' ON YOU NOW...
"...AND THAT'S REALLY ALL I NEED."
MY CLOAK-- FLOWING ABOUT ME LIKE A LIQUID!
LITERALLY IN THE BLINK OF AN EYE, STORM FINDS HERSELF FROZEN WITHIN A PILLAR OF AMBER...
ORORO!!
IF THAT HUNK O' CRYSTAL IS AS SOLID AS IT LOOKS, SHE'LL SUFFOCATE IN SECONDS!
BUT IF I TRY TO SAVE HER, I'LL BE LEAVIN' MYSELF WIDE OPEN TO PROTEUS -- JUST THINKIN' ABOUT THAT TURNS MY GUTS TO ICE.
BUT I CAN'T LET HER DIE...
HANG ON, BABE--THESE ADAMANTIUM CLAWS O' MINE WILL CUT THROUGH ANYTHING.
I'LL GETCHA OUT-- I SWEAR IT!

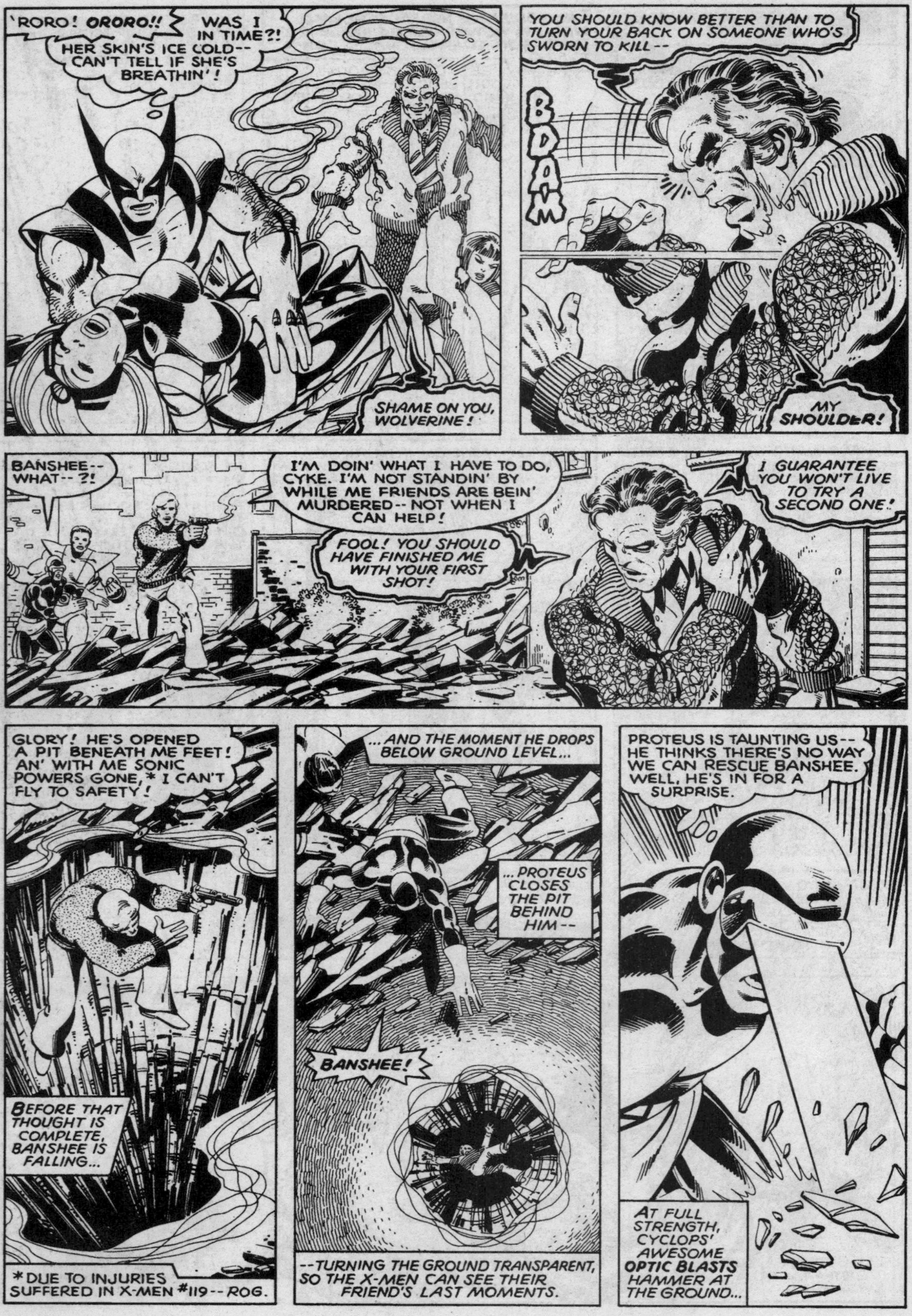
'RORO! ORORO!!
WAS I IN TIME?!
HER SKIN'S ICE COLD-- CAN'T TELL IF SHE'S BREATHIN'!
SHAME ON YOU, WOLVERINE!
YOU SHOULD KNOW BETTER THAN TO TURN YOUR BACK ON SOMEONE WHO'S SWORN TO KILL--
BDAM
MY SHOULDER!
BANSHEE-- WHAT-- ?!
I'M DOIN' WHAT I HAVE TO DO, CYKE. I'M NOT STANDIN' BY WHILE ME FRIENDS ARE BEIN' MURDERED-- NOT WHEN I CAN HELP!
FOOL! YOU SHOULD HAVE FINISHED ME WITH YOUR FIRST SHOT!
I GUARANTEE YOU WON'T LIVE TO TRY A SECOND ONE!
GLORY! HE'S OPENED A PIT BENEATH ME FEET! AN' WITH ME SONIC POWERS GONE,* I CAN'T FLY TO SAFETY!
BEFORE THAT THOUGHT IS COMPLETE, BANSHEE IS FALLING...
*DUE TO INJURIES SUFFERED IN X-MEN #119-- ROG.
...AND THE MOMENT HE DROPS BELOW GROUND LEVEL...
...PROTEUS CLOSES THE PIT BEHIND HIM--
BANSHEE!
--TURNING THE GROUND TRANSPARENT, SO THE X-MEN CAN SEE THEIR FRIEND'S LAST MOMENTS.
PROTEUS IS TAUNTING US-- HE THINKS THERE'S NO WAY WE CAN RESCUE BANSHEE. WELL, HE'S IN FOR A SURPRISE.
AT FULL STRENGTH, CYCLOPS' AWESOME OPTIC BLASTS HAMMER AT THE GROUND...

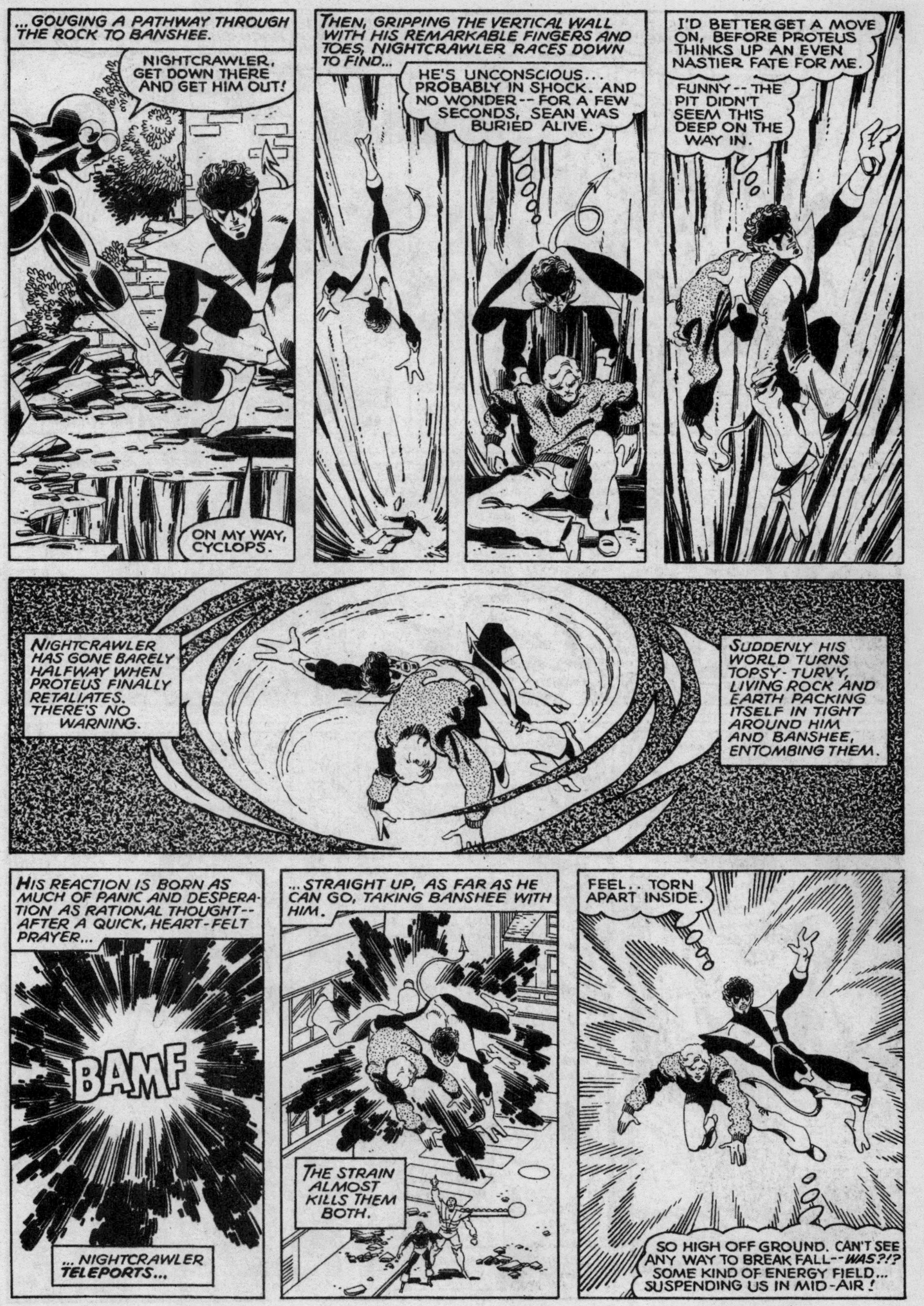
...GOUGING A PATHWAY THROUGH THE ROCK TO BANSHEE.
NIGHTCRAWLER, GET DOWN THERE AND GET HIM OUT!
ON MY WAY, CYCLOPS.
THEN, GRIPPING THE VERTICAL WALL WITH HIS REMARKABLE FINGERS AND TOES, NIGHTCRAWLER RACES DOWN TO FIND...
HE'S UNCONSCIOUS... PROBABLY IN SHOCK. AND NO WONDER -- FOR A FEW SECONDS, SEAN WAS BURIED ALIVE.
I'D BETTER GET A MOVE ON, BEFORE PROTEUS THINKS UP AN EVEN NASTIER FATE FOR ME.
FUNNY -- THE PIT DIDN'T SEEM THIS DEEP ON THE WAY IN.
NIGHTCRAWLER HAS GONE BARELY HALFWAY WHEN PROTEUS FINALLY RETALIATES. THERE'S NO WARNING.
SUDDENLY HIS WORLD TURNS TOPSY-TURVY, LIVING ROCK AND EARTH PACKING ITSELF IN TIGHT AROUND HIM AND BANSHEE, ENTOMBING THEM.
HIS REACTION IS BORN AS MUCH OF PANIC AND DESPERATION AS RATIONAL THOUGHT-- AFTER A QUICK, HEART-FELT PRAYER...
BAMF
...NIGHTCRAWLER TELEPORTS...
...STRAIGHT UP, AS FAR AS HE CAN GO, TAKING BANSHEE WITH HIM.
THE STRAIN ALMOST KILLS THEM BOTH.
FEEL.. TORN APART INSIDE.
SO HIGH OFF GROUND. CAN'T SEE ANY WAY TO BREAK FALL--WAS?!? SOME KIND OF ENERGY FIELD... SUSPENDING US IN MID-AIR!

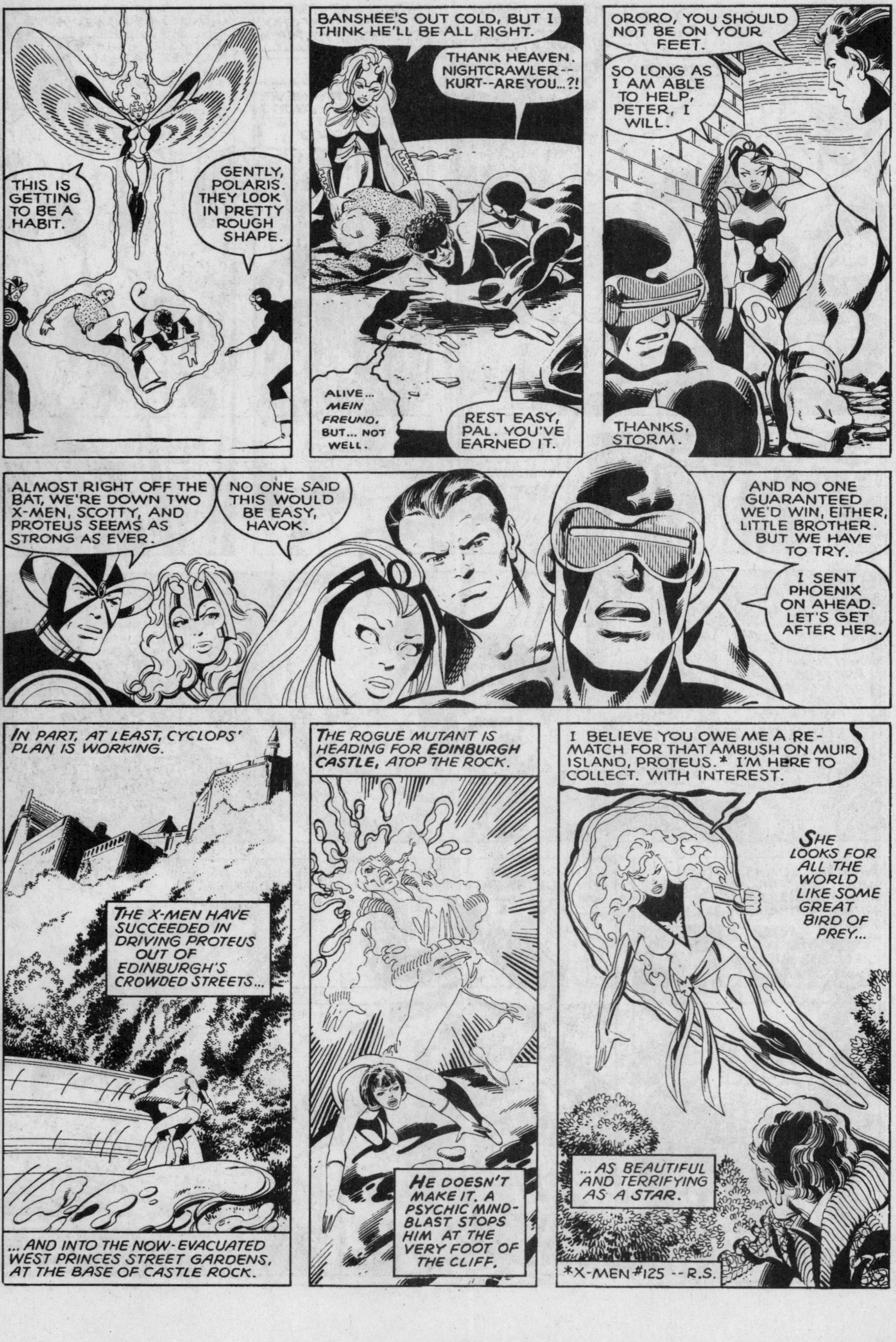
THIS IS GETTING TO BE A HABIT.
GENTLY, POLARIS. THEY LOOK IN PRETTY ROUGH SHAPE.
BANSHEE'S OUT COLD, BUT I THINK HE'LL BE ALL RIGHT.
THANK HEAVEN. NIGHTCRAWLER--KURT--ARE YOU...?!
ALIVE... MEIN FREUND. BUT... NOT WELL.
REST EASY, PAL. YOU'VE EARNED IT.
ORORO, YOU SHOULD NOT BE ON YOUR FEET.
SO LONG AS I AM ABLE TO HELP, PETER, I WILL.
THANKS, STORM.
ALMOST RIGHT OFF THE BAT, WE'RE DOWN TWO X-MEN, SCOTTY, AND PROTEUS SEEMS AS STRONG AS EVER.
NO ONE SAID THIS WOULD BE EASY, HAVOK.
AND NO ONE GUARANTEED WE'D WIN, EITHER, LITTLE BROTHER. BUT WE HAVE TO TRY.
I SENT PHOENIX ON AHEAD. LET'S GET AFTER HER.
IN PART, AT LEAST, CYCLOPS' PLAN IS WORKING.
THE X-MEN HAVE SUCCEEDED IN DRIVING PROTEUS OUT OF EDINBURGH'S CROWDED STREETS...
... AND INTO THE NOW-EVACUATED WEST PRINCES STREET GARDENS, AT THE BASE OF CASTLE ROCK.
THE ROGUE MUTANT IS HEADING FOR EDINBURGH CASTLE, ATOP THE ROCK.
HE DOESN'T MAKE IT. A PSYCHIC MIND-BLAST STOPS HIM AT THE VERY FOOT OF THE CLIFF.
I BELIEVE YOU OWE ME A RE-MATCH FOR THAT AMBUSH ON MUIR ISLAND, PROTEUS.* I'M HERE TO COLLECT. WITH INTEREST.
SHE LOOKS FOR ALL THE WORLD LIKE SOME GREAT BIRD OF PREY...
... AS BEAUTIFUL AND TERRIFYING AS A STAR.
*X-MEN #125 -- R.S.

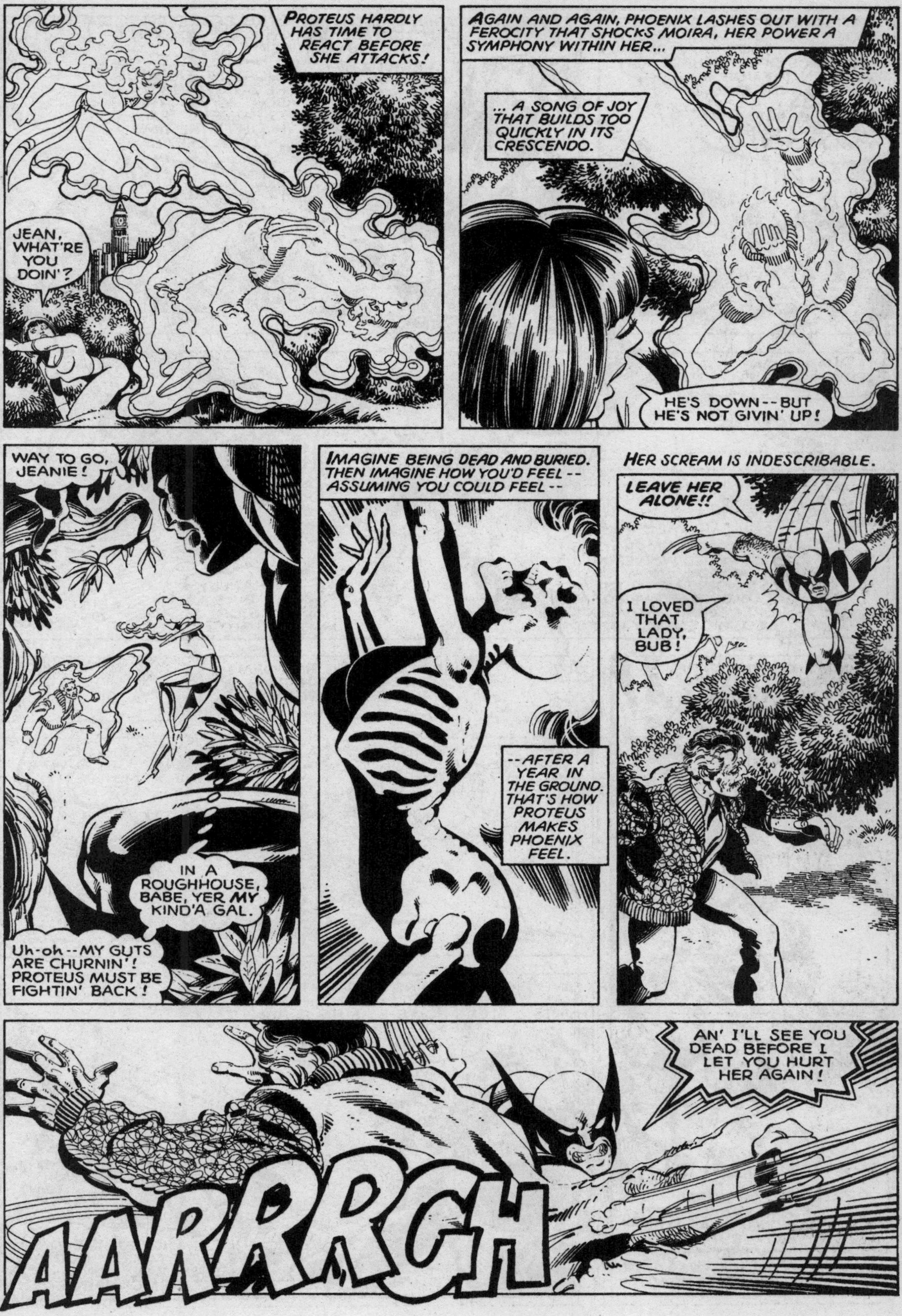
PROTEUS HARDLY HAS TIME TO REACT BEFORE SHE ATTACKS!
JEAN, WHAT'RE YOU DOIN'?
AGAIN AND AGAIN, PHOENIX LASHES OUT WITH A FEROCITY THAT SHOCKS MOIRA, HER POWER A SYMPHONY WITHIN HER...
... A SONG OF JOY THAT BUILDS TOO QUICKLY IN ITS CRESCENDO.
HE'S DOWN -- BUT HE'S NOT GIVIN' UP!
WAY TO GO, JEANIE!
IN A ROUGHHOUSE, BABE, YER MY KIND'A GAL.
Uh-oh -- MY GUTS ARE CHURNIN'! PROTEUS MUST BE FIGHTIN' BACK!
IMAGINE BEING DEAD AND BURIED. THEN IMAGINE HOW YOU'D FEEL -- ASSUMING YOU COULD FEEL --
-- AFTER A YEAR IN THE GROUND. THAT'S HOW PROTEUS MAKES PHOENIX FEEL.
HER SCREAM IS INDESCRIBABLE.
LEAVE HER ALONE!!
I LOVED THAT LADY, BUB!
AN' I'LL SEE YOU DEAD BEFORE I LET YOU HURT HER AGAIN!
AARRRCH

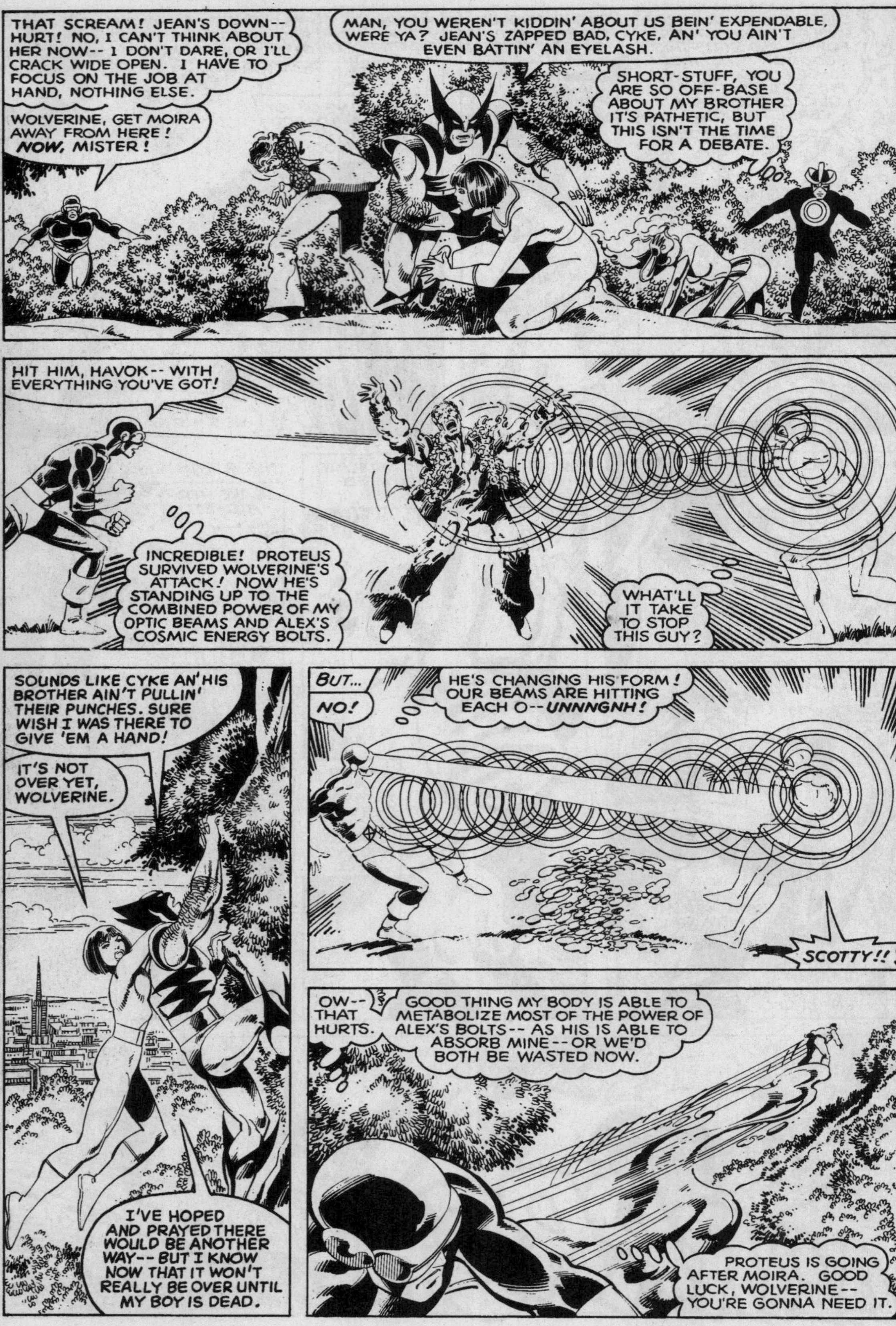
THAT SCREAM! JEAN'S DOWN-- HURT! NO, I CAN'T THINK ABOUT HER NOW-- I DON'T DARE, OR I'LL CRACK WIDE OPEN. I HAVE TO FOCUS ON THE JOB AT HAND, NOTHING ELSE.
WOLVERINE, GET MOIRA AWAY FROM HERE! NOW, MISTER!
MAN, YOU WEREN'T KIDDIN' ABOUT US BEIN' EXPENDABLE, WERE YA? JEAN'S ZAPPED BAD, CYKE, AN' YOU AIN'T EVEN BATTIN' AN EYELASH.
SHORT-STUFF, YOU ARE SO OFF-BASE ABOUT MY BROTHER IT'S PATHETIC, BUT THIS ISN'T THE TIME FOR A DEBATE.
HIT HIM, HAVOK-- WITH EVERYTHING YOU'VE GOT!
INCREDIBLE! PROTEUS SURVIVED WOLVERINE'S ATTACK! NOW HE'S STANDING UP TO THE COMBINED POWER OF MY OPTIC BEAMS AND ALEX'S COSMIC ENERGY BOLTS.
WHAT'LL IT TAKE TO STOP THIS GUY?
SOUNDS LIKE CYKE AN' HIS BROTHER AIN'T PULLIN' THEIR PUNCHES. SURE WISH I WAS THERE TO GIVE 'EM A HAND!
IT'S NOT OVER YET, WOLVERINE.
I'VE HOPED AND PRAYED THERE WOULD BE ANOTHER WAY-- BUT I KNOW NOW THAT IT WON'T REALLY BE OVER UNTIL MY BOY IS DEAD.
BUT...
NO!
HE'S CHANGING HIS FORM! OUR BEAMS ARE HITTING EACH O--UNNNGNH!
SCOTTY!!
OW-- THAT HURTS.
GOOD THING MY BODY IS ABLE TO METABOLIZE MOST OF THE POWER OF ALEX'S BOLTS-- AS HIS IS ABLE TO ABSORB MINE-- OR WE'D BOTH BE WASTED NOW.
PROTEUS IS GOING AFTER MOIRA. GOOD LUCK, WOLVERINE-- YOU'RE GONNA NEED IT.

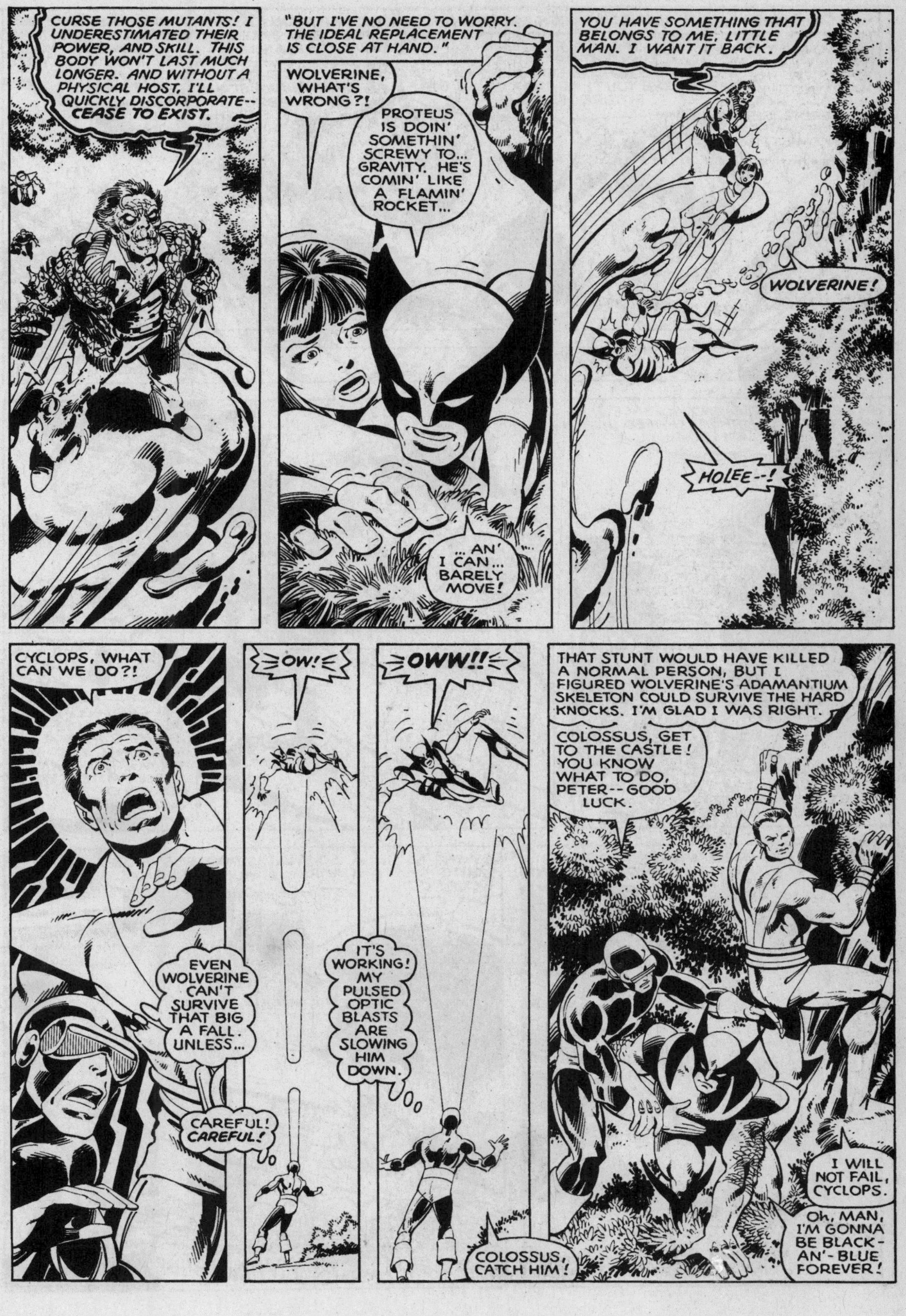
CURSE THOSE MUTANTS! I UNDERESTIMATED THEIR POWER, AND SKILL. THIS BODY WON'T LAST MUCH LONGER. AND WITHOUT A PHYSICAL HOST, I'LL QUICKLY DISCORPORATE-- CEASE TO EXIST.
"BUT I'VE NO NEED TO WORRY. THE IDEAL REPLACEMENT IS CLOSE AT HAND."
WOLVERINE, WHAT'S WRONG?!
PROTEUS IS DOIN' SOMETHIN' SCREWY TO... GRAVITY. HE'S COMIN' LIKE A FLAMIN' ROCKET...
... AN' I CAN... BARELY MOVE!
YOU HAVE SOMETHING THAT BELONGS TO ME, LITTLE MAN. I WANT IT BACK.
WOLVERINE!
HOLEE--!
CYCLOPS, WHAT CAN WE DO?!
EVEN WOLVERINE CAN'T SURVIVE THAT BIG A FALL. UNLESS...
CAREFUL! CAREFUL!
OW!
OWW!!
IT'S WORKING! MY PULSED OPTIC BLASTS ARE SLOWING HIM DOWN.
COLOSSUS, CATCH HIM!
THAT STUNT WOULD HAVE KILLED A NORMAL PERSON, BUT I FIGURED WOLVERINE'S ADAMANTIUM SKELETON COULD SURVIVE THE HARD KNOCKS. I'M GLAD I WAS RIGHT.
COLOSSUS, GET TO THE CASTLE! YOU KNOW WHAT TO DO, PETER--GOOD LUCK.
I WILL NOT FAIL, CYCLOPS.
Oh, MAN, I'M GONNA BE BLACK-AN'-BLUE FOREVER!

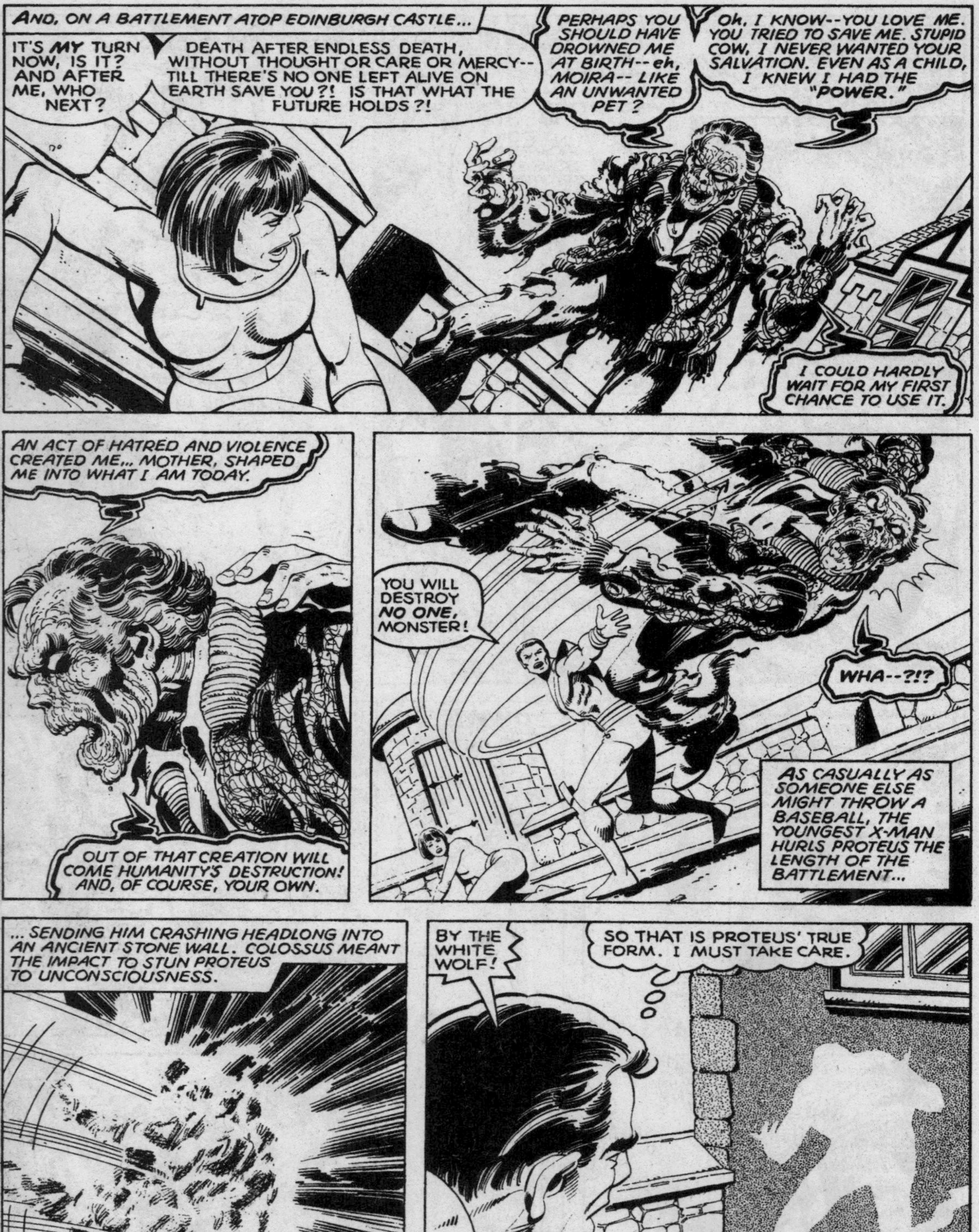
AND, ON A BATTLEMENT ATOP EDINBURGH CASTLE...
IT'S MY TURN NOW, IS IT? AND AFTER ME, WHO NEXT?
DEATH AFTER ENDLESS DEATH, WITHOUT THOUGHT OR CARE OR MERCY-- TILL THERE'S NO ONE LEFT ALIVE ON EARTH SAVE YOU?! IS THAT WHAT THE FUTURE HOLDS?!
PERHAPS YOU SHOULD HAVE DROWNED ME AT BIRTH--eh, MOIRA-- LIKE AN UNWANTED PET?
Oh, I KNOW--YOU LOVE ME. YOU TRIED TO SAVE ME. STUPID COW, I NEVER WANTED YOUR SALVATION. EVEN AS A CHILD, I KNEW I HAD THE "POWER."
I COULD HARDLY WAIT FOR MY FIRST CHANCE TO USE IT.
AN ACT OF HATRED AND VIOLENCE CREATED ME... MOTHER, SHAPED ME INTO WHAT I AM TODAY.
OUT OF THAT CREATION WILL COME HUMANITY'S DESTRUCTION! AND, OF COURSE, YOUR OWN.
YOU WILL DESTROY NO ONE, MONSTER!
WHA--?!?
AS CASUALLY AS SOMEONE ELSE MIGHT THROW A BASEBALL, THE YOUNGEST X-MAN HURLS PROTEUS THE LENGTH OF THE BATTLEMENT...
... SENDING HIM CRASHING HEADLONG INTO AN ANCIENT STONE WALL. COLOSSUS MEANT THE IMPACT TO STUN PROTEUS TO UNCONSCIOUSNESS.
INSTEAD, IT SHATTERS HIS DECAYING HOST BODY INTO POWDER.
BY THE WHITE WOLF!
SO THAT IS PROTEUS' TRUE FORM. I MUST TAKE CARE.
CYCLOPS SAID THAT IN THIS STATE, PROTEUS WILL BE BOTH THE MOST VULNERABLE AND THE MOST DANGEROUS. HE WILL BE DESPERATE TO STEAL ANOTHER HOST BODY. I MUST NOT LET HIM.

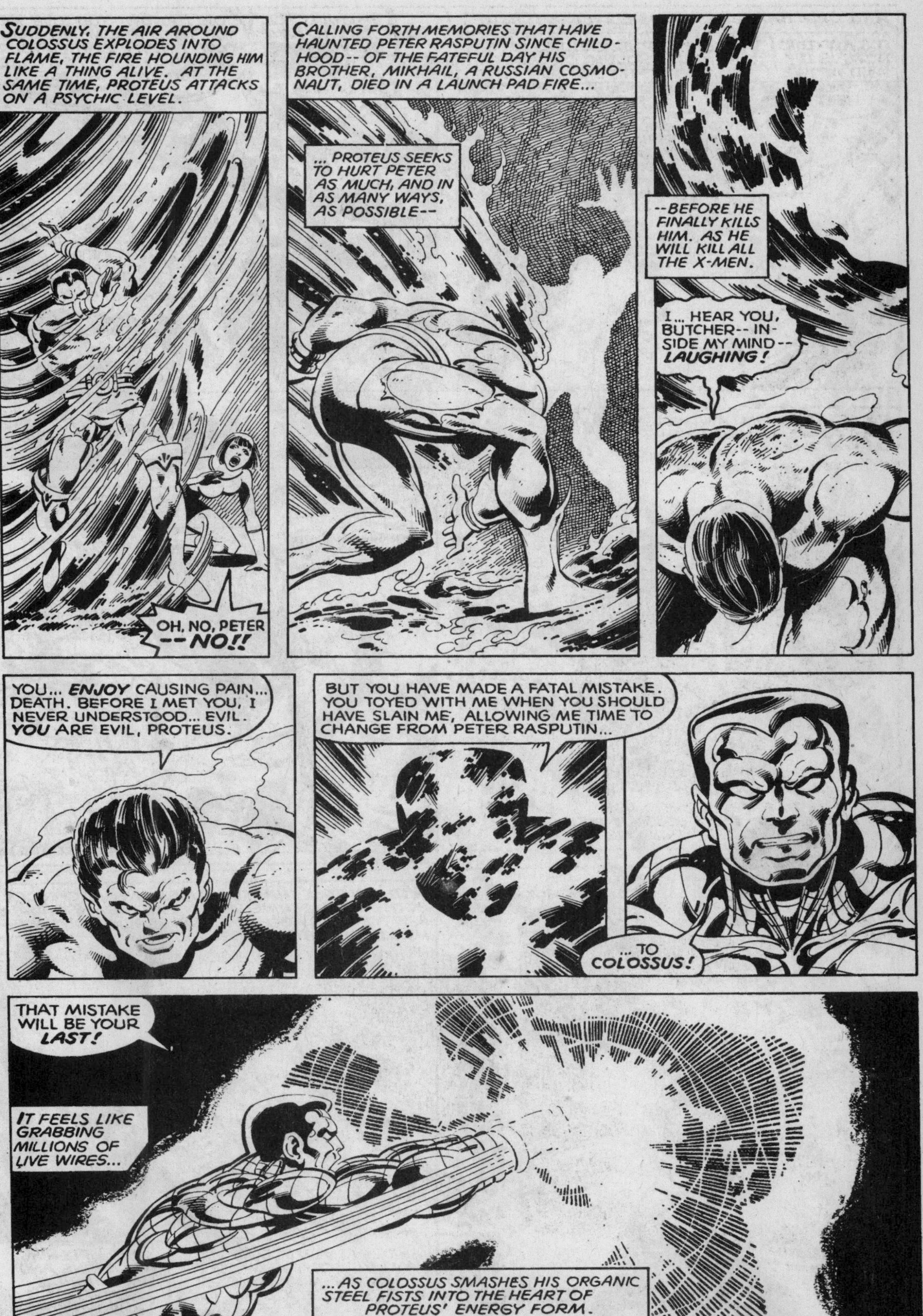

SUDDENLY, THE AIR AROUND COLOSSUS EXPLODES INTO FLAME, THE FIRE HOUNDING HIM LIKE A THING ALIVE. AT THE SAME TIME, PROTEUS ATTACKS ON A PSYCHIC LEVEL.
OH, NO, PETER --NO!!
CALLING FORTH MEMORIES THAT HAVE HAUNTED PETER RASPUTIN SINCE CHILDHOOD-- OF THE FATEFUL DAY HIS BROTHER, MIKHAIL, A RUSSIAN COSMONAUT, DIED IN A LAUNCH PAD FIRE...
... PROTEUS SEEKS TO HURT PETER AS MUCH, AND IN AS MANY WAYS, AS POSSIBLE--
--BEFORE HE FINALLY KILLS HIM. AS HE WILL KILL ALL THE X-MEN.
I... HEAR YOU, BUTCHER-- INSIDE MY MIND-- LAUGHING!
YOU... ENJOY CAUSING PAIN... DEATH. BEFORE I MET YOU, I NEVER UNDERSTOOD... EVIL. YOU ARE EVIL, PROTEUS.
BUT YOU HAVE MADE A FATAL MISTAKE. YOU TOYED WITH ME WHEN YOU SHOULD HAVE SLAIN ME, ALLOWING ME TIME TO CHANGE FROM PETER RASPUTIN...
... TO COLOSSUS!
THAT MISTAKE WILL BE YOUR LAST!
IT FEELS LIKE GRABBING MILLIONS OF LIVE WIRES...
...AS COLOSSUS SMASHES HIS ORGANIC STEEL FISTS INTO THE HEART OF PROTEUS' ENERGY FORM.

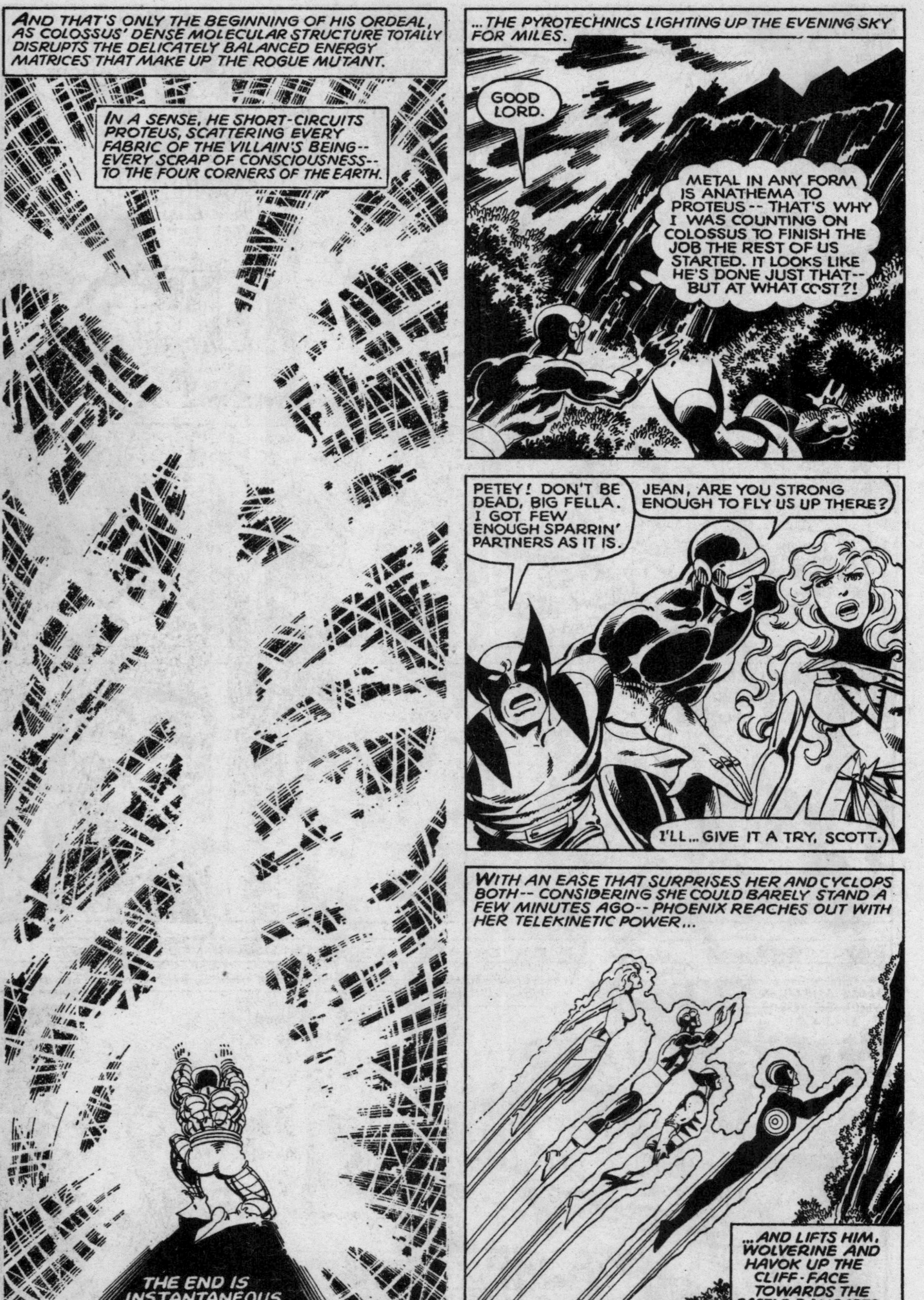
AND THAT'S ONLY THE BEGINNING OF HIS ORDEAL, AS COLOSSUS' DENSE MOLECULAR STRUCTURE TOTALLY DISRUPTS THE DELICATELY BALANCED ENERGY MATRICES THAT MAKE UP THE ROGUE MUTANT.
IN A SENSE, HE SHORT-CIRCUITS PROTEUS, SCATTERING EVERY FABRIC OF THE VILLAIN'S BEING-- EVERY SCRAP OF CONSCIOUSNESS-- TO THE FOUR CORNERS OF THE EARTH.
THE END IS INSTANTANEOUS...
...THE PYROTECHNICS LIGHTING UP THE EVENING SKY FOR MILES.
GOOD LORD.
METAL IN ANY FORM IS ANATHEMA TO PROTEUS -- THAT'S WHY I WAS COUNTING ON COLOSSUS TO FINISH THE JOB THE REST OF US STARTED. IT LOOKS LIKE HE'S DONE JUST THAT-- BUT AT WHAT COST?!
PETEY! DON'T BE DEAD, BIG FELLA. I GOT FEW ENOUGH SPARRIN' PARTNERS AS IT IS.
JEAN, ARE YOU STRONG ENOUGH TO FLY US UP THERE?
I'LL... GIVE IT A TRY, SCOTT.
WITH AN EASE THAT SURPRISES HER AND CYCLOPS BOTH-- CONSIDERING SHE COULD BARELY STAND A FEW MINUTES AGO-- PHOENIX REACHES OUT WITH HER TELEKINETIC POWER...
...AND LIFTS HIM, WOLVERINE AND HAVOK UP THE CLIFF-FACE TOWARDS THE CASTLE RAMPARTS.

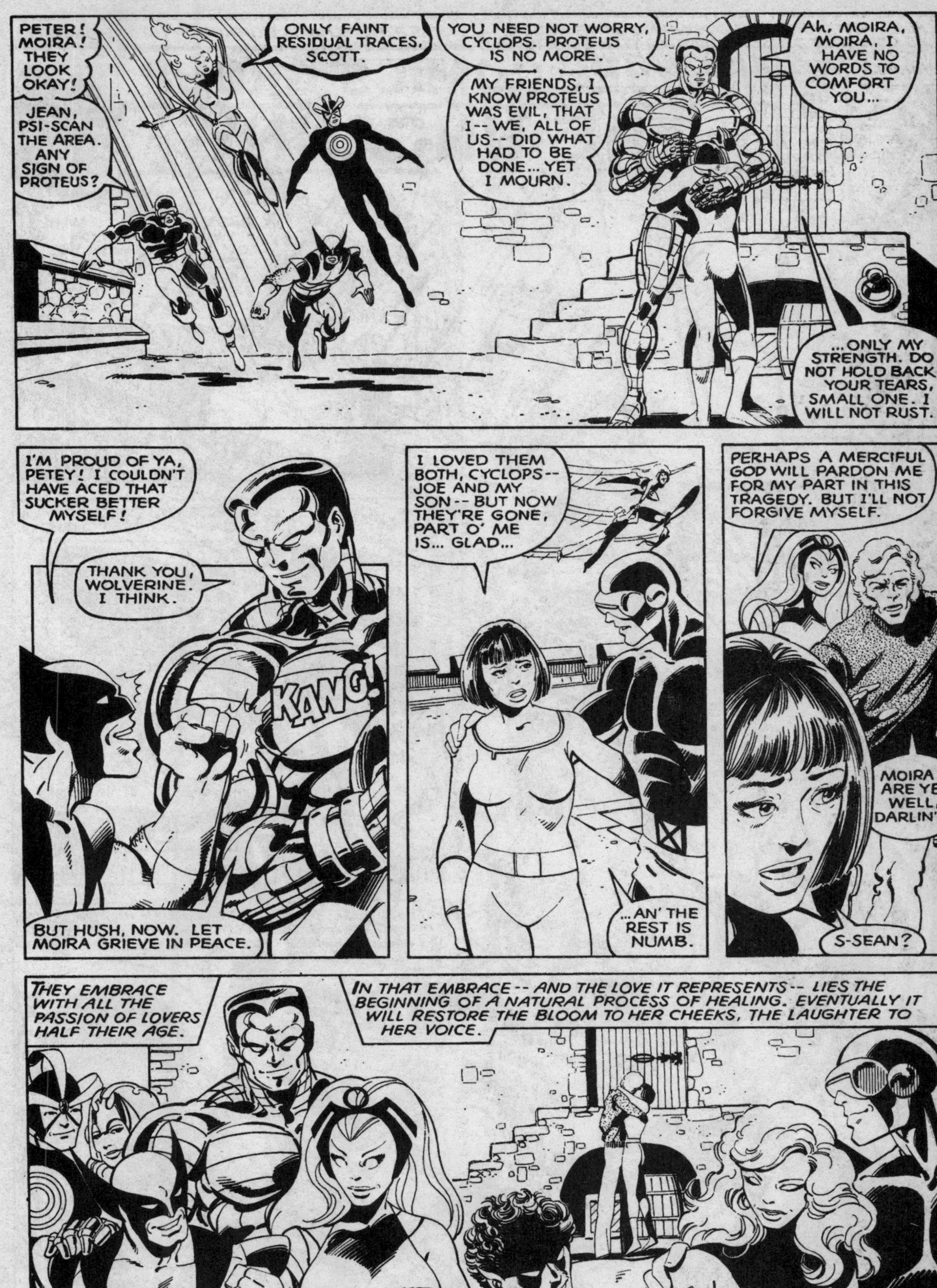

PETER! MOIRA! THEY LOOK OKAY!
JEAN, PSI-SCAN THE AREA. ANY SIGN OF PROTEUS?
ONLY FAINT RESIDUAL TRACES, SCOTT.
YOU NEED NOT WORRY, CYCLOPS. PROTEUS IS NO MORE.
MY FRIENDS, I KNOW PROTEUS WAS EVIL, THAT I-- WE, ALL OF US-- DID WHAT HAD TO BE DONE... YET I MOURN.
Ah, MOIRA, MOIRA, I HAVE NO WORDS TO COMFORT YOU...
...ONLY MY STRENGTH. DO NOT HOLD BACK YOUR TEARS, SMALL ONE. I WILL NOT RUST.
I'M PROUD OF YA, PETEY! I COULDN'T HAVE ACED THAT SUCKER BETTER MYSELF!
THANK YOU, WOLVERINE. I THINK.
KANG!
BUT HUSH, NOW. LET MOIRA GRIEVE IN PEACE.
I LOVED THEM BOTH, CYCLOPS-- JOE AND MY SON-- BUT NOW THEY'RE GONE, PART O' ME IS... GLAD...
...AN' THE REST IS NUMB.
PERHAPS A MERCIFUL GOD WILL PARDON ME FOR MY PART IN THIS TRAGEDY. BUT I'LL NOT FORGIVE MYSELF.
MOIRA! ARE YE WELL, DARLIN'?
S-SEAN?
THEY EMBRACE WITH ALL THE PASSION OF LOVERS HALF THEIR AGE.
IN THAT EMBRACE -- AND THE LOVE IT REPRESENTS -- LIES THE BEGINNING OF A NATURAL PROCESS OF HEALING. EVENTUALLY IT WILL RESTORE THE BLOOM TO HER CHEEKS, THE LAUGHTER TO HER VOICE.
WHEN THAT HAPPENS, THE X-MEN'S BATTLE HERE TODAY...
...CAN FINALLY, TRULY, BE CALLED A VICTORY.
Fin

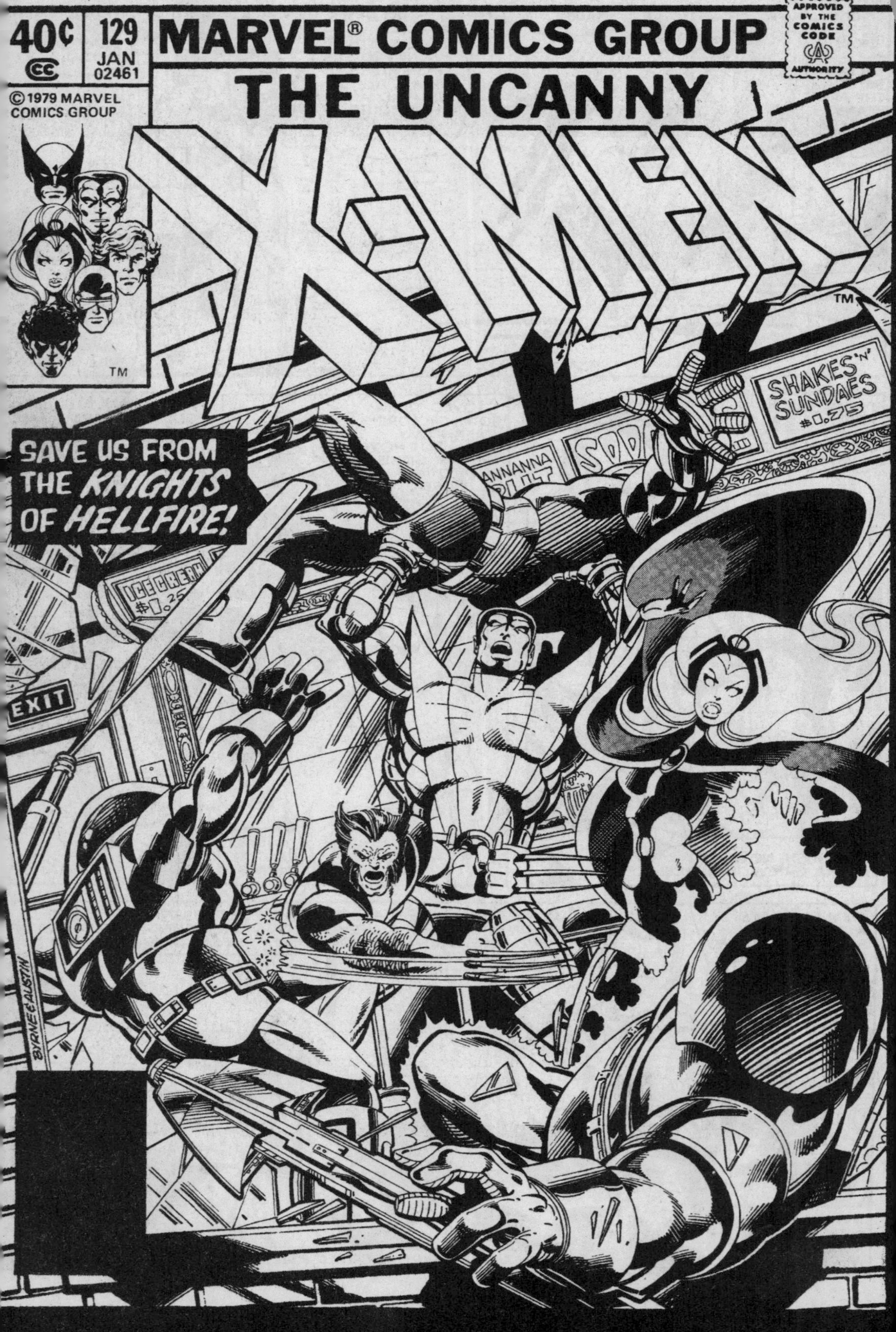

40¢
129
JAN
02461
MARVEL® COMICS GROUP
APPROVED BY THE COMICS CODE AUTHORITY
© 1979 MARVEL COMICS GROUP
THE UNCANNY
X-MEN
TM
SAVE US FROM THE KNIGHTS OF HELLFIRE!
SHAKES 'N' SUNDAES $1.75
EXIT

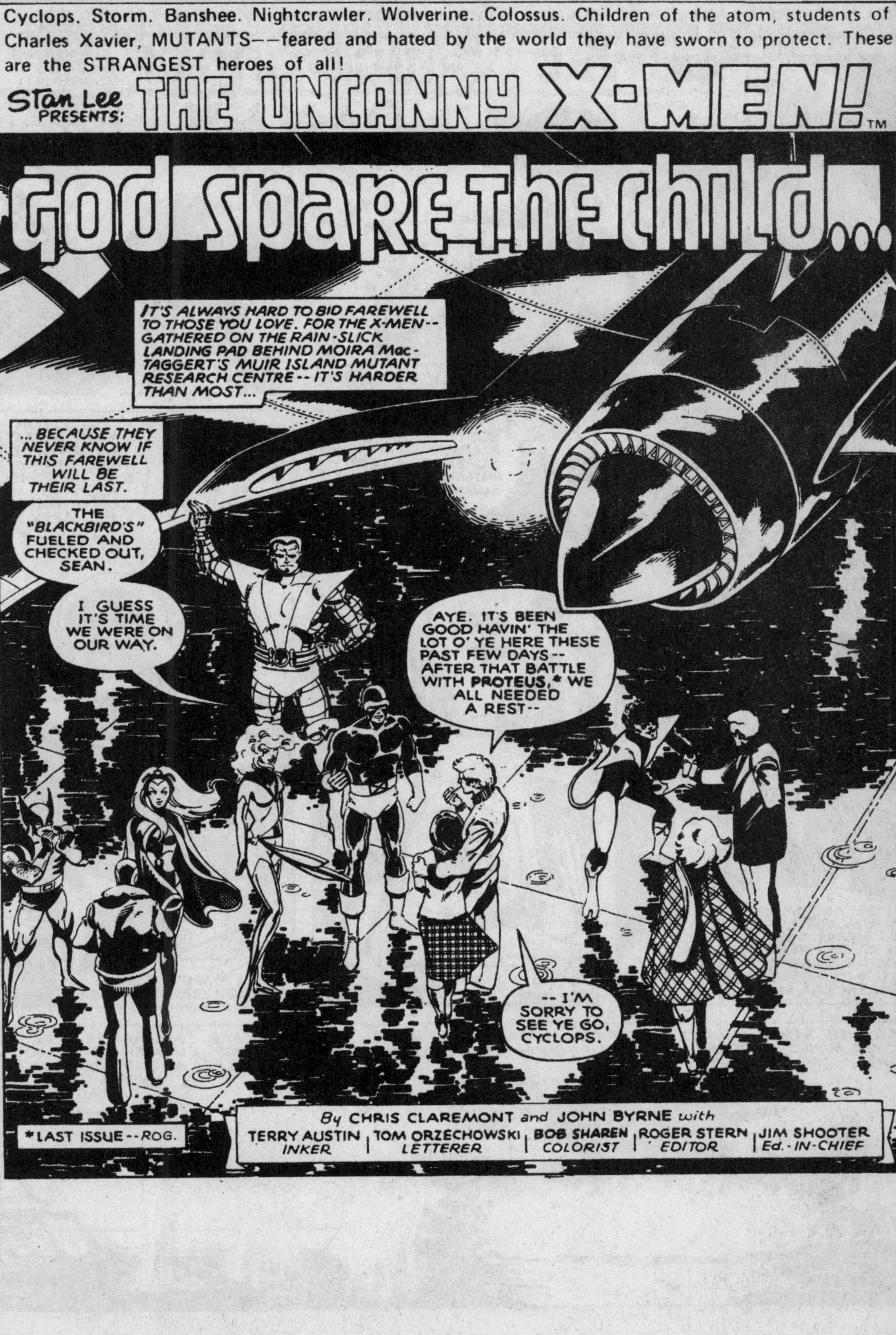
Cyclops. Storm. Banshee. Nightcrawler. Wolverine. Colossus. Children of the atom, students of Charles Xavier, MUTANTS--feared and hated by the world they have sworn to protect. These are the STRANGEST heroes of all!
Stan Lee PRESENTS: THE UNCANNY X-MEN! TM
GOD SPARE THE CHILD...
IT'S ALWAYS HARD TO BID FAREWELL TO THOSE YOU LOVE. FOR THE X-MEN--GATHERED ON THE RAIN-SLICK LANDING PAD BEHIND MOIRA MacTAGGERT'S MUIR ISLAND MUTANT RESEARCH CENTRE--IT'S HARDER THAN MOST...
...BECAUSE THEY NEVER KNOW IF THIS FAREWELL WILL BE THEIR LAST.
THE "BLACKBIRD'S" FUELED AND CHECKED OUT, SEAN.
I GUESS IT'S TIME WE WERE ON OUR WAY.
AYE. IT'S BEEN GOOD HAVIN' THE LOT O' YE HERE THESE PAST FEW DAYS--AFTER THAT BATTLE WITH PROTEUS,* WE ALL NEEDED A REST--
--I'M SORRY TO SEE YE GO, CYCLOPS.
*LAST ISSUE--ROG.
By CHRIS CLAREMONT and JOHN BYRNE with
TERRY AUSTIN INKER | TOM ORZECHOWSKI LETTERER | BOB SHAREN COLORIST | ROGER STERN EDITOR | JIM SHOOTER Ed.-IN-CHIEF

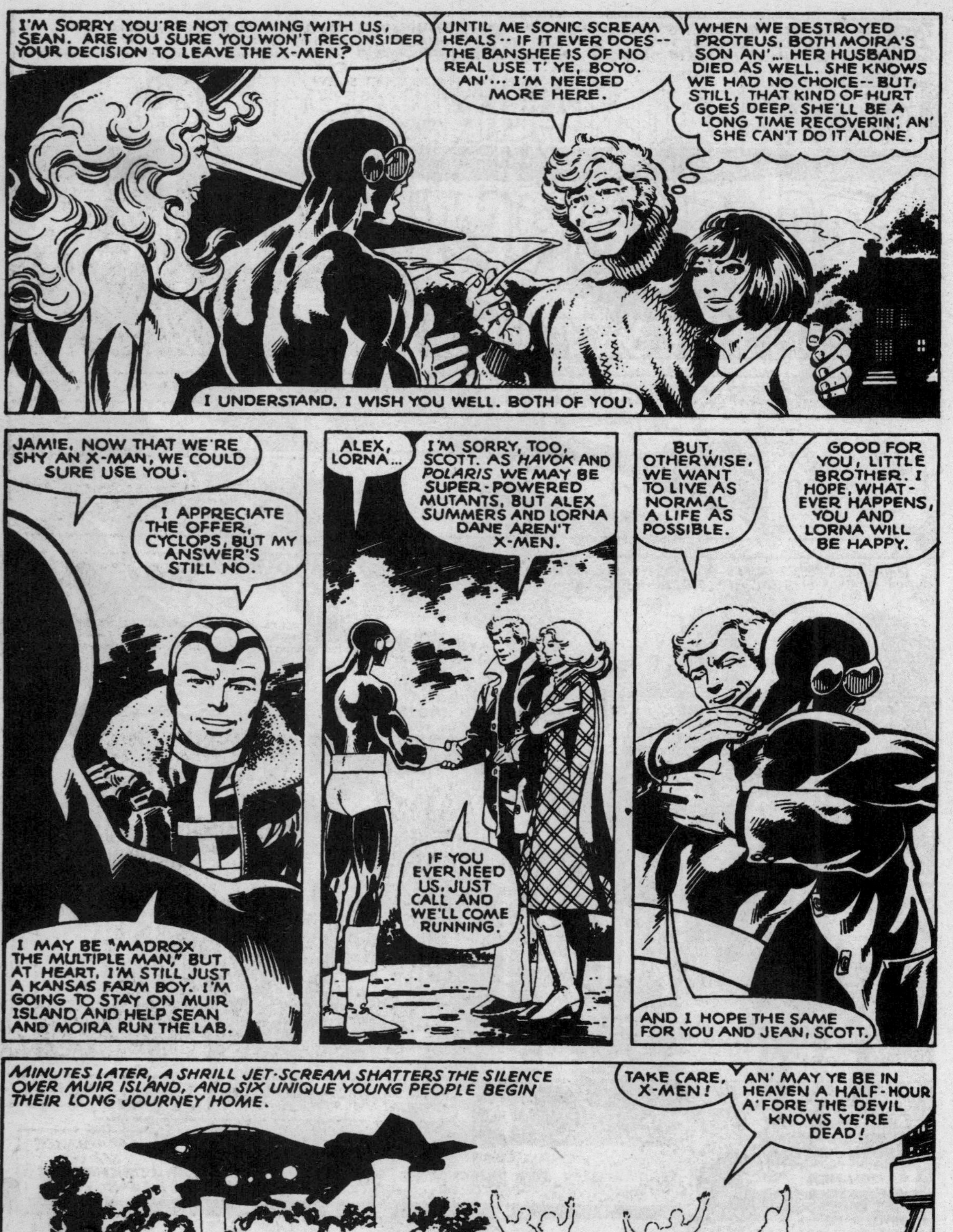

I'M SORRY YOU'RE NOT COMING WITH US, SEAN. ARE YOU SURE YOU WON'T RECONSIDER YOUR DECISION TO LEAVE THE X-MEN?
UNTIL ME SONIC SCREAM HEALS -- IF IT EVER DOES -- THE BANSHEE IS OF NO REAL USE T' YE, BOYO. AN'... I'M NEEDED MORE HERE.
WHEN WE DESTROYED PROTEUS, BOTH MOIRA'S SON AN'... HER HUSBAND DIED AS WELL. SHE KNOWS WE HAD NO CHOICE -- BUT, STILL, THAT KIND OF HURT GOES DEEP. SHE'LL BE A LONG TIME RECOVERIN', AN' SHE CAN'T DO IT ALONE.
I UNDERSTAND. I WISH YOU WELL. BOTH OF YOU.
JAMIE, NOW THAT WE'RE SHY AN X-MAN, WE COULD SURE USE YOU.
I APPRECIATE THE OFFER, CYCLOPS, BUT MY ANSWER'S STILL NO.
I MAY BE "MADROX THE MULTIPLE MAN," BUT AT HEART, I'M STILL JUST A KANSAS FARM BOY. I'M GOING TO STAY ON MUIR ISLAND AND HELP SEAN AND MOIRA RUN THE LAB.
ALEX, LORNA...
I'M SORRY, TOO, SCOTT. AS HAVOK AND POLARIS WE MAY BE SUPER-POWERED MUTANTS, BUT ALEX SUMMERS AND LORNA DANE AREN'T X-MEN.
IF YOU EVER NEED US, JUST CALL AND WE'LL COME RUNNING.
BUT, OTHERWISE, WE WANT TO LIVE AS NORMAL A LIFE AS POSSIBLE.
GOOD FOR YOU, LITTLE BROTHER. I HOPE, WHATEVER HAPPENS, YOU AND LORNA WILL BE HAPPY.
AND I HOPE THE SAME FOR YOU AND JEAN, SCOTT.
MINUTES LATER, A SHRILL JET-SCREAM SHATTERS THE SILENCE OVER MUIR ISLAND, AND SIX UNIQUE YOUNG PEOPLE BEGIN THEIR LONG JOURNEY HOME.
TAKE CARE, X-MEN!
AN' MAY YE BE IN HEAVEN A HALF-HOUR A'FORE THE DEVIL KNOWS YE'RE DEAD!

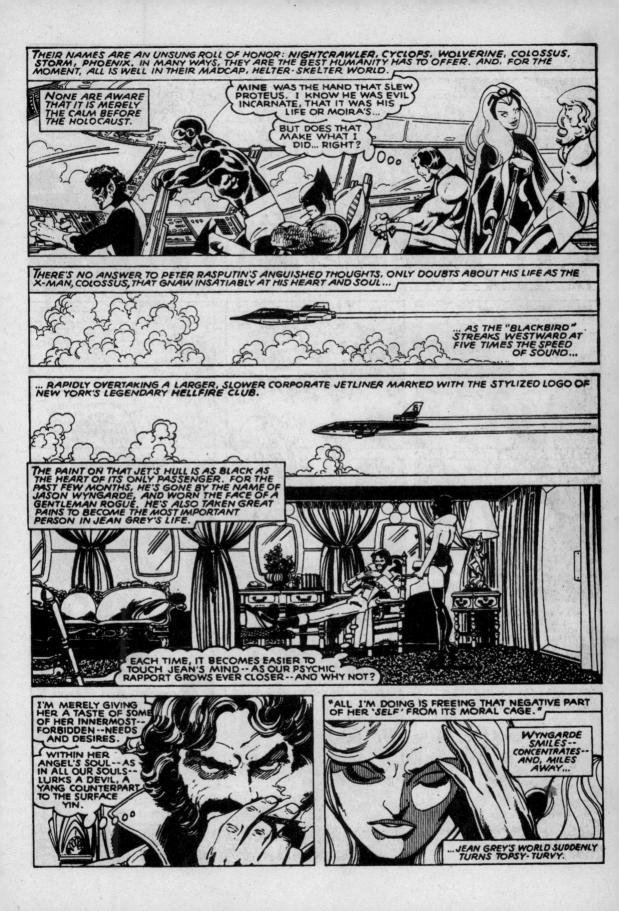

THEIR NAMES ARE AN UNSUNG ROLL OF HONOR: NIGHTCRAWLER, CYCLOPS, WOLVERINE, COLOSSUS, STORM, PHOENIX. IN MANY WAYS, THEY ARE THE BEST HUMANITY HAS TO OFFER. AND, FOR THE MOMENT, ALL IS WELL IN THEIR MADCAP, HELTER-SKELTER WORLD.

NONE ARE AWARE THAT IT IS MERELY THE CALM BEFORE THE HOLOCAUST.

MINE WAS THE HAND THAT SLEW PROTEUS. I KNOW HE WAS EVIL INCARNATE, THAT IT WAS HIS LIFE OR MOIRA'S...

BUT DOES THAT MAKE WHAT I DID... RIGHT?

THERE'S NO ANSWER TO PETER RASPUTIN'S ANGUISHED THOUGHTS, ONLY DOUBTS ABOUT HIS LIFE AS THE X-MAN, COLOSSUS, THAT GNAW INSATIABLY AT HIS HEART AND SOUL...

...AS THE "BLACKBIRD" STREAKS WESTWARD AT FIVE TIMES THE SPEED OF SOUND...

... RAPIDLY OVERTAKING A LARGER, SLOWER CORPORATE JETLINER MARKED WITH THE STYLIZED LOGO OF NEW YORK'S LEGENDARY HELLFIRE CLUB.

THE PAINT ON THAT JET'S HULL IS AS BLACK AS THE HEART OF ITS ONLY PASSENGER. FOR THE PAST FEW MONTHS, HE'S GONE BY THE NAME OF JASON WYNGARDE, AND WORN THE FACE OF A GENTLEMAN ROGUE. HE'S ALSO TAKEN GREAT PAINS TO BECOME THE MOST IMPORTANT PERSON IN JEAN GREY'S LIFE.

EACH TIME, IT BECOMES EASIER TO TOUCH JEAN'S MIND -- AS OUR PSYCHIC RAPPORT GROWS EVER CLOSER -- AND WHY NOT?

I'M MERELY GIVING HER A TASTE OF SOME OF HER INNERMOST-- FORBIDDEN --NEEDS AND DESIRES.

WITHIN HER ANGEL'S SOUL-- AS IN ALL OUR SOULS-- LURKS A DEVIL, A YANG COUNTERPART TO THE SURFACE YIN.

"ALL I'M DOING IS FREEING THAT NEGATIVE PART OF HER 'SELF' FROM ITS MORAL CAGE."

WYNGARDE SMILES-- CONCENTRATES-- AND, MILES AWAY...

...JEAN GREY'S WORLD SUDDENLY TURNS TOPSY-TURVY.

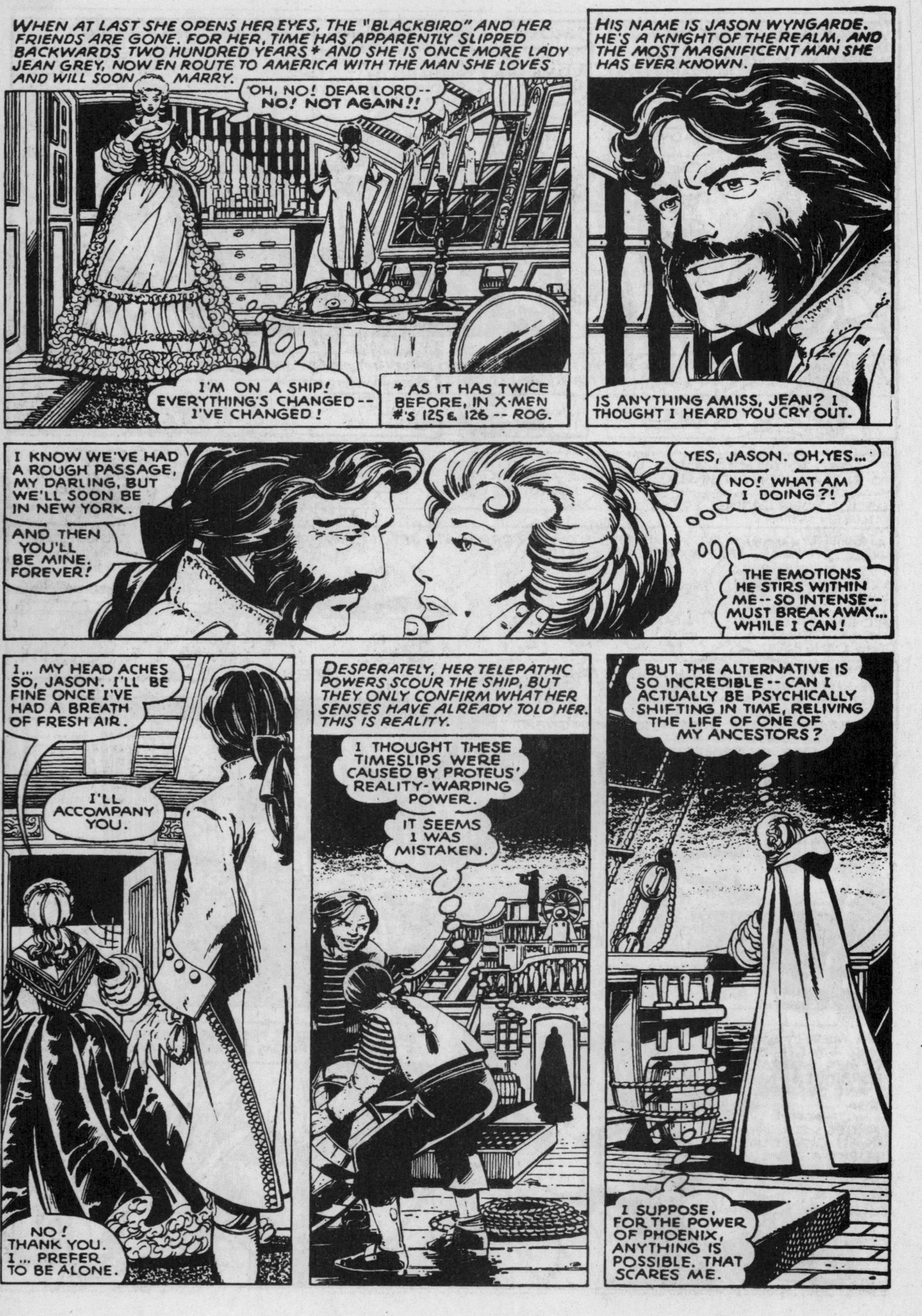
WHEN AT LAST SHE OPENS HER EYES, THE "BLACKBIRD" AND HER FRIENDS ARE GONE. FOR HER, TIME HAS APPARENTLY SLIPPED BACKWARDS TWO HUNDRED YEARS* AND SHE IS ONCE MORE LADY JEAN GREY, NOW EN ROUTE TO AMERICA WITH THE MAN SHE LOVES AND WILL SOON MARRY.
OH, NO! DEAR LORD-- NO! NOT AGAIN!!
I'M ON A SHIP! EVERYTHING'S CHANGED-- I'VE CHANGED!
* AS IT HAS TWICE BEFORE, IN X-MEN #'S 125 & 126 -- ROG.
HIS NAME IS JASON WYNGARDE. HE'S A KNIGHT OF THE REALM, AND THE MOST MAGNIFICENT MAN SHE HAS EVER KNOWN.
IS ANYTHING AMISS, JEAN? I THOUGHT I HEARD YOU CRY OUT.
I KNOW WE'VE HAD A ROUGH PASSAGE, MY DARLING, BUT WE'LL SOON BE IN NEW YORK.
AND THEN YOU'LL BE MINE. FOREVER!
YES, JASON. OH, YES...
NO! WHAT AM I DOING?!
THE EMOTIONS HE STIRS WITHIN ME-- SO INTENSE-- MUST BREAK AWAY... WHILE I CAN!
I... MY HEAD ACHES SO, JASON. I'LL BE FINE ONCE I'VE HAD A BREATH OF FRESH AIR.
I'LL ACCOMPANY YOU.
NO! THANK YOU. I... PREFER TO BE ALONE.
DESPERATELY, HER TELEPATHIC POWERS SCOUR THE SHIP, BUT THEY ONLY CONFIRM WHAT HER SENSES HAVE ALREADY TOLD HER. THIS IS REALITY.
I THOUGHT THESE TIMESLIPS WERE CAUSED BY PROTEUS' REALITY-WARPING POWER.
IT SEEMS I WAS MISTAKEN.
BUT THE ALTERNATIVE IS SO INCREDIBLE-- CAN I ACTUALLY BE PSYCHICALLY SHIFTING IN TIME, RELIVING THE LIFE OF ONE OF MY ANCESTORS?
I SUPPOSE, FOR THE POWER OF PHOENIX, ANYTHING IS POSSIBLE. THAT SCARES ME.

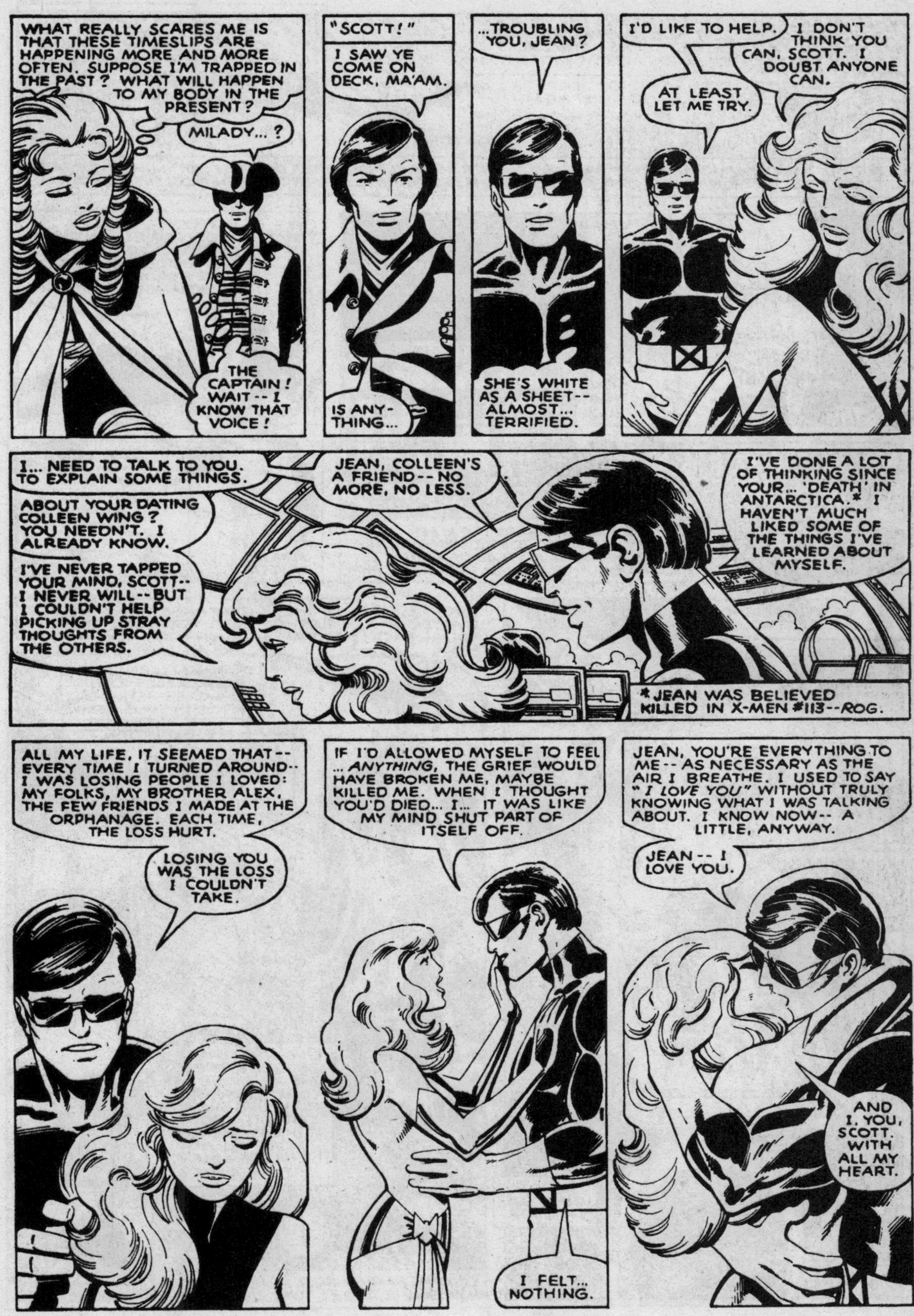

WHAT REALLY SCARES ME IS THAT THESE TIMESLIPS ARE HAPPENING MORE AND MORE OFTEN. SUPPOSE I'M TRAPPED IN THE PAST? WHAT WILL HAPPEN TO MY BODY IN THE PRESENT?
MILADY...?
THE CAPTAIN! WAIT -- I KNOW THAT VOICE!
"SCOTT!"
I SAW YE COME ON DECK, MA'AM.
IS ANYTHING...
...TROUBLING YOU, JEAN?
SHE'S WHITE AS A SHEET-- ALMOST... TERRIFIED.
I'D LIKE TO HELP.
I DON'T THINK YOU CAN, SCOTT. I DOUBT ANYONE CAN.
AT LEAST LET ME TRY.
I... NEED TO TALK TO YOU. TO EXPLAIN SOME THINGS.
ABOUT YOUR DATING COLLEEN WING? YOU NEEDN'T. I ALREADY KNOW.
I'VE NEVER TAPPED YOUR MIND, SCOTT-- I NEVER WILL--BUT I COULDN'T HELP PICKING UP STRAY THOUGHTS FROM THE OTHERS.
JEAN, COLLEEN'S A FRIEND-- NO MORE, NO LESS.
I'VE DONE A LOT OF THINKING SINCE YOUR... 'DEATH' IN ANTARCTICA.* I HAVEN'T MUCH LIKED SOME OF THE THINGS I'VE LEARNED ABOUT MYSELF.
*JEAN WAS BELIEVED KILLED IN X-MEN #113--ROG.
ALL MY LIFE, IT SEEMED THAT-- EVERY TIME I TURNED AROUND-- I WAS LOSING PEOPLE I LOVED: MY FOLKS, MY BROTHER ALEX, THE FEW FRIENDS I MADE AT THE ORPHANAGE. EACH TIME, THE LOSS HURT.
LOSING YOU WAS THE LOSS I COULDN'T TAKE.
IF I'D ALLOWED MYSELF TO FEEL ... ANYTHING, THE GRIEF WOULD HAVE BROKEN ME, MAYBE KILLED ME. WHEN I THOUGHT YOU'D DIED... I... IT WAS LIKE MY MIND SHUT PART OF ITSELF OFF.
I FELT... NOTHING.
JEAN, YOU'RE EVERYTHING TO ME-- AS NECESSARY AS THE AIR I BREATHE. I USED TO SAY "I LOVE YOU" WITHOUT TRULY KNOWING WHAT I WAS TALKING ABOUT. I KNOW NOW-- A LITTLE, ANYWAY.
JEAN -- I LOVE YOU.
AND I, YOU, SCOTT. WITH ALL MY HEART.

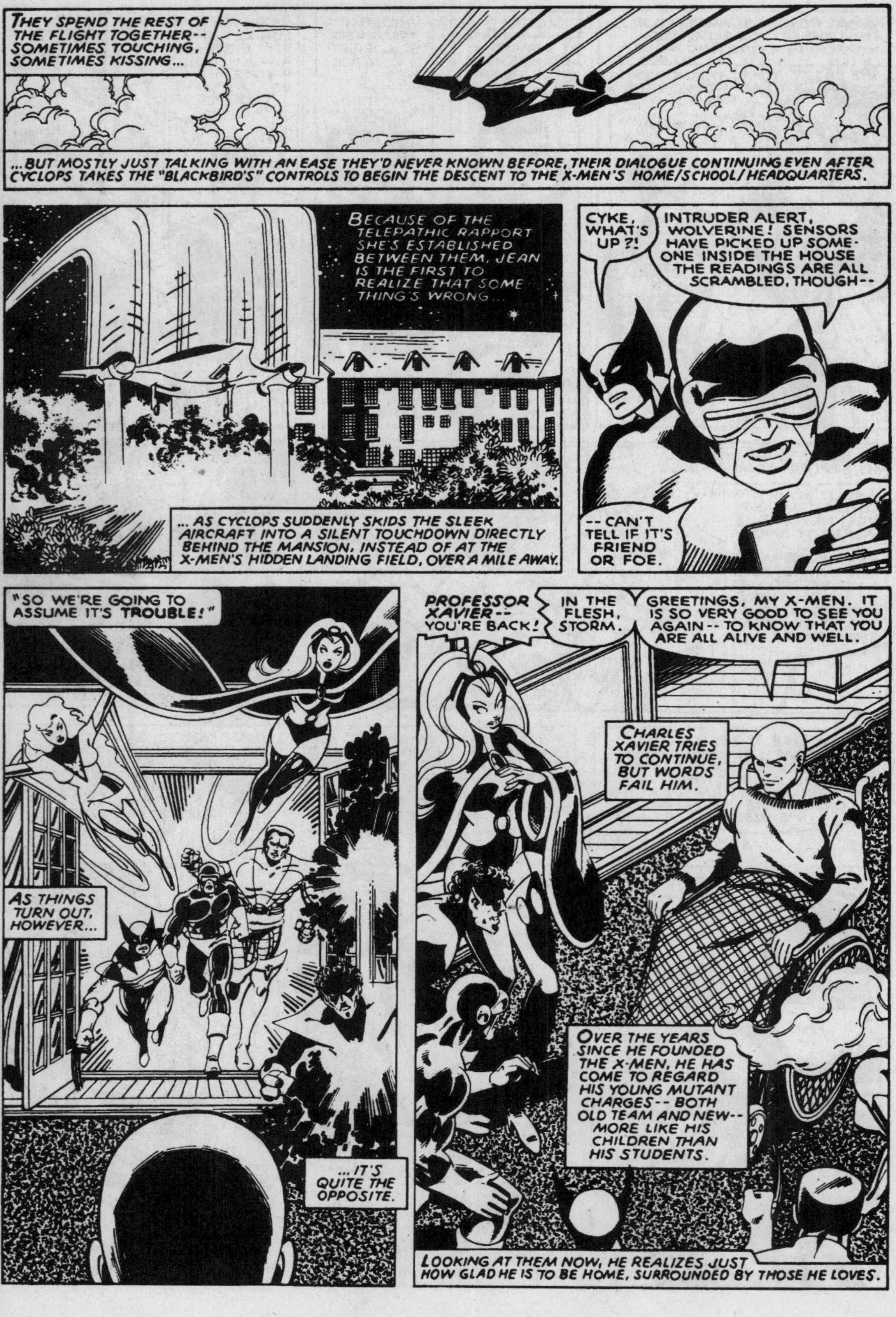

THEY SPEND THE REST OF THE FLIGHT TOGETHER-- SOMETIMES TOUCHING, SOMETIMES KISSING...
...BUT MOSTLY JUST TALKING WITH AN EASE THEY'D NEVER KNOWN BEFORE, THEIR DIALOGUE CONTINUING EVEN AFTER CYCLOPS TAKES THE "BLACKBIRD'S" CONTROLS TO BEGIN THE DESCENT TO THE X-MEN'S HOME/SCHOOL/HEADQUARTERS.
BECAUSE OF THE TELEPATHIC RAPPORT SHE'S ESTABLISHED BETWEEN THEM, JEAN IS THE FIRST TO REALIZE THAT SOMETHING'S WRONG...
...AS CYCLOPS SUDDENLY SKIDS THE SLEEK AIRCRAFT INTO A SILENT TOUCHDOWN DIRECTLY BEHIND THE MANSION, INSTEAD OF AT THE X-MEN'S HIDDEN LANDING FIELD, OVER A MILE AWAY.
CYKE, WHAT'S UP?!
INTRUDER ALERT, WOLVERINE! SENSORS HAVE PICKED UP SOMEONE INSIDE THE HOUSE THE READINGS ARE ALL SCRAMBLED, THOUGH--
--CAN'T TELL IF IT'S FRIEND OR FOE.
"SO WE'RE GOING TO ASSUME IT'S TROUBLE!"
AS THINGS TURN OUT, HOWEVER...
...IT'S QUITE THE OPPOSITE.
PROFESSOR XAVIER-- YOU'RE BACK!
IN THE FLESH, STORM.
GREETINGS, MY X-MEN. IT IS SO VERY GOOD TO SEE YOU AGAIN-- TO KNOW THAT YOU ARE ALL ALIVE AND WELL.
CHARLES XAVIER TRIES TO CONTINUE, BUT WORDS FAIL HIM.
OVER THE YEARS SINCE HE FOUNDED THE X-MEN, HE HAS COME TO REGARD HIS YOUNG MUTANT CHARGES-- BOTH OLD TEAM AND NEW-- MORE LIKE HIS CHILDREN THAN HIS STUDENTS.
LOOKING AT THEM NOW, HE REALIZES JUST HOW GLAD HE IS TO BE HOME, SURROUNDED BY THOSE HE LOVES.

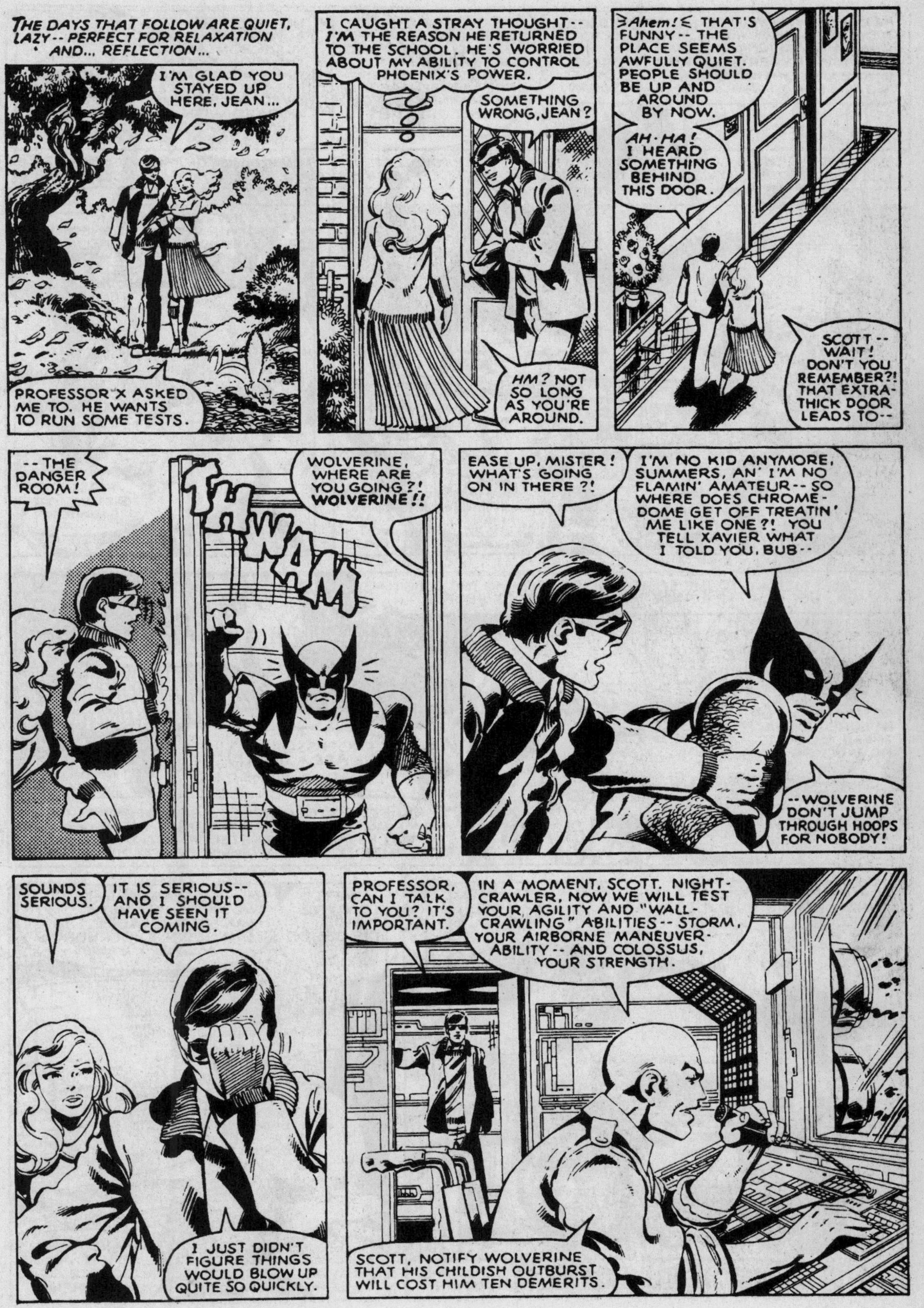
THE DAYS THAT FOLLOW ARE QUIET, LAZY -- PERFECT FOR RELAXATION AND... REFLECTION...
I'M GLAD YOU STAYED UP HERE, JEAN...
PROFESSOR X ASKED ME TO. HE WANTS TO RUN SOME TESTS.
I CAUGHT A STRAY THOUGHT -- I'M THE REASON HE RETURNED TO THE SCHOOL. HE'S WORRIED ABOUT MY ABILITY TO CONTROL PHOENIX'S POWER.
SOMETHING WRONG, JEAN?
HM? NOT SO LONG AS YOU'RE AROUND.
Ahem! THAT'S FUNNY -- THE PLACE SEEMS AWFULLY QUIET. PEOPLE SHOULD BE UP AND AROUND BY NOW.
AH-HA! I HEARD SOMETHING BEHIND THIS DOOR.
SCOTT -- WAIT! DON'T YOU REMEMBER?! THAT EXTRA-THICK DOOR LEADS TO--
-- THE DANGER ROOM!
THWAM
WOLVERINE, WHERE ARE YOU GOING?! WOLVERINE!!
EASE UP, MISTER! WHAT'S GOING ON IN THERE?!
I'M NO KID ANYMORE, SUMMERS, AN' I'M NO FLAMIN' AMATEUR -- SO WHERE DOES CHROME-DOME GET OFF TREATIN' ME LIKE ONE?! YOU TELL XAVIER WHAT I TOLD YOU, BUB--
-- WOLVERINE DON'T JUMP THROUGH HOOPS FOR NOBODY!
SOUNDS SERIOUS.
IT IS SERIOUS -- AND I SHOULD HAVE SEEN IT COMING.
I JUST DIDN'T FIGURE THINGS WOULD BLOW UP QUITE SO QUICKLY.
PROFESSOR, CAN I TALK TO YOU? IT'S IMPORTANT.
IN A MOMENT, SCOTT. NIGHT-CRAWLER, NOW WE WILL TEST YOUR AGILITY AND "WALL-CRAWLING" ABILITIES -- STORM, YOUR AIRBORNE MANEUVER-ABILITY -- AND COLOSSUS, YOUR STRENGTH.
SCOTT, NOTIFY WOLVERINE THAT HIS CHILDISH OUTBURST WILL COST HIM TEN DEMERITS.

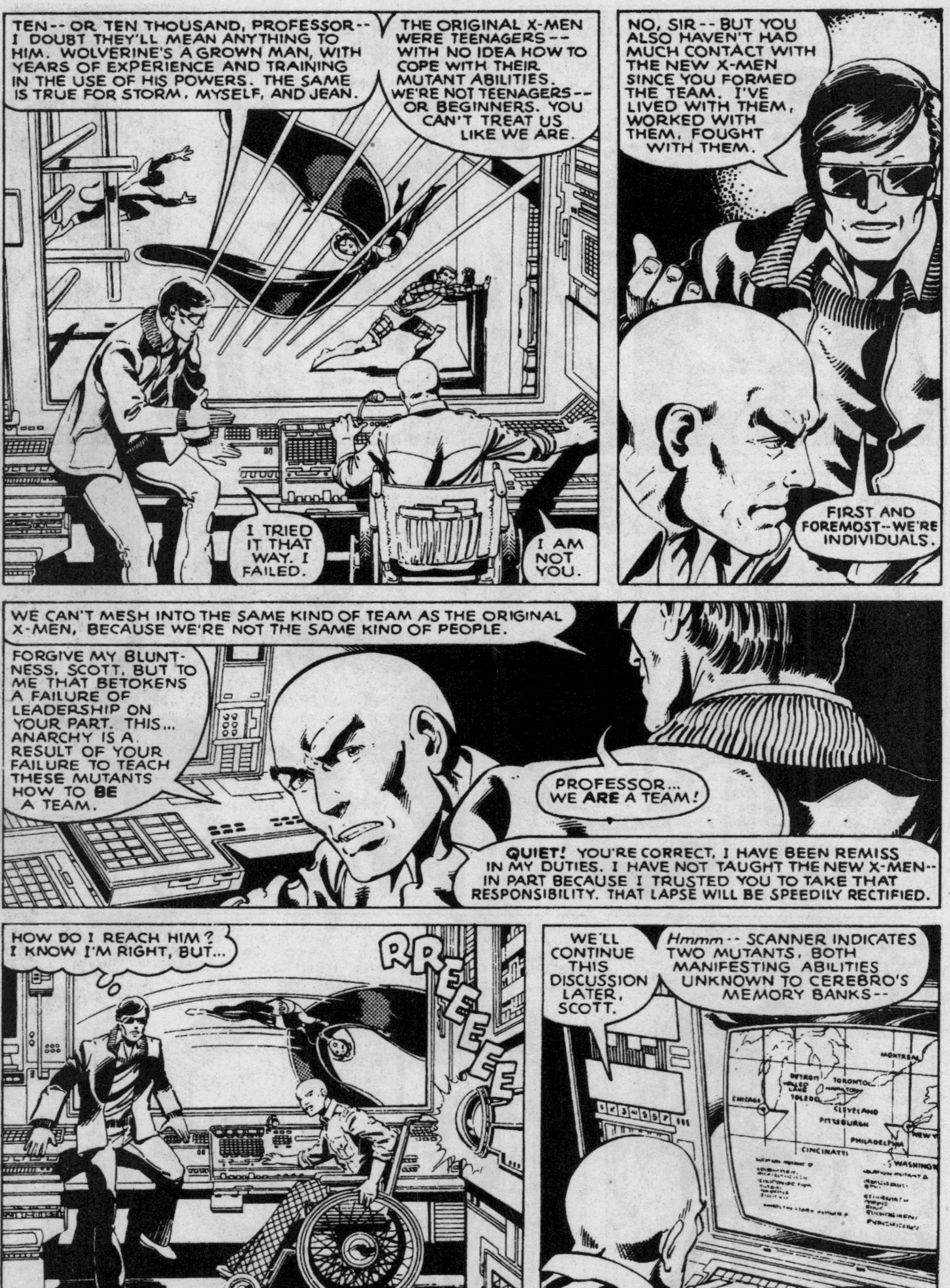

TEN-- OR TEN THOUSAND, PROFESSOR-- I DOUBT THEY'LL MEAN ANYTHING TO HIM. WOLVERINE'S A GROWN MAN, WITH YEARS OF EXPERIENCE AND TRAINING IN THE USE OF HIS POWERS. THE SAME IS TRUE FOR STORM, MYSELF, AND JEAN.
THE ORIGINAL X-MEN WERE TEENAGERS-- WITH NO IDEA HOW TO COPE WITH THEIR MUTANT ABILITIES. WE'RE NOT TEENAGERS-- OR BEGINNERS. YOU CAN'T TREAT US LIKE WE ARE.
I TRIED IT THAT WAY. I FAILED.
I AM NOT YOU.
NO, SIR-- BUT YOU ALSO HAVEN'T HAD MUCH CONTACT WITH THE NEW X-MEN SINCE YOU FORMED THE TEAM. I'VE LIVED WITH THEM, WORKED WITH THEM, FOUGHT WITH THEM.
FIRST AND FOREMOST--WE'RE INDIVIDUALS.
WE CAN'T MESH INTO THE SAME KIND OF TEAM AS THE ORIGINAL X-MEN, BECAUSE WE'RE NOT THE SAME KIND OF PEOPLE.
FORGIVE MY BLUNTNESS, SCOTT, BUT TO ME THAT BETOKENS A FAILURE OF LEADERSHIP ON YOUR PART. THIS... ANARCHY IS A RESULT OF YOUR FAILURE TO TEACH THESE MUTANTS HOW TO **BE** A TEAM.
PROFESSOR... WE **ARE** A TEAM!
QUIET! YOU'RE CORRECT. I HAVE BEEN REMISS IN MY DUTIES. I HAVE NOT TAUGHT THE NEW X-MEN-- IN PART BECAUSE I TRUSTED YOU TO TAKE THAT RESPONSIBILITY. THAT LAPSE WILL BE SPEEDILY RECTIFIED.
HOW DO I REACH HIM? I KNOW I'M RIGHT, BUT...
RREEEEE
CEREBRO'S CONTACT ALARM! MY SCANNING DEVICE HAS DISCOVERED A NEW MUTANT!
WE'LL CONTINUE THIS DISCUSSION LATER, SCOTT.
Hmmm-- SCANNER INDICATES TWO MUTANTS, BOTH MANIFESTING ABILITIES UNKNOWN TO CEREBRO'S MEMORY BANKS--
MONTREAL
DETROIT
TORONTO
WALLED LAKE
HAMILTON
CHICAGO
TOLEDO
CLEVELAND
PITTSBURGH
PHILADELPHIA
NEW Y
CINCINATTI
WASHINGT
--AND BOTH POTENTIALLY QUITE POWERFUL!

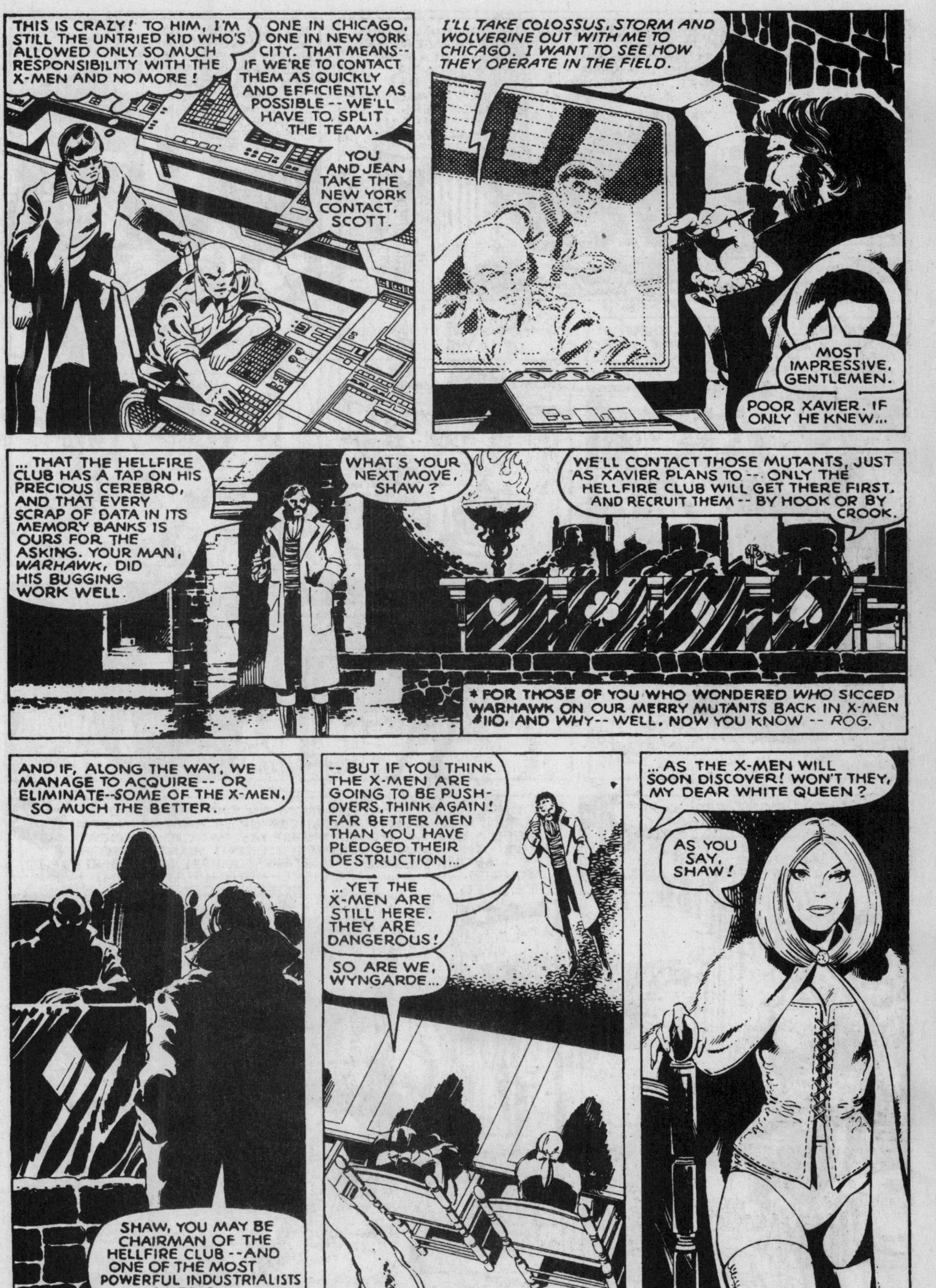
THIS IS CRAZY! TO HIM, I'M STILL THE UNTRIED KID WHO'S ALLOWED ONLY SO MUCH RESPONSIBILITY WITH THE X-MEN AND NO MORE!
ONE IN CHICAGO, ONE IN NEW YORK CITY. THAT MEANS-- IF WE'RE TO CONTACT THEM AS QUICKLY AND EFFICIENTLY AS POSSIBLE -- WE'LL HAVE TO SPLIT THE TEAM.
YOU AND JEAN TAKE THE NEW YORK CONTACT, SCOTT.
I'LL TAKE COLOSSUS, STORM AND WOLVERINE OUT WITH ME TO CHICAGO. I WANT TO SEE HOW THEY OPERATE IN THE FIELD.
MOST IMPRESSIVE, GENTLEMEN.
POOR XAVIER. IF ONLY HE KNEW...
... THAT THE HELLFIRE CLUB HAS A TAP ON HIS PRECIOUS CEREBRO, AND THAT EVERY SCRAP OF DATA IN ITS MEMORY BANKS IS OURS FOR THE ASKING. YOUR MAN, WARHAWK, DID HIS BUGGING WORK WELL.
WHAT'S YOUR NEXT MOVE, SHAW?
WE'LL CONTACT THOSE MUTANTS, JUST AS XAVIER PLANS TO -- ONLY THE HELLFIRE CLUB WILL GET THERE FIRST, AND RECRUIT THEM -- BY HOOK OR BY CROOK.
* FOR THOSE OF YOU WHO WONDERED WHO SICCED WARHAWK ON OUR MERRY MUTANTS BACK IN X-MEN #110, AND WHY-- WELL, NOW YOU KNOW -- ROG.
AND IF, ALONG THE WAY, WE MANAGE TO ACQUIRE -- OR ELIMINATE--SOME OF THE X-MEN, SO MUCH THE BETTER.
SHAW, YOU MAY BE CHAIRMAN OF THE HELLFIRE CLUB --AND ONE OF THE MOST POWERFUL INDUSTRIALISTS IN AMERICA--
-- BUT IF YOU THINK THE X-MEN ARE GOING TO BE PUSH-OVERS, THINK AGAIN! FAR BETTER MEN THAN YOU HAVE PLEDGED THEIR DESTRUCTION...
... YET THE X-MEN ARE STILL HERE. THEY ARE DANGEROUS!
SO ARE WE, WYNGARDE...
... AS THE X-MEN WILL SOON DISCOVER! WON'T THEY, MY DEAR WHITE QUEEN?
AS YOU SAY, SHAW!

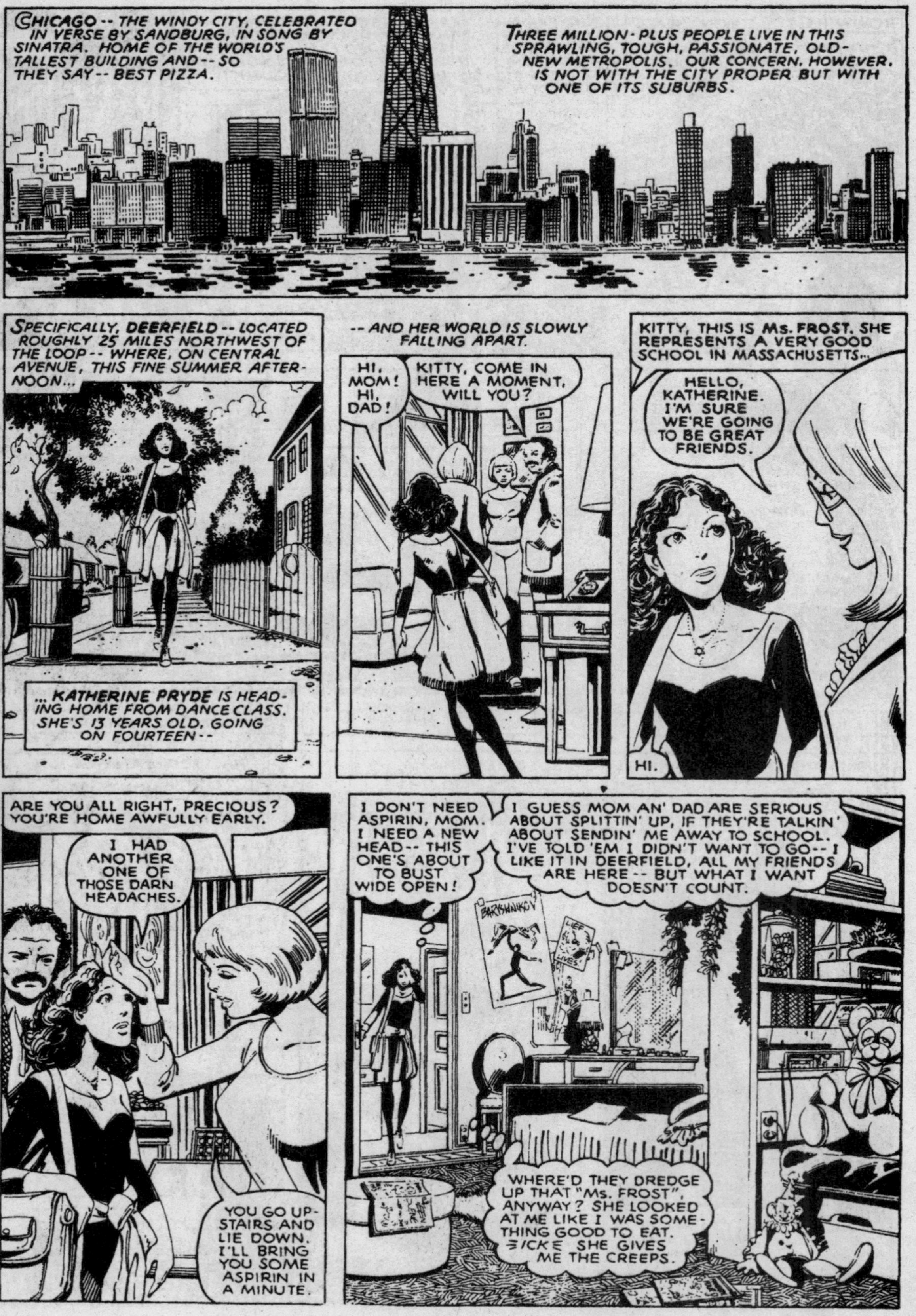
CHICAGO -- THE WINDY CITY, CELEBRATED IN VERSE BY SANDBURG, IN SONG BY SINATRA. HOME OF THE WORLD'S TALLEST BUILDING AND -- SO THEY SAY -- BEST PIZZA.
THREE MILLION-PLUS PEOPLE LIVE IN THIS SPRAWLING, TOUGH, PASSIONATE, OLD-NEW METROPOLIS. OUR CONCERN, HOWEVER, IS NOT WITH THE CITY PROPER BUT WITH ONE OF ITS SUBURBS.
SPECIFICALLY, DEERFIELD -- LOCATED ROUGHLY 25 MILES NORTHWEST OF THE LOOP -- WHERE, ON CENTRAL AVENUE, THIS FINE SUMMER AFTERNOON...
... KATHERINE PRYDE IS HEADING HOME FROM DANCE CLASS. SHE'S 13 YEARS OLD, GOING ON FOURTEEN--
-- AND HER WORLD IS SLOWLY FALLING APART.
HI, MOM! HI, DAD!
KITTY, COME IN HERE A MOMENT, WILL YOU?
KITTY, THIS IS Ms. FROST. SHE REPRESENTS A VERY GOOD SCHOOL IN MASSACHUSETTS...
HELLO, KATHERINE. I'M SURE WE'RE GOING TO BE GREAT FRIENDS.
HI.
ARE YOU ALL RIGHT, PRECIOUS? YOU'RE HOME AWFULLY EARLY.
I HAD ANOTHER ONE OF THOSE DARN HEADACHES.
YOU GO UPSTAIRS AND LIE DOWN. I'LL BRING YOU SOME ASPIRIN IN A MINUTE.
I DON'T NEED ASPIRIN, MOM. I NEED A NEW HEAD -- THIS ONE'S ABOUT TO BUST WIDE OPEN!
I GUESS MOM AN' DAD ARE SERIOUS ABOUT SPLITTIN' UP, IF THEY'RE TALKIN' ABOUT SENDIN' ME AWAY TO SCHOOL. I'VE TOLD 'EM I DIDN'T WANT TO GO -- I LIKE IT IN DEERFIELD, ALL MY FRIENDS ARE HERE -- BUT WHAT I WANT DOESN'T COUNT.
WHERE'D THEY DREDGE UP THAT "Ms. FROST", ANYWAY? SHE LOOKED AT ME LIKE I WAS SOMETHING GOOD TO EAT. ICK SHE GIVES ME THE CREEPS.

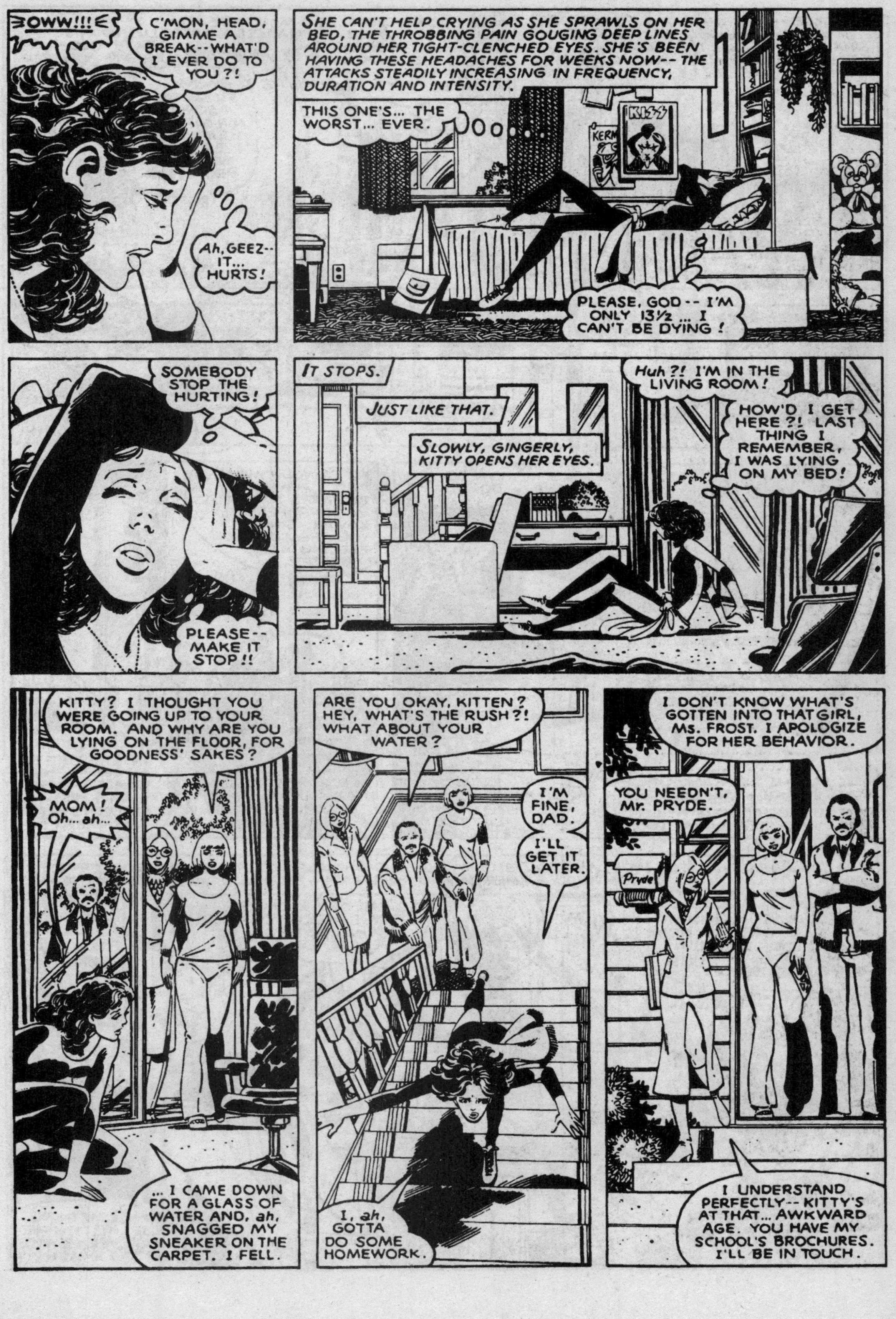
OWW!!!
C'MON, HEAD, GIMME A BREAK--WHAT'D I EVER DO TO YOU?!
Ah, GEEZ-- IT... HURTS!
SHE CAN'T HELP CRYING AS SHE SPRAWLS ON HER BED, THE THROBBING PAIN GOUGING DEEP LINES AROUND HER TIGHT-CLENCHED EYES. SHE'S BEEN HAVING THESE HEADACHES FOR WEEKS NOW-- THE ATTACKS STEADILY INCREASING IN FREQUENCY, DURATION AND INTENSITY.
THIS ONE'S... THE WORST... EVER.
KISS
PLEASE, GOD -- I'M ONLY 13½ ... I CAN'T BE DYING!
SOMEBODY STOP THE HURTING!
PLEASE-- MAKE IT STOP!!
IT STOPS.
JUST LIKE THAT.
SLOWLY, GINGERLY, KITTY OPENS HER EYES.
Huh?! I'M IN THE LIVING ROOM!
HOW'D I GET HERE?! LAST THING I REMEMBER, I WAS LYING ON MY BED!
KITTY? I THOUGHT YOU WERE GOING UP TO YOUR ROOM. AND WHY ARE YOU LYING ON THE FLOOR, FOR GOODNESS' SAKES?
MOM! Oh... ah...
... I CAME DOWN FOR A GLASS OF WATER AND, ah, SNAGGED MY SNEAKER ON THE CARPET. I FELL.
ARE YOU OKAY, KITTEN? HEY, WHAT'S THE RUSH?! WHAT ABOUT YOUR WATER?
I'M FINE, DAD.
I'LL GET IT LATER.
I, ah, GOTTA DO SOME HOMEWORK.
I DON'T KNOW WHAT'S GOTTEN INTO THAT GIRL, Ms. FROST. I APOLOGIZE FOR HER BEHAVIOR.
YOU NEEDN'T, Mr. PRYDE.
Pryde
I UNDERSTAND PERFECTLY-- KITTY'S AT THAT... AWKWARD AGE. YOU HAVE MY SCHOOL'S BROCHURES. I'LL BE IN TOUCH.

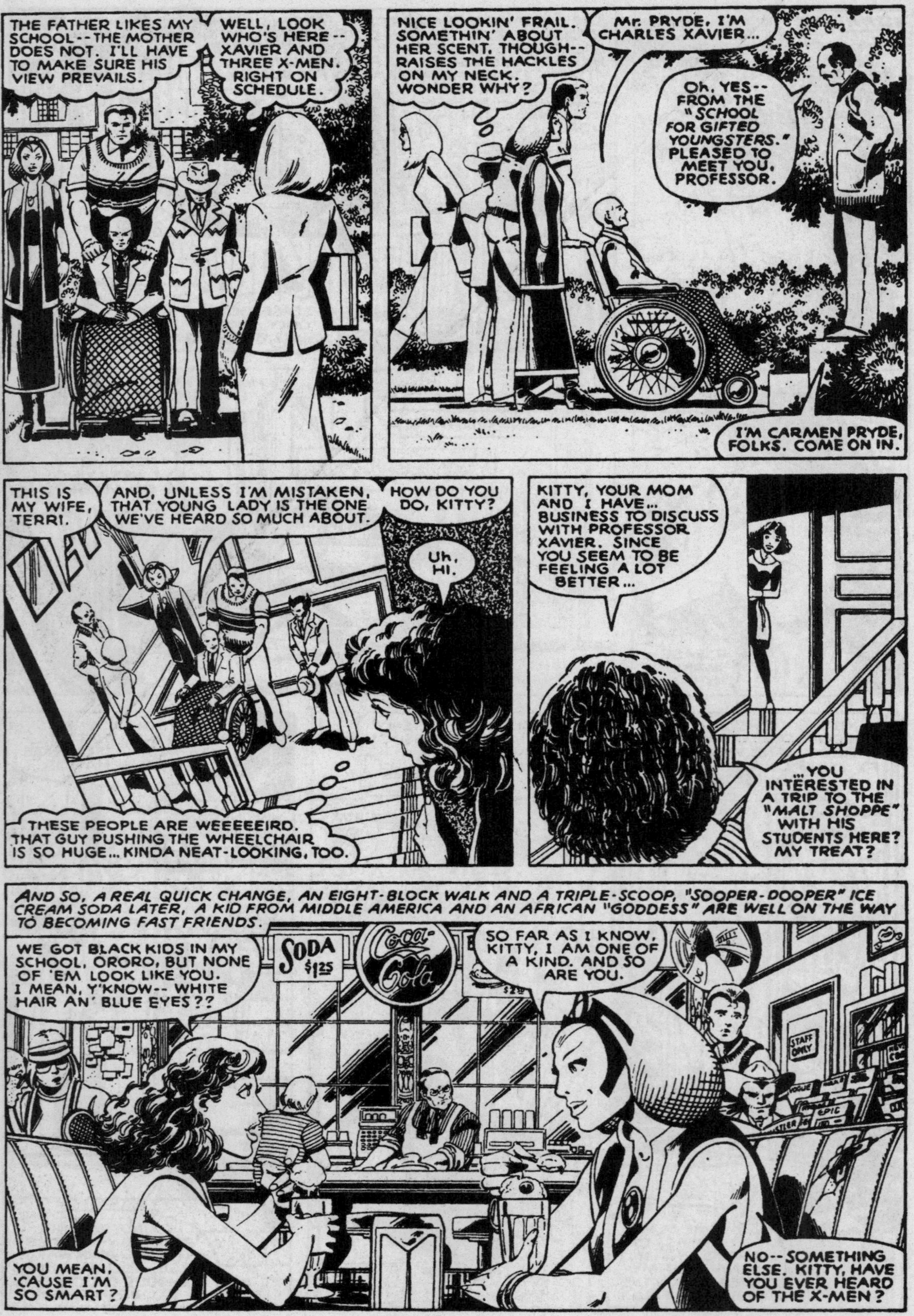
THE FATHER LIKES MY SCHOOL--THE MOTHER DOES NOT. I'LL HAVE TO MAKE SURE HIS VIEW PREVAILS.
WELL, LOOK WHO'S HERE--XAVIER AND THREE X-MEN. RIGHT ON SCHEDULE.
NICE LOOKIN' FRAIL. SOMETHIN' ABOUT HER SCENT, THOUGH--RAISES THE HACKLES ON MY NECK. WONDER WHY?
Mr. PRYDE, I'M CHARLES XAVIER...
Oh, YES--FROM THE "SCHOOL FOR GIFTED YOUNGSTERS." PLEASED TO MEET YOU, PROFESSOR.
I'M CARMEN PRYDE, FOLKS. COME ON IN.
THIS IS MY WIFE, TERRI.
AND, UNLESS I'M MISTAKEN, THAT YOUNG LADY IS THE ONE WE'VE HEARD SO MUCH ABOUT.
HOW DO YOU DO, KITTY?
Uh, HI.
THESE PEOPLE ARE WEEEEEIRD. THAT GUY PUSHING THE WHEELCHAIR IS SO HUGE... KINDA NEAT-LOOKING, TOO.
KITTY, YOUR MOM AND I HAVE... BUSINESS TO DISCUSS WITH PROFESSOR XAVIER. SINCE YOU SEEM TO BE FEELING A LOT BETTER...
...YOU INTERESTED IN A TRIP TO THE "MALT SHOPPE" WITH HIS STUDENTS HERE? MY TREAT?
AND SO, A REAL QUICK CHANGE, AN EIGHT-BLOCK WALK AND A TRIPLE-SCOOP, "SOOPER-DOOPER" ICE CREAM SODA LATER, A KID FROM MIDDLE AMERICA AND AN AFRICAN "GODDESS" ARE WELL ON THE WAY TO BECOMING FAST FRIENDS.
WE GOT BLACK KIDS IN MY SCHOOL, ORORO, BUT NONE OF 'EM LOOK LIKE YOU. I MEAN, Y'KNOW-- WHITE HAIR AN' BLUE EYES??
SODA $1.25
Coca-Cola
SO FAR AS I KNOW, KITTY, I AM ONE OF A KIND. AND SO ARE YOU.
STAFF ONLY
YOU MEAN, 'CAUSE I'M SO SMART?
NO--SOMETHING ELSE. KITTY, HAVE YOU EVER HEARD OF THE X-MEN?

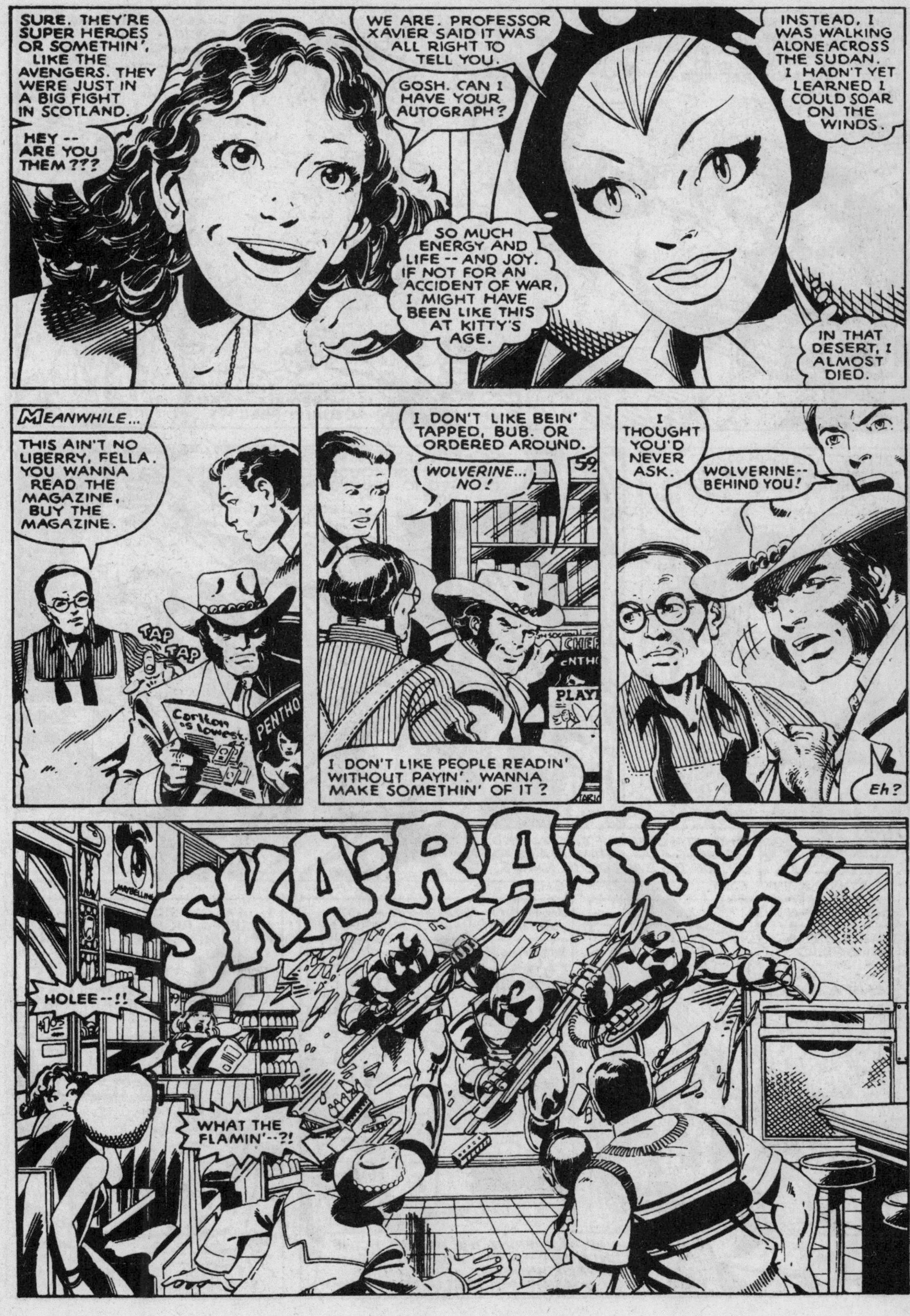
SURE. THEY'RE SUPER HEROES OR SOMETHIN', LIKE THE AVENGERS. THEY WERE JUST IN A BIG FIGHT IN SCOTLAND.
HEY -- ARE YOU THEM???
WE ARE. PROFESSOR XAVIER SAID IT WAS ALL RIGHT TO TELL YOU.
GOSH. CAN I HAVE YOUR AUTOGRAPH?
SO MUCH ENERGY AND LIFE -- AND JOY. IF NOT FOR AN ACCIDENT OF WAR, I MIGHT HAVE BEEN LIKE THIS AT KITTY'S AGE.
INSTEAD, I WAS WALKING ALONE ACROSS THE SUDAN. I HADN'T YET LEARNED I COULD SOAR ON THE WINDS.
IN THAT DESERT, I ALMOST DIED.
MEANWHILE...
THIS AIN'T NO LIBERRY, FELLA. YOU WANNA READ THE MAGAZINE, BUY THE MAGAZINE.
TAP TAP
I DON'T LIKE BEIN' TAPPED, BUB. OR ORDERED AROUND.
WOLVERINE... NO!
I DON'T LIKE PEOPLE READIN' WITHOUT PAYIN'. WANNA MAKE SOMETHIN' OF IT?
I THOUGHT YOU'D NEVER ASK.
WOLVERINE-- BEHIND YOU!
Eh?
SKA-RASSH
HOLEE--!!
WHAT THE FLAMIN'--?!

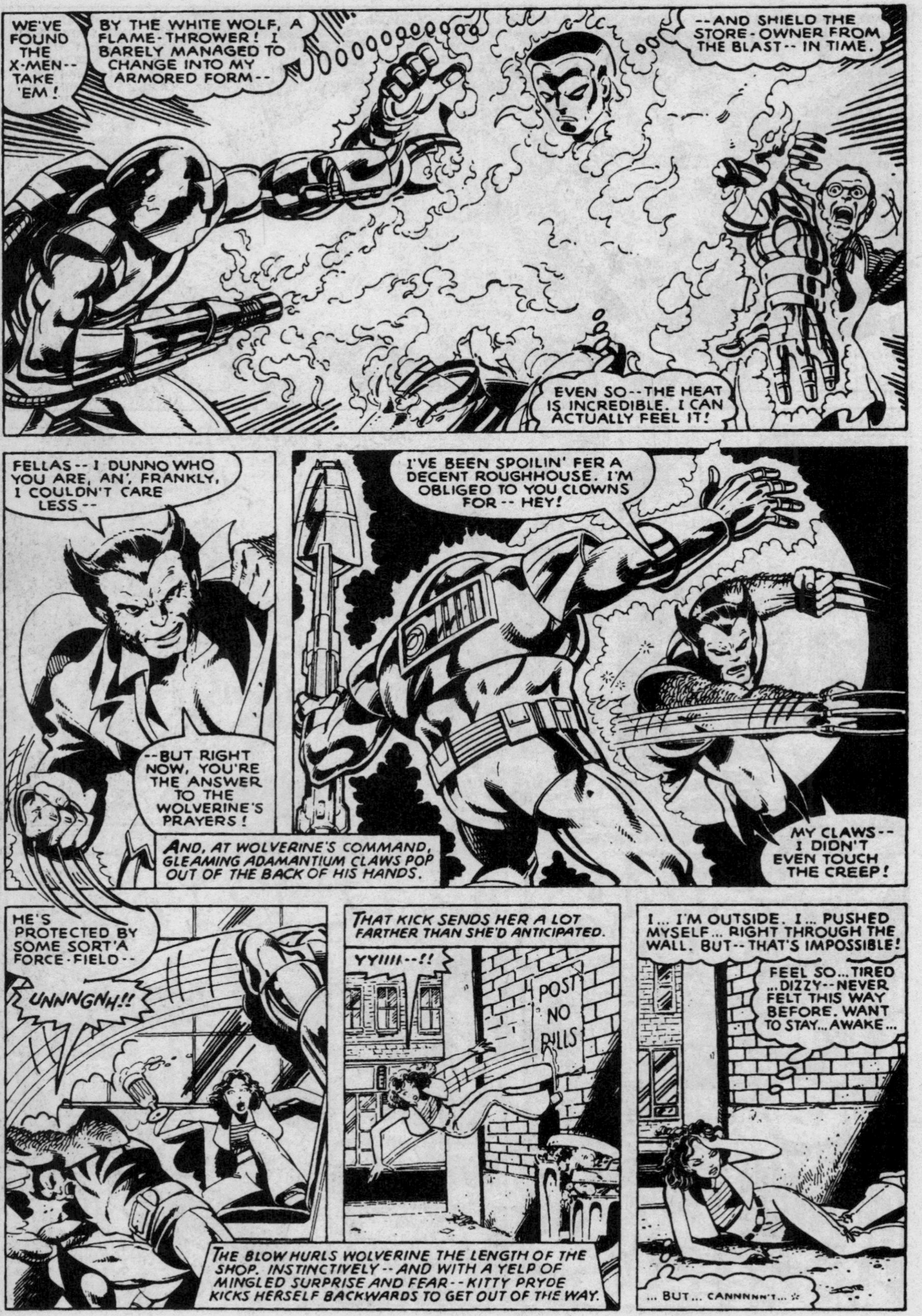
WE'VE FOUND THE X-MEN-- TAKE 'EM!
BY THE WHITE WOLF, A FLAME-THROWER! I BARELY MANAGED TO CHANGE INTO MY ARMORED FORM--
--AND SHIELD THE STORE-OWNER FROM THE BLAST-- IN TIME.
EVEN SO--THE HEAT IS INCREDIBLE. I CAN ACTUALLY FEEL IT!
FELLAS-- I DUNNO WHO YOU ARE, AN', FRANKLY, I COULDN'T CARE LESS--
--BUT RIGHT NOW, YOU'RE THE ANSWER TO THE WOLVERINE'S PRAYERS!
AND, AT WOLVERINE'S COMMAND, GLEAMING ADAMANTIUM CLAWS POP OUT OF THE BACK OF HIS HANDS.
I'VE BEEN SPOILIN' FER A DECENT ROUGHHOUSE. I'M OBLIGED TO YOU CLOWNS FOR-- HEY!
MY CLAWS-- I DIDN'T EVEN TOUCH THE CREEP!
HE'S PROTECTED BY SOME SORT'A FORCE-FIELD--
UNNNGNH!!
THAT KICK SENDS HER A LOT FARTHER THAN SHE'D ANTICIPATED.
YYIIII--!!
POST NO BILLS
THE BLOW HURLS WOLVERINE THE LENGTH OF THE SHOP. INSTINCTIVELY-- AND WITH A YELP OF MINGLED SURPRISE AND FEAR--KITTY PRYDE KICKS HERSELF BACKWARDS TO GET OUT OF THE WAY.
I... I'M OUTSIDE. I... PUSHED MYSELF... RIGHT THROUGH THE WALL. BUT--THAT'S IMPOSSIBLE!
FEEL SO... TIRED ...DIZZY--NEVER FELT THIS WAY BEFORE. WANT TO STAY... AWAKE...
... BUT... CANNNNN'T...

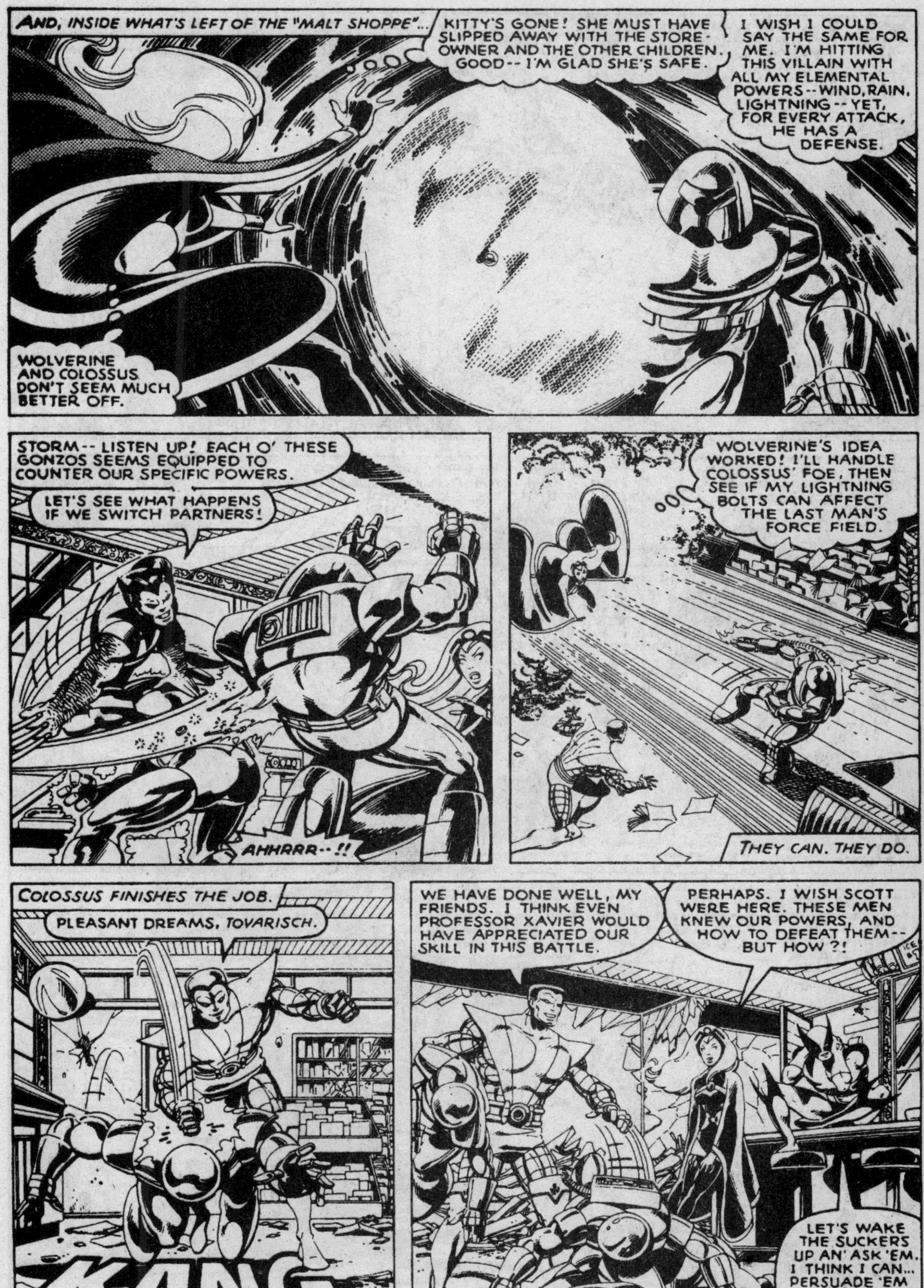
AND, INSIDE WHAT'S LEFT OF THE "MALT SHOPPE"...
KITTY'S GONE! SHE MUST HAVE SLIPPED AWAY WITH THE STORE-OWNER AND THE OTHER CHILDREN. GOOD-- I'M GLAD SHE'S SAFE.
I WISH I COULD SAY THE SAME FOR ME. I'M HITTING THIS VILLAIN WITH ALL MY ELEMENTAL POWERS--WIND, RAIN, LIGHTNING--YET, FOR EVERY ATTACK, HE HAS A DEFENSE.
WOLVERINE AND COLOSSUS DON'T SEEM MUCH BETTER OFF.
STORM-- LISTEN UP! EACH O' THESE GONZOS SEEMS EQUIPPED TO COUNTER OUR SPECIFIC POWERS.
LET'S SEE WHAT HAPPENS IF WE SWITCH PARTNERS!
AHHRRR--!!
WOLVERINE'S IDEA WORKED! I'LL HANDLE COLOSSUS' FOE, THEN SEE IF MY LIGHTNING BOLTS CAN AFFECT THE LAST MAN'S FORCE FIELD.
THEY CAN. THEY DO.
COLOSSUS FINISHES THE JOB.
PLEASANT DREAMS, TOVARISCH.
KANG
WE HAVE DONE WELL, MY FRIENDS. I THINK EVEN PROFESSOR XAVIER WOULD HAVE APPRECIATED OUR SKILL IN THIS BATTLE.
PERHAPS. I WISH SCOTT WERE HERE. THESE MEN KNEW OUR POWERS, AND HOW TO DEFEAT THEM-- BUT HOW?!
LET'S WAKE THE SUCKERS UP AN' ASK 'EM. I THINK I CAN... PERSUADE 'EM TO TELL US ALL THEY KNOW.

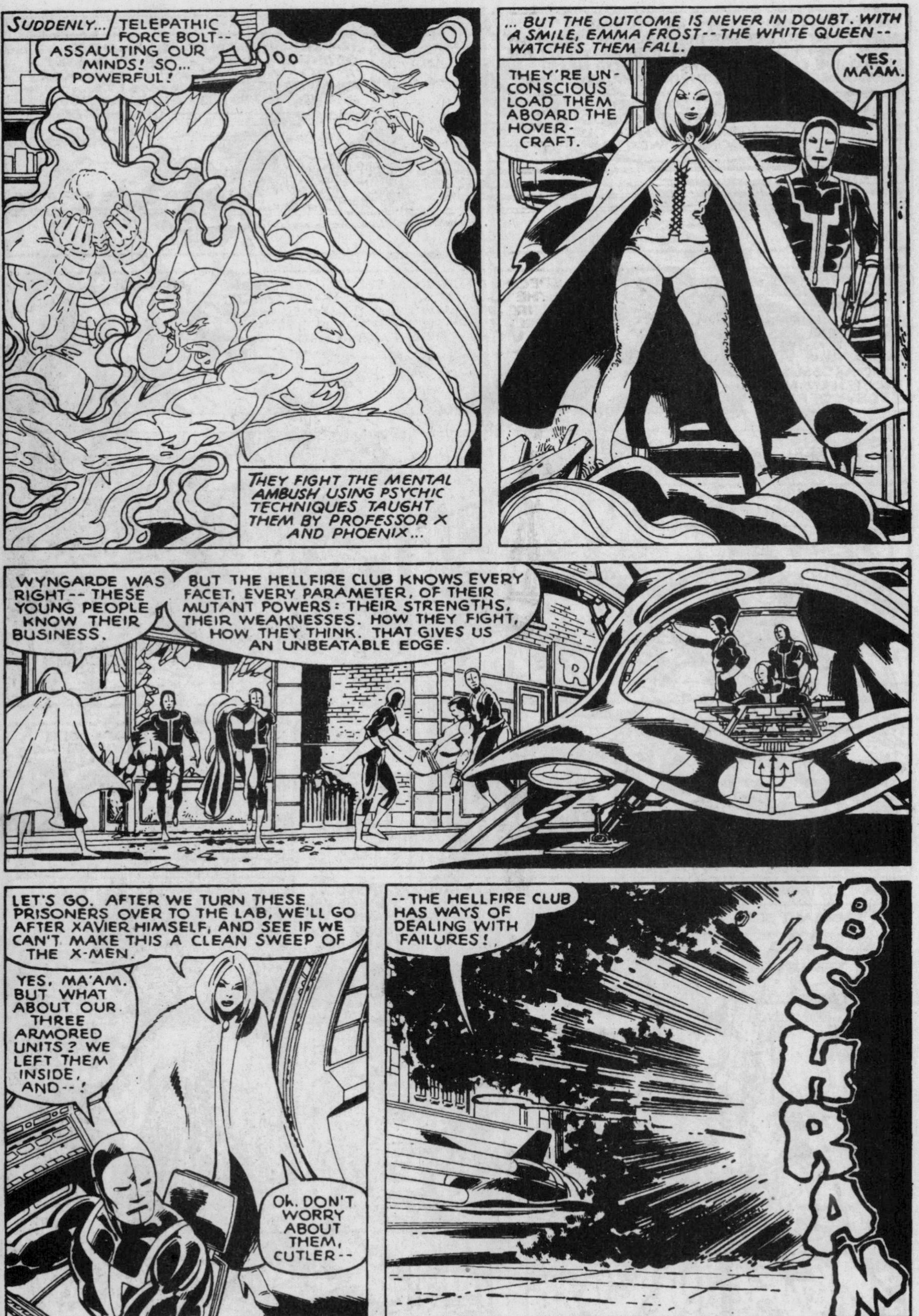
SUDDENLY...
TELEPATHIC FORCE BOLT-- ASSAULTING OUR MINDS! SO... POWERFUL!
THEY FIGHT THE MENTAL AMBUSH USING PSYCHIC TECHNIQUES TAUGHT THEM BY PROFESSOR X AND PHOENIX...
... BUT THE OUTCOME IS NEVER IN DOUBT. WITH A SMILE, EMMA FROST-- THE WHITE QUEEN-- WATCHES THEM FALL.
THEY'RE UN-CONSCIOUS LOAD THEM ABOARD THE HOVER-CRAFT.
YES, MA'AM.
WYNGARDE WAS RIGHT-- THESE YOUNG PEOPLE KNOW THEIR BUSINESS.
BUT THE HELLFIRE CLUB KNOWS EVERY FACET, EVERY PARAMETER, OF THEIR MUTANT POWERS: THEIR STRENGTHS, THEIR WEAKNESSES. HOW THEY FIGHT, HOW THEY THINK. THAT GIVES US AN UNBEATABLE EDGE.
LET'S GO. AFTER WE TURN THESE PRISONERS OVER TO THE LAB, WE'LL GO AFTER XAVIER HIMSELF, AND SEE IF WE CAN'T MAKE THIS A CLEAN SWEEP OF THE X-MEN.
YES, MA'AM. BUT WHAT ABOUT OUR THREE ARMORED UNITS? WE LEFT THEM INSIDE, AND--!
Oh. DON'T WORRY ABOUT THEM, CUTLER--
--THE HELLFIRE CLUB HAS WAYS OF DEALING WITH FAILURES!
BSHRAM

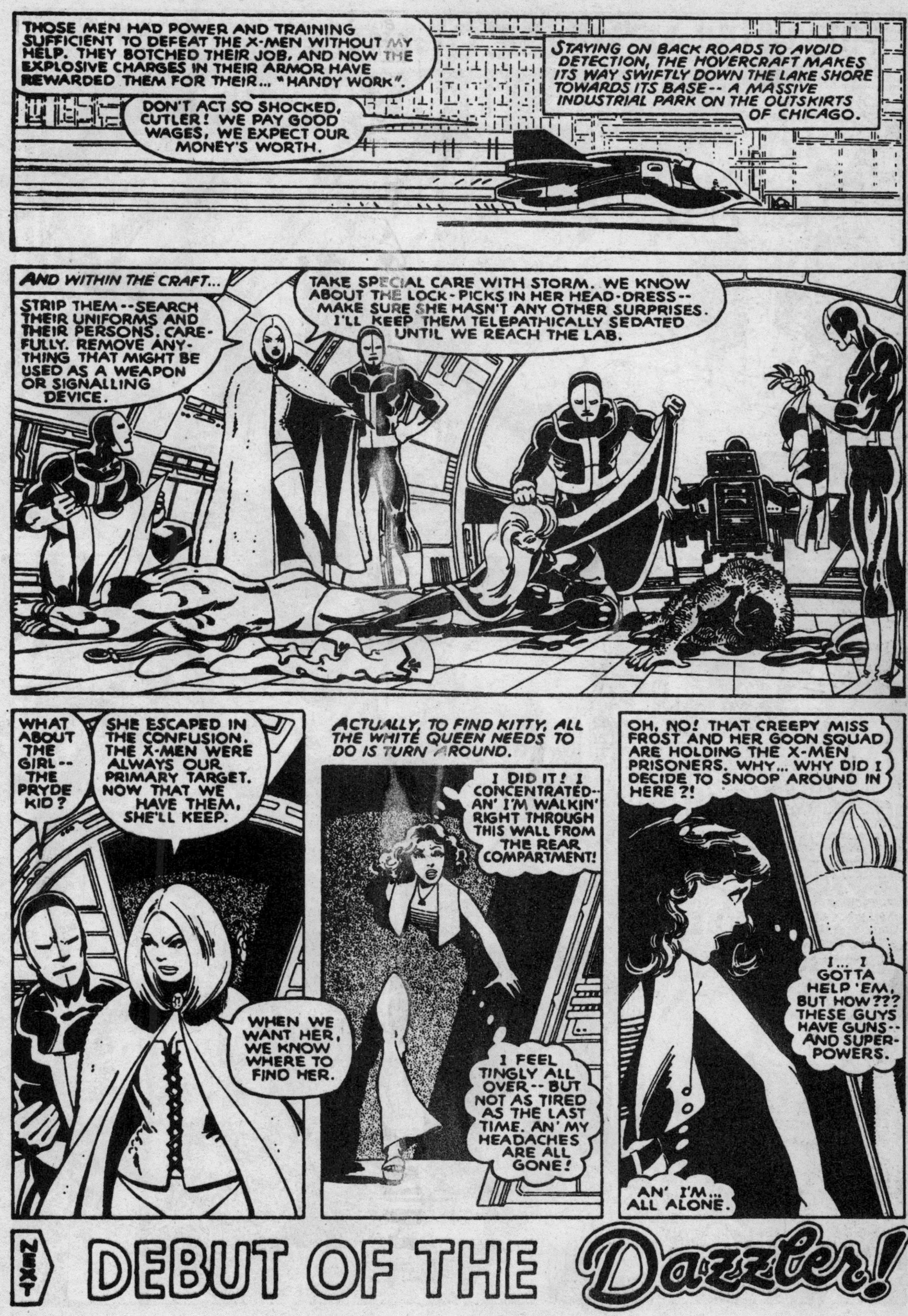
THOSE MEN HAD POWER AND TRAINING SUFFICIENT TO DEFEAT THE X-MEN WITHOUT MY HELP. THEY BOTCHED THEIR JOB, AND NOW THE EXPLOSIVE CHARGES IN THEIR ARMOR HAVE REWARDED THEM FOR THEIR... "HANDY WORK".
DON'T ACT SO SHOCKED, CUTLER! WE PAY GOOD WAGES, WE EXPECT OUR MONEY'S WORTH.
STAYING ON BACK ROADS TO AVOID DETECTION, THE HOVERCRAFT MAKES ITS WAY SWIFTLY DOWN THE LAKE SHORE TOWARDS ITS BASE-- A MASSIVE INDUSTRIAL PARK ON THE OUTSKIRTS OF CHICAGO.
AND WITHIN THE CRAFT...
STRIP THEM --SEARCH THEIR UNIFORMS AND THEIR PERSONS. CAREFULLY. REMOVE ANYTHING THAT MIGHT BE USED AS A WEAPON OR SIGNALLING DEVICE.
TAKE SPECIAL CARE WITH STORM. WE KNOW ABOUT THE LOCK-PICKS IN HER HEAD-DRESS-- MAKE SURE SHE HASN'T ANY OTHER SURPRISES. I'LL KEEP THEM TELEPATHICALLY SEDATED UNTIL WE REACH THE LAB.
WHAT ABOUT THE GIRL-- THE PRYDE KID?
SHE ESCAPED IN THE CONFUSION. THE X-MEN WERE ALWAYS OUR PRIMARY TARGET. NOW THAT WE HAVE THEM, SHE'LL KEEP.
WHEN WE WANT HER, WE KNOW WHERE TO FIND HER.
ACTUALLY, TO FIND KITTY, ALL THE WHITE QUEEN NEEDS TO DO IS TURN AROUND.
I DID IT! I CONCENTRATED-- AN' I'M WALKIN' RIGHT THROUGH THIS WALL FROM THE REAR COMPARTMENT!
I FEEL TINGLY ALL OVER-- BUT NOT AS TIRED AS THE LAST TIME. AN' MY HEADACHES ARE ALL GONE!
OH, NO! THAT CREEPY MISS FROST AND HER GOON SQUAD ARE HOLDING THE X-MEN PRISONERS. WHY... WHY DID I DECIDE TO SNOOP AROUND IN HERE?!
I... I GOTTA HELP 'EM, BUT HOW??? THESE GUYS HAVE GUNS-- AND SUPER-POWERS.
AN' I'M... ALL ALONE.
NEXT
DEBUT OF THE Dazzler!

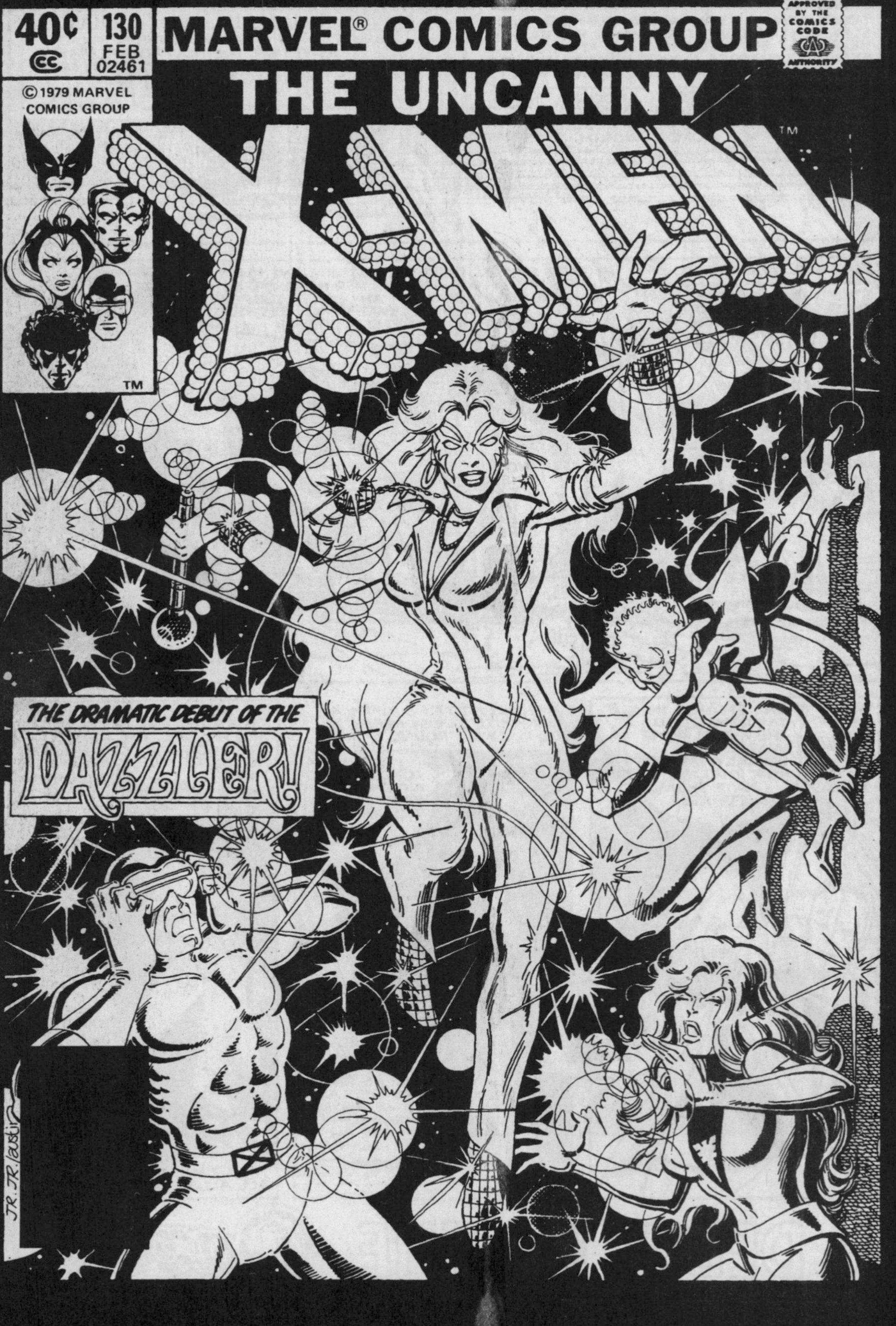

40¢
130
FEB
02461
MARVEL® COMICS GROUP
APPROVED BY THE COMICS CODE AUTHORITY
© 1979 MARVEL COMICS GROUP
THE UNCANNY
X-MEN™
THE DRAMATIC DEBUT OF THE
DAZZLER!

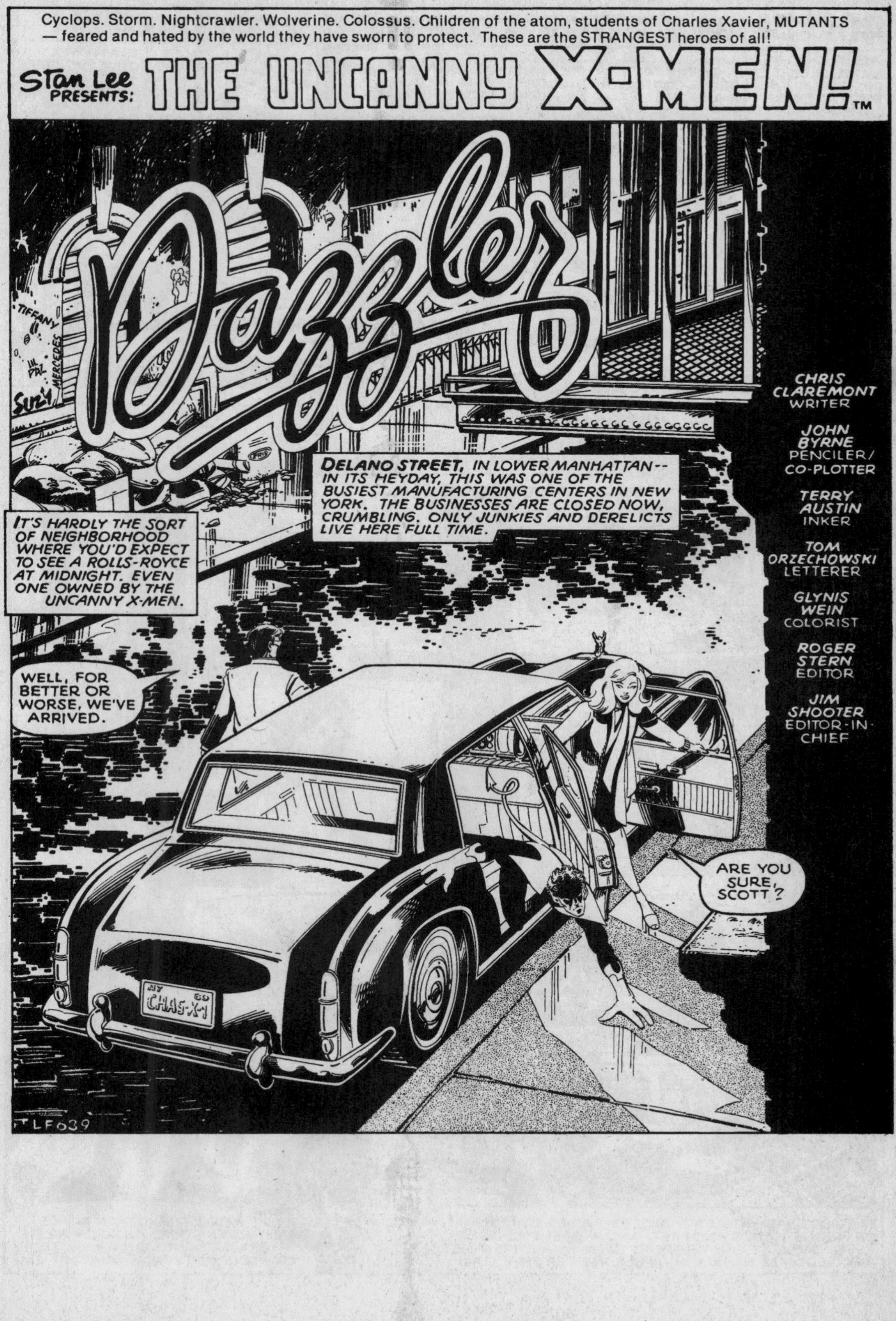
Cyclops. Storm. Nightcrawler. Wolverine. Colossus. Children of the atom, students of Charles Xavier, MUTANTS — feared and hated by the world they have sworn to protect. These are the STRANGEST heroes of all!
Stan Lee PRESENTS: THE UNCANNY X-MEN!™
Dazzler
CHRIS CLAREMONT WRITER
JOHN BYRNE PENCILER/CO-PLOTTER
TERRY AUSTIN INKER
TOM ORZECHOWSKI LETTERER
GLYNIS WEIN COLORIST
ROGER STERN EDITOR
JIM SHOOTER EDITOR-IN-CHIEF
DELANO STREET, IN LOWER MANHATTAN-- IN ITS HEYDAY, THIS WAS ONE OF THE BUSIEST MANUFACTURING CENTERS IN NEW YORK. THE BUSINESSES ARE CLOSED NOW, CRUMBLING. ONLY JUNKIES AND DERELICTS LIVE HERE FULL TIME.
IT'S HARDLY THE SORT OF NEIGHBORHOOD WHERE YOU'D EXPECT TO SEE A ROLLS-ROYCE AT MIDNIGHT. EVEN ONE OWNED BY THE UNCANNY X-MEN.
WELL, FOR BETTER OR WORSE, WE'VE ARRIVED.
ARE YOU SURE, SCOTT?
CHAS-X-1
TLF639

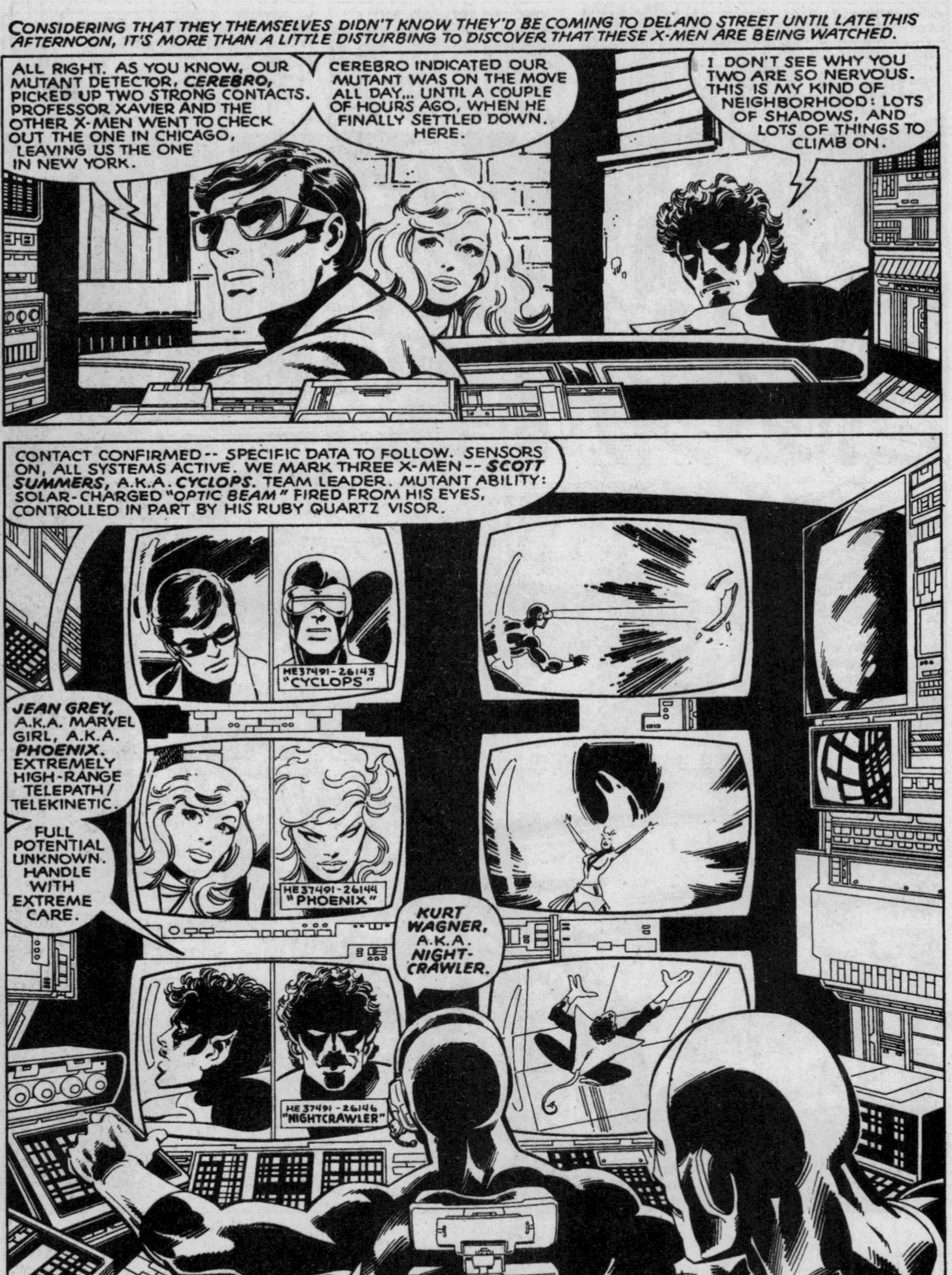
CONSIDERING THAT THEY THEMSELVES DIDN'T KNOW THEY'D BE COMING TO DELANO STREET UNTIL LATE THIS AFTERNOON, IT'S MORE THAN A LITTLE DISTURBING TO DISCOVER THAT THESE X-MEN ARE BEING WATCHED.
ALL RIGHT. AS YOU KNOW, OUR MUTANT DETECTOR, CEREBRO, PICKED UP TWO STRONG CONTACTS. PROFESSOR XAVIER AND THE OTHER X-MEN WENT TO CHECK OUT THE ONE IN CHICAGO, LEAVING US THE ONE IN NEW YORK.
CEREBRO INDICATED OUR MUTANT WAS ON THE MOVE ALL DAY... UNTIL A COUPLE OF HOURS AGO, WHEN HE FINALLY SETTLED DOWN. HERE.
I DON'T SEE WHY YOU TWO ARE SO NERVOUS. THIS IS MY KIND OF NEIGHBORHOOD: LOTS OF SHADOWS, AND LOTS OF THINGS TO CLIMB ON.
CONTACT CONFIRMED -- SPECIFIC DATA TO FOLLOW. SENSORS ON, ALL SYSTEMS ACTIVE. WE MARK THREE X-MEN -- SCOTT SUMMERS, A.K.A. CYCLOPS. TEAM LEADER. MUTANT ABILITY: SOLAR-CHARGED "OPTIC BEAM" FIRED FROM HIS EYES, CONTROLLED IN PART BY HIS RUBY QUARTZ VISOR.
HE37491-26143
"CYCLOPS"
JEAN GREY, A.K.A. MARVEL GIRL, A.K.A. PHOENIX. EXTREMELY HIGH-RANGE TELEPATH/ TELEKINETIC.
FULL POTENTIAL UNKNOWN. HANDLE WITH EXTREME CARE.
HE37491-26144
"PHOENIX"
KURT WAGNER, A.K.A. NIGHT-CRAWLER.
HE 37491-26146
"NIGHTCRAWLER"
EXTRAORDINARY ATHLETIC ABILITIES -- AIDED BY UNUSUALLY DEXTROUS HANDS AND FEET, AND A PREHENSILE TAIL. ALSO, SUBJECT CAN TELEPORT OVER SMALL DISTANCES, AND BECOMES NEARLY INVISIBLE IN DEEP SHADOW.
ALERT THE ATTACK FORCE. WE'LL STRIKE AS SOON AS WE GET THE WORD FROM BASE. THOSE POOR FOOLS WON'T KNOW WHAT HIT 'EM.

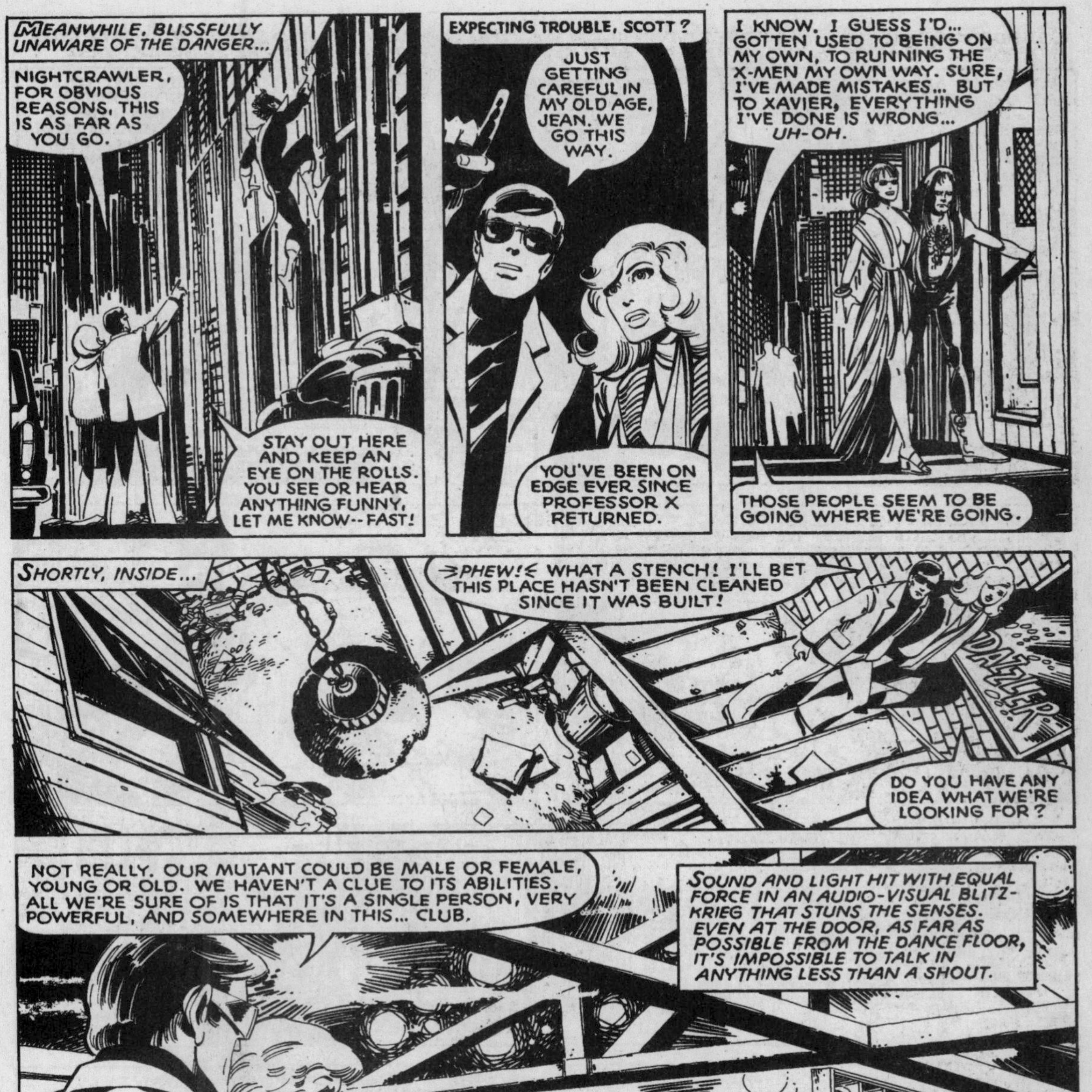
MEANWHILE, BLISSFULLY UNAWARE OF THE DANGER...
NIGHTCRAWLER, FOR OBVIOUS REASONS, THIS IS AS FAR AS YOU GO.
STAY OUT HERE AND KEEP AN EYE ON THE ROLLS. YOU SEE OR HEAR ANYTHING FUNNY, LET ME KNOW--FAST!
EXPECTING TROUBLE, SCOTT?
JUST GETTING CAREFUL IN MY OLD AGE, JEAN. WE GO THIS WAY.
YOU'VE BEEN ON EDGE EVER SINCE PROFESSOR X RETURNED.
I KNOW. I GUESS I'D... GOTTEN USED TO BEING ON MY OWN, TO RUNNING THE X-MEN MY OWN WAY. SURE, I'VE MADE MISTAKES... BUT TO XAVIER, EVERYTHING I'VE DONE IS WRONG... UH-OH.
THOSE PEOPLE SEEM TO BE GOING WHERE WE'RE GOING.
SHORTLY, INSIDE...
PHEW! WHAT A STENCH! I'LL BET THIS PLACE HASN'T BEEN CLEANED SINCE IT WAS BUILT!
DAZZLER
DO YOU HAVE ANY IDEA WHAT WE'RE LOOKING FOR?
NOT REALLY. OUR MUTANT COULD BE MALE OR FEMALE, YOUNG OR OLD. WE HAVEN'T A CLUE TO ITS ABILITIES. ALL WE'RE SURE OF IS THAT IT'S A SINGLE PERSON, VERY POWERFUL, AND SOMEWHERE IN THIS... CLUB.
SOUND AND LIGHT HIT WITH EQUAL FORCE IN AN AUDIO-VISUAL BLITZ-KRIEG THAT STUNS THE SENSES. EVEN AT THE DOOR, AS FAR AS POSSIBLE FROM THE DANCE FLOOR, IT'S IMPOSSIBLE TO TALK IN ANYTHING LESS THAN A SHOUT.
TELL ME, JEAN, IS THIS WHERE OLD DISCOS GO TO DIE?
AUTOMATICALLY, JEAN SHIFTS INTO A TELEPATHIC RAPPORT WITH SCOTT, USING THE MIND-LINK TO COMMUNICATE WITH HIM IN COMPLETE PRIVACY.

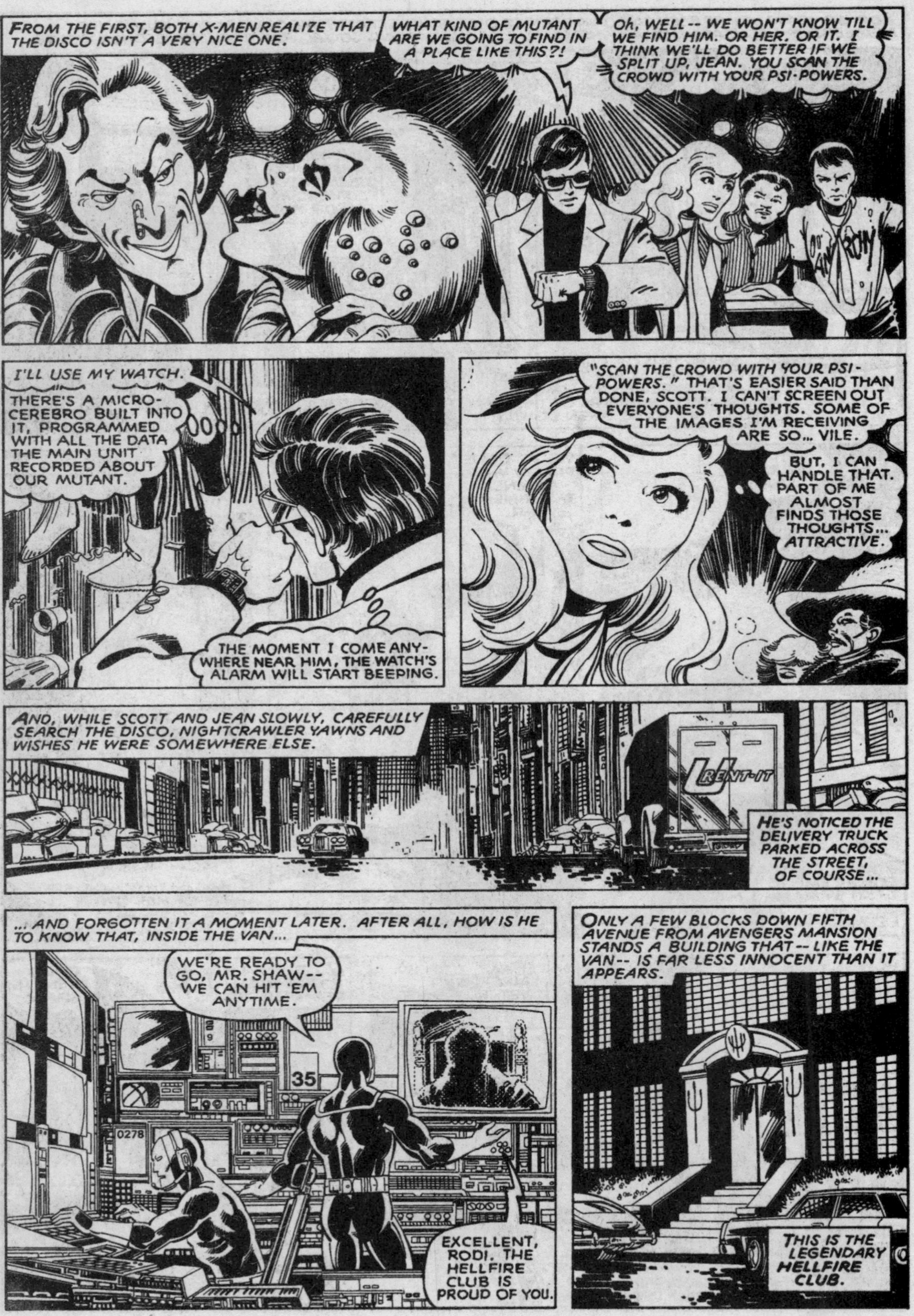
FROM THE FIRST, BOTH X-MEN REALIZE THAT THE DISCO ISN'T A VERY NICE ONE.
WHAT KIND OF MUTANT ARE WE GOING TO FIND IN A PLACE LIKE THIS?!
Oh, WELL -- WE WON'T KNOW TILL WE FIND HIM. OR HER. OR IT. I THINK WE'LL DO BETTER IF WE SPLIT UP, JEAN. YOU SCAN THE CROWD WITH YOUR PSI-POWERS.
I'LL USE MY WATCH.
THERE'S A MICRO-CEREBRO BUILT INTO IT, PROGRAMMED WITH ALL THE DATA THE MAIN UNIT RECORDED ABOUT OUR MUTANT.
THE MOMENT I COME ANYWHERE NEAR HIM, THE WATCH'S ALARM WILL START BEEPING.
"SCAN THE CROWD WITH YOUR PSI-POWERS." THAT'S EASIER SAID THAN DONE, SCOTT. I CAN'T SCREEN OUT EVERYONE'S THOUGHTS. SOME OF THE IMAGES I'M RECEIVING ARE SO... VILE.
BUT, I CAN HANDLE THAT. PART OF ME ALMOST FINDS THOSE THOUGHTS... ATTRACTIVE.
AND, WHILE SCOTT AND JEAN SLOWLY, CAREFULLY SEARCH THE DISCO, NIGHTCRAWLER YAWNS AND WISHES HE WERE SOMEWHERE ELSE.
U-RENT-IT
HE'S NOTICED THE DELIVERY TRUCK PARKED ACROSS THE STREET, OF COURSE...
... AND FORGOTTEN IT A MOMENT LATER. AFTER ALL, HOW IS HE TO KNOW THAT, INSIDE THE VAN...
WE'RE READY TO GO, MR. SHAW-- WE CAN HIT 'EM ANYTIME.
35
0278
EXCELLENT, RODI. THE HELLFIRE CLUB IS PROUD OF YOU.
ONLY A FEW BLOCKS DOWN FIFTH AVENUE FROM AVENGERS MANSION STANDS A BUILDING THAT -- LIKE THE VAN -- IS FAR LESS INNOCENT THAN IT APPEARS.
THIS IS THE LEGENDARY HELLFIRE CLUB.

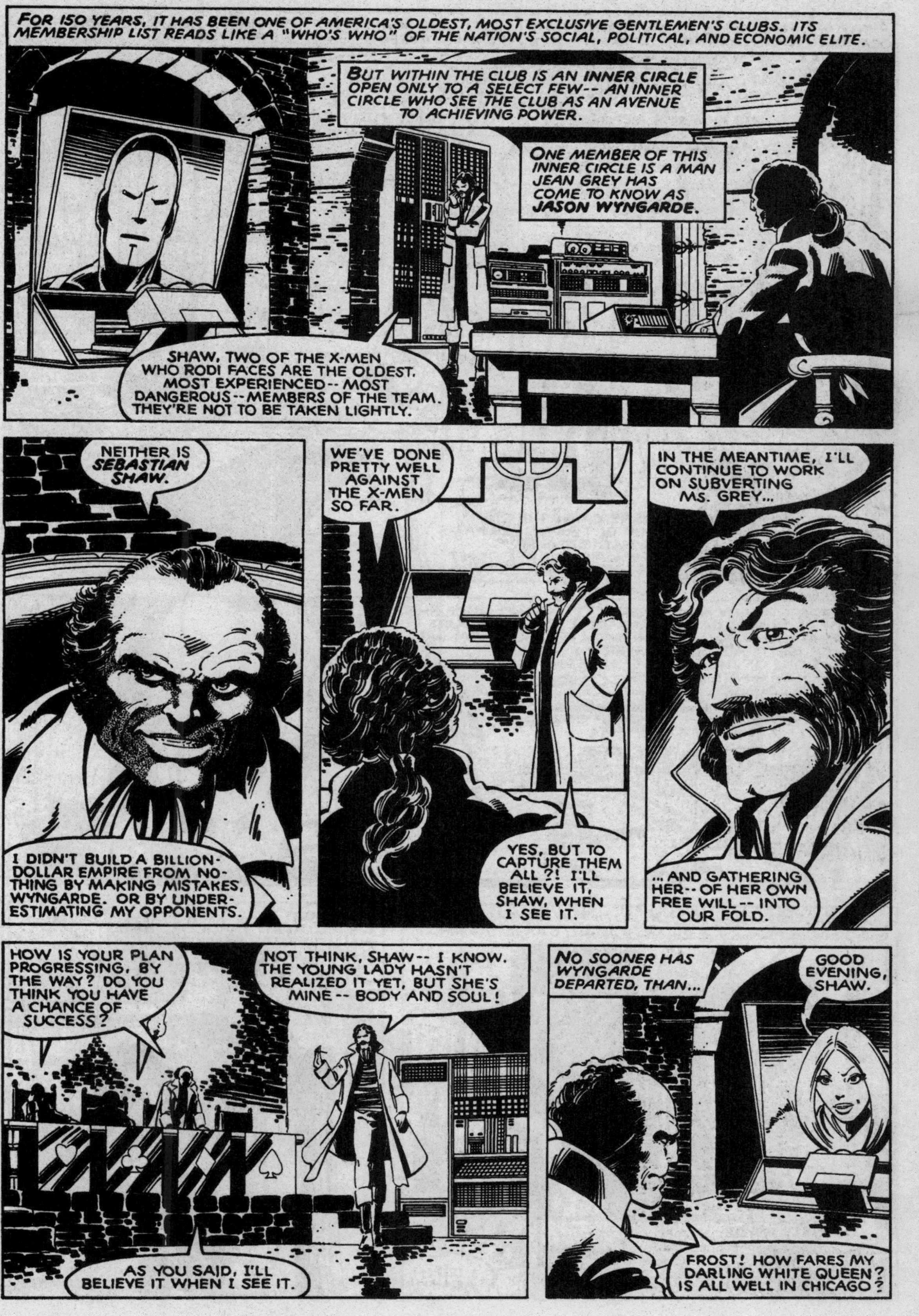
FOR 150 YEARS, IT HAS BEEN ONE OF AMERICA'S OLDEST, MOST EXCLUSIVE GENTLEMEN'S CLUBS. ITS MEMBERSHIP LIST READS LIKE A "WHO'S WHO" OF THE NATION'S SOCIAL, POLITICAL, AND ECONOMIC ELITE.
BUT WITHIN THE CLUB IS AN INNER CIRCLE OPEN ONLY TO A SELECT FEW-- AN INNER CIRCLE WHO SEE THE CLUB AS AN AVENUE TO ACHIEVING POWER.
ONE MEMBER OF THIS INNER CIRCLE IS A MAN JEAN GREY HAS COME TO KNOW AS JASON WYNGARDE.
SHAW, TWO OF THE X-MEN WHO RODI FACES ARE THE OLDEST. MOST EXPERIENCED-- MOST DANGEROUS--MEMBERS OF THE TEAM. THEY'RE NOT TO BE TAKEN LIGHTLY.
NEITHER IS SEBASTIAN SHAW.
I DIDN'T BUILD A BILLION-DOLLAR EMPIRE FROM NOTHING BY MAKING MISTAKES, WYNGARDE. OR BY UNDERESTIMATING MY OPPONENTS.
WE'VE DONE PRETTY WELL AGAINST THE X-MEN SO FAR.
YES, BUT TO CAPTURE THEM ALL?! I'LL BELIEVE IT, SHAW, WHEN I SEE IT.
IN THE MEANTIME, I'LL CONTINUE TO WORK ON SUBVERTING MS. GREY...
...AND GATHERING HER-- OF HER OWN FREE WILL-- INTO OUR FOLD.
HOW IS YOUR PLAN PROGRESSING, BY THE WAY? DO YOU THINK YOU HAVE A CHANCE OF SUCCESS?
NOT THINK, SHAW-- I KNOW. THE YOUNG LADY HASN'T REALIZED IT YET, BUT SHE'S MINE-- BODY AND SOUL!
AS YOU SAID, I'LL BELIEVE IT WHEN I SEE IT.
NO SOONER HAS WYNGARDE DEPARTED, THAN...
GOOD EVENING, SHAW.
FROST! HOW FARES MY DARLING WHITE QUEEN? IS ALL WELL IN CHICAGO?

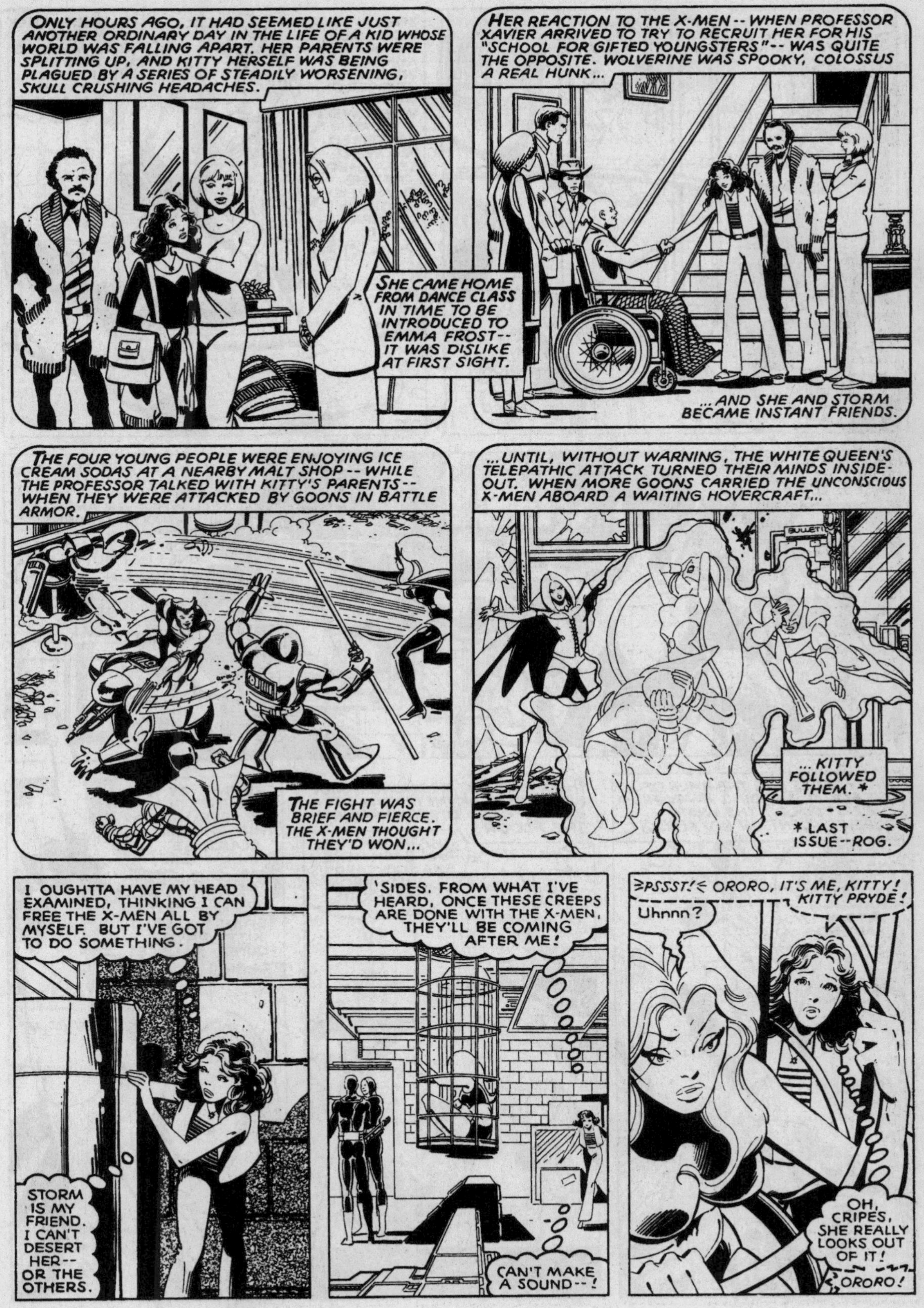
ONLY HOURS AGO, IT HAD SEEMED LIKE JUST ANOTHER ORDINARY DAY IN THE LIFE OF A KID WHOSE WORLD WAS FALLING APART. HER PARENTS WERE SPLITTING UP, AND KITTY HERSELF WAS BEING PLAGUED BY A SERIES OF STEADILY WORSENING, SKULL CRUSHING HEADACHES.
SHE CAME HOME FROM DANCE CLASS IN TIME TO BE INTRODUCED TO EMMA FROST-- IT WAS DISLIKE AT FIRST SIGHT.
HER REACTION TO THE X-MEN -- WHEN PROFESSOR XAVIER ARRIVED TO TRY TO RECRUIT HER FOR HIS "SCHOOL FOR GIFTED YOUNGSTERS" -- WAS QUITE THE OPPOSITE. WOLVERINE WAS SPOOKY, COLOSSUS A REAL HUNK...
...AND SHE AND STORM BECAME INSTANT FRIENDS.
THE FOUR YOUNG PEOPLE WERE ENJOYING ICE CREAM SODAS AT A NEARBY MALT SHOP -- WHILE THE PROFESSOR TALKED WITH KITTY'S PARENTS -- WHEN THEY WERE ATTACKED BY GOONS IN BATTLE ARMOR.
THE FIGHT WAS BRIEF AND FIERCE. THE X-MEN THOUGHT THEY'D WON...
...UNTIL, WITHOUT WARNING, THE WHITE QUEEN'S TELEPATHIC ATTACK TURNED THEIR MINDS INSIDE-OUT. WHEN MORE GOONS CARRIED THE UNCONSCIOUS X-MEN ABOARD A WAITING HOVERCRAFT...
... KITTY FOLLOWED THEM. *
* LAST ISSUE--ROG.
I OUGHTTA HAVE MY HEAD EXAMINED, THINKING I CAN FREE THE X-MEN ALL BY MYSELF. BUT I'VE GOT TO DO SOMETHING.
STORM IS MY FRIEND. I CAN'T DESERT HER-- OR THE OTHERS.
'SIDES, FROM WHAT I'VE HEARD, ONCE THESE CREEPS ARE DONE WITH THE X-MEN, THEY'LL BE COMING AFTER ME!
CAN'T MAKE A SOUND--!
PSSST! ORORO, IT'S ME, KITTY! KITTY PRYDE!
Uhnnn?
OH, CRIPES, SHE REALLY LOOKS OUT OF IT!
ORORO!

AT THAT MOMENT, BACK IN THE DISCO, JEAN GREY HAS JUST FINISHED HER SECOND CIRCUIT OF THE CROWDED DANCE FLOOR.

SHE'S NOT EVEN A QUARTER-CENTURY OLD, YET SHE'S FALLEN IN LOVE, DIED, RESURRECTED HERSELF AND SAVED THE UNIVERSE. SHE KNOWS SHE ONCE POSSESSED THE POWER OF... A GOD.

THAT MEMORY STILL TERRIFIES-- AND TANTALIZES -- HER.

SO FAR, I'VE NOTHING TO SHOW FOR TONIGHT BUT THREE DRUNKEN PASSES AND A COMMENT THAT MY DRESS IS TACKY. SCOTT ISN'T DOING ANY BETTER.

I WONDER IF CEREBRO COULD HAVE MADE A MISTAKE.

EXCUSE ME, MISS, I-- I WAS RIGHT! IT IS YOU! HULLO, AGAIN.

DO YOU REMEMBER ME? I'M JASON WYN-GARDE. WE MET IN STORNOWAY.

OH! YES, I...

THEIR EYES MEET--

-- AND SUDDENLY, REALITY... CHANGES AROUND JEAN.

THE 20TH CENTURY GIVES WAY TO THE 18TH, A LOWER-MANHATTAN DISCO...

... TO A BURNED-OUT CHURCH IN A WOODLAND GLADE THAT WILL ONE DAY BECOME PART OF FIFTH AVENUE.

UNLIKE THE PREVIOUS TIME-SLIPS, JEAN DOESN'T TRY TO FIGHT HER WAY OUT OF THE PAST. THIS TIME, SHE ACCEPTS WHAT'S HAPPENING...

... AS SHE'S LED TO THE ALTAR AND HER WAITING HUSBAND-TO-BE. AS ALWAYS, HIS MANLY BEAUTY TAKES HER BREATH AWAY.

DEARLY BELOVED, WE ARE GATHERED TOGETHER IN THE FACE OF THIS CONGRE-GATION, TO JOIN TOGETHER THIS MAN AND THIS WOMAN IN HOLY MATRIMONY.

IT TAKES ALL HER STRENGTH OF WILL TO STAND DEMURELY AND LISTEN TO THE VICAR'S SERVICE...

... WHEN SHE WOULD RATHER BE IN SIR JASON WYNGARDE'S ARMS.

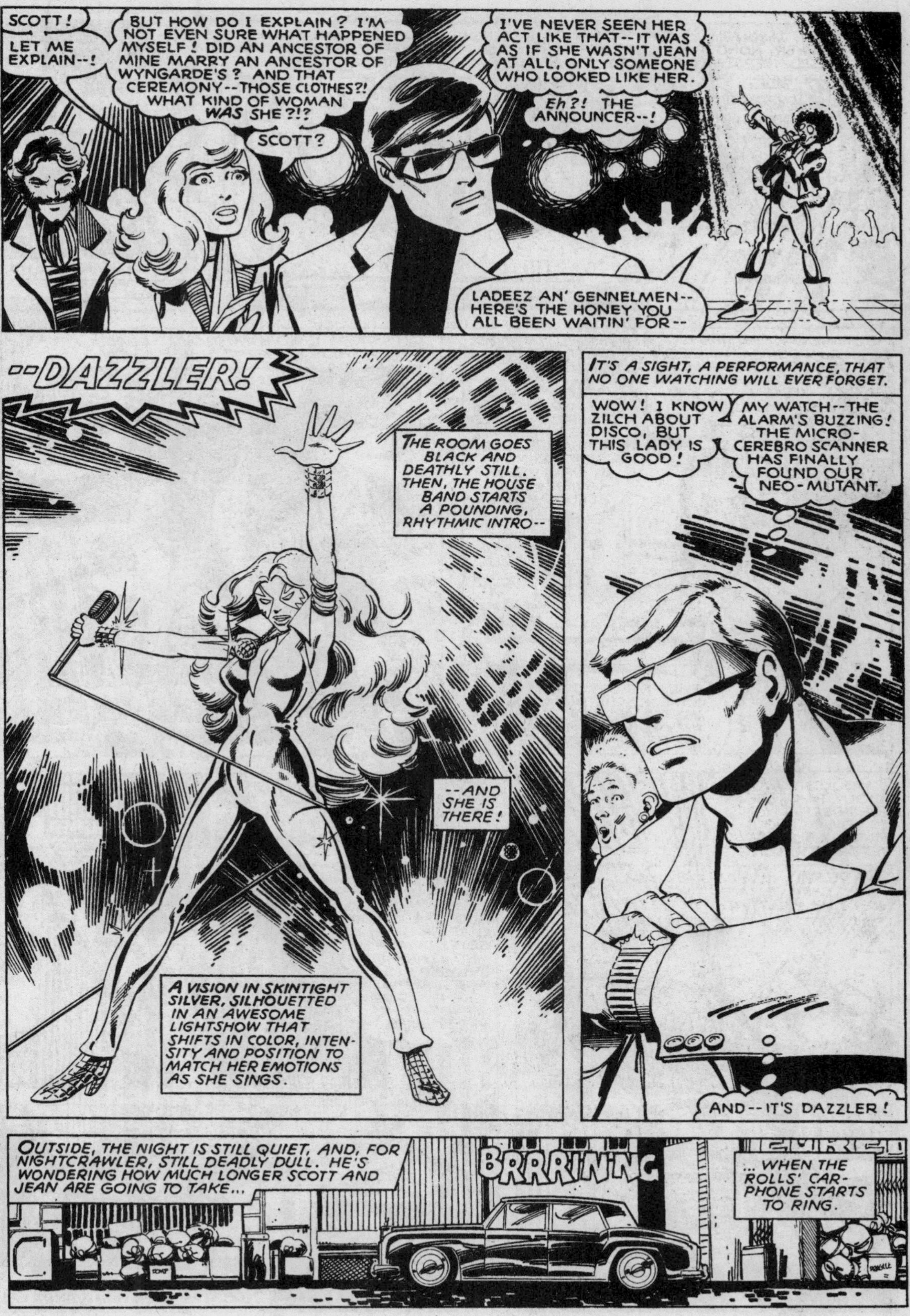
SCOTT! LET ME EXPLAIN--!
BUT HOW DO I EXPLAIN? I'M NOT EVEN SURE WHAT HAPPENED MYSELF! DID AN ANCESTOR OF MINE MARRY AN ANCESTOR OF WYNGARDE'S? AND THAT CEREMONY--THOSE CLOTHES?! WHAT KIND OF WOMAN WAS SHE?!?
SCOTT?
I'VE NEVER SEEN HER ACT LIKE THAT--IT WAS AS IF SHE WASN'T JEAN AT ALL, ONLY SOMEONE WHO LOOKED LIKE HER.
Eh?! THE ANNOUNCER--!
LADEEZ AN' GENNELMEN--HERE'S THE HONEY YOU ALL BEEN WAITIN' FOR--
--DAZZLER!
THE ROOM GOES BLACK AND DEATHLY STILL. THEN, THE HOUSE BAND STARTS A POUNDING, RHYTHMIC INTRO--
--AND SHE IS THERE!
A VISION IN SKINTIGHT SILVER, SILHOUETTED IN AN AWESOME LIGHTSHOW THAT SHIFTS IN COLOR, INTENSITY AND POSITION TO MATCH HER EMOTIONS AS SHE SINGS.
IT'S A SIGHT, A PERFORMANCE, THAT NO ONE WATCHING WILL EVER FORGET.
WOW! I KNOW ZILCH ABOUT DISCO, BUT THIS LADY IS GOOD!
MY WATCH--THE ALARM'S BUZZING! THE MICRO-CEREBRO SCANNER HAS FINALLY FOUND OUR NEO-MUTANT.
AND--IT'S DAZZLER!
OUTSIDE, THE NIGHT IS STILL QUIET, AND, FOR NIGHTCRAWLER, STILL DEADLY DULL. HE'S WONDERING HOW MUCH LONGER SCOTT AND JEAN ARE GOING TO TAKE...
BRRRINNG
...WHEN THE ROLLS' CAR-PHONE STARTS TO RING.

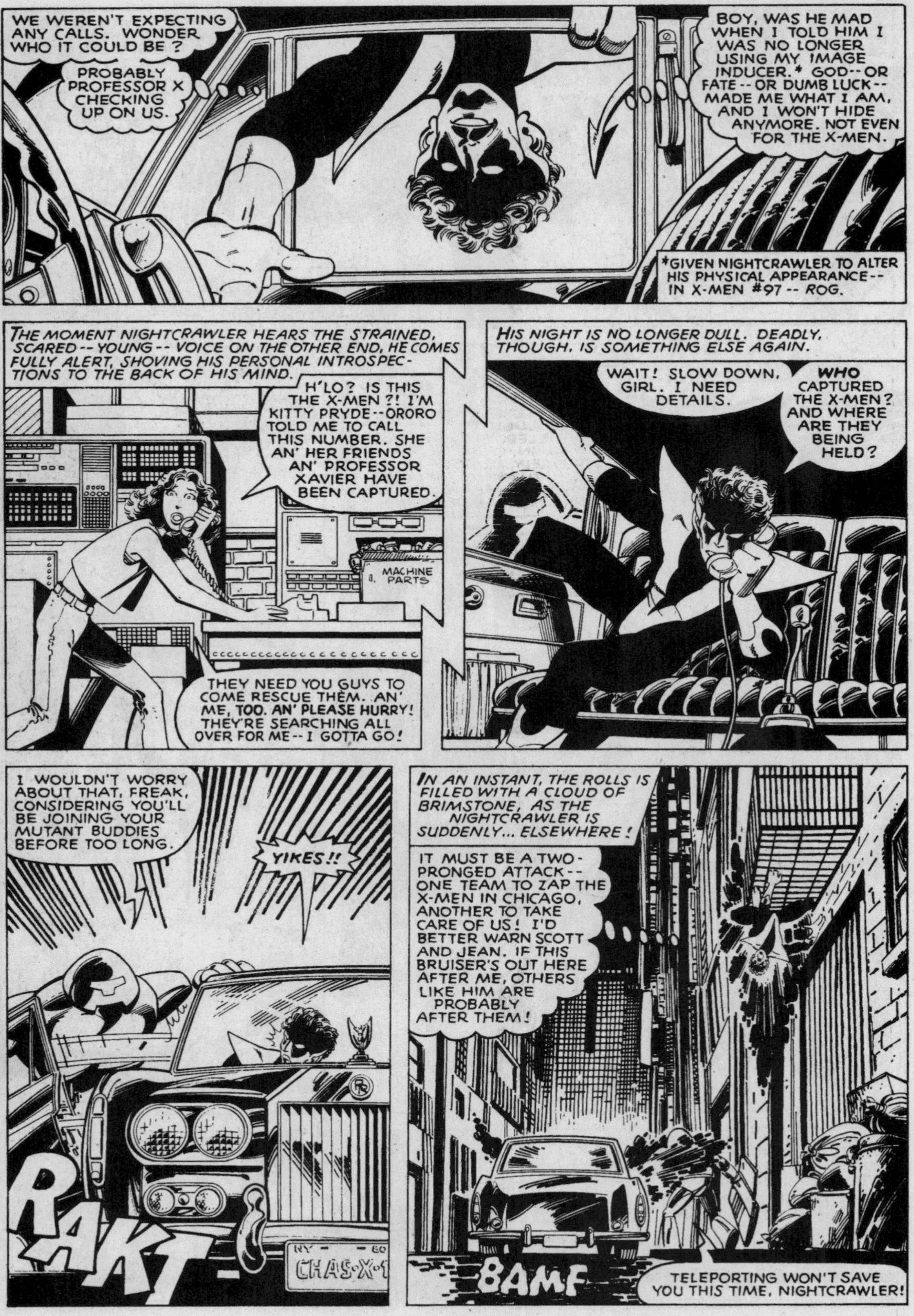

WE WEREN'T EXPECTING ANY CALLS. WONDER WHO IT COULD BE?
PROBABLY PROFESSOR X CHECKING UP ON US.
BOY, WAS HE MAD WHEN I TOLD HIM I WAS NO LONGER USING MY IMAGE INDUCER.* GOD--OR FATE--OR DUMB LUCK--MADE ME WHAT I AM, AND I WON'T HIDE ANYMORE. NOT EVEN FOR THE X-MEN.
*GIVEN NIGHTCRAWLER TO ALTER HIS PHYSICAL APPEARANCE--IN X-MEN #97 -- ROG.
THE MOMENT NIGHTCRAWLER HEARS THE STRAINED, SCARED--YOUNG--VOICE ON THE OTHER END, HE COMES FULLY ALERT, SHOVING HIS PERSONAL INTROSPECTIONS TO THE BACK OF HIS MIND.
H'LO? IS THIS THE X-MEN?! I'M KITTY PRYDE--ORORO TOLD ME TO CALL THIS NUMBER. SHE AN' HER FRIENDS AN' PROFESSOR XAVIER HAVE BEEN CAPTURED.
MACHINE PARTS
THEY NEED YOU GUYS TO COME RESCUE THEM. AN' ME, TOO. AN' PLEASE HURRY! THEY'RE SEARCHING ALL OVER FOR ME--I GOTTA GO!
HIS NIGHT IS NO LONGER DULL. DEADLY, THOUGH, IS SOMETHING ELSE AGAIN.
WAIT! SLOW DOWN, GIRL. I NEED DETAILS.
WHO CAPTURED THE X-MEN? AND WHERE ARE THEY BEING HELD?
I WOULDN'T WORRY ABOUT THAT, FREAK, CONSIDERING YOU'LL BE JOINING YOUR MUTANT BUDDIES BEFORE TOO LONG.
YIKES!!
RAKT
NY 80
CHAS-X-1
IN AN INSTANT, THE ROLLS IS FILLED WITH A CLOUD OF BRIMSTONE, AS THE NIGHTCRAWLER IS SUDDENLY... ELSEWHERE!
IT MUST BE A TWO-PRONGED ATTACK--ONE TEAM TO ZAP THE X-MEN IN CHICAGO, ANOTHER TO TAKE CARE OF US! I'D BETTER WARN SCOTT AND JEAN. IF THIS BRUISER'S OUT HERE AFTER ME, OTHERS LIKE HIM ARE PROBABLY AFTER THEM!
BAMF
TELEPORTING WON'T SAVE YOU THIS TIME, NIGHTCRAWLER!

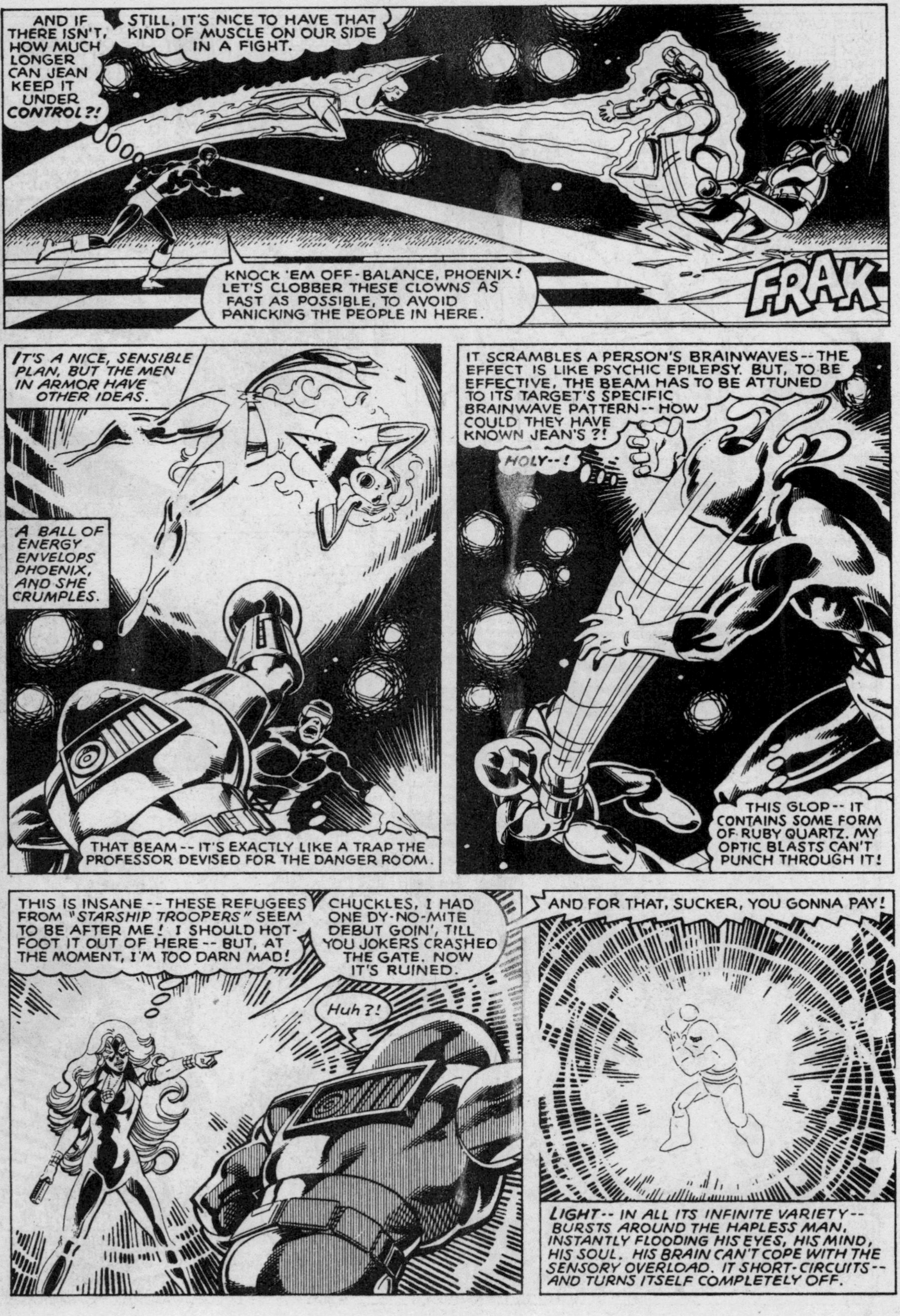

AND IF THERE ISN'T, HOW MUCH LONGER CAN JEAN KEEP IT UNDER CONTROL?!
STILL, IT'S NICE TO HAVE THAT KIND OF MUSCLE ON OUR SIDE IN A FIGHT.
KNOCK 'EM OFF-BALANCE, PHOENIX! LET'S CLOBBER THESE CLOWNS AS FAST AS POSSIBLE, TO AVOID PANICKING THE PEOPLE IN HERE.
FRAK
IT'S A NICE, SENSIBLE PLAN, BUT THE MEN IN ARMOR HAVE OTHER IDEAS.
A BALL OF ENERGY ENVELOPS PHOENIX, AND SHE CRUMPLES.
THAT BEAM -- IT'S EXACTLY LIKE A TRAP THE PROFESSOR DEVISED FOR THE DANGER ROOM.
IT SCRAMBLES A PERSON'S BRAINWAVES -- THE EFFECT IS LIKE PSYCHIC EPILEPSY. BUT, TO BE EFFECTIVE, THE BEAM HAS TO BE ATTUNED TO ITS TARGET'S SPECIFIC BRAINWAVE PATTERN -- HOW COULD THEY HAVE KNOWN JEAN'S?!
HOLY--!
THIS GLOP -- IT CONTAINS SOME FORM OF RUBY QUARTZ. MY OPTIC BLASTS CAN'T PUNCH THROUGH IT!
THIS IS INSANE -- THESE REFUGEES FROM "STARSHIP TROOPERS" SEEM TO BE AFTER ME! I SHOULD HOT-FOOT IT OUT OF HERE -- BUT, AT THE MOMENT, I'M TOO DARN MAD!
CHUCKLES, I HAD ONE DY-NO-MITE DEBUT GOIN', TILL YOU JOKERS CRASHED THE GATE. NOW IT'S RUINED.
Huh?!
AND FOR THAT, SUCKER, YOU GONNA PAY!
LIGHT -- IN ALL ITS INFINITE VARIETY -- BURSTS AROUND THE HAPLESS MAN, INSTANTLY FLOODING HIS EYES, HIS MIND, HIS SOUL. HIS BRAIN CAN'T COPE WITH THE SENSORY OVERLOAD. IT SHORT-CIRCUITS -- AND TURNS ITSELF COMPLETELY OFF.

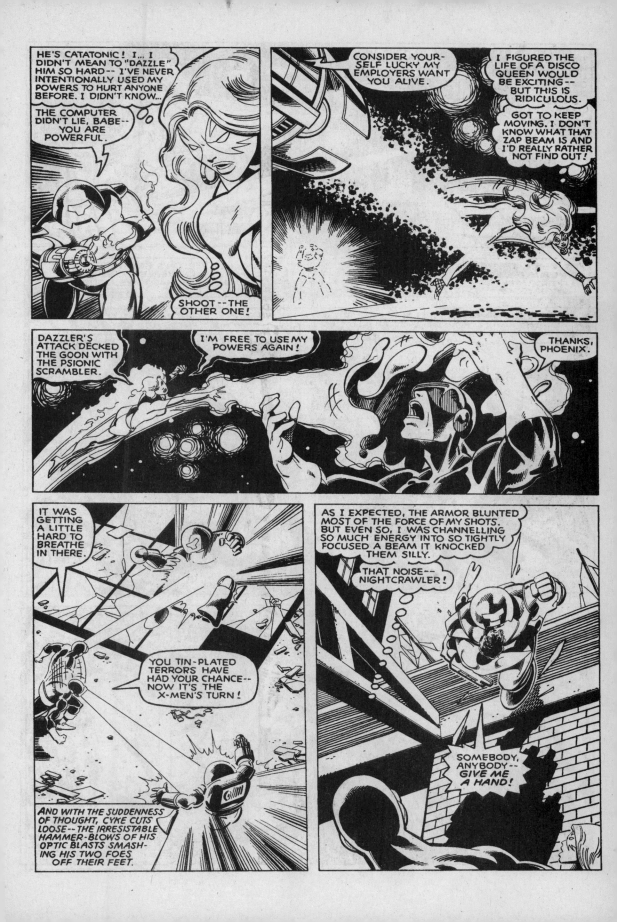

AS THEY REACH THE STREET, A SERIES OF EXPLOSIONS SHATTER THE TOP FLOOR OF THE BUILDING.

THE DISCO! INSIDE -- QUICK! I'LL PROTECT THE CAR FROM FALLING DEBRIS WITH A TELEPATHIC SHIELD.

CYCLOPS, I'M NOT PICKING UP OUR ATTACKERS' THOUGHTS ANYMORE. THEY JUST... CUT OUT.

I WAS PLANNING TO HAVE JEAN TELE-PATHICALLY INTERROGATE ONE OF THOSE GOONS.

I GUESS THEIR MASTERS WANTED TO MAKE SURE I COULDN'T. NICE PEOPLE.

THEY SEEM TO KNOW AN AWFUL LOT ABOUT THE X-MEN -- TOO MUCH. BUT HOW?! WHO ARE WE UP AGAINST?! WHAT ARE THEY AFTER?!

IT'S THE MAN JEAN KISSED IN THE DISCO.

IS HE PART OF THIS PUZZLE, TOO? OR SIMPLY MY RIVAL FOR JEAN'S AFFECTIONS? THE FIRST I CAN DEAL WITH. THE SECOND... I'M NOT SO SURE.

EITHER WAY, I DON'T LIKE HIM.

CYCLOPS -- A MAN, WAITING AT THE CORNER.

THE ROLLS' HEAD-LIGHTS TOUCH JASON WYNGARDE FOR A MOMENT, THROWING HIS SHADOW ACROSS THE WALL BEHIND HIM. CYCLOPS AUTOMATICALLY NOTES THE IMAGE...

...BUT HIS MIND -- PREOCCUPIED WITH A HOST OF FAR-MORE-PRESSING CONCERNS -- DOESN'T REGISTER IT. PERHAPS, ONE DAY, HE WILL REMEMBER -- AND RECOGNIZE -- WHO HE PASSED THIS NIGHT.

BY THEN, HOWEVER, IT MAY WELL BE FAR TOO LATE. FOR HIM, FOR THE X-MEN --

-- AND, MOST IMPORTANTLY, FOR THE WOMAN HE LOVES.

HA HA HA HA HA HA HA HA HA HA

IT'S CYCLOPS, PHOENIX, NIGHTCRAWLER AND DAZZLER TO THE RESCUE. BUT WILL THEY REACH CHICAGO IN TIME TO SAVE KITTY PRYDE? FIND OUT IN...

NEXT ▷ "RUN FOR YOUR LIFE!"

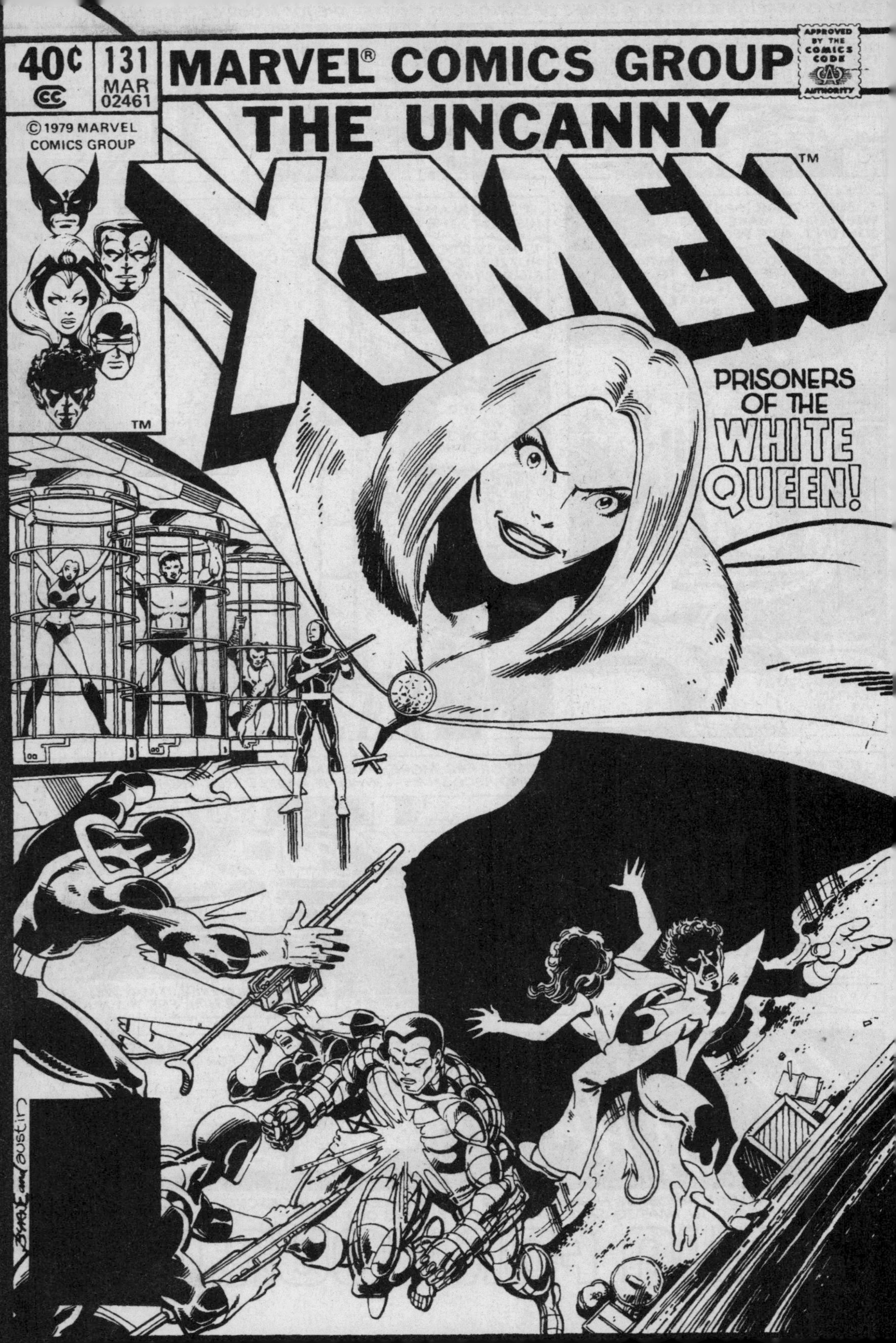

40¢
CC
131
MAR
02461
MARVEL® COMICS GROUP
APPROVED BY THE COMICS CODE AUTHORITY
© 1979 MARVEL COMICS GROUP
THE UNCANNY
X-MEN™
TM
PRISONERS OF THE WHITE QUEEN!

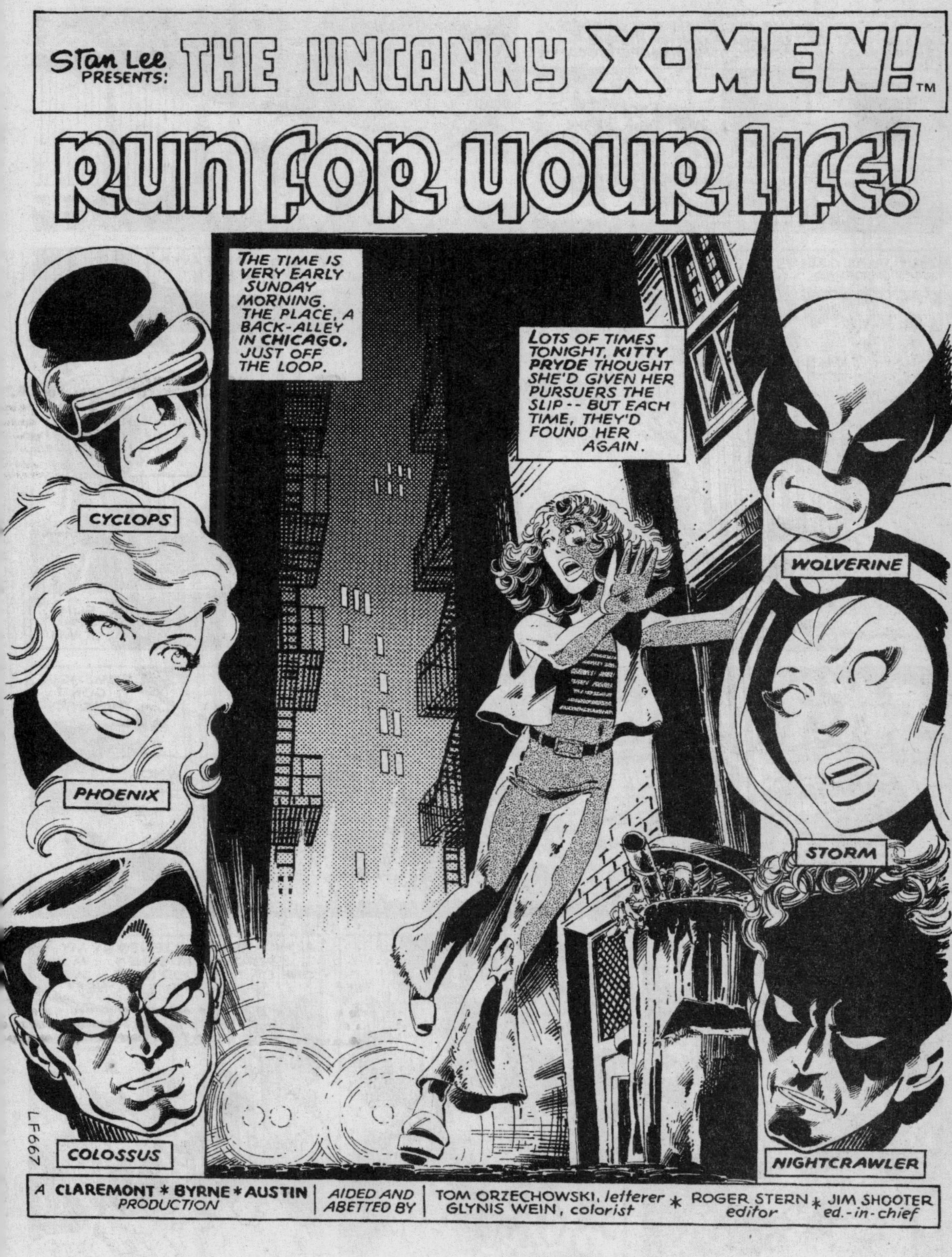
Stan Lee PRESENTS: THE UNCANNY X-MEN!™
RUN FOR YOUR LIFE!
THE TIME IS VERY EARLY SUNDAY MORNING. THE PLACE, A BACK-ALLEY IN CHICAGO. JUST OFF THE LOOP.
LOTS OF TIMES TONIGHT, KITTY PRYDE THOUGHT SHE'D GIVEN HER PURSUERS THE SLIP -- BUT EACH TIME, THEY'D FOUND HER AGAIN.
CYCLOPS
PHOENIX
COLOSSUS
WOLVERINE
STORM
NIGHTCRAWLER
A CLAREMONT * BYRNE * AUSTIN PRODUCTION
AIDED AND ABETTED BY
TOM ORZECHOWSKI, letterer
GLYNIS WEIN, colorist
* ROGER STERN editor
* JIM SHOOTER ed.-in-chief

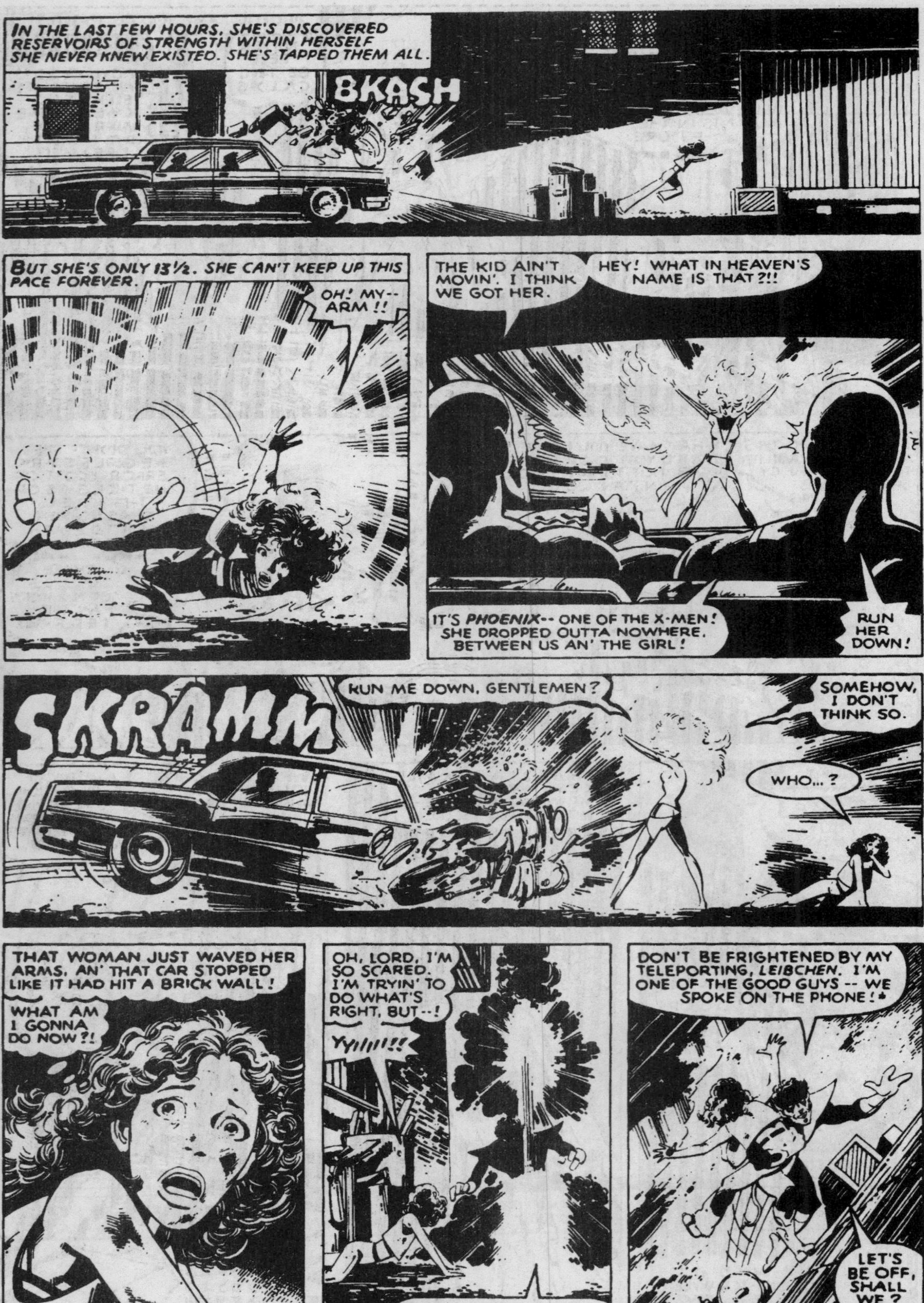

IN THE LAST FEW HOURS, SHE'S DISCOVERED RESERVOIRS OF STRENGTH WITHIN HERSELF SHE NEVER KNEW EXISTED. SHE'S TAPPED THEM ALL.
BKASH
BUT SHE'S ONLY 13½. SHE CAN'T KEEP UP THIS PACE FOREVER.
OH! MY-- ARM!!
THE KID AIN'T MOVIN'. I THINK WE GOT HER.
HEY! WHAT IN HEAVEN'S NAME IS THAT?!!
IT'S PHOENIX-- ONE OF THE X-MEN! SHE DROPPED OUTTA NOWHERE. BETWEEN US AN' THE GIRL!
RUN HER DOWN!
SKRAMM
RUN ME DOWN, GENTLEMEN?
SOMEHOW, I DON'T THINK SO.
WHO...?
THAT WOMAN JUST WAVED HER ARMS, AN' THAT CAR STOPPED LIKE IT HAD HIT A BRICK WALL!
WHAT AM I GONNA DO NOW?!
OH, LORD, I'M SO SCARED. I'M TRYIN' TO DO WHAT'S RIGHT, BUT--!
YYIIIII!!
GUTEN ABEND, FRAULEIN PRYDE, I ASSUME?
DON'T BE FRIGHTENED BY MY TELEPORTING, LEIBCHEN. I'M ONE OF THE GOOD GUYS -- WE SPOKE ON THE PHONE!*
LET'S BE OFF, SHALL WE?
*LAST ISSUE --ROG.

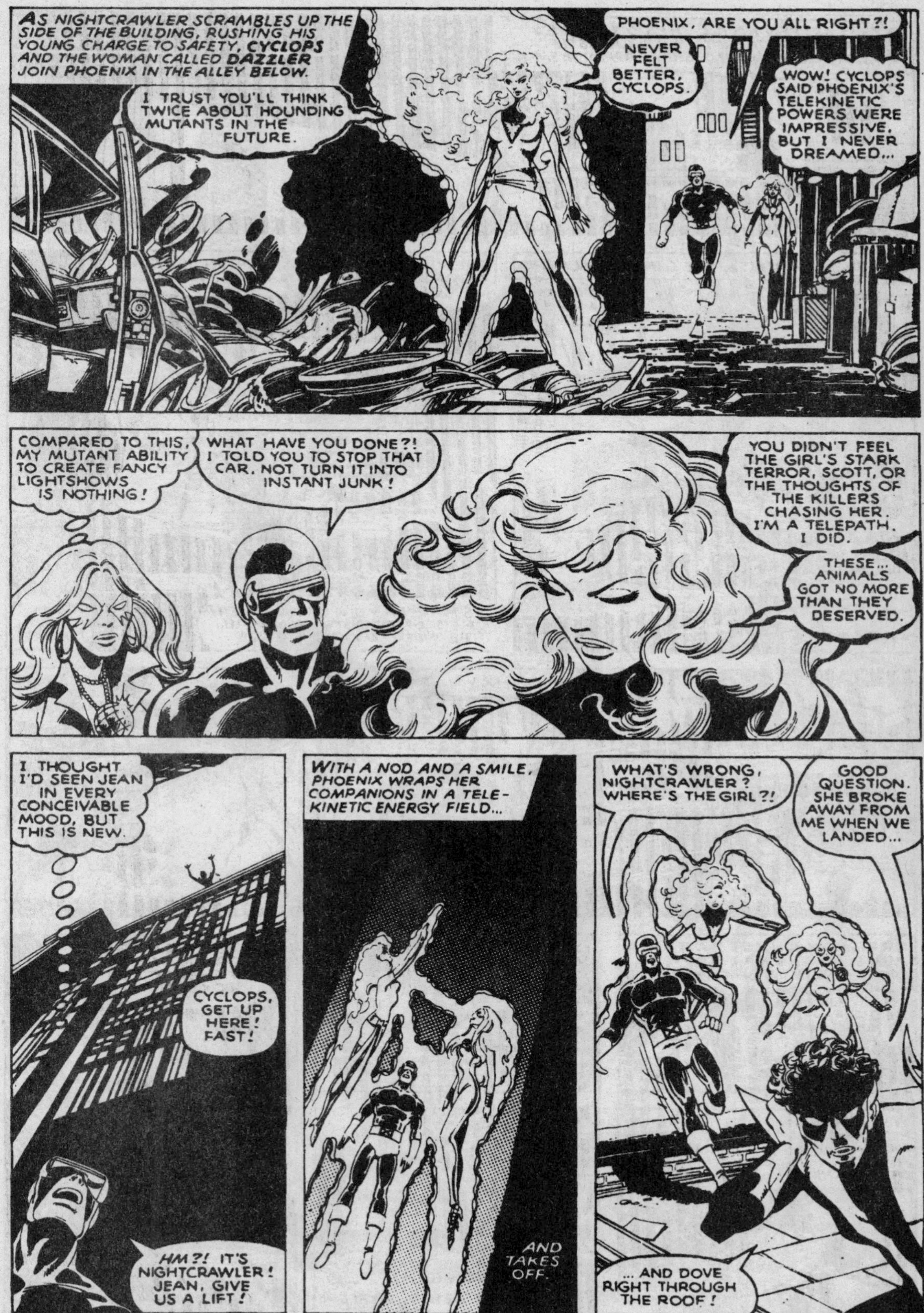

AS NIGHTCRAWLER SCRAMBLES UP THE SIDE OF THE BUILDING, RUSHING HIS YOUNG CHARGE TO SAFETY, CYCLOPS AND THE WOMAN CALLED DAZZLER JOIN PHOENIX IN THE ALLEY BELOW.
I TRUST YOU'LL THINK TWICE ABOUT HOUNDING MUTANTS IN THE FUTURE.
PHOENIX, ARE YOU ALL RIGHT?!
NEVER FELT BETTER, CYCLOPS.
WOW! CYCLOPS SAID PHOENIX'S TELEKINETIC POWERS WERE IMPRESSIVE, BUT I NEVER DREAMED...
COMPARED TO THIS, MY MUTANT ABILITY TO CREATE FANCY LIGHTSHOWS IS NOTHING!
WHAT HAVE YOU DONE?! I TOLD YOU TO STOP THAT CAR, NOT TURN IT INTO INSTANT JUNK!
YOU DIDN'T FEEL THE GIRL'S STARK TERROR, SCOTT, OR THE THOUGHTS OF THE KILLERS CHASING HER. I'M A TELEPATH. I DID.
THESE... ANIMALS GOT NO MORE THAN THEY DESERVED.
I THOUGHT I'D SEEN JEAN IN EVERY CONCEIVABLE MOOD, BUT THIS IS NEW.
CYCLOPS, GET UP HERE! FAST!
HM?! IT'S NIGHTCRAWLER! JEAN, GIVE US A LIFT!
WITH A NOD AND A SMILE, PHOENIX WRAPS HER COMPANIONS IN A TELEKINETIC ENERGY FIELD...
AND TAKES OFF.
WHAT'S WRONG, NIGHTCRAWLER? WHERE'S THE GIRL?!
GOOD QUESTION. SHE BROKE AWAY FROM ME WHEN WE LANDED...
... AND DOVE RIGHT THROUGH THE ROOF!

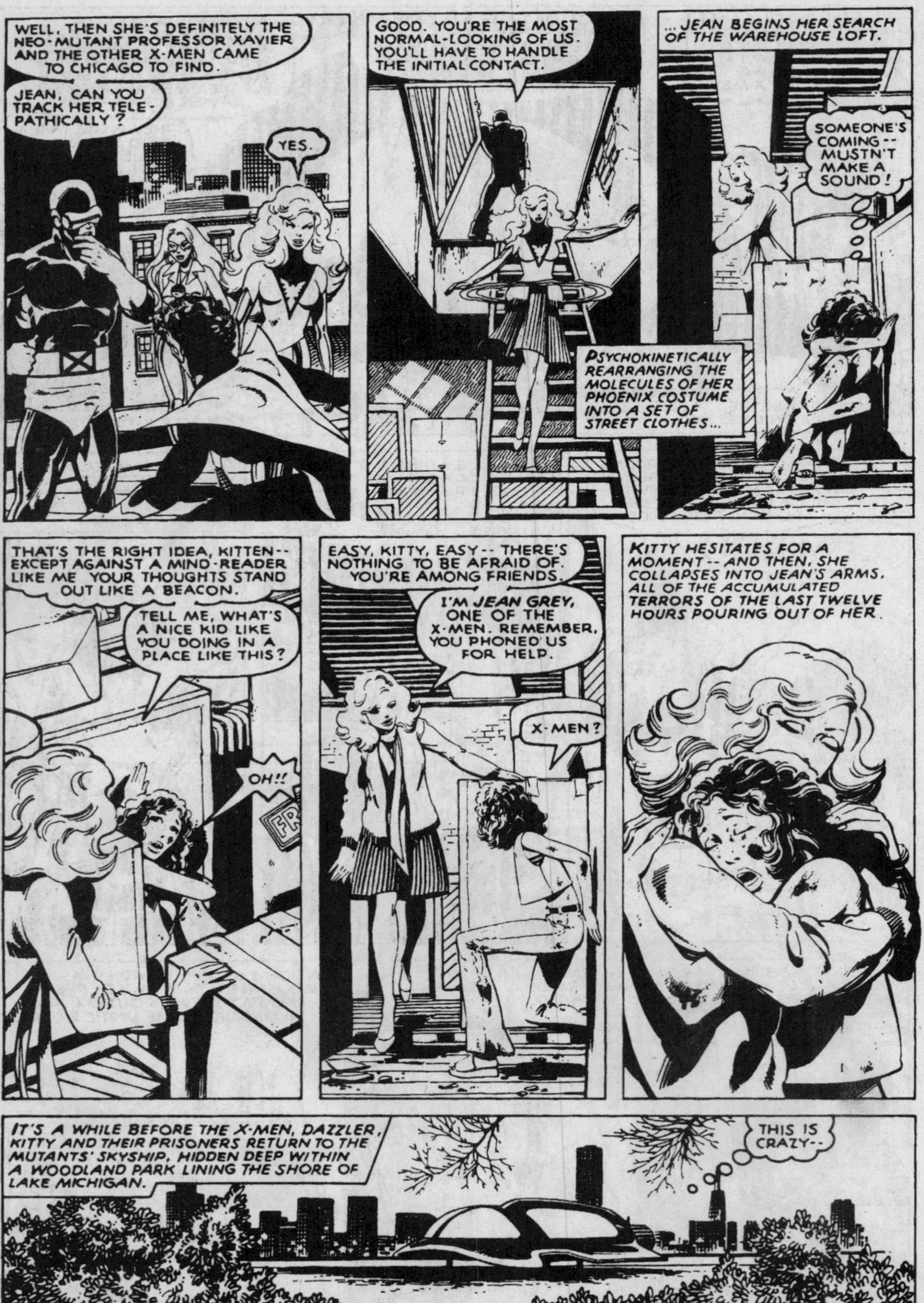
WELL, THEN SHE'S DEFINITELY THE NEO-MUTANT PROFESSOR XAVIER AND THE OTHER X-MEN CAME TO CHICAGO TO FIND.
JEAN, CAN YOU TRACK HER TELEPATHICALLY?
YES.
GOOD. YOU'RE THE MOST NORMAL-LOOKING OF US. YOU'LL HAVE TO HANDLE THE INITIAL CONTACT.
PSYCHOKINETICALLY REARRANGING THE MOLECULES OF HER PHOENIX COSTUME INTO A SET OF STREET CLOTHES...
...JEAN BEGINS HER SEARCH OF THE WAREHOUSE LOFT.
SOMEONE'S COMING -- MUSTN'T MAKE A SOUND!
THAT'S THE RIGHT IDEA, KITTEN -- EXCEPT AGAINST A MIND-READER LIKE ME YOUR THOUGHTS STAND OUT LIKE A BEACON.
TELL ME, WHAT'S A NICE KID LIKE YOU DOING IN A PLACE LIKE THIS?
OH!!
EASY, KITTY, EASY -- THERE'S NOTHING TO BE AFRAID OF. YOU'RE AMONG FRIENDS.
I'M JEAN GREY, ONE OF THE X-MEN. REMEMBER, YOU PHONED US FOR HELP.
X-MEN?
KITTY HESITATES FOR A MOMENT -- AND THEN, SHE COLLAPSES INTO JEAN'S ARMS, ALL OF THE ACCUMULATED TERRORS OF THE LAST TWELVE HOURS POURING OUT OF HER.
IT'S A WHILE BEFORE THE X-MEN, DAZZLER, KITTY AND THEIR PRISONERS RETURN TO THE MUTANTS' SKYSHIP, HIDDEN DEEP WITHIN A WOODLAND PARK LINING THE SHORE OF LAKE MICHIGAN.
THIS IS CRAZY--

-- I STARTED OUT LAST NIGHT TO BREAK INTO THE NEW YORK DISCO SCENE... AND NOW I'M SUDDENLY FIGHTING ALONGSIDE THE X-MEN.

MOST OF THESE ARE ONLY SCRAPES -- THEY LOOK A LOT WORSE THAN THEY REALLY ARE -- BUT SOME OF THESE CUTS ARE PRETTY DEEP. SING OUT IF I HURT YOU, KITTY.

OKAY.

ANYWAY, ORORO -- AN' COLOSSUS AN' WOLVERINE -- AN' I WERE AT THE MALT SHOP, WHEN THESE CREEPS BUSTED IN ON US. I GOT AWAY, BUT THE X-MEN AND PROFESSOR XAVIER GOT CAPTURED.

THEY WERE TAKEN TO THIS BIG INDUSTRIAL PARK JUST OUTSIDE THE CITY. I KIND'A TAGGED ALONG. *

I DON'T THINK THE LITTLE *FRAULEIN* LIKES ME.

*SEE X-MEN #129.--ROG.

ORORO GAVE ME YOUR PHONE NUMBER, TOLD ME TO CALL YOU GUYS TO COME RESCUE EVERY-ONE. I DID, AN' I'VE BEEN RUNNIN' EVER SINCE.

WE WERE ATTACKED, TOO, IN NEW YORK. *

*LAST ISSUE --R.

I'M THROUGH TANGLING WITH SHADOWS. MIND-SCAN OUR PRISONERS, JEAN, AND FIND OUT WHO WE'RE UP AGAINST.

AS GOOD AS DONE.

THE GOONS' MINDS ARE SHIELDED, BUT, WITH AN EASE THAT DEFIES DESCRIPTION, PHOENIX SLIPS PAST THEIR MENTAL DEFENSES.

... AND, IN THE BLINK OF AN EYE, LEARNS WHERE THE OTHER X-MEN ARE BEING HELD AND HOW WELL THAT COMPLEX IS DEFENDED. SHE LEARNS THAT THEY WERE STRUCK DOWN BY ANOTHER TELEPATH, A WOMAN NAMED EMMA FROST --

-- ONE OF A GROUP OF WEALTHY INDUSTRIALISTS WHO SEEK PRE-EMINENT SOCIAL, POLITICAL AND ECONOMIC POWER IN THE WORLD.

FROST INC.

THE HELLFIRE CLUB FOUNDED 1780

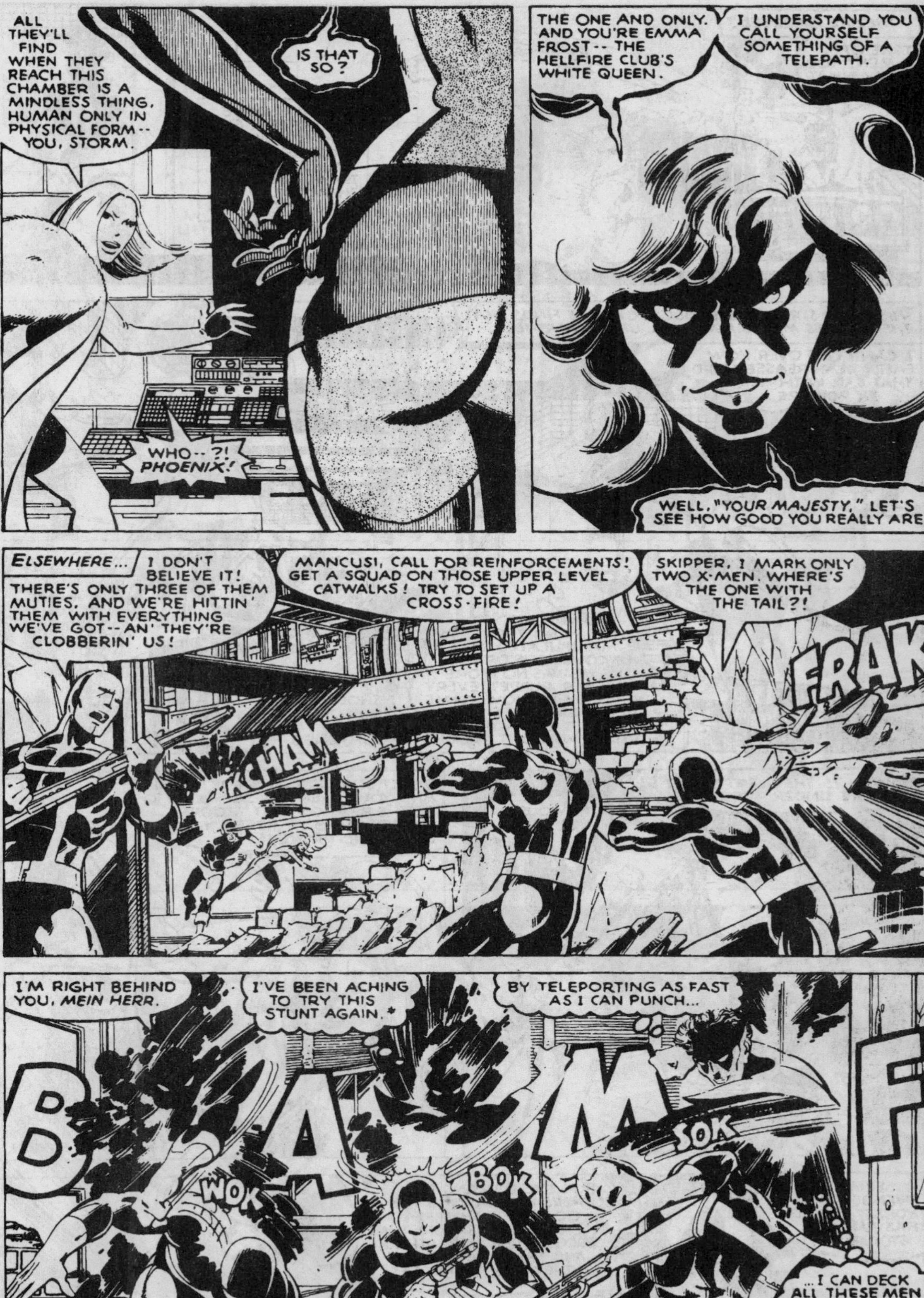
ALL THEY'LL FIND WHEN THEY REACH THIS CHAMBER IS A MINDLESS THING, HUMAN ONLY IN PHYSICAL FORM -- YOU, STORM.
IS THAT SO?
WHO--?! PHOENIX!
THE ONE AND ONLY. AND YOU'RE EMMA FROST -- THE HELLFIRE CLUB'S WHITE QUEEN.
I UNDERSTAND YOU CALL YOURSELF SOMETHING OF A TELEPATH.
WELL, "YOUR MAJESTY," LET'S SEE HOW GOOD YOU REALLY ARE.
ELSEWHERE...
I DON'T BELIEVE IT! THERE'S ONLY THREE OF THEM MUTIES, AND WE'RE HITTIN' THEM WITH EVERYTHING WE'VE GOT--AN' THEY'RE CLOBBERIN' US!
MANCUSI, CALL FOR REINFORCEMENTS! GET A SQUAD ON THOSE UPPER LEVEL CATWALKS! TRY TO SET UP A CROSS-FIRE!
SKIPPER, I MARK ONLY TWO X-MEN. WHERE'S THE ONE WITH THE TAIL?!
FRAK
KCHAM
I'M RIGHT BEHIND YOU, MEIN HERR.
I'VE BEEN ACHING TO TRY THIS STUNT AGAIN.*
BY TELEPORTING AS FAST AS I CAN PUNCH...
BAMF
WOK
BOK
SOK
...I CAN DECK ALL THESE MEN BEFORE THE FIRST ONE EVEN HITS THE GROUND!
*LAST USED IN X-MEN #111 -- ROG.

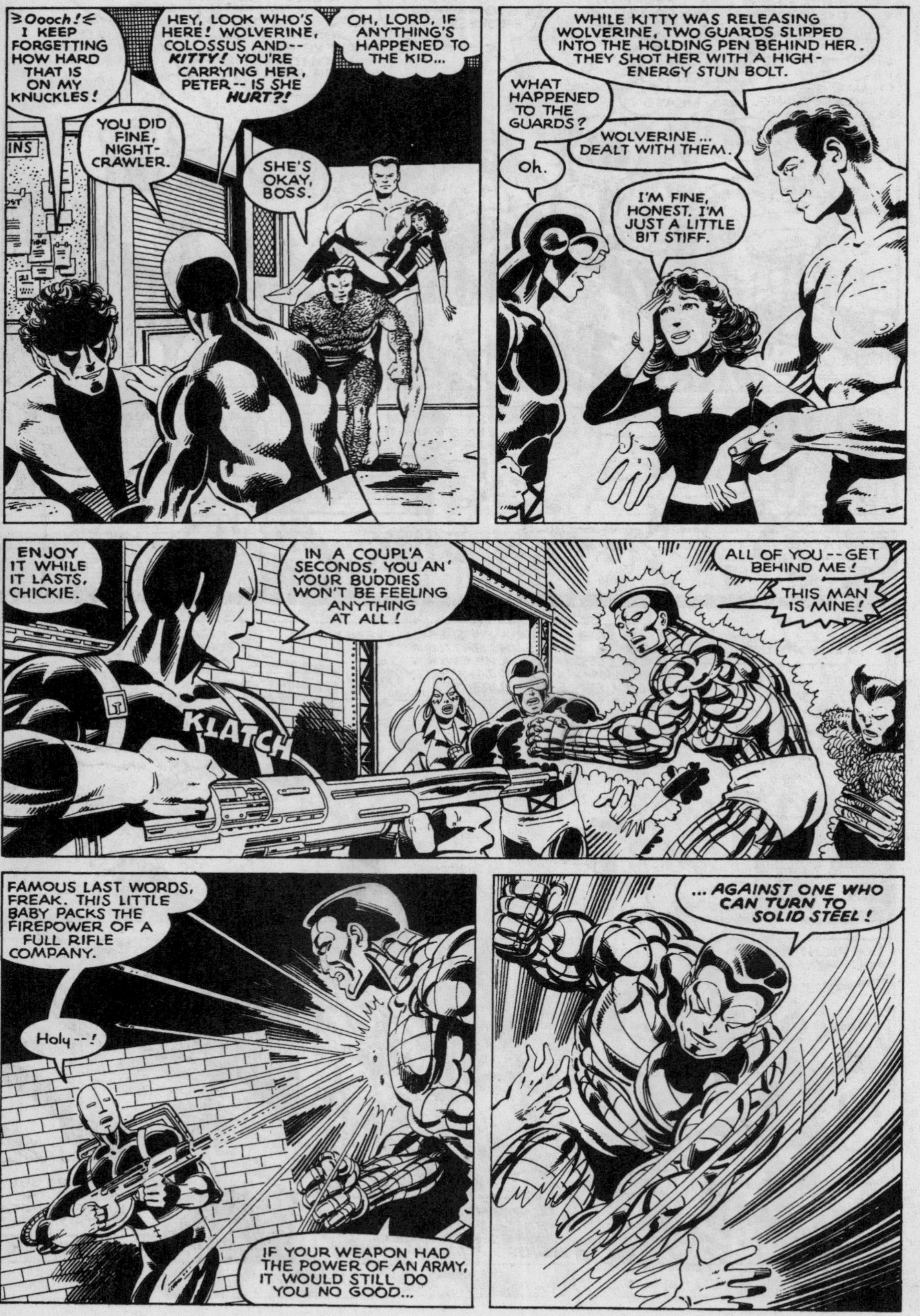
Oooch! I KEEP FORGETTING HOW HARD THAT IS ON MY KNUCKLES!
HEY, LOOK WHO'S HERE! WOLVERINE, COLOSSUS AND-- KITTY! YOU'RE CARRYING HER, PETER-- IS SHE HURT?!
OH, LORD, IF ANYTHING'S HAPPENED TO THE KID...
YOU DID FINE, NIGHT-CRAWLER.
SHE'S OKAY, BOSS.
WHILE KITTY WAS RELEASING WOLVERINE, TWO GUARDS SLIPPED INTO THE HOLDING PEN BEHIND HER. THEY SHOT HER WITH A HIGH-ENERGY STUN BOLT.
WHAT HAPPENED TO THE GUARDS?
WOLVERINE... DEALT WITH THEM.
Oh.
I'M FINE, HONEST. I'M JUST A LITTLE BIT STIFF.
ENJOY IT WHILE IT LASTS, CHICKIE.
IN A COUPL'A SECONDS, YOU AN' YOUR BUDDIES WON'T BE FEELING ANYTHING AT ALL!
KLATCH
ALL OF YOU--GET BEHIND ME!
THIS MAN IS MINE!
FAMOUS LAST WORDS, FREAK. THIS LITTLE BABY PACKS THE FIREPOWER OF A FULL RIFLE COMPANY.
Holy--!
IF YOUR WEAPON HAD THE POWER OF AN ARMY, IT WOULD STILL DO YOU NO GOOD...
...AGAINST ONE WHO CAN TURN TO SOLID STEEL!

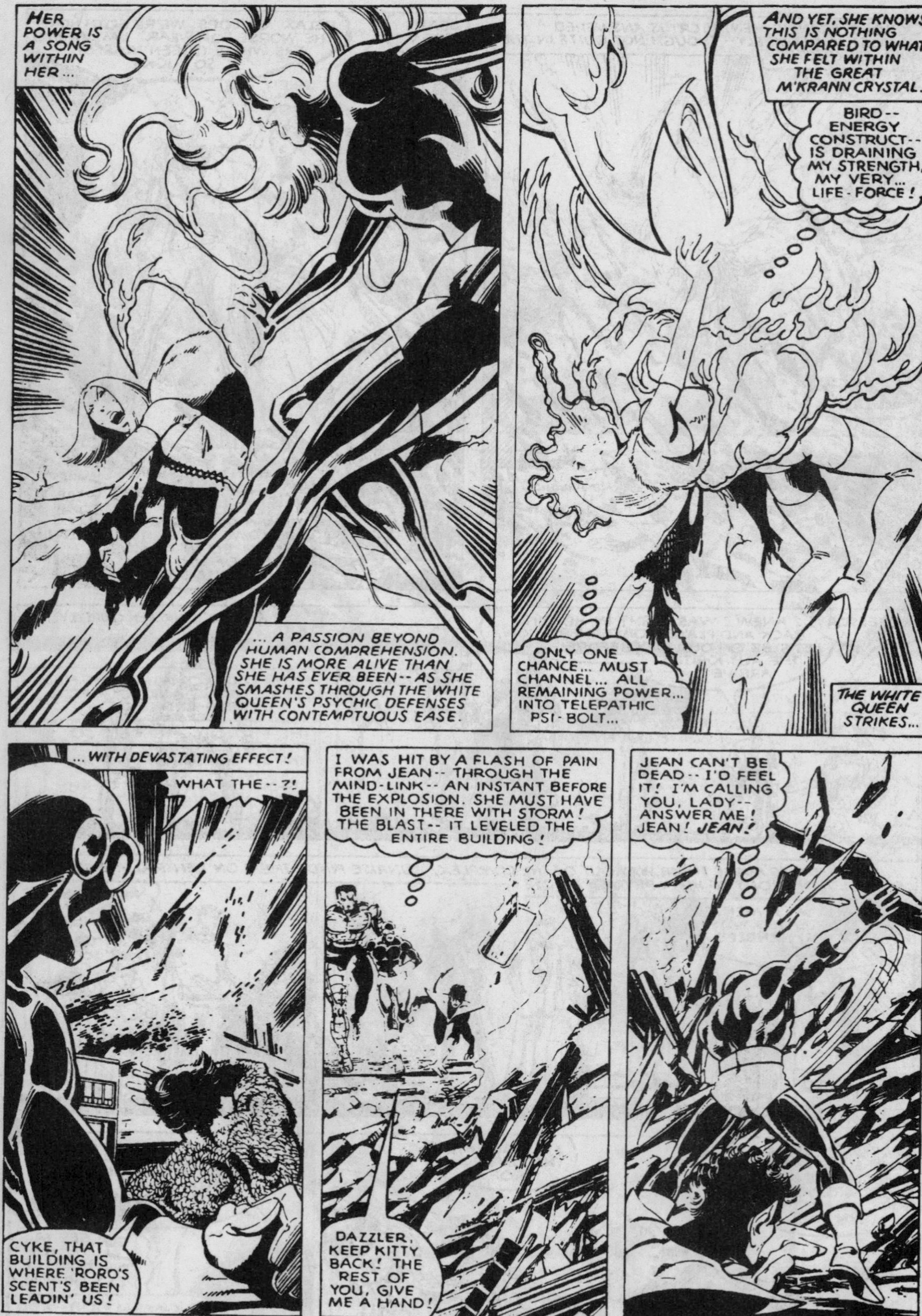
HER POWER IS A SONG WITHIN HER...
... A PASSION BEYOND HUMAN COMPREHENSION. SHE IS MORE ALIVE THAN SHE HAS EVER BEEN -- AS SHE SMASHES THROUGH THE WHITE QUEEN'S PSYCHIC DEFENSES WITH CONTEMPTUOUS EASE.
AND YET, SHE KNOWS THIS IS NOTHING COMPARED TO WHAT SHE FELT WITHIN THE GREAT M'KRANN CRYSTAL.
BIRD -- ENERGY CONSTRUCT -- IS DRAINING MY STRENGTH, MY VERY... LIFE-FORCE!
ONLY ONE CHANCE... MUST CHANNEL... ALL REMAINING POWER... INTO TELEPATHIC PSI-BOLT...
THE WHITE QUEEN STRIKES...
... WITH DEVASTATING EFFECT!
WHAT THE -- ?!
CYKE, THAT BUILDING IS WHERE 'RORO'S SCENT'S BEEN LEADIN' US!
I WAS HIT BY A FLASH OF PAIN FROM JEAN -- THROUGH THE MIND-LINK -- AN INSTANT BEFORE THE EXPLOSION. SHE MUST HAVE BEEN IN THERE WITH STORM! THE BLAST -- IT LEVELED THE ENTIRE BUILDING!
DAZZLER, KEEP KITTY BACK! THE REST OF YOU, GIVE ME A HAND!
JEAN CAN'T BE DEAD -- I'D FEEL IT! I'M CALLING YOU, LADY -- ANSWER ME! JEAN! JEAN!

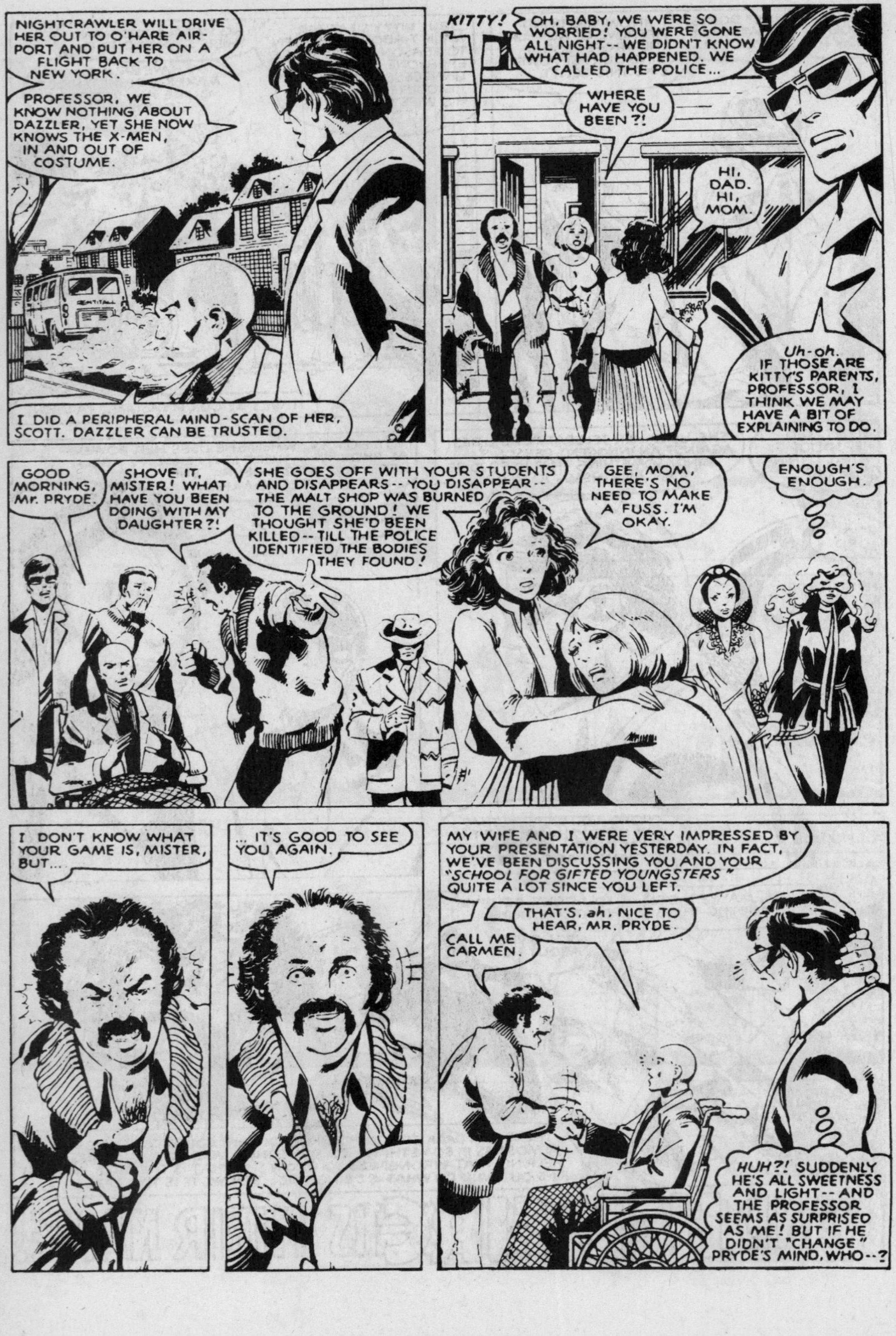

NIGHTCRAWLER WILL DRIVE HER OUT TO O'HARE AIRPORT AND PUT HER ON A FLIGHT BACK TO NEW YORK.
PROFESSOR, WE KNOW NOTHING ABOUT DAZZLER, YET SHE NOW KNOWS THE X-MEN, IN AND OUT OF COSTUME.
I DID A PERIPHERAL MIND-SCAN OF HER, SCOTT. DAZZLER CAN BE TRUSTED.
KITTY!
OH, BABY, WE WERE SO WORRIED! YOU WERE GONE ALL NIGHT-- WE DIDN'T KNOW WHAT HAD HAPPENED. WE CALLED THE POLICE...
WHERE HAVE YOU BEEN?!
HI, DAD. HI, MOM.
Uh-oh. IF THOSE ARE KITTY'S PARENTS, PROFESSOR, I THINK WE MAY HAVE A BIT OF EXPLAINING TO DO.
GOOD MORNING, Mr. PRYDE.
SHOVE IT, MISTER! WHAT HAVE YOU BEEN DOING WITH MY DAUGHTER?!
SHE GOES OFF WITH YOUR STUDENTS AND DISAPPEARS-- YOU DISAPPEAR-- THE MALT SHOP WAS BURNED TO THE GROUND! WE THOUGHT SHE'D BEEN KILLED-- TILL THE POLICE IDENTIFIED THE BODIES THEY FOUND!
GEE, MOM, THERE'S NO NEED TO MAKE A FUSS. I'M OKAY.
ENOUGH'S ENOUGH.
I DON'T KNOW WHAT YOUR GAME IS, MISTER, BUT...
...IT'S GOOD TO SEE YOU AGAIN.
MY WIFE AND I WERE VERY IMPRESSED BY YOUR PRESENTATION YESTERDAY. IN FACT, WE'VE BEEN DISCUSSING YOU AND YOUR "SCHOOL FOR GIFTED YOUNGSTERS" QUITE A LOT SINCE YOU LEFT.
THAT'S, ah, NICE TO HEAR, MR. PRYDE.
CALL ME CARMEN.
HUH?! SUDDENLY HE'S ALL SWEETNESS AND LIGHT-- AND THE PROFESSOR SEEMS AS SURPRISED AS ME! BUT IF HE DIDN'T "CHANGE" PRYDE'S MIND, WHO--?

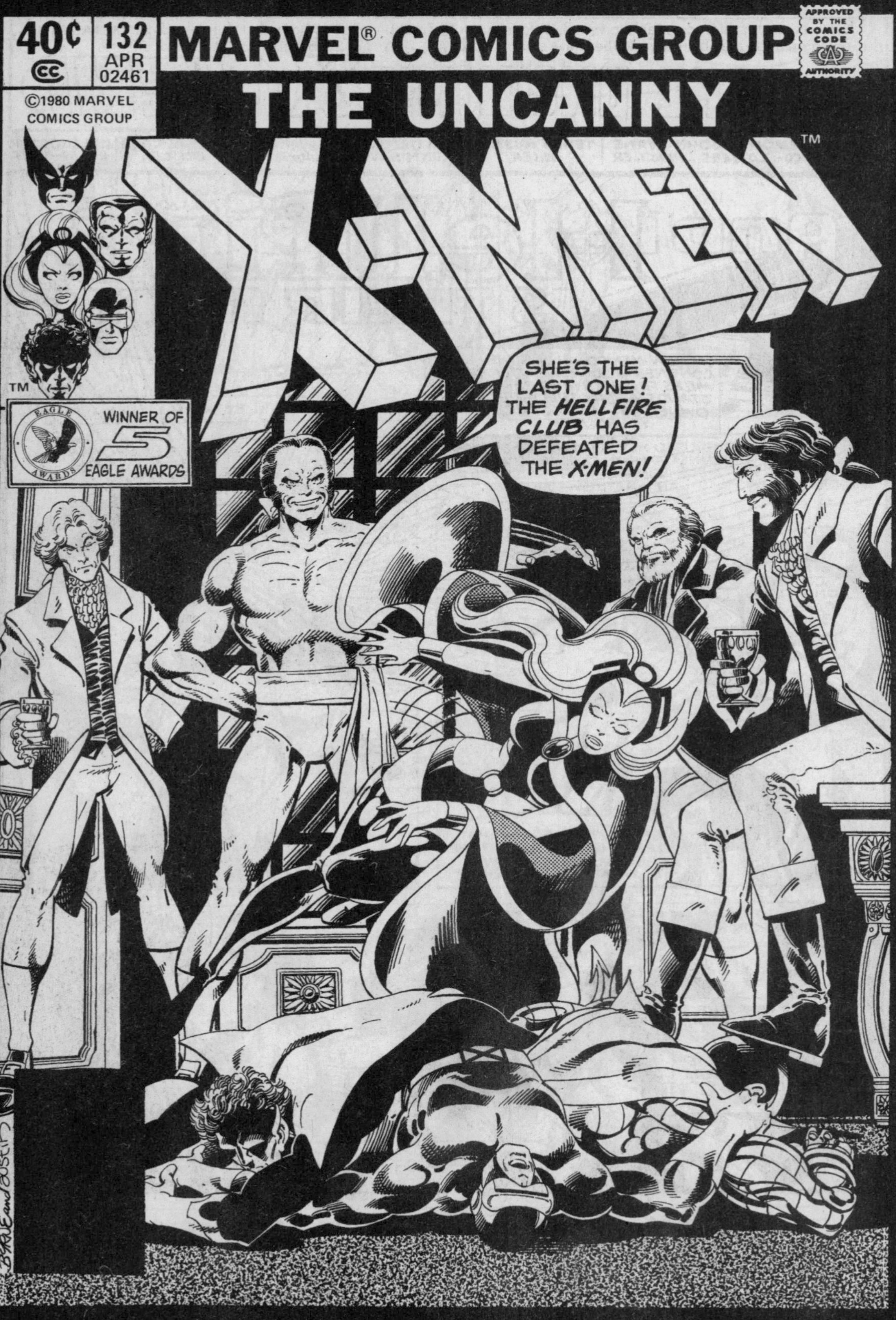
40¢
132
APR
02461
MARVEL® COMICS GROUP
APPROVED BY THE COMICS CODE AUTHORITY
©1980 MARVEL COMICS GROUP
THE UNCANNY
X-MEN™
WINNER OF 5 EAGLE AWARDS
SHE'S THE LAST ONE! THE HELLFIRE CLUB HAS DEFEATED THE X-MEN!
BYRNE and AUSTIN

Cyclops. Storm. Nightcrawler. Wolverine. Colossus. Children of the atom, students of Charles Xavier, MUTANTS — feared and hated by the world they have sworn to protect. These are the STRANGEST heroes of all!

Stan Lee PRESENTS: THE UNCANNY X-MEN!™

CHRIS CLAREMONT · JOHN BYRNE WRITER / CO-PLOTTERS / PENCILER | TERRY AUSTIN INKER | TOM ORZECHOWSKI, letterer GLYNIS WEIN, colorist | JIM SALICRUP EDITOR | JIM SHOOTER Ed.-IN-CHIEF

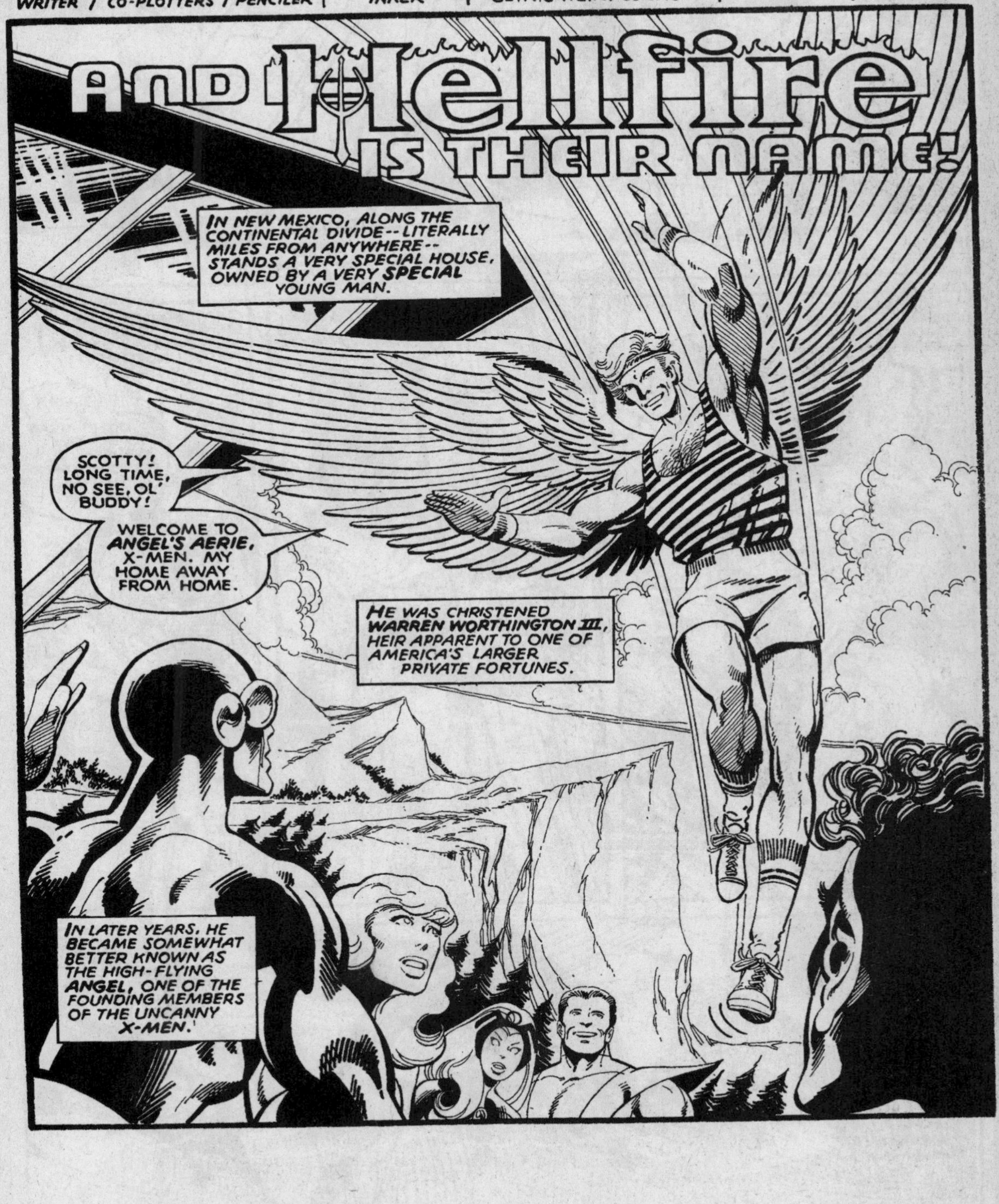
AND HELLFIRE IS THEIR NAME!
IN NEW MEXICO, ALONG THE CONTINENTAL DIVIDE--LITERALLY MILES FROM ANYWHERE--STANDS A VERY SPECIAL HOUSE, OWNED BY A VERY SPECIAL YOUNG MAN.
SCOTTY! LONG TIME, NO SEE, OL' BUDDY!
WELCOME TO ANGEL'S AERIE, X-MEN. MY HOME AWAY FROM HOME.
HE WAS CHRISTENED WARREN WORTHINGTON III, HEIR APPARENT TO ONE OF AMERICA'S LARGER PRIVATE FORTUNES.
IN LATER YEARS, HE BECAME SOMEWHAT BETTER KNOWN AS THE HIGH-FLYING ANGEL, ONE OF THE FOUNDING MEMBERS OF THE UNCANNY X-MEN.

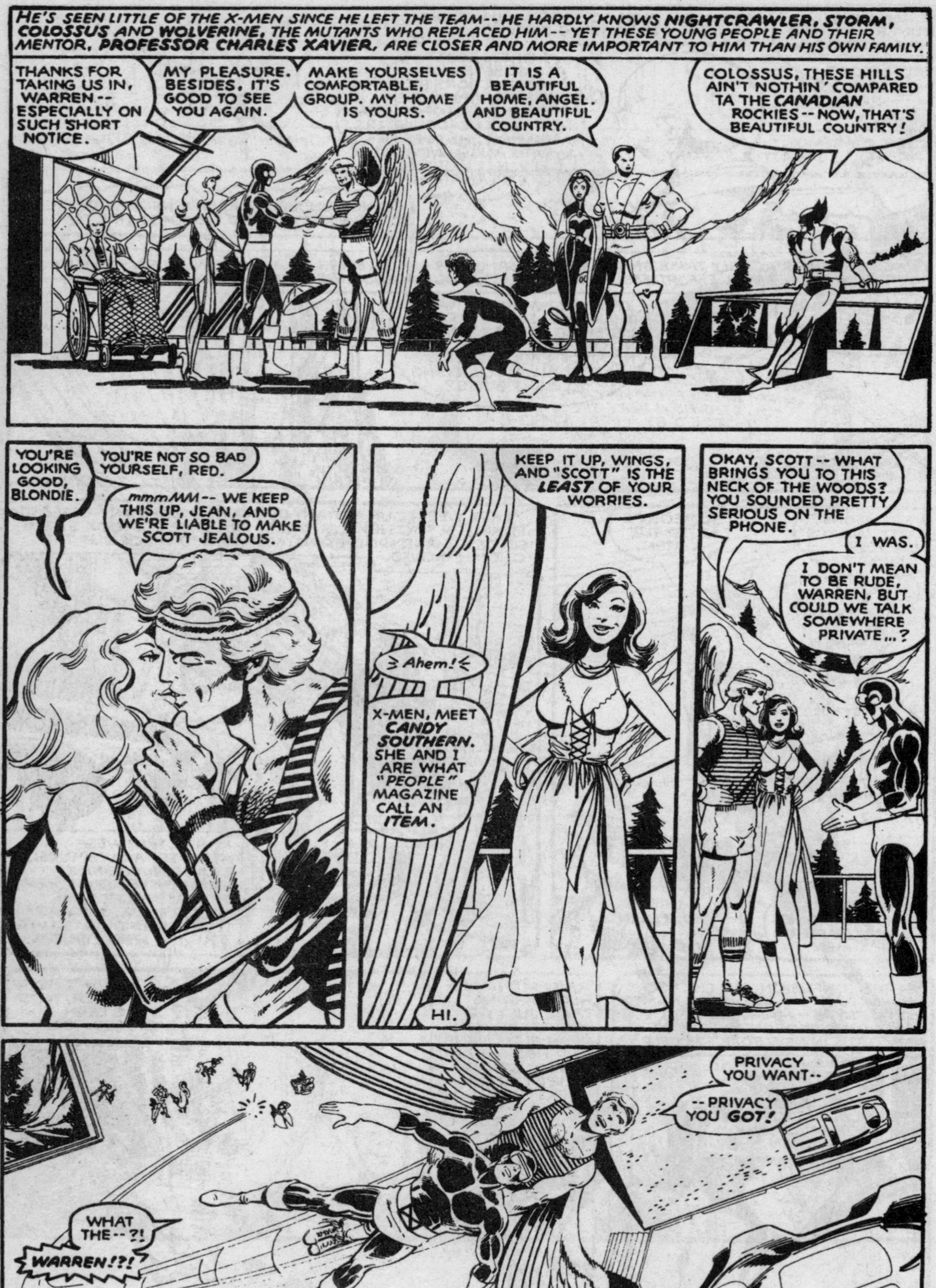
HE'S SEEN LITTLE OF THE X-MEN SINCE HE LEFT THE TEAM-- HE HARDLY KNOWS NIGHTCRAWLER, STORM, COLOSSUS AND WOLVERINE, THE MUTANTS WHO REPLACED HIM-- YET THESE YOUNG PEOPLE AND THEIR MENTOR, PROFESSOR CHARLES XAVIER, ARE CLOSER AND MORE IMPORTANT TO HIM THAN HIS OWN FAMILY.
THANKS FOR TAKING US IN, WARREN-- ESPECIALLY ON SUCH SHORT NOTICE.
MY PLEASURE. BESIDES, IT'S GOOD TO SEE YOU AGAIN.
MAKE YOURSELVES COMFORTABLE, GROUP. MY HOME IS YOURS.
IT IS A BEAUTIFUL HOME, ANGEL. AND BEAUTIFUL COUNTRY.
COLOSSUS, THESE HILLS AIN'T NOTHIN' COMPARED TA THE CANADIAN ROCKIES -- NOW, THAT'S BEAUTIFUL COUNTRY!
YOU'RE LOOKING GOOD, BLONDIE.
YOU'RE NOT SO BAD YOURSELF, RED.
mmmMM -- WE KEEP THIS UP, JEAN, AND WE'RE LIABLE TO MAKE SCOTT JEALOUS.
KEEP IT UP, WINGS, AND "SCOTT" IS THE LEAST OF YOUR WORRIES.
Ahem!
X-MEN, MEET CANDY SOUTHERN. SHE AND I ARE WHAT "PEOPLE" MAGAZINE CALL AN ITEM.
HI.
OKAY, SCOTT -- WHAT BRINGS YOU TO THIS NECK OF THE WOODS? YOU SOUNDED PRETTY SERIOUS ON THE PHONE.
I WAS.
I DON'T MEAN TO BE RUDE, WARREN, BUT COULD WE TALK SOMEWHERE PRIVATE...?
PRIVACY YOU WANT--
--PRIVACY YOU GOT!
WHAT THE--?!
WARREN!?!

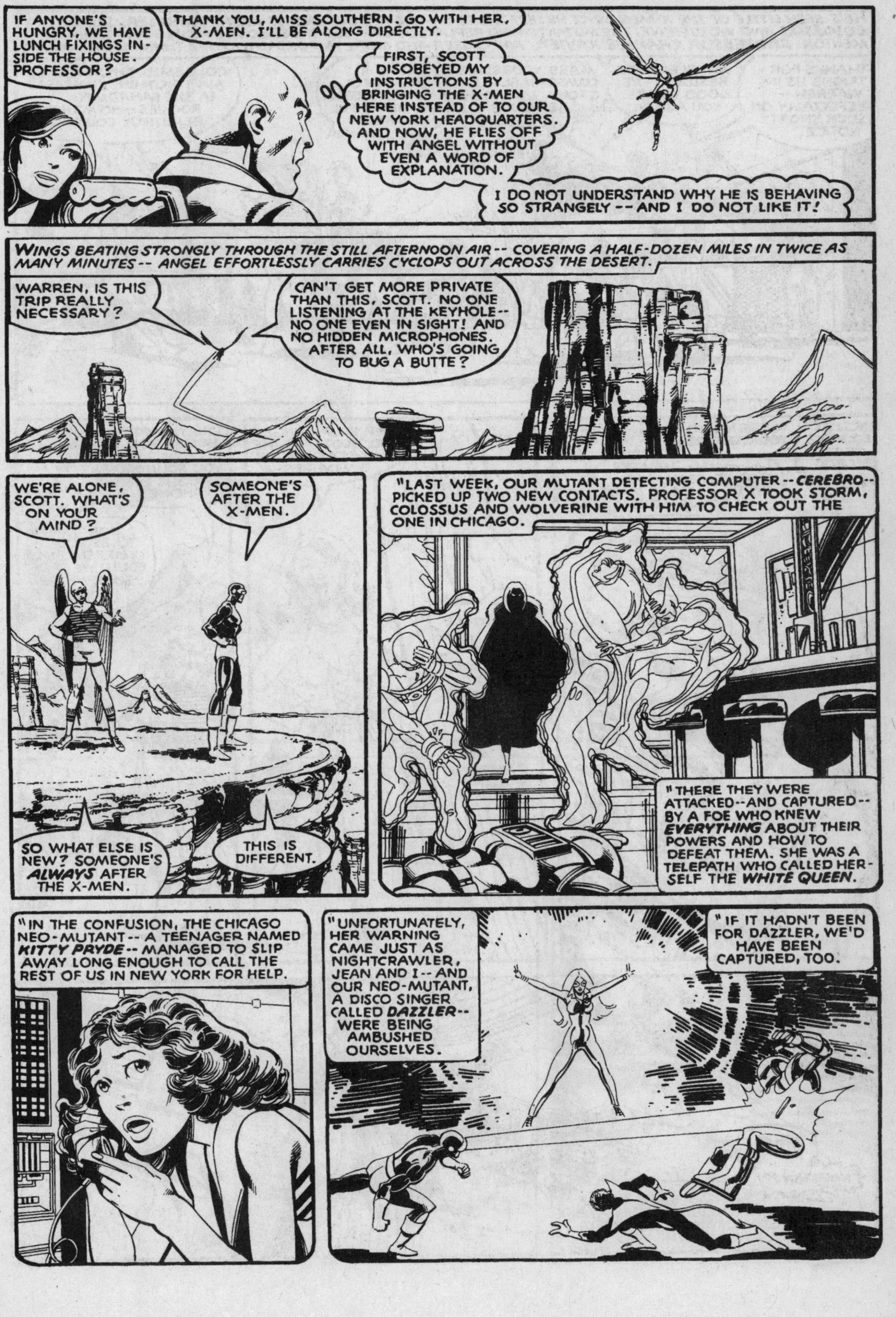
IF ANYONE'S HUNGRY, WE HAVE LUNCH FIXINGS INSIDE THE HOUSE. PROFESSOR?
THANK YOU, MISS SOUTHERN. GO WITH HER, X-MEN. I'LL BE ALONG DIRECTLY.
FIRST, SCOTT DISOBEYED MY INSTRUCTIONS BY BRINGING THE X-MEN HERE INSTEAD OF TO OUR NEW YORK HEADQUARTERS. AND NOW, HE FLIES OFF WITH ANGEL WITHOUT EVEN A WORD OF EXPLANATION.
I DO NOT UNDERSTAND WHY HE IS BEHAVING SO STRANGELY -- AND I DO NOT LIKE IT!
WINGS BEATING STRONGLY THROUGH THE STILL AFTERNOON AIR -- COVERING A HALF-DOZEN MILES IN TWICE AS MANY MINUTES -- ANGEL EFFORTLESSLY CARRIES CYCLOPS OUT ACROSS THE DESERT.
WARREN, IS THIS TRIP REALLY NECESSARY?
CAN'T GET MORE PRIVATE THAN THIS, SCOTT. NO ONE LISTENING AT THE KEYHOLE-- NO ONE EVEN IN SIGHT! AND NO HIDDEN MICROPHONES. AFTER ALL, WHO'S GOING TO BUG A BUTTE?
WE'RE ALONE, SCOTT. WHAT'S ON YOUR MIND?
SOMEONE'S AFTER THE X-MEN.
SO WHAT ELSE IS NEW? SOMEONE'S ALWAYS AFTER THE X-MEN.
THIS IS DIFFERENT.
"LAST WEEK, OUR MUTANT DETECTING COMPUTER -- CEREBRO -- PICKED UP TWO NEW CONTACTS. PROFESSOR X TOOK STORM, COLOSSUS AND WOLVERINE WITH HIM TO CHECK OUT THE ONE IN CHICAGO.
"THERE THEY WERE ATTACKED--AND CAPTURED-- BY A FOE WHO KNEW EVERYTHING ABOUT THEIR POWERS AND HOW TO DEFEAT THEM. SHE WAS A TELEPATH WHO CALLED HERSELF THE WHITE QUEEN.
"IN THE CONFUSION, THE CHICAGO NEO-MUTANT -- A TEENAGER NAMED KITTY PRYDE -- MANAGED TO SLIP AWAY LONG ENOUGH TO CALL THE REST OF US IN NEW YORK FOR HELP.
"UNFORTUNATELY, HER WARNING CAME JUST AS NIGHTCRAWLER, JEAN AND I -- AND OUR NEO-MUTANT, A DISCO SINGER CALLED DAZZLER -- WERE BEING AMBUSHED OURSELVES.
"IF IT HADN'T BEEN FOR DAZZLER, WE'D HAVE BEEN CAPTURED, TOO.

"WE HEADED FOR CHICAGO AND -- WITH KITTY AND DAZZLER'S AID-- RESCUED THE OTHERS.

PHOENIX MIND-SCANNED A GUARD AND WE LEARNED THAT THE WHITE QUEEN BELONGED TO A GROUP OF INDUSTRIAL-ISTS OUT TO RULE THE WORLD. THEY SEE MUTANT-KIND -- AND THE X-MEN-- AS A MEANS TO ACHIEVING THAT GOAL.

"JEAN-- *PHOENIX*-- FOUGHT THE WHITE QUEEN IN A PSYCHIC DUEL. I WANTED THE WOMAN TAKEN ALIVE, FOR QUESTIONING. BUT, IN THE END, SHE PREFERRED SUICIDE TO CAPTURE." *

*A VERY ABBREVIATED RECAP OF THE EVENTS OF X-MEN #129-131-- JIM.

THEY CALL THEMSELVES THE *HELLFIRE CLUB.*

ARE YOU SURE?! I'M A *MEMBER* OF THE HELLFIRE CLUB. SO'S CANDY.

I INHERITED THE MEMBERSHIP, ALONG WITH WORTHINGTON INDUSTRIES, WHEN MY FOLKS PASSED AWAY. IT'S AN OLD, VERY STUFFY-- YET RISQUE-- ESTABLISHMENT CLUB.

CANDY AND I VISITED IT ONCE...

...BEFORE I TOLD THE WORLD I WAS THE ANGEL. WE DIDN'T LIKE IT. WE NEVER WENT BACK.

WHATEVER YOUR WHITE QUEEN LEARNED ABOUT THE X-MEN, IT WASN'T FROM ME.

THERE HAS TO BE A LEAK SOMEWHERE. WARREN, THESE PEOPLE KNEW OUR POWERS, OUR PLANS, THE WAY WE FIGHT-- THE WAY WE THINK!

THAT'S WHY I BROUGHT THE X-MEN HERE INSTEAD OF HOME-- PARTLY TO THROW OUR FOES OFF-BALANCE AND BUY US SOME BREATHING SPACE, PARTLY BECAUSE I DON'T THINK THE MANSION'S SAFE ANYMORE.

AND, AS IF THAT WASN'T ENOUGH TO WORRY ABOUT, SOME-THING ODD HAS BEEN HAPPENING TO JEAN LATELY...

SOMEONE MENTION MY NAME?

YOU FELLAS HAVE BEEN TALKING FOR HOURS. TIME FOR A BREAK.

WHA--? *JEAN!*

NICE ENTRANCE, RED.

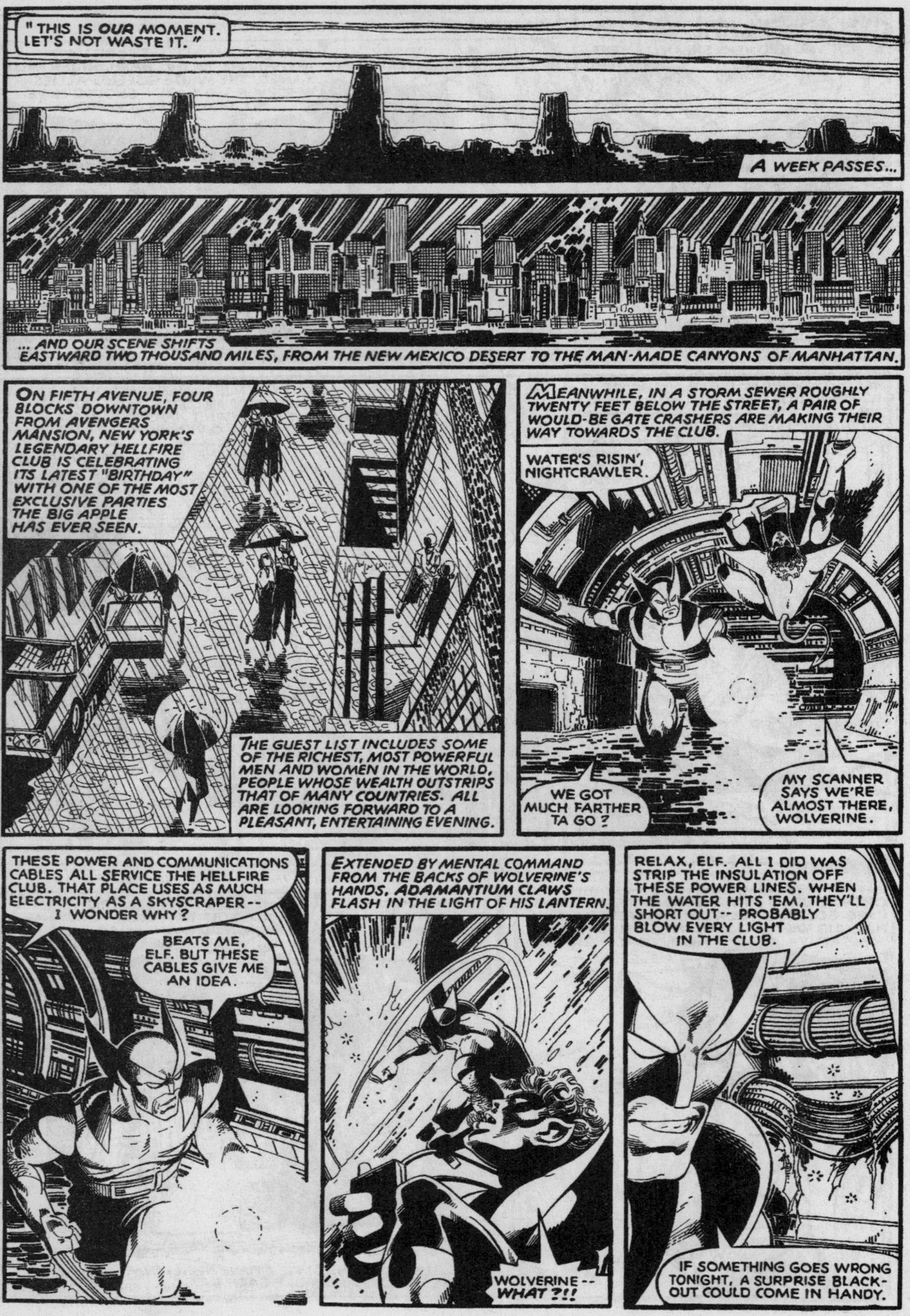

"THIS IS OUR MOMENT. LET'S NOT WASTE IT."
A WEEK PASSES...
... AND OUR SCENE SHIFTS EASTWARD TWO THOUSAND MILES, FROM THE NEW MEXICO DESERT TO THE MAN-MADE CANYONS OF MANHATTAN.
ON FIFTH AVENUE, FOUR BLOCKS DOWNTOWN FROM AVENGERS MANSION, NEW YORK'S LEGENDARY HELLFIRE CLUB IS CELEBRATING ITS LATEST "BIRTHDAY" WITH ONE OF THE MOST EXCLUSIVE PARTIES THE BIG APPLE HAS EVER SEEN.
THE GUEST LIST INCLUDES SOME OF THE RICHEST, MOST POWERFUL MEN AND WOMEN IN THE WORLD, PEOPLE WHOSE WEALTH OUTSTRIPS THAT OF MANY COUNTRIES. ALL ARE LOOKING FORWARD TO A PLEASANT, ENTERTAINING EVENING.
MEANWHILE, IN A STORM SEWER ROUGHLY TWENTY FEET BELOW THE STREET, A PAIR OF WOULD-BE GATE CRASHERS ARE MAKING THEIR WAY TOWARDS THE CLUB.
WATER'S RISIN', NIGHTCRAWLER.
WE GOT MUCH FARTHER TA GO?
MY SCANNER SAYS WE'RE ALMOST THERE, WOLVERINE.
THESE POWER AND COMMUNICATIONS CABLES ALL SERVICE THE HELLFIRE CLUB. THAT PLACE USES AS MUCH ELECTRICITY AS A SKYSCRAPER -- I WONDER WHY?
BEATS ME, ELF. BUT THESE CABLES GIVE ME AN IDEA.
EXTENDED BY MENTAL COMMAND FROM THE BACKS OF WOLVERINE'S HANDS, ADAMANTIUM CLAWS FLASH IN THE LIGHT OF HIS LANTERN.
WOLVERINE -- WHAT?!!
RELAX, ELF. ALL I DID WAS STRIP THE INSULATION OFF THESE POWER LINES. WHEN THE WATER HITS 'EM, THEY'LL SHORT OUT -- PROBABLY BLOW EVERY LIGHT IN THE CLUB.
IF SOMETHING GOES WRONG TONIGHT, A SURPRISE BLACK-OUT COULD COME IN HANDY.

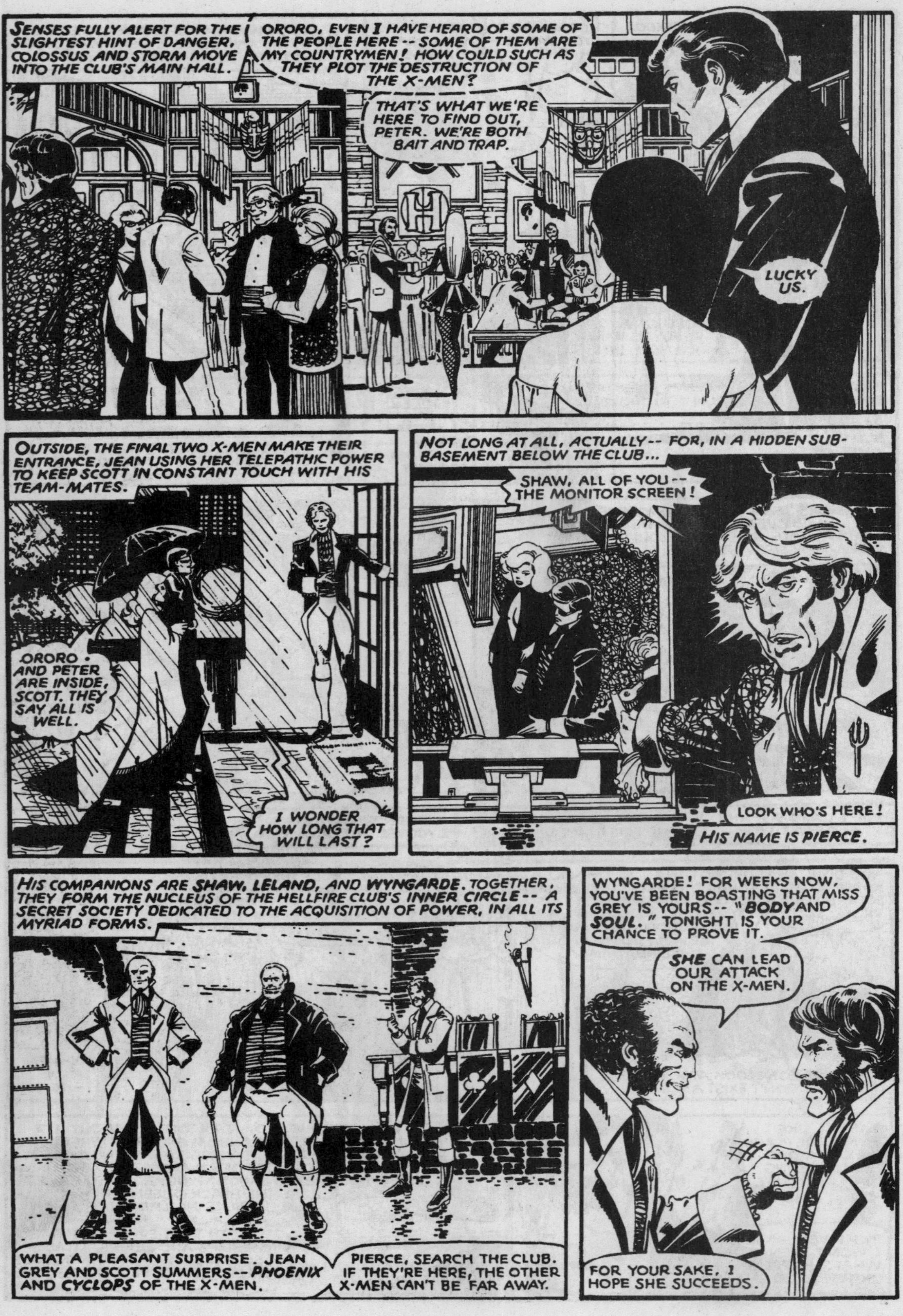

SENSES FULLY ALERT FOR THE SLIGHTEST HINT OF DANGER, COLOSSUS AND STORM MOVE INTO THE CLUB'S MAIN HALL.
ORORO, EVEN I HAVE HEARD OF SOME OF THE PEOPLE HERE -- SOME OF THEM ARE MY COUNTRYMEN! HOW COULD SUCH AS THEY PLOT THE DESTRUCTION OF THE X-MEN?
THAT'S WHAT WE'RE HERE TO FIND OUT, PETER. WE'RE BOTH BAIT AND TRAP.
LUCKY US.
OUTSIDE, THE FINAL TWO X-MEN MAKE THEIR ENTRANCE, JEAN USING HER TELEPATHIC POWER TO KEEP SCOTT IN CONSTANT TOUCH WITH HIS TEAM-MATES.
ORORO AND PETER ARE INSIDE, SCOTT. THEY SAY ALL IS WELL.
I WONDER HOW LONG THAT WILL LAST?
NOT LONG AT ALL, ACTUALLY -- FOR, IN A HIDDEN SUB-BASEMENT BELOW THE CLUB...
SHAW, ALL OF YOU -- THE MONITOR SCREEN!
LOOK WHO'S HERE!
HIS NAME IS PIERCE.
HIS COMPANIONS ARE SHAW, LELAND, AND WYNGARDE. TOGETHER, THEY FORM THE NUCLEUS OF THE HELLFIRE CLUB'S INNER CIRCLE -- A SECRET SOCIETY DEDICATED TO THE ACQUISITION OF POWER, IN ALL ITS MYRIAD FORMS.
WHAT A PLEASANT SURPRISE. JEAN GREY AND SCOTT SUMMERS -- PHOENIX AND CYCLOPS OF THE X-MEN.
PIERCE, SEARCH THE CLUB. IF THEY'RE HERE, THE OTHER X-MEN CAN'T BE FAR AWAY.
WYNGARDE! FOR WEEKS NOW, YOU'VE BEEN BOASTING THAT MISS GREY IS YOURS -- "BODY AND SOUL." TONIGHT IS YOUR CHANCE TO PROVE IT.
SHE CAN LEAD OUR ATTACK ON THE X-MEN.
FOR YOUR SAKE, I HOPE SHE SUCCEEDS.

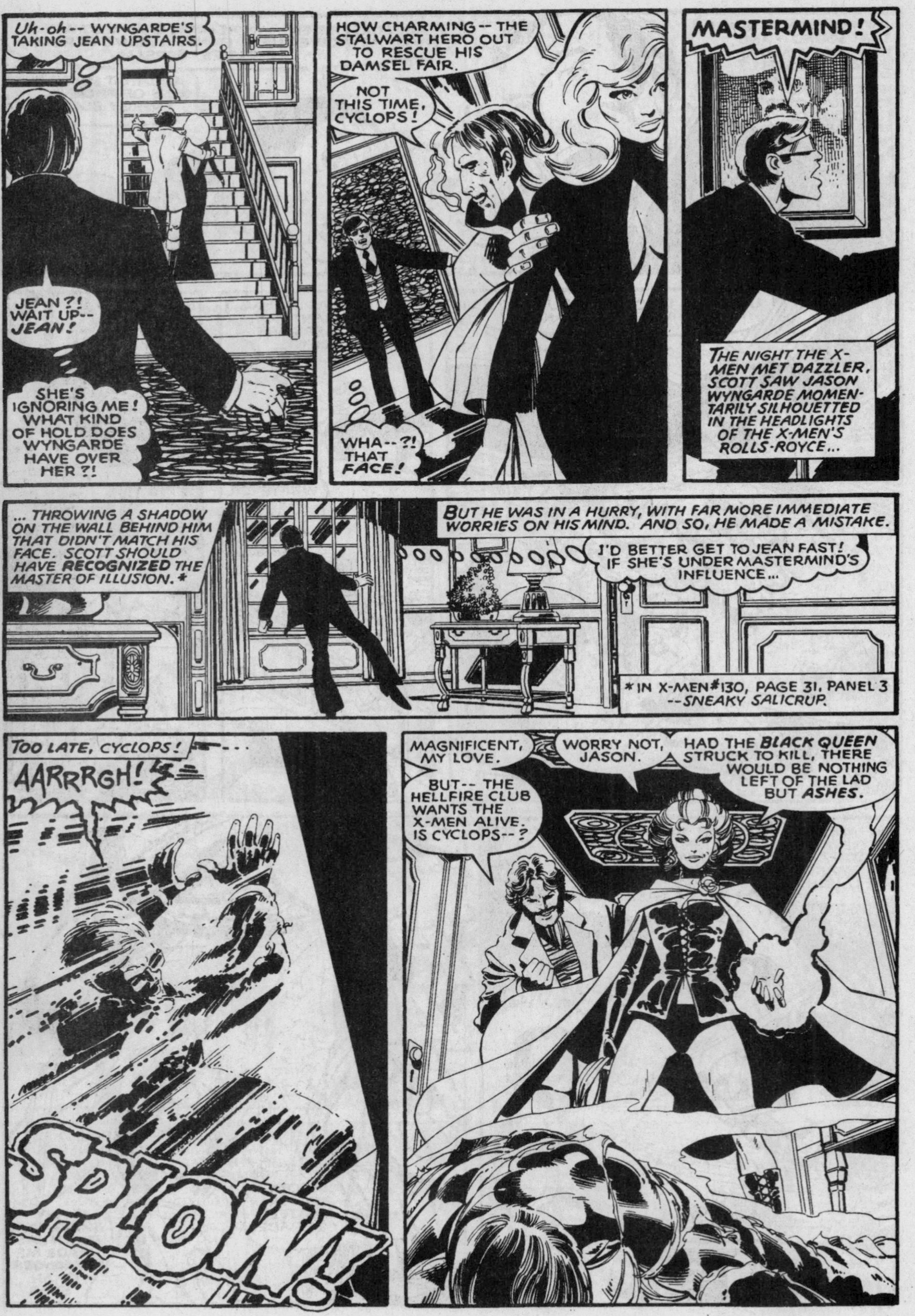
Uh-oh -- WYNGARDE'S TAKING JEAN UPSTAIRS.
JEAN?! WAIT UP-- JEAN!
SHE'S IGNORING ME! WHAT KIND OF HOLD DOES WYNGARDE HAVE OVER HER?!
HOW CHARMING -- THE STALWART HERO OUT TO RESCUE HIS DAMSEL FAIR.
NOT THIS TIME, CYCLOPS!
WHA--?! THAT FACE!
MASTERMIND!
THE NIGHT THE X-MEN MET DAZZLER, SCOTT SAW JASON WYNGARDE MOMENTARILY SILHOUETTED IN THE HEADLIGHTS OF THE X-MEN'S ROLLS-ROYCE...
... THROWING A SHADOW ON THE WALL BEHIND HIM THAT DIDN'T MATCH HIS FACE. SCOTT SHOULD HAVE RECOGNIZED THE MASTER OF ILLUSION.*
BUT HE WAS IN A HURRY, WITH FAR MORE IMMEDIATE WORRIES ON HIS MIND. AND SO, HE MADE A MISTAKE.
I'D BETTER GET TO JEAN FAST! IF SHE'S UNDER MASTERMIND'S INFLUENCE...
*IN X-MEN #130, PAGE 31, PANEL 3 --SNEAKY SALICRUP.
TOO LATE, CYCLOPS!
AARRRGH!
SPLOW!
MAGNIFICENT, MY LOVE.
BUT-- THE HELLFIRE CLUB WANTS THE X-MEN ALIVE. IS CYCLOPS--?
WORRY NOT, JASON.
HAD THE BLACK QUEEN STRUCK TO KILL, THERE WOULD BE NOTHING LEFT OF THE LAD BUT ASHES.

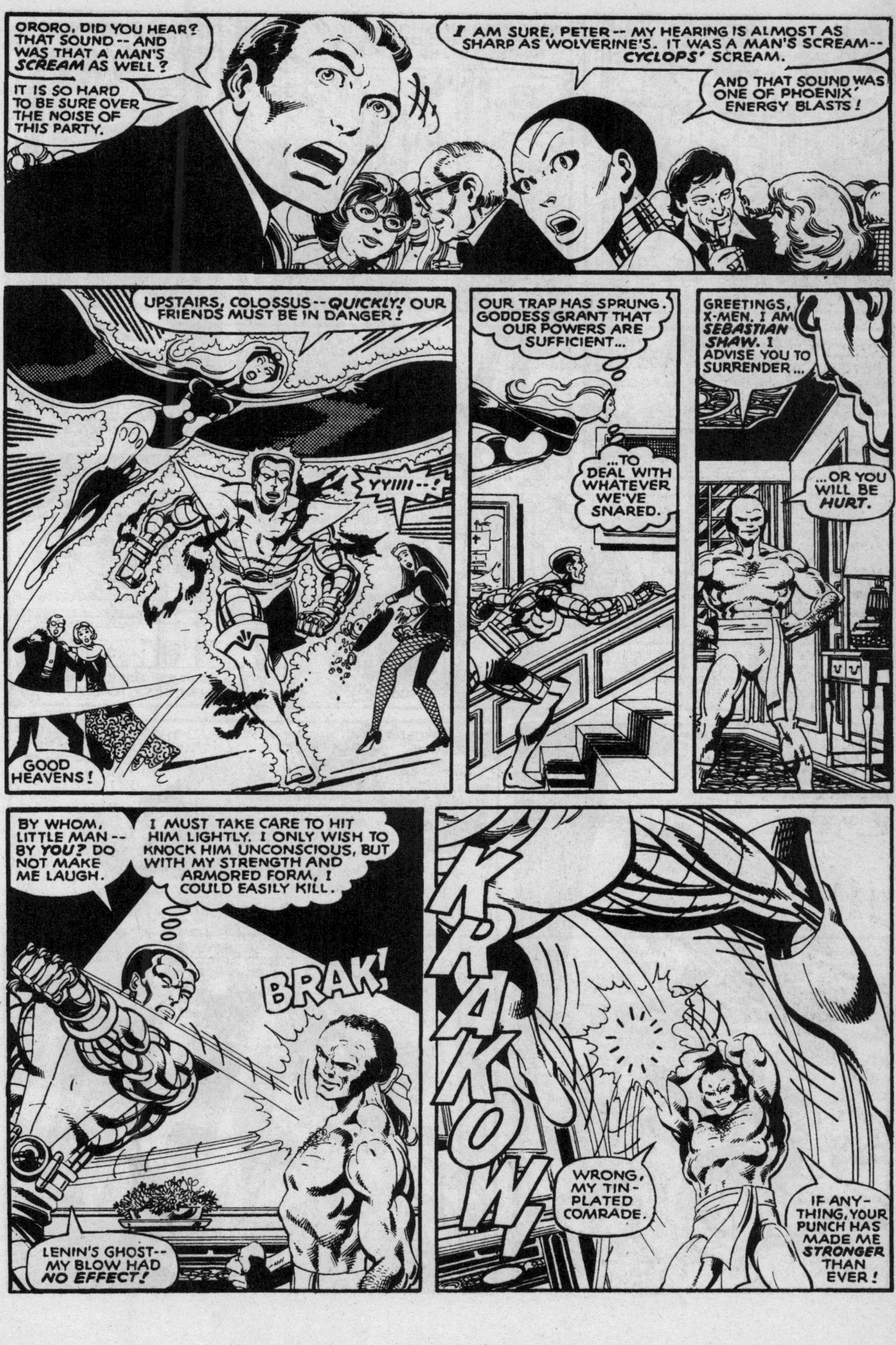
ORORO, DID YOU HEAR? THAT SOUND -- AND WAS THAT A MAN'S SCREAM AS WELL?
IT IS SO HARD TO BE SURE OVER THE NOISE OF THIS PARTY.
I AM SURE, PETER -- MY HEARING IS ALMOST AS SHARP AS WOLVERINE'S. IT WAS A MAN'S SCREAM -- CYCLOPS' SCREAM.
AND THAT SOUND WAS ONE OF PHOENIX' ENERGY BLASTS!
UPSTAIRS, COLOSSUS -- QUICKLY! OUR FRIENDS MUST BE IN DANGER!
YYIIII--!
GOOD HEAVENS!
OUR TRAP HAS SPRUNG. GODDESS GRANT THAT OUR POWERS ARE SUFFICIENT...
...TO DEAL WITH WHATEVER WE'VE SNARED.
GREETINGS, X-MEN. I AM SEBASTIAN SHAW. I ADVISE YOU TO SURRENDER...
...OR YOU WILL BE HURT.
BY WHOM, LITTLE MAN -- BY YOU? DO NOT MAKE ME LAUGH.
I MUST TAKE CARE TO HIT HIM LIGHTLY. I ONLY WISH TO KNOCK HIM UNCONSCIOUS, BUT WITH MY STRENGTH AND ARMORED FORM, I COULD EASILY KILL.
BRAK!
LENIN'S GHOST-- MY BLOW HAD NO EFFECT!
KRAKOW!
WRONG, MY TIN-PLATED COMRADE.
IF ANY-THING, YOUR PUNCH HAS MADE ME STRONGER THAN EVER!

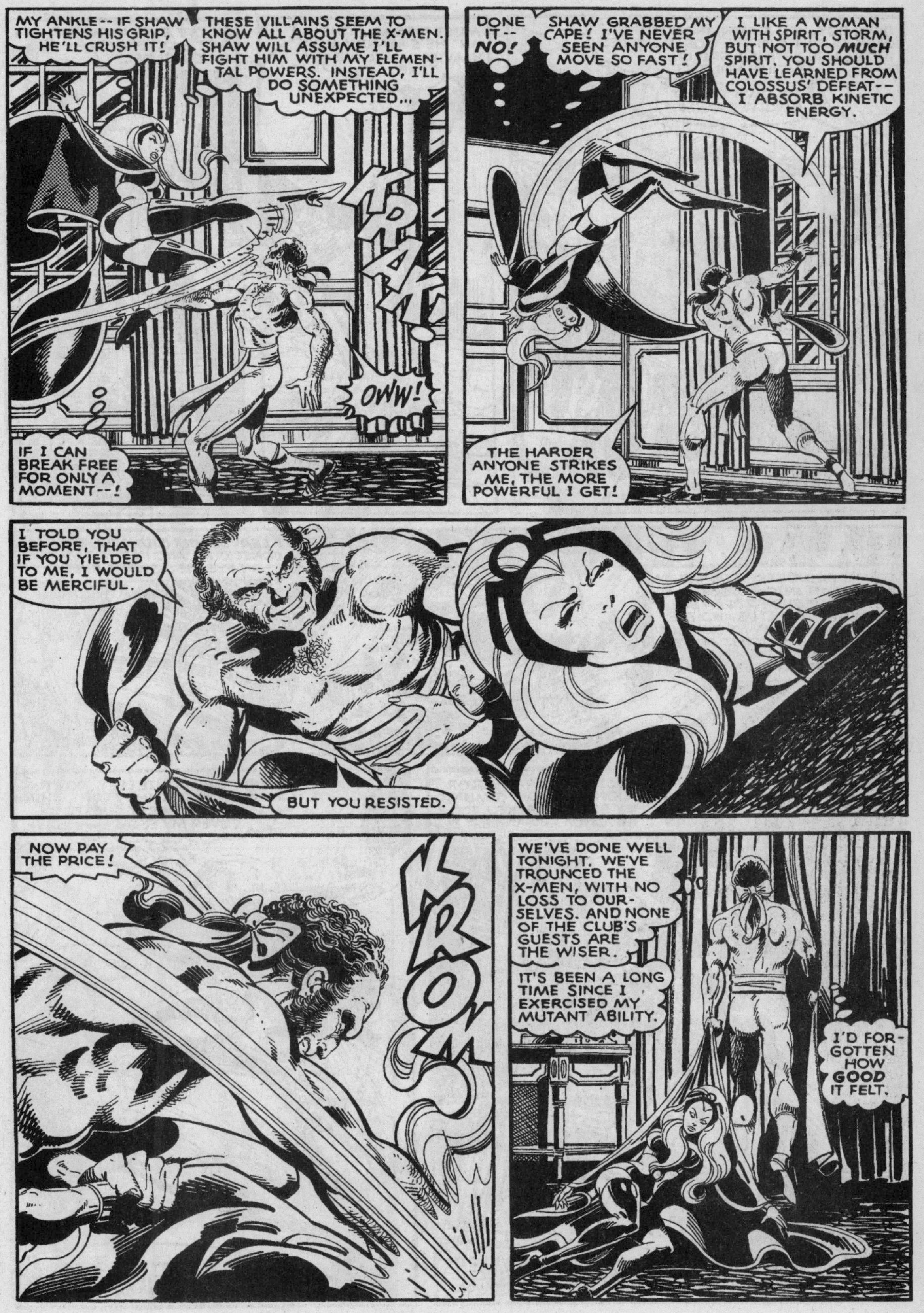
MY ANKLE-- IF SHAW TIGHTENS HIS GRIP, HE'LL CRUSH IT!
THESE VILLAINS SEEM TO KNOW ALL ABOUT THE X-MEN. SHAW WILL ASSUME I'LL FIGHT HIM WITH MY ELEMENTAL POWERS. INSTEAD, I'LL DO SOMETHING UNEXPECTED...
KRAK!
OWW!
IF I CAN BREAK FREE FOR ONLY A MOMENT--!
DONE IT-- NO!
SHAW GRABBED MY CAPE! I'VE NEVER SEEN ANYONE MOVE SO FAST!
I LIKE A WOMAN WITH SPIRIT, STORM, BUT NOT TOO MUCH SPIRIT. YOU SHOULD HAVE LEARNED FROM COLOSSUS' DEFEAT-- I ABSORB KINETIC ENERGY.
THE HARDER ANYONE STRIKES ME, THE MORE POWERFUL I GET!
I TOLD YOU BEFORE, THAT IF YOU YIELDED TO ME, I WOULD BE MERCIFUL.
BUT YOU RESISTED.
NOW PAY THE PRICE!
KROOM
WE'VE DONE WELL TONIGHT. WE'VE TROUNCED THE X-MEN, WITH NO LOSS TO OURSELVES. AND NONE OF THE CLUB'S GUESTS ARE THE WISER.
IT'S BEEN A LONG TIME SINCE I EXERCISED MY MUTANT ABILITY.
I'D FORGOTTEN HOW GOOD IT FELT.

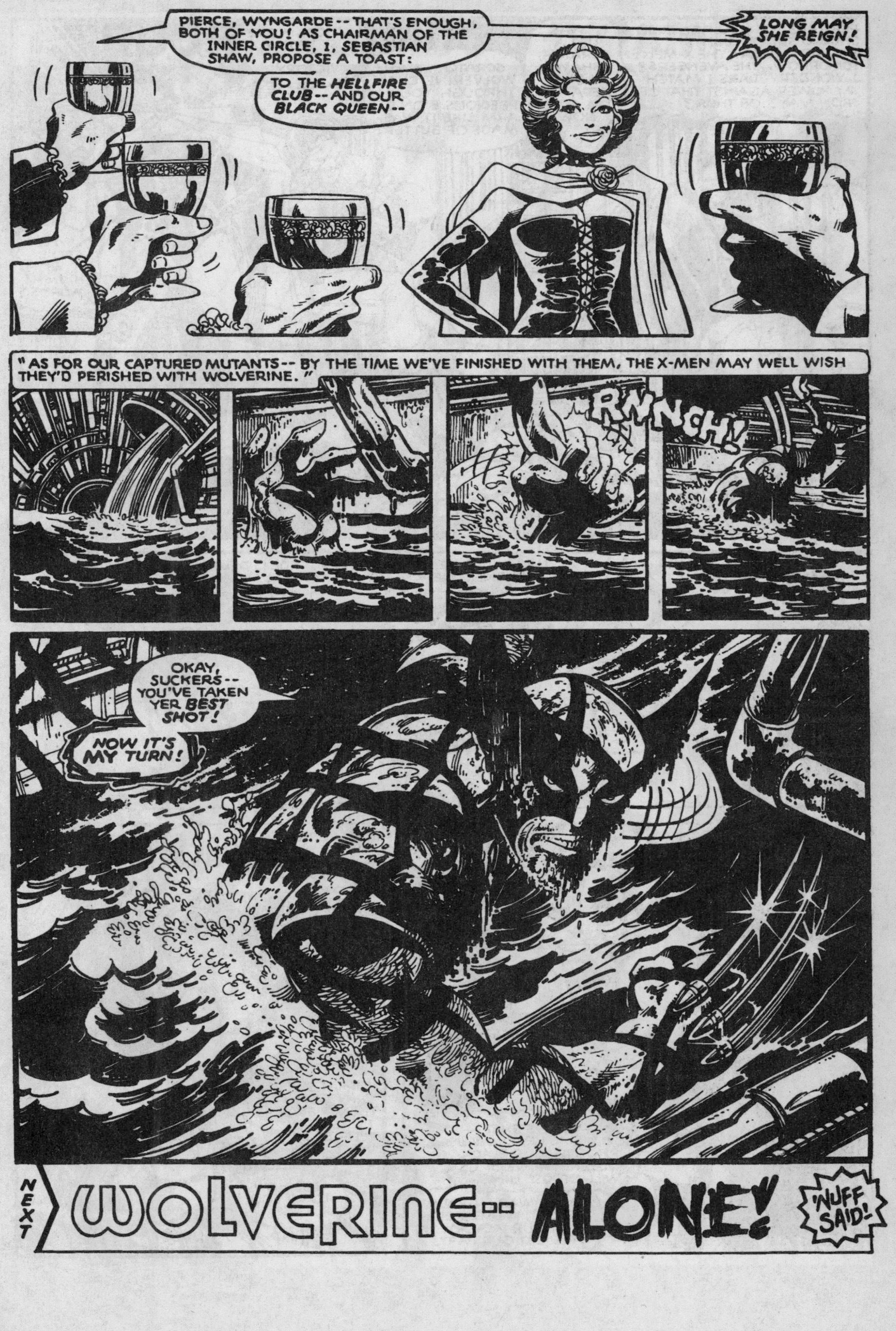
PIERCE, WYNGARDE -- THAT'S ENOUGH, BOTH OF YOU! AS CHAIRMAN OF THE INNER CIRCLE, I, SEBASTIAN SHAW, PROPOSE A TOAST:
TO THE HELLFIRE CLUB -- AND OUR BLACK QUEEN --
LONG MAY SHE REIGN!
"AS FOR OUR CAPTURED MUTANTS -- BY THE TIME WE'VE FINISHED WITH THEM, THE X-MEN MAY WELL WISH THEY'D PERISHED WITH WOLVERINE."
RNNCH!
OKAY, SUCKERS -- YOU'VE TAKEN YER BEST SHOT!
NOW IT'S MY TURN!
NEXT
WOLVERINE -- ALONE!
'NUFF SAID!

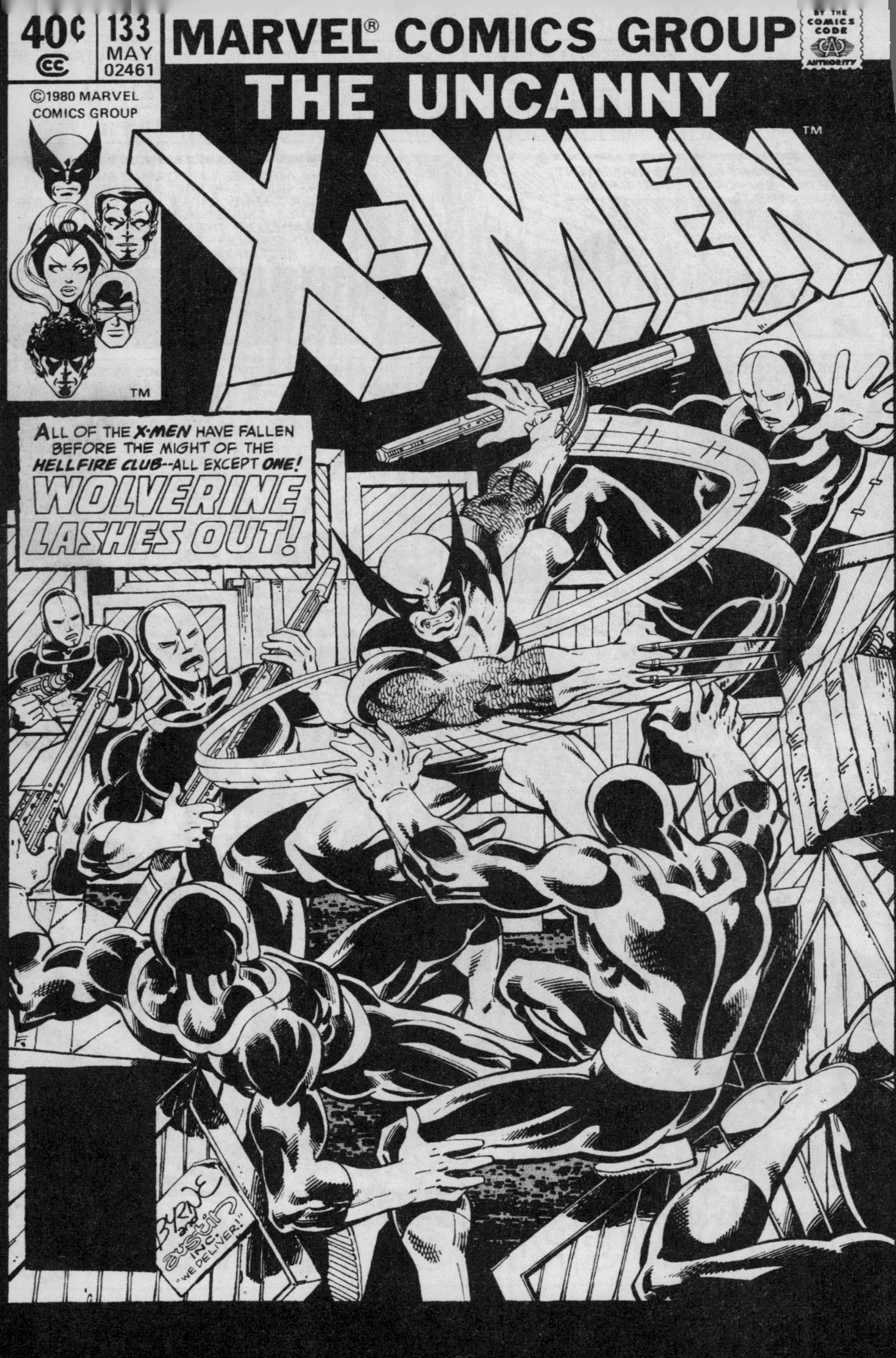

40¢
133
MAY
02461
MARVEL® COMICS GROUP
BY THE COMICS CODE AUTHORITY
THE UNCANNY
X-MEN™
©1980 MARVEL COMICS GROUP
ALL OF THE X-MEN HAVE FALLEN BEFORE THE MIGHT OF THE HELLFIRE CLUB--ALL EXCEPT ONE!
WOLVERINE LASHES OUT!
BYRNE and AUSTIN INC. "WE DELIVER!"

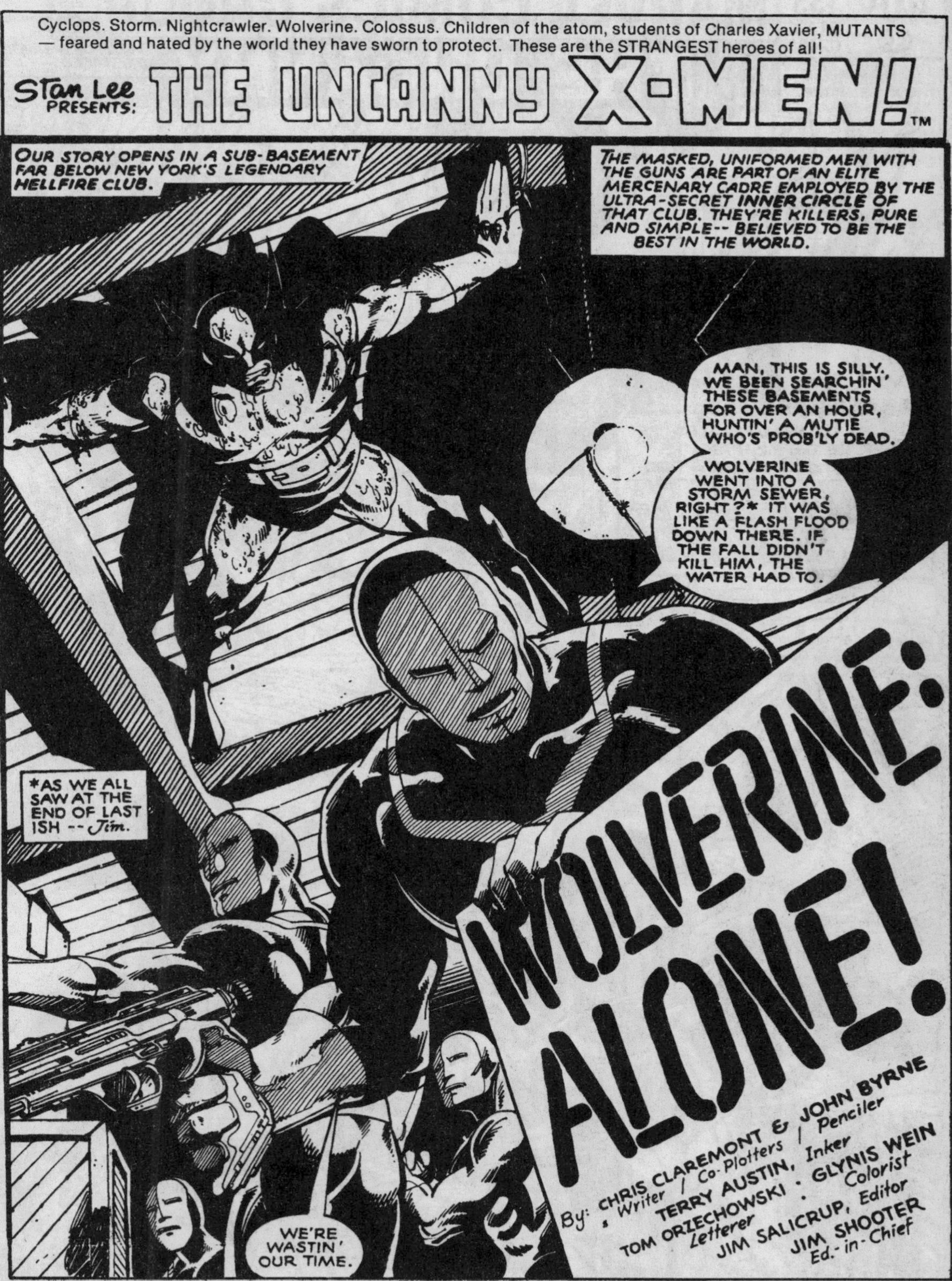
Cyclops. Storm. Nightcrawler. Wolverine. Colossus. Children of the atom, students of Charles Xavier, MUTANTS — feared and hated by the world they have sworn to protect. These are the STRANGEST heroes of all!
Stan Lee PRESENTS: THE UNCANNY X-MEN! TM
OUR STORY OPENS IN A SUB-BASEMENT FAR BELOW NEW YORK'S LEGENDARY HELLFIRE CLUB.
THE MASKED, UNIFORMED MEN WITH THE GUNS ARE PART OF AN ELITE MERCENARY CADRE EMPLOYED BY THE ULTRA-SECRET INNER CIRCLE OF THAT CLUB. THEY'RE KILLERS, PURE AND SIMPLE-- BELIEVED TO BE THE BEST IN THE WORLD.
MAN, THIS IS SILLY. WE BEEN SEARCHIN' THESE BASEMENTS FOR OVER AN HOUR, HUNTIN' A MUTIE WHO'S PROB'LY DEAD.
WOLVERINE WENT INTO A STORM SEWER, RIGHT?* IT WAS LIKE A FLASH FLOOD DOWN THERE. IF THE FALL DIDN'T KILL HIM, THE WATER HAD TO.
*AS WE ALL SAW AT THE END OF LAST ISH -- Jim.
WOLVERINE: ALONE!
By: CHRIS CLAREMONT & JOHN BYRNE
Writer / Co-Plotters / Penciler
TERRY AUSTIN, Inker
TOM ORZECHOWSKI · GLYNIS WEIN
Letterer · Colorist
JIM SALICRUP, Editor
JIM SHOOTER Ed.-in-Chief
WE'RE WASTIN' OUR TIME.

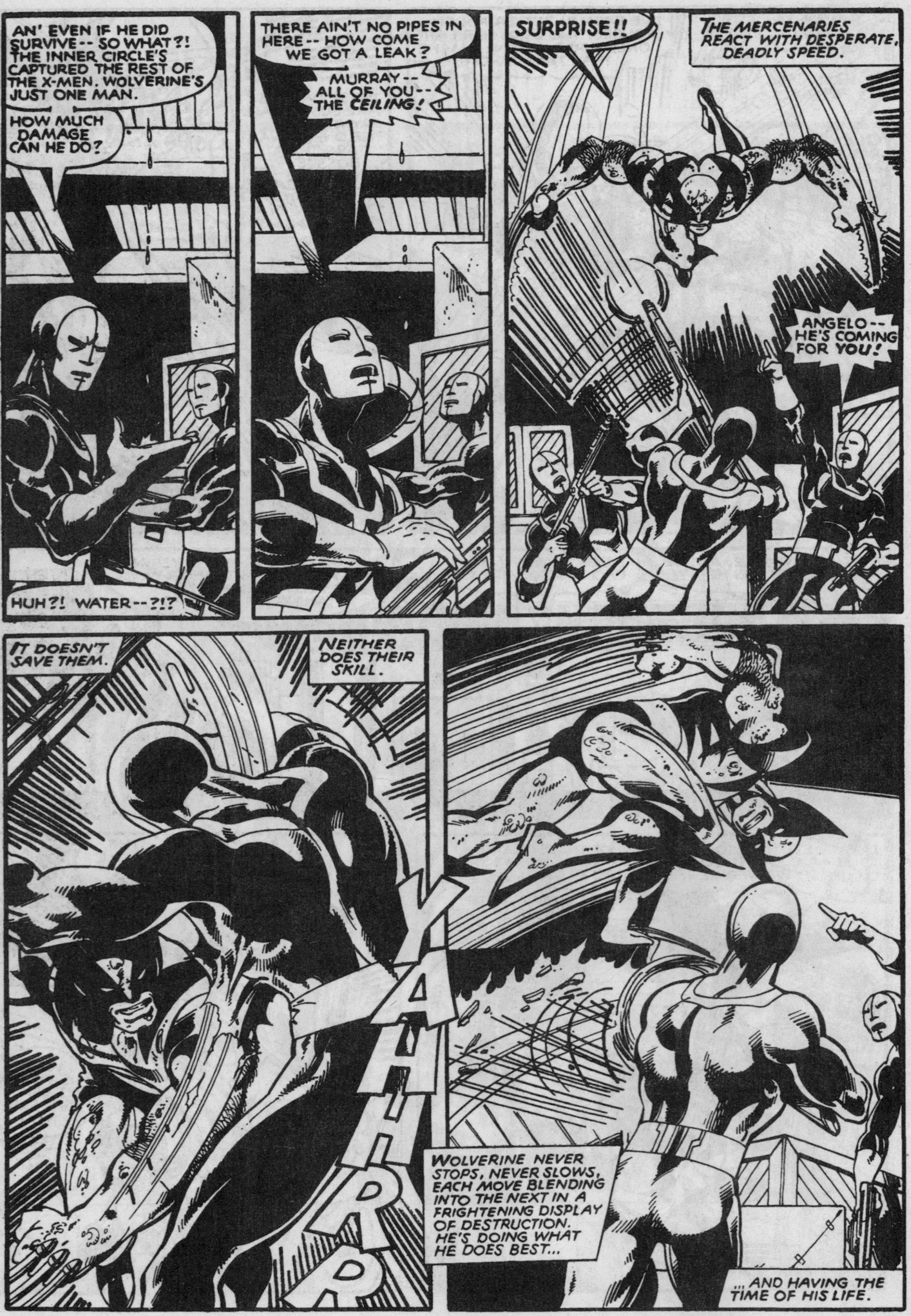
AN' EVEN IF HE DID SURVIVE -- SO WHAT?! THE INNER CIRCLE'S CAPTURED THE REST OF THE X-MEN. WOLVERINE'S JUST ONE MAN.
HOW MUCH DAMAGE CAN HE DO?
HUH?! WATER --?!?
THERE AIN'T NO PIPES IN HERE -- HOW COME WE GOT A LEAK?
MURRAY -- ALL OF YOU -- THE CEILING!
SURPRISE!!
THE MERCENARIES REACT WITH DESPERATE, DEADLY SPEED.
ANGELO -- HE'S COMING FOR YOU!
IT DOESN'T SAVE THEM.
NEITHER DOES THEIR SKILL.
YAAHHRRR
WOLVERINE NEVER STOPS, NEVER SLOWS, EACH MOVE BLENDING INTO THE NEXT IN A FRIGHTENING DISPLAY OF DESTRUCTION. HE'S DOING WHAT HE DOES BEST...
...AND HAVING THE TIME OF HIS LIFE.

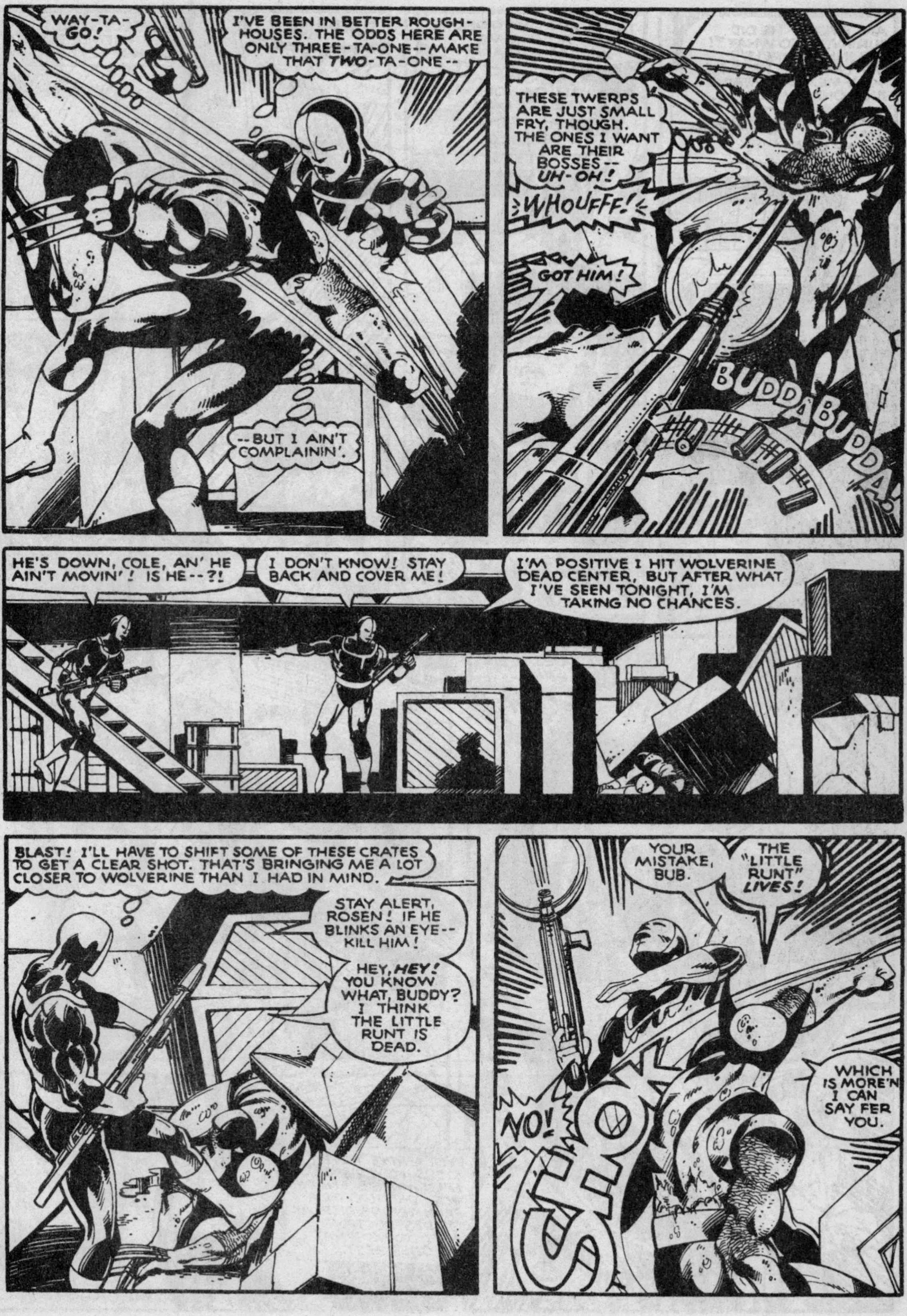
WAY-TA-GO!
I'VE BEEN IN BETTER ROUGH-HOUSES. THE ODDS HERE ARE ONLY THREE-TA-ONE--MAKE THAT TWO-TA-ONE--
--BUT I AIN'T COMPLAININ'.
THESE TWERPS ARE JUST SMALL FRY, THOUGH. THE ONES I WANT ARE THEIR BOSSES-- UH-OH!
WHOUFFF!
GOT HIM!
BUDDABUDDA!
HE'S DOWN, COLE, AN' HE AIN'T MOVIN'! IS HE--?!
I DON'T KNOW! STAY BACK AND COVER ME!
I'M POSITIVE I HIT WOLVERINE DEAD CENTER, BUT AFTER WHAT I'VE SEEN TONIGHT, I'M TAKING NO CHANCES.
BLAST! I'LL HAVE TO SHIFT SOME OF THESE CRATES TO GET A CLEAR SHOT. THAT'S BRINGING ME A LOT CLOSER TO WOLVERINE THAN I HAD IN MIND.
STAY ALERT, ROSEN! IF HE BLINKS AN EYE-- KILL HIM!
HEY, HEY! YOU KNOW WHAT, BUDDY? I THINK THE LITTLE RUNT IS DEAD.
YOUR MISTAKE, BUB.
THE "LITTLE RUNT" LIVES!
NO!
SHOK
WHICH IS MORE'N I CAN SAY FER YOU.

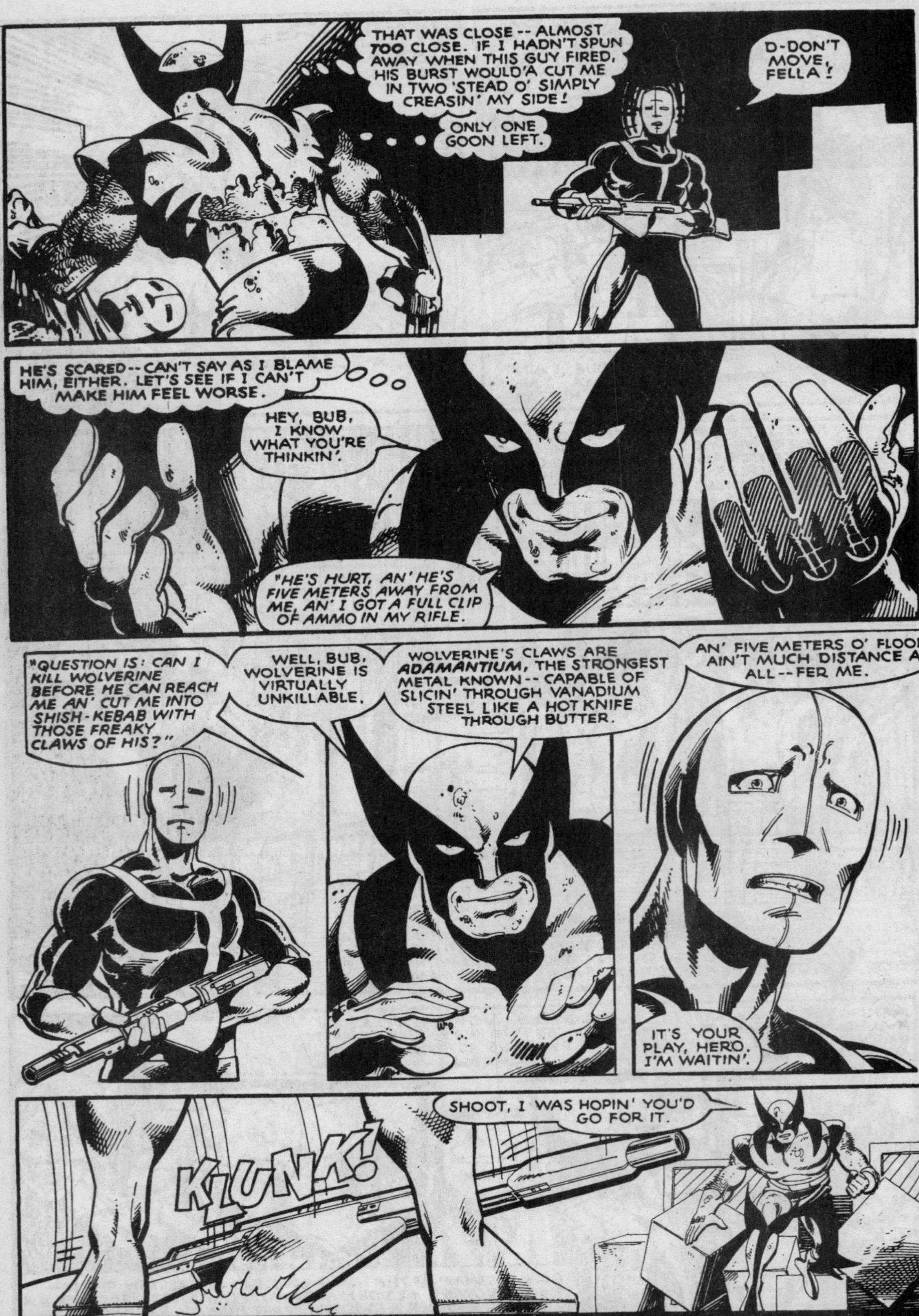
THAT WAS CLOSE -- ALMOST TOO CLOSE. IF I HADN'T SPUN AWAY WHEN THIS GUY FIRED, HIS BURST WOULD'A CUT ME IN TWO 'STEAD O' SIMPLY CREASIN' MY SIDE!
ONLY ONE GOON LEFT.
D-DON'T MOVE, FELLA!
HE'S SCARED -- CAN'T SAY AS I BLAME HIM, EITHER. LET'S SEE IF I CAN'T MAKE HIM FEEL WORSE.
HEY, BUB, I KNOW WHAT YOU'RE THINKIN'.
"HE'S HURT, AN' HE'S FIVE METERS AWAY FROM ME, AN' I GOT A FULL CLIP OF AMMO IN MY RIFLE.
"QUESTION IS: CAN I KILL WOLVERINE BEFORE HE CAN REACH ME AN' CUT ME INTO SHISH-KEBAB WITH THOSE FREAKY CLAWS OF HIS?"
WELL, BUB, WOLVERINE IS VIRTUALLY UNKILLABLE.
WOLVERINE'S CLAWS ARE ADAMANTIUM, THE STRONGEST METAL KNOWN -- CAPABLE OF SLICIN' THROUGH VANADIUM STEEL LIKE A HOT KNIFE THROUGH BUTTER.
AN' FIVE METERS O' FLOOR AIN'T MUCH DISTANCE AT ALL -- FER ME.
IT'S YOUR PLAY, HERO. I'M WAITIN'.
SHOOT, I WAS HOPIN' YOU'D GO FOR IT.
KLUNK!

Panel 1:

CONGRATULATIONS, WYNGARDE. WE HAVE DONE WELL TONIGHT.

THIS KNAVE'S ARROGANCE IS MATCHED ONLY BY HIS AMBITION. THROUGH HIS PRECIOUS BLACK QUEEN, WYNGARDE THINKS TO EVENTUALLY *SEIZE* CONTROL OF THE INNER CIRCLE. BUT IF HE THINKS SEBASTIAN SHAW WILL BE AS EASY A CONQUEST AS THE X-MEN...

...HE IS IN FOR A SURPRISE.

Panel 2:

DESPITE HIS PLEASANT WORDS, SHAW SUSPECTS ME. BUT I WILL DEAL WITH HIM -- AND FAR SOONER THAN HE EXPECTS.

FOR THE MOMENT, HOWEVER, I INTEND TO FULLY ENJOY THE FRUITS OF *MY* VICTORY.

WYNGARDE AND THE BLACK QUEEN EMBRACE LIKE LONG-LOST LOVERS. WHEN THEY FINALLY PART, JEAN'S EYES ARE LIT WITH A CRUEL, WANTON PASSION SHE'S NEVER SHOWN BEFORE.

Panel 3:

STORM -- ALL OF YOU -- I DO NOT UNDERSTAND. IN MY HEART, I KNOW THAT IS JEAN GREY...

YET SHE ISN'T, COLOSSUS.

WHAT HAVE THEY DONE TO HER?!

IF I COULD SPEAK, NIGHTCRAWLER, I'D TELL YOU.

Panel 4:

THANKS TO MASTERMIND, JEAN BELIEVES SHE'S PHYSICALLY SHIFTING IN TIME, RELIVING THE LIFE OF AN 18TH CENTURY ANCESTOR. EVERYTHING SHE SEES -- INCLUDING US -- IS IN TERMS OF THE 1700'S.

THIS "ANCESTOR" -- LADY JEAN GREY, WIFE OF SIR JASON WYNGARDE -- KNOWS *NOTHING* OF THE X-MEN. HER ALLEGIANCE IS TO THE HELLFIRE CLUB. IF THEY ASK HER TO KILL US...

...I'VE A NASTY FEELING SHE'LL DO IT WITHOUT A SECOND THOUGHT.

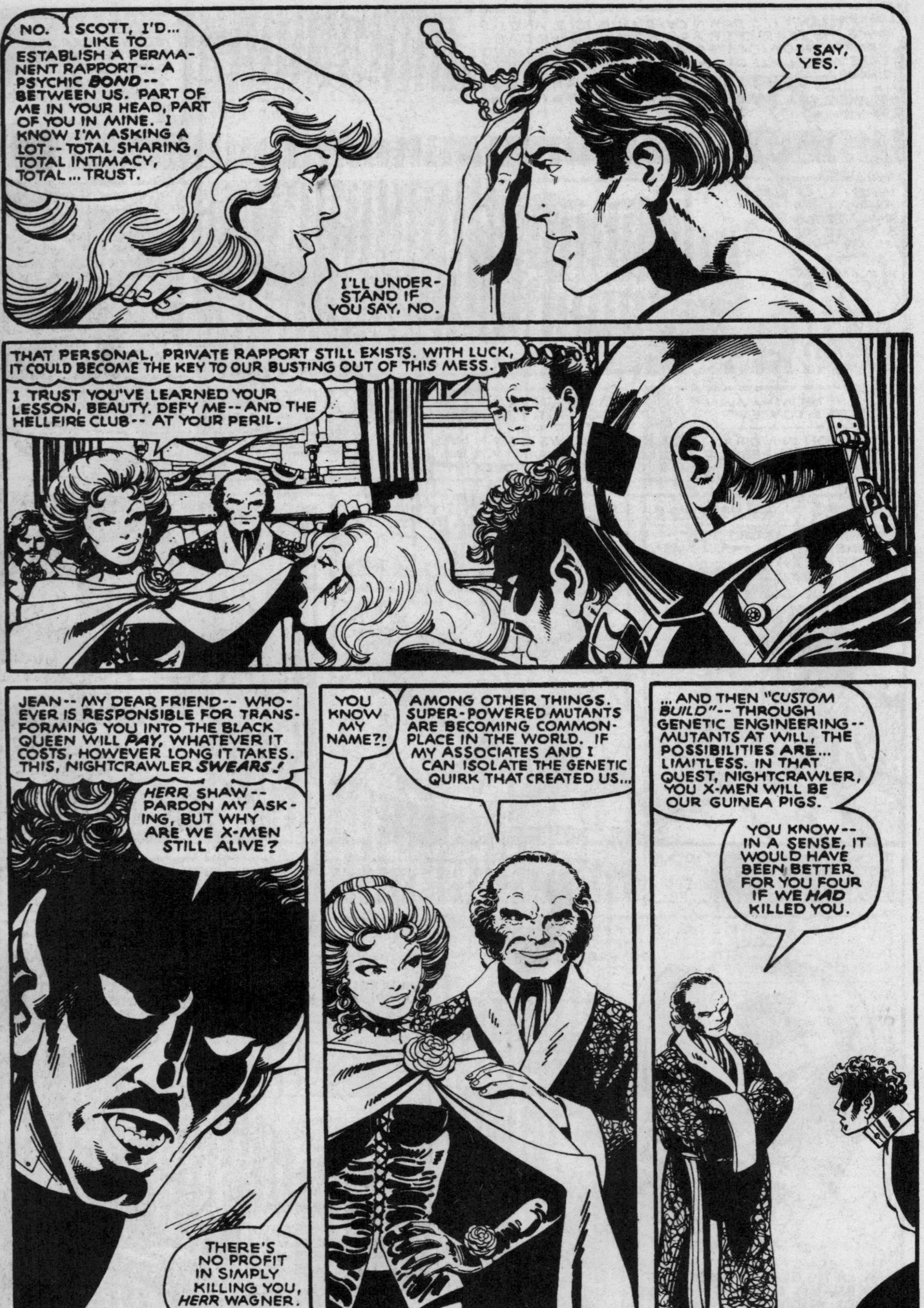

NO.
SCOTT, I'D... LIKE TO ESTABLISH A PERMANENT RAPPORT -- A PSYCHIC BOND -- BETWEEN US. PART OF ME IN YOUR HEAD, PART OF YOU IN MINE. I KNOW I'M ASKING A LOT -- TOTAL SHARING, TOTAL INTIMACY, TOTAL... TRUST.
I'LL UNDERSTAND IF YOU SAY, NO.
I SAY, YES.
THAT PERSONAL, PRIVATE RAPPORT STILL EXISTS. WITH LUCK, IT COULD BECOME THE KEY TO OUR BUSTING OUT OF THIS MESS.
I TRUST YOU'VE LEARNED YOUR LESSON, BEAUTY. DEFY ME -- AND THE HELLFIRE CLUB -- AT YOUR PERIL.
JEAN -- MY DEAR FRIEND -- WHOEVER IS RESPONSIBLE FOR TRANSFORMING YOU INTO THE BLACK QUEEN WILL PAY, WHATEVER IT COSTS, HOWEVER LONG IT TAKES. THIS, NIGHTCRAWLER SWEARS!
HERR SHAW -- PARDON MY ASKING, BUT WHY ARE WE X-MEN STILL ALIVE?
THERE'S NO PROFIT IN SIMPLY KILLING YOU, HERR WAGNER.
YOU KNOW MY NAME?!
AMONG OTHER THINGS. SUPER-POWERED MUTANTS ARE BECOMING COMMONPLACE IN THE WORLD. IF MY ASSOCIATES AND I CAN ISOLATE THE GENETIC QUIRK THAT CREATED US...
...AND THEN "CUSTOM BUILD" -- THROUGH GENETIC ENGINEERING -- MUTANTS AT WILL, THE POSSIBILITIES ARE... LIMITLESS. IN THAT QUEST, NIGHTCRAWLER, YOU X-MEN WILL BE OUR GUINEA PIGS.
YOU KNOW -- IN A SENSE, IT WOULD HAVE BEEN BETTER FOR YOU FOUR IF WE HAD KILLED YOU.

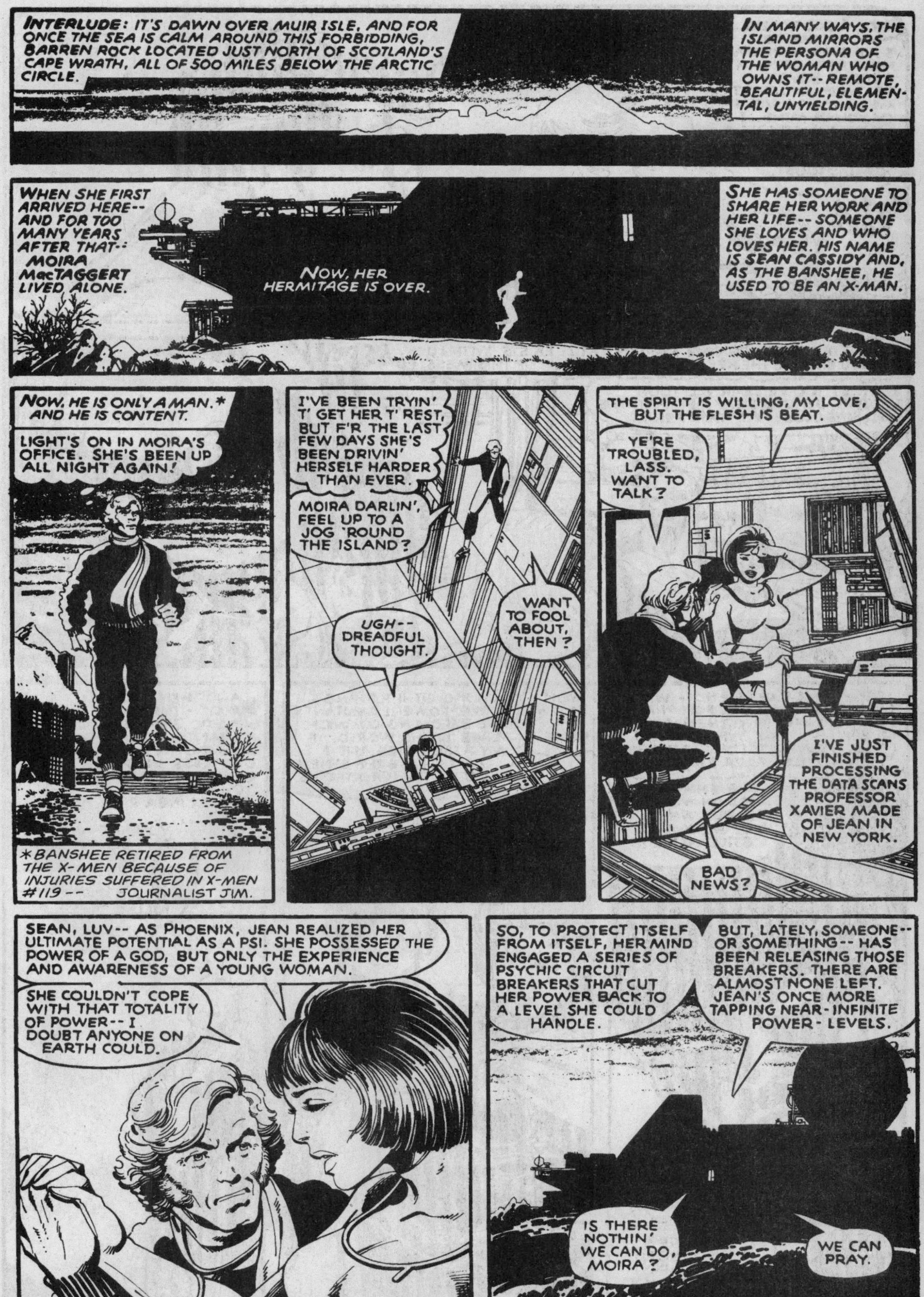
INTERLUDE: IT'S DAWN OVER MUIR ISLE, AND FOR ONCE THE SEA IS CALM AROUND THIS FORBIDDING, BARREN ROCK LOCATED JUST NORTH OF SCOTLAND'S CAPE WRATH, ALL OF 500 MILES BELOW THE ARCTIC CIRCLE.
IN MANY WAYS, THE ISLAND MIRRORS THE PERSONA OF THE WOMAN WHO OWNS IT-- REMOTE, BEAUTIFUL, ELEMENTAL, UNYIELDING.
WHEN SHE FIRST ARRIVED HERE-- AND FOR TOO MANY YEARS AFTER THAT-: MOIRA MacTAGGERT LIVED ALONE.
NOW, HER HERMITAGE IS OVER.
SHE HAS SOMEONE TO SHARE HER WORK AND HER LIFE-- SOMEONE SHE LOVES AND WHO LOVES HER. HIS NAME IS SEAN CASSIDY AND, AS THE BANSHEE, HE USED TO BE AN X-MAN.
NOW, HE IS ONLY A MAN.* AND HE IS CONTENT.
LIGHT'S ON IN MOIRA'S OFFICE. SHE'S BEEN UP ALL NIGHT AGAIN!
*BANSHEE RETIRED FROM THE X-MEN BECAUSE OF INJURIES SUFFERED IN X-MEN #119 -- JOURNALIST JIM.
I'VE BEEN TRYIN' T' GET HER T' REST, BUT F'R THE LAST FEW DAYS SHE'S BEEN DRIVIN' HERSELF HARDER THAN EVER.
MOIRA DARLIN', FEEL UP TO A JOG 'ROUND THE ISLAND?
UGH-- DREADFUL THOUGHT.
WANT TO FOOL ABOUT, THEN?
THE SPIRIT IS WILLING, MY LOVE, BUT THE FLESH IS BEAT.
YE'RE TROUBLED, LASS. WANT TO TALK?
I'VE JUST FINISHED PROCESSING THE DATA SCANS PROFESSOR XAVIER MADE OF JEAN IN NEW YORK.
BAD NEWS?
SEAN, LUV-- AS PHOENIX, JEAN REALIZED HER ULTIMATE POTENTIAL AS A PSI. SHE POSSESSED THE POWER OF A GOD, BUT ONLY THE EXPERIENCE AND AWARENESS OF A YOUNG WOMAN.
SHE COULDN'T COPE WITH THAT TOTALITY OF POWER-- I DOUBT ANYONE ON EARTH COULD.
SO, TO PROTECT ITSELF FROM ITSELF, HER MIND ENGAGED A SERIES OF PSYCHIC CIRCUIT BREAKERS THAT CUT HER POWER BACK TO A LEVEL SHE COULD HANDLE.
BUT, LATELY, SOMEONE-- OR SOMETHING-- HAS BEEN RELEASING THOSE BREAKERS. THERE ARE ALMOST NONE LEFT. JEAN'S ONCE MORE TAPPING NEAR-INFINITE POWER-LEVELS.
IS THERE NOTHIN' WE CAN DO, MOIRA?
WE CAN PRAY.

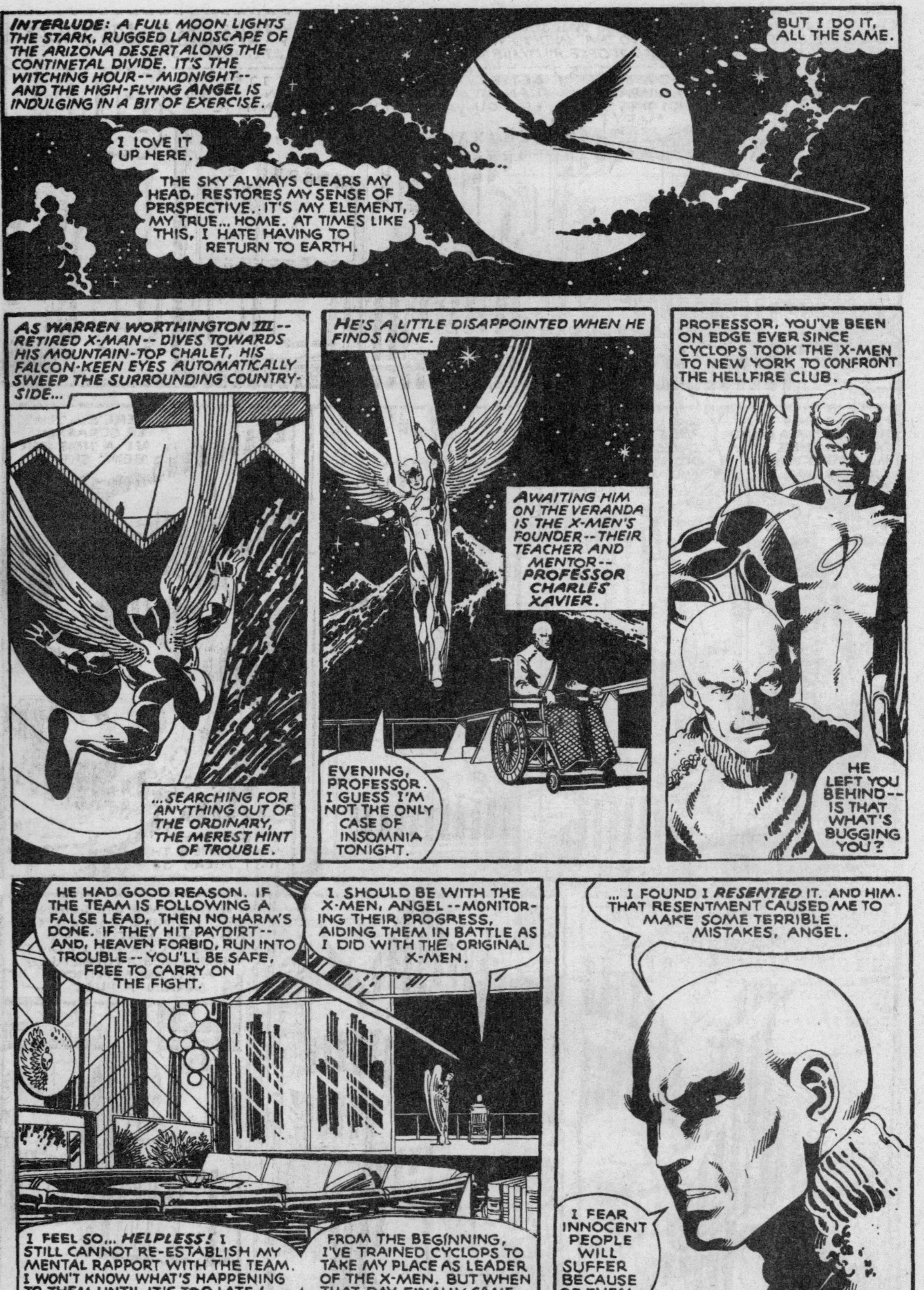

INTERLUDE: A FULL MOON LIGHTS THE STARK, RUGGED LANDSCAPE OF THE ARIZONA DESERT ALONG THE CONTINETAL DIVIDE. IT'S THE WITCHING HOUR-- MIDNIGHT-- AND THE HIGH-FLYING ANGEL IS INDULGING IN A BIT OF EXERCISE.
I LOVE IT UP HERE.
THE SKY ALWAYS CLEARS MY HEAD, RESTORES MY SENSE OF PERSPECTIVE. IT'S MY ELEMENT, MY TRUE... HOME. AT TIMES LIKE THIS, I HATE HAVING TO RETURN TO EARTH.
BUT I DO IT, ALL THE SAME.
AS WARREN WORTHINGTON III -- RETIRED X-MAN-- DIVES TOWARDS HIS MOUNTAIN-TOP CHALET, HIS FALCON-KEEN EYES AUTOMATICALLY SWEEP THE SURROUNDING COUNTRY-SIDE...
...SEARCHING FOR ANYTHING OUT OF THE ORDINARY, THE MEREST HINT OF TROUBLE.
HE'S A LITTLE DISAPPOINTED WHEN HE FINDS NONE.
AWAITING HIM ON THE VERANDA IS THE X-MEN'S FOUNDER--THEIR TEACHER AND MENTOR-- PROFESSOR CHARLES XAVIER.
EVENING, PROFESSOR. I GUESS I'M NOT THE ONLY CASE OF INSOMNIA TONIGHT.
PROFESSOR, YOU'VE BEEN ON EDGE EVER SINCE CYCLOPS TOOK THE X-MEN TO NEW YORK TO CONFRONT THE HELLFIRE CLUB.
HE LEFT YOU BEHIND-- IS THAT WHAT'S BUGGING YOU?
HE HAD GOOD REASON. IF THE TEAM IS FOLLOWING A FALSE LEAD, THEN NO HARM'S DONE. IF THEY HIT PAYDIRT-- AND, HEAVEN FORBID, RUN INTO TROUBLE-- YOU'LL BE SAFE, FREE TO CARRY ON THE FIGHT.
I SHOULD BE WITH THE X-MEN, ANGEL--MONITORING THEIR PROGRESS, AIDING THEM IN BATTLE AS I DID WITH THE ORIGINAL X-MEN.
I FEEL SO... HELPLESS! I STILL CANNOT RE-ESTABLISH MY MENTAL RAPPORT WITH THE TEAM. I WON'T KNOW WHAT'S HAPPENING TO THEM UNTIL IT'S TOO LATE!
FROM THE BEGINNING, I'VE TRAINED CYCLOPS TO TAKE MY PLACE AS LEADER OF THE X-MEN. BUT WHEN THAT DAY FINALLY CAME...
... I FOUND I RESENTED IT. AND HIM. THAT RESENTMENT CAUSED ME TO MAKE SOME TERRIBLE MISTAKES, ANGEL.
I FEAR INNOCENT PEOPLE WILL SUFFER BECAUSE OF THEM.

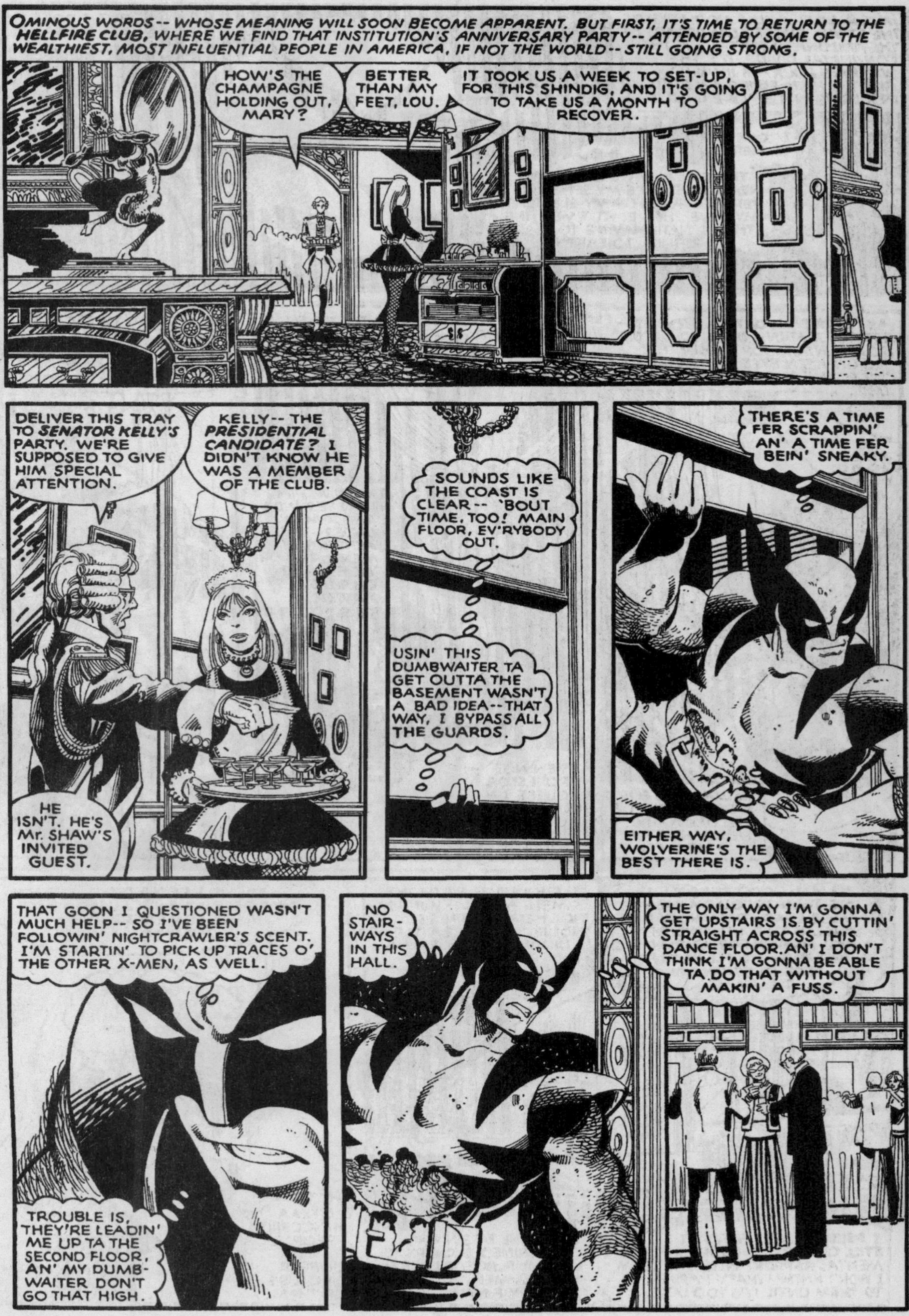
OMINOUS WORDS -- WHOSE MEANING WILL SOON BECOME APPARENT. BUT FIRST, IT'S TIME TO RETURN TO THE HELLFIRE CLUB, WHERE WE FIND THAT INSTITUTION'S ANNIVERSARY PARTY -- ATTENDED BY SOME OF THE WEALTHIEST, MOST INFLUENTIAL PEOPLE IN AMERICA, IF NOT THE WORLD -- STILL GOING STRONG.
HOW'S THE CHAMPAGNE HOLDING OUT, MARY?
BETTER THAN MY FEET, LOU.
IT TOOK US A WEEK TO SET-UP, FOR THIS SHINDIG, AND IT'S GOING TO TAKE US A MONTH TO RECOVER.
DELIVER THIS TRAY TO SENATOR KELLY'S PARTY. WE'RE SUPPOSED TO GIVE HIM SPECIAL ATTENTION.
KELLY -- THE PRESIDENTIAL CANDIDATE? I DIDN'T KNOW HE WAS A MEMBER OF THE CLUB.
HE ISN'T. HE'S Mr. SHAW'S INVITED GUEST.
SOUNDS LIKE THE COAST IS CLEAR -- 'BOUT TIME, TOO! MAIN FLOOR, EV'RYBODY OUT.
USIN' THIS DUMBWAITER TA GET OUTTA THE BASEMENT WASN'T A BAD IDEA -- THAT WAY, I BYPASS ALL THE GUARDS.
THERE'S A TIME FER SCRAPPIN' AN' A TIME FER BEIN' SNEAKY.
EITHER WAY, WOLVERINE'S THE BEST THERE IS.
THAT GOON I QUESTIONED WASN'T MUCH HELP -- SO I'VE BEEN FOLLOWIN' NIGHTCRAWLER'S SCENT. I'M STARTIN' TO PICK UP TRACES O' THE OTHER X-MEN, AS WELL.
TROUBLE IS, THEY'RE LEADIN' ME UP TA THE SECOND FLOOR. AN' MY DUMB-WAITER DON'T GO THAT HIGH.
NO STAIR-WAYS IN THIS HALL.
THE ONLY WAY I'M GONNA GET UPSTAIRS IS BY CUTTIN' STRAIGHT ACROSS THIS DANCE FLOOR. AN' I DON'T THINK I'M GONNA BE ABLE TA DO THAT WITHOUT MAKIN' A FUSS.

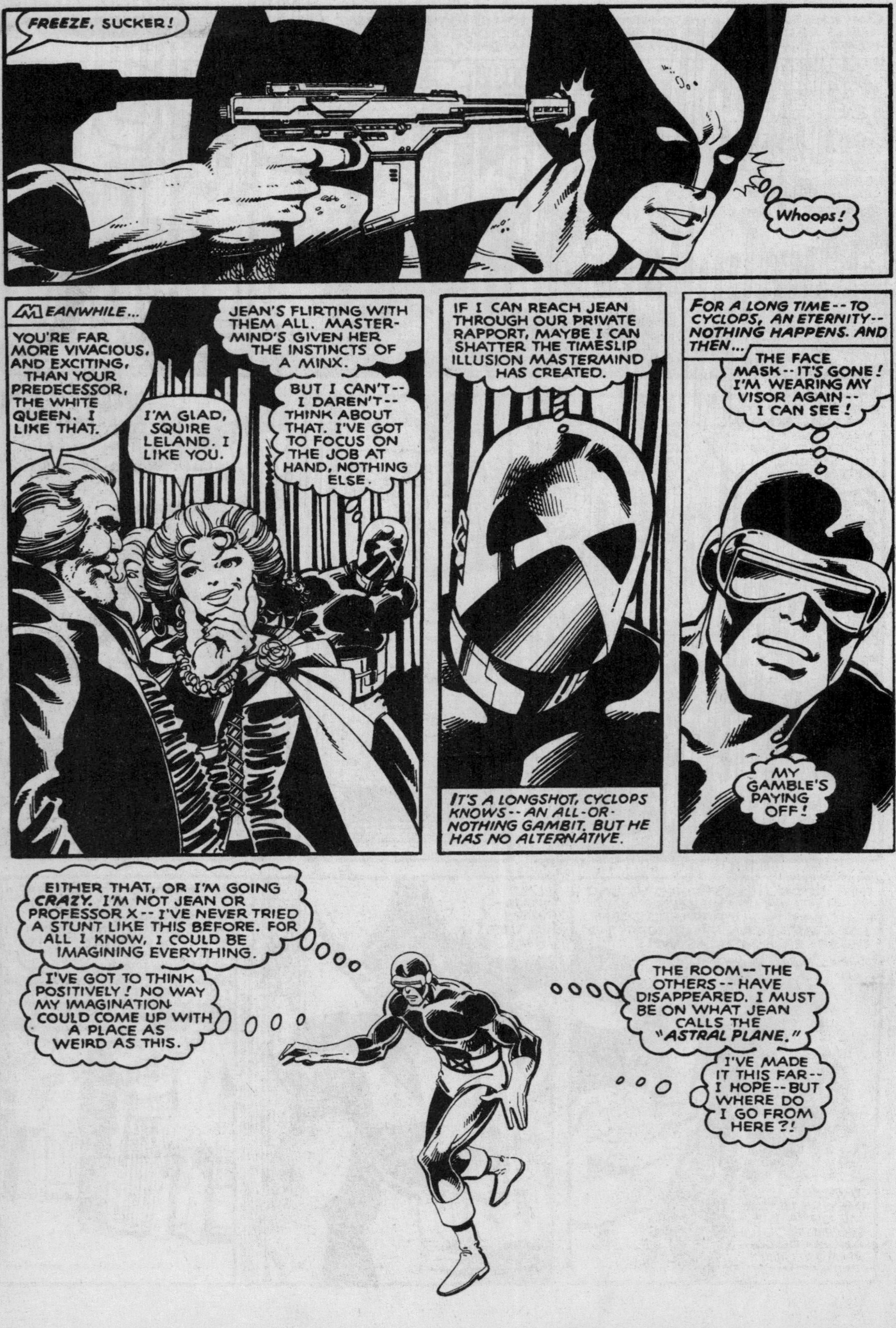
FREEZE, SUCKER!
Whoops!
MEANWHILE...
YOU'RE FAR MORE VIVACIOUS, AND EXCITING, THAN YOUR PREDECESSOR, THE WHITE QUEEN. I LIKE THAT.
I'M GLAD, SQUIRE LELAND. I LIKE YOU.
JEAN'S FLIRTING WITH THEM ALL. MASTERMIND'S GIVEN HER THE INSTINCTS OF A MINX.
BUT I CAN'T-- I DAREN'T-- THINK ABOUT THAT. I'VE GOT TO FOCUS ON THE JOB AT HAND, NOTHING ELSE.
IF I CAN REACH JEAN THROUGH OUR PRIVATE RAPPORT, MAYBE I CAN SHATTER THE TIMESLIP ILLUSION MASTERMIND HAS CREATED.
IT'S A LONGSHOT, CYCLOPS KNOWS-- AN ALL-OR-NOTHING GAMBIT. BUT HE HAS NO ALTERNATIVE.
FOR A LONG TIME-- TO CYCLOPS, AN ETERNITY-- NOTHING HAPPENS. AND THEN...
THE FACE MASK-- IT'S GONE! I'M WEARING MY VISOR AGAIN-- I CAN SEE!
MY GAMBLE'S PAYING OFF!
EITHER THAT, OR I'M GOING CRAZY. I'M NOT JEAN OR PROFESSOR X-- I'VE NEVER TRIED A STUNT LIKE THIS BEFORE. FOR ALL I KNOW, I COULD BE IMAGINING EVERYTHING.
I'VE GOT TO THINK POSITIVELY! NO WAY MY IMAGINATION COULD COME UP WITH A PLACE AS WEIRD AS THIS.
THE ROOM-- THE OTHERS-- HAVE DISAPPEARED. I MUST BE ON WHAT JEAN CALLS THE "ASTRAL PLANE."
I'VE MADE IT THIS FAR-- I HOPE-- BUT WHERE DO I GO FROM HERE?!

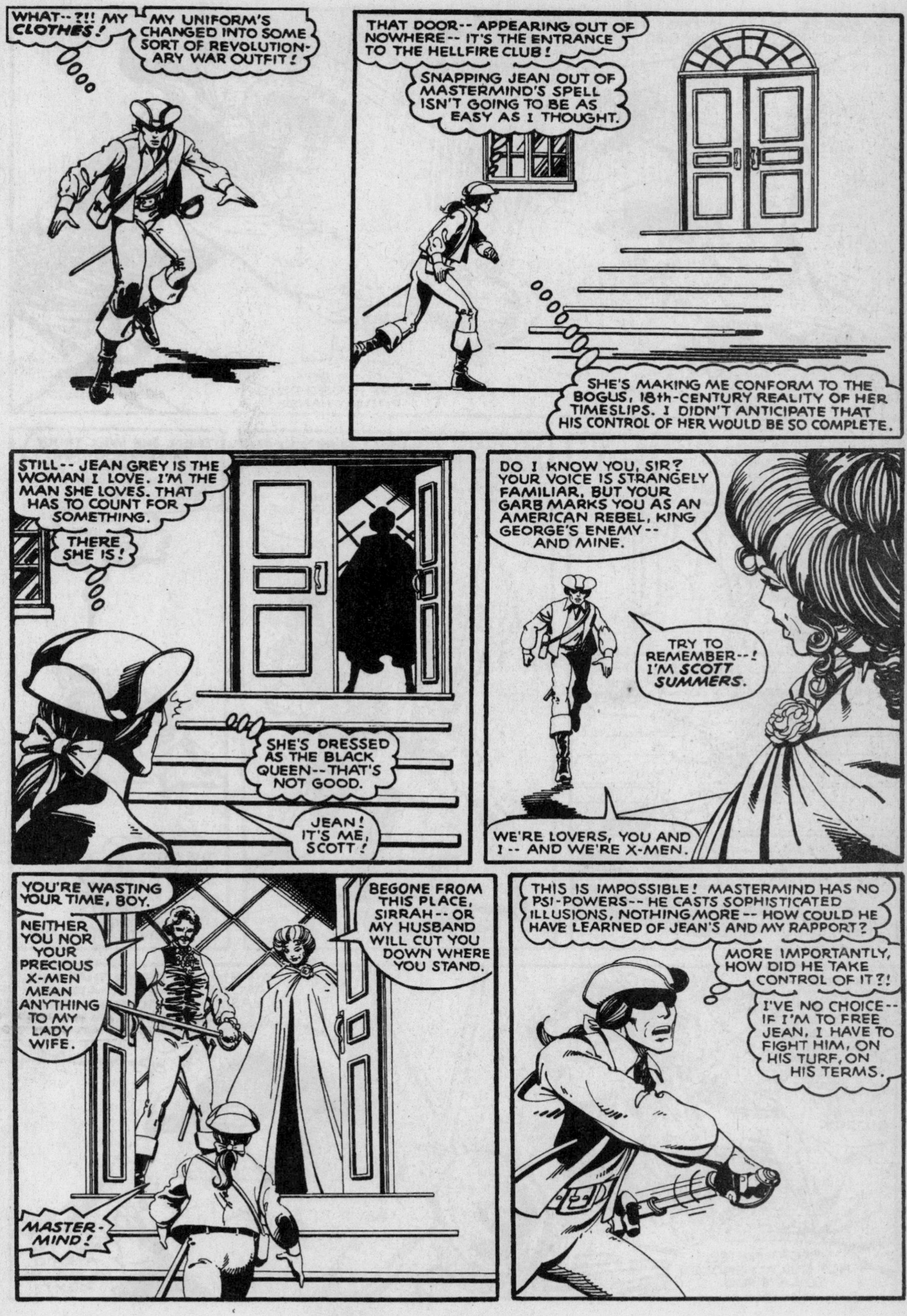
WHAT--?!! MY CLOTHES!
MY UNIFORM'S CHANGED INTO SOME SORT OF REVOLUTIONARY WAR OUTFIT!
THAT DOOR-- APPEARING OUT OF NOWHERE-- IT'S THE ENTRANCE TO THE HELLFIRE CLUB!
SNAPPING JEAN OUT OF MASTERMIND'S SPELL ISN'T GOING TO BE AS EASY AS I THOUGHT.
SHE'S MAKING ME CONFORM TO THE BOGUS, 18th-CENTURY REALITY OF HER TIMESLIPS. I DIDN'T ANTICIPATE THAT HIS CONTROL OF HER WOULD BE SO COMPLETE.
STILL-- JEAN GREY IS THE WOMAN I LOVE. I'M THE MAN SHE LOVES. THAT HAS TO COUNT FOR SOMETHING.
THERE SHE IS!
SHE'S DRESSED AS THE BLACK QUEEN--THAT'S NOT GOOD.
JEAN! IT'S ME, SCOTT!
DO I KNOW YOU, SIR? YOUR VOICE IS STRANGELY FAMILIAR, BUT YOUR GARB MARKS YOU AS AN AMERICAN REBEL, KING GEORGE'S ENEMY-- AND MINE.
TRY TO REMEMBER--! I'M SCOTT SUMMERS.
WE'RE LOVERS, YOU AND I-- AND WE'RE X-MEN.
YOU'RE WASTING YOUR TIME, BOY.
NEITHER YOU NOR YOUR PRECIOUS X-MEN MEAN ANYTHING TO MY LADY WIFE.
BEGONE FROM THIS PLACE, SIRRAH-- OR MY HUSBAND WILL CUT YOU DOWN WHERE YOU STAND.
MASTERMIND!
THIS IS IMPOSSIBLE! MASTERMIND HAS NO PSI-POWERS-- HE CASTS SOPHISTICATED ILLUSIONS, NOTHING MORE-- HOW COULD HE HAVE LEARNED OF JEAN'S AND MY RAPPORT?
MORE IMPORTANTLY, HOW DID HE TAKE CONTROL OF IT?!
I'VE NO CHOICE-- IF I'M TO FREE JEAN, I HAVE TO FIGHT HIM, ON HIS TURF, ON HIS TERMS.

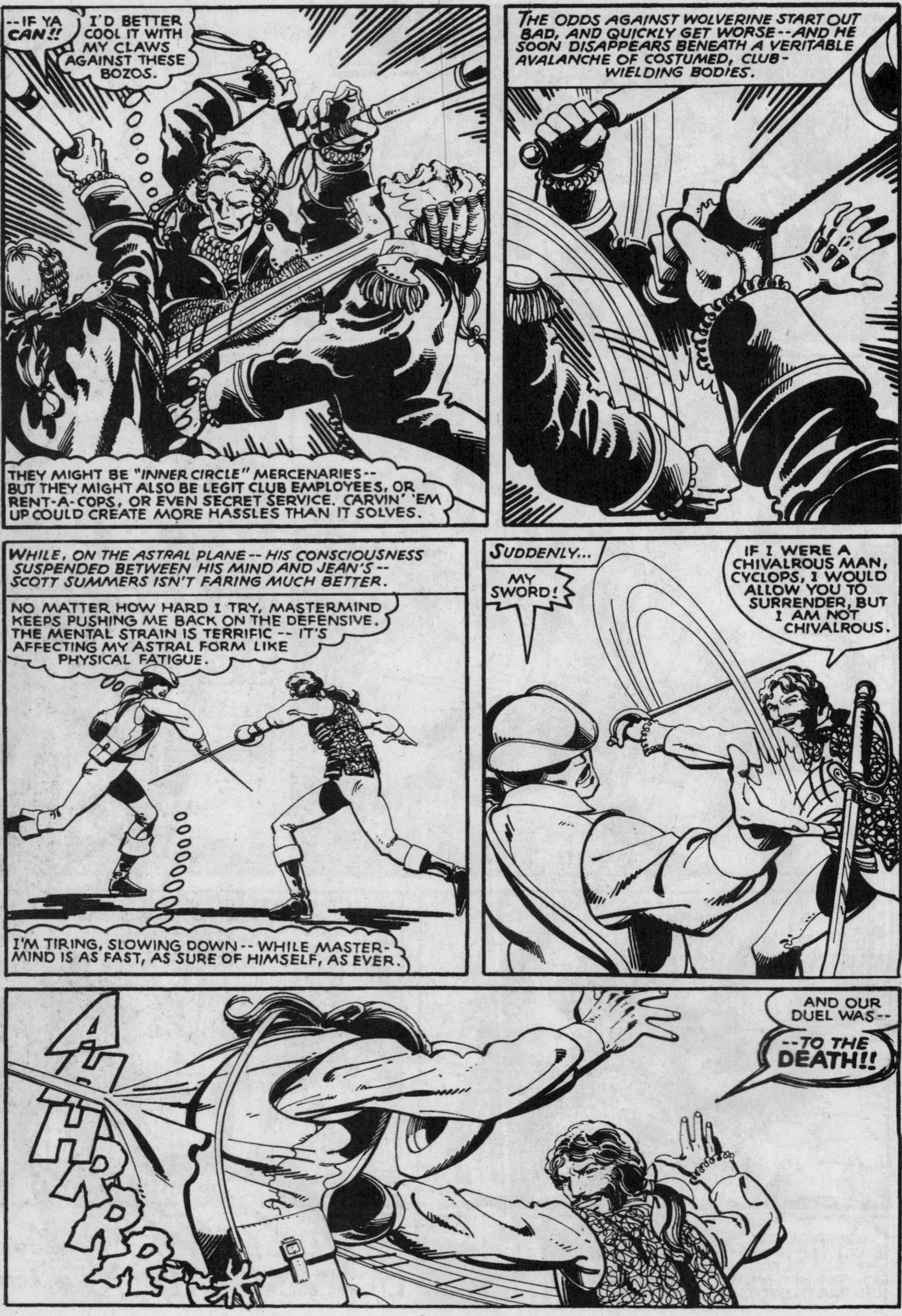
--IF YA CAN!!
I'D BETTER COOL IT WITH MY CLAWS AGAINST THESE BOZOS.
THEY MIGHT BE "INNER CIRCLE" MERCENARIES-- BUT THEY MIGHT ALSO BE LEGIT CLUB EMPLOYEES, OR RENT-A-COPS, OR EVEN SECRET SERVICE. CARVIN' 'EM UP COULD CREATE MORE HASSLES THAN IT SOLVES.
THE ODDS AGAINST WOLVERINE START OUT BAD, AND QUICKLY GET WORSE--AND HE SOON DISAPPEARS BENEATH A VERITABLE AVALANCHE OF COSTUMED, CLUB-WIELDING BODIES.
WHILE, ON THE ASTRAL PLANE--HIS CONSCIOUSNESS SUSPENDED BETWEEN HIS MIND AND JEAN'S--SCOTT SUMMERS ISN'T FARING MUCH BETTER.
NO MATTER HOW HARD I TRY, MASTERMIND KEEPS PUSHING ME BACK ON THE DEFENSIVE. THE MENTAL STRAIN IS TERRIFIC -- IT'S AFFECTING MY ASTRAL FORM LIKE PHYSICAL FATIGUE.
I'M TIRING, SLOWING DOWN--WHILE MASTERMIND IS AS FAST, AS SURE OF HIMSELF, AS EVER.
SUDDENLY...
MY SWORD!
IF I WERE A CHIVALROUS MAN, CYCLOPS, I WOULD ALLOW YOU TO SURRENDER, BUT I AM NOT CHIVALROUS.
AHHRRR
AND OUR DUEL WAS--
--TO THE DEATH!!

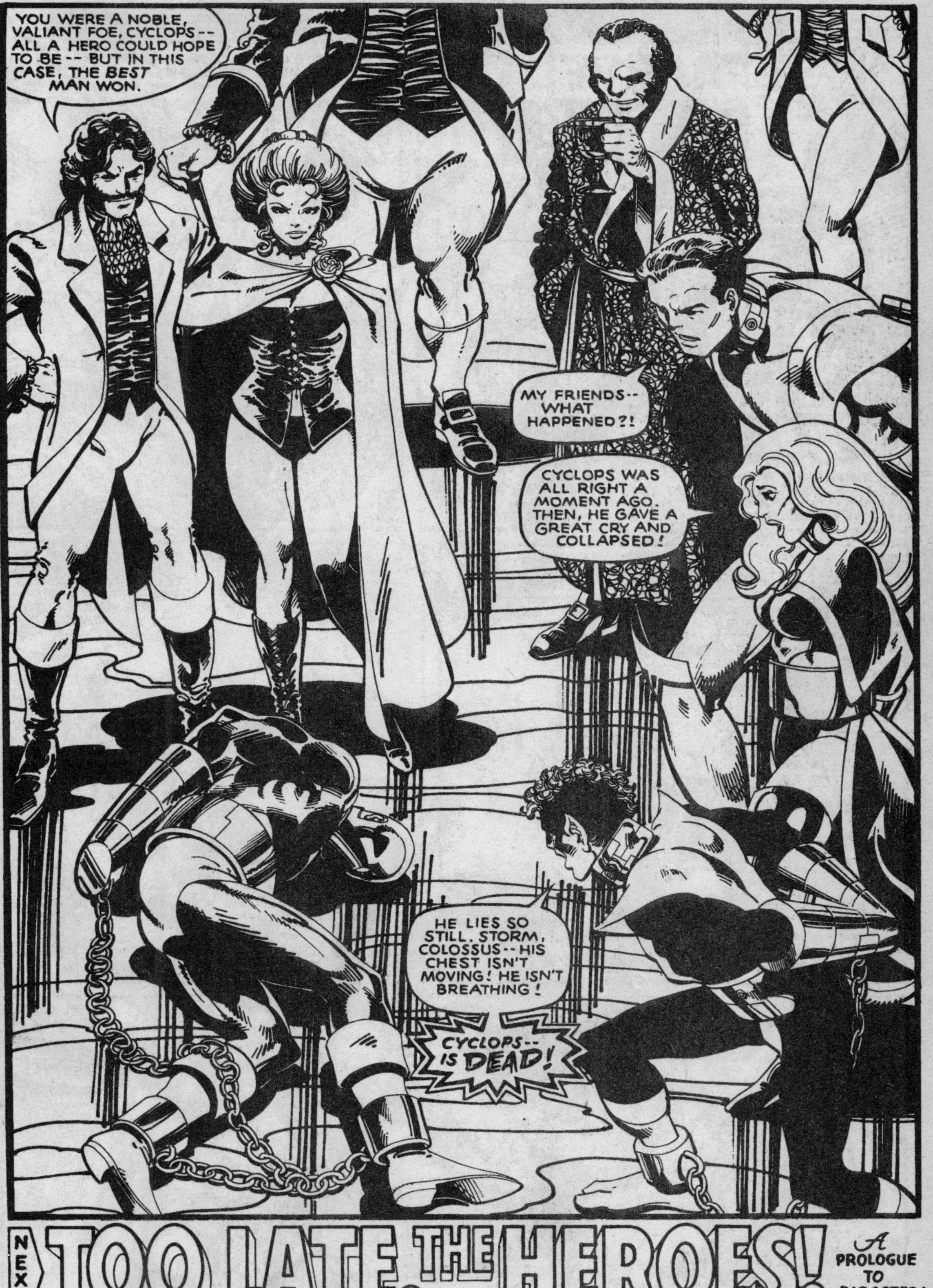
YOU WERE A NOBLE, VALIANT FOE, CYCLOPS -- ALL A HERO COULD HOPE TO BE -- BUT IN THIS CASE, THE BEST MAN WON.
MY FRIENDS-- WHAT HAPPENED?!
CYCLOPS WAS ALL RIGHT A MOMENT AGO. THEN, HE GAVE A GREAT CRY AND COLLAPSED!
HE LIES SO STILL, STORM, COLOSSUS--HIS CHEST ISN'T MOVING! HE ISN'T BREATHING!
CYCLOPS-- IS DEAD!
NEXT TOO LATE, THE HEROES!
A PROLOGUE TO DISASTER!

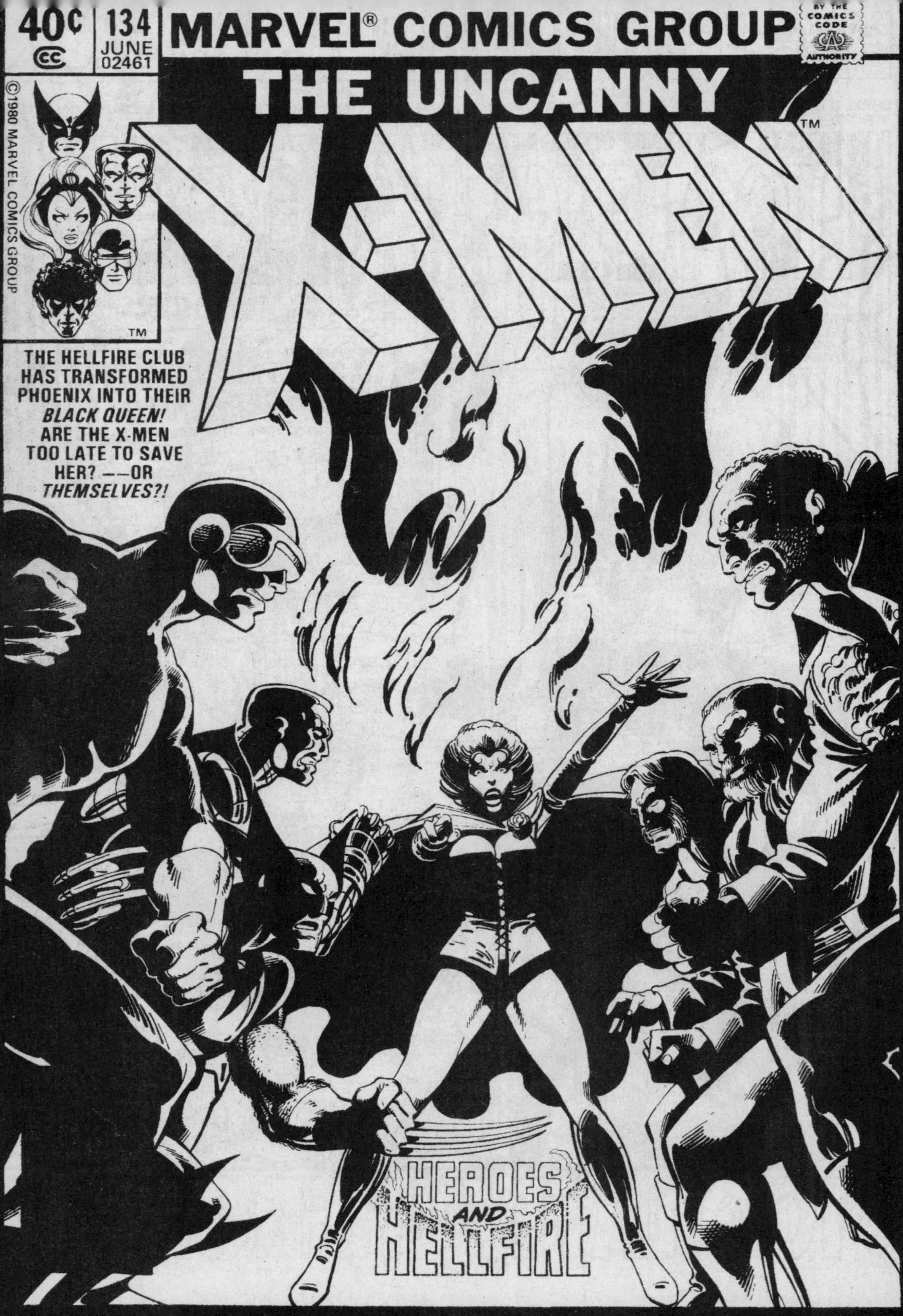
40¢
CC
134
JUNE
02461
MARVEL® COMICS GROUP
APPROVED BY THE COMICS CODE AUTHORITY
THE UNCANNY
X-MEN™
©1980 MARVEL COMICS GROUP
™
THE HELLFIRE CLUB HAS TRANSFORMED PHOENIX INTO THEIR *BLACK QUEEN!* ARE THE X-MEN TOO LATE TO SAVE HER? ——OR *THEMSELVES?!*
HEROES AND HELLFIRE

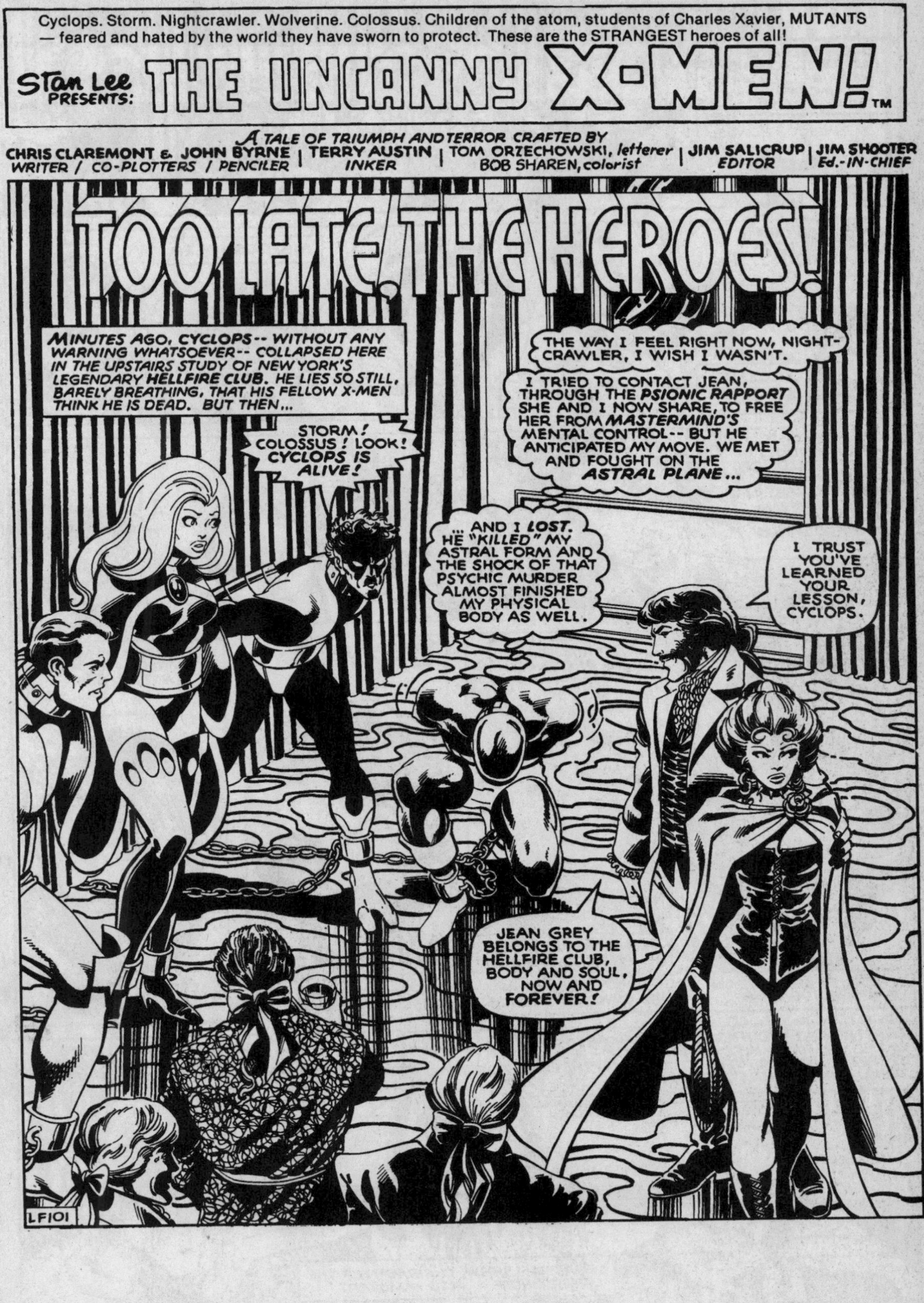
Cyclops. Storm. Nightcrawler. Wolverine. Colossus. Children of the atom, students of Charles Xavier, MUTANTS — feared and hated by the world they have sworn to protect. These are the STRANGEST heroes of all!
Stan Lee PRESENTS: THE UNCANNY X-MEN!™
A TALE OF TRIUMPH AND TERROR CRAFTED BY
CHRIS CLAREMONT & JOHN BYRNE WRITER / CO-PLOTTERS / PENCILER | TERRY AUSTIN INKER | TOM ORZECHOWSKI, letterer BOB SHAREN, colorist | JIM SALICRUP EDITOR | JIM SHOOTER Ed.-IN-CHIEF
TOO LATE, THE HEROES!
MINUTES AGO, CYCLOPS -- WITHOUT ANY WARNING WHATSOEVER -- COLLAPSED HERE IN THE UPSTAIRS STUDY OF NEW YORK'S LEGENDARY HELLFIRE CLUB. HE LIES SO STILL, BARELY BREATHING, THAT HIS FELLOW X-MEN THINK HE IS DEAD. BUT THEN...
STORM! COLOSSUS! LOOK! CYCLOPS IS ALIVE!
THE WAY I FEEL RIGHT NOW, NIGHTCRAWLER, I WISH I WASN'T.
I TRIED TO CONTACT JEAN, THROUGH THE PSIONIC RAPPORT SHE AND I NOW SHARE, TO FREE HER FROM MASTERMIND'S MENTAL CONTROL -- BUT HE ANTICIPATED MY MOVE. WE MET AND FOUGHT ON THE ASTRAL PLANE...
... AND I LOST. HE "KILLED" MY ASTRAL FORM AND THE SHOCK OF THAT PSYCHIC MURDER ALMOST FINISHED MY PHYSICAL BODY AS WELL.
I TRUST YOU'VE LEARNED YOUR LESSON, CYCLOPS.
JEAN GREY BELONGS TO THE HELLFIRE CLUB, BODY AND SOUL, NOW AND FOREVER!
LF101

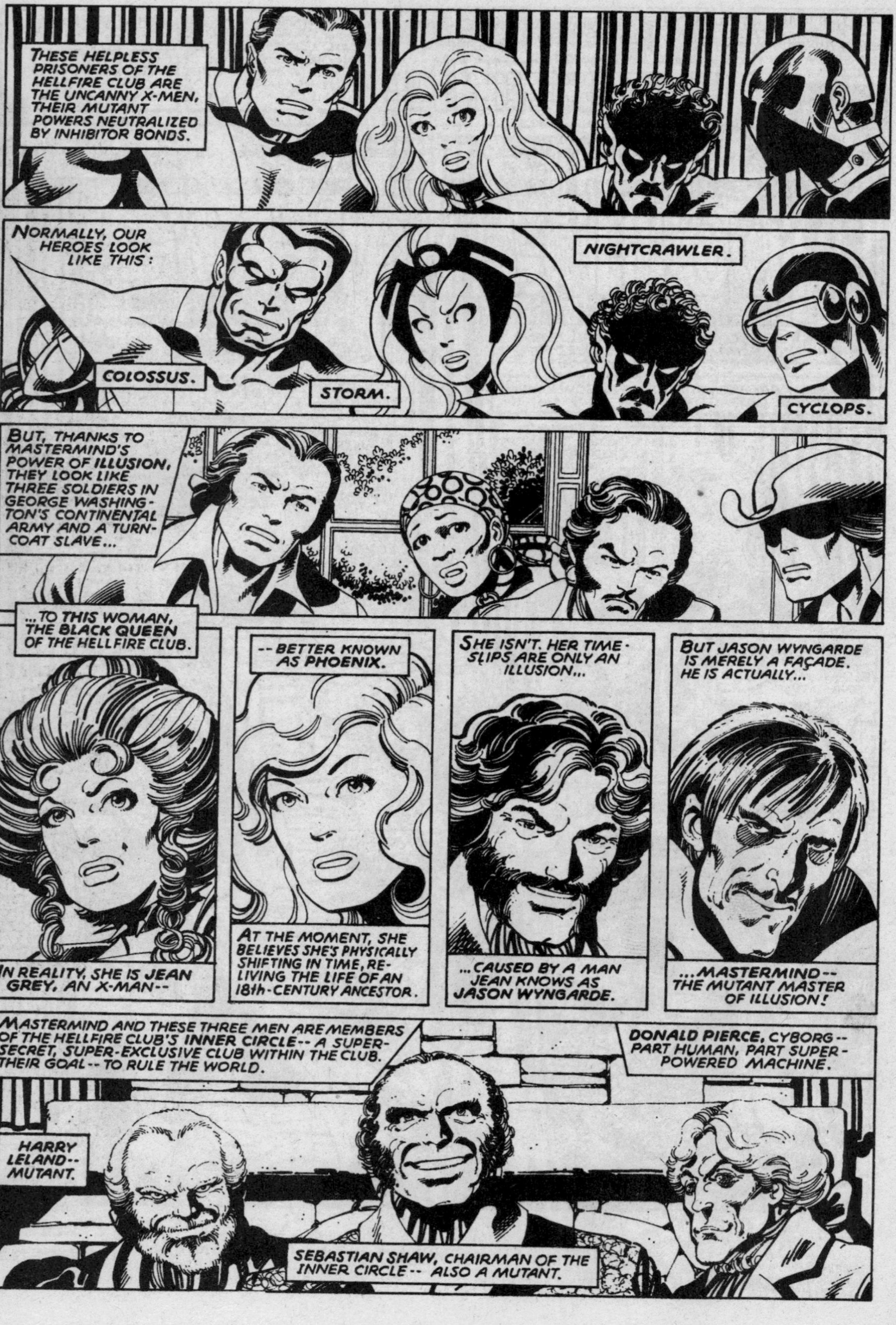

THESE HELPLESS PRISONERS OF THE HELLFIRE CLUB ARE THE UNCANNY X-MEN, THEIR MUTANT POWERS NEUTRALIZED BY INHIBITOR BONDS.
NORMALLY, OUR HEROES LOOK LIKE THIS:
COLOSSUS.
STORM.
NIGHTCRAWLER.
CYCLOPS.
BUT, THANKS TO MASTERMIND'S POWER OF ILLUSION, THEY LOOK LIKE THREE SOLDIERS IN GEORGE WASHINGTON'S CONTINENTAL ARMY AND A TURNCOAT SLAVE...
...TO THIS WOMAN, THE BLACK QUEEN OF THE HELLFIRE CLUB.
IN REALITY, SHE IS JEAN GREY, AN X-MAN--
--BETTER KNOWN AS PHOENIX.
AT THE MOMENT, SHE BELIEVES SHE'S PHYSICALLY SHIFTING IN TIME, RELIVING THE LIFE OF AN 18th-CENTURY ANCESTOR.
SHE ISN'T. HER TIME-SLIPS ARE ONLY AN ILLUSION...
...CAUSED BY A MAN JEAN KNOWS AS JASON WYNGARDE.
BUT JASON WYNGARDE IS MERELY A FAÇADE. HE IS ACTUALLY...
...MASTERMIND-- THE MUTANT MASTER OF ILLUSION!
MASTERMIND AND THESE THREE MEN ARE MEMBERS OF THE HELLFIRE CLUB'S INNER CIRCLE-- A SUPER-SECRET, SUPER-EXCLUSIVE CLUB WITHIN THE CLUB. THEIR GOAL-- TO RULE THE WORLD.
DONALD PIERCE, CYBORG-- PART HUMAN, PART SUPER-POWERED MACHINE.
HARRY LELAND-- MUTANT.
SEBASTIAN SHAW, CHAIRMAN OF THE INNER CIRCLE-- ALSO A MUTANT.

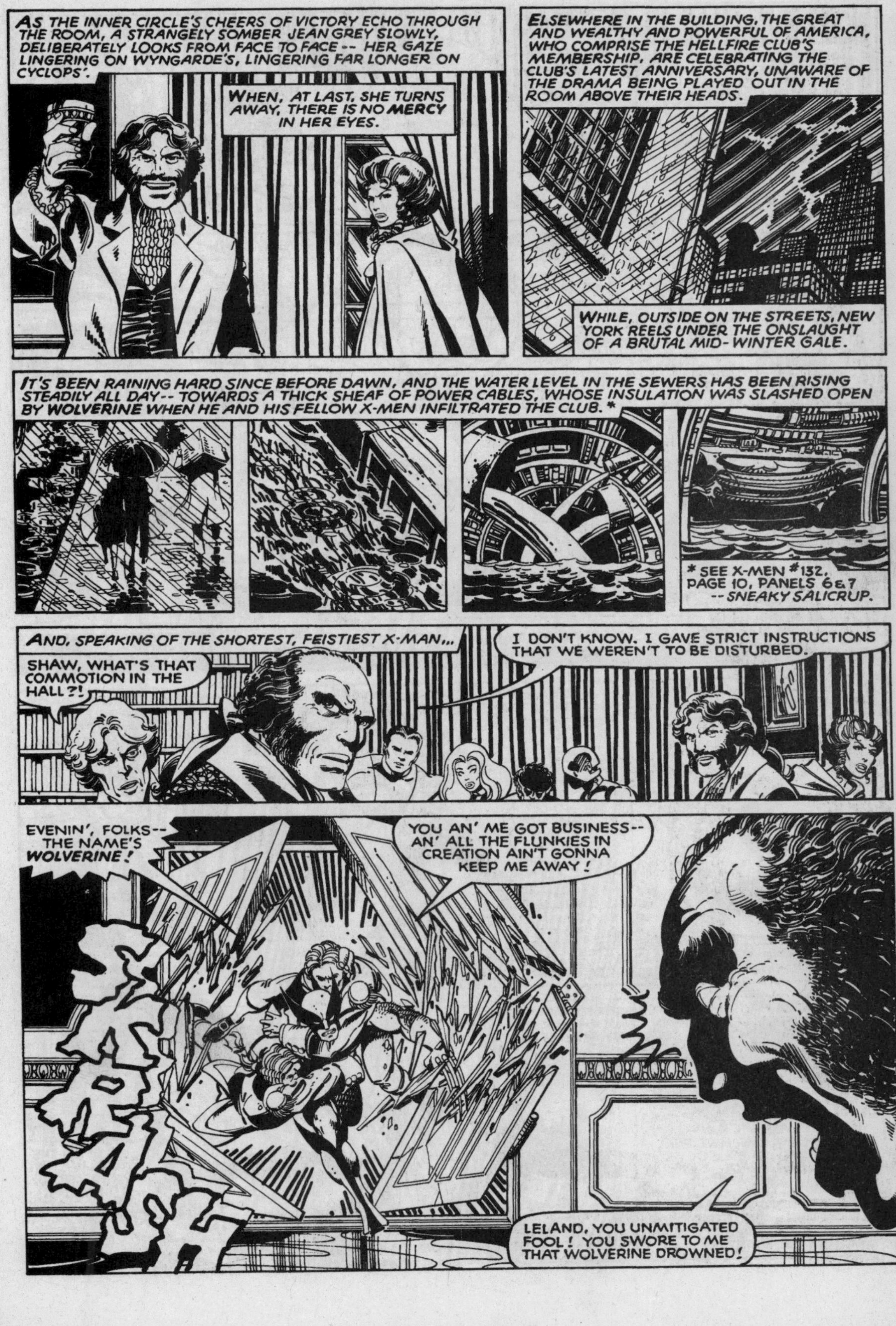
AS THE INNER CIRCLE'S CHEERS OF VICTORY ECHO THROUGH THE ROOM, A STRANGELY SOMBER JEAN GREY SLOWLY, DELIBERATELY LOOKS FROM FACE TO FACE -- HER GAZE LINGERING ON WYNGARDE'S, LINGERING FAR LONGER ON CYCLOPS'.
WHEN, AT LAST, SHE TURNS AWAY, THERE IS NO MERCY IN HER EYES.
ELSEWHERE IN THE BUILDING, THE GREAT AND WEALTHY AND POWERFUL OF AMERICA, WHO COMPRISE THE HELLFIRE CLUB'S MEMBERSHIP, ARE CELEBRATING THE CLUB'S LATEST ANNIVERSARY, UNAWARE OF THE DRAMA BEING PLAYED OUT IN THE ROOM ABOVE THEIR HEADS.
WHILE, OUTSIDE ON THE STREETS, NEW YORK REELS UNDER THE ONSLAUGHT OF A BRUTAL MID-WINTER GALE.
IT'S BEEN RAINING HARD SINCE BEFORE DAWN, AND THE WATER LEVEL IN THE SEWERS HAS BEEN RISING STEADILY ALL DAY-- TOWARDS A THICK SHEAF OF POWER CABLES, WHOSE INSULATION WAS SLASHED OPEN BY WOLVERINE WHEN HE AND HIS FELLOW X-MEN INFILTRATED THE CLUB. *
* SEE X-MEN #132, PAGE 10, PANELS 6&7 -- SNEAKY SALICRUP.
AND, SPEAKING OF THE SHORTEST, FEISTIEST X-MAN...
SHAW, WHAT'S THAT COMMOTION IN THE HALL?!
I DON'T KNOW. I GAVE STRICT INSTRUCTIONS THAT WE WEREN'T TO BE DISTURBED.
EVENIN', FOLKS-- THE NAME'S WOLVERINE!
YOU AN' ME GOT BUSINESS-- AN' ALL THE FLUNKIES IN CREATION AIN'T GONNA KEEP ME AWAY!
SPAK
LELAND, YOU UNMITIGATED FOOL! YOU SWORE TO ME THAT WOLVERINE DROWNED!

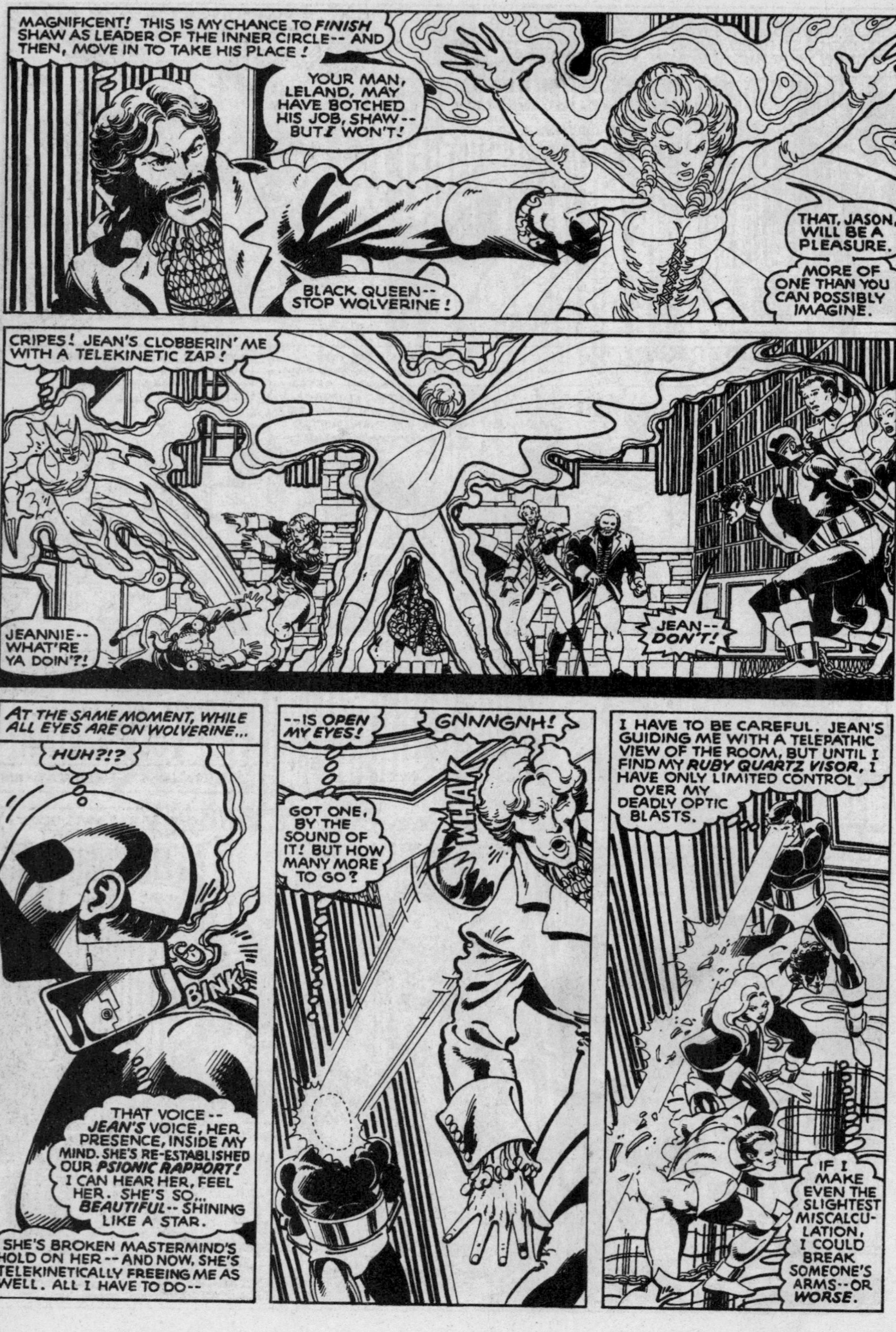
MAGNIFICENT! THIS IS MY CHANCE TO FINISH SHAW AS LEADER OF THE INNER CIRCLE-- AND THEN, MOVE IN TO TAKE HIS PLACE!
YOUR MAN, LELAND, MAY HAVE BOTCHED HIS JOB, SHAW-- BUT I WON'T!
BLACK QUEEN-- STOP WOLVERINE!
THAT, JASON, WILL BE A PLEASURE.
MORE OF ONE THAN YOU CAN POSSIBLY IMAGINE.
CRIPES! JEAN'S CLOBBERIN' ME WITH A TELEKINETIC ZAP!
JEANNIE-- WHAT'RE YA DOIN'?!
JEAN-- DON'T!
AT THE SAME MOMENT, WHILE ALL EYES ARE ON WOLVERINE...
HUH?!?
BINK!
THAT VOICE-- JEAN'S VOICE, HER PRESENCE, INSIDE MY MIND. SHE'S RE-ESTABLISHED OUR PSIONIC RAPPORT! I CAN HEAR HER, FEEL HER. SHE'S SO... BEAUTIFUL-- SHINING LIKE A STAR.
SHE'S BROKEN MASTERMIND'S HOLD ON HER-- AND NOW, SHE'S TELEKINETICALLY FREEING ME AS WELL. ALL I HAVE TO DO--
--IS OPEN MY EYES!
GNNNGNH!
WHAK
GOT ONE, BY THE SOUND OF IT! BUT HOW MANY MORE TO GO?
I HAVE TO BE CAREFUL. JEAN'S GUIDING ME WITH A TELEPATHIC VIEW OF THE ROOM, BUT UNTIL I FIND MY RUBY QUARTZ VISOR, I HAVE ONLY LIMITED CONTROL OVER MY DEADLY OPTIC BLASTS.
IF I MAKE EVEN THE SLIGHTEST MISCALCULATION, I COULD BREAK SOMEONE'S ARMS--OR WORSE.

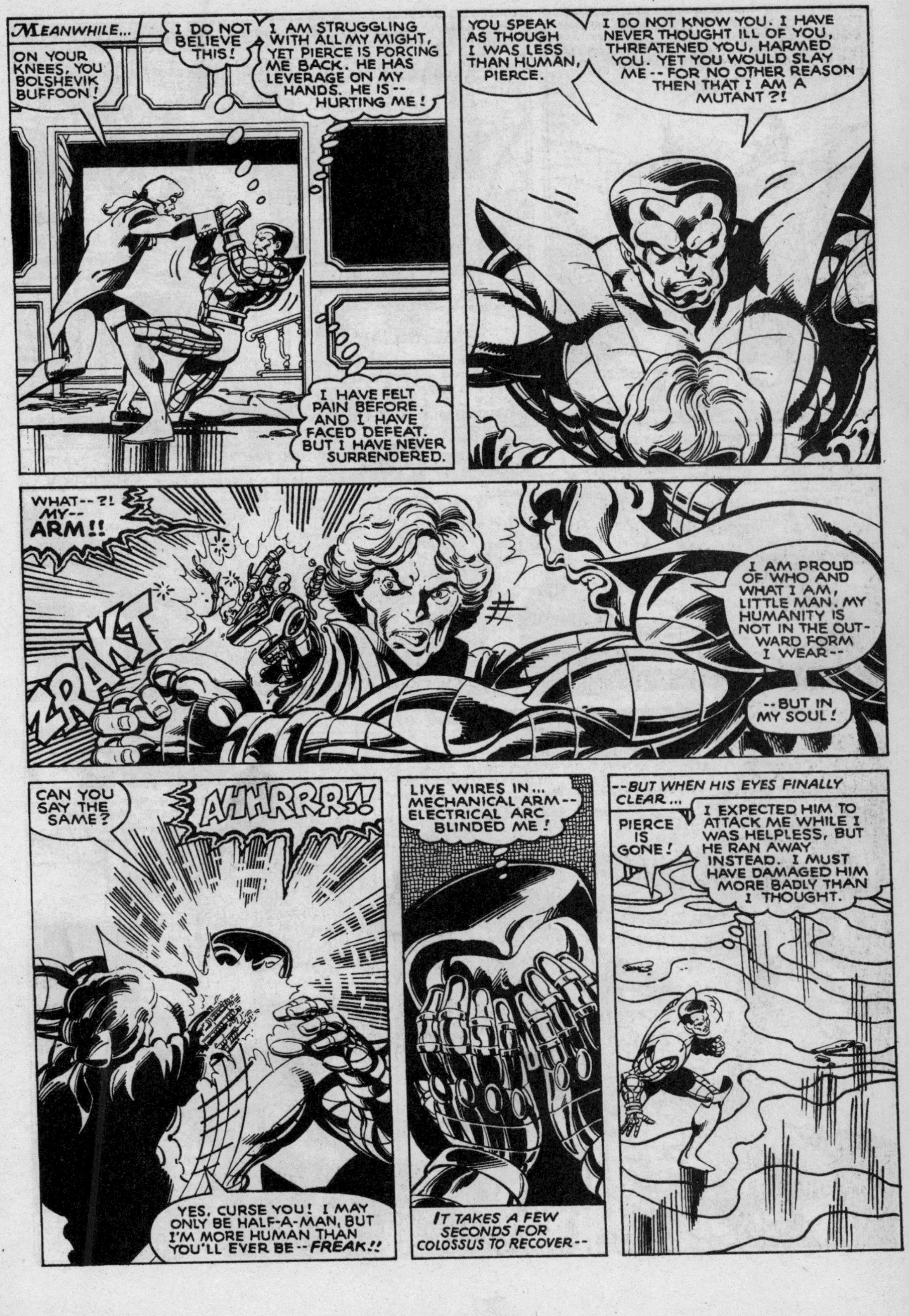
MEANWHILE...
ON YOUR KNEES, YOU BOLSHEVIK BUFFOON!
I DO NOT BELIEVE THIS!
I AM STRUGGLING WITH ALL MY MIGHT, YET PIERCE IS FORCING ME BACK. HE HAS LEVERAGE ON MY HANDS. HE IS -- HURTING ME!
I HAVE FELT PAIN BEFORE. AND I HAVE FACED DEFEAT. BUT I HAVE NEVER SURRENDERED.
YOU SPEAK AS THOUGH I WAS LESS THAN HUMAN, PIERCE.
I DO NOT KNOW YOU. I HAVE NEVER THOUGHT ILL OF YOU, THREATENED YOU, HARMED YOU. YET YOU WOULD SLAY ME -- FOR NO OTHER REASON THEN THAT I AM A MUTANT ?!
WHAT--?! MY-- ARM!!
ZRAKT
I AM PROUD OF WHO AND WHAT I AM, LITTLE MAN. MY HUMANITY IS NOT IN THE OUTWARD FORM I WEAR--
--BUT IN MY SOUL!
CAN YOU SAY THE SAME?
AHHRRR!!
YES, CURSE YOU! I MAY ONLY BE HALF-A-MAN, BUT I'M MORE HUMAN THAN YOU'LL EVER BE -- FREAK!!
LIVE WIRES IN... MECHANICAL ARM -- ELECTRICAL ARC BLINDED ME!
IT TAKES A FEW SECONDS FOR COLOSSUS TO RECOVER --
-- BUT WHEN HIS EYES FINALLY CLEAR...
PIERCE IS GONE!
I EXPECTED HIM TO ATTACK ME WHILE I WAS HELPLESS, BUT HE RAN AWAY INSTEAD. I MUST HAVE DAMAGED HIM MORE BADLY THAN I THOUGHT.

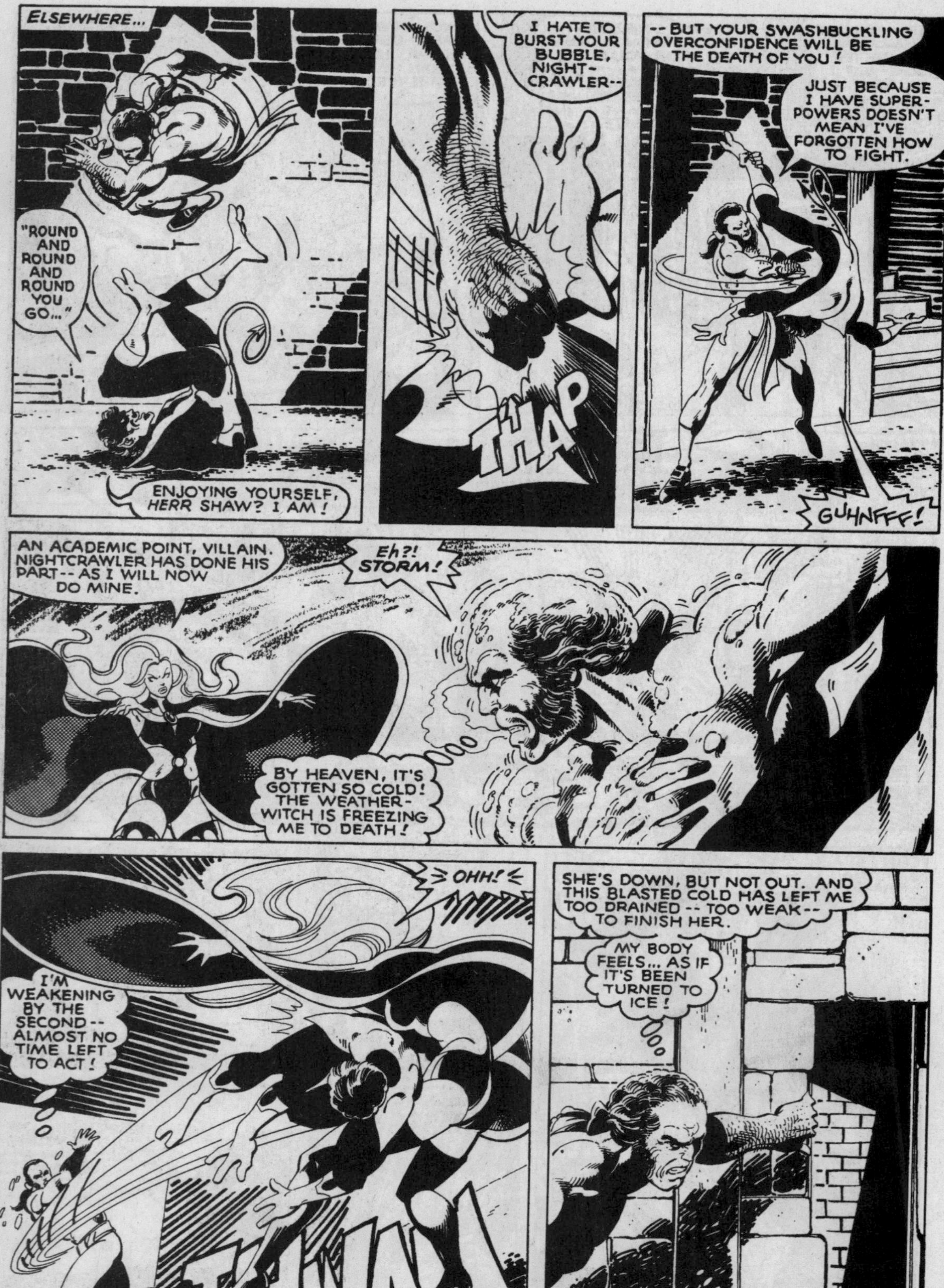
ELSEWHERE...
"ROUND AND ROUND AND ROUND YOU GO..."
ENJOYING YOURSELF, HERR SHAW? I AM!
I HATE TO BURST YOUR BUBBLE, NIGHT-CRAWLER--
THAP
--BUT YOUR SWASHBUCKLING OVERCONFIDENCE WILL BE THE DEATH OF YOU!
JUST BECAUSE I HAVE SUPER-POWERS DOESN'T MEAN I'VE FORGOTTEN HOW TO FIGHT.
GUHNFFF!
AN ACADEMIC POINT, VILLAIN. NIGHTCRAWLER HAS DONE HIS PART-- AS I WILL NOW DO MINE.
Eh?! STORM!
BY HEAVEN, IT'S GOTTEN SO COLD! THE WEATHER-WITCH IS FREEZING ME TO DEATH!
OHH!
I'M WEAKENING BY THE SECOND-- ALMOST NO TIME LEFT TO ACT!
THWAK
SHE'S DOWN, BUT NOT OUT. AND THIS BLASTED COLD HAS LEFT ME TOO DRAINED -- TOO WEAK-- TO FINISH HER.
MY BODY FEELS... AS IF IT'S BEEN TURNED TO ICE!
I WANT TO STAY-- TO FIGHT-- BUT I DARE NOT.

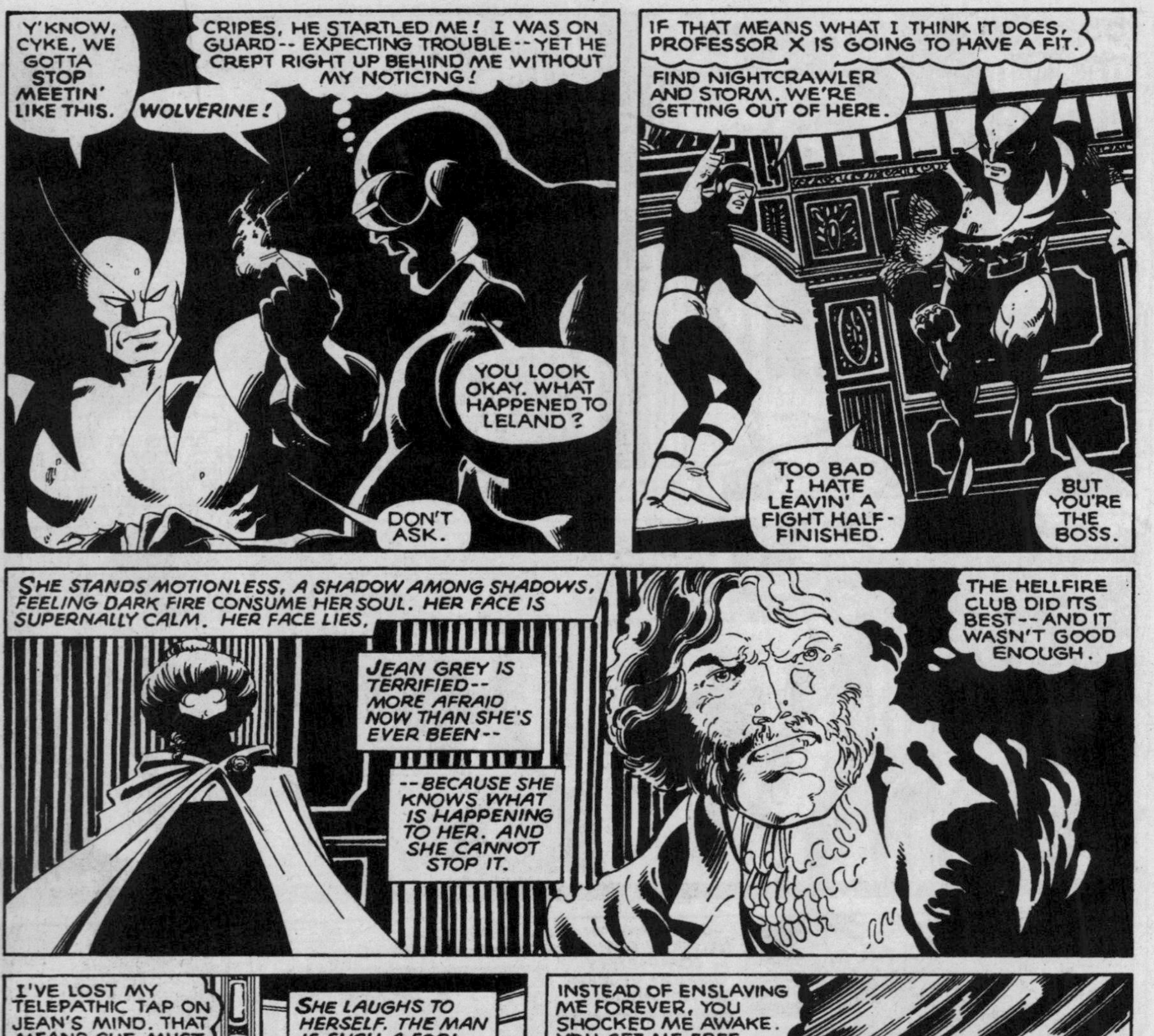
Y'KNOW, CYKE, WE GOTTA STOP MEETIN' LIKE THIS.
WOLVERINE!
CRIPES, HE STARTLED ME! I WAS ON GUARD-- EXPECTING TROUBLE--YET HE CREPT RIGHT UP BEHIND ME WITHOUT MY NOTICING!
YOU LOOK OKAY. WHAT HAPPENED TO LELAND?
DON'T ASK.
IF THAT MEANS WHAT I THINK IT DOES, PROFESSOR X IS GOING TO HAVE A FIT.
FIND NIGHTCRAWLER AND STORM. WE'RE GETTING OUT OF HERE.
TOO BAD I HATE LEAVIN' A FIGHT HALF-FINISHED.
BUT YOU'RE THE BOSS.
SHE STANDS MOTIONLESS, A SHADOW AMONG SHADOWS, FEELING DARK FIRE CONSUME HER SOUL. HER FACE IS SUPERNALLY CALM. HER FACE LIES.
JEAN GREY IS TERRIFIED-- MORE AFRAID NOW THAN SHE'S EVER BEEN--
--BECAUSE SHE KNOWS WHAT IS HAPPENING TO HER. AND SHE CANNOT STOP IT.
THE HELLFIRE CLUB DID ITS BEST--AND IT WASN'T GOOD ENOUGH.
I'VE LOST MY TELEPATHIC TAP ON JEAN'S MIND. THAT MEANS SHE MUST HAVE BROKEN MY CONTROL--BUT HOW? I ANTICIPATED EVERY CONTINGENCY.
SHE LAUGHS TO HERSELF. THE MAN IS SUCH A FOOL. SHE WILL ENJOY WHAT HAPPENS NEXT.
AND, REALIZING THAT, SHE WEEPS.
YOU MADE A MISTAKE, JASON. YOU "SLEW" THE MAN I LOVED BEFORE MY EYES. INSTEAD OF SEVERING MY LAST CONNECTION WITH THE X-MEN, THAT ACTED LIKE A BUCKET OF ICE WATER IN MY FACE.
INSTEAD OF ENSLAVING ME FOREVER, YOU SHOCKED ME AWAKE. YOU SET ME FREE.
TOO LATE.
NO! I COMPENSATED FOR THAT REACTION--MY POWER SHOULD HAVE...
YOUR POWER IS NOTHING!

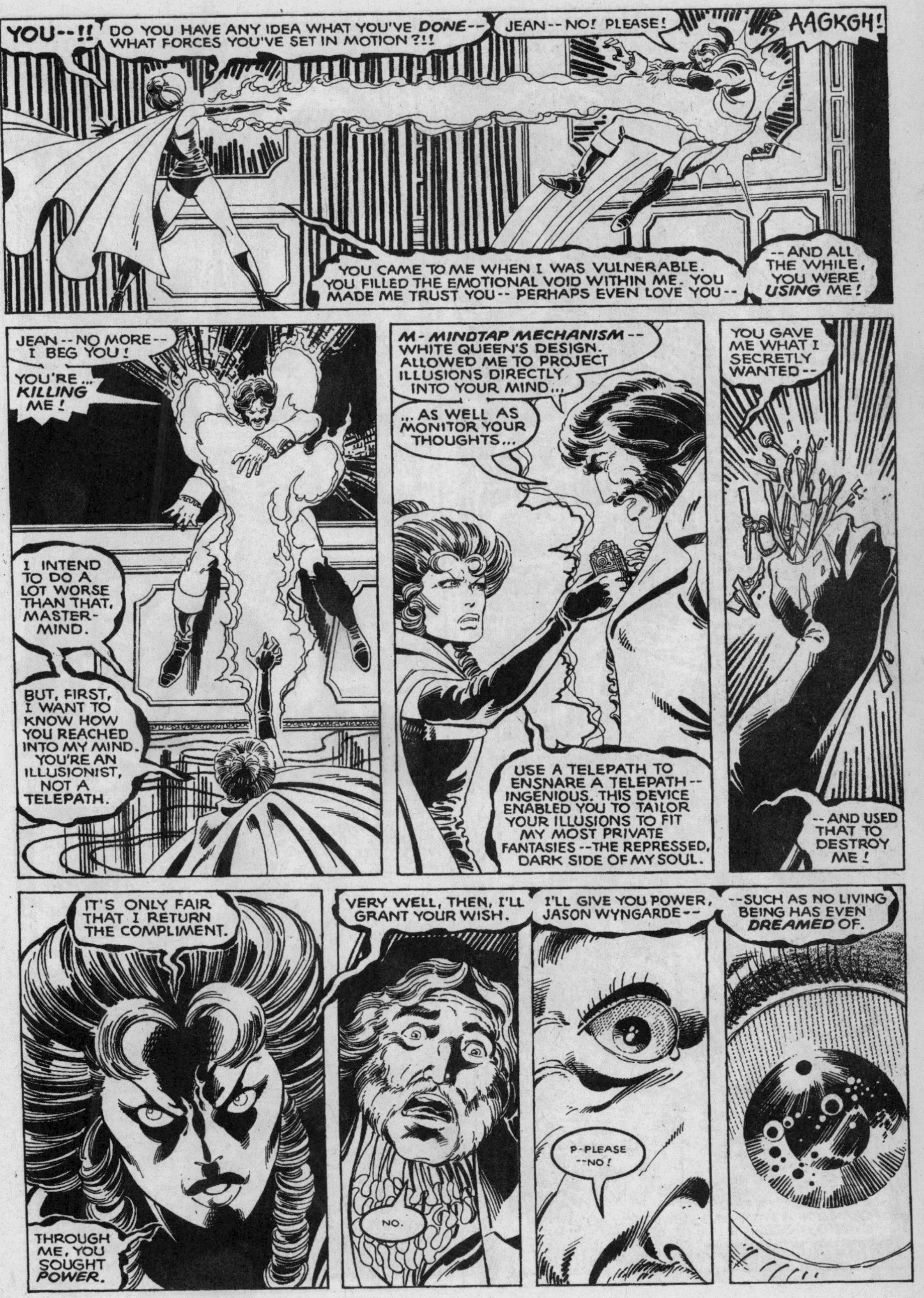

YOU--!!
DO YOU HAVE ANY IDEA WHAT YOU'VE DONE-- WHAT FORCES YOU'VE SET IN MOTION?!!
JEAN--NO! PLEASE!
AAGKGH!
YOU CAME TO ME WHEN I WAS VULNERABLE. YOU FILLED THE EMOTIONAL VOID WITHIN ME. YOU MADE ME TRUST YOU-- PERHAPS EVEN LOVE YOU--
--AND ALL THE WHILE, YOU WERE USING ME!
JEAN--NO MORE-- I BEG YOU!
YOU'RE... KILLING ME!
I INTEND TO DO A LOT WORSE THAN THAT, MASTER-MIND.
BUT, FIRST, I WANT TO KNOW HOW YOU REACHED INTO MY MIND. YOU'RE AN ILLUSIONIST, NOT A TELEPATH.
M-MINDTAP MECHANISM-- WHITE QUEEN'S DESIGN. ALLOWED ME TO PROJECT ILLUSIONS DIRECTLY INTO YOUR MIND...
...AS WELL AS MONITOR YOUR THOUGHTS...
USE A TELEPATH TO ENSNARE A TELEPATH-- INGENIOUS. THIS DEVICE ENABLED YOU TO TAILOR YOUR ILLUSIONS TO FIT MY MOST PRIVATE FANTASIES--THE REPRESSED, DARK SIDE OF MY SOUL.
YOU GAVE ME WHAT I SECRETLY WANTED--
--AND USED THAT TO DESTROY ME!
IT'S ONLY FAIR THAT I RETURN THE COMPLIMENT.
THROUGH ME, YOU SOUGHT POWER.
VERY WELL, THEN, I'LL GRANT YOUR WISH.
NO.
I'LL GIVE YOU POWER, JASON WYNGARDE--
P-PLEASE --NO!
--SUCH AS NO LIVING BEING HAS EVEN DREAMED OF.

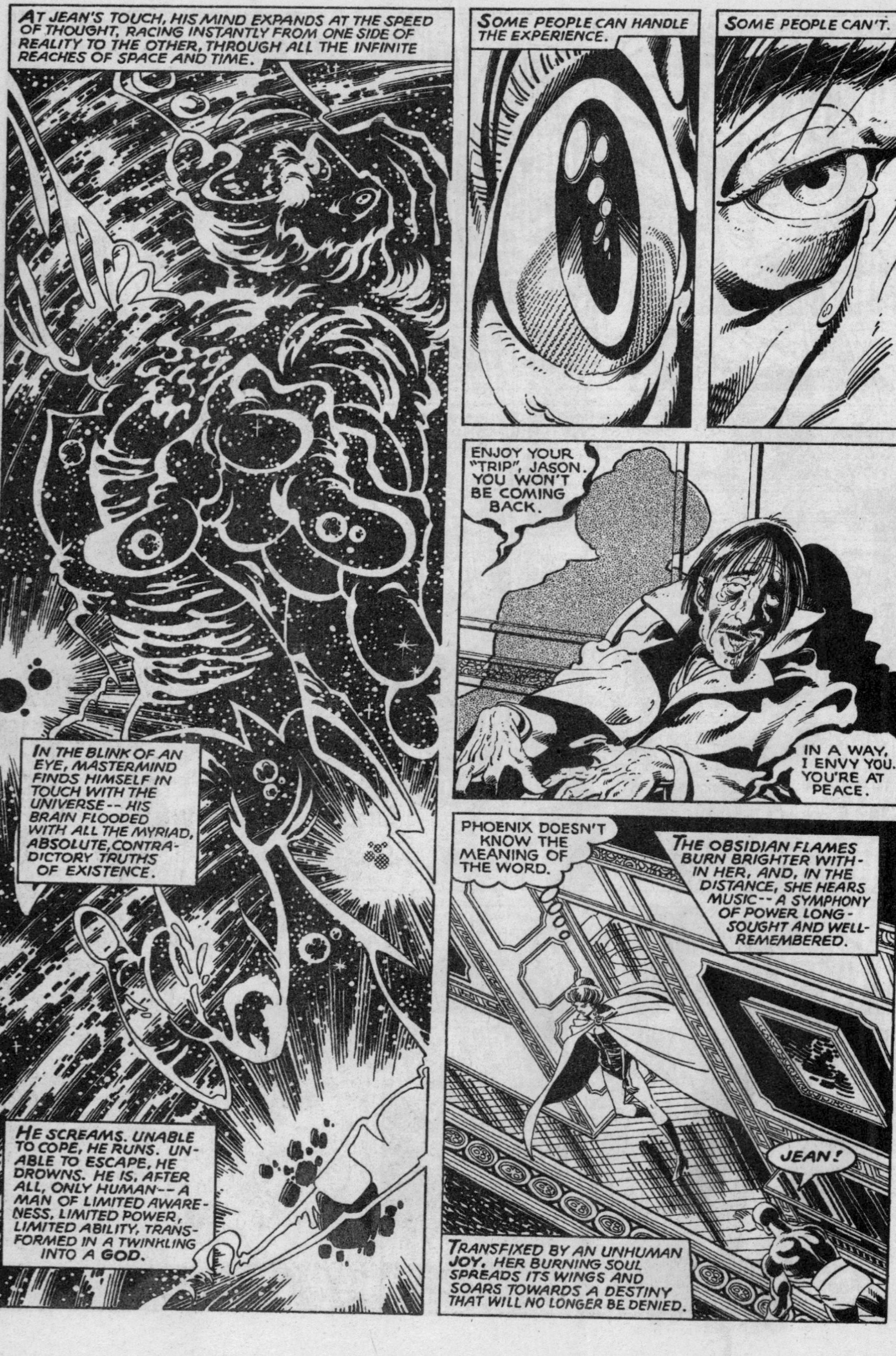

AT JEAN'S TOUCH, HIS MIND EXPANDS AT THE SPEED OF THOUGHT, RACING INSTANTLY FROM ONE SIDE OF REALITY TO THE OTHER, THROUGH ALL THE INFINITE REACHES OF SPACE AND TIME.
IN THE BLINK OF AN EYE, MASTERMIND FINDS HIMSELF IN TOUCH WITH THE UNIVERSE-- HIS BRAIN FLOODED WITH ALL THE MYRIAD, ABSOLUTE, CONTRADICTORY TRUTHS OF EXISTENCE.
HE SCREAMS. UNABLE TO COPE, HE RUNS. UNABLE TO ESCAPE, HE DROWNS. HE IS, AFTER ALL, ONLY HUMAN-- A MAN OF LIMITED AWARENESS, LIMITED POWER, LIMITED ABILITY, TRANSFORMED IN A TWINKLING INTO A GOD.
SOME PEOPLE CAN HANDLE THE EXPERIENCE.
SOME PEOPLE CAN'T.
ENJOY YOUR "TRIP", JASON. YOU WON'T BE COMING BACK.
IN A WAY, I ENVY YOU. YOU'RE AT PEACE.
PHOENIX DOESN'T KNOW THE MEANING OF THE WORD.
THE OBSIDIAN FLAMES BURN BRIGHTER WITHIN HER, AND, IN THE DISTANCE, SHE HEARS MUSIC-- A SYMPHONY OF POWER LONG-SOUGHT AND WELL-REMEMBERED.
JEAN!
TRANSFIXED BY AN UNHUMAN JOY, HER BURNING SOUL SPREADS ITS WINGS AND SOARS TOWARDS A DESTINY THAT WILL NO LONGER BE DENIED.

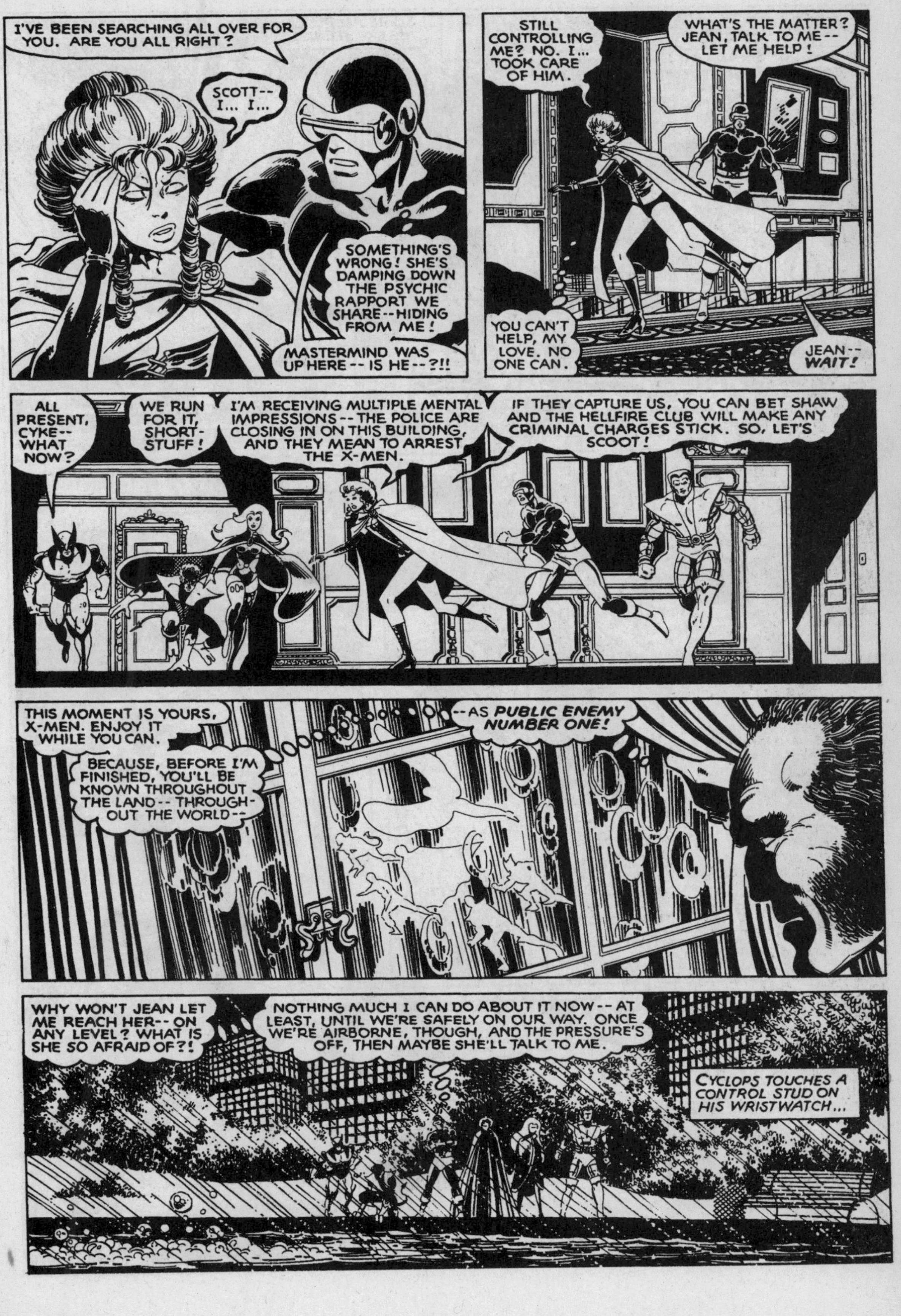
I'VE BEEN SEARCHING ALL OVER FOR YOU. ARE YOU ALL RIGHT?
SCOTT-- I... I...
SOMETHING'S WRONG! SHE'S DAMPING DOWN THE PSYCHIC RAPPORT WE SHARE--HIDING FROM ME!
MASTERMIND WAS UP HERE -- IS HE --?!!
STILL CONTROLLING ME? NO. I... TOOK CARE OF HIM.
WHAT'S THE MATTER? JEAN, TALK TO ME -- LET ME HELP!
YOU CAN'T HELP, MY LOVE. NO ONE CAN.
JEAN-- WAIT!
ALL PRESENT, CYKE-- WHAT NOW?
WE RUN FOR IT, SHORT-STUFF!
I'M RECEIVING MULTIPLE MENTAL IMPRESSIONS -- THE POLICE ARE CLOSING IN ON THIS BUILDING, AND THEY MEAN TO ARREST THE X-MEN.
IF THEY CAPTURE US, YOU CAN BET SHAW AND THE HELLFIRE CLUB WILL MAKE ANY CRIMINAL CHARGES STICK. SO, LET'S SCOOT!
THIS MOMENT IS YOURS, X-MEN. ENJOY IT WHILE YOU CAN.
BECAUSE, BEFORE I'M FINISHED, YOU'LL BE KNOWN THROUGHOUT THE LAND -- THROUGH-OUT THE WORLD--
--AS PUBLIC ENEMY NUMBER ONE!
WHY WON'T JEAN LET ME REACH HER-- ON ANY LEVEL? WHAT IS SHE SO AFRAID OF?!
NOTHING MUCH I CAN DO ABOUT IT NOW -- AT LEAST, UNTIL WE'RE SAFELY ON OUR WAY. ONCE WE'RE AIRBORNE, THOUGH, AND THE PRESSURE'S OFF, THEN MAYBE SHE'LL TALK TO ME.
CYCLOPS TOUCHES A CONTROL STUD ON HIS WRISTWATCH...

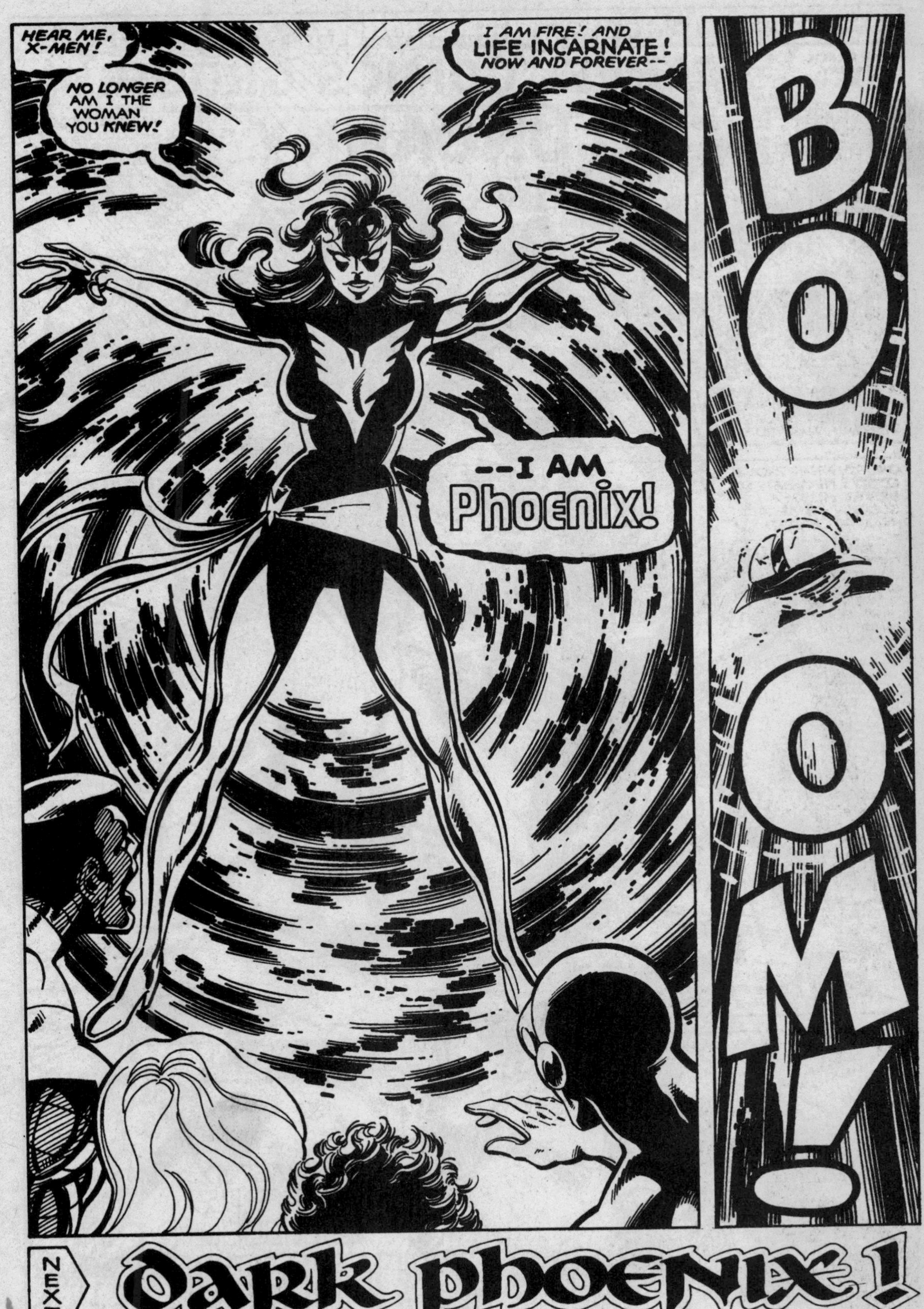

HEAR ME, X-MEN!
NO LONGER AM I THE WOMAN YOU KNEW!
I AM FIRE! AND LIFE INCARNATE! NOW AND FOREVER--
--I AM Phoenix!
BOOM!

NEXT Dark Phoenix!

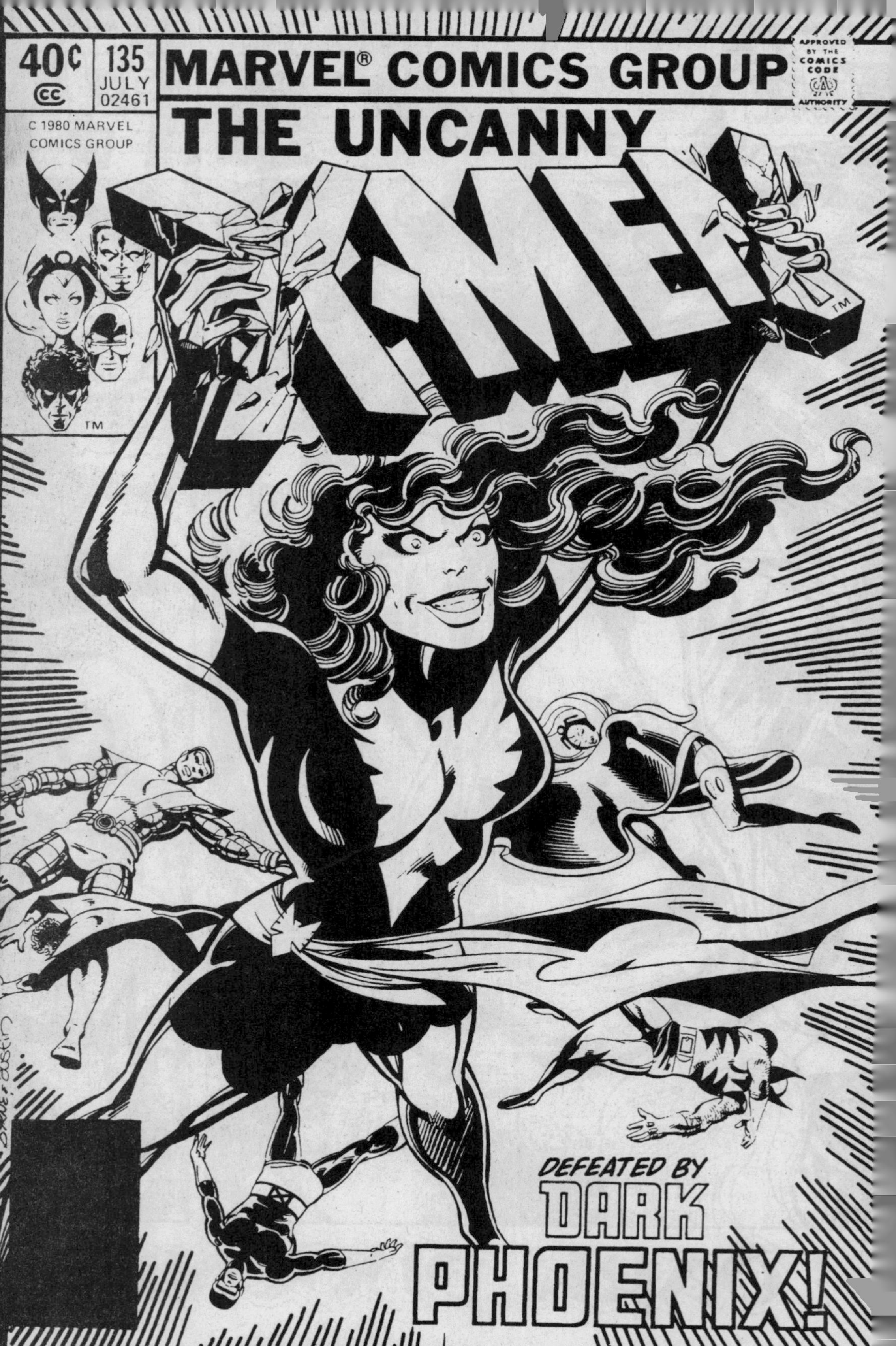

40¢
135
JULY
02461
MARVEL® COMICS GROUP
APPROVED BY THE COMICS CODE AUTHORITY
C 1980 MARVEL COMICS GROUP
THE UNCANNY
X-MEN TM
DEFEATED BY
DARK
PHOENIX!

Cyclops. Storm. Nightcrawler. Wolverine. Colossus. Children of the atom, students of Charles Xavier, MUTANTS — feared and hated by the world they have sworn to protect. These are the STRANGEST heroes of all!

Stan Lee PRESENTS: THE UNCANNY X-MEN!™

CHRIS CLAREMONT & JOHN BYRNE WRITER / CO-PLOTTERS / PENCILER | TERRY AUSTIN INKER | TOM ORZECHOWSKI, letterer BOB SHAREN, colorist | JIM SALICRUP EDITOR | JIM SHOOTER Ed.-IN-CHIEF

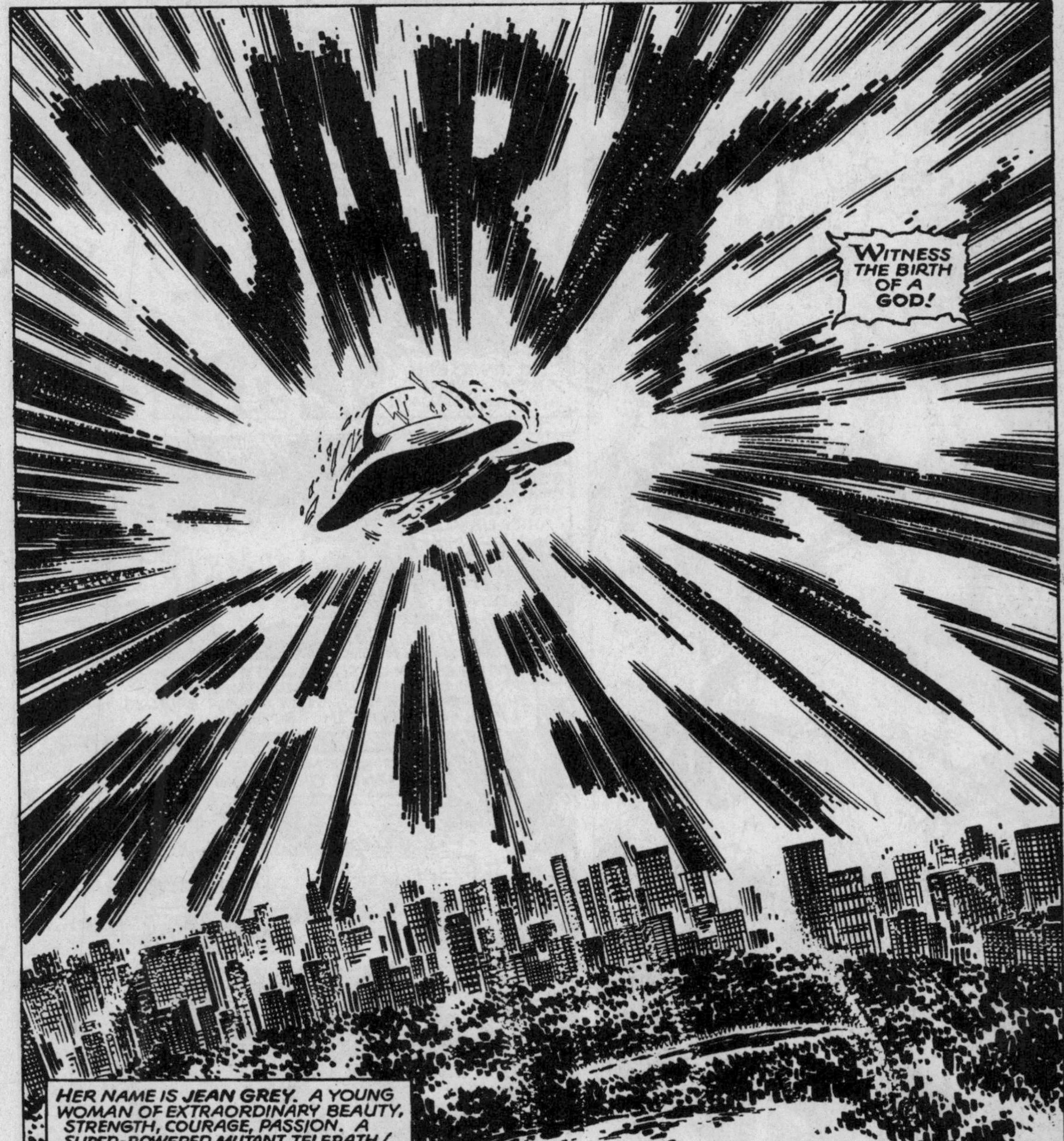
WITNESS THE BIRTH OF A GOD!
HER NAME IS JEAN GREY. A YOUNG WOMAN OF EXTRAORDINARY BEAUTY, STRENGTH, COURAGE, PASSION. A SUPER-POWERED MUTANT TELEPATH/ TELEKINETIC. A CHARTER MEMBER OF THE UNCANNY X-MEN.
NONE OF THAT HAS CHANGED. AND YET-- EVERYTHING HAS CHANGED.

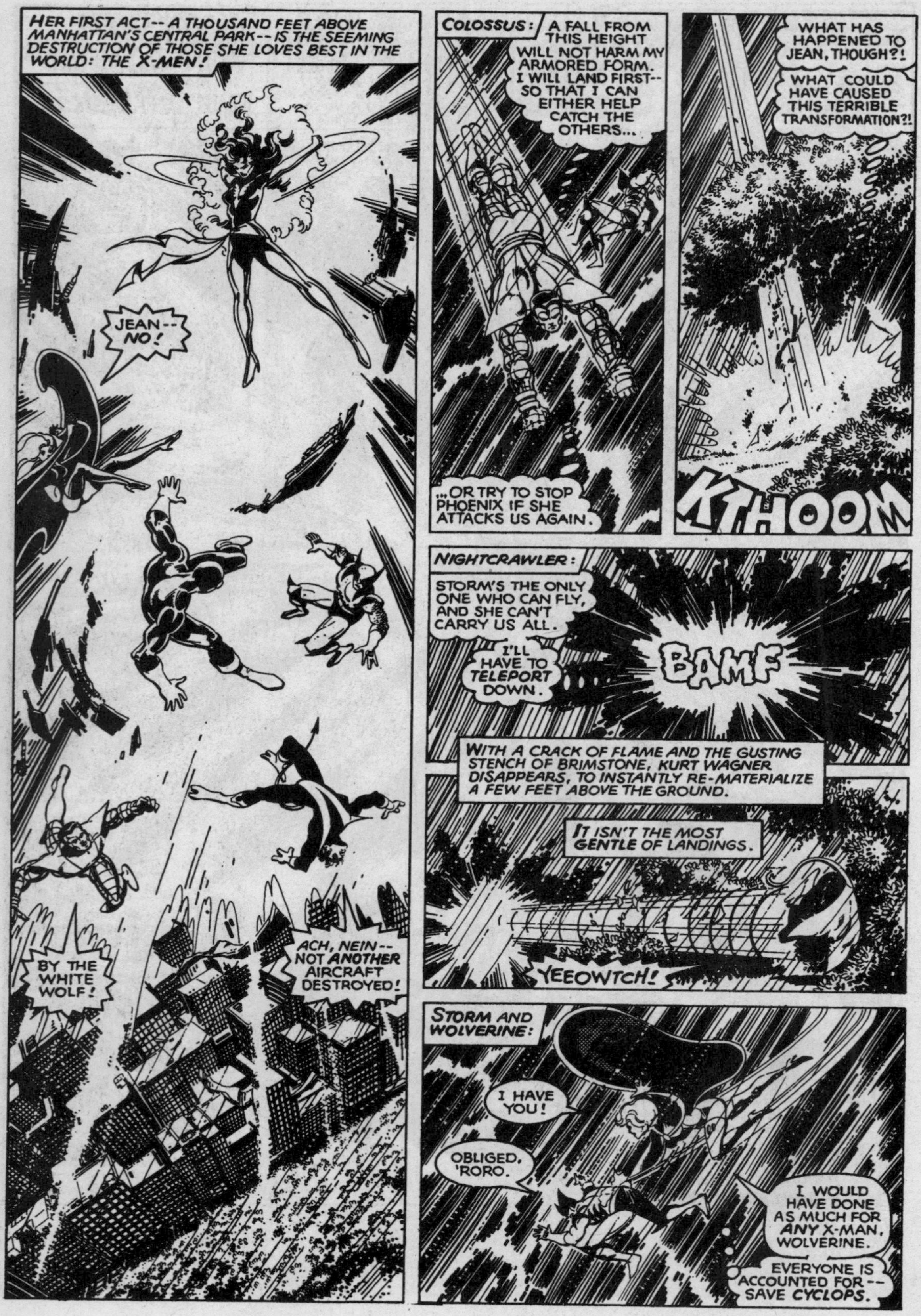
HER FIRST ACT-- A THOUSAND FEET ABOVE MANHATTAN'S CENTRAL PARK-- IS THE SEEMING DESTRUCTION OF THOSE SHE LOVES BEST IN THE WORLD: THE X-MEN!
JEAN-- NO!
BY THE WHITE WOLF!
ACH, NEIN-- NOT ANOTHER AIRCRAFT DESTROYED!
COLOSSUS: A FALL FROM THIS HEIGHT WILL NOT HARM MY ARMORED FORM. I WILL LAND FIRST-- SO THAT I CAN EITHER HELP CATCH THE OTHERS...
...OR TRY TO STOP PHOENIX IF SHE ATTACKS US AGAIN.
WHAT HAS HAPPENED TO JEAN, THOUGH?!
WHAT COULD HAVE CAUSED THIS TERRIBLE TRANSFORMATION?!
KTHOOM
NIGHTCRAWLER: STORM'S THE ONLY ONE WHO CAN FLY, AND SHE CAN'T CARRY US ALL.
I'LL HAVE TO TELEPORT DOWN.
BAMF
WITH A CRACK OF FLAME AND THE GUSTING STENCH OF BRIMSTONE, KURT WAGNER DISAPPEARS, TO INSTANTLY RE-MATERIALIZE A FEW FEET ABOVE THE GROUND.
IT ISN'T THE MOST GENTLE OF LANDINGS.
YEEOWTCH!
STORM AND WOLVERINE:
I HAVE YOU!
OBLIGED, 'RORO.
I WOULD HAVE DONE AS MUCH FOR ANY X-MAN, WOLVERINE.
EVERYONE IS ACCOUNTED FOR-- SAVE CYCLOPS.

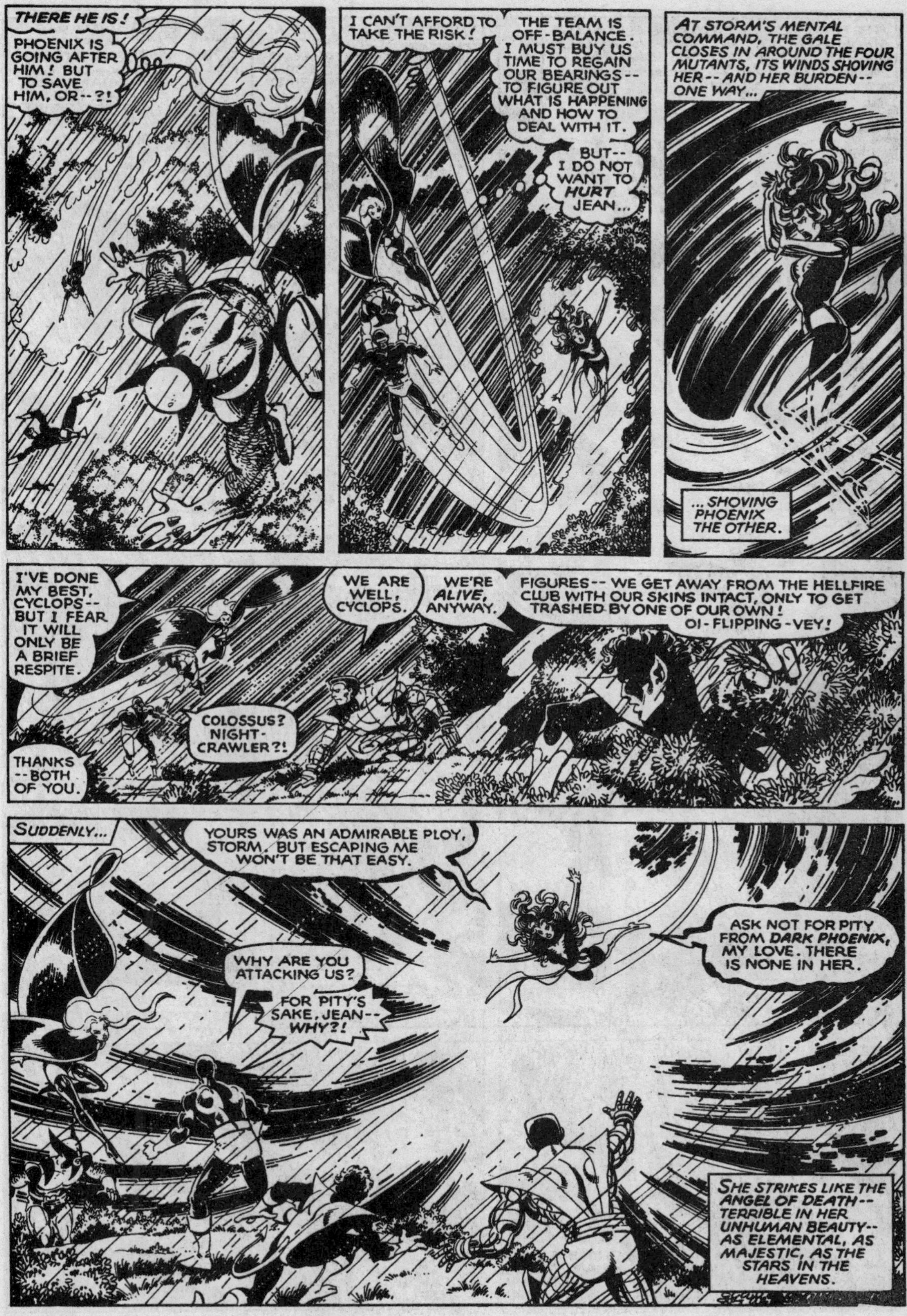
THERE HE IS!
PHOENIX IS GOING AFTER HIM! BUT TO SAVE HIM, OR--?!
I CAN'T AFFORD TO TAKE THE RISK!
THE TEAM IS OFF-BALANCE. I MUST BUY US TIME TO REGAIN OUR BEARINGS -- TO FIGURE OUT WHAT IS HAPPENING AND HOW TO DEAL WITH IT.
BUT-- I DO NOT WANT TO HURT JEAN...
AT STORM'S MENTAL COMMAND, THE GALE CLOSES IN AROUND THE FOUR MUTANTS, ITS WINDS SHOVING HER -- AND HER BURDEN -- ONE WAY...
...SHOVING PHOENIX THE OTHER.
I'VE DONE MY BEST, CYCLOPS -- BUT I FEAR IT WILL ONLY BE A BRIEF RESPITE.
WE ARE WELL, CYCLOPS.
WE'RE ALIVE, ANYWAY.
FIGURES -- WE GET AWAY FROM THE HELLFIRE CLUB WITH OUR SKINS INTACT, ONLY TO GET TRASHED BY ONE OF OUR OWN!
OI-FLIPPING-VEY!
COLOSSUS? NIGHT-CRAWLER?!
THANKS -- BOTH OF YOU.
SUDDENLY...
YOURS WAS AN ADMIRABLE PLOY, STORM. BUT ESCAPING ME WON'T BE THAT EASY.
WHY ARE YOU ATTACKING US?
FOR PITY'S SAKE, JEAN-- WHY?!
ASK NOT FOR PITY FROM DARK PHOENIX, MY LOVE. THERE IS NONE IN HER.
SHE STRIKES LIKE THE ANGEL OF DEATH -- TERRIBLE IN HER UNHUMAN BEAUTY -- AS ELEMENTAL, AS MAJESTIC, AS THE STARS IN THE HEAVENS.

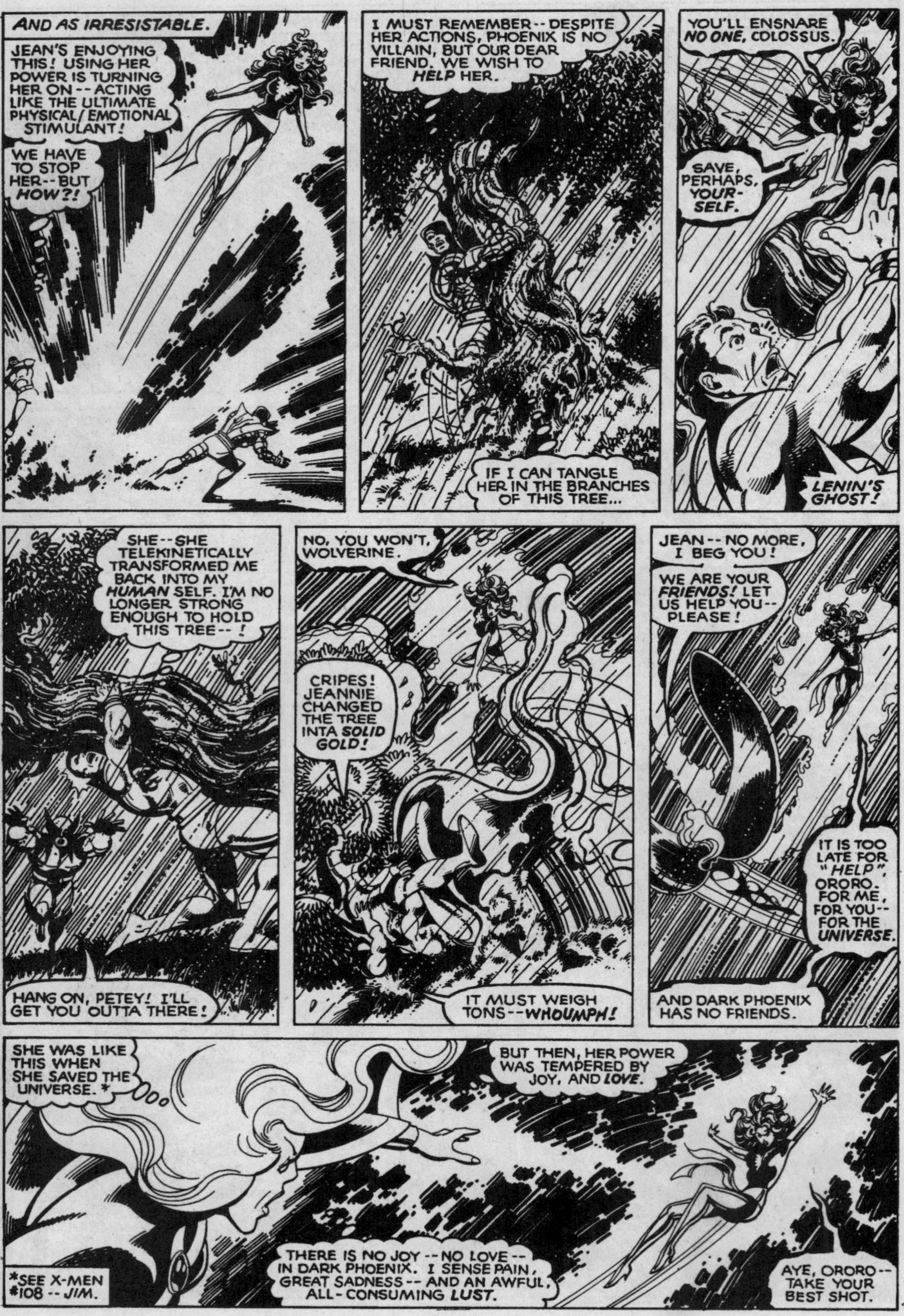
AND AS IRRESISTABLE.
JEAN'S ENJOYING THIS! USING HER POWER IS TURNING HER ON -- ACTING LIKE THE ULTIMATE PHYSICAL/EMOTIONAL STIMULANT!
WE HAVE TO STOP HER -- BUT HOW?!
I MUST REMEMBER -- DESPITE HER ACTIONS, PHOENIX IS NO VILLAIN, BUT OUR DEAR FRIEND. WE WISH TO HELP HER.
IF I CAN TANGLE HER IN THE BRANCHES OF THIS TREE...
YOU'LL ENSNARE NO ONE, COLOSSUS.
SAVE, PERHAPS, YOURSELF.
LENIN'S GHOST!
SHE -- SHE TELEKINETICALLY TRANSFORMED ME BACK INTO MY HUMAN SELF. I'M NO LONGER STRONG ENOUGH TO HOLD THIS TREE -- !
HANG ON, PETEY! I'LL GET YOU OUTTA THERE!
NO, YOU WON'T, WOLVERINE.
CRIPES! JEANNIE CHANGED THE TREE INTA SOLID GOLD!
IT MUST WEIGH TONS -- WHOUMPH!
JEAN -- NO MORE, I BEG YOU!
WE ARE YOUR FRIENDS! LET US HELP YOU -- PLEASE!
IT IS TOO LATE FOR "HELP", ORORO. FOR ME, FOR YOU -- FOR THE UNIVERSE.
AND DARK PHOENIX HAS NO FRIENDS.
SHE WAS LIKE THIS WHEN SHE SAVED THE UNIVERSE.*
BUT THEN, HER POWER WAS TEMPERED BY JOY, AND LOVE.
THERE IS NO JOY -- NO LOVE -- IN DARK PHOENIX. I SENSE PAIN, GREAT SADNESS -- AND AN AWFUL, ALL-CONSUMING LUST.
AYE, ORORO -- TAKE YOUR BEST SHOT.
*SEE X-MEN #108 -- JIM.

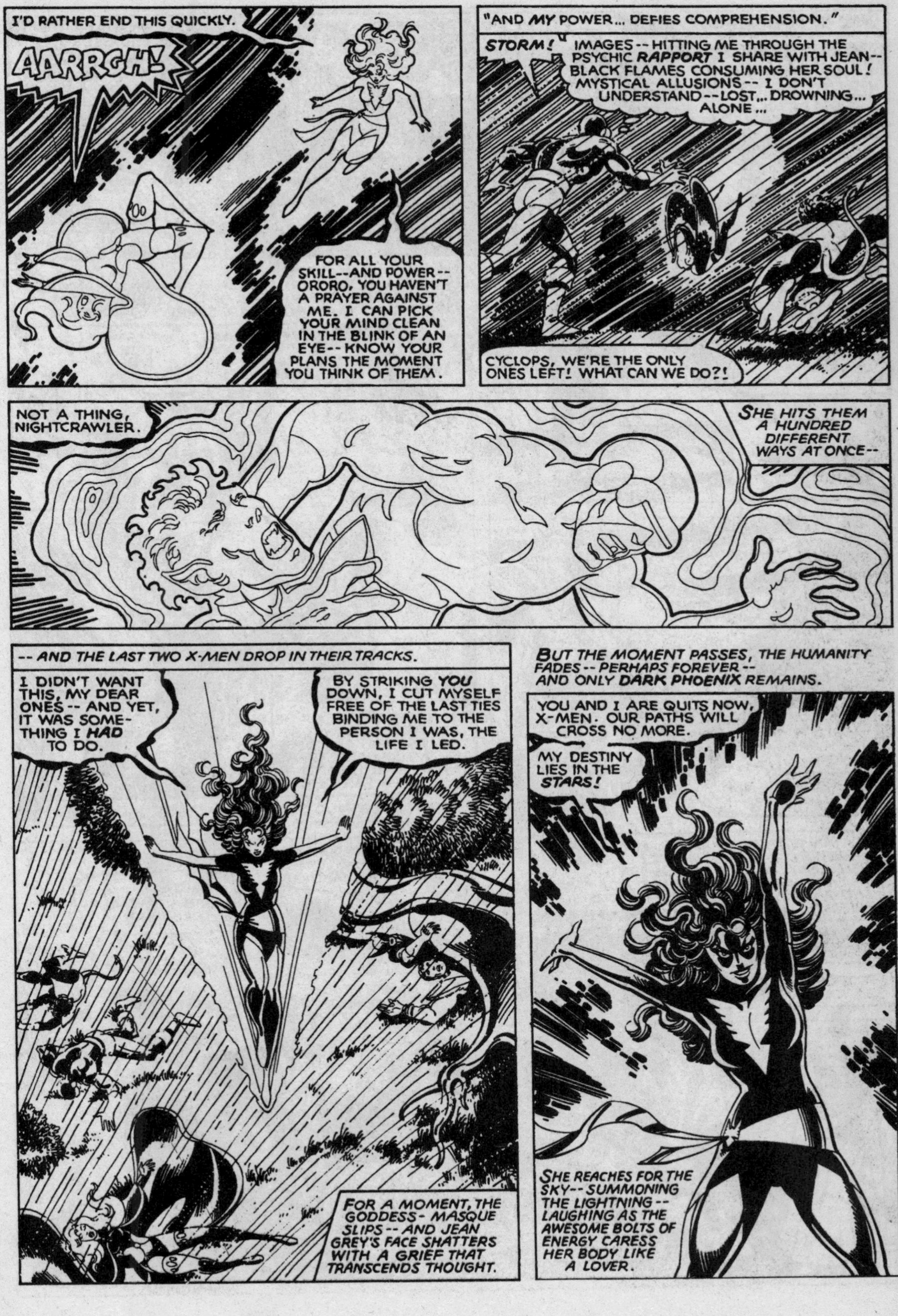

I'D RATHER END THIS QUICKLY.
AARRGH!
FOR ALL YOUR SKILL--AND POWER-- ORORO, YOU HAVEN'T A PRAYER AGAINST ME. I CAN PICK YOUR MIND CLEAN IN THE BLINK OF AN EYE--KNOW YOUR PLANS THE MOMENT YOU THINK OF THEM.
"AND MY POWER... DEFIES COMPREHENSION."
STORM!
IMAGES--HITTING ME THROUGH THE PSYCHIC RAPPORT I SHARE WITH JEAN-- BLACK FLAMES CONSUMING HER SOUL! MYSTICAL ALLUSIONS--I DON'T UNDERSTAND--LOST... DROWNING... ALONE...
CYCLOPS, WE'RE THE ONLY ONES LEFT! WHAT CAN WE DO?!
NOT A THING, NIGHTCRAWLER.
SHE HITS THEM A HUNDRED DIFFERENT WAYS AT ONCE--
--AND THE LAST TWO X-MEN DROP IN THEIR TRACKS.
I DIDN'T WANT THIS, MY DEAR ONES--AND YET, IT WAS SOMETHING I HAD TO DO.
BY STRIKING YOU DOWN, I CUT MYSELF FREE OF THE LAST TIES BINDING ME TO THE PERSON I WAS, THE LIFE I LED.
FOR A MOMENT, THE GODDESS-MASQUE SLIPS--AND JEAN GREY'S FACE SHATTERS WITH A GRIEF THAT TRANSCENDS THOUGHT.
BUT THE MOMENT PASSES, THE HUMANITY FADES--PERHAPS FOREVER-- AND ONLY DARK PHOENIX REMAINS.
YOU AND I ARE QUITS NOW, X-MEN. OUR PATHS WILL CROSS NO MORE.
MY DESTINY LIES IN THE STARS!
SHE REACHES FOR THE SKY--SUMMONING THE LIGHTNING-- LAUGHING AS THE AWESOME BOLTS OF ENERGY CARESS HER BODY LIKE A LOVER.

TIME: FIVE MINUTES EARLIER. PLACE: THE HELLFIRE CLUB, ON NEW YORK'S FASHIONABLE FIFTH AVENUE.

THE X-MEN HAVE JUST FLED INTO THE GALE-SWEPT NIGHT, A STEP AHEAD OF THE POLICE UNITS ASSEMBLED TO ARREST THEM.

ON THE SURFACE, THE CASE LOOKS CUT AND DRIED. THE X-MEN BROKE INTO THE CLUB DURING A PARTY CELEBRATING ITS ANNIVERSARY.

THEY RAMPAGED THROUGH THE BUILDING, TERRORIZING THE GUESTS AND LEAVING TWO CLUB MEMBERS-- HARRY LELAND AND JASON WYNGARDE-- IN NEED OF IMMEDIATE HOSPITALIZATION.

TO ALL CONCERNED, THE X-MEN ARE OBVIOUSLY CRIMINALS.

BUT, IN REALITY, THEY ARE NOT.

IF ANYTHING, THEY ARE VICTIMS-- OF A PLOT HATCHED BY SEBASTIAN SHAW, HEAD OF THE CLUB'S SECRET INNER CIRCLE, A GROUP OUT, SIMPLY, TO RULE THE WORLD.

SEBASTIAN, I... I AM SORRY ABOUT LELAND.

THANK YOU, ROBERT. THAT'S VERY KIND.

THE X-MEN WERE OUR HELPLESS PRISONERS YET STILL THEY ESCAPED AND DEFEATED US. WE UNDERESTIMATED THEM-- AND LELAND AND WYNGARDE PAID THE PRICE. *

* FOR FULL DETAILS, SEE THE LAST THREE ISSUES--JIM.

THE MAN WITH SHAW IS U.S. SENATOR ROBERT KELLY-- PRESIDENTIAL CANDIDATE-- INTELLIGENT, ARTICULATE, DECENT, POPULAR, GIVEN A GOOD CHANCE OF WINNING IN NOVEMBER. HE AND SHAW ARE OLD FRIENDS.

MR. SHAW, SENATOR KELLY...

...MY MEN HAVE SEARCHED THE CLUB. THERE'S NO SIGN OF THE MUTIES.

OBVIOUSLY, CAPTAIN -- BECAUSE THE X-MEN ARE NO LONGER INSIDE THE BUILDING !

MR. SHAW SAW THEM RUNNING TOWARDS CENTRAL PARK.

I SUGGEST YOU SHOW SOME INIATIVE AND GET YOUR PEOPLE IN THERE AFTER THEM-- BEFORE THEY GET AWAY !

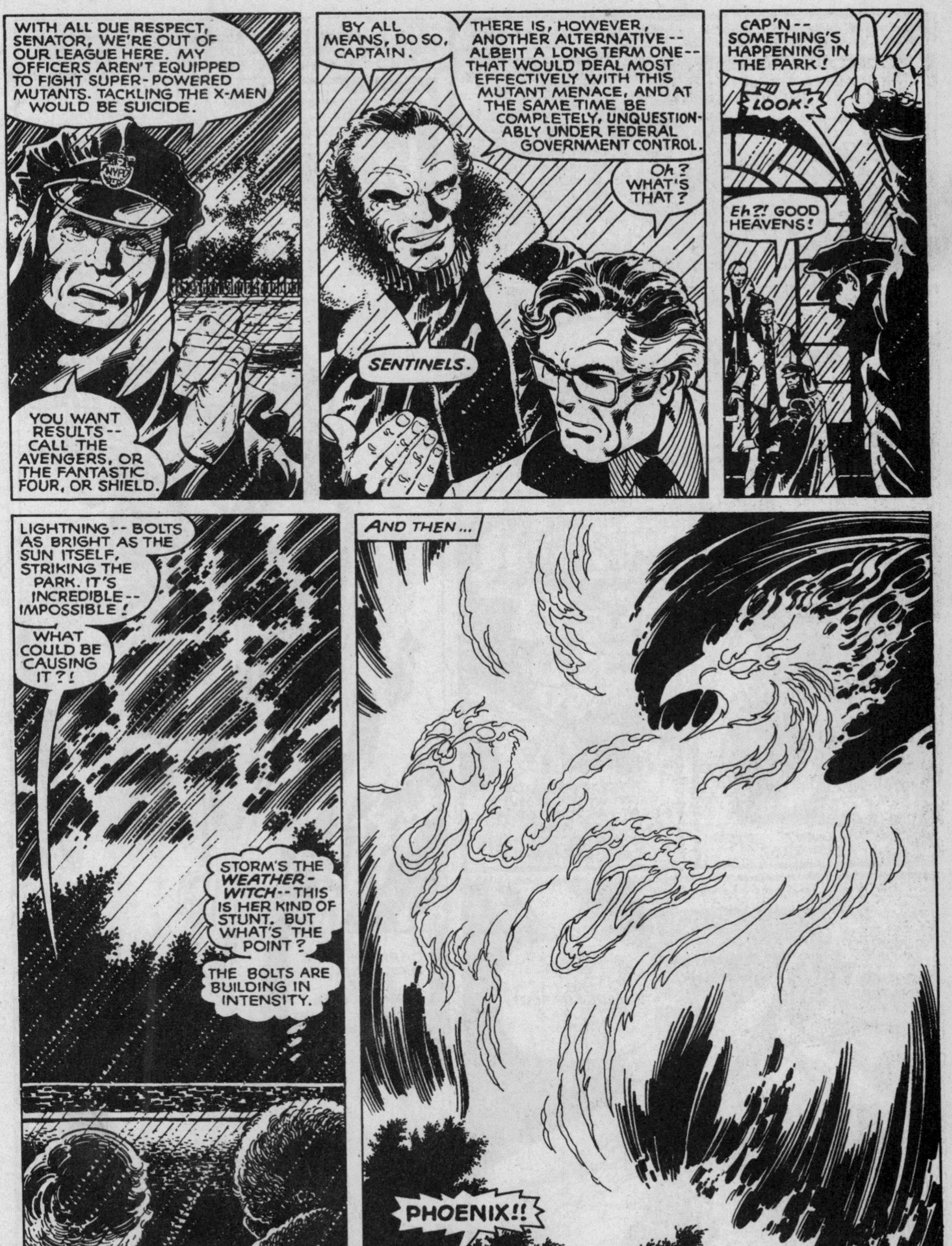
WITH ALL DUE RESPECT, SENATOR, WE'RE OUT OF OUR LEAGUE HERE. MY OFFICERS AREN'T EQUIPPED TO FIGHT SUPER-POWERED MUTANTS. TACKLING THE X-MEN WOULD BE SUICIDE.
YOU WANT RESULTS -- CALL THE AVENGERS, OR THE FANTASTIC FOUR, OR SHIELD.
BY ALL MEANS, DO SO, CAPTAIN.
THERE IS, HOWEVER, ANOTHER ALTERNATIVE -- ALBEIT A LONG TERM ONE -- THAT WOULD DEAL MOST EFFECTIVELY WITH THIS MUTANT MENACE, AND AT THE SAME TIME BE COMPLETELY, UNQUESTIONABLY UNDER FEDERAL GOVERNMENT CONTROL.
Oh? WHAT'S THAT?
SENTINELS.
CAP'N -- SOMETHING'S HAPPENING IN THE PARK!
LOOK!
Eh?! GOOD HEAVENS!
LIGHTNING -- BOLTS AS BRIGHT AS THE SUN ITSELF, STRIKING THE PARK. IT'S INCREDIBLE -- IMPOSSIBLE!
WHAT COULD BE CAUSING IT?!
STORM'S THE WEATHER-WITCH -- THIS IS HER KIND OF STUNT. BUT WHAT'S THE POINT?
THE BOLTS ARE BUILDING IN INTENSITY.
AND THEN...
PHOENIX!!
SAINTS PRESERVE US!

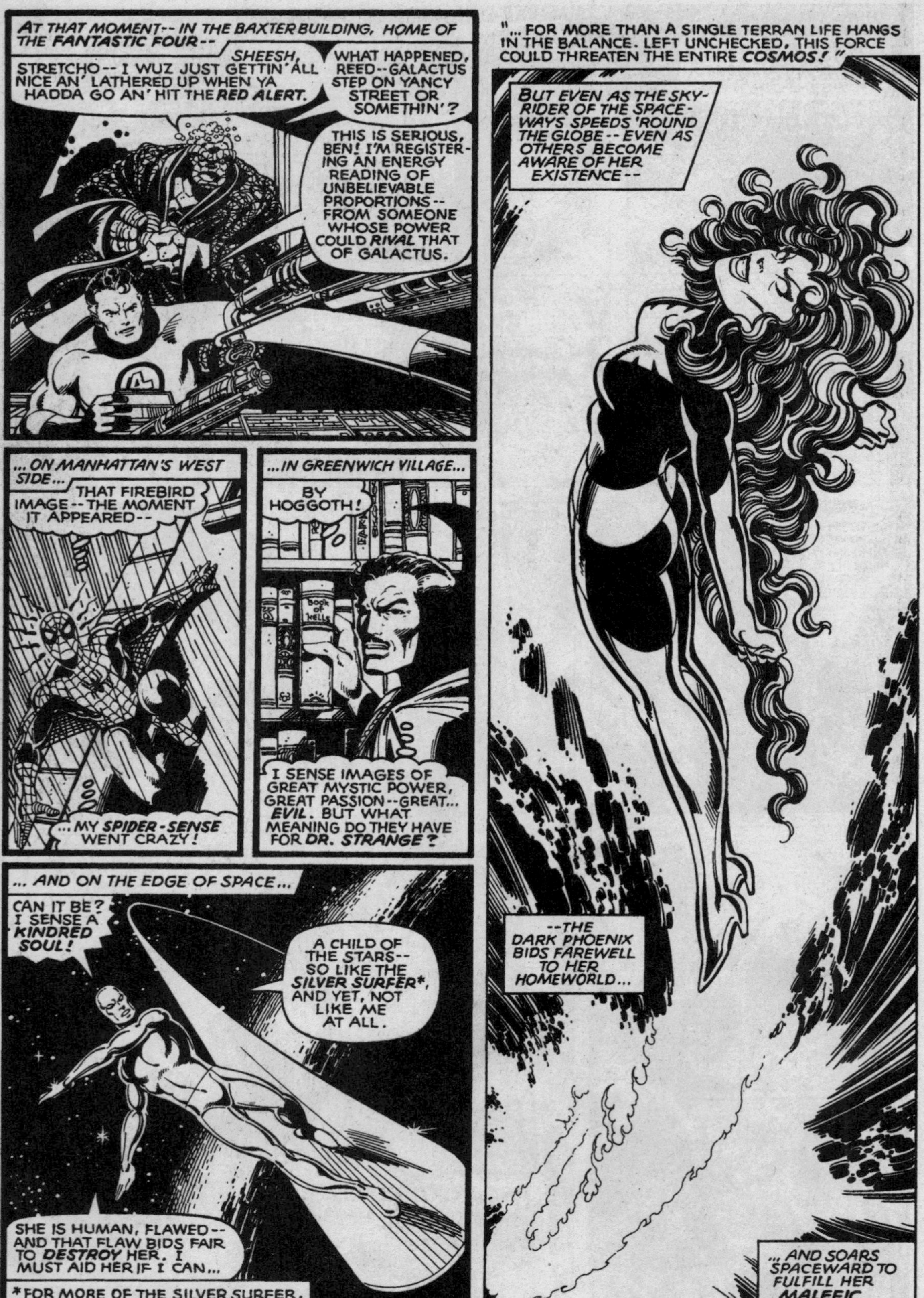
AT THAT MOMENT-- IN THE BAXTER BUILDING, HOME OF THE FANTASTIC FOUR--
SHEESH, STRETCHO-- I WUZ JUST GETTIN' ALL NICE AN' LATHERED UP WHEN YA HADDA GO AN' HIT THE RED ALERT.
WHAT HAPPENED, REED--GALACTUS STEP ON YANCY STREET OR SOMETHIN'?
THIS IS SERIOUS, BEN! I'M REGISTERING AN ENERGY READING OF UNBELIEVABLE PROPORTIONS-- FROM SOMEONE WHOSE POWER COULD RIVAL THAT OF GALACTUS.
...ON MANHATTAN'S WEST SIDE...
THAT FIREBIRD IMAGE--THE MOMENT IT APPEARED--
...MY SPIDER-SENSE WENT CRAZY!
...IN GREENWICH VILLAGE...
BY HOGGOTH!
I SENSE IMAGES OF GREAT MYSTIC POWER, GREAT PASSION--GREAT... EVIL. BUT WHAT MEANING DO THEY HAVE FOR DR. STRANGE?
... AND ON THE EDGE OF SPACE...
CAN IT BE? I SENSE A KINDRED SOUL!
A CHILD OF THE STARS-- SO LIKE THE SILVER SURFER*, AND YET, NOT LIKE ME AT ALL.
SHE IS HUMAN, FLAWED-- AND THAT FLAW BIDS FAIR TO DESTROY HER. I MUST AID HER IF I CAN...
*FOR MORE OF THE SILVER SURFER, SEE EPIC ILLUSTRATED #1 -- JIM.
"... FOR MORE THAN A SINGLE TERRAN LIFE HANGS IN THE BALANCE. LEFT UNCHECKED, THIS FORCE COULD THREATEN THE ENTIRE COSMOS!"
BUT EVEN AS THE SKY-RIDER OF THE SPACE-WAYS SPEEDS 'ROUND THE GLOBE-- EVEN AS OTHERS BECOME AWARE OF HER EXISTENCE--
--THE DARK PHOENIX BIDS FAREWELL TO HER HOMEWORLD...
...AND SOARS SPACEWARD TO FULFILL HER MALEFIC DESTINY.

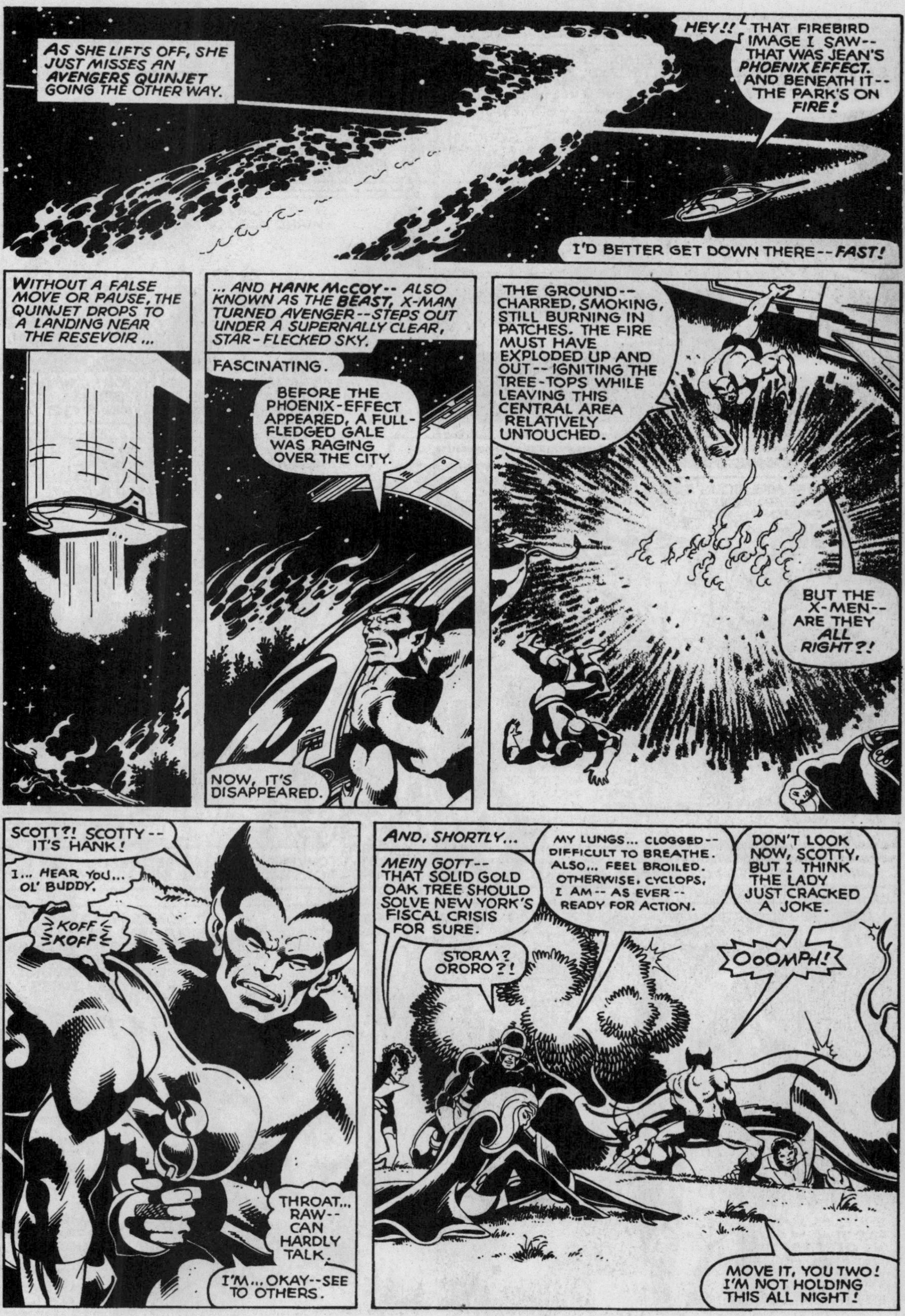

AS SHE LIFTS OFF, SHE JUST MISSES AN AVENGERS QUINJET GOING THE OTHER WAY.
HEY!! THAT FIREBIRD IMAGE I SAW-- THAT WAS JEAN'S PHOENIX EFFECT. AND BENEATH IT-- THE PARK'S ON FIRE!
I'D BETTER GET DOWN THERE--FAST!
WITHOUT A FALSE MOVE OR PAUSE, THE QUINJET DROPS TO A LANDING NEAR THE RESEVOIR...
...AND HANK McCOY-- ALSO KNOWN AS THE BEAST, X-MAN TURNED AVENGER--STEPS OUT UNDER A SUPERNALLY CLEAR, STAR-FLECKED SKY.
FASCINATING.
BEFORE THE PHOENIX-EFFECT APPEARED, A FULL-FLEDGED GALE WAS RAGING OVER THE CITY.
NOW, IT'S DISAPPEARED.
THE GROUND-- CHARRED, SMOKING, STILL BURNING IN PATCHES. THE FIRE MUST HAVE EXPLODED UP AND OUT--IGNITING THE TREE-TOPS WHILE LEAVING THIS CENTRAL AREA RELATIVELY UNTOUCHED.
BUT THE X-MEN-- ARE THEY ALL RIGHT?!
SCOTT?! SCOTTY-- IT'S HANK!
I... HEAR YOU... OL' BUDDY.
KOFF KOFF
THROAT... RAW-- CAN HARDLY TALK.
I'M...OKAY--SEE TO OTHERS.
AND, SHORTLY...
MEIN GOTT-- THAT SOLID GOLD OAK TREE SHOULD SOLVE NEW YORK'S FISCAL CRISIS FOR SURE.
STORM? ORORO?!
MY LUNGS... CLOGGED-- DIFFICULT TO BREATHE. ALSO... FEEL BROILED. OTHERWISE, CYCLOPS, I AM--AS EVER-- READY FOR ACTION.
DON'T LOOK NOW, SCOTTY, BUT I THINK THE LADY JUST CRACKED A JOKE.
OOOMPH!!
MOVE IT, YOU TWO! I'M NOT HOLDING THIS ALL NIGHT!

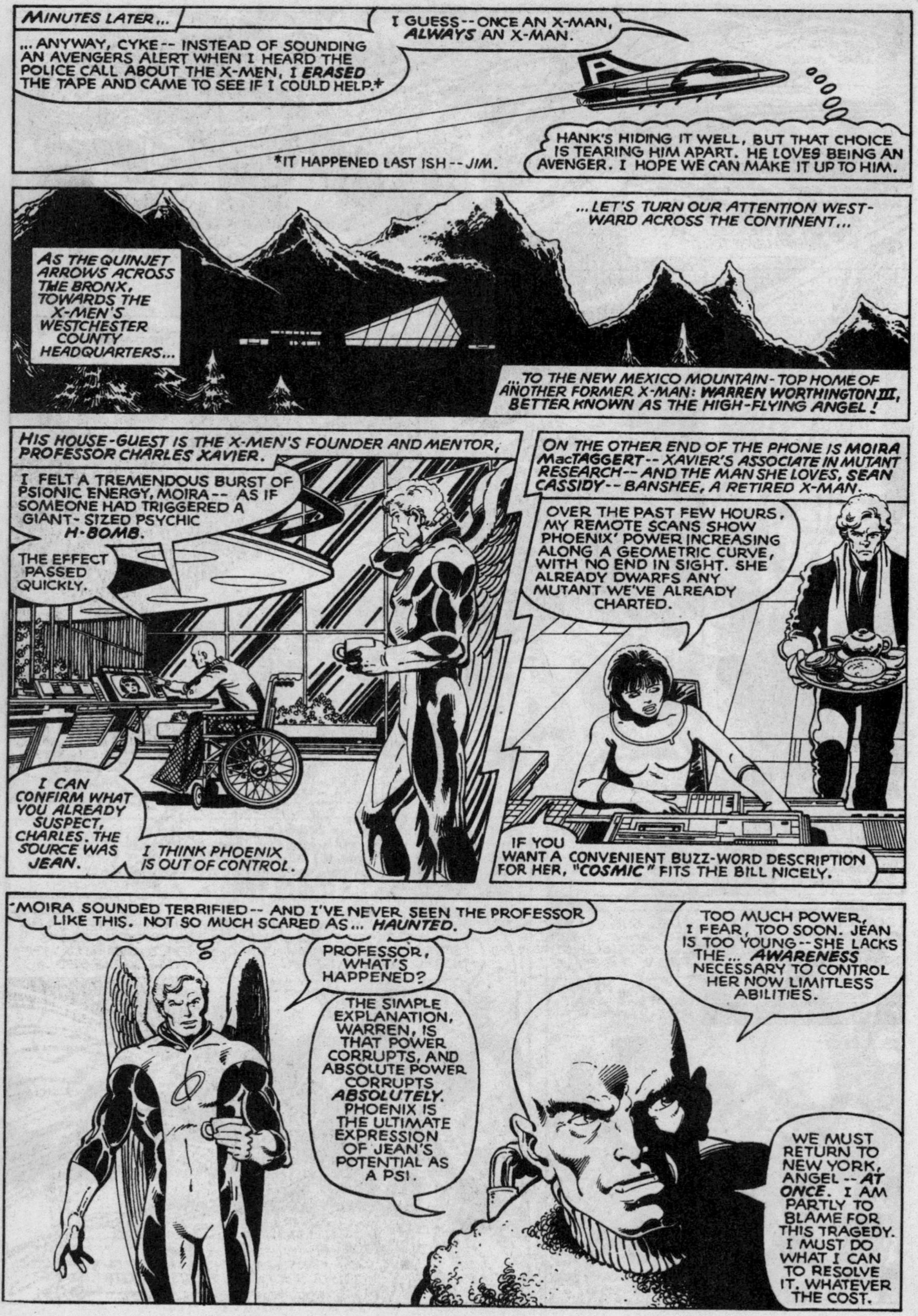

MINUTES LATER...
... ANYWAY, CYKE -- INSTEAD OF SOUNDING AN AVENGERS ALERT WHEN I HEARD THE POLICE CALL ABOUT THE X-MEN, I ERASED THE TAPE AND CAME TO SEE IF I COULD HELP.*
I GUESS -- ONCE AN X-MAN, ALWAYS AN X-MAN.
HANK'S HIDING IT WELL, BUT THAT CHOICE IS TEARING HIM APART. HE LOVES BEING AN AVENGER. I HOPE WE CAN MAKE IT UP TO HIM.
*IT HAPPENED LAST ISH -- JIM.
AS THE QUINJET ARROWS ACROSS THE BRONX, TOWARDS THE X-MEN'S WESTCHESTER COUNTY HEADQUARTERS...
... LET'S TURN OUR ATTENTION WESTWARD ACROSS THE CONTINENT...
... TO THE NEW MEXICO MOUNTAIN-TOP HOME OF ANOTHER FORMER X-MAN: WARREN WORTHINGTON III, BETTER KNOWN AS THE HIGH-FLYING ANGEL!
HIS HOUSE-GUEST IS THE X-MEN'S FOUNDER AND MENTOR, PROFESSOR CHARLES XAVIER.
I FELT A TREMENDOUS BURST OF PSIONIC ENERGY, MOIRA -- AS IF SOMEONE HAD TRIGGERED A GIANT-SIZED PSYCHIC H-BOMB.
THE EFFECT PASSED QUICKLY.
I CAN CONFIRM WHAT YOU ALREADY SUSPECT, CHARLES. THE SOURCE WAS JEAN.
I THINK PHOENIX IS OUT OF CONTROL.
ON THE OTHER END OF THE PHONE IS MOIRA MacTAGGERT -- XAVIER'S ASSOCIATE IN MUTANT RESEARCH -- AND THE MAN SHE LOVES, SEAN CASSIDY -- BANSHEE, A RETIRED X-MAN.
OVER THE PAST FEW HOURS, MY REMOTE SCANS SHOW PHOENIX' POWER INCREASING ALONG A GEOMETRIC CURVE, WITH NO END IN SIGHT. SHE ALREADY DWARFS ANY MUTANT WE'VE ALREADY CHARTED.
IF YOU WANT A CONVENIENT BUZZ-WORD DESCRIPTION FOR HER, "COSMIC" FITS THE BILL NICELY.
MOIRA SOUNDED TERRIFIED -- AND I'VE NEVER SEEN THE PROFESSOR LIKE THIS. NOT SO MUCH SCARED AS... HAUNTED.
PROFESSOR, WHAT'S HAPPENED?
THE SIMPLE EXPLANATION, WARREN, IS THAT POWER CORRUPTS, AND ABSOLUTE POWER CORRUPTS ABSOLUTELY. PHOENIX IS THE ULTIMATE EXPRESSION OF JEAN'S POTENTIAL AS A PSI.
TOO MUCH POWER, I FEAR, TOO SOON. JEAN IS TOO YOUNG -- SHE LACKS THE... AWARENESS NECESSARY TO CONTROL HER NOW LIMITLESS ABILITIES.
WE MUST RETURN TO NEW YORK, ANGEL -- AT ONCE. I AM PARTLY TO BLAME FOR THIS TRAGEDY. I MUST DO WHAT I CAN TO RESOLVE IT, WHATEVER THE COST.

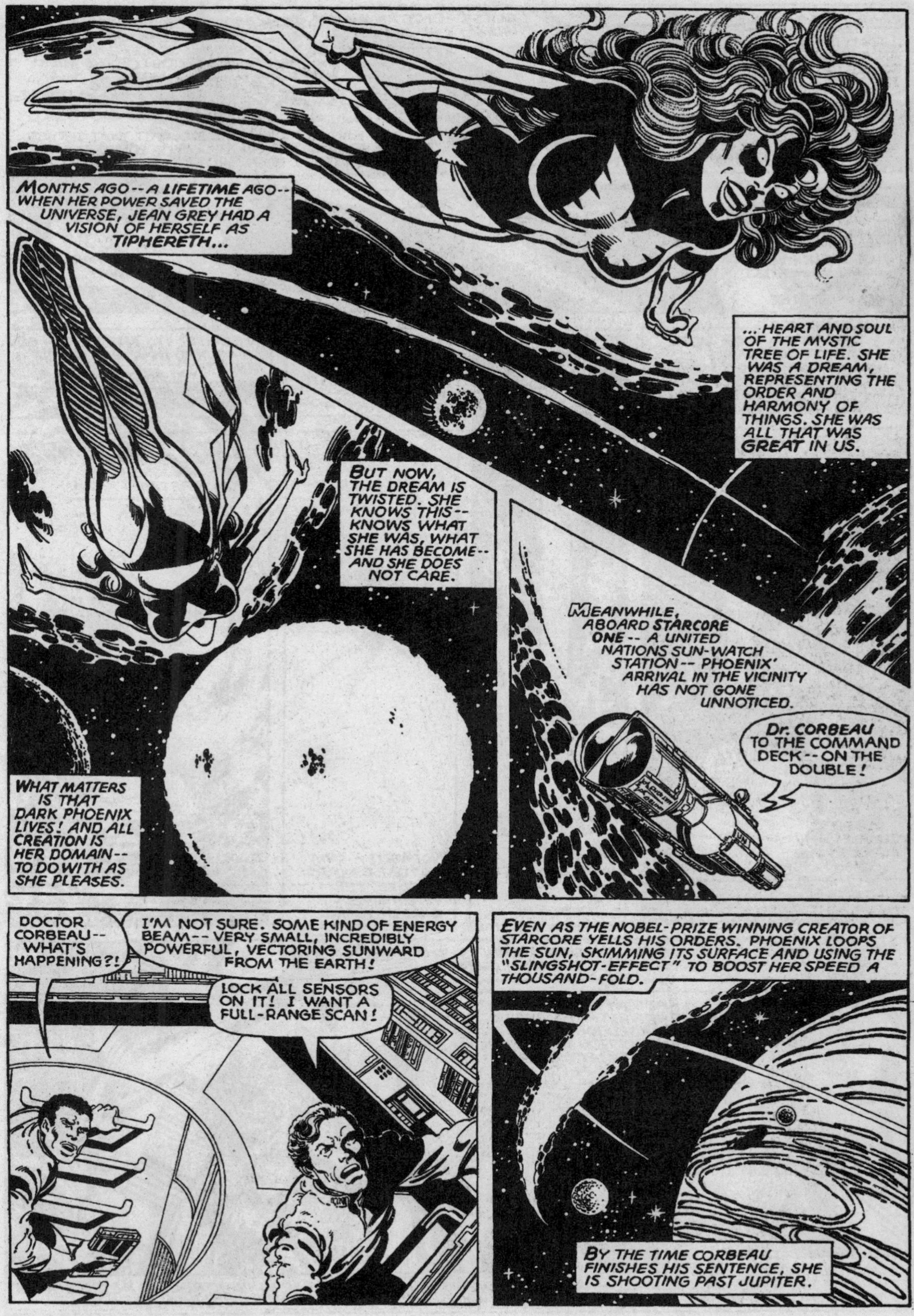
MONTHS AGO -- A LIFETIME AGO -- WHEN HER POWER SAVED THE UNIVERSE, JEAN GREY HAD A VISION OF HERSELF AS TIPHERETH...
...HEART AND SOUL OF THE MYSTIC TREE OF LIFE. SHE WAS A DREAM, REPRESENTING THE ORDER AND HARMONY OF THINGS. SHE WAS ALL THAT WAS GREAT IN US.
BUT NOW, THE DREAM IS TWISTED. SHE KNOWS THIS -- KNOWS WHAT SHE WAS, WHAT SHE HAS BECOME -- AND SHE DOES NOT CARE.
WHAT MATTERS IS THAT DARK PHOENIX LIVES! AND ALL CREATION IS HER DOMAIN -- TO DO WITH AS SHE PLEASES.
MEANWHILE, ABOARD STARCORE ONE -- A UNITED NATIONS SUN-WATCH STATION -- PHOENIX' ARRIVAL IN THE VICINITY HAS NOT GONE UNNOTICED.
Dr. CORBEAU TO THE COMMAND DECK -- ON THE DOUBLE!
DOCTOR CORBEAU -- WHAT'S HAPPENING?!
I'M NOT SURE. SOME KIND OF ENERGY BEAM -- VERY SMALL, INCREDIBLY POWERFUL, VECTORING SUNWARD FROM THE EARTH!
LOCK ALL SENSORS ON IT! I WANT A FULL-RANGE SCAN!
EVEN AS THE NOBEL-PRIZE WINNING CREATOR OF STARCORE YELLS HIS ORDERS, PHOENIX LOOPS THE SUN, SKIMMING ITS SURFACE AND USING THE "SLINGSHOT-EFFECT" TO BOOST HER SPEED A THOUSAND-FOLD.
BY THE TIME CORBEAU FINISHES HIS SENTENCE, SHE IS SHOOTING PAST JUPITER.

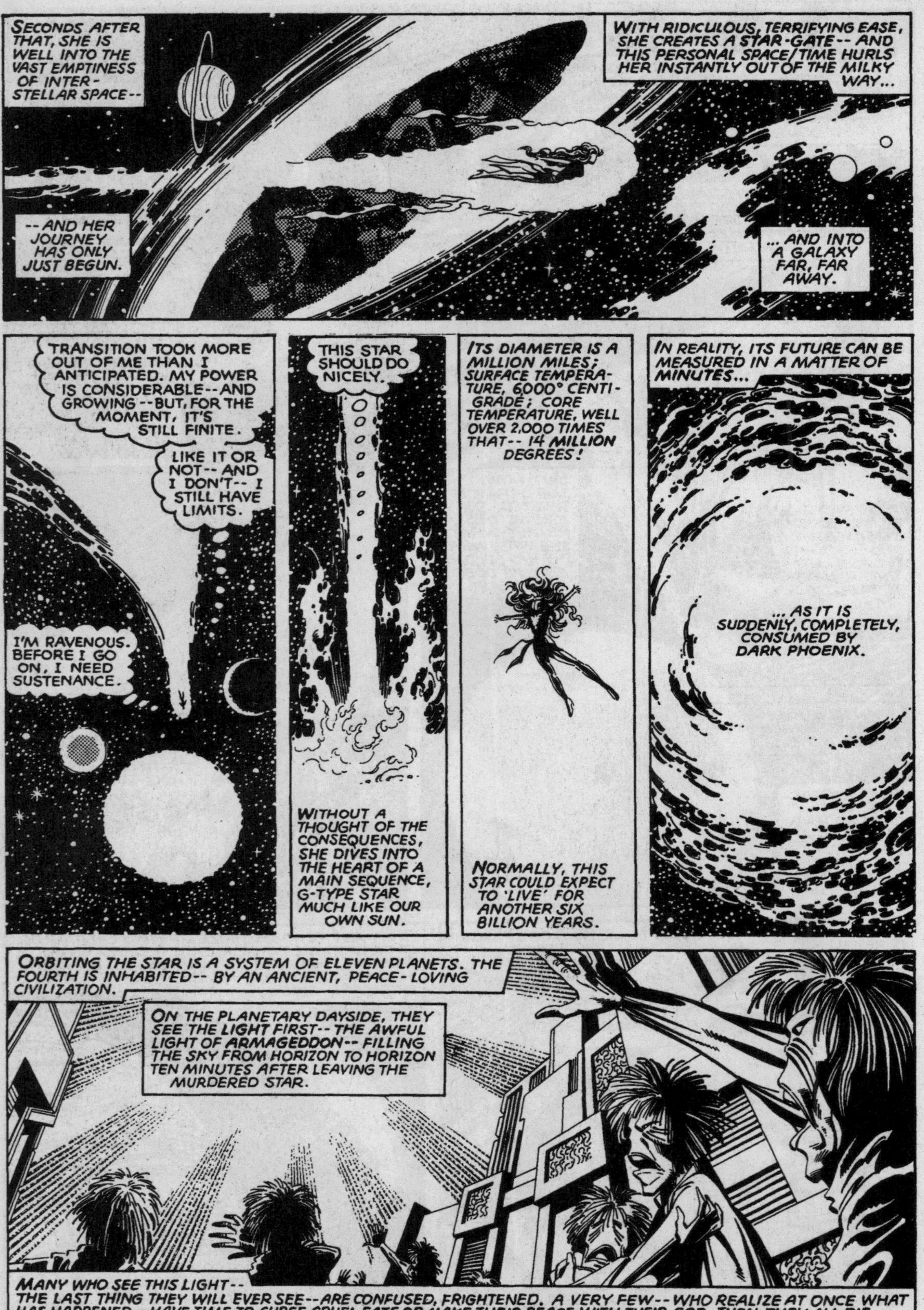
SECONDS AFTER THAT, SHE IS WELL INTO THE VAST EMPTINESS OF INTER-STELLAR SPACE--
WITH RIDICULOUS, TERRIFYING EASE, SHE CREATES A STAR-GATE-- AND THIS PERSONAL SPACE/TIME HURLS HER INSTANTLY OUT OF THE MILKY WAY...
--AND HER JOURNEY HAS ONLY JUST BEGUN.
...AND INTO A GALAXY FAR, FAR AWAY.
TRANSITION TOOK MORE OUT OF ME THAN I ANTICIPATED. MY POWER IS CONSIDERABLE--AND GROWING--BUT, FOR THE MOMENT, IT'S STILL FINITE.
LIKE IT OR NOT-- AND I DON'T-- I STILL HAVE LIMITS.
I'M RAVENOUS. BEFORE I GO ON, I NEED SUSTENANCE.
THIS STAR SHOULD DO NICELY.
WITHOUT A THOUGHT OF THE CONSEQUENCES, SHE DIVES INTO THE HEART OF A MAIN SEQUENCE, G-TYPE STAR MUCH LIKE OUR OWN SUN.
ITS DIAMETER IS A MILLION MILES; SURFACE TEMPERATURE, 6,000° CENTIGRADE; CORE TEMPERATURE, WELL OVER 2,000 TIMES THAT-- 14 MILLION DEGREES!
NORMALLY, THIS STAR COULD EXPECT TO 'LIVE' FOR ANOTHER SIX BILLION YEARS.
IN REALITY, ITS FUTURE CAN BE MEASURED IN A MATTER OF MINUTES...
...AS IT IS SUDDENLY, COMPLETELY, CONSUMED BY DARK PHOENIX.
ORBITING THE STAR IS A SYSTEM OF ELEVEN PLANETS. THE FOURTH IS INHABITED-- BY AN ANCIENT, PEACE-LOVING CIVILIZATION.
ON THE PLANETARY DAYSIDE, THEY SEE THE LIGHT FIRST-- THE AWFUL LIGHT OF ARMAGEDDON-- FILLING THE SKY FROM HORIZON TO HORIZON TEN MINUTES AFTER LEAVING THE MURDERED STAR.
MANY WHO SEE THIS LIGHT-- THE LAST THING THEY WILL EVER SEE--ARE CONFUSED, FRIGHTENED. A VERY FEW-- WHO REALIZE AT ONCE WHAT HAS HAPPENED-- HAVE TIME TO CURSE CRUEL FATE OR MAKE THEIR PEACE WITH THEIR GOD. THEN, THEY ALL DIE.

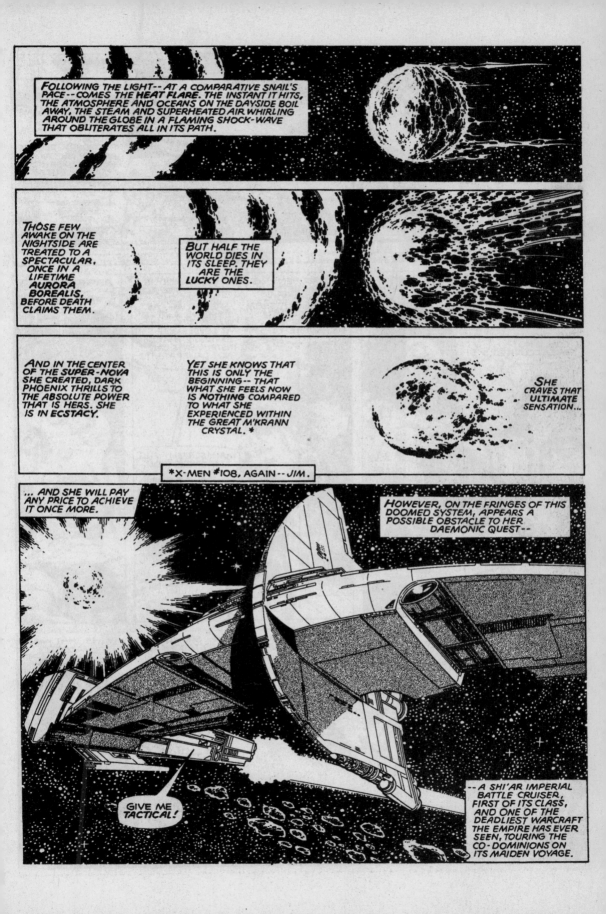

FOLLOWING THE LIGHT-- AT A COMPARATIVE SNAIL'S PACE--COMES THE *HEAT FLARE.* THE INSTANT IT HITS, THE ATMOSPHERE AND OCEANS ON THE DAYSIDE BOIL AWAY, THE STEAM AND SUPERHEATED AIR WHIRLING AROUND THE GLOBE IN A FLAMING SHOCK-WAVE THAT OBLITERATES ALL IN ITS PATH.

THOSE FEW AWAKE ON THE NIGHTSIDE ARE TREATED TO A SPECTACULAR, ONCE IN A LIFETIME AURORA BOREALIS, BEFORE DEATH CLAIMS THEM.

BUT HALF THE WORLD DIES IN ITS SLEEP. THEY ARE THE LUCKY ONES.

AND IN THE CENTER OF THE *SUPER-NOVA* SHE CREATED, DARK PHOENIX THRILLS TO THE ABSOLUTE POWER THAT IS HERS. SHE IS IN ECSTACY.

YET SHE KNOWS THAT THIS IS ONLY THE BEGINNING-- THAT WHAT SHE FEELS NOW IS NOTHING COMPARED TO WHAT SHE EXPERIENCED WITHIN THE GREAT M'KRANN CRYSTAL. *

SHE CRAVES THAT ULTIMATE SENSATION...

*X-MEN #108, AGAIN--JIM.

... AND SHE WILL PAY ANY PRICE TO ACHIEVE IT ONCE MORE.

HOWEVER, ON THE FRINGES OF THIS DOOMED SYSTEM, APPEARS A POSSIBLE OBSTACLE TO HER DAEMONIC QUEST--

GIVE ME TACTICAL!

--A *SHI'AR IMPERIAL BATTLE CRUISER,* FIRST OF ITS CLASS, AND ONE OF THE DEADLIEST WARCRAFT THE EMPIRE HAS EVER SEEN, TOURING THE CO-DOMINIONS ON ITS MAIDEN VOYAGE.

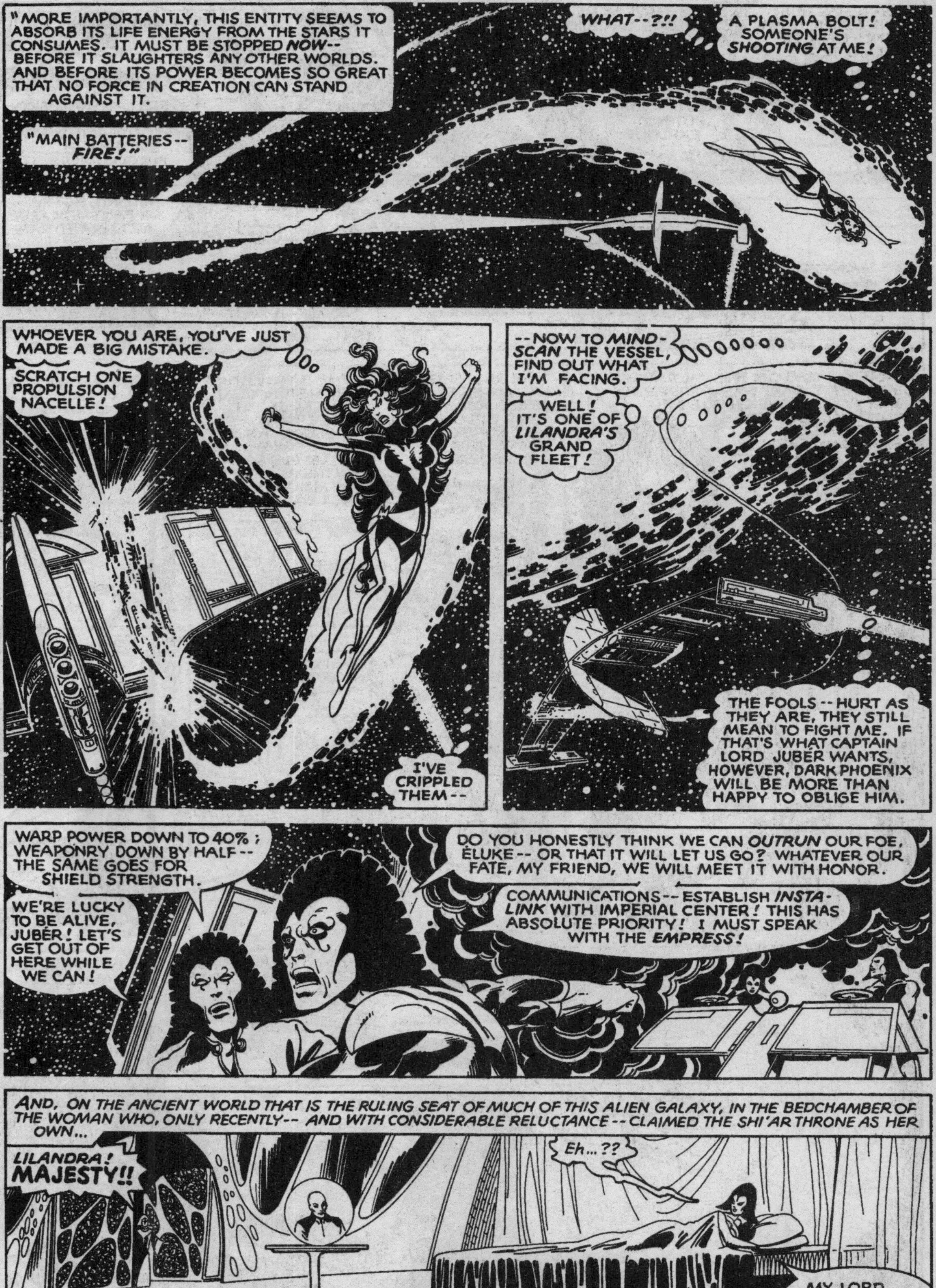
"MORE IMPORTANTLY, THIS ENTITY SEEMS TO ABSORB ITS LIFE ENERGY FROM THE STARS IT CONSUMES. IT MUST BE STOPPED NOW-- BEFORE IT SLAUGHTERS ANY OTHER WORLDS. AND BEFORE ITS POWER BECOMES SO GREAT THAT NO FORCE IN CREATION CAN STAND AGAINST IT.
"MAIN BATTERIES-- FIRE!"
WHAT--?!!
A PLASMA BOLT! SOMEONE'S SHOOTING AT ME!
WHOEVER YOU ARE, YOU'VE JUST MADE A BIG MISTAKE.
SCRATCH ONE PROPULSION NACELLE!
I'VE CRIPPLED THEM--
--NOW TO MIND-SCAN THE VESSEL, FIND OUT WHAT I'M FACING.
WELL! IT'S ONE OF LILANDRA'S GRAND FLEET!
THE FOOLS--HURT AS THEY ARE, THEY STILL MEAN TO FIGHT ME. IF THAT'S WHAT CAPTAIN LORD JUBÉR WANTS, HOWEVER, DARK PHOENIX WILL BE MORE THAN HAPPY TO OBLIGE HIM.
WARP POWER DOWN TO 40%; WEAPONRY DOWN BY HALF-- THE SAME GOES FOR SHIELD STRENGTH.
WE'RE LUCKY TO BE ALIVE, JUBÉR! LET'S GET OUT OF HERE WHILE WE CAN!
DO YOU HONESTLY THINK WE CAN OUTRUN OUR FOE, ÉLUKE-- OR THAT IT WILL LET US GO? WHATEVER OUR FATE, MY FRIEND, WE WILL MEET IT WITH HONOR.
COMMUNICATIONS-- ESTABLISH INSTA-LINK WITH IMPERIAL CENTER! THIS HAS ABSOLUTE PRIORITY! I MUST SPEAK WITH THE EMPRESS!
AND, ON THE ANCIENT WORLD THAT IS THE RULING SEAT OF MUCH OF THIS ALIEN GALAXY, IN THE BEDCHAMBER OF THE WOMAN WHO, ONLY RECENTLY-- AND WITH CONSIDERABLE RELUCTANCE--CLAIMED THE SHI'AR THRONE AS HER OWN...
LILANDRA! MAJESTY!!
Eh...??
MY LORD CHAMBERLAIN? WHAT'S THE MATTER?!

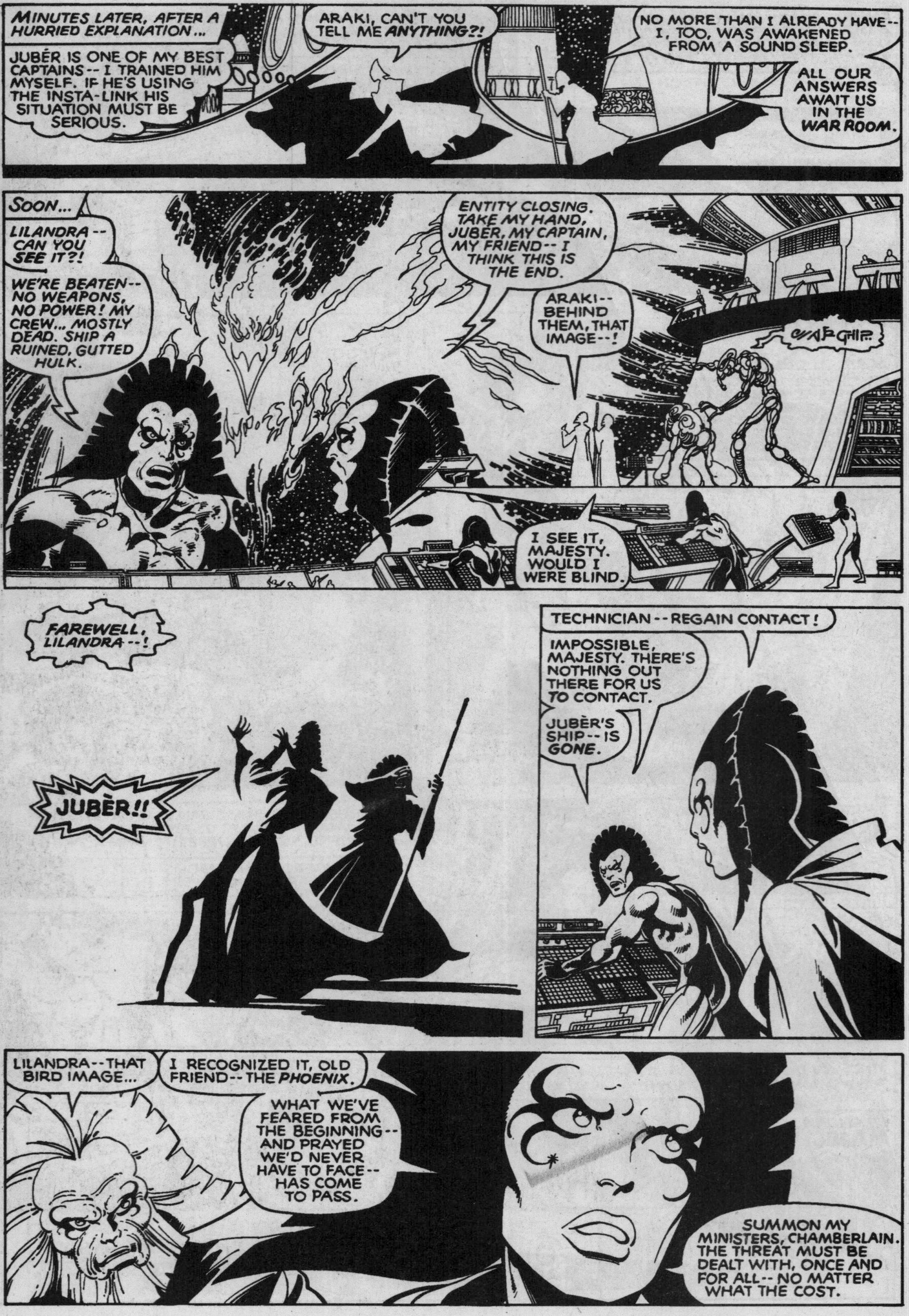
MINUTES LATER, AFTER A HURRIED EXPLANATION...
JUBÉR IS ONE OF MY BEST CAPTAINS -- I TRAINED HIM MYSELF. IF HE'S USING THE INSTA-LINK HIS SITUATION MUST BE SERIOUS.
ARAKI, CAN'T YOU TELL ME ANYTHING?!
NO MORE THAN I ALREADY HAVE -- I, TOO, WAS AWAKENED FROM A SOUND SLEEP.
ALL OUR ANSWERS AWAIT US IN THE WAR ROOM.
SOON...
LILANDRA -- CAN YOU SEE IT?!
WE'RE BEATEN -- NO WEAPONS, NO POWER! MY CREW... MOSTLY DEAD. SHIP A RUINED, GUTTED HULK.
ENTITY CLOSING. TAKE MY HAND, JUBER, MY CAPTAIN, MY FRIEND -- I THINK THIS IS THE END.
ARAKI -- BEHIND THEM, THAT IMAGE --!
I SEE IT, MAJESTY. WOULD I WERE BLIND.
FAREWELL, LILANDRA --!
JUBÈR!!
TECHNICIAN -- REGAIN CONTACT!
IMPOSSIBLE, MAJESTY. THERE'S NOTHING OUT THERE FOR US TO CONTACT.
JUBÈR'S SHIP -- IS GONE.
LILANDRA -- THAT BIRD IMAGE...
I RECOGNIZED IT, OLD FRIEND -- THE PHOENIX.
WHAT WE'VE FEARED FROM THE BEGINNING -- AND PRAYED WE'D NEVER HAVE TO FACE -- HAS COME TO PASS.
SUMMON MY MINISTERS, CHAMBERLAIN. THE THREAT MUST BE DEALT WITH, ONCE AND FOR ALL -- NO MATTER WHAT THE COST.

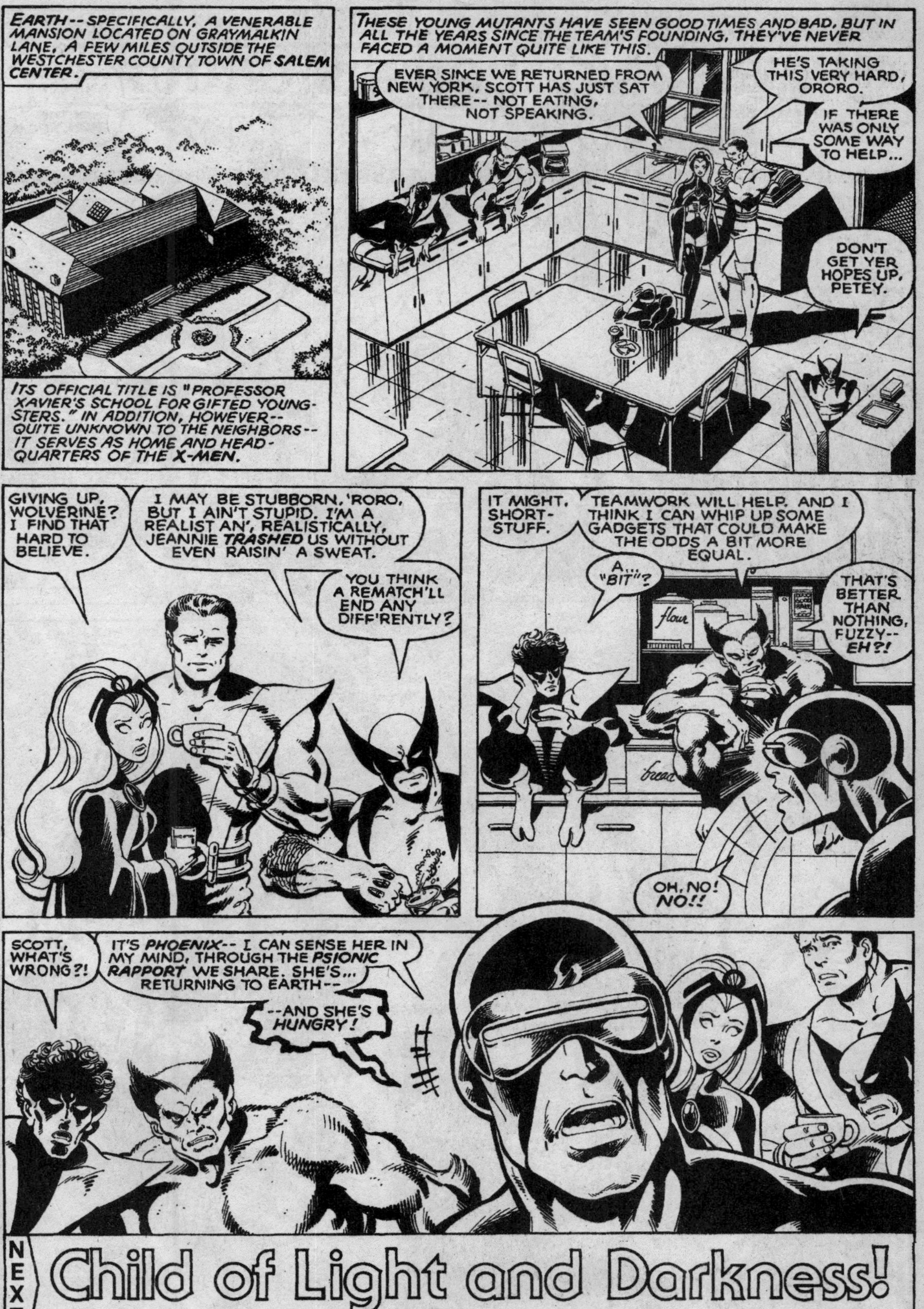
EARTH -- SPECIFICALLY, A VENERABLE MANSION LOCATED ON GRAYMALKIN LANE, A FEW MILES OUTSIDE THE WESTCHESTER COUNTY TOWN OF SALEM CENTER.
ITS OFFICIAL TITLE IS "PROFESSOR XAVIER'S SCHOOL FOR GIFTED YOUNGSTERS." IN ADDITION, HOWEVER -- QUITE UNKNOWN TO THE NEIGHBORS -- IT SERVES AS HOME AND HEADQUARTERS OF THE X-MEN.
THESE YOUNG MUTANTS HAVE SEEN GOOD TIMES AND BAD, BUT IN ALL THE YEARS SINCE THE TEAM'S FOUNDING, THEY'VE NEVER FACED A MOMENT QUITE LIKE THIS.
EVER SINCE WE RETURNED FROM NEW YORK, SCOTT HAS JUST SAT THERE -- NOT EATING, NOT SPEAKING.
HE'S TAKING THIS VERY HARD, ORORO.
IF THERE WAS ONLY SOME WAY TO HELP...
DON'T GET YER HOPES UP, PETEY.
GIVING UP, WOLVERINE? I FIND THAT HARD TO BELIEVE.
I MAY BE STUBBORN, 'RORO, BUT I AIN'T STUPID. I'M A REALIST AN', REALISTICALLY, JEANNIE TRASHED US WITHOUT EVEN RAISIN' A SWEAT.
YOU THINK A REMATCH'LL END ANY DIFF'RENTLY?
IT MIGHT, SHORT-STUFF.
TEAMWORK WILL HELP. AND I THINK I CAN WHIP UP SOME GADGETS THAT COULD MAKE THE ODDS A BIT MORE EQUAL.
A... "BIT"?
THAT'S BETTER THAN NOTHING, FUZZY -- EH?!
flour
bread
OH, NO! NO!!
SCOTT, WHAT'S WRONG?!
IT'S PHOENIX -- I CAN SENSE HER IN MY MIND, THROUGH THE PSIONIC RAPPORT WE SHARE. SHE'S... RETURNING TO EARTH --
-- AND SHE'S HUNGRY!
NEXT
Child of Light and Darkness!

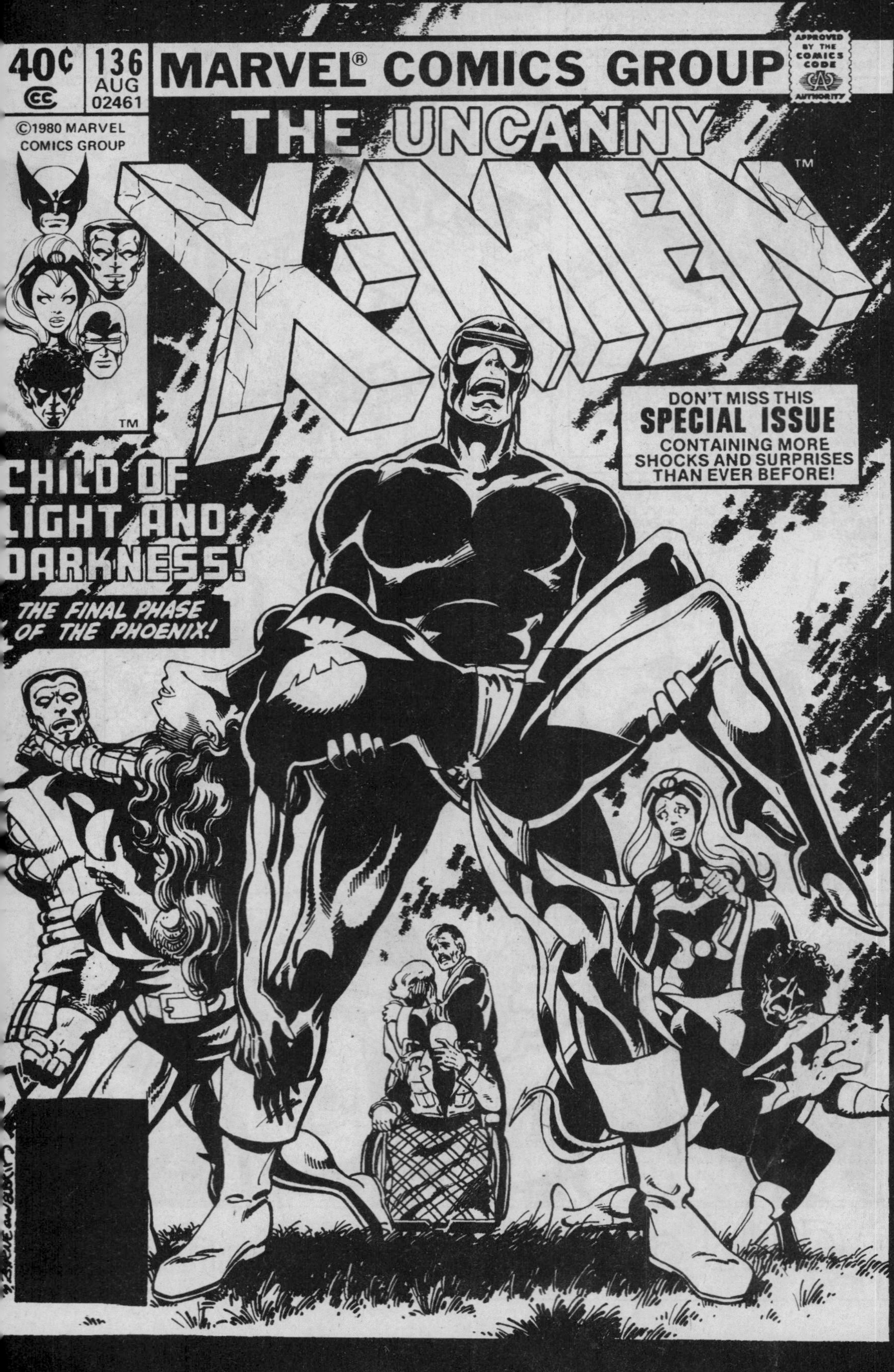
40¢
136
AUG
02461
MARVEL® COMICS GROUP
APPROVED BY THE COMICS CODE AUTHORITY
©1980 MARVEL COMICS GROUP
THE UNCANNY
X-MEN™
DON'T MISS THIS
SPECIAL ISSUE
CONTAINING MORE SHOCKS AND SURPRISES THAN EVER BEFORE!
CHILD OF LIGHT AND DARKNESS!
THE FINAL PHASE OF THE PHOENIX!

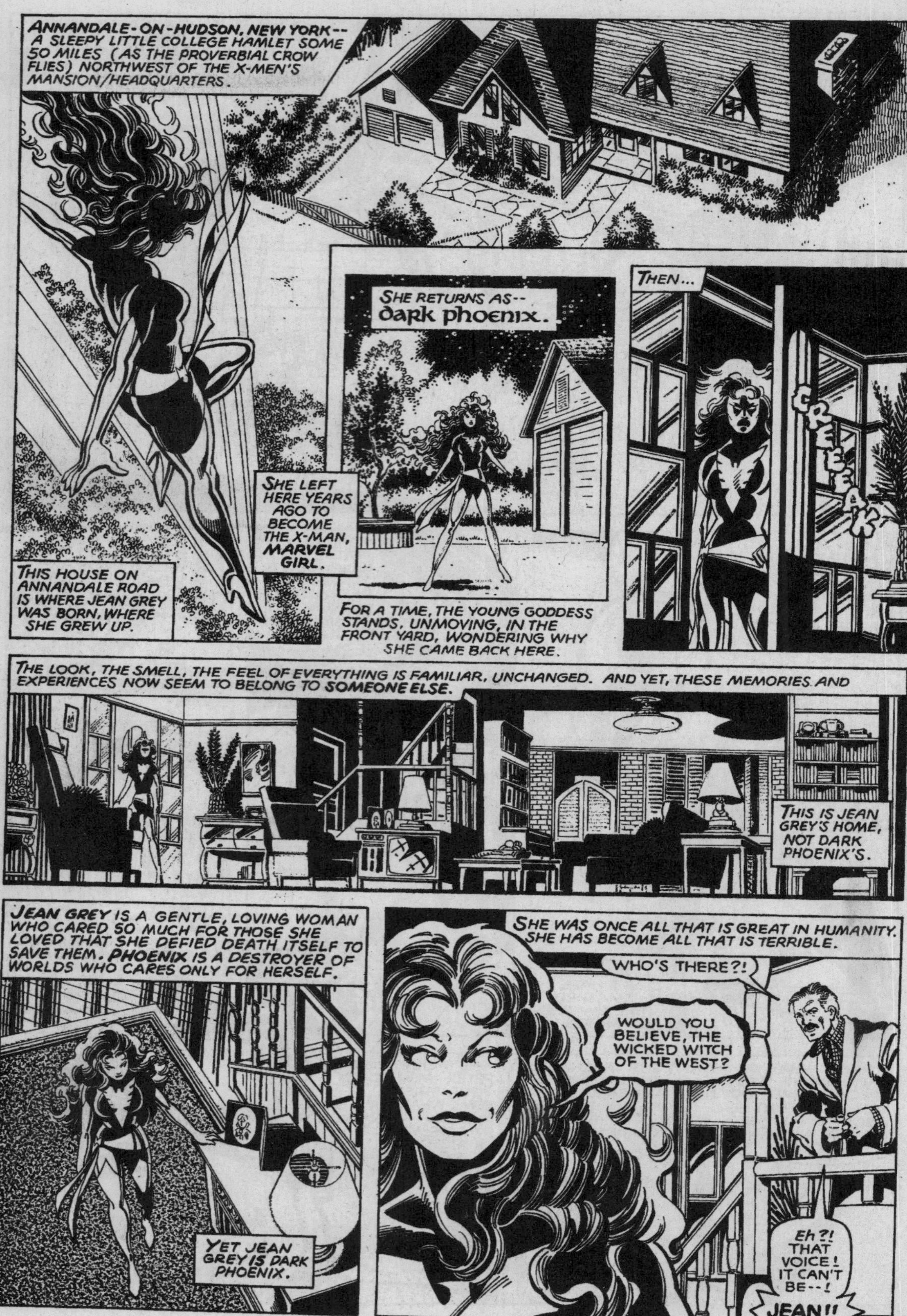
ANNANDALE-ON-HUDSON, NEW YORK-- A SLEEPY LITTLE COLLEGE HAMLET SOME 50 MILES (AS THE PROVERBIAL CROW FLIES) NORTHWEST OF THE X-MEN'S MANSION/HEADQUARTERS.
THIS HOUSE ON ANNANDALE ROAD IS WHERE JEAN GREY WAS BORN, WHERE SHE GREW UP.
SHE LEFT HERE YEARS AGO TO BECOME THE X-MAN, MARVEL GIRL.
SHE RETURNS AS-- dark phoenix.
FOR A TIME, THE YOUNG GODDESS STANDS, UNMOVING, IN THE FRONT YARD, WONDERING WHY SHE CAME BACK HERE.
THEN...
CREEEAK
THE LOOK, THE SMELL, THE FEEL OF EVERYTHING IS FAMILIAR, UNCHANGED. AND YET, THESE MEMORIES AND EXPERIENCES NOW SEEM TO BELONG TO SOMEONE ELSE.
THIS IS JEAN GREY'S HOME, NOT DARK PHOENIX'S.
JEAN GREY IS A GENTLE, LOVING WOMAN WHO CARED SO MUCH FOR THOSE SHE LOVED THAT SHE DEFIED DEATH ITSELF TO SAVE THEM. PHOENIX IS A DESTROYER OF WORLDS WHO CARES ONLY FOR HERSELF.
YET JEAN GREY IS DARK PHOENIX.
SHE WAS ONCE ALL THAT IS GREAT IN HUMANITY. SHE HAS BECOME ALL THAT IS TERRIBLE.
WHO'S THERE?!
WOULD YOU BELIEVE, THE WICKED WITCH OF THE WEST?
Eh?! THAT VOICE! IT CAN'T BE--!
JEAN!!

NOT LONG AGO, YET FOR JEAN, A *LIFETIME* AGO, PHOENIX BOUND A ROGUE NEUTRON GALAXY WITHIN A STASIS-FIELD OF LIVING ANTI-ENERGY, THEREBY PREVENTING THAT ULTIMATE *BLACK HOLE* FROM DESTROYING THE ENTIRE UNIVERSE.

NOW, IN MUCH THE SAME WAY, CHARLES XAVIER SEEKS TO BIND DARK PHOENIX ONCE MORE...

...WITHIN AN *UNBREACHABLE* NETWORK OF PSIONIC CIRCUIT BREAKERS.

THE END COMES SUDDENLY. ONE MOMENT, THE PHOENIX-EFFECT IS LIGHTING UP THE COUNTRYSIDE LIKE A SMALL SUN.

JEAN!!

THE NEXT, JEAN GREY COLLAPSES TO THE GROUND LIKE A PUPPET WITH ITS STRINGS CUT.

..WOULD... HAVE LOST -- BUT I ... SENSED JEAN... FIGHTING HER PHOENIX-SELF... *HELPING* ME...

BLESS YOU, CHILD. I AM SO *PROUD* ...OF YOU...

JEAN? SHE'S SO STILL. I'M NOT EVEN SURE SHE'S ALIVE. I WANT HER TO LIVE --

-- BUT WHAT IF SHE HASN'T CHANGED? WHAT IF SHE'S STILL DARK PHOENIX?!

I'LL *LOVE* HER JUST THE SAME.

FOR BETTER, WORSE, RICHER, POORER, SICKNESS, HEALTH -- TILL DEATH DO US PART.

HI.

H-HI, YOUR-SELF.

IF I DIDN'T KNOW BETTER, I'D SAY THOSE THOUGHTS I JUST PICKED UP SOUNDED LIKE A *PROPOSAL.*

THEY DID, DIDN'T THEY?

WHAT DO YOU SAY, RED?

I SAY, YES!

NEXT ISSUE: THE END OF AN EPIC -- A 35-PAGE MASTERWORK!

The FATE of THE PHOENIX!

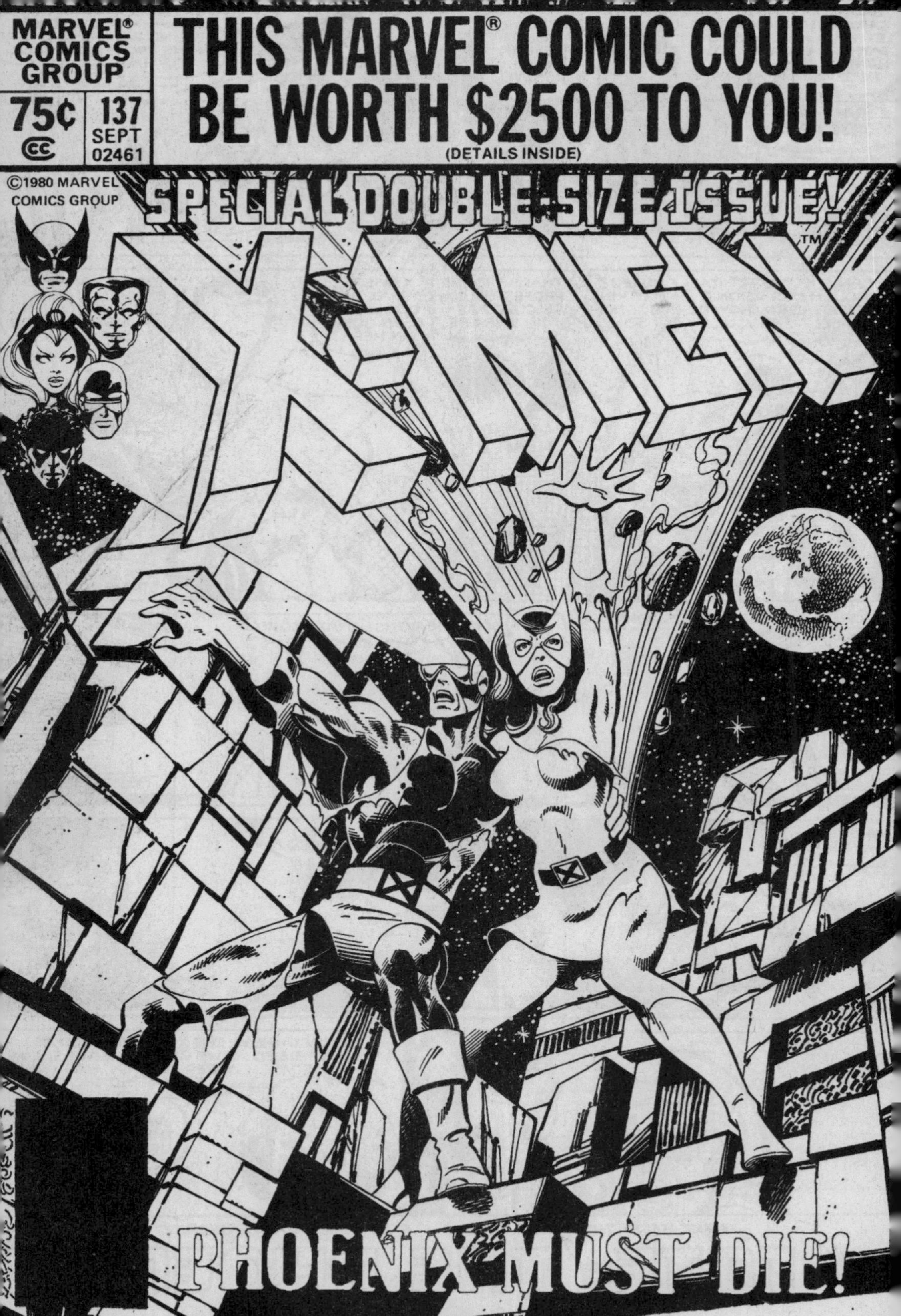

MARVEL® COMICS GROUP
75¢
137 SEPT 02461
THIS MARVEL® COMIC COULD BE WORTH $2500 TO YOU!
(DETAILS INSIDE)
©1980 MARVEL COMICS GROUP
SPECIAL DOUBLE-SIZE ISSUE!
X-MEN™
PHOENIX MUST DIE!

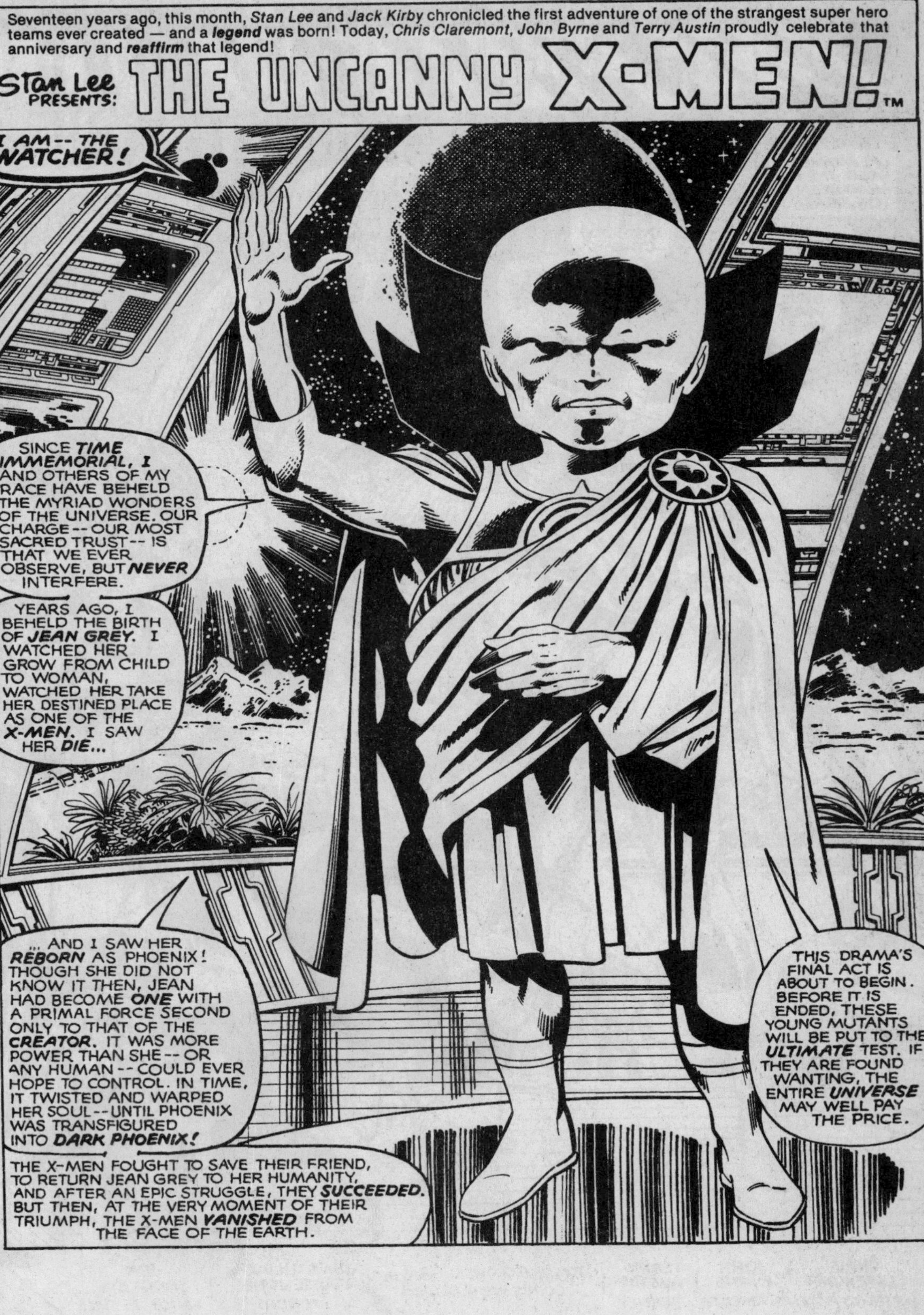
Seventeen years ago, this month, *Stan Lee* and *Jack Kirby* chronicled the first adventure of one of the strangest super hero teams ever created — and a **legend** was born! Today, *Chris Claremont, John Byrne* and *Terry Austin* proudly celebrate that anniversary and **reaffirm** that legend!
STAN LEE PRESENTS: THE UNCANNY X-MEN!™
I AM-- THE WATCHER!
SINCE TIME IMMEMORIAL, I AND OTHERS OF MY RACE HAVE BEHELD THE MYRIAD WONDERS OF THE UNIVERSE. OUR CHARGE--OUR MOST SACRED TRUST-- IS THAT WE EVER OBSERVE, BUT NEVER INTERFERE.
YEARS AGO, I BEHELD THE BIRTH OF JEAN GREY. I WATCHED HER GROW FROM CHILD TO WOMAN, WATCHED HER TAKE HER DESTINED PLACE AS ONE OF THE X-MEN. I SAW HER DIE...
...AND I SAW HER REBORN AS PHOENIX! THOUGH SHE DID NOT KNOW IT THEN, JEAN HAD BECOME ONE WITH A PRIMAL FORCE SECOND ONLY TO THAT OF THE CREATOR. IT WAS MORE POWER THAN SHE--OR ANY HUMAN--COULD EVER HOPE TO CONTROL. IN TIME, IT TWISTED AND WARPED HER SOUL--UNTIL PHOENIX WAS TRANSFIGURED INTO DARK PHOENIX!
THIS DRAMA'S FINAL ACT IS ABOUT TO BEGIN. BEFORE IT IS ENDED, THESE YOUNG MUTANTS WILL BE PUT TO THE ULTIMATE TEST. IF THEY ARE FOUND WANTING, THE ENTIRE UNIVERSE MAY WELL PAY THE PRICE.
THE X-MEN FOUGHT TO SAVE THEIR FRIEND, TO RETURN JEAN GREY TO HER HUMANITY, AND AFTER AN EPIC STRUGGLE, THEY SUCCEEDED. BUT THEN, AT THE VERY MOMENT OF THEIR TRIUMPH, THE X-MEN VANISHED FROM THE FACE OF THE EARTH.

COLOSSUS.

≥YawwwWWWWWNN!≤

IS IT DAWN, ALREADY? HAVE I SLEPT THE WHOLE NIGHT THROUGH?

THE MOMENT OF TRUTH FAST APPROACHES. I KNOW DARK PHOENIX IS EVIL; I HAVE FELT HER POWER. YET, I ALSO KNOW JEAN GREY; I HAVE FELT HER LOVE. I OWE HER MY LIFE! WHEN WE X-MEN FOUGHT DARK PHOENIX, WE WERE NOT TRYING TO DESTROY HER...

...BUT *CURE* HER WE FOUGHT OUT OF LOVE. THAT HAS NOT CHANGED.

TO LEAVE JEAN TO PHOENIX'S FATE NOW--AFTER HAVING STRUGGLED SO HARD TO SAVE HER--WOULD BE A DENIAL OF THAT LOVE. SUCH A BETRAYAL, I CANNOT--I WILL NOT--COMMIT.

HE CONCENTRATES --AND IN THE BLINK OF AN EYE A BODY OF FLESH AND BLOOD AND BONE AND SINEW BECOMES ONE OF NIGH-INVINCIBLE *ORGANIC STEEL!*

STORM.

DAWN. ON EARTH, THAT IS MARKED BY THE ETERNAL BEAUTY OF A *SUNRISE.*

HERE, BY THE CHIME OF AN ALARM. I PREFER THE SUNRISE.

Oh, FOR THOSE HAPPY DAYS WHEN I WAS SIMPLY *ORORO,* WIND-RIDER.

I WAS ALONE, THEN.

I WAS *FREE.*

NOW, I AM NEITHER ALONE NOR FREE. AND RARELY HAPPY.

YET, I CHOSE TO JOIN THE X-MEN, TO LEAVE MY AFRICAN HOME OF MY OWN FREE WILL. THE X-MEN HAVE BECOME MY FAMILY, AND JEAN GREY THE BELOVED *SISTER* I NEVER HAD.

HOW IRONIC. DARK PHOENIX SYMBOLIZES ALL I ABHOR. BUT-- KNOWING THAT SHE IS JEAN, I FIND... THAT I CAN NO MORE DENY HER THAN I CAN MYSELF. I... *LOVE* JEAN. AS PART AND PARCEL OF THAT LOVE, I SHALL USE MY ELEMENTAL POWERS TO DEFEND HER TO THE DEATH.

IT HAPPENED SO FAST-- NO TIME TO STOP HERSELF, NO TIME EVEN FOR THOUGHT. SHE SAW CYCLOPS CUT DOWN, AND THE CRY OF SHOCK AND GRIEF AND TERROR THAT WELLED WITHIN HER *SHATTERED* THE PSYCHIC RESTRAINTS THAT PROFESSOR XAVIER HAD PLACED AROUND HER POWER.

OH, JEAN-- NO!

EH?! PROFESSOR X, CONTACTING ME *TELEPATHICALLY!*

CYCLOPS, ATTACK PHOENIX NOW! WHILE SHE IS STILL COMPARA- TIVELY WEAK!

PROFESSOR, THERE HAS TO BE SOME OTHER WAY! PLEASE!

"IF THERE WAS, LAD, DON'T YOU THINK I'D BE USING IT?"

GOOD, SCOTT. YOU'RE DOING EXACTLY WHAT I PRAYED YOU WOULD.

FORGIVE ME, MY LOVE.

HE OPENS HIS RUBY QUARTZ VISOR WIDE, SCYTHING HIS OPTIC BLASTS--AT FULL POWER--ACROSS THE BASE OF A NEARBY BUILDING.

A MILLION TONS OF MASONRY AND STEEL TOPPLE TOWARDS PHOENIX. SHE MANAGES TO SAVE HERSELF WITH A TELEKINETIC SHIELD, BUT THE IMPACT STILL HAMMERS HER TO HER KNEES.

HER POWER IS AWESOME, BUT, FOR THE PRESENT, IT HAS LIMITS, AND SHE HAS REACHED THEM.

CYCLOPS-- PROFESSOR'S VOICE... INSIDE MY MIND... FORCING ME AWAKE...

JEAN'S BECOME PHOENIX AGAIN.

GODDESS, NO!

IT'S UP TO *US* TO STOP HER.

IS SUCH A THING POSSIBLE?

I DON'T KNOW, ORORO, BUT WE HAVE TO TRY.

WE HAVE TO KEEP HER OFF-BALANCE-- MAKE HER USE UP HER POWER, BURN HERSELF OUT.

I... WILL DO WHAT I CAN.

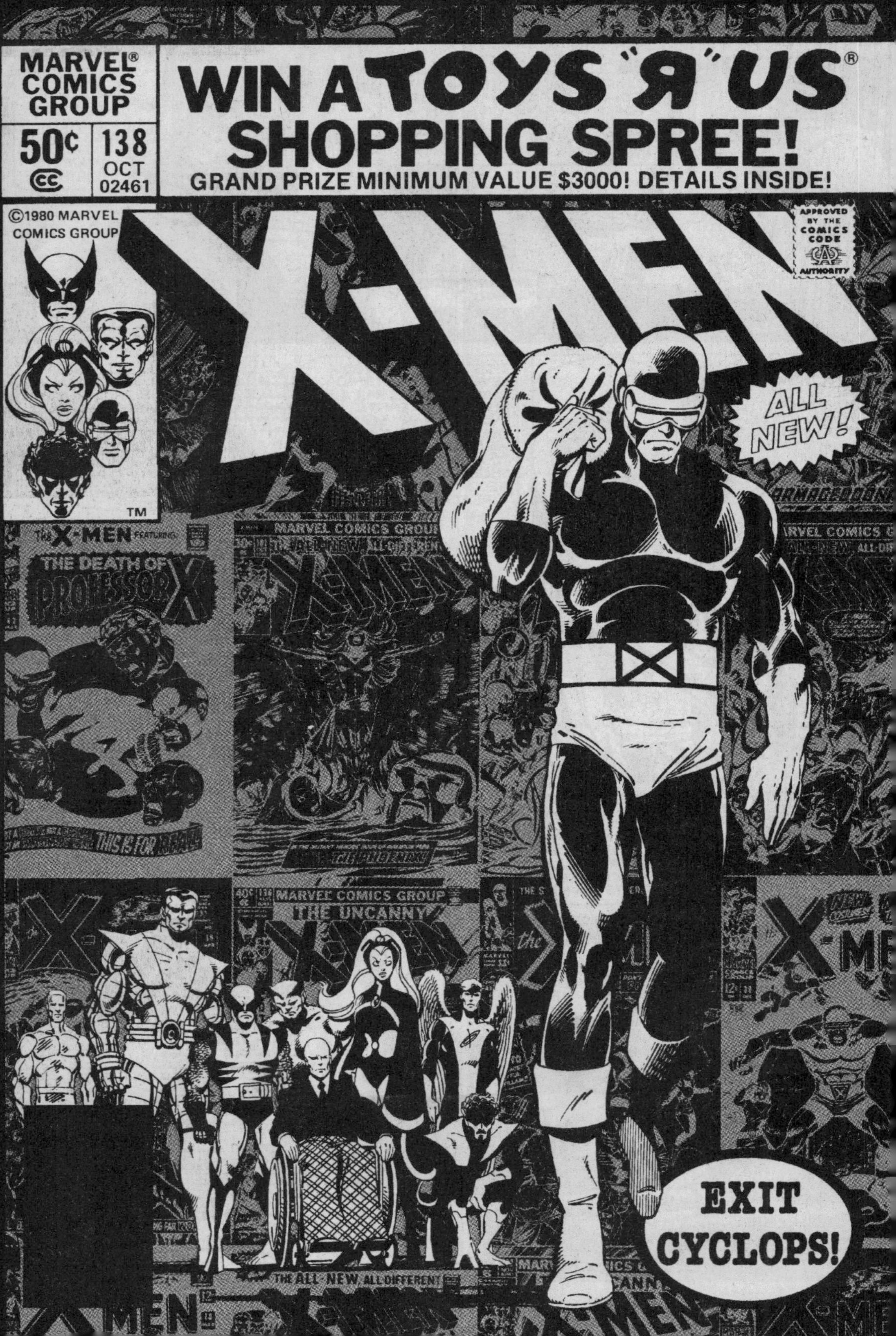

MARVEL® COMICS GROUP
50¢
138
OCT
02461
WIN A TOYS "R" US® SHOPPING SPREE!
GRAND PRIZE MINIMUM VALUE $3000! DETAILS INSIDE!
©1980 MARVEL COMICS GROUP
APPROVED BY THE COMICS CODE AUTHORITY
X-MEN
ALL NEW!
THE DEATH OF PROFESSOR X
MARVEL COMICS GROUP
THE UNCANNY X-MEN
EXIT CYCLOPS!

WE THOUGHT WE WERE PRETTY HOT STUFF-- UNTIL WE FOUGHT THE *VANISHER.* FOR ALL OUR VAUNTED PROWESS, IT STILL TOOK PROFESSOR X'S *PSI-POWERS* TO DEFEAT HIM. GOOD AS WE WERE, WE STILL HAD A *LOT* TO LEARN.

AS TIME PASSED, I BECAME INCREASINGLY ATTRACTED TO JEAN -- YET I SAID NOTHING, DID NOTHING. I'D BEEN HURT TOO OFTEN, TOO DEEPLY, IN THE STATE ORPHANAGE WHERE I GREW UP. I WAS DETERMINED NOT TO BE HURT AGAIN.

ALSO, I FELT I HAD NO RIGHT TO LOVE *ANYONE* SO LONG AS MY OPTIC BLASTS REMAINED UNCONTROLLABLE.

THEN, MAGNETO RE-APPEARED.

THIS TIME, HE WASN'T ALONE. TOGETHER WITH QUICKSILVER, THE SCARLET WITCH, MASTERMIND AND THE TOAD, HE FORMED A *BROTHERHOOD OF EVIL MUTANTS.*

THE BATTLE LEFT THE PROFESSOR BADLY INJURED, HIS PSI-ABILITIES APPARENTLY *GONE.* WHEN MAGNETO AMBUSHED US IN NEW YORK, WE WERE ON OUR OWN FOR THE FIRST TIME.

THAT FIGHT RAGED FROM THE LEXINGTON AVENUE SUBWAY, THROUGH GRAND CENTRAL STATION, WHERE ANGEL WAS CAPTURED--

--TO *ASTEROID M,* MAGNETO'S ORBITING HEADQUARTERS. AGAIN, AS THEY HAD BEFORE, QUICKSILVER AND HIS SISTER SURREPTITIOUSLY *HELPED* US. THEY WERE TORN BY CONFLICTING LOYALTIES.

THEY TRIED TO OVERTHROW THE SOUTH AMERICAN REPUBLIC OF *SAN MARCO.* WE STOPPED THEM, BUT OURS WAS A *PYRRHIC* VICTORY.

THEY OWED MAGNETO THEIR LIVES. YET IN THEIR HEARTS, THEY *HATED* WHAT HE MADE THEM DO.

MONTHS LATER, THEY LEFT MAGNETO TO BECOME HONORED MEMBERS OF THE *AVENGERS.*

WE RESCUED ANGEL, DESTROYED ASTEROID M, AND RETURNED TO EARTH RELATIVELY UNSCATHED. IN RETROSPECT, I MARVEL AT OUR LUCK.

MAGNETO, OF COURSE, *ESCAPED.*

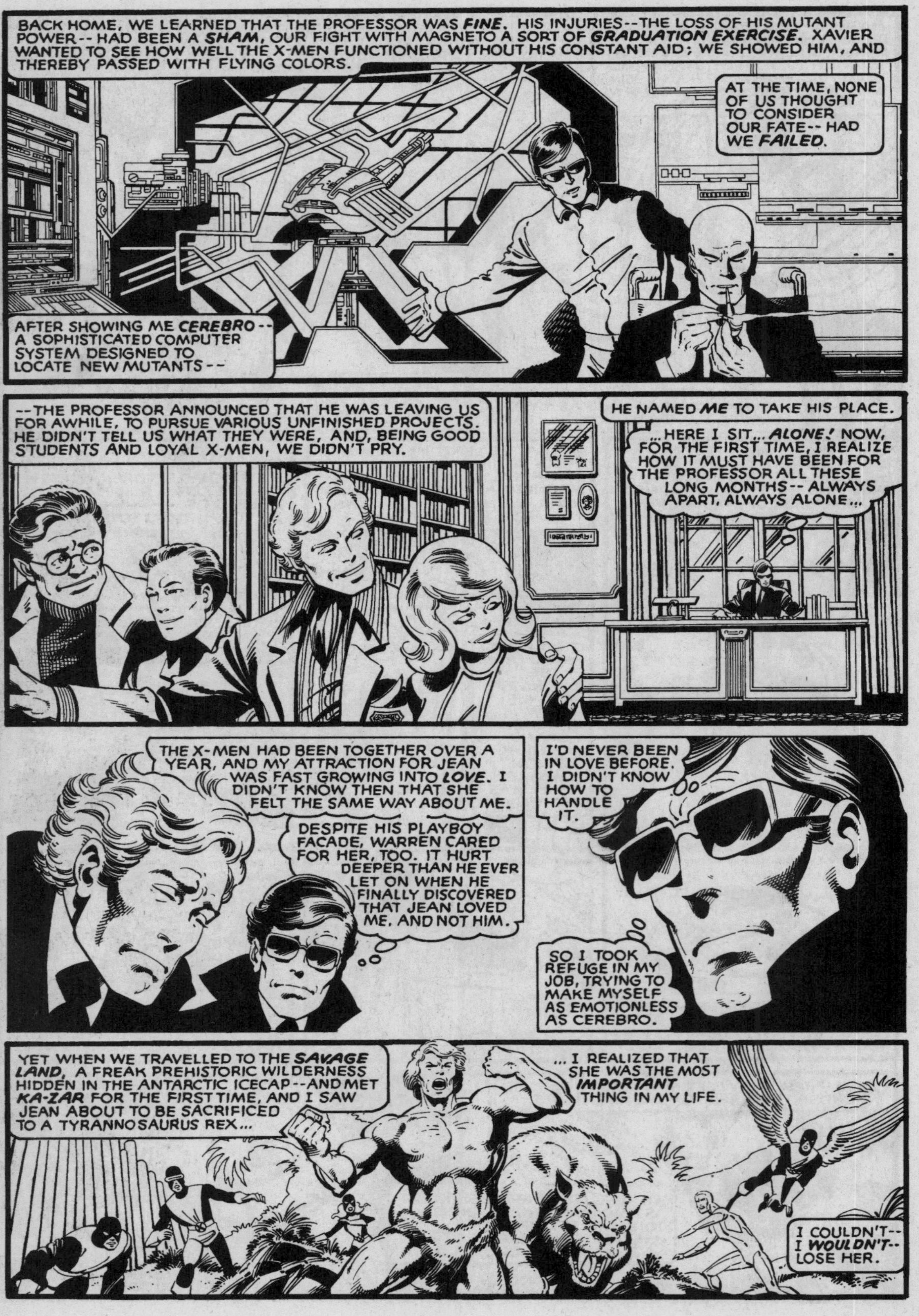
BACK HOME, WE LEARNED THAT THE PROFESSOR WAS FINE. HIS INJURIES--THE LOSS OF HIS MUTANT POWER--HAD BEEN A SHAM, OUR FIGHT WITH MAGNETO A SORT OF GRADUATION EXERCISE. XAVIER WANTED TO SEE HOW WELL THE X-MEN FUNCTIONED WITHOUT HIS CONSTANT AID; WE SHOWED HIM, AND THEREBY PASSED WITH FLYING COLORS.
AT THE TIME, NONE OF US THOUGHT TO CONSIDER OUR FATE--HAD WE FAILED.
AFTER SHOWING ME CEREBRO--A SOPHISTICATED COMPUTER SYSTEM DESIGNED TO LOCATE NEW MUTANTS--
--THE PROFESSOR ANNOUNCED THAT HE WAS LEAVING US FOR AWHILE, TO PURSUE VARIOUS UNFINISHED PROJECTS. HE DIDN'T TELL US WHAT THEY WERE, AND, BEING GOOD STUDENTS AND LOYAL X-MEN, WE DIDN'T PRY.
HE NAMED ME TO TAKE HIS PLACE.
...HERE I SIT... ALONE! NOW, FOR THE FIRST TIME, I REALIZE HOW IT MUST HAVE BEEN FOR THE PROFESSOR ALL THESE LONG MONTHS--ALWAYS APART, ALWAYS ALONE...
THE X-MEN HAD BEEN TOGETHER OVER A YEAR, AND MY ATTRACTION FOR JEAN WAS FAST GROWING INTO LOVE. I DIDN'T KNOW THEN THAT SHE FELT THE SAME WAY ABOUT ME.
DESPITE HIS PLAYBOY FACADE, WARREN CARED FOR HER, TOO. IT HURT DEEPER THAN HE EVER LET ON WHEN HE FINALLY DISCOVERED THAT JEAN LOVED ME. AND NOT HIM.
I'D NEVER BEEN IN LOVE BEFORE. I DIDN'T KNOW HOW TO HANDLE IT.
SO I TOOK REFUGE IN MY JOB, TRYING TO MAKE MYSELF AS EMOTIONLESS AS CEREBRO.
YET WHEN WE TRAVELLED TO THE SAVAGE LAND, A FREAK PREHISTORIC WILDERNESS HIDDEN IN THE ANTARCTIC ICECAP--AND MET KA-ZAR FOR THE FIRST TIME, AND I SAW JEAN ABOUT TO BE SACRIFICED TO A TYRANNOSAURUS REX...
...I REALIZED THAT SHE WAS THE MOST IMPORTANT THING IN MY LIFE.
I COULDN'T--I WOULDN'T--LOSE HER.

MAGNETO WAS NEVER ONE TO SUFFER DEFEAT LIGHTLY. EACH SETBACK MERELY STRENGTHENED HIS DETERMINATION TO DESTROY US. FINALLY, HE CONTACTED A MYSTERIOUS BEING WHO CALLED HIMSELF THE *"STRANGER"* AND TRIED TO ENLIST HIS AID...

... ONLY TO DISCOVER THAT HE'D BITTEN OFF FAR MORE THAN HE COULD CHEW. BOTH HE AND PROFESSOR X ASSUMED THE STRANGER TO BE A MUTANT. THEY WERE WRONG.

HE WAS AN *ALIEN.*

HE TOOK MAGNETO AND THE TOAD WITH HIM TO HIS HOME AMONG THE STARS. HE SAID THEY WOULD NEVER RETURN.

I CAN'T SAY I WAS SORRY TO SEE THEM GO.

BUT IF WE THOUGHT OUR LIVES WOULD GET ANY EASIER WITH MAGNETO'S ABRUPT DEPARTURE, WE WERE SOON RUDELY DISILLUSIONED. ALMOST IMMEDIATELY, CEREBRO'S MUTANT ALARM HERALDED THE ARRIVAL OF A FOE WHOSE RAW POWER AND FEROCITY WERE AS AWESOME AS HIS *HATE.*

HIS NAME WAS *CAIN MARKO.* HE WAS PROFESSOR XAVIER'S HALF-BROTHER.

WE CAME TO KNOW HIM BETTER AS-- **JUGGERNAUT!**

WE THREW EVERYTHING WE HAD AT HIM. NOTHING WORKED. AFTER A DESPERATE FIGHT, ANGEL, WITH THE AID OF THE *HUMAN TORCH,* MANAGED TO REMOVE MARKO'S HELMET, THEREBY RENDERING JUGGERNAUT VULNERABLE TO THE PROFESSOR'S TELEPATHIC ATTACK.

WE'D SURVIVED, WE'D TRIUMPHED, BY THE SKIN OF OUR TEETH. WE DIDN'T KNOW THAT THERE WAS FAR *WORSE* YET TO COME.

AN ANTHROPOLOGIST NAMED *BOLIVAR TRASK* SPOKE OUT AGAINST THE "MUTANT MENACE", AND, SEEMINGLY OVERNIGHT, THE X-MEN BECAME VIRTUAL PUBLIC ENEMIES. TRASK HAD CREATED GIANT ROBOTIC *SENTINELS* TO COMBAT THIS "MENACE", BUT THINGS QUICKLY GOT OUT OF HAND. INSTEAD OF PROTECTING HUMANITY, THE SENTINELS -- LED BY THEIR *MASTER MOLD* -- SET OUT TO CONQUER IT.

LOOKING BACK ON THOSE DAYS, IT SEEMS LIKE WE WERE CONSTANTLY FIGHTING SOME NEW MUTANT MENACE OR SUPER-VILLAIN.

TRASK SACRIFICED HIS LIFE TO DESTROY HIS REBELLIOUS CREATIONS -- AND THAT EPIC BATTLE ALMOST KILLED *ICEMAN* AS WELL.

NO MATTER HOW HARD WE TRIED TO LIVE OUR OWN LIVES, BEING AN X-MAN ALWAYS SEEMED TO TAKE PRECEDENCE. I DIDN'T MIND, THEN. PERHAPS I SHOULD HAVE.

JEAN WAS AN UNDERGRADUATE STUDENT AT METRO UNIVERSITY. I WAS DESPERATELY AFRAID OF LOSING HER, YET TERRIFIED OF TELLING HER SO. THE NIGHT OF BOBBY'S 18th BIRTHDAY, I RESOLVED TO LET HER KNOW HOW I FELT. I THINK I'D HAVE RATHER FACED JUGGERNAUT SINGLE-HANDED.

A *SURPRISE PARTY* -- IN GREENWICH VILLAGE! HOW LUCKY CAN A GUY *BE*?!

HI, CREW! I WANT YOU TO MEET A VERY GOOD FRIEND OF MINE -- *CANDY SOUTHERN*!

HEADS UP, GROUP! WARREN'S HERE!

AND LOOK AT THE GAL HE BROUGHT WITH HIM!

I'M VERY GLAD TO MEET ALL OF YOU!

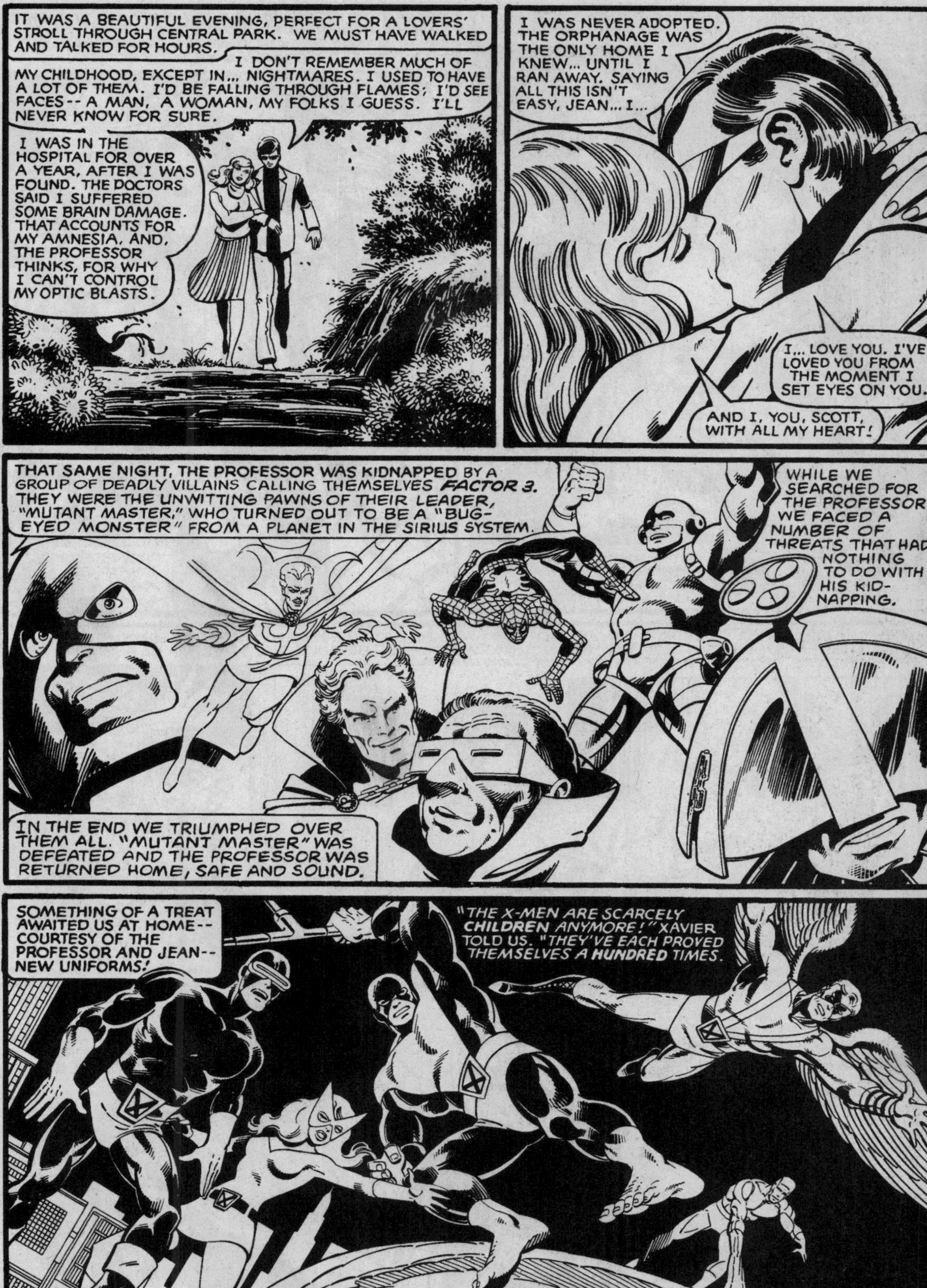

IT WAS A BEAUTIFUL EVENING, PERFECT FOR A LOVERS' STROLL THROUGH CENTRAL PARK. WE MUST HAVE WALKED AND TALKED FOR HOURS.
I DON'T REMEMBER MUCH OF MY CHILDHOOD, EXCEPT IN... NIGHTMARES. I USED TO HAVE A LOT OF THEM. I'D BE FALLING THROUGH FLAMES; I'D SEE FACES -- A MAN, A WOMAN, MY FOLKS I GUESS. I'LL NEVER KNOW FOR SURE.
I WAS IN THE HOSPITAL FOR OVER A YEAR, AFTER I WAS FOUND. THE DOCTORS SAID I SUFFERED SOME BRAIN DAMAGE. THAT ACCOUNTS FOR MY AMNESIA, AND, THE PROFESSOR THINKS, FOR WHY I CAN'T CONTROL MY OPTIC BLASTS.
I WAS NEVER ADOPTED. THE ORPHANAGE WAS THE ONLY HOME I KNEW... UNTIL I RAN AWAY. SAYING ALL THIS ISN'T EASY, JEAN... I...
I... LOVE YOU. I'VE LOVED YOU FROM THE MOMENT I SET EYES ON YOU.
AND I, YOU, SCOTT, WITH ALL MY HEART!
THAT SAME NIGHT, THE PROFESSOR WAS KIDNAPPED BY A GROUP OF DEADLY VILLAINS CALLING THEMSELVES *FACTOR 3*. THEY WERE THE UNWITTING PAWNS OF THEIR LEADER, "MUTANT MASTER," WHO TURNED OUT TO BE A "BUG-EYED MONSTER" FROM A PLANET IN THE SIRIUS SYSTEM.
WHILE WE SEARCHED FOR THE PROFESSOR WE FACED A NUMBER OF THREATS THAT HAD NOTHING TO DO WITH HIS KID-NAPPING.
IN THE END WE TRIUMPHED OVER THEM ALL. "MUTANT MASTER" WAS DEFEATED AND THE PROFESSOR WAS RETURNED HOME, SAFE AND SOUND.
SOMETHING OF A TREAT AWAITED US AT HOME -- COURTESY OF THE PROFESSOR AND JEAN -- NEW UNIFORMS!
*"THE X-MEN ARE SCARCELY **CHILDREN** ANYMORE!"* XAVIER TOLD US. *"THEY'VE EACH PROVED THEMSELVES A **HUNDRED** TIMES.*
*"IT'S TIME THEY LOOKED LIKE **INDIVIDUALS**-- NOT PRODUCTS OF AN **ASSEMBLY LINE**!"*

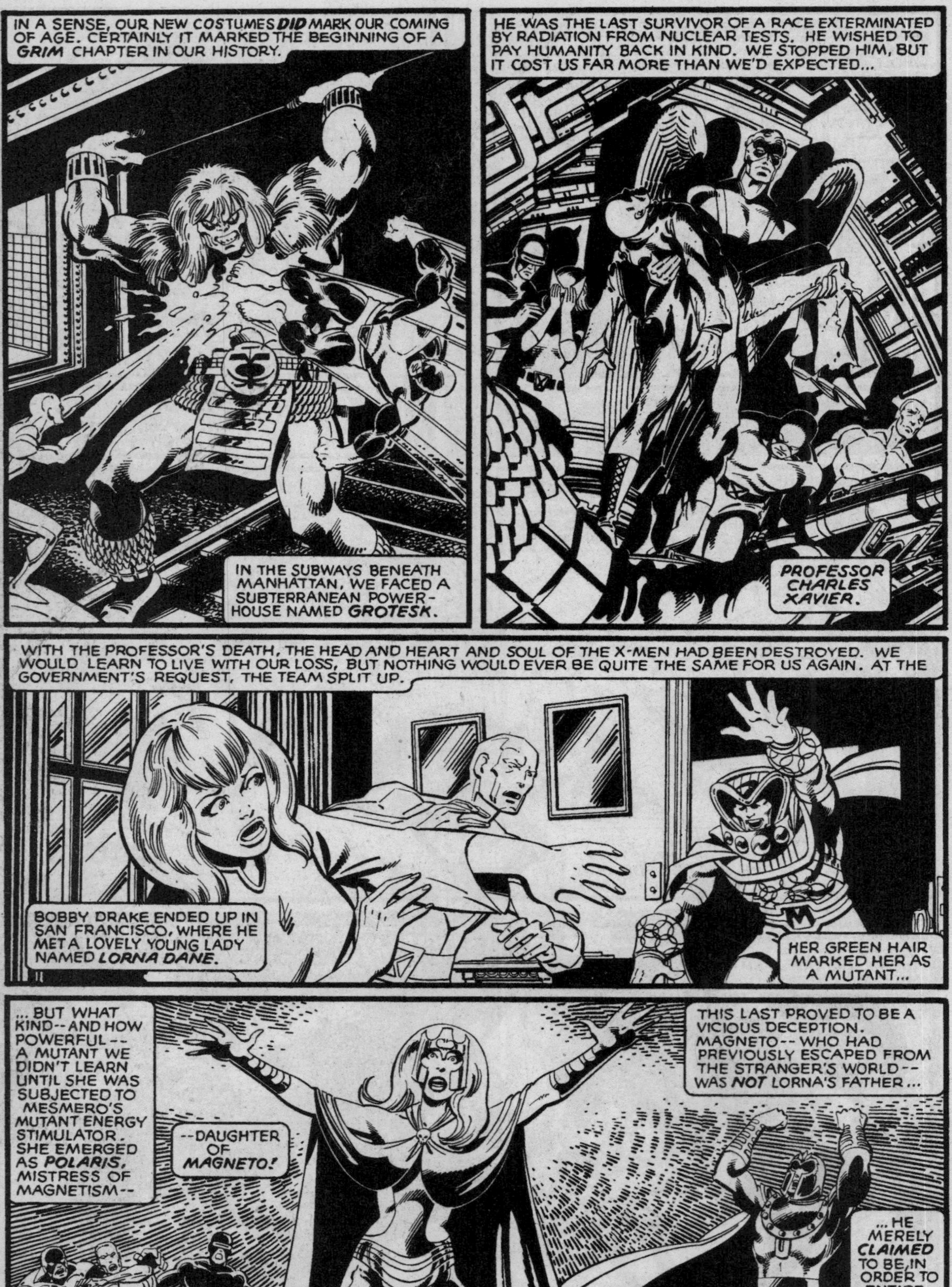
IN A SENSE, OUR NEW COSTUMES DID MARK OUR COMING OF AGE. CERTAINLY IT MARKED THE BEGINNING OF A GRIM CHAPTER IN OUR HISTORY.
IN THE SUBWAYS BENEATH MANHATTAN, WE FACED A SUBTERRANEAN POWER-HOUSE NAMED GROTESK.
HE WAS THE LAST SURVIVOR OF A RACE EXTERMINATED BY RADIATION FROM NUCLEAR TESTS. HE WISHED TO PAY HUMANITY BACK IN KIND. WE STOPPED HIM, BUT IT COST US FAR MORE THAN WE'D EXPECTED...
PROFESSOR CHARLES XAVIER.
WITH THE PROFESSOR'S DEATH, THE HEAD AND HEART AND SOUL OF THE X-MEN HAD BEEN DESTROYED. WE WOULD LEARN TO LIVE WITH OUR LOSS, BUT NOTHING WOULD EVER BE QUITE THE SAME FOR US AGAIN. AT THE GOVERNMENT'S REQUEST, THE TEAM SPLIT UP.
BOBBY DRAKE ENDED UP IN SAN FRANCISCO, WHERE HE MET A LOVELY YOUNG LADY NAMED LORNA DANE.
HER GREEN HAIR MARKED HER AS A MUTANT...
... BUT WHAT KIND-- AND HOW POWERFUL -- A MUTANT WE DIDN'T LEARN UNTIL SHE WAS SUBJECTED TO MESMERO'S MUTANT ENERGY STIMULATOR. SHE EMERGED AS POLARIS, MISTRESS OF MAGNETISM--
--DAUGHTER OF MAGNETO!
THIS LAST PROVED TO BE A VICIOUS DECEPTION. MAGNETO-- WHO HAD PREVIOUSLY ESCAPED FROM THE STRANGER'S WORLD-- WAS NOT LORNA'S FATHER...
...HE MERELY CLAIMED TO BE, IN ORDER TO ENTICE HER INTO JOINING HIS CAUSE. HE FAILED.

FBI EDICT OR NO, WE BEGAN TO DRIFT BACK TOGETHER. SEPARATING THE X-MEN HADN'T REALLY WORKED OUT. IT MERELY PROVED WHAT WE ALREADY KNEW, THAT THE WHOLE OF THE TEAM WAS GREATER THAN THE SUM OF THE PARTS.

WE WERE MORE THAN A SIMPLE FIGHTING TEAM. THE X-MEN WERE A *FAMILY.* IN MY CASE, THE ONLY FAMILY I HAD--

-- SAVE FOR MY YOUNGER BROTHER, ALEX.

I INTRODUCED THE X-MEN TO HIM--AND HIM TO THEM--THE DAY HE GRADUATED FROM LANDON COLLEGE.

WE'D BEEN SEPARATED IN THE ORPHANAGE-- HE'D BEEN ADOPTED WHILE I'D BEEN IN THE HOSPITAL, IN A COMA. PROFESSOR X HELPED ME TRACK HIM DOWN, AND WE'D STAYED IN CLOSE TOUCH EVER SINCE. I KNEW HE WAS A MUTANT, BUT-- AS WITH LORNA-- WE DIDN'T DISCOVER THE NATURE AND EXTENT OF HIS POWERS...

...UNTIL HE WAS KIDNAPPED BY THE *LIVING PHARAOH.*

THE TWO WERE *SYMBIOTES,* EACH DRAWING POWER FROM COSMIC RAYS AND FROM EACH OTHER.

AS ALEX'S ABILITY WAXED, THE PHARAOH'S WANED-- AND VICE VERSA. A FULL CHARGE TRANSFORMED THAT EGYPTIAN MADMAN INTO THE *LIVING MONOLITH.*

BUT WHEN HE WAS DEFEATED, ALL THAT RAW ENERGY FLOWED INTO ALEX. AND WHAT I FEARED MOST CAME TO PASS.

HE COULDN'T CONTROL IT.

IN HIS OWN WAY, HE WAS AS POTENTIALLY DANGEROUS AS I. UNABLE TO COPE WITH THAT DREAD REALIZATION--AND, TO BE HONEST, I CAN'T SAY I BLAME HIM-- HE FLED FROM THE X-MEN... RIGHT INTO THE ARMS OF A *SENTINEL.*

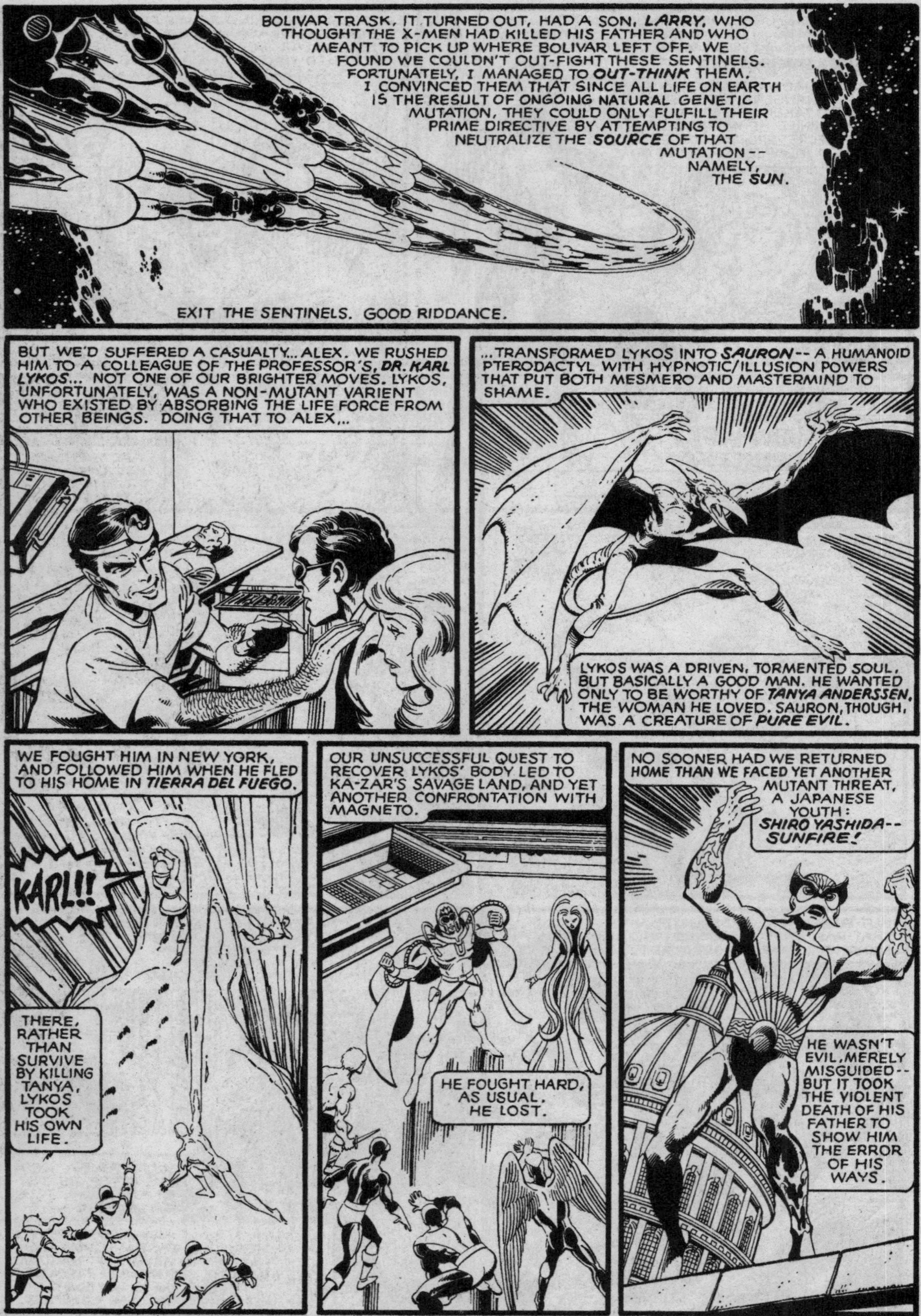
BOLIVAR TRASK, IT TURNED OUT, HAD A SON, LARRY, WHO THOUGHT THE X-MEN HAD KILLED HIS FATHER AND WHO MEANT TO PICK UP WHERE BOLIVAR LEFT OFF. WE FOUND WE COULDN'T OUT-FIGHT THESE SENTINELS. FORTUNATELY, I MANAGED TO OUT-THINK THEM. I CONVINCED THEM THAT SINCE ALL LIFE ON EARTH IS THE RESULT OF ONGOING NATURAL GENETIC MUTATION, THEY COULD ONLY FULFILL THEIR PRIME DIRECTIVE BY ATTEMPTING TO NEUTRALIZE THE SOURCE OF THAT MUTATION -- NAMELY, THE SUN.
EXIT THE SENTINELS. GOOD RIDDANCE.
BUT WE'D SUFFERED A CASUALTY... ALEX. WE RUSHED HIM TO A COLLEAGUE OF THE PROFESSOR'S, DR. KARL LYKOS... NOT ONE OF OUR BRIGHTER MOVES. LYKOS, UNFORTUNATELY, WAS A NON-MUTANT VARIENT WHO EXISTED BY ABSORBING THE LIFE FORCE FROM OTHER BEINGS. DOING THAT TO ALEX,..
...TRANSFORMED LYKOS INTO SAURON -- A HUMANOID PTERODACTYL WITH HYPNOTIC/ILLUSION POWERS THAT PUT BOTH MESMERO AND MASTERMIND TO SHAME.
LYKOS WAS A DRIVEN, TORMENTED SOUL, BUT BASICALLY A GOOD MAN. HE WANTED ONLY TO BE WORTHY OF TANYA ANDERSSEN, THE WOMAN HE LOVED. SAURON, THOUGH, WAS A CREATURE OF PURE EVIL.
WE FOUGHT HIM IN NEW YORK, AND FOLLOWED HIM WHEN HE FLED TO HIS HOME IN TIERRA DEL FUEGO.
KARL!!
THERE, RATHER THAN SURVIVE BY KILLING TANYA, LYKOS TOOK HIS OWN LIFE.
OUR UNSUCCESSFUL QUEST TO RECOVER LYKOS' BODY LED TO KA-ZAR'S SAVAGE LAND, AND YET ANOTHER CONFRONTATION WITH MAGNETO.
HE FOUGHT HARD, AS USUAL. HE LOST.
NO SOONER HAD WE RETURNED HOME THAN WE FACED YET ANOTHER MUTANT THREAT, A JAPANESE YOUTH: SHIRO YASHIDA-- SUNFIRE!
HE WASN'T EVIL, MERELY MISGUIDED-- BUT IT TOOK THE VIOLENT DEATH OF HIS FATHER TO SHOW HIM THE ERROR OF HIS WAYS.

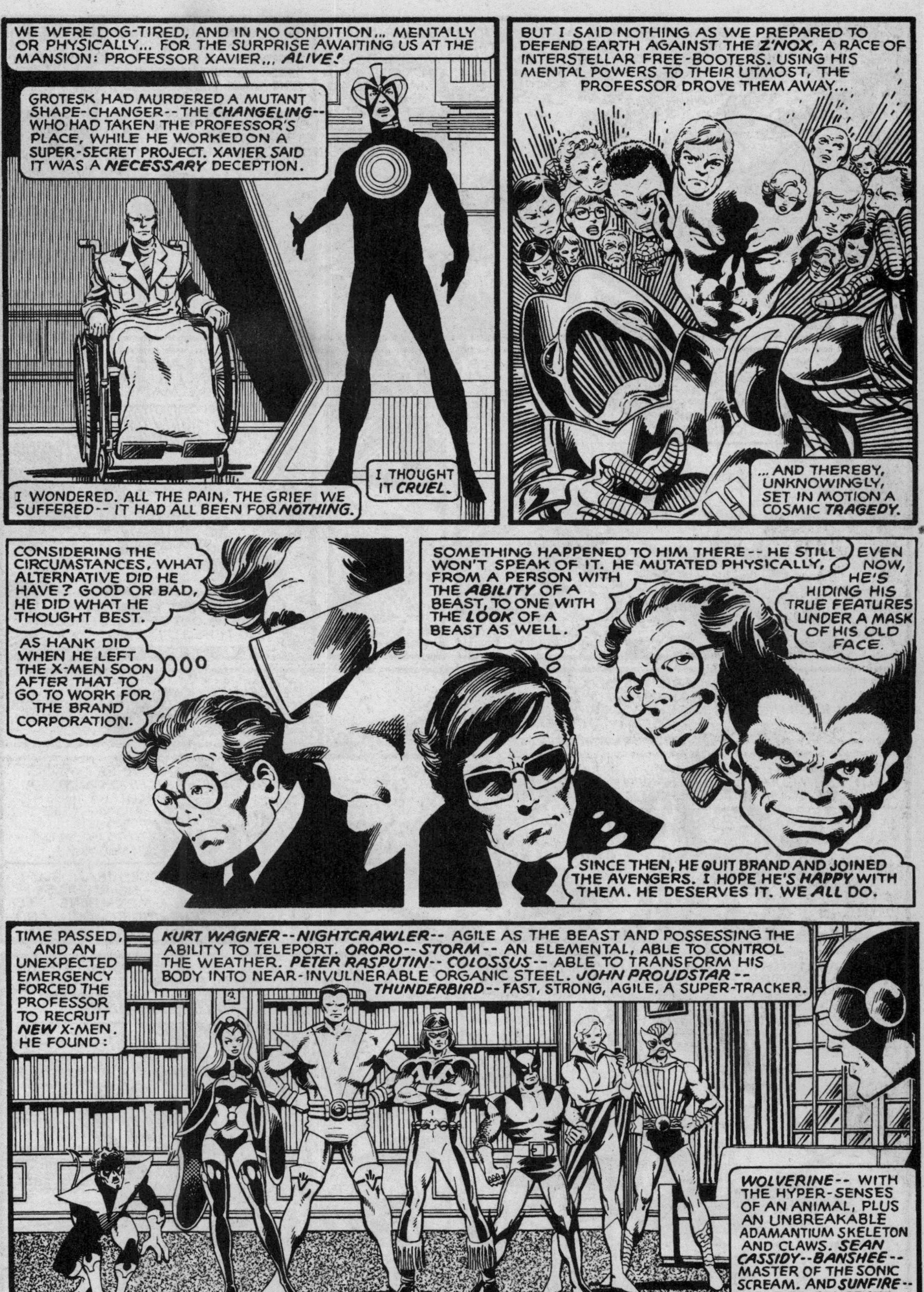
WE WERE DOG-TIRED, AND IN NO CONDITION... MENTALLY OR PHYSICALLY... FOR THE SURPRISE AWAITING US AT THE MANSION: PROFESSOR XAVIER... ALIVE!
GROTESK HAD MURDERED A MUTANT SHAPE-CHANGER--THE CHANGELING--WHO HAD TAKEN THE PROFESSOR'S PLACE, WHILE HE WORKED ON A SUPER-SECRET PROJECT. XAVIER SAID IT WAS A NECESSARY DECEPTION.
I THOUGHT IT CRUEL.
I WONDERED. ALL THE PAIN, THE GRIEF WE SUFFERED-- IT HAD ALL BEEN FOR NOTHING.
BUT I SAID NOTHING AS WE PREPARED TO DEFEND EARTH AGAINST THE Z'NOX, A RACE OF INTERSTELLAR FREE-BOOTERS. USING HIS MENTAL POWERS TO THEIR UTMOST, THE PROFESSOR DROVE THEM AWAY...
...AND THEREBY, UNKNOWINGLY, SET IN MOTION A COSMIC TRAGEDY.
CONSIDERING THE CIRCUMSTANCES, WHAT ALTERNATIVE DID HE HAVE? GOOD OR BAD, HE DID WHAT HE THOUGHT BEST.
AS HANK DID WHEN HE LEFT THE X-MEN SOON AFTER THAT TO GO TO WORK FOR THE BRAND CORPORATION.
SOMETHING HAPPENED TO HIM THERE-- HE STILL WON'T SPEAK OF IT. HE MUTATED PHYSICALLY, FROM A PERSON WITH THE ABILITY OF A BEAST, TO ONE WITH THE LOOK OF A BEAST AS WELL.
EVEN NOW, HE'S HIDING HIS TRUE FEATURES UNDER A MASK OF HIS OLD FACE.
SINCE THEN, HE QUIT BRAND AND JOINED THE AVENGERS. I HOPE HE'S HAPPY WITH THEM. HE DESERVES IT. WE ALL DO.
TIME PASSED, AND AN UNEXPECTED EMERGENCY FORCED THE PROFESSOR TO RECRUIT NEW X-MEN. HE FOUND:
KURT WAGNER--NIGHTCRAWLER-- AGILE AS THE BEAST AND POSSESSING THE ABILITY TO TELEPORT. ORORO--STORM-- AN ELEMENTAL, ABLE TO CONTROL THE WEATHER. PETER RASPUTIN--COLOSSUS-- ABLE TO TRANSFORM HIS BODY INTO NEAR-INVULNERABLE ORGANIC STEEL. JOHN PROUDSTAR--THUNDERBIRD-- FAST, STRONG, AGILE, A SUPER-TRACKER.
WOLVERINE-- WITH THE HYPER-SENSES OF AN ANIMAL, PLUS AN UNBREAKABLE ADAMANTIUM SKELETON AND CLAWS. SEAN CASSIDY--BANSHEE-- MASTER OF THE SONIC SCREAM. AND SUNFIRE-- ABLE TO GENERATE NUCLEAR FIREBOLTS.

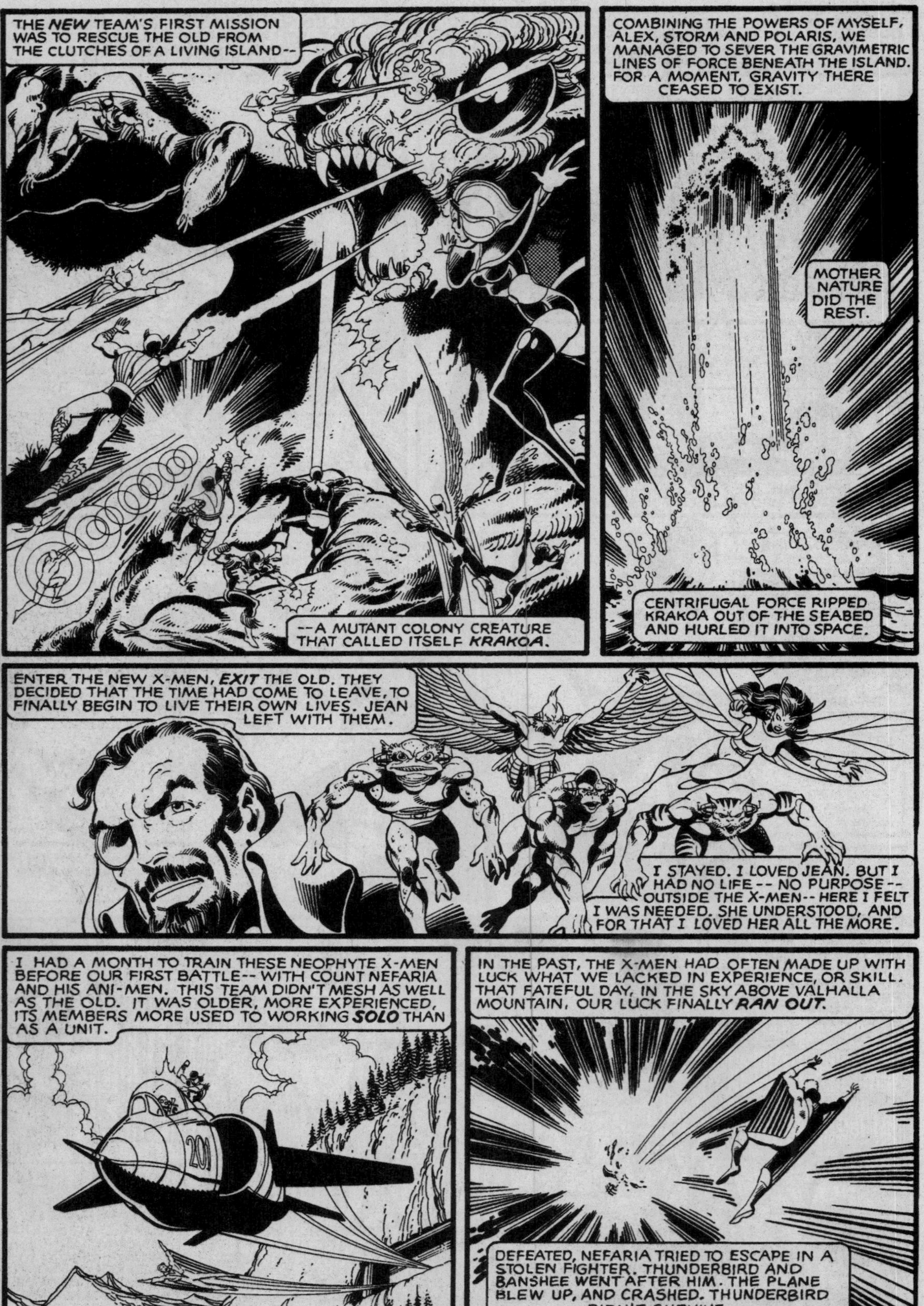
THE NEW TEAM'S FIRST MISSION WAS TO RESCUE THE OLD FROM THE CLUTCHES OF A LIVING ISLAND--
--A MUTANT COLONY CREATURE THAT CALLED ITSELF KRAKOA.
COMBINING THE POWERS OF MYSELF, ALEX, STORM AND POLARIS, WE MANAGED TO SEVER THE GRAVIMETRIC LINES OF FORCE BENEATH THE ISLAND. FOR A MOMENT, GRAVITY THERE CEASED TO EXIST.
MOTHER NATURE DID THE REST.
CENTRIFUGAL FORCE RIPPED KRAKOA OUT OF THE SEABED AND HURLED IT INTO SPACE.
ENTER THE NEW X-MEN, EXIT THE OLD. THEY DECIDED THAT THE TIME HAD COME TO LEAVE, TO FINALLY BEGIN TO LIVE THEIR OWN LIVES. JEAN LEFT WITH THEM.
I STAYED. I LOVED JEAN. BUT I HAD NO LIFE -- NO PURPOSE -- OUTSIDE THE X-MEN-- HERE I FELT I WAS NEEDED. SHE UNDERSTOOD, AND FOR THAT I LOVED HER ALL THE MORE.
I HAD A MONTH TO TRAIN THESE NEOPHYTE X-MEN BEFORE OUR FIRST BATTLE-- WITH COUNT NEFARIA AND HIS ANI-MEN. THIS TEAM DIDN'T MESH AS WELL AS THE OLD. IT WAS OLDER, MORE EXPERIENCED, ITS MEMBERS MORE USED TO WORKING SOLO THAN AS A UNIT.
201
IN THE PAST, THE X-MEN HAD OFTEN MADE UP WITH LUCK WHAT WE LACKED IN EXPERIENCE, OR SKILL. THAT FATEFUL DAY, IN THE SKY ABOVE VALHALLA MOUNTAIN, OUR LUCK FINALLY RAN OUT.
DEFEATED, NEFARIA TRIED TO ESCAPE IN A STOLEN FIGHTER. THUNDERBIRD AND BANSHEE WENT AFTER HIM. THE PLANE BLEW UP, AND CRASHED. THUNDERBIRD DIDN'T SURVIVE.

IS THAT WHEN I BEGAN TO QUESTION -- TOO LITTLE, TOO LATE?

DID IT TAKE THUNDER-BIRD'S *DEATH* TO MAKE ME REALIZE THE TRUE COST OF A MISTAKE?

I KEEP REMEMBERING WHAT ORORO ASKED ME NOT LONG AGO -- IF *THIS* WAS THE LIFE I IMAGINED FOR MYSELF WHEN I WAS YOUNG?

WAS THIS THE LIFE *ANY* OF US IMAGINED FOR OURSELVES?

THINGS WERE RELATIVELY PEACEFUL FOR THE X-MEN AFTER THAT. THE PROFESSOR LEFT ON A VACATION. I SPENT MORE AND MORE TIME WITH JEAN. WE WERE HAPPY, CONTENT.

IT WAS TOO GOOD TO LAST. IT DIDN'T.

PREPARE TO FACE YOUR *DOOM*, MUTANTS -- -- FOR THE SENTINELS HAVE RETURNED!

I'LL NEVER FORGET THE 72 HOURS THAT FOLLOWED. THESE NEO-SENTINELS WERE THE BRAINCHILD OF A GOVERNMENT WACKO NAMED *STEVEN LANG*. WE FOUGHT HIM IN AN ABANDONED AMERICAN SPACE STATION, AND WON. BUT DURING RE-ENTRY, WE WERE CAUGHT IN A *SOLAR FLARE*.

THE FLARE -- THE RADIATION -- IT'S STARTING TO *GET THROUGH*!

SCOTT!

EVERYONE BUT JEAN WAS IN THE SHUTTLE'S SHIELDED ANTI-RADIATION CELL. SHE WAS ON THE UNPROTECTED FLIGHT DECK, PILOTING THE SPACE-CRAFT. SHE USED HER TELEKINETIC POWER TO BLOCK THE SOLAR RADIATION AS LONG AS POSSIBLE. BUT EVEN SHE COULDN'T HOLD OUT INDEFIN

WE ALL THOUGHT SHE'D DIED. CERTAINLY NOTHING EVEN REMOTELY *HUMAN* COULD HAVE SURVIVED.

NOTHING REMOTELY HUMAN *DID*.

HEAR ME, X-MEN!

NO LONGER AM I, THE WOMAN YOU *KNEW*!

I AM FIRE! AND *LIFE INCARNATE*! NOW AND FOREVER --

-- I AM phœnix!

PART OF ME WISHES JEAN HAD... DIED IN THAT CRASH. AND YET... I WOULDN'T HAVE MISSED THIS LAST MONTH -- OUR LAST WEEKS TOGETHER -- FOR THE WORLD.

XAVIER SENT THE X-MEN TO IRELAND FOR A VACATION -- WHILE I STAYED WITH JEAN IN NEW YORK. SOME VACA-TION. FIRST THEY FOUGHT JUGGERNAUT AND HIS NEW PARTNER -- BANSHEE'S VILLAINOUS COUSIN, *BLACK TOM CASSIDY* -- AND THEN MAGNETO.

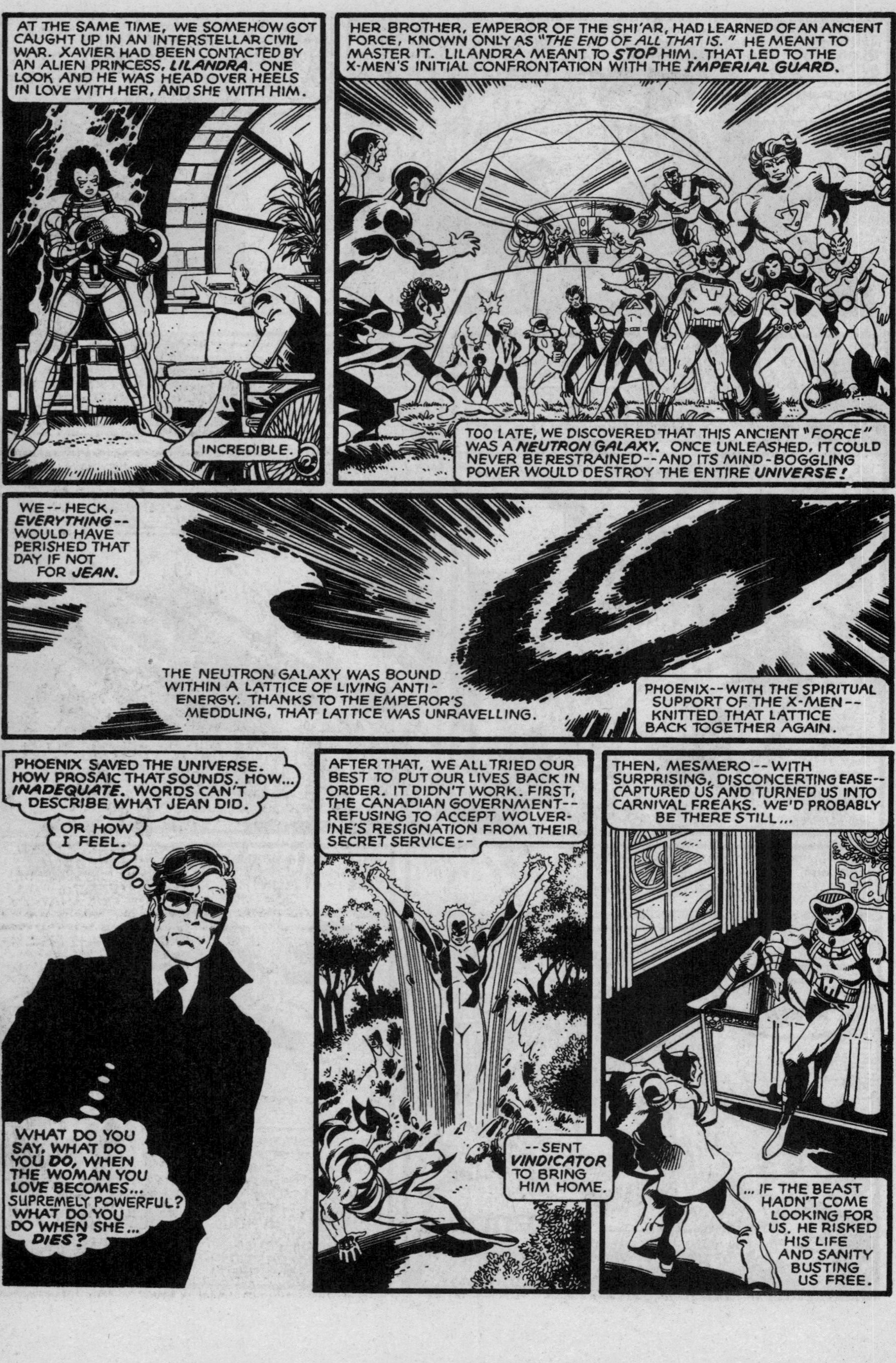
AT THE SAME TIME, WE SOMEHOW GOT CAUGHT UP IN AN INTERSTELLAR CIVIL WAR. XAVIER HAD BEEN CONTACTED BY AN ALIEN PRINCESS, LILANDRA. ONE LOOK AND HE WAS HEAD OVER HEELS IN LOVE WITH HER, AND SHE WITH HIM.
INCREDIBLE.
HER BROTHER, EMPEROR OF THE SHI'AR, HAD LEARNED OF AN ANCIENT FORCE, KNOWN ONLY AS "THE END OF ALL THAT IS." HE MEANT TO MASTER IT. LILANDRA MEANT TO STOP HIM. THAT LED TO THE X-MEN'S INITIAL CONFRONTATION WITH THE IMPERIAL GUARD.
TOO LATE, WE DISCOVERED THAT THIS ANCIENT "FORCE" WAS A NEUTRON GALAXY. ONCE UNLEASHED, IT COULD NEVER BE RESTRAINED--AND ITS MIND-BOGGLING POWER WOULD DESTROY THE ENTIRE UNIVERSE!
WE--HECK, EVERYTHING--WOULD HAVE PERISHED THAT DAY IF NOT FOR JEAN.
THE NEUTRON GALAXY WAS BOUND WITHIN A LATTICE OF LIVING ANTI-ENERGY. THANKS TO THE EMPEROR'S MEDDLING, THAT LATTICE WAS UNRAVELLING.
PHOENIX--WITH THE SPIRITUAL SUPPORT OF THE X-MEN--KNITTED THAT LATTICE BACK TOGETHER AGAIN.
PHOENIX SAVED THE UNIVERSE. HOW PROSAIC THAT SOUNDS. HOW... INADEQUATE. WORDS CAN'T DESCRIBE WHAT JEAN DID.
OR HOW I FEEL.
WHAT DO YOU SAY, WHAT DO YOU DO, WHEN THE WOMAN YOU LOVE BECOMES... SUPREMELY POWERFUL? WHAT DO YOU DO WHEN SHE... DIES?
AFTER THAT, WE ALL TRIED OUR BEST TO PUT OUR LIVES BACK IN ORDER. IT DIDN'T WORK. FIRST, THE CANADIAN GOVERNMENT--REFUSING TO ACCEPT WOLVERINE'S RESIGNATION FROM THEIR SECRET SERVICE--
--SENT VINDICATOR TO BRING HIM HOME.
THEN, MESMERO--WITH SURPRISING, DISCONCERTING EASE--CAPTURED US AND TURNED US INTO CARNIVAL FREAKS. WE'D PROBABLY BE THERE STILL...
...IF THE BEAST HADN'T COME LOOKING FOR US. HE RISKED HIS LIFE AND SANITY BUSTING US FREE.

BUT MASTERMIND HAD MADE A *FATAL* MIS-CALCULATION. HE ASSUMED THAT PHOENIX WAS MERELY MARVEL GIRL WITH A DIFFERENT NAME AND FLASHIER COSTUME.

SHE WASN'T.

IT WAS INCREASINGLY EVIDENT TO JEAN -- AND TO *MOIRA MacTAGGERT,* XAVIER'S LONG-TIME COLLEAGUE IN MUTANT RESEARCH -- THAT THERE WAS NO COMPARI-SON BETWEEN MARVEL GIRL AND PHOENIX.

IT'S EASY TO PLAY *"WHAT IF"* GAMES, TO THINK OF WHAT *MIGHT* HAVE BEEN. MOIRA FEARED THAT JEAN'S POWER COULD GET OUT OF CONTROL. SHE MIGHT HAVE FOUND A WAY TO PREVENT THAT...

... HAD HER -- AND OUR -- ATTENTION NOT BEEN DIVERTED BY THE MENACE OF HER SON, *PROTEUS.*

TO EXIST, HE POSSESSED PEOPLE -- CONSUMING A LIFETIME'S WORTH OF BIO-ENERGY IN A MATTER OF HOURS. HE THOUGHT OF PEOPLE THE WAY WE THINK OF COWS -- AS *FOOD.* IF HE HUNGERED FOR A LIFE, HE *TOOK* IT.

HE WAS THE KIND OF MUTANT THE X-MEN HAD BEEN FORMED TO COMBAT.

THINGS HAVE A WAY OF *BALANCING* OUT, THOUGH. WE'D FOUND A TRULY EVIL MUTANT IN PROTEUS. BUT SOON AFTER THAT WE FOUND A TRULY GOOD ONE -- INDEED, A POTENTIAL X-MAN --

-- IN *KITTY PRYDE.*

SHE'S 13½, CUTE, BRIGHT, SPUNKY -- AND SHE WALKS THROUGH WALLS.

MY ONE REGRET WAS THAT OUR BATTLE WITH PROTEUS WAS TO THE *DEATH.* IT WAS NECESSARY, BUT I WISH THERE'D BEEN ANOTHER WAY.

THEN... CAME THE HELLFIRE CLUB. MASTERMIND HAD SUCCEEDED IN SUBVERTING JEAN BY MAKING HER BELIEVE THAT SHE WAS PSYCHICALLY SLIPPING IN TIME, RELIVING AN ANCESTOR'S LIFE. THE WORLD SHE SAW WAS THAT OF *1780,* NOT 1980.

BY THE TIME SHE BROKE HIS CONTROL OVER HER, THE DAMAGE HAD BEEN DONE.

NO LONGER WAS SHE PHOENIX, CHILD OF LIGHT AND LAUGHTER. SHE WAS *DARK PHOENIX*, THE BLACK ANGEL, CHAOS-BRINGER.

RAVAGER OF WORLDS.

AT HER HANDS, AN ENTIRE STAR SYSTEM-- FIVE BILLION PEOPLE -- DIED. SHE WAS DRIVEN BY NEEDS, DESIRES, PASSIONS THAT NONE OF US CAN COMPREHEND-- AFTER ALL, WE'RE ONLY HUMAN. PHOENIX WAS A STEP BEYOND.

BUT... SHE WAS STILL THE WOMAN I LOVED. I HAD TO TRY TO SAVE HER. I TRIED TO TALK HER DOWN. I WAS REACHING HER WHEN PROFESSOR X STEPPED IN. I USED REASON...HE USED *FORCE*. WHO'S TO SAY WHICH OF US HAD THE *BETTER* WAY?

HE AND PHOENIX FACED OFF IN A *PSI-WAR*. HE WON. JEAN WAS *"CURED,"* THE POWER OF THE PHOENIX ONCE MORE UNDER CONTROL. I ASKED HER TO MARRY ME. SHE SAID, YES. HAPPY ENDING.

NOT SO.

ENTER LILANDRA, DETERMINED TO ELIMINATE PHOENIX AS A THREAT ONCE AND FOR ALL.

WHEN HER IMPERIAL GUARD FAILED JEAN FINISHED THE JOB HERSELF.

SCOTT!

JEAN!

THIS... IS PAIN BEYOND PAIN. I NEVER KNEW A BODY COULD HURT SO MUCH AND STILL... FUNCTION.

I'M NOT SURE I WANT TO CALL THIS *"LIVING."*

HOW ARE YOU BEARING UP, SCOTT? I KNOW HOW MUCH YOU LOVED JEAN, AND SHE YOU. I KNOW HOW HARD ALL THIS MUST BE...

PROFESSOR GREY, I SPEAK FOR ALL SHI'AR WHEN I SAY HOW... SORRY WE ARE AT YOUR DAUGHTER'S DEATH. YOUR GRIEF IS OURS.

THANK YOU, YOUR... MAJESTY. THAT'S VERY KIND.

SO LONG AS I RULE, SO LONG AS SHI'AR ENDURES, JEAN GREY'S NAME AND MEMORY WILL BE

DON'T WORRY ABOUT ME, SIR. I'LL BE FINE. BUT HOW ARE *YOU*? AND *MRS. GREY*?

SURVIVING.

SHE GAVE HER LIFE, THAT THE *UNIVERSE* MIGHT LIVE.

PLEASE ACCEPT THIS GIFT. IT IS A HOLEMPATHIC MATRIX CRYSTAL. TOUCH IT, AND YOU WILL NOT ONLY SEE A 3-DIMENSIONAL IMAGE OF JEAN, BUT FEEL THE ESSENCE OF HER PERSONALITY AS WELL. THIS WAY, A PART OF HER WILL BE WITH YOU, ALWAYS.

Th- thank you.

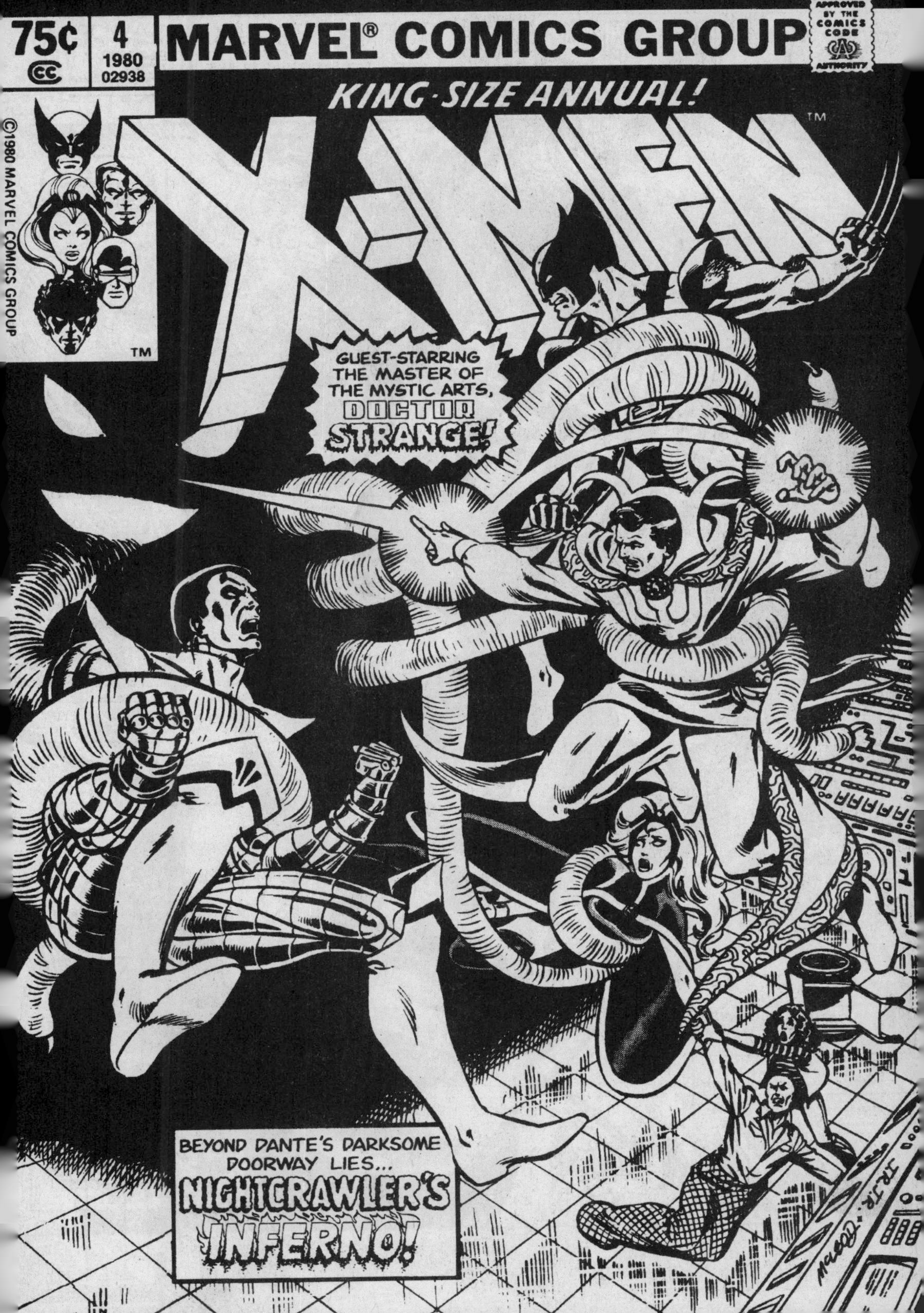
75¢
4
1980
02938
MARVEL® COMICS GROUP
APPROVED BY THE COMICS CODE AUTHORITY
KING-SIZE ANNUAL!
X-MEN™
©1980 MARVEL COMICS GROUP
™
GUEST-STARRING THE MASTER OF THE MYSTIC ARTS, DOCTOR STRANGE!
BEYOND DANTE'S DARKSOME DOORWAY LIES...
NIGHTCRAWLER'S INFERNO!

Stan Lee PRESENTS: THE UNCANNY X-MEN!™

CHRIS CLAREMONT WRITER | JOHN ROMITA, Jr. & BOB McLEOD ARTISTS | TOM ORZECHOWSKI, letterer GLYNIS WEIN, colorist | LOUISE JONES EDITOR | JIM SHOOTER Ed.-in-CHIEF

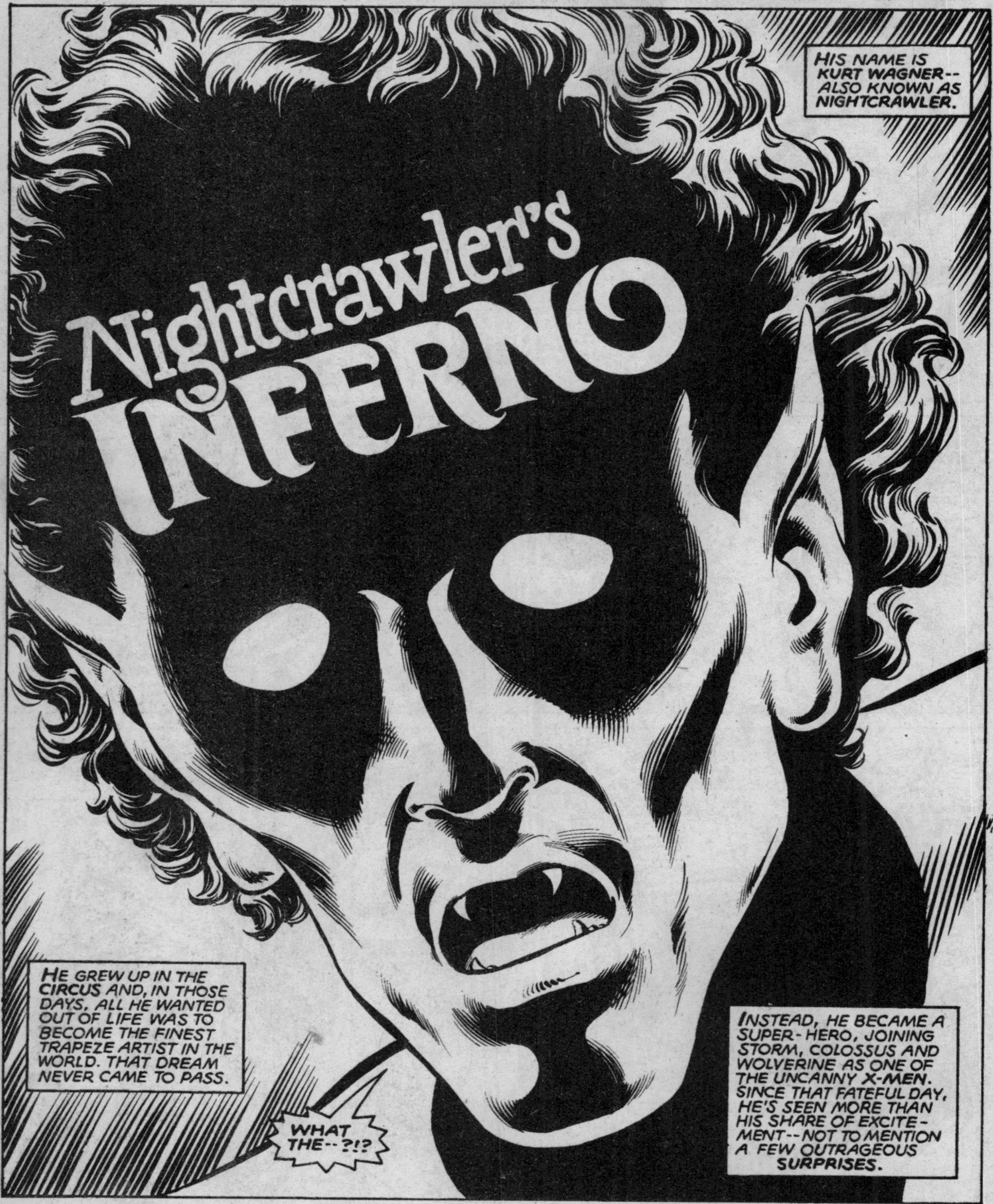
HIS NAME IS KURT WAGNER-- ALSO KNOWN AS NIGHTCRAWLER.
Nightcrawler's INFERNO
HE GREW UP IN THE CIRCUS AND, IN THOSE DAYS, ALL HE WANTED OUT OF LIFE WAS TO BECOME THE FINEST TRAPEZE ARTIST IN THE WORLD. THAT DREAM NEVER CAME TO PASS.
WHAT THE--?!?
INSTEAD, HE BECAME A SUPER-HERO, JOINING STORM, COLOSSUS AND WOLVERINE AS ONE OF THE UNCANNY X-MEN. SINCE THAT FATEFUL DAY, HE'S SEEN MORE THAN HIS SHARE OF EXCITEMENT--NOT TO MENTION A FEW OUTRAGEOUS SURPRISES.

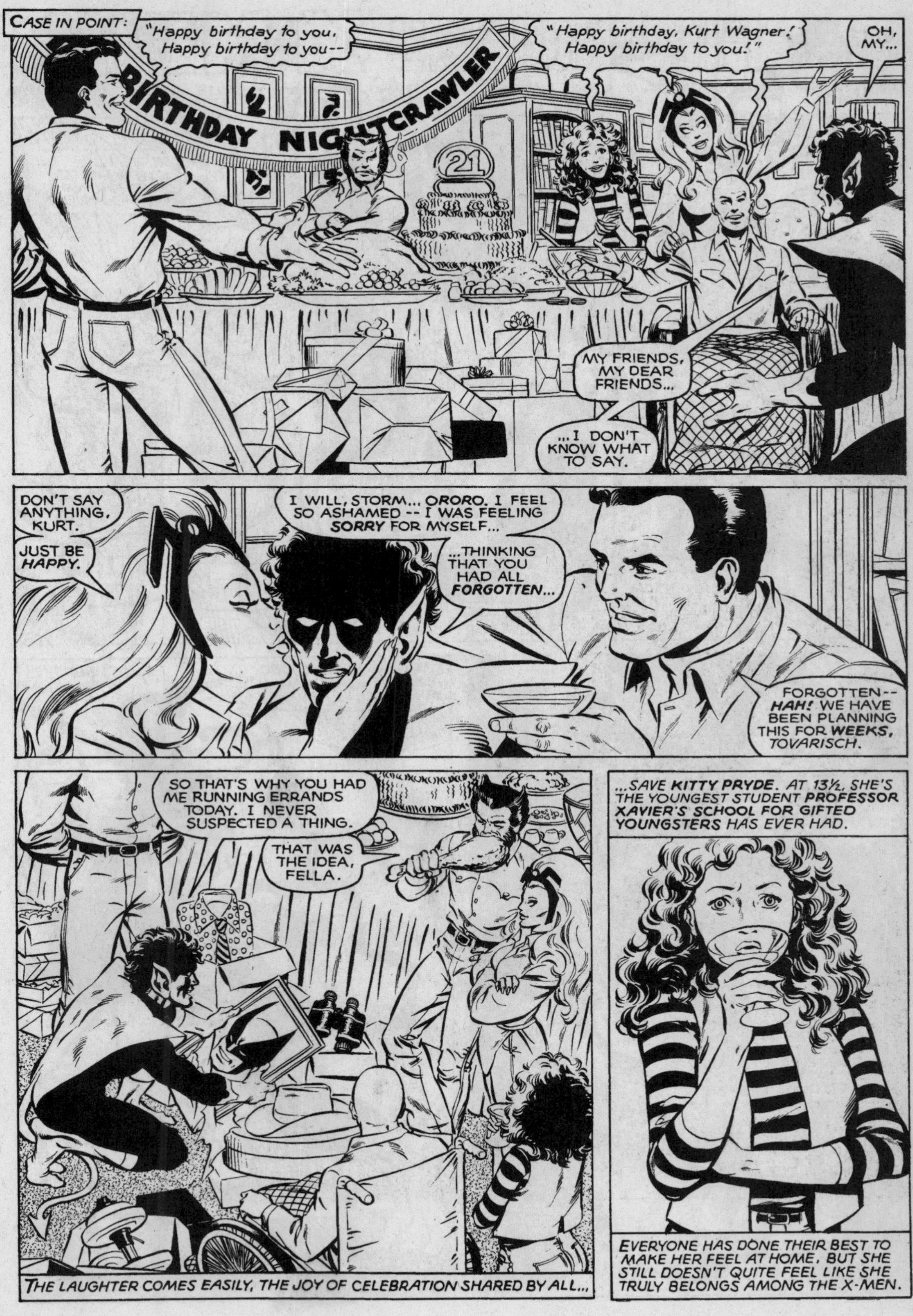

CASE IN POINT:
"Happy birthday to you, Happy birthday to you--
BIRTHDAY NIGHTCRAWLER
21
"Happy birthday, Kurt Wagner! Happy birthday to you!"
OH, MY...
MY FRIENDS, MY DEAR FRIENDS...
...I DON'T KNOW WHAT TO SAY.
DON'T SAY ANYTHING, KURT.
JUST BE HAPPY.
I WILL, STORM... ORORO. I FEEL SO ASHAMED -- I WAS FEELING SORRY FOR MYSELF...
...THINKING THAT YOU HAD ALL FORGOTTEN...
FORGOTTEN-- HAH! WE HAVE BEEN PLANNING THIS FOR WEEKS, TOVARISCH.
SO THAT'S WHY YOU HAD ME RUNNING ERRANDS TODAY. I NEVER SUSPECTED A THING.
THAT WAS THE IDEA, FELLA.
THE LAUGHTER COMES EASILY, THE JOY OF CELEBRATION SHARED BY ALL...
...SAVE KITTY PRYDE. AT 13½, SHE'S THE YOUNGEST STUDENT PROFESSOR XAVIER'S SCHOOL FOR GIFTED YOUNGSTERS HAS EVER HAD.
EVERYONE HAS DONE THEIR BEST TO MAKE HER FEEL AT HOME, BUT SHE STILL DOESN'T QUITE FEEL LIKE SHE TRULY BELONGS AMONG THE X-MEN.

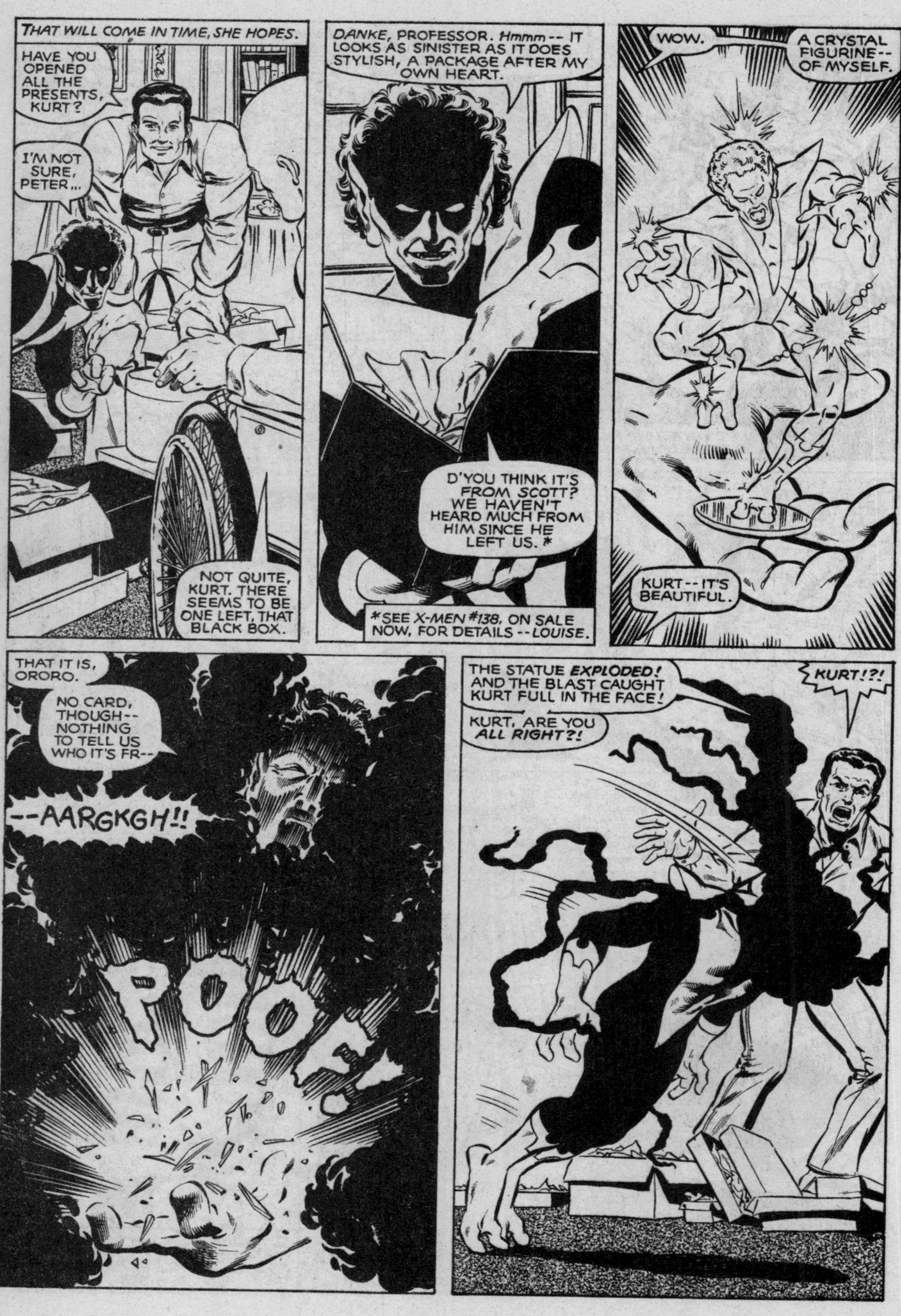
THAT WILL COME IN TIME, SHE HOPES.
HAVE YOU OPENED ALL THE PRESENTS, KURT?
I'M NOT SURE, PETER...
NOT QUITE, KURT. THERE SEEMS TO BE ONE LEFT, THAT BLACK BOX.
DANKE, PROFESSOR. Hmmm -- IT LOOKS AS SINISTER AS IT DOES STYLISH, A PACKAGE AFTER MY OWN HEART.
D'YOU THINK IT'S FROM SCOTT? WE HAVEN'T HEARD MUCH FROM HIM SINCE HE LEFT US.*
*SEE X-MEN #138, ON SALE NOW, FOR DETAILS --LOUISE.
WOW.
A CRYSTAL FIGURINE -- OF MYSELF.
KURT -- IT'S BEAUTIFUL.
THAT IT IS, ORORO.
NO CARD, THOUGH -- NOTHING TO TELL US WHO IT'S FR--
--AARGKGH!!
POOF
THE STATUE EXPLODED! AND THE BLAST CAUGHT KURT FULL IN THE FACE!
KURT, ARE YOU ALL RIGHT?!
KURT!?!

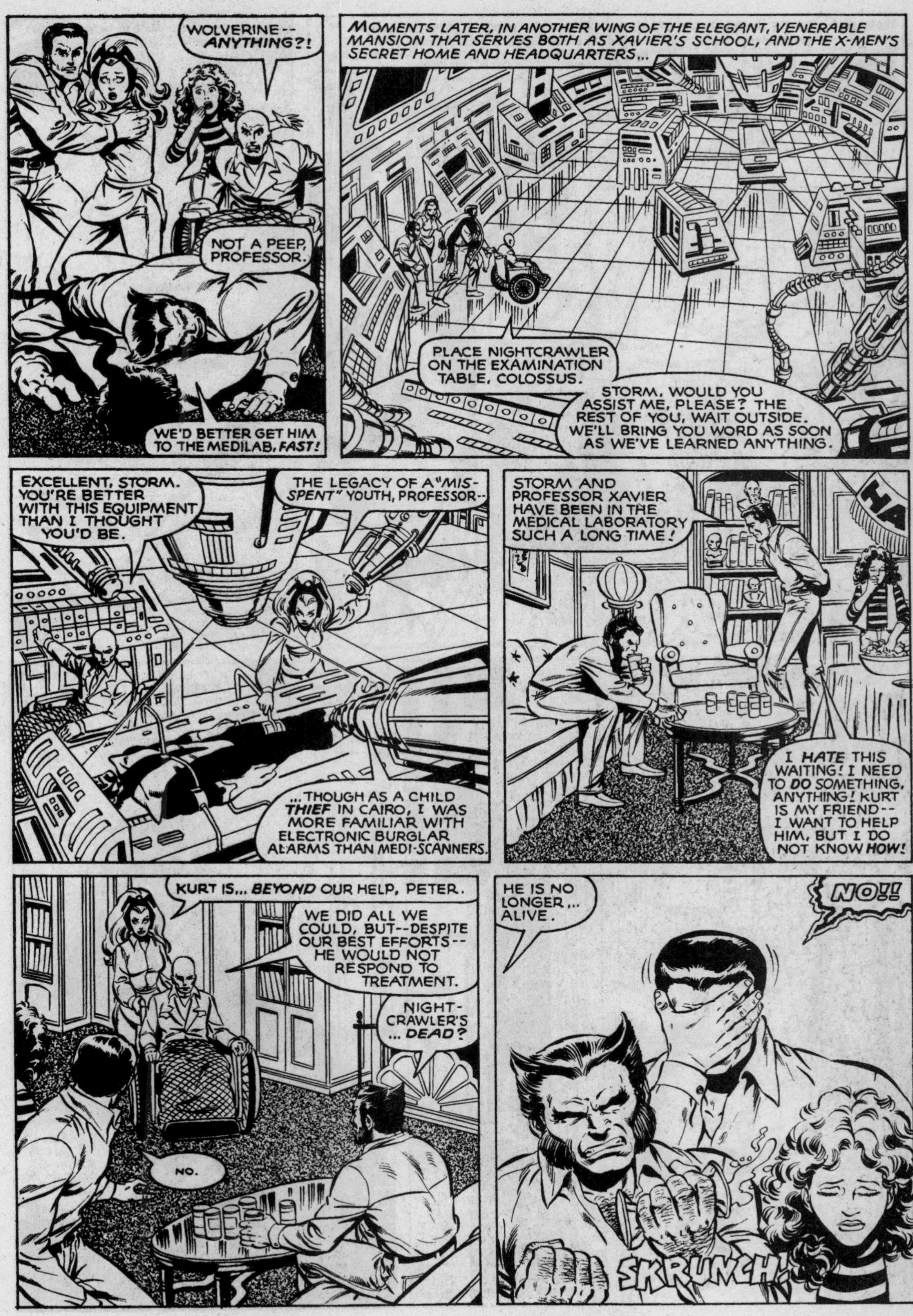
WOLVERINE-- ANYTHING?!
NOT A PEEP, PROFESSOR.
WE'D BETTER GET HIM TO THE MEDILAB, FAST!
MOMENTS LATER, IN ANOTHER WING OF THE ELEGANT, VENERABLE MANSION THAT SERVES BOTH AS XAVIER'S SCHOOL, AND THE X-MEN'S SECRET HOME AND HEADQUARTERS...
PLACE NIGHTCRAWLER ON THE EXAMINATION TABLE, COLOSSUS.
STORM, WOULD YOU ASSIST ME, PLEASE? THE REST OF YOU, WAIT OUTSIDE. WE'LL BRING YOU WORD AS SOON AS WE'VE LEARNED ANYTHING.
EXCELLENT, STORM. YOU'RE BETTER WITH THIS EQUIPMENT THAN I THOUGHT YOU'D BE.
THE LEGACY OF A "MIS-SPENT" YOUTH, PROFESSOR--
...THOUGH AS A CHILD THIEF IN CAIRO, I WAS MORE FAMILIAR WITH ELECTRONIC BURGLAR ALARMS THAN MEDI-SCANNERS.
STORM AND PROFESSOR XAVIER HAVE BEEN IN THE MEDICAL LABORATORY SUCH A LONG TIME!
I HATE THIS WAITING! I NEED TO DO SOMETHING, ANYTHING! KURT IS MY FRIEND-- I WANT TO HELP HIM, BUT I DO NOT KNOW HOW!
KURT IS... BEYOND OUR HELP, PETER.
WE DID ALL WE COULD, BUT--DESPITE OUR BEST EFFORTS-- HE WOULD NOT RESPOND TO TREATMENT.
NIGHT-CRAWLER'S ... DEAD?
NO.
HE IS NO LONGER... ALIVE.
NO!!
SKRUNCH!

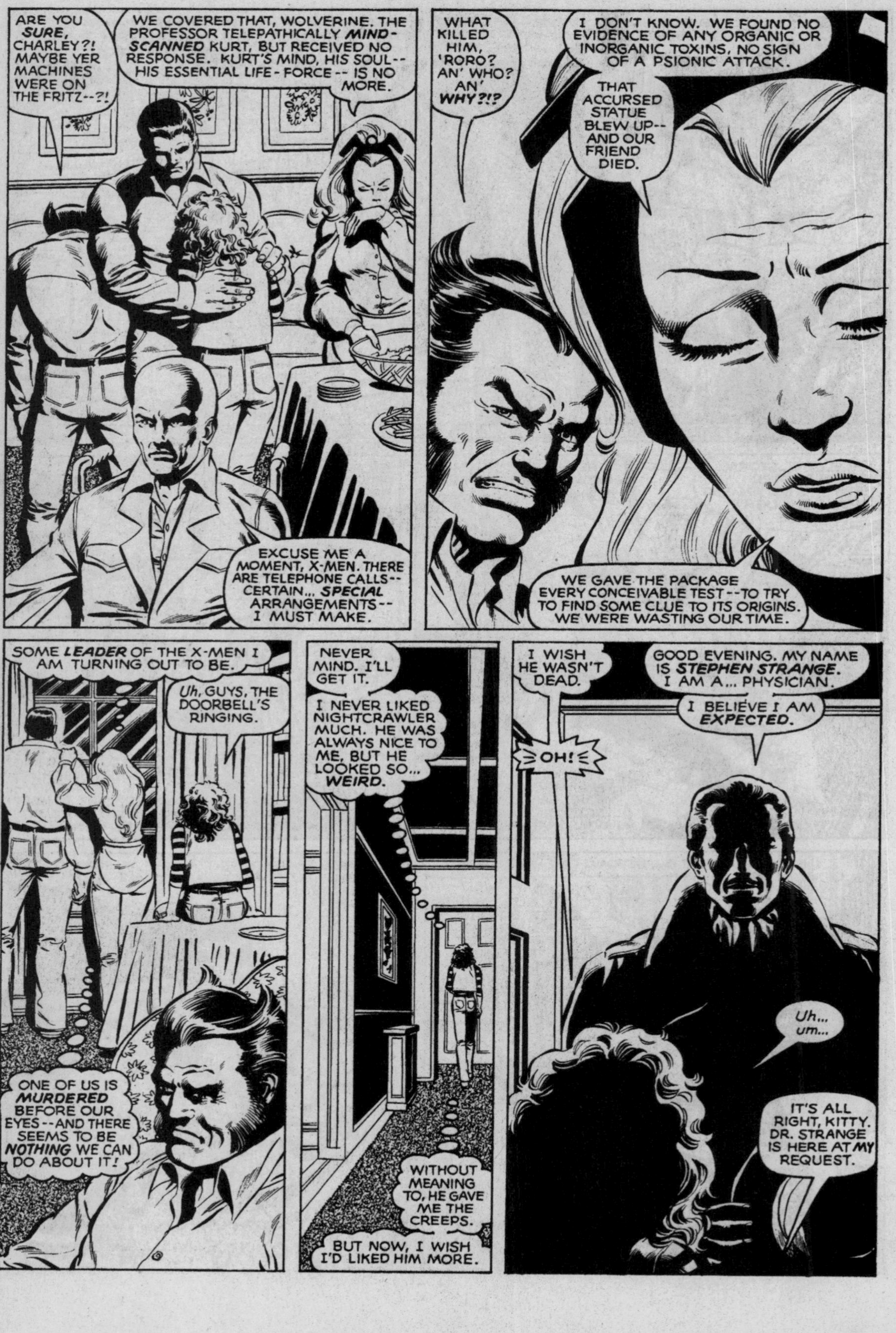
ARE YOU SURE, CHARLEY?! MAYBE YER MACHINES WERE ON THE FRITZ--?!
WE COVERED THAT, WOLVERINE. THE PROFESSOR TELEPATHICALLY MIND-SCANNED KURT, BUT RECEIVED NO RESPONSE. KURT'S MIND, HIS SOUL--HIS ESSENTIAL LIFE-FORCE--IS NO MORE.
EXCUSE ME A MOMENT, X-MEN. THERE ARE TELEPHONE CALLS--CERTAIN... SPECIAL ARRANGEMENTS--I MUST MAKE.
WHAT KILLED HIM, 'RORO? AN' WHO? AN' WHY?!?
I DON'T KNOW. WE FOUND NO EVIDENCE OF ANY ORGANIC OR INORGANIC TOXINS, NO SIGN OF A PSIONIC ATTACK.
THAT ACCURSED STATUE BLEW UP--AND OUR FRIEND DIED.
WE GAVE THE PACKAGE EVERY CONCEIVABLE TEST--TO TRY TO FIND SOME CLUE TO ITS ORIGINS. WE WERE WASTING OUR TIME.
SOME LEADER OF THE X-MEN I AM TURNING OUT TO BE.
Uh, GUYS, THE DOORBELL'S RINGING.
ONE OF US IS MURDERED BEFORE OUR EYES--AND THERE SEEMS TO BE NOTHING WE CAN DO ABOUT IT!
NEVER MIND. I'LL GET IT.
I NEVER LIKED NIGHTCRAWLER MUCH. HE WAS ALWAYS NICE TO ME, BUT HE LOOKED SO... WEIRD.
WITHOUT MEANING TO, HE GAVE ME THE CREEPS.
BUT NOW, I WISH I'D LIKED HIM MORE.
I WISH HE WASN'T DEAD.
GOOD EVENING. MY NAME IS STEPHEN STRANGE. I AM A... PHYSICIAN.
I BELIEVE I AM EXPECTED.
OH!
Uh... um...
IT'S ALL RIGHT, KITTY. DR. STRANGE IS HERE AT MY REQUEST.

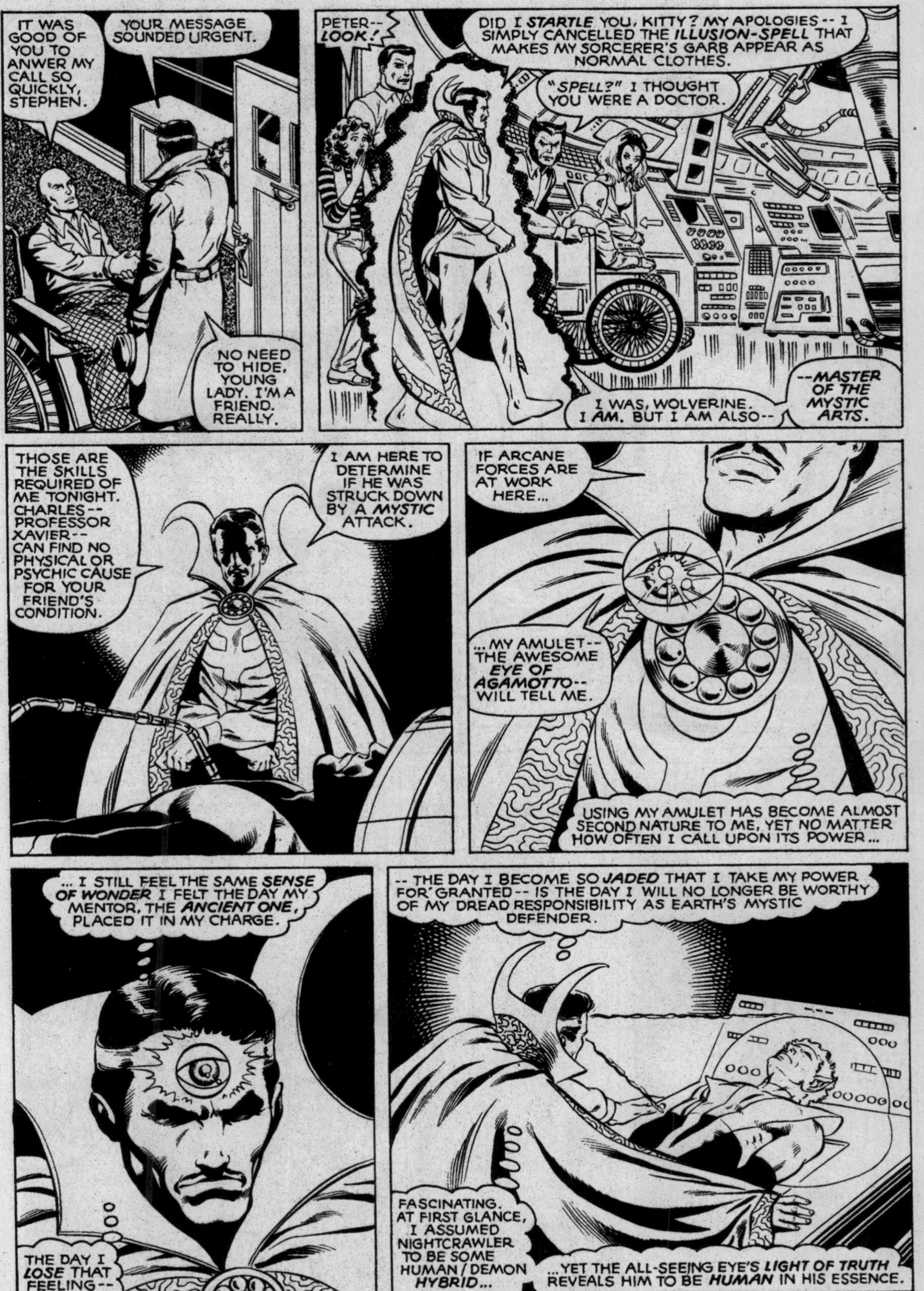

IT WAS GOOD OF YOU TO ANWER MY CALL SO QUICKLY, STEPHEN.
YOUR MESSAGE SOUNDED URGENT.
NO NEED TO HIDE, YOUNG LADY. I'M A FRIEND. REALLY.
PETER-- LOOK!
DID I STARTLE YOU, KITTY? MY APOLOGIES -- I SIMPLY CANCELLED THE ILLUSION-SPELL THAT MAKES MY SORCERER'S GARB APPEAR AS NORMAL CLOTHES.
"SPELL?" I THOUGHT YOU WERE A DOCTOR.
I WAS, WOLVERINE. I AM. BUT I AM ALSO--
--MASTER OF THE MYSTIC ARTS.
THOSE ARE THE SKILLS REQUIRED OF ME TONIGHT. CHARLES-- PROFESSOR XAVIER-- CAN FIND NO PHYSICAL OR PSYCHIC CAUSE FOR YOUR FRIEND'S CONDITION.
I AM HERE TO DETERMINE IF HE WAS STRUCK DOWN BY A MYSTIC ATTACK.
IF ARCANE FORCES ARE AT WORK HERE...
...MY AMULET-- THE AWESOME EYE OF AGAMOTTO-- WILL TELL ME.
USING MY AMULET HAS BECOME ALMOST SECOND NATURE TO ME, YET NO MATTER HOW OFTEN I CALL UPON ITS POWER...
... I STILL FEEL THE SAME SENSE OF WONDER I FELT THE DAY MY MENTOR, THE ANCIENT ONE, PLACED IT IN MY CHARGE.
THE DAY I LOSE THAT FEELING--
-- THE DAY I BECOME SO JADED THAT I TAKE MY POWER FOR GRANTED -- IS THE DAY I WILL NO LONGER BE WORTHY OF MY DREAD RESPONSIBILITY AS EARTH'S MYSTIC DEFENDER.
FASCINATING. AT FIRST GLANCE, I ASSUMED NIGHTCRAWLER TO BE SOME HUMAN / DEMON HYBRID...
...YET THE ALL-SEEING EYE'S LIGHT OF TRUTH REVEALS HIM TO BE HUMAN IN HIS ESSENCE.

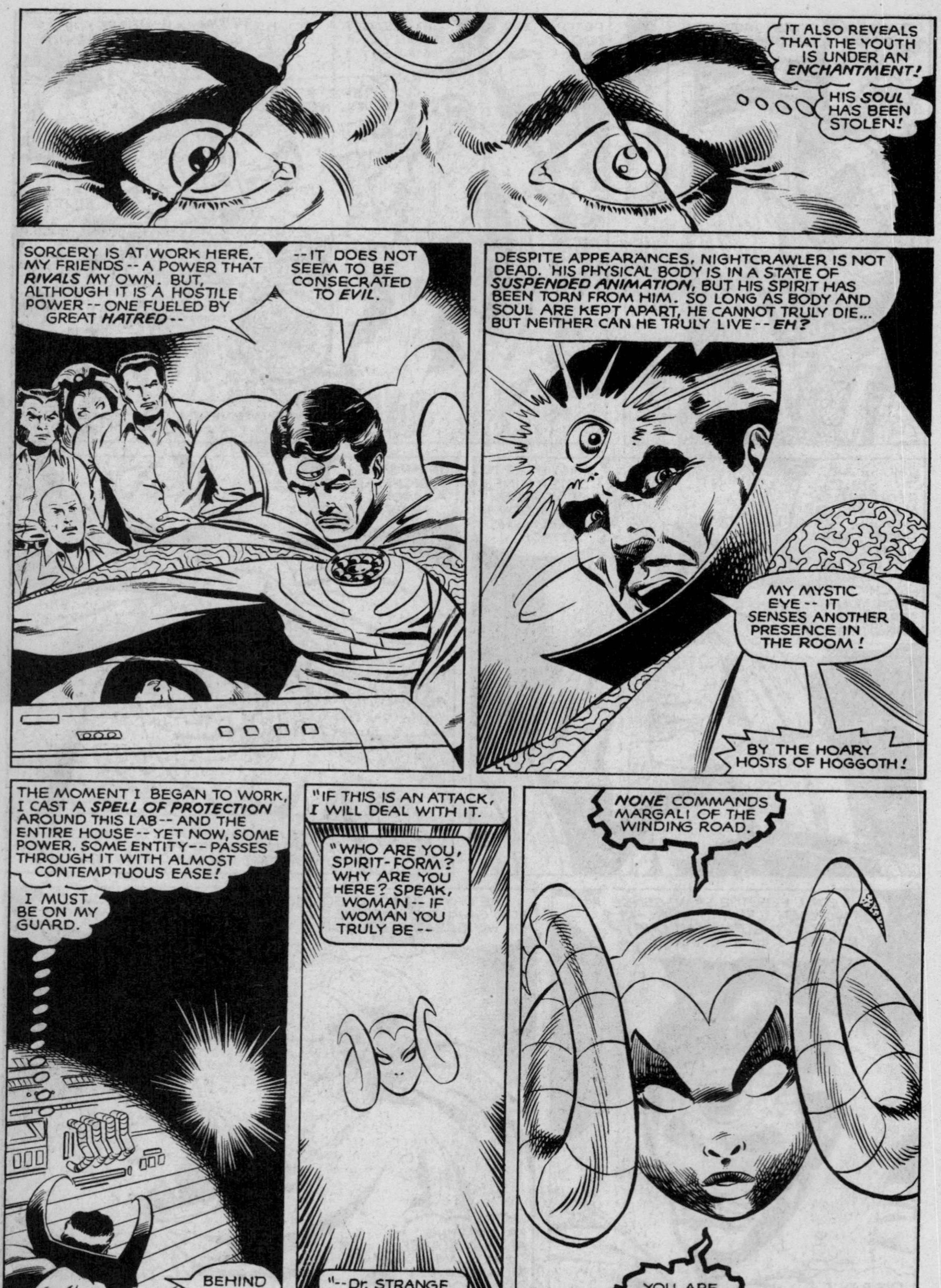
IT ALSO REVEALS THAT THE YOUTH IS UNDER AN ENCHANTMENT!
HIS SOUL HAS BEEN STOLEN!
SORCERY IS AT WORK HERE, MY FRIENDS -- A POWER THAT RIVALS MY OWN. BUT, ALTHOUGH IT IS A HOSTILE POWER -- ONE FUELED BY GREAT HATRED --
--IT DOES NOT SEEM TO BE CONSECRATED TO EVIL.
DESPITE APPEARANCES, NIGHTCRAWLER IS NOT DEAD. HIS PHYSICAL BODY IS IN A STATE OF SUSPENDED ANIMATION, BUT HIS SPIRIT HAS BEEN TORN FROM HIM. SO LONG AS BODY AND SOUL ARE KEPT APART, HE CANNOT TRULY DIE... BUT NEITHER CAN HE TRULY LIVE -- EH?
MY MYSTIC EYE -- IT SENSES ANOTHER PRESENCE IN THE ROOM!
BY THE HOARY HOSTS OF HOGGOTH!
THE MOMENT I BEGAN TO WORK, I CAST A SPELL OF PROTECTION AROUND THIS LAB -- AND THE ENTIRE HOUSE -- YET NOW, SOME POWER, SOME ENTITY -- PASSES THROUGH IT WITH ALMOST CONTEMPTUOUS EASE!
I MUST BE ON MY GUARD.
BEHIND ME, X-MEN!
"IF THIS IS AN ATTACK, I WILL DEAL WITH IT.
"WHO ARE YOU, SPIRIT-FORM? WHY ARE YOU HERE? SPEAK, WOMAN -- IF WOMAN YOU TRULY BE --
"--Dr. STRANGE COMMANDS IT!"
NONE COMMANDS MARGALI OF THE WINDING ROAD.
YOU ARE KNOWN TO ME, MAGE.

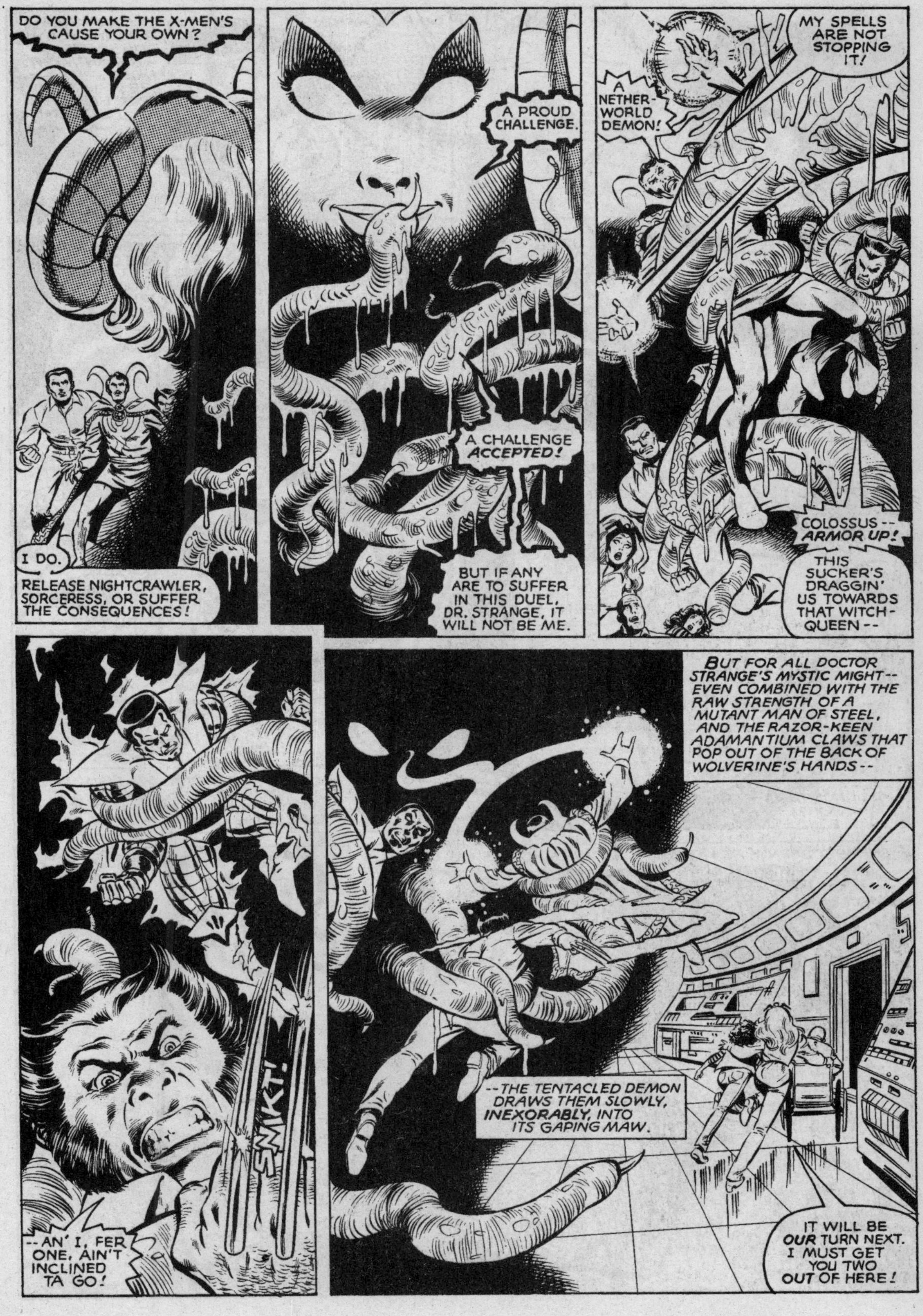

DO YOU MAKE THE X-MEN'S CAUSE YOUR OWN?
I DO.
RELEASE NIGHTCRAWLER, SORCERESS, OR SUFFER THE CONSEQUENCES!
A PROUD CHALLENGE.
A CHALLENGE ACCEPTED!
BUT IF ANY ARE TO SUFFER IN THIS DUEL, DR. STRANGE, IT WILL NOT BE ME.
A NETHER-WORLD DEMON!
MY SPELLS ARE NOT STOPPING IT!
COLOSSUS -- ARMOR UP!
THIS SUCKER'S DRAGGIN' US TOWARDS THAT WITCH-QUEEN --
SNIKT!
--AN' I, FER ONE, AIN'T INCLINED TA GO!
BUT FOR ALL DOCTOR STRANGE'S MYSTIC MIGHT-- EVEN COMBINED WITH THE RAW STRENGTH OF A MUTANT MAN OF STEEL, AND THE RAZOR-KEEN ADAMANTIUM CLAWS THAT POP OUT OF THE BACK OF WOLVERINE'S HANDS--
--THE TENTACLED DEMON DRAWS THEM SLOWLY, INEXORABLY, INTO ITS GAPING MAW.
IT WILL BE OUR TURN NEXT. I MUST GET YOU TWO OUT OF HERE!

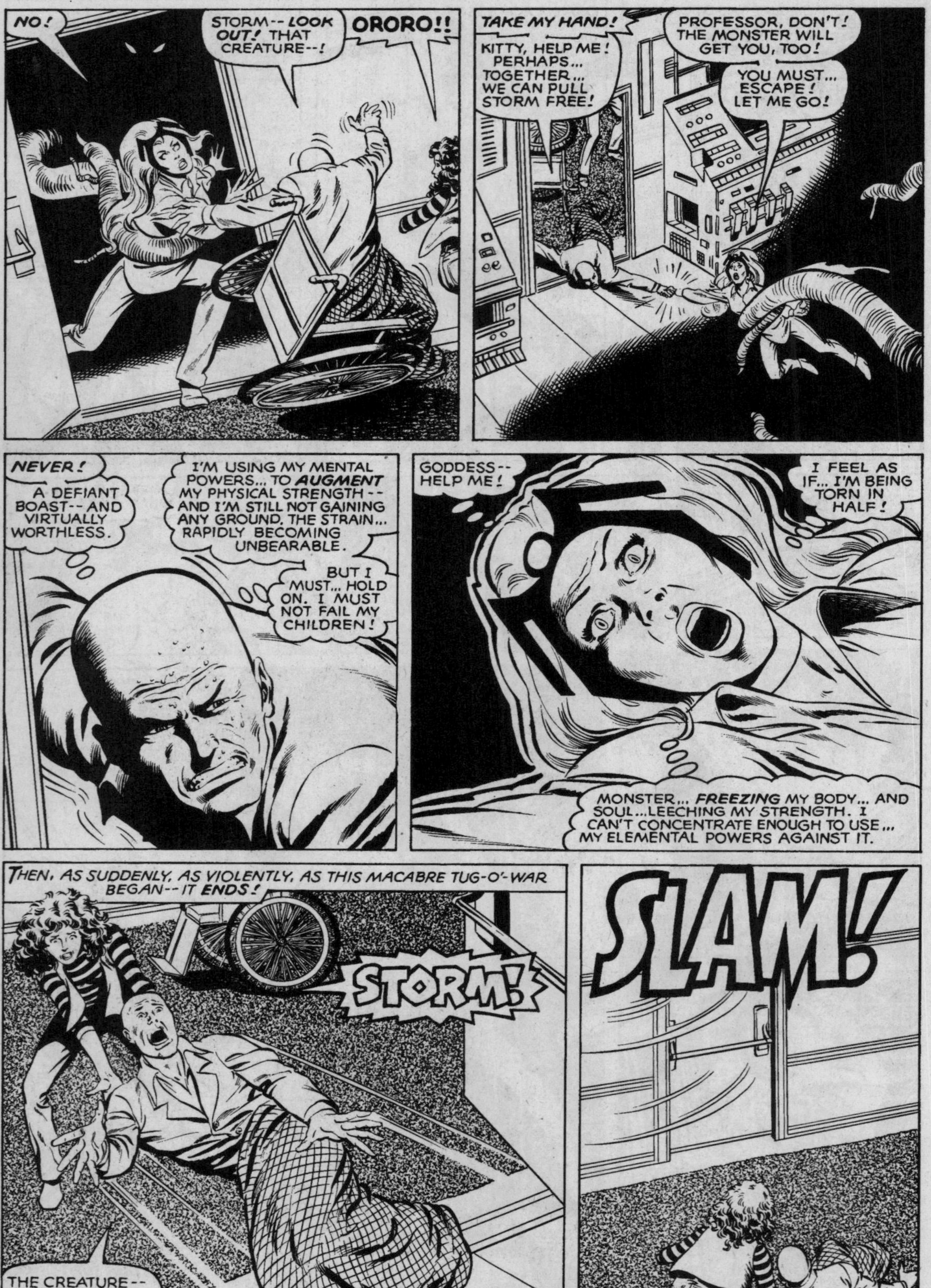
NO!
STORM-- LOOK OUT! THAT CREATURE--!
ORORO!!
TAKE MY HAND!
KITTY, HELP ME! PERHAPS... TOGETHER... WE CAN PULL STORM FREE!
PROFESSOR, DON'T! THE MONSTER WILL GET YOU, TOO!
YOU MUST... ESCAPE! LET ME GO!
NEVER!
A DEFIANT BOAST-- AND VIRTUALLY WORTHLESS.
I'M USING MY MENTAL POWERS... TO AUGMENT MY PHYSICAL STRENGTH -- AND I'M STILL NOT GAINING ANY GROUND. THE STRAIN... RAPIDLY BECOMING UNBEARABLE.
BUT I MUST... HOLD ON. I MUST NOT FAIL MY CHILDREN!
GODDESS-- HELP ME!
I FEEL AS IF... I'M BEING TORN IN HALF!
MONSTER... FREEZING MY BODY... AND SOUL...LEECHING MY STRENGTH. I CAN'T CONCENTRATE ENOUGH TO USE... MY ELEMENTAL POWERS AGAINST IT.
THEN, AS SUDDENLY, AS VIOLENTLY, AS THIS MACABRE TUG-O'-WAR BEGAN-- IT ENDS!
STORM!
THE CREATURE-- PULLED HER OUT OF MY GRASP!
SLAM!

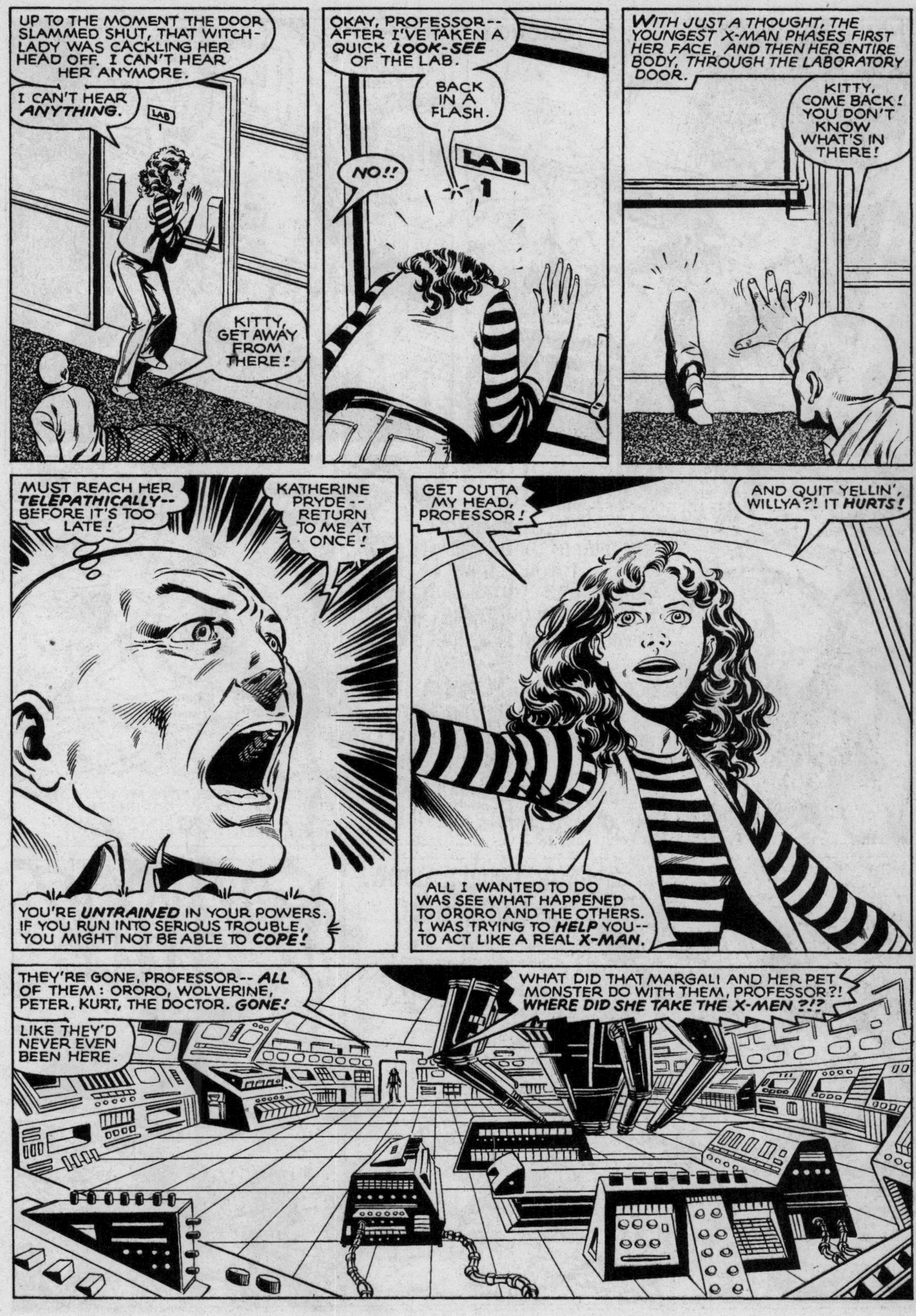
UP TO THE MOMENT THE DOOR SLAMMED SHUT, THAT WITCH-LADY WAS CACKLING HER HEAD OFF. I CAN'T HEAR HER ANYMORE.
I CAN'T HEAR ANYTHING.
LAB 1
KITTY, GET AWAY FROM THERE!
OKAY, PROFESSOR-- AFTER I'VE TAKEN A QUICK LOOK-SEE OF THE LAB.
BACK IN A FLASH.
NO!!
LAB 1
WITH JUST A THOUGHT, THE YOUNGEST X-MAN PHASES FIRST HER FACE, AND THEN HER ENTIRE BODY, THROUGH THE LABORATORY DOOR.
KITTY, COME BACK! YOU DON'T KNOW WHAT'S IN THERE!
MUST REACH HER TELEPATHICALLY-- BEFORE IT'S TOO LATE!
KATHERINE PRYDE-- RETURN TO ME AT ONCE!
YOU'RE UNTRAINED IN YOUR POWERS. IF YOU RUN INTO SERIOUS TROUBLE, YOU MIGHT NOT BE ABLE TO COPE!
GET OUTTA MY HEAD, PROFESSOR!
AND QUIT YELLIN', WILLYA?! IT HURTS!
ALL I WANTED TO DO WAS SEE WHAT HAPPENED TO ORORO AND THE OTHERS. I WAS TRYING TO HELP YOU-- TO ACT LIKE A REAL X-MAN.
THEY'RE GONE, PROFESSOR-- ALL OF THEM: ORORO, WOLVERINE, PETER, KURT, THE DOCTOR. GONE!
LIKE THEY'D NEVER EVEN BEEN HERE.
WHAT DID THAT MARGALI AND HER PET MONSTER DO WITH THEM, PROFESSOR?! WHERE DID SHE TAKE THE X-MEN?!?

Part the Second

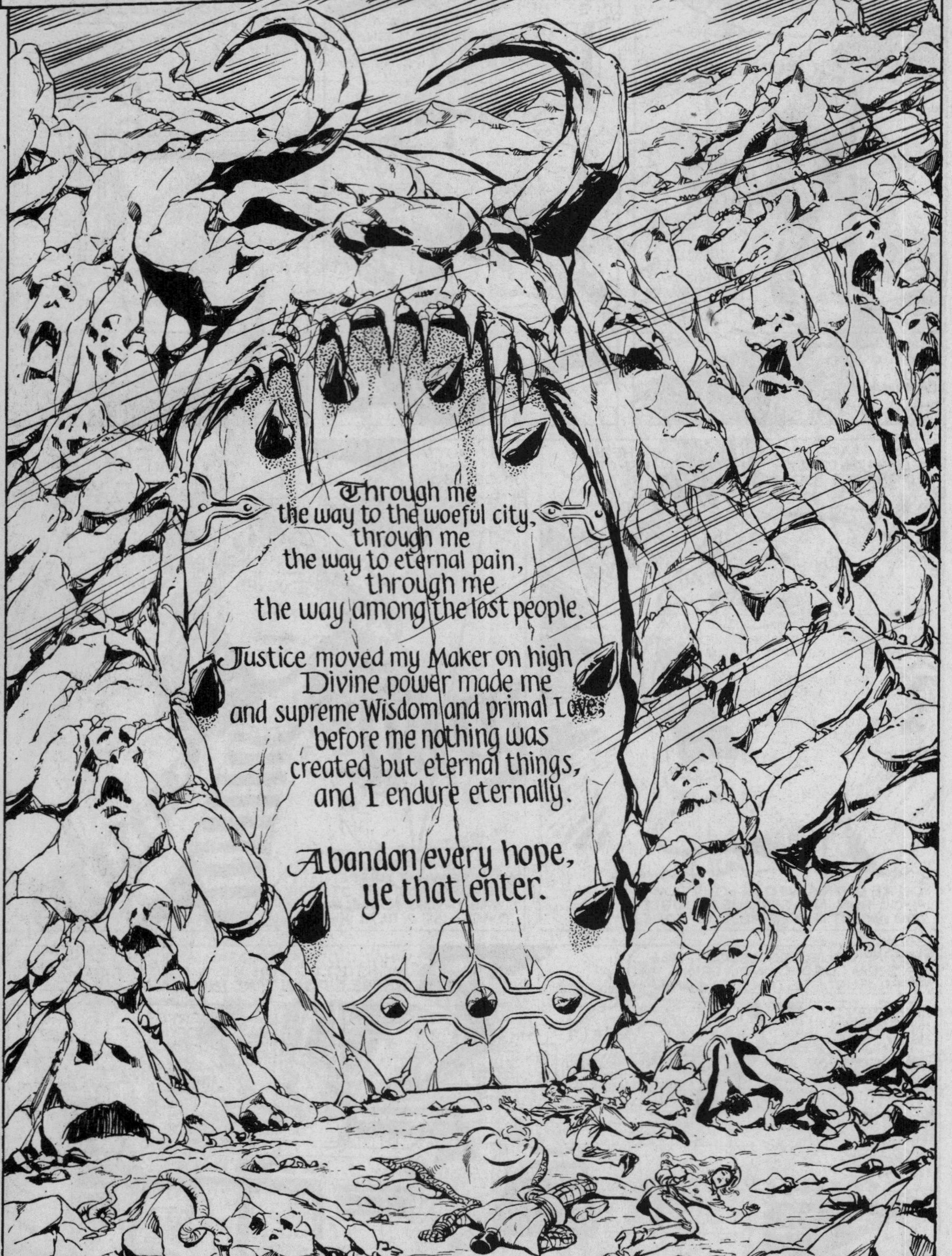
Through me
the way to the woeful city,
through me
the way to eternal pain,
through me
the way among the lost people.
Justice moved my Maker on high
Divine power made me
and supreme Wisdom and primal Love;
before me nothing was
created but eternal things,
and I endure eternally.
Abandon every hope,
ye that enter.

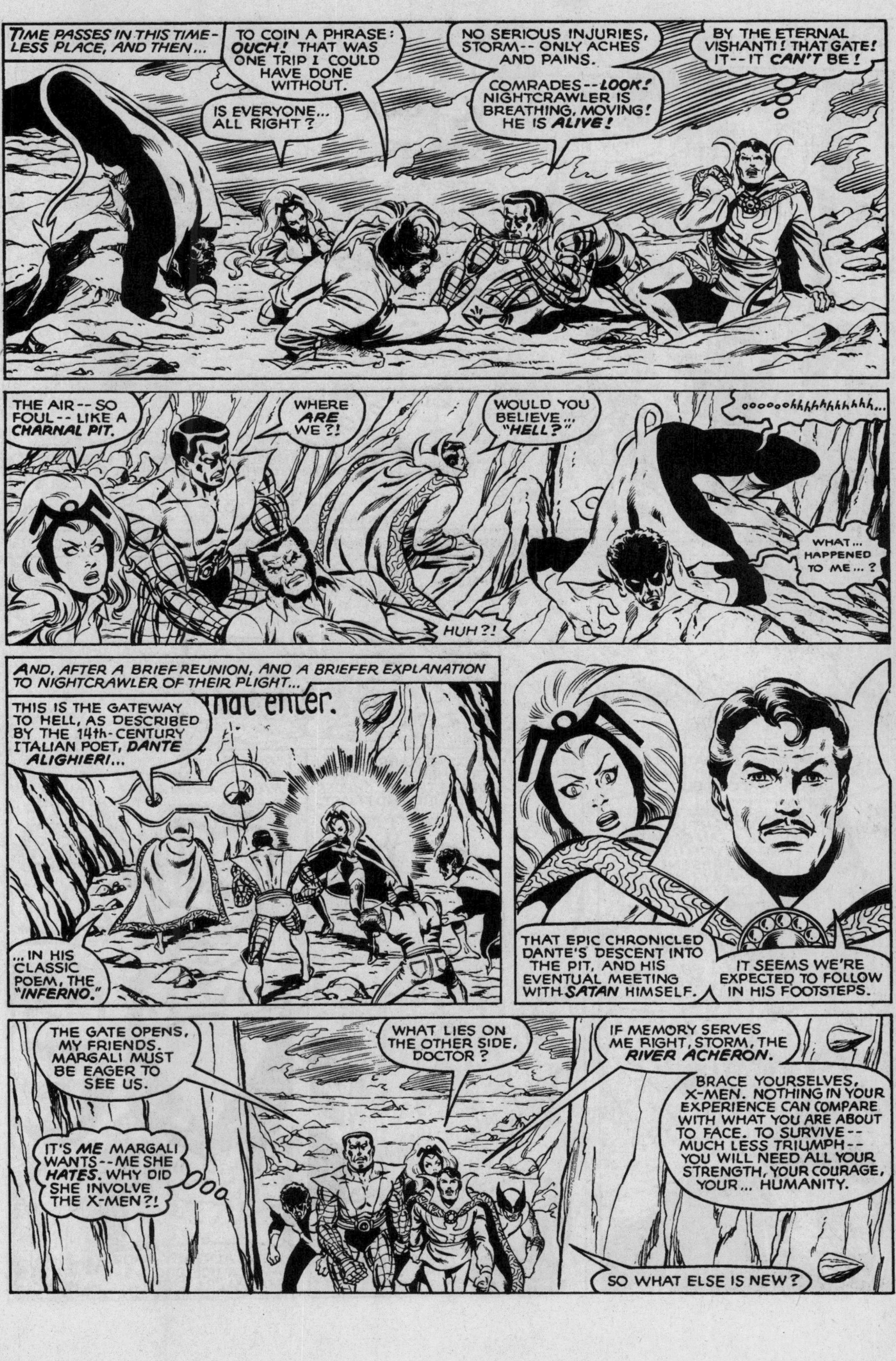
TIME PASSES IN THIS TIMELESS PLACE, AND THEN...
TO COIN A PHRASE: OUCH! THAT WAS ONE TRIP I COULD HAVE DONE WITHOUT.
IS EVERYONE... ALL RIGHT?
NO SERIOUS INJURIES, STORM-- ONLY ACHES AND PAINS.
COMRADES--LOOK! NIGHTCRAWLER IS BREATHING, MOVING! HE IS ALIVE!
BY THE ETERNAL VISHANTI! THAT GATE! IT--IT CAN'T BE!
THE AIR--SO FOUL--LIKE A CHARNAL PIT.
WHERE ARE WE?!
WOULD YOU BELIEVE... "HELL?"
ooooooohhhhhhhhhh...
WHAT... HAPPENED TO ME...?
HUH?!
AND, AFTER A BRIEF REUNION, AND A BRIEFER EXPLANATION TO NIGHTCRAWLER OF THEIR PLIGHT...
THIS IS THE GATEWAY TO HELL, AS DESCRIBED BY THE 14th-CENTURY ITALIAN POET, DANTE ALIGHIERI...
...IN HIS CLASSIC POEM, THE "INFERNO."
THAT EPIC CHRONICLED DANTE'S DESCENT INTO THE PIT, AND HIS EVENTUAL MEETING WITH SATAN HIMSELF.
IT SEEMS WE'RE EXPECTED TO FOLLOW IN HIS FOOTSTEPS.
THE GATE OPENS, MY FRIENDS. MARGALI MUST BE EAGER TO SEE US.
IT'S ME MARGALI WANTS--ME SHE HATES. WHY DID SHE INVOLVE THE X-MEN?!
WHAT LIES ON THE OTHER SIDE, DOCTOR?
IF MEMORY SERVES ME RIGHT, STORM, THE RIVER ACHERON.
BRACE YOURSELVES, X-MEN. NOTHING IN YOUR EXPERIENCE CAN COMPARE WITH WHAT YOU ARE ABOUT TO FACE. TO SURVIVE--MUCH LESS TRIUMPH--YOU WILL NEED ALL YOUR STRENGTH, YOUR COURAGE, YOUR... HUMANITY.
SO WHAT ELSE IS NEW?

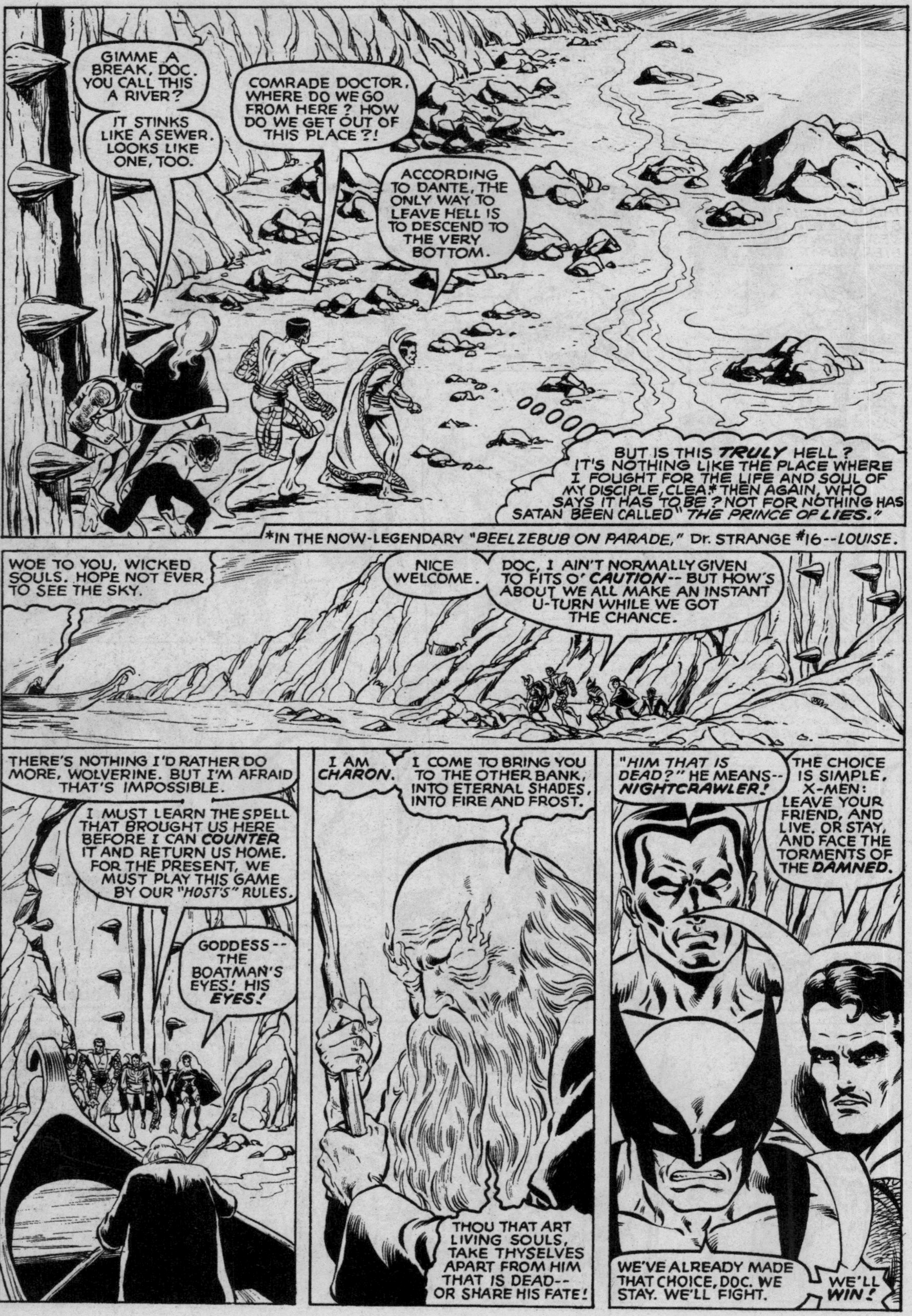
GIMME A BREAK, DOC. YOU CALL THIS A RIVER?
IT STINKS LIKE A SEWER. LOOKS LIKE ONE, TOO.
COMRADE DOCTOR, WHERE DO WE GO FROM HERE? HOW DO WE GET OUT OF THIS PLACE?!
ACCORDING TO DANTE, THE ONLY WAY TO LEAVE HELL IS TO DESCEND TO THE VERY BOTTOM.
BUT IS THIS TRULY HELL? IT'S NOTHING LIKE THE PLACE WHERE I FOUGHT FOR THE LIFE AND SOUL OF MY DISCIPLE, CLEA.* THEN AGAIN, WHO SAYS IT HAS TO BE? NOT FOR NOTHING HAS SATAN BEEN CALLED "THE PRINCE OF LIES."
*IN THE NOW-LEGENDARY "BEELZEBUB ON PARADE," Dr. STRANGE #16--LOUISE.
WOE TO YOU, WICKED SOULS. HOPE NOT EVER TO SEE THE SKY.
NICE WELCOME.
DOC, I AIN'T NORMALLY GIVEN TO FITS O' CAUTION-- BUT HOW'S ABOUT WE ALL MAKE AN INSTANT U-TURN WHILE WE GOT THE CHANCE.
THERE'S NOTHING I'D RATHER DO MORE, WOLVERINE. BUT I'M AFRAID THAT'S IMPOSSIBLE.
I MUST LEARN THE SPELL THAT BROUGHT US HERE BEFORE I CAN COUNTER IT AND RETURN US HOME. FOR THE PRESENT, WE MUST PLAY THIS GAME BY OUR "HOST'S" RULES.
GODDESS-- THE BOATMAN'S EYES! HIS EYES!
I AM CHARON.
I COME TO BRING YOU TO THE OTHER BANK, INTO ETERNAL SHADES, INTO FIRE AND FROST.
THOU THAT ART LIVING SOULS, TAKE THYSELVES APART FROM HIM THAT IS DEAD-- OR SHARE HIS FATE!
"HIM THAT IS DEAD?" HE MEANS-- NIGHTCRAWLER!
THE CHOICE IS SIMPLE, X-MEN: LEAVE YOUR FRIEND, AND LIVE. OR STAY, AND FACE THE TORMENTS OF THE DAMNED.
WE'VE ALREADY MADE THAT CHOICE, DOC. WE STAY. WE'LL FIGHT.
WE'LL WIN!

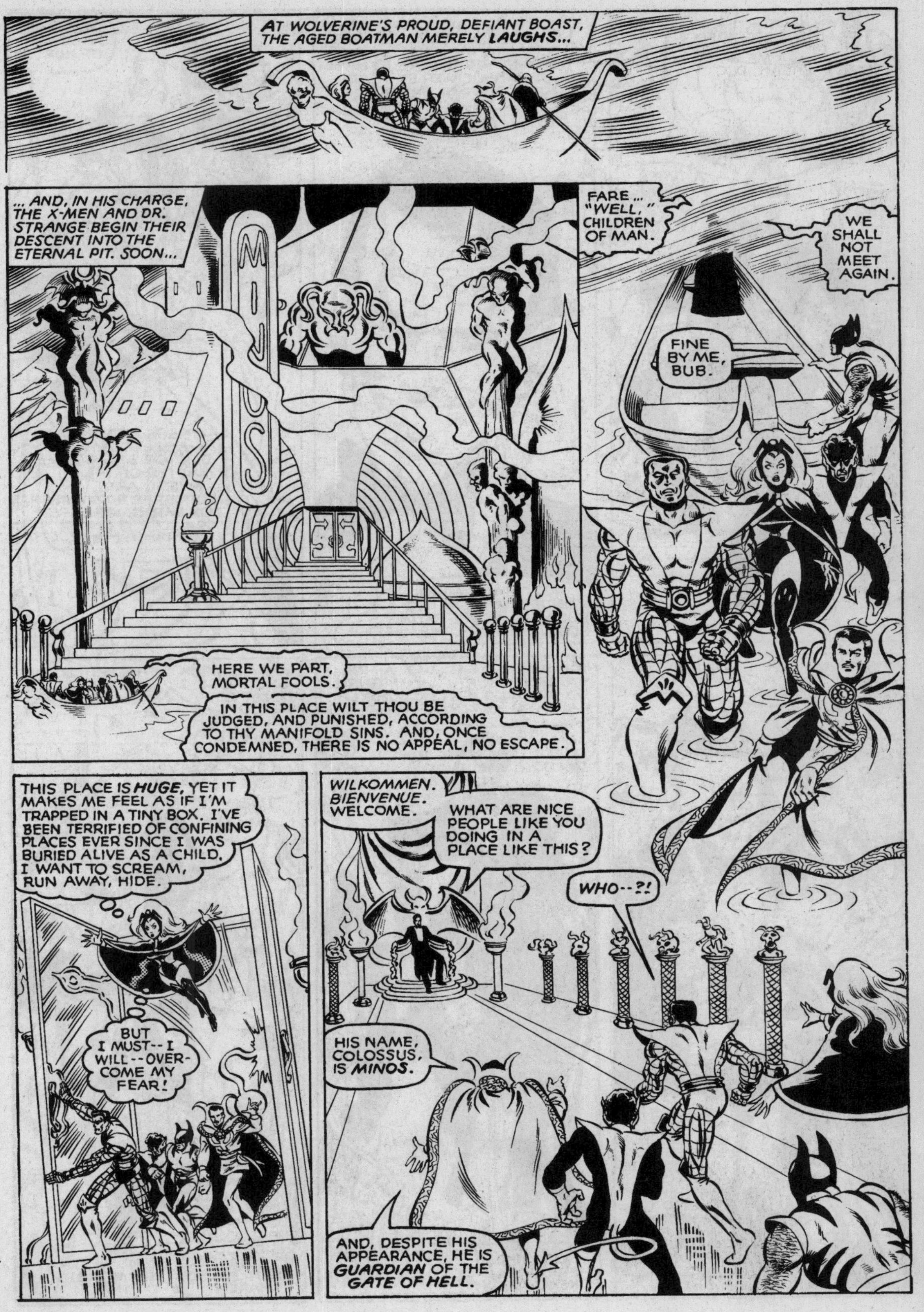
AT WOLVERINE'S PROUD, DEFIANT BOAST, THE AGED BOATMAN MERELY LAUGHS...
... AND, IN HIS CHARGE, THE X-MEN AND DR. STRANGE BEGIN THEIR DESCENT INTO THE ETERNAL PIT. SOON...
MINOS
HERE WE PART, MORTAL FOOLS.
IN THIS PLACE WILT THOU BE JUDGED, AND PUNISHED, ACCORDING TO THY MANIFOLD SINS. AND, ONCE CONDEMNED, THERE IS NO APPEAL, NO ESCAPE.
FARE... "WELL," CHILDREN OF MAN.
WE SHALL NOT MEET AGAIN.
FINE BY ME, BUB.
THIS PLACE IS HUGE, YET IT MAKES ME FEEL AS IF I'M TRAPPED IN A TINY BOX. I'VE BEEN TERRIFIED OF CONFINING PLACES EVER SINCE I WAS BURIED ALIVE AS A CHILD. I WANT TO SCREAM, RUN AWAY, HIDE.
BUT I MUST-- I WILL--OVERCOME MY FEAR!
WILKOMMEN. BIENVENUE. WELCOME.
WHAT ARE NICE PEOPLE LIKE YOU DOING IN A PLACE LIKE THIS?
WHO--?!
HIS NAME, COLOSSUS, IS MINOS.
AND, DESPITE HIS APPEARANCE, HE IS GUARDIAN OF THE GATE OF HELL.

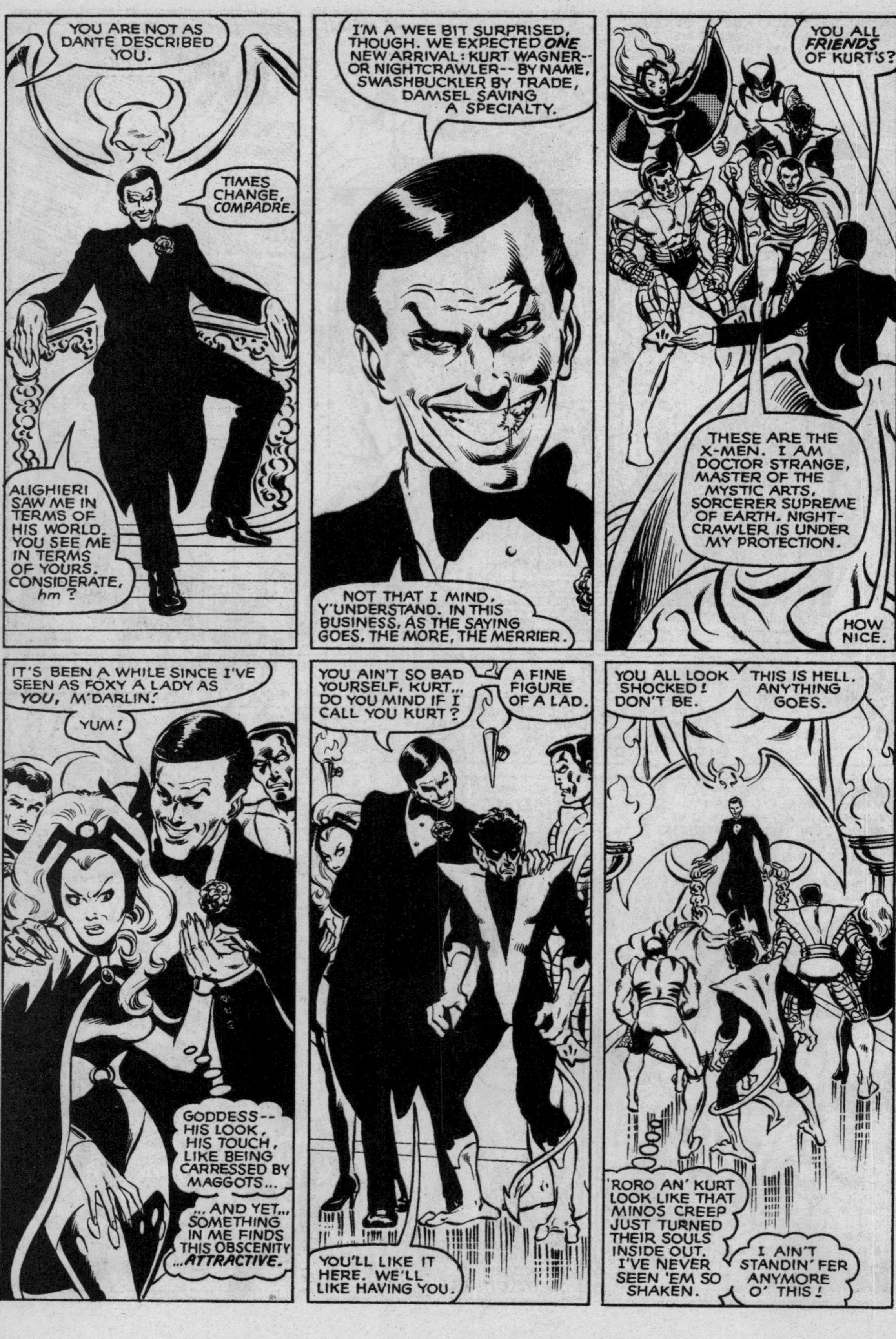
YOU ARE NOT AS DANTE DESCRIBED YOU.
TIMES CHANGE, COMPADRE.
ALIGHIERI SAW ME IN TERMS OF HIS WORLD. YOU SEE ME IN TERMS OF YOURS. CONSIDERATE, hm?
I'M A WEE BIT SURPRISED, THOUGH. WE EXPECTED ONE NEW ARRIVAL: KURT WAGNER-- OR NIGHTCRAWLER-- BY NAME, SWASHBUCKLER BY TRADE, DAMSEL SAVING A SPECIALTY.
NOT THAT I MIND, Y'UNDERSTAND. IN THIS BUSINESS, AS THE SAYING GOES, THE MORE, THE MERRIER.
YOU ALL FRIENDS OF KURT'S?
THESE ARE THE X-MEN. I AM DOCTOR STRANGE, MASTER OF THE MYSTIC ARTS, SORCERER SUPREME OF EARTH. NIGHT-CRAWLER IS UNDER MY PROTECTION.
HOW NICE.
IT'S BEEN A WHILE SINCE I'VE SEEN AS FOXY A LADY AS YOU, M'DARLIN'.
YUM!
GODDESS-- HIS LOOK, HIS TOUCH, LIKE BEING CARRESSED BY MAGGOTS...
... AND YET... SOMETHING IN ME FINDS THIS OBSCENITY ...ATTRACTIVE.
YOU AIN'T SO BAD YOURSELF, KURT... DO YOU MIND IF I CALL YOU KURT?
A FINE FIGURE OF A LAD.
YOU'LL LIKE IT HERE. WE'LL LIKE HAVING YOU.
YOU ALL LOOK SHOCKED! DON'T BE.
THIS IS HELL. ANYTHING GOES.
'RORO AN' KURT LOOK LIKE THAT MINOS CREEP JUST TURNED THEIR SOULS INSIDE OUT. I'VE NEVER SEEN 'EM SO SHAKEN.
I AIN'T STANDIN' FER ANYMORE O' THIS!

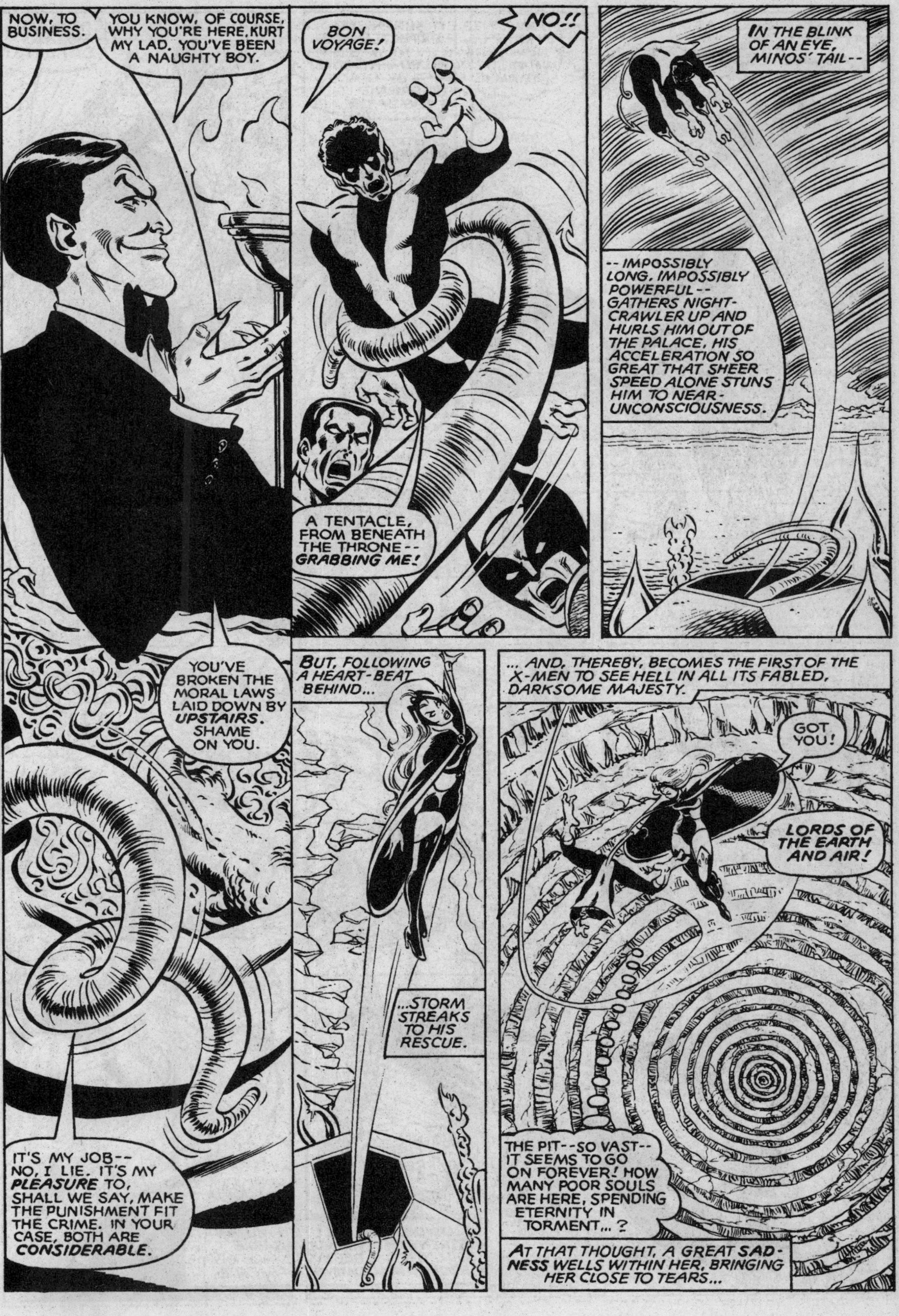
NOW, TO BUSINESS.
YOU KNOW, OF COURSE, WHY YOU'RE HERE, KURT MY LAD. YOU'VE BEEN A NAUGHTY BOY.
BON VOYAGE!
NO!!
A TENTACLE, FROM BENEATH THE THRONE-- GRABBING ME!
IN THE BLINK OF AN EYE, MINOS' TAIL--
--IMPOSSIBLY LONG, IMPOSSIBLY POWERFUL-- GATHERS NIGHT-CRAWLER UP AND HURLS HIM OUT OF THE PALACE, HIS ACCELERATION SO GREAT THAT SHEER SPEED ALONE STUNS HIM TO NEAR-UNCONSCIOUSNESS.
YOU'VE BROKEN THE MORAL LAWS LAID DOWN BY UPSTAIRS. SHAME ON YOU.
IT'S MY JOB-- NO, I LIE. IT'S MY PLEASURE TO, SHALL WE SAY, MAKE THE PUNISHMENT FIT THE CRIME. IN YOUR CASE, BOTH ARE CONSIDERABLE.
BUT, FOLLOWING A HEART-BEAT BEHIND...
...STORM STREAKS TO HIS RESCUE.
...AND, THEREBY, BECOMES THE FIRST OF THE X-MEN TO SEE HELL IN ALL ITS FABLED, DARKSOME MAJESTY.
GOT YOU!
LORDS OF THE EARTH AND AIR!
THE PIT--SO VAST-- IT SEEMS TO GO ON FOREVER! HOW MANY POOR SOULS ARE HERE, SPENDING ETERNITY IN TORMENT...?
AT THAT THOUGHT, A GREAT SADNESS WELLS WITHIN HER, BRINGING HER CLOSE TO TEARS...

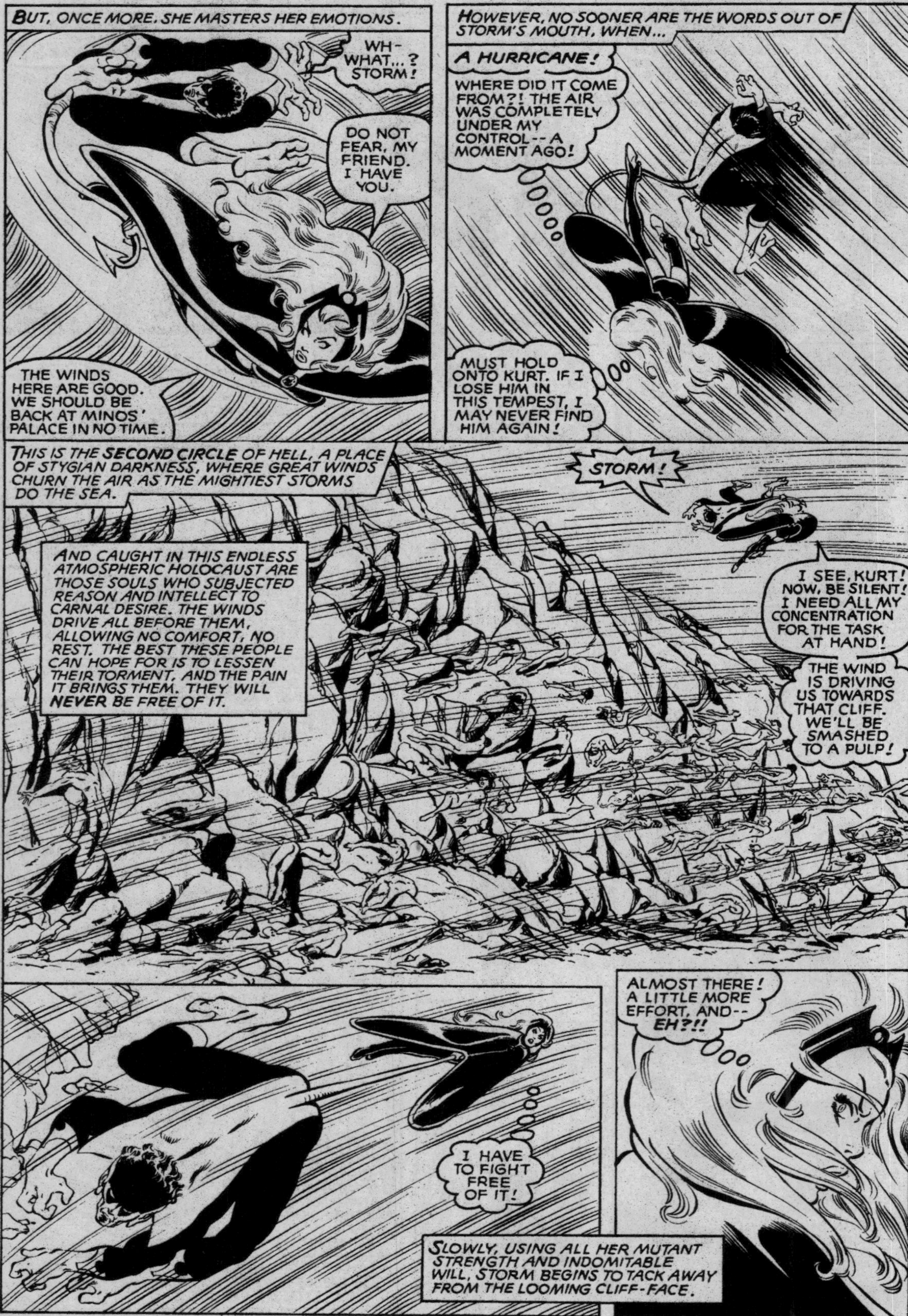
BUT, ONCE MORE. SHE MASTERS HER EMOTIONS.
WH-WHAT...? STORM!
DO NOT FEAR, MY FRIEND. I HAVE YOU.
THE WINDS HERE ARE GOOD. WE SHOULD BE BACK AT MINOS' PALACE IN NO TIME.
HOWEVER, NO SOONER ARE THE WORDS OUT OF STORM'S MOUTH, WHEN...
A HURRICANE!
WHERE DID IT COME FROM?! THE AIR WAS COMPLETELY UNDER MY CONTROL-- A MOMENT AGO!
MUST HOLD ONTO KURT. IF I LOSE HIM IN THIS TEMPEST, I MAY NEVER FIND HIM AGAIN!
THIS IS THE SECOND CIRCLE OF HELL, A PLACE OF STYGIAN DARKNESS, WHERE GREAT WINDS CHURN THE AIR AS THE MIGHTIEST STORMS DO THE SEA.
STORM!
AND CAUGHT IN THIS ENDLESS ATMOSPHERIC HOLOCAUST ARE THOSE SOULS WHO SUBJECTED REASON AND INTELLECT TO CARNAL DESIRE. THE WINDS DRIVE ALL BEFORE THEM, ALLOWING NO COMFORT, NO REST. THE BEST THESE PEOPLE CAN HOPE FOR IS TO LESSEN THEIR TORMENT, AND THE PAIN IT BRINGS THEM. THEY WILL NEVER BE FREE OF IT.
I SEE, KURT! NOW, BE SILENT! I NEED ALL MY CONCENTRATION FOR THE TASK AT HAND!
THE WIND IS DRIVING US TOWARDS THAT CLIFF. WE'LL BE SMASHED TO A PULP!
I HAVE TO FIGHT FREE OF IT!
ALMOST THERE! A LITTLE MORE EFFORT, AND-- EH?!!
SLOWLY, USING ALL HER MUTANT STRENGTH AND INDOMITABLE WILL, STORM BEGINS TO TACK AWAY FROM THE LOOMING CLIFF-FACE.

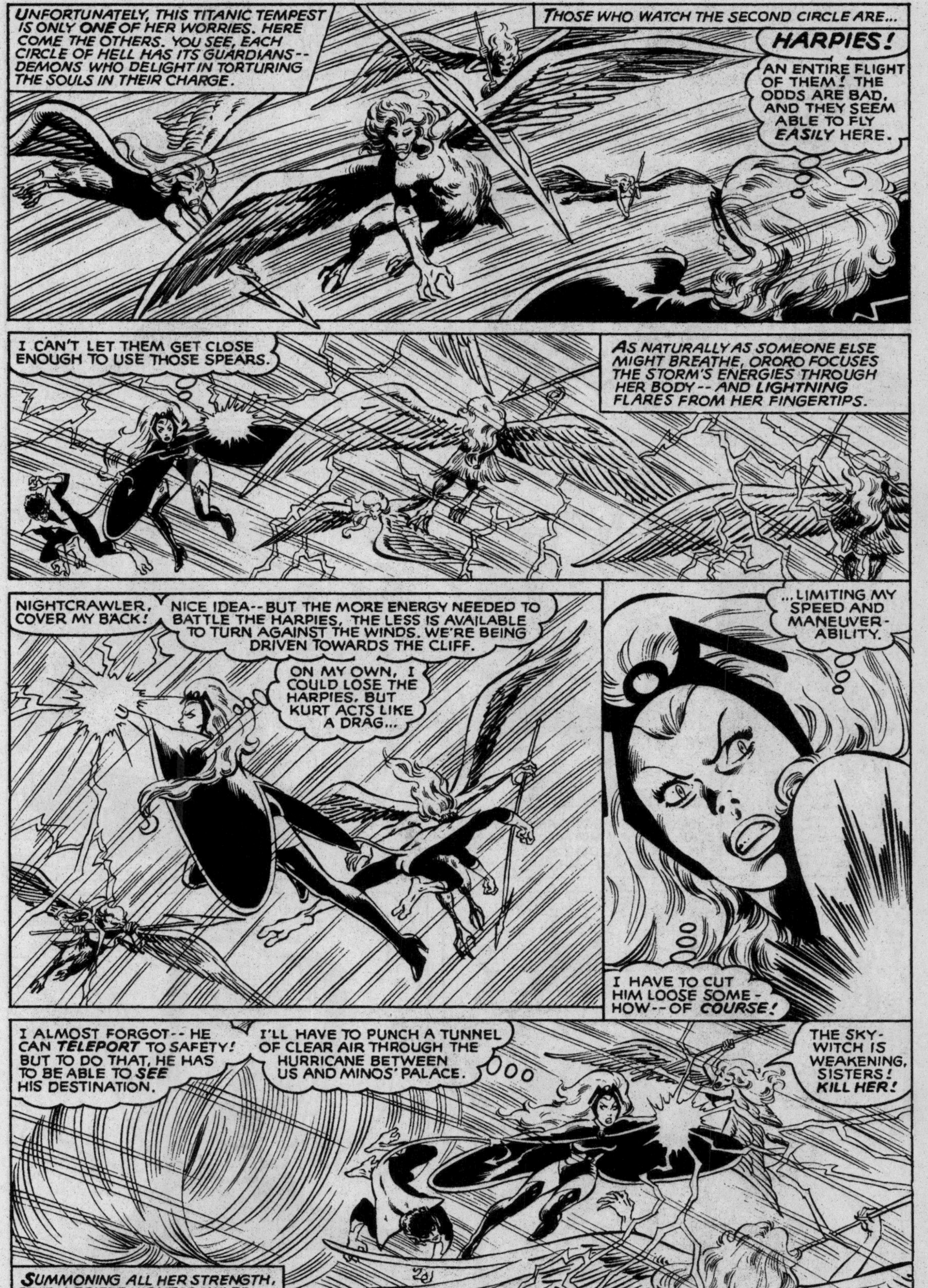
UNFORTUNATELY, THIS TITANIC TEMPEST IS ONLY ONE OF HER WORRIES. HERE COME THE OTHERS. YOU SEE, EACH CIRCLE OF HELL HAS ITS GUARDIANS-- DEMONS WHO DELIGHT IN TORTURING THE SOULS IN THEIR CHARGE.
THOSE WHO WATCH THE SECOND CIRCLE ARE...
HARPIES!
AN ENTIRE FLIGHT OF THEM! THE ODDS ARE BAD, AND THEY SEEM ABLE TO FLY EASILY HERE.
I CAN'T LET THEM GET CLOSE ENOUGH TO USE THOSE SPEARS.
AS NATURALLY AS SOMEONE ELSE MIGHT BREATHE, ORORO FOCUSES THE STORM'S ENERGIES THROUGH HER BODY -- AND LIGHTNING FLARES FROM HER FINGERTIPS.
NIGHTCRAWLER, COVER MY BACK!
NICE IDEA-- BUT THE MORE ENERGY NEEDED TO BATTLE THE HARPIES, THE LESS IS AVAILABLE TO TURN AGAINST THE WINDS. WE'RE BEING DRIVEN TOWARDS THE CLIFF.
ON MY OWN, I COULD LOSE THE HARPIES. BUT KURT ACTS LIKE A DRAG...
...LIMITING MY SPEED AND MANEUVER-ABILITY.
I HAVE TO CUT HIM LOOSE SOME-HOW-- OF COURSE!
I ALMOST FORGOT-- HE CAN TELEPORT TO SAFETY! BUT TO DO THAT, HE HAS TO BE ABLE TO SEE HIS DESTINATION.
I'LL HAVE TO PUNCH A TUNNEL OF CLEAR AIR THROUGH THE HURRICANE BETWEEN US AND MINOS' PALACE.
THE SKY-WITCH IS WEAKENING, SISTERS! KILL HER!
SUMMONING ALL HER STRENGTH, STORM BRIEFS NIGHTCRAWLER...

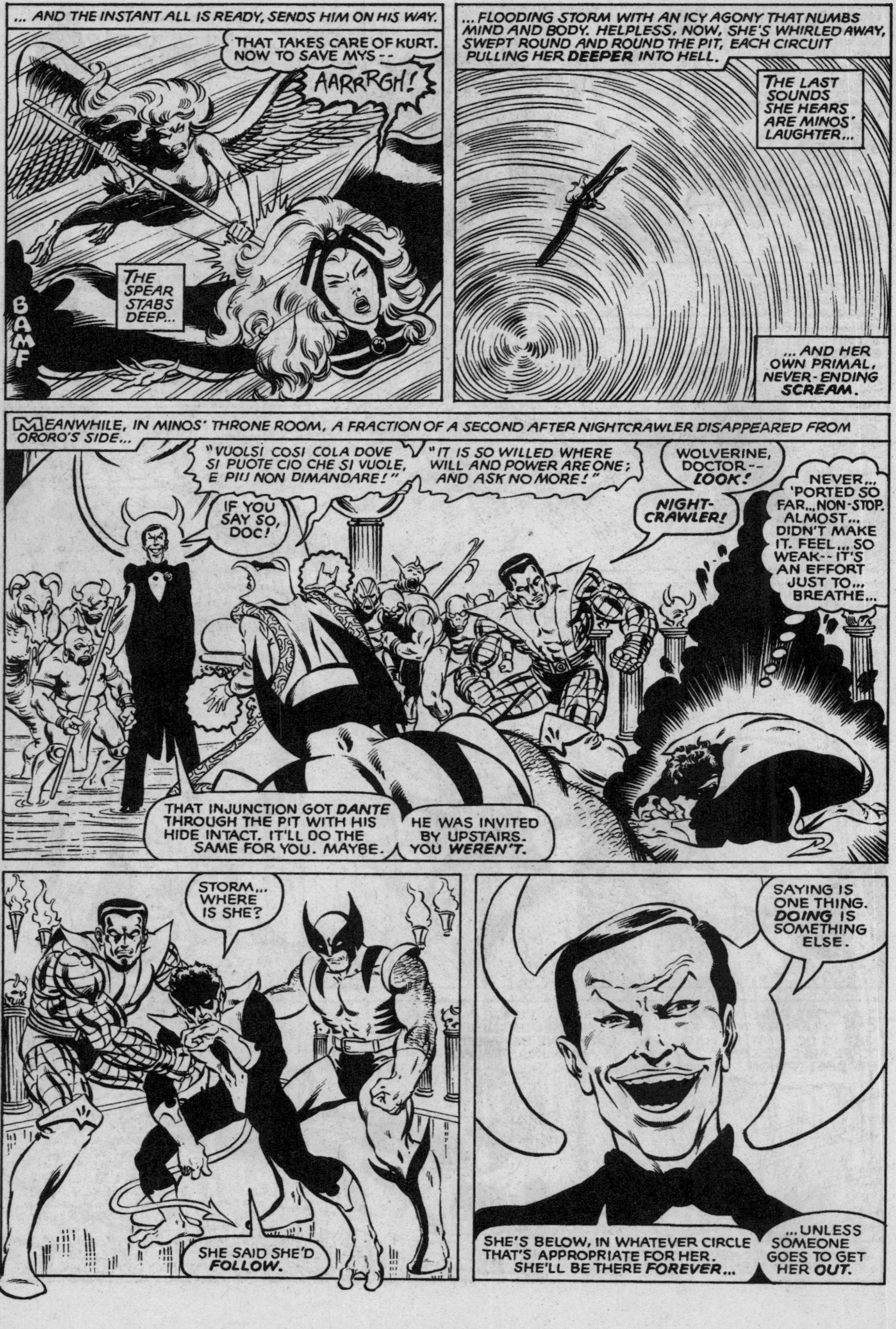
... AND THE INSTANT ALL IS READY, SENDS HIM ON HIS WAY.
THAT TAKES CARE OF KURT. NOW TO SAVE MYS--
AARRRGH!
THE SPEAR STABS DEEP...
BAMF
...FLOODING STORM WITH AN ICY AGONY THAT NUMBS MIND AND BODY. HELPLESS, NOW, SHE'S WHIRLED AWAY, SWEPT ROUND AND ROUND THE PIT, EACH CIRCUIT PULLING HER DEEPER INTO HELL.
THE LAST SOUNDS SHE HEARS ARE MINOS' LAUGHTER...
...AND HER OWN PRIMAL, NEVER-ENDING SCREAM.
MEANWHILE, IN MINOS' THRONE ROOM, A FRACTION OF A SECOND AFTER NIGHTCRAWLER DISAPPEARED FROM ORORO'S SIDE...
"VUOLSI COSI COLA DOVE SI PUOTE CIO CHE SI VUOLE, E PIU NON DIMANDARE!"
"IT IS SO WILLED WHERE WILL AND POWER ARE ONE; AND ASK NO MORE!"
IF YOU SAY SO, DOC!
WOLVERINE, DOCTOR-- LOOK!
NIGHT-CRAWLER!
NEVER... 'PORTED SO FAR... NON-STOP. ALMOST... DIDN'T MAKE IT. FEEL... SO WEAK-- IT'S AN EFFORT JUST TO... BREATHE...
THAT INJUNCTION GOT DANTE THROUGH THE PIT WITH HIS HIDE INTACT. IT'LL DO THE SAME FOR YOU. MAYBE.
HE WAS INVITED BY UPSTAIRS. YOU WEREN'T.
STORM... WHERE IS SHE?
SHE SAID SHE'D FOLLOW.
SAYING IS ONE THING. DOING IS SOMETHING ELSE.
SHE'S BELOW, IN WHATEVER CIRCLE THAT'S APPROPRIATE FOR HER. SHE'LL BE THERE FOREVER...
...UNLESS SOMEONE GOES TO GET HER OUT.

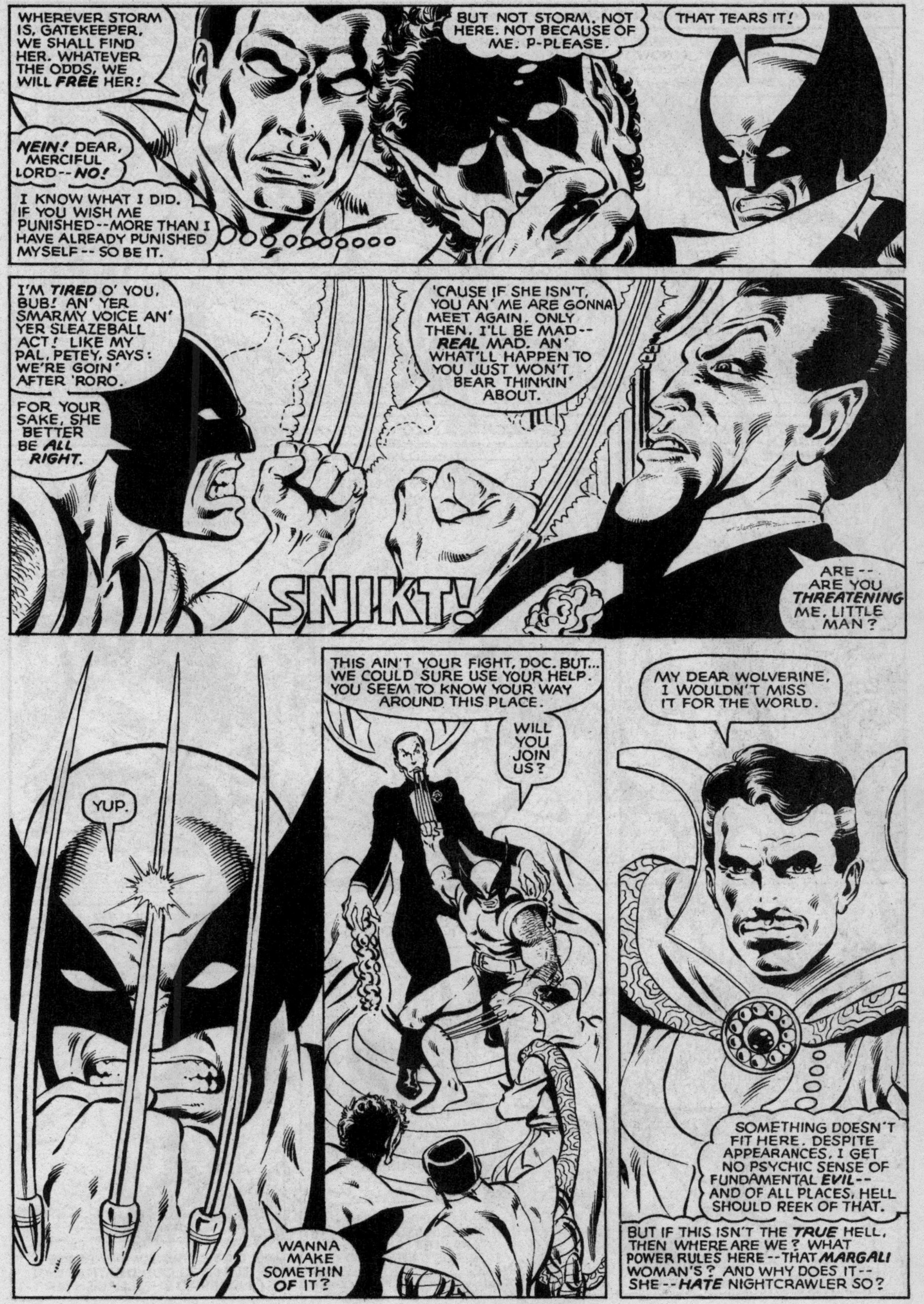
WHEREVER STORM IS, GATEKEEPER, WE SHALL FIND HER. WHATEVER THE ODDS, WE WILL FREE HER!
NEIN! DEAR, MERCIFUL LORD--NO!
I KNOW WHAT I DID. IF YOU WISH ME PUNISHED--MORE THAN I HAVE ALREADY PUNISHED MYSELF--SO BE IT.
BUT NOT STORM. NOT HERE. NOT BECAUSE OF ME. P-PLEASE.
THAT TEARS IT!
I'M TIRED O' YOU, BUB! AN' YER SMARMY VOICE AN' YER SLEAZEBALL ACT! LIKE MY PAL, PETEY, SAYS: WE'RE GOIN' AFTER 'RORO.
FOR YOUR SAKE, SHE BETTER BE ALL RIGHT.
'CAUSE IF SHE ISN'T, YOU AN' ME ARE GONNA MEET AGAIN. ONLY THEN, I'LL BE MAD--REAL MAD. AN' WHAT'LL HAPPEN TO YOU JUST WON'T BEAR THINKIN' ABOUT.
SNIKT!
ARE--ARE YOU THREATENING ME, LITTLE MAN?
YUP.
WANNA MAKE SOMETHIN OF IT?
THIS AIN'T YOUR FIGHT, DOC. BUT... WE COULD SURE USE YOUR HELP. YOU SEEM TO KNOW YOUR WAY AROUND THIS PLACE.
WILL YOU JOIN US?
MY DEAR WOLVERINE, I WOULDN'T MISS IT FOR THE WORLD.
SOMETHING DOESN'T FIT HERE. DESPITE APPEARANCES, I GET NO PSYCHIC SENSE OF FUNDAMENTAL EVIL--AND OF ALL PLACES, HELL SHOULD REEK OF THAT.
BUT IF THIS ISN'T THE TRUE HELL, THEN WHERE ARE WE? WHAT POWER RULES HERE--THAT MARGALI WOMAN'S? AND WHY DOES IT--SHE--HATE NIGHTCRAWLER SO?

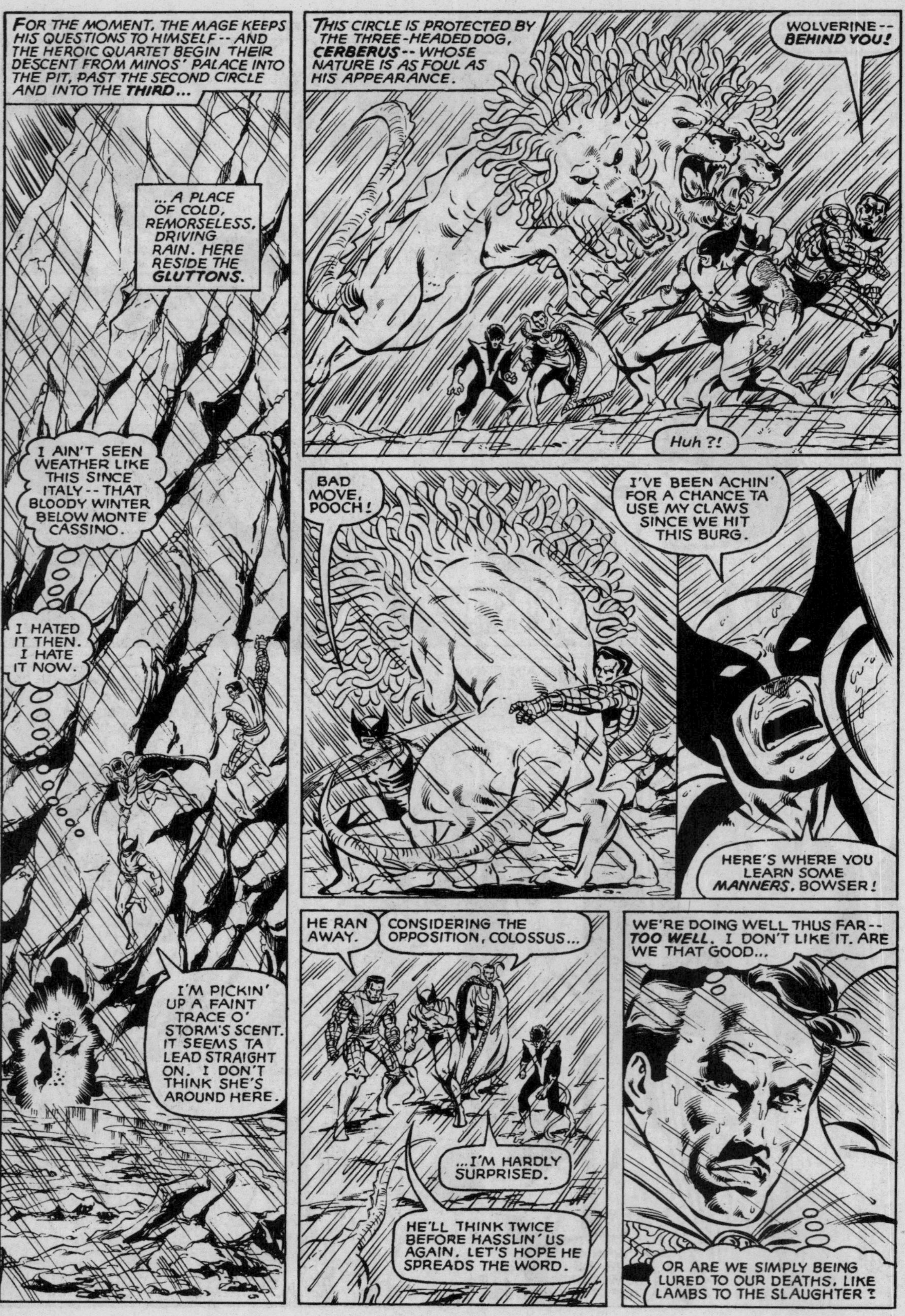
FOR THE MOMENT, THE MAGE KEEPS HIS QUESTIONS TO HIMSELF -- AND THE HEROIC QUARTET BEGIN THEIR DESCENT FROM MINOS' PALACE INTO THE PIT, PAST THE SECOND CIRCLE AND INTO THE THIRD...
...A PLACE OF COLD, REMORSELESS, DRIVING RAIN. HERE RESIDE THE GLUTTONS.
I AIN'T SEEN WEATHER LIKE THIS SINCE ITALY -- THAT BLOODY WINTER BELOW MONTE CASSINO.
I HATED IT THEN. I HATE IT NOW.
I'M PICKIN' UP A FAINT TRACE O' STORM'S SCENT. IT SEEMS TA LEAD STRAIGHT ON. I DON'T THINK SHE'S AROUND HERE.
THIS CIRCLE IS PROTECTED BY THE THREE-HEADED DOG, CERBERUS -- WHOSE NATURE IS AS FOUL AS HIS APPEARANCE.
WOLVERINE -- BEHIND YOU!
Huh?!
BAD MOVE, POOCH!
I'VE BEEN ACHIN' FOR A CHANCE TA USE MY CLAWS SINCE WE HIT THIS BURG.
HERE'S WHERE YOU LEARN SOME MANNERS, BOWSER!
HE RAN AWAY.
CONSIDERING THE OPPOSITION, COLOSSUS...
...I'M HARDLY SURPRISED.
HE'LL THINK TWICE BEFORE HASSLIN' US AGAIN. LET'S HOPE HE SPREADS THE WORD.
WE'RE DOING WELL THUS FAR -- TOO WELL. I DON'T LIKE IT. ARE WE THAT GOOD...
OR ARE WE SIMPLY BEING LURED TO OUR DEATHS, LIKE LAMBS TO THE SLAUGHTER?

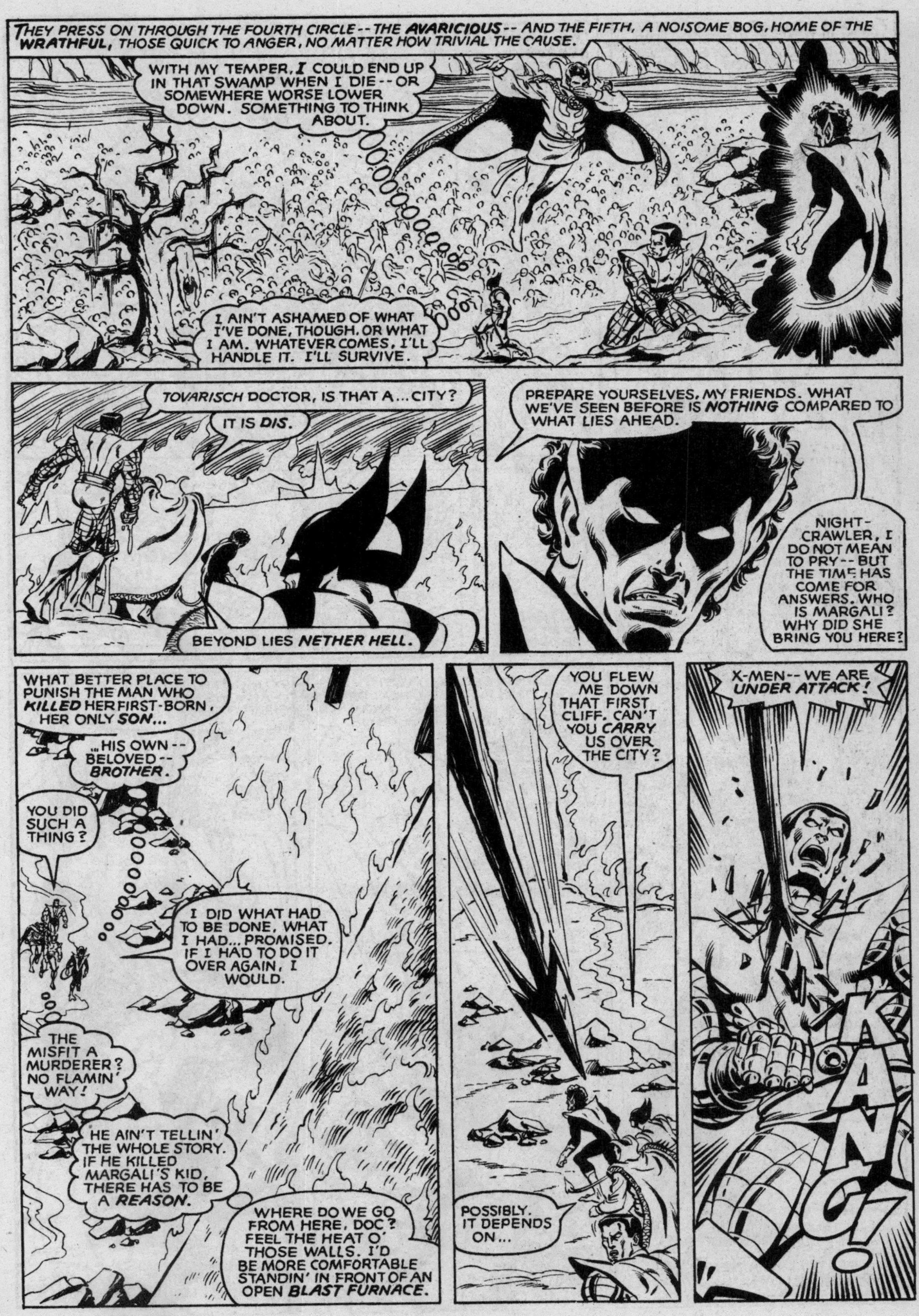
THEY PRESS ON THROUGH THE FOURTH CIRCLE -- THE AVARICIOUS -- AND THE FIFTH, A NOISOME BOG, HOME OF THE WRATHFUL, THOSE QUICK TO ANGER, NO MATTER HOW TRIVIAL THE CAUSE.
WITH MY TEMPER, I COULD END UP IN THAT SWAMP WHEN I DIE -- OR SOMEWHERE WORSE LOWER DOWN. SOMETHING TO THINK ABOUT.
I AIN'T ASHAMED OF WHAT I'VE DONE, THOUGH, OR WHAT I AM. WHATEVER COMES, I'LL HANDLE IT. I'LL SURVIVE.
TOVARISCH DOCTOR, IS THAT A... CITY?
IT IS DIS.
BEYOND LIES NETHER HELL.
PREPARE YOURSELVES, MY FRIENDS. WHAT WE'VE SEEN BEFORE IS NOTHING COMPARED TO WHAT LIES AHEAD.
NIGHT-CRAWLER, I DO NOT MEAN TO PRY -- BUT THE TIME HAS COME FOR ANSWERS. WHO IS MARGALI? WHY DID SHE BRING YOU HERE?
WHAT BETTER PLACE TO PUNISH THE MAN WHO KILLED HER FIRST-BORN, HER ONLY SON...
...HIS OWN -- BELOVED -- BROTHER.
YOU DID SUCH A THING?
I DID WHAT HAD TO BE DONE, WHAT I HAD... PROMISED. IF I HAD TO DO IT OVER AGAIN, I WOULD.
THE MISFIT A MURDERER? NO FLAMIN' WAY!
HE AIN'T TELLIN' THE WHOLE STORY. IF HE KILLED MARGALI'S KID, THERE HAS TO BE A REASON.
WHERE DO WE GO FROM HERE, DOC? FEEL THE HEAT O' THOSE WALLS. I'D BE MORE COMFORTABLE STANDIN' IN FRONT OF AN OPEN BLAST FURNACE.
YOU FLEW ME DOWN THAT FIRST CLIFF. CAN'T YOU CARRY US OVER THE CITY?
POSSIBLY. IT DEPENDS ON...
X-MEN -- WE ARE UNDER ATTACK!
KANG!

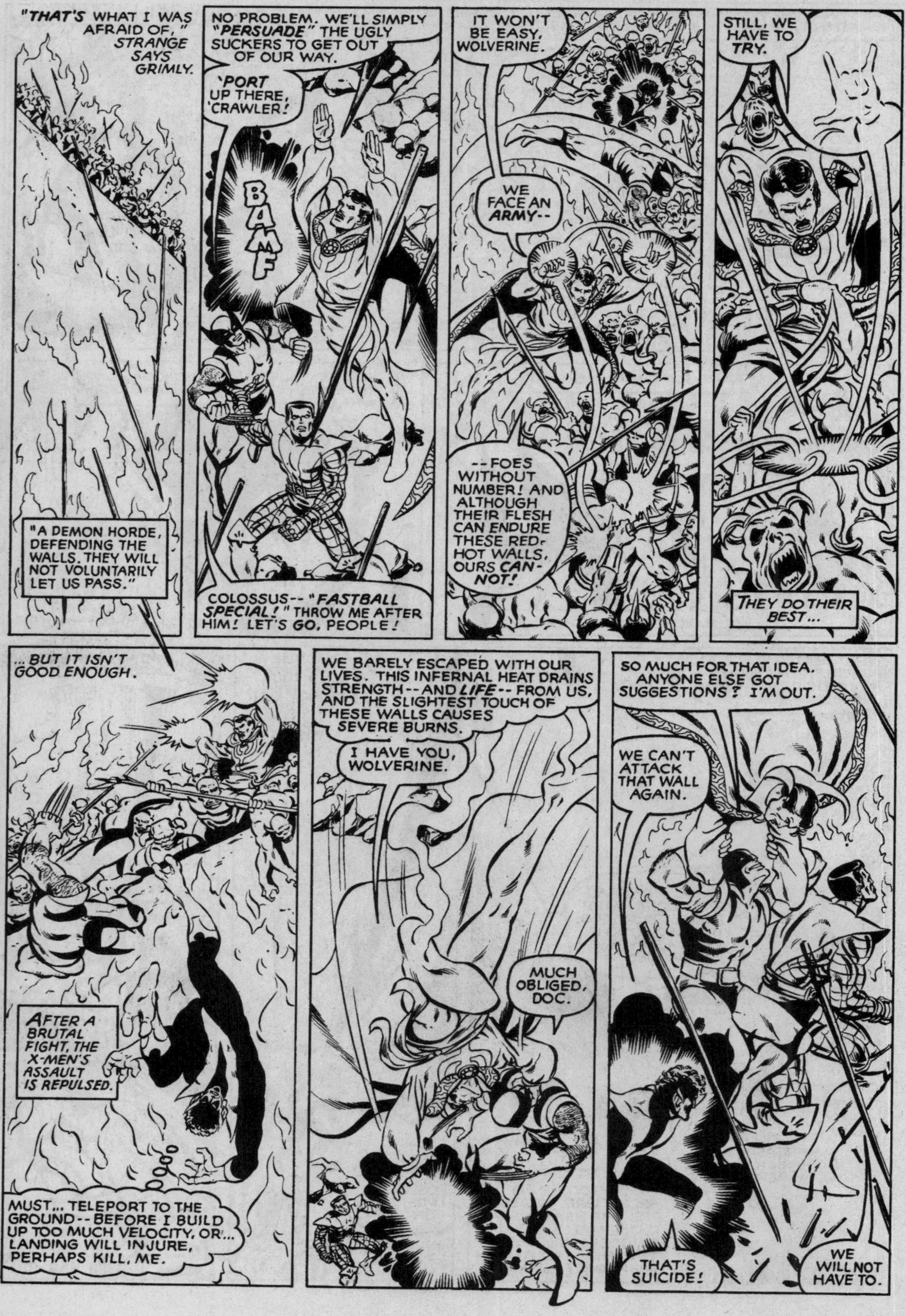
"THAT'S WHAT I WAS AFRAID OF," STRANGE SAYS GRIMLY.
"A DEMON HORDE, DEFENDING THE WALLS. THEY WILL NOT VOLUNTARILY LET US PASS."
NO PROBLEM. WE'LL SIMPLY "PERSUADE" THE UGLY SUCKERS TO GET OUT OF OUR WAY.
'PORT UP THERE, 'CRAWLER!
BAMF
COLOSSUS-- "FASTBALL SPECIAL!" THROW ME AFTER HIM! LET'S GO, PEOPLE!
IT WON'T BE EASY, WOLVERINE.
WE FACE AN ARMY--
--FOES WITHOUT NUMBER! AND ALTHOUGH THEIR FLESH CAN ENDURE THESE RED-HOT WALLS, OURS CANNOT!
STILL, WE HAVE TO TRY.
THEY DO THEIR BEST...
...BUT IT ISN'T GOOD ENOUGH.
AFTER A BRUTAL FIGHT, THE X-MEN'S ASSAULT IS REPULSED.
MUST... TELEPORT TO THE GROUND--BEFORE I BUILD UP TOO MUCH VELOCITY, OR... LANDING WILL INJURE, PERHAPS KILL, ME.
WE BARELY ESCAPED WITH OUR LIVES. THIS INFERNAL HEAT DRAINS STRENGTH--AND LIFE--FROM US, AND THE SLIGHTEST TOUCH OF THESE WALLS CAUSES SEVERE BURNS.
I HAVE YOU, WOLVERINE.
MUCH OBLIGED, DOC.
SO MUCH FOR THAT IDEA. ANYONE ELSE GOT SUGGESTIONS? I'M OUT.
WE CAN'T ATTACK THAT WALL AGAIN.
THAT'S SUICIDE!
WE WILL NOT HAVE TO.

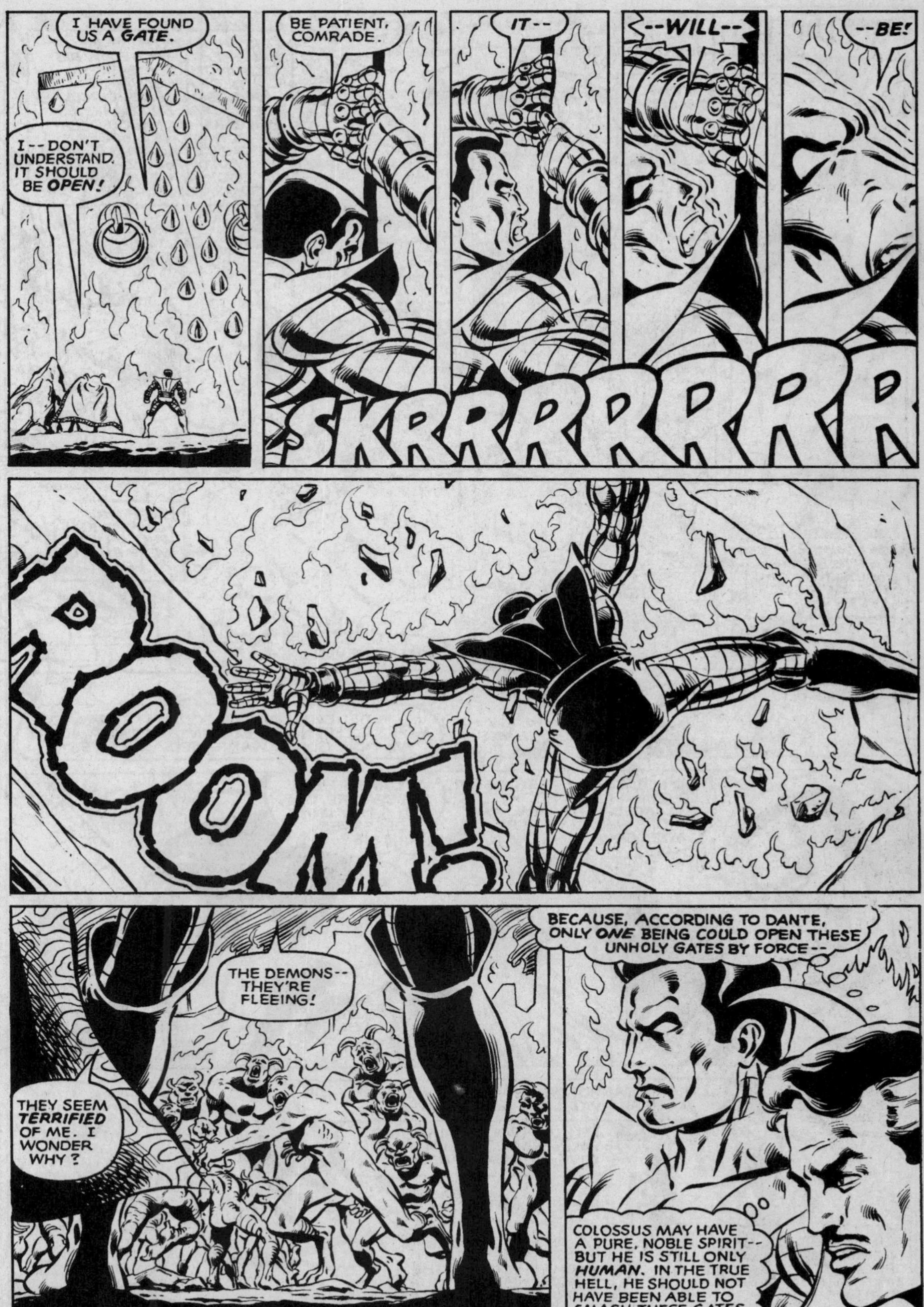
I HAVE FOUND US A GATE.
I--DON'T UNDERSTAND. IT SHOULD BE OPEN!
BE PATIENT, COMRADE.
IT--
--WILL--
--BE!
SKRRRRRRR
BOOM!
THE DEMONS--THEY'RE FLEEING!
THEY SEEM TERRIFIED OF ME. I WONDER WHY?
BECAUSE, ACCORDING TO DANTE, ONLY ONE BEING COULD OPEN THESE UNHOLY GATES BY FORCE--
COLOSSUS MAY HAVE A PURE, NOBLE SPIRIT--BUT HE IS STILL ONLY HUMAN. IN THE TRUE HELL, HE SHOULD NOT HAVE BEEN ABLE TO SMASH THESE GATES.

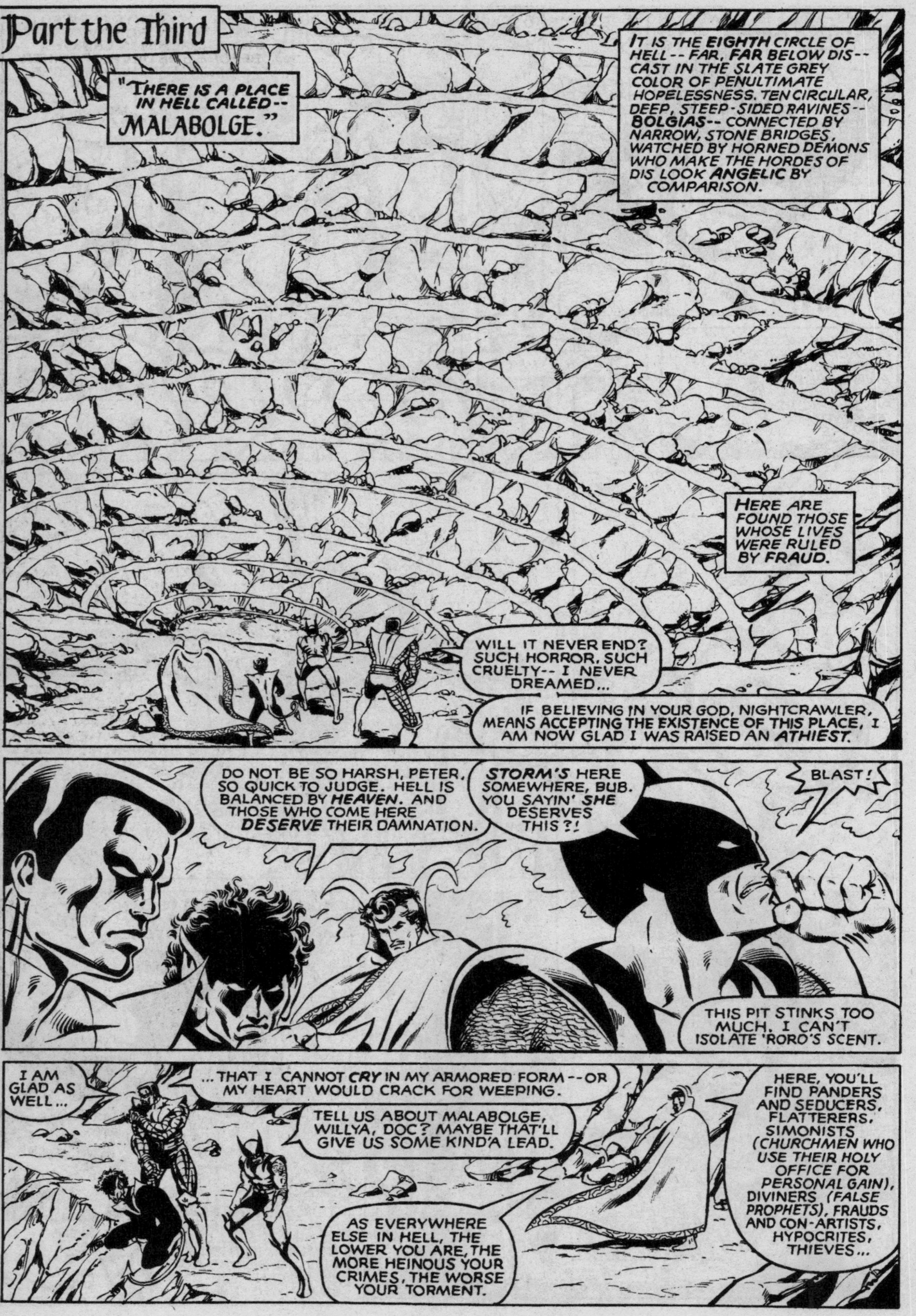
Part the Third
"THERE IS A PLACE IN HELL CALLED-- MALABOLGE."
IT IS THE EIGHTH CIRCLE OF HELL -- FAR, FAR BELOW DIS -- CAST IN THE SLATE GREY COLOR OF PENULTIMATE HOPELESSNESS. TEN CIRCULAR, DEEP, STEEP-SIDED RAVINES -- BOLGIAS -- CONNECTED BY NARROW, STONE BRIDGES, WATCHED BY HORNED DEMONS WHO MAKE THE HORDES OF DIS LOOK ANGELIC BY COMPARISON.
HERE ARE FOUND THOSE WHOSE LIVES WERE RULED BY FRAUD.
WILL IT NEVER END? SUCH HORROR, SUCH CRUELTY-- I NEVER DREAMED...
IF BELIEVING IN YOUR GOD, NIGHTCRAWLER, MEANS ACCEPTING THE EXISTENCE OF THIS PLACE, I AM NOW GLAD I WAS RAISED AN ATHIEST.
DO NOT BE SO HARSH, PETER, SO QUICK TO JUDGE. HELL IS BALANCED BY HEAVEN. AND THOSE WHO COME HERE DESERVE THEIR DAMNATION.
STORM'S HERE SOMEWHERE, BUB. YOU SAYIN' SHE DESERVES THIS?!
BLAST!
THIS PIT STINKS TOO MUCH. I CAN'T ISOLATE 'RORO'S SCENT.
I AM GLAD AS WELL...
...THAT I CANNOT CRY IN MY ARMORED FORM -- OR MY HEART WOULD CRACK FOR WEEPING.
TELL US ABOUT MALABOLGE, WILLYA, DOC? MAYBE THAT'LL GIVE US SOME KIND'A LEAD.
AS EVERYWHERE ELSE IN HELL, THE LOWER YOU ARE, THE MORE HEINOUS YOUR CRIMES, THE WORSE YOUR TORMENT.
HERE, YOU'LL FIND PANDERS AND SEDUCERS, FLATTERERS, SIMONISTS (CHURCHMEN WHO USE THEIR HOLY OFFICE FOR PERSONAL GAIN), DIVINERS (FALSE PROPHETS), FRAUDS AND CON-ARTISTS, HYPOCRITES, THIEVES...

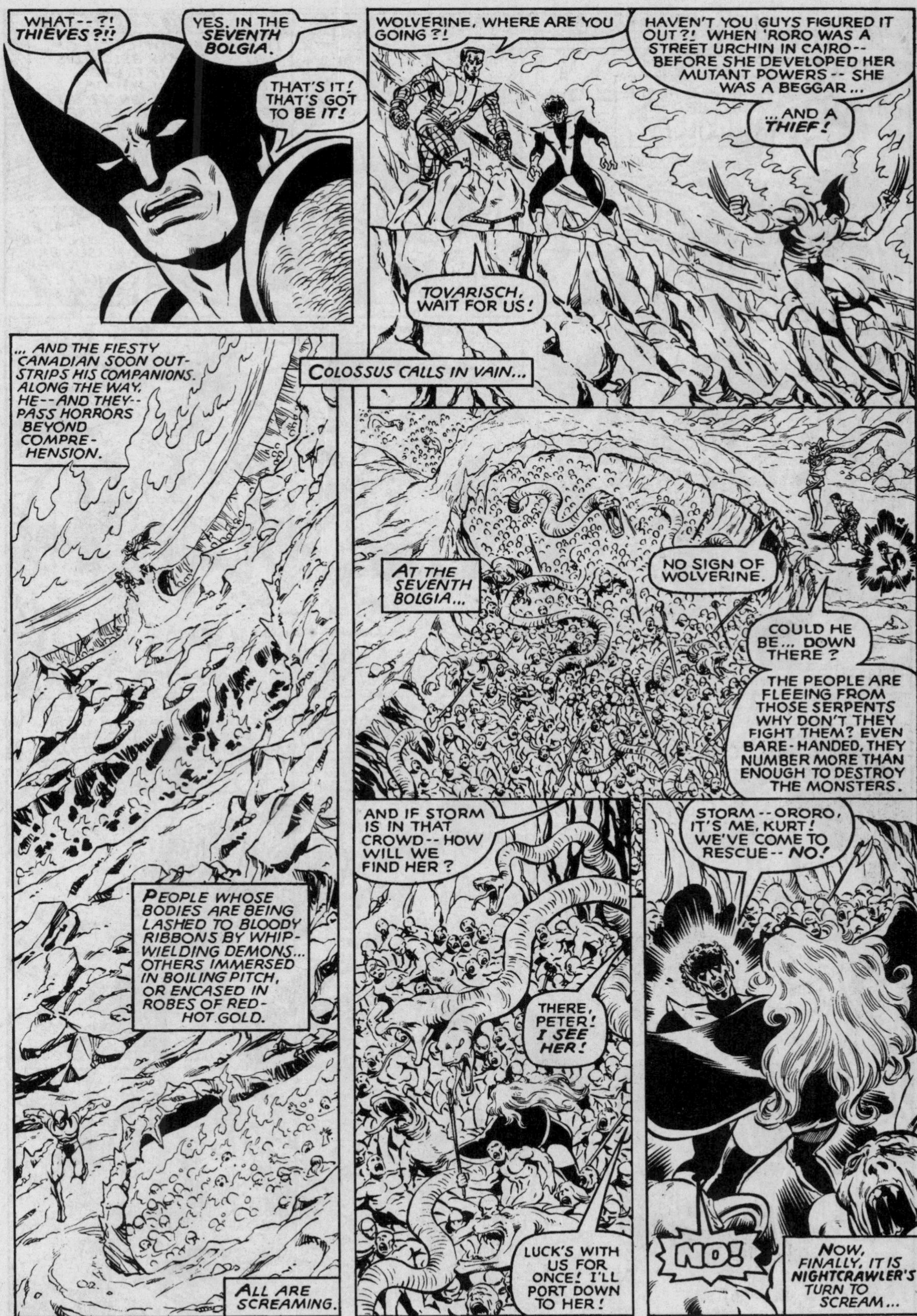
WHAT--?! THIEVES?!!
YES. IN THE SEVENTH BOLGIA.
THAT'S IT! THAT'S GOT TO BE IT!
WOLVERINE, WHERE ARE YOU GOING?!
HAVEN'T YOU GUYS FIGURED IT OUT?! WHEN 'RORO WAS A STREET URCHIN IN CAIRO-- BEFORE SHE DEVELOPED HER MUTANT POWERS-- SHE WAS A BEGGAR...
...AND A THIEF!
TOVARISCH, WAIT FOR US!
COLOSSUS CALLS IN VAIN...
... AND THE FIESTY CANADIAN SOON OUT-STRIPS HIS COMPANIONS. ALONG THE WAY, HE--AND THEY-- PASS HORRORS BEYOND COMPRE-HENSION.
PEOPLE WHOSE BODIES ARE BEING LASHED TO BLOODY RIBBONS BY WHIP-WIELDING DEMONS... OTHERS IMMERSED IN BOILING PITCH, OR ENCASED IN ROBES OF RED-HOT GOLD.
ALL ARE SCREAMING.
AT THE SEVENTH BOLGIA...
NO SIGN OF WOLVERINE.
COULD HE BE... DOWN THERE?
THE PEOPLE ARE FLEEING FROM THOSE SERPENTS WHY DON'T THEY FIGHT THEM? EVEN BARE-HANDED, THEY NUMBER MORE THAN ENOUGH TO DESTROY THE MONSTERS.
AND IF STORM IS IN THAT CROWD-- HOW WILL WE FIND HER?
THERE, PETER! I SEE HER!
LUCK'S WITH US FOR ONCE! I'LL PORT DOWN TO HER!
STORM--ORORO, IT'S ME, KURT! WE'VE COME TO RESCUE-- NO!
NO!
NOW, FINALLY, IT IS NIGHTCRAWLER'S TURN TO SCREAM...

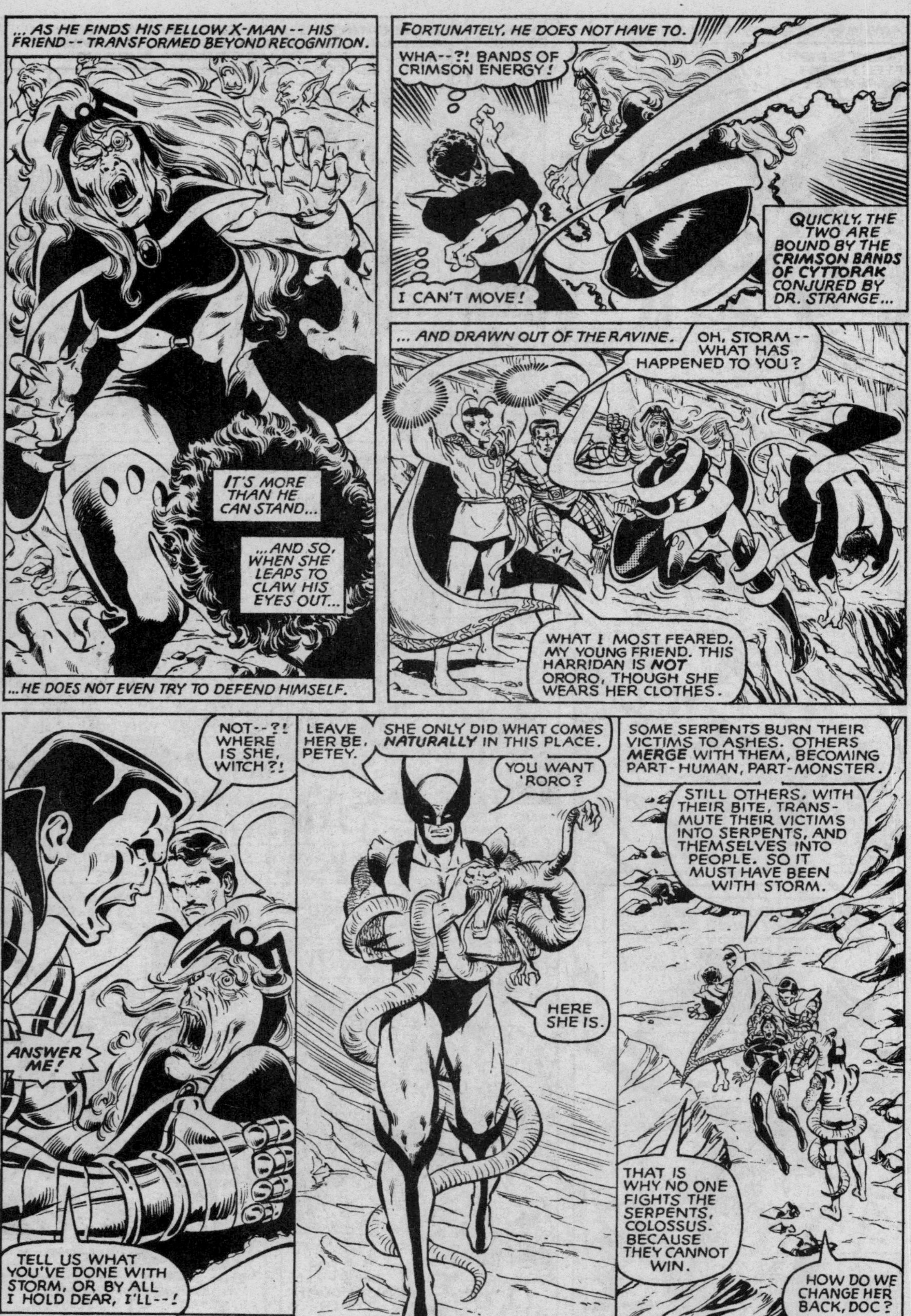
... AS HE FINDS HIS FELLOW X-MAN -- HIS FRIEND -- TRANSFORMED BEYOND RECOGNITION.
IT'S MORE THAN HE CAN STAND...
...AND SO, WHEN SHE LEAPS TO CLAW HIS EYES OUT...
...HE DOES NOT EVEN TRY TO DEFEND HIMSELF.
FORTUNATELY, HE DOES NOT HAVE TO.
WHA--?! BANDS OF CRIMSON ENERGY!
I CAN'T MOVE!
QUICKLY, THE TWO ARE BOUND BY THE CRIMSON BANDS OF CYTTORAK CONJURED BY DR. STRANGE...
... AND DRAWN OUT OF THE RAVINE.
OH, STORM -- WHAT HAS HAPPENED TO YOU?
WHAT I MOST FEARED, MY YOUNG FRIEND. THIS HARRIDAN IS NOT ORORO, THOUGH SHE WEARS HER CLOTHES.
NOT--?! WHERE IS SHE, WITCH?!
ANSWER ME!
TELL US WHAT YOU'VE DONE WITH STORM, OR BY ALL I HOLD DEAR, I'LL--!
LEAVE HER BE, PETEY.
SHE ONLY DID WHAT COMES NATURALLY IN THIS PLACE.
YOU WANT 'RORO?
HERE SHE IS.
SOME SERPENTS BURN THEIR VICTIMS TO ASHES. OTHERS MERGE WITH THEM, BECOMING PART-HUMAN, PART-MONSTER.
STILL OTHERS, WITH THEIR BITE, TRANSMUTE THEIR VICTIMS INTO SERPENTS, AND THEMSELVES INTO PEOPLE. SO IT MUST HAVE BEEN WITH STORM.
THAT IS WHY NO ONE FIGHTS THE SERPENTS, COLOSSUS. BECAUSE THEY CANNOT WIN.
HOW DO WE CHANGE HER BACK, DOC?

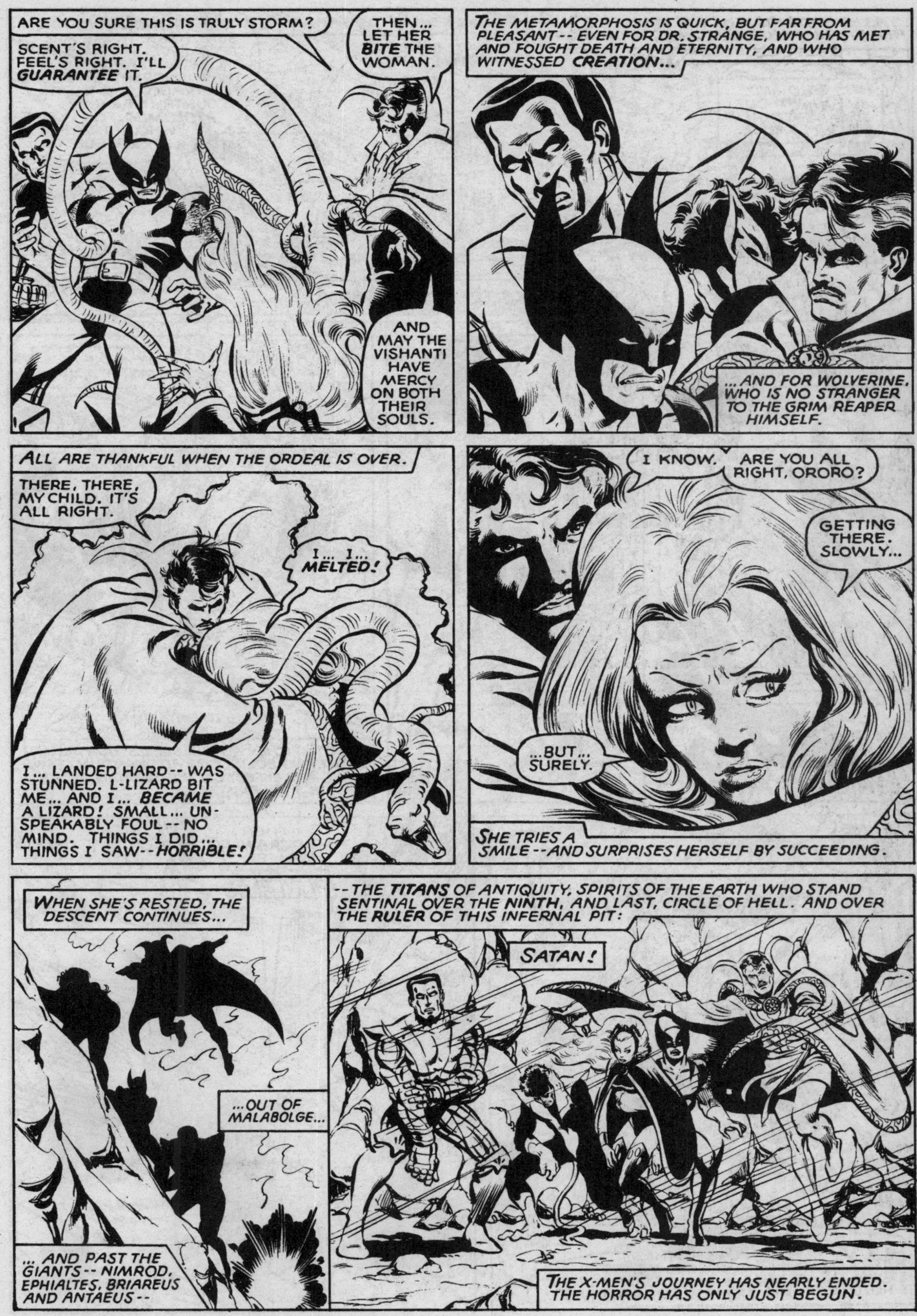
ARE YOU SURE THIS IS TRULY STORM?
SCENT'S RIGHT. FEEL'S RIGHT. I'LL GUARANTEE IT.
THEN... LET HER BITE THE WOMAN.
AND MAY THE VISHANTI HAVE MERCY ON BOTH THEIR SOULS.
THE METAMORPHOSIS IS QUICK, BUT FAR FROM PLEASANT -- EVEN FOR DR. STRANGE, WHO HAS MET AND FOUGHT DEATH AND ETERNITY, AND WHO WITNESSED CREATION...
...AND FOR WOLVERINE, WHO IS NO STRANGER TO THE GRIM REAPER HIMSELF.
ALL ARE THANKFUL WHEN THE ORDEAL IS OVER.
THERE, THERE, MY CHILD. IT'S ALL RIGHT.
I... I... MELTED!
I... LANDED HARD -- WAS STUNNED. L-LIZARD BIT ME... AND I... BECAME A LIZARD! SMALL... UN-SPEAKABLY FOUL -- NO MIND. THINGS I DID... THINGS I SAW -- HORRIBLE!
I KNOW.
ARE YOU ALL RIGHT, ORORO?
GETTING THERE. SLOWLY...
...BUT... SURELY.
SHE TRIES A SMILE -- AND SURPRISES HERSELF BY SUCCEEDING.
WHEN SHE'S RESTED, THE DESCENT CONTINUES...
...OUT OF MALABOLGE...
... AND PAST THE GIANTS -- NIMROD, EPHIALTES, BRIAREUS AND ANTAEUS --
-- THE TITANS OF ANTIQUITY, SPIRITS OF THE EARTH WHO STAND SENTINAL OVER THE NINTH, AND LAST, CIRCLE OF HELL. AND OVER THE RULER OF THIS INFERNAL PIT:
SATAN!
THE X-MEN'S JOURNEY HAS NEARLY ENDED. THE HORROR HAS ONLY JUST BEGUN.

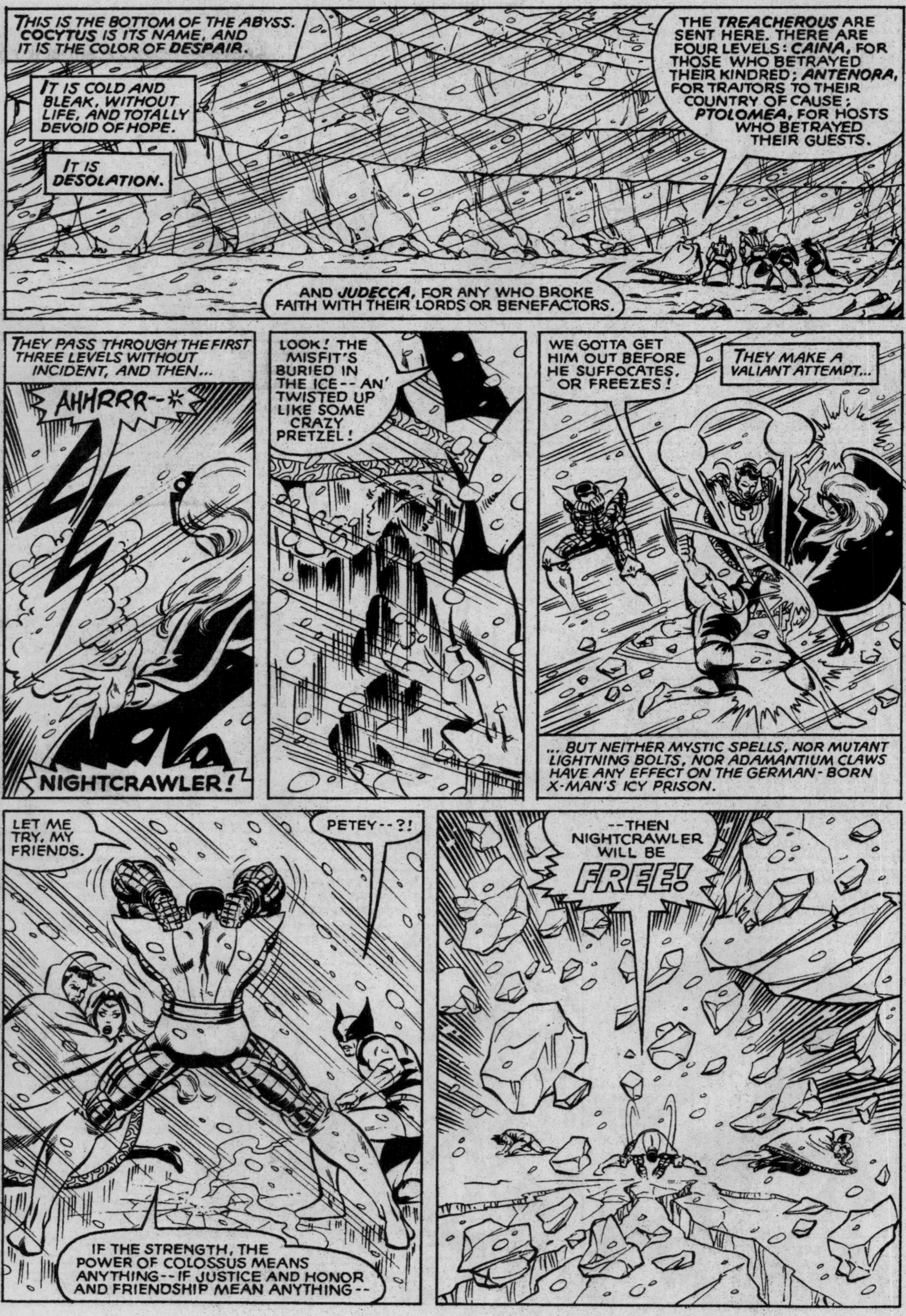

THIS IS THE BOTTOM OF THE ABYSS. COCYTUS IS ITS NAME, AND IT IS THE COLOR OF DESPAIR.
IT IS COLD AND BLEAK, WITHOUT LIFE, AND TOTALLY DEVOID OF HOPE.
IT IS DESOLATION.
THE TREACHEROUS ARE SENT HERE. THERE ARE FOUR LEVELS: CAINA, FOR THOSE WHO BETRAYED THEIR KINDRED; ANTENORA, FOR TRAITORS TO THEIR COUNTRY OF CAUSE; PTOLOMEA, FOR HOSTS WHO BETRAYED THEIR GUESTS.
AND JUDECCA, FOR ANY WHO BROKE FAITH WITH THEIR LORDS OR BENEFACTORS.
THEY PASS THROUGH THE FIRST THREE LEVELS WITHOUT INCIDENT, AND THEN...
AHHRRR--
NIGHTCRAWLER!
LOOK! THE MISFIT'S BURIED IN THE ICE-- AN' TWISTED UP LIKE SOME CRAZY PRETZEL!
WE GOTTA GET HIM OUT BEFORE HE SUFFOCATES, OR FREEZES!
THEY MAKE A VALIANT ATTEMPT...
... BUT NEITHER MYSTIC SPELLS, NOR MUTANT LIGHTNING BOLTS, NOR ADAMANTIUM CLAWS HAVE ANY EFFECT ON THE GERMAN-BORN X-MAN'S ICY PRISON.
LET ME TRY, MY FRIENDS.
PETEY--?!
IF THE STRENGTH, THE POWER OF COLOSSUS MEANS ANYTHING--IF JUSTICE AND HONOR AND FRIENDSHIP MEAN ANYTHING--
--THEN NIGHTCRAWLER WILL BE FREE!

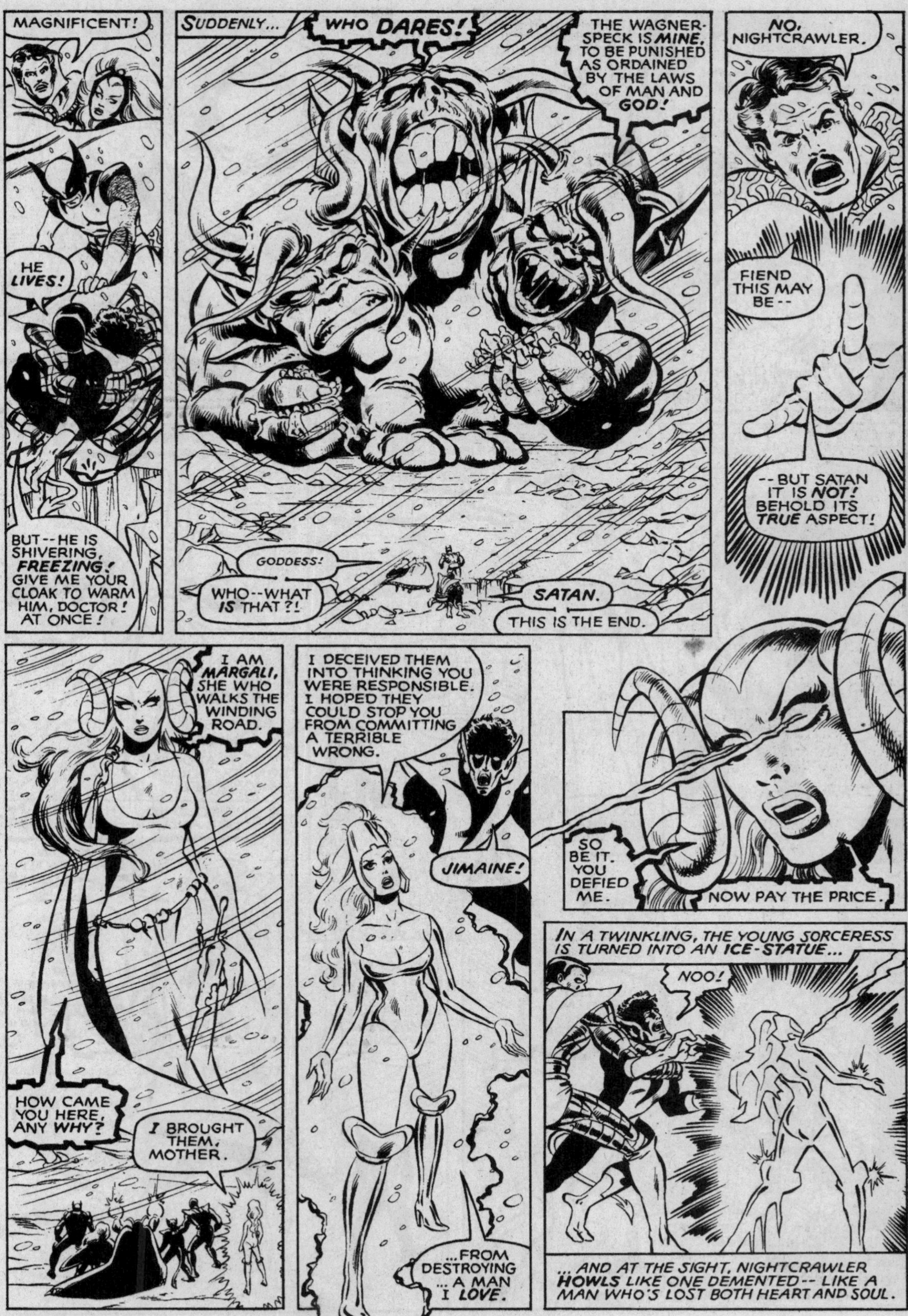

MAGNIFICENT!
HE LIVES!
BUT--HE IS SHIVERING, FREEZING! GIVE ME YOUR CLOAK TO WARM HIM, DOCTOR! AT ONCE!
SUDDENLY...
WHO DARES!
THE WAGNER-SPECK IS MINE, TO BE PUNISHED AS ORDAINED BY THE LAWS OF MAN AND GOD!
GODDESS!
WHO--WHAT IS THAT?!
SATAN.
THIS IS THE END.
NO, NIGHTCRAWLER.
FIEND THIS MAY BE--
--BUT SATAN IT IS NOT! BEHOLD ITS TRUE ASPECT!
I AM MARGALI, SHE WHO WALKS THE WINDING ROAD.
HOW CAME YOU HERE, ANY WHY?
I BROUGHT THEM, MOTHER.
I DECEIVED THEM INTO THINKING YOU WERE RESPONSIBLE. I HOPED THEY COULD STOP YOU FROM COMMITTING A TERRIBLE WRONG.
JIMAINE!
...FROM DESTROYING ...A MAN I LOVE.
SO BE IT. YOU DEFIED ME.
NOW PAY THE PRICE.
IN A TWINKLING, THE YOUNG SORCERESS IS TURNED INTO AN ICE-STATUE...
NOO!
...AND AT THE SIGHT, NIGHTCRAWLER HOWLS LIKE ONE DEMENTED--LIKE A MAN WHO'S LOST BOTH HEART AND SOUL.

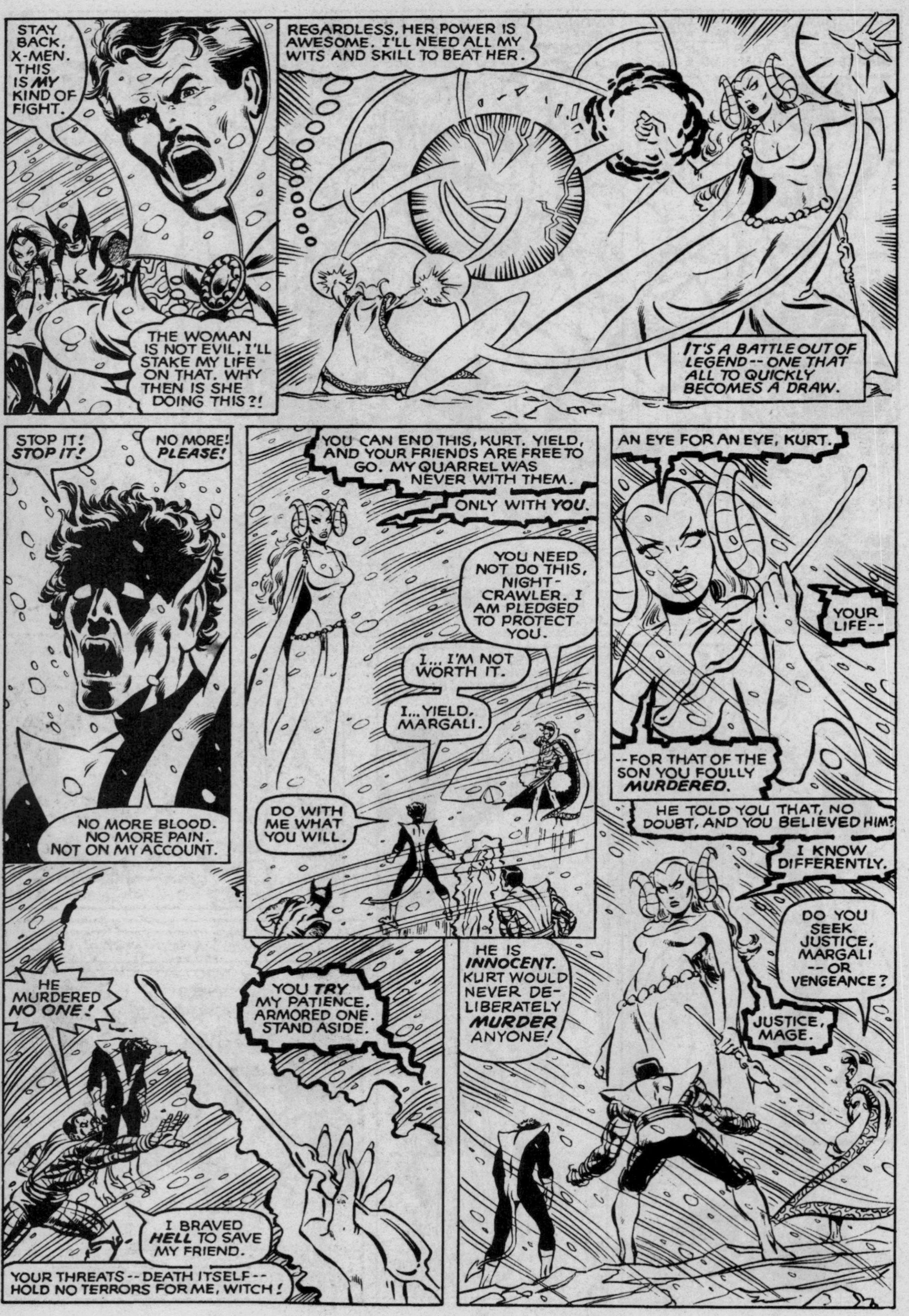
STAY BACK, X-MEN. THIS IS MY KIND OF FIGHT.
THE WOMAN IS NOT EVIL, I'LL STAKE MY LIFE ON THAT. WHY THEN IS SHE DOING THIS?!
REGARDLESS, HER POWER IS AWESOME. I'LL NEED ALL MY WITS AND SKILL TO BEAT HER.
IT'S A BATTLE OUT OF LEGEND -- ONE THAT ALL TO QUICKLY BECOMES A DRAW.
STOP IT! STOP IT!
NO MORE! PLEASE!
NO MORE BLOOD. NO MORE PAIN. NOT ON MY ACCOUNT.
YOU CAN END THIS, KURT. YIELD, AND YOUR FRIENDS ARE FREE TO GO. MY QUARREL WAS NEVER WITH THEM.
ONLY WITH YOU.
YOU NEED NOT DO THIS, NIGHT-CRAWLER. I AM PLEDGED TO PROTECT YOU.
I... I'M NOT WORTH IT.
I... YIELD, MARGALI.
DO WITH ME WHAT YOU WILL.
AN EYE FOR AN EYE, KURT.
YOUR LIFE--
--FOR THAT OF THE SON YOU FOULLY MURDERED.
HE TOLD YOU THAT, NO DOUBT, AND YOU BELIEVED HIM?
I KNOW DIFFERENTLY.
HE MURDERED NO ONE!
YOU TRY MY PATIENCE, ARMORED ONE. STAND ASIDE.
I BRAVED HELL TO SAVE MY FRIEND.
YOUR THREATS -- DEATH ITSELF -- HOLD NO TERRORS FOR ME, WITCH!
HE IS INNOCENT. KURT WOULD NEVER DE-LIBERATELY MURDER ANYONE!
DO YOU SEEK JUSTICE, MARGALI -- OR VENGEANCE?
JUSTICE, MAGE.

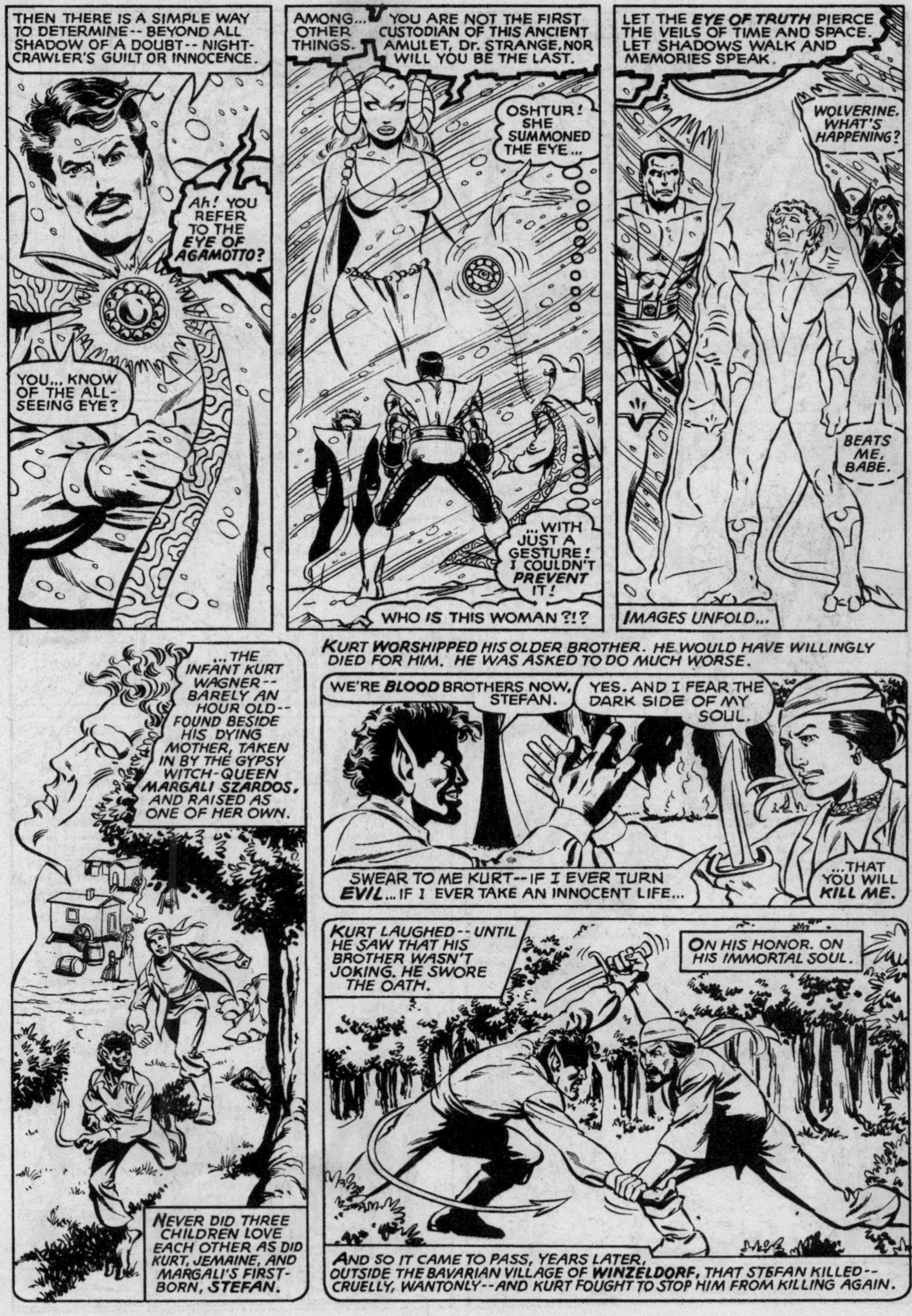
THEN THERE IS A SIMPLE WAY TO DETERMINE-- BEYOND ALL SHADOW OF A DOUBT-- NIGHT-CRAWLER'S GUILT OR INNOCENCE.
Ah! YOU REFER TO THE EYE OF AGAMOTTO?
YOU... KNOW OF THE ALL-SEEING EYE?
AMONG... OTHER THINGS.
YOU ARE NOT THE FIRST CUSTODIAN OF THIS ANCIENT AMULET, Dr. STRANGE, NOR WILL YOU BE THE LAST.
OSHTUR! SHE SUMMONED THE EYE...
...WITH JUST A GESTURE! I COULDN'T PREVENT IT!
WHO IS THIS WOMAN?!?
LET THE EYE OF TRUTH PIERCE THE VEILS OF TIME AND SPACE. LET SHADOWS WALK AND MEMORIES SPEAK.
WOLVERINE. WHAT'S HAPPENING?
BEATS ME, BABE.
IMAGES UNFOLD...
...THE INFANT KURT WAGNER-- BARELY AN HOUR OLD-- FOUND BESIDE HIS DYING MOTHER, TAKEN IN BY THE GYPSY WITCH-QUEEN MARGALI SZARDOS, AND RAISED AS ONE OF HER OWN.
NEVER DID THREE CHILDREN LOVE EACH OTHER AS DID KURT, JEMAINE, AND MARGALI'S FIRST-BORN, STEFAN.
KURT WORSHIPPED HIS OLDER BROTHER. HE WOULD HAVE WILLINGLY DIED FOR HIM. HE WAS ASKED TO DO MUCH WORSE.
WE'RE BLOOD BROTHERS NOW, STEFAN.
YES. AND I FEAR THE DARK SIDE OF MY SOUL.
SWEAR TO ME KURT-- IF I EVER TURN EVIL... IF I EVER TAKE AN INNOCENT LIFE...
...THAT YOU WILL KILL ME.
KURT LAUGHED-- UNTIL HE SAW THAT HIS BROTHER WASN'T JOKING. HE SWORE THE OATH.
ON HIS HONOR. ON HIS IMMORTAL SOUL.
AND SO IT CAME TO PASS, YEARS LATER, OUTSIDE THE BAVARIAN VILLAGE OF WINZELDORF, THAT STEFAN KILLED-- CRUELLY, WANTONLY-- AND KURT FOUGHT TO STOP HIM FROM KILLING AGAIN.

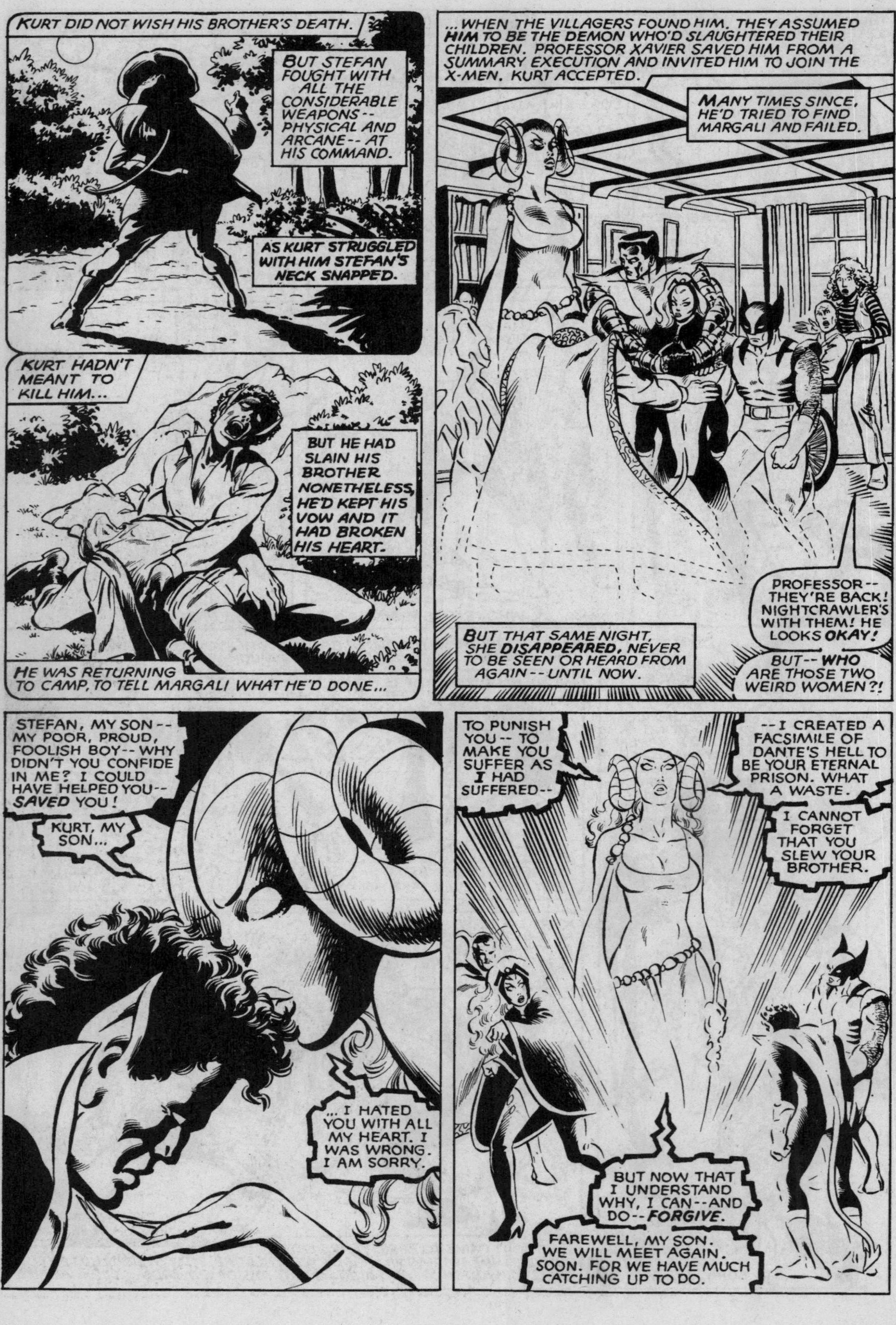
KURT DID NOT WISH HIS BROTHER'S DEATH.
BUT STEFAN FOUGHT WITH ALL THE CONSIDERABLE WEAPONS -- PHYSICAL AND ARCANE -- AT HIS COMMAND.
AS KURT STRUGGLED WITH HIM STEFAN'S NECK SNAPPED.
KURT HADN'T MEANT TO KILL HIM...
BUT HE HAD SLAIN HIS BROTHER NONETHELESS. HE'D KEPT HIS VOW AND IT HAD BROKEN HIS HEART.
HE WAS RETURNING TO CAMP, TO TELL MARGALI WHAT HE'D DONE...
... WHEN THE VILLAGERS FOUND HIM, THEY ASSUMED HIM TO BE THE DEMON WHO'D SLAUGHTERED THEIR CHILDREN. PROFESSOR XAVIER SAVED HIM FROM A SUMMARY EXECUTION AND INVITED HIM TO JOIN THE X-MEN. KURT ACCEPTED.
MANY TIMES SINCE, HE'D TRIED TO FIND MARGALI AND FAILED.
PROFESSOR -- THEY'RE BACK! NIGHTCRAWLER'S WITH THEM! HE LOOKS OKAY!
BUT THAT SAME NIGHT, SHE DISAPPEARED, NEVER TO BE SEEN OR HEARD FROM AGAIN -- UNTIL NOW.
BUT -- WHO ARE THOSE TWO WEIRD WOMEN?!
STEFAN, MY SON -- MY POOR, PROUD, FOOLISH BOY -- WHY DIDN'T YOU CONFIDE IN ME? I COULD HAVE HELPED YOU -- SAVED YOU!
KURT, MY SON...
... I HATED YOU WITH ALL MY HEART. I WAS WRONG. I AM SORRY.
TO PUNISH YOU -- TO MAKE YOU SUFFER AS I HAD SUFFERED --
-- I CREATED A FACSIMILE OF DANTE'S HELL TO BE YOUR ETERNAL PRISON. WHAT A WASTE.
I CANNOT FORGET THAT YOU SLEW YOUR BROTHER.
BUT NOW THAT I UNDERSTAND WHY, I CAN -- AND DO -- FORGIVE.
FAREWELL, MY SON. WE WILL MEET AGAIN. SOON. FOR WE HAVE MUCH CATCHING UP TO DO.

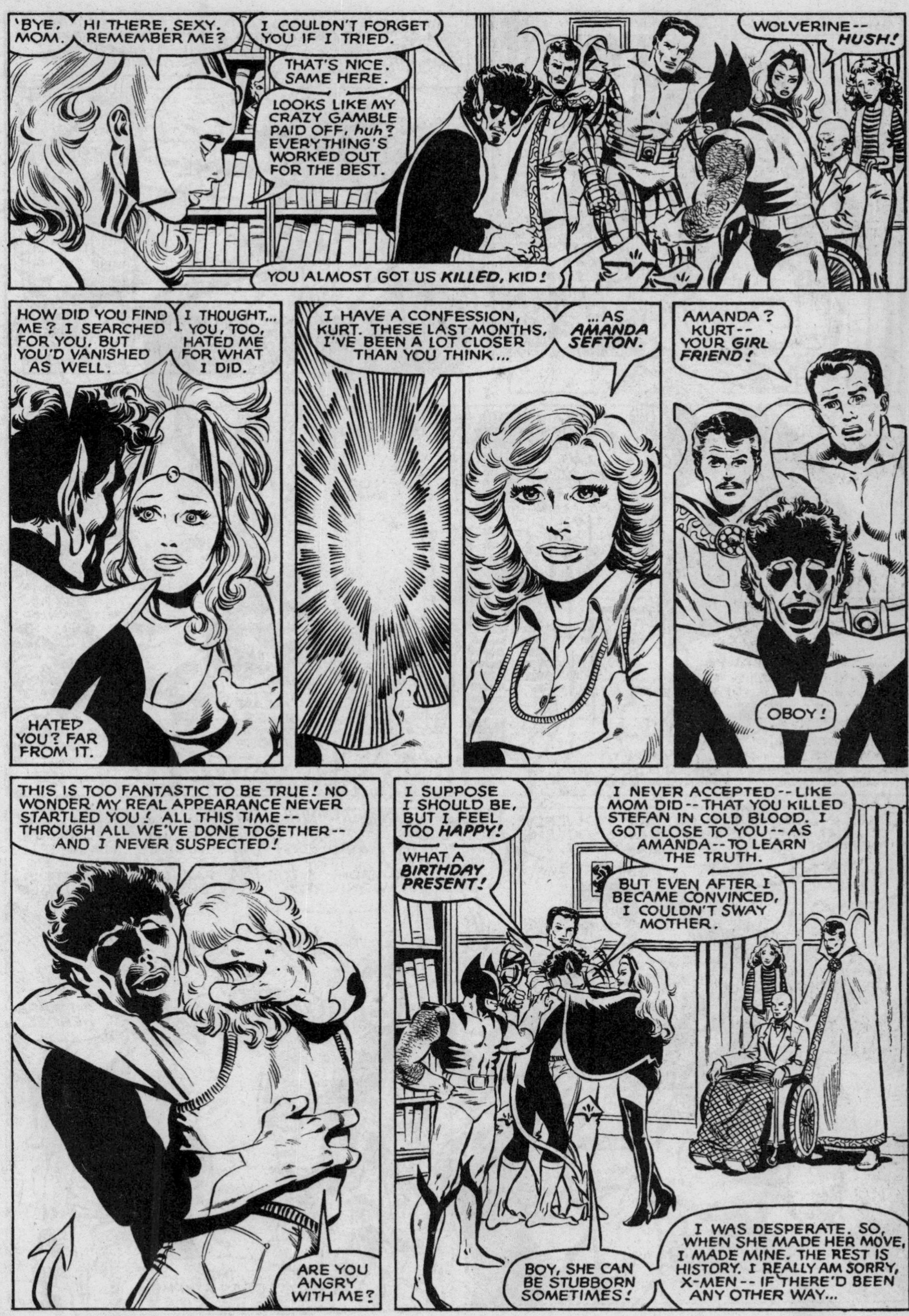
'BYE, MOM.
HI THERE, SEXY. REMEMBER ME?
I COULDN'T FORGET YOU IF I TRIED.
THAT'S NICE. SAME HERE.
LOOKS LIKE MY CRAZY GAMBLE PAID OFF, *huh*? EVERYTHING'S WORKED OUT FOR THE BEST.
WOLVERINE-- ***HUSH!***
YOU ALMOST GOT US ***KILLED***, KID!
HOW DID YOU FIND ME? I SEARCHED FOR YOU, BUT YOU'D VANISHED AS WELL.
I THOUGHT... YOU, TOO, HATED ME FOR WHAT I DID.
HATED YOU? FAR FROM IT.
I HAVE A CONFESSION, KURT. THESE LAST MONTHS, I'VE BEEN A LOT CLOSER THAN YOU THINK...
...AS ***AMANDA SEFTON.***
AMANDA? KURT-- YOUR ***GIRL FRIEND!***
OBOY!
THIS IS TOO FANTASTIC TO BE TRUE! NO WONDER MY REAL APPEARANCE NEVER STARTLED YOU! ALL THIS TIME-- THROUGH ALL WE'VE DONE TOGETHER-- AND I NEVER SUSPECTED!
ARE YOU ANGRY WITH ME?
I SUPPOSE I SHOULD BE, BUT I FEEL TOO ***HAPPY!***
WHAT A ***BIRTHDAY PRESENT!***
I NEVER ACCEPTED--LIKE MOM DID--THAT YOU KILLED STEFAN IN COLD BLOOD. I GOT CLOSE TO YOU--AS AMANDA--TO LEARN THE TRUTH.
BUT EVEN AFTER I BECAME CONVINCED, I COULDN'T SWAY MOTHER.
BOY, SHE CAN BE STUBBORN SOMETIMES!
I WAS DESPERATE. SO, WHEN SHE MADE HER MOVE, I MADE MINE. THE REST IS HISTORY. I REALLY AM SORRY, X-MEN--IF THERE'D BEEN ANY OTHER WAY...

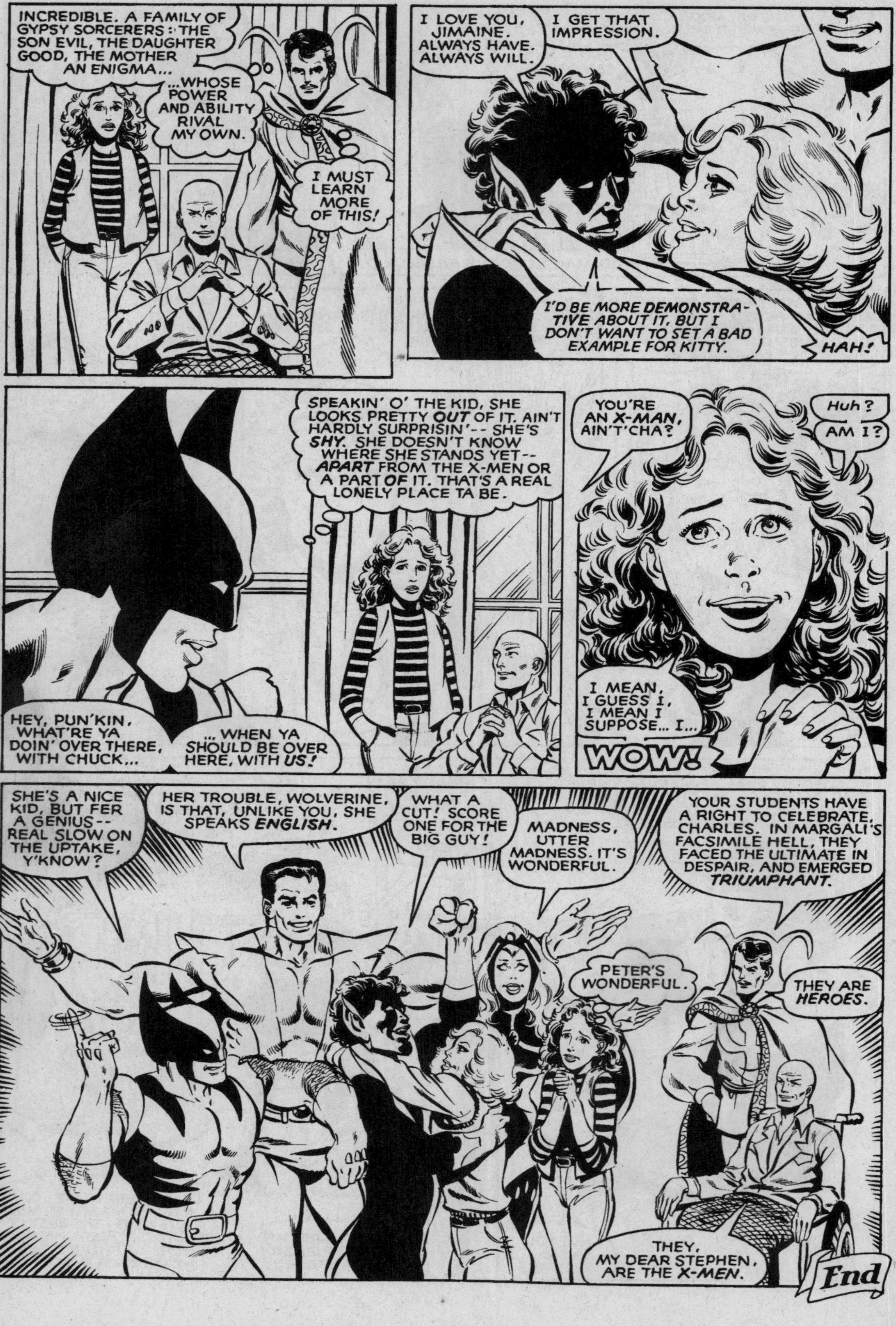
INCREDIBLE. A FAMILY OF GYPSY SORCERERS: THE SON EVIL, THE DAUGHTER GOOD, THE MOTHER AN ENIGMA...
...WHOSE POWER AND ABILITY RIVAL MY OWN.
I MUST LEARN MORE OF THIS!
I LOVE YOU, JIMAINE. ALWAYS HAVE. ALWAYS WILL.
I GET THAT IMPRESSION.
I'D BE MORE DEMONSTRATIVE ABOUT IT, BUT I DON'T WANT TO SET A BAD EXAMPLE FOR KITTY.
HAH!
HEY, PUN'KIN, WHAT'RE YA DOIN' OVER THERE, WITH CHUCK...
SPEAKIN' O' THE KID, SHE LOOKS PRETTY OUT OF IT. AIN'T HARDLY SURPRISIN'-- SHE'S SHY. SHE DOESN'T KNOW WHERE SHE STANDS YET-- APART FROM THE X-MEN OR A PART OF IT. THAT'S A REAL LONELY PLACE TA BE.
... WHEN YA SHOULD BE OVER HERE, WITH US!
YOU'RE AN X-MAN, AIN'T'CHA?
Huh?
AM I?
I MEAN, I GUESS I, I MEAN I SUPPOSE... I...
WOW!
SHE'S A NICE KID, BUT FER A GENIUS-- REAL SLOW ON THE UPTAKE, Y'KNOW?
HER TROUBLE, WOLVERINE, IS THAT, UNLIKE YOU, SHE SPEAKS ENGLISH.
WHAT A CUT! SCORE ONE FOR THE BIG GUY!
MADNESS, UTTER MADNESS. IT'S WONDERFUL.
YOUR STUDENTS HAVE A RIGHT TO CELEBRATE, CHARLES. IN MARGALI'S FACSIMILE HELL, THEY FACED THE ULTIMATE IN DESPAIR, AND EMERGED TRIUMPHANT.
PETER'S WONDERFUL.
THEY ARE HEROES.
THEY, MY DEAR STEPHEN, ARE THE X-MEN.
End

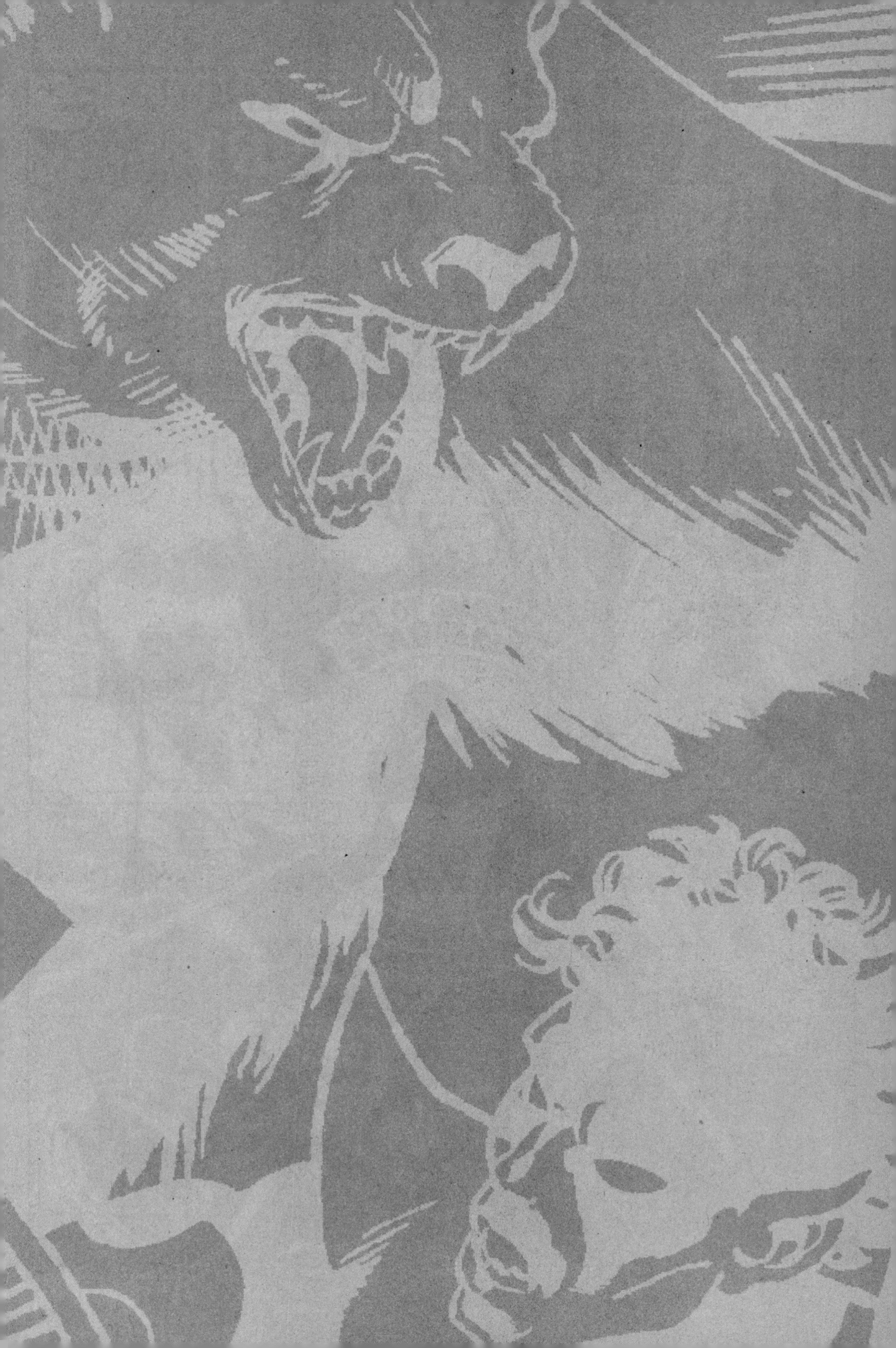

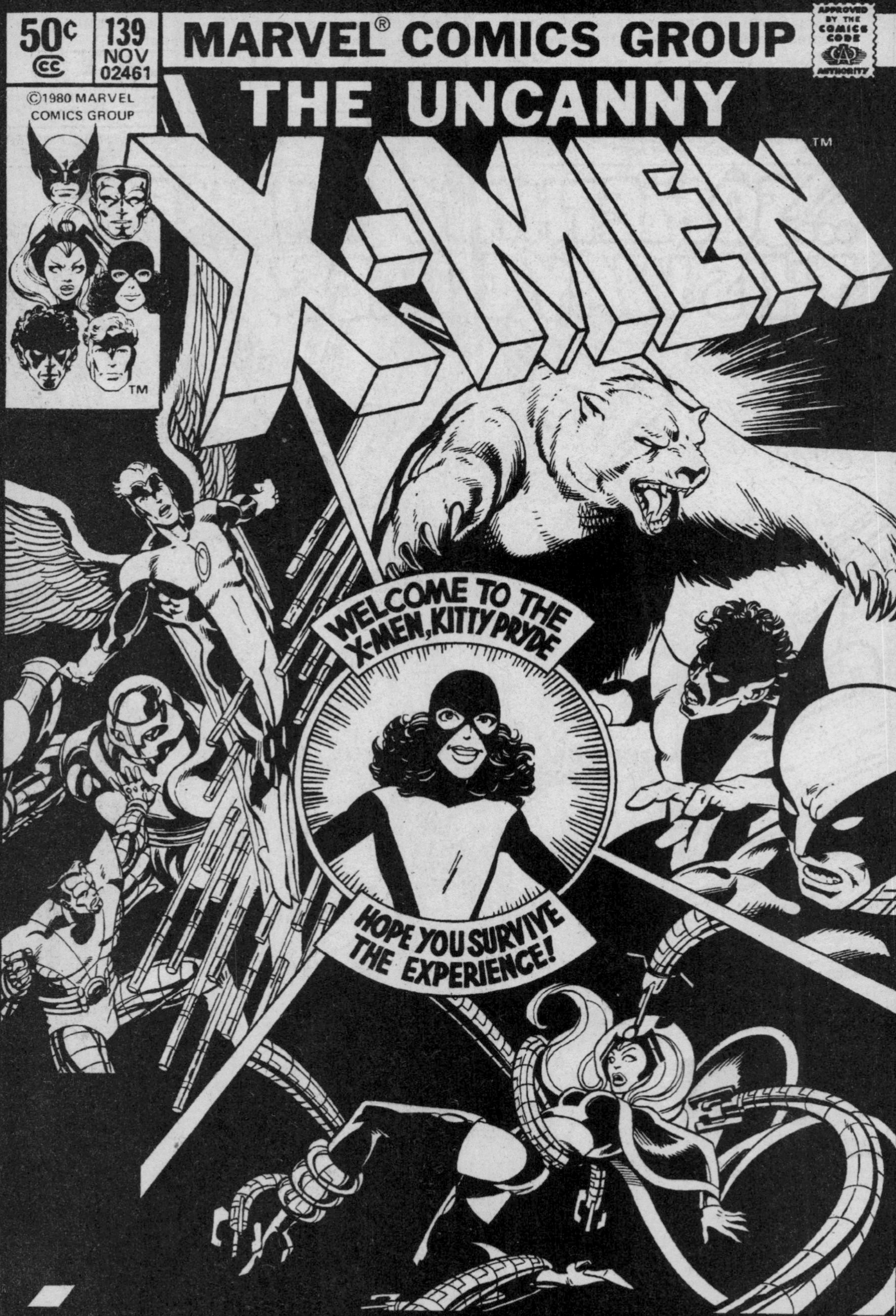
50¢
CC
139
NOV
02461
MARVEL® COMICS GROUP
APPROVED BY THE COMICS CODE AUTHORITY
©1980 MARVEL COMICS GROUP
THE UNCANNY
X-MEN™
WELCOME TO THE X-MEN, KITTY PRYDE
HOPE YOU SURVIVE THE EXPERIENCE!

YOUR FRIEND IS ONE OF THE X-MEN, RIGHT? JAMIE TOLD ME ABOUT THEM AFTER YOU HAD THAT SCRAP IN CALGARY.* THIS IS... NIGHT-CREEPER?

NIGHT-CRAWLER. TAKE A BOW, PAL, AN' MAKE NICE WITH THE LADY. 'TILL I MET YOU CLOWNS, SHE AN' MAC WERE THE ONLY TRUE FRIENDS I EVER HAD.

ENCHANTÉ, MADAME. WITH FRIENDS LIKE YOU, I CAN'T IMAGINE WHERE WOLVERINE DEVELOPED HIS "DELIGHTFUL" PERSONALITY.

CAN IT, FUZZY. OR ELSE.

LOGAN, YOU'RE NOT HERE TO FIGHT MAC AGAIN, ARE YOU?

*X-MEN #'s 120 & 121 -- LOUISE.

I CAME TO MAKE PEACE, HEATHER, IF I CAN.

GOOD. WE THREE HAVE BEEN APART TOO LONG.

HE'S IN THE NORTH COUNTRY-- HUDSON BAY. THERE'S SERIOUS TROUBLE UP THERE, SOMETHING SO DANGEROUS THAT THE MINISTER CALLED IN DEPARTMENT H, AND ALPHA FLIGHT.

TIME PASSES -- AND ALONG THE SHORELINE OF A BAY THAT'S BIGGER THAN MANY STATES, A BALL OF SCARLET FIRE STREAKS ACROSS THE EARLY EVENING SKY...

...SHATTERING THE SUMMERTIME SERENITY OF ONE OF THE MOST BEAUTIFUL WILDERNESS AREAS IN NORTH AMERICA.

IT IS A MAN -- JAMES MacDONALD HUDSON, BY NAME -- WHO, AS VINDICATOR, FORMED AND NOW HEADS THE TEAM OF CANADIAN SUPER-HEROES KNOWN AS ALPHA FLIGHT.

HE HADN'T WANTED THE JOB. THAT HONOR HAD BEEN INTENDED FOR HIS PROTEGE, WOLVERINE.

BUT THINGS HADN'T WORKED OUT THE WAY HE'D INTENDED. THAT FAILURE STILL RANKLES.

I'M BACK IN RECORD TIME. THIS BATTLE SUIT WORKS LIKE A DREAM. I DESIGNED IT AND ITS CAPABILITIES STILL CONTINUALLY AMAZE AND SURPRISE ME.

I ENJOY USING IT, TOO. IT'S BECOME LIKE AN EXTENSION OF MY OWN BODY.

IT'S PUTTING MY LIFE ON THE LINE, AS A MEMBER OF ALPHA FLIGHT, THAT GIVES ME THE WILLIES.

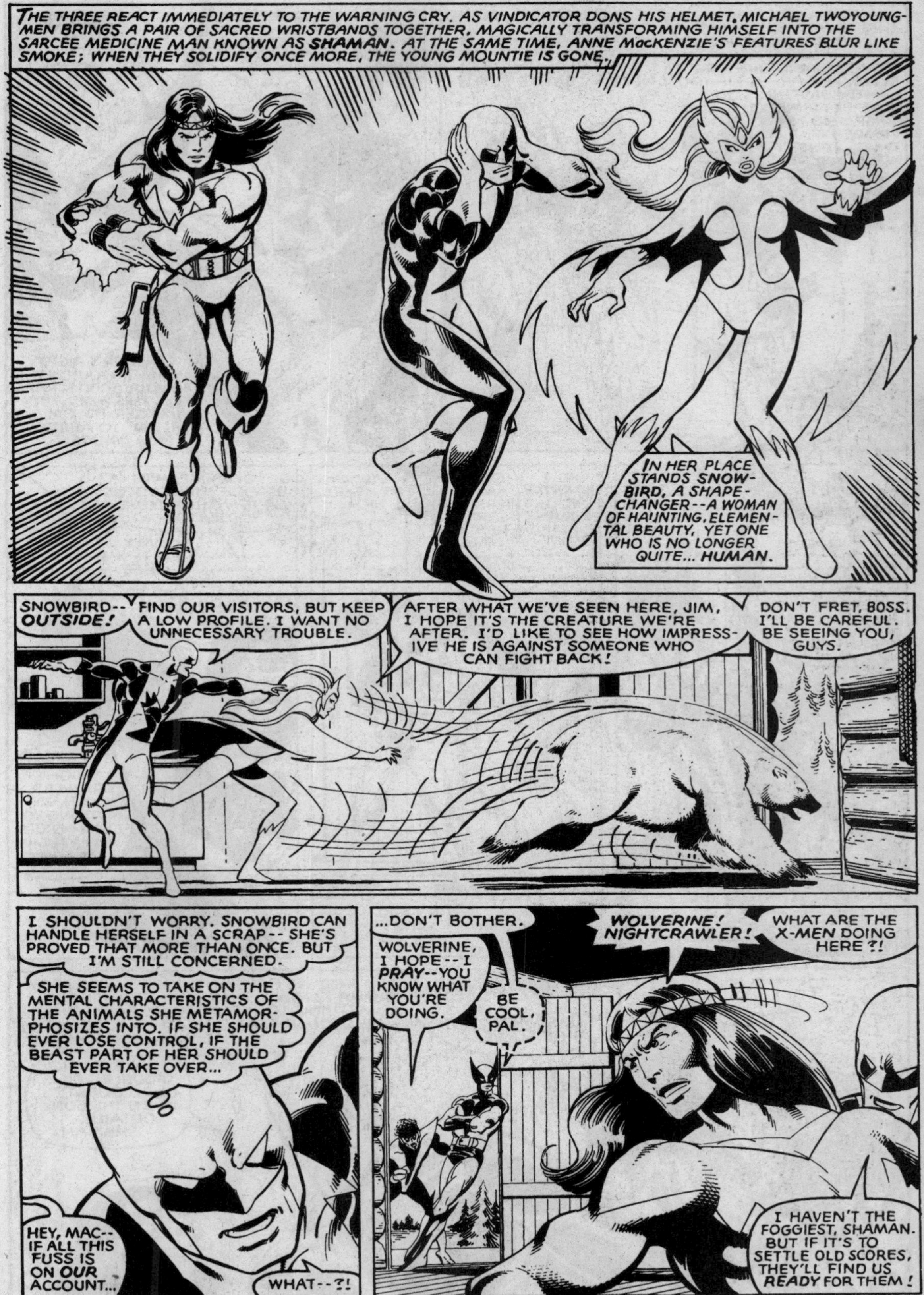
THE THREE REACT IMMEDIATELY TO THE WARNING CRY. AS VINDICATOR DONS HIS HELMET, MICHAEL TWOYOUNGMEN BRINGS A PAIR OF SACRED WRISTBANDS TOGETHER, MAGICALLY TRANSFORMING HIMSELF INTO THE SARCEE MEDICINE MAN KNOWN AS SHAMAN. AT THE SAME TIME, ANNE MacKENZIE'S FEATURES BLUR LIKE SMOKE; WHEN THEY SOLIDIFY ONCE MORE, THE YOUNG MOUNTIE IS GONE...
IN HER PLACE STANDS SNOWBIRD, A SHAPE-CHANGER--A WOMAN OF HAUNTING, ELEMENTAL BEAUTY, YET ONE WHO IS NO LONGER QUITE... HUMAN.
SNOWBIRD-- OUTSIDE!
FIND OUR VISITORS, BUT KEEP A LOW PROFILE. I WANT NO UNNECESSARY TROUBLE.
AFTER WHAT WE'VE SEEN HERE, JIM, I HOPE IT'S THE CREATURE WE'RE AFTER. I'D LIKE TO SEE HOW IMPRESSIVE HE IS AGAINST SOMEONE WHO CAN FIGHT BACK!
DON'T FRET, BOSS. I'LL BE CAREFUL. BE SEEING YOU, GUYS.
I SHOULDN'T WORRY. SNOWBIRD CAN HANDLE HERSELF IN A SCRAP-- SHE'S PROVED THAT MORE THAN ONCE. BUT I'M STILL CONCERNED.
SHE SEEMS TO TAKE ON THE MENTAL CHARACTERISTICS OF THE ANIMALS SHE METAMORPHOSIZES INTO. IF SHE SHOULD EVER LOSE CONTROL, IF THE BEAST PART OF HER SHOULD EVER TAKE OVER...
HEY, MAC-- IF ALL THIS FUSS IS ON OUR ACCOUNT...
WHAT--?!
...DON'T BOTHER.
WOLVERINE, I HOPE--I PRAY--YOU KNOW WHAT YOU'RE DOING.
BE COOL, PAL.
WOLVERINE! NIGHTCRAWLER!
WHAT ARE THE X-MEN DOING HERE?!
I HAVEN'T THE FOGGIEST, SHAMAN. BUT IF IT'S TO SETTLE OLD SCORES, THEY'LL FIND US READY FOR THEM!

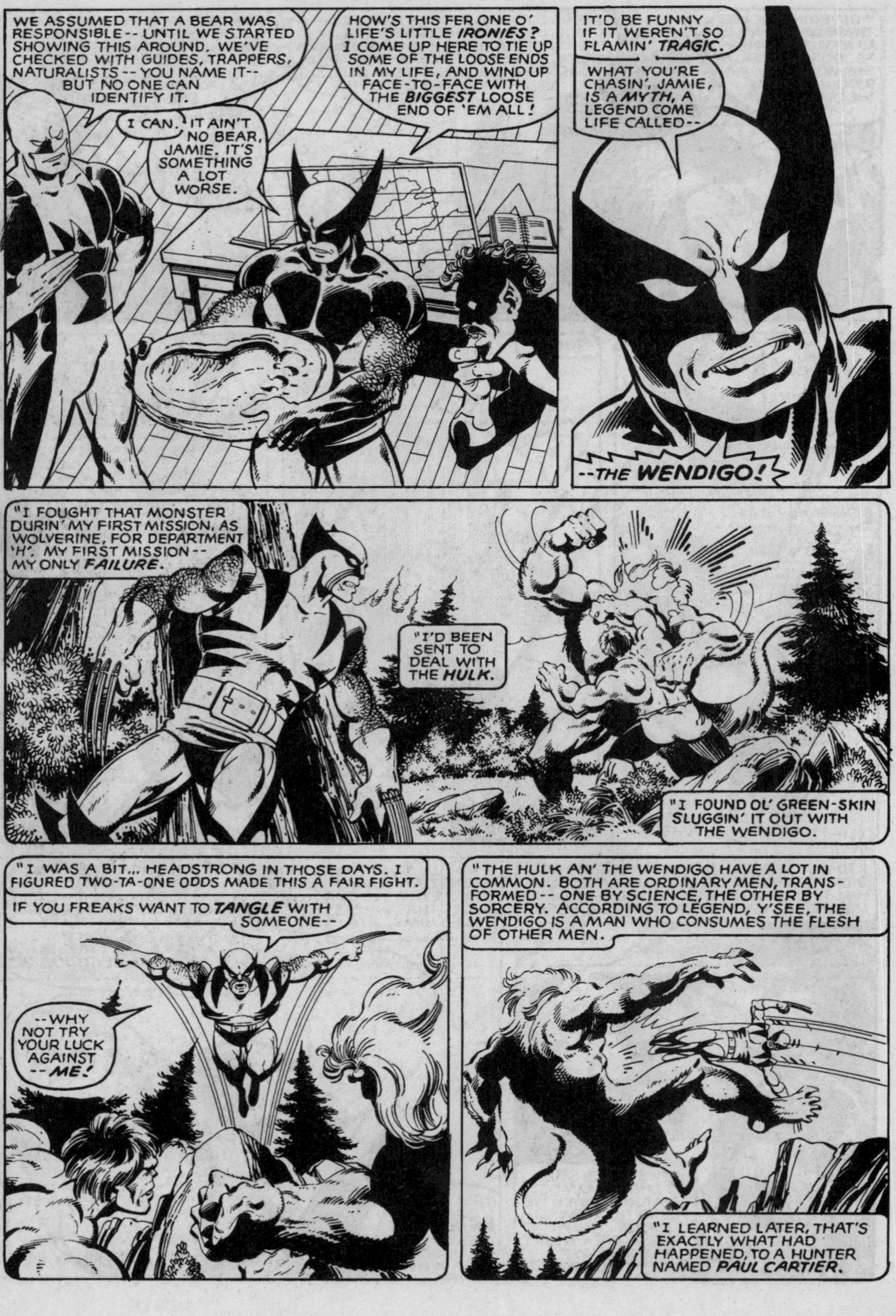
WE ASSUMED THAT A BEAR WAS RESPONSIBLE -- UNTIL WE STARTED SHOWING THIS AROUND. WE'VE CHECKED WITH GUIDES, TRAPPERS, NATURALISTS -- YOU NAME IT -- BUT NO ONE CAN IDENTIFY IT.
I CAN.
IT AIN'T NO BEAR, JAMIE. IT'S SOMETHING A LOT WORSE.
HOW'S THIS FER ONE O' LIFE'S LITTLE IRONIES? I COME UP HERE TO TIE UP SOME OF THE LOOSE ENDS IN MY LIFE, AND WIND UP FACE-TO-FACE WITH THE BIGGEST LOOSE END OF 'EM ALL!
IT'D BE FUNNY IF IT WEREN'T SO FLAMIN' TRAGIC.
WHAT YOU'RE CHASIN', JAMIE, IS A MYTH, A LEGEND COME LIFE CALLED--
--THE WENDIGO!
"I FOUGHT THAT MONSTER DURIN' MY FIRST MISSION, AS WOLVERINE, FOR DEPARTMENT 'H'. MY FIRST MISSION -- MY ONLY FAILURE.
"I'D BEEN SENT TO DEAL WITH THE HULK.
"I FOUND OL' GREEN-SKIN SLUGGIN' IT OUT WITH THE WENDIGO.
"I WAS A BIT... HEADSTRONG IN THOSE DAYS. I FIGURED TWO-TA-ONE ODDS MADE THIS A FAIR FIGHT.
IF YOU FREAKS WANT TO TANGLE WITH SOMEONE--
--WHY NOT TRY YOUR LUCK AGAINST --ME!
"THE HULK AN' THE WENDIGO HAVE A LOT IN COMMON. BOTH ARE ORDINARY MEN, TRANSFORMED -- ONE BY SCIENCE, THE OTHER BY SORCERY. ACCORDING TO LEGEND, Y'SEE, THE WENDIGO IS A MAN WHO CONSUMES THE FLESH OF OTHER MEN.
"I LEARNED LATER, THAT'S EXACTLY WHAT HAD HAPPENED, TO A HUNTER NAMED PAUL CARTIER.

"HE AND SOME FRIENDS HAD BEEN TRAPPED BY WOLVES. ONE OF THE PARTY DIED. THEY HAD NO FOOD. FACED WITH STARVATION, CARTIER TURNED *CANNIBAL*-- AN' THE ANCIENT CURSE O' THE NORTH WOODS TRANSFORMED HIM INTO THE WENDIGO:"

"WHAT I DIDN'T KNOW THEN WAS THAT CARTIER'S *SISTER* WAS TRYING TO SAVE HIM. WITH THE HELP OF HIS BEST FRIEND, *GEORGES BAPTISTE*, SHE INTENDED TO USE BLACK MAGIC TO SHIFT THE WENDIGO-CURSE FROM CARTIER TO THE HULK."

KROOM!

WEN-DI-GO!

"IT WAS A CRAZY FIGHT. I WAS HACKIN' AWAY LIKE A MAD-MAN, CONSUMED BY ONE O' MY *BERSERKER RAGES*."

"BETWEEN ME AN' THE HULK, WE MANAGED TO KNOCK WENDIGO UNCONSCIOUS. WITH HIM OUT OF THE WAY, I WAS FREE TO COMPLETE MY ORIGINAL MISSION: TO STOP THE HULK, ANY WAY I COULD."

"IN THE END, ALL I DID WAS MAKE HIM ANGRY."

"BY RIGHTS, I SHOULD HAVE BEATEN THOSE TWO FREAKS TO A PULP, OR CUT 'EM INTO SHISH-KEBAB. BUT NO MATTER HOW HARD I TRIED, I COULDN'T HURT EITHER OF 'EM. THEY WERE BOTH DARN NEAR *INVULNERABLE*."

"WE NEVER FINISHED THAT FIGHT. MARIE CARTIER HIT US WITH SOME SORT OF MAGIC WHAMMY-- INSTANT DREAMLAND. SHE NEVER GOT HER CHANCE TO ZAP THE HULK, THOUGH. BAPTISTE CAST THE BIG SPELL, INSTEAD OF HER, TAKING THE HULK'S PLACE FOR THE TRANSFORMATION."

"WHEN THE DUST SETTLED, CARTIER WAS CURED, MARIE INSANE, AND BAPTISTE HAD BE-CALLED BY DEPARTMENT H; THE HULK AND WENDIGO ESCAPED. *

*PRECEEDING FLASHBACK COURTESY OF HULK #'S 162, 180 & 181 -- LOUISE.

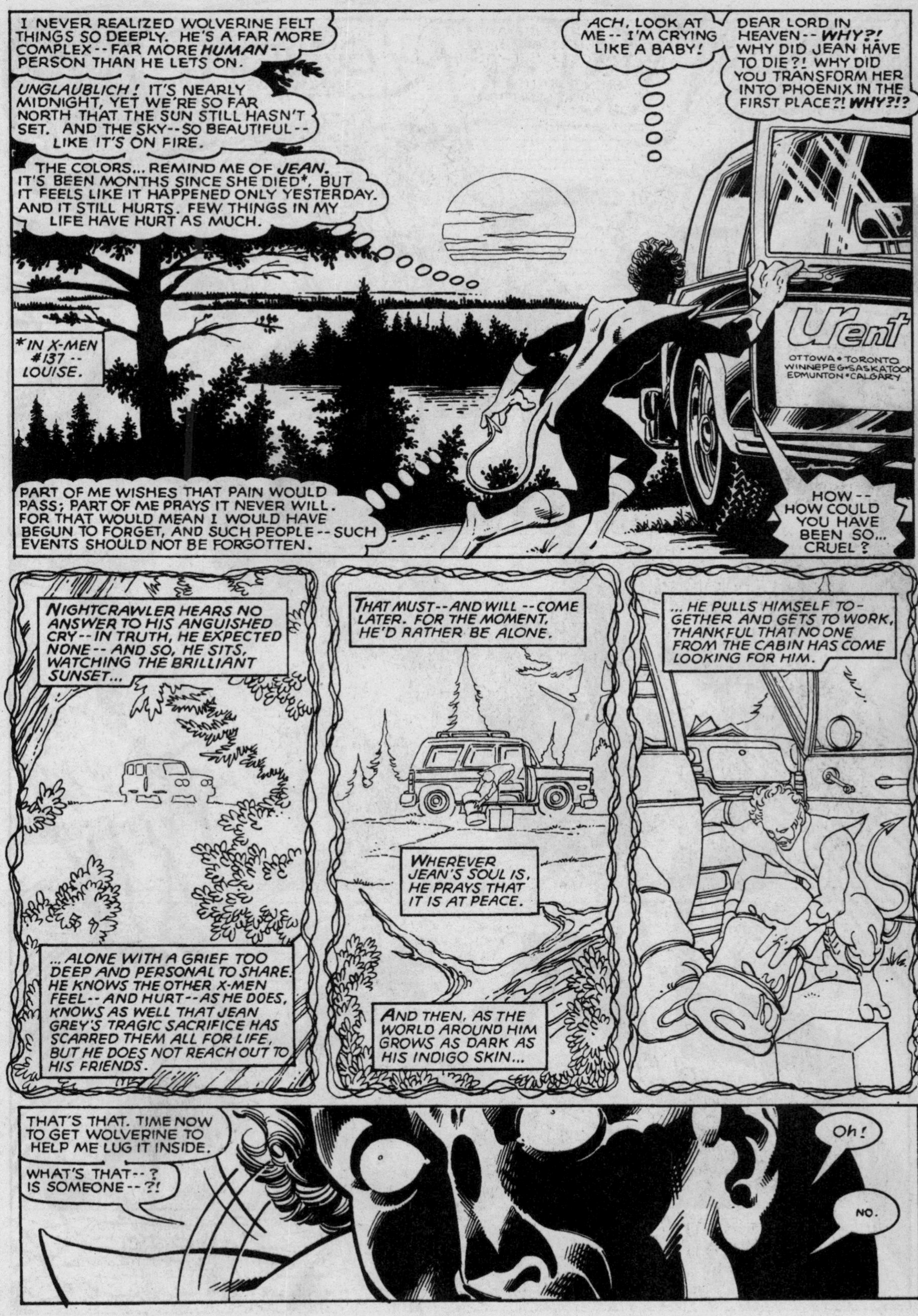

I NEVER REALIZED WOLVERINE FELT THINGS SO DEEPLY. HE'S A FAR MORE COMPLEX -- FAR MORE HUMAN -- PERSON THAN HE LETS ON.
UNGLAUBLICH! IT'S NEARLY MIDNIGHT, YET WE'RE SO FAR NORTH THAT THE SUN STILL HASN'T SET. AND THE SKY -- SO BEAUTIFUL -- LIKE IT'S ON FIRE.
THE COLORS... REMIND ME OF JEAN. IT'S BEEN MONTHS SINCE SHE DIED*, BUT IT FEELS LIKE IT HAPPENED ONLY YESTERDAY. AND IT STILL HURTS. FEW THINGS IN MY LIFE HAVE HURT AS MUCH.
ACH, LOOK AT ME -- I'M CRYING LIKE A BABY!
DEAR LORD IN HEAVEN -- WHY?! WHY DID JEAN HAVE TO DIE?! WHY DID YOU TRANSFORM HER INTO PHOENIX IN THE FIRST PLACE?! WHY?!?
*IN X-MEN #137 -- LOUISE.
URent
OTTOWA • TORONTO WINNEPEG • SASKATOON EDMUNTON • CALGARY
PART OF ME WISHES THAT PAIN WOULD PASS; PART OF ME PRAYS IT NEVER WILL. FOR THAT WOULD MEAN I WOULD HAVE BEGUN TO FORGET, AND SUCH PEOPLE -- SUCH EVENTS SHOULD NOT BE FORGOTTEN.
HOW -- HOW COULD YOU HAVE BEEN SO... CRUEL?
NIGHTCRAWLER HEARS NO ANSWER TO HIS ANGUISHED CRY -- IN TRUTH, HE EXPECTED NONE -- AND SO, HE SITS, WATCHING THE BRILLIANT SUNSET...
...ALONE WITH A GRIEF TOO DEEP AND PERSONAL TO SHARE. HE KNOWS THE OTHER X-MEN FEEL -- AND HURT -- AS HE DOES, KNOWS AS WELL THAT JEAN GREY'S TRAGIC SACRIFICE HAS SCARRED THEM ALL FOR LIFE, BUT HE DOES NOT REACH OUT TO HIS FRIENDS.
THAT MUST -- AND WILL -- COME LATER. FOR THE MOMENT, HE'D RATHER BE ALONE.
WHEREVER JEAN'S SOUL IS, HE PRAYS THAT IT IS AT PEACE.
AND THEN, AS THE WORLD AROUND HIM GROWS AS DARK AS HIS INDIGO SKIN...
...HE PULLS HIMSELF TOGETHER AND GETS TO WORK, THANKFUL THAT NO ONE FROM THE CABIN HAS COME LOOKING FOR HIM.
THAT'S THAT. TIME NOW TO GET WOLVERINE TO HELP ME LUG IT INSIDE.
WHAT'S THAT --? IS SOMEONE --?!
Oh!
NO.

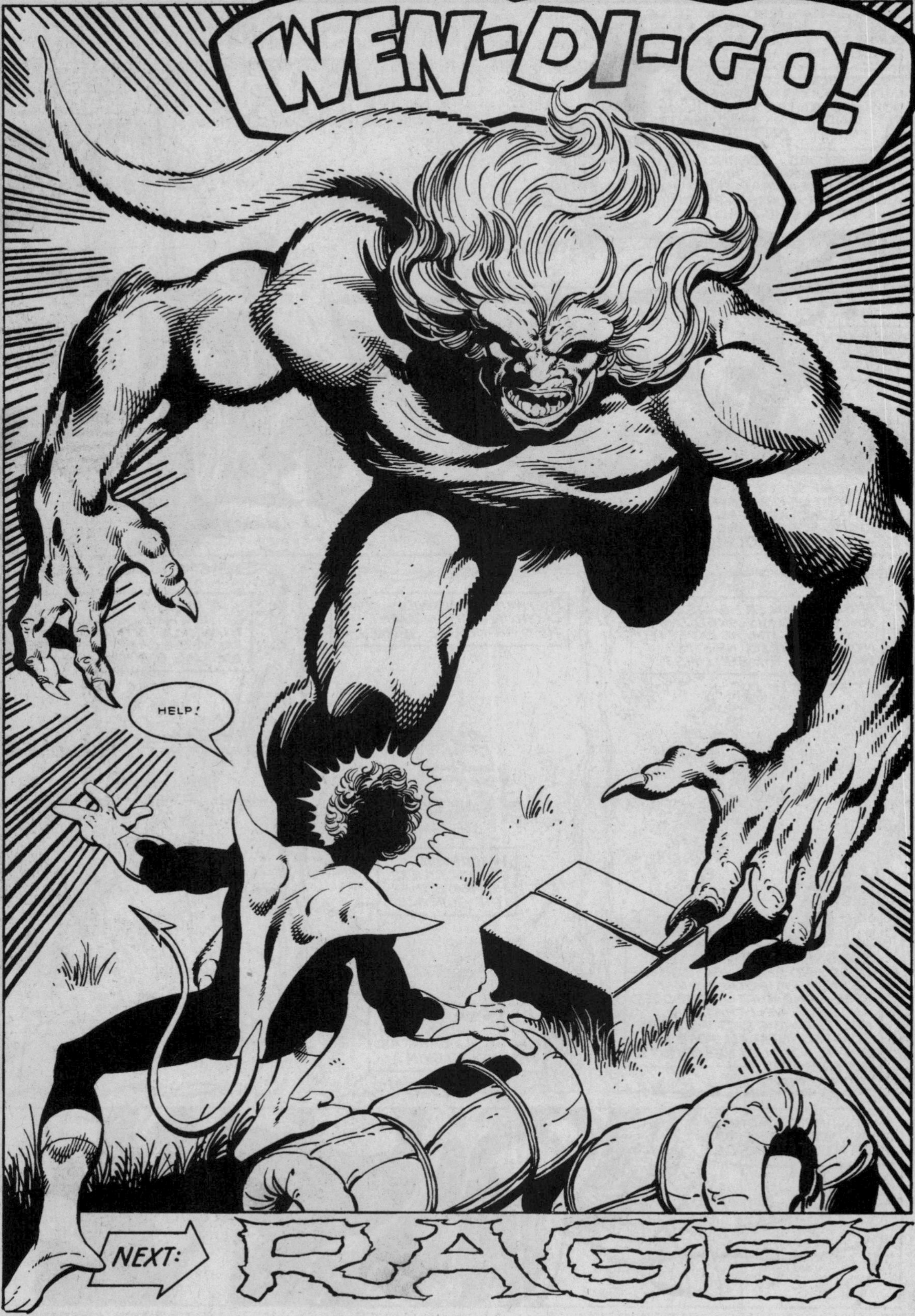
WEN-DI-GO!
HELP!
NEXT:
RAGE!

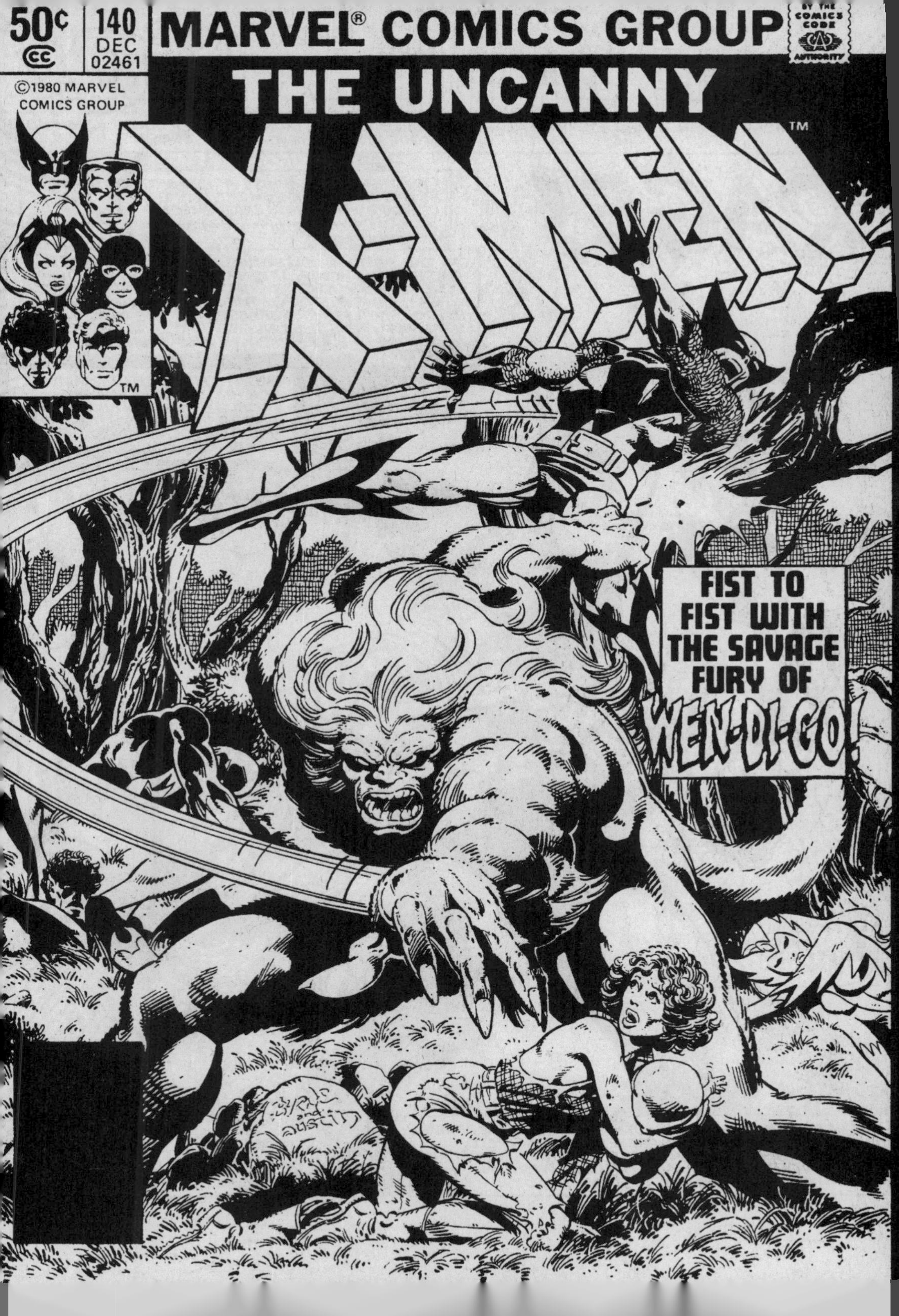
50¢
CC
140
DEC
02461
MARVEL® COMICS GROUP
BY THE COMICS CODE AUTHORITY
©1980 MARVEL COMICS GROUP
THE UNCANNY
X-MEN™
TM
FIST TO FIST WITH THE SAVAGE FURY OF
WEN-DI-GO!

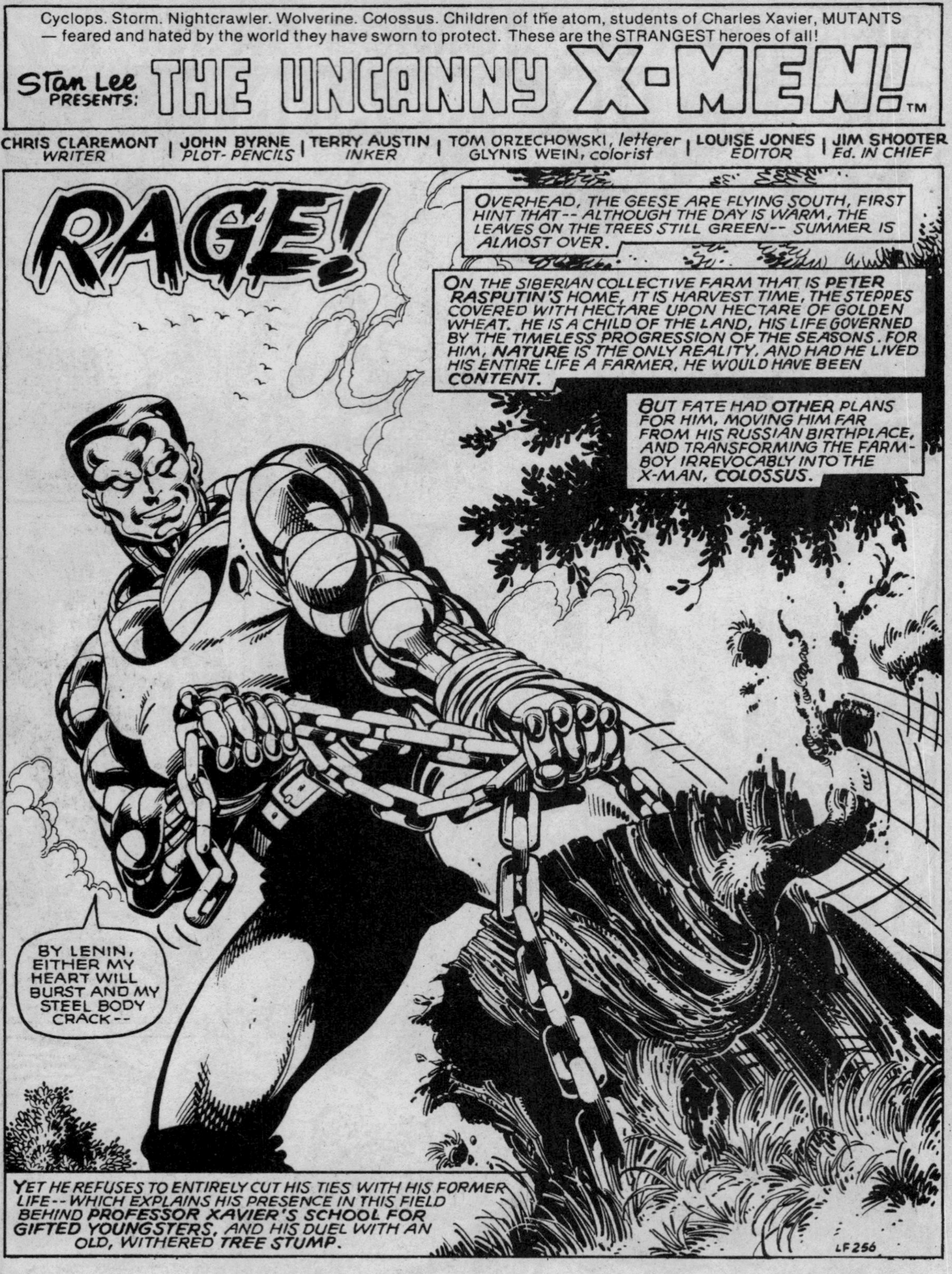
Cyclops. Storm. Nightcrawler. Wolverine. Colossus. Children of the atom, students of Charles Xavier, MUTANTS — feared and hated by the world they have sworn to protect. These are the STRANGEST heroes of all!
Stan Lee PRESENTS:
THE UNCANNY X-MEN!™
CHRIS CLAREMONT WRITER | JOHN BYRNE PLOT-PENCILS | TERRY AUSTIN INKER | TOM ORZECHOWSKI, letterer GLYNIS WEIN, colorist | LOUISE JONES EDITOR | JIM SHOOTER Ed. IN CHIEF
RAGE!
OVERHEAD, THE GEESE ARE FLYING SOUTH, FIRST HINT THAT-- ALTHOUGH THE DAY IS WARM, THE LEAVES ON THE TREES STILL GREEN-- SUMMER IS ALMOST OVER.
ON THE SIBERIAN COLLECTIVE FARM THAT IS PETER RASPUTIN'S HOME, IT IS HARVEST TIME, THE STEPPES COVERED WITH HECTARE UPON HECTARE OF GOLDEN WHEAT. HE IS A CHILD OF THE LAND, HIS LIFE GOVERNED BY THE TIMELESS PROGRESSION OF THE SEASONS. FOR HIM, NATURE IS THE ONLY REALITY, AND HAD HE LIVED HIS ENTIRE LIFE A FARMER, HE WOULD HAVE BEEN CONTENT.
BUT FATE HAD OTHER PLANS FOR HIM, MOVING HIM FAR FROM HIS RUSSIAN BIRTHPLACE, AND TRANSFORMING THE FARM-BOY IRREVOCABLY INTO THE X-MAN, COLOSSUS.
BY LENIN, EITHER MY HEART WILL BURST AND MY STEEL BODY CRACK--
YET HE REFUSES TO ENTIRELY CUT HIS TIES WITH HIS FORMER LIFE-- WHICH EXPLAINS HIS PRESENCE IN THIS FIELD BEHIND PROFESSOR XAVIER'S SCHOOL FOR GIFTED YOUNGSTERS, AND HIS DUEL WITH AN OLD, WITHERED TREE STUMP.
LF 256

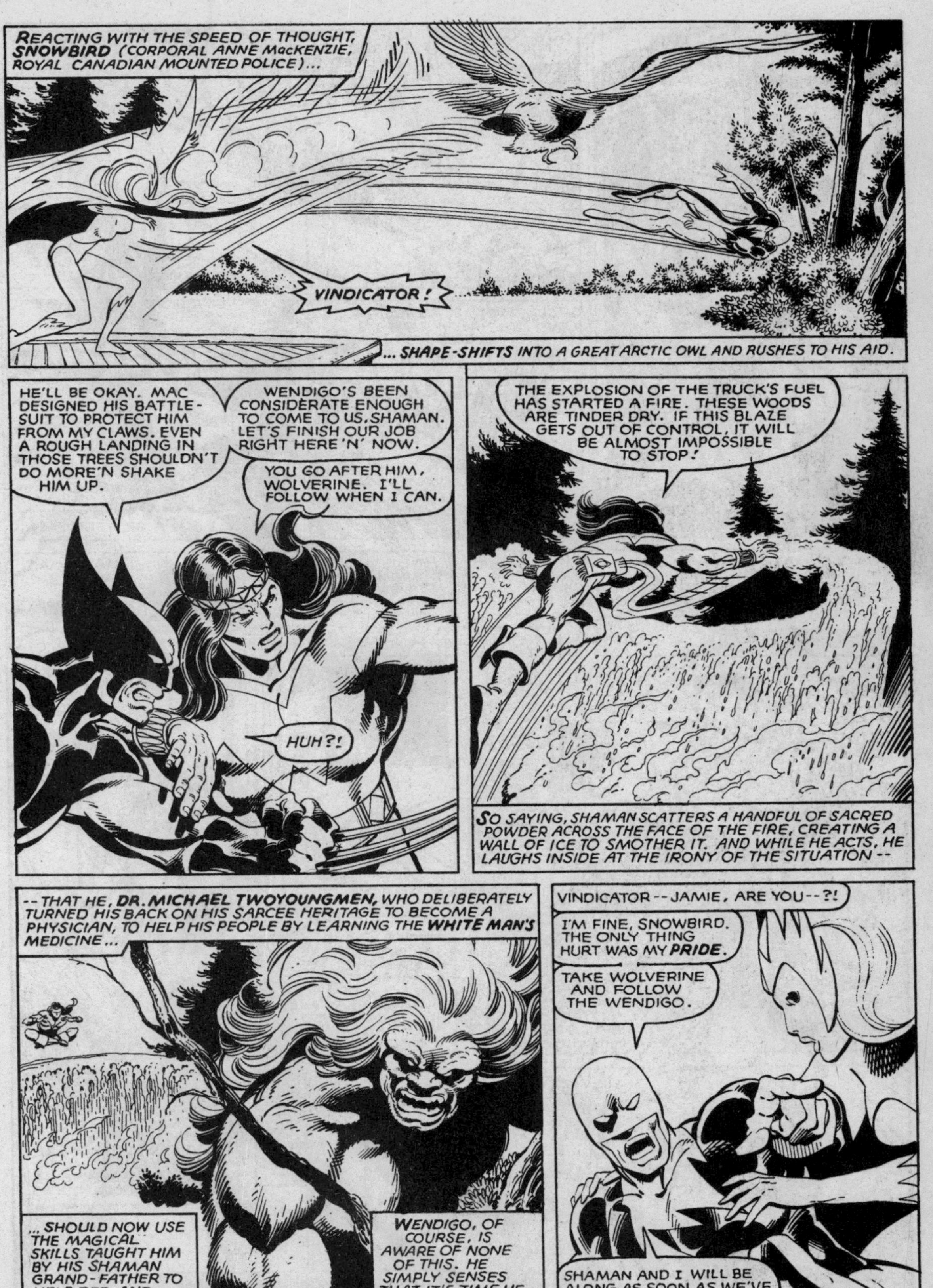
REACTING WITH THE SPEED OF THOUGHT, SNOWBIRD (CORPORAL ANNE MacKENZIE, ROYAL CANADIAN MOUNTED POLICE)...
VINDICATOR!
...SHAPE-SHIFTS INTO A GREAT ARCTIC OWL AND RUSHES TO HIS AID.
HE'LL BE OKAY. MAC DESIGNED HIS BATTLE-SUIT TO PROTECT HIM FROM MY CLAWS. EVEN A ROUGH LANDING IN THOSE TREES SHOULDN'T DO MORE'N SHAKE HIM UP.
WENDIGO'S BEEN CONSIDERATE ENOUGH TO COME TO US, SHAMAN. LET'S FINISH OUR JOB RIGHT HERE 'N' NOW.
YOU GO AFTER HIM, WOLVERINE. I'LL FOLLOW WHEN I CAN.
HUH?!
THE EXPLOSION OF THE TRUCK'S FUEL HAS STARTED A FIRE. THESE WOODS ARE TINDER DRY. IF THIS BLAZE GETS OUT OF CONTROL, IT WILL BE ALMOST IMPOSSIBLE TO STOP!
SO SAYING, SHAMAN SCATTERS A HANDFUL OF SACRED POWDER ACROSS THE FACE OF THE FIRE, CREATING A WALL OF ICE TO SMOTHER IT. AND WHILE HE ACTS, HE LAUGHS INSIDE AT THE IRONY OF THE SITUATION --
-- THAT HE, DR. MICHAEL TWOYOUNGMEN, WHO DELIBERATELY TURNED HIS BACK ON HIS SARCEE HERITAGE TO BECOME A PHYSICIAN, TO HELP HIS PEOPLE BY LEARNING THE WHITE MAN'S MEDICINE...
...SHOULD NOW USE THE MAGICAL SKILLS TAUGHT HIM BY HIS SHAMAN GRAND-FATHER TO HELP RED AND WHITE MEN BOTH!
WENDIGO, OF COURSE, IS AWARE OF NONE OF THIS. HE SIMPLY SENSES THAT IT'S TIME HE MADE HIS EXIT.
VINDICATOR -- JAMIE, ARE YOU --?!
I'M FINE, SNOWBIRD. THE ONLY THING HURT WAS MY PRIDE.
TAKE WOLVERINE AND FOLLOW THE WENDIGO.
SHAMAN AND I WILL BE ALONG AS SOON AS WE'VE EXTINGUISHED THE FIRE.

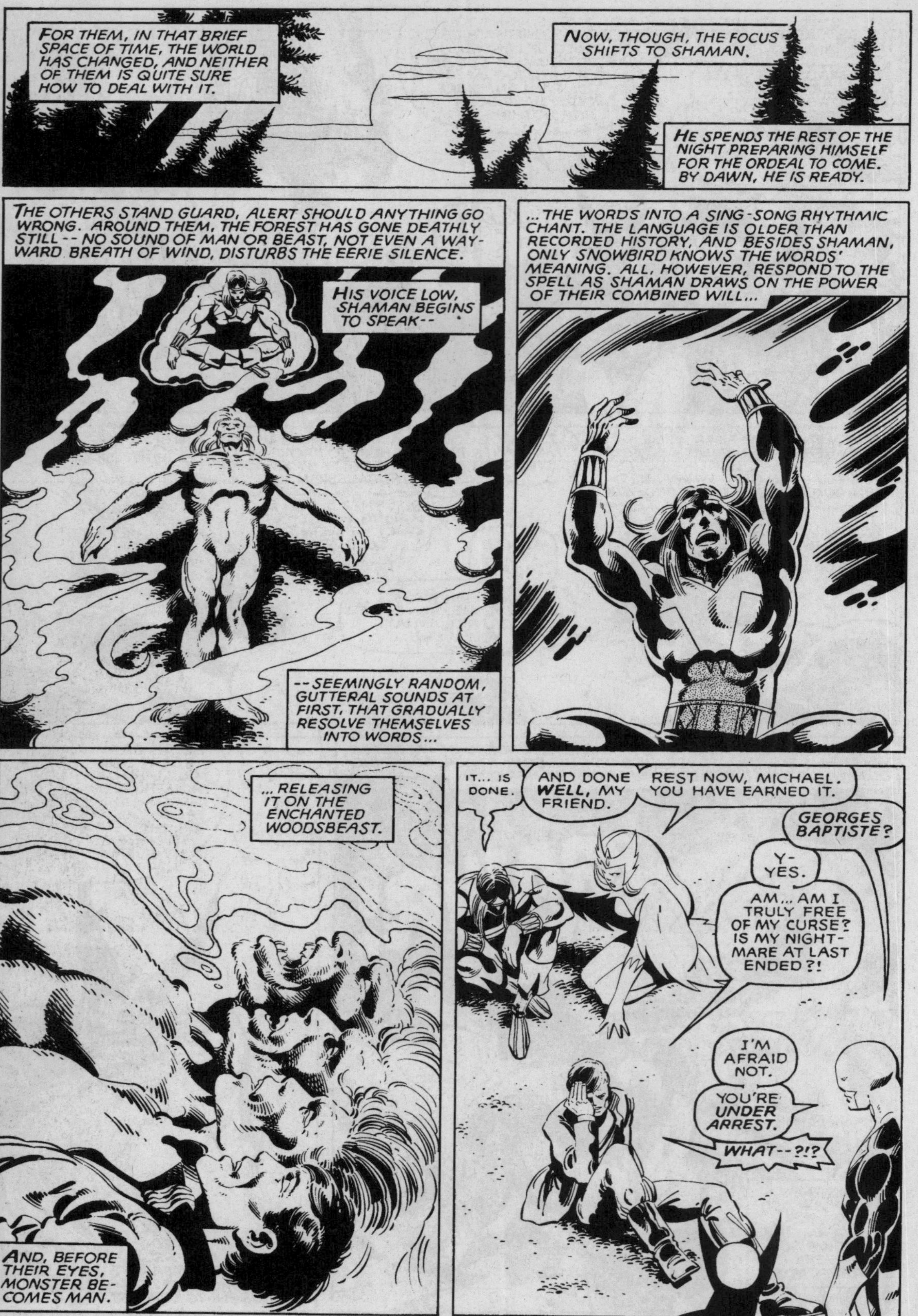
FOR THEM, IN THAT BRIEF SPACE OF TIME, THE WORLD HAS CHANGED, AND NEITHER OF THEM IS QUITE SURE HOW TO DEAL WITH IT.
NOW, THOUGH, THE FOCUS SHIFTS TO SHAMAN.
HE SPENDS THE REST OF THE NIGHT PREPARING HIMSELF FOR THE ORDEAL TO COME. BY DAWN, HE IS READY.
THE OTHERS STAND GUARD, ALERT SHOULD ANYTHING GO WRONG. AROUND THEM, THE FOREST HAS GONE DEATHLY STILL -- NO SOUND OF MAN OR BEAST, NOT EVEN A WAYWARD BREATH OF WIND, DISTURBS THE EERIE SILENCE.
HIS VOICE LOW, SHAMAN BEGINS TO SPEAK--
--SEEMINGLY RANDOM, GUTTERAL SOUNDS AT FIRST, THAT GRADUALLY RESOLVE THEMSELVES INTO WORDS...
...THE WORDS INTO A SING-SONG RHYTHMIC CHANT. THE LANGUAGE IS OLDER THAN RECORDED HISTORY, AND BESIDES SHAMAN, ONLY SNOWBIRD KNOWS THE WORDS' MEANING. ALL, HOWEVER, RESPOND TO THE SPELL AS SHAMAN DRAWS ON THE POWER OF THEIR COMBINED WILL...
...RELEASING IT ON THE ENCHANTED WOODSBEAST.
AND, BEFORE THEIR EYES, MONSTER BECOMES MAN.
IT... IS DONE.
AND DONE WELL, MY FRIEND.
REST NOW, MICHAEL. YOU HAVE EARNED IT.
GEORGES BAPTISTE?
Y-YES.
AM... AM I TRULY FREE OF MY CURSE? IS MY NIGHTMARE AT LAST ENDED?!
I'M AFRAID NOT.
YOU'RE UNDER ARREST.
WHAT--?!?

... AND THE FEW TIMES HE DOES SPEAK, DURING THEIR LEISURELY MEANDER -- A VACATION BY ANY OTHER NAME -- HOME, HIS TONE IS THOUGHTFUL. NIGHTCRAWLER'S WORDS -- HIS FINAL QUESTION -- STRUCK DEEP.

NOW -- LIKE IT OR NOT, FOR BETTER OR WORSE -- WOLVERINE MUST DEAL WITH THEM.

MEANWHILE, IN THE PARLIAMENT BUILDING IN OTTAWA ...

YOU WANTED TO SEE ME, PRIME MINISTER?

YES, Dr. HUDSON. FIRSTLY, I'D LIKE TO CONGRATULATE ALPHA FLIGHT FOR YOUR HANDLING OF THIS "WENDIGO" BUSINESS. YOU DID WELL. I WISH I HAD A ... BETTER REWARD.

SIR?

THERE'S NO EASY WAY TO SAY THIS. I'M AFRAID DEPARTMENT H AND ALPHA FLIGHT ARE BEING DISBANDED.

TIMES ARE HARD. MONEY IS IN SHORT SUPPLY. THE HOUSE FELT THAT SUPER-HEROES WERE A LUXURY THE FEDERAL GOVERNMENT COULD NO LONGER AFFORD.

MANY MEMBERS -- LIKE THEIR CONSTITUENTS -- HAVE NEVER FELT ENTIRELY ... COMFORTABLE WITH THE IDEA OF SUPER-BEINGS. THE CURRENT ANTI-MUTANT SENTIMENT IN THE UNITED STATES IS A GOOD EXAMPLE OF THAT.

REGRETTABLY, IGNORING YOUR EXISTENCE -- AS MANY ARE TRYING TO DO -- WILL NOT MAKE YOU DISAPPEAR.

THE GENIE IS OUT OF THE BOTTLE. PANDORA'S BOX IS OPEN. WE MUST LIVE WITH THIS REALITY AS BEST WE CAN. IF FOR NO OTHER REASON THAN THAT WE HAVE NO OTHER CHOICE.

I'M SORRY, JAMES. I WILL GIVE YOU AND ALPHA FLIGHT WHAT AID I CAN. YOU CAN KEEP YOUR SECURITY CLEARANCES AND YOUR STATUS AS R.C.M.P. AUXILIARIES. I WISH I COULD DO MORE.

I KNOW, SIR. DON'T WORRY, THOUGH. WE'LL MANAGE. SOMEHOW. WE'VE WORKED AND FOUGHT TOO HARD TO CHUCK EVERY-THING NOW.

THAT'S THE SPIRIT.

VINDICATOR -- WHATEVER HAPPENS, I PRAY YOU'LL KEEP THE WELFARE OF CANADA AND HER PEOPLE FOREMOST IN YOUR THOUGHTS AND ACTIONS.

I WILL, PRIME MINISTER. AND I HOPE YOU'RE RIGHT. GOOD-BYE.

IN TIME, THEY WILL COME TO RESPECT -- AND HONOR -- YOU AND ALPHA FLIGHT, AS I DO.

AN ENDING OF SORTS, YET ALSO A BEGINNING -- OF A NEW, POSSIBLY BRIGHTER CHAP-TER IN THE LIFE OF ALPHA FLIGHT.

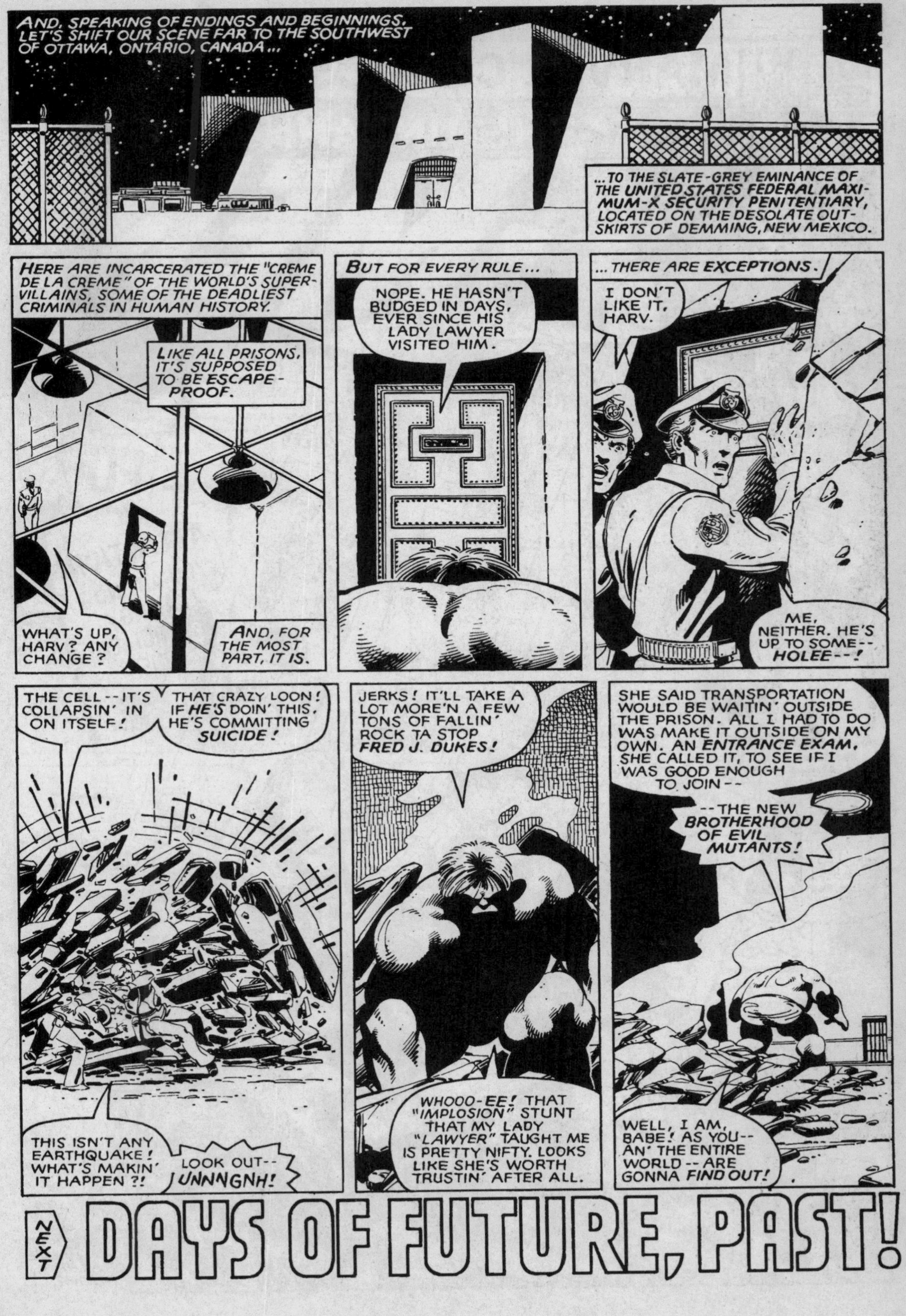

AND, SPEAKING OF ENDINGS AND BEGINNINGS, LET'S SHIFT OUR SCENE FAR TO THE SOUTHWEST OF OTTAWA, ONTARIO, CANADA...
...TO THE SLATE-GREY EMINANCE OF THE UNITED STATES FEDERAL MAXIMUM-X SECURITY PENITENTIARY, LOCATED ON THE DESOLATE OUTSKIRTS OF DEMMING, NEW MEXICO.
HERE ARE INCARCERATED THE "CREME DE LA CREME" OF THE WORLD'S SUPER-VILLAINS, SOME OF THE DEADLIEST CRIMINALS IN HUMAN HISTORY.
LIKE ALL PRISONS, IT'S SUPPOSED TO BE ESCAPE-PROOF.
WHAT'S UP, HARV? ANY CHANGE?
AND, FOR THE MOST PART, IT IS.
BUT FOR EVERY RULE...
NOPE. HE HASN'T BUDGED IN DAYS, EVER SINCE HIS LADY LAWYER VISITED HIM.
...THERE ARE EXCEPTIONS.
I DON'T LIKE IT, HARV.
ME, NEITHER. HE'S UP TO SOME-- HOLEE--!
THE CELL--IT'S COLLAPSIN' IN ON ITSELF!
THAT CRAZY LOON! IF HE'S DOIN' THIS, HE'S COMMITTING SUICIDE!
THIS ISN'T ANY EARTHQUAKE! WHAT'S MAKIN' IT HAPPEN?!
LOOK OUT-- UNNNGNH!
JERKS! IT'LL TAKE A LOT MORE'N A FEW TONS OF FALLIN' ROCK TA STOP FRED J. DUKES!
WHOOO-EE! THAT "IMPLOSION" STUNT THAT MY LADY "LAWYER" TAUGHT ME IS PRETTY NIFTY. LOOKS LIKE SHE'S WORTH TRUSTIN' AFTER ALL.
SHE SAID TRANSPORTATION WOULD BE WAITIN' OUTSIDE THE PRISON. ALL I HAD TO DO WAS MAKE IT OUTSIDE ON MY OWN. AN ENTRANCE EXAM, SHE CALLED IT, TO SEE IF I WAS GOOD ENOUGH TO JOIN--
--THE NEW BROTHERHOOD OF EVIL MUTANTS!
WELL, I AM, BABE! AS YOU-- AN' THE ENTIRE WORLD--ARE GONNA FIND OUT!
NEXT
DAYS OF FUTURE, PAST!

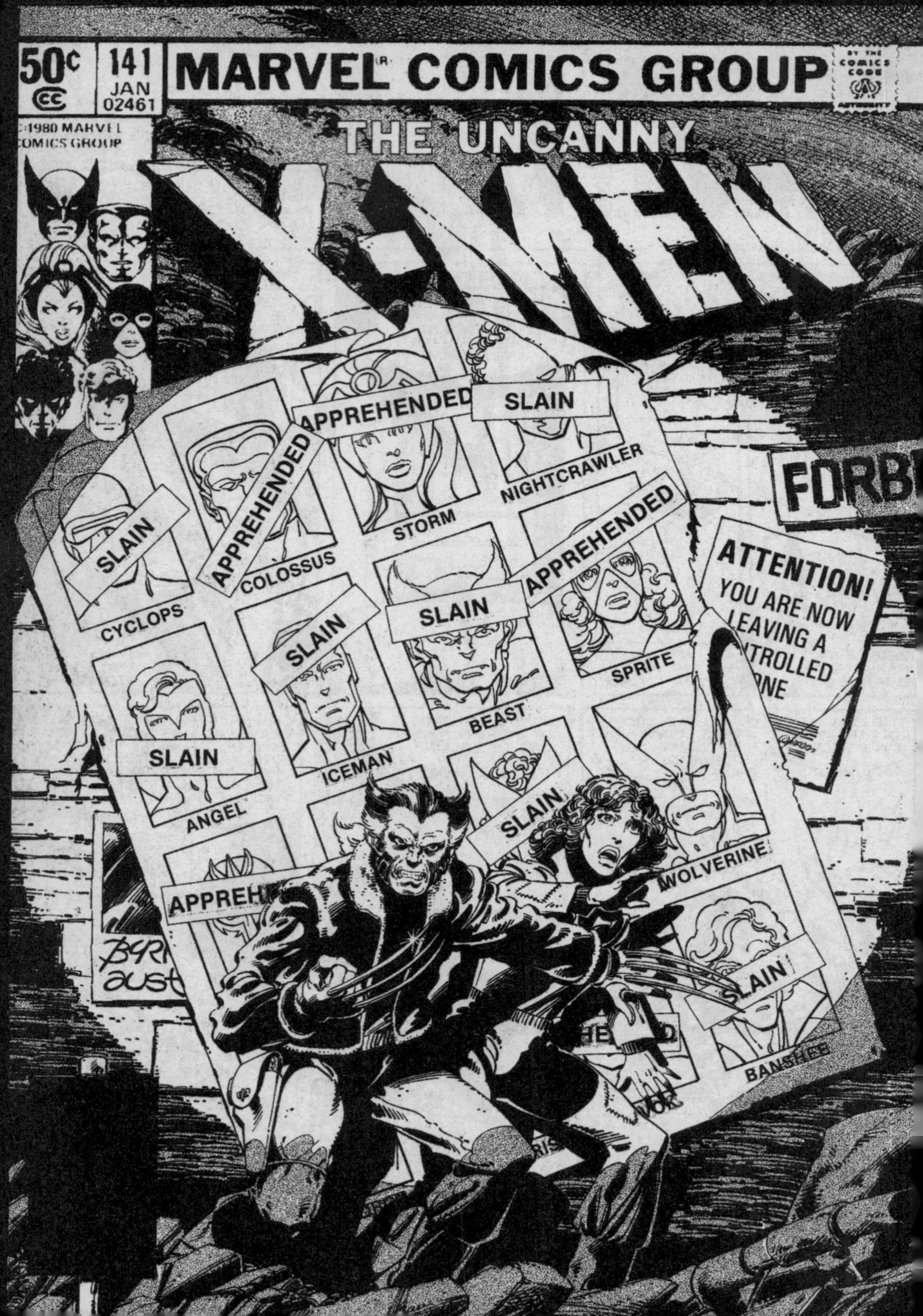

50¢
141
JAN
02461
MARVEL COMICS GROUP
©1980 MARVEL COMICS GROUP
THE UNCANNY
X-MEN
APPREHENDED
SLAIN
NIGHTCRAWLER
STORM
APPREHENDED
SLAIN
COLOSSUS
CYCLOPS
FORB
ATTENTION!
YOU ARE NOW
LEAVING A
TROLLED
ONE
APPREHENDED
SLAIN
SLAIN
SPRITE
BEAST
SLAIN
ICEMAN
ANGEL
SLAIN
WOLVERINE
APPREH
SLAIN
BANSHEE

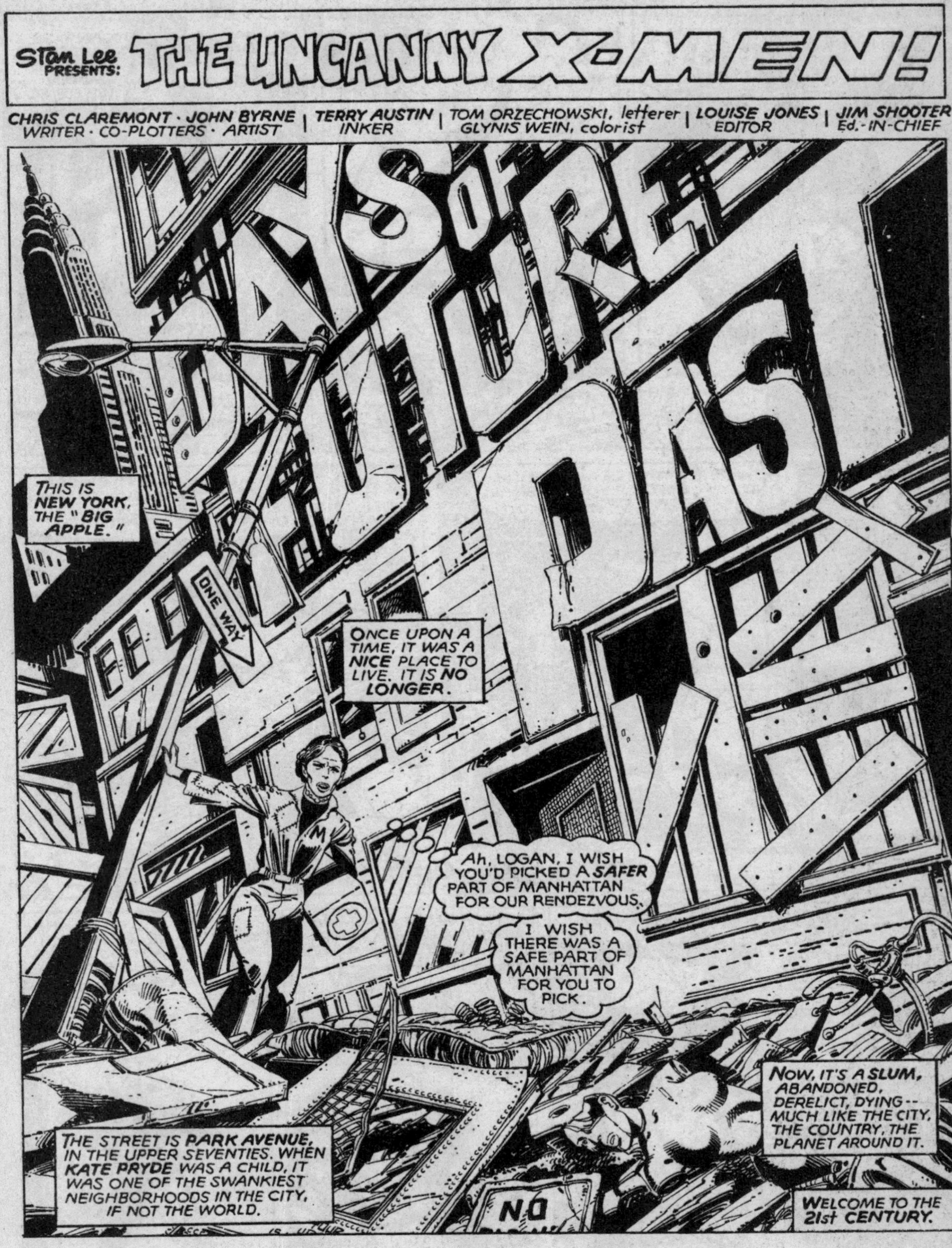

Stan Lee PRESENTS: THE UNCANNY X-MEN!
CHRIS CLAREMONT · JOHN BYRNE WRITER · CO-PLOTTERS · ARTIST | TERRY AUSTIN INKER | TOM ORZECHOWSKI, letterer GLYNIS WEIN, colorist | LOUISE JONES EDITOR | JIM SHOOTER Ed.-IN-CHIEF
DAYS OF FUTURE PAST
THIS IS NEW YORK, THE "BIG APPLE."
ONE WAY
ONCE UPON A TIME, IT WAS A NICE PLACE TO LIVE. IT IS NO LONGER.
Ah, LOGAN, I WISH YOU'D PICKED A SAFER PART OF MANHATTAN FOR OUR RENDEZVOUS.
I WISH THERE WAS A SAFE PART OF MANHATTAN FOR YOU TO PICK.
THE STREET IS PARK AVENUE, IN THE UPPER SEVENTIES. WHEN KATE PRYDE WAS A CHILD, IT WAS ONE OF THE SWANKIEST NEIGHBORHOODS IN THE CITY, IF NOT THE WORLD.
NOW, IT'S A SLUM, ABANDONED, DERELICT, DYING-- MUCH LIKE THE CITY, THE COUNTRY, THE PLANET AROUND IT.
NO
WELCOME TO THE 21st CENTURY.

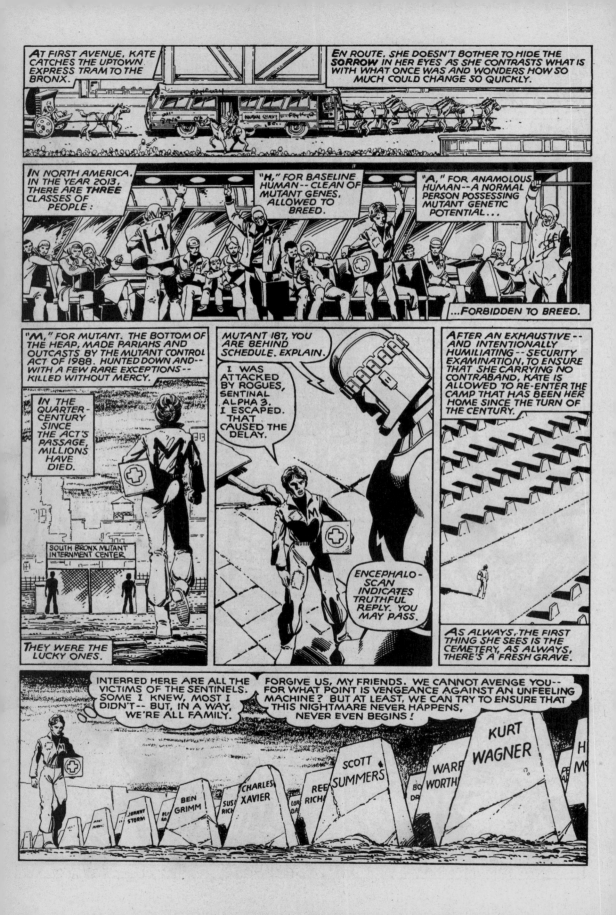

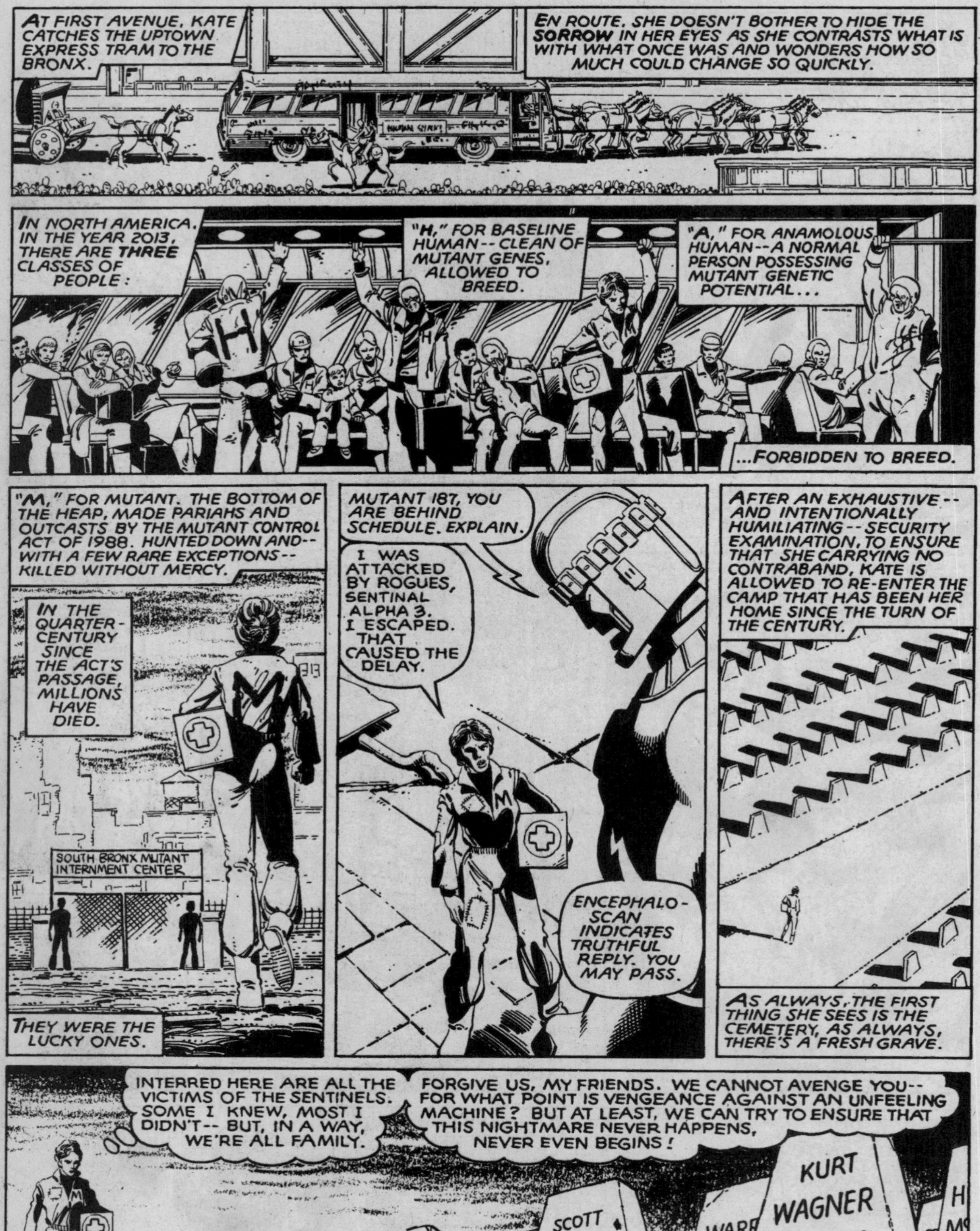
AT FIRST AVENUE, KATE CATCHES THE UPTOWN EXPRESS TRAM TO THE BRONX.
EN ROUTE, SHE DOESN'T BOTHER TO HIDE THE SORROW IN HER EYES AS SHE CONTRASTS WHAT IS WITH WHAT ONCE WAS AND WONDERS HOW SO MUCH COULD CHANGE SO QUICKLY.
IN NORTH AMERICA, IN THE YEAR 2013, THERE ARE THREE CLASSES OF PEOPLE:
"H," FOR BASELINE HUMAN--CLEAN OF MUTANT GENES, ALLOWED TO BREED.
"A," FOR ANAMOLOUS HUMAN--A NORMAL PERSON POSSESSING MUTANT GENETIC POTENTIAL...
...FORBIDDEN TO BREED.
"M," FOR MUTANT. THE BOTTOM OF THE HEAP, MADE PARIAHS AND OUTCASTS BY THE MUTANT CONTROL ACT OF 1988. HUNTED DOWN AND--WITH A FEW RARE EXCEPTIONS--KILLED WITHOUT MERCY.
IN THE QUARTER-CENTURY SINCE THE ACT'S PASSAGE, MILLIONS HAVE DIED.
SOUTH BRONX MUTANT INTERNMENT CENTER
THEY WERE THE LUCKY ONES.
MUTANT 187, YOU ARE BEHIND SCHEDULE. EXPLAIN.
I WAS ATTACKED BY ROGUES, SENTINAL ALPHA 3. I ESCAPED. THAT CAUSED THE DELAY.
ENCEPHALO-SCAN INDICATES TRUTHFUL REPLY. YOU MAY PASS.
AFTER AN EXHAUSTIVE--AND INTENTIONALLY HUMILIATING--SECURITY EXAMINATION, TO ENSURE THAT SHE CARRYING NO CONTRABAND, KATE IS ALLOWED TO RE-ENTER THE CAMP THAT HAS BEEN HER HOME SINCE THE TURN OF THE CENTURY.
AS ALWAYS, THE FIRST THING SHE SEES IS THE CEMETERY, AS ALWAYS, THERE'S A FRESH GRAVE.
INTERRED HERE ARE ALL THE VICTIMS OF THE SENTINELS. SOME I KNEW, MOST I DIDN'T--BUT, IN A WAY, WE'RE ALL FAMILY.
FORGIVE US, MY FRIENDS. WE CANNOT AVENGE YOU--FOR WHAT POINT IS VENGEANCE AGAINST AN UNFEELING MACHINE? BUT AT LEAST, WE CAN TRY TO ENSURE THAT THIS NIGHTMARE NEVER HAPPENS, NEVER EVEN BEGINS!
JOHNNY STORM
BEN GRIMM
CHARLES XAVIER
SCOTT SUMMERS
KURT WAGNER

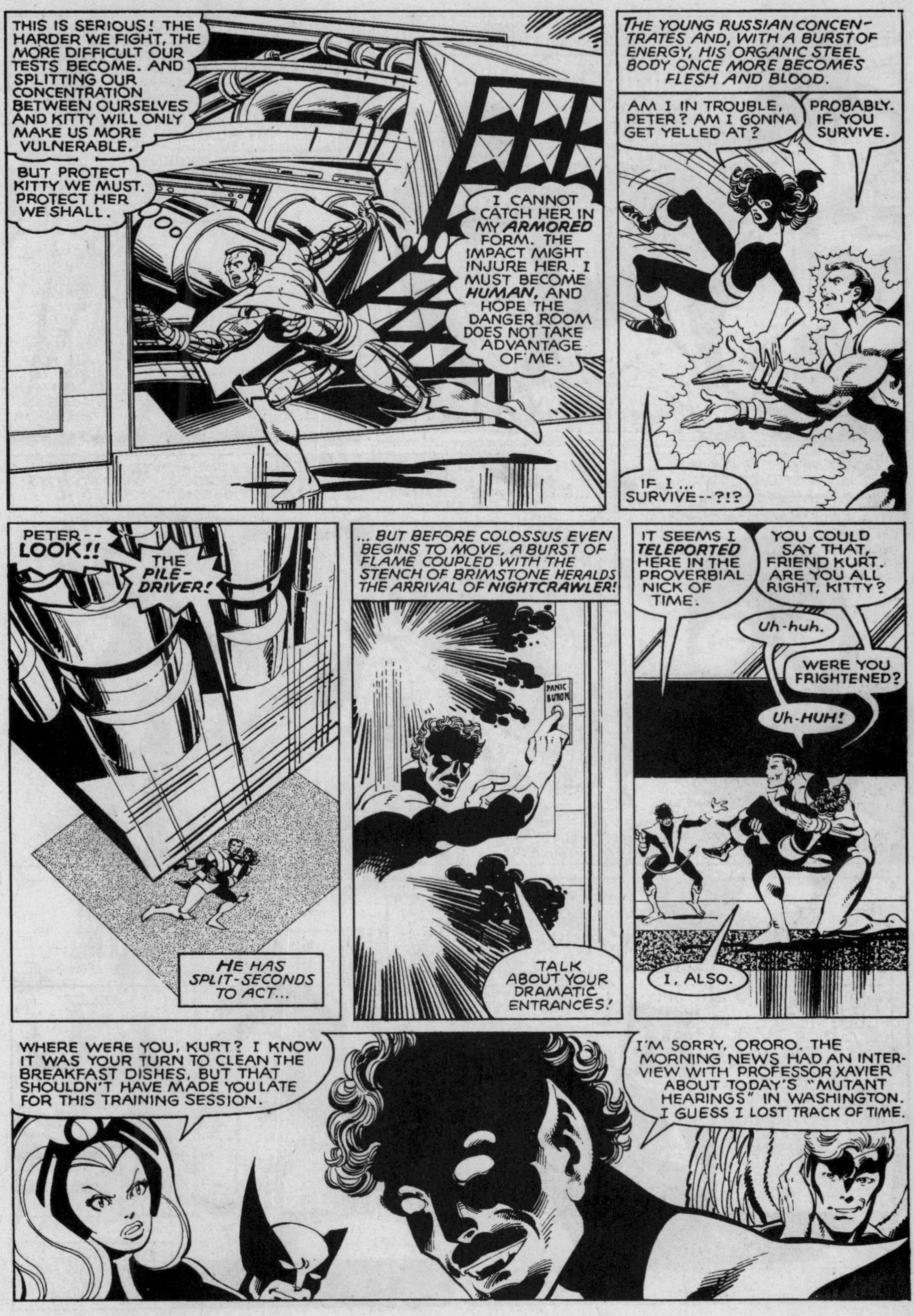
THIS IS SERIOUS! THE HARDER WE FIGHT, THE MORE DIFFICULT OUR TESTS BECOME. AND SPLITTING OUR CONCENTRATION BETWEEN OURSELVES AND KITTY WILL ONLY MAKE US MORE VULNERABLE.
BUT PROTECT KITTY WE MUST. PROTECT HER WE SHALL.
I CANNOT CATCH HER IN MY ARMORED FORM. THE IMPACT MIGHT INJURE HER. I MUST BECOME HUMAN, AND HOPE THE DANGER ROOM DOES NOT TAKE ADVANTAGE OF ME.
THE YOUNG RUSSIAN CONCENTRATES AND, WITH A BURST OF ENERGY, HIS ORGANIC STEEL BODY ONCE MORE BECOMES FLESH AND BLOOD.
AM I IN TROUBLE, PETER? AM I GONNA GET YELLED AT?
PROBABLY. IF YOU SURVIVE.
IF I... SURVIVE--?!?
PETER-- LOOK!!
THE PILE-DRIVER!
HE HAS SPLIT-SECONDS TO ACT...
... BUT BEFORE COLOSSUS EVEN BEGINS TO MOVE, A BURST OF FLAME COUPLED WITH THE STENCH OF BRIMSTONE HERALDS THE ARRIVAL OF NIGHTCRAWLER!
PANIC BUTTON
TALK ABOUT YOUR DRAMATIC ENTRANCES!
IT SEEMS I TELEPORTED HERE IN THE PROVERBIAL NICK OF TIME.
YOU COULD SAY THAT, FRIEND KURT. ARE YOU ALL RIGHT, KITTY?
Uh-huh.
WERE YOU FRIGHTENED?
Uh-HUH!
I, ALSO.
WHERE WERE YOU, KURT? I KNOW IT WAS YOUR TURN TO CLEAN THE BREAKFAST DISHES, BUT THAT SHOULDN'T HAVE MADE YOU LATE FOR THIS TRAINING SESSION.
I'M SORRY, ORORO. THE MORNING NEWS HAD AN INTERVIEW WITH PROFESSOR XAVIER ABOUT TODAY'S "MUTANT HEARINGS" IN WASHINGTON. I GUESS I LOST TRACK OF TIME.

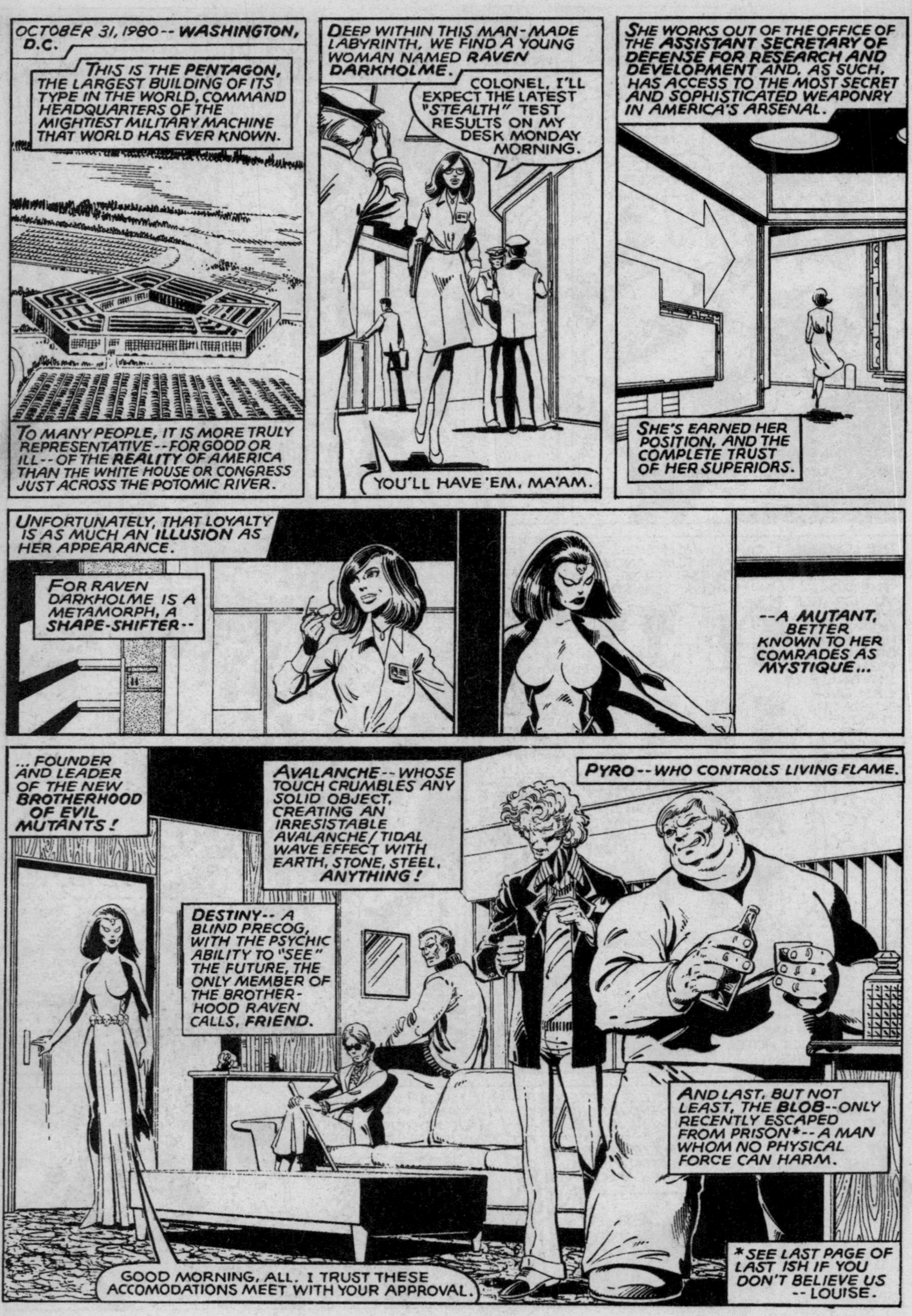
OCTOBER 31, 1980-- WASHINGTON, D.C.
THIS IS THE PENTAGON, THE LARGEST BUILDING OF ITS TYPE IN THE WORLD, COMMAND HEADQUARTERS OF THE MIGHTIEST MILITARY MACHINE THAT WORLD HAS EVER KNOWN.
TO MANY PEOPLE, IT IS MORE TRULY REPRESENTATIVE--FOR GOOD OR ILL--OF THE REALITY OF AMERICA THAN THE WHITE HOUSE OR CONGRESS JUST ACROSS THE POTOMIC RIVER.
DEEP WITHIN THIS MAN-MADE LABYRINTH, WE FIND A YOUNG WOMAN NAMED RAVEN DARKHOLME.
COLONEL, I'LL EXPECT THE LATEST "STEALTH" TEST RESULTS ON MY DESK MONDAY MORNING.
YOU'LL HAVE 'EM, MA'AM.
SHE WORKS OUT OF THE OFFICE OF THE ASSISTANT SECRETARY OF DEFENSE FOR RESEARCH AND DEVELOPMENT AND, AS SUCH, HAS ACCESS TO THE MOST SECRET AND SOPHISTICATED WEAPONRY IN AMERICA'S ARSENAL.
SHE'S EARNED HER POSITION, AND THE COMPLETE TRUST OF HER SUPERIORS.
UNFORTUNATELY, THAT LOYALTY IS AS MUCH AN ILLUSION AS HER APPEARANCE.
FOR RAVEN DARKHOLME IS A METAMORPH, A SHAPE-SHIFTER--
--A MUTANT, BETTER KNOWN TO HER COMRADES AS MYSTIQUE...
...FOUNDER AND LEADER OF THE NEW BROTHERHOOD OF EVIL MUTANTS!
AVALANCHE--WHOSE TOUCH CRUMBLES ANY SOLID OBJECT, CREATING AN IRRESISTABLE AVALANCHE/TIDAL WAVE EFFECT WITH EARTH, STONE, STEEL, ANYTHING!
PYRO--WHO CONTROLS LIVING FLAME.
DESTINY-- A BLIND PRECOG, WITH THE PSYCHIC ABILITY TO "SEE" THE FUTURE, THE ONLY MEMBER OF THE BROTHER-HOOD RAVEN CALLS, FRIEND.
AND LAST, BUT NOT LEAST, THE BLOB--ONLY RECENTLY ESCAPED FROM PRISON*-- A MAN WHOM NO PHYSICAL FORCE CAN HARM.
GOOD MORNING, ALL. I TRUST THESE ACCOMODATIONS MEET WITH YOUR APPROVAL.
*SEE LAST PAGE OF LAST ISH IF YOU DON'T BELIEVE US --LOUISE.

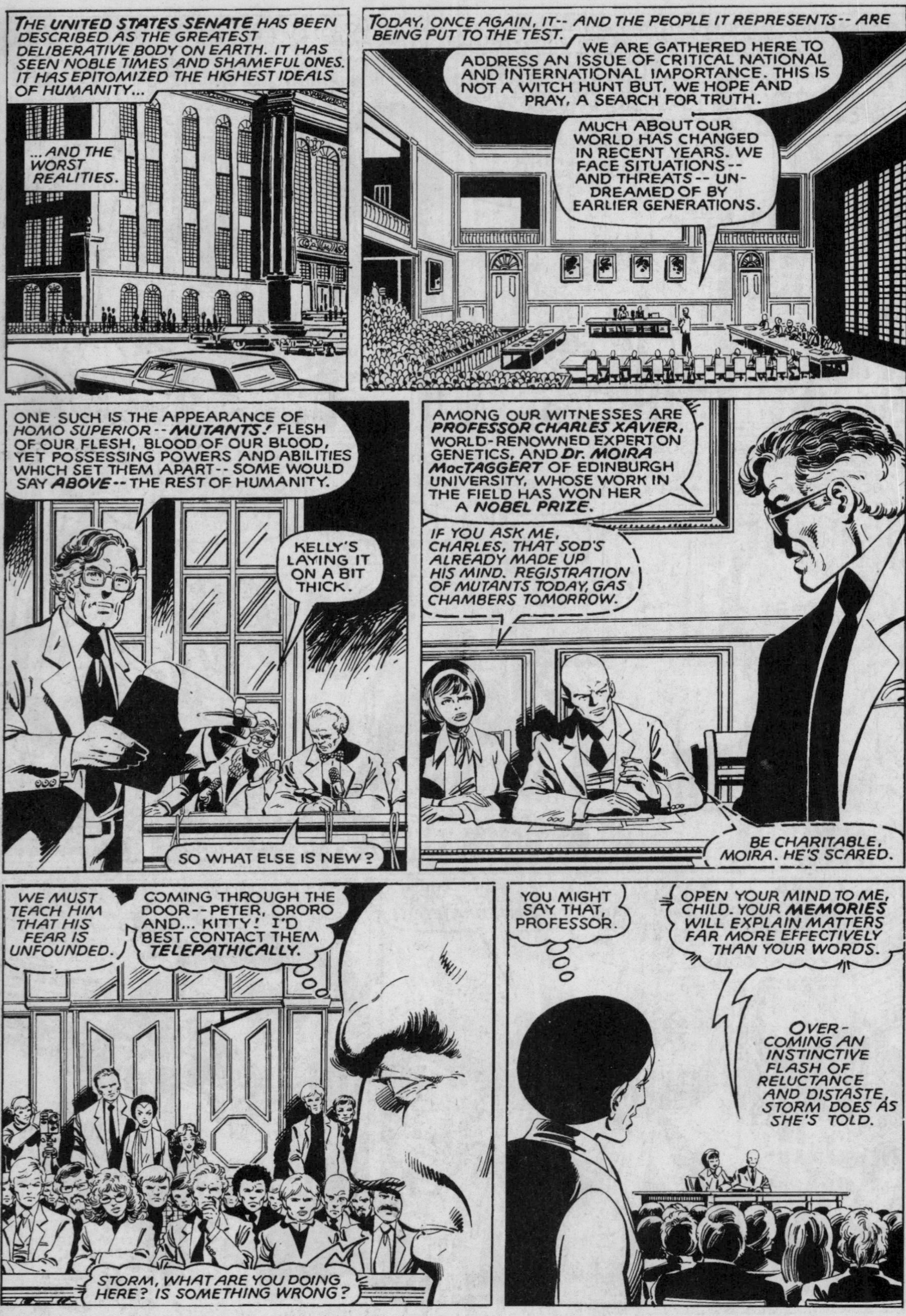
THE UNITED STATES SENATE HAS BEEN DESCRIBED AS THE GREATEST DELIBERATIVE BODY ON EARTH. IT HAS SEEN NOBLE TIMES AND SHAMEFUL ONES. IT HAS EPITOMIZED THE HIGHEST IDEALS OF HUMANITY...
...AND THE WORST REALITIES.
TODAY, ONCE AGAIN, IT-- AND THE PEOPLE IT REPRESENTS-- ARE BEING PUT TO THE TEST.
WE ARE GATHERED HERE TO ADDRESS AN ISSUE OF CRITICAL NATIONAL AND INTERNATIONAL IMPORTANCE. THIS IS NOT A WITCH HUNT BUT, WE HOPE AND PRAY, A SEARCH FOR TRUTH.
MUCH ABOUT OUR WORLD HAS CHANGED IN RECENT YEARS. WE FACE SITUATIONS-- AND THREATS-- UNDREAMED OF BY EARLIER GENERATIONS.
ONE SUCH IS THE APPEARANCE OF HOMO SUPERIOR-- MUTANTS! FLESH OF OUR FLESH, BLOOD OF OUR BLOOD, YET POSSESSING POWERS AND ABILITIES WHICH SET THEM APART-- SOME WOULD SAY ABOVE-- THE REST OF HUMANITY.
KELLY'S LAYING IT ON A BIT THICK.
SO WHAT ELSE IS NEW?
AMONG OUR WITNESSES ARE PROFESSOR CHARLES XAVIER, WORLD-RENOWNED EXPERT ON GENETICS, AND Dr. MOIRA MacTAGGERT OF EDINBURGH UNIVERSITY, WHOSE WORK IN THE FIELD HAS WON HER A NOBEL PRIZE.
IF YOU ASK ME, CHARLES, THAT SOD'S ALREADY MADE UP HIS MIND. REGISTRATION OF MUTANTS TODAY, GAS CHAMBERS TOMORROW.
BE CHARITABLE, MOIRA. HE'S SCARED.
WE MUST TEACH HIM THAT HIS FEAR IS UNFOUNDED.
COMING THROUGH THE DOOR--PETER, ORORO AND... KITTY! I'D BEST CONTACT THEM TELEPATHICALLY.
STORM, WHAT ARE YOU DOING HERE? IS SOMETHING WRONG?
YOU MIGHT SAY THAT, PROFESSOR.
OPEN YOUR MIND TO ME, CHILD. YOUR MEMORIES WILL EXPLAIN MATTERS FAR MORE EFFECTIVELY THAN YOUR WORDS.
OVERCOMING AN INSTINCTIVE FLASH OF RELUCTANCE AND DISTASTE, STORM DOES AS SHE'S TOLD.

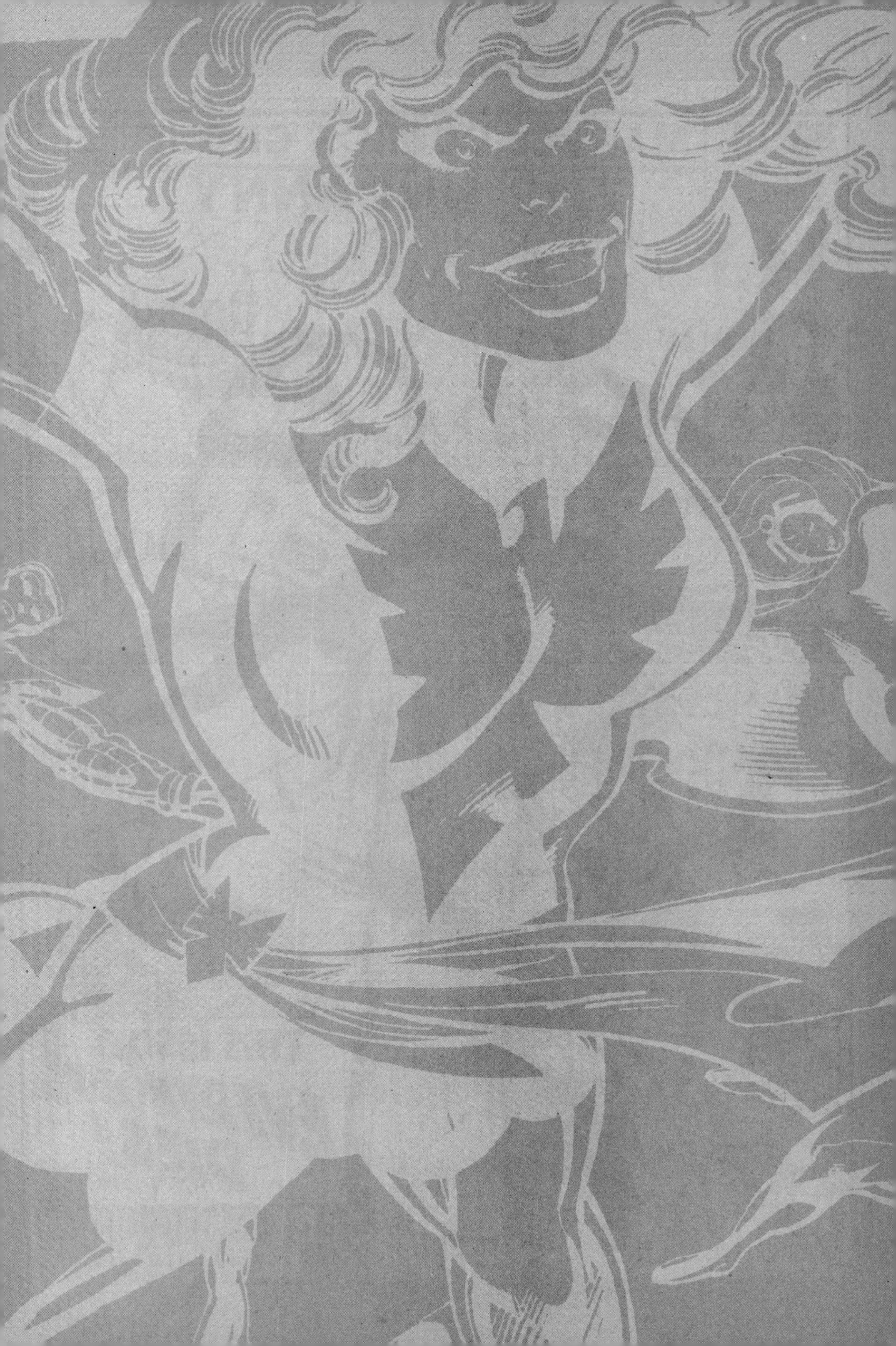

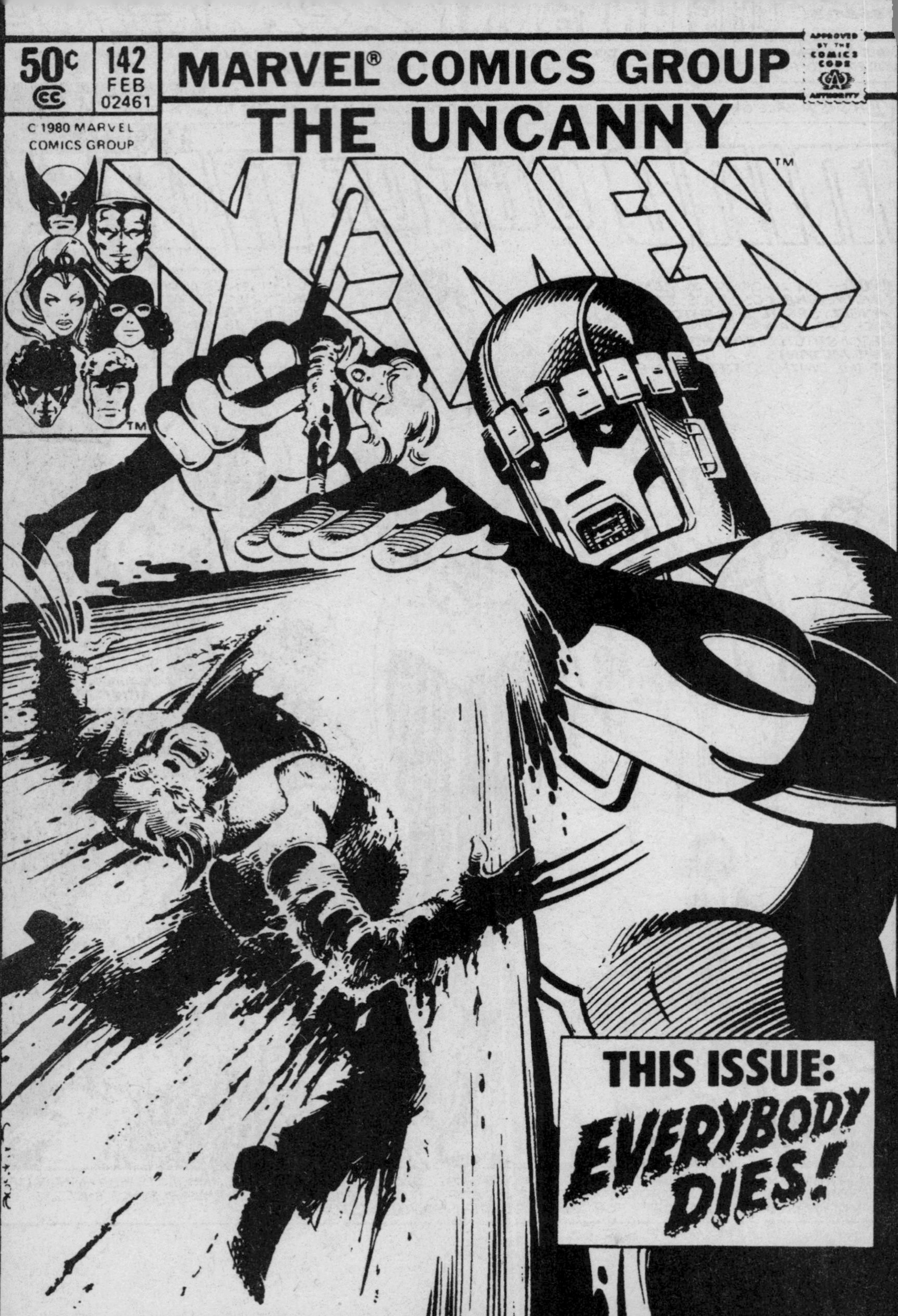
50¢
142
FEB
02461
MARVEL® COMICS GROUP
APPROVED BY THE COMICS CODE AUTHORITY
C 1980 MARVEL COMICS GROUP
THE UNCANNY
X-MEN™
THIS ISSUE:
EVERYBODY DIES!

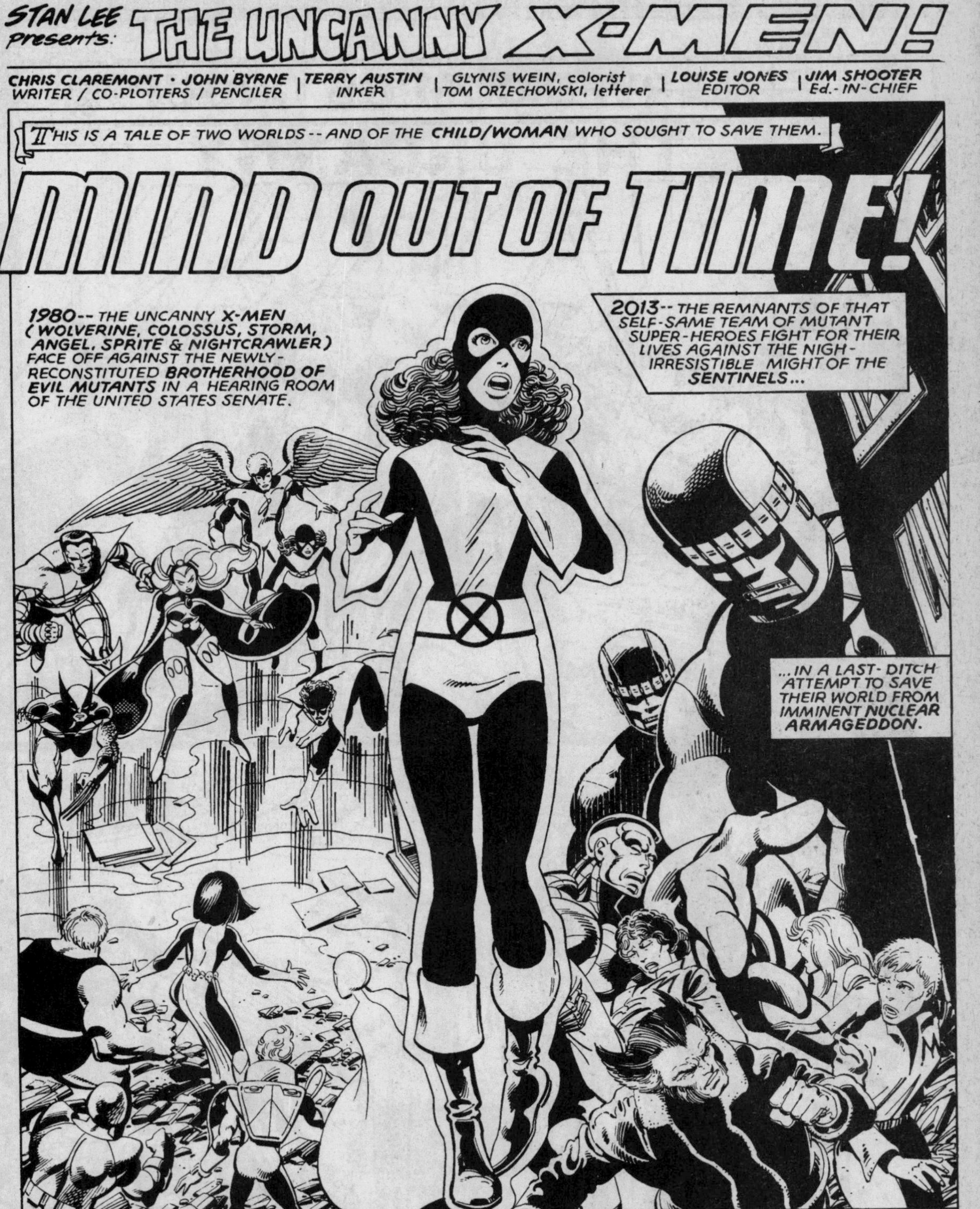
STAN LEE presents: THE UNCANNY X-MEN!
CHRIS CLAREMONT · JOHN BYRNE WRITER / CO-PLOTTERS / PENCILER
TERRY AUSTIN INKER
GLYNIS WEIN, colorist TOM ORZECHOWSKI, letterer
LOUISE JONES EDITOR
JIM SHOOTER Ed.-IN-CHIEF
THIS IS A TALE OF TWO WORLDS -- AND OF THE CHILD/WOMAN WHO SOUGHT TO SAVE THEM.
MIND OUT OF TIME!
1980-- THE UNCANNY X-MEN (WOLVERINE, COLOSSUS, STORM, ANGEL, SPRITE & NIGHTCRAWLER) FACE OFF AGAINST THE NEWLY-RECONSTITUTED BROTHERHOOD OF EVIL MUTANTS IN A HEARING ROOM OF THE UNITED STATES SENATE.
2013-- THE REMNANTS OF THAT SELF-SAME TEAM OF MUTANT SUPER-HEROES FIGHT FOR THEIR LIVES AGAINST THE NIGH-IRRESISTIBLE MIGHT OF THE SENTINELS...
...IN A LAST-DITCH ATTEMPT TO SAVE THEIR WORLD FROM IMMINENT NUCLEAR ARMAGEDDON.
AND LINKING THESE TWO WORLDS, THESE TWO DESPERATE BATTLES, IS KATHERINE PRYDE. IN HER HANDS LIES THE FATE OF MUTANTKIND, OF HUMANITY, OF THE EARTH ITSELF. FAILURE IS UNTHINKABLE, YET SUCCESS MAY WELL BE IMPOSSIBLE -- FOR SHE SEEKS TO CHANGE HISTORY.

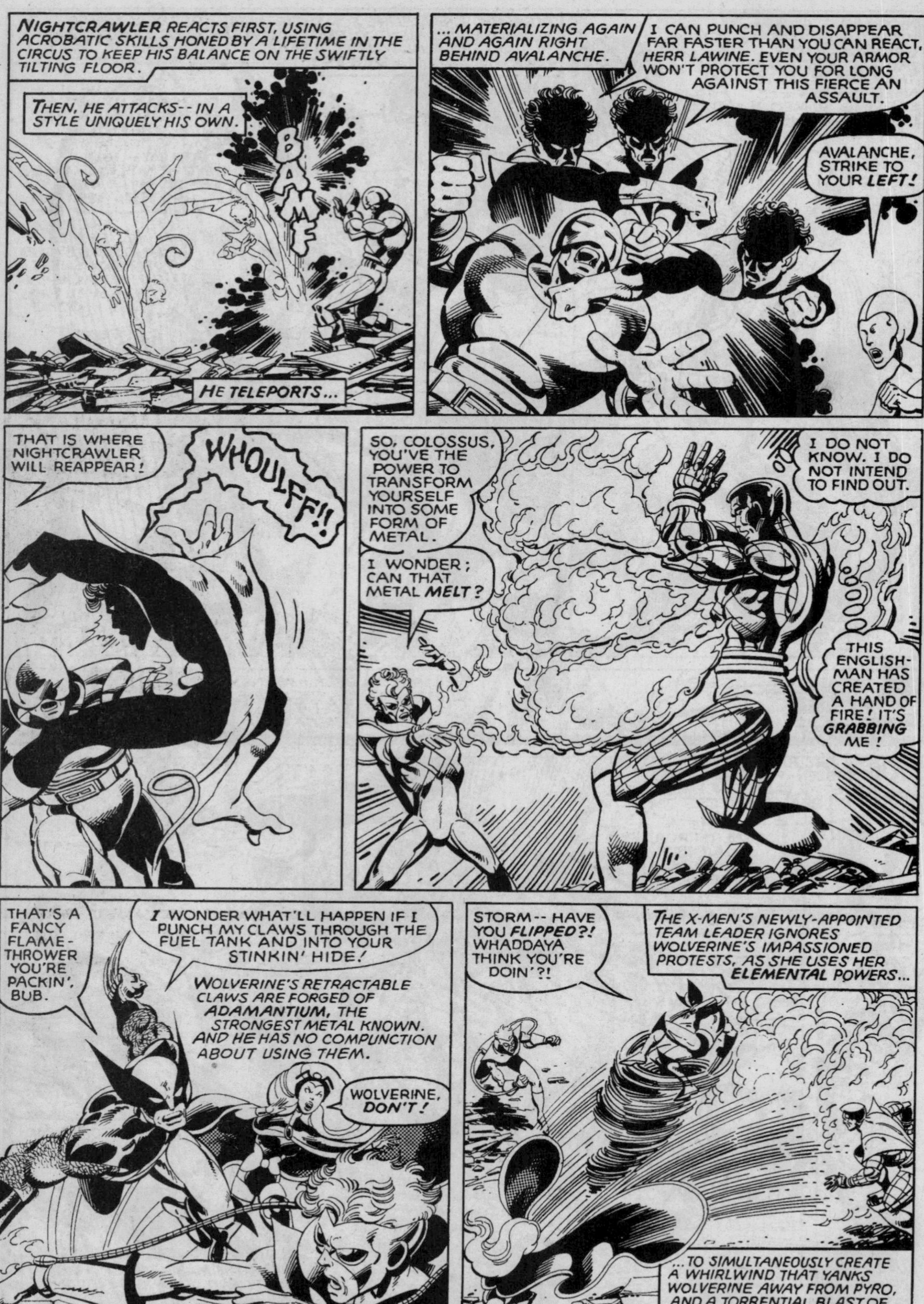

NIGHTCRAWLER REACTS FIRST, USING ACROBATIC SKILLS HONED BY A LIFETIME IN THE CIRCUS TO KEEP HIS BALANCE ON THE SWIFTLY TILTING FLOOR.
THEN, HE ATTACKS-- IN A STYLE UNIQUELY HIS OWN.
BAMF
HE TELEPORTS...
...MATERIALIZING AGAIN AND AGAIN RIGHT BEHIND AVALANCHE.
I CAN PUNCH AND DISAPPEAR FAR FASTER THAN YOU CAN REACT, HERR LAWINE. EVEN YOUR ARMOR WON'T PROTECT YOU FOR LONG AGAINST THIS FIERCE AN ASSAULT.
AVALANCHE, STRIKE TO YOUR LEFT!
THAT IS WHERE NIGHTCRAWLER WILL REAPPEAR!
WHOULFF!!
SO, COLOSSUS, YOU'VE THE POWER TO TRANSFORM YOURSELF INTO SOME FORM OF METAL.
I WONDER; CAN THAT METAL MELT?
I DO NOT KNOW. I DO NOT INTEND TO FIND OUT.
THIS ENGLISHMAN HAS CREATED A HAND OF FIRE! IT'S GRABBING ME!
THAT'S A FANCY FLAME-THROWER YOU'RE PACKIN', BUB.
I WONDER WHAT'LL HAPPEN IF I PUNCH MY CLAWS THROUGH THE FUEL TANK AND INTO YOUR STINKIN' HIDE!
WOLVERINE'S RETRACTABLE CLAWS ARE FORGED OF ADAMANTIUM, THE STRONGEST METAL KNOWN. AND HE HAS NO COMPUNCTION ABOUT USING THEM.
WOLVERINE, DON'T!
STORM-- HAVE YOU FLIPPED?! WHADDAYA THINK YOU'RE DOIN'?!
THE X-MEN'S NEWLY-APPOINTED TEAM LEADER IGNORES WOLVERINE'S IMPASSIONED PROTESTS, AS SHE USES HER ELEMENTAL POWERS...
...TO SIMULTANEOUSLY CREATE A WHIRLWIND THAT YANKS WOLVERINE AWAY FROM PYRO, AND A TORRENTIAL BLAST OF RAIN TO DOUSE THE FLAME HAND AROUND COLOSSUS.

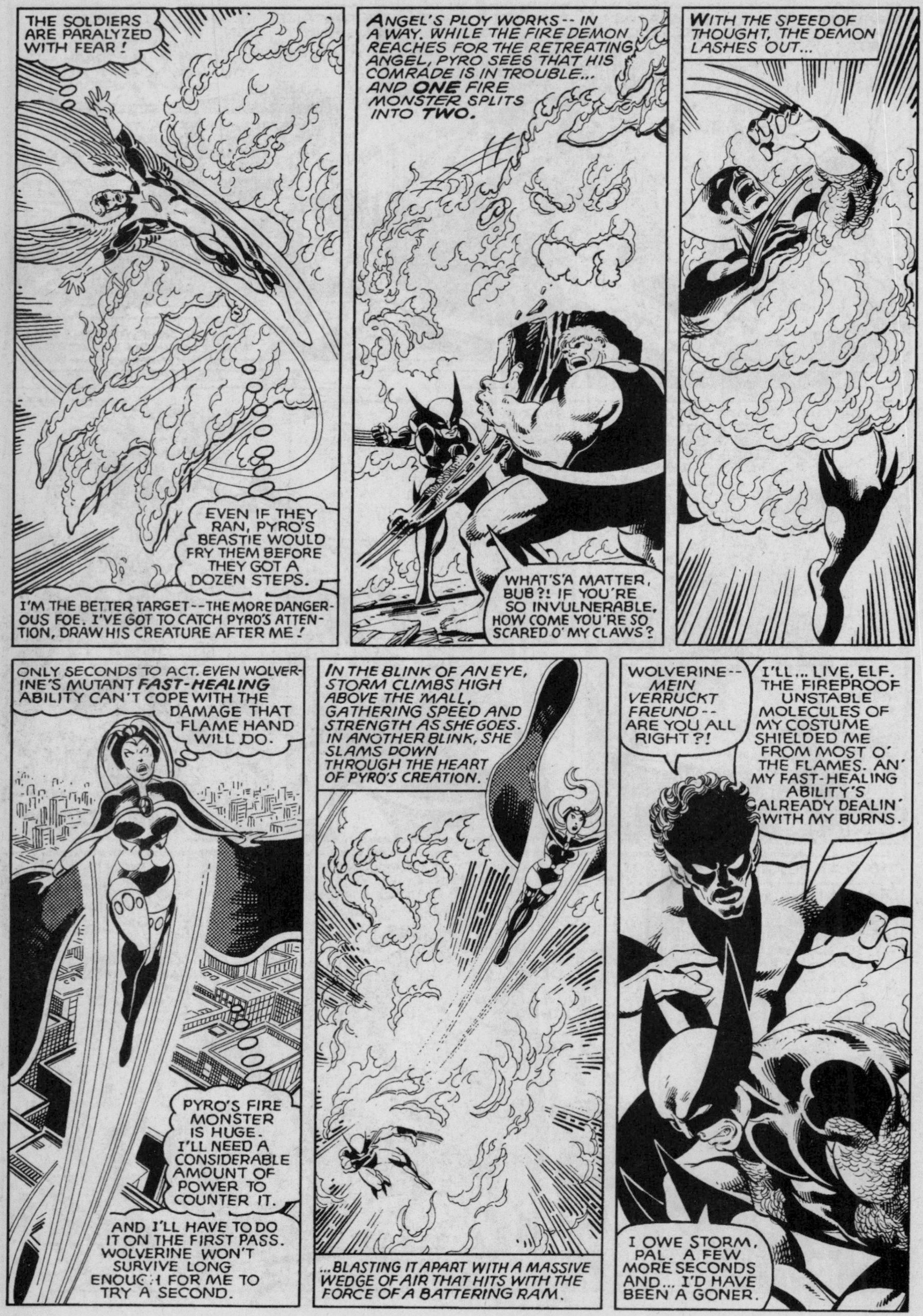

THE SOLDIERS ARE PARALYZED WITH FEAR!
EVEN IF THEY RAN, PYRO'S BEASTIE WOULD FRY THEM BEFORE THEY GOT A DOZEN STEPS.
I'M THE BETTER TARGET--THE MORE DANGEROUS FOE. I'VE GOT TO CATCH PYRO'S ATTENTION, DRAW HIS CREATURE AFTER ME!
ANGEL'S PLOY WORKS-- IN A WAY. WHILE THE FIRE DEMON REACHES FOR THE RETREATING ANGEL, PYRO SEES THAT HIS COMRADE IS IN TROUBLE... AND ONE FIRE MONSTER SPLITS INTO TWO.
WHAT'S'A MATTER, BUB?! IF YOU'RE SO INVULNERABLE, HOW COME YOU'RE SO SCARED O' MY CLAWS?
WITH THE SPEED OF THOUGHT, THE DEMON LASHES OUT...
ONLY SECONDS TO ACT. EVEN WOLVERINE'S MUTANT FAST-HEALING ABILITY CAN'T COPE WITH THE DAMAGE THAT FLAME HAND WILL DO.
PYRO'S FIRE MONSTER IS HUGE. I'LL NEED A CONSIDERABLE AMOUNT OF POWER TO COUNTER IT.
AND I'LL HAVE TO DO IT ON THE FIRST PASS. WOLVERINE WON'T SURVIVE LONG ENOUGH FOR ME TO TRY A SECOND.
IN THE BLINK OF AN EYE, STORM CLIMBS HIGH ABOVE THE MALL, GATHERING SPEED AND STRENGTH AS SHE GOES. IN ANOTHER BLINK, SHE SLAMS DOWN THROUGH THE HEART OF PYRO'S CREATION.
...BLASTING IT APART WITH A MASSIVE WEDGE OF AIR THAT HITS WITH THE FORCE OF A BATTERING RAM.
WOLVERINE-- MEIN VERRUCKT FREUND-- ARE YOU ALL RIGHT?!
I'LL... LIVE, ELF. THE FIREPROOF UNSTABLE MOLECULES OF MY COSTUME SHIELDED ME FROM MOST O' THE FLAMES. AN' MY FAST-HEALING ABILITY'S ALREADY DEALIN' WITH MY BURNS.
I OWE STORM, PAL. A FEW MORE SECONDS AND... I'D HAVE BEEN A GONER.

1980: THE BLIND PRECOG, *DESTINY*, HAS SENATOR KELLY CORNERED. BUT... IF SHE CAN PSYCHICALLY SCAN THE FUTURE, WHY HASN'T SHE SPOTTED ME?! UNLESS...

...THE TIMESWITCH HAS MADE ME SOMEHOW *INVISIBLE* TO HER PRESCIENT ABILITIES!

MY COLLEAGUES HAVE BEEN DEFEATED, YET VICTORY WILL STILL BE OURS-- WITH YOUR DEATH.

MURDERING ME WILL ACCOMPLISH *NOTHING.* TRUE, PEOPLE WILL FEAR MUTANTS, AS THEY FEAR *ALL* TERRORISTS--

--BUT THEY WON'T BE *COWED* BY THAT FEAR. THEY'LL FIGHT BACK. THEY'LL *DESTROY* YOU, DESTINY!

POSSIBLY. BUT YOU ARE A GREATER THREAT ALIVE.

DO NOT TRY TO EVADE MY CROSSBOW BOLT, SENATOR. I WILL SENSE YOUR PLANS A HEARTBEAT BEFORE YOU EVEN FORMULATE THEM, AND FIRE WHERE YOU ARE *GOING* TO BE.

I WOULDN'T GIVE YOU THAT SATISFACTION. IF I GOT MY HANDS ON YOU, MUTANT, I'D PROBABLY BREAK YOUR NECK...

...BUT I WON'T RUN.

DESTINY LAUGHS SOFTLY, AND TIGHTENS HER FINGER ON THE TRIGGER.

BUT, AS DESTINY FIRES, KATE "PHASES" WRAITH-LIKE THROUGH HER, CALLING UPON HER DECADES OF TRAINING AND EXPERIENCE TO ACT AS HER CHILD SELF COULD NOT...

MY--MY-- *MIND!*

THE TEMPORAL ANOMALY-- A PART OF ME-- CONSUMING ME!

SHE WILLS HER SHOULDERS TO BECOME SOLID, BASHING THE OTHER WOMAN'S ARM AND THROWING OFF HER AIM.

SENATOR-- *DUCK!*

IN THAT SPLIT-SECOND, AN ABYSS OPENS WITHIN KATE PRYDE. REALITY TWISTS INSIDE-OUT AND, SUDDENLY, SHE COMES FACE-TO-FACE WITH HERSELF AS A CHILD:-- SO INNOCENT, SO VULNERABLE, SO YOUNG.

IMPULSIVELY, SHE GIVES HERSELF A KISS...

...AND LETS THE WINDS OF ETERNITY SWEEP HER HOME.

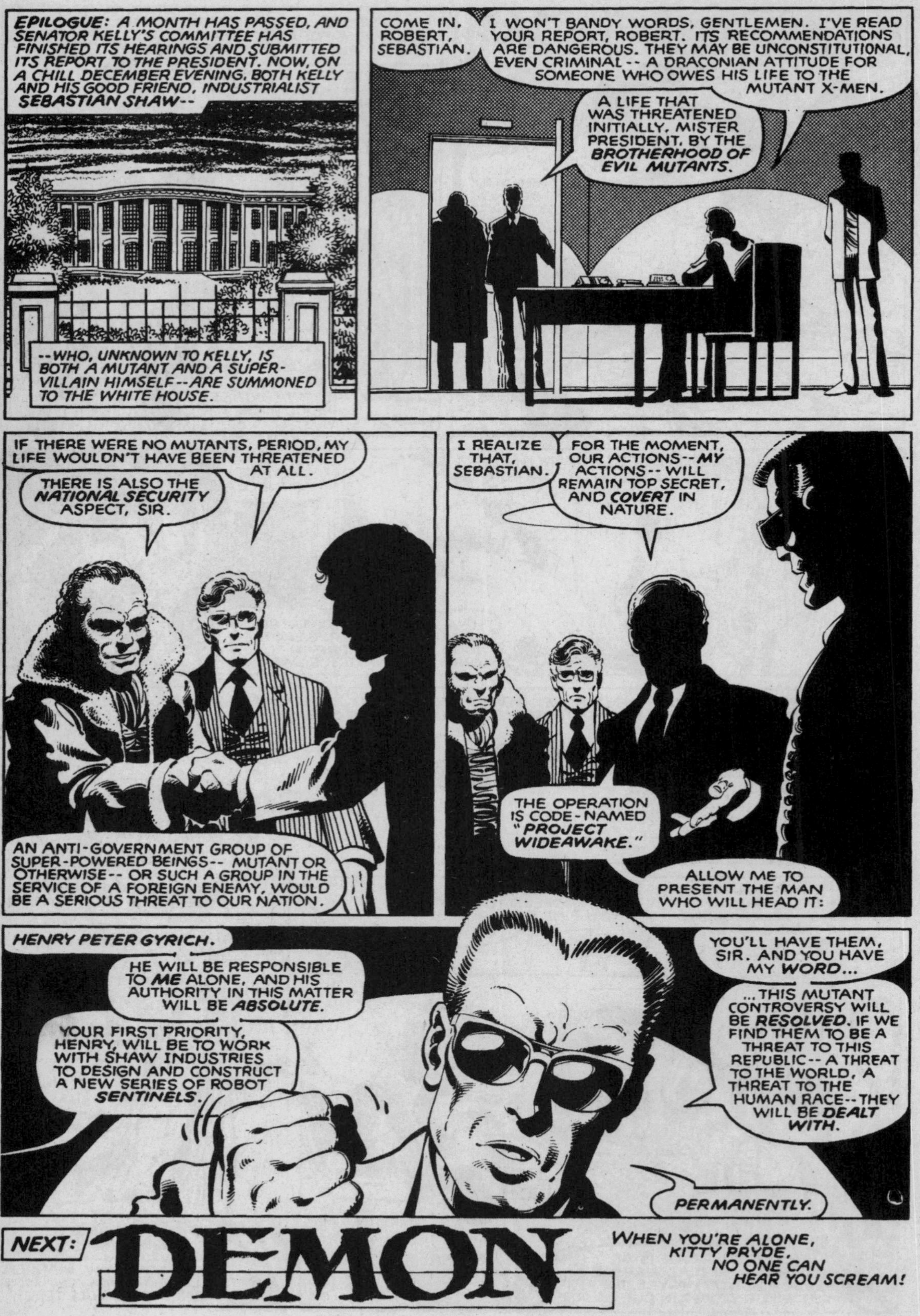
EPILOGUE: A MONTH HAS PASSED, AND SENATOR KELLY'S COMMITTEE HAS FINISHED ITS HEARINGS AND SUBMITTED ITS REPORT TO THE PRESIDENT. NOW, ON A CHILL DECEMBER EVENING, BOTH KELLY AND HIS GOOD FRIEND, INDUSTRIALIST SEBASTIAN SHAW--
--WHO, UNKNOWN TO KELLY, IS BOTH A MUTANT AND A SUPER-VILLAIN HIMSELF--ARE SUMMONED TO THE WHITE HOUSE.
COME IN, ROBERT, SEBASTIAN.
I WON'T BANDY WORDS, GENTLEMEN. I'VE READ YOUR REPORT, ROBERT. ITS RECOMMENDATIONS ARE DANGEROUS. THEY MAY BE UNCONSTITUTIONAL, EVEN CRIMINAL -- A DRACONIAN ATTITUDE FOR SOMEONE WHO OWES HIS LIFE TO THE MUTANT X-MEN.
A LIFE THAT WAS THREATENED INITIALLY, MISTER PRESIDENT, BY THE BROTHERHOOD OF EVIL MUTANTS.
IF THERE WERE NO MUTANTS, PERIOD, MY LIFE WOULDN'T HAVE BEEN THREATENED AT ALL.
THERE IS ALSO THE NATIONAL SECURITY ASPECT, SIR.
AN ANTI-GOVERNMENT GROUP OF SUPER-POWERED BEINGS-- MUTANT OR OTHERWISE-- OR SUCH A GROUP IN THE SERVICE OF A FOREIGN ENEMY, WOULD BE A SERIOUS THREAT TO OUR NATION.
I REALIZE THAT, SEBASTIAN.
FOR THE MOMENT, OUR ACTIONS--MY ACTIONS-- WILL REMAIN TOP SECRET, AND COVERT IN NATURE.
THE OPERATION IS CODE-NAMED "PROJECT WIDEAWAKE."
ALLOW ME TO PRESENT THE MAN WHO WILL HEAD IT:
HENRY PETER GYRICH.
HE WILL BE RESPONSIBLE TO ME ALONE, AND HIS AUTHORITY IN THIS MATTER WILL BE ABSOLUTE.
YOUR FIRST PRIORITY, HENRY, WILL BE TO WORK WITH SHAW INDUSTRIES TO DESIGN AND CONSTRUCT A NEW SERIES OF ROBOT SENTINELS.
YOU'LL HAVE THEM, SIR. AND YOU HAVE MY WORD...
...THIS MUTANT CONTROVERSY WILL BE RESOLVED. IF WE FIND THEM TO BE A THREAT TO THIS REPUBLIC-- A THREAT TO THE WORLD, A THREAT TO THE HUMAN RACE--THEY WILL BE DEALT WITH.
PERMANENTLY.
NEXT:
DEMON
WHEN YOU'RE ALONE, KITTY PRYDE, NO ONE CAN HEAR YOU SCREAM!

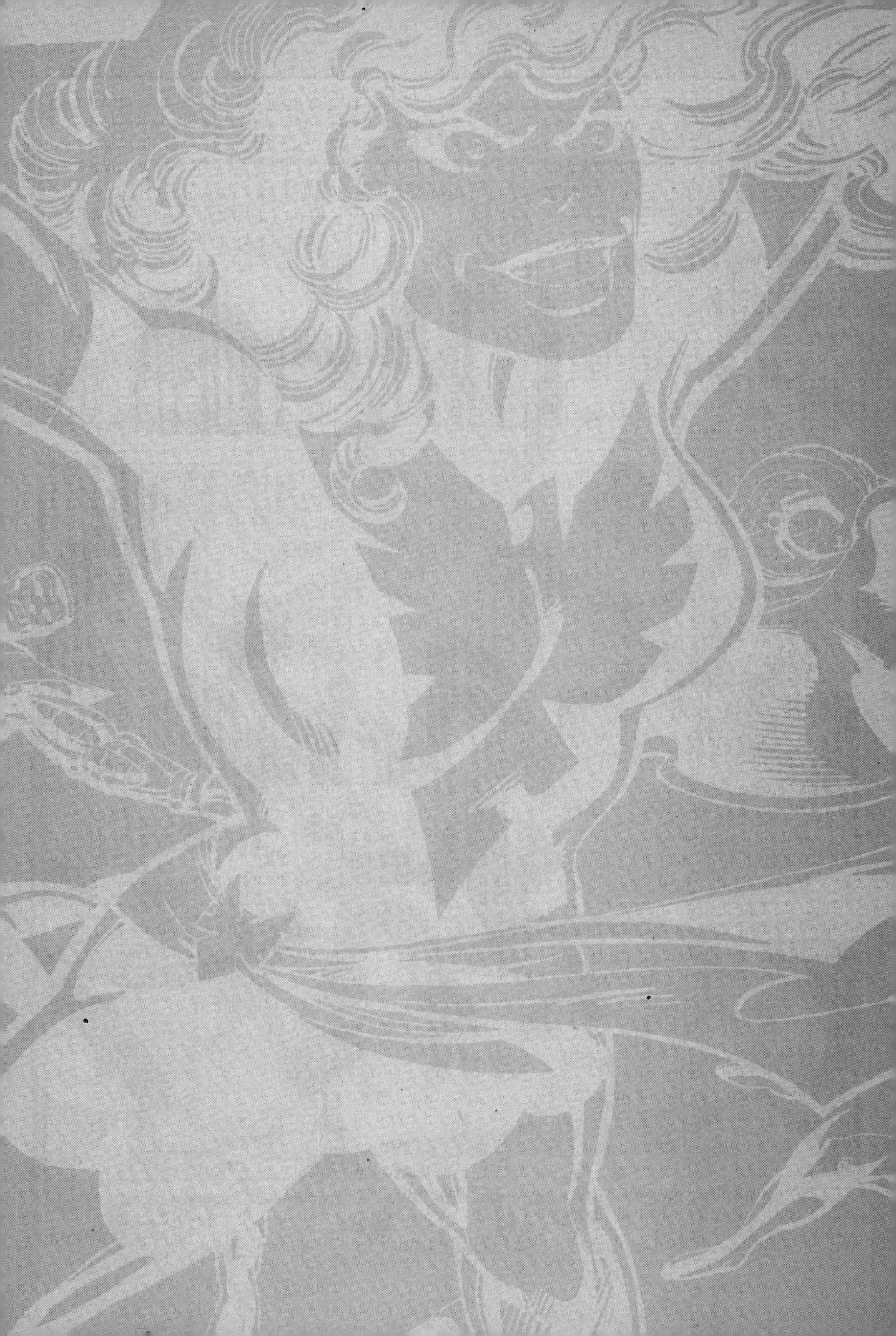

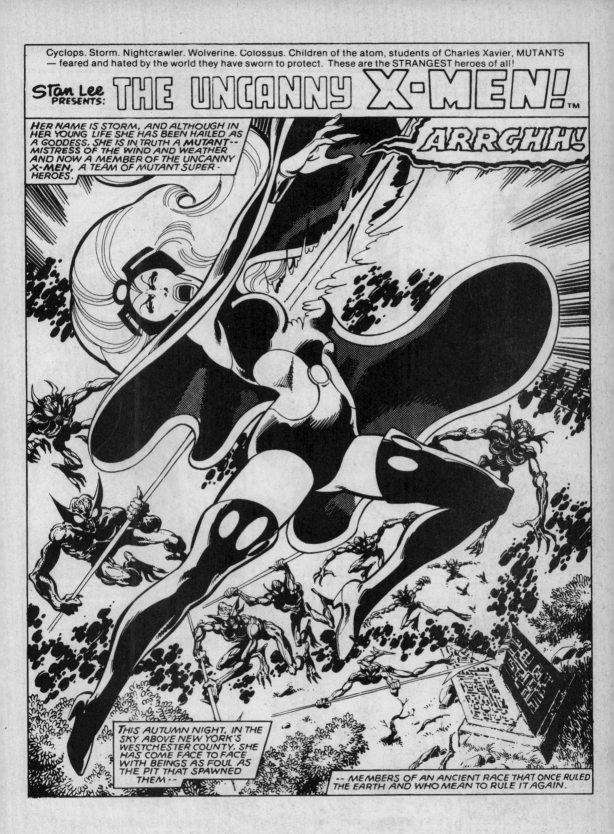

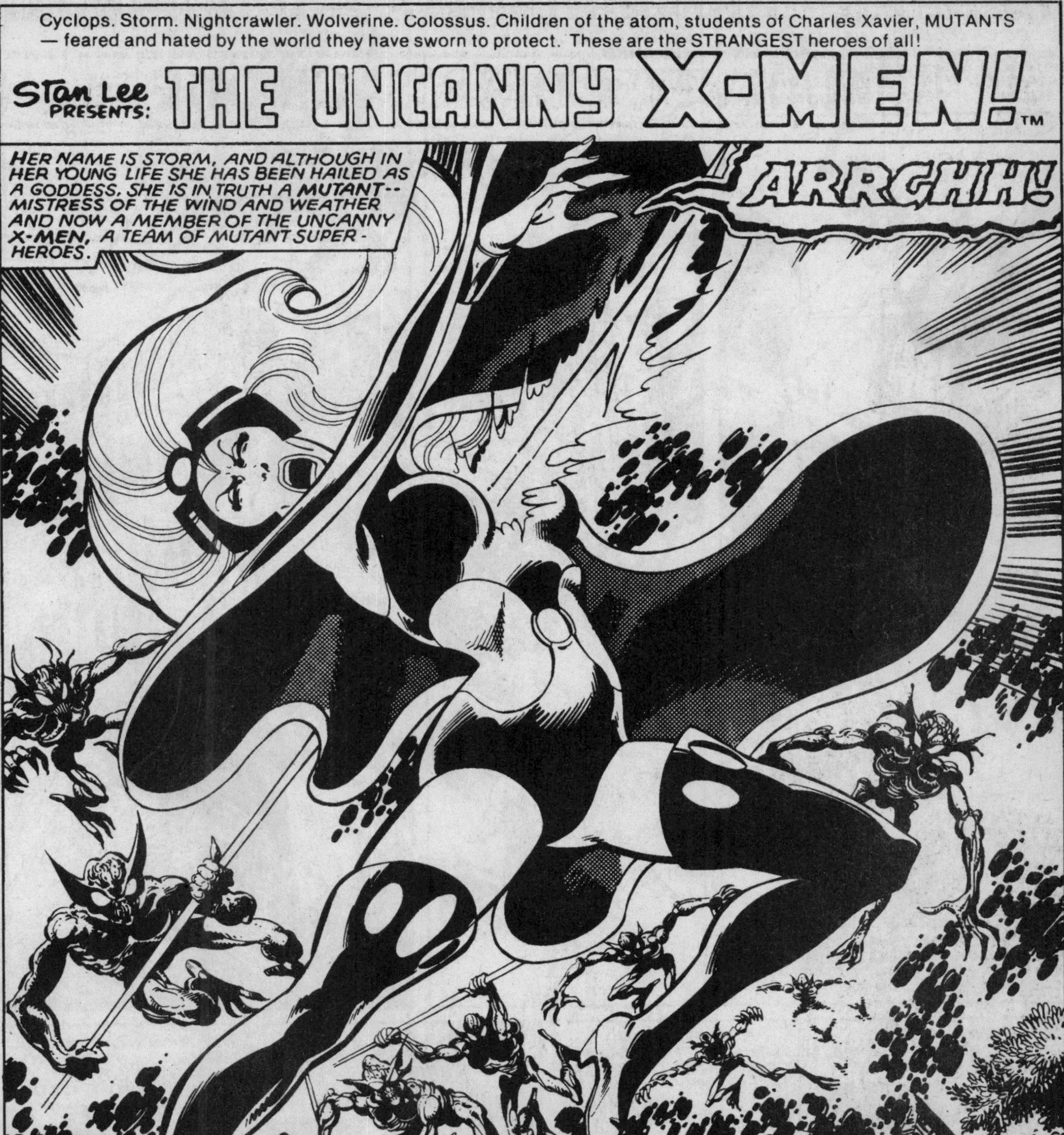
Cyclops. Storm. Nightcrawler. Wolverine. Colossus. Children of the atom, students of Charles Xavier, MUTANTS — feared and hated by the world they have sworn to protect. These are the STRANGEST heroes of all!
STAN LEE PRESENTS: THE UNCANNY X-MEN!™
HER NAME IS STORM, AND ALTHOUGH IN HER YOUNG LIFE SHE HAS BEEN HAILED AS A GODDESS, SHE IS IN TRUTH A MUTANT-- MISTRESS OF THE WIND AND WEATHER AND NOW A MEMBER OF THE UNCANNY X-MEN, A TEAM OF MUTANT SUPER-HEROES.
ARRGHH!
THIS AUTUMN NIGHT, IN THE SKY ABOVE NEW YORK'S WESTCHESTER COUNTY, SHE HAS COME FACE TO FACE WITH BEINGS AS FOUL AS THE PIT THAT SPAWNED THEM --
-- MEMBERS OF AN ANCIENT RACE THAT ONCE RULED THE EARTH AND WHO MEAN TO RULE IT AGAIN.

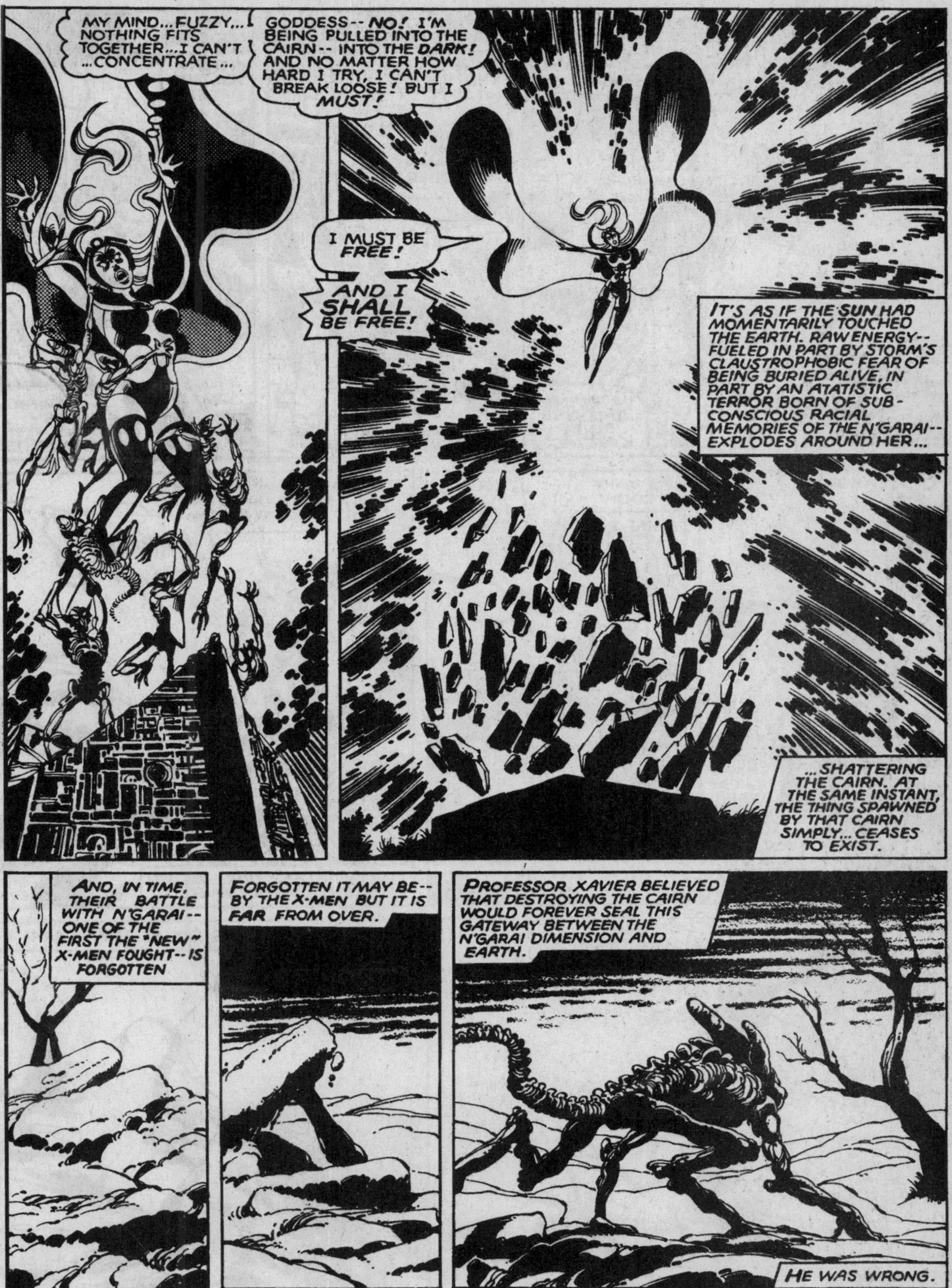

MY MIND... FUZZY... NOTHING FITS TOGETHER... I CAN'T ...CONCENTRATE...
GODDESS-- NO! I'M BEING PULLED INTO THE CAIRN-- INTO THE DARK! AND NO MATTER HOW HARD I TRY, I CAN'T BREAK LOOSE! BUT I MUST!
I MUST BE FREE!
AND I SHALL BE FREE!
IT'S AS IF THE SUN HAD MOMENTARILY TOUCHED THE EARTH. RAW ENERGY-- FUELED IN PART BY STORM'S CLAUSTROPHOBIC FEAR OF BEING BURIED ALIVE, IN PART BY AN ATATISTIC TERROR BORN OF SUB-CONSCIOUS RACIAL MEMORIES OF THE N'GARAI-- EXPLODES AROUND HER...
...SHATTERING THE CAIRN. AT THE SAME INSTANT, THE THING SPAWNED BY THAT CAIRN SIMPLY... CEASES TO EXIST.
AND, IN TIME, THEIR BATTLE WITH N'GARAI-- ONE OF THE FIRST THE "NEW" X-MEN FOUGHT-- IS FORGOTTEN
FORGOTTEN IT MAY BE-- BY THE X-MEN BUT IT IS FAR FROM OVER.
PROFESSOR XAVIER BELIEVED THAT DESTROYING THE CAIRN WOULD FOREVER SEAL THIS GATEWAY BETWEEN THE N'GARAI DIMENSION AND EARTH.
HE WAS WRONG.

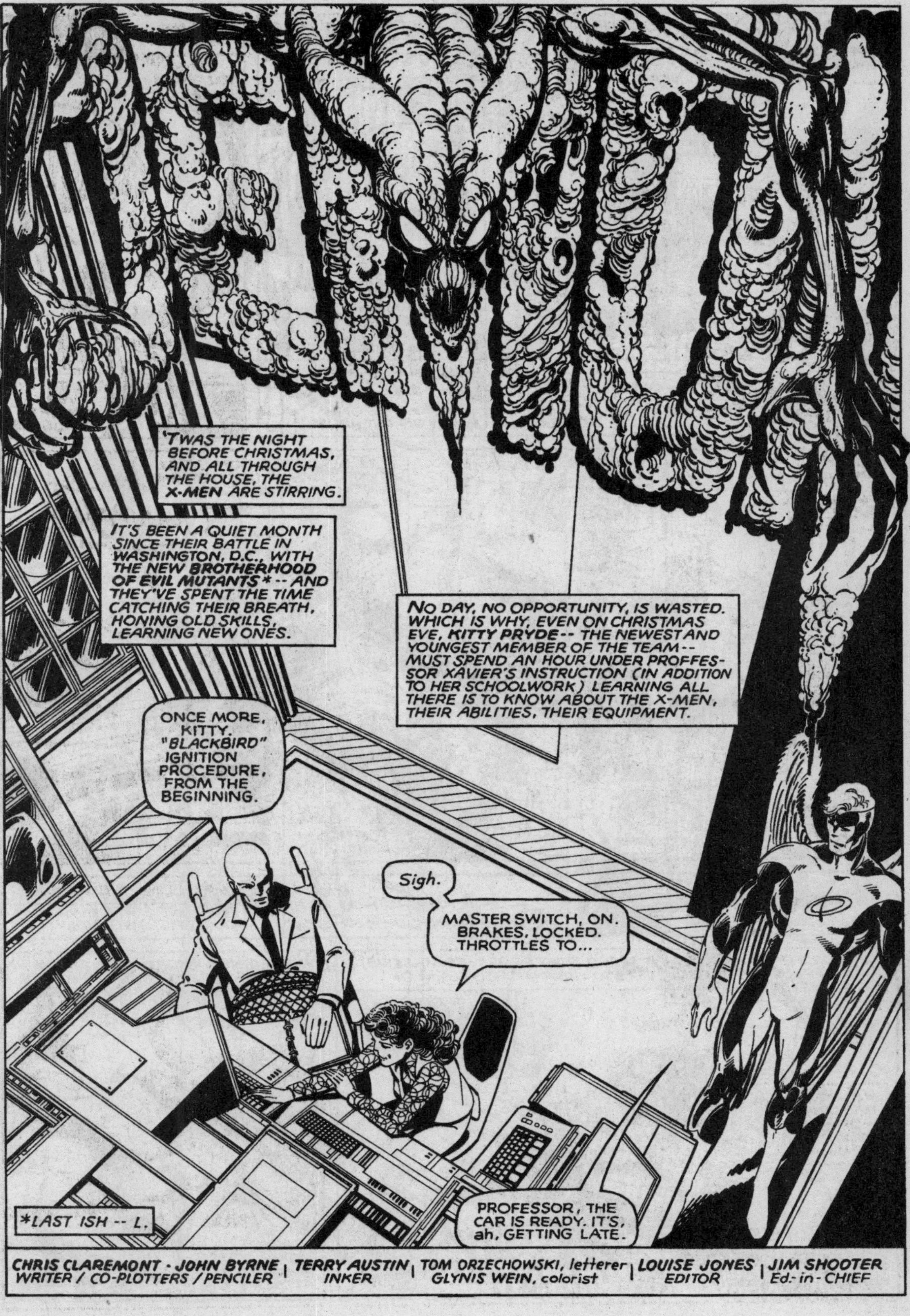

'TWAS THE NIGHT BEFORE CHRISTMAS, AND ALL THROUGH THE HOUSE, THE X-MEN ARE STIRRING.
IT'S BEEN A QUIET MONTH SINCE THEIR BATTLE IN WASHINGTON, D.C., WITH THE NEW BROTHERHOOD OF EVIL MUTANTS* -- AND THEY'VE SPENT THE TIME CATCHING THEIR BREATH, HONING OLD SKILLS, LEARNING NEW ONES.
NO DAY, NO OPPORTUNITY, IS WASTED. WHICH IS WHY, EVEN ON CHRISTMAS EVE, KITTY PRYDE -- THE NEWEST AND YOUNGEST MEMBER OF THE TEAM -- MUST SPEND AN HOUR UNDER PROFFESSOR XAVIER'S INSTRUCTION (IN ADDITION TO HER SCHOOLWORK) LEARNING ALL THERE IS TO KNOW ABOUT THE X-MEN, THEIR ABILITIES, THEIR EQUIPMENT.
ONCE MORE, KITTY. "BLACKBIRD" IGNITION PROCEDURE, FROM THE BEGINNING.
Sigh.
MASTER SWITCH, ON. BRAKES, LOCKED. THROTTLES TO...
PROFESSOR, THE CAR IS READY. IT'S, ah, GETTING LATE.
*LAST ISH -- L.

CHRIS CLAREMONT · JOHN BYRNE WRITER / CO-PLOTTERS / PENCILER | TERRY AUSTIN INKER | TOM ORZECHOWSKI, letterer GLYNIS WEIN, colorist | LOUISE JONES EDITOR | JIM SHOOTER Ed.-in-CHIEF

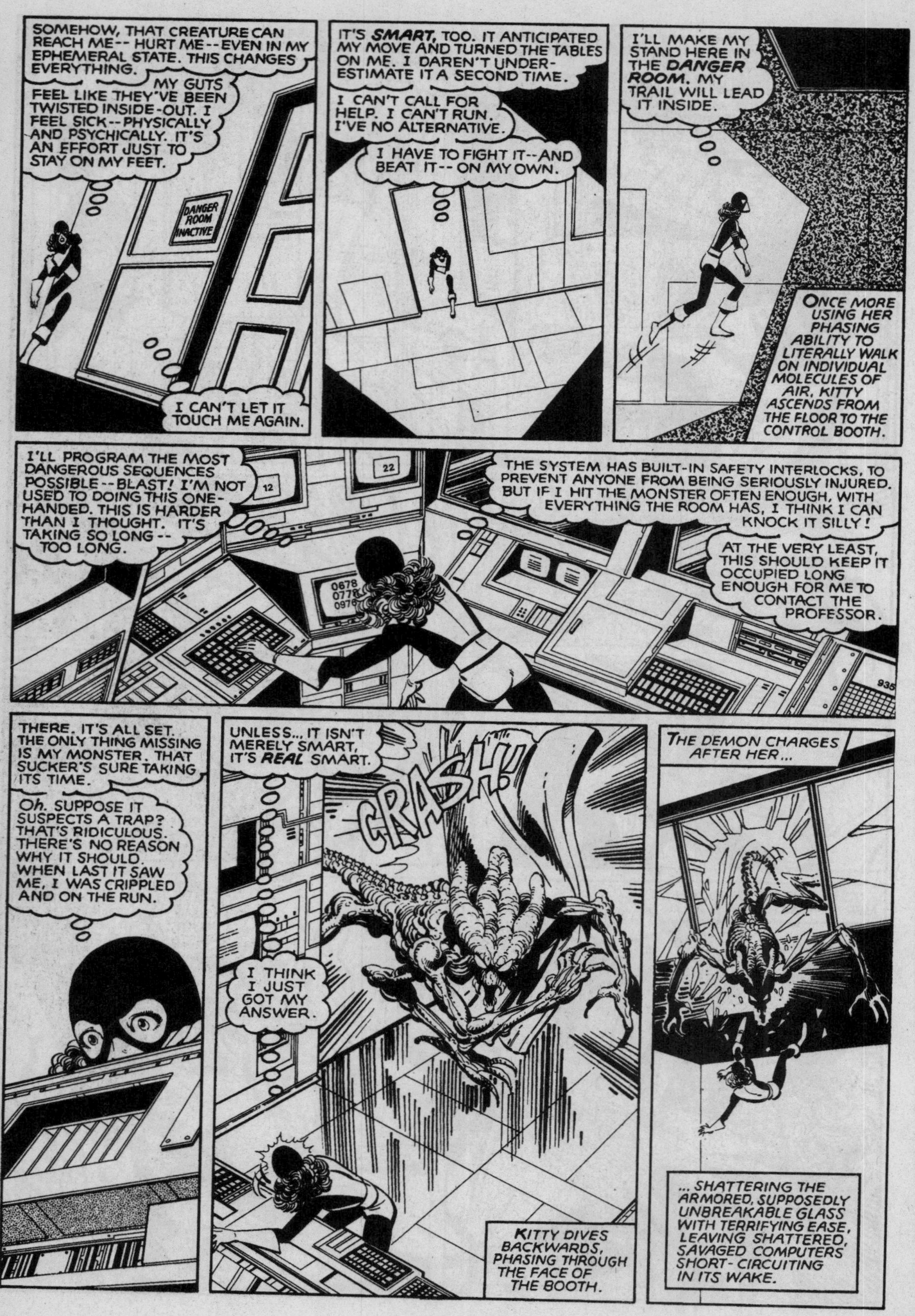
SOMEHOW, THAT CREATURE CAN REACH ME-- HURT ME--EVEN IN MY EPHEMERAL STATE. THIS CHANGES EVERYTHING.
MY GUTS FEEL LIKE THEY'VE BEEN TWISTED INSIDE-OUT. I FEEL SICK--PHYSICALLY AND PSYCHICALLY. IT'S AN EFFORT JUST TO STAY ON MY FEET.
DANGER ROOM INACTIVE
I CAN'T LET IT TOUCH ME AGAIN.
IT'S SMART, TOO. IT ANTICIPATED MY MOVE AND TURNED THE TABLES ON ME. I DAREN'T UNDER-ESTIMATE IT A SECOND TIME.
I CAN'T CALL FOR HELP. I CAN'T RUN. I'VE NO ALTERNATIVE.
I HAVE TO FIGHT IT--AND BEAT IT-- ON MY OWN.
I'LL MAKE MY STAND HERE IN THE DANGER ROOM. MY TRAIL WILL LEAD IT INSIDE.
ONCE MORE USING HER PHASING ABILITY TO LITERALLY WALK ON INDIVIDUAL MOLECULES OF AIR, KITTY ASCENDS FROM THE FLOOR TO THE CONTROL BOOTH.
I'LL PROGRAM THE MOST DANGEROUS SEQUENCES POSSIBLE--BLAST! I'M NOT USED TO DOING THIS ONE-HANDED. THIS IS HARDER THAN I THOUGHT. IT'S TAKING SO LONG -- TOO LONG.
THE SYSTEM HAS BUILT-IN SAFETY INTERLOCKS, TO PREVENT ANYONE FROM BEING SERIOUSLY INJURED. BUT IF I HIT THE MONSTER OFTEN ENOUGH, WITH EVERYTHING THE ROOM HAS, I THINK I CAN KNOCK IT SILLY!
AT THE VERY LEAST, THIS SHOULD KEEP IT OCCUPIED LONG ENOUGH FOR ME TO CONTACT THE PROFESSOR.
THERE. IT'S ALL SET. THE ONLY THING MISSING IS MY MONSTER. THAT SUCKER'S SURE TAKING ITS TIME.
Oh. SUPPOSE IT SUSPECTS A TRAP? THAT'S RIDICULOUS. THERE'S NO REASON WHY IT SHOULD. WHEN LAST IT SAW ME, I WAS CRIPPLED AND ON THE RUN.
UNLESS... IT ISN'T MERELY SMART, IT'S REAL SMART.
CRASH!
I THINK I JUST GOT MY ANSWER.
KITTY DIVES BACKWARDS, PHASING THROUGH THE FACE OF THE BOOTH.
THE DEMON CHARGES AFTER HER...
... SHATTERING THE ARMORED, SUPPOSEDLY UNBREAKABLE GLASS WITH TERRIFYING EASE, LEAVING SHATTERED, SAVAGED COMPUTERS SHORT-CIRCUITING IN ITS WAKE.

IN THE DANGER ROOM, IT ALMOST CAUGHT ME, BUT *FIRE* FORCED IT AWAY. IS IT VULNERABLE TO INTENSE HEAT? TOO BAD I DON'T HAVE SOME KING-SIZED *FLAME-THROWERS* HANDY!

THEY USED *THEM* TO FIGHT THE MONSTER IN THAT *MOVIE!* IT DIDN'T WORK, THOUGH--

--BUT I REMEMBER WHAT *DID!* OH BOY! I JUST HOPE IT WORKS AS WELL FOR *ME!*

THE UNDERGROUND HANGAR COMPLEX IS A MILE FROM THE MANSION, CONNECTED BY A HIGH-SPEED SUBWAY. THIS MONOCAR CAN MAKE IT IN LESS THAN A MINUTE.

BUT, THOUGH IT DOESN'T SEEM LIKE MUCH...

...A MINUTE CAN SOMETIMES BE A *VERY* LONG TIME.

KITTY HASN'T EVEN GONE HALFWAY...

...BEFORE THE DEMON DERAILS HER MONOCAR.

SHE FINISHES THE JOURNEY ON FOOT -- NINE HUNDRED METERS IN THREE MINUTES* IGNORING THE WHITE HOT POKERS STABBING THROUGH HER CHEST WITH EVERY GASPING BREATH, AND THE BLINDING SHARDS OF PAIN FROM HER LEFT KNEE THAT REDUCE HER TO A HOBBLE BY THE TIME SHE REACHES THE HANGAR.

*1 METER = 3.3 FEET -- L.

THERE, IN THE LAUNCH BAY -- ON THE ELEVATOR THAT LIFTS IT TO THE SURFACE FOR TAKE-OFF -- SITS THE X-MEN'S MODIFIED *SR-71 BLACKBIRD.* PROBABLY THE MOST POWERFUL AIRCRAFT ON EARTH, IT IS CAPABLE OF CIRCLING THE GLOBE WITHOUT REFUELING, OR SOARING TO THE EDGE OF SPACE, OF FLYING AT HYPERSONIC SPEEDS, OVER FIVE TIMES THE SPEED OF SOUND.

IF THE MONSTER WANTS ME, IT'LL HAVE TO COME DOWN THE TRANSIT TUNNEL. THERE'S NO OTHER ENTRANCE TO THE HANGAR COMPLEX FROM THE MANSION.

THE HANGAR IS CONSTRUCTED OF STEEL AND CONCRETE -- A COUPLE OF METERS THICK. EVEN THAT CREATURE WOULD HAVE A HARD TIME DIGGING ITS WAY IN HERE.

I'M COUNTING ON IT BEING TOO ANGRY TO TRY...

...OR WANTING ME SO BADLY THAT IT'LL FOLLOW THE PATH OF LEAST RESISTANCE, CERTAIN THAT I CAN DO NOTHING TO DESTROY IT.

SUPPOSE IT'S RIGHT?

I DON'T SEE IT YET, IN THE TAIL CAMERA. NOW TO RUN THROUGH THE IGNITION CHECK LIST. PLEASE, LORD, DON'T LET ME FORGET ANYTHING.

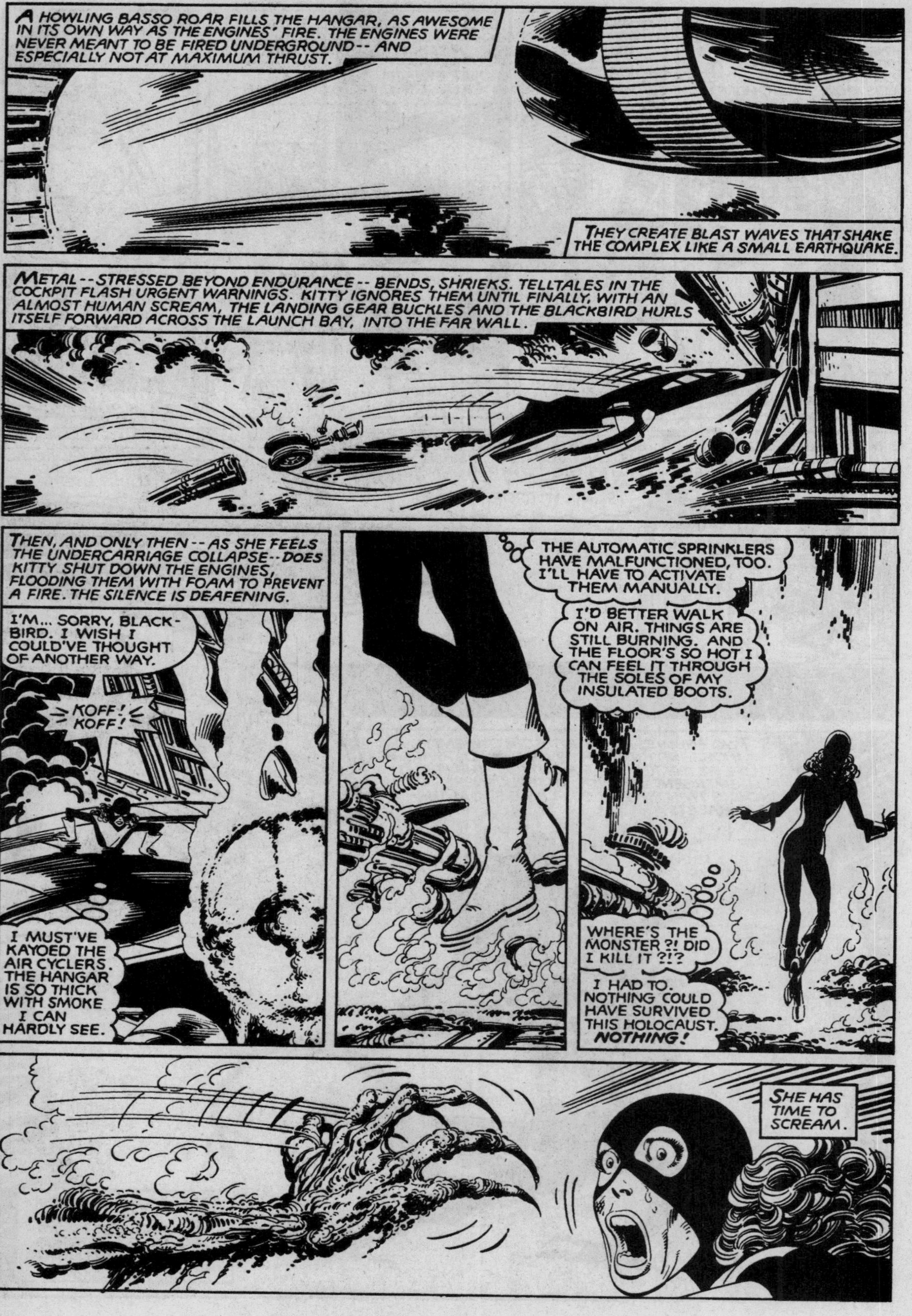
A HOWLING BASSO ROAR FILLS THE HANGAR, AS AWESOME IN ITS OWN WAY AS THE ENGINES' FIRE. THE ENGINES WERE NEVER MEANT TO BE FIRED UNDERGROUND -- AND ESPECIALLY NOT AT MAXIMUM THRUST.
THEY CREATE BLAST WAVES THAT SHAKE THE COMPLEX LIKE A SMALL EARTHQUAKE.
METAL -- STRESSED BEYOND ENDURANCE -- BENDS, SHRIEKS. TELLTALES IN THE COCKPIT FLASH URGENT WARNINGS. KITTY IGNORES THEM UNTIL FINALLY, WITH AN ALMOST HUMAN SCREAM, THE LANDING GEAR BUCKLES AND THE BLACKBIRD HURLS ITSELF FORWARD ACROSS THE LAUNCH BAY, INTO THE FAR WALL.
THEN, AND ONLY THEN -- AS SHE FEELS THE UNDERCARRIAGE COLLAPSE -- DOES KITTY SHUT DOWN THE ENGINES, FLOODING THEM WITH FOAM TO PREVENT A FIRE. THE SILENCE IS DEAFENING.
I'M... SORRY, BLACKBIRD. I WISH I COULD'VE THOUGHT OF ANOTHER WAY.
KOFF! KOFF!
I MUST'VE KAYOED THE AIR CYCLERS. THE HANGAR IS SO THICK WITH SMOKE I CAN HARDLY SEE.
THE AUTOMATIC SPRINKLERS HAVE MALFUNCTIONED, TOO. I'LL HAVE TO ACTIVATE THEM MANUALLY.
I'D BETTER WALK ON AIR. THINGS ARE STILL BURNING. AND THE FLOOR'S SO HOT I CAN FEEL IT THROUGH THE SOLES OF MY INSULATED BOOTS.
WHERE'S THE MONSTER ?! DID I KILL IT ?!?
I HAD TO. NOTHING COULD HAVE SURVIVED THIS HOLOCAUST. NOTHING!
SHE HAS TIME TO SCREAM.

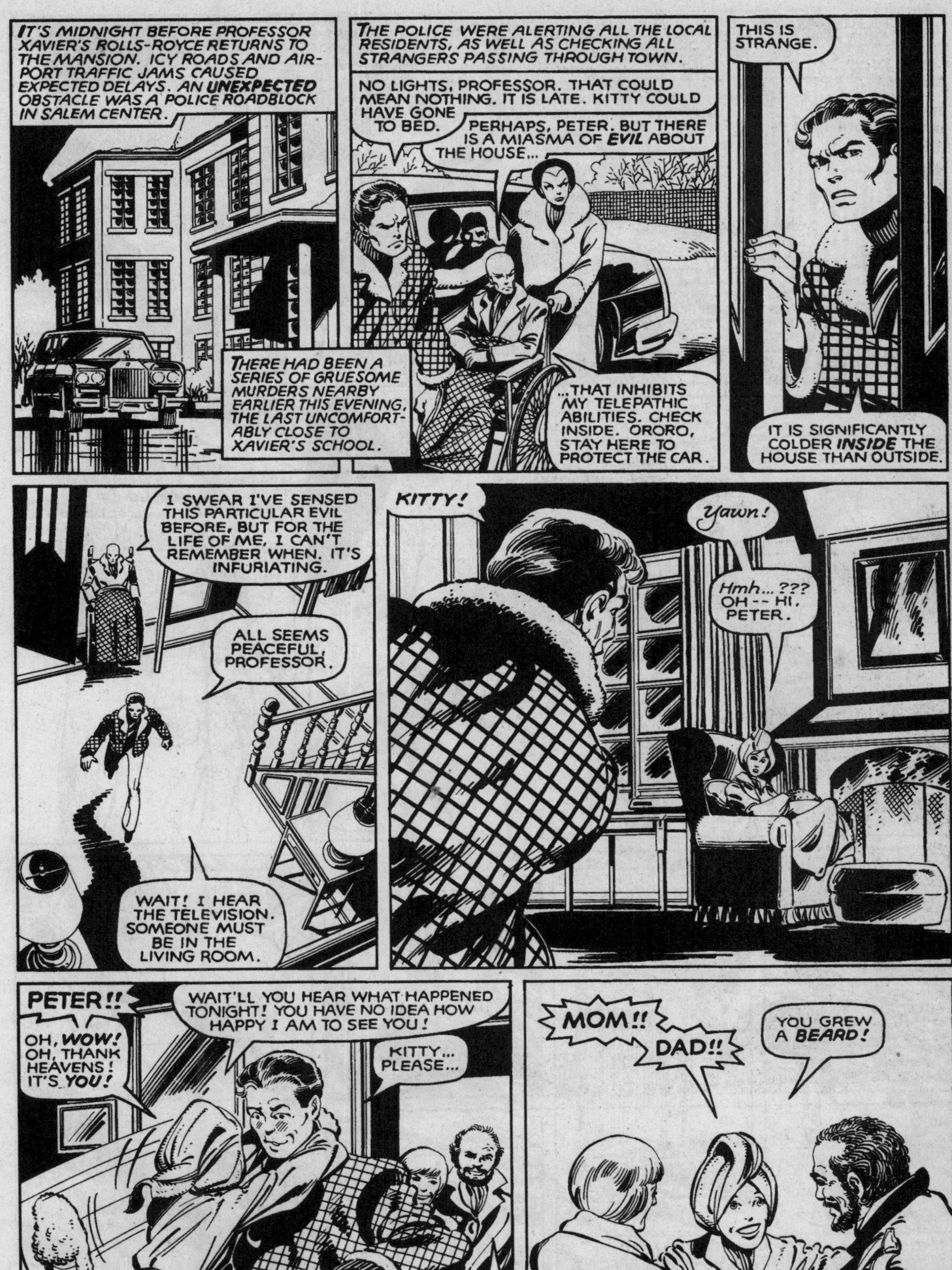

IT'S MIDNIGHT BEFORE PROFESSOR XAVIER'S ROLLS-ROYCE RETURNS TO THE MANSION. ICY ROADS AND AIRPORT TRAFFIC JAMS CAUSED EXPECTED DELAYS. AN UNEXPECTED OBSTACLE WAS A POLICE ROADBLOCK IN SALEM CENTER.
THERE HAD BEEN A SERIES OF GRUESOME MURDERS NEARBY EARLIER THIS EVENING, THE LAST UNCOMFORTABLY CLOSE TO XAVIER'S SCHOOL.
THE POLICE WERE ALERTING ALL THE LOCAL RESIDENTS, AS WELL AS CHECKING ALL STRANGERS PASSING THROUGH TOWN.
NO LIGHTS, PROFESSOR. THAT COULD MEAN NOTHING. IT IS LATE. KITTY COULD HAVE GONE TO BED.
PERHAPS, PETER. BUT THERE IS A MIASMA OF EVIL ABOUT THE HOUSE...
...THAT INHIBITS MY TELEPATHIC ABILITIES. CHECK INSIDE. ORORO, STAY HERE TO PROTECT THE CAR.
THIS IS STRANGE.
IT IS SIGNIFICANTLY COLDER INSIDE THE HOUSE THAN OUTSIDE.
I SWEAR I'VE SENSED THIS PARTICULAR EVIL BEFORE, BUT FOR THE LIFE OF ME, I CAN'T REMEMBER WHEN. IT'S INFURIATING.
ALL SEEMS PEACEFUL, PROFESSOR.
WAIT! I HEAR THE TELEVISION. SOMEONE MUST BE IN THE LIVING ROOM.
KITTY!
Yawn!
Hmh...??? OH -- HI, PETER.
PETER!!
OH, WOW! OH, THANK HEAVENS! IT'S YOU!
WAIT'LL YOU HEAR WHAT HAPPENED TONIGHT! YOU HAVE NO IDEA HOW HAPPY I AM TO SEE YOU!
KITTY... PLEASE...
MOM!!
DAD!!
YOU GREW A BEARD!
IF YOU'RE HAPPY TO SEE PETER, KITTEN, HOW D'YOU FEEL ABOUT US?

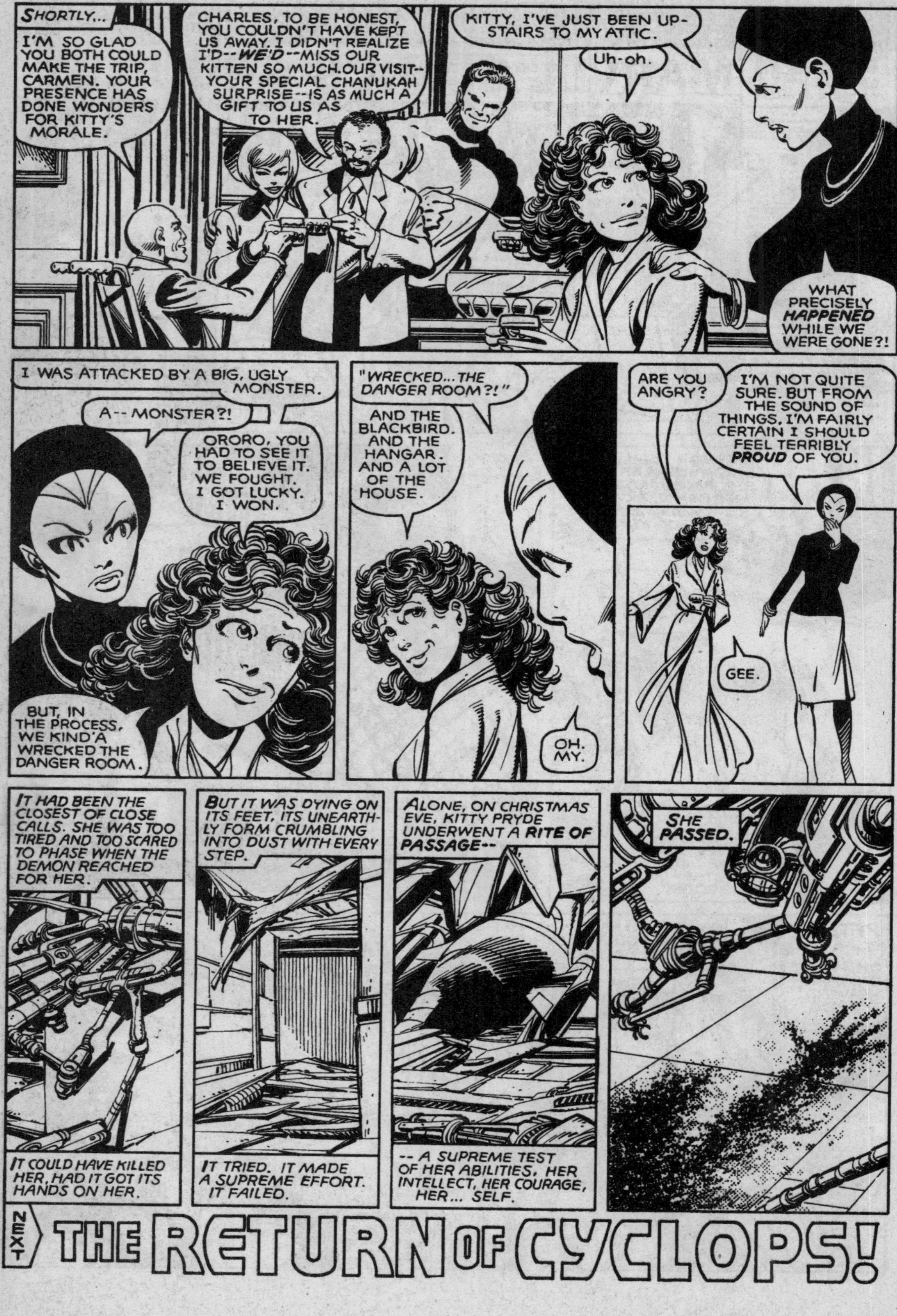
SHORTLY...
I'M SO GLAD YOU BOTH COULD MAKE THE TRIP, CARMEN. YOUR PRESENCE HAS DONE WONDERS FOR KITTY'S MORALE.
CHARLES, TO BE HONEST, YOU COULDN'T HAVE KEPT US AWAY. I DIDN'T REALIZE I'D--WE'D--MISS OUR KITTEN SO MUCH. OUR VISIT--YOUR SPECIAL CHANUKAH SURPRISE--IS AS MUCH A GIFT TO US AS TO HER.
KITTY, I'VE JUST BEEN UP-STAIRS TO MY ATTIC.
Uh-oh.
WHAT PRECISELY HAPPENED WHILE WE WERE GONE?!
I WAS ATTACKED BY A BIG, UGLY MONSTER.
A-- MONSTER?!
ORORO, YOU HAD TO SEE IT TO BELIEVE IT. WE FOUGHT. I GOT LUCKY. I WON.
BUT, IN THE PROCESS, WE KIND'A WRECKED THE DANGER ROOM.
"WRECKED... THE DANGER ROOM?!"
AND THE BLACKBIRD. AND THE HANGAR. AND A LOT OF THE HOUSE.
OH. MY.
ARE YOU ANGRY?
I'M NOT QUITE SURE. BUT FROM THE SOUND OF THINGS, I'M FAIRLY CERTAIN I SHOULD FEEL TERRIBLY PROUD OF YOU.
GEE.
IT HAD BEEN THE CLOSEST OF CLOSE CALLS. SHE WAS TOO TIRED AND TOO SCARED TO PHASE WHEN THE DEMON REACHED FOR HER.
IT COULD HAVE KILLED HER, HAD IT GOT ITS HANDS ON HER.
BUT IT WAS DYING ON ITS FEET, ITS UNEARTHLY FORM CRUMBLING INTO DUST WITH EVERY STEP.
IT TRIED. IT MADE A SUPREME EFFORT. IT FAILED.
ALONE, ON CHRISTMAS EVE, KITTY PRYDE UNDERWENT A RITE OF PASSAGE--
-- A SUPREME TEST OF HER ABILITIES, HER INTELLECT, HER COURAGE, HER... SELF.
SHE PASSED.
NEXT
THE RETURN OF CYCLOPS!

Cyclops. Storm. Nightcrawler. Wolverine. Colossus. Children of the atom, students of Charles Xavier, MUTANTS — feared and hated by the world they have sworn to protect. These are the STRANGEST heroes of all!

STAN LEE PRESENTS: **THE UNCANNY X-MEN!** ™

CHRIS CLAREMONT WRITER | BRENT ANDERSON, GUEST PENCILER | GLYNIS WEIN, colorist | LOUISE JONES EDITOR | JIM SHOOTER Ed.-IN-CHIEF
JOSEF RUBENSTEIN, INKER | TOM ORZECHOWSKI, letterer

Even in death....

THE DOCTOR WAS HONEST, AND AS GENTLE AS A PERSON CAN BE WHEN SHE TELLS AN OLD FRIEND THAT HE'S GOING TO DIE.

DIAGNOSIS: CANCER -- INOPERABLE, INCURABLE. PROGNOSIS: EVER-INCREASING ENFEEBLEMENT OF PHYSICAL AND MENTAL FACULTIES, EVER-INCREASING PAIN, DEATH WITHIN A YEAR.

FROM THE HOSPITAL, JOCK FORRESTER CAME HERE TO THE SWAMP HE'D KNOWN AND LOVED SINCE CHILDHOOD, TO MAKE THE MOST IMPORTANT DECISION OF HIS LIFE: TO FIGHT THIS DISEASE -- AND PRAY THAT SOME MIRACLE MIGHT SAVE HIM -- OR END THINGS, QUICKLY, CLEANLY, IN HIS OWN WAY, HIS OWN TIME.

JOCK DOES NOT REALIZE THAT, THE MOMENT HE ENTERED THIS GLADE, HIS DECISION WAS MADE FOR HIM.

NEARBY, UNNOTICED IN THE SHADOWS, SOMETHING STIRS. ONCE, THIS WAS A BIOLOGIST NAMED *TED SALLIS*...

HE IS AN EMPATH.

Ah, Mary my darling, why couldn't I have died with you? I wanted to.

Why now, Lord? Why...THIS WAY? IT...IT'S SO UNFAIR!

...TRANSFORMED BY A FREAK ACCIDENT INTO A MINDLESS, MISSHAPEN MOCKERY OF HUMANITY CALLED THE MAN-THING.

HE RESPONDS TO THE EMOTIONAL RESONANCES OF THE BEINGS AROUND HIM. NEGATIVE -- AND VIOLENT -- EMOTIONS CAUSE HIM PAIN...FEAR, THE WORST PAIN OF ALL. DRAWN BY JOCK'S SORROW, HE MEANS TO END IT -- IF NECESSARY, BY DESTROYING THE SOURCE.

BUT, AS HE APPROACHES THE MAN, HIS ATTENTION IS SNAGGED BY A PATCH OF OILY BLACK SMOKE SWIRLING ACROSS THE GROUND.

ITS TENDRILS REACH TOWARDS JOCK--THE ELDRITCH CLOUD RADIATING AN ALMOST PALPABLE AURA OF EVIL--

--AND THE MAN RESPONDS.

SKRIK!

KLATCH!

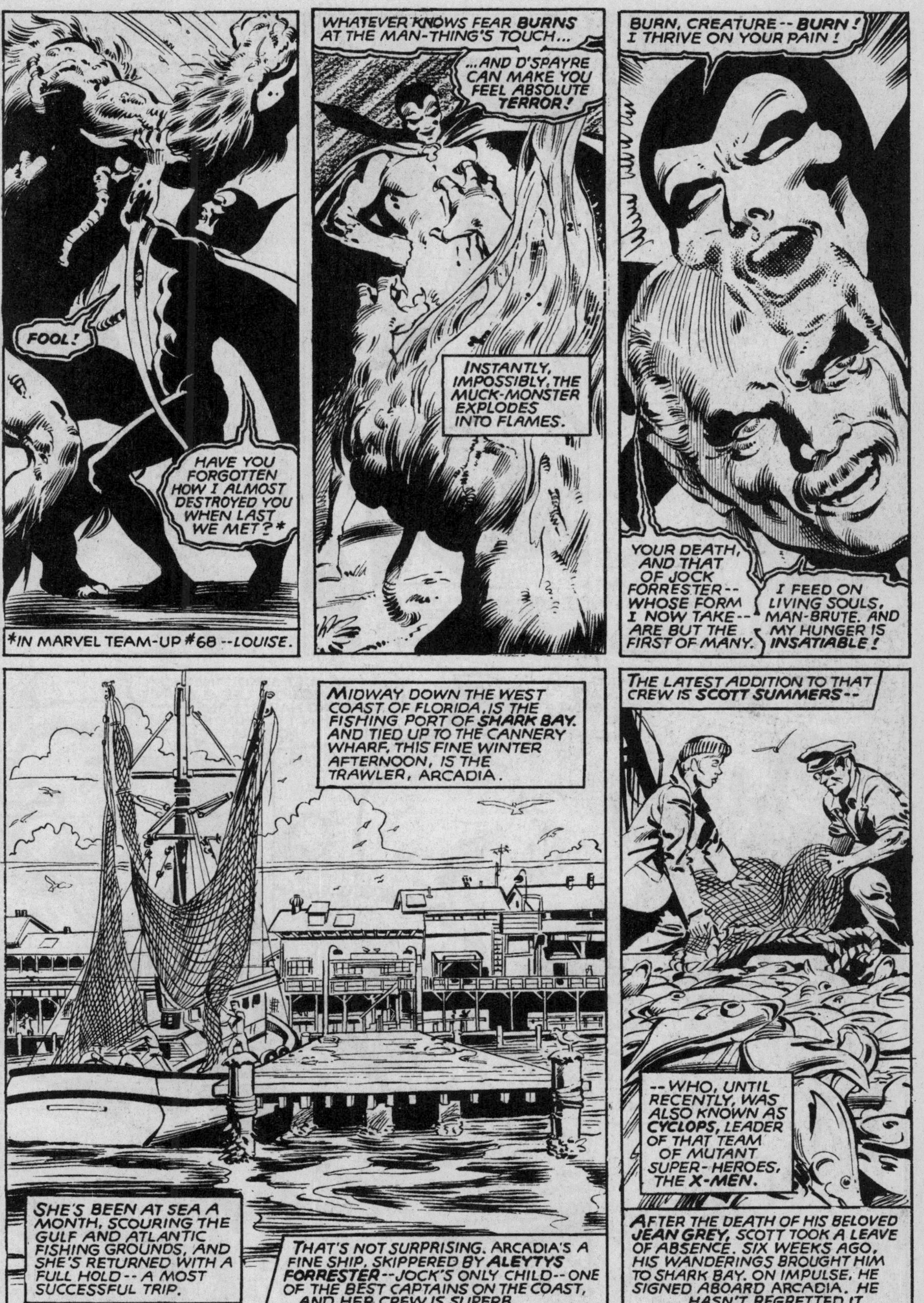
FOOL!
HAVE YOU FORGOTTEN HOW I ALMOST DESTROYED YOU WHEN LAST WE MET?*
*IN MARVEL TEAM-UP #68 --LOUISE.
WHATEVER KNOWS FEAR BURNS AT THE MAN-THING'S TOUCH...
...AND D'SPAYRE CAN MAKE YOU FEEL ABSOLUTE TERROR!
INSTANTLY, IMPOSSIBLY, THE MUCK-MONSTER EXPLODES INTO FLAMES.
BURN, CREATURE -- BURN! I THRIVE ON YOUR PAIN!
YOUR DEATH, AND THAT OF JOCK FORRESTER -- WHOSE FORM I NOW TAKE -- ARE BUT THE FIRST OF MANY.
I FEED ON LIVING SOULS, MAN-BRUTE. AND MY HUNGER IS INSATIABLE!
MIDWAY DOWN THE WEST COAST OF FLORIDA, IS THE FISHING PORT OF SHARK BAY. AND TIED UP TO THE CANNERY WHARF, THIS FINE WINTER AFTERNOON, IS THE TRAWLER, ARCADIA.
SHE'S BEEN AT SEA A MONTH, SCOURING THE GULF AND ATLANTIC FISHING GROUNDS, AND SHE'S RETURNED WITH A FULL HOLD -- A MOST SUCCESSFUL TRIP.
THAT'S NOT SURPRISING. ARCADIA'S A FINE SHIP, SKIPPERED BY ALEYTYS FORRESTER -- JOCK'S ONLY CHILD -- ONE OF THE BEST CAPTAINS ON THE COAST, AND HER CREW IS SUPERB.
THE LATEST ADDITION TO THAT CREW IS SCOTT SUMMERS --
-- WHO, UNTIL RECENTLY, WAS ALSO KNOWN AS CYCLOPS, LEADER OF THAT TEAM OF MUTANT SUPER-HEROES, THE X-MEN.
AFTER THE DEATH OF HIS BELOVED JEAN GREY, SCOTT TOOK A LEAVE OF ABSENCE. SIX WEEKS AGO, HIS WANDERINGS BROUGHT HIM TO SHARK BAY. ON IMPULSE, HE SIGNED ABOARD ARCADIA. HE HASN'T REGRETTED IT.

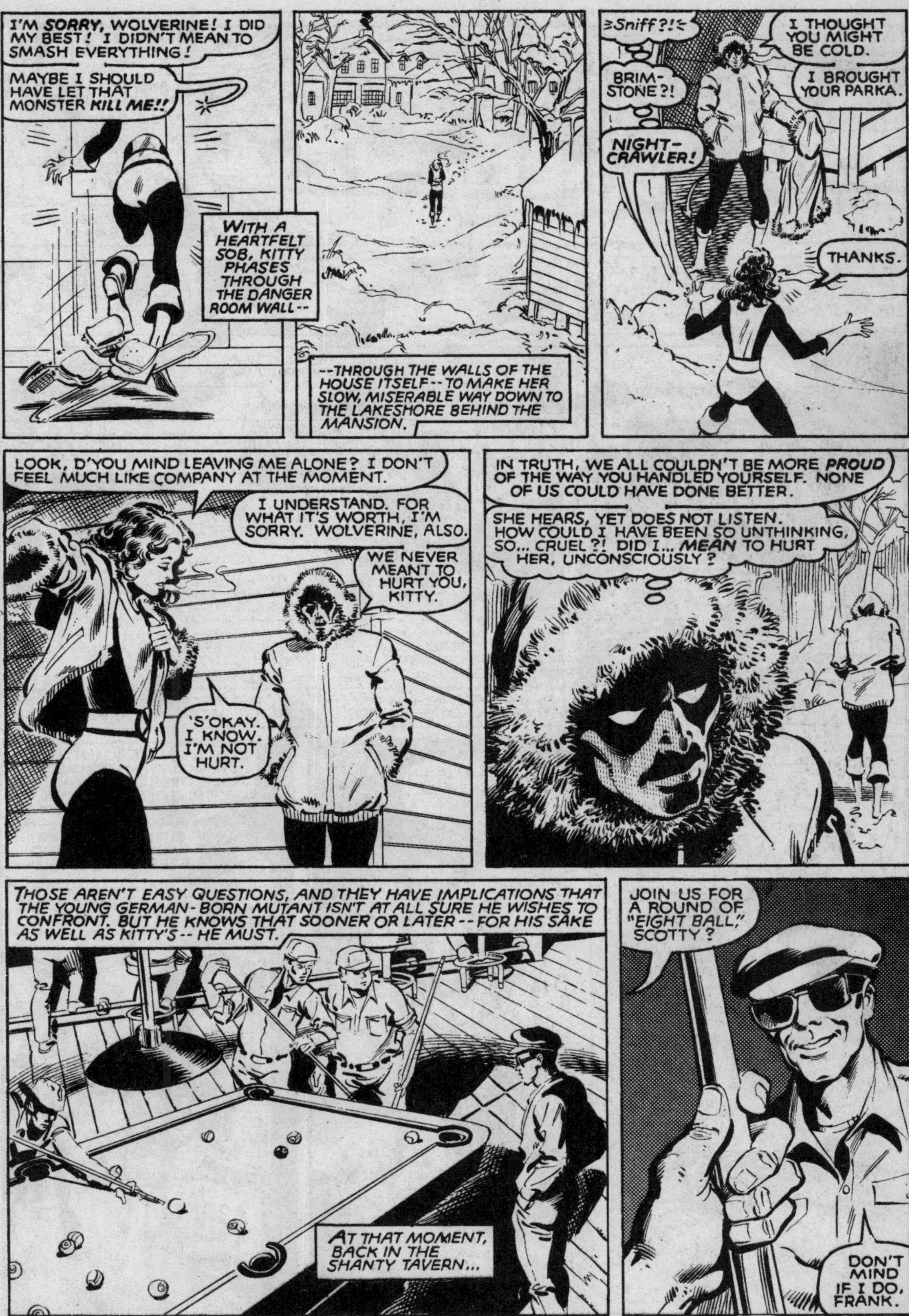

I'M SORRY, WOLVERINE! I DID MY BEST! I DIDN'T MEAN TO SMASH EVERYTHING!
MAYBE I SHOULD HAVE LET THAT MONSTER KILL ME!!
WITH A HEARTFELT SOB, KITTY PHASES THROUGH THE DANGER ROOM WALL--
--THROUGH THE WALLS OF THE HOUSE ITSELF--TO MAKE HER SLOW, MISERABLE WAY DOWN TO THE LAKESHORE BEHIND THE MANSION.
Sniff?!
BRIM-STONE?!
NIGHT-CRAWLER!
I THOUGHT YOU MIGHT BE COLD.
I BROUGHT YOUR PARKA.
THANKS.
LOOK, D'YOU MIND LEAVING ME ALONE? I DON'T FEEL MUCH LIKE COMPANY AT THE MOMENT.
I UNDERSTAND. FOR WHAT IT'S WORTH, I'M SORRY. WOLVERINE, ALSO.
WE NEVER MEANT TO HURT YOU, KITTY.
'S'OKAY. I KNOW. I'M NOT HURT.
IN TRUTH, WE ALL COULDN'T BE MORE PROUD OF THE WAY YOU HANDLED YOURSELF. NONE OF US COULD HAVE DONE BETTER.
SHE HEARS, YET DOES NOT LISTEN. HOW COULD I HAVE BEEN SO UNTHINKING, SO... CRUEL?! DID I... MEAN TO HURT HER, UNCONSCIOUSLY?
THOSE AREN'T EASY QUESTIONS, AND THEY HAVE IMPLICATIONS THAT THE YOUNG GERMAN-BORN MUTANT ISN'T AT ALL SURE HE WISHES TO CONFRONT. BUT HE KNOWS THAT SOONER OR LATER--FOR HIS SAKE AS WELL AS KITTY'S--HE MUST.
AT THAT MOMENT, BACK IN THE SHANTY TAVERN...
JOIN US FOR A ROUND OF "EIGHT BALL," SCOTTY?
DON'T MIND IF I DO, FRANK.

L-LORNA. OH, LORNA...

M-MY VISOR... THIS IS MY *OLD* COSTUME! AND... I *KNOW* THIS PLACE! IT'S THE MOUNTAIN HEADQUARTERS OF *LARRY TRASK*!

WHAT IS *HAPPENING* TO ME?!!

HE STANDS SURROUNDED BY THE ORIGINAL X-MEN. ALL SAVE HIS BROTHER, ALEX--THE SUPERHERO HAVOK--ARE DEAD.

AND, ECHOING THROUGH THE VAST UNDERGROUND COMPLEX...

...HE CAN HEAR THE LEAD-FOOTED APPROACH OF THEIR MURDERERS.

ALEX...?

SCOTT, I... I LOVED HER. NOW SHE'S...

SENTINELS!

AM I *DREAMING*?! AM I *INSANE*?!

THOSE ROBOTS LOOK LIKE THE X-MEN!

THEY *BUTCHERED* OUR FRIENDS, SCOTT, AND THE WOMAN I LOVE.

AND HAVOK IS GOING TO PAY THEM BACK IN KIND!

DRAWING ON THE INFINITE POWER OF COSMIC RAYS -- AS CYCLOPS DRAWS ON SUNLIGHT -- HAVOK UNLEASHES AN ENERGY BLAST OF AWESOME PROPORTIONS.

BESIDE HIM-- HIS MIND DENYING WHAT HIS HEART ACCEPTS AS TRUTH-- CYCLOPS FOLLOWS HIS LEAD.

D'SPAYRE! THE SWAMP MONSTER! FORGET IT. IF THEY'RE STILL INSIDE THAT HOLOCAUST, THEY'RE BOTH DEAD. LEE AND I CAME CLOSE--TOO CLOSE--TO JOINING THEM.

ONCE I REALIZED THAT...

...I KNEW I'D DIE BEFORE I'D LET YOU HAVE THAT KIND OF VICTORY. AT THAT MOMENT, YOU WERE BEATEN.

THE DEMON'S FATAL MISTAKE WAS ATTACKING ME THROUGH MY MEMORIES OF JEAN. THROUGH HER, I FACED THE BEST AND WORST OF HUMANITY. I LEARNED THE TRUE MEANING OF COURAGE-- AND OF LOVE.

YIELDING TO YOU, D'SPAY WOULD HAVE BEEN THE ULTIMATE DENIAL--AND BETRAYAL--OF THAT LOVE.

SCOTT LEAVES WITHOUT A BACK-WARDS GLANCE, QUICKLY CHANGING FROM COS-TUME TO STREET CLOTHES BEFORE RUSHING LEE IN THE AIRBOAT TO COUNTY HOSPITAL. THERE, THE DOCTORS TELL HIM SHE'LL BE FINE. HE'S... GLAD.

BY DAWN, THE FIRE IS OUT...

...THE MAN-THING RISES, WHOLE AND UNHARMED.

THE SWAMP GAVE HIM BIRTH. THE SWAMP SUSTAINS HIM.

SO LONG AS HE REMAINS WITHIN ITS VAST CONFINES, HE IS VIRTUALLY IMMORTAL.

HE PAUSES, SEEKING SOME SENSE OF D'SPAYRE AND, FINDING NONE, DEPARTS. FOR A TIME, SILENCE REIGNS.

THEN, SOFT MALEFIC LAUGHTER BREAKS THE STILLNESS...

...TO ECHO OUT ACROSS THE FACE OF THE WORLD.

...THE HOUSE REDUCED TO SMOULDERING REMAINS. THEN, AMID THE ASHES...

TRUE, HE WAS TRAPPED IN THE HEART OF THE FIRE. TRUE, IT CONSUMED HIM AS IT DID THE MANSION. BUT THE QUAG-BEAST WAS CREATED AS MUCH BY SORCERY AS SCIENCE.

JOCK FORRESTER'S HOUSE WAS BUILT WITHIN THE SWAMP. SO, WHEN THE FIRE INCINERATED MAN-THING, THE SWAMP RESURRECTED HIM. AS IT HAS DONE BEFORE AND WILL DO AGAIN.

"...SO LONG AS THERE IS HOPE, IT MUST BE BALANCED... BY DESPAIR. WE CAN REDUCE HIM FOR A TIME, BUT WHILE THERE IS LIFE ITSELF, HE WILL EXIST." -- DAKIMH THE ENCHANTER.

SPECIAL BONUS:

Frank Miller's cover to *X-Men Annual #3* was intended to print with a host of barbarians as a color overlay; however, the overlay was left out by the printer in its original printing. It is presented here from the original artwork.

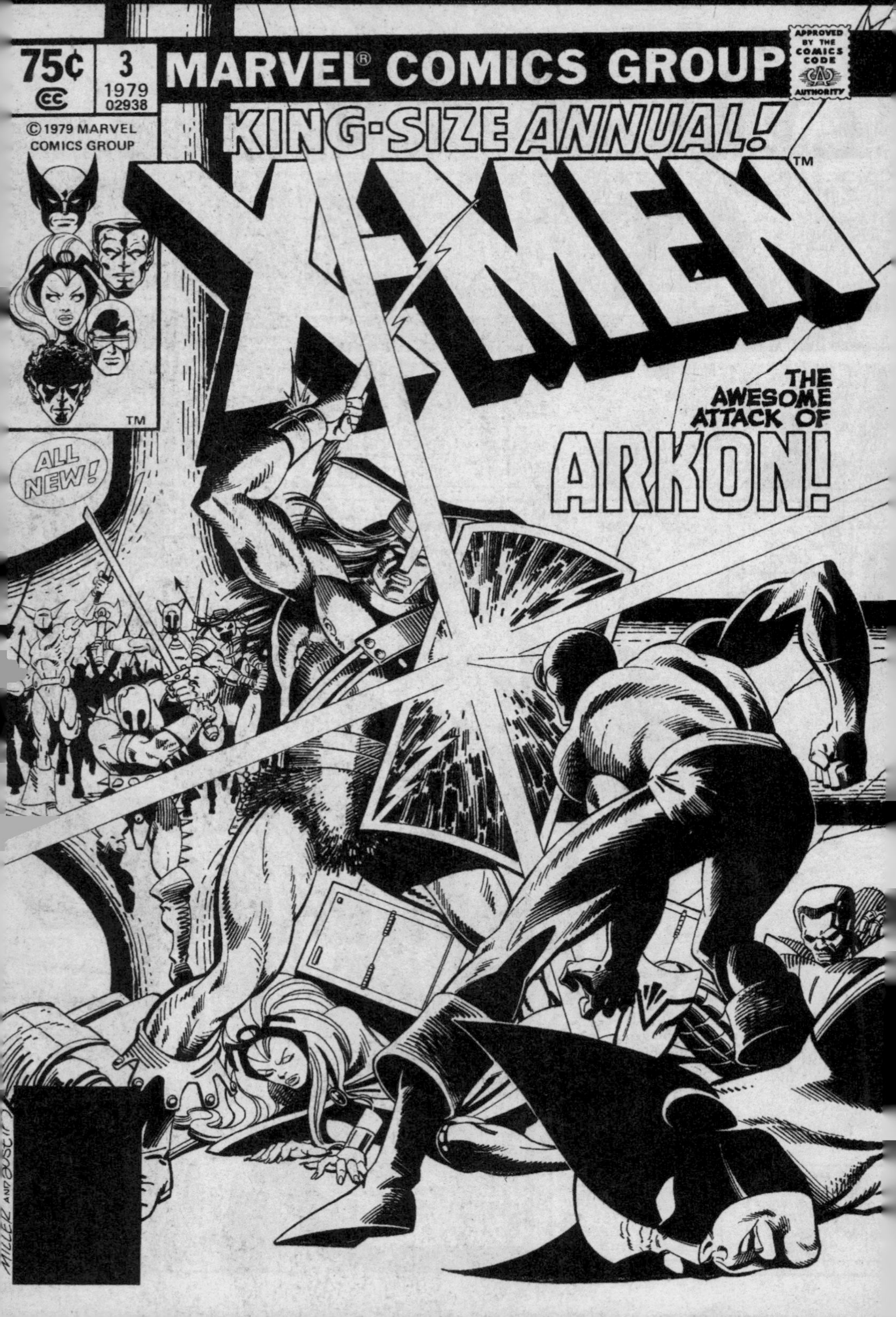

75¢
3
1979
02938
MARVEL® COMICS GROUP
APPROVED BY THE COMICS CODE AUTHORITY
© 1979 MARVEL COMICS GROUP
KING-SIZE ANNUAL!
X-MEN™
THE AWESOME ATTACK OF
ARKON!
ALL NEW!
TM

The *X-Men #132* page 6 original art by John Byrne and Terry Austin

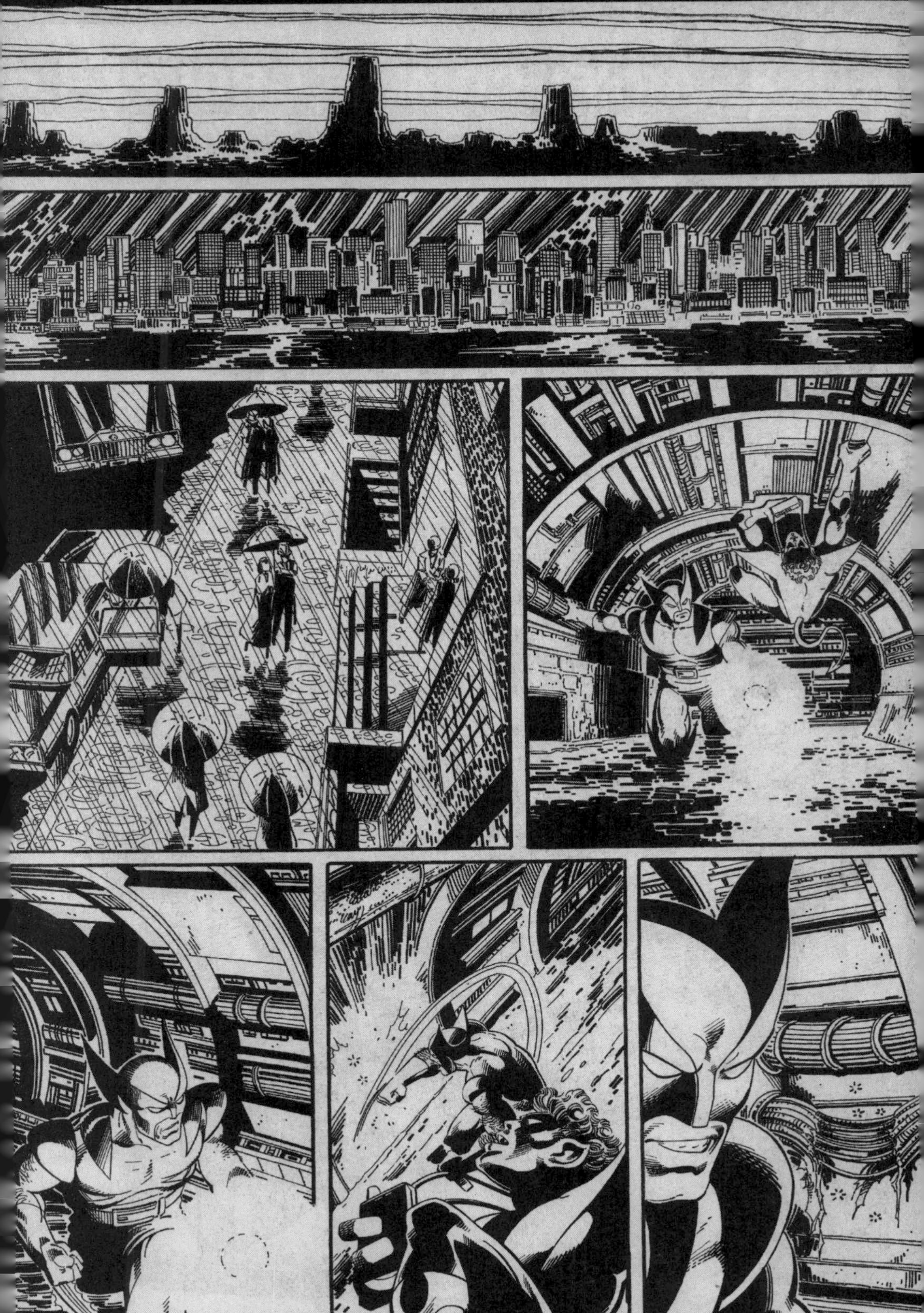

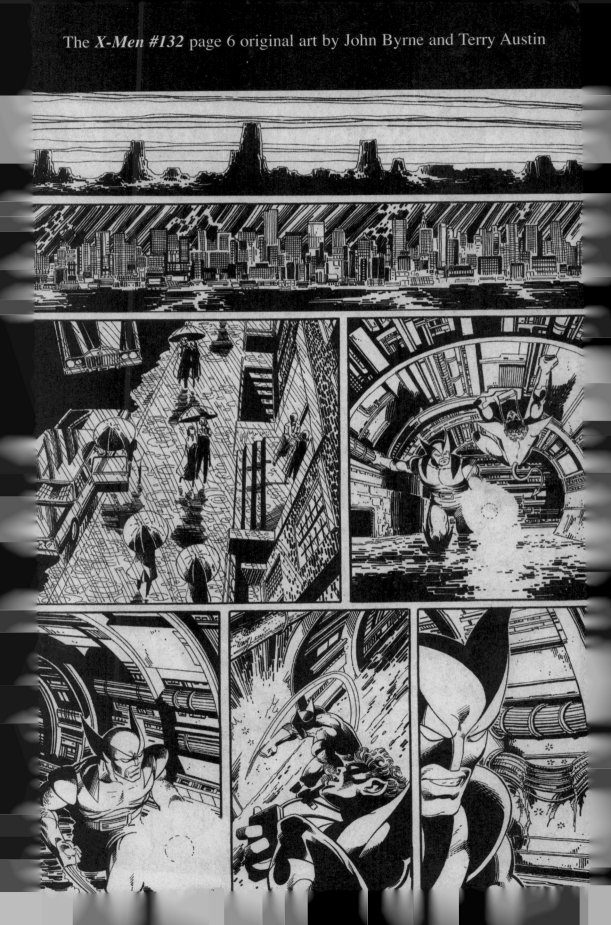

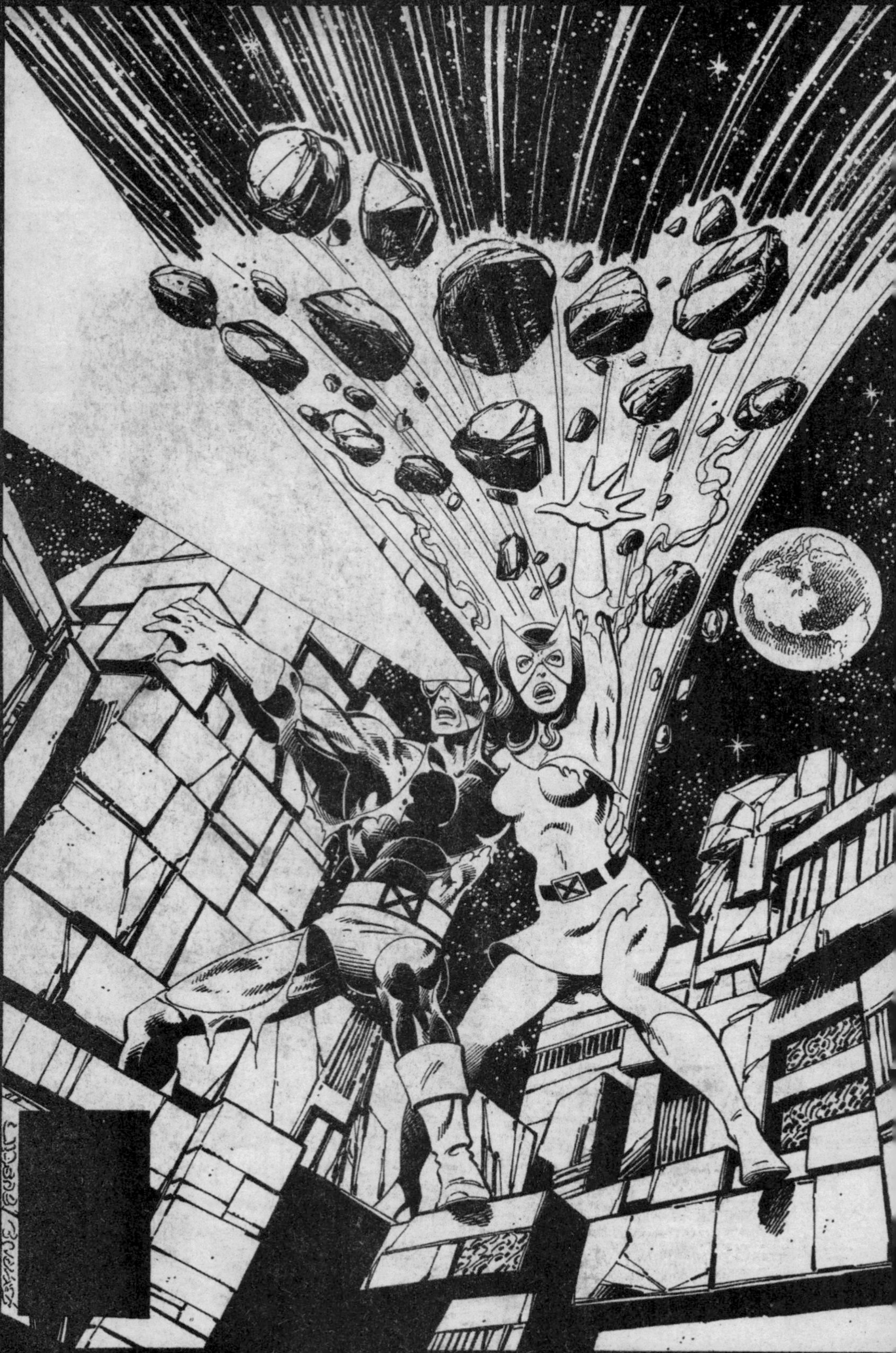

The *X-Men #137* original cover art by John Byrne and Terry Austin

If Jean Grey had lived, *The X-Men #138* would have begun with this splash page instead of the graveyard scene which was used instead.

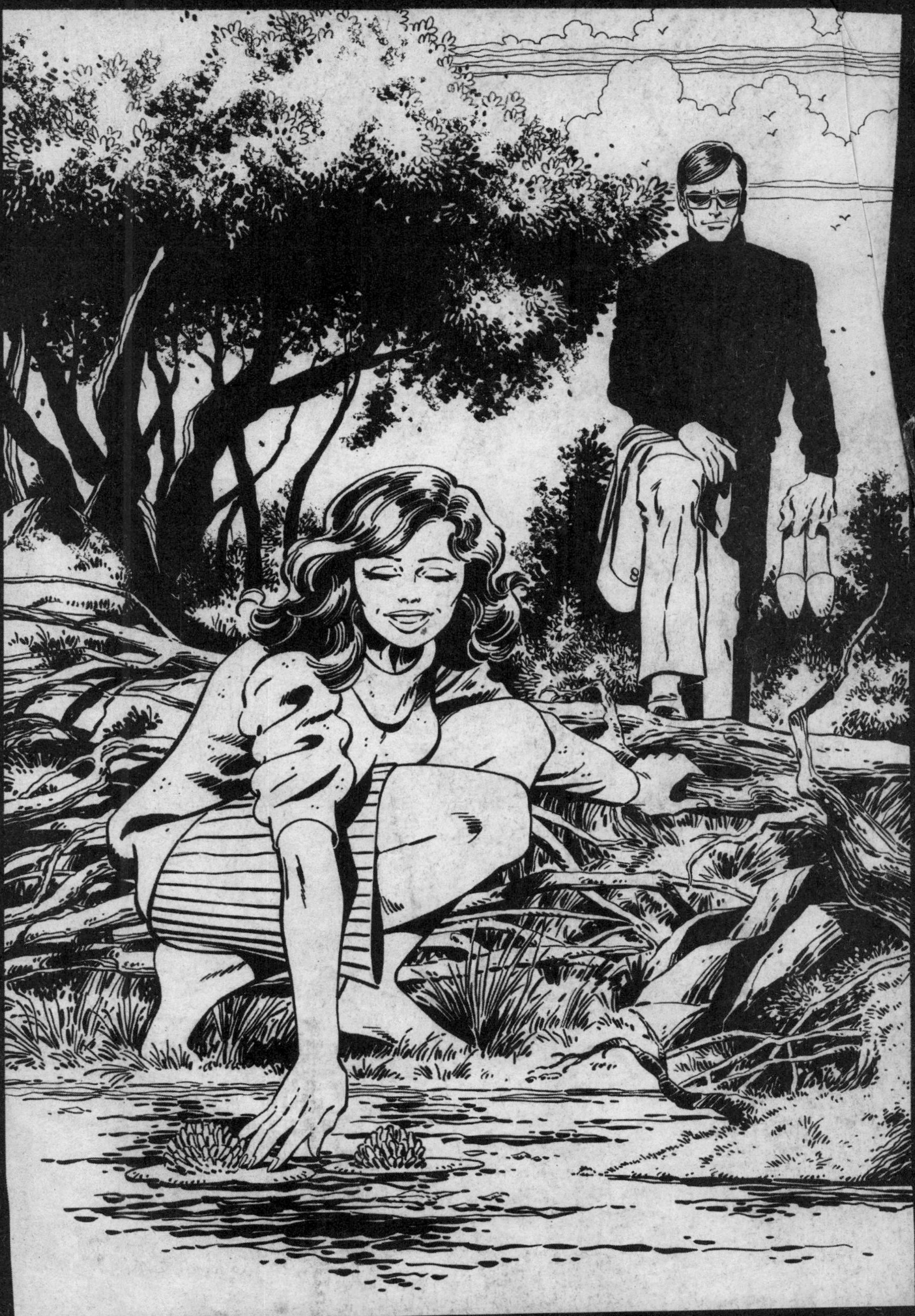

Uncanny X-Men #142 original cover art by John Byrne and Terry Austin

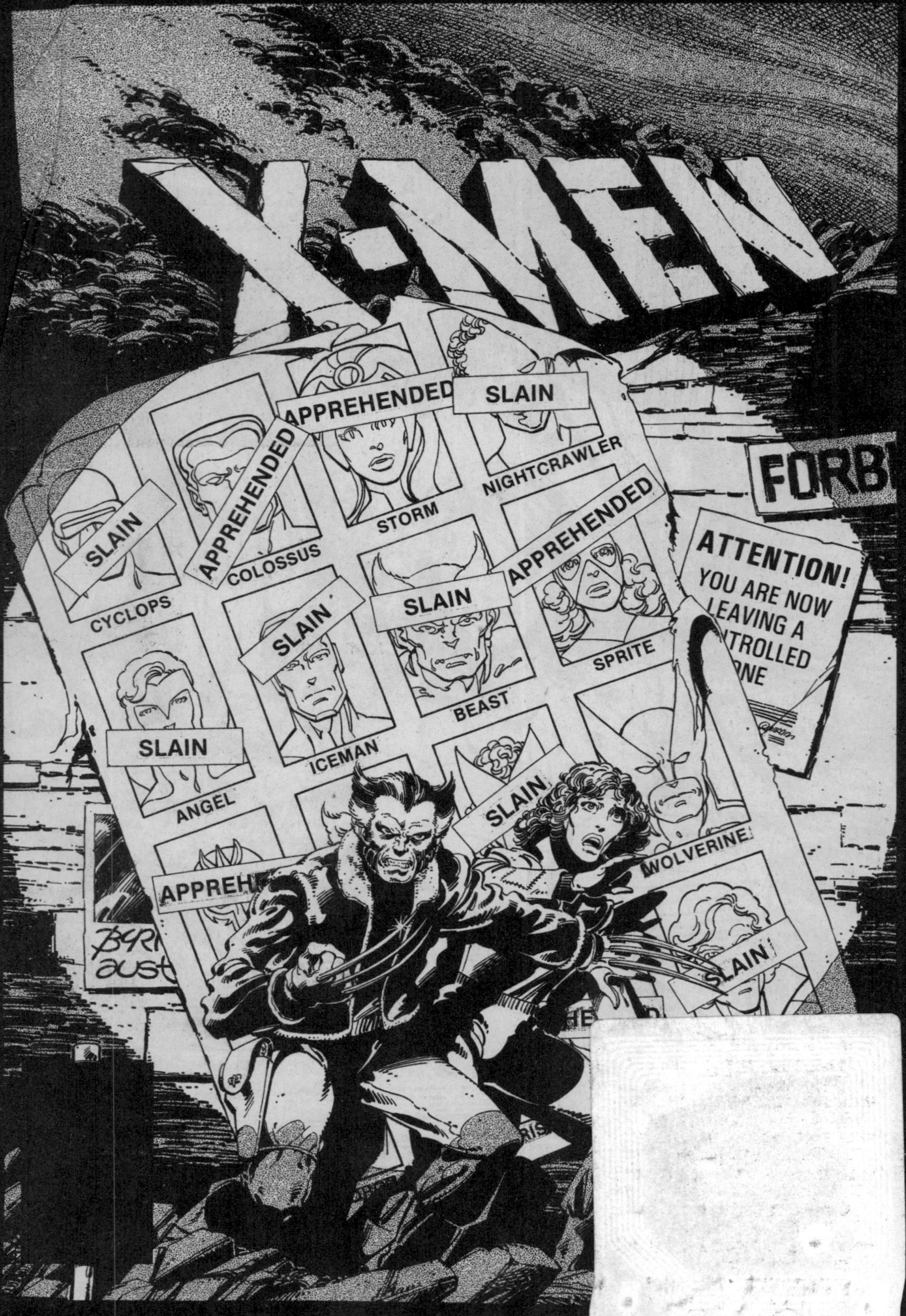
X-MEN
SLAIN
CYCLOPS
APPREHENDED
COLOSSUS
APPREHENDED
STORM
SLAIN
NIGHTCRAWLER
SLAIN
ANGEL
SLAIN
ICEMAN
SLAIN
BEAST
APPREHENDED
SPRITE
SLAIN
WOLVERINE
SLAIN
ATTENTION!
YOU ARE NOW